Guiding Children's Social Development & Learning

Sixth Edition

Join us on the web at
EarlyChildEd.delmar.com

Guiding Children's Social Development & Learning

Sixth Edition

Marjorie J. Kostelnik, Ph.D.
UNIVERSITY OF NEBRASKA–LINCOLN

Alice Phipps Whiren, Ph.D.

Anne K. Soderman, Ph.D.

Kara M. Gregory, Ph.D.
MICHIGAN STATE UNIVERSITY

DELMAR
CENGAGE Learning™

Australia • Brazil • Japan • Korea • Mexico • Singapore • Spain • United Kingdom • United States

Guiding Children's Social Development and Learning, 6th. Edition
Marjorie J. Kostelnik, Ph.D., Alice Phipps Whiren, Ph.D., Anne K. Soderman, Ph.D., Kara M. Gregory, Ph.D.

Vice President, Career Education SBU: Dawn Gerrain

Director of Learning Solutions: John Fedor

Acquisitions Editor: Christopher Shortt

Managing Editor: Robert Serenka

Product Manager: Philip I. Mandl

Editorial Assistant: Alison Archambault

Marketing Director: Wendy Mapstone

Marketing Manager: Kristin McNary

Marketing Coordinator: Scott Chrysler

Production Director: Wendy Troeger

Production Manager: Mark Bernard

Content Project Manager: Jeffery Varecka

Art Director: David Arsenault

Technology Project Manager: Sandy Charette

For product information and technology assistance, contact us at
Cengage Learning Customer & Sales Support, 1-800-354-9706

For permission to use material from this text or product, submit all requests online at **cengage.com/permissions**.
Further permissions questions
can be e-mailed to **permissionrequest @cengage.com**

Library of Congress Control Number: 2007942957

ISBN-13: 978-1-4283-3694-0

ISBN-10: 1-4283-3694-X

Delmar
5 Maxwell Drive
Clifton Park, NY 12065-2919
USA

Cengage Learning is a leading provider of customized learning solutions with office locations around the globe, including Singapore, the United Kingdom, Australia, Mexico, Brazil, and Japan. Locate your local office at:
international.cengage.com/region

Cengage Learning products are represented in Canada by Nelson Education, Ltd.

For your lifelong learning solutions, visit **delmar.cengage.com**

Visit our corporate website at **www.cengage.com**

Printed in the United States of America
2 3 4 5 6 7 12 11 10 09

Contents

Preface

Generosity
Self-confidence
Helpfulness
Responsibility
Trustworthiness
Independence
Caring for Others
Respect
Sense of Belongingness

These are just some of the values and character traits adults hope young children will acquire over time.

Early childhood educators play a central role in helping children explore these values and enact them in their daily lives. Every day, young children in early childhood programs interact with peers and practitioners, learning valuable lessons about themselves and the people around them. Adults too are learning, as they watch and interact with the children and with each other.

As someone who aspires to work with young children professionally, you are about to enter a remarkable world in which you will be both teacher and learner at the same time. What you say and do with the young children in your charge will have a tremendous impact on them, and may shape them for good or ill in ways you will never fully know. At the same time, the children will be teaching you new things about child development, family life, social learning in early childhood, and yourself. *Guiding Children's Social Development and Learning*, Sixth Edition, is designed to help you make the most of these learning opportunities.

Our original purpose in writing this book was to do something to improve the quality of life for children and their families and to contribute to the professional development of practitioners in training.

That continues to be our goal. We believe helping professionals have a primary role in providing emotional support and guidance to the youngsters with whom they work. This includes helping children develop positive feelings about themselves, increasing their ability to interact effectively with others, and teaching them socially acceptable means of behavior.

We also know that this type of learning is facilitated when children view the adult as a wellspring of comfort and encouragement as well as a source of behavioral guidance. How proficiently adults perform these roles is affected by the extent to which they understand child development, their ability to establish positive relationships with children, and their grasp of principles related to behavior management.

It is our premise that helping professionals must first learn about children's social development and then become adept in relationship enhancement skills and behavior-management techniques. Unfortunately, in the literature and in practice, a dichotomy often is assumed between relationship enhancement and behavior management. For example, approaches that focus on the former teach students how to demonstrate warmth and respect, acceptance and empathy, but leave them to their own devices in figuring out how to deal with typical childhood behaviors such as spitting, hitting, teasing, or making friends. Conversely, approaches that focus on behavior control address the latter circumstances but often neglect to teach students how to build rapport with children, how to help children develop coping strategies, or how to assist them in better understanding themselves and others.

We have decided to tackle these issues by including research, information, and skills associated with both relationship enhancement and behavior management. We have pulled together a unique blend of developmental and mechanistic theory and practice that establishes common ground between the two while maintaining the integrity of each. In doing so, we demonstrate that there is a factual knowledge base that can be brought to bear on how aspiring professionals think about children's social development and how they respond to it.

Additionally, too often, we have encountered students and practitioners who treat their interactions with children as wholly intuitive. They rely on "gut level" responses, adhering to no explicit or comprehensive principles. These adults frequently view child guidance as a series of tricks that they use indiscriminately to meet short-range objectives, such as getting a child to stop interrupting. They have no purposeful or integrated set of strategies that address long-range goals, such as teaching a child to delay gratification.

Other adults have more knowledge about broad principles regarding relationship building and behavior management but have difficulty integrating those principles into a systematic, consistent plan of action. Most distressing to us are those adults whose lack of training leads them to conclude that the normal behaviors children exhibit as they engage in the socialization process somehow are abnormal or malicious. These people also fail to recognize the impact of their own behavior on their interactions with children. As a result, when children do not comply with their expectations, they think condemnation rather than teaching is appropriate for the situation.

Guiding Children's Social Development and Learning has been written to address these shortcomings. It is our goal to eliminate much of the guesswork and frustration experienced by professionals in the field as well as to improve the conditions under which children are socialized in formal group settings. To accomplish this, we have provided a solid foundation of child development information. In addition, we have shown how to translate that information into related skills and procedures that support children's social development.

NEW TO THIS EDITION

Instructor and student feedback have helped to shape the sixth edition of *Guiding Children's Social Development and Learning*. If you have used this book before, you will note a small, but important change in the title—the word "learning." We believe this more accurately captures the comprehensive nature of the text. Edition six has been extensively updated. Every chapter also contains new figures as well as examples and guidelines to help students better understand how to adapt the material to working with children with special needs. Although the content of Chapter 1 remains basically the same, we have included several new figures depicting key concepts. Some of these include: multicultural ideas about social competence, learning standards associated with social competence from preschool through the elementary grades, and the process by which supporting social competence proceeds from developing personal relationships to individualized intervention as needed. We have also included

stronger evidence of how social skills provide the foundations for later academic success.

Chapter 2 includes a new section on strategies for working with very young children having special needs. Chapter 3 includes a brief description of baby sign, which is increasingly used by caregivers and families.

Chapter 4 expands the discussion of self and others to include fuller discussion of the role of language, experience, and adults in children's understanding of self. A new figure has been added to illustrate the role of the adult's tone on children's development

We have streamlined the theory portions of Chapter 5 and laid it out in such a way that the developmental sequences should be easier for readers to grasp. This chapter also includes a case study example of a gifted child whose lively imagination contributes to vivid fears. In Chapter 6 we have inserted new material about the developmental aspects of stress coping in infants, toddlers, preschoolers, and elementary children as well as a new table regarding children's understanding of death. Tips for parents on talking about terrorism with children have also been added.

Chapter 7 includes a new section on supporting play of special needs children in an integrated setting. Chapter 8 has expanded its discussion to include not only friends, but peer relationships. A section on the multiple influences on children's friendship has been added with a corresponding figure to illustrate the combination of variables. Finally, there is a new table highlighting the role of friendship in the lives of children with special needs.

Chapter 9 has been shortened to facilitate student reading. It maintains its focus on organizing physical space to enhance relationships between children and adults as well as among children in the group.

Chapter 10 now includes a case study depicting one teacher's decision making regarding how to help a child with cerebral palsy become more fully integrated in the classroom community through compliance with certain classroom rules. Within Chapter 11 we have created a new section describing guidance strategies for children with disabilities. Students are encouraged to consider the whole child as they accommodate children's special needs using strategies outlined throughout the text.

New research on gender differences relative to childhood aggression has been added to Chapter 12. Also, we have extensively reworked the sections on physical punishment to take into account new legislation in the states and to make it clearer to readers why spanking is not a viable option for early childhood professionals.

Chapter 13 extends the discussion of the variables impacting children's prosocial behavior to include social experiences. The influence of the adult on prosocial behavior has also been expanded. In Chapter 14, there is added content about inclusion of children with special needs into group settings with typically developing children as well as more information about temperament and individuality. The priority principles in Chapter 15 have been reduced from seven to six and are now presented in a chart. We have also included more material on child abuse and neglect and have expanded the section on ethical judgments with family members. The portion of this chapter devoted to child abuse and neglect has also been expanded in accordance with the most recent NCANDS findings.

The online resource that supports better understanding of concepts and skills presented in *Guiding Children's Social Development and Learning* has been completely updated. All exercises have been field tested and revised in accordance with student learning outcomes.

Lists of children's literature, adult books, and relevant Web sites for each chapter have been revised and updated as online resources for instructor and reader use.

These revisions are meant to address current issues in child development and early intervention, and further aid in student comprehension. They should better prepare students to face the realities of working with children on a day-to-day basis.

PRESENTATION

Together, the chapters in this book comprise a thorough picture of children's social development and behavior, and the classroom practices professionals use to enhance children's social competence. We have been careful to include traditional areas of study such as self-esteem, aggression, routines, rules, and consequences.

We also have addressed more current topics of interest such as infant communication, stress, friendship, bullying, and prosocial behavior. Considered individually, each chapter offers an in-depth literature review in which findings from many fields have been integrated (psychology, physiology, education, medicine, sociology, family and consumer sciences, personnel management, interior design).

Thus, even within the confines of a single subject, there is breadth.

The sequence of chapters also has been thoughtfully planned so that each serves as a foundation for the next—simple concepts and/or skills precede more complex ones; chapters that focus on relationship enhancement and strategies for enhancing children social skills come before those that discuss behavior management and intensive interventions for challenging behaviors

Throughout the text, we have tried to establish a lucid, straightforward writing style, which we hope makes the book easy to read and interesting. Although many research findings have been cited, we have purposely used parenthetical notation rather than constantly referring to the researchers by name. We want students to remember the concepts those findings represent rather than to simply memorize names and dates.

In addition, we have made liberal use of real-life examples to illustrate concepts and related skills. This is to assist students in making the connection between what they read and "flesh-and blood" children. Furthermore, we have described many different settings in which adults find themselves working with children so that, regardless of their professional intents, students can relate to what we have written. Another reason for multiple-setting scenarios is to demonstrate that the content is not situation bound and that the knowledge and skills can be generalized from one setting to another.

Our scope of study encompasses the social development of children from birth to 12 years of age. We have targeted this period of childhood because it is during the formative years that the foundation for all socialization takes place. Furthermore, the skills taught have been specially designed to take into account the cognitive structures and social abilities particular to children of this age. Because children live and develop within the context of a family, a community, a nation, and a world, they are constantly influenced by, and in turn affect, the people and events around them. Thus, our perspective is an ecological one in which children are viewed as dynamic, ever-changing beings in an equally dynamic, ever-changing context. This ecological perspective is incorporated into each chapter in the literature review and in many of the examples provided.

Additionally, in most chapters, at least one and sometimes more of the discussion questions raise these issues for students to think about. It has been our experience that students learn professional behavior best when they are given clear, succinct directions for how to carry out a procedure. Defining a procedure, offering examples, and giving a rationale for its use are necessary, but not sufficient. Thus, our approach to skill training is to point out to the student research-based strategies related to chapter content. We then break those strategies down into a series of discrete, observable skills that students can implement. We have been direct, rather than circumspect, in articulating the specific steps involved.

This forthrightness should not be taken to imply that our directions are in stone or that there is no room for students to use the skills creatively. Rather, we anticipate that students will internalize and modify skills according to their own needs, personality, interaction style, and circumstance once they have learned them. We recognize that an important component of using skills correctly is determining which alternatives from the entire available array are best suited for a given situation. Hence, knowing when to use a particular skill and when to refrain from using it is as important as knowing how to use it. For this reason, we discuss these issues throughout each chapter, both in the body of the text and in the "pitfalls to avoid" section at the end. We also have incorporated specific guidelines for how the skills can be adapted for use with youngsters of varying ages and differing cultural backgrounds. Finally, all of Chapter 15 is devoted to various aspects of decision-making.

LEARNING AIDS

This book incorporates a number of features aimed at enhancing student learning. Each chapter is introduced by a statement of objectives, which tells students what they should know on completion of that segment of the book. This alerts them to the primary foci of that chapter. All chapters open with a discussion of theory and research related to a particular social development topic. Implications of the research for both children and adults also are described. A major portion of each chapter is devoted to presenting the professional skills relevant to the topic under discussion.

Each skill is broken down into a series of observable behaviors that students can learn and instructors can evaluate directly. This section also makes extensive use of examples to further illustrate the skills under consideration. Strategies for use with children as well as family communication techniques are offered. Near the end of each chapter is a description of pitfalls or common mistakes students make when first learning to use the skills. Suggestions for how to avoid these difficulties are provided.

All chapters include a summary that gives a brief overview of the material presented. This is a useful synopsis for student review of important concepts.

An added feature of each chapter is a listing of topics for discussion. These are thought-provoking questions aimed at helping students synthesize and apply, through conversations with classmates, what they have read. Each chapter concludes with a suggested list of field assignments students may use to practice and perfect the skills described. These assignments may be carried out independently or under the direction of the instructor.

SUPPLEMENTARY MATERIALS

Instructor's e.Resource CD-ROM   The new e.Resource component provides instructors with all the tools they need in one convenient CD-ROM. Instructors will find that this resource provides them with a turnkey solution to help them teach by making available PowerPoint® slides for each chapter, a Computerized Test Bank, and an electronic version of the Instructor's Manual.

The Instructor's Manual found on the e.Resource CD is comprehensive and further supplements the textbook. In it, we describe how to organize a course using the textbook; how to search out, select, and maintain appropriate field placements for students; how to model skills for students to imitate; and how to provide feedback to students assigned to field placements. In addition, we have included a series of rehearsal exercises, which are role-play activities meant to be carried out in class. They are aimed at acquainting students with how to use particular skills prior to implementing them with children and at clarifying basic concepts as they emerge during discussion or interaction. There are at least five overhead guides per chapter to help instructor's highlight key lecture topics or to enhance the hands-on exercises instructors may carry out in class. A third section of the instructor's manual provides sample field assignments that can be for student use.

The field assignments enable students to practice skills presented in each chapter of *Guiding Children's Social Development and Learning,* Sixth Edition, in their field placement or practicum setting. Finally, the instructor's manual contains a criterion-referenced observational tool, the PSI (Professional Skills Inventory). This is a unique feature of our instructional package. It can be used by instructors and/or practitioners to evaluate the degree to which students demonstrate the skills taught.

The Computerized Test Bank, included on the e.Resource CD, consists of multiple-choice, true/false, short answer, and essay questions for each chapter.

Professional Enhancement Text A new supplement to accompany this text is the Guidance and Behavior Management Professional Enhancement handbook for students. This resource, which is part of Delmar Cengage Learning's Early Childhood Education Professional Enhancement series, focuses on key topics of interest for future early childhood directors, teachers, and caregivers. Becoming a teacher is a process of continuing to grow, learn, reflect, and discover through experience. The Professional Enhancement text helps tomorrow's teachers along their way. Students will keep this informational supplement and use it for years to come in their early childhood practices.

In addition to the textbook, we have designed an online resource to help students master the skills presented in the textbook and an instructor's manual for the teacher.

The **Online Companion**™ is an online study guide available to help students understand and master the skills presented in the textbook. The companion includes modules that correspond to each chapter in the textbook. Every module contains performance objectives, a rationale for the skills, an outline of key points regarding skill performance, a review of key terms, and a series of exercises focused on skill development.

A list of books and Web sites that reflect the content of the chapter is provided for each module as well. The online study guide enables students to practice and apply, in both hypothetical and real

situations, skills they have learned. Skills are broken down into manageable segments and are presented in a sequence ranging from simple to more complex.

In addition, students can gauge their own progress via an answer key. All of these features increase students' ability to incorporate the skills into their professional behavior. Note that a prototype of the material contained in the Online Companion™ was extensively field tested with college students and practitioners (Kostelnik, 1983; Peters & Kostelnik, 1981). Data from those studies showed that students who complete the activities significantly increase their ability to use the skills and to maintain them over time. Moreover, many of the items that have been included in this online study guide are ones that students have recommended. The terms covered in the online study guide are set in boldface throughout the textbook. The Online Companion™ icon appears at the end of each chapter, to prompt you to go online and take advantage of the many features provided.

The Online Companion™ can be found at www. EarlyChildEd.delmar.com.

TO THE STUDENT

This book will give you a foundation of knowledge and skills necessary for guiding children's social development and behavior in professional practice. We hope it will contribute to your enthusiasm about the field and to your confidence in working with young children and their families. Although what you read here will not encompass everything you will need to know, it will serve as a secure base from which you can begin to develop your own professional style. You will have the advantage of learning, in one course, information and strategies that otherwise might take many years to discover. Through examples, you will be able to accumulate a background of experience that you may not yet have had a chance to develop or learn by other means.

Finally, you will be reading a book authored by people with extensive practical experience in working with children, engaging in research, and teaching this content to learners much like yourselves. As a result, we are well aware of the issues related to children's social development that are important to students, and we have focused on those. We also have anticipated some of the questions you might ask and some of the difficulties you might encounter in working with this material. Consequently, we have made a conscious effort to discuss these in relevant places throughout the book.

HINTS FOR USING THE MATERIALS

1. Read each chapter of the textbook carefully. Plan to read them more than once. Use the first reading to gain a broad grasp of the subject matter; then, read a second time, paying particular attention to the sequence of development presented. Identify major concepts regarding adult behavior and focus on the actual procedures related to each skill. Use subsequent readings to recall the material in more detail.
2. Jot notes in the margin and underline points you wish to remember.
3. Go beyond simply memorizing terminology. Concentrate on how you might recognize the concepts you are studying in real children's behavior and how you might apply this knowledge in your interactions with children. Not only will this expand your understanding of the material, but also both levels of information are likely to appear on quizzes and exams.
4. Ask questions. Share with classmates and the instructor your experiences in using the material. Participate fully in class discussions and role-play exercises.
5. Try out what you are learning with children. If you are in a field placement, are volunteering, or are employed in a program, take full advantage of that opportunity. Do not hesitate to practice your skills simply because they are new to you and you are not sure how well you will perform them. Persist in spite of your awkwardness or mistakes, and make note of what you might do to improve. Focus on your successes and your increasing skill, not just on things that don't go perfectly. Allow yourself to enjoy the children even as you are learning from them.

ACKNOWLEDGMENTS AND THANKS

We thank the following persons for their contributions to our work: Louise F. Guerney, professor emeritus, The Pennsylvania State University; and Steven J. Danish, Commonwealth University of Virginia, were original sources of information regarding the philosophy and skills presented here. Laura C. Stein, coauthor and master teacher of children and students at Michigan State University, worked hand-in-hand with us to develop the first edition of this book and the several editions that followed. We owe her much for her insights and for helping our ideas come alive on the page. Her influence continues. We wish to thank Sara Mietzner, who helped us develop book lists for children and adults for the Web site and student guide. The following reviewers provided valuable feedback throughout the revision process for this edition:

Carolyn Bush, MA, Ed
Hazard Community and Technical College
Kentucky

Amy Huffman, BS, MA,
Guilford Technical Community College
North Carolina

Judith A. Lindman, BS, MEd
Rochester Community & Technical College
Minnesota

Mabel T. Himel, EdD
University of Memphis
Tennessee

Nancy Baptiste, EdD
New Mexico State University
New Mexico

Kathleen E. Fite, MEd, EdD
Texas State University
Texas

Ellen Lynch, MEd, EdD
University of Cincinnati
Ohio

Finally, over the years, we have worked with many students whose enthusiasm and excitement have invigorated us. Simultaneously, we have been privileged to know hundreds of children during their formative years. From them we have gained insight and the motivation to pursue this project. We dedicate this book to them.

Chapter 1

MAKING A DIFFERENCE IN CHILDREN'S LIVES

OBJECTIVES

On completion of this chapter, you should be able to describe:

- Social competence and how it affects children's lives.

- How child development and learning influence children's social competence.

- The contexts within which children develop socially.

- Differences between laypersons and early childhood professionals in promoting children's social competence.

- Your role in supporting children's social competence.

Walk into any early childhood program and you might hear children singing this song to the tune of "Did You Ever See a Lassie?"

> The more we get together,
> together, together.
> The more we get together,
> the happier we'll be.

This classic song highlights the important fact that children are social beings. They need productive relationships with other people to lead happy, satisfying lives.

Think about the aspects of everyday living that are most important to you—family life, time with friends, school, work, and play. They all involve human relationships. In fact, from the moment we are born, we spend a lifetime actively engaged with others. Through social interactions we gain knowledge of who we are and how the world works. We develop social skills and become familiar with the expectations and values of the society in which we live. Although people never stop learning, the social experiences we have in childhood provide the foundation on which all future human relations are developed.

CHILDREN IN THE SOCIAL WORLD

The social environment is complicated. There is a lot to know and many things you must be able to do to function successfully in society. Take the simple act of greeting someone you meet. To interact effectively, you need to know a variety of scripts and what physical actions others will interpret as friendly. You have to make judgments about what is polite or impolite based on how well you know the person, that person's status, your status, the time, the place, and the culture in which you are operating. For instance, you will probably address someone you know well differently from someone you are meeting for the first time. Likewise, you will adopt a very different manner greeting someone at a football game than you might use greeting that same person at a funeral. Although this seems like common sense to adults, children are new to the world and many of the social understandings and behaviors we take for granted are things children are just learning.

CHILDREN'S SOCIAL KNOWLEDGE AND SKILLS

Imagine that you are working with children in a child care setting or elementary classroom. You observe the following behaviors among three six-year-olds in your group: Dennis, Rosalie, and Sarah Jo.

Dennis is an active child. He has strong reactions to the people and things around him. He is imaginative, with many ideas for how to play. In an effort to translate his ideas into action, Dennis spends a lot of time telling the other children what to do and what to say. When peers suggest alternate play themes or strategies, Dennis tends to resist their ideas and yell to make things go his way. When other children ask if they can play with something he is using, Dennis often answers, "No." If they persist, it is not unusual for him to push or hit to keep things for himself.

Rosalie is a quiet child who seldom misbehaves. Typically, she wanders from one activity to the next without talking to the other children. Rosalie responds when spoken to, but rarely initiates social interactions with peers or adults. She cannot name anyone in the group who is her friend and no other children identify her as a favorite playmate. Although children do not actively reject her, they have come to ignore her and seldom include her in their activities. Most days, Rosalie is a solitary figure in the room.

Sarah Jo is keenly interested in the other children and often invites them to interact with her. Frequently she is willing to try games or play in ways proposed by peers, yet she also expresses ideas of her own. Sarah Jo shares easily and can usually figure out how to keep the play going. Although she has her ups and downs, she is generally cheerful. Other children seek her out as a playmate and notice when Sarah Jo is absent from the group.

As you can see, each of these children is exhibiting a variety of social behaviors. Unfortunately, Dennis and Rosalie are displaying certain interaction patterns that are not serving them well. In fact, if they maintain these patterns over time, their prospects for life success will be hampered (Goleman, 2006). On the other hand, Sarah Jo has skills that predict a positive future.

As an early childhood professional, you could help Dennis and Rosalie develop better ways of getting along with others. You could also support Sarah Jo in expanding her skills. In doing these things you would be contributing to each child's social competence.

SOCIAL COMPETENCE

Social competence is the ability to integrate thinking, feeling, and behaving to achieve interpersonal goals and social outcomes that are valued within a given context and culture (Dundee University, 1999;

Early childhood professionals should observe the behavior of the children they are working with to evaluate the social skills they are exhibiting. What social behaviors are being exhibited by these children?

McCay & Keyes, 2002). Typical categories of behavior associated with social competence include:

- social values
- personal identity
- interpersonal skills
- self-regulation
- planning, organizing, and decision making
- cultural competence

This array of behaviors is depicted in more detail in Figure 1-1. As you can tell by examining the figure,

social competence encompasses a broad range of values, attitudes, knowledge, and skills involving both self and others.

Definitions of social competence vary from one society to another. Certain qualities may be emphasized more or less (e.g., cooperation versus independence), and the same value may be demonstrated through different behaviors in different groups (e.g., words and actions that constitute **respect**). Yet, many of the behaviors identified in Figure 1-1 are commonly regarded as important. Check this out

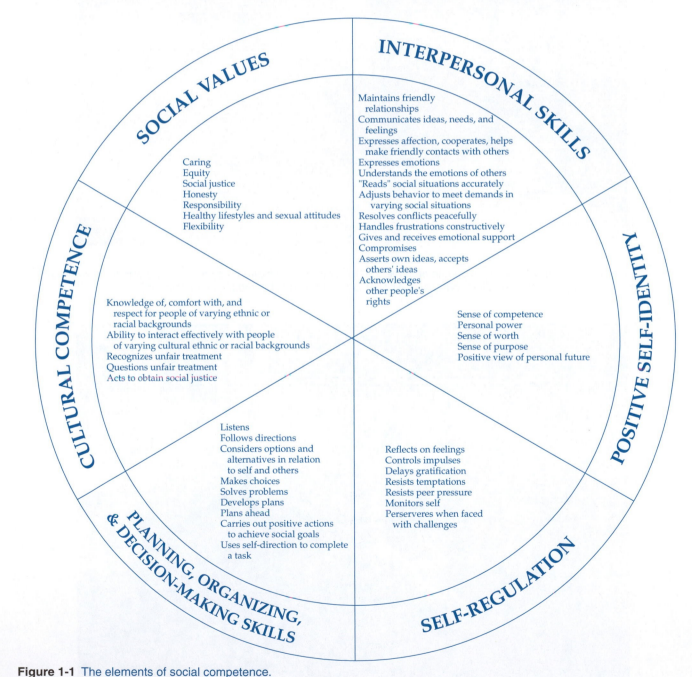

Figure 1-1 The elements of social competence.

yourself. Compare Figure 1-1 to the depiction of social competence derived from a Sioux Nation orientation to life illustrated in Figure 1-2. The latter is presented visually as a wheel with four spokes that work together to keep the wheel strong, resulting in a socially competent person (Brendtro, Brokenleg & Van Bockern, 1992). A third version of social competence, describing Russian ideals, is offered in Discussion Question 2 at the end of this chapter. Again, you will see many overlapping elements with those identified in Figure 1-1.

In the United States, many people tend to view children as more socially competent when they are responsible rather than irresponsible; independent versus suggestible; friendly, not hostile; cooperative instead of resistive; purposeful rather than aimless; and self-controlled, not impulsive (Baumrind, 1995;

Landy, 2002). Based on this perspective, Art, who notices that Gary is unhappy and attempts to comfort him, is more socially competent than Ralph, who walks by unaware of Gary's distress. Dinah, who often blurts out whatever comes to mind the instant it occurs to her, is less socially competent than if she were able to wait without interrupting. When Chip uses verbal reasoning to persuade his friends to give him a turn with a video game, he is demonstrating more social competence than a classmate who whines or relies on physical force to make his point. Diane McClellan and Lillian Katz (2001) have created a profile of the socially competent child. This profile is presented in Figure 1-3 and will give you a sense of what social competence looks like in action.

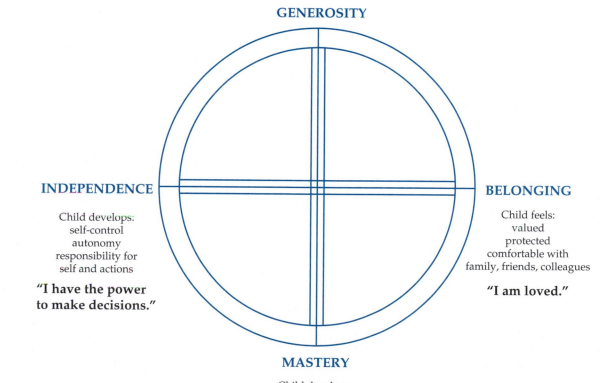

"I have a purpose."

Child develops:
empathy
desire to help others
desire to share time, work, play and resources

GENEROSITY

INDEPENDENCE

Child develops:
self-control
autonomy
responsibility for
self and actions

**"I have the power
to make decisions."**

BELONGING

Child feels:
valued
protected
comfortable with
family, friends, colleagues

"I am loved."

MASTERY

Child develops:
interest in seeking new skills and knowledge
willingness to fail
sense of competence

"I can succeed."

Figure 1-2 The depiction of social competence derived from a Sioux Nation orientation.

INDIVIDUAL ATTRIBUTES

The child

1. is usually in a positive mood
2. is not excessively dependent on the teacher
3. usually comes to the program willingly
4. usually copes with rebuffs adequately
5. shows the capacity to empathize
6. has positive relationships with one or two peers; shows the capacity to really care about them and misses them if they are absent
7. displays a capacity for humor
8. does not seem to be acutely lonely

SOCIAL SKILLS

The child usually

1. approaches others positively
2. expresses wishes and preferences clearly; gives reasons for actions and positions
3. asserts own rights and needs appropriately
4. is not easily intimidated by bullies
5. expresses frustration and anger effectively and without escalating disagreements or harming others
6. gains access to ongoing groups at play and work

7. enters ongoing discussions; makes relevant contributions to ongoing activities
8. takes turns fairly easily
9. shows interest in others; exchanges information with and requests information from others appropriately
10. negotiates and compromises with others appropriately
11. does not draw inappropriate attention to self or disrupt the play or work of others
12. accepts and enjoys peers and adults of ethnic groups other than his or her own
13. interacts nonverbally with other children using smiles, waves, nods, etc.

PEER RELATIONSHIPS

The child is

1. usually accepted rather than neglected or rejected by other children
2. sometimes invited by other children to join them in play, friendship, and work
3. named by other children as someone they are friends with or like to play and work with

Figure 1-3 Observable behaviors of socially competent children.

Source: Reprinted with permission from *Assessing Young Children's Social Competence*, by D. McClellan and L. Katz, 2001, ERIC Clearinghouse on Elementary and Early Childhood Education, Champaign, IL. (ERIC Document Reproduction Service No. ED450953.)

Note that the words *usually, frequently,* and *sometimes* best describe socially competent children's behavior. Children will not always be in a positive mood nor will they always experience success in asserting their rights appropriately. "Childhood is, by definition, a time for learning and testing many ways of responding to social situations" (Katz & McClellan, 1997, p. 104). Thus, we can assume that all children will explore the social environment with differing degrees of success from one situation to the next. Over time, however, children develop patterns of behavior that can be described as more or less competent. Such outcomes have a powerful influence on children's lives.

The Benefits of Being Socially Competent

. . . the single best childhood predictor of adult adaptation is not IQ nor school grades, but rather the adequacy with which a child gets along with others.

Children who are generally disliked, who are aggressive and disruptive, who are unable to sustain close relationships with others . . . are seriously "at risk."

Willard Hartup (childhood researcher, 1992)

Social competence is not a luxury. It makes a tremendous difference in how children feel about themselves and in how others perceive them. Research tells us that socially competent children are happier than their less competent peers. They are more successful in their interactions with others, more popular, and more satisfied with life. In addition, children's social relations have been linked to academic achievement, with positive social skills being associated with greater success in school (NASP, 2002). See Figure 1-4.

As a result of these favorable outcomes, socially competent children tend to see themselves as worthwhile human beings who can make a difference in the world. Other people perceive them as desirable

Socially competent children are more successful in their interactions with others.

companions and competent members of society. The same cannot be said for children whose social competence is poor. Youngsters unable to function successfully in the social world often experience anguish and loneliness, even in the early years. They frequently are rejected by peers, suffer low self-esteem, and do more poorly in their studies (Crockenburg, Jackson, & Langrock, 1996; NASP, 2002). To make matters worse, socially incompetent children are at risk of continuing these problematic behavior patterns as they mature (Ladd, 2000; Goleman, 2006).

Whether children eventually become more or less socially competent is influenced by many factors, including child development, childhood learning, and the contexts in which children function.

DEVELOPMENT AND SOCIAL COMPETENCE

The best thing about the future is that it comes one day at a time.

Abraham Lincoln (U.S. president, 1809–1865)

As children mature, developmental changes gradually occur that increase their social capacities.

Such changes are governed by certain developmental principles that help us recognize commonalities among children and characteristics typical within age ranges. These principles remind us that children's social development is a complicated business, requiring the support of knowledgeable adults who appreciate the unique qualities of the children they serve.

All Development Is Interrelated

All threads of development (social, emotional, cognitive, language, and physical) interweave and exist simultaneously. No aspect of development is more important than another, nor can any single thread exist independent of the rest. The truth of this principle is illustrated as children try to make friends. Their ability to establish relations with peers is dependent on a whole host of developmental skills and understandings.

Social—negotiating the rules of a game; waiting to take a turn; working out who will go first.

Emotional—having confidence to approach another child; responding with enthusiasm when invited to play by a peer; expressing empathy toward another child.

Cognitive—remembering another child's name; developing alternate strategies for how to solve conflicts that arise during play; knowing which scripts fit which social situations.

Language—using words to greet another child or to describe how a game could be played; responding with appropriate comments to questions from a potential friend.

Physical—making room for a new player; having the motor skills necessary to play a video game, a game of chase, or a game of catch with a potential friend.

Recognizing that all development is inter-related will enable you to better appreciate the complex social behaviors children are striving to master. It will also help you identify opportunities to guide children's social development throughout the day. Such chances come up as children play in

---

"LEARNING IS A SOCIAL PROCESS"

Academic success in the early school years is based on social and emotional skills. Young children can't learn to read, do their sums or solve a science problem if they have difficulty getting along with others and controlling their emotions, if they are impulsive, and if they have no idea about how to consider options, carry out a plan, or get help.

Students who demonstrate strong social and emotional skills also tend to exhibit:

- greater academic motivation
- more positive attitudes toward school
- fewer absences
- more classroom participation
- higher math achievement
- higher language arts achievement
- higher social studies achievement
- higher grades
- fewer suspensions
- less tendency to drop out in high school

Figure 1-4 Social competence contributes to academic success.

Source: Zins, J., Bloodworth, M., Weissberg, R. & Walberg, H. (2004). "The scientific base linking social and emotional learning to school success." In J. Zins, R. Weissberg, M. Wang, & H. J. Walberg (Eds.), *Building academic success on social and emotional learning: What does the research say?* New York: Teachers College Press, Columbia University (pp. 1–22).

the housekeeping area, as children discuss rules for building with blocks, as they proceed through the steps in a science experiment, or as they work out a math problem in a group. These opportunities can occur indoors, outside, at the lunch table, in the gym, on the bus, during a field trip, or at a home visit. Social development is happening all the time and everywhere children are.

There Is an Orderly Sequence to Social Development

Try putting these developmental milestones related to self-awareness in the order in which they tend to appear during childhood:

- Children define themselves by comparing them-selves to others. (I ride bikes better than Susan. I am shorter than Mark.)
- Children define themselves based on their per-sonality traits. (I am honest. I am fun to be with.)
- Children define themselves based on what they look like. (I am a boy. I have brown eyes.)

What did you decide? In their proper order, benchmarks such as these illustrate the principle of developmental sequence.

Social development proceeds in a stepwise fash-ion and is relatively predictable. Scientists world-wide have identified typical sequences of behavior or understanding related to various aspects of social development and social competence (Berk, 2006; Case & Okamoto, 1996). For instance, children de-velop their concept of self over several years.

Preschoolers tend to focus primarily on physical traits. As they grow older, children gradually incor-porate comparisons into their definition of self. By age 8 or 9 children become more conscious of the internal characteristics that comprise their personal-ity. Although children spend differing amounts of time on each step, and sometimes skip steps alto-gether, self-awareness seems to progress in roughly the same order for everyone.

There are developmental sequences for many aspects of social competence—self-regulation, empathy, prosocial behavior, moral understanding, ideas about friendship, and so forth. As you learn these sequences you will gain insights into what comes first, second, and third in social maturation. Such knowledge will help you to determine reasonable expectations for in-dividual children and decide what new understand-ings or behaviors might logically expand children's current levels of functioning. For example, knowing that three- and four-year olds are becoming aware of the physical traits that characterize who they are, you might plan classroom activities such as self-portraits or body tracings to enhance their self-awareness. On the other hand, you might ask early elementary-aged children, whose physical sense of self is more established, to tell or write stories focused on the personal qualities they value in themselves, such as honesty or being a good friend.

Rates of Development Vary Among Children

Darlene is 4 years old; so is Emma. Darlene was walking at 9 months and could use whole phrases to describe her feelings by age 2. She has numerous strategies for getting what she wants, including taking turns and making plans for the order in which children will get to use a favored toy. Emma did not walk until she was 14 months old and only began using multiword sentences around age 3. Her approaches to getting something she wants include asking a child who has it if she can have it next or getting the teacher to help her find another one like it. Darlene and Emma are alike in many ways, but they are different from one another as well. Both children are developing in a typical manner.

As illustrated by Darlene and Emma, all children develop according to their own timetable. No two children are exactly alike. Although the principle of orderly sequences still applies, the pace at which individuals go through the various sequences differs.

This explains why Darlene could express her feelings in words by age 2 and Emma accomplished the same skill several months later. Both children are exhibiting typical development, but the timing is different.

Based on the principle of varying rates, you can presume that children the same age will exhibit a wide range of social abilities. Some will be in the early developmental phases of a particular skill and others will be further along in the sequence. These variations are not a question of bad or good, worse or better, but simply typical differences in children's social development. Understanding this will help you to be more patient with children and more realistic in what you expect of them.

There Are Optimal Periods of Social Development

There are certain moments in childhood when the door opens and lets the future in.

Graham Greene (novelist, 1904–1991)

Certain times in people's lives provide critical foundations for future development (Bailey, 2002;

Johnson et al., 1997). It is during these periods that children are developmentally primed to acquire new understandings and skills. Conversely, if children are denied the kinds of experiences that will enhance development during this time, it may be harder for them to acquire certain skills or abilities later on. This is the principle of optimal periods of development.

Between the ages of birth and 12 years, children are eager, motivated social learners. They want to connect—to become socially engaged. Concurrently, negative behavior patterns are not so entrenched that they cannot be changed. This makes the childhood years an ideal time for enhancing many essential attitudes and behaviors related to social competence. Some of these include:

- trust
- self-awareness and self-esteem
- interpersonal communication skills
- prosocial attitudes and behaviors
- friendship dispositions and skills
- problem-solving strategies
- coping skills
- self-discipline and self-regulation

If the preceding developmental tasks are ignored, it is harder for children to become socially adept as adolescents or adults. The principle of optimal periods therefore compels us to focus on children's social development beginning when they are babies and well into the second decade of life.

Social Development Has Cumulative and Delayed Effects

An experience that has a minimal effect on a child's development if it occurs once in a while may have a positive or harmful influence if it happens repeatedly over a long period of time (Katz & Chard, 2000). This is the principle of cumulative effects. For instance, being the target of occasional criticism is not likely to cause permanent damage to children's self-esteem; however, youngsters who are subjected to steady fault finding are likely to develop lasting feelings of inferiority and pessimism (Seligman, 1995). On the other hand, reasoning with a child only once will not have a lasting impact on that child. However, adults who make a habit of reasoning with children will gradually see those children become better able to reason for themselves.

In addition to these accumulated impacts, developmental outcomes may be delayed. That is, some early experiences influence children's functioning in ways that only appear much later in life (Wieder & Greenspan, 1993). For instance, children's development of self-regulation takes years to accomplish. The delayed nature of this process may prompt adults to wonder if their early efforts at reasoning with children will ever yield positive results. However, research shows that children do eventually become better able to monitor their behavior without constant supervision when adults consistently explain their point of view while also considering the child's perspective (Shaffer & Kipp, 2006). These strategies must be used for a long time before children can reason on their own.

Knowing the principle of cumulative and delayed effects will help you to consider the long-range implications of your efforts to guide children's social development and behavior. As a result there will be times when you reject a quick solution because it could undermine your long-term goals. For instance, even though it is faster to simply tell children "No," when they disobey, if you want children to develop self regulation, you will take the time to talk to them about their actions. In doing so, both the cumulative and delayed effects of reasoning support children's eventual development of social competence.

As you can see, development plays a significant role in the extent to which children gain social competence. Understanding developmental principles will influence your interpretations of child behavior as well as your professional practices. Childhood learning is another factor to consider.

LEARNING AND SOCIAL COMPETENCE

Cooperation, generosity, loyalty and honesty are not inborn. They must be passed on to the child by older people, whether they are parents, other adults or older youngsters.

Urie Bronfenbrenner (learning theorist, 1998)

Some of the social learning we pass on to children includes saying, "Excuse me" when they bump into someone, crossing streets at the corner, and deriving pleasure from sharing with a friend. We communicate such lessons through our words and our deeds. How well children learn these lessons is governed by several principles.

Children Are Active Social Learners
Consider the following Chinese proverb:

> *I hear, and I forget,*
> *I see, and I remember,*
> *I do, and I understand.*

This saying captures a central truth about childhood learning: Children are doers. They do not wait passively for others to load them up with information. Children have active bodies and minds, which they use to make sense of social experiences everywhere they go. They do this by observing, acting on objects, and interacting with other people (Bredekamp & Copple, 1997). As a result of their experiences, children form hypotheses about how the social world works. (For instance, Cory might think, "If I say 'Please' Mohammed will give me the scissors right now.") Sometimes children's ideas are confirmed (Mohammed says, "Okay"). Sometimes children encounter evidence that is contrary to what they believe (Mohammed says "No" because he still needs the scissors). By observing, experimenting, and reflecting on what happens, children gradually make adjustments in their thinking (Cory decides, "I will have to wait for the scissors, but I'll get them next"). Through hundreds of experiences like these, children construct ideas about codes of behavior to follow and strategies to use (Piaget, 1962; Vygotsky, 1978).

Because children are active learners, they need many opportunities to experience the social world firsthand. For instance, children become more skillful at sharing when they practice sharing with others in their daily encounters, rather than simply hearing or talking about sharing. Figuring out how to divide the crackers at snack, how two people can use the computer together, or how to fit an extra person into a game are tangible problems children can solve on their own or with support from you. Such natural opportunities for social learning become teachable moments, in which children are motivated to learn new strategies to achieve their aims. A typical teachable moment occurs when Celia wants to jump rope with a group of children already jumping. Her teacher uses this chance to help Celia figure out words she might use to approach the other children. On-the-spot mini-lessons like these are powerful. Children have immediate opportunities to practice relevant new skills as well as get feedback on the strategies they use. As you guide children's social development and behavior,

Children benefit from having many opportunities to interact with minimal adult intervention.

you will need to look for teachable moments such as these and take advantage of the learning opportunities they offer.

Children Have Multiple Ways of Learning About the Social World

Although all children are active learners, there are many ways in which they perceive, act on, and process social information. Consider the following examples:

> Gary has a real feel for music and uses that medium as a way to express his feelings. When a problem comes up, he likes to figure it out on his own.
>
> Samantha has a way with words. It's easy for her to communicate needs and feelings to others verbally. In problem situations, she prefers strategizing with a friend.

Gary and Samantha are demonstrating different combinations of knowing and learning. Howard Gardner has coined the phrase **multiple intelligences** to describe these multilearning capabilities. His research suggests that there are at least eight ways of learning (Gardner, 2003):

Intrapersonal: Children learn on their own through self-paced activities.

Interpersonal: Children learn through relating to others and collaborating.

Kinesthetic: Children learn through touch and movement.

Linguistic: Children learn by seeing, saying, and using language.

Logical-mathematical: Children learn by looking for patterns and relationships among objects and events.

Musical: Children learn through rhythm and melody.

Naturalist: Children learn through observations and interactions with plants and animals.

Spatial: Children learn through visualizing something in their mind's eye and then translating what they see in some tangible way.

All children have all these intelligences, but each type is not developed equally in each child. Thus children learn best when they have access to learning opportunities that match the learning modes they favor. Because you cannot always be sure which manner of learning suits an individual child best, children benefit when you use a variety of modes in your social teaching. For instance, assume you want children to learn about helping. Some children may find it useful to:

- carry out a classroom job on their own or read a book to themselves about helpful people. (intrapersonal)
- interact with another child to carry out a classroom job. (interpersonal)
- rehearse a helpful act before trying it out for real. (kinesthetic)
- talk about helpful actions they observed or carried out. (linguistic)
- consider patterns that characterize helpful behaviors. (logical-mathematical)
- sing or make up a catchy song about helping. (musical)
- help to care for a pet in the classroom. (naturalist)
- reflect on a helpful act they have seen or heard about (spatial).

Most children combine such experiences, extracting important information from the ones that match their preferred ways of learning. As you guide children's social development you will have to be sensitive to these different learning styles and make use of strategies that address each of them.

Social Competence Involves Continuous Challenge and Mastery

Children enjoy the challenge of learning what they nearly understand, but do not quite grasp, and of trying things they can almost do, but not quite do on their own. This means they benefit from tackling concepts and skills just slightly beyond their current levels of proficiency and from working at them until they achieve greater competence (Bodrova & Leong, 1996). At the same time, research shows that children need to successfully negotiate learning tasks most of the time if they are to remain motivated to learn. Youngsters who are overwhelmed will fail. If failure becomes routine, most children will simply stop trying (Bredekamp & Copple, 1997). Thus, positive social learning is most likely to occur when children feel both stimulated and successful. Knowing this, your role is to monitor social situations, challenge children to stretch their understandings, support children as they attempt new social skills, and help children figure out more successful approaches. At times, peers may provide these supports instead.

As children become more adept, you will gradually withdraw from the scene, allowing them to pursue mastery on their own.

Two-year-old Callie wants more snack, but does not know how to ask for it—this example can be used to illustrate the process of challenge and mastery. Some on-the-spot coaching by you or a more knowledgeable peer could facilitate Callie's learning. Such coaching might involve suggesting a simple script for Callie to use to get her peers to pass the cracker basket. If your words are too complex or too abstract, Callie will not absorb the lesson. If the script is just slightly more involved than Callie is used to, however, she may stretch her thinking to encompass the new words. Chances are, Callie will not learn the new script in a single episode, but this interaction may prompt her to try the new script in a variety of situations, practicing until she eventually gains mastery without prompting from someone else. In doing this, she will actually move to a higher order of social learning.

Social Learning Takes Time

There is more to life than simply increasing its speed.

Mahatma Gandhi (political and spiritual leader, 1869–1948)

Social learning is a gradual process. Although children are social beings at birth, they are not born socially competent. Nor do they attain mature levels of competence quickly. Thus, when they come to preschool, kindergarten, or even fifth grade, youngsters are not yet socially mature. Throughout the preschool and elementary years, children spend much of their time exploring social ideas, experimenting with various strategies, and seeking clues about what works in the social world and what does not. This social learning cannot be unduly hurried. Youngsters need numerous opportunities to engage in social interactions to perfect their concepts and skills. This is true for typically developing children as well as for children with special needs. While all young children need time and guidance to develop social skills, some children require extra help in this regard. Consider this as you think about Patrick who is described in Figure 1-5.

As an early childhood professional, you have the responsibility to see that children, including youngsters like Patrick, get the time and opportunity to develop their social skills. In line with this task, you will need to exercise patience and provide support

MEET PATRICK

Four-year-old Patrick is enrolled in Head Start. He likes to build with blocks, create things at the art table, ride trikes on the playground and jump on the trampoline at home. He is a high-energy child with a charming smile. Patrick is also very curious. However, his attention moves from one thing to the next quickly and he is easily distracted. It is hard for Patrick to listen to a story the whole way through, to pay attention when an adult is giving directions, to sit in his chair at snack, or to follow along when someone is explaining what will happen next. Although most young children fidget and squirm sometimes, Patrick is in perpetual motion most of the time. His impulsivity is very high and his ability to deal with frustration is extremely low. These behaviors contribute to poor social relations with peers. Recently, Patrick's parents, caregiver, and pediatrician have been exploring the idea that Patrick may have ADHD.

Children with ADHD (attention-deficit hyperactive disorder) are hyper alert, responding to everything they see or hear. This leads to impulsiveness and the inability to attend to any one thing very long. These behaviors are present at levels much higher than expected for the child's developmental stage and actually interfere with the child's daily functioning. ADHD affects approximately 3–7% of the U.S. population and is diagnosed three times more often in boys than in girls (CDC, 2006). Because of their distracted, impulsive nature, children with ADHD need ongoing assistance from caring adults to develop greater social competence.

Figure 1-5 Meet Patrick.

as children practice new techniques. That practice will take place in a variety of social contexts.

THE CONTEXTS IN WHICH SOCIAL COMPETENCE IS ACQUIRED

Home, Grandma's house, the child care center, school, playground, peer group, synagogue, and neighborhood—these are some of the many settings where children form ideas and behaviors associated with social competence. Things that happen in any one or all of these environments affect children in various ways, ultimately influencing the degree of social competence they achieve. To effectively guide children's social development and behavior, you must consider how such forces combine to affect children's lives (Bronfenbrenner, 1993; Horowitz, Darling-Hammond & Bransford, 2005).

Begin by envisioning the contexts in which children live as a series of concentric rings, with the child at the center. Figure 1-6 shows four distinct social systems: the microsystem, mesosystem, exosystem, and macrosystem. Moving outward from the child, microsystems are embedded within mesosystems, mesosystems are contained within exosystems, and exosystems function within macrosystems. Let us consider each system separately and then how they function together.

Microsystems

The most basic social system is the **microsystem**. Such a system includes the people, materials, activities, and interpersonal relationships children experience directly in face-to-face settings such as home or school. At various times in their lives, children may participate in some or all of the following microsystems:

- immediate or extended family setting
- child care program or Head Start center
- school
- 4-H group
- church, synagogue, temple, or mosque
- doctor's office
- recreation center

Each of these is its own environment in which children gain social practice through interactions with people and things. Evidence shows that children are significantly influenced by the microsystems in which they live. For example, when adults at home balance warmth with control and fondness with firmness, children's social competence blossoms. When adults are predominately negative or intrusive, positive outcomes are less likely to occur (NICHD Early Child Care Research Network, 2001; Goleman, 2006). Similar results are reported for extrafamilial microsystems such as child care settings

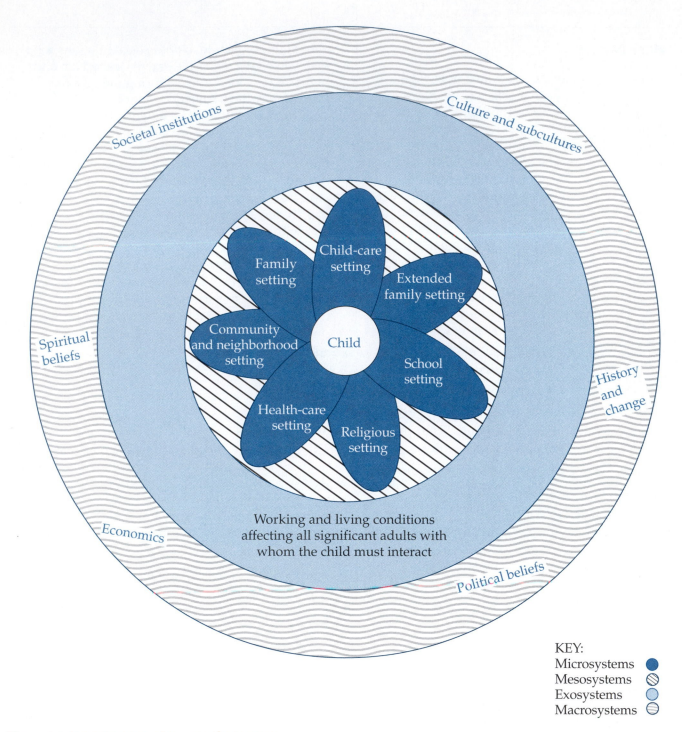

Figure 1-6 Nested ecology of human development.

and elementary classrooms (Mill and Romano-White, 1999; Peisner-Feinberg et al., 2001). Findings such as these illustrate the important role microsystems play in shaping children's behavior; however, such shaping is not a one-way process.

Children also influence people and events around them. Sometimes this is a function of children's bio-logical characteristics such as temperament or ap-pearance. Sometimes it happens as a result of child behaviors. For instance, Baby Thomas has been cry-ing nonstop for an hour. Nothing his caregiver does comforts him. This lack of positive response prompts her to feel harried and inadequate. As she communi-cates these feelings to the child through her strained voice and tense body, his negative demeanor intensifies. At this point, the caregiver takes a moment to engage in some quiet breathing exercises. When she reenters the interaction with Thomas, she is less tense. Her more mellow behavior helps Thomas settle more easily, and she feels more confident as a result. Such reciprocal interactions underscore the fact that microsystems are dynamic environments in which each person influences and is influenced by other people in the system.

Before we leave this discussion of microsystems, let us take a moment to consider more specifically how the people in children's families, the peer group, and childhood programs contribute to children's social competence. These three microsystems are especially important to children in the early years.

Family Influences

Families throughout the world bear primary responsibility for meeting children's physical needs, nurturing children, and socializing them (Turnbull, Turnbull, Erwin & Soodak, 2005). Family members have long-term attachments to children, providing links to their past as well as visions for their future (Gonzalez-Mena & Eyer, 2006). Parents and sometimes grandparents, aunts and uncles, or brothers and sisters are children's first teachers. They provide children with their earliest social relationships, models for behaviors and roles, a framework of values and beliefs, and intellectual stimulation. The initial attitudes toward other people, education, work, and society that children encounter are in the family. These functions take place through direct and indirect teaching, in constructive and sometimes destructive ways, more or less successfully. In addition, most environmental influences are channeled through the family. For instance, it is through their families that children gain access to economic resources and learn the customs of their culture groups. Family members arrange for out-of-home care and make the initial entry into a school for their children. Family members also promote or inhibit opportunities for children's interactions with peers and the greater community by organizing informal contacts with peers and by enrolling their children in formal activities such as 4-H or scouts (DeWolfe & Benedict, 1997). Through their actions and choices, families play the lead role in transmitting to children the manners, views, beliefs, and ideas held and accepted by the society in which they live. Eventually, however, children's social worlds expand to include microsystems beyond the home or extended family. In these settings peers, caregivers, teachers, and other adults provide additional opportunities for social learning.

Peer Group Influences

As youngsters interact with peers in child care settings, at school, and in the neighborhood, a significant amount of social learning occurs. Within peer relationships, children learn concepts of reciprocity and fairness through the give and take that happens among equals. The social negotiation, discussion, and conflict found among peers help children learn to understand others' thoughts, emotions, motives, and intentions. This understanding enables children to think about the consequences of their behavior both for themselves and for others (Doll, Zucker & Brehm, 2004). Youngsters explore various roles, such as "leadership" and "followership," in ways not possible to achieve with adults. Then, as they receive feedback from their peers, children begin to evaluate the appropriateness of their actions and modify their behavior accordingly (McCay & Keyes, 2002; Santrock, 2006). Consequently, peer relations provide critical contexts for social cognition (i.e., thinking about social phenomena) and social action. Such thinking and acting may result in either negative or positive social outcomes. This process is illustrated when 7-year-old Marvin has a "meltdown" each time he strikes out in T-ball. At first, his peers say nothing, but after a few instances, they tell him to stop and complain that he is acting like a baby. Marvin eventually stops protesting so loudly if his turn at bat goes poorly. He wants the other children to accept him and comes to realize that they are more tolerant of his striking out than of his tantrums. Chances are you can think of many additional examples of how the peer group provides an important context for social learning.

Caregiver and Teacher Influences

Caregivers and teachers are also crucial in promoting children's social competence (Berns, 2006). They do this when they engage in a variety of social behaviors.

- They form relationships with children.
- They communicate values to children.
- They instruct children.
- They model social behaviors and attitudes.
- They design activities that highlight and give children practice in relevant knowledge and skills.

- They plan the physical environment.
- They formulate routines.
- They communicate rules to children.
- They enact positive or corrective consequences to help children comply with societal expectations.

Social competence is so crucial that it is addressed in the formal learning standards designated for Head Start, state-sponsored early childhood programs, and elementary education programs throughout the United States. These standards describe what children should know and be able to do in the program. Although each state has its own standards, all of the states address social competence in some way. See Figure 1-7 for examples.

How childhood professionals carry out these responsibilities either enhances or inhibits the degree to which children develop attitudes and behaviors associated with social competence.

Now that we have explored the three primary microsystems in which most young children function, it is time to examine their joint impact.

Mesosystems

All the different microsystems in which a child participates combine to form that child's **mesosystem**. Rachel may be involved in a mesosystem that includes home, school, peer group, after-school child care program, synagogue, and Aunt Mabel's apartment. Jason's mesosystem may include some of the same elements as well as other microsystems specific to his life. As children's mesosystems expand, influences from each setting also affect the others. Thus, the home environment affects children's social learning at school and vice versa. Children's social competence is enhanced when they experience connections between the microsystems that make up their mesosystem. Such connections are made stronger when the people in each microsystem communicate with one another (family members talk to teachers, teachers talk to child care providers, and so forth). Connections are also enhanced when the social values prized in one microsystem are honored in another and when social expectations in each setting are more congruent than dissimilar (Berger, 2005; Shaffer & Kipp, 2006).

Exosystems

Exosystems represent settings and relationships people do not experience directly but that ultimately affect them. For instance, children do not serve on town councils, but the policies made by town councils influence children's home, education, and recreational experiences.

Another common exosystem for children is their parent's workplace. What happens to Mom or Dad on the job affects children too. The parent's mood, level of stress, income, and time available for leisure are exosystem-related factors that influence children. Conversely, a child's scout troop, elementary classroom, and ballet class function as an exosystem for the parent whose child participates in these settings. In due course, what goes on in such places comes home with the child. And, in the end, all of these elements have an impact on children's social development and behavior.

Macrosystems

The larger context in which all other systems operate is the macrosystem. **Macrosystems** are dominated by cultural influences. They are defined not by physical environments, but by the values, beliefs, laws, and traditions shared among people and groups of people. As a result, people may share certain values, traditions, and beliefs because they

- speak the same language.
- have certain historic experiences in common.
- trace their ancestors to the same country or region.
- share a common religion.
- live in the same place.
- see themselves as members of a particular generation.
- consider themselves to be of a particular economic/social class.

Macrosystem beliefs vary from society to society and within societies among various subcultures. Some examples of typical variations among groups are depicted in Figure 1-8.

Macrosystem beliefs are transmitted from generation to generation. Children learn them explicitly through direct teaching and implicitly through the behavior of those around them (Bredekamp & Copple, 1997). As a result of the way different groups approach these issues, children learn different things. For instance, in some societies children learn that competition is good; in others, children learn to value cooperation more highly. In one group, time may be treated as a finite commodity not to be wasted; in another group, time may be seen as more fluid and less pressing. One subculture might interpret a child's loud behavior as a positive sign of exuberance, whereas another might construe the

EARLY LEARNING STANDARDS: EXAMPLES RELATED TO SOCIAL COMPETENCE

State	Level	Expectations	Benchmarks/Learning Outcomes
Georgia	Two-Year Olds	Children will begin to develop relationships with adults	• Child seeks out adults with whom to interact and play • Child goes to adult for help and comfort
	Preschool Ages 4–5	Children will increase their capacity for self-control	• Child helps to establish classroom rules and routines • Child follows rules and routines within the learning environment • Child uses classroom materials purposefully and respectfully • Child expresses feelings through appropriate gestures, actions and language
Arizona	Preschool Ages 3–5	Children acknowledge the rights and property of self and others	• Child asks permission before using items that belong to others • Child defends own rights and the rights of others • Child uses courteous words and actions • Child participates in cleaning up the learning environment
Illinois	Early Elementary	Children recognize the feelings and perspectives of others	• Child recognizes that others may experience situations differently than oneself • Child uses listening skill to identify the feelings and perspectives of others
	Later Elementary	Children recognize the feelings and perspectives of others	• Child identifies verbal, physical and situational cues that indicate how others might feel • Child describes the expressed feelings and perspectives of others
New Jersey	K-4th Grade	Children demonstrate effective interpersonal communication	• Child uses positive social skills to interact with others • Child uses language appropriate to the situation • Child practices steps for effective conflict resolution • Child works with others cooperatively to accomplish a task

Figure 1-7 Early learning standards: Examples related to social competence.

Sources: *Bright from the Start: Georgia's Pre-K Program Content Standards*, Georgia Department of Early Care and Learning 2006, Atlanta, GA; *Arizona Early Learning Standards*, Arizona Department of Education 2005, Phoenix, AZ; *Illinois Learning Standards*, Illinois State Board of Education 2006, Springfield, IL; *Academic and Professional Standards*, State of New Jersey Department of Education 2006, Trenton, NJ.

Cultural Variations

People vary in their beliefs, values, and behaviors regarding:

- the way human beings relate to one another
- how people think about time and personal space
- what personality traits are highly prized
- fundamental notions of whether human beings are naturally good or bad
- how to show respect
- how to interact with people you know as well as people you just met
- how to dress
- what and when to eat
- ways positive and negative feelings are to be expressed
- when, how, and with whom affection, anger, resistance, and other feelings are appropriate or inappropriate
- what may be shared and how much
- in what ways individuals may touch each other
- what may and may not be communicated directly
- how to worship
- how to respond to life transitions and celebrations

Figure 1-8 Cultural variations.

Sources: Berns, 2006; Bredekamp & Copple, 1997; Katz & McClellan, 1997.

same action as impolite. In these ways, macrosystems broadly define how people believe children should be treated, what they should be taught, and what behaviors and attitudes represent social competence (Berns, 2006).

Thinking about Children Contextually

Microsystems, mesosystems, exosystems, and macrosystems combine to form a total social context within which children develop and learn. None of these systems exists in isolation. For instance, although macrosystem elements are pictured as the outermost ring in Figure 1-6, their influence does not remain at the outer edges of people's experiences. Eventually, the impact of societal beliefs, laws, economic conditions, religious concerns, and

political positions filter down to the microsystem level. This happens, for example, when society's tolerance of media violence works its way into the classroom through children's imitation of the violent actions they see on television—pretending to shoot one another or to kill the dolls in a fiery crash. On the other hand, microsystem influences also can be felt at the macrosystem's level. This happens, for instance, when families demand certain business services or community structures to support their changing needs. Because all of these systems interact and influence one another, you should keep the following ideas in mind as you work with children, their families, and your colleagues.

- **Many factors influence children's beliefs and social behaviors.** Making a deliberate effort to see the big picture will make it easier for you to consider the many different variables that influence children's social behavior. For instance, when Gordon hits another child, he may be hungry or ill or unsure of how to enter a game. He may have witnessed someone using physical force to achieve a goal and, thus, is imitating what he has seen. He may simply have run out of strategies to try. How effectively you react to Gordon will be influenced by your ability to recognize and sort out such factors.
- **Communication among microsystems fosters children's social competence.** When there is communication among the settings that comprise a child's mesosystem, the people in each microsystem get a more complete understanding of the child and the circumstances surrounding his or her social behavior. It also becomes possible to coordinate efforts so that children experience similar expectations in each setting and a cohesive approach to the development of social competence. Children benefit when this occurs. For instance, if Alfreda's mesosystem includes home, school, and after-school care, her social competence would be enhanced if the adults in those settings were to confer periodically and share information with one another. These mesosystem dynamics underscore how important it is for you to communicate with the central people in children's lives, providing them with relevant information and inviting them to offer their perspectives to further your understandings.
- **System influences are distinctive for each child.** A group as a whole may share some understandings (e.g., everyone in the 4-year-old room is aware that the guinea pig died). Yet, the total

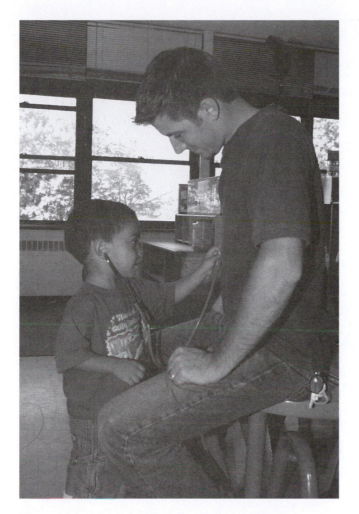

When children have positive relationships with their caregivers, they become more socially competent.

context for every youngster is unlike that of any other (e.g., Stanley has never before experienced death; Ramona saw her dog killed on the road in front of her home). Understanding these variations will increase your sensitivity to the individual strengths, needs, and interests that each child brings to the classroom, the playground, or the 4-H group.

- **There is no single best family form, value system, tradition, or lifestyle.** Families come in all shapes and sizes with all manner of beliefs. Children may live in two-parent families, single-parent families, blended families, interracial families, families in which parents are of different genders, families in which parents are of the same gender, families headed by grandparents, families whose members live near one another in the same community, family members separated by great distances, adoptive families, and foster

families. Families also differ from one another in terms of ethnicity, their access to resources, the languages they speak, their beliefs, and the values they pass on to their children. To work effectively with children, you must make a conscious effort to interact with all families in ways that communicate respect and openness even when their perspectives are very different from your own.

- **Programs for children complement, but do not replace, families in enhancing children's social competence.** Keeping in mind that families are children's first teachers, your job is not to replace parents or family caregivers, but to supplement their efforts at socializing their children. This is best achieved when you treat families as partners in the socialization process. Such partnerships are enhanced when you establish respectful relationships with families and when you recognize that they have valuable insights from which you will learn and benefit.

- **Adults in programs for children can moderate some of the negative circumstances children experience in other social contexts.** For example, in 2005, children in Martin County, Florida, experienced the chaos of Hurricane Francis. Buildings were damaged, trees were toppled, and daily activity was totally interrupted for months. Professionals in the area quickly rose to the challenge, reestablishing programs in which children could receive services while members of the community attempted to restore reasonable living conditions. Practitioners focused on helping children feel safe and secure while their families did what they had to do. They did this by providing children with safe environments, loving adults, and predictable routines. These conditions were in great contrast to the upheaval children were experiencing in their community at the time. Similar strategies for enhancing children's feelings of security were employed in childhood programs throughout New York City following the 9/11 tragedy in 2001. These two examples are particularly dramatic. However, there are daily ways in which people in child care settings, schools, and other children's programs lessen the impact of negative conditions children experience elsewhere in the social system. Some examples are listed in Figure 1-9.

As you can see, social contexts play a significant part in children's social development. Now it is time to consider more specifically the role you will play in this network of influence.

IF CHILDREN / FAMILIES EXPERIENCE . . .	YOU CAN PROVIDE . . .
Rejection	Acceptance
Feelings of isolation	Support and connections
Uncertainty due to divorce, death, changing family relationships	Consistent relationships, information for family members about these issues
Chaos in the environment	Predictable settings and routines
Fear, anger, shame	Safety, empathy, acceptance
Stress and pressure	Calm, patient interactions; time to explore and think; strategies for coping and handling stress more effectively
Poverty	Access to human resources and learning opportunities
Homelessness	A sense of safety, security, stability, and belonging within the classroom community
Violence at home, in the community, in the media	Nonviolent classrooms, peaceful strategies for dealing with conflict
Abuse or neglect	Protection, care, and compassion
Bias and discrimination	Equitable treatment, support in developing positive self-identity, awareness of others and anti-bias behaviors

Figure 1-9 Program conditions that offset system pressures.

YOUR ROLE IN FOSTERING CHILDREN'S SOCIAL COMPETENCE

If a job interviewer asked you: Why do you want to work with children? Think of what you would answer.

Chances are, no matter what else you might say, your dreams for the future include making a positive difference in children's lives. There is no place where that difference will be more felt than in the social domain. Every day you will be faced with situations in which you will have to make judgments about how to support and guide the children in your charge. These are challenging tasks. On any given occasion, you may wonder about the following:

Should I pick up the crying baby or should I let her cry it out?

What should I do about a child who bites others?

When is it reasonable to expect children to know how to share?

How can children learn better ways to resolve their differences?

Where can I turn if I suspect a child is being sexually abused?

How you answer such questions and what actions you take can be more or less helpful to children and their families. Some responses may even be harmful. For instance, your actions could enhance children's feelings of self-worth or detract from them. They could increase children's interpersonal abilities or leave children at a loss about how to interact effectively. Your response could either promote or inhibit children's development of self-control.

Although there is no one right answer for any situation, the things you say and do will make a real difference in children's lives. So, what resources will you tap to formulate effective responses?

As a caring person interested in supporting children's development, you could draw on your past experiences with children, information you have read, advice provided by colleagues, and your intuition about what is best. Indeed, such sources might provide valuable insights. However, none of them is sufficient to help you formulate a truly professional reaction to such situations. For that, you will need a greater array of knowledge and skills than can be accrued based solely on life experience. This is truly the case, even if others say you are naturally gifted when it comes to working with infants, toddlers, preschoolers, or elementary-age children. Although it is true that some people have certain personality traits and previous experiences that enhance their ability to guide children's social development and behavior, that background must be supplemented by additional knowledge and competencies if you are to make the journey from talented novice to bona fide professional.

Working with Children as a Professional

Think of the qualities adults need to relate well to young children. Perhaps you think adults need to be:

- patient
- caring
- respectful
- open-minded
- humorous and fun

Such qualities are ones that anyone could possess to interact with children effectively. However, whether your title is teacher, caregiver, counselor, group leader, social worker, or child life specialist, there are certain other characteristics that will differentiate you as a professional. These include specialized knowledge, demonstrated competence, formalized standards of practice, lifelong education, and adoption of an ethical code of conduct.

Specialized knowledge.   Professionals have access to a body of knowledge that goes beyond what is known by the average layperson. This knowledge base is derived from a combination of theories and research that professionals gain through reading, reflection, observation, and experience. It includes terms, facts, principles, and concepts that help us understand why children behave as they do. It also provides guidance regarding which intervention strategies might be useful and which are not. Acquisition of relevant content happens as a result of prolonged education and specialized training (Morrison, 2006; Horowitz, Darling-Hammond & Bransford, 2005). The American Association of Colleges of Teacher Education (AACTE), the

Association of Childhood Education International (ACEI), and the National Association for the Education of Young Children (NAEYC) have all made recommendations for training professionals in a variety of fields involving children. They recommend a knowledge base that includes: general studies (humanities, mathematics, technology, social sciences, biological and physical sciences, the arts, physical health, and fitness), child development, teaching and learning; curriculum development and implementation; family and community relationships; assessment, documentation and evaluation; and, field experiences with young children under appropriate supervision. Other professional groups such as the Child Life Specialist Association (CLSA) advocate similar content with the addition of specific information about health care settings.

Demonstrated competence.   Another way to distinguish professionals from laypeople is that the former have to demonstrate competencies related to their field in order to enter the profession. The most formalized evidence of mastery involves licensing or certification, which are usually governed by state or national standards. Less formal monitoring occurs when aspiring professionals take tests, pass courses, and demonstrate effective practices either in a practicum setting or on the job. These experiences take place under the supervision of qualified members of the profession.

Regardless of how competence is assessed, the hallmark of being a professional goes beyond simply memorizing facts for a test; it requires you to translate the knowledge base into effective practices or skills. **Skills** consist of observable actions that, when used in combination, represent mastery of certain strategies. They can be observed, learned, and evaluated (Gazda, Balzer, Childers, & Nealy, 2005). For example, research tells us that an effective strategy for enhancing children's emotional development is to label children's emotions in a variety of situations (Dettore, 2002). Although this sounds simple enough to do, it requires adults to use a broad feeling word vocabulary, to accurately interpret children's moods, to make nonjudgmental statements to children, and to determine when and where to best use the strategy. These actions fit the definition of a skill. First, they are all observable. You can see and hear the extent to which people use different feeling words and whether their statements are objective. Second, if individuals have limited vocabularies, they can learn additional feeling words; if they speak to children in judgmental ways, they can learn to be more objective. Third, a qualified observer could evaluate the person's use of the skill as well as provide feedback that would contribute to improved performance.

It is only when a person performs the entire combination of strategies correctly that it can be said that he or she has demonstrated the skill. Most aspiring professionals find that it takes time and practice to achieve this.

Some skills are simple to understand and easy to learn; others are more complex and difficult. In all cases, skill mastery will require you to know what to do, why to do it, and how to do it. Even when all this is accomplished, true mastery is attained only when you can carry out strategies in the setting for which they were intended. It is not enough to understand the importance of children's emotions or even to use feeling words in role-playing situations in class or at a workshop. You must also label children's emotions accurately in the center, on the playground, or in the classroom. This transfer of training from practice situations to real-life encounters is the ultimate demonstration of professional competence.

Standards of practice. Professionals perform their duties in keeping with standards of practice generally accepted for the field (Feeney & Freeman, 1999; Business Roundtable, 2004). Such standards come about through research and professional discourse. They are enforced through self-monitoring within the profession as well as governmental regulation. In early childhood education, for instance, practices have been identified that support and assist children's social, emotional, cognitive, language, and physical development. Some of these include health and safety provisions that ensure children's well-being; staff-to-child ratios that enable frequent personal interactions between each child and staff member; requiring adults to have special training in child development and early education; stable staffing so children have chances to develop trusting relationships with adults; and programming that is appropriate for children's developmental levels and interests (Doherty-Derkowski, 1997). Professionals who strive to maintain such standards are more likely to provide high-quality programs for the children in their charge. Deviation from these standards has detrimental effects on children, and

is considered undesirable within the profession. Knowing the professional standards that govern the field provides a gauge by which practitioners assess their own performance as well as the overall quality of the services they offer children and families.

Continuing education. To keep up with the standards in their field, professionals participate in continuing education throughout their careers. They constantly upgrade their knowledge and skills by attending workshops, consulting with colleagues, participating in professional organizations, reading professional journals, and pursuing additional schooling. Thus, professionals treat learning as a lifelong process that continues throughout the course of their careers.

Adopting a code of ethics. All professions have an ethical code that guides the behavior of their members on the job. These codes include statements of professional values as well as standards of conduct to help people distinguish good from evil, right from wrong, and proper from improper professional behavior (Kenyon, 1999; CSEP, 2006). Such codes supplement the personal morals people bring with them to the profession.

Although having strong moral character is an important asset to your professional development, knowing right from wrong in a professional sense requires more than personal judgment (Brophy-Herb, Kostelnik, & Stein, 2001). It requires us to know the agreed-upon ethical standards within the field. Thus, professionalism requires adoption of an ethical code of conduct that has been formally approved by the members of a profession. One such code prepared by NAEYC is presented in Appendix A.

A code of ethics provides a guide for decision making and a standard against which we can judge the appropriateness of our actions in different circumstances.

It gives us a tool for talking about ethical dilemmas with others and gives us access to the collective wisdom of our colleagues even when no one else is available in person. Laypersons do not have access to these same ethical supports.

Take a moment to consider how the five elements of professionalism just outlined influence your response to the question, "What should I do about a child who bites others?" Examples of what professionals might think about, know, and do related

WHAT SHOULD I DO ABOUT A CHILD WHO BITES OTHERS?

ELEMENTS OF PROFESSIONALISM	THINGS TO THINK ABOUT, KNOW, AND DO
Specialized Knowledge	Awareness of age-related characteristics of young children.
	Theoretical explanations for why children bite.
	Research related to various strategies aimed at reducing-biting among children.
Demonstrated Competence	Intervene with children who bite using redirection, substitution, logical consequences, and/or stress reduction strategies.
	Address the needs of victims through restitution, selftalk, and/or assertiveness strategies.
	Utilize conflict mediation strategies to reduce aggression.
	Use prevention and assertion strategies with onlookers.
	Demonstrate effective communication skills in working with the families of children who bite and their victims.
Standards of Practice	State licensing requirements.
	Accreditation criteria and procedures of the National Academy of Early Childhood programs.
	Accreditation criteria for family group homes.
	Developmentally appropriate practices in early childhood programs.
	National Council of Teacher Education accreditation standards.
	State guidelines for teacher certification.
	Child development associate criteria. Schoolwide discipline policies.
Continuing Education	Learn the latest information on emotional self-regulation.
	Become familiar with recent research on biting among toddlers.
Ethical Code of Conduct	Consider and act on ethical guidelines related to safety, confidentiality, and responsibility to children and families.

Figure 1-10 Elements of professionalism.

to each element are presented in Figure 1-10. As you can see, professionals have a rich background of knowledge, skills, and standards they call on to enhance children's social development. Evidence indicates that practitioners who have this kind of professional background are most likely to engage in practices that foster children's social competence (Gestwicki, 2006; McCay & Keyes, 2002). Such practices are often described as being developmentally appropriate.

DEVELOPMENTALLY APPROPRIATE PRACTICES AND SOCIAL COMPETENCE

Developmentally appropriate practices are associated both with professionalism and high-quality programs for children (Horowitz, Darling-Hammond & Bransford, 2005). To engage in developmentally appropriate practices, you will make decisions based on the following information (Copple & Bredekamp, 2006):

- what you know about how all children develop and learn
- what you know about the strengths, needs, and interests of individual children
- what you know about the social and cultural contexts in which children live

These three criteria help to ensure that your approaches to guiding children's social development and learning are age appropriate, individually appropriate, and socially and culturally appropriate.

Age-Appropriate Practices

Jack is 2. Amy is 10. Both want to play a game. Would you select the same game for each of them? Would you expect them to have similar skills or the same understanding of how games are played?

As someone who is familiar with child development, you undoubtedly answered "No" to these questions because you are aware that age makes a difference in what children know and what they can do. Consequently, to choose games that would be fun and doable for Jack and Amy, you must take into account the age-appropriateness of the different games available for them to play. For instance, a simple game of stacking blocks, then pushing them over might please Jack, but quickly bore Amy. Conversely, Amy might enthusiastically engage in an action game with other children outdoors that Jack would find too difficult to play. In both cases, your idea of a suitable game would be influenced by your knowledge of Jack's and Amy's motor skills, their cognitive understandings, their language abilities, and their social skills (such as their ability to wait, to follow rules, to take turns, to accommodate other people's needs, and to share). Although chronological age is not a foolproof indicator of children's thoughts and abilities, it does serve as a helpful gauge. This, in turn, allows us to make reasonable assumptions of what might be safe, interesting, achievable, and challenging for children at different times in their lives (Bredekamp & Copple, 1997). Therefore, we recognize that children's social competencies are influenced by age-related variables and that children at different ages will demonstrate different understandings and levels of skill.

Individually Appropriate Practices

The children are visiting a farm. Walter runs to the fence calling out, "Here horsy. Come here!" Margaret hangs back from the group, unsure of how close she wants to get to the big, hairy creatures. Carlos moves to the fence with Ms. Lopez. He is happy to watch as long as she is nearby.

Three different children—three different reactions. Each calls for an individualized response from you.

Every child who comes into this world is a unique being, the result of a combination of tens of thousands of genes inherited from his or her parents. Each child has a distinctive voiceprint, fingerprint, lip print, and footprint—and a natural odor singular enough for a bloodhound to follow. Even the size, shape, and operation of a child's brain are slightly different from those of all other children. Children's temperaments are so distinct at birth that family members often make remarks such as, "Lucida has been that way ever since she was a baby." These biological differences are complemented by experiential factors that further differentiate one child from another. Each child in any group setting brings a backlog of experiences and understandings that influence social competence. A child who has few group experiences will have different needs and strengths than a child who has been in group care since birth. Likewise, youngsters who have a certain game at home will be more capable of explaining the rules to others than children who have never played the game before. The kinds of experiences children have, the amount of experience they acquire, the quality of that experience, and its outcomes all combine to yield a different result for each child.

Thinking about children as individuals enables you to adapt programs and strategies appropriately and to be responsive to the variations that exist among children in a group (Copple & Bredekamp, 2006). You can see the notion of individually appropriate practice at work during the children's visit to the farm. One adult walks up to the fence with

Walter, sharing his pleasure in the horses and helping him to control the impulse to immediately stick his hand through the fence to pet them. Another adult stands back with Margaret and Carlos, providing emotional support as they watch the animals from a comfortable distance. These individualized responses take into account the children's differing reactions and needs. Requiring all the children to stand far back would deny Walter the opportunity to examine the horses more closely, and making everyone stand up close would force Carlos and Margaret into a situation they fear. Thus, treating all the children in exactly the same way would be inappropriate under the circumstances. The concept of individually appropriate practice reminds us that treating children fairly requires us to treat them as individuals and sometimes that means treating them differentially according to their needs.

Socially and Culturally Appropriate Practices

In addition to considering age and individuality, we have to look at children within the context of their family, community, and culture to effectively support their development of social competence. Consider the following classroom scenes:

Scene 1

Ms. Hayes notices two children arguing over a doll in the pretend play area. She carefully separates the children and begins to talk with them about their disagreement. Juanita looks down at the floor. Ms. Hayes says, "Now Juanita, I want you to listen carefully. Look at me when I'm talking to you." Juanita keeps her eyes on the floor. Ms. Hayes gently raises Juanita's chin and insists that Juanita look her in the eye to show that she is listening to what is being said.

Scene 2

Ms. Freelander notices two children arguing over a steam shovel in the block area. She carefully separates the children and begins to talk with them about their disagreement. Carlos looks down at the floor. Ms. Freelander continues talking with the children. Eventually they agree to look for another vehicle so both children can have one to use.

In both cases, the adults were trying to help children resolve their differences within the context of a typical classroom disagreement. Both teachers relied on reasoning to support the children's efforts to solve the problem. These are accepted standards within the profession. Yet, Ms. Hayes insisted that Juanita look at her to show she was being attentive;

Ms. Freelander did not make the same demand of Carlos. Ms. Freelander was engaging in socially and culturally appropriate practices; Ms. Hayes was not. What Ms. Freelander realized, and Ms. Hayes did not, was that in Carlos's and Juanita's families, children are taught to cast their eyes downward in the presence of adults, especially if they are being scolded. To do otherwise is to demonstrate lack of respect (Trawick-Smith, 2005).

Without realizing she was doing so, Ms. Hayes had ignored the social context in which Juanita lives. The adult presumed that because her own upbringing taught her to look at someone directly as a sign of attentiveness, the children in her group had been taught the same. This assumption was inaccurate.

When we ignore the cultural contexts of children's lives, we lose access to the rich background children bring with them from home. We also convey a message to children that they are unacceptable and less valued than other children might be (Chipman, 1997). To avoid these problematic outcomes, you will have to make a special effort to learn about the social contexts that surround the children in your charge. By interacting with children and families in ways that demonstrate appreciation and interest, you will learn more about what they interpret as meaningful and respectful. You will discover what expectations families have regarding their children's social development. You will find out more about what is happening in children's lives at home.

These understandings will go a long way toward helping you interpret children's behaviors, emotions, and needs more accurately and respectfully.

Keeping the idea of developmentally appropriate practice in mind, let us now focus on the first steps you will take to guide children's social development.

Foundations of Social Competence

Children flourish in a classroom where they sense that the teacher cares deeply about them—as people, about what they are learning, and about the skills they are developing.

Eliason and Jenkins
(early childhood educators, 2003)

Communicating to children that you care about them is fundamental to enhancing their social competence. This is called the **facilitation dimension** of guiding children's social development (Gazda, Balzer, Childers, & Nealy, 2005).

Chao is 3 years old. What are some things that might be true about Chao, based on what you know about children his age? How might Chao be different from other three year-olds in the program?

The facilitation dimension. Establishing emotionally supportive adult–child relationships is the function of facilitation. Children learn best when they feel psychologically safe and secure (Goleman, 2006). For young children, this translates into being with people they like and trust. Security also comes from consistent relationships with loving adults. Children who know that their mistakes will be tolerated and that their efforts to learn will be supported are more open to learning new things. On the other hand, children who are frightened and suspicious are not likely to absorb social lessons of any kind. Thus, facilitation is fundamental to helping children achieve greater social competence. Five key elements that contribute to positive relationships are empathy, warmth, respect, acceptance, and authenticity.

Empathy. The single most important manifestation of caring is **empathy** (Carkhuff, 2000; Goleman,

1995). Empathy is the act of recognizing and understanding another person's perspective even when that perspective is different from your own.

An empathic person responds to another's affective or emotional state by experiencing some of the same emotion. Empathy, therefore, involves the cognitive processes of examining and knowing, as well as the affective process of feeling. This idea is captured in such sayings as "walking in someone else's shoes" or "seeing the world through another person's eyes." Thinking about this definition, take a moment to contrast two teacher's reactions to Emily, a third grader, who spent an hour gluing and nailing a creation made entirely from wood (Steiner & Whelan, 1995).

> *Emily:* "It's a wishing tree. You talk to it and things come true."
>
> *Mr. Daley:* "Don't get slivers from that thing. Did you finish your math assignment?"
>
> *Later in the afternoon, Mr. Bewick stops by the after-school program. Emily shyly shows him the wishing tree.*
>
> *Mr. Bewick:* "Wow, a wishing tree. I've never seen a wishing tree before. Can I make a wish?"

Mr. Bewick's response was empathic; Mr. Daley's was not. Mr. Daley focused on his agenda and was insensitive to the value of Emily's creation to her. Mr. Bewick, on the other hand, recognized the importance of Emily's message and let her know that he felt some of her same excitement. It is likely that of the two teachers, Emily sees Mr. Bewick as the more friendly and caring adult.

Warmth. Showing interest in children, being friendly toward them, and being responsive to them are all aspects of **warmth** (Berk & Winsler, 1995). Early childhood professionals who are warmhearted help children feel comfortable, supported, and valued. Ms. Hamouz is demonstrating warmth when she greets 3-year-old Sarah by squatting down to the child's eye level, smiling, and touching her shoulder gently as Sarah tells her about last night.

Respect. Respect involves believing that children are capable of learning and making self-judgments. You show **respect** when you allow children to think for themselves, make decisions, work toward their own solutions, and communicate

The teacher's laughter, gentle touch and available lap all signal warmth.

ideas (Morrison, 2006). Lack of respect is evident when adults tell children how to think and feel, ignore their point of view, or deprive them of genuine opportunities to grow and learn. Disrespect is also apparent when adults believe that children cannot learn because of their culture or socioeconomic background.

Acceptance. Closely related to respect is acceptance. **Acceptance** refers to every human being's need for self-validation from others. Without acceptance, constructive social development is impossible. To be accepted fully means to be valued unconditionally. Adults who demonstrate acceptance toward children care about them regardless of their personal attributes, family background, or behavior. They do not require children to earn their caring through good grades, compliance, charm, or beauty. Rather, they believe all children are worthy of acceptance simply because

of who they are. Thus, "acceptance does not judge" (Egan, 2007).

Unfortunately, acceptance is a component of the facilitation dimension that is widely misunderstood. Some adults assume that acceptance translates into condoning all child behaviors, even the antisocial ones. That is inaccurate. As you will discover throughout this text, there are ways to communicate caring and acceptance to children while at the same time guiding them toward adopting more appropriate behaviors. This dual agenda is illustrated when Ms. Chigubu moves quickly over to two children who are hitting each other with sticks on the playground. They are obviously angry. She communicates acceptance by acknowledging their anger. At the same time she makes it clear that hitting is not permitted and helps the children put the sticks down.

Authenticity. Positive adult–child relationships are also characterized by **authenticity** (Curry & Johnson, 1990). Authentic adults are genuine with children. That is, what they say to children is truthful, yet also reasonable and encouraging. As a result, youngsters receive balanced, informative, helpful feedback that enables them to more accurately assess their ideas, values, and behaviors.

Authentic adults gain children's trust because children know their words are believable. Mrs. Tashima demonstrates authenticity when she takes time to point out something particularly interesting about each child's painting ("You used a lot of bright colors" or, "You found a way to make the house look far away") rather than simply telling each child, "Good job."

Empathy, warmth, respect, acceptance, and authenticity all provide a foundation for positive adult–child relationships. Children who experience such relationships generally demonstrate increased social competence and positive behavior adjustment (Elicker & Fortner-Wood, 1997). When adult–child relationships lack these key elements, children are more likely to display behavior problems, have a lower tolerance for frustration, and exhibit poorer social skills with peers. It is therefore important to make positive interactions with children a high priority on your list of professional goals. You will learn many ways to establish and maintain positive relationships as you read this textbook. Now let us look at the action dimension of guiding children's social development.

The action dimension. The **action dimension** focuses on teaching children to maintain desirable behaviors and to change inappropriate ones to more acceptable alternatives. Supporting children as they work their way through a verbal conflict and reminding children to "Walk, don't run" are examples of strategies related to the action dimension. Depending on the situation, what you do to implement the action phase of child guidance will be more or less direct. In either case, your aim is to help children achieve desirable standards of behavior, rather than simply restricting or punishing them for inappropriate conduct. To do this, you will use verbal and nonverbal communications, direct physical actions, or a combination of the two to help children maintain or change their behavior. Typical action strategies include modeling, on-the-spot coaching, redirecting, discussing, implementing consequences, and instructing. What strategies to use, how to use them, when to use them, and what variations to employ are all things to consider in guiding children's social development and behavior.

Expert practitioners blend the facilitative and action dimensions in their interactions with children. They understand when and how to use each component and are skilled in effectively implementing them with children individually and in groups. Their professional practices range from the basics of relationship building, to preventing problem behaviors, to supporting children's social skill development, to engaging in intensive individualized interventions as necessary. (See Figure 1-11) All of this is what you will be learning in the remaining chapters of this text.

CHAPTER STRUCTURE

Guiding Children's Social Development and learning is designed to help you acquire the necessary knowledge, skills, and attitudes to function as a professional working with children. Therefore, every chapter that follows is structured around the five elements of professionalism.

Specialized Knowledge

A statement of objectives opens each chapter to guide you in your learning. The body of the chapter begins with a discussion of the latest empirical findings and research regarding a particular topic, such as children's emotional development or play.

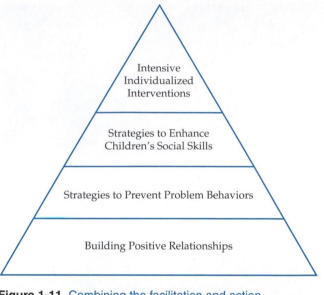

Figure 1-11 Combining the facilitation and action dimensions to guide children's' social development and behavior.

Source: Fox, Dunlap, Hemmeter, Joseph and Strain (2003).

This opener constitutes the knowledge base for the chapter.

Demonstrated Competence

Next comes a section that describes specific techniques related to the research outlined at the start. These strategies are presented as skills that can be observed, learned, and evaluated. The majority of skills are directly applicable to your work with children.

However, some skills for communicating with family members about the topic are included as well to enhance home/program connections. To help you improve your performance, we also report on pitfalls you may experience as you begin to incorporate the new skills into your interactions with children and families.

Standards of Practice

The skills outlined in each chapter represent standards of practice commonly accepted for the field. They have their basis in developmentally appropriate practice and address the competencies expected of professionals working with young children.

Continuing Education

All chapters conclude with a summary that provides a brief overview of the chapter's topic. Discussion questions follow to help you assess your understanding of the material. Field assignments give you an opportunity to apply what you have learned with real children in early childhood programs. These sections are designed to help you generalize what you are learning beyond the college classroom and to provide a base for future practice. As you become more involved in the field, we assume you will update what you have learned in these pages by reading journals, attending conferences, and pursuing additional modes of continuing education.

Code of Ethics

Because ethics are so integral to professionalism, there are ethics-related discussion questions in each chapter. Although there is no single correct answer for any of the questions, talking them over with peers and supervisors will hone your ethical judgments.

Throughout the course of the book, every aspect of the NAEYC Code of Ethics will be covered. Our expectation is that you will be thoroughly familiar with the code by the time you complete Chapter 15.

SUMMARY

Social competence refers to a person's ability to recognize, interpret, and respond to social situations in ways deemed appropriate by society. The acquisition of social competence begins in childhood and occurs as a result of both development and learning.

Children acquire social competence within an interdependent network of systems—the microsystem, mesosystem, exosystem, and macrosystem. Considering how these systems combine to affect children's lives involves adopting a contextual perspective.

Maintaining this perspective enables you to see children holistically, to appreciate how various systems affect children's lives, and to communicate more successfully with other people in the microsystems in which children participate. The most basic microsystem is the family. As children mature, other microsystems such as the peer group, child care or educational settings play an ever-increasing role in their lives. As children engage in such settings they often come in contact with professionals in the field. Professionals demonstrate five characteristics that differentiate them from laypersons: specialized knowledge, demonstrated competence, standards of performance, continuing education, and a code of ethics.

Professionals who work with children ideally demonstrate empathy, warmth, respect, acceptance, and authenticity. These are all facets of the facilitation dimension of guiding children's social development.

Once positive adult–child relationships have been established, professionals move into the action phase of fostering children's social competence. This phase teaches children how to adapt their behavior to meet societal expectations. As you learn to carry out both the facilitation and action dimensions effectively, you will be on your way to making a positive difference in children's lives.

KEY TERMS

acceptance	exosystem	professionals
action dimension	facilitation dimension	respect
authenticity	macrosystem	skills
developmentally appropriate practice	mesosystem	social competence
empathy	microsystem	warmth

DISCUSSION QUESTIONS

1. Refer to Figure 1-1. Define social competence. Randomly select one of the elements of social competence to discuss. Describe examples of behaviors that would illustrate the knowledge, skills, and values encompassed by that element.

2. A recent study involving Russian parents and early childhood professionals revealed that the following elements of social competence were ones they particularly valued:

   kindness
   good manners

respect for individual differences
independent thinking and acting
self-confidence
self-direction
spontaneity
happiness

Discuss how these behaviors/values compare with the elements of social competence described in relation to children in the United States identified in this chapter.

3. There is evidence that approximately 75% of students with learning disabilities manifest social skills deficits during the early years. In addition, children with mental retardation are much more likely to experience problems in socialization and communication than their nondisabled peers (McCay & Keyes, 2002). Discuss what implications this has for families and early childhood professionals working with young children.

4. There is a saying that goes, "Remember that children are whole people in their own right, not deficient adults." Based on your knowledge of child development and learning as well as the content of this chapter, what significance does this have in relation to children's development of social competence?

5. Using Figure 1-6 as a reference, draw a picture of the social systems in your life. Label the elements that are contained in each of the systems that influence you.

6. Imagine that you have been invited to speak to a group of families whose children are newly enrolled in your program. What are the three key things you would want to communicate to them about children's social competence and ways in which your program supports the development of social competence in children?

7. Consider the five characteristics of a professional—specialized knowledge, demonstrated competence, standards of practice, continuing education, and a code of ethics. List these on a piece of paper and then discuss various ways in which you are involved in acquiring these characteristics.

8. Refer to the NAEYC Code of Ethical Conduct outlined in Appendix A. Read Section I: Ethical Responsibilities to Children. Identify principles and concepts described in Chapter 1 text that support the ideals and principles covered in this section of the code.

9. Not all children develop typically; some children experience challenges or delays in their development and learning. Discuss how you would adapt the notion of developmentally appropriate practice to take this into account.

10. List the five elements of the facilitation dimension: empathy, warmth, respect, acceptance, and authenticity. Discuss examples of adult behavior that would correspond to these five elements.

FIELD ASSIGNMENTS

1. Make a diagram of the classroom or other childhood setting in which you will be practicing your skills this semester. Be sure to include details related to doors, windows, and furniture. Write a daily schedule for the formal group setting in which you will be participating and identify your role at each time of the day. Name at least 3 adults with whom you will interact and briefly describe each person's role in the program. Name at least 10 of the children in your setting. What are two goals you believe the supervisor has for the children in the setting and what evidence did you use to determine this?

2. Select one principle of development or learning described in this chapter. Name the principle and give an example of children demonstrating that principle in your field placement or practicum site. Remember to write objectively, focusing on observable behaviors.

3. Refer to Figure 1-9. Make a copy of this figure and share it with a childhood professional. Ask him or her what elements of the figure may represent his or her program. Invite him or her to offer examples of how the program provides children with the conditions that offset system pressures.

4. Observe an early childhood setting. Write out examples of age-appropriate, individually appropriate, and socially/culturally appropriate practices you observe in the setting.

5. Consider the five elements of the facilitation dimension: empathy, warmth, respect, acceptance, and authenticity. Observe in a childhood program and provide examples of adult behaviors that demonstrate each of the five elements.

Chapter 2

INITIATING SOCIAL RELATIONSHIPS IN INFANCY

OBJECTIVES

On completion of this chapter, you should be able to describe:

- Infant behavioral states and how to respond effectively to each one.

- The role of motor development, sensory abilities, and temperament in social interaction.

- Attachment behavior of infants and the role of caregivers in supporting it.

- The process of identity development.

- Social competencies displayed by infants and toddlers with peers and adults.

- Strategies to support healthy social-emotional development in infants.

- Communication strategies for interacting with family members.

- Pitfalls to avoid in interacting with infants and their families.

Now, don't spoil the baby.
Please shut that baby up!
Oh, babies are no trouble for me!

These comments may represent the view of family members or other caregivers with whom you may come in contact as you begin working professionally with infants and their families in a newborn nursery of a hospital, in a child care center, or in any other infant development program.

When a baby is born, he or she immediately is a member of a social group: a family, who lives in a community, which is contained within a larger culture. As adults respond to infant posture, gazes, vocalizations, they modify their own behavior accordingly and treat the infant as a member of the intimate social group of the family, helping the child to fit into the cultural group. Fortunately, other family members, friends, and helping professionals often participate in the early child rearing in ways that can support and enhance the efforts of parents. This includes you.

INFANT CHARACTERISTICS AS FACTORS IN SOCIAL RELATIONSHIPS

Infants are appealing to adults. Newborns have large heads and trunks with relatively smaller arms and legs. They may or may not have much hair, but their heads smell nice. Their skin, in the beginning, may be discolored and wrinkly, but is always soft and soon fills out. Eyes are large in a face that may be quite flat, and, in the beginning, they have no tears. Rounded cheeks are characteristic of the first year. Newborns grow rapidly, gaining in both length and weight so that a one-year-old seems heavy in comparison. Initially fairly still, they become intrepid travelers. The physical appeal and rapid change is attractive to adults who engage them in a multitude of interactions every day. One of the many factors that will influence those interactions is the child's behavioral state.

Behavioral States

Ms. Dennis entered the infant room on the first day of her student placement. Paul was sleeping soundly in his crib. Lily was sitting on the floor with her back to everyone else. Robbie was crying gustily in Ms. Griffore's arms. Lena was alert and awake in her car seat. Elly was sitting in her crib, with her eyebrows pulled together, looking unhappy. Ms. Luster was greeting the last infant to arrive in the doorway. Ms. Dennis washed her hands and approached Elly with a smile and a greeting.

The earliest behaviors are *organized*, (typical body movements and vocalizations occurring during each state), *predictable* (state changes occur in sequence), and *rhythmic* (in a daily pattern) after the first few days. As infants mature, the duration of each state alters. Every infant establishes a unique and routine style of function that fits into larger patterns and cycles. Thus, even from the beginning, infants participate in their own development. Adults who quickly recognize each of these states and learn the infant's typical pattern of behavior are able to select and time their responses most effectively. Such synchronous caregiving is often called sensitive caregiving (see Table 2-1).

Sleep states. Infants who are in any of the sleep or drowsy states should not be interrupted or stimulated. Only the infant who is waking up slowly from a long sleep and is still drowsy should be picked up. Allow typically developing babies to sleep and do not wake them to be changed, fed, or engaged in social interaction.

Newborns spend much of their time sleeping, with frequent episodes of wakefulness for feeding. Sleep lasts only two to three hours for newborns, with infants gradually sleeping more at night than during the day by 8 weeks. Periods of sleep gradually decline over the first year with some infants sleeping through the night by 6 months and most doing so by one year. There is a corresponding increase in the amount of time an infant is in one of the alert states. The amount of time infants are asleep or alert varies widely from child to child. By the end of the first year, infants generally sleep through the night and take naps during the morning and afternoon and before two may need only one nap during the day.

Alert states. In the quiet alert or alert inactive state, the infant may appear to stare and is more likely to be responsive to stimulation and social contact. States of quiet alert are both brief and rare initially but increase noticeably over the first few months.

Caregivers should take advantage of moments when infants are displaying alert inactivity by talking to them, touching them, and presenting objects for them to enjoy. Caregivers should not conclude that quiet infants will entertain themselves or do not require stimulation just because they are not obviously demanding attention. However, if the amount of stimulation is too great, the infant will increase its activity, cry, or go to sleep as a way to avoid over-stimulation.

Table 2-1 Infant Behavioral States and Appropriate Adult Responses.

	Respiration	Facial Expression	Action	Adult Response
Regular sleep	Regular; 36 per minute	Eyes closed and still; face relaxed	Little movement; fingers slightly curled, thumbs extended	Do not disturb
Irregular sleep	Uneven, faster; 48 per minute	Eyes closed; occasional rapid eye movement; smiles and grimaces	Gentle movement	Do not disturb
Periodic sleep	Pattern varies	Alternates between regular and irregular sleep		Do not disturb
Drowsiness	Even	Eyes open and close or remain halfway open; eyes dull/ glazed	Less movement than in irregular sleep; hands open and relaxed; fingers extended	Pick up if drowsiness follows sleeping; do not disturb if drowsiness follows awake periods
Quiet alert	Constant; faster than in regular sleep	Bright eyes; fully open; face relaxed; eyes focused	Slight activity; hands open, fingers extended, arms bent at elbow, stares	Talk to infant; present objects; perform any assessment
Waking activity	Irregular	Face flushed; less able to focus than in quiet alert	Extremities and body move; vocalizes, makes noises	Interact with infant; provide basic care
Crying		Red skin; facial grimaces; eyes partially or fully open	Vigorous activity, crying vocalizations; fists are clenched	Pick up immediately; try to identify source of discomfort and remedy it; soothe infant

Crying.   Crying is one of the infant's earliest means of communicating needs to the caregiver and has the expected effect of drawing an adult near. In the first 3 to 4 months, crying is usually physiological in nature due to hunger, digestive problems, or a pain. Later, crying increasingly becomes psychological and is used to indicate fear, boredom, and anger (Kopp, 1994). Babies of about 4 months of age may cry because they have not been placed in the preferred sleeping position. Others in the second half of the first year may cry from rage at having tossed a toy out of reach. Frequently, crying between 9 and 15 months is accompanied by gestures. Once the source of the distress is identified and attended to, the infant usually can be soothed and the crying stopped.

Infant cries range from general fussiness to intense fear, anger, or pain (Gustafson, Wood, & Green, 2000). Hunger, discomfort, and sleepiness apparently tend to increase in intensity over time if the source of distress is not removed. Harry woke hungry and made a few fussy noises. His caregiver did not come immediately, so he began to cry. By the time his caregiver prepared his bottle, he was wailing; the loud, gusty cries stopping when the bottle was offered. Usually caregivers use the context of the situation as well as auditory cues and their knowledge of the individual infant to determine the probable cause of the cry.

The cry caused by pain is a long, piercing wail followed by a long silence, and then gasping. This cry is a signal that something is wrong (Gustafson et al., 2000). It is quite different from speech sounds and is an extremely effective signal in getting the attention of the caregiver. Some family members may not be able to reliably distinguish their infant's cries initially, but over time most increase in their ability to distinguish between the child's bid for attention and distress, anger, or pain. Likewise, other caregivers who are familiar with individual infants learn to identify and respond appropriately to these varying cries.

Babies crying fluctuates in duration and intensity at predictable periods during the first 20 months (Heimann, 2003). There are 10 periods of time (at 5, 8, 12, 17, 26, 36, 44, 52, 61–62, and 72–73 weeks) when the baby cries and fusses more, which in turn draws the caregiver near. These displays of emotion appear to regulate contacts and relationships with other people just as the child needs to reorganize his or her internal structures. These periods are thought to indicate the need for increased contact with the primary caregiver, which then affects neural pathways and eventual learning.

Jackie, who was only 4 months old, was crying hard when his caregiver picked him up and carried him to the refrigerator to get his formula. He sniffled and stopped his loud cries gradually, but when the phone rang, she put him down to answer it. His crying resumed loudly.

Hanna, at 7 months, woke up hungry and crying. Her caregiver, who was reliably prompt in feeding and changing her, started walking toward her and she stopped her crying even before being picked up.

At about 12:15 P.M., Alberto toddled to the refrigerator and pointed. His mother was cleaning another room and did not see him. He began jabbering, pointing, and crying until she came to investigate. Alberto stopped crying as soon as he saw her walk into the kitchen.

Thus, though behavioral states are largely controlled by internal, physiological functions, babies learn to self-regulate crying gradually from their social contacts with the adults caring for them. Infants learn that they will be comforted, fed, changed, or attended when prompt care is quickly forthcoming. Ignoring the cries of infants in the first six months is not effective in reducing the duration or frequency of crying. In general, the longer the infant has been crying, the longer and more difficult the soothing time. Each behavioral state elicits potential responses from caregivers. Once the physical needs of infants are addressed, the most typical behavior elicited in caregivers to a crying infant is soothing.

Soothing. Crying is a signal that demands action. Caregivers must first guess the likely source of stress, and then attempt to address it. Once crying

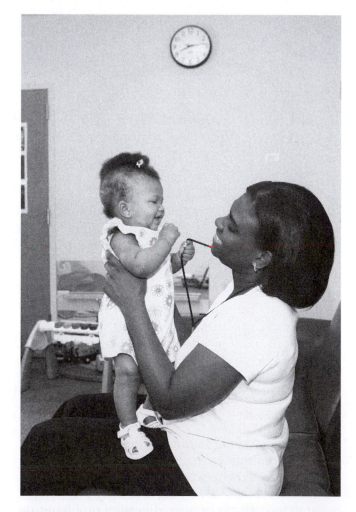

Infants whose caregivers are most responsive to their needs learn that the environment is predictable and the caregiver can be counted on.

has begun, however, some babies need soothing before, during, and after the initial cause has been identified and addressed. The most effective strategy is picking them up and holding them to the shoulder. Other strategies include the following:

- offering a pacifier, as sucking often calms the baby
- stimulating the baby in a rhythmic way, such as through soft music or walking
- firmly wrapping the baby in a blanket
- changing the baby's position
- changing the room temperature or putting on or taking off the child's clothing
- taking the infant for a stroller or wagon ride
- massaging the child's body, even if the crying goes on a little while
- asking someone to take the baby if you are upset, as babies respond to adult stress by crying (Papalia, et al., 2006)

In fact, the more senses that receive continuous stimulation, the calmer babies become (Brackbill, 1979). Thus, picking up crying babies, swaddling them, walking or rocking them, and singing lullabies continue to be effective. Older babies prefer the soothing strategy with which they are familiar, so individual preferences may be influenced by cultural patterns. Infants whose caregivers are most responsive to cries in the first few months of life cry least. These children also become more effective in noncrying communication later (Bell & Ainsworth, 1972).

Atypical crying and difficult soothing.   Infants may excessively cry when they experience overly stimulating events such as the first day of child care or a large family gathering. Disturbances in sleep and feeding patterns may also produce excessive crying when the infant's familiar routine is disrupted. Infants also cry excessively when their caregivers are experiencing a lot of stress (Poole & Magilner, 2000).

In recent years, caregivers have had increasing contact with infants who have experienced physical or emotional stress. These infants do not display expected crying patterns. Adults who care for them should seek specific information about each child's condition and crying patterns as some cry for long periods of time and others do not cry at all.

Colic is excessive crying that is not amenable to soothing by typical means. This begins during the first three weeks of life and increases through the second month then decreases rapidly to more normal levels by the fourth month (Barr & Gunnar, 2000). Such infants have recurrent crying spells that last more than three hours per day and at least three days a week; they cry at predictable times of day and are otherwise well nourished and healthy. Additional soothing strategies include reducing stimulation when the crying bout is expected, placing the infant in a quiet and dark room with minimal handling, and introducing monotonous sounds in the infant environment (Poole & Magilner, 2000). At this time, there is no cure or prevention for colic, and caregivers need support for the difficulty they experience and stress such a condition triggers in adults.

When adults use soothing strategies, infants learn that the caregiver can be counted on to respond to their signals of distress predictably. This is an important element of trust that is developed early in life.

Sensory Ability and Social Interaction

Human infants are born with billions of neurons. After birth, a process of making connections will strengthen some, but others will fade (Puckett & Black, 2004). When the environment offers what babies need—physical contact with a caregiver, communication, and play that engages all the senses—the physical structure of the brain itself is molded into an increasingly complex network. Some pathways in the brain are strengthened as a result of many repetitions of similar behaviors by the caregiver. The opportunity to develop social attachment and the ability to cope with stress are physically structured in the brain during infancy as a result of warm responsive care. Essential experiences such as child-focused guidance and appropriate play produce neural pathways leading to the ability to regulate and control of emotion (Puckett & Black, 2004). Thus, the rapidly growing and developing brain is molded by social experience while the young child is learning how to engage in increasingly complex interactions with people and the environment.

The first information about the world is based on sensations infants receive while being handled. They smell the adult's hands, hair, and body. They taste his or her skin. They see the adult's face when being fed, bathed, clothed, and changed. They feel the caregiver's body directly as they are held close, so they sense muscular tension or relaxation as well as the rhythm of movement. Caregivers who are comfortable with their own bodies and can accept infants' ways of knowing about them through body exploration have taken the first step in establishing a relationship.

Perceptual capacities are critical to social development as babies are remarkably well equipped to respond to the social environment—particularly human faces, voices, and smells. Newborns turn their heads toward their mother when she speaks and are able to recognize her by smell, and by 6 months they are able to recognize familiar people by sight.

Babies are highly responsive to touch, showing distress with extremes of temperature and moisture, texture and pain. Both adults and infants appear to enjoy holding, stroking, rocking, walking, and other positive physical contacts (Klaus, Kennell, & Klaus, 1995). Infants can be comforted by being swaddled, having a hand placed on the abdomen, sensing a change of position, or being held. When caregivers are both firm and gentle during feeding, bathing, and diapering, silent messages of comfort, approval, and affection are conveyed. Regular rough or painful handling causes distress and may influence the infant's view of the environment as a risky place.

Hearing is well developed before birth. Very young infants are attuned to speech sounds, particularly those high in pitch with exaggerated contours (Aslin, Jurczyk, & Pisoni, 1998). Between 3 and 5 months of age, infants can imitate the changes of pitch in an adult's voice, and when they are sung to, they can "sing" back. Infants of 6 months can distinguish melodies, regardless of the scale, and tend to prefer infant-directed play songs and lullabies over other singing between 4 and 7 months of age (Aslin et al., 1998; Trainor, 1996). They tend to prefer complex sounds to pure tones, soft rather than loud sounds, and those that have a longer duration rather than short, sharp sounds. Between 3 and 6 months of age, they may startle at noises previously ignored. By the sixth month, infants recognize their parents or other caregivers by the sound of their voices alone or by the familiar sound of their footsteps as they approach the child.

By the sixth week, babies appear to look directly at the faces of the caregivers, with eye brightening and eye widening, and by 3 months of age, infants can distinguish photographs of their parents from same sexed strangers (Walton, Bower, & Bower, 1992). Infants prefer to look at people rather than objects during

the first year, and by 6 months of age recognize all the people with whom they have regular contact.

Using each of the senses independently, infants recognize the important people in their lives. Using the senses together, they go further, establishing basic social relationships such as preferences for particular caregivers. As infants mature, their sensory competencies become more complex and support language acquisition.

Attachment

The function of **attachment** behavior is to keep an adult, who provides food, protection, and comfort close to the infant (Hinde, 2006). In the beginning, it is the rooting, grasping, crying, and vocalizing which at first tend to maintain physical contact and later maintain the proximity of the adult. As children mature, their attachment behaviors might include smiling, pointing, following, or offering toys. Later, with language, they ask the adult to look at something, to come, or to help. Older children also use the attachment behaviors of touching, snuggling, or seeking a favored adult to hold them. Young children use their sensory abilities to recognize the adults in the environment and to elicit caregiving behavior from them. Adults generally find the child's recognition, smile, or lifted arms satisfying.

A mother who provides consistent, responsive care is frequently the person to whom the child is attached. However, this person may be a father, grandparent, or sibling as long as the person who is regularly meeting the needs of the baby is available and responsive to the baby's cues as to what is needed. We typically refer to this person as the primary caregiver. Attachment figures may also be caregivers outside of the immediate family. Children may have multiple attachment figures but it is essential that they have one. The attachment behaviors of the infant stimulates the adult caregiving. Sensitive caregiving elicits attachment behaviors in the child. These behaviors cycle repeatedly every day (see Figure 2-1).

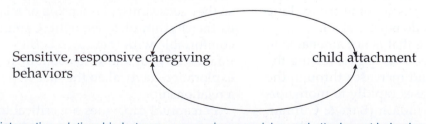

Figure 2-1 The interactive relationship between responsive caregiving and attachment behavior.

The child builds up mental models of the environment and the self within it as a result of accumulated experiences. If children have many positive encounters, they tend to approach the world with confidence and seek help if they cannot manage on their own, with the expectation that help will be provided. Children who do not experience predictable, responsive care learn that they cannot count on adults to respond to their needs. They are likely to view the world as precarious, unpredictable, and the adults in it as unreliable (Bretherton, 2006).

Needless to say, attachment relationships form the foundation of future social engagement. The adult to whom the child is attached forms the secure base from which he or she can explore, which in turn influences the child's overall development and social experiences. Children who have two securely attached adults seem to be particularly advantaged in a number of developmental outcomes. There are individual differences in the quality of attachments, with children having disorganized attachment behavior at greater risk. They appear not to have experienced predictable care as a response to their expressed needs. Professionals who work with infants and toddlers can remedy avoidant, ambivalent, or disorganized attachment to varying degrees during the first two years by providing predictable, responsive, and appropriate care with consistency and by responding rapidly to children's bids for assistance or attention. Professionals can be an additional attachment figures while children are in care.

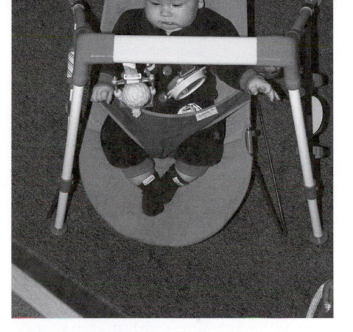

With the gradual increase in control of the head, arms, and shoulders, infants are able to manipulate the amount of stimulation they receive.

Motor Control and Social Interaction

With the gradual increase in control of the head, arms, and shoulders, infants are able to manipulate their social interaction. By 3 months of age, they use their head position and gaze as a means of influencing communication with the caregiver. In the face-to-face position, infants are fully engaged in gazing at their caregivers. When infants turn their heads slightly, they maintain contact but signal that the play may be too fast or too slow.

When the head is fully turned and the gaze lowered, contact is completely broken (Beebe & Stern, 1977). When infants are completely overwhelmed by interactions that are too intense, they go to sleep, cry, or go limp. A summary of infant behaviors relating to head, gaze, and facial expression and corresponding typical meanings to the caregiver is presented in Table 2-2. By the third month, infants are capable of tracking people as they move around the room. They stare at other people for long periods and, as they get older, will shift into a better position to watch what others are doing. For many sensitive caregivers, this is an invitation for conversation or play.

Once infants can sit up, between 7 and 10 months of age, they develop greater eye–hand coordination skills and a corresponding increase of interest in objects. They also may turn completely away from the caregiver to focus on an object. This is not a rejection of the caregiver, but is the exploration of the environment made possible by a comfortable relationship with a trustworthy adult. At about the same time babies can creep successfully and follow their caregivers from room to room.

With increased mobility, infants' social horizons are greatly expanded. So are the opportunities to encounter unsafe objects and environments, get into

Table 2-2 Infant Gaze and Social Meaning to Caregivers.

POSITION AND EXPRESSION	TYPICAL INTERPRETATION
Face to face, sober	Fully, engaged, intent
Face to face, smiling	Pleased, interested
Head turned slightly away	Maintaining interest; interaction too fast or too slow
Complete head rotation	Uninterested; stop for awhile
Head lowered	Stop!
Rapid head rotation	Dislikes something
Glances away, tilts head up; partial head aversion	Stop or change strategy
Head lowered, body limp	Has given up fighting off over-stimulation

others' things and explore their world. In doing so, they also need consistent, sensitive guidance that will keep them safe and encourage them to learn at the same time.

Temperament

Infants have unique personalities, and from the moment of birth, have genetically based temperaments that affect their development throughout life (Rothbart & Bates, 1998). **Temperament** involves the individual differences infants display in their affect and motoric expression. **Affect** is the general mood of the child, which varies from high tone (inflation) to low tone (depression) (Rochat & Striano, 1999). Expression of emotion is how the children behave in response to the environment and the people in it. It does not explain why they do something, or how well they accomplish it. Temperament then is the style of behavior that children display when they show affect (Kristal, 2005).

Characteristics of the child's temperament influence interaction with the caregiver right from the beginning. An infant may be timid or intrepid, quick-tempered or slow to anger, passive or actively curious, rhythmic or irregular. Some infants respond to every event, whereas others ignore loud noises, bright lights, and other sensations. Temperamental differences, then, are differences in the degree, or intensity, of emotional behavior and in timing and duration of responses. Some temperament trait clusters are challenging to caregivers and will influence the quality of social experiences between caregivers and children as well as their adjustment to group settings (Coplan, Bowker, & Cooper, 2003).

Negative affect includes emotional reactivity and difficulty in affect regulation. These babies are very likely to respond strongly to stimulation and appear to have a negative mood (grumpy). A second cluster, **resistance to control**, encompasses lack of attention, low agreeableness, and strong attention to rewarding stimuli. These children are challenging to manage. The third group includes those who show **shyness and inhibition**. These babies are wary of new situations and people.

Three distinctive types of temperament have been described and appear to be useful to understand how children might respond to their world (Thomas & Chess, 1986). The easy child (about 40% of children) is generally happy, friendly, predictable, and adaptable. The slow-to-warm-up child (about 15% of children) is mildly **responsive** affectively, predictable in schedule, but hesitant in new situations. Eventually this child will engage with new people or in new situations after repeated exposures. The difficult child (about 10% of children) is likely to laugh loudly and long, or throw a tantrum. Affective intensity is strong, the pattern of sleeping and waking is irregular and unpredictable, and the child is frequently irritable and generally very active. Some children (about 35%) do not fall into one of the three clear types of temperament but demonstrate unique combinations of activity level, positive affect, and the degree of regularity in their behavior pattern.

The four constellations of these patterns are normal, and are apparently stable over time (Rothbart & Bates, 1998); however, the way such consistency is expressed changes as the child matures. For practical purposes, professionals might use the perspective of viewing these characteristics as having both assets and challenges for the caregiver that require differing strategies to attain desirable child outcomes.

Table 2-3 illustrates potential assets and challenges inherent in high scores on the following measures (Rothbart & Bates, 1998).

1. **positive affect:** cooperativeness, manageability, and amount of laughter and smiling
2. **irritable distress:** fussiness, frustration, anger over limit-setting; general irritability

3. **fearful distress:** withdrawal, difficulty in adjusting to new situations, adaptability
4. **activity level:** more or less active
5. **attention span/persistence:** length of time the child remains engaged and focused
6. **rhythmicity:** predictability of the child's behavior pattern

In infancy, persistence might be seen as the length of time the baby looks at a toy, whereas in an older preschooler it would be seen as the length of time the child works at a puzzle or builds with blocks.

Table 2-3 Assets and Challenges of Temperamental Characteristics.

TRAIT(S)	DEGREE	POTENTIAL STRENGTH	POTENTIAL CHALLENGE
Positive affect: cooperativeness, manageability, amount of smiling and laughter	High	Child will likely engage in a lot of pleasant social exchanges with adults and children.	Child might be vulnerable to strangers. He or she will need help in learning when trust is appropriate.
Irritable distress: fussiness, frustration, anger over limit-setting, irritability	High	Child will likely get his or her needs met, even when resources are limited.	Child will need assistance in maintaining social interactions and developing empathy for others.
Fearful distress: withdrawal, difficulty in adjusting to new situations, adaptability	High	Child is likely to stay in proximity of the primary caregiver, getting more support for interactions with others and hearing more language.	Child will need help in accepting a new child care provider and will need a slow entry into a new setting with lots of support.
Activity level	High	Will encounter more objects in the environment in a specific period of time. Will have bountiful exercise.	Child is likely to need help in focusing on one activity until complete. This child may be vulnerable to injuries due to the challenge in supervision.
Attention span/persistence: length of time the child remains focused	High	Usually this trait is associated with children who become good problem solvers and attend to detail.	Child may need to explore wider into the environment; his or her exposure may be self-limited with little variety.
Rhythmicity: predictability of the child's behavior pattern	High	Child is likely going to learn to use the toilet more easily.	Child may need help when the patterns of the day do not conform to his or her routine or biological rhythm.

During the middle of childhood, persistence is often seen in task completion or the return to an unfinished self-determined goal. In older children and adults, temperament is often described in terms of emotionality. The congruity of temperament over time is seen when fussy, active, irritable infants become intense, irregular, highly active 12-year-olds. Inhibited, hesitant toddlers appear to become extremely shy adolescents (Kagan, 1997). Supportive, sensitive care can help youngsters cope with their own temperaments, modifying their natural tendencies, as more timid children are encouraged to engage with new people and situations and the most exuberant explorer is taught about appropriate social restraint and caution (Kristal, 2005).

Mutual influences of temperament between infants and caregivers. The culture in which a particular child is born shapes the temperament of the child, just as it shapes the expectations and values of the caregivers who care for the infant (Day & Parlakian, 2004). Different groups of people value different personality characteristics, and thereby influence how the caregivers might view the temperaments of individual children. Temperament differences make the infant easy or difficult to care for, and more or less pleasant and interesting to play with, influencing the amount and quality of social interaction he or she is likely to receive. Difficult temperaments seem to require extreme amounts of patient, persistent care from adults who have little other stress and much time to devote. Consequently, the difficult baby seems to challenge the resources of overtaxed caregivers. Fortunately, some adults are able to cope effectively with difficult infants and provide the support, patience, and interaction necessary for good development.

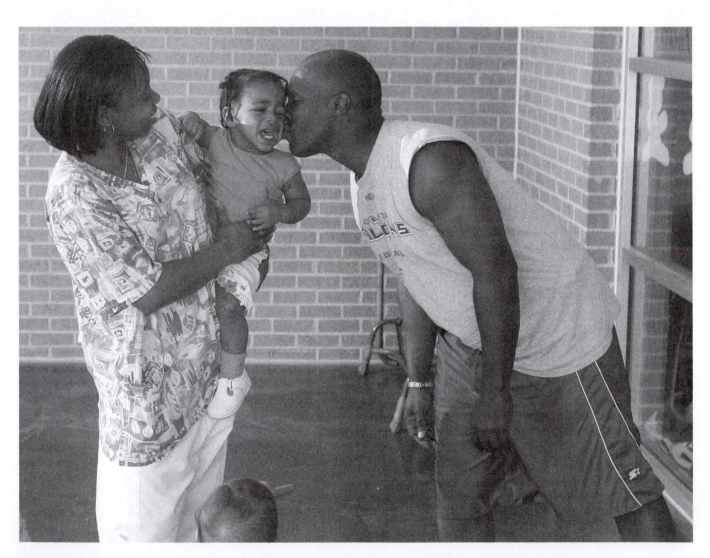

Understanding and warmth are key to supporting the social development of children with difficult temperaments.

For example, two children who differ markedly in activity and impulsiveness elicit different responses from adults.

> Mike moves slowly, watches what is going on, seldom cries, and plays in his crib contentedly for long periods after awakening. Todd, on the other hand, is distracted by every movement or noise; moves quickly from one part of the room to another; always seems to be underfoot; cries vigorously, long, and frequently, and rarely is content to play in his crib after awakening. Both boys are 8 months old. Mr. McIntyre, who takes care of them, interacts less frequently with Mike but finds him satisfying and restful, though slightly boring to play with. Todd gets much more attention, although Mr. McIntyre frequently feels irritated with him. The only time Todd seems to settle down is when he plays with an adult. Mr. McIntyre is aware of his tendency to ignore Mike and pursue Todd, so he carefully remembers to check on Mike regularly and involve him in play.

As patterns of interaction between adults and children emerge and become habitual, each child's social context becomes unique, influencing the organization of personality. **"Goodness of fit"** between the temperament of the adult and that of the child is important because both parties of the relationship have characteristic styles of handling affect, feelings, and **emotions**. The experience of an infant like Mike, who is somewhat inactive and not very sociable, with an adult who is impulsive, impatient, and expects quick social responses from him would be very different from his experience with an easygoing, patient adult who is willing to wait for him to respond in his own good time.

The goodness of fit between the infant, the caregiver's temperament and expectations, and the infant's general living environment may be more important to the long-term outcome for the child than temperament alone. Even infants with difficult temperaments can be happy and successful if their caregivers are easygoing, if the caregivers' expectations for the child are clear and suitable for the child's age, and if caregivers use skills that enable them to be sensitive and responsive.

INDIVIDUATION AND SOCIALIZATION

Two functions of social development begin to operate from the beginning of life. **Socialization** is the process that includes one's capacity to cooperate in a group, to regulate one's behavior according to society, and, in general, to get along with others. **Individuation** is the process by which the self or personal identity is developed and one's individual place in the social order is acquired. Individuation integrates the emerging perceptual, memory, cognitive, and emotional capacities to form a unified personality or self-identity in the young child. Individuation differentiates the self from others and takes place in a social context. Individuation must occur if attachment, or preference for specific adults, is to take place. Both individuation and socialization are absolutely essential to successful adaptation to life and occur gradually over time. Table 2-4 summarizes the process of individuation, including infant capabilities; social actions that stem from these capabilities; and appropriate adult responses that support individuation.

During the neonatal period, babies show an innate attunement to people, paying acute attention to them with all sensory modalities. By the end of the second month, self-awareness unfolds as the infant becomes an agent in the environment. During this phase, the infant molds to the parent's body when held, engages in mutual cueing with the parent, is most easily soothed by the preferred adult, and responds to signals contingently with another. **Contingent behavior** is like a conversation with turn taking, but using only gesture, facial expressions, touching, or playing, often with vocalizing.

Between 2 and 6 months, the infant is able to engage in reciprocal (give-and-take) relationships with caregivers that require an understanding of self and other. Routine care and predictable adult–child face-to-face interactions lead to social expectations in the infant. The distress–relief sequence contains all the components necessary for the infant to accomplish the following (Lamb, 1981):

> Learn that relief quickly follows distress.
>
> Recognize the person who provides relief.
>
> Gradually develop a complex concept of the caregiver.
>
> Associate the caregiver with the pleasurable outcomes he or she produces.

Apparently, the more promptly adults respond, the more likely infants will learn associations between their own and another person's behavior. They are capable of learning and remembering positive social behavior from 6 months of age and are likely to show surprise if their caregivers behave unexpectedly. If, for some reason, the primary caregiver alters the typical patterns and timing of responses, the infant becomes sober, agitated, and then distressed.

Table 2-4 The Individuation Process and Appropriate Adult Responses.

AGE OF ONSET IN MONTHS	INFANT CAPABILITIES	SOCIAL OUTCOME	ROLE IN INDIVIDUATION PROCESS	ADULT BEHAVIORS THAT SUPPORT INDIVIDUATION
0–1	Sucking; visual tracking; grasping; cuddling; vocalizes; social attunement	Reflexes; shared gazing; orienting toward caregiver	Proximity to caregiver	Observation of states; prompt basic care
1–2	More time quietly alert; sensory learning about people and objects; molding to caregiver's body; continues interesting activities; coos and goos	Beginning social responsiveness; mutual cueing	Begins differentiation between self and objects; more ways of maintaining proximity	Provide objects; engage in turntaking play; give prompt basic care; respond sensitively to different states
4–8	Sits, grasps; creeps; increased interest in objects; sensory learning: mouthing, manipulating, examining, banging; laughs, yells, and squeals; babbling	Recognizes familiar people; shows clear preferences among people; intentionality limited to previously learned actions; playful; social smile, laughter	Beginnings of social expectations; stranger fear; maintains proximity by following, checking back on caregiver after short excursions	Provide a safe environment for floor exploration; establish limits for child; respond predictably
9–14	Walking, climbing, running; joyful exploration; curious excited; beginning use of language and gesture; person and object permanence becoming clearer; trial-and-error problem solving; intentions conveyed by language, gesture, and action; makes requests; comprehends words; complex babbling	Strong desire for approval, inclined to comply; self-willed; increased self-control; variety of emotions; social play with adults; interest in events	Maintains proximity by following and calling caregiver; strong preferences for particular people; protests separation; uses caregiver as a "base of operations" and moves outward; recognizes that others act; beginning to cooperate	Protect from hazards (child has mobility without judgment); respond promptly to communicative acts; set and maintain routines and limits; provide opportunity for independence; use language to comfort; explain leaving child with familiar adults; have patience

AGE OF ONSET IN MONTHS	INFANT CAPABILITIES	SOCIAL OUTCOME	ROLE IN INDIVIDUATION PROCESS	ADULT BEHAVIORS THAT SUPPORT INDIVIDUATION
15–24	Increase of all motor tasks; skillful exploration; rapid increase in language and nonverbal communication skills; offers objects to preferred adults; self-recognition and person permanence; pointing, says words then word combinations	Is likely to cling, then run away; plays "mother chase me!"; self-willed: "No" before compliance; considerable amount of self-control; self-comforting; may show sudden fear after departure from caregiver; may cry from relief at caregiver's return	Realizes caregiver's goals are not own goals; may be ambivalent about dependence/independence; can play happily in absence of preferred person; uses "gifts" of toys in seeking proximity, more language	Verbalize about departures, reassure; tolerate rapid changes in approach and withdrawal; use language to discuss events, relationships, objects, etc.; allow child to control some holding on, letting go; make social expectations clear over and over; have patience
24–30	Good understanding of ordinary language; intentionality well developed; mental problem solving; ability to ask for help based on need; goal-directed behavior; self-definition of gender and age	Increasing interest in other children; peer play and communication stronger; mutually regulated social interactions; pretend play	Realistic sense of self and others; uses a wide array of techniques to maintain proximity (helping, conversation, play stories); can cope well with separations	Continue to reassure, support, and provide affection; praise efforts at self-control and independent behavior; provide experience with another toddler

Between 4 and 6 months babies detect increasingly subtle cues and remember more from previous experiences, thereby acquiring the ability to act intentionally. At about 8 months babies not only figure out that they can do things but that other people can also. For example, Randy could not get into a box, so she reached over to pull her caregiver's hand to the box (with the expectation that help was at hand). At 9 months children appear to detect "who is doing what to whom," identifying a process as well as perceiving the person and objects affected.

By the age of 1, the baby is able to cooperate with a caregiver, such as by lifting his or her legs when a diaper is being changed. Babies begin to read subtle differences between people and begin to understand the dispositional world in which peoples' feelings and inclinations are revealed. They act with the clear intention of influencing the behavior of the adult. The foundation of social cognition emerges as a result of the intimate encounters repeated daily in which adults and infants respond synchronously to one another (Rochat & Striano, 1999). Regular, frequent contact is essential to this process. Otherwise, social expectations are not rewarded. Infants can cope with a few caregivers such as the parents and the child care worker, but they give up trying to build social connectedness if they encounter several adults a day or over a week. Infants in group caregiving environments are capable of developing expectations of their regular caregivers who are consistently with them. However if there is inconsistency in adults, the babies do not have the opportunities to learn what to expect from so many different adults.

The toddler is practicing being a separate person and having a will, and is beginning to develop a sense of autonomy. Creeping and walking enable these older infants to experiment with new ways to achieve desired goals. The exploits of this period require persistence and patience in adults. Barriers that previously protected children from falls are surmounted. Climbing makes forbidden objects high on shelves accessible. The emergence of self-will is accompanied by the gradual development of enough self-control to enable the child to act, to do. From the necessity of controlling body movements emerges the sense of autonomy (Erikson, 1963). If toddlers can control their own bodies, then they can exert their will over their own actions. However, children who are not permitted to exert control over their own movement will feel doubt about their ability to do so. This is probably why floor freedom

and appropriate independence is related to the ability to internalize self-control (Stayton, Hogan, & Ainsworth, 1971).

Sometime in the middle of the second year of life children develop an objective self-awareness, and conscious, self-reflective behavior is possible (Lewis, 1999). Assertions of "mine" reflect this capability.

The conscious monitoring, control, and prediction of people's behavior is based on the intimate one-to-one relationships and an emerging understanding of the affective determinants of people's behavior, which is sometimes called the child's theory of mind (Legerstee, 2005). Verbalizations of "I want" signify that the child can think about thoughts and feelings that he or she has experienced.

Although the process of becoming a person and then becoming a member of a group begins in infancy, it is never really finished. The development of self-control, identity, and the place of the individual within the group continue to challenge each person as he or she is socialized as a member of the culture.

Coping with Adult–Child Separation

Wariness of strangers tends to occur at 7 months and again around the time the child turns 1 for those children reared only at home. They are less fearful with a family member or in their familiar surroundings. The age when stranger-anxiety occurs varies, as does its intensity and duration, and some babies never seem to experience it. However, when a child is first introduced to an unfamiliar caregiver, especially when stranger-fears exist, it can be a very stressful experience for everyone.

Parents can handle separations best by first allowing the child to become familiar with an alternative adult, then explaining that the parent is leaving soon, having the familiar adult help the child to start an activity, then quickly departing. Helping professionals must, of course, provide comfort and reassurance and support the child in exploration as soon as possible. Practices such as lying to or deceiving the child, encouraging parents to sneak out, or pulling a screaming infant from the parent's arms are to be avoided because the infant is quite capable of associating these terrifying and painful experiences with the caregiver as a person.

Wanting to be self-willed and independent, children often are frightened by the accompanying sense of separateness and aloneness. Toddlers can hold opposing emotional feelings—such as loving a caregiver and feeling angry—at the same time.

This beginning of constancy helps toddlers come to terms with their own and adults' wishes. This ambivalence of feelings often is observed in behavior; a child might cling one minute and dart away the next; he or she may show a toy and then turn abruptly away.

Because toddlers have developed a considerable amount of self-control and can maintain a mental image of the absent parent, they might be able to tolerate several hours of separation. However, because holding back crying still is difficult, they might burst into tears at the moment of return. Parents may need help to understand that the child contained the desire to cry as long as possible and that this behavior should not be misinterpreted as the infant not wanting the parent.

Two-and-ahalf-year-olds engage in mutually regulated conversation, conveying their intentions and understanding well the verbalized intentions of others. They cope well with the loneliness and distress of separation and are capable of using a variety of behaviors to achieve closeness to preferred adults. Language plays an important role as they begin to attend to adult verbal reasoning as a guide to behavior. Goal-directed partnerships with adults are possible.

The presence and reassurance of a family member continue to be important. As the child reaches out into the neighborhood and community and meets the challenge of interacting with peers, behaviors seen in earlier phases are likely to reappear and be worked through again.

When children are away from parents for substantial periods of time, or when parents are under such stress that they are emotionally unavailable to the child, a helping professional may become the child's primary nurturer. Infant–childcare provider attachments appear to be independent of infant–mother and infant–father attachments, with the provider having a secure relationship with some infants whose relationships with their parents are insecure (Goossens & Ijzendoorn, 1990). Apparently the urgent needs of infants can be met if the provider does not have too many infants at once. The attachment figure can be anyone, but it must be someone if healthy development is to occur. Therefore, caregivers should act as if they were the preferred adults with all their young charges. Children prefer a parent when exposed to several caring adults, so this does not entail competing with the family for the child's affection and loyalty.

Individual Differences in Outcome

Developing a wholesome sense of trust is central to the process of individuation (Erikson, 1963). If feelings from the sensory world are typically pleasant, the infant will develop a sense of trust. However, if sensory stimulation is harsh, the child will develop a sense of mistrust or a sense that the world is a dangerous place. The discomforts infants experience from hunger, gas, wet diapers, cold, or excessive heat are typical, as are the pleasures of being dry and warm and being fed, cuddled, or played with. Trust and mistrust are the endpoints of a continuum, with each child needing some of both.

Complete trust is as maladaptive as complete mistrust. On one hand, a completely trusting child may be oblivious to the real dangers of the world, such as rapidly moving cars, because of the inappropriate expectation that she or he will always be taken care of. On the other hand, a completely mistrustful child may be unable to interact with the things or people because nothing but pain and danger are expected.

The ideal is to have children on the trusting end of the continuum so that they can risk exploration and learn to tolerate frustration and delay gratification. Such children expect to be safe and comfortable most of the time, and their view of the world is hopeful. Trust is acquired through communication. The interaction between the infant's behavior and the caregiver's response is the basis of affective bonds, security, and the confidence felt by the infant, all of which help determine the degree to which children thrive.

Another outcome of the process of socialization and individuation is the child's self-concept. If adults are available, responsive, and loving, children perceive themselves as endearing, worthy, and lovable. However, if adults are inaccessible, unresponsive, or unloving, infants perceive themselves as disgusting, unworthy, or unlovable. The adult's general pattern of expressing affection and rejection will influence how well a baby's strong need for affection and comfort are met (Tracy & Ainsworth, 1981). Most infants' worldviews and self-perceptions are a blend of these continua (endearing, disgusting; worthy, unworthy; lovable, unlovable).

From this discussion, it can be seen that no two infants emerge from the early individuation process alike. Differences in temperament, daily relationships with the parents and other caregivers, and the comparative amounts of pleasant or unpleasant experiences they accrue influence the degree of trust,

As more infants and toddlers experience group care, more of them have the opportunity for true peer interaction.

the quality of attachment, and the perception of self they develop.

Friendliness

Adults may not think of babies as being friendly with one another, but as more infants are experiencing group care, more of them have the opportunity for true peer interaction. It seems that infants acquire social styles and an enduring orientation toward other people from their families.

Babies show more interest than fear when babies unknown to them approach. Prior experience with others helps when unfamiliar children of the same age are encountered. Babies initiate more interactions and more complex interactions with familiar peers (Field & Ignatoff, 1980). They cannot engage in complex play with more than one other child at a time, however. Play episodes in which babies interact are typically short in time and consist of careful watching, sometimes with toys being offered and retrieved or observation with vocalization.

Toddlers in a group setting use three types of social bids to initiate interaction with their peers.

Distal contact such as watching from more than 3 or 4 feet away, or glancing or smiling at another, is used infrequently and rarely results in positive social engagement. Proximal nonverbal contact such as touching another child or leaning over to see what another is doing is often more successful, but rejections of such approaches do occur.

Proximal contact combined with child verbalizations is about as effective as nonverbal contact for these youngest players in a group setting, although ignoring and rejecting are more common than a positive response (Honig, 1993). Sometimes when toddlers are attracted to an object or a person, they gather rapidly together, tumbling over one another in an effort to get near the person or obtain the object. This group approach has been described as "swarming" and is most frequently an unsuccessful social interaction.

Toys attract children and bring babies together, but they also may draw attention away from another player. Toddlers usually can start a friendly approach, but have difficulty keeping the interaction going. Toddlers 15 to 20 months old are capable of engaging in an activity that involves taking turns, repetition, and imitation along with much smiling and laughing. Going around and around the table is a typical example. As toddlers mature, their interactions with age mates become longer and their ability to share intentions and purpose increases the scope of their play (Ross & Conant, 1992). Typical early peer behavior is summarized in Table 2-5.

EMERGENCE OF COMMUNICATIVE COMPETENCE

Neonates are innately prepared to learn language. They are capable of a limited array of signals that engage caregivers in social interactions. Neonates make pleasure sounds, and adults respond with satisfaction. An infant gazes into the adult's eyes for prolonged intervals and the adult begins to talk as though the infant understood the message, even pausing when it would be the infant's turn to speak. Infants turn their heads toward the speaker, are calmed by the voice of the caregiver, and show preferences for their own parent's voice (Gleason, 2004). It is in this early beginning that babies learn to signal nonverbally and begin to learn the rudiments of oral communication, with voice variations in pitch and volume and turn-taking.

Nearly all adult speech directed toward preverbal infants is used to convey social connectedness. The melody is important—rise-and-fall phrasing communicates warmth and loving approval, and short, staccato bursts signal "stop," "pay attention," or "don't touch." Soft murmurs are used to comfort and soothe. These patterns are true of all language speakers (Otto, 2006).

Between 1 and 3 months of age, babies make cooing sounds in response to speech, smile and laugh, and make speechlike sounds when elicited. As the length of the quiet alert state increases, opportunities for communication with people increase. When adults talk to babies of this age, they frequently do so around some referent object in the near environment: "You are ready for your bottle, aren't you?" Between 3 and 7 months, babies respond distinctly to different intonations in people's speech.

By 8 months of age, they repeat some simple babbling sounds such as "bababa" or "mamama" and may attempt to imitate sounds produced by adults. Though much of the babble practice occurs when infants are alone or resting before and after a nap, they will also babble when an older child or adult speaks to them. Babbling also draws caregivers into conversations. Solitary babbling is different from the vocalizations heard when infants are "talking" in a "conversation" with their caregivers. Throughout the infancy period, babies need the back-and-forth patterning of face-to-face speech in the context of joint activity (Barnet & Barnet, 1998). The baby and the caregiver are constantly influencing one another during these conversation-like interactions well before the child uses words (Masataka, 1993).

The range of communication skills expands considerably in the middle of the first year. They show pleasure in simple games such as "tug the blanket"; cry in rage when disappointed; and express caution by looking away, knitting the brows, and having a sober facial expression. Caregivers have many more cues to interpret that allow them to understand the feelings of these young babies. Thus, the flow of social interaction between the caregiver and the infant depends on regular contact, detailed observations of each of the partners, and the time and commitment for such engagements for communication to be effective. Adults bear most of the burden of the social interaction, with infants gradually taking greater part during the course of the first two years.

Table 2-5 Peer Relationships in Infancy.

AGE	INFANT BEHAVIOR
0–2 months	Contagious peer crying; intense visual regard between familiar infants
2–6 months	Mutual touching
6–9 months	Smiling; approaching and following; vocalizing; watching
9–12 months	Giving and accepting toys; simple games: "chase," "peek-a-boo," waving
12–15 months	Vocal exchanges with turn-taking; social imitation; conflicts over toys; "swarming" may occur with groups of infants
15–24 months	Early words; mutual roles: "hide and seek"; "offer and receive"; imitates others; aware of being imitated
24–36 months	Communicate about play events; wide range of play

Even quite young infants are able to read, decode, and interpret the facial expressions of their caregivers (Camaras, Malatesta, & Izard, 1991). They improve greatly in the understanding and use of gestures (Fogel, 1993). They exert some limited control in the turn-taking patterns and respond expressively to communications directed to them. Thus, they gradually learn the patterns of social engagement.

When a child is about 6 months of age, infant–adult interactions become focused on joint object involvement. Adults briefly point out and offer objects while commenting on them. However, babies may turn their backs toward the adult when their interest is engaged in a toy in order to concentrate on the object. This behavior should not be interpreted as dislike; instead, it can be explained by the fact that the infant cannot focus on several things at the same time.

Between 9 and 15 months of age, infants gradually develop increasing ability to deliberately initiate communication that influences the behavior of their caregivers (Carpenter, Nagell, & Tomasello, 1998). They first engage in **shared attention**. The most typical example is when the baby looks at the toy and then looks at the adult face to see that the caregiver is also looking at the toy. **Communicative gestures** such as pointing to an object desired with an urgent vocalization may be an imperative demand for the object, or the baby may point to an object with a vocalization indicating "isn't this interesting?" Regardless, the child will check if the adult is apparently responding to the overture. **Gaze following** occurs when the infant notices that the adult is focused elsewhere in the distance and the child orients to the same place. By 12 months, babies will look to where the caregiver is pointing. Babies continue to try to communicate when the caregiver does not respond appropriately and may modify or elaborate gestures. For example, Harry wanted the revolving holiday ornament on the table. He opened and closed his hands and vocalized, "Eh, Eh!" with increasing volume. Unsuccessful, he pointed and increased the length of the vocalization and "Eehh. . . !" Finally his caregiver came over to him, picked him up, and then moved the ornament from view while telling him why he could not have it.

At a year or so, children develop some alternative ways of handling certain emotions. They might appraise a new situation before responding to it instead of responding immediately. One means of evaluating a situation is called **social referencing**. Babies use their developing communication abilities to read the caregiver's facial expression and tone of voice. If the adult responds to a new situation with comfortable posture and a neutral or smiling face, the infant will respond by exploratory behavior. On the other hand, if the caregiver appears fretful or upset, the infant is likely to behave warily (Clymen et al., 1986). Social referencing continues throughout childhood as children pick up emotional cues from other children and adults when determining how to act in an unfamiliar situation or with an unexpected occurrence.

They can send messages, too. Babies clearly can "tell" the caregiver when they want to do something, using combinations of gesture, gaze, and vocalization. Most adults quickly recognize lifted arms as a request to be picked up. Older infants and toddlers have a variety of noncrying sounds that get and keep attention, gradually developing words. At about 13 months of age, symbolic communication emerges, and toddlers and their partners become increasingly ritualized as they repeat and expand upon their ways to interact (Adamson, 1995).

Imitative learning begins to appear at the end of this period. Toddlers show awareness when either an adult or another toddler imitates what they are doing. They often gaze and smile at the person imitating them before continuing their play. Earliest forms of pretend play (such as a baby washing his face in the living room) are examples of imitative behaviors separated in time and place from the playing child. The emotional displays one sees in other people are also eventually imitated. Thus the older infant and toddler are likely to display pleasure, interest, anger, or fear in ways similar to the important adults in their environments.

Between 18 and 24 months of age, the infant learns to use both referential speech and expressive speech. **Referential speech** is about concrete objects, actions, and locations. Sometimes the names of objects of interest are spoken after only one or two exposures with children learning very rapidly (Otto, 2006). Occasionally a made up word is used, such as "babish" instead of diaper, which may function as a real word if the caregivers also use the word, "Come, let me change your babish." **Expressive speech** is about emotional content, feelings, and social experiences. Less dependent on gestures to convey feelings, the baby uses words that express possession ("Mine"), negation or defiance ("No!"), and goals ("Want down"). Two-word sentences appear with little attention to details, such as "Me cookie." With the increased competence of the baby to send and receive messages that can be understood by anyone, and the ability to mentally formulate intentions, the baby achieves a milestone in social relationships. By the end of the second year, the infant can function as a social partner and can communicate intentionally to influence the behavior of others. For some children this occurs earlier.

Sign language is increasingly used by some families after their infants can sit up and are being fed with a spoon. Parents teach simple signs such as the one for "more" or "all done" which allows the baby to communicate more specifically and eliminates some mealtime stress. Babies may use between 50 and 100 signs before they begin to speak the oral language of the family, and use it in social interactions with the people around them.

Books illustrating American Sign Language(ASL) for infants and toddlers are readily available in bookstores. Generally, professionals find this strategy very useful as well. If caregivers are fluent in sign, the child becomes bilingual as they would if there were two languages spoken by caregivers.

Simultaneous bilingualism is the acquisition of more than one language before the age of 2. Both languages are acquired the same way, and children become fluent at approximately the same age as they would with only one language. These tots may take a little longer than with one language as there is a lot more vocabulary to learn, but the delay is not substantial (Otto, 2006).

Successive bilingualism is when children acquire a second language after 3. The older toddler or preschooler learns the language of the childcare environment in much the same way as when the original home language is learned. Therefore, professionals should make sure that common objects are clearly named (chair, toilet) and verbs demonstrated (wash, put) as soon as possible in the program. As with home language, children understand a lot well before they speak much (Otto, 2006). The importance of connecting the vocabulary to clear meanings cannot be overstated. It is usually easier to support the learning of a second language when the child is a competent communicator for his or her age in the home language. Some caregivers outside the home have successfully used key sign words in the interim (come, clean up, stop, toilet, rest, etc.).

The two-year-old group had half of the children whose home language was English. The other children's families were speakers of Finnish, Korean, and Chinese. Miss Eppinger taught all of the children American sign from the beginning to ease their social interactions with signs for "stop,", "help,", and "look" among the first. She used both the sign and the English words to assist them in following routines and resolving conflicts. All of the children used the signs months before the second language speakers actually spoke English, enabling them to engage in social play successfully.

Supporting communicative competence. Children learn the communication skills of the caregivers with whom they interact. Sensitive and effective caregivers learn how each infant engages in social bouts and respects signals for disengagement. Observation of infant state, gaze, spatial positioning, posture, and distance from the adult will provide cues to the adult of whether to initiate social activity. Forcing social interaction on an infant who is tired or otherwise engaged leads to tears and irritability.

Adults who talk to infants within the routine settings of the day about ordinary things that are happening tend to increase the amount of vocalization of babies. Turn-taking conversations, lullabies and songs, and comments on the task at hand are all effective. Speech directed to other adults or general talking in the room is not effective.

Words and gestures have meaning for babies long before they begin to use words. Therefore, when caregivers begin to label an infant's feelings according to how they are interpreting a particular event, they are providing appropriate vocabulary while simultaneously providing cues to the child as to the appropriate social response. "Oh, you don't know Uncle David, do you? It's a little scary. Come here and we will talk to him together," when murmured in a soothing voice and acted upon will both calm a baby and describe what is happening.

Adults must use the context of the situation to interpret the meaning of one-word utterances. In addition, a particular baby may have a unique meaning for "words" that are composed of easily produced sounds. Oftentimes, even then, caregivers must guess and observe the infant carefully to see that they have responded appropriately. Repeating the word often helps as children recognize the meaning of a much larger vocabulary than the one they are able to produce.

When adults use precise language for objects, actions, locations, and people, toddlers will also use precise words by the end of the second year. Early in their development, they tend to over generalize. "Dada" may be applied to all males indiscriminately. However, when adults use only the correct names for objects and actions, babies soon learn correct vocabulary (Gruendel, 1977). "Dada" will be applied to one important male and "Bompa" to the grandfather. Because some sounds are difficult to produce, babies typically substitute easier sounds until the necessary speech sounds are acquired.

Toddlers: Transition from Infancy

Toddlers have left the conspicuous dependency of their first year of life. In a very short time they have achieved significant progress in becoming socially competent persons. Walking is usually the criteria for becoming a toddler and may occur as early as 9 months, but it is more typical between 12 and 14 months. With the increased mobility typical of the toddler period, they are active, intrepid explorers of the physical environment, where every object is felt, tasted, smelled, examined, and manipulated. Adults must actively protect toddlers, as children do not have the judgment to determine what is safe and what is not.

Self-regulation.   The youngest toddlers are still very much dependent upon their biological rhythms for eating, sleeping, and eliminating, though these are usually regular and predictable. They are able to wait longer to be fed, especially as they perceive someone getting the food ready. Never patient, they do delay protest if the wait is not too long. As this period progresses, they are able to adapt to the time schedules of center or home so as to share in family meals, especially if appropriate snacks or bottles are offered between meals.

Toddlers are quite adept at soothing themselves. Sucking pacifiers or thumbs supports this purpose. Soft objects such as a blanket or soft toy are saturated with familiar scents and textures that remind the toddler of the comfort of home and primary caregiver.

These are frequently sucked or rubbed near the face so that the full sensory impact is available. (Needless to say, washing these objects generates great distress for the child, as the smells are gone.) This strategy is used to support sleep or soothing when youngsters are experiencing other forms of distress. Toddlers who do not have a transitional object and who are entering child care may find comfort in using of the unwashed pillowcase of a family member as a cover in the crib to support the child's self control. Physical contact with a preferred adult continues to be the favored source of comfort for most toddlers.

Toddlers apparently are able to distract themselves by directing their attention to objects when they are feeling distressed if their caregivers have consistently used this tactic previously (Grolnick, Bridges, & Connell, 1996). Thus, they are somewhat

able to delay gratification, maintain behavioral control, or moderate their feelings of distress. The degree of distress, the child's temperament, and gender all play a role in this process (Raver, 1996). Offering an appealing toy or activity distracts the child from the source of distress and may assist the toddler in moderating negative affect to a neutral or positive emotional state. When adults use this strategy consistently, toddlers imitate it themselves on their own.

Toddlers are not patient; they cannot delay gratification very long and are notable for the total lack of control when they throw tantrums. Even given this, they show the beginnings of self-regulation, particularly when rested and in safe and supportive conditions. Tantrums sometimes are a result of the inability to communicate with others or of experiencing frustration. As greater skills are achieved, there are usually fewer and fewer outbursts.

Toilet learning.   With mobility and the development of enough language to communicate about toileting needs, older toddlers are increasingly able to learn sufficient control of bladder and bowel to use the toilet. Once toddlers have learned what they are supposed to do (remove clothing, get in position, eliminate, wipe themselves, wash hands), they are capable of carrying out this routine. Toddlers need the support of adults who provide calm, straightforward instruction and a reachable toilet, who treat this function of self-regulation in a low-key, matter-of fact way, and who give the reminders necessary for them to be successful. Power struggles between the toddler and adult over this issue are unproductive.

Positive self-identity.   Toddlers learn words such as "me" and "mine" and happily claim ownership of desirable toys. They know their names or nicknames and call family members by name. In this sense, they assert their own identity. Toddlers show pride in their ability to climb, jump, run, or engage in an increasingly varied set of large- and small-motor skills. A healthy sense of worth and power may develop as the child achieves success in learning to use the toilet, dress and undress, and eat independently. They also have the amazing capacity to change from the very independent doer of things to a person who wishes to retreat to the more dependent stages of infancy without a moment's notice. Caregivers support the toddler's emerging self-identity by allowing appropriate independence and cuddling.

Toddlers do not have the experience to judge risk. They might try to climb too high, jump on the furniture,

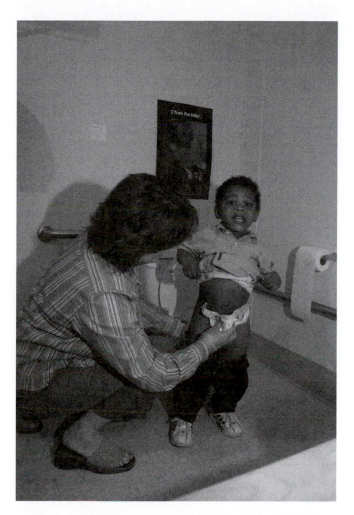

Toddlers need calm, loving support as they learn basic life skills such as toileting.

preferred caregivers exist even if not present. They improve rapidly in all cognitive abilities if they have opportunities to explore safely. They learn about causal relations (Oakes, 1994) and rapidly acquire problem-solving skills (Chen, Sanchez, & Campbell, 1997). Toddlers 18 to 30 months of age use several problem-solving strategies, continuing some less successful ones even when they have learned more successful approaches, with their selected strategies becoming increasingly adaptive with experience. In fact, children who are coached with hints or who observe a demonstration are able to transfer their strategies to similar problems and even continue to use the more effective strategies on their own (Chen & Siegler, 2000).

Gwennie and Kirk were both about 14 months old. Kirk had a large ball and Gwennie was holding a large, metal truck. Gwennie pointed to the ball and vocalized. Kirk looked up and frowned. Then Gwennie stood up, waddled over to Kirk, and dropped the truck on his head. He wailed loudly and let the ball go and she hurried after it. The caregiver did not allow Gwennie to keep the ball and brought her back to Kirk to comfort him. Gwennie seemed to be surprised that he was crying and patted him. Though Gwennie had solved the problem of how to obtain a desired object, the strategy was not acceptable to the caregiver and she was not ultimately successful.

About four months later Gwennie was observed staring at Lizbet, who was astride a toy horse mounted on rollers. She pointed to the horse and jabbered at Lizbet, who continued to push the rolling toy across the room. Gwennie grabbed the handlebars and pointed to the horse and continued her insistent sounding vocalizations. Lizbet looked at her and stayed on the horse. Then Gwennie walked over to Lizbet's diaper bag, which had been left on the floor. She removed Lizbet's bottle and held it out to her. Lizbet protested "No!" got off the horse, and hurried over to Gwennie to retrieve her bottle. Gwennie gave up the bottle quickly, and climbed on the rolling horse, smiling. Because both children seemed very satisfied with the outcome of Gwennie's problem-solving strategy, she was able to continue her play with the rolling horse. Gwennie had experienced many more opportunities of seeing one object substituted for another in the intervening four months and was able to learn from this.

eat food from another child's plate, or otherwise violate what adults think they should do. Clear, firm limit-setting with consistent follow-through helps children of this age define a sense of self with a clear understanding of what can and cannot be within their control. The process of setting limits and following through is developed fully in Chapters 10 and 11.

With toddlers, caregivers should expect to repeat these guides many times a day as the youngsters truly forget or treat each situation as a new experience. Regular, consistent caregiving is important in learning. In the process of socialization, children develop identity and autonomy within the limits of the social context.

Planning and decision-making skills.   Cognitive processes are present in rudimentary forms in toddlers (Chen & Siegler, 2000). They are able to imitate, plan (Willatts, 1990), form expectations of future events (Haith, 1993), and remember that their

Once older toddlers acquire language skills, the scope of their social problem-solving abilities widens immeasurably, as asking for things is so effective in getting them. They thus become more like preschool-age children in this regard.

Interpersonal skills. Toddlers show affection to parents, familiar adults, and regular caregivers. The child's temperament and other individual characteristics shape the nature of these relationships. Most of the responsibility of the relationship remains with the adult, though toddlers may offer toys or share materials with adults readily. Toddlers may comfort a child who has been injured, or cry because another child is crying. Many early displays of caring for another occur when one child experiences what they themselves have experienced previously. For example, Todd walked over to Sammy who had tripped and fallen hard on his knees. He patted him, looked up to see if the caregiver was coming, and remained nearby until Sammy was comforted.

Toddlers show interest in other children, may offer toys occasionally, and engage in short episodes of play with materials near others. The youngest toddlers have difficulty in maintaining an interaction, but with guided experience and better language

Toddlers enjoy one another's company.

skills, older children less than 2 years of age can engage in longer play bouts. They may be more successful with an older child who is able to lead the interaction.

Infants and Toddlers with Special Needs

Up to this point, the discussion and description of infants and toddlers has been based on typical development. Some infants are identified at birth as having conditions that will alter the speed or the outcome in their growth and development, and others as having high risk of not developing typically. Sometimes the challenges they face may not become apparent until later. For example, children experiencing delays in language development generally are not identified until well into the second year or even later. The helping professionals who work with infants and their families have a responsibility to refer children for special services or to cooperate with the intervention team in providing optimal conditions for their development. Physicians and child care workers are most likely to be among the first to identify irregularities in the child's developmental progress because they see children regularly during their first two years. Early intervention has moderate and positive effects on the developmental progress of many children with disabilities who are less than 3 years of age. Special services are free to the family if they meet one of the following criteria (Solomon, 1995, p. 40):

- identifiable condition (e.g., Down syndrome, cerebral palsy)
- physical disability (e.g., visual or hearing impairment)
- developmental delay
- need for early intervention indicated by clinical judgment

In some states infants and toddlers who are at high risk are also eligible for services. High risk is defined by the states but is likely to include infants born to chemically dependent mothers, abused and neglected youngsters, children who have had lead poisoning, and low-birth-weight infants. Language problems are among the most frequent and have substantial impact on children's social development.

Professional roles. Early childhood professionals who also have background in special education are usually involved directly in developing the early intervention plan for infants and their families. Caregivers in programs providing child care or other services to infants and their families are likely to encounter special needs children in the course of their practice. The role of the specialist is to devise and support the intervention plan around the special needs of the child. This plan, which is called the **Individualized Family Service Plan (IFSP)**, is developed with parents, any professionals who can contribute specialized knowledge to implementing the plan, and those people involved in day-to-day work with the baby. However, the role of the general practitioner is to deliver a quality program typical for the age and development of a group of children, taking the intervention plan of the child with special needs into account and cooperating as much as possible with the specialists.

General practitioners also have the significant role of surveillance of all the children in their programs. They must observe skillfully, communicate with parents, and refer children for assessment when necessary. Consulting with the administrators of the program and sharing concerns with the family are necessary prerequisites for making a referral to the appropriate agency in the community. (Local public schools will be able to identify the specific agency in any community.) A referral means that someone with specialized skill will make a detailed assessment of a child. Some youngsters are on the edge of normal ranges and may not require specialized interventions, and other children may be missed because caregivers and families continue to think that the problem will correct itself in time.

Problem recognition. Caregivers can recognize when referral would be appropriate by identifying some of the cues. Table 2-6 lists guidelines that are based on language development, as it is the most frequent diagnosis for special intervention (Solomon, 1995). Table 2-7 is a listing of signs of emotional distress and/or mental health troubles of infants and toddlers (Honig, 1993). These signs are diffuse, and sometimes children do not get the help they need in this area in a timely manner because adults in their environment do not recognize the signals. When caregivers observe a clustering of characteristics of concern that persist over time and are not helped by high-quality responses, then they should seek assistance, first through supervisors and then with families and other professionals.

Many early child care professionals do not recognize that the skills they have may be applied to infants and toddlers who have special needs. Many special needs are mild to moderate, and the children can fit into a program with typically developing peers with minimal alteration of the environment and strategies used to guide children. For example, children with Down syndrome learn more slowly than others. They will need more repetition and will achieve milestones of self-feeding and toileting later than their age-mates. Often they are brought into a group of children younger than they are as the primary program adjustment. However, their social development will progress in the same direction, but more slowly.

Table 2-6 Referral Guidelines for Children with Speech Delay.

12 months	Exhibits no differentiated babbling ("bababa") or vocal imitation; exhibits no recognition of familiar names or words ("mama, bye-bye")
18 months	Exhibits no use of single words; is not following simple commands ("Give it to me"); does not wave "bye-bye" or point to familiar objects
24 months	Has single-word vocabulary of less than 10 words; does not point to body parts when requested (eyes, nose, mouth, or ear); does not point to pictures in a book or when they are named
30 months	Uses fewer than 100 words; shows no evidence of two-word combinations; is unintelligible; does not follow simple directions ("Put it on the table," "Pick up the book," "Go get your shoes")
36 months	Uses fewer than 200 words; has no use of telegraphic sentences; has clarity less than half the time
48 months	Uses fewer than 600 words; has no use of simple sentences; has clarity less than 80% of the time

Source: Data from "Pediatricians and Early Intervention: Everything You Need to Know But Are Too Busy to Ask" by R. Solomon, 1995, *Infants and Young Children*, 7, no. 3, p. 44.

Table 2-7 Signs of Emotional Distress in Infants and Toddlers.

BODY CUES	SOCIAL CUES
Dull eyes without sparkle	Lack of fluency in the older toddler who is already verbal
Back arching and body stiffening as a regular response, especially in the latter third of the first year	Reverse emotions such as giggling hysterically when frightened
Eye gaze avoidance	Impassive or angry when peer becomes hurt or distressed
Pushing away rather than relaxed molding onto the adult	Lack of friendliness to loving adult overtures
Limp, floppy, listless body when without illness	Echoic verbalizations: repeats the end of the adult statement or phrases rather than responding to what is said
Smiles are rare despite tender adult elicitation, after adjustment to the program	Fearful withdrawal or flinching when caregiver tries to touch or caress
Diarrhea or very hard stools, without infection present	Regular avoidance of or indifference to parent at pickup time
Difficulties in sinking into deep, refreshing sleep	Anxious "shadowing" of caregiver without letup
Regular rocking of body back and forth, even when rested	Continuous biting or hitting of others with no prior aggressive provocation
Inconsolable crying for hours	Strong aversion to limit-setting and explanations of caregiver over time
Scattered attention rather than attention flowing freely between caregiver and baby during intimate exchanges	Little if any interest in peers or persons
Head banging against crib persistently	Constant masturbation daily even when not tired or at nap
Grimaces of despair	Other children let toddler be strongly aggressive, in deference to the "disabled" status, but then mostly avoid this toddler in play
Frozen affect (apathetic look)	
Wild, despairing, thrashing tantrums	
Banging headlong into furniture or hurting self often, without turning to caregiver for comfort	

Source: Data from "Toddler Strategies for Social Engagement with Peers," by A. Honig, December 1993, paper presented at the Biennial National Training Institute of the National Center for Clinical Infant Programs (8th), Washington, D.C.

SKILLS FOR INITIATING POSITIVE SOCIAL RELATIONSHIPS IN INFANCY

You have read about the importance of being a responsive, loving adult in the lives of infants. Feelings of concern, affection, and attraction for infants seem to come naturally to many adults, but the skills to help infants grow and develop must be learned. Many of the skills first presented here will be more fully developed for older children in later chapters. All the skills focus on the quality of sensitivity.

 Providing Prompt Basic Care

1. Respond promptly to infants' bids for aid. When an infant 6 months of age or younger cries, pick up the infant quickly and attend to his or her needs. Older infants have an increased ability to wait and will respond to speech and other signs of attention while waiting for care, but their patience is limited. No child under a year of age should wait long for routine care such as feeding, diapering, or being put to bed for a nap. Infants who cry a great deal, and conversely, infants whose caregivers do not wait for them to cry, do not associate their communication behavior with the caregiver's response. The pattern of prompt response to infant cries enables the infant to learn that adult help is an outcome of their distress signals.

2. Establish a regular pattern in giving care when responding to infant signals. Timing is important, as is developing a particular pattern of picking up, talking, soothing, changing diapers, feeding, or holding the infant. Consistent adult behavior allows children to learn to expect a particular kind of response to their bids for aid. Although some general consistencies in common procedures among caregivers in the child care center are highly desirable, infants are able to distinguish among potential caregivers with whom they are familiar and can develop preferences for specific individuals by 6 months of age.

3. Confer with parents about the child's routine. Avoid undue stress by finding out the child's particular pattern of sleeping, playing, and eating at home. There are often cultural differences in how families provide routine care. Listen carefully, and when possible within the group setting, adapt your patterns of care to more closely conform to the parents'. In addition, ask adult family members simple, direct questions: "What do you usually do to soothe Terry when he cries?" or "Show me how you usually place Terry on the bed for sleeping" for children 4 months or more of age.

4. Handle infants gently but firmly, moving them so they can see your face or other interesting sights. Infants will not "break" and should be held securely, with the head supported during the first weeks until head control is attained. Place them at your shoulder when walking so they can see the environment. Support them in the crook of your arm for feeding so they can gaze into your face. Carry older infants at your side with their backs supported so that when they pull away from your body, they will not fall backward out of your arms. At the end of the first year, some infants may protest at being carried at all. In such a case, if for any reason you must carry the child, hold her closely and firmly to your body, wrapping the arms and legs with your arms so the child does not strike you in the process of protesting. When held, an infant should be safe and secure, and should not experience falling, being squeezed too tightly, or other discomfort.

5. Ensure that the infant experiences tactile comfort.
   a. Change wet diapers and clothing promptly. Babies who urinate several times in a disposable diaper before being changed get a painful rash.
   b. Pat gently when burping the baby; a thump is not required.
   c. Wash the baby's skin as needed.

continued

SKILLS FOR INITIATING POSITIVE SOCIAL RELATIONSHIPS IN INFANCY—continued

d. Caress the infant whenever opportunities arise. Loving touches are pleasurable to them. Back rubs or massage also may be effective in helping infants to relax.

6. Adjust the environment to keep it safe and sanitary as infants begin to move on their own. Protect babies from harm. As babies begin to roll, crawl, or walk, it is better to keep space orderly, safe, and clean than it is to restrict the baby or engage in rounds of limit-setting and upset. Remove breakables, keep floors free of clutter, cupboards securely fastened, and gate stairways are examples.

 Detecting Individual Needs

1. Use all your senses to gain information about the children. Scan all the infants under your supervision regularly. Look for signs of drowsiness, level of activity, degree of involvement with objects, potential opportunities for social engagement, and possible safety hazards. Listen to their vocalizations as well as their cries. Intent observation helps you to become knowledgeable about an individual child and often facilitates understanding and even liking between adults and the children in their care.

2. Write down the time and date of developmental milestones, such as the first step, or of a behavior that concerns you, such as the appearance of apathy in an infant. Noting an infant's eating and elimination patterns are not as useful as noting changes or irregularities in such patterns. Describe specifics of the circumstances and how adults and children acted rather than writing your conclusions about such experiences.

3. Use your knowledge of development and the infant's typical behavior to interpret events. Your knowledge can help you understand what babies' behaviors mean. For example, Juan, 4 months old, awakened quietly and has been staring blank-faced into distant space for the last 10 minutes. Saba, at

8 months of age, has tossed all her toys onto the floor and is looking at them with an angry expression, waving her arms and vocalizing loudly. Alexis, 10 months old, is rapidly crawling toward the discarded toys. Bridget, only 1 month old, is sleeping restlessly.

Miss Zimmerman knows that Juan usually takes a long time to become interested in exploration after he wakes up. She promptly removes Saba from the crib, offers a toy, and changes her diaper. Attending to another child, Miss Zimmerman did not know the reason for Saba's displeasure. Bridget's need obviously is to be left alone, and Alexis is clearly attending to her own needs to move in space and to explore objects. Finished with diapering Saba, Miss Zimmerman places her on the floor near Alexis, offers her a plastic bowl and balls, and moves to speak to Juan.

This example demonstrates how knowledge of child development in general and of individual children in particular can enable adults to respond with greater sensitivity and skill.

4. Take into account the temperament and experience of all the children in your care. Be sure to provide adequate stimulation for the very quiet child as well as the fussy baby. If you are more comfortable with peaceful babies, do not ignore the frequent crying of infants whose responses are less satisfying to you. In working with infants, preferences are almost always inevitable. These feelings are legitimate, but they should not alter your standards of professional practice. As a caregiver, you will have to exert self-control and self-discipline. You must distribute your attention among all the infants under your supervision.

5. Keep pace with the changing needs of children as they mature. During the first year of life, infants' abilities and interests change rapidly, and a response appropriate to an infant only a short time ago now may be outdated. Turning the head away when a new food is offered and promptly spitting it out is not unusual for an infant between 4 and 6 months

SKILLS FOR INITIATING POSITIVE SOCIAL RELATIONSHIPS IN INFANCY

of age who is just learning to eat pureed foods. The appropriate response is to continue offering the food if at the beginning of a feeding or discontinue if the child is at the end of a feeding. However, when the infant is only a few months older, head-turning, arm-waving interference, and spitting may signal the infant's emerging motor competencies, and offering a curved-handled spoon for the infant's participation in the feeding process might be messier but more appropriate.

6. Encourage older infants to participate in their own care. Adults can do practically anything faster and easier themselves, and infant participation usually is inefficient and messier. The purpose of participation is to support the infant's emerging concept of the self as an actor, a person who can do something, not just experience something done by another. For instance, an infant who can sit can participate in diaper changes, altering his or her body and leg position as necessary; one who can sit, reach, grasp, and let go can put at least one object into a storage container; an older infant who has sufficient eye and hand coordination to easily move objects to the mouth and who can sit independently may be ready to hold a bottle and, later, a spoon.

Once basic finger control is achieved, undressing is possible. The removal of socks and shoes is common at about 12 months of age, with other articles of clothing coming within the range of the older toddler. Children need to learn the appropriate time and place to remove clothing, as they are likely to practice this interesting skill indiscriminately. Putting clothing back on usually is more difficult.

7. Report new skills and abilities to adult family members as soon as they are observed. This is particularly important to parents who are away from the infant all day. Parents may have little time with the infant while he or she is awake and may not have the opportunity to observe the new abilities as soon as the caregiver can. Help them understand each day's achievement.

 Establishing and Maintaining Effective Communication

1. Respond to infant's signals in a way that is consistent with your interpretation of the meaning and appropriate for the development level of the child. If a young infant is in the quiet alert state, provide something to look at such as your face, a mirror, a mobile toy, or a leaf on the tree outside the window. If the same child becomes drowsy after a period of wakefulness, settle him or her for a nap. Immediately respond to a crying infant less than 6 months old. However, if a child 19 months old cries in similar circumstances, she or he may be signaling for attention and wanting to play, which can be delayed for a few minutes while the younger child's needs are attended to. Explain your behavior to the older child: "It seems that you want to play, Hanna. I will come as soon as I change Billy's diaper." The behavioral state of the infant; the nonverbal cues of facial expression, pointing, and vocalization; and the child's typical behavior are useful in determining appropriate responses.

2. Talk to every baby of any age. Words are never wasted on infants. Maintain a face-to-face position and eye contact while speaking. Use short, simple sentences or phrases.

Use a higher-pitched voice, emphasizing vowel sounds, and allow time for the infant to respond.

To 7-month-old Brandy Marie, her caregiver said, "Hel-l-o-o-o. Hel-l-o-o, Brandy, h-e-l-l-o little girl." Brandy smiled openly and waved her arms. "So you want to play . . . want to play," Brandy's caregiver continued in a lyrical tone of voice, repeating many phrases to the delight of the infant.

To 15-month-old Kevin, the caregiver said, "Here's the ball. It's here, by the crib," pointing to the ball when he didn't find it. In a higher pitch she repeated, "Look here (pointing). The ball is by the crib." Kevin responded by running unsteadily toward the ball. Imitate

continued

SKILLS FOR INITIATING POSITIVE SOCIAL RELATIONSHIPS IN INFANCY—continued

the infant's vocalizations, facial expressions, and gestures in playlike conversations.

Once you begin to converse with a baby, she or he will respond with coos, smiles, laughter, babbling, and attentiveness, depending on the baby's age. Pause for the child to respond in much the same way that you would carry on an adult conversation. Allow older infants enough time to respond to your speech with words or gestures.

3. Comment during routine care about objects, positions, or actions that concern the infant and are immediately observable. Use specific vocabulary, simple grammar, and short sentences. Speak slowly and distinctly (Otto, 2006). The following script is based on an interaction between a 3-month-old child and his caregiver.

> *Charlie begins to cry and Ms. Nu approaches. "Charlie, are you hungry? The bottle is warming." (She picks the infant up and walks toward the changing table.) "I'll bet you are wet . . . a diaper, yes . . . " (Charlie has stopped crying and appears to be watching her hands.) "Lay you down . . . now, unfasten this diaper . . . take it off, oooofff, ooooff." (She smiles and looks into Charlie's face as he wiggles his body and moves his arms.) Ms. Nu continues to tell Charlie what she is doing as she completes the diaper change, puts him in an infant seat near the sink, and washes her hands.*

4. Slow down or discontinue the interaction if the infant looks away for a few seconds, lowers the head, or cries. He may be experiencing over-stimulation. Going to sleep or shutting the eyes is another means for younger infants to terminate an interaction. Older babies may simply crawl or walk away.

5. Use language to respond to older infants' gestures. When a toddler points to a cookie, say, "Cookie?" Or, when an older infant bangs the cup after drinking juice, say, "Looks like you're finished." Name actions that the child is doing. For example, when Jeff was bobbing up and down while music was playing, his caregiver smiled and said, "Gee, Jeff, you're

dancing!" Simple, short, direct statements are best.

6. Wait for a physical response to key phrases for babies who don't talk yet. Before toddlers begin to talk, they understand many words and phrases such as "Bye-bye," "So high," or "All gone." They may, however, take a little time to respond before waving the hand, putting the arms up, or looking into the cup.

7. Tell infants and toddlers what you are going to do before you do it and wait a second or two before acting. Engage children in participating in their own care whenever possible. Announce, "I am going to pick you up now" before you do it. Allow the baby time to reach for you. "It looks like your nose is runny. I will wipe it with a Kleenex." For babies 7 months and older the caregiver might say, "Lift up your legs now, so I can put the diaper under you." In each case, provide opportunities for the child to participate as much as possible in the social event. Avoid quick, impersonal actions that treat the baby as an object rather than a social person.

8. Repeat and expand toddler utterances. At the end of the first year, infants may begin to say their first words. Simply use their word in a way that seems to make sense: "Mama!" exclaims Diedra. Her caregiver responds, "Mama's gone to work." Sometimes people outside the family do not readily recognize a baby's word; family members must be consulted if the word is used regularly. "Manky" may mean a particular blanket; "Doe" may mean, "Look at that." In either case, respond with words such as "Do you want your blanket?" or "Blanket?" This skill is further developed in Chapter 4.

 Encouraging Exploration and Learning

1. Provide play materials and interaction experiences that encourage infants to explore the environment. Allow young infants

SKILLS FOR INITIATING POSITIVE SOCIAL RELATIONSHIPS IN INFANCY

to explore your body by touching your hair or skin or by patting your clothing. Provide toys and materials that are within children's developmental range but that challenge their awakening interest in objects.

Demonstrate how toys work, such as how a pull toy chimes when dragged across the floor. Place toys and materials where older infants can reach them. Periodically remove the clutter of toys on the floor and replace two or three so that children can more readily perceive them.

Entice slower-developing babies into play with toys by offering them and demonstrating play. Play impromptu interactive games such as "peek-a-boo" or "where's the toy" with young toddlers or "making faces" with younger infants. Allow babies to set the pace. Do not intrude on their activities.

2. Praise each success. Rejoice in the infant's accomplishments. Finding a toy that has rolled behind a box is a significant achievement for an 8-month-old. Getting food from the plate onto the spoon and into the mouth is a feat for a 1-year-old. The first time to sit, to crawl, or to walk is the result of concentration, effort, and practice for the developing infant. Let children know you are proud of their successes. Laugh with them.

Hug them. Talk to them. Let them know how glad you are that they can do something new.

3. Encourage exploration by being physically available to children during play. Infants not asleep or engaged in other routine care should be on the floor for play. Stay in close proximity as infants move out into the world of objects. Do not walk away as soon as they are engaged or leave them alone in a strange environment or with strange people without giving them a chance to acclimate themselves to the new situation. Timid infants especially need patient support because, to them, the world may appear to be a frightening, dangerous place. Be aware that older infants can "read" your fear, pleasure, anger,

or joy from the tone of your voice, your facial expression, and your body tension.

This social referencing helps the exploring baby to determine if he or she should cry after a fall or other painful event.

4. Play with toddlers and organize playtime so that more than one adult at a time is sitting on the floor and interacting with toddlers in groups. Nothing is more appealing to a toddler than an adult who is doing something that they can play too. They hurry over to play, all of them, all at once. In their desire to engage they crawl over, squeeze between, step on, fall over, or push down their peers. As mentioned, this is sometimes called swarming. Often a child is hurt or frightened, so the best prevention is to have more than one adult at a time prepared to sit on the floor to play.

 Helping Infants Comply with Adult Requests

1. Use simple, common verbs to make requests of older infants. Say things like "Come here," "Look," and "Show me." A baby can understand and comply with these oral requests sometime between 8 and 10 months of age. Sign language, if used by the adults in an appropriate context, can be imitated by children sooner than they can speak the words. Use a warm tone of voice that is relaxed and in your usual pitch and make requests or suggestions in a conversational volume, and children will be more likely to comply. Avoid harsh voices and physical force. They are ineffective and will generate only fear and withdrawal.

2. Show infants what to do. Demonstrate the action that you wish the infant to perform.

At the same time, describe it in words. For example, if you want an infant to place a toy in a storage box, you might sit on the floor, pick up a toy, place it in the box, offer another toy to the infant, and, pointing to the box, ask her to put it in. Infants learn by imitation. They

continued

SKILLS FOR INITIATING POSITIVE SOCIAL RELATIONSHIPS IN INFANCY—continued

are likely to do what they see others doing. Do not expect infants or toddlers to already "know how to behave." They are just beginning to learn social behavior and must experience many appropriate interactions with adults who patiently demonstrate what is to be done.

3. Repeat suggestions or requests. Babies need to hear directions and see demonstrations more than once. Infants generally comply with requests for behaviors that are made with a warm voice by an adult who has taken into account their needs and interests. Children under the age of 2 cannot really stop an action in progress on their own, but a simple repetition of the request with a few moments of delay is likely to be effective. Sometimes toddlers respond with "No!" when asked to so something. Wait a moment or so and repeat the request. This assertion of self is not the same as defiance, and many toddlers will happily comply a minute or so later. Try not to be impatient or convey urgency or hurry. All toddlers take many repetitions, and youngsters with special needs take even more.

4. Distract an infant's attention by offering a substitute action or object. Getting the child's attention is the first step. Offer an alternative object or point something out that might be of interest. An exploring infant may readily give up a pair of glasses if offered an appealing toy. Use simple substitution; infants often let go of what they are holding in order to get something else. Verbal demands and pulling objects out of the infants' hands are less effective and lead to angry confrontations that need not occur. Use proactive controls such as engaging the infant's attention, distracting her or him from less appropriate actions or objects, making suggestions about what to do, and showing how to do it. These will avoid power struggles and are likely to achieve compliant behavior.

5. Physically pick up and move an infant who does not comply with your requests when safety or orderly function is at stake. Never delay action when safety is involved!

Simple, firm, friendly physical removal with appropriate redirection of the child's interest is both appropriate and effective. Quietly voiced explanations, such as "It's not safe for you outside all by yourself" or "You can play in the tub of water when it's out, not the toilet," should accompany the removal and be followed by helping the child into another exploratory experience.

 Supporting the Beginnings of Peer Relationships

1. Arrange social experiences between infants when they are comfortable and alert. Place small infants in seats for short periods of time, arranging the seats so they can see other children. Provide opportunities for creeping infants to explore objects in the same area. Usually, any social overtures between infants occur when there are only two children in close proximity and when each child is comfortable and unafraid. Even then, infants in the first 12 months of life will not be able to maintain an interaction for very long. Peer play skills are slowly acquired in the second year of life.

2. Provide adequate space and material for toddlers to use while playing together. Toddlers are unable to stop quickly and often have poor balance as they acquire locomotor skills and are therefore likely to inadvertently lurch into other children.

They should have enough uncluttered space to avoid getting into one another's way. Duplicate play materials are useful in minimizing conflict over toys and for increasing social play. Sharing toys is unrealistic before the age of 3. Toddlers are just beginning to act on their own goals and are unable to comprehend that others also have goals. Quick action that prevents interpersonal stress between infants supports the eventual development of more positive relationships.

SKILLS FOR INITIATING POSITIVE SOCIAL RELATIONSHIPS IN INFANCY

3. Demonstrate simple actions or words that can extend peer play. One strategy is to "talk for the baby" or explain nonverbal play bids to the other child. "When Cassandra points to the dough, she is letting you know that she wants to play with some of it here beside you." In another instance Spencer walked into the housekeeping area and picked up a doll, looking at Austin. Their teacher said, "Austin, you are fixing food to eat. I think Spencer's baby might be hungry. Do you think that you could fix something good for the baby to eat?" Austin brought the high chair to the table and began to prepare food as Spencer placed the doll in the high chair. The teacher observes carefully and expresses the toddler's wishes and intentions in words so the social exchange can get started or be maintained for a few minutes.

 Being Available to Interact with Infants

Even though you know what to do and how to do it, there inevitably will be times when you are unavailable to respond promptly. You will experience time and energy constraints. Infants whose caregivers usually respond sensitively receive the beneficial effects of developing expectations of adults, acquiring a sense of effectiveness, and associating their own actions with the outcome. Being available is not always the same as being present.

1. Do housekeeping chores when infants are asleep or when another caregiver is available to interact with the children. Any task that diminishes your attentiveness to the children makes you unavailable.

2. Limit the frequency and duration of adult-to-adult conversations. People who are unfamiliar with infants sometimes consider them unsocial or uncommunicative and seek to engage other caregivers in conversation to meet their own needs for social interaction.

Helping professionals must focus their attention on the children and meet their own needs in other social contexts. Telephone conversations should be limited to short, essential messages and emergencies. Only parents need the phone number in the child care room; personal cell phones should be off.

3. Send long-distance cues to cruising babies that you are available for a hug, a lap, or general sharing of delight. Smile at them from across the room. Outdoors, hold your arms open to be run into. Clap your hands when you see a new accomplishment. Nod your head when they look up at you when they finish a task. Offer your lap for a rest spot after a quick run. All of these specific actions let the child know that you are there for them. You are present wholly for them.

4. Limit the number of infants cared for by one adult. The adult-to-child ratio should be established after taking into account the age distribution of the infants in the group, the skill of the caregivers, the physical setting, and other resources. For all practical purposes, an adult-to-child ratio of 1:3 or 1:4 is needed to implement the skills previously described. When an adult is involved with one infant, he or she is essentially unavailable to all the others. The probability of giving adequate, sensitive, supportive nurturance necessary for healthy social and emotional development decreases as the number of infants for each caregiver increases.

 Supporting Children Who Have Special Needs

1. Read the individualized family service plan that has been prepared by the local agency providing specialized services. Babies who have been identified as having specialized needs prior to entry into the program will have a written plan of intervention.

In addition, some babies have particular medical or dietary needs with which you must

continued

SKILLS FOR INITIATING POSITIVE SOCIAL RELATIONSHIPS IN INFANCY—continued

be familiar. Find out as much information as you can from family members or other professionals working with the family.

2. Ask for and participate in any specific training that will enable you to provide safe, healthy care of a specific child enrolled in the program. Occasionally infants wear breathing monitors, hearing aides or devices, foot and leg braces, or must use other equipment and materials with which you must be familiar to be effective in providing basic care. Ask a knowledgeable person to demonstrate the use and care of any such devices before the infant is left in your custody. Find out about the specialized needs of these infants and understand clearly your responsibilities.

3. Cooperate with the parents and other professionals by communicating regularly about the infant who is receiving special services. Often a journal that travels with the child is used to keep everyone informed about the child's normal progress. Parents, special intervention professionals, and child care providers often need to share information. Babies cannot speak for themselves. Additionally, they frequently will not perform for an occasional visitor those behaviors that are more frequent in settings with adults they see daily.

4. Follow the process of your agency or program for obtaining written consent to share information with others, or to refer families for special services. Share information with others outside the program only with the consent of the parents. Community resources to serve infants and toddlers with special needs are available in the United States. There is a process for initiating and maintaining these services. Avoid chatting about any child with coworkers, other parents, or even other professionals.

Information should only be shared among the team and program administrators who are responsible for the care of the child and with others only with the consent of the parents. The behavior of all children should be treated as confidential information.

5. Collect detailed written observations on the child's behavior and development as you see it. Be objective in describing what you see. Organize such observations in a way that is meaningful to you so that you may contribute to the plan for intervention for the infant. Note things that are typical for any infant as well as those that seem to you to be unusual or atypical. Seek counsel of administrative leadership or experienced professionals in your program if the behavior seems atypical before conferring with parents. There is considerable variation in the rates of development.

6. Participate in new and renewed individualized family service plans as appropriate. A group of professionals and family members meet together initially, and thereafter annually, to plan for the interventions to support children having special needs. The members of the group always include the parents and those professionals whose specific skills might contribute to the child's successful functioning. If an infant is receiving child care, the director and the regular caregiver or teacher should be included in this group. Details of the child's performance or progress are shared and plans developed for the following year. A summary of observations of development, supported by the detailed observations as needed, is relevant and should be contributed at this time.

7. Implement interventions that come within the scope of the program and that are meaningful to the child's progress. Each profession has specific skills that might be useful for an individual child. Caregivers often incorporate into their routines specific strategies that other professionals proscribe or initiate if they are possible to do so within the routine of the program. Occasionally, the strategies needed are so time consuming or require so much one-to-one intervention that an aide is hired specifically to deliver these interventions. The developmental professional is responsible for integrating the adult

SKILLS FOR INITIATING POSITIVE SOCIAL RELATIONSHIPS IN INFANCY

aide into the program in such a way as to allow for group experience for the child as well as for the interventions.

 Supporting the Adult Family Members of Infants

1. Listen to what family members tell you about their infant. Adults who are caring for an infant full time since birth know a lot about that particular baby. They will tell you about what the child can do at this point, what other professionals have said regarding the child's development, how well the baby sleeps or eats, and if there is a change in the baby's behavior.

2. Record pertinent information for other adults who provide care for the child in the program. If a parent reports that a child has had a poor rest during the night or if stressful family events or other experiences have disrupted the tranquility of the home, make a note for other staff members who will be providing care when you leave for the day. Many infants and toddlers are in care for 9 or 10 hours. Be sure that private information is communicated only to those who need to know and is not shared indiscriminately.

3. Allow parents opportunities to discuss how they feel about leaving their infant or toddler with a caregiver. Nearly all parents feel some misgivings and many are ambivalent about child care. Mrs. Walinsak brought her 7-month-old son into the center looking a little worried. "I think he is feeling cranky," she commented, as she started to give him to the caregiver. Ms. Biggs took Kelvin and smiled. He reached out for his mother and began to howl. Mrs. Walinsak began to tear up, looking as if she were about to cry. She said, "Good-bye Kelvin" and hurried out the door as Ms. Biggs assured her she would let her know how Kelvin was doing. Mrs. Walinsak went to her car, sat a moment, and came back to a window to peek in. Kelvin was still whimpering

but no longer crying so gustily. She hesitated, then went to the car and drove off. Ms. Biggs waited for about 45 minutes before phoning Mrs. Walinsak at work: "I just wanted you to know that Kelvin started playing just after you left. He's rolling balls right now and laughing." Mrs. Walinsak sighed, "I really need to work, but it is hard you know." "Yes, most parents find it hard. You want to stay and go at the same time," replied Ms. Biggs. "You can say that again!" responded Mrs. Walinsak.

4. Periodically provide opportunities for parents to talk privately. Some centers have regularly scheduled parent conferences. Some offer the parents opportunities to schedule them based on their perceived needs. Generally speaking, the head teacher should address major concerns at a time when children are not competing for attention. If the major concerns about the child's development are addressed to program support people, they should follow through by arranging for the head teacher and the parent to talk. However, if parents ask if the child had a good day or slept well, any staff member could answer this question.

5. Ask questions periodically so that parents will have an opportunity to share concerns or inquire about typical behavior. Simple questions can be asked, such as:

"What changes have you seen in Aida recently?"

"What are you finding most difficult about caring for Ian just now?"

"What are Kala's favorite play activities at home?" or

"Do you have anything that you are wondering about in regard to Sandra's development?"

When eliciting parental concerns, take their questions and answers seriously.

Never deny their feelings or they will cease to share with you. For example, Mrs. Mir may indicate that Faizan is 13 months old and has not started walking, but that her sister's

continued

SKILLS FOR INITIATING POSITIVE SOCIAL RELATIONSHIPS IN INFANCY—continued

daughter is younger and is already cruising the furniture. If you think that Faizan is doing well in motor development, then let the mother know that this is not unusual: "Toddlers start to walk sometime from 9 months to about 14 or 15 months. Have you noticed that Faizan can pull himself up and stand for a few moments? Babies do that just before they begin to walk around things." Once reassurance is provided, make a note to tell the parent as the child acquires the new skill.

6. Provide accurate developmental information based on observations of the child to parents. Inform parents of typically developing behavior. Parents who are away from their infants and toddlers are interested in hearing about the developmental milestones and daily events of the child. As necessary, share the atypical behavior that you have observed so that parents may adjust their own care accordingly. This may be as simple as noting fussiness or fretfulness.

Other observations may be more serious. If you have noted that a baby does not babble between 5 and 7 months, and rarely responds to noises that appear to surprise other infants, share this information with the parents. The behavior may be caused by recurring ear infections or be a result of other problems. Regardless, the responsibility of the head teacher is to share these observations with the parents and recommend that someone qualified examine the child.

7. Demonstrate respect for the families' cultures and languages by becoming informed.

If necessary, seek a translator if no adult member of the family speaks English.

Learn the correct form of address for both the mother and father, as women in some societies do not take the name of the husband. Use the name of the child that the family uses; do not rename Ja-Young to June or any other more familiar name. Seek out additional written resources to help you to understand the patterns of family behavior that will aide you in communicating with a family who has entrusted a child in your care. Keep in mind that individual differences within a cultural group are as varied as those between cultural groups.

8. Know resources for information about child development and parenting as well as community resources. Most adults enter the parenting role with little information about being a parent, raising a child, or performing ordinary tasks such as taking a temperature, changing a diaper, or spoon-feeding a baby. They frequently know even less about normal development or how to use this information to guide them in supporting their child's daily life. Various local, state, and government agencies and professional groups provide free or low-cost written materials that are very useful to parents. Sometimes commercial organizations such as insurance companies provide safety information. The child care sections of local bookstores have many titles, some more useful than others. Increasingly, materials related to health and to concerns of parents are available on the World Wide Web.

PITFALLS TO AVOID

Regardless of whether you are working with infants individually or in groups, informally or in structured activities, there are certain pitfalls you should avoid.

Ignoring infant cries. Such notions as "Let him cry it out" or "You'll spoil the baby if you pick her up when she cries" are not true and do not work. The infant continues to cry because crying is the only signal for pain, hunger, or distress that is available. Infants cannot be spoiled in the first six months of life (Santrock, 2006b). Providing quick, responsive, sensitive care to infants is likely to produce a compliant, cooperative, competent infant rather than one with unacceptable behavior.

Attributing intentionality to infants' behavior before age 2. Infants do not cry to make you run; they cry because of some discomfort. Infants do not get into things to annoy you; they are exploring the environment and are mentally incapable of planning to aggravate an adult. In the second half of the first year, intentional behavior begins when the child notes the effects of his or her behavior on adults. Children stumble on these behaviors through trial and error, so ignoring whining or screeching and suggesting another alternative to get your attention is fine.

Attributing moral characteristics to infants. Certain infants are easy to care for whereas others are very difficult or challenging. These babies are neither "good" nor "bad." Sometimes, adults project their feelings onto a baby. An infant is born with a temperament not of his or her choosing. Colic is a painful condition that makes life as difficult for the infant as for the caregiver. A sunny, happy temperament does not make an infant an "angel," nor does an intestinal complaint make a baby a "perfect devil." The ability to make choices based on a value system is not acquired for several years. Avoid the trap of "good child–bad child" by focusing on actual infant behavior and emerging competencies.

Focusing your attention only on the attractive, cuddly, or responsive infants. Distribute attention to all children and be sure that infants who are slow to warm up or who are not cuddlers get reasonable and appropriate care. The more passive, less demanding infant should not be left alone in the crib for more than 15 minutes after awakening. Give this child the encouragement to explore and to socialize even if she or he appears content to do nothing at all.

Assuming that nonspeakers cannot communicate. Communication includes a wide range of verbal and nonverbal behaviors that allow us to send and receive messages. Speech is universally understood, but infants have an array of abilities to both send and receive information long before they develop speech.

Ignoring cues that development is not progressing well and/or discounting parental concerns. Nothing is less helpful than the phrase, "He will out-grow that." Infants and toddlers grow out of shoes and clothing with little intervention, but language, cognitive, motor, and social development usually require adjustments in adult behavior to facilitate improvement in problem behavior. Sometimes simple adjustments are not enough and children need more intensive intervention from specialists. No concern of a parent is trivial to the parent, so each concern should be treated respectfully. If concerns are treated as insignificant, parents will stop expressing them.

Communicating important information or significant concerns about the child's behavior or development casually or in a hurry. Sometimes caregivers do not want to see parents become upset, and other times they are so busy with children, they do not have time to interact. However, casual, fast communications that may be difficult or stressful for the parent to handle must be avoided. Think of how a parent would feel if the only thing you said was, "Mitchell had a bad day today. He bit four other children hard enough to leave tooth marks," and then went on to do something else. Instead, ask the parent to stay until you are free for about 15 minutes, try to set up an appointment, or arrange to talk to the parent by phone later. Rapid communications that are positive, "K. C. and Carl played in the blocks for a half hour today," or statements that affirm the parent, "The book you sent with Peter was really enjoyed by the other children," are always appropriate.

Treating all families alike. Families are no more alike than are a group of children. An outstanding feature of the United States is its collection of diverse people. Families vary in composition, economic resources, religion, and education as well as in cultural affiliation or language of preference. Developing a relationship with families requires the same sensitivity to individual differences as developing a relationship with children. A variety of approaches and provisions of opportunities for interactions face to face, in writing or on the phone, in group settings or individually usually will provide a means of contact that will reach most families. If you have been unsuccessful with one strategy, never assume that the parents are uninterested.

SUMMARY

Infants begin life in the context of their families. They are biologically equipped to be responsive to human interactions through all sensory modalities as well as being particularly attuned to language. Having the capacity to communicate their emotions and degree of alertness, they interact with caregivers and the environment from early life. Gradually, they increase their social awareness of themselves, and correspondingly understand that others also have goals of their own. During the second year, they become increasingly socialized and act independently, with increasing ability to regulate their own feelings and behavior. Some children encounter challenges from the beginning of life and may need the intervention of specialists as well as the cooperation of teachers of typically developing children to support their development.

Skills that will enable you to become a sensitive, responsive adult who can support the child's individuation process were presented so that children in your care may establish a system of maintaining proximity to you, of exploring the environment, of establishing an identity, and of beginning social relationships with adults and other children. Basic skills of communicating with the adult family members can support continuity and understanding between professionals and the home.

Using these skills, you can recognize individual differences among children, quickly perceive their needs, accurately interpret their signals, and select appropriate alternatives for action. Integrating social interaction into the basic care of infants and using an array of communication skills will help you to nurture the infant's development of basic social relationships.

Now that you understand some of the foundations of building a social relationship during the earliest part of life, you are ready to concentrate on building and maintaining positive relationships with children as they mature. You will begin by examining the role of nonverbal communication in the next chapter.

KEY TERMS

affect	goodness of fit	shared attention
attachment	imitative learning	shyness and inhibition
behavioral state	individuation	social referencing
communicative gestures	negative affect	socialization
inhibition	referential speech	temperament
contingent behavior	resistance to control	Individual Family Service Plan
emotions	responsive	simultaneous bilingualism
expressive speech	self-regulate	successive bilingualism
gaze following		

DISCUSSION QUESTIONS

1. Explain what is meant by the statement, "Infants participate in their own development."

2. How should adults respond to each of the infants' behavioral states: drowsiness, quiet alert, vigorous crying, and sound sleeping?

3. Describe the techniques that are most effective in soothing a crying infant.

4. When would it be reasonable to expect that an infant would recognize a person by sight or voice?

5. How do babies develop a transitional object and what function does it serve?

6. Look at Table 2-3. Without repeating concepts suggested as assets or challenges, generate an asset and a challenge for each temperament trait. Now select any two traits, and describe how that combination might prove advantageous or disadvantages to the child's interaction with his or her caregiver.

7. How does the way in which basic care is given to an infant influence the course of the child's development?

8. Describe the process of individuation, clarifying how and when self-awareness is displayed.

9. What peer relationships can be expected of infants between 9 and 12 months of age? Would you say that they could react to an experience as a group or simply as a collection of individuals? Why?

10. Describe how infants 6, 9, 12, and 18 months of age are likely to communicate. How are they similar; how are they different?

11. What behaviors would you expect to see or not see in a twelve-month-old who has an undiagnosed language delay?

12. Trevor is a timid, fearful child at a year and a half who is truly frightened when his mother leaves him at the center. Your efforts at distracting him seem to fail and he withdraws into a corner and weeps alone daily. What choices of strategies do you have in working directly with Trevor and with his family? How would you alter your strategies if this pattern persists?

13. Mick is a fast-acting, rapidly moving explorer. He usually perceives possibilities for play and exploration that you do not anticipate. He approaches other children eagerly and is sometimes successful and sometimes not. When he is angry, he is furious and may bite or hit. Rarely still or quiet, he is difficult to get to sleep and naps only a short time. He wriggles away when an adult tries to pick him up and protests loudly. At 18 months of age, he seems to have the ability to exhaust all of the adults in the program, though his general disposition seems to be cheerful eagerness. Generate a plan to help Mick develop his social skills.

14. Patsy is 9 months old and does not babble and does not appear to respond much to environmental noise. You are concerned about her ability to hear. List in order what you should do to approach this problem.

FIELD ASSIGNMENTS

1. Visit a child care center or a family child care home and observe how children respond to routine events of the day, such as being brought to the center and left by their parents, being fed, being diapered, and being put down for a nap. Record the caregiver communication to the child and the infant's responses in these situations.

2. Note at least two instances of infant crying. How did the caregiver respond? What cues were there as to the meaning or message of the cry? Sometimes adults have difficulty in interpreting a cry and try several responses. If you observed this, note what the baby did in reaction to the adult behaviors on each occasion. What soothing techniques worked for each infant?

3. Describe incidents in which older babies responded to simple directions and gestures from the caregivers. Compare the instances of compliance and noncompliance. What strategies did adults use when the children did not comply? How did this vary with the age of the child?

4. Watch an older infant play with a toy and then play with the baby yourself. Take cues from the infant, imitate the baby, and then elaborate on what the child has previously done. Note what you say and do and how the infant responds to your behavior.

5. Select one toddler to observe intently during the day. Watch how the child approaches other children. Under what conditions does he or she just observe a peer playing? Note how the toddler responds to the social approaches of other children and adults, and the duration and quality of social engagements with adults and peers. After the session, write three descriptions of the child engaging in some social or communicative event.

Chapter 3

BUILDING POSITIVE RELATIONSHIPS THROUGH NONVERBAL COMMUNICATION

OBJECTIVES

On completion of this chapter, you should be able to describe:

- The channels of nonverbal communication.

- Cultural differences in nonverbal communication.

- The function of nonverbal communication in working with children.

- The means by which children acquire nonverbal skills.

- How nonverbal behaviors communicate messages about relationships between adults and children.

- Adult skills related to nonverbal behaviors that support interpersonal relationships, positive self-identity, and cultural competence.

- Pitfalls to avoid in interacting nonverbally with children and parents.

Don't look at me in that tone of voice!

Shari, age 5, clearly understood the message conveyed by her mother, who stood stiffly with feet apart, hands on hips, scowling from the doorway as she viewed a clutter of baking supplies spilled on the counters and shelves where Shari was playing. Like most children, Shari could quickly interpret the meaning of her caregiver's stance and facial expression.

Such nonverbal messages rarely are discussed but usually are understood by people sharing the same culture. Unlike spoken language, in which words are explicitly defined, nonverbal codes are implicit, with the meaning derived from the context of the situation and the flow of the interaction. For this reason, nonverbal messages may be ambiguous or confusing. However, they allow people to convey feelings, as well as information (Doherty-Sneddon, 2004).

Nonverbal communication is composed of actions rather than words. It includes facial expressions, gazing, hand and arm gestures, postures, positions in space, and various movements of the body, legs, and feet. In addition, nonverbal communication includes paralinguistic, or vocal, behaviors such as the frequency range of the voice, its intensity range, speech errors or pauses, speech rate, and speech duration (Gazda, 2006).

The meaning of all nonverbal communication is derived from specific behaviors within a specific context. Thus, the same act in a new context may have a very different intent.

FUNCTIONS OF NONVERBAL COMMUNICATION

Some of the functions of implicit behavior have been described (Knapp & Hall, 2005). Gestures such as handshaking, nodding the head, or waving the hand are used as **emblems**. Such gestures can be directly translated into words but are efficient, meaningful signals by themselves. Increasingly, infants are being taught American sign as their first language to facilitate communication day to day with their families and may enter a program with an array of meaningful gestures as young as 6 months.

Young children most often use **illustrator gestures** to supplement the spoken word, especially when the child has a limited vocabulary (Doherty-Sneddon, 2004). Tommy, age 3, pointed to the spot where a game was stored, whereas an older child

might explain that the game is in the lower cupboard inside the closet. Tommy "drew pictures in the air" to indicate the relative size and shape of the box. He also indicated that it was heavy by dropping down his arm as if he were carrying it. His hands moved rhythmically, with words indicating the emphasis of his spoken communication.

Usually, emotional or evaluative content is conveyed nonverbally and is more accurate than communication by verbal means alone. Feelings of pleasure, surprise, happiness, anger, interest, disgust, sadness, and fear are expressed in interactions and may be expressed with or without accompanying speech. However, words alone cannot convey the depth of meaning present in a verbal message enriched by nonverbal cues. For example, compare a written note with a telephone conversation, which has both words and intonations, and then with an interpersonal experience, in which words, intonations, and visual information are available simultaneously. The amount of meaning that can be derived from a message increases as the number of nonverbal behavioral cues increases, either complementing the spoken word or reinforcing it.

Nonverbal communication acts as a regulator of social interaction. For example, turn taking in a conversation is indicated by changes in eye contact, voice pitch, and body position. The person speaking may involve the receiver in the communication by signaling a message such as "As you know," with the hands or acknowledging the listener's response with a nod to indicate, "I see you understood me." Other gestures such as tapping the forehead are information-seeking gestures: "Now what is that person's name?" (Bavelas, Chovil, Coates, & Roe, 1995).

Nonverbal cues may serve a **metacommunication** function; that is, they may communicate about the message itself. For example, facial expressions can convey a notion about the way the total message is to be interpreted, such as, "I'm only kidding" or "Now, seriously speaking." Social context and environmental setting cues communicate social expectations. For example, a large space such as a gym might invite vigorous play, whereas a similarly large space, such as a theater auditorium, may invite quiet, passive observation and listening. A room with soft furnishings and a homelike atmosphere is more conducive for conversation than a similarly sized space set up as an office waiting room. Adults generally accept that children under 5 will not necessarily understand appropriate behavior in all settings and are quite lenient with them, whereas the same behavior is likely to get a reprimand in a 6-to-8-year-old in the same situation.

Some nonverbal behaviors also may serve an adaptive need rather than function as a communication signal. For example, a person may scratch the scalp because the skin is dry and it itches, or the gesture may indicate bewilderment or confusion. Some actions related to satisfying body needs can, in other circumstances, indicate an emotional state. Nonetheless, the receiver may misinterpret unintended signals.

Another function of nonverbal communication is the presentation of personality, personal identity, and sometimes a person's role. This has been referred to as *the process of impression formation and management*. A person's clothing, posture, tone of voice, facial expressions, gestures, and so forth provide information to others about social position, temperament, disposition, and other characteristics of personality. However, it is difficult to interpret these nonverbal cues without understanding culture, race, and gender expectations (O'Hair & Ropo, 1994; Ting-Toomey, 1999).

> *Miss Kitchen generally wore tee shirts and hipster blue jeans with holes in the knees when she was in the child care setting during her internship. She was dismayed that other adults coming into the setting for the first time ignored her for an equally youthful aide who generally wore slacks with a collared shirt.*

Clothing can be selected to suggest that an individual is a worker, a student, or a professional.

Older children who have learned to use nonverbal cues as suggestions may adopt an amazed look of innocence when a misdeed has been discovered. The "Who, me?" expression is not usually considered to be a falsehood, as a verbal denial would be. The "Who Me?" expression requires that they be able to suppress their natural feelings of anxiety in that type of situation.

Nonverbal cues represent the most suitable vehicle for suggestion. Because nonverbal cues are not explicit and can potentially be misinterpreted, they also may be denied. Adults may use these deliberately as they try to "act a part" in a socially uncomfortable situation. Such "acting" requires that the adult perform as though he or she is at ease in the situation. There is some evidence that if children deliberately act in a way that they think would be socially appropriate for an unfamiliar situation, their feelings actually become modified (Saarni & Weber, 1999). Typical situations include giving a demonstration at a county

fair, playing in a recital, or even answering questions in a classroom.

A clear relationship exists between the level of development of an individual's social skills and his or her successful use and interpretation of nonverbal behavior. Having a broad array of nonverbal skills is important to social success and psychological wellbeing (Riggio, 2006). Children who monitor and understand other's nonverbal behaviors are perceived as being sensitive and are highly desired as playmates by their peers (Doherty-Sneddon, 2004).

Children become adept at nonverbal communication by interacting with skillful adults. In addition, children are more likely to learn from people who show them acceptance, genuine sincerity, warmth, and respect and who show sincere interest in them. All of these attitudes are made tangible to children by nonverbal means.

CHANNELS OF NONVERBAL COMMUNICATION

A **channel of communication** is one of the modes or types of nonverbal communication. For example, the tone of voice itself is one mode, or channel; posture and position in space are others. Each channel of nonverbal communication may function independently and may be congruent with the verbal message sent. Under ordinary circumstances, nonverbal messages are not likely to be under conscious control.

Nonverbal communication is a major medium of communication in everyday life (Richmond & McCroskey, 2003). From infancy onward, nonverbal communication links children to the adults in their world (Butterfield, Martin & Prairie, 2004). With or without words, people within visual range still send and receive messages through nonverbal cues. Monitoring, regulating, and control of nonverbal communication influence the flow and outcome of human interactions and contribute to interpersonal effectiveness (Riggio, 2006). For example, a person may "look daggers" at another, "deliberately ignore" someone, or perhaps give the appearance of mental abstraction or boredom. On a more subtle level, the relationships of people interacting in a group can be discerned by observation of nonverbal cues. Noting the body orientations, head tilt, and arm gestures of all the group members usually can identify the leader or speaker. For example, when observing a group of children on the other side of the playground, one could pick out the leader by watching the children interact. One child is gesturing; her head is tilted up and she is looking at the others in sequence. The others in the group are looking and nodding in response to her gesturing. There is little doubt as to which child is the center of attention, even though the conversation cannot be heard.

In the following section, selected components of nonverbal behavior will be described as they relate to the helping professional's ability to deliberately send and receive messages while working with children.

Position in Space

Personal space, radiating from the center of the body, has specific boundaries. Comfortable distances for interacting with others are from 0 to 1½ feet for intimate distance, 1½ to 4 feet for casual interaction or personal contact, from 4 to 10 feet for social or consultive contact, and 10 feet or more for public interaction (Krannich & Krannich, 2001). Another description of personal space places the boundaries in relation to body parts or functions (Machotka & Spiegel, 1982).

Internal space is the area between the inner core of the body and the skin and is the most intimate and personal of all spaces. Openings to the body, such as the mouth, ears, nostrils, anus, vagina, and urethra, all represent access to internal space. Internal space also is entered when the skin is broken in injury or when a hypodermic needle is inserted. To illustrate, Nick protested and pulled away when Ms. Payne took out the sharp, pointed tweezers even though the sliver in his hand was painful.

Proximal space is the area between the body and its covering of clothing, hair, or ornament. Uncovered body parts, such as the face, are not physically restricted but are psychologically restricted. For example casual acquaintances do not touch one another's arms, legs, or face, even though they are uncovered. Some uncovered sections of proximal space, such as the hands, are freely accessible to entry unless otherwise protected by countermoves such as crossing the arms or turning away. This means that, ordinarily, people do not touch portions of another's body that are clothed and limit touching the skin of others except when invited, as in shaking hands or giving a hug. A child sitting close to you on a sofa while you read a book is in your proximal space.

Axial space is bounded by the full extension of the arms and legs in all directions. Invitation to enter the axial space is indicated by open arms, in contrast to crossed arms or legs. Children are in your axial space when seated at a small table where you are also seated, for example.

Distal space is located between the axial boundary and the outer limits that the eye or ear can scan. The knowable world, or the impersonal world, exists in distal space. Usually young boys run and chase each other on the playground in your distal space. Children are also in your distal space when engaging in activities in a gym or lunchroom.

Figure 3-1 illustrates internal, proximal, axial, and distal space.

It is important for professionals to understand the implicit rules of interpersonal space for three reasons. First, violation of personal space generates negative feelings (Hall, 1966; Knapp & Hall, 2005). These negative feelings may be only mild irritation, such as that experienced in overcrowded church pews or elevators. Adults in these situations carefully refrain from inadvertently touching one another. Children, however, may poke or shove, violating both the axial space and the proximal space of another, resulting in vocal protest.

Negative feelings increase as successive boundaries of personal space are crossed. Young children defend themselves when they perceive that their proximal space has been violated, or they try to avoid the person or situation. For example, when crammed close together in a line, children are likely to push other children who unavoidably touch them, leave the line, or call for help because such experiences are interpreted as aggression. In addition, even young children may move away if an adult strokes their hair.

Rage and violent protest are common when internal space is entered without permission. Medical personnel can expect to meet with severe protest when patients have not accepted that nurses and doctors have special roles that permit them to invade internal space. People prefer to have only their most intimate companions—the ones they prefer the most—to have any access to internal space. In fact, this is why children want their mothers or preferred caregivers to take care of them when they are sick. Extrusions (feces or vomit) from internal space also are considered to be intimate.

The second reason for understanding the rules of personal space is that a message is considered more remote, impersonal, or inapplicable as the distance between the communicators increases. For example, Sally, age 7, was stirring the water in a

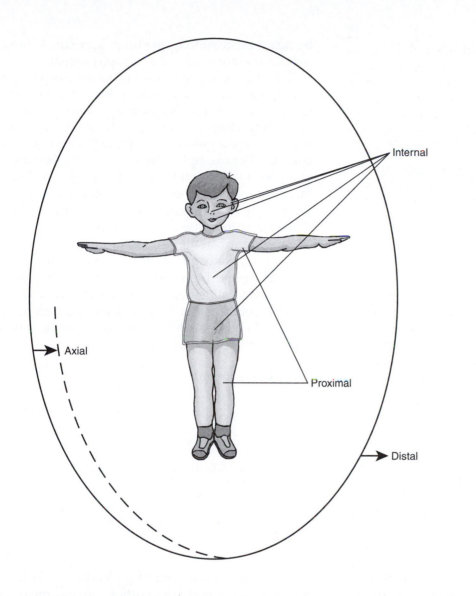

Figure 3-1 Personal space.

Internal

Axial

Proximal

Distal

mud puddle on the playground with the toe of her shoe. She looked up to see the playground attendant shaking her head and shouting "No!" while looking in her direction. Sally was aware that a lot of children were in her vicinity and ignored the signal. However, when the attendant walked up to her and suggested that she use a stick for playing in the water rather than her shoe, Sally willingly complied because she then knew the message was meant for her. The power or potency of a message is greater at lesser distances and more remote and impersonal at greater distances.

The third reason for understanding the concept of personal space is that the definitions of intimate space, personal space, and general social or public space vary by culture and subculture. Children learn the rules of interpersonal space from their parents, and helping professionals must recognize cultural differences as they interpret children's behaviors. Adults may misinterpret the meaning of a behavior because it is different from their cultural expectations. Although cultural differences exist for all channels of nonverbal communication, variations in the distance factor may be the most apparent. For example, a child who stands very close to an adult, speaks in a slightly louder voice than typical children, orients the body in a face-to-face position, and maintains eye contact longer than expected may be considered by a teacher of European ancestry to be pushy, brassy, or aggressive, when the behavior actually is rather typical for an Arabic male child. Another child who also stands close to the adult while conversing, but maintains less eye contact than expected and speaks in a softer voice, may inaccurately be considered clingy or dependent. Such behavior reflects simple courtesy in Asian cultures.

Body Motion

Torey was a little confused when she moved from the room for toddlers to the room where 3-year-olds engaged in their daily routine. Seemingly quiet and shy for the first two hours, she smiled and ran rapidly toward Ms. Cross when the caregiver came into the center at nine o'clock. Ms. Cross returned her smile, knelt down, and opened her arms wide to receive a big hug. Torey had known Ms. Cross from other encounters in her earlier experience in the center.

People do not remain stationary. They move through space toward or away from others. An approach into one's axial space may be met by accepting it, either by standing still or by extending the hands or arms. An approach may be reinforced by a mutual approach, with each person moving toward the other. However, an approach may be refused by moving away slightly, by simply avoiding the person approaching, or by closing the axial space by folding the arms.

Grasping the person is one way to control contact. To submit to an undesired contact remain immobile and passive. There is no reciprocity in this passive resistance. To avert the grasp throw it off, shake it off, or push the person away. For example, when Marta tried holding hands with Kevin, he moved slightly away and shook his hand free of her grasp without saying a word.

When adults unfamiliar to one another make contact, the asserting and accepting movements usually are ritualized, such as a handshake, a salutation, or other formal introduction or greeting. Frequently, adults are much less polite to children, particularly when the children are in a group. Children may experience being shoved into a line by a strange adult or may be patted on the head, pinched on the cheek, or chucked under the chin. Often, children correctly interpret these as hostile invasions of proximal space and attempt to avoid the approach or avert the contact as best they can. Sometimes the child is then chastised for improper behavior!

Accepting the separation involves moving away simultaneously or one person moving while the other remains; both terminate an interaction. On the other hand, advancing while the other retreats may refuse a separation. When a separation is desired by one person but not another, pushing the person away may be the only choice. To avoid a separation, a person may slow down his or her retreat, turn and stand, or show defiance against the other's intentions by facial expression or posture. Sometimes, forced separations are accepted by a rapid retreat.

Difficulties in separation often are seen as parents leave their very young children with caregivers. This particular situation was discussed in the preceding chapter. Younger children frequently experience exclusion from the activities of older children. For example, Mike, age 6, was listening to older boys talk about their marbles. Mike had some marbles, too; so, when the others decided to play a game, he bent down to join them. They told him that he was too little and didn't know how to play. Mike stood up, in the way of the other players. One of them pushed him slightly. Mike moved a step back. The older boys formed a circle with Mike on the outside. Mike took a step back and watched for a while before going to join other children on the climber. In this case, Mike tried to refuse the separation, and then accepted it.

Body Orientation

Cheryl, age 2, picks up the new manipulative toy and carries it to a quiet corner, which she faces while investigating the toy carefully.

Ryan and Dillon, both age 7, face each other, each having an angry face and hands fisted and high.

Vicki turns slightly toward Betty when Kate comes near the pretend play area and continues the play as though Kate were not attempting to enter the area.

The position of the front of the body in relation to the front of the body of another conveys meaningful information. The face-to-face position is the most confronting body orientation. This is the position used in greeting, comforting, fighting, and conversing intimately. Avoidance of this position usually indicates evasion or the desire to conceal. When people are facing the backs of others, they are proceeding in turn, following, or chasing. The side-by-side position implies companionship, togetherness, or a united front. The back-to-back position is associated with disengagement that is not simple separation, but hostility or protection in a hostile situation. Rotating the body around is simply a display. Slight turns of the body usually are a transition from one position to another, but may convey lack of interest or distrust or indicate impending separation.

The relationship between body orientations of people who are interacting also has a vertical dimension. The term one-upmanship is descriptive both visually and in meaning. The position of being higher, or on the top, denotes status, authority, or power. The position of being lower denotes incapacity, humility, or servility. In the natural course of things, adults are big and powerful and children are small and weak. Movement to diminish the vertical space between adults and children signals that an important message is about to be conveyed. This leveling can be done by squatting to the child's level or by lifting the child into a face-to-face position with the adult, as is commonly done with babies and very young toddlers. Between adults, leveling may be accomplished by sitting down, as height differentials among adults are usually in the legs. Squatting down may indicate friendliness or a willingness to interact on a cooperative basis.

Body orientation has other dimensions as well. Leaning toward another implies interest or regard, and leaning away suggests interpersonal distancing, offense, or lack of interest. An inclusion, in which another surrounds the axial space of a person, usually is either an emotionally positive experience, such as an embrace, or a negative one, such as a struggle.

Professionals who work with children use inclusion in giving affection or comfort or when they use their bodies to keep children from harming themselves or others. The intersecting of the axial spaces of two persons indicates togetherness or friendship, but this also occurs in fighting. When two children are angry at each other, one child approaching the other within two child-sized arm lengths usually indicates that physical battle is about to begin.

Gesture

Movements of the hands, arms, and body, or **gestures**, accompany speech and may be used to illustrate a word, such as moving the hands apart to show how large a fish was; to emphasize a statement, such as bringing the fist down on the table; and to replace speech, such as pointing to where the missing truck went. Gestures may be used as insults, such as in raising the middle finger from a clenched fist, or as terms of endearment, such as a caress. They also convey attitudes of the speaker about the content of the message and about the listener (Feyereisen & deLannoy, 1991).

Most gestures occur in the axial space of the sender and may be made without any speech. Although gestures commonly are learned with spoken language, young children frequently use illustrative gestures

Infants and toddlers use sign before their oral language is well developed, if taught. A toddler is signing 'fish' in response to observing gold fish in a pond at the butterfly house.

when they don't know the words to use. Intentional messages are sent by older babies through gestures such as pointing to a cup to indicate the need to drink. Hearing children who know sign use these emblems in combination with oral language when communicating. Likewise, preschool children resort to pantomime. Gesturing increases in efficiency throughout childhood. Even 11-year-olds are more effective in giving directions when the listener can see as well as hear them (Doherty-Sneedon, 2004).

Communication problems occur whenever a person's gestures suggest a meaning different from the verbal message (O'Hair & Ropo, 1994). These are occasionally deliberate, but frequently they are a result of differing cultural patterns. People in lower social positions gesture more, and more vividly, than people of higher social status in all cultural groups. There are, however, distinct differences between ethnic groups in the amount and expansiveness of the gestures commonly used. People from Asian countries use fewer and subtler gestures than persons of either European or African culture. People from northern Europe tend to be more restrictive as well, with southern Europeans using more expansive gestures and using them more frequently. Thus, North American children of English or Swedish descent are likely to make less expansive gestures than children of Latino(a) descent. Youngsters of Chinese background move their hands and body even less while speaking. The longer children participate in the mixed American culture, the more they tend to move their bodies at a moderate level of activity (Ting-Toomey, 1999).

Some gestures are widely used and understood, such as the finger click or snap for attention. Others, such as the fingers in a claw position (contempt in Saudi Arabia), are used only in one country. These emblems are cultural-specific gestures that have direct verbal referents (Ting-Toomey, 1999). Every cultural group has a wide variety of emblems understood by members of that particular group; but this leaves much room for error because the same movement may mean a vastly different thing to other cultural groups. For example, moving the head from side to side means "no" to Bulgarians but "yes" to several other cultures. The gesture meaning "OK," made by holding up the hand and forming a circle with the first finger and the thumb, means "money" in Japan, is a sexual insult in Brazil, is a vulgar gesture in Russia, and means "zero" in France. There is much potential for misunderstanding and confusion, especially for adults working in multicultural settings.

Touch

Situations in which touching occurs may be the most intimate, loving experiences, or the most hostile, angry, or hurtful ones. Situations in which touching is least likely to occur also are the most emotionally neutral. The probability of touch occurring is implied in the discussions of position in space (nearness to one another) and body orientation (face-to-face encounters).

The skin is both a communication sender and receiver. The role of touch in soothing and stimulating infants was discussed in Chapter 2. Other affective messages also can be conveyed. Feelings related to mothering, fear, detachment, anger, and

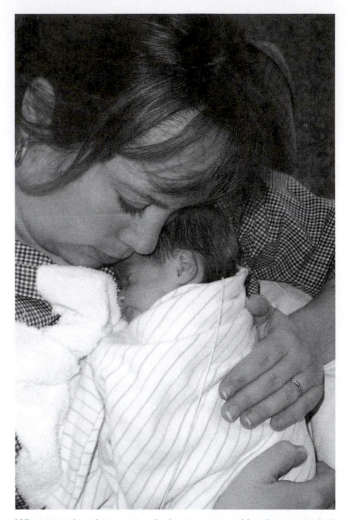

What emotional tones are being expressed by the nonverbal messages that you can see? Note that the neonate has experienced an intrusion with a feeding tube to the nose, and is in the proximal space of the mother, whose gestures with head and hands form an enclosure for the baby.

playfulness can be conveyed between adults by touch. Although little research has been done with children, gentle strokes, cuddling, caresses, and pats of affection are associated with nurturance. Games of walking fingers up a child's arm or "buzzing the bee to the tummy" illustrate playful touches. Slaps, kicks, pinches, and pokes that hurt are clearly understood as being hostile.

Touch is used to control or to influence others, such as grasping the hand of a child who is about to hit another. Touch is used less forcefully in getting a child's attention by gently tapping on the shoulder, or a child getting attention by tugging on the teacher's clothing. Touch also indicates the level of

Touch is an important means for establishing personal regard.

involvement or interpersonal responsiveness in the communication. Both adults and children use touch this way (Knapp & Hall, 2005).

Two factors influence the quality of tactile communication: the quantity (how much touching takes place) and the region of the body where one is touched. People touch friends and family more than casual acquaintances. People tend to touch peers or younger persons more than those older than themselves (Hall, 1996). Touching is more likely to occur in less formal situations, with higher-status individuals using more relaxed and affectionate strategies and lower-status persons using more formal strategies such as handshaking (Hall, 1996).

The accessibility of the body to touch is limited by age, relationship, and gender. Obviously, infants must be changed, fed, and otherwise handled extensively by caregivers of either sex. As children

mature, direct touch of the skin between the chest and the knees is taboo. In adulthood, most direct touching of the skin is limited to the hands, arms, neck, and face for parents and same-sexed friends. Mothers and other close relatives are more likely to touch children than are other people. However, caregivers who have established a relationship with a child also have more freedom to touch or be touched by a child.

Touching the clothed body of a child in an appropriate public situation is acceptable for caregivers of either sex. For example, lifting a child so that a climber can be reached, putting an arm around a child who has suffered a mishap, or cleaning a cut are acceptable regardless of the age and sex of child or adult.

Men frequently initiate backslapping and handshaking, but the regions of the body that are acceptable to touch are more limited (Richmond & McCroskey, 2003). Women touch both children and other adults more frequently as well as receive more touching from them (Hall, 2006). The touching behavior of children less than 6 years old is prevalent but decreases steadily through later childhood, with marked sex differences emerging gradually until adult patterns are reached in adolescence.

The channel of touch may be the primary mode of establishing a sense of identity in the first three years, and physical contact may be necessary for the development of satisfactory interpersonal relationships (Sansone, 2004). Therefore, appropriate physical contact with adult caregivers, especially for children under 6, should be available to them.

Touch is an important means for establishing personal regard. The concept of "being touched" by a story implies emotional involvement. Being "close" to someone implies being close enough to touch, as well as having strong affectionate bonds.

In addition to expressing ritualistic interactions (shaking hands) and playfulness (tag), and expressing affect (cuddling) and a task-related function (cleaning a scraped knee), touch may also be used as a control function (firmly grasping the hand of a young child who is crossing the street). The amount and frequency of touch as well as the rules about who may touch whom are also culturally specific, though much of the caregiving adult–child touching is more general. Both adults and children have personal preferences as to how much they touch others and the amount of touching that is comfortable for them to receive.

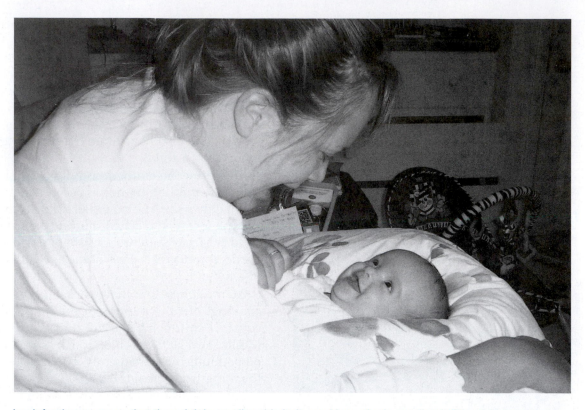

Look for the message that the adult is sending this baby and how she is sending it. The child is in the proximal space of the adult, with partial physical contact and a face-to-face position. There is a mutual gaze and laughter.

Facial Expression

Mark marched around the tree in the playground. His face was pulled downward and the muscles were very tight.

Mr. Decker approached him saying, "You look upset, Mark." Mark glowered at him and answered. "Not upset, mad! I wanted to stay home!"

Facial expression is the most obvious component of body language. In dialogues, speakers use facial expression and gesture integrated into oral language to convey information as well as feelings (Bavelas & Chovil, 2006). Facial expressions can be consciously controlled and used to deceive. Ordinarily, facial expressions supplement and complement the verbal message and both the sender and receiver benefit from it (Fridlund & Russell, 2006).

Many dimensions of meaning can be communicated by facial expression. The face communicates evaluative judgments, the degree of interest, and the intensity or degree of involvement through pleasant and unpleasant expressions. Although the face can clearly convey specific emotions—happiness, surprise, fear, anger, sadness, disgust, contempt, and interest—it is very mobile, and combinations of affect also may be displayed. Younger children are more open in showing feelings by their facial expressions that older children and adults, though the differences are a matter of degree, not of kind. Adults have more control and sometimes subdue their facial expressions using more subtle expressions.

Children display affect through facial expressions from early infancy onward. Pouting is a well-known expression of displeasure, and sticking out the tongue is a widely known expression of insult in Western cultures. Wrinkling of the nose when smelling an unpleasant odor and the disgust displayed when children taste new or different foods are readily understood. More subtle expressions, such as surprise quickly followed by interest or anger, sometimes are more difficult to detect.

Generally even young children are fairly accurate in understanding facial expressions. However, peers reject playmates whose facial expression is not appropriate for the situation (Doherty-Sneddon, 2004). Some children do not seem to know when to smile, look serious, or appear concerned. Such children can be coached so that they are more responsive in their expressions.

Smile. The smile is one of the earliest facial expressions acquired. The simple smile, the broad open smile, and the grin convey different meanings and use different muscles. When the smile is broad and lines form at the corners of the eyes, the person is amused or very pleased. A grin frequently is associated with mischief, and may also indicate pleasure with oneself. A simple smile, sometimes called a social smile, is the gesture of slight pleasure, greeting, and appeasement or obligation in that situation. It may be used to avert aggression or to indicate submissiveness—the display of the lower-status person is intended to placate the higher-status person (LaFrance & Hecht, 1999). The simple smile with an otherwise neutral expression is called a **mask smile** (Key, 1975) because it is used to hide unpleasant or unacceptable feelings. The mask smile often has been described as being "painted on the face" or "plastered on" and has a rather immobile quality.

The combination of a mask smile or a habitual smile and either very serious or emotionally negative verbal content is particularly offensive to children (Bugental, Love, & Gianetto, 1971). This insincere smile lacks warmth and feeling.

The cultural meaning of the smile varies. For example, children of western European descent traditionally smile when greeting another person, and Japanese children offer greetings with a sober face. As with other nonverbal communications, cultural variations in the use of the smile are modified as children interact in the context of the larger society. Use of the mask face, or the face with no expression at all, makes communication with children more difficult. A nonexpressive face used with children may be interpreted as lack of interest, lack of caring, or phoniness, and may become a serious hindrance to real communication. Unsuccessful attempts at using a mask face result in a display of an expression that represents neither what the sender feels nor what they want people to perceive. Usually this comes across as a blend of emotions and frequently misleads and confuses the receiver (O'Hair & Friedrich, 2001).

Finally, adults must be careful in interpreting children's facial expressions as well as in using their own expressiveness to highlight the message they intend to convey. For example, a young child may smile when a person slips on the ice and falls because the movements of the arms and legs are unusual, not because the child is amused that someone has been hurt.

Eye contact. Gaze is associated with dominance, power, or aggression and also with attachment and nurturing (Matsumoto, 2006). Eye contact between two persons is a special kind of communication that can rapidly move an interaction to a personal or intimate level even though considerable physical space may separate the communicators. Latino(a) white Americans tend to engage in longer eye contact during conversations than Europeans and African-Americans (Ting-Toomey, 1999). The eye lock, or prolonged gaze, implies a more intimate holding or communication. The very long gaze between an infant and an adult is normal communication, but a similarly long eye lock between an older child and an adult is a glare and may be interpreted as hostility or aggression. The glance also holds meaning between persons who know each other well. A shared moment of eye contact may mean anything from "Have you ever seen anything so ridiculous?" to "Let's go!" Culturally appropriate eye contact denotes interest and the willingness to engage in social contact.

Eye aversion also is used to indicate turn taking in normal conversation. In Western cultures, people tend to look more when listening than when speaking (Krannich & Krannich, 2001). Speakers glance away briefly at the end of an utterance, and then return the gaze to the other. They expect the listener to be looking at them at this point. This pattern is essentially reversed in African cultures and modified in mixed racial interaction (LaFrance & Mayo, 1976). In mixed racial interaction, African-American listeners gaze less at the speaker than do white listeners. In fact, African-Americans consider eye-to-eye gazing as rude, a put-down, or a confrontation (Scheflen, 1972). The pattern of looking down to show respect also is common to Japanese, Puerto Ricans, and Mexican-Americans (Johnson, 1998).

Unfortunately, adults sometimes become very angry when a child violates the rules of establishing rapport through eye contact and may not recognize that the child is behaving correctly within a different set of culturally defined rules. There are normal variations among families as well as regional variations in the same cultural group.

Paralinguistics

Paralinguistics are the sounds people make that carry meaning but are not used as regular words in

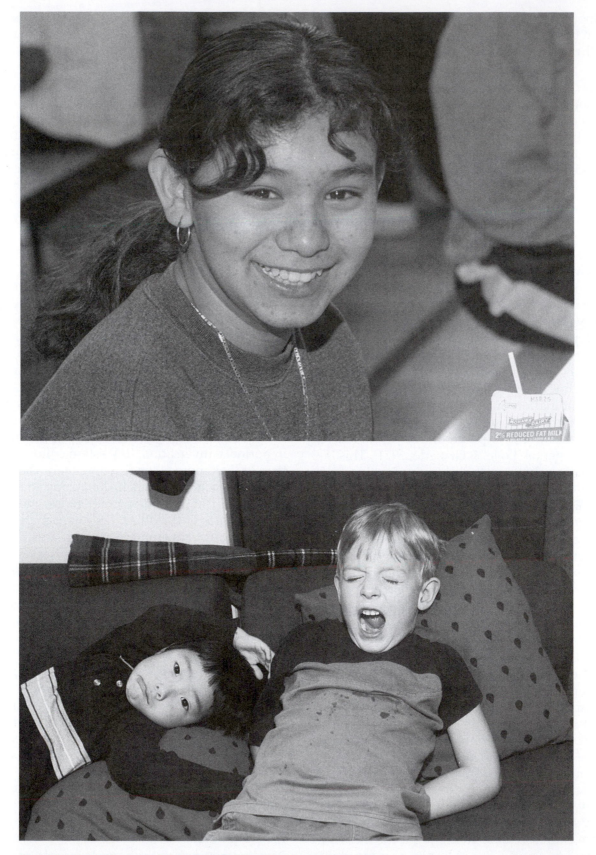

Facial expression is the most obvious component of body language.

a sentence, or the way in which a speaker says something. Paralinguistics provide additional meaning so that the listener will understand the intent of the speaker better. Usually these communicate affective content as well. Some types of parlinguistic behaviors are listed in Table 3-1.

Nonlexical sounds, or sounds that are not words, are produced by everyone and can serve all the functions of nonverbal speech. Physiological acts such as coughing, clearing the throat, sneezing, spitting, belching, sucking the teeth, hiccupping, swallowing, choking, yawning, and sighing can be used solely as adaptive mechanisms or to demonstrate affect. For example, the cough, besides clearing

the throat, may be used to communicate tension, anxiety, criticism, doubt, surprise, a prompting to pay attention, or recognition of one's own lies while talking. Several familiar sounds are used as emblems, or in place of words, such as "Uh, uh" (no), "Ah, ah" (warning), "Mmhmm" (yes), "Mmm-mmmmm" (good!), "Psst" (look here), and "Ugh!" (how unpleasant!). Intonation is used to denote the end of a sentence, an exclamation, or a question and serves as an indicator in conversational turn taking. In addition, much of the affective content of a message is conveyed by particular vocal qualities expressed simultaneously with speech. These include rhythmicity, intensity, volume, pitch, and tone.

Table 3-1 Common Paralinguistic Behaviors and Examples.

TYPE OF BEHAVIOR	EXAMPLES	MEANINGS
Nonlexical sounds	Cough	Physiological need or tension, surprise, or doubt
Nonlexical sounds/emblems	Uh, uh	No
Rhythm of speech	Stresses and pauses	Emphasis on stressed words
	Elongating a consonant	Dramatic effect, fear
Rhythm provided by listener	Repetitious phrases such, as "Yes, maam," "Right on"	Confirms speaker's meanings, agreement
Hesitations	Um, ah	Fills up time between words allowing the speaker to get his or her thoughts together
	Repetition of a consonant when the speaker does not usually stutter	Excitement
Intensity	Force and volume of speech: Loud and forceful	High intensity usually means very strong feelings such as joy or terror or rage
	Softer, may be more or less forceful	Whispering usually means secrecy or private communication
Silence	No movement, no sound, direct eye contact	Provocation, resistance
	No sound	Being polite, avoiding embarrassment for self or other
	No sound	Used before or after to stress words
Pitch and Tone	High pitch, light or strong tone	Panic
	Medium tone, medium pitch	In control, firmness
	Fluctuating pitches and tones	Speaker is unpredictable in that beyond typical use circumstance
	Lower tones and pitches	May be soothing or commanding

The **rhythm** of speech is composed of differential stress on words, the length of time sounds are held while speaking, and pauses. The stress given to each part of a sentence can determine its meaning. For example, when different words are stressed in the following sentence, the meaning of the pure lexical, or word, content is altered. "*Philip* is sharing the book with Harriet" implies that it is truly Philip, not someone else, who is interacting with Harriet. However, "Philip is sharing the *book* with Harriet" indicates that the book is the focus of attention.

In the English language, the lengthening of consonants gives a terrifying or dramatic effect. "Runnnnnnn!" is a serious, urgent, frightened demand for haste. Adults are likely to lengthen sounds for dramatic appeal when reading stories to children. Variations in the lengths of vowel sounds in ordinary speech, though, simply may reflect dialectal patterns.

Another aspect of rhythm is interpersonal, synchronous interaction. As one person speaks, the conversation partner may vocalize, "That's true," "Right on," or "Um hum" in rhythm with the other's spoken words. This is not interruption, but confirmation of the speaker's meaning. Nodding of the head and other gestures and body motions may all be used. African-American and Latin American cultures that are highly sensitive to context are much more likely to use this rhythmic manner of total communication than are European Americans.

Hesitations, or pauses in speech, allow the speaker to retain the floor or a speaking turn while gathering the next thought. People may pause to think when they have been interrupted or react to an external disturbance such as a slamming door. Pauses may be filled with verbalizations such as "Er," "Um," or "Ah," nonlexical sounds such as a cough, or unvoiced expressions such as swallowing. Major pauses in children's speech to adults usually occur because the child needs time to organize his or her thoughts. The tempo of a child's speech may be fast or slow, and the total rhythm smooth, jerky, or abrupt. Adults should allow plenty of time for children to complete their thoughts, should refrain from jumping in to finish the sentence for them, and should suppress the urge to take a talking turn prematurely. Such restraint shows respect for the child.

An increase in **intensity**, the force and volume with which something is said, usually is associated with strong feelings such as excitement, joy, eager anticipation, terror, rage, and coercion. However,

how loud is "too loud" usually is situationally and culturally determined. For example, speaking intensely and loudly may be perfectly appropriate in a gym or on the street, but speech of the same volume would be inappropriate in a classroom or movie theater. High-volume speech in situations that call for moderate-to-low volume is considered by adults to be boorish, inappropriate, and annoying. Adults on cell phones tend not to monitor their volume for the situation in their physical environment and therefore often offend other people nearby.

Whispering or simply mouthing words may be interpreted as attempts at secrecy or intimacy. When a voiced utterance dwindles to a whisper, it may be embarrassment that is being expressed. In any case, because a whisper lacks pitch and volume, a listener must attend to it more intently than to regular speech to receive the message.

Silence, the absence of sound when sound is expected, also is a powerful communicator. Deliberate silence in response to a question may be an insult or a provocation or may indicate resistance. Silence may also be used selectively in an attempt to be polite, to avoid an imposition on another, or to allow someone else to avoid embarrassment (Sifianou, 1995). Silence also stresses the utterance following it, making the message stand out as being of extreme importance. A relaxed, attentive silence from an adult to a beginning speaker or a second language speaker is simple wait time for the child to speak.

Variations in **pitch and tone** convey a variety of emotional messages. High-pitched voices are associated with strong emotions such as great excitement or panic. Fluctuations in pitch are characteristic of the angry tone of voice. The pitch and tone of the voice are difficult to control; therefore, subtle interpersonal attitudes and emotions can "leak through" (Bugental, Caporeal, & Shennum, 1980; Zuckerman, Larrance, Spiegel, Klorman 1981). The quality of the voice itself conveys meaning to the listener, often adding emotional content to the message. Voice quality can be described as follows (Key, 1975, p. 61)

raspy   heavy   gruff   shrill   dull   full   resonant
gravelly reedy   squeaky soft   moaning deep rough
thin   harsh   smooth   breaking guttural groaning
singing

In an emergency situation, an adult who is distraught may speak rapidly in a shrill, fluctuating tone. Such speech is not likely to instill confidence in his or her ability to handle the problem. On the other hand, an adult's voice that is within the normal range of speech tone and volume enhances the message that the adult can cope with the circumstances (Mehrabian, 1972).

Read the scenario below and then try to answer the questions posed at the end. Keep in mind that nonverbal communication is continuous, fast and changes rapidly throughout an interaction. The nonverbal communications contain strong identity and relational messages that may be misinterpreted.

> *Jenny's mother admonished her to pay attention to the teacher and to not talk back to her before helping Jenny, in her clean, unpressed dress, onto the Head Start bus. Trying to comply, Jenny, brushing her fine, flyaway blond hair from her face, stood close to her teacher. Careful to be still and quiet and gazing steadily at Ms. Sable, her African-American teacher, she listened intently, with an immobile expression, to her teacher's greeting and directions.*
>
> *Ms. Sable smiled at Jenny and tried to reassure her, but with the distinct impression that this youngster might be difficult to deal with this year. The notion that the child seemed resentful and maybe difficult flitted through her mind as she gazed at the rest of the mostly African- American children in the class. She hoped the family would not create problems because she was an African- American teacher.*
>
> 1. *What nonverbal cues about Jenny's identity did Ms. Sable probably process quickly?*
>
> 2. *What more subtle cues left the impression that Jenny might be resentful and difficult?*
>
> 3. *Why do you think this first impression might be made on a busy first day?*

All interactions between people occur in a specific time and place with a host of contextual features. Both senders and receivers need to understand some common principles to communicate effectively. Communications are inferential—that is, meanings are based on what is actually said and the nonverbal signals that accompany the message. Communications are intentional—people generally send the messages that they intend to send. Communications are conventional—within a culture group, the same nonverbal signals have consistent meanings. Usually communication is negotiated between the listener and the speaker, is sequential with turn taking, is systematic, and varies according to the participant's social relationships (Haslett & Samter, 1997).

Nonverbal messages clearly convey messages about friendliness and hostility as well as about dominance and submissiveness. Most of the time, these are taken for granted and do not come under conscious control. It is through the effective receiving of children's nonverbal messages that the sensitive caregiver comes to understand the child's meanings and feelings and is thereby able to be more effectively responsive.

ADULT ABUSES OF NONVERBAL BEHAVIOR

Some forms of paralinguistics, body motion, and gesture are not appropriate for adults who work professionally with children. The use of these behaviors communicates that adults cannot be trusted or that they do not like the child.

Baby Talk

Baby talk, a stylized form of adult speech, does not imitate any developmental stage of infant speech. It is used to establish an intimate relationship, a status relationship, or a nurturing relationship or is used to control behavior. Puckering the lips produces it, which alters the sounds of the words. Use of a falsetto voice, a high pitch, or an unusually low pitch is common. Use of the diminutive form of words is also common (doggie, dolly, horsie), as are sound substitutions (twain instead of train). The plural first person pronoun is used improperly. For example, a nurse might say: "How are we today?" or "Did we shower yet?" Other pronouns either are not used or are used improperly: "Is you going bye-bye?" (Are you going outside?); "Let teacher carry Davie" (Let me carry you).

Adults often use baby talk when talking to pets, children, persons considered inferior in status, mentally incompetent persons, and sick persons. Baby talk is disrespectful. Professionals should not use baby talk in interacting with children because it is insulting to the child and confuses meaning. For example, the statement "We must put away the toys" can legitimately be interpreted to include the adult speaker. Particularly offensive is the habit of adults to fix diminutives on personal names, such as "Ralphie" instead of Ralph or "Annie" instead of Ann, particularly when the family uses the regular form.

Yells

> Mrs. Daily walked into the entry of the local elementary school in the district where the family just moved.

She heard the shrill demand for children to be quiet and complete their assignment emanating from room 133, far down the hall. Entering the principal's office to enroll her child, she asked specifically to not have her shy son Sam placed in room 133.

Screams, shouts, roars, howls, bellows, squeals, shrieks, or screeches have unique qualities of volume, pitch, and tone that demand attention. Adults who work with children may hear these frequently in the course of play as children express their exuberance.

However, adults should never scream or yell at children. Shouting across a room for children to be quiet, although common, is particularly ineffective and inappropriate. When these unique paralinguistic forms are used by an adult, children surmise that the adult has lost self-control and is potentially dangerous or, at best, ineffective.

Hurtful Touching

Adults should never physically injure children. Yanking children by the arms, dragging them by the legs, pulling their hair, twisting their arms or wrists, biting, pinching, kicking, or even hitting them under the chin, or otherwise causing the child bodily pain or injury, are always inappropriate. In many states, such behavior is illegal. It is definitely inconsistent with the NAEYC code of ethics that affirms that professionals first do no harm. Family members, the community, and the profession expect that children will be safe while in care. Because adults provide guidance and support to children, they should never abuse their authority.

Sometimes children are unintentionally hurt, such as when an adult steps back and lands on a child's foot. This is an accident and is unrelated to the misuse of authority. Safety is discussed in Chapter 9. Precautions that prevent hurting children require both planning and vigilance.

COMMUNICATING ABOUT THE RELATIONSHIP

People communicate specific messages nonverbally in the course of everyday interaction. In addition, through a combination of various nonverbal channels, people convey impressions about their overall relationships with others. Messages that communicate authority, warmth, and caring, or the relative importance of another person, are mostly nonverbal.

When adults are mindful of their own nonverbal messages, children with whom they are communicating are more likely to feel understood, respected, and supported. When nonverbal communication is unfamiliar or unexpected, children feel vulnerable. When it is predictable and familiar, they feel secure. Adults who think about their own nonverbal behaviors, and those of the children with whom they work, can monitor and possibly modify their actions to provide a more secure and comfortable climate.

Time

Many social expectations are based on the shared meaning of time. Helping professionals must be aware of their own concept of time so that they can more easily understand their responses to children's behavior. In addition, they must learn how others, particularly people of different cultural backgrounds, interpret time. Otherwise, misunderstandings about time between adults and children will be inevitable. An adult may interpret that an 8-year-old is late for a Cub Scout meeting because the child arrived several minutes after the scheduled meeting time. However, the child may consider himself "on time" because he arrived before the major activities that were important to him had begun.

Children must learn a complex set of rules for the use of time in American culture. Children from Native American and Hispanic cultures may perceive clock time as less important than **subjective time**, which may cause additional misunderstanding (Hall, 1981; DeCapua & Wintergerst, 2007). Subjective time, in contrast to clock time, is ambiguous. It is based on an internal feeling of the people using it. Native American adults attending a powwow may know the dancing will be done on a particular weekend, but it may be at any hour during that period. It is the timing of the event that is important rather than the specific time of day.

Many Americans treat time as a material resource: It can be bought, saved, wasted, and segmented. Time is future-oriented, but very short. The focus is on the minutes, hours, and days, not on months, seasons, or generations. The control of time is an indicator of status. This means that adults are likely to become angry with children who are slow, who dawdle, or who use what the adult perceives as too much time for a task. On the other hand, adults get angry with children who are impatient and do not wait for them for "just a minute." The **duration** of an event may be either too long or too short depending upon the perspective of the people involved.

In American culture, being fast is equated with being intelligent or being efficient. Adults who take the time to listen to a child demonstrate that the child is important and the conversation is interesting. Adults who interrupt children, who are obviously ready to leave the interaction at the first opportunity, or who are excessively distracted by the events around them demonstrate a lack of interest. Attending to children promptly, keeping appointments or commitments, and taking the time to observe the child's work or play communicate to the child that she or he is important. On the other hand, adults must keep in mind that although children understand these cues in others, they are just learning to adopt such actions in their own behavior. As a result, their own use of time to convey respect and interest is not fully developed.

Warmth

How do children know that you like them? Only a small portion of the message of liking a child is conveyed by words; much more of the message is communicated by vocal characteristics and most by facial expression. Warmth is communicated entirely nonverbally (Gazda, 2006).

Adults who want to communicate caring and concern are more likely to approach the child and interact close to them. They will maintain frequent but not continuous eye contact and will face the child directly, keeping their head at about the same level as the child's. They may lean or reach toward the child while gesturing or speaking. Smiling, nodding, and a relaxed facial expression and body also indicate warmth and interest. Speech is at normal pitch, speed, and volume, and the tone is relaxed and melodious. Statements that express agreement, approval, or validation contribute as well. Warm adults appear willing to take time with the child (Andersen, Guerrero & Jones, 2006). The overall impression is smooth, comfortable, and relaxed. These behaviors also tend to reduce the power differential between adults and children.

Fidgeting, turning away, a mask expression, a sharp tone of voice, or standing up and looking or moving far away communicates coolness, aloofness, or the absence of warmth. Crossing the arms or legs and either staring or failing to maintain normal conversational eye contact communicates maximum coldness. The overall impression is either tense or carelessly offhand. Unfortunately, adults such as students who are unsure of themselves or who are afraid of doing the wrong thing also may behave in this manner. Children and other adults may misinterpret this behavior as uncaring and uninterested.

Power

Fortunately, adults have the legitimate power, or authority, to provide for the safety, security, and well-being of the children in their care. Obviously, adults control the resources needed for survival, learning, or play, and the ability to reward appropriate behavior. Adults have power in that they have skills and knowledge that children need. Most adults working with children have power based on warm, positive relationships with children and the children's desire to please. In addition, they have greater strength and size, which may be necessary to pick up and move a child who may be in dangerous place or situation (Guerrero & Floyd, 2006). Perhaps less obvious is the fact that adults also provide for the order, safety, and feeling of security that children need.

Much of this sense of authority is conveyed to children nonverbally. Adults demonstrate their assertiveness when they interact in close physical

What message is the adult conveying to this child through her body orientation and gestures?

proximity, maintain eye contact, and use a firm, even, confident tone of voice. They may need to grasp a child firmly to prevent an injury to the child or someone else. Socially skilled dominant behavior that displays confidence and energy is more successful in influencing behavior in the long term than coercive (physical or verbal) strategies (Guerrero & Floyd, 2006).

Nonassertiveness implies lack of control of the situation or unwillingness to act responsibly. Both of these are communicated nonverbally, and even very young children can detect the fluctuating, intense, loud voice of anger and the weak, wavering, hesitant voice of the timid adult. As a result, they are likely to respond to these aspects of that adult message rather than to the words that are used.

Young children appear to display status and power through control of space or toys, through size and strength; by using vigorous, energetic movements; and through arguments with one another (Burgoon & Dunbar, 2006). Dominant children are more successful in getting other children to do what they want them to do, and submissive children tend to avoid arguments in favor of using more polite requests. The strategies that appear to work for the dominant child to gain power include leaning close to the other or invading the play area, standing up while the opponent is sitting and exerting superior strength while pulling or struggling, or offering empty compromises. Such interchanges do not necessarily lead to violence or personal injury and may be necessary for children to learn how to deal with a social system in which individuals have incompatible goals.

Rudy entered the block area that he had left 15 minutes previously and asserted, "I didn't say you could move these blocks," as he moved in closely and loomed over the players. David, Devan, and Forrest initially tried to ignore him. Rudy moved forward, scowled, and said, "Put those back, over there . . . Don't you hear me?" as he grasped one of the offending blocks and moved it. Devan protested and told Rudy that he had left and they were building. Rudy responded in a firm, loud voice, "I left and came right back." More softly and casually he continued, "You can do it when I am not here." Since Rudy is rarely absent, this compromise offer is essentially meaningless. The play continued with Rudy directing, asserting, and demanding, and the other three complying. This is essentially a collaborative arrangement between the ones who dominate and the ones who submit, as all the children know that adults would intervene if a vigorous altercation took place.

Rudy used the following strategies to exert dominance over his playmates: elevation, spatial violations, loud voice, conversational control, and control of materials. The other children attempted withdrawal to avoid conflict, then submitted. Rudy also offered a compromise or a solution to the problem, which, if sincere, would be an effective strategy to minimize injuring other's feelings.

THE IMPACT OF MIXED MESSAGES

One or all channels of nonverbal communication transmit unspoken messages. In addition, it is possible to communicate one message in one **channel of communication,** such as facial expression, while communicating something quite different in another channel, such as the tone of voice. Neither of these may correspond to the meaning of the actual words spoken, resulting in a **mixed message.** For instance, an adult may smile and say, "Sure, have another helping," while displaying a rigid posture, a tense voice tone, and a clenched hand, which clearly demonstrate disapproval. Discrepant messages can be detected from what is said and can be linked to four nonverbal processes: control, arousal, negative affect, and cognitive complexity. The untruthful communicator tends to select words carefully and use grammar differently than when being truthful. In addition, the voice is more controlled while the body is tense. Often, unnecessary detail is added. Apparently, it is much easier to be an accurate, honest communicator (Zuckerman, Driver, & Guadagno, 1985).

By 9 months of age infants can both identify when words and feelings of a speaker are discrepant and apply this confusing message to a social context (Blanck & Rosenthal, 1982). Children of preschool age are sensitive to and wary of messages when the facial expression and tone of voice do not match (Volkmar & Siegel, 1982). When modalities are discrepant, young children tend to trust the tone of voice more than gestures or facial expressions. The qualities of what they hear are more important than what they see when they are young (Blanck & Rosenthal, 1982). Children as young as 1 year of age are capable of weighing and interpreting discrepant affective messages. Little children seem to know who really likes them and who does not.

As children get older, they show greater accuracy and speed in decoding facial expressions. They shift from depending mostly on what they hear to using facial expression as the primary key to understanding without losing their previously developed skills. As they become more skilled, children are able to extract more subtle emotional messages from the nonverbal communications, and their dependence on the words that people use is decreased. They are less easily fooled, more accurate, and more competent in receiving the totality of the communication.

However, children with learning disabilities are substantially less accurate in interpreting emotions in others. Boys, in particular, may not use facial cues to judge another's feelings, relying instead on motion cues (large gestures and movement through space). Although the trend of greater accuracy is maintained over time, many of these youngsters may be still confused as they enter adolescence (Nabuzoka & Smith, 1995). This can be especially serious; for example, a smiling child who is running fast toward another who is disabled in this way may be seen as an aggressor rather than a potential playmate. Nearly all social interactions will pose potential problems of misinterpretation for children who are playing with their more skilled age-mates.

Sarcasm combines negative lexical (word) content and a scathing tone of voice with a pleasant facial expression. Sarcasm is a strategy used to convey contempt, that the other person is incompetent and is at the least a put down (Guerrero & Floyd, 2006). Young children are disturbed by it because the words and tone of voice are both strongly negative, and these are the cues they rely on to interpret the affective meaning of a message. Preadolescents interpret such behavior as negative in tone or a bad joke (Blanck & Rosenthal, 1982). Even between parent and child, sarcastic "joking" by the adult is perceived as ridicule by the child (Bugental, Kaswan, & Love, 1970). Adults may perceive this markedly mixed message as funny or a joke.

CHILDREN'S ACQUISITION OF NONVERBAL COMMUNICATION SKILLS

Children learn from the adults in their families, schools, and neighborhoods and acquire nonverbal communication skills gradually. Content of nonverbal messages as well as style and degree of expressiveness are socialized by families from birth to adulthood (Halberstadt, 1991). Children of families who use overtly expressive nonverbal behavior decode these cues accurately earlier than children whose families are less expressive. However, when families use subtler, less overtly expressive nonverbal cues, the children's decoding abilities are keener and more skilled as they mature because they have more practice in decoding nuances (Halberstadt, 1991). This means that by imitation children learn the specifics of the communication strategies of their families and their immediate neighborhoods. It also means that from the earliest years, children pick up the nonverbal behaviors typical of their gender and cultural group. Viewing media also enhances decoding skills (Feldman, Coats, & Philippot, 1999).

Not surprisingly, Americans vary systematically by racial groups, cultural heritage, gender, and even region of the country (Richmond & McCroskey, 2003). In fact, although adults may speak the same language, nonverbal patterns may be still closely linked to the country of origin of the family. For example, an individual may use the gestures more typical of Italians while speaking American English as a primary language.

The same variations are true for Spanish-speaking families. For example, although comfortable communicating distances are closer for all Spanish-speaking adults than for North Americans of northern European descent, there is a considerable difference between groups coming from different Spanish-speaking countries. Professionals who are aware that systematic differences in nonverbal communication exist should observe carefully the adults close to the child to pick up the typical nonverbal behavioral cues that they use. In this way, they will more quickly understand the total message that the child is communicating.

Children tend to imitate the patterns of behavior of adults with whom they interact. This means that youngsters who interact with skillful, expressive adults also will eventually become skilled in nonverbal communication. Also, a child who has a cultural experience at home that differs from the larger culture at school or in other community settings will gradually modify his or her nonverbal communications, in essence becoming nonverbally bilingual.

Adults share in the responsibility for learning the meaning of the child's nonverbal environment, particularly for children under 6 years of age. Some rules of nonverbal behavior are pointed out by admonition. When adults see a child doing something that "everyone" finds inappropriate, like spitting on the floor, they respond with a strong statement such as "You spit on the floor. That spreads germs. Use a tissue."

Cultural expectations are learned when a child makes an error and is corrected. Americans have firm rules about nudity and all interactions with internal space. Children simply cannot urinate in public! Rarely are these nonverbal rules formally explained.

A third way children learn nonverbal behavior is through instruction. Adults may give children suggestions on how to "be friendly" or how to stand up for their rights. Family members may also provide scripts and coaching for younger children with cues as to nonverbal congruence: "Say, 'Thank you very much'" or "Tell him you are sorry if you mean it" (Halberstadt, 1991). Children receive formal instruction in English in schools and in caregiving settings. However, they seldom receive similar instruction for nonverbal behaviors except when they are engaged in theatrical experiences and must assume a role unfamiliar to them. Adults may give formal instruction as to nonverbal communications when children attend a performance ("Sit still. Don't whisper during the play.").

The pattern of the development of nonverbal language is very similar to that of speech. Children become increasingly skillful as they get older. Their messages become more complex and come increasingly under their control. Understanding of discrepant messages becomes easier with age and experience. Children can successfully tell a white lie in a politeness situation (Talwar & Lee, 2002). Comprehension precedes expression, and children shift from reliance on the verbal channel to the adult pattern of major reliance on facial expression between 7 and 10 years of age.

Display rules are guidelines that govern the display of nonverbal behavior. Children learn to exaggerate, minimize, or mask expressions of their feelings depending on the setting and the social situation. Preschool-age children learn from their parents, teachers, and friends about what is and is not polite or acceptable to express.

> *Mickey, who is only 3, made a face when tasting a new food at home, and said "Yuck!" as he pushed his plate away. Later in the week when Mickey ate at the child care center and encountered a disliked food, he tasted it, refrained from comment, managing to keep his expression more subdued, almost neutral, and avoided eating it thereafter.*

By the time children are 8 years of age they can explain the use of display rules to others (Saarni & Weber, 1999).

> *When Martha was embarrassed by falling on the ice just after bragging to some other 8-year-old girls, she got up, smiled, and tried the fall again deliberately to make the others laugh. To her best friend, she admitted later that she was hurt but did not want to look "stupid" in front of the other girls.*

Social learning influences communication of emotional content. Boys are less likely to spontaneously express their feelings as they get older, and girls are less likely to be aggressive or show an achievement orientation (Buck, 1982). Girls also are more likely to be tolerant of mixed messages or "white lies" than are boys (Blanck & Rosenthal, 1982). Children who are better at decoding and more expressive are more popular with peers and demonstrate greater social competence (Haslett & Samter, 1997).

GUIDING CHILDREN WITH ADULT NONVERBAL BEHAVIOR

Usually human beings do not think about their nonverbal messages. Yet, unconsciously, they observe and interpret the nonverbal messages of others, which influence all social interactions taking place.

Professionals who are mindful of their own and other's nonverbal messages think about these deliberately, and consider culture, the specific setting and situation, and the developmental level of children involved. Thoughtful observation and deliberate choices of nonverbal messages enable the adult to be more sensitive to children and more effective when communicating emotions and expectations.

When adults use nonverbal communication that repeats, complements, or accents the lexical meaning of their messages to children, they clarify the total meaning of the message. Thus, children are more likely to understand and respond to what is being said. People usually display subtle differences in their styles of nonverbal communication, and an individual may communicate differently in varying circumstances. These differences in communication style also influence the flow of communication with children and affect the probability of them responding appropriately. The following guidelines will help you increase the effectiveness and accuracy of your nonverbal communication.

SKILLS FOR BUILDING POSITIVE RELATIONSHIPS WITH CHILDREN THROUGH NONVERBAL COMMUNICATION

 Tuning into Children

1. Observe the nonverbal behavior of the children in your care. Observing your typical interactions with a child, those between the child and other children, and those between the child and other adults will help you understand various movements and gestures for that particular child. For example, Anne Janette's teacher checked for a fever when she had been playing quietly by herself at the puzzle table. Ordinarily, Anne Janette was noisy, boisterous, social, and physically active. Her temperature was over 100°F. The teacher was alert to the change in the child's typical behavior.

2. Recognize and learn cultural and family variations in children's nonverbal behavior. With so many variations among cultural groups, only direct observation within an appropriate context will provide enough information to understand the meanings of particular behaviors. Does the child usually look toward the speaker or away from the speaker when listening? Does the quiet wriggling of a 3-year-old when listening to a story mean that the child is uncomfortable, is bored, or has to go to the bathroom? Be alert for consistent sequences of behavior in individual children to learn what these cues mean. Respect children's nonverbal indications of violations of personal space.

3. Recognize children's self-identifying nonverbal messages and markers and treat them respectfully. Both adults and children use a variety of nonverbal signals to show group membership and to exert their individuality. Clothing such as a team baseball cap or a scout uniform is a typical marker. Sometimes other markers, such as haircut and styling, change so frequently that adults who are 22 years old may not recognize markers for children in their care. For example, boys who wear very long hair hanging loose, long hair bound on top with tight curls on the sides, moderately long styled haircuts, braids (of various numbers), very short haircuts, or clean-shaven heads are generally denoting a group membership. Except for those suggesting religious groups, the hairstyles mean different things for different generations and in different circumstances. To illustrate, the clean-shaven head may indicate that the child is demonstrating solidarity with a peer who has lost hair as a result of cancer treatment, or that it is summer and the child chooses an inexpensive way to stay cool, or that the child is a member of a group that shares a set of political beliefs and racial attitudes. Thoughtful adults take the time to understand the meaning of the specific marker for the child within the current context.

Gender is also marked nonverbally, though it is less distinctive now than in former generations. Clothing styles and types selected, hairstyles, and the number and placement of body piercings and tattoos (as well as content) chosen may indicate group membership or the values of the person displaying decorative and functional pieces.

Auditory cues also denote gender. Although certain physical characteristics determine the speaking-voice pitch, the differences in range are notably culturally reinforced and exaggerated so as to enhance gender differences. Body movements, such as hip movements when walking, and selected hand gestures are also gender related. Every nonverbal channel has gender identity markers in all cultures. Adults must use context cues and knowledge of children's culture in interpreting gender cues.

Social status, economic background, education, and ethnicity are also conveyed by nonverbal means. Clothing choice, care of nails, shoes, and speech may denote economic and social position. Membership in cultural subgroups is conveyed by proximity control and eye contact as well as display rules. Dialect and speech tones may provide cues as to ethnicity and region of the country. Sometimes older youngsters deliberately misuse such

continued

cues solely to confuse adults. Professionals, however, treat all children and their families with respect regardless of their interpretations of the family social background.

Children 10 to 12 years old may begin to exert independence typical of adolescence. Putting on makeup is characteristic of girls in this age group. If an adult should laugh and make fun of the child, or treat the child as something disgusting, then the child's identity as a maturing female is challenged. If the adult notices and provides guidance as to what makeup to wear on which occasions and how to put it on, the child's identity is supported while the specific display rules are being learned.

When adults recognize the multilayered meanings of nonverbal signals as part of the children's self perception, as signs of identity, they may more thoughtfully and respectfully interact with the child.

4. Respect children's proximal space. Pat children on the back; shake their hands; give them congratulatory hugs. Avoid absent-minded fondling or patting children on the head or buttocks. These gestures communicate patronization or disrespect.

5. Use nonverbal signals to gain the attention of a group of children who are engaged in an activity or who are dispersed in space. Indoors, signals such as playing a chord on a piano, flicking the lights on and off, singing a specific tune, clapping of hands, sitting quietly and waiting for children to join you, change in your tone of voice, or other signals are effective in getting the attention of the children. Then, you may signal for silence by putting a finger over your pursed lips or beckoning the children nearer with your hand. Outdoors, signals such as whistling, waving a hand or flag, holding an arm high with flattened palm toward the children, ringing a bell, or blowing a whistle are effective for getting children's attention.

Children cannot be expected to receive and understand spoken messages if they do not know that you are trying to communicate with them. You can tell that they have received a signal if they turn toward you or begin to quiet down. Your spoken message should begin after you have gained their attention. Very young children will need to be taught the meaning of nonverbal signals such as those mentioned in the preceding paragraph, as they are seldom used by families: "When I turn the lights on and off like this (demonstrate), stop what you are doing, stop talking, and look at me. Let's practice it once."

6. Walk up to children with whom you want to communicate and orient yourself in a face-to-face position at their eye level. Move your body into the axial space of the child to get the child's attention before trying to deliver a message. For example, Paul was concentrating on gluing together a model airplane. The recreation leader, standing about 10 feet away from him, said: "Put newspaper down on the table before gluing. That stuff won't wash off." Paul continued with his task, completely unaware that someone had spoken to him. The message would have been effective if the adult had walked over, stooped down, and looked directly at Paul when speaking to him.

Thus, when children are engaged in activities, move from child to child and speak to them individually. You will have to squat down to achieve face-to-face communication with small children. Children should be able to see your face. Verbal messages can otherwise go literally "over their heads"! Facial expressions that reinforce your words help children to understand what you are saying.

7. Keep all channels of communication consistent when communicating about your feelings. When expressing your feelings to a child, your words should match your behavior. During the course of working with children, you are likely to experience a variety of feelings such as joy, amusement, annoyance, anger, surprise, puzzlement, and interest.

SKILLS FOR BUILDING POSITIVE RELATIONSHIPS WITH CHILDREN THROUGH NONVERBAL COMMUNICATION

Communications that are consistent across all channels are authentic, genuine, and honest. You can achieve clarity and understanding by using all channels to convey one message. Multiple feelings can be expressed in rapid sequence and still be genuine.

When adults try to suppress, mask, or simulate feelings, they are not being authentic, genuine, or honest. If you are angry, you should look and sound angry, without loss of self-control; if you are happy, your face, body, and voice should reflect your joy.

8. Touch the child. The younger the child, the more likely it is that he or she will find physical touching acceptable. Frequently, boys over 8 years of age resent being touched. The adult must, of course, respect the child's preference. However, when trust has been established, touching or patting a child in a friendly or congratulatory manner is acceptable regardless of age. When used appropriately, touch is soothing, comforting, and emotionally healing because it is a tangible link between you and the child. Something as simple as a nurse holding a child's hand while someone else is drawing a blood sample can reduce the child's anxiety.

 Showing Warmth and Caring

1. Stand, sit, or squat close to the child, not more than an arm's length away. Do not allow furniture or materials to act as a barrier between you and the child.

2. Sit or stand so that your head is at the same level as the child's. This avoids the appearance of talking down to the child. It minimizes the natural dominance in the interaction and is more comfortable for the child.

3. Maintain frequent but not continuous eye contact. This is normal listening behavior and demonstrates your interest in the child.

4. Face the child so that your shoulders and the child's are parallel. When your upper body is at an angle to another's, you are in an unstable position that usually implies that you are going to move. Therefore, your upper body as well as your face should be in a front-to-front position with the child.

5. Lean slightly toward the child. Leaning toward the child communicates interest and also helps you hear what the child is saying. Maintain a relaxed body posture. Slouching or rigidity does not convey interest or concern. Your body should not appear "ready to leave immediately." The arms and legs should be open, not tightly closed or crossed. Use movements that convey alertness. Nod your head or use other gestures to indicate your understanding. This should not be confused with fidgeting, which usually indicates lack of interest or boredom. Feet should be unobtrusive, not moving about. Mannerisms (hair flicking, lint picking, or table tapping) should be unobtrusive or absent. None of your movements should compete for attention with the child's words.

6. Convey a generally positive facial expression in neutral situations. Smile when greeting the child. Relax and enjoy everyday interactions with the child.

7. Respond as quickly as possible when spoken to, and take the time to listen. Taking time to really listen to a child is sometimes very difficult to do. If you do not have time to listen to what a child has to say, let the child know that you are interested and will be able to attend more fully later. Then, be sure to do so. For example, Mr. Wardlich had begun reading a story aloud to the class when Carrie announced that she was going to Florida during spring break. Mr. Wardlich told her that she could tell him about it when the children were working on their penmanship, but that now it was time to read a story.

continued

SKILLS FOR BUILDING POSITIVE RELATIONSHIPS WITH CHILDREN THROUGH NONVERBAL COMMUNICATION—continued

8. Reflect on the child's nonverbal messages and make every effort to demonstrate that you are attempting to understand. Avoid being dismissive and rushing to interpretation, particularly when the child is relatively unfamiliar to you or a member of another culture group. Pay close attention to what they say and how they say it as well as what they do. Make judgments about displays of emotion, appropriate behavior, and the message intent using what you understand about culture, gender, age, and skills of the child. When people believe that you are attempting to understand (whether you do or not), they feel your care and warmth.

9. Try to be understood by the children. Take the child's abilities into account. Stick to the point and give neither too much nor too little information for the circumstances.

Assume that the child is trying to understand what you are trying to convey. For example, the directions given to a 24-month-old child may include all nonverbal channels, repetition, and demonstration with clear verbalization as you guide the child on how to climb a short ladder to go down the slide. You might say, "Put your hands here" while showing exactly where to put them, then, "Lift your foot up here and move one hand up." During this guidance the adult would be standing behind the child, perhaps grasping the waist as the climb progresses. "Now sit here and hold the sides. Wait and I will catch you." The adult then moves to the catching position. Avoid chattering between statements. Your presence, closeness, and attempt to truly communicate are sufficient to convey caring. To provide the same level of support to a typical 9-year-old would not convey the same meaning. Instead, the same behavior would likely be interpreted as demeaning by the older child. An adult would stand 3 to 9 feet from the slide and might remind the children, "Allow the child ahead of you to sit down before you start to climb." Only if the child asked for assistance or the adult perceived a potential danger to the youngsters

would a move to close physical proximity be appropriate.

10. Use voice tones that are normal to soft in loudness and normal to low in pitch, and a voice quality that is relaxed, serious, and concerned. Your voice should be clear, audible, and free of many filled pauses such as "Ah" or "Um." The speech should be regular and even in tempo, not impatient or excessively slow. Your speech should be fluent when answering simple questions or commenting on a topic rather than staccato or full of hesitations.

 Demonstrating Authority and Security

1. Dress appropriately. Clothing, grooming, hairstyle, and general appearance convey messages, particularly of power and authority. A person responsible for the supervision of children, especially those younger than the children's parents, may be ignored. Unfamiliar young children will not approach you for assistance, and the 10- to 12-year-old is likely to treat you as a peer if your appearance suggests a peer relationship. Because appropriate dress varies from setting to setting, the easiest guide is to observe the dress of the highest-status adults in the group.

2. Maintain a tone of voice that is firm, warm, and confident. The pitch should be even and the volume normal. Avoid shouting or using an overly loud voice. Tonal quality should be open (sound is full and melodious) and the speed steady. Dropping the jaw, relaxing the throat, and projecting through the mouth rather than the nose can achieve the desired tonal quality. Variations in pitch during a sentence or very rapid speech give the impression of uncertainty. A weak, distant, wavering, or very soft voice is nonassertive and may convey the message, "I am telling you to do this, but I don't think you will. And if you don't, I won't follow through." Adults whose normal voices are very soft or very high

SKILLS FOR BUILDING POSITIVE RELATIONSHIPS WITH CHILDREN
THROUGH NONVERBAL COMMUNICATION

may need to add extra depth or intensity to their very important messages in order to be taken seriously.

3. Look directly at the child when speaking and maintain regular eye contact. Eye contact may be maintained while speaking firmly to a child for longer periods than is typical of usual conversation, but staring or glaring at a child usually is not necessary. A steady, firm look at a child who is misbehaving sometimes is sufficient to remind the child to redirect the behavior in question. Aversion of eye contact or a pleading look is nonassertive. Because some adults are shorter than tall 11- and 12-year-olds, serious messages will be more effective if both child and adult are seated. Differences in height are usually differences in leg length. When a child towers over an adult, assertive messages are unusually difficult to deliver. Face-to-face interaction is more effective.

4. Relax, maintain close physical proximity, and maintain arms and legs in either an open or semi-open position. You are in a naturally authoritative role. It is unnecessary to display aggressiveness, as demonstrated by hands on hips, feet apart, and a tense body, to achieve compliance. However, having a stooped or dejected-looking posture or leaning on something for support certainly is not assertive and children may not comply with requests when they detect a nonassertive stance.

5. Use your hands to gesture appropriately or, if necessary, to hold the child until the communication is complete. Little children are quite capable of darting away when they do not want to hear what you have to say. They may also twist about, turn their backs toward you, or put their hands over their ears. The child can be held firmly and steadily without pinching or excessive force until the message is completed. Gestures that enumerate points, that describe the meanings of the words used, or that indicate position in space are appropriate. Avoid wagging a finger in the face.

 Applying Nonverbal Communication Skills to Informal Interactions with Family Members

1. Approach family members with a relaxed body posture and a smile of welcome. Family members may come to the program for a variety of reasons. If the safety of children is not jeopardized by your doing so, walk up to the parents, greet them, and ask if you can be of assistance. Some beginning professionals may appear to be cold and indifferent when they are feeling a little shy or timid in initial interactions with parents, so remember that the professional role is to help parents feel at ease and comfortable.

2. Orient your body for a face-to-face interaction in close proximity to the family member with whom you are interacting. This is the normal pattern for personal interaction between adults and should be comfortable for both of you. However, if you are observing children at the same time, ask the parent to step further inside the room or position yourself so that you can continue to supervise children, and explain this to the parent.

3. Maintain eye contact for brief interactions or alternate between child focus and adult focus. For example, shift your focus from the parent to the child as appropriate to maintain the interaction while assisting children to enter and leave. In a classroom, you might seat yourself while the parent is seated or stand as necessary to maintain eye contact.

4. Speak with normal to soft volume and normal to low pitch. Try to achieve a voice quality that is relaxed, serious, and concerned. The nonverbal communication strategies for warmth and respect are the same for adults and children. Many relaxed, friendly encounters help to establish rapport between adult family members and the staff.

continued

5. When family members communicate, pay attention to their nonverbal behavior and maintain your nonverbal channels appropriately for their message to you and the message you wish them to receive. For a worried family member, a look of confidence in the professional is reassuring. When someone is distressed or angered, a serious expression and a firm, quiet tone is appropriate; a nervous giggle or laugh would irritate them even more. A smiling face and general tone of friendliness are appropriate when a child tells a funny story but probably would not be appropriate if a parent of the opposite sex told an off-color joke at pickup time. The nonverbal messages that you send parents are much better communicators about your professionalism and your feelings about them than any other mode of communication.

PITFALLS TO AVOID

Regardless of whether you are using nonverbal communication techniques with children individually or in groups, informally or in structured activities, there are certain pitfalls you should avoid.

Giving inconsistent nonverbal messages or nonverbal messages inconsistent with the verbal content. Do not smile when you are angry, stating a rule, or trying to convey an admonition or your displeasure. Do not use a loving tone of voice while giving an admonition, or use a cold, distant tone while expressing approval or affection. These classic double-bind messages result in confusion or distrust on the part of children.

Acting before thinking. Uninformed, unthinking adults sometimes behave nonverbally in ways that may be insensitive or insulting to others. Using a loud voice and speaking slowly will not help a non-English-speaking person understand. Quickly judging a 12-year-old with purple spiked hair and responding angrily toward him is more likely to elicit rebellion than cooperation. Though genuine, honest responses are appropriate, thoughtful responses are also necessary to move toward positive relationships and understanding others. This is one of the differences between professionals and untrained persons. Professionals have and use information that will enable them to be more effective than do others who must rely solely on their own life experiences.

Hurting or threatening to hurt children. Some nonverbal means of getting attention, such as rapping children on the head with a pencil, yanking them to get into line, or using excessive force to hold them in place so you can talk, are aggressive and inappropriate. Imminent violence is signaled by a raised hand or fist, looming over, forceful grasping, or glaring in extremely close proximity—and is inappropriate and inconsistent with ethical practice.

Using "baby talk." Parents and intimates may use baby talk as a form of affection. Professionals who work with children must establish clear communication based on respect for the child.

Interrupting children. Allow children the chance to speak. Do not complete sentences for them even if you think you know what they mean. Do not try to fill the normal hesitations of a child's speech with your own words. Allowing children time to speak their own thoughts shows respect. Interrupting children and finishing sentences for them is intrusive, patronizing, and disrespectful. Let children choose the words to use, and do not hurry them along. This demonstrates good listening skills, providing a positive example for children to follow.

Shouting, bellowing, shrieking, or screaming at children. More effective ways have been described for getting the attention of children. In addition, loud or shrill voices can be frightening. Such behavior in adults usually indicates that the adult has lost self-control.

Calling to children from across the room. In neutral or positive situations, adults usually remember to walk over to children and speak to them directly. However, in emergencies or when danger threatens, this procedure often is forgotten. In such a situation, you may attempt to regulate a child by calling out a warning. Unfortunately, this usually is ineffective because children do not always know the message is directed toward them. In addition, they may startle and thereby get hurt. Take a few seconds and move toward the child to deliver the message.

Placing your hand over your mouth, on the chin, or otherwise covering your face and mouth. If you are covering part of your face when speaking, your speech may be unclear or misunderstood, and your facial expressions may not be fully visible. Wearing hats such as baseball caps indoors may shadow your face so much that your expressions cannot be readily seen. Give children the chance to see your face clearly.

Ignoring family members who are in reasonably close proximity. When any adult approaches a caregiver, simple courtesy is always appropriate. Ignoring them gives the impression of indifference or of being rude. Adults may or may not be parents, so identifying them appropriately is also a safety issue for the children in your care.

SUMMARY

People use nonverbal behaviors to efficiently and subtly communicate their feelings about a relationship as well as to convey the substance of the verbal message they are sending. Nonverbal messages usually are implicit and often fleeting and therefore can be denied or misinterpreted.

Each of the channels, or modes, of nonverbal communication can work independently of the others and can complement or contradict the lexical message. Messages that are consistent across all channels are more easily understood; in addition, the speaker sends the general message of honesty, genuineness, and integrity. Mixed messages—those that are not consistent across channels—are confusing to children, convey a general sense of deception or disinterest, cause children to distrust the adult, and are less likely to elicit the desired response.

Children learn to interpret nonverbal messages before they learn to deliberately send them. Most of their learning is based on imitation. Therefore, children exposed to effective communicators will themselves become more effective communicators. Infants are able to detect mixed messages, and they rely substantially on the paralinguistic features of the message. As children get older, they become more skillful in understanding and sending nonverbal messages. They also tend to rely more on facial expressions in decoding messages, except when they detect deception.

Adults who understand the meanings of nonverbal messages can deliberately use them to enhance their effectiveness in communication. Skills have been presented that will increase your ability to nonverbally convey warmth and concern as well as authority. Using these skills will help you to communicate clearly and develop positive relationships with children and their families built on respect and concern.

Pitfalls have been identified that should be avoided. These will either prove ineffective or interfere with building positive relationships with children. Now that you understand some of the most basic components of communication with children, you are ready to explore ways in which these can be combined with verbal communication skills to facilitate the development of positive, growth-enhancing relationships with children and their adult family members.

KEY TERMS

axial space	illustrator gestures	nonverbal communication
channel of communication	intensity	paralinguistics
display rules	internal space	personal space
distal space	mask smile	pitch and tone
duration	metacommunication	proximal space
emblems	mixed message	rhythm
gestures	nonlexical sounds	subjective time
hesitations		

DISCUSSION QUESTIONS

1. Describe the functions of nonverbal communication and how each is used in ordinary interactions.
2. How does nonverbal communication regulate social interaction?
3. Why is it necessary to describe how the different channels of nonverbal communication operate when discussing building relationships with young children?

4. Imagine watching two 10-year-olds in a face-to-face situation in which one is thrusting a stick at the other. What would be your interpretation of this event if the children were 12 feet apart; 3 feet apart; quite close together? Why would you interpret these differently?

5. Answer question 4 in relation to internal, proximal, axial, and distal space.

6. Why is it important to know something about the cultural heritage of children when interpreting the meaning of their nonverbal behaviors?

7. How do age, relationship, and gender affect nonverbal communication behaviors? Give examples.

8. Why should helping professionals use congruent verbal and nonverbal communications with children and strictly avoid incongruent messages?

9. Nonverbal communication, unlike language arts, is not taught in school. How do children learn about it?

10. How does your use of time in interactions with other people denote your social relationship to them?

11. Which nonverbal behaviors are most likely to convey warmth? Assertiveness?

12. Recall a time when you have been misinterpreted or when you misinterpreted someone else. Did you send or receive a mixed message (whether intentional or not)? Were cultural differences involved in the misunderstanding?

13. How do the nonverbal communications of adults contribute to building positive relationships with children?

14. Describe how nonverbal skills for adults compare with those for children.

FIELD ASSIGNMENTS

1. Observe two adults anywhere you can see them, but not hear them. This may be in a mall, grocery store, or restaurant. Watch them and describe what you see. Record what you think the emotional tone or content of the interaction is. Include a description of the setting, position in space of each participant, body motions and orientation, gestures, and facial expressions.

2. Reread the guides for behavior to demonstrate warmth and caring as well as to demonstrate authority. Practice each one with one or two children in your field placement. Describe what you did and how the children responded. Evaluate how well you were able to use these skills.

3. In a group of children, practice smiling, keeping eye contact on a face-to-face level, and using strategies for conveying warmth. Observe the response of the children to your behavior. Describe their nonverbal behaviors as a response to your own.

4. Listen to a skilled adult giving directions to children. Note position in space, gestures, facial expression, tone of voice, and eye contact with the children. What did this person actually do? Compare to any other person interacting with children.

5. Compare the dress of any two adults in group situations with children. Listing all things that the people wore, determine whether or not the apparel was functional, and what you think it communicated to children and their parents.

6. Imagine that you are describing the behavior of a coworker. Use the following sentences below in quotation marks and speak them aloud to another classmate to convey (1) your respect and admiration for this person and then (2) your disdain and disrespect for the person. Use gestures, facial expression, paralinguistics, or other strategies to convey your meanings. Ask your listener if they could easily tell which message was which. "Ms Reardson is a real professional. She knows a lot about the families. The children know that she means what she says. I could tell you a lot more if I had the time." What articles of the NAEYC Code of Ethics would you select to judge whether these communications are appropriate?

Chapter 4

PROMOTING CHILDREN'S DEVELOPING SENSE OF SELF THROUGH VERBAL COMMUNICATION

OBJECTIVES

On completion of this chapter, you should be able to describe:

- Self-awareness.

- The relationship between self-awareness and social understanding.

- How children develop a concept of self over time.

- Self-esteem.

- Characteristics of a negative verbal environment.

- Characteristics of a positive verbal environment.

- Adult communication strategies associated with a positive verbal environment.

- Positive communication strategies for interacting with family members.

- Pitfalls to avoid in communicating verbally with children and their families.

One day, Maddie was busy drawing this picture (Figure 4-1) at the table. She squinted her eyes, pursed her lips, and worked a long time. She carefully placed the parts of her body and those of her family on her drawing. When she finished, she put down her marker with a satisfied, "There." Followed by, "Want to see my picture? It's me and my family. See, here I am, and here is V and here are the twinnies, and Mommy and Daddy. I'm big cause I'm special. I am the second baby and a big sister . . . and that's important."

Maddie has a happy sense of self. As a preschooler, she is already beginning to define who she is and who she is not and where she fits in her social world, which currently consists primarily of her family. It is within Maddie's social context, through the interactions with the people in her environment, that she will continue to expand upon her sense of self and develop greater self-awareness.

Figure 4-1 Maddie and her family.

THE CHILD'S EVOLVING SENSE OF SOCIAL UNDERSTANDING AND SELF

The roots of children's social behaviors lie within their overall developing concept of how the social world works, their **social understanding.** This understanding begins with children's awareness of themselves (Lewis & Carpendale, 2004). The manner in which children see themselves as individuals directly influences how they will interact with others now and in the future. It sets up expectations for successful interactions or rejection. And it contributes to how well the child feels he or she can make a significant contribution to society.

Self-Awareness and Social Understanding

The understanding of self is both a social and cognitive construction (Harter, 2006). Children's interactions with people in the environment, along with their cognitive interpretation of these interactions, contributes to each child's understanding of self as both an independent being and in relation to others. This understanding contributes to children's overall social competence. Let's take a closer look at the progression from awareness of self towards increased social understanding (see Figure 4-2).

Based on Chapter 2, you already know that infants begin life with a very general awareness of self. Over time and through numerous interactions, this general awareness deepens to a greater understanding that oneself is different from others (Laible & Thompson, 2007). Thus, **self-awareness** evolves from a very concrete beginning to a much more abstract awareness through cognitive maturity, social experience, and the development of language.

At first, children are involved in becoming aware of their existence as separate from others. They move from knowing "I am" (baby crying, intention: "Hey, look at me!") to an awareness that "I can make things happen" (the bouncy toy moves as it the child kicks it over and over again) to "I can get a reaction from others" (Mom smiles across the room at the latest "trick" of crawling) to "I have thoughts and ideas" ("No! I don't want that!") (Thompson, 2006).

As children become aware of their own ideas, they eventually begin to develop a theory that other people have ideas too. Some have called the children's evolving theory about their own and others' thoughts, desires, emotions, and beliefs **theory of mind** (Wellman & Liu, 2004). Whether called theory of mind, perception of others' thoughts, or understanding states of mind, the research is demonstrating that children do move through a predictable progression in thinking of and understanding others' social actions in relation to the thoughts and intentions of others. In turn, this progression is connected to children's interpretation of events relative to themselves and to future prediction of how their actions will impact others.

When children are first considering the thoughts of others, in true egocentric fashion they initially theorize that other people think exactly the same as they do. For example, Sara doesn't like brussel

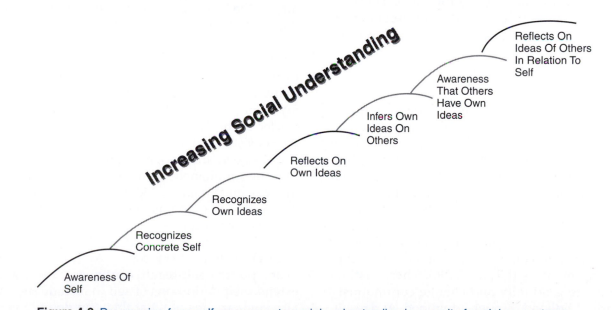

Figure 4-2 Progression from self-awareness to social understanding in pursuit of social competence.

sprouts. She sees them being served at lunch and loudly proclaims, "No way. No one likes those," honestly believing that to be the truth because she does not care for them. From this egocentric thinking emerges the idea that others can have desires, thoughts, beliefs, and emotions that are different from those of the child. This can happen as early as age 3 or 4, depending upon social, cognitive, and language experiences (Astington, 2001).

Finally, children begin to be able to *predict* or *reflect* upon the beliefs of others as different from their own. This can occur for children at a most basic level by age 4 or 5 (Wellman, Cross, & Watson, 2001). This ability to predict others' thinking in social situations helps children adjust their behavior to fit the perceived possible reaction of others.

> Jonathan observed his caregiver scowling at the water on the floor. He interpreted the look on her face to be one of displeasure (contrary to his elation over the water balloon play). He decided to get a towel and wipe up the spilled water before the adult reacted unfavorably.

Throughout the entire process from self-awareness to social awareness to social understanding, children actively expand their social competence. Of course, the process of coming to understand others is a lifelong endeavor. It expands over time as the child grows in cognitive, language, and social abilities. Children cycle through this process not in a linear fashion, but in a more cyclical, tornado-shaped manner in which each "cycle" generates more experience in the social world. Beyond self-awareness, two other aspects of self relate closely to children's social understanding and subsequent social competence: self-concept and self-esteem.

Self-Concept

Whereas self-awareness is an understanding that the self is distinct from others in the environment, **self-concept** is the manner in which children define themselves using a combination of attributes, abilities, behaviors, attitudes, and values that children believe represent themselves and make them different from everyone else (Shaffer, 2006). Because the construction of "Who am I?" is both cognitively and socially constructed, as children's cognitive thinking changes, the child comes to view and define self in more complex ways (Harter, 2006). These distinctions emerge gradually and change continuously from early childhood through adulthood. As a result,

children's view of themselves becomes more differentiated and more complex as they mature.

Toddlerhood. By about 18 months of age, children clearly differentiate between themselves and others (Harter, 1999). Part of this self-understanding occurs as they are able to name and describe themselves with words (Thompson, 2006). Toddlers, realizing they are distinct from other people, are quick to verbalize "Mine" when claiming a favored possession and "Me" when referring to their image in a looking glass or photograph. They notice the impact of their behavior on others (Laible & Thompson, 2007). By the end of their second year, children have a well-established sense that they are their own person, with the power to influence the people, things, and events around them.

As children acquire more language ability, they become better at thinking about self (Harter, 2006). Their earliest descriptions focus on categorical attributes of age and sex. These little ones proudly announce: "Me two." "I a girl."

Preschool age. Building on concepts developed in toddlerhood, children ages 2, 3, and 4 define themselves in very concrete, observable terms (Harter, 2006). Their self-descriptions include physical attributes ("I have brown hair"), abilities ("I can climb the ramp"), possessions ("I have a bike"), social affiliation ("I have a big sister"), and preferences ("I like ice cream and chocolate"). When possible, children will demonstrate these attributes on the spot, such as by climbing the ramp or "showing off" on the bike. These immediate actions highlight the concrete nature of their thinking. During this same period, children's self-concept also includes simple emotions and attitudes regarding what they like or do not like about certain objects or activities, for example: "I am happy when I play with my friends" and "I don't like peas" (Griffin, 1992; Harter, 2006). Twos, threes, and fours can't imagine the coexistence of both positive and negative traits such as good and bad, nor can they describe experiencing simultaneous emotions such as scared and overwhelmed (Harter, 2006). Overall, children aged 2, 3, and 4 view themselves in an overly positive light (Harter, 2006).

Early elementary age. At 5, 6, and 7, this overly positive self-regard continues. Now, children extend their definitions of self to include rudimentary comparisons of what they can do now versus

To describe himself, this preschooler says, "I have brown hair and a yellow shirt. I jump high."

what they could do at earlier ages (Frey & Ruble, 1990). Typical statements are "I can run faster now than I used to" or "When I was little I was scared of the dark, but I'm not scared anymore." These comparisons occur as they see the growth in themselves, not as boasts. Comparisons also occur as children this age worry about fairness: "He's got more than me!" (Frey & Ruble, 1990). Simple categories to define self such as "athletic" are created by combining individual attributes such as kicking, running, and batting. However, children at this age remain unable to put opposite categories or emotions together and thus cannot yet express having two competing emotions simultaneously, such as furious and joyful. However, they are able to describe two complementary emotions together (e.g., I'm excited for the game and content that we can go together!) (Harter, 2006).

Middle elementary age.   By ages 7 and 8, children become more aware of their private selves and begin self-description in a more abstract manner. They use trait labels that focus on abilities and interpersonal characteristics, such as smart and dumb, nice and mean. Their comparisons now revolve around what one can do in relation to what

another peer can do (Harter, 2006): "I run faster than Jonathan. Mary spells better than me." These comparisons are not meant to be harmful; they are the children's way of differentiating themselves from others. Age, gender, and material goods are convenient, observable features for grouping "me" and "not me."

Later elementary age.   While children's definition of self continues to incorporate the concrete features from former stages (as evident in Figure 4-3), a significant shift in children's thinking occurs with children ages 8 to 11. Less concrete and more abstract adjectives are used to describe themselves. They begin to mention personality traits, such as "I am popular." They continue to refer to competencies, but they are now able to categorize them into specific areas and differentiate between them. This enables them to see variations within their performance. Unlike earlier stages, perception of self tends to become much more negative at this age (Harter, 2006). In addition, interpersonal relationships are more critical to their ideas of self-identity: "I am Sarah and Josie's friend"; "I'm Jerome's sister's friend." This more sophisticated view is possible because their perceptions are influenced by what they have

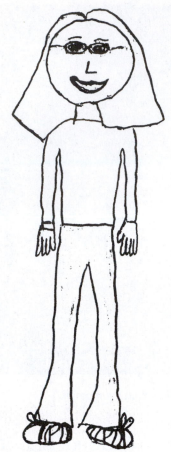

Figure 4-3 Cauleen's self-portrait at age 11, representing the physical attributes of self within her self-concept.

done in the past as well as by what they might do or be like in the future. Self-descriptions often refer to patterns of behavior that have been established over time and that children perceive will continue (I am smart; I am shy; I am a hard worker). Thinking of the self in these terms represents a more abstract orientation, which has become possible through increased experience and more advanced cognitive powers. Hence, they enter adolescence with much greater self-awareness than was possible at earlier points in their lives.

Self-Esteem

With growth in self-knowledge comes the ability to evaluate that knowledge, making positive and negative judgments about self-worth. As with self-awareness and self-concept, this ability to evaluate self develops over time. Children use the information (gained from words and actions) that one perceives that others are sending about one's overall value (Harter, 2006). These judgments are made in comparison to some internalized standard or expectation (Harter, 2006). For instance:

I am good looking.	I am not very good looking.
I am someone people like.	I am not someone people like much.
I am smart.	I am not very smart.
I can do things well.	I can't do many things well.
I am agile.	I am clumsy.
I like myself.	I don't like myself.

This evaluative component of the self is called **self-esteem.** Self-esteem has three broad dimensions: worth, competence, and control (Curry & Johnson, 1990; Marion, 2007). The extent to which people value and like themselves as well as perceive that they are valued (and loved) by others is a measure of their **worth. Competence** involves the belief that one is able to accomplish tasks and achieve one's goals. **Control** refers to the degree to which individuals believe they can influence outcomes and events in the world. People who judge their worth, competence, and control mostly in positive terms are said to have high self-esteem, and those whose self-evaluations are primarily poor are described as having low self-esteem (Damon & Hart, 1982).

The importance of self-esteem. Whether people's self-esteem is generally high or low, favorable or unfavorable, has a tremendous impact on their ability to derive joy and satisfaction from life. Self-esteem is strongly related to happiness (Furnham & Cheng, 2000). It affects how people feel about themselves, how they anticipate others will respond to them, and what they think they can accomplish (Baumeister, Campbell, Krueger, & Vohs, 2003). In addition, there is a high correlation between self-esteem and interpersonal relationships (Leary & McDonald, 2003). People who have high self-esteem are more likely to have healthy, positive relationships with peers and friends. Those with low self-esteem are more likely to be lonely and experience fewer friendship opportunities. Low self-esteem may hurt relationships because the person feels a lack of satisfaction with the relationship and constantly is looking for more acceptance (Leary & McDonald, 2003). People with high self-esteem are more likely to behave more prosocially and less antisocially (Leary & McDonald, 2003; Simons, Paternite, & Shore, 2001).

Youngsters whose self-esteem is high feel good about themselves and evaluate their abilities highly (Harter 2006). They have higher social confidence. They are more sociable, outgoing, and assertive

(Leary & McDonald, 2003). They consider themselves to be competent and likeable. They have a sense of control, believing that their own actions usually determine their fate. Thus, they expect to do well and are able to prevail in challenging circumstances (Baumeister et al. 2003). In social interactions, they anticipate that their encounters with others will be rewarding and that they will have a positive influence on the outcome of the exchange (Leary & Baumeister, 2000). These optimistic feelings make it easier for them both to give and to receive love. Such children also have confidence in their own judgments. As a result, they are able to express and defend ideas they believe in, even when faced with opposition from others. When confronted with obstacles, they draw on positive feelings from the past to help them get through difficult times. In addition, with age and experience they tend to appraise their abilities and limitations realistically and can separate weaknesses in one area from successes in others (Harter, 2006). When not successful, they are able to focus on personal strengths to overcome the situation and keep positive feelings about themselves intact. For these reasons, high self-esteem is related to positive life satisfaction, good mental health and happiness.

Low self-esteem, on the other hand, is often associated with depression, anxiety, suicidal and violent thinking and maladjustment (Baumeister et al., 2003; Harter, 2006, Leary&McDonald, 2003). It is also related to aggression, antisocial behavior, and delinquency (Donnellan, Trzesniewski, Robins, Moffitt, and Caspi, 2005). Children whose estimations of self-worth are entirely negative experience feelings of inadequacy, incompetence, fear, and rejection. They also are less likely to be objective about their capabilities, and more likely to focus on their weaknesses (Brown, 1998). This is not a balanced view but one that focuses primarily on failings. Such youngsters have little hope that they can influence others and anticipate that most interactions will be costly for them. They see that what happens to them is governed largely by factors beyond their control and are convinced that no matter how hard they try, their efforts will mostly go unrewarded unless they are lucky. Consequently, children may hesitate to express their opinions, lack independence, and tend to feel isolated or alone (Baumeister et al., 2003). Their gloomy outlook often leads them to build elaborate defenses as a way to protect their fragile egos or to ward off expected rejection (Dreikurs, 1991). Typical means of self-protection include putting themselves

By the early elementary years, children make differing judgments about their abilities in one area, such as music versus another, such as athletics.

down, keeping people at a distance, or building themselves up by tearing others down. Low self-esteem takes away from their quality of life.

Although most of the research to date has treated self-esteem as a totally "either/or" concept, in reality almost everybody falls somewhere between the two extremes (Curry & Johnson, 1990). In addition, there are times in each person's life when he or she experiences temporary feelings of high or low self-esteem depending on the circumstance (Brown, 1998). These variations are in keeping with the dynamic nature of human development. Therefore, it may be most accurate to think of high self-esteem as involving predominantly positive self-judgments across many life areas, interspersed with some negative self-evaluations. Low self-esteem represents the opposite combination of personal perceptions.

The Evolution of Self-Esteem

Just as the development of self-concept follows a normative sequence, so does the development of self-esteem. Toddlers and young preschoolers tend to make assessments of their self-worth that are all encompassing (Harter, 2006). That is, they make no distinctions among the various aspects of the self (e.g., the cognitive self versus the physical self). Instead, they think of themselves as either competent or incompetent across all areas. However, self-evaluation at this age tends to be overly positive. This may be due to the fact that young children cannot tell the difference between the behavior/performance they desire and the actual one (Harter, 2003).

Because their self-concept is rooted in the here and now, children's assessments change as circumstances change. For instance, 3-year-old Jessica, who has mastered opening and closing the screen door entirely on her own, may feel quite pleased with her newfound prowess. She announces, "I can do anything." Yet moments later, she may be plunged into tears when her older brother says she's too little to join him in a game in the backyard. Her self-evaluation at that point may be "I can't do anything."

Older preschoolers and early-elementary-age children begin to compartmentalize their notions of self-worth. They make different evaluations of the self in different categories—social, physical, and intellectual (Harter, 2006). More often than not, 5- to 7-year-olds tend to overestimate their abilities, seeing themselves in a very favorable light (Harter, 2006; see Figure 4-4). However, if children

Figure 4-4 Veronica's view of self at age five.

have experienced some extreme negative socialization, they may see themselves as all bad (Harter, 2006). By age 8, most youngsters make essential distinctions about their abilities in each realm. From then on, self-esteem represents a multifaceted combination of perceptions (Harter, 1999, 2006). Hence a child may have positive feelings about himself or herself in relation to academics, while simultaneously feeling inadequate athletically. However, simply recognizing perceived inadequacies in a particular realm does not automatically result in low self-esteem (Harter, 2006). The relative significance of a particular category to an individual child also factors into his or her self-judgment. Consequently, a child may truly conclude, "I'm not good at fixing things and that's okay." Seeing the positive aspects of self alongside the limitations makes it more likely that children's self-perception is more closely aligned with the opinions others have of them (Harter, 2003).

One final factor that comes into play as children evaluate themselves is the role of stress. Children experiencing emotional distress are more likely to underestimate their abilities. They see less positive attributes in themselves and thus experience lowered self-esteem (Pomerantz & Rudolph, 2003).

As children collect life experiences, their self-perceptions become more enduring. Rather than shifting dramatically from situation to situation, children begin to identify patterns related to their social, physical, and intellectual abilities and make self-judgments with those in mind. This is demonstrated when a child concludes, "I'm good at spelling. I have a hard time making friends." Such perceptions also serve as the basis for projecting a future/possible self, as when the child states, "Probably they won't like me. I never have been good at making friends," or "I'm good at math. If I keep practicing, I should be able to do these problems," (Harter, 2006). There is evidence that such patterns of thinking tend to last and may become difficult to change (Bee, 1999). For instance, a child who has high self-esteem at age 10 is likely to have high self-esteem as a teenager and even as an adult. Likewise, low self-esteem in middle childhood often predicts negative self-judgments as a person matures. Having said this, it must also be noted that the evolution of self-esteem never really ends (Brown, 1998; Harter, 2006). People's self-perceptions continue to be influenced by their interactions with one another and the environment throughout their lifetimes. See Table 4-1 for view of development of self over time.

Influences on self-esteem. There are multiple things that influence children's self-esteem: people's behaviors and language, cultural messages, and the gender of the child. Most influential are the significant people children interact with on a daily basis: parents, teachers, peers, and siblings. Through the accepting and rejecting behavior of these important people, children receive answers to the questions "Who am I?," "What kind of person am I?," and "How valued am I?" (Harter, 2006). All of these influential people serve as mirrors through which children see themselves and then evaluate what they see . If the image is perceived by the child to be negative, rejecting, or punitive, then children experience feelings of being unloveable, incompetent, and unworthy. The opposite is also possible: given caring and sensitive adults, children feel loveable, competent and capable. The more important that the "judge" is to the child, the more influential that person's judgment is on the child's attitude toward self (Harter, 1999). Children are sensitive to the attitudes that they *perceive* these significant people have toward them and often adopt those opinions as their own (Harter, 2006).

The language that is used in communication between adults and the child serves to create a story for the child of his/her life. Of particular consequence is the manner in which adults narrate children's worlds: "You're so helpful. We needed your hands to get the clean up done!" or "You really fell short today on the soccer field when you missed that goal." The content that adults include in this ongoing narrative (whether selecting to ignore or expand upon positive or negative events) scaffolds children's understanding and future evaluation of self (Nelson & Fivush, 2004; Thompson, 2006). Further, this type of **narrative talk** formulates a large portion of children's autobiographical memory. **Autobiographical memory** is not necessarily an accurate account of events, but rather a child created memory based on specific perceptions of events. Children use this type of memory when they encounter situations. They compare the current experience with past memories from their "autobiographical bank." These memories are then used to further assist the child in assessing whether the current situation will be a successful or unsuccessful event (Laible &

Table 4-1 Children's Developmental Progression of Self.

BIRTH–AGE 1	2–4	5–7	8–11
General awareness of self separate from caregiver Beginning to recognize ME!	Describes self in concrete terms, one thing at a time (I'm a girl! I have blue eyes.).	Chunks concrete descriptions to form self-description (I can run fast, jump high, swim far . . . I'm an athlete!).	Sets of descriptions of self grouped into traits: I'm social (lots of friends, outgoing, popular), or I'm shy (when I don't know others).
Beginning awareness.	Overall positive view of self. Doesn't see negatives.	Overall positive view of self; may ignore negative aspects to keep positive frame.	Aware of and acknowledges positive and negative aspects of self.
No comparisons.	Typically doesn't make comparisons with others, unless about fairness (He got more!).	Temporal comparisons: comparisons are typically concerned with fairness and with what self could do in the past (When I was 4, I could only make my first name. Now I write Jessica Marie Jacoby!).	Social comparisons: Comparisons are between self and what others can do. These help child understand self better (I can't do math like Jeremy, but I can figure out the word puzzle each day before anyone else!).
Notices reactions of others to self (cries, gets picked up).	Aware of reactions of others to self (puts head down when spills milk).	Aware of the evaluations of others of self. Begins to use the evaluations of others to regulate self.	Evaluates self. Continues to use evaluations of others to guide behavior.

Source: Based on Harter, 2003.

Thompson, 2007). We will discuss more about narrative talk later in this chapter.

Part of the narrative talk that occurs with children focuses on transmitting cultural messages, which in turn contribute to children's sense of cultural self and evaluation of self within his/her culture (Nelson, 2003). How children define themselves typically follows cultural definitions. For instance, American children often define themselves as independent and assertive while Chinese children are likely to pride themselves on being more cooperative and obedient (Laible & Thompson, 2007). Of particular interest are the comparisons between African-Americans and European Americans. In reports of self-esteem, African-Americans consistently

attest to possessing higher self-esteem than European Americans. It is hypothesized that part of this is directly related to the narrative talk that parents provide in the early years as to how to be successful and happy in America, with the former being more supportive and positive in how to fit within the African-American culture (Harter, 2006).

Finally, gender also seems to play a role in self-esteem. There is consistent evidence that beginning in middle childhood, boys report higher self-esteem than girls in both overall self-esteem and in area specific self-evaluations (such as academics or athletics). Cultural expectations for females, particularly in reference to appearance may account for this difference (Harter, 2006).

HOW ADULT PRACTICES RELATE TO SELF-ESTEEM

Messages that impact children's self-esteem can be conveyed to children both nonverbally (as discussed in Chapter 3) and verbally. Many adults believe self-esteem is something they grant to children by telling them they're wonderful (Hendrick & Weissman, 2006). Others hope children will acquire high self-esteem by participating in "feel good" activities during special times set aside in the day. This latter, direct instruction technique has been increasingly tied to the use of commercially prepared self-esteem programs in which children and helping professionals make their way through a prescribed set of experiences or a workbook (Beane, 1991). Neither of these approaches takes into account the holistic, complex nature of child development. Instead, self-esteem is isolated from all other developmental domains and treated as something children acquire in doses rather than develop continuously over time. Over-inflating children with artificial undue praise can lead to narcissism (Leary, 2004). Short, 15-minute activities or the adult's gushing remarks will not give children a sense of well-being or prevent negative self-perceptions. Because esteem-influencing experiences are vital parts of children's lives, authentic esteem-enhancing efforts must be present.

When adults demonstrate that they can be trusted; when they are loving, caring, and respectful of children, they provide the "right" kind of socioemotional support that children need in order to be able to venture into new situations and engage and persist in learning. These experiences help children develop a positive value of self, higher self-esteem, a sense of belonging, and emotional comfort at school and in child care (Eccles, 2007). This is the emotional climate. When children and adults mutually respect and value each other, children's social, emotional and cognitive development thrives (Eisenberg, 2006). It is the emotional tone demonstrated through words and in actions that influences all areas of children's development. Healthy supportive relationships lead to positive outcomes in children's healthy development. Unfortunately, unhealthy relationships in which the adult is not viewed by the child as supportive will lead to less success for the child (See Figure 4-5). Key adult behaviors can be grouped into two major categories: nurturance and guidance. **Nurturance** refers to the types of relationships adults establish with children; **guidance** involves the discipline and instruction approaches adults use.

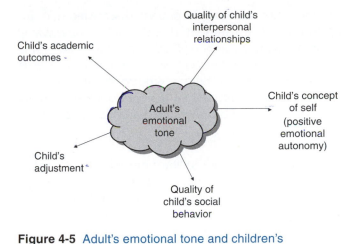

Figure 4-5 Adult's emotional tone and children's development.

Source: Based on work by Bugental & Grusec, 2006; Collins & Steinberg, 2006; Dodge, Coie, & Lynam, 2006; Eisenberg, Fabes, & Spinrad, 2006; Parke & Buriel, 2006; Rubin, Bukowski, & Parker, 2006; Thompson, 2006.

Nurturance

Adults who demonstrate warmth, acceptance, genuineness (authenticity), empathy, and respect are most likely to foster positive self-judgments in children (Marion, 2007; NICHD Early Child Care Research Network, 2001). How sensitive teachers and caregivers are to children's needs predicts how they will feel towards future teachers. Children who feel supported and valued in their current environment are more likely to do well cognitively and socially and approach new events with hope for success (NICHD, 2002). Adults who show approval, provide positive nurturance, and respond appropriately to children's needs are more likely to have children with higher self-esteem than adults who show disapproval and are not interested or fail to respond to children's needs (Harter, 2006). Recall that these are the very qualities that mark the facilitative dimension of the helping relationship and that have been identified as the primary components of positive adult–child relationships. When adults treat children sensitively, children feel they have an impact on their environment and experience a greater sense of control (Eccles, 2007). These same children are likely to believe that they are lovable and competent (Harter, 2006). Children who experience the opposite, whose caregiving adults are rejecting, uninterested, or insensitive, find it difficult to feel good about themselves and will form a model of themselves as unworthy (Thompson, 2006). Adults manifest these attitudes when they ignore children or when they are aloof, impatient, discourteous, or inappropriate toward them. If adults act in these ways, youngsters often conclude that because the adult finds them unworthy and incompetent, it must be so. This is the case with abused children who believe that they deserve the maltreatment they receive from their parents because they must be inherently bad (Harter, 2006).

Guidance

Adults who help children learn the skills they need to achieve social competence contribute to the development of positive self-esteem in those children. These are adults who: have high standards for children's behavior; consistently enforce reasonable rules, and who encourage children to participate in developing some of those rules. Adults are likely to encourage feelings of competence, worth, and control when they provide a combination of acceptance, limits, and meaningful, realistic expectations concerning behavior and effort (Deci & Flaste, 1995; Lamborn, Mounts, Steinberg, & Dornbusch, 1991). When adults use encouraging initiatives, give meaningful rationales for requests, and limit their use of controlling language, they support children's development of autonomy (Deci & Ryan, 2000). When adult expectations are appropriate: not too high or too low, children experience greater competence (Eccles, 2007). Further, when practices are used that support children's autonomy, children are more likely to have the intrinsic motivation to learn (Lepper & Henderlong, 2000). Adults who do little to increase children's sense of competence, who are harsh, who employ unreasonable rules, or who enforce no rules at all contribute to children's negative self-judgments (Curry & Johnson, 1990). Moreover, when adults use primarily extrinsic rewards to shape and control children's behavior, children are likely to develop a lower sense of well-being (Kasser & Ryan, 1996). However, when teachers reduce the amount of external rewards, competition, and comparisons between students, then children's motivation, persistence on difficult tasks, and overall socioemotional development increases (Midgley, 2002). Exactly why this is so and what it means to helping professionals is fully explained in Chapters 10 through 15.

Relating the Environment to Adult Talk

Whether adults convey esteem-enhancing or esteem damaging attitudes frequently is determined by what they say to children and how they say it. In fact, adult verbalizations are a major contributor to the perceptions children form about themselves (Marion, 2007). Consider the following scenario.

SITUATION: You are invited to visit a program for children.

When you arrive, you are asked to wait until the youngsters return from a field trip. As you survey your surroundings, you notice brightly colored furniture comfortably arranged, sunlight softly streaming through the windows, children's artwork pleasingly displayed, attractive materials that look well cared for, green plants placed about the room, and a large, well-stocked aquarium bubbling in a corner. You think to yourself, "What a pleasant place for children!" Just then, a child bursts into the room crying. She is followed by an adult who snaps: "Rose, you're being a big baby. Now, hush." As the other youngsters file in, you hear another child say, "Look what I found outside!" An adult replies: "Can't you see I'm busy? Show it to me later." After a while, you overhear a child ask, "When do we get to take these home?" He is told, "If you'd been listening earlier, you'd know."

Your favorable impression is shattered. Despite the lovely surroundings, the ways in which adults are talking to children has made the setting unpleasant. Adult comments have caused you to question whether it is possible for children to feel good about themselves in this program and whether the adult–child relationships can be anything but distant and unfavorable. What you have overheard has unlocked an invisible but keenly felt component of every program—the verbal environment.

THE VERBAL ENVIRONMENT

The manner in which adults speak to children reveals their attitude toward children as well as the tenor of their relationship (Stone, 1993). The **verbal environment** encompasses all verbal exchanges that take place within a given setting. The language of the environment is a crucial element on which to focus. Language directly contributes to children's sense of self, current and future self-esteem, and overall social competence. Its elements include words and silence—how much is said, what is said, how it is stated, who talks, and who listens. The way in which these elements are used and combined dictates whether the environment is one in which children's self-evaluations are favorable or unfavorable. Thus, verbal environments can be characterized as being either positive or negative.

The Negative Verbal Environment

Negative verbal environments are ones in which children feel unworthy, unlovable, insignificant, or incompetent as a result of what adults do or do not say to them. You could readily identify the most extreme illustrations of these. Adults screaming at children, ridiculing them, cursing at them, or subjecting them to ethnic slurs are blatant examples. Yet there are less obvious, more common adult behaviors that also contribute to negative verbal environments, and hence detract from children's self-esteem. These are summarized in Table 4-2. As you read the table, notice how the adult's use of language impacts the three key components of self-esteem: worth, competence, and control.

Table 4-2 The Negative Verbal Environment and Its Impact on Children.

ADULT BEHAVIOR/INTERACTION	REASON FOR ACTION	CHILD'S REACTION/ INTERPRETATION MAY BE
Shows little or no interest • Doesn't acknowledge child's presence • Doesn't talk when child is nearby • Barely responds to child's attempts	Adult is hurried or busy or thinking	Adult is not interested in ME I'm not important, something else is I'm not WORTH time
Pays insincere attention • Doesn't actively listen • Asks irrelevant or closed-ended questions • Responds inappropriately • Doesn't use eye contact • Cuts off child's words	Adult is lost in own thoughts	Adult is not interested in ME My ideas are not important I am not important I'm not WORTH the time My ideas are not COMPETENT
Speaks discourteously to children • Interrupts child's conversations with other children • Interrupts child talking with adult • Insists child respond immediately to requests • Tone is inappropriate to situation • Neglects social niceties such as please, thank you, excuse me . . .	Adult is not thinking Adult is looking for short-term fix, not thinking of long-term impact on child	Things I have to say are not important or relevant or interesting The adult is more important I'm not WORTH time I have no CONTROL I am not COMPETENT
Uses sarcasm with children • Uses negative tone • Uses negative words • Makes child butt of joke • Puts child "in his place" ("She thinks she is so smart that she doesn't have to pay attention.")	Adult wants to gain control of the situation Adult uses the sarcasm to establish power Adult may think it is humorous	How embarrassing! I'm not important I am stupid I have negative WORTH I have no CONTROL I won't talk/participate with this adult I must have no COMPETENCE
Uses judgmental vocabulary to describe children • Labels children with negative terms: hyper, selfish, lazy, pushy, etc. • Uses labels for children directly or within their hearing	Adult is trying to control the situation Adult is NOT THINKING of the children's feelings	I am not important I have no WORTH
Discourages children from expressing ideas • Tells child to "Tell me later," but later doesn't come • Shushes children, "Shshhhhh" • Tells children, "Not now"	Adult is following the adult agenda Adult may be trying to "get everything done" Adult is hurried or feels pressured	I have ideas, but they aren't important I must not be important I have no WORTH I have no CONTROL My ideas aren't good enough I have no COMPETENCE

continued

Table 4-2 The Negative Verbal Environment and Its Impact on Children——continued

ADULT BEHAVIOR/INTERACTION	REASON FOR ACTION	CHILD'S REACTION/ INTERPRETATION MAY BE
Ignores children's interests • Tells children to talk about something else, "I'm tired of hearing you tell me about Rorey and your troubles. Talk about something else, or be quiet." • Tells children to stop what they are doing to follow the adult agenda, "You've seen the butterfly long enough. Now come sit down." • Ignores child's statement or question to follow own agenda	Adult is following the adult agenda Adult may be hurried or pressured to complete prescribed amount of work Adult is not interested	I am not interesting My needs/desires don't have value I am not WORTH the time Her story is more important than my story I'm not in CONTROL I'm bothering her I must have bad ideas I'm not COMPETENT
Uses words primarily to control children's behavior, not for conversation • Gives directions, "Sit in your chair. Open your book to the first blank page. Draw a line. Draw your picture . . ." • States rules, "NO fighting!" • Engages in very little conversations with children	Adult wants to control the children's behavior Adult heard that words are important, so is using many words at children (instead of with)	I better behave I am not important I have no WORTH I am not COMPETENT (If I were, she wouldn't have to tell me everything) I have no CONTROL
Asks rhetorical questions • Uses empty questions, "What is your problem today?" • Uses sarcastic tone, "Did you leave your brain at home?"	Adult is controlling the children's behavior with words Adult is frustrated or unhappy with situation	I am not important My response (if I give one) is not wanted and is not liked I am not valuable (no WORTH)
Uses names of children to mean NO and DON'T and STOP	Adult is controlling the children's behavior Adult is angry or frustrated or unhappy with the situation	I am not important The very essence of me, my name, is BAD . . . I must be BAD
Criticizes children • Focuses on what children can't do, not what they can do • Decreases opportunities for improvement by denying option ("You're too little, too dumb, too unskilled, etc.") • Expects perfection • Ignores approximations of behaviors • Makes fun of what children can't do • Scolds children for what they can't do	Adult is controlling children's behavior Adult may think this helps motivate child (in reality it demotivates most)	I am not WORTHwhile I am not successful. I may never be successful. I can't even try. I am not COMPETENT Since the targeted behavior is not broken into manageable pieces, I can't even CONTROL the situation No one takes the time to help me, I must not be WORTHwhile

Table 4-2 The Negative Verbal Environment and Its Impact on Children.

ADULT BEHAVIOR/INTERACTION	REASON FOR ACTION	CHILD'S REACTION/ INTERPRETATION MAY BE
Uses insincere or destructive praise • Links positive behavior with negative put-down ("I'm glad you are sitting now. You've been out of your seat all day.")	Adult is trying to control children's behavior Adult is trying to motivate children Adult may think it is useful	I don't trust this adult I don't believe what she says I don't want her to notice me (whether I've been "good" or "bad"—either is bad)
• Uses the same compliments with everyone, "Nice job," "Good," "Great" • Builds up one child at the expense of the others, "Jenna, you did so well; too bad no one else studied." • Uses fake sweet voice		I'm not important enough to notice true accomplishments I'm no different than everyone else I'm not WORTHwhile I'm not in CONTROL I must not have COMPETENCE

All of the negative verbal behaviors convey to children adult attitudes of aloofness, disrespect, lack of acceptance, and insensitivity. They cause the program setting to be dominated by adult talk and make it clear to youngsters that adult agendas take precedence over their own. In addition, children quickly learn that their ideas, thoughts, and concerns are not valued, nor are the children important enough as persons to be afforded the courtesy and respect one would anticipate if held in high regard. The aversive encounters that occur in a negative verbal environment tend to make children feel inadequate, confused, or angry (Kontos & Wilcox-Herzog, 1997). If interactions such as these become the norm, then children's self-esteem is likely to suffer. A different set of circumstances exists in programs characterized by a positive verbal environment.

The Positive Verbal Environment

In a **positive verbal environment**, children experience socially rewarding interactions with the adults present. Adult verbalizations are purposefully aimed at satisfying children's needs and making the children feel valued. At all times when speaking to children, adults concern themselves not only with the informational content of their words, but with the emotional impact their speech will have as well. Adults create a positive verbal environment by following the principles shown in Table 4-3 in their verbal exchanges with children. As you read this table, notice the impact on competence, worth, and control.

The importance of a positive verbal environment. Positive verbal environments are beneficial to both the adults and children who participate in them.

The principles outlined here provide concrete ways for adults to communicate warmth, acceptance, genuineness, empathy, and respect to children. This makes it more likely that youngsters will view adults as sources of comfort and encouragement.

Demonstration of such attitudes also creates the facilitative base from which adults can more confidently take appropriate future action. Simultaneously, children benefit because there are people in the program with whom they feel comfortable and secure. In addition, the adult–child interaction patterns enable children to learn more about themselves and to feel good about the self they come to know. Thus, a positive verbal environment is associated favorably with self-awareness, self-concept, and self-esteem (Harter, 2006).

Establishing a Positive Verbal Environment

Helping professionals would not knowingly act in ways to damage children's self-esteem. Observations of early childhood settings, however, show that at times adults unintentionally slip into verbal patterns that produce negative verbal environments. Over the years it has become increasingly clear that positive verbal environments do not happen by chance. Their creation is the result of purposeful planning and implementation. Adults pay careful attention to the principles shown in Table 4-3. They incorporate, as part of their daily interactions, such simple but telling behaviors as greeting the children as they arrive, making time for children, addressing children by name, inviting children to talk, speaking politely to children, and listening carefully to what children have to say.

These basic actions convey fundamental attitudes of affection, interest, and involvement. Together,

Table 4-3 The Positive Verbal Environment and Its Impact on Children.

ADULT BEHAVIOR/INTERACTION	REASON FOR ACTION	CHILD'S REACTION/ INTERPRETATION MAY BE
Actively engages with children • Saves nonessential housekeeping until children are not present • Engages socially with other adults when children are not present	Adult wants to be actively available to the children	I am important I am WORTH the time She noticed ME!
Uses language to demonstrate interest in children • Notices children with reflections ("You've been working hard on that puzzle.") • Notices children's accomplishments ("You've been waiting so patiently for a turn on the computer. Now it's time!") • Laughs with the children • Answers children's questions • Acknowledges children's invitations to participate with them and tries to accommodate ("That sounds fun—thanks for asking me.")	Adult wants children to know she is GENUINELY interested in them Adult communicates WARMTH and availability to children Adult communicates ACCEPTANCE of children Adult wants children to know she RESPECTS their ideas and activities	I am important I have WORTH She noticed my work/ideas/me I am COMPETENT I trust this adult
Actively listens to children • Replies thoughtfully to children's ideas • Accepts children's ideas • Remembers to ask children later on what their idea was when there truly wasn't time to hear it • Invites children to elaborate on ideas	Adult wants child to experience WARMTH and ACCEPTANCE, GENUINENESS, EMPATHY, and RESPECT	I am important She's interested in my ideas and in me I have COMPETENCE I have WORTH I have some CONTROL over what we will talk about I have COMPETENCE, my ideas are pretty good I trust this adult
Speaks courteously to children • Allows children to complete thoughts without interrupting • Demonstrates patience • Uses accepting tone of voice • Uses social amenities such as, please, thank you, and excuse me	Adult wants to build the relationship with the children Adult wants children to feel WARMTH and ACCEPTANCE and to share ideas now and in the future Adult wants children to know she GENUINELY is interested Wants to demonstrate respect for children	I am important My ideas are valuable I have WORTH I am interesting I am COMPETENT I can choose to CONTROL some of the conversation I trust this adult
Discusses children professionally in professionally appropriate situations • Avoids labeling children • Refrains from discussing children • Discusses issues in private with only appropriate parties	Adult wants children and their families to feel valued and RESPECTED Adult practices confidentiality Adult recognizes the impact of negative words or innuendos on children	I must be fine . . . no one is saying bad things about me I have WORTH I trust this adult

Table 4-3 The Positive Verbal Environment and Its Impact on Children.

Speaks with children informally throughout the day • Focuses on individual children and their current needs/interests (eating, toileting, anxiety about upcoming test, the bus, etc.)	Adult wants to know the children and what is important to them Adult wants to GENUINELY communicate with children Adult wants children to feel RESPECTED and ACCEPTED Adult wants children to know she is WARM and has EMPATHY for them	She wants to hear about me Whatever I say is interesting I am important She likes me I have WORTH I have some CONTROL in my world because I can talk about things I can share my COMPETENCE with her I trust this adult
Uses children's ideas and interests to guide the conversation • Follows children's lead in conversations • Brings up subjects that are known to be interesting to individual children	Adult wants children to know they are GENUINELY VALUED; that their ideas are RESPECTED and ACCEPTED Wants children to feel warm relationship	I am interesting I have WORTH I have CONTROL in the conversation I have COMPETENCE, my ideas are important enough to discuss
Uses questions to gain answers • Asks thought-provoking questions	Adult wants children to know that their ideas and opinions are GENUINELY RESPECTED and ACCEPTED Wants to increase children's competence at problem solving	I am interesting I have WORTH I have CONTROL in the length of my answers and content of my ideas I have COMPETENCE because she wants to hear my thoughts
Uses children's names in positive circumstances, never in place of negative commands	Adult thoughtfully considers that children's sense of self is most crucially tied to their name and strives to preserve only good feelings toward it	I have WORTH
Uses words to guide children's behavior • Uses words to encourage • Uses words to assist with frustrations • Carefully selects words to help children change their behavior without damaging their sense of self	Adult is constantly aware of the power of language and children's sense of self Adult wants to guide behavior in a positive manner, to increase prosocial behavior and decrease antisocial behavior, not to punish or control. Wants children to feel WARMTH, ACCEPTANCE, GENUINENESS, EMPATHY, and RESPECT	I am valuable enough for her to make the effort I can learn new behaviors I am worth teaching I have WORTH I have COMPETENCE I can CONTROL my behavior

the adult and the children co-construct the child's social experiences. Children encounter the social world experientially. The adult in a positive verbal environment scaffolds that experience with language through narration and discussions to increase each child's social competence. One such scaffolding strategy is the behavior reflection.

Behavior Reflections

Behavior reflections are nonjudgmental statements made to children regarding some aspect of their behavior or person. The adult observes a child and then comments to the child about her or his attributes or activities. Such statements do not express opinion or evaluation but are exactly about what the adult sees, keeping the child as the focal point.

SITUATION: A child is coming down a slide on his stomach.

> *Adult:* You're sliding down the slide. (Or: You found a new way to come down—you're sliding head first.)

SITUATION: Joe and Melissa are drawing a mural together.

> *Adult:* You two are working together. (Or: Each of you has figured out a way to contribute to the mural; You're concentrating on what you are doing; You are cooperating—each of you has a part in the picture.)

SITUATION: A child arrives at a child care center.

> *Adult:* You're wearing your tennis shoes today. (Or: You look all ready to go; You look like you're carrying a heavy load!)

The value to children of using behavior reflections. Behavior reflections are a powerful way to show interest in children and to narrate their world. When adults reflect what children are doing, they talk about actions and experiences that have the most meaning for youngsters—those in which they themselves are involved. Verbal observations such as these increase children's self-awareness and make them feel valued because the adult notices them and takes the time to note aloud something they have done. As mentioned earlier, these narratives of children's actions contribute to their autobiographical memory and definition of self (Thompson, 2006). Behavior reflections can have a positive influence on children's views of themselves (Tice & Wallace, 2003).

From these reflections, children learn that their everyday actions are important enough to be noticed and that extreme behavior is not needed to gain appropriate attention. This is an important concept for children to understand, because they sometimes assume that adults will only notice

Adults create a positive verbal environment for children by making themselves available to interact with the children upon their arrival at school.

behavior that is out of the ordinary (Dreikurs & Cassel, 1992). Youngsters' interpretations of "out of the ordinary" might include excelling in a particular area or acting out. Such conclusions are not surprising because in many group settings, one has to be the birthday child, the one who gets all A's, or the child who pinches a lot in order to receive individual attention from adults. By reflecting, adults instead make note of such commonplace events as: "You're sharing the paint with Wally," or "You're trying hard to tie your shoes," or "You noticed our math books are brand new." Simple comments such as these say to the child, "You are important." Because each takes only a few seconds to say, these comments are particularly useful to helping professionals who must work with more than one child at a time. Thus, while helping Nakita with her coat, the caregiver also can attend to Micah and Leon by saying: "Micah, you have almost every single button done," and "Leon, you wore your brown coat today," and to Nakita, "You figured out which arm to put in first." This spreads the attention around and helps Micah and Leon as well as Nakita feel that the adult has taken them into account.

Because reflections do not evaluate behavior, children learn not to feel threatened by adult attention. The nonevaluative nature of the reflection enables adults to actively and concretely demonstrate acceptance of children; youngsters interpret reflections as the adults trying to understand them better.

Further, when used appropriately, behavior reflections call on adults to take the child's perspective within an interaction. Understanding what is important to a child about a particular activity by seeing it through the child's eyes sets the stage for adults to be more empathic in their responses to children (Rogers, 1961). Also, observing closely and taking cues from the children makes it more likely that youngsters will feel good about the interactions that take place with the adult. Thus, an adult watching children dancing in a conga line might reflect: "You formed a really long conga line," or "Everybody's figured out a way to hang on," or "Everyone's smiling. You look like you're having fun." These are child-centered remarks that correspond to the youngsters' agenda in that situation rather than the adult's.

All too often, adults in group settings feel more comfortable supervising children than actually interacting with them. Within this mode, their remarks might have been: "What's that you're doing?" or "That's a hopscotch outline, not a conga pattern," or "You forgot to put the kickstep in. It goes like this." Even if these observations were meant to show adult interest, they do not match the children's perception of what is important in their game. Such comments only disrupt the activity and tell children that the adult knows better. Neither outcome promotes favorable self-judgments in children or positive adult–child relationships.

Behavior reflections can also increase children's receptive language skills because children learn word meanings from hearing the words used to describe their immediate experiences (Sharp, 1987). This type of contextual learning occurs when youngsters hear new words and new ways of putting words together to describe day-to-day events. For instance, young children who hear the child care provider observe on different occasions: "You are walking to the door," "You and Jeremy walked into the coatroom together," and "We were walking along and found a ladybug" will begin to comprehend the meanings of different verb forms based on their own direct involvement in each situation. Similarly, words children already know help them figure out the definitions of new words they hear. Thus, a child may realize that gargantuan means "big" because a helping professional reflects, "You found the most gargantuan dinosaur of all" as the child points to an Apatosaurus, which he already considers a large animal. New words add to children's store of knowledge about themselves and the world around them. Becoming better able to understand the words directed toward them contributes to positive self-esteem.

New vocabulary expands children's concepts as well as their language. As language grows, so does children's ability to describe self and think of self (Thompson, 2006). For instance, an adult who describes the child's action in the following way: "Tonia, you are building with all the square blocks. You've figured out how to balance them on edge," adds the additional concepts of "square" and "balance" for Tonia to consider, if she is ready. Such scaffolding by the adult facilitates the child's competence at a higher level than would be possible without the adult's comments (Berk & Winsler, 1995). **Scaffolding** is a term used to describe the process of linking what the child already knows or can do with new information or skills that he or she is ready to acquire.

In cases when children are not prepared to move forward, they simply ignore the new ideas. Further, the sheer act of directing language at the child about that child increase the number of words in the child's world. The more language children experience directly, the easier it is for them to acquire new language and concepts, and the better they will do in future cognitive and social endeavors (Hart & Risley, 2000).

An added benefit of using behavior reflections is that they may serve as an opening for children to talk to adults if they wish. Often, youngsters respond to the adult's reflections with comments of their own. Thus, a verbal exchange may develop that is centered on the child's interests. On the other hand, children do not feel compelled to answer every reflection they hear. For this reason, reflecting does not interrupt children's activities or make them stop what they are doing in order to respond to an adult query. Even when youngsters remain silent, they benefit by being made aware of the adult's interest in them.

When to use behavior reflections. Behavior reflections can be used singly, in succession, and with other skills you will learn about in later chapters. When interacting with toddlers, preschoolers, youngsters whose primary language is not English,

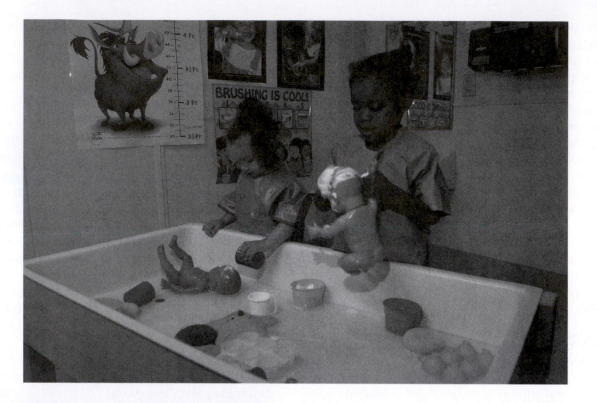

What behavior reflections might you use with these children?

and with children whose receptive language development has been delayed, it is appropriate to use a series of behavior reflections. For example, in a 10-minute interaction at the water table, the teacher might say: "You're pouring the water down the hose and watching it come out the other end," "You found a funnel to use," "You all remembered to put your smocks on," "Lucy, you're churning the water with an eggbeater," and "Mimi, you're getting the water to move with your hands." Such remarks could be addressed to one child, to more than one child, or to the group as a whole. Regardless of whether they answer, children of this age and ability appreciate knowing the adult is nearby and attentive.

School-age children, on the other hand, may feel self-conscious having that many remarks directed their way. For them, a single behavior reflection acts as an appropriate signal that the adult is interested in them and is available for further involvement if they wish it. Thus, out on the playground, children would consider it a friendly overture for an adult to say: "That was some catch!" or "You figured out the rules all by yourselves." In each case, if the child were to reply, the adult would have a clear invitation to continue the interaction. Were children to remain engrossed in their activity or direct remarks to others, this would be a cue to the adult that a prolonged interaction was not desired at that time.

Both children and adults benefit when helping professionals use behavior reflections in their repertoire of communication techniques. Most importantly, behavior reflections afford adults an excellent means to show children they care about them and are interested in their activities. Behavior reflections are particularly effective with young children, children who are just learning to speak English, or children who are mentally impaired; they are also useful as an entree to more involved interactions with older youngsters. Yet, to build relationships with children over time, it is necessary to implement additional skills that eventually will lead to more prolonged verbal exchanges.

Using Conversations to Support Children's Development of Sense of Self and Social Understanding and to Build the Relationship

In conversations, the emotional tone, the content, and the style of the message all contribute to children's development of emotions, morality and understanding of self (Thompson, 2006). One of the most basic ways for adults to show their concern for and interest in children is to carry on conversations

with them. Adult–child conversations contribute to children's positive feelings about themselves. When adults are attentive and respond meaningfully, they are demonstrating interest in the youngsters with whom they interact. Because adults represent authority figures, this clear sign of the adult's respect, caring, and acceptance conveys a powerful message to children about their value (Goffin; 1989; Kontos & Wilcox-Herzog, 1997).

Attitudes such as these increase children's self-respect and self-acceptance. In addition, conversations that center on topics in which children are interested are more likely to produce spontaneous and lengthy discussions than those focusing on adult topics. In such an atmosphere, youngsters begin to feel more confident about expressing their own thoughts, ideas, and feelings. As adults become actively involved with children in this manner, children come to view them as people worthy of receiving their trust and as potential sources of information and guidance. Thus, the foundations for positive adult–child relationships are extended and built.

Conversations are also a powerful context in which children can enhance their social understanding (Lewis & Carpendale, 2004). When adults model mental-state talk (talk about beliefs, desires, feelings), it helps children begin to understand and interpret the behavior of others (Jenkins, Turrell, Kogushi, Lollis, & Ross, 2003). It also helps the children see how they can also use mental-state talk to explain themselves and their actions to others. Adults can assist with this by doing three important things: talking about mental states as rationale for actions (e.g., I was wondering how Jana was feeling, so I thought I'd give her a call); pointing out how others feel in relation to the child's action (e.g., Kamie is crying and feels frustrated that you took away the puzzle piece); and reflecting on the mental state of others (e.g., You look perplexed . . .) (Lewis & Carpendale, 2004). Through conversations, adults can draw out and enhance upon important aspects of the social context that assist the child in a better understanding of the given situation (and self within the situation) which impacts their behavior in current and future social situations (Thompson, 2006).

Conversation stoppers. Unfortunately, in our haste to manage the day or accomplish our curriculum objectives, adults often inadvertently send out the unintended message to children that we either don't have time or don't care what they have to offer. We do this in a variety of ways. Most often we kill conversation by missing children's cues, correcting grammar, giving facts, offering unsolicited opinions, or suggesting advice when not asked. See Table 4-4 for common mistakes for these conversation stoppers.

All conversation stoppers listed in Table 4-4 should be avoided. There are a variety of ways in which adults can invite children to participate in conversation. In Chapter 3, nonverbal cues such as eye contact, facial expression, and paralinguistics were discussed as possibilities to invite or extend

conversations with children. In addition, the use of open-ended questions and paraphrase reflections can increase the likelihood that a child will engage in a conversation.

Using Questions to Invite Conversation

Questions can be a powerful way to open the door to invite a child into a conversation if they are used thoughtfully and skillfully. However, as discussed in Table 4-4, all too often, the questions serve as a

Table 4-4 Conversation Stoppers.

CHILDREN'S BEHAVIOR	ADULT BEHAVIOR	CHILD'S INTERPRETATION
1. Makes comments that appear unrelated or off-topic. Example: A robin's nest is found. Child responds, "I had eggs for breakfast."	*Missing children's conversational cues* Adult ignores the comments or makes an offhand remark such as, "That's nice."	You aren't interested in my ideas or me.
2. Use language inappropriately (grammatical mistakes, omitting words, mispronouncing words) in eagerness to share ideas with others. Example: "I helded the disk very carefully, but it slipped."	*Correcting grammar* Interrupts and/or insists child fix the error (repeat correctly or repronounce a word). Example: "You mean you HELD the disk—Say held . . ."	You didn't hear me. My ideas aren't interesting to you. If I talk, you won't like what I say. I don't talk right. I won't talk next time.
3. States facts incorrectly in excitement to share an idea or story. Example: "I bet Michael Jordan would love Mom's cherry pie. He'd jump right out of the TV to get a bite."	*Supplying facts and giving opinions* Instead of enjoying the story or conversation, the adult corrects the fact. Example response: "People don't jump out of TVs."	You aren't interested in my story or me. I need to be perfect to talk to you. I may not be right, so perhaps I'd better not try to talk to you.
4. Approaches adult with a problem. Example: "J.J. took my lunchbox."	*Advising* Adult wants to fix the problem, but if the child doesn't get to help work out the problem, the true source of the problem may not surface and the child may not like the adult's solution. Example response: "J.J., give it back."	You may not know the true problem, but I guess you aren't interested in hearing it. The child probably won't elaborate further, and unfortunately probably won't explore possible solutions. A learning opportunity is missed.
5. Child hears lots of questions.	*Inappropriate Questioning* Too many questions or ill-timed questions end talk by the other party. Control rests in the hands of the adult. A one-way monologue ensues.	You aren't actually interested in my ideas. You want to do all the talking. OR, You are asking about things I just don't want to talk about. OR, You don't really want an answer, you just want to talk.

means to close the door to conversation. The kinds of questions adults ask dictate the quality of the answers they receive (Cassidy, 2003; Trepanier-Street, 1991). To stimulate verbal exchanges, the best questions are those that draw people out and prompt them to elaborate. These are sometimes called open-ended questions or **creative questions** (Hendrick & Weissman, 2006). **Open-ended questions** have many possible answers but no single correct answer. Their purpose is to get children to talk about their ideas, thoughts, and emotions, not to quiz them or test their powers of memorization. Open-ended questions ask children to:

- predict ("What will happen next?")
- reconstruct a previous experience ("What happened when you visited your grandma?")
- make comparisons ("How are these animals the same/different?")
- make decisions ("What do you think we should do after lunch?")
- evaluate ("Which story was your favorite? Why?")
- imagine something ("What would it be like if the dinosaurs were alive today?")
- propose alternatives ("What is another way you could cross the beam?")
- apply factual knowledge ("Where do you suppose we might find a caterpillar at this time of year?")
- solve problems ("What can we do to find out how many marbles are in this jar?")
- generalize ("Now that you saw what happened when we heated the ice cube, what do you think will happen when we heat this snowball?")
- transform ("How could we make muffins from all these ingredients?")
- reason ("How did you decide those went together?")

All of these questions are open to a wide variety of answers and allow children to express whatever is on their mind. As a result, children are able to choose the direction the dialogue will go. They gain control of the conversation. This increases the likelihood that they will remain interested and involved in the give and take of true conversation.

In addition, challenging, well-timed, open-ended questions promote children's thinking and problem-solving skills (Cassidy, 2003). Using open-ended questions communicates acceptance of the child, thereby enhancing children's self-esteem and promoting positive adult–child relationships (Marion, 2007).

The opposite of an open-ended question is a closed-ended question. **Closed-ended questions** call for one-word answers. Though useful in many venues, they are typically conversation stoppers. The following are examples of closed-ended questions: "Are you rooting for the Tigers?" "Do you like peaches?" "What kind of bird is this?" Although the intention of the adult is often to use the questions to show interest in a subject presumably favored by the child, once the answer is given, the child often has nothing else to say. There are obviously proper times to use both open-ended and closed-ended questions. When selecting which is most useful for the given situation, consider the purpose of the question. See Table 4-5 for a comparison of these two types of questions. The intent of using open-ended questions is to enhance children's sense of worth, competence, and control. Paraphrase reflections are another powerful resource to enhance children's sense of self and to invite children into a conversation.

Paraphrase Reflections

A **paraphrase reflection** is a restatement, in an adult's words, of something a child has said. The adult listens carefully to what the child is saying, then repeats the statement to the child in words slightly different from those she or he had originally used. As with behavior reflections, paraphrase reflections are nonjudgmental statements. Adults DO NOT express personal opinions about what the child is trying to communicate in paraphrase reflections. Rather, they are signals to the children that the adult is listening attentively. Examples might include:

Child: Teacher, see my new dress and shoes!

Adult: You have a new outfit on today. (Or either of the following: You wanted me to see your new clothes; you sound pleased about your new things.)

Child: (At lunch table) Oh no! Macaroni again.

Adult: You've had more macaroni than you can stand. (Or: Macaroni's not your favorite; you thought it was time to have something else.)

Child: Is it almost time for us to get going?

Adult: You think we should be leaving soon. (Or: You're wondering if it's time to go yet; you'd like to get started.)

In each of the preceding situations, the adult first listened to the child, and then paraphrased the child's

Table 4-5 Comparison of Closed-Ended and Open-Ended Questions.

CHARACTERISTICS	
Closed-Ended Questions	**Open-Ended Questions**
Require a nonverbal response, or a one- or two-word answer from children	Promote multi-word, multi-phrase responses from children
Tend to have right or wrong answers	Have more than one correct answer
Are ones for which adults already know the answers	Are ones for which adults do not know what children's answers might be
Require a "quick" response	Allow children time to formulate and collect their thoughts
Focus on facts and similarity in thinking	Focus on ideas and originality in thinking
Ask for information	Ask for reasoning
Focus on labeling or naming	Focus on thinking and problem solving
Require the child to recall something from memory	Require the child to use his or her imagination

EXAMPLES	
Closed-Ended Questions	**Open-Ended Questions**
What shape is this? . . . Square.	What do you think will happen next?
How many cows did you see? . . . None.	How else could we . . . ?
What street do you live on? . . . Gunson.	What's your idea?
How are you? . . . Fine.	How did you . . . ?
Who brought you to school today? . . . Mom.	What would happen if . . . ?
Where is your knapsack? . . . . Home.	What do you think about . . . ?
Do you know what this is? . . .Yes.	What do you suppose would explain . . . ?

statement or inquiry. You will note that there was more than one appropriate way to reflect in each situation.

Although paraphrase reflections are all similar in form, the content of each depends on the adult's interpretation of the child's message. Thus, there is no one reflection that is most correct in every situation, many are possible.

Why paraphrase reflections benefit children. For true conversations to take place, it is important that adults listen to what children have to say. Real listening involves more than simply remaining silent. It means responding to children's words with words of one's own that imply, "I hear you; I understand you" (Gordon, 1990). Paraphrase reflections are an ideal way to get this message across.

Sometimes called active, reflective, or emphatic listening, paraphrase reflections are widely used in the helping professions to indicate positive regard and involvement. People who employ this technique often are perceived by those with whom they interact as sensitive, interested, and accurate listeners (Gazda, 2000). The result is that people talk more freely and that conversations are more rewarding

Taking the time to sit with a child and engage in conversation tells the child she is valuable.

for both participants. This favorable outcome occurs for several reasons (Gazda, 2000). Paraphrasing:

1. Gives the impression that the listener is carefully considering his or her ideas and is trying to understand the sender's frame of reference. Even though the listener may not agree with the other person, paraphrasing demonstrates an awareness and a comprehension of the message. Such understanding is critical if miscommunication is to be avoided.

2. Assists the listener in being more empathic toward the message sender. To accurately paraphrase another person's words, one must not only listen to the words and the meaning behind them. Using both aspects of the message, the listener gains a better understanding of how the sender is seeing and interpreting the world. This is particularly critical when the listener and the message sender have different opinions or goals within the interaction.

3. Allows for the sender to restate the original message in different words if the listener has not quite grasped the point, or to correct a mistaken reflection if the listener's interpretation was not accurate. Also, senders may elaborate and provide further information that they think is important for the listener to know.

4. Emphasizes what the message sender really said. Often, people are surprised to hear what someone else has understood by their words and are rewarded by a deeper insight into their own thoughts on hearing a reiteration of them.

5. Places control for the direction of the conversation with the message sender. She or he determines what to reveal and what channels to pursue. This is particularly advantageous to children because the nature of the instructional and socialization process often requires them to follow the adult's lead in a discussion rather than determining it themselves. Use of paraphrase reflections enables children to discuss topics adults might never think of or might consider too silly, too gory, or too sensitive to talk about.

6. Can prompt the speaker to answer some questions or solve some problems on his or her own. Children are more likely to rely on their own ideas if the adult helps them clarify the issue via a paraphrase reflection rather than immediately furnishing a fact or solution (Hendrick & Weissman, 2006). For example:

Helene: Is it snack time yet?

Adult: You're not sure when we'll be having a snack.

Helene: Must be soon. There's the cups out already.

In this situation, Helene used the evidence available to her in the physical environment to determine that it was almost time for a snack. The adult's response prompted Helene to think more than if the question had been answered directly.

7. Can have a positive influence on children's language development, particularly through the age of 7. This added benefit occurs when adults expand children's verbal messages. **Expansion** means to fill in or extend what the child is saying. This type of paraphrasing is slightly different from and more complex than the youngster's speech and has been shown to stimulate children to produce lengthier, more varied sentences (Kontos & Wilcox-Herzog, 1997). Between the ages of 18 and 36 months, simple expansions work well (Educational Products Inc., 1988).

Child: Kitty sleep.

Adult: Yes, the kitty is sleeping.

Child: Me eat.

Adult: You are eating a sandwich.

In each of these examples, the adult has expanded the child's telegraphic message to include appropriate connecting words in the same tense as the child's.

Children aged 4 and older profit from a more elaborate variation termed **recasting** (Educational Products Inc., 1988). Recasting refers to actually restructuring the child's sentence into a new grammatical form:

Child: The cat is sleeping.

Adult: Snowball is asleep on the windowsill.

Child: This car goes fast.

Adult: Your car is going very fast around the track. Soon it will have gone the whole way around.

Recasting preserves the child's meaning, but rephrases it in a way that is moderately novel. **Novelty** can be introduced by changing the sentence structure, by adding auxiliary verbs, or by using relevant synonyms. This helps the child to notice the more complex grammatical form. Recasting works best when adults make modest changes in the child's words but do not alter them entirely. If the restatement is too complex, children will overlook the new grammatical or syntactical structure, making it unlikely that they will use it themselves.

The strategy of scaffolding can be applied when adults paraphrase two children, as in the following example: Jeffrey and Andy, both 7 years old, are playing with some blocks and having a discussion about how to put the blocks in a particular configuration. Jeffrey is holding two flat, narrow boards, trying to make them stand on end. Each time he tries to balance them, they fall. "It won't stay up! My castle needs a pointy tower." Andy says, "Wait. If you put this other block there, they won't fall over," as he demonstrates how to make a tripod. Ms. Haas, who has been listening and watching, paraphrases, "Jeffrey, you were trying to make a tower. Andy, you figured out how to use a third block as a brace. That's one way to solve the problem." In this way, the teacher's words have reflected Andy's more sophisticated approach to solving the dilemma. These comments, to which Jeffrey has access, serve as a scaffold or a bridge between what he knows and what Andy has seen as a solution. If Jeffrey is ready to use the information, he can apply it to his building at the moment or in the future.

Using paraphrase reflections. Paraphrase reflections can be used any time a child addresses a comment to an adult. They may consist of a simple phrase or multiple statements. Sometimes, a simple verbal acknowledgment of something a child has said is all that is required:

Child: I'm up to page 15.

Adult: You've gotten pretty far in a short time. (Child resumes reading.)

Even when program pressures preclude the feasibility of involved adult–child interactions, a single paraphrase can indicate interest in the child while minimally interrupting the flow of events. However, when time permits, paraphrase reflections are excellent conversation starters and powerful at prolonging an interaction once it begins.

Consider the following two conversations. The first involves Chris, who is 5; the second, his 6-year-old brother, Kyle. Both discussions were spontaneous.

Chris: We got a new dog over the weekend!

Adult: You sound excited. Tell me more.

Chris: Well, he's got a flat nose . . . well, ah . . . he's been biting a lot . . . and, he's ah, he's cute . . . you know, he's ugly and homely. He's cute . . . and, ah . . . he's in a biting mood . . . you know, he has to chew on something a lot of times, he's just, he's going to be . . . ah, October . . . um, August seventh was his birthday! Not his real birthday. His real birthday was . . . what was his real birthday? His real birthday . . .was February seventh, I think.

Adult: Ah, but you celebrated his birthday at a different time even though it wasn't his real one.

Chris: August, uh huh, August. He's only 6 months old. Six months. . . .

Adult: Oh, he's only 6 months old. He's just a small dog.

Chris: No, he's not a small dog. He's about, you know, from here to here (child spreads arms to indicate size) . . . you know . . .he's. . . .

Adult: Oh, he's a pretty large dog.

Chris: Yeah. He's pretty large, all right! He's got a fat stomach and tiny legs! (Laughs)

Adult: (Laughing) He sounds comical, with a flat nose too.

Chris: Yeah, and . . . you know, he has knots on his head . . . and he has a face like he's real sad, and . . . um. . . .

Adult: Sad-faced.

Chris: Uh huh.

Adult: Sad-faced dogs are really cute sometimes.

Chris: Yeah.

End of conversation one.

Kyle: Know what? Our dog's really cute, and . . .we keep him in one of those kinds of pens where you keep, like, babies when you want to keep them from falling down the steps or something. Well, we . . . we keep him in one of those. We keep him in our laundry room and, uh . . . we got him from North Carolina. My dad says that he was . . . he, his father, um, was registered as Nathan Hale. Well . . . he was the champion bulldog of the nation . . . and, uh . . .we got him for free, because we know the people who know the owner of Nathan Hale.

Adult: Sounds like you were pretty lucky to get such a special dog.

Kyle: Yeah. We are. . . .We got him from North Carolina.

Adult: He came from far away.

Kyle: Yeah. We, they took him . . . they took him on a trip for eight hours . . . and, he threw up about four times. That must have been a long trip.

Kyle: Yeah, when he got out, um. . . . he just sorta layed there, and he was . . .he really looked sick, and um. . . this is the stage when he has long legs, bu you should see his stomach!

Adult: It's really something else.

Kyle: Yeah.

As demonstrated, youngsters may pursue the same topic in very different ways. Each child talked about the same dog, but chose a different feature to discuss. By paraphrasing, the adult was able to respond to Chris and Kyle individually. She also was able to key in on what interested them most. If she had led the conversation by asking a series of questions, such as: "What kind of dog did you get?" "How big is he?" "What's his name?" "What color is he?" and "Where did you get him?" the two interactions would have been similar, rather than unique as they were. In addition, it is unlikely that the adult would have thought to inquire about the knots on the dog's head or how many times it threw up, important considerations to the boys. Note, too, that Chris felt comfortable enough to correct an inaccurate response. This occurred when the adult's interpretation that a 6-month-old dog was small (meaning "young") did not match what Chris wished to convey. Because paraphrase reflections are tentative statements of what the adult thinks she or he heard, children learn that the reflections are correctable. Directing the conversation in these ways makes children feel important and worthwhile.

Effective Praise

Finally, the verbal strategy of effective praise statements can have a positive impact on children's evaluation of themselves. Everyone knows children need lots of positives Therefore, it is logical to assume that praise favorably influences children's self-esteem; but past research makes it clear that this is not always so. For instance, if teachers laud children indiscriminately, children discount the praise (Parsons, Kaczala, & Meece, 1982). Children may also treat the adult offering insincere praise with suspicion, thus negatively impacting the adult–child relationship (Damon, 1995). When children experience excessive praise, their intrinsic motivation and interest is reduced and their overall sense of autonomy is undermined (Lepper & Henderlong, 2000). Furthermore, certain kinds of praise actually have the potential to lower children's self-confidence, to inhibit achievement, and to make children reliant on external rather than internal controls (Leary & McDonald, 2003). All of these conditions contribute to low self-esteem. The overuse of praise can also contribute to children's overly inflated views of self, which can also be quite unhealthy (Leary, 2004; Harter 2006).

In contrast, meaningful feedback pertinent to the task at hand in the form of appreciation or **effective praise** is more likely to foster healthy self-esteem (Katz, 1993). For this reason, educators have investigated the characteristics that distinguish effective praise from ineffective praise.

For praise to be considered effective, it must meet three criteria. It must be selective, specific, and positive. **Selective praise** is reserved for situations in which it is genuinely deserved. It is not given in all situations nor in general blanket statements to all children. It is more likely to be directed at an individual or small groups of children at a given moment in time, rather than at the entire class. **Specific praise** refers to providing explicit information to the children about what is being praised. Finally, it must be **positive praise.** There are no negative comparisons and no one is being put down as a result of someone else being elevated. A comparison of ineffective praise versus effective praise is summarized in Table 4-6. As you read through the examples of effective praise, you will probably notice that most are either reflections or simple informational statements to children. None make any reference to the teacher's feelings or evaluate the child in any way. When used skillfully, effective praise is a powerful contributor to children's developing sense of self and social understanding because it helps children see themselves from someone else's perspective.

The verbal strategies discussed here are appropriate for all children, regardless of their primary language, to both further the relationship between adult and child as well as to assist children in better understanding themselves and others. In fact, for children whose first language is not English, the verbal strategies of behavior reflections, open-ended questions, paraphrase reflections, and effective praise are powerful strategies to assist in enhancing all areas of development.

Supporting Linguistically Diverse Children with Verbal Strategies

Although many Americans speak English, the population of people who speak English as a second language has been increasing over time. In

Table 4-6 Comparison of Ineffective and Effective Praise.

INEFFECTIVE PRAISE	EFFECTIVE PRAISE
Evaluates children "You draw beautifully."	Acknowledges children "You used a lot of colors in your picture."
Is general "Good job." "Nice work."	Is specific "You worked hard on your painting." "You spent a lot of time deciding what to draw."
Compares children with one another "You wrote the most interesting story of anyone."	Compares children's progress with their past performance "You wrote two words in this story that you have never used before."
Links children's actions to external rewards "You read three books. Pick a sticker from the box."	Links children's actions to the enjoyment and satisfaction they experience "You read three books. You seem pleased to have read so many."
Attributes children's success to luck or to ease of task "That was a lucky catch."	Attributes children's success to effort and ability "You tracked that ball and caught it."
Is offhand in content and tone	Is thoughtful
Is offered in a falsetto or deadpan tone	Is offered in a natural-sounding tone
Is always the same	Is individualized to fit the child and situation
Is intrusive—interrupts the child's work or concentration	Is nonintrusive

children 5 and older within the population, 47 million people in the United States speak a language other than English as their home language. This accounts for 18% of the population (National Council for Teachers of English [NCTE], 2003). Estimates also indicate that by 2025, more than half of the children in elementary schools will be from non-Caucasian backgrounds (U.S. Bureau of the Census, 2000. The term **English Language Learners** (ELL) is used to describe those children enrolled in educational programs who speak a language other than English at home and who are variously proficient in English (Genishi, 2002; Soderman, Gregory, & O'Neill, 2005). The notion of home language is also important for speakers of English who have regional or ethnic dialects or other distinct speech patterns. In every case, children's self-concept and self-esteem are strongly tied to their home language (McGroarty, 1992). The language that a child speaks serves as the mediator between children's development in social, emotional, and cognitive areas (Bloom, 1998). Long before children ever enter formal schooling, they are busy using their home language for interactions with others (Genishi, 2002). Children whose home language is treated with respect feel valued. Those who receive the message that their home language is unimportant or, even worse, a "problem" are less likely to feel good about themselves. Thus, it is potentially harmful to deny children access to their home language in the formal group setting of child care or school. This has sometimes been done in the mistaken belief that "English only" rules promote speedier acquisition. The research does not support this assumption. A more natural approach to second-language acquisition makes better sense. Such an approach is based on three major assumptions (Wolfe, 1992, pp. 144–145):

- If we want to help children develop a positive self-concept and a real sense of belonging, "We need to integrate the language and culture of each child in our classrooms." Children need many opportunities to encounter both their home language and English in their day-to-day interactions with adults, peers, and materials.
- "We must adopt a non-deficit perspective in relation to linguistic diversity." Children who are just learning to speak English, but are fluent in their home language, have demonstrated strengths in language acquisition. Thus, a child may be Mandarin proficient with some English proficiency. Such youngsters are not simply limited-English speakers.
- Parents and community members are important resources for assisting children's transitions into the program. They can underscore the importance of the children's home language at the same time that children are learning to speak English as a second language.

Helping professionals can better support **linguistic diversity** in children when they are sensitive to variations in how children acquire English as a second language. Some children may experience a silent period (of six or more months) while they acquire English; other children may practice their knowledge by mixing or combining languages (for example, "Mi mama me put on mi coat"); still other children may seem to have acquired English language skills (appropriate accent, use of vernacular, vocabulary, and grammatical rules) but are not truly proficient; yet some children will quickly acquire standard English-language proficiency. Each child's way of learning language should be viewed as acceptable (Genishi, 2002).

One of the most concrete ways formal group settings demonstrate acceptance is to have people who speak children's home languages on staff or as volunteers in the program. When staff is bilingual or when the staff includes both English-speaking members as well as persons who speak the children's home language, children have many opportunities to speak and hear speech that is familiar to them (Chang, Muckelroy, & Pulido-Tobiassen, 1996). In addition, they have the chance to hear languages other than their own. This increases children's involvement in learning and validates the importance of the children's home language as well as English (Berk, 2006). Other visible signs of acceptance include making available an assortment of multilingual story tapes, song tapes, books, wall hangings, signs, and posters. Singing and reciting in a variety of languages are additional strategies that convey the value of children's home languages. Additional ideas for celebrating the cultural and ethnic heritage of linguistically diverse children are presented in Chapter 14. In addition, it is advisable to learn a few key words in the children's own language, even if you are not fluent in that language. Words of greeting and farewell, words that describe family relations, and those that indicate basic needs such as hunger, thirst, and toileting are useful to know.

Exposing children to English in the formal group setting can be carried out through a combination of formal instruction and informal conversation. All of the skills outlined in this chapter are useful in the latter approach. Behavior and paraphrase reflections extend children's language skills and also indicate interest in and acceptance of all children. Behavior reflections are particularly effective when working with children who are in the early phases of English proficiency. Simple words and phrases accompanied by gestures and demonstrations help to get the message across. Teaching children simple scripts in English, such as "my turn," "I'm next," or "show me" provide children with basic words they need to function socially. This contributes to children's feelings of competence and worth.

A variety of techniques have been discussed that, when used in combination, contribute to the development of a positive verbal environment, thus increasing the likelihood that children's understanding of self and others will be beneficially supported. These techniques include fundamental strategies, such as greeting children and calling them by name, as well as the more complex skills of behavior reflections, paraphrase reflections, open-ended questions, and effective praise. Let us now examine ways to formulate and adapt these skills.

"What will you do if your baby gets hungry while you're at the grocery store?" is an open-ended question you might ask this child.

SKILLS FOR PROMOTING CHILDREN'S SELF-AWARENESS AND SELF-ESTEEM THROUGH VERBAL COMMUNICATION

 Using the Skills Associated with a Positive Verbal Environment

1. Greet children when they arrive. Say "Hello" to youngsters at the beginning of the day and when they enter an activity in which you are participating. Show obvious pleasure in their presence through the nonverbal communication skills you learned in Chapter 3.

2. Use names. When speaking to children, say their names. This lets children know that you have remembered them from one day to

the next; that you perceive them as individuals, unique from others in the group; and that your message is aimed especially at them. Take care to pronounce each child's name correctly.

3. Invite children to interact with you. Use phrases such as: "We're making tuna melts. Come and join us," "There's a place for you right next to Sylvia," "Let's take a minute to talk. I wanted to find out more about your day," or "You look pretty upset. If you want to talk, I'm available." These remarks create

SKILLS FOR PROMOTING CHILDREN'S SELF-AWARENESS AND SELF-ESTEEM THROUGH VERBAL COMMUNICATION

openings for children to approach you or to join an activity and make it easier for shy or hesitant children to interact with you.

4. Speak politely to children. Allow children to finish talking before you begin your remarks. If you must interrupt a child who is speaking to you or to another person, remember to say, "Excuse me," "Pardon me," or "I'm sorry to interrupt." Remember also to thank children when they are thoughtful or when they comply with your requests. If you are making a request, preface it with, "Please." Use a conversational, friendly voice tone rather than one that is impatient and demanding.

5. Use ACTIVE listening. Show your interest through eye contact, smiling, nodding, and allowing children to talk uninterrupted. Verbally indicate interest by periodically saying, "Mmm-hm," "Uhhuh," or "Yes." If the child has more to say than you can listen to at the moment, indicate a desire to hear more, explain why you cannot, and assure the child that you will resume the conversation at a specific point later in the day.

6. Invite children to elaborate on what they are saying. Prolong verbal exchanges with children by saying: "Tell me something about that," "Then what happened?" or "I'd like to hear more about what you did." Such comments make children feel interesting and valued.

7. Consider conversation openers in advance. Generate ideas ahead of time for one or two topics that might interest children. ("Tell me about last night's game," "How's that new brother of yours?" or "I was really interested in your report on Martin Luther King. Tell me what you liked best about him.") Comments or questions like these can be answered in any number of ways and have no right or wrong answers, thus opening the door for further communication.

8. Use silence to invite conversation. Remain silent long enough for children to gather their thoughts. Ask or comment, then pause (at least to the count of five). Children need time to think of what they are going to say next, especially if they have been listening carefully to what you were saying, because their attention was on your words, not on formulating their subsequent reply. Don't rush into your next statement or question. This overwhelms children and gives them the impression that the adult has taken over completely rather than becoming involved with them in a more participatory way.

9. Engage children in conversation frequently. Spontaneously converse with children. Look for times when you can talk with children individually, both planned and unplanned. Informal times or transitions are great times for true conversations.

10. Use silence too! Refrain from speaking when talk would destroy the mood of the interaction. Remember that silence is the other component of the verbal environment.

Talk can sometimes take away from the positive verbal environment. When you see children deeply absorbed in their activity or engrossed in their conversations with one another, allow the natural course of their interaction to continue. Keep quiet. These are times when the entry of an adult into the picture could be disruptive or could change the entire tone of the interchange. Speak to benefit the child, not just to speak.

The absence of talk in situations like these is also a sign of warmth and respect.

11. Provide verbal encouragement to children as they refine and expand their skills. Do this by giving children relevant information such as, "Just one more piece and you'll have the whole puzzle complete." Share your confidence in their ability with them. "This project will be challenging, but I'm sure you can do it."

continued

SKILLS FOR PROMOTING CHILDREN'S SELF-AWARENESS AND SELF-ESTEEM THROUGH VERBAL COMMUNICATION—continued

12. Choose your language carefully. Listen to yourself. Listen carefully to what you say and how you say it. Consider how children may interpret your message. If unsure, ask your colleagues to give you feedback about how you sound. Another strategy is to carry a tape recorder with you for a short time as a means of self-monitoring.

 Formulating Behavior Reflections

1. Use appropriate behavior reflections. After observing a child carefully, select an attribute or behavior that seems important to him or her and remark on it. At all times, focus on the child's perspective of the situation, not your own. Thus, an appropriate behavior reflection to Manny, who is tying his shoes, would be any of the following: "You're working on your left shoe," "You know how to make a bow," or "Those are the new shoes Grandma bought you." The following statements would not constitute behavior reflections: "I wish you'd hurry up," "I'm glad you're putting those on all by yourself," or "If you don't hurry, we'll be late." Although the latter remarks may be accurate statements of what is important to the adult in the interaction, they do not mirror the child's point of view.

2. Use statements. Phrase behavior reflections as simple statements, never as questions. Questions imply that children must respond; reflections do not. The purpose of this skill is to enable adults to show interest in children without pressuring them to answer.

3. Direct reflections to the child. Use the word "you" somewhere in your statement so that the child recognizes that your reflection is aimed at her or him. This makes each reflection more personal.

4. Use descriptive vocabulary as part of your reflection. Including adverbs, adjectives, and specific object names as part of the reflection makes them more meaningful and valuable to children. Children's contextual learning is more favorably enhanced when you say, "You put the pencil on the widest shelf" than when you say, "You put it on the shelf."

5. Use a nonjudgmental vocabulary and tone when reflecting children's behavior. Reflect only what you see, not how you feel about it. It does not matter whether your evaluation is good or bad; reflections are not the appropriate vehicles through which to express opinions. Therefore, "You're using lots of colors in your painting" is a reflection; "What a nice picture" or "You used too much gray" is not. This is because evaluations represent the adult's point of view; the reflection represents the child's.

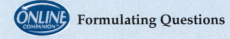 **Formulating Questions**

1. Ask open-ended questions.

2. Monitor the questions you ask. Check yourself to be sure you are asking the appropriate type of question for the situation. Do you want to invite conversation? Use a open-ended question. Are you looking for a specific answer? Perhaps use a closed-ended one.

3. Carefully judge when to use open-ended questions. Consider both the time available and the circumstances under which the question is to be asked. Pick an unhurried time, giving children ample opportunity to respond to avoid frustration (yours or the child's). If you catch yourself saying, "Okay, okay," "Fine, fine, fine," "That's enough," or "I get the idea" in the middle of a child's response, your question should have been saved for later. Use child choice time and transitions to ask open-ended questions rather than times when you are managing groups of children. For instance, it would be inappropriate to initiate a prolonged conversation with a child

SKILLS FOR PROMOTING CHILDREN'S SELF-AWARENESS AND SELF-ESTEEM THROUGH VERBAL COMMUNICATION

while you are counting heads during a fire drill, proctoring a spelling test, or when the rest of the children are waiting for you to lead them in the next activity.

4. Emphasize quality over quantity in using questions in conversations with children. Measure the effectiveness of the questions you ask by listening to children's answers in regard to both content and tone. If responses become monosyllabic or the child sounds weary of answering, stop. If answers are lively and lead to elaboration, continue.

5. WAIT for the answer. Give children a minimum of three minutes to respond to your questions. The time is often well spent when you hear the thoughtful reply.

 Formulating Paraphrase Reflections

1. Listen actively to the child's words. Consciously pay attention to the child's message. Look at the child and listen to his or her entire verbalization without interrupting. Concentrate. Momentarily set aside other thoughts; think more about what the child is saying than what you are going to say in response.

2. Restate in your own words what the child has said. Make sure that your rewording maintains the child's original intent. Don't include your opinion or extraneous things.

3. Rephrase erroneous reflections. At times, children give signs that your reflection was not in keeping with their intent. They may correct you directly by saying, "No" or "That's not what I meant." Other, subtler cues are children repeating themselves, adding new information, or sighing in exasperation. Be alert for these, and if they occur, try a variation of your statement. Do this conversationally, with no implication that the child was at fault for communicating inaccurately. This is not the time to insist that you heard

correctly based on the child's words. Focus on more acutely perceiving the child's message.

4. Match your reflection to each child's ability to understand language. Use simple, short reflections with toddlers. Construct these by adding one or two connecting words to the child's telegraphic utterances. Go beyond simple expansions, however, when working with children aged 4 and older. Recast the child's message by adding auxiliary verbs or relevant synonym phrases. Periodically, use multiple phrase reflections when working with school-age children:

Child: There's Webelos on Tuesday and all the guys are going. Me too.

Adult: Sounds like you've got a special meeting coming up. Lots of your friends are going.

Be aware of how well children understand spoken English. Accompany your words with gestures and demonstrations if some children seem confused. These adaptations demonstrate respect for children's varying communication abilities and make your reflections more interesting and comprehensible to them.

5. Use a conversational tone when reflecting. Use an expressive voice tone when reflecting either children's behavior or language. Adults who reflect in a monotone or singsong voice sound condescending and disrespectful. Children do not respond well when they perceive these attitudes.

6. Summarize children's actions and words. Summarizing is more effective than reflecting each individual behavior or idea expressed. Formulate reflections that tie together a series of actions or statements. For instance, if Malcolm is playing with colored blocks, do not say, "You have a red block. You have a green block. Now you're picking up a blue block." Do say, "You're using many colors in your building."

continued

7. Select one idea at a time to paraphrase. Children may express many ideas, focus on one at a time. There will be times when children spend several minutes describing a particular event or expressing their thoughts, ideas, or concerns. It is neither feasible nor desirable to reflect everything, because this would take too much time from the child, who might be anxious to say more. Pick one main idea that stands out to you and reflect that. If this is not the child's major focus, he or she will tell you or restate the intent.

An example of this was evident in the previous adult conversation with Kyle about his dog. Initially, Kyle made several comments regarding where the dog was kept and how his family got it. Based on his building excitement when describing the dog's championship lineage, it was this part of the description the adult reflected. Had Kyle wanted to talk more about the laundry room, he might have said: "Yeah, he's special. We keep him in the laundry room" as a way to return to his main interest.

8. Add interest to your reflections by periodically phrasing them in a form opposite from that used by the child. Thus, if Sue says, "I want the door open," it would be appropriate to say, "You don't want the door closed." If Mark announces, "I want another helping of everything," you could say, "You don't want to miss anything."

9. Reflect first when children ask you a question. Reflect children's wonder, uncertainty, confusion, or interest before offering an answer or solution to their queries. This helps children clarify what it is they are really asking and gives them an opportunity to answer some questions themselves. If the child repeats the question, asks a second, more pointed question, or waits expectantly for an answer, provide it.

Situation: Miss Drobney is tenderizing meat with a meat pounder. Audrey approaches and asks, "What are you doing?" The adult reflects, "You noticed I'm using a special tool."

At this point, it is possible that Audrey might say, "It makes holes in meat." This provides an opportunity for Miss Drobney to reflect again.

"You've figured out one thing this tool can do—it makes holes." This could be the beginning of a verbal exchange in which Audrey discovers for herself the various attributes of a meat pounder. On the other hand, it is also possible that when the adult reflects, "You noticed I'm using a special tool," Audrey would remain quiet, waiting for more, or would respond, "Yeah, what is that?" Miss Drobney would then have a choice of simply answering, "This is a meat pounder" or pointing out attributes of the tool that might help Audrey discover some of its characteristics on her own: "Look at the bumps on the end. See what they do when I pound the meat," or "See how it puts holes in the meat? That makes it easier to chew."

 ### Formulating Effective Praise Statements

1. Use behavior reflections to acknowledge children's efforts and accomplishments. Make nonevaluative comments such as, "You've been working on that a long time," "You found a new way to make a tunnel," or "You did it." These statements show children you are aware of their expanding competencies while allowing them to judge for themselves the adequacy of their efforts. They also help children recognize that they can influence outcomes and events in their daily lives. This realization contributes to children's increasing sense of control, which promotes positive self-judgments.

2. Note positive changes you've observed in children's abilities over time. "Last time you

SKILLS FOR PROMOTING CHILDREN'S SELF-AWARENESS AND SELF-ESTEEM THROUGH VERBAL COMMUNICATION

climbed to the first platform. Now you've made it all the way to the top," "You've been practicing a lot and now you can make it across the whole beam without falling off," or "You're getting a lot faster at matching those shapes."

3. Point out to children the positive effects their actions have on others. "You noticed Marcel was having a hard time getting the computer going. You gave him some help and now it's working fine."

4. Focus on some positive aspect of children's efforts to do something, not simply the product they achieve. It is better to say, "Look at how you made those brush strokes sweep across the page. You've worked for 10 minutes on that" than to say, "Nice picture."

5. Be honest in your praise and offer children authentic feedback. Behavior reflections are a good tool to help you achieve this. For instance, if Elliot has just struggled through reading a page aloud, say something like, "You're learning to read some new words" or "You read that whole page by yourself." This is more honest than "Great reading" or "That was terrific." Elliot is probably quite aware that his reading is not yet fluent. The latter comments lack credibility and may sound patronizing to the child. Adult praise means more when it is believable. Because behavior reflections describe rather than evaluate the child's performance, they fit this criterion well.

 Supporting Linguistically Diverse Children

1. Evaluate your sensitivity to children's use of home language. Ask yourself the following questions: Do I know what home languages are represented within the group of children with whom I am working? Do I respond respectfully to children when they talk to me in their home language? Do I feel confident interacting with children whose language I do not speak fluently? If you are answering "no" to any of these items, review the skills you have learned so far. Identify specific strategies you can use to interact more sensitively with linguistically diverse children.

2. Learn relevant words in the home languages of the children in your group. Look up such phrases or ask colleagues and parents to help you. Ask children to teach you a few key words if possible. Find poems, songs, and riddles in a variety of languages to share with children in the group. Refer to books, audiotapes, colleagues, or family members as necessary.

3. Monitor how you interact with the children when using their home language. Ask yourself the following questions: Do I use the children's home language for more than simply giving children directions? Do I use the children's home language for more than simply correcting children's behavior? If your honest answer to either of these queries is "No," review the skills associated with a positive verbal environment. Plan to incorporate those skills as you speak to children in their home language. Also make sure to use that language to provide positive reinforcement to children, to soothe and comfort them, and to simply engage them in enjoyable, supportive interactions. Adopt the skills you are learning in this chapter and others to the children's home language as well.

4. Become familiar with ways in which the formal group setting can be designed to better support children's linguistic diversity. Observe ways in which the formal group setting encourages the use of home language by both children and parents. Notice ways in which the helping professionals in your setting provide opportunities for different languages to be used in day-to-day activities.

continued

SKILLS FOR PROMOTING CHILDREN'S SELF-AWARENESS AND SELF-ESTEEM THROUGH VERBAL COMMUNICATION—continued

Survey your setting for materials that reflect children's home languages. Think about how you might strengthen the program's support of linguistically diverse children and families. Discuss your ideas with colleagues and make a plan to put some of these into action.

 Communicating with Children's Families

1. Apply the principles of a positive verbal environment in your interactions with family members. Greet family members. Take time to learn the names of the families in your program. Use adults' last names, unless you have a relationship outside of the program, as well as their appropriate title, such as Mr., Ms., or Mrs., when addressing them. If you aren't familiar with family names, greet them as the parent/guardian/grandparent of their specific child. Then, introduce yourself. For instance, "You must be with Elise. I'm Ms.____." If the child is with his or her family, remember to greet him or her as well. It is proper to speak about the child in this circumstance, but only if you include the child in the conversation. In other words, avoid talking "above the child's head." Get to know family members as individuals.

Treat family members as people whose lives are multidimensional. Convey friendly interest in these facets of people's lives. Remember, in addition to talking about the child, to comment on day-to-day living or on upcoming events that family members have mentioned to you. Invite family members to enter the room, to watch their child, and to speak with you. Use such phrases as, "You've come to see Jose. He's in the group area looking at books. You are welcome to join him there" or "Welcome to the classroom. We're almost finished with story time. Here is a comfortable place to wait" or "Thank you for coming in to speak with me. Let's watch

Jose for awhile and then I'd be happy to answer any questions you have about his time at school." Speak politely at all times. Parents and other family members, in their efforts to communicate with you, may not always express themselves calmly or politely or with good grammar. They may seem brusque, hurried, demanding, or timid. Furthermore, family members may speak in a manner that is comfortable for them but that sounds unfamiliar to you in terms of word usage or grammatical syntax. It is the professional's responsibility to decipher the intent of the message without necessarily responding in kind to its mode of delivery.

Part of your role is to build relationships with every family member. Just as you do with children, allow these adults to finish their requests or comments before introducing your own. Remember to include everyone in the conversation, using appropriate eye contact and facial expressions. Use polite language, such as "please" and "thank you," and speak in an even, conversational tone, independent of the manner in which you are addressed.

2. Use paraphrase reflections and open-ended questions while interacting with family members. Adapt your use of paraphrase reflections to demonstrate respect for and interest in adults. Paraphrase reflections can be very effective with adults when used carefully. First, mix your reflections with other verbal strategies. Second, make sure not to "mirror" an adult's words or exact style of speech. Vary your word choice using some of the techniques outlined earlier in this chapter, such as reversing the word order, saying the opposite of what the speaker has stated, and using multiple sentences. Although reflecting is suitable for all kinds of interactions, it is particularly useful when family members are expressing concern. This strategy helps to clarify the information they are attempting to convey, so that you can respond to needs and desires more effectively.

SKILLS FOR PROMOTING CHILDREN'S SELF-AWARENESS AND SELF-ESTEEM THROUGH VERBAL COMMUNICATION

Rephrase the speaker's sentences to demonstrate your awareness of the message being delivered. Do not hesitate to correct yourself if the speaker indicates that you interpreted his or her intent inaccurately. Respond positively to the inquiries of family members regarding their children. Use paraphrase reflections and open-ended questions as appropriate to obtain information and to indicate interest. If you do not know the information they are seeking, direct family members to a teacher or director in charge of the program. Offer to find that individual, if you are in a position to do so (that is, if you have no other responsibilities at the moment). Use commonly understood language, not jargon. An important element of verbal communication is that the participants feel acknowledged and respected. When speaking with family members, clearly describe the issue at hand in natural, unaffected vocabulary and sentences. Use the principles of good verbal and nonverbal communication to both talk and listen. If you sense a misunderstanding, find alternate words or phrases to clarify your meaning. If you think you have misunderstood what others are saying, verify your perception with phrases, such as, "What I think you are saying is . . ." or "It sounds as if you think . . ." In addition, it is best to avoid using evaluative or overly "gushing" language in talking with family members about their own children or in reference to other children.

Allow sufficient time for family members to gather their thoughts. It is not always easy for parents and other family members to come to a program to speak with professionals about their children. They may therefore be hesitant in their speech, fumble for words, or stammer. Be patient and refrain from finishing their sentences or interrupting them.

Use all of your best verbal and nonverbal skills to indicate interest, warmth, caring, and respect while you wait for the person to complete his or her message. Use open-ended questions and continuing responses to encourage their verbalizations. Respond appropriately when they do tell you about their concern or interest.

3. Use honest praise and authentic feedback to acknowledge family participation in the program. Respond genuinely to helpful family involvement. When parents and other family members help on a field trip, bring something of special interest to share with the children, or simply assist in the classroom, acknowledge their efforts honestly and specifically. Use phrases such as, "Thank you for driving on the trip. Having you along made it possible for everyone to participate," or "The children really enjoyed the story you told about your mother's first days in America. It gave them a real understanding of what life must have been like for her at that time," or "I really appreciated your helping us work on the journal project. It meant that more of the children were able to write their ideas down."

4. Collaborate with family members in supporting linguistically diverse children. Ask family members to teach you some words and phrases that could be useful in interacting with their child. Invite family members to the program to tell stories, sayings, and riddles in their home language and to share other oral traditions typical of their family. Ask families to bring music, artifacts, or foods into the classroom to share and discuss. Have family members who are literate in their home language read storybooks aloud to the children or make audiotapes for children to hear at school or take home (Soderman et al., 2005). Ask families to provide newspapers and magazines that feature the home language in print for use in the classroom. When working with older children, provide ways in which family members can use their primary language to help their children with program-related assignments/activities at home. Create a school-to-home library from which families can check out resources to share with their children.

continued

SKILLS FOR PROMOTING CHILDREN'S SELF-AWARENESS AND SELF-ESTEEM THROUGH VERBAL COMMUNICATION—continued

Make clear the importance of the child's home language to the child and, therefore, to you. Stress that although children will be learning English in the formal group setting, such learning does not require children to abandon or reject the language at home. On the contrary, respect for and practice in the home language will assist the child in developing not only a positive view of self but also in all aspects of learning English (Genishi, 2002).

PITFALLS TO AVOID

Whether your words are aimed at demonstrating your interest in children, or whether you are using your speech to become more involved in children's activities, there are certain hazards to avoid.

Parroting. A common way in which adults paraphrase children is to respond by mirroring exactly the child's words and voice tone. Parroting is often offensive to children because it makes the adult sound insincere or condescending. Although parroting is a natural first step for people just learning how to paraphrase, adults should learn to vary their responses as quickly as possible. Several techniques can be used. Listen to children who are talking to one another and silently formulate paraphrases for statements they make. Although you are not actually saying anything, this provides good mental practice. A second tactic is to listen to children talking or remember things they have said throughout the day, and then later write down several alternate paraphrases. Finally, students have reported that it is helpful to practice paraphrasing the speech of family members and friends. In many cases, this involves paraphrasing adults, which may prompt the student to work harder at sounding original because mimicking someone's words is not part of natural conversation.

Reflecting incessantly. It is a mistake to reflect everything children do or say. The purpose of behavior and paraphrase reflecting is to give adults opportunities to observe children, to listen to them, to understand their point of view, and to provide them with more information about themselves. None of these goals can be accomplished if adults are talking nonstop. Using summary reflections is a good way to avoid overpowering children with excessive verbiage.

Perfunctory reflecting. Reflecting without thinking is not appropriate; it is another form of parroting. Adults who find themselves simply "going through the motions" or responding absentmindedly to children just to have something to say should stop, then intensify their efforts at attending more closely to what children are really saying or indicating through their actions. A good reflection increases children's **self-understanding rather than merely serving as a placeholder in a conversation.**

Another form of perfunctory reflecting occurs when adults reflect children's questions but neglect to follow up on them. For example, Ralph asks Mr. Wu, "When are we going to have music?" Mr. Wu responds, "You're wondering when we're going to have music," and then immediately turns to talk to Alicia. In this case, his response was not wholly correct, because he did not attend to the entirety of the child's message. He should have waited to determine if Ralph was going to answer the question himself or if he needed additional information. The best way to avoid such a dilemma is to think while reflecting and to pay attention to how children react to the reflections.

Treating children as objects. There are many times when adults speak to children in the third person. That is, they make comments about the child that they intend for the child to hear but that are not personally addressed to the child. For instance, Miss Long is playing with 2-year-old Curtis in the block area. No one else is nearby. She says things like: "Curtis is building with square blocks. Curtis is making a tall tower. Oops, Curtis' tower fell." If other youngsters were close at hand, her remarks might be interpreted as information aimed at them. But, as the situation stands, her impersonal running commentary on his activity is not conversational and leaves no real openings for a response from Curtis should he choose to make one. Miss Long's remarks could be turned into reflections by the insertion of "you" in each one: "Curtis, you're building with square blocks. You're making a tall tower. Oops, your tower fell."

Correcting children's overestimation of their abilities. Sometimes in an attempt to be factual, adults feel compelled to correct children's inaccurate statements about themselves. For instance, when Johnny states, "I am a perfect speller," the adult replies, "Well, most of the time you do fine, but you do get some words wrong." Through the age of 7, it is very common for children to overestimate their own abilities. It is a developmental stepping-stone in self-esteem. Correcting children does not assist them in developing a more accurate picture of themselves. It is more helpful to reflect the emotional content of the statement. In this situation, the adult could respond, "You are proud of your spelling ability" or "You believe you can really spell."

Turning reflections into questions. Phrases such as "aren't you?," "didn't you?," "don't you?," "right?," or "okay?" tacked to the end of a sentence transform reflections into questions. A similar result occurs when the adult allows his or her voice to rise at the end of a sentence. Using this habit, the nature of verbal exchanges with children changes from unintrusive interest and involvement to a tone that is interruptive and demanding. This is one of the most common misuses of the reflecting technique and occurs because adults would like some confirmation regarding the accuracy of their reflection. They want some sign from the child that what they have said is right. Yet, rarely does one hear:

Child: I'm at the top.

Adult: You're excited to be so high, aren't you?

Child: You're right, Teacher.

The real confirmation of appropriate reflecting is that children continue their activity or conversation. If they stop or correct the adult, these are signs that the original reflection was not on target. Adults who find themselves questioning rather than reflecting must consciously work to eliminate this behavior. If you notice that you have done this in conversation with a child, it helps to stop and repeat the reflection correctly.

Answering one's own questions rather than allowing children to answer. Adults frequently answer many of their own questions. For instance,

Ms. Cooper asks, "Who remembered to bring their permission slips back?" Without a moment's hesitation, she says: "John, you've got one. Mary, you've got one, too." Later, she inquires, "Why do you think birds fly south for the winter?" Before children have a chance to even think about the question, she supplies an answer: "Usually, they're looking for food." In both instances, Ms. Cooper precluded children answering by responding too quickly herself. Unfortunately, as this becomes a pattern, Ms. Cooper may well conclude that children are incapable of answering her questions, while the youngsters translate her actions as lack of interest in what they have to say. If you detect this habit in yourself, deliberately work to eliminate it. When you answer prematurely, verbally make note of it; then, repeat your question: "Oops. I didn't give you a chance to answer. What do you think about . . . ?"

Habitually answering children's questions with your own. Sometimes, when children ask a question, adults automatically echo the question back to them:

Child: Where do bears sleep in the winter?

Adult: Where do you think they sleep?

Echoing causes children to form negative impressions of adults. The question sounds like a putdown; youngsters translate it to mean: "You're dumb. You should know that," "I know and I'm not going to tell you," or "I'm going to let you make a fool of yourself by giving the wrong answer. Then, I'll tell you what the real answer is." Although this may not be the adult's intent, it is often the result. To avoid these unfavorable impressions, either supply the needed fact or reflect the children's questions and then help them discover the answer by working with them.

Using ineffective praise. When adults catch themselves praising children indiscriminately or falling back on overused, pat phrases, the best strategy is to stop talking, then refocus on what the child is actually doing. Rephrase your statement so it conforms to the guidelines for effective praise presented earlier in this chapter. If an on-the-spot correction seems too difficult, simply remember the situation and during a quiet moment later in the day, reconsider what you might have said. On another day, in a similar activity, see whether any of the alternatives you thought about might fit. If so, use one or a variation of it.

Interrupting children's activities. Reflecting or asking a question when a child is obviously engrossed in an activity or is absorbed in conversation is intrusive. At times like these, adults can exhibit interest in children by observing quietly nearby and responding with nonverbal signs such as smiles, nods, or laughter at appropriate moments. When children are working very hard at something, an occasional reflection that corresponds to their point of view is appreciated; constant interruptions are not. Children who are speaking to someone else and give no indication of wanting to include the adult should not be reflected or questioned at all. If, for a legitimate reason, the adult must get the child's attention or enter the conversation, he or she should just say, "Excuse me."

Failing to vary your responses. It is common when learning new skills to find a tactic with which one is comfortable and then to use that to the exclusion of all others. For instance, after reading this chapter, you might be tempted to use a behavior reflection in response to every situation that arises. This would be a mistake; certain skills meet certain needs. When one skill is developed to the exclusion of others, the benefits offered by the other skills will not be available to children. In addition, overuse of one form of verbal communication becomes monotonous and uninteresting for adults and children alike. For this reason, it is best to utilize all of the skills presented thus far rather than only one or two.

Hesitating to speak. Individuals new to the helping professions, as well as those who have worked with children before, may experience awkward moments in which they find themselves fumbling for the right words when trying to implement the skills presented in this chapter. By the time they think of a response, the opportunity may have slipped by or the words that come out may sound stilted. When this happens, some find it tempting to abandon these techniques and revert to old verbal habits. Others stop talking altogether. Both of these reactions arise from adult efforts to avoid embarrassment or discomfort with unfamiliar verbal skills. Such experiences are to be expected, and every student goes through these uncertain times. Yet, the key to attaining facility with reflections, appropriate questioning techniques, and effective praise statements is to use them frequently so that they become a more natural part of your everyday interac-

tions. In fact, in the beginning, it is better to talk too much than to neglect practicing these skills. Once the mechanics are mastered, you can turn your attention to appropriate timing.

Sounding mechanical and unnatural while using the skills. Implementing reflections and open-ended questions feels awkward and uncomfortable at first. Beginners complain that they do not sound like themselves and that they have to think about what they are saying more than they ever have in the past. They become discouraged when their responses sound repetitive and lack the warmth and spontaneity they have come to expect from themselves. Again, at this point some people give up, reverting to old verbal habits. As with any new skill, however, proficiency develops only after much practice.

Learning these techniques can be likened to learning to roller-skate. Beginning skaters have a hard time keeping their balance, shuffle along, and fall down periodically. They have enough trouble going forward, let alone going backward, doing turns, or making spins. Stopping also is a major hurdle. If people only roller-skate a few times, chances are they will continue to struggle and feel conspicuous. If these feelings cause them to give up skating, their progress is halted and they will never improve. However, should they keep on practicing, not only will their skill increase, but they will be able to get beyond the mechanics and develop an individualized style.

The process is the same for the skills taught in this chapter. When readers are willing to practice and continue working through the difficulties, noticeable improvement occurs. The artificial speech that marks the early stages of acquisition of verbal skills gradually gives way to more natural-sounding responses.

SUMMARY

Children's developing sense of self and subsequent social understanding directly contributes to their level of social competence. As they come to better understand themselves and the relationship that their thoughts and actions have on others (and vice versa), they are more able to purposefully choose their actions and reactions with others.

Beginning with self-awareness, children come to know more about themselves and others in their environment. They develop their definition of who they really are. This definition, which changes over time, is their self-concept. Self-esteem is the evaluation of one's self-concept.

Children at each age utilize their current cognitive ability in combination with experiences in their environment to formulate their sense of self. Beginning with toddlerhood, children describe themselves in physical and concrete ways. As children approach middle childhood, around 7 and 8 years of age, they begin to use more abstract adjectives in their description. By the end of middle childhood, children's self-concepts are primarily described by psychological traits and are characteristic of more abstract thinking.

Children who judge their competence, worth, and control positively have high self-esteem; those who do not have low self-esteem. Individuals with high self-esteem lead happier lives than those whose self-judgments are negative. The development of self-esteem follows a normative sequence, evolving from assessing oneself in the here and now as a preschooler to a more compartmentalized view of the self as a young grade-schooler to a general index of one's value as a person by middle-school age. This predominantly positive or negative view remains relatively constant throughout life.

This view is impacted greatly by the adults within the children's world. Adult behaviors prompt children to make either positive or negative judgments about themselves. Self-judgments of competence, worth, and control are likeliest in children who interact with adults who demonstrate warmth, acceptance, genuineness, respect, and empathy. What adults say to children conveys these or the opposite messages to children and therefore is a key factor in the degree to which children develop high or low self-esteem.

The atmosphere adults create by their verbalizations to children is called the verbal environment. It can be either positive or negative. Continual exposure to a negative verbal environment diminishes children's self-esteem, whereas exposure to a positive verbal environment enhances children's self-awareness and perceptions of self-worth.

Behavior reflections are a specific verbal strategy adults can use to help create a positive verbal environment. Behavior reflections are nonjudgmental statements made to children about some aspect of their behavior or person. Using behavior reflections increases children's self-awareness and self-esteem; it helps adults look at situations from children's perspectives; it demonstrates interest, acceptance, and empathy for children; and it helps children increase their receptive language skills. Behavior reflections also help children see how others see them, which aids them in their social understanding.

Conversing with children is another way for adults to demonstrate affection, interest, and involvement. Using a more sensitive approach to verbal interactions increases children's self-respect and self-acceptance. However, certain common errors, such as missing children's cues, correcting grammar, supplying facts and rendering opinions prematurely, advising, and using unnecessary or unskillful questioning act as conversation stoppers. On the other hand, open-ended questions and paraphrase reflections are effective conversation sustainers. Paraphrase reflections help clarify communication, help the listener to be more empathic toward the message sender, allow the message sender to control the direction of the conversation, provide the message sender an opportunity to solve his or her own problems, and have a positive influence on the language development and autobiographical memory of young children. In addition, appropriate use of effective praise also adds to the creation of a positive verbal environment.

Each of the behaviors described to support a positive verbal environment are powerful tools for work with all children, regardless of their primary language. In fact, the strategies described are very effective for not only assisting in developing children's understanding of self and others, but also in scaffolding language development for native and non-native English speakers. Furthermore, it is useful to tailor these strategies in interactions with family members as a means of developing and maintaining positive relationships.

Finally, certain pitfalls are to be avoided, such as parroting, reflecting incessantly or perfunctorily, treating children as objects, using inappropriate questioning methods, interrupting children, and failing to vary one's responses. Hesitating to speak and sounding mechanical at first also are common problems encountered by individuals who are just beginning to learn these skills.

All children can become socially competent members of society. From self-awareness to self-concept to self-esteem—the messages that we as adults send to the children contribute significantly to who they become.

KEY TERMS

autobiographical memory
behavior reflections
closed-ended questions
competence
control
creative questions
effective praise
English Language Learner (ELL)
expansions
guidance

linguistic diversity
narrative talk
negative verbal environment
nurturance
open-ended questions
paraphrase reflections
positive praise
positive verbal environment
recasting
scaffolding

selective praise
self-awareness
self-concept
self-esteem
social understanding
specific praise
theory of mind
verbal environment
worth

DISCUSSION QUESTIONS

1. Describe the normative sequence of the development of self-concept in children from birth to early adolescence.

2. Describe an incident from your childhood that enhanced your self-esteem. Describe another that detracted from it. How did the first incident enhance your self-esteem? What does it say to you about your behavior with children? Use the information in the chapter to assess the negative incident and how it could have been transformed into a positive experience.

3. Review the characteristics of the positive and negative verbal environments. Discuss any additional variables that should be added to both lists.

4. Describe three ways in which you could improve the verbal environment of a setting in which you currently interact with children.

5. Refer to Appendix A, the NAEYC Code of Ethical Conduct, when responding to the following: One of your colleagues talks about "those children" when referring to youngsters who are just beginning to learn English. Consider her point of view as well as what she is communicating to children.

6. Describe at least four benefits of using behavior reflections with young children.

7. Describe how the adult's use of paraphrase reflections affects children's self-awareness and self-esteem.

8. Describe the characteristics of an open-ended question and discuss how the use of this technique relates to self-awareness and self-esteem in children.

9. Describe how interaction strategies that are used with children can be applied to interactions with adults.

10. Talk about the differences between effective and ineffective praise. Using examples from your past experience, describe times when you were praised effectively and/or ineffectively. What was your reaction at the time? What do you think about it now?

FIELD ASSIGNMENTS

1. Identify three strategies you used with children that are associated with the creation of a positive verbal environment. For each situation, briefly describe what the children were doing. Summarize the strategy you used. (Describe it and quote the words you said.) Discuss the children's reaction in each case.

2. Keep a record of the behavior reflections and paraphrase reflections you use with children. When you have a chance, record at least four of your responses. Begin by describing what the child(ren) did or said that prompted your response. Next, quote the words you used. Correct any inaccurate reflections as necessary. Finally, write at least two alternate reflections that fit the situations you described.

3. Focus on using open-ended questions and effective praise as you work with the children. Describe at least four situations in which you used these skills. Begin by describing what the child(ren) said or did to prompt your response. Next, record your exact words. Correct any mistaken responses by rewriting them. Finally, write at least two alternate ways of phrasing your remarks, regardless of their accuracy.

4. Describe an interaction you heard or observed involving a child's adult family member. Include positive verbal strategies that were used, including behavior and paraphrase reflections, open-ended questions, and conversation extenders. Give a summary of your assessment of the interaction.

Chapter 5

SUPPORTING CHILDREN'S EMOTIONAL DEVELOPMENT

OBJECTIVES

On completion of this chapter, you should be able to describe:

- What emotions are and how they affect people's lives.

- Children's emotional development from birth through middle childhood.

- How children differ from one another emotionally.

- Emotional challenges children face.

- Strategies for supporting children's emotional development.

- Family communication strategies related to emotions.

- Pitfalls to avoid when responding to children's emotions.

A butterfly lands on Sean's hand—his eyes widen in *amazement*.

On her first day at the center, Maureen sobs *miserably* as her mother attempts to leave.

Emily makes a diving catch and is *elated* to find the ball in her mitt.

Tony is *frightened* by the escalating sounds of angry adult voices in the other room.

When Larry calls her stupid, Jennifer yells *furiously*, "No, I'm not!"

Children experience hundreds of different emotions each day. Emotions are linked to everything children do and are prompted by numerous happenings, both large and small. They are what cause children to be affected by the people and events around them. How well children express their emotions and understand the emotions of others are key elements of social competence.

Where Do Emotions Come From?

People in all cultures experience emotions. Joy, sadness, disgust, anger, surprise, interest, and fear seem universal (Ekman, 2003; Cole, Bruschi & Tamang, 2002). Although there are obvious differences among these emotional states, they all have certain characteristics in common. Each is triggered by *internal or external events* that *send signals to the brain* and central nervous system.

As a result of these signals, people become aroused and their bodies respond with physiological changes. Their hearts may beat faster, their palms may sweat, or their throats might become dry. This is the *physical* part of emotion. Such sensations usually are accompanied by observable alterations in facial expression, posture, voice, and body movement.

Smiling, frowning, or laughing are visible signs of how people feel. Actions like these represent the *expressive* side of emotion. As this is going on, individuals interpret what is happening to them. Their interpretations are influenced by the context of the situation, their goals, and by past experience (Lewis, 1999). Considering all of these factors, people make a judgment about whether they are experiencing some degree of happiness, sadness, anger, or fear. This is the *cognitive* part of emotion.

Although scientists vary in their beliefs about the order in which physical sensations, expressive reactions, and cognitive interpretations occur, they generally agree that all three combine to create emotions (Messinger, Fogel & Dickson, 2001; Stein

& Levine, 1999). To understand how these elements work together, consider what happens when Kitty, age 8, is called on to read her report aloud:

Signals to Kitty's brain: Teacher speaking Kitty's name; the other children's silence; a giggle from the back of the room.

Physical response: Kitty's mouth dries up; her pulse beats rapidly; her stomach contracts.

Expressive response: Kitty scowls; her shoulders slump.

Cognitive response: Kitty thinks about past difficulties in front of an audience as well as her desire to do well in class.

Emotion: Kitty feels nervous.

If Kitty's cognitive response had focused on past public speaking triumphs, she might determine that the emotion she is experiencing is excitement, not nervousness. In either case, Kitty makes the ultimate judgment about how she feels. Even if others expect Kitty to do well, if she perceives the situation as threatening, she will be nervous. Different cognitive responses explain why two people may have opposite emotional reactions to the same event. While Kitty feels nervous, another child in the group may be eager to read his or her report to the class. No one interpretation is right or wrong; each simply defines that child's current reality.. Because emotions are tied to everything people do, emotional episodes like this are repeated many times each day.

Why Emotions Are Important

Children's emotions run the gamut from joy and affection to anger and frustration. Some emotions are pleasant, some are not, but all emotions play an essential role in children's lives.

At their most fundamental level, *emotions help children to survive*. Jumping out of the way of a speeding tricycle or forming attachments with the important people in their lives are instances in which expressive reactions overshadow one's cognitive response. In these cases, emotions instinctively propel children toward self-preservation without their having to "think" about what is happening (Ekman & Davidson, 1994). When they do have a chance to think, *emotions provide children with information about their well-being*. This often results in children taking some action to maintain or change their emotional state (Frijda, 2000). Feelings such as happiness and trust give children a sense of safety and security.

Affectionate feelings tell children they are loveable and that their love is valued by others. Feelings of pride suggest that they are competent. All these positive emotions indicate that all is right with the world and prompt children to continue or repeat pleasurable experiences. On the other hand, some emotions signal discontent, misfortune, or danger. They alert children that something is wrong. Anger prompts children to try to overcome obstacles. Sadness brings a drop in energy, allowing children time to adjust to loss or disappointment. Fear prompts children to avoid, escape, or otherwise protect themselves from something (Witherington, Campos & Hertenstein, 2001). In every case, emotions help children interpret what is happening to them and cue them to adapt to changing circumstances. These interpretations are depicted in Table 5-1.

In addition, emotions serve as a form of communication.Emotional displays, such a smiling or crying, provide the first language with which infants and adults communicate before babies learn to talk. This communication function continues over the lifespan as people use words and nonverbal cues to express what they are feeling and to better understand the feelings of others (Eisenberg et al., 1994; Saarni, Mumme, & Campos, 1998; Hyson, 2004).

Table 5-1 What Emotions Signal to Children About Their Well-Being.

EMOTION	MESSAGE TO CHILD
Happiness	I am safe. This is a good place. This is a good thing to do. I need to continue or repeat this.
Affection	I am capable and worthy of giving and receiving love.
Pride	I am competent.
Anger	Something is wrong. I need to overcome this obstacle.
Sadness	Something is wrong. I have suffered a loss. I need to adjust to this loss.
Fear	Something is wrong. I am in danger. I must escape. I need to protect myself.

Emotions also influence children's cognitive functioning (Zins, Weissberg, Wang & Walberg, 2004). Recent scientific evidence shows that the neural circuits in the brain that regulate emotion are highly interactive with those associated with intellectual activities such as attending to details, setting goals, planning, problem-solving and decision-making (National Scientific Council on the Developing Child, 2006). As a result, emotions can either support or interfere with these cognitive tasks. Poorly controlled emotions and negative feelings tend to detract from intellectual functioning; strong positive emotions and emotions that are well regulated support more advanced cognitive activity (Shonkoff & Phillips, 2000; Bush, Luu & Posner, 2000).

Because emotions are such an important part of children's lives, adults have a special responsibility to help children:

Better understand their emotions.
Become more sensitive to the emotions of others.
Find effective ways to manage the many different emotions they experience.

This begins at birth and continues throughout the elementary years. To carry out this role well, adults must first understand the developmental aspects of children's emotions.

CHILDREN'S EMOTIONAL DEVELOPMENT

Children's emotional development is characterized by five developmental sequences. These include the predictable phases through which

- children's emotions emerge.
- children develop emotional self-awareness.
- children come to recognize other people's emotions.
- children learn to regulate what they are feeling.
- children address the emotional tasks of childhood.

All of these developmental processes are influenced by both maturation and experience. Understanding them will help you to respond to children with sensitivity and in ways that promote children's social competence.

How Children's Emotions Develop

Nadia was born two days ago. She grimaces when her older brother quickly shifts from holding her upright to laying her down in his lap. Some scientists argue that Nadia is showing true emotion (Izard, 1994; Izard et al., 1995). Others believe that the newborn's grimace is just a reflex. They contend that real emotions do not appear until weeks later when children's cognitive processes are developed enough to allow them to interpret what they are experiencing (Sullivan & Lewis, 2003). Despite these differing points of view, researchers agree that within their first year, babies will experience varying emotions. However, infants will not display all the emotions they will ever have. Instead, emotions increase in number and complexity as children mature. This emotional maturation emerges according to developmental sequences as predictable as those associated with language and physical development. Before she is 12 months old, baby Nadia will clearly express joy (at about 6 weeks), anger (at approximately 4 to 6 months), sadness (around 5 to 7 months), and fear (between 6 and 12 months).

Joy, anger, sadness, and fear are considered **primary emotions,** from which other, more differentiated emotions eventually develop (Izard et al., 1995; Witherington, Campos, & Hertenstein, 2001). For example, joy is seen in the baby's first social smile. This is an unmistakable sign of infant pleasure, usually prompted by the face of a primary caregiver and welcomed by families worldwide as a significant social event (see Figure 5-1).

A Laughing Baby
In the traditional Navajo culture, custom dictates that the friend or family member who witnesses a baby's first laugh has the honor of hosting a celebration called "The First Laugh Ceremony." This festive event, honoring the appearance of joy in a baby's life, marks his or her birth as a true social being.

Figure 5-1 The appearance of joy is celebrated in traditional Navajo families.

Gradually, joy branches out to include surprise, affection, and pride. Likewise, the primary emotion of anger serves as a foundation for the eventual development of frustration, annoyance, envy, fury, and disgust. Combinations of these feelings produce more complex reactions, as when annoyance and disgust together lead to feelings of contempt. Four primary emotions and their corresponding emotional clusters are listed in Table 5-2.

Even as later emotions are surfacing, earlier ones are becoming more differentiated. Thus, by the end of the first year, a child's repertoire of emotions has moved beyond the primary four to include surprise, elation, frustration, separation anxiety, and stranger distress. Further diversity and greater specificity of emotion is seen in the second year. At that age, children are more self-conscious, and emotions such as embarrassment, affection, envy, defiance, and contempt enter the picture. By 3 years of age, children become increasingly focused on others, exhibiting initial signs of empathy and a difference between their affection for children and for adults.

Around age 3, children also start to make judgments about their actions, demonstrating signs of pride when they succeed (smiling, clapping, or shouting "I did it"), as well as shame when they are not successful (slumped posture, averted eyes, declaring "I'm no good at this.") (Lewis, Alessandri, & Sullivan, 1992; Sroufe, 1996; Tangney & Dearing, 2002). The general order in which emotions appear during the first three years is depicted in Figure 5-2. By the time children are in elementary school, the number of emotions they experience is even greater.

Early in life, the primary emotions are very intense. The dramatic outbursts so common among infants and toddlers underscore that intensity.

Table 5-2 Primary Emotions and Corresponding Emotional Clusters.

JOY	ANGER	SADNESS	FEAR
Happiness	Frustration	Dejection	Wariness
Delight	Jealousy	Unhappiness	Anxiety
Contentment	Disgust	Distress	Suspicion
Satisfaction	Annoyance	Grief	Dread
Pleasure	Fury	Discouragement	Dismay
Elation	Boredom	Shame	Anguish
Pride	Defiance	Guilt	Panic

However, as children's emotions become more differentiated, their reactions also become more varied.

Thus, as children mature, rather than relying on screaming to express every variation of anger, they may shout in fury, pout in disappointment, whimper in frustration, or express their upset feelings in words. This expanded repertoire of emotional expression is a result of several interacting factors—the presence of the primary emotions, the context of each situation, and children's developing cognitive and language capacities. These elements also contribute to children's understanding of emotions in themselves and in others.

How Children Develop Emotional Self-Awareness

"I'm mad at you, Teacher—go away!"

Alec – 3 years old

" All the children look at me and say: Look at that ugly boy with a bump. That annoys me and makes me sad. Just because I have a hunchback it does not mean that my ears don't hear and my heart doesn't ache."

John – 11 years old

These comments illustrate the dramatic change that occurs in children's understanding of their emotions during childhood. Over time, the simplistic declarations of the toddler give way to more complex reasoning and greater breadth of understanding. It all begins with children thinking that their emotions happen one at a time. When toddlers and preschoolers are angry, they are completely angry; when they are pleased, they are entirely pleased (Harter, 1998). These emotional responses alternate rapidly. One minute a child may scream, "No!" and a few minutes later he or she may laugh at something else that has happened. The

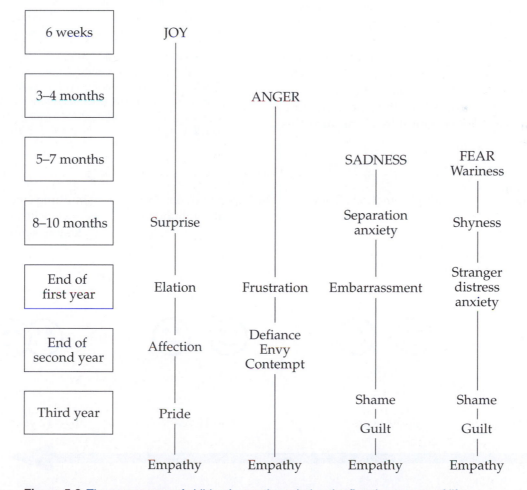

Figure 5-2 The emergence of children's emotions during the first three years of life.

quick changes children make from one emotional state to another are universally recognized as typical for children of this age (Gonzalez-Mena & Eyer, 2006).

By ages 5 or 6, youngsters report that they can hold more than one feeling at a time as long as those feelings come from the same emotional cluster. Thus, a kindergartner might say that he is feeling happy as well as excited about going to a birthday party (Wintre & Vallance, 1994). In contrast, he would not suggest that he could feel both happy and nervous about the party because he would expect such opposing feelings to be directed toward different things.

Sometime between the ages of 8 and 11, children come to understand that multiple and contrasting feelings toward the same event are feasible. With this new thinking, a child might suggest that staying home alone prompts both scary feelings and proud ones (Brown & Dunn, 1996). Initially, children perceive these feelings as occurring in succession, not simultaneously. One feeling replaces another rather than coexisting with it. So it is possible to be both happy and sad about the same event, but not at the same time.

By ages 10 to 12 years, children recognize that they can hold two or more very different feelings toward the same object or situation at the same time. This marks the first time that they become consciously aware of "mixed emotions." Initially, this mix can produce confusion. As a result, children this age often express anxiety about such feelings or distress that their emotions are "arguing with one another" (Whitesell & Harter, 1989). Learning to sort out mixed feelings accurately requires additional maturity and experience. It isn't until later adolescence that young people are able to do this reasonably well. Another emotional characteristic of children in the later elementary grades is that they do not shift emotional states as rapidly as toddlers and preschoolers. Their emotions last longer and are rooted in the past and future, as well as in the here and now. In fact, older youngsters often describe themselves as being in a good or bad mood, meaning they expect their general emotional state to remain relatively stable for some period of time. The developmental sequence described here is depicted in Figure 5-3.

How Children Learn to Identify Other People's Emotions

Three year-old Maggie notices another child sobbing, with tears running down her face. Pointing to the crying child she says, "Teacher, look at Rosie. She's sad."

A mother leaves her toddler with Max, her 6-year-old, while she goes to get a soft drink from the ice chest at a family picnic. The 2-year-old begins to whimper. Max surveys the situation, grasps the younger child's hand and says, "Oh, that's all right. She isn't going far. She'll be right back. Don't be afraid. I'm here."

All one emotion	Multiple emotions from the same emotional cluster	Multiple emotions from opposite emotional clusters in succession	Multiple emotions from opposite emotional clusters simultaneously

Below 5 years	5 to 7 years	8 to 11 years	10 to 12 years and older

Figure 5-3 Developmental sequence of children's understanding of emotion.

These boys can't imagine being happy and nervous at the same time.

The ability to recognize and interpret other people's emotions is an important skill that becomes more fine-tuned over time. As illustrated by Maggie and Max, in just a few short years, children shift from focusing on obvious physical cues to more subtle contextual ones to interpret other people's emotions and respond to them. Beginning slowly in the first three years of life, emotion recognition progresses rapidly during the preschool and grade-school years.

Prior to age 3 Infants and toddlers are not very adept at accurately interpreting other people's emotions (Widen & Russell, 2003). Their lack of experience and limited vocabulary contribute to this circumstance.

Ages 3 through 5 Preschoolers become increasingly accurate at identifying other people's positive and negative emotions (Widen & Russell, 2003).

In doing so, they rely mostly on facial expressions and tone of voice to tell them how someone else is feeling. Their assessments are based more on how a person looks and sounds than on the context of the situation (Boone & Cunningham, 1998). Relying on expressive cues, preschoolers are likely to decide that a crying peer is sad based on the tears streaming down her face rather than on knowing what happened. Not too surprisingly, the primary emotions are consistently easier for preschoolers to identify than emotions characterized by more subtle cues (Levine, 1995). Younger children also focus on only one emotion at a time in others, just as they do in themselves. This makes it hard for them to recognize the complex blend of emotions that other people experience.

The primary years During the primary years, children combine physical, situational, and historic information to understand and interpret emotions (Shaffer, 2005). With maturity and experience, children come to recognize that a child may be sad because her toy is broken or because her dog is lost, not simply because she is crying. They also discover that the same child's feelings could change to happiness if the toy were repaired or if the lost pet found its way home. Gradually, children learn that the source of a person's feelings may be internal as well as physical and situational (Lagattuta & Wellman, 2001; Stein & Levine, 1999). For instance, they become aware that memories may produce feelings even though the original event is long past. When 10-year-old Janelle says, "Tom's sad. He's lonesome for the dog he used to have," she is demonstrating an increasingly mature concept of how and why emotions occur. Furthermore, by this age, Janelle can imagine the succession of emotions or even the mixed emotions that Tom may experience, such as feeling sad about his lost dog but also pleased that his family is talking about getting a new puppy soon (Brown & Dunn, 1996). By the end of this period, most children realize that the same events do not always lead to the same outcomes. Similar situations may prompt different responses in different people or different responses from the same person on separate occasions. For example, loud music may prompt happy feelings in Tricia but make Katrina feel overwhelmed. The same music may cause Janet to feel exuberant on Monday, but on edge Tuesday. Because of these variations, even though children increase in their ability to recognize another person's emotions, doing so continues to be a challenge throughout this period.

Figure 5-4 Children focus on facial expressions to signal emotion. Can you find "angry" Maddie in this picture, drawn by Maddie herself?

How Children Learn to Regulate Their Emotions

At the same time that children are developing greater emotional understanding, they are also becoming better able to regulate what they feel. That is, children gradually learn to manage their emotions so they are not totally overwhelmed by them and so they can interact with others more effectively. Emotional regulation requires putting emotional awareness to work in real-life situations that may be upsetting, frustrating, or embarrassing (National Research Council and the Institute of Medicine, 2000; Eisenberg & Spinrad, 2004). Even positive emotions require regulation: exuberance, for example, is appropriate in some situations, but not in others. At times emotional regulation involves suppressing certain emotions (such as getting one's anger under control in order to deal with an unfair situation). At other times it involves intensifying them (as when a child marshals his anger to stand up to a bully).

As discussed in Chapter 2, the process of emotional regulation begins in infancy. Babies learn to elicit comfort from a caregiver through the sounds they make or to turn away if an interaction is too emotionally intense. Toddlers can be seen rocking themselves when they are upset and distracting themselves in frustrating circumstances or when they have to wait (Grolnick, Bridges, & Connell, 1996). By the time children go to kindergarten, they have many more strategies at their disposal and are more proficient in using them. Words become more central to their repertoire and children become better able to use internal strategies to moderate their feelings in various situations. Typical emotion-regulating strategies children may acquire over time include:

Suppressing the expression of certain emotions (Tom doesn't show his disappointment over not coming in first as he congratulates the winner).

Soothing one's self (Gloria talks to herself as she goes into a dark part of the basement; Spencer carries around his teddy whenever he feels tired or sad).

Seeking comfort (a toddler crawls up in the lap of her caregiver after another child takes her toy).

Avoiding or ignoring certain emotionally arousing events (Connie covers her eyes with her hands during an unpleasant part of the movie).

Changing goals that have been stymied (Khalil abandons his efforts to make the wrestling team and concentrates on his scouting badges instead).

Interpreting emotionally arousing events in alternate ways (When his brother is abrupt with him, Calvin doesn't take it personally because he assumes his brother is still upset over a recent argument with their mom).

Emotional IQ

Children's emotional self-awareness, their understanding of other people's feelings, and their ability to

manage what they feel all contribute to their social competence. This combination of knowledge and action is popularly termed **emotional IQ** (Goleman, 1995, 1999). The fundamental lessons associated with emotional IQ are learned during childhood and are summarized in Figure 5-5.

We have become increasingly aware that children who have well-developed emotional understandings and skills (or high emotional IQ) are more successful in life than children who do not (Hyson, 2004). For instance, when children exhibit a high degree of emotional awareness, peers and adults view them as likeable, cooperative, and friendly. Children who lack these understandings are not perceived in the same positive light (Belsky, Friedman, & Hsieh, 2001; Dunn, Brown, & Maguire, 1995). Similarly, children who

1. *Everyone has emotions.* I feel happy this morning. So does Nicole, and so does Lisa. Ms. Bernaro, my teacher, has feelings too. Sometimes she is excited or pleased and sometimes she is unhappy or annoyed.

2. *Emotions are prompted by different situations.* Lots of things make me happy: wearing my favorite shirt, getting an extra cookie at snack, having all the blocks I need to build a road that goes all around the rug. When someone walks through my road, or when I fall on the playground, I get angry or sad.

3. *There are different ways to express emotions.* Sometimes when I am happy I sing a little song, sometimes I laugh, sometimes I just sit and smile to myself.

4. *Other people may not feel the same way I do about everything.* When the garbage truck came to school, I wanted to climb right up and sit on the seat behind the wheel. It felt exciting. Janice stayed back with Ms. Klein. She thought it was scary.

5. *I can do things to affect how I feel and how others feel.* When I'm sad, I can go sit on Aunt Sophie's lap or in the big chair and after a while I feel better. Sometimes when baby Camilla is fussing, I make funny faces at her and she starts to laugh.

Figure 5-5 The emotional lessons of early childhood.
Source: Adapted from Hyson, 2004.

lack the ability to regulate their emotions are more prone to emotional outbursts, to elicit negative responses from others, and to experience lack of satisfaction in their emotional lives. On the other hand, children who learn how to manage their emotions constructively have an easier time with the disappointments, frustrations, and hurt feelings that are a natural part of growing up. Such children also tend to feel happier overall (National Research Council and the Institute of Medicine, 2000).

The degree to which children develop their emotional IQ is influenced to a great extent by how well they address the emotional tasks of childhood.

The Emotional Tasks of Childhood

Currently, many people believe that human beings work through a series of emotional tasks over the course of their lives. The person who has most influenced our understanding of what these tasks are is Erik Erikson (1950, 1963). He has identified eight emotional stages through which people progress.

Each stage is characterized by positive and negative emotions as well as a central emotional task. This task is to resolve the conflict that arises between the two emotional extremes. Although all children experience a ratio between both poles of a given stage, optimal emotional development occurs when the proportion is weighted toward the positive. These stages build on one another, each serving as the foundation for the next. Refer to Table 5-3 for a list of all eight of Erikson's stages.

Four of the stages outlined in Table 5-3 take place during the childhood years. Let's look at these more closely.

Trust versus mistrust.   The first stage of emotional development takes place during infancy and was described in Chapter 2. The emotional conflict during this stage is whether children will develop self-confidence and trust in the world or feelings of hopelessness, uncertainty, and suspicion. Children who develop positive feelings in this stage learn, "I am lovable and my world is safe and secure." They are supported in this learning when adults develop positive relationships with them and attend to their needs from the earliest days.

Autonomy versus shame and doubt.   Sometime during their second year, toddlers who have developed a strong sense of trust begin to move away from the total dependency of infancy toward having a mind and will of their own. The struggle throughout this period is whether the child will emerge with a sense of being an independent, self-directed human being, or one who has fundamental misgivings about self-worth. Autonomous children do what they can for themselves, whereas nonautonomous youngsters doubt their ability to control their world or themselves and so become overly dependent on other people. Children who develop a dominant sense of shame and doubt are those who have few opportunities to explore, to do for themselves, to experiment with objects, or to make decisions. Their attempts at exploration and independence are met with impatience, harsh criticism, ridicule, physical restraint, or resistance. In contrast, children who develop a healthy sense of autonomy are given numerous opportunities for mastery, are permitted to make choices, and are given clear, positive messages regarding limits to their behavior. Youngsters who successfully navigate this stage learn, "I can make decisions; I can do some things on my own."

Initiative versus guilt.   During their fourth or fifth year, children develop a new sense of energy. The emotional conflict during this stage is whether this energy will be directed constructively and be valued by others, or whether it will be nonproductive and rejected. Throughout the preschool and early grade-school years, children have experiences with both initiative and guilt by

putting plans and ideas into action.

attempting to master new skills and goals.

striving to gain new information.

exploring ideas through fantasy.

experiencing the sensations of their bodies.

figuring out ways to maintain their behavior within bounds considered appropriate by society.

Youngsters who have opportunities to engage in such experiences with adult support and acceptance are more likely to develop a strong sense of initiative. They take pleasure in their increasing competence and find ways to use their energy constructively. They become better able to cooperate and to accept help from others. They also learn that they can work for the things they want without jeopardizing their developing sense of correct behavior. On the other

Table 5-3 Summary of Erikson's Stages of Development.

APPROXIMATE AGE	STAGE	TASK	KEY SOCIAL AGENTS
Birth to 1 year	Trust versus mistrust	To establish a trusting relationship with a primary caregiver—to develop trust in self, others, and the world as a place where needs are met.	Parents/Family
1 to 3 years	Autonomy versus shame and doubt	To strive for independence.	Parents/Family/ Caregivers
3 to 6 years	Initiative versus guilt	To plan and carry out activities and learn society's boundaries.	Family/Caregivers
6 to 12 years	Industry versus inferiority	To be productive and successful.	Teachers/Peers
12 to 20 years	Identity versus role confusion	To establish social and occupational identities.	Peers
20 to 40 years	Intimacy versus isolation	To form strong friendships and to achieve a sense of love and companionship.	Friends/Lovers/ Spouse/Partner
40 to 65 years	Generativity versus stagnation	To be productive in terms of family and work.	Spouse/Partner/ Children/Culture
65 + years	Ego integrity versus despair	To look back at life as meaningful and productive.	Family/Friends/ Society

hand, children whose efforts fall short of their own expectations or adult expectations develop a sense of guilt. Adults compound this sense of guilt when they make children feel that their physical activity is bad, that their fantasy play is silly, that their exaggerations are lies, that their tendency to begin projects but not complete them is irresponsible, and that their exploration of body and language is totally objectionable. Which kinds of experiences dominate children's interactions with others and the world strongly influences children's self-judgments. The optimal outcome of this stage is a child who thinks, "I can do, and I can make."

Industry versus inferiority.   The fourth stage of emotional development takes place throughout middle childhood (approximately 6 to 12 years of age). During this phase, children become preoccupied with producing things and with adult-like tasks. They also are more interested in joining with others to get things done and in contributing to society as a whole. The central emotional issue is whether youngsters will come away feeling competent and able, or whether they will believe that their best efforts are inadequate. Although all children have times when they are incapable of mastering what they set out to accomplish, some experience a pervasive sense of failure. This happens when adult, peer, or school standards are clearly beyond their abilities or when they have an unrealistic view of what is possible to achieve. Strong feelings of inferiority also arise when children believe that mastery only counts in areas in which they are not skilled.

School-age children enjoy mastering new tools and skills.

ied forms, (2) how children come to understand what they are feeling, (3) how children recognize other people's emotions, (4) how children come to regulate their emotions, and (5) the emotional tasks of early childhood. All of these processes underscore emotional similarities among children. Now we will look at ways in which children differ from one another emotionally.

Individual Variations in Children's Expressive Styles

If you were to use feeling words to describe some of the children you know, you might say things like: Tanya is usually "quiet and shy"; Georgio is generally "exuberant and eager to try new things"; Brandon tends to be "prickly and easily offended." Descriptions such as these are referring to children's patterns of emotional responsiveness, or their **expressive style** (National Scientific Council on the Developing Child, 2006; Hyson, 2004). Children's expressive style is influenced by their temperament and results from unique combinations of the following factors.

The proportion of positive and negative emotions children typically exhibit. Some children are more optimistic, some are more neutral, and some are more downhearted much of the time. Though, everyone experiences many different emotions each day, all of us have a certain emotional tenor that determines how we handle most emotion-arousing events.

The frequency with which children show certain emotions. Children have certain ways they tend to react from one situation to another. For instance, Felix may react with caution each time he encounters something new. His brother may have the opposite reaction, responding with eagerness to novel circumstances.

The intensity with which children express their emotions. Although two children may respond with a similar feeling to a particular situation, the intensity of their responses may vary. Sue and Ricardo are both pleased to have been invited to another child's party. Sue claps her hands and giggles with joy. Ricardo gives a slow smile to show his pleasure.

How long certain emotional states last. Some children hang on to their emotional reactions longer

Industriousness is fostered when adults recognize and praise children's success, when they encourage children to explore their skills in a variety of areas, when they help children set realistic goals, and when they set up tasks so children experience mastery. Providing guidance and support to children whose efforts fail eases the pain and gives children the confidence to try again. This is also an important time for adults to encourage children to work with one another in order to experience the satisfaction of working in a group as well as to learn the skills necessary to do so. When feelings of industry outweigh those of inferiority, children emerge into adolescence thinking, "I can learn; I can contribute; I can work with others."

In this portion of the chapter we have considered five sequences that characterize children's emotional development: (1) how emotions evolve from the primary emotions to their more var-

Young children take pleasure in their increasing competence.

than others do. For instance, Sarah may become up-set over not getting to go first in line, then quickly move on to enjoying a game of catch outdoors. Lisa, on the other hand, may remain unhappy for most of the afternoon, brooding over not being chosen as line-leader.

The degree to which children's emotional responses are dominated by primary or mixed emotions. Although all children become capable of more complex emotional expression as they ma-ture, some continue to exhibit the primary emotions most frequently, whereas others generally exhibit more complicated combinations of feelings. This ex-plains why Kyle's parents describe the 7-year-old as an "easy read." You know he is happy or angry just by looking at his face. His brother Raymond, on the other hand, is harder to decipher because he often displays a complicated mix of feelings that are not so readily interpreted.

How quickly children's emotions are activated. Some children are quick to exhibit an emotional response. Others take much more time to show any emotional reaction. These distinctions are exemplified by Sandra, who has a "short fuse,"

reacting with anger at minor provocations; and Bethany, who is slow to anger and is seldom out of sorts.

Such variations in emotional responsiveness are not inherently good or bad, just different. Adults who are tuned-in to the children in their care rec-ognize and respect each child's unique expressive style. They understand that such differences give clues as to what each child is feeling and a basis for determining the kinds of emotional support each child needs.

Gender Differences in Children's Emotional Expression

Conventional wisdom says that females are more emotionally expressive than males and that females are the more sensitive of the two genders to other people's feelings. Current research tends to support these popular beliefs (Weinberg, Tronick, Cohn, & Olson, 1999; Bajgar, Ciarrochi, Lane & Deane, 2005). From their first year, girls smile more and cry more than boys do. Girls use more emotion-related words in their conversations with peers and adults, and girls are more likely than boys to figure out what other people are feeling. These tendencies continue throughout the teenage years.

Although biology likely plays a role in gender differences, scientists believe that many of these variations are taught directly and modeled from the first days of life. Throughout the United States, parents use more expressive facial expressions with their infant daughters than with their infant sons. Also, they use feeling words more often in conversations with girls than with boys. Adults encourage little girls to express a wide range of emotions, but they are less likely to do this with young boys (Bukatko & Daehler, 2004; Kuebli, Butler, & Fivush, 1995). These outcomes suggest that adults need to pay careful attention to how they interact with boys and girls if their goal is for all children to become comfortable and adept at dealing with emotions effectively.

Family and Cultural Variations in Children's Emotional Expression

> *Two 8-year-olds are racing down the hall. A teacher stops them and tells them she is disappointed that they forgot the rule about walking inside. Andrew stops laughing and says, "Sorry." Wu Fang smiles, says nothing, then walks slowly to his classroom. Both boys are expressing regret according to the customs of their family and culture.*

To become successfully integrated into society, children must learn certain display rules regarding how emotions are exhibited and which emotions are acceptable in certain situations and which are not. Such learning is influenced by family expectations and by culture. For instance, in many European-American families, when children are being reprimanded, they are expected to maintain eye contact to show respect and to adopt a solemn expression to communicate remorse. Mexican-American and African-American children, on the other hand, often are taught to avert their gaze to indicate respect. Chinese children learn to smile as an expression of apology when being scolded by an elder, whereas Korean children develop a demeanor referred to as *myupojung*, or lack of facial expression, which they are expected to display in similar situations (Lynch & Hanson, 2004).

Children learn these expressive variations at home and in the community. They absorb them through observing and interacting with others. At first, children obey display rules to avoid negative reactions or to gain approval from the important people in their lives. Gradually, they come to accept them as the natural order of things in the family and culture in which they live (Saarni, 1995; Bosacki & Moore 2004).

Imitation. At the lunch following her grandmother's funeral, 3-year-old Meridith turns to see her mother grimace and begin to cry. Mom searches for her handkerchief, sobs, and blows her nose. Meridith runs to the buffet table. Grabbing a paper napkin, she begins to cry and blow her nose. In this case, Meridith was clearly imitating her mother's emotional expression to guide her own actions in a situation she had never encountered before.

A similar but more subtle form of **social referencing** occurs when Jorge falls down while running across the playground. He looks up to see how the nearby adult reacts to his fall. If the adult's face registers alarm, the child may determine that this is a worrisome event and begin to cry in response. If the adult's reaction is matter-of-fact, Jorge may register the idea that the fall is no big deal and simply pick himself up to continue his play. As children gain experience in the world, they use circumstances like these to experiment with various forms of emotional expression.

Feedback. Adults also provide feedback to children regarding the appropriateness of the ways they choose to express their emotions. Such feedback is offered through gestures and sounds. For instance, when a baby's smile is greeted with the excited voice of the caregiver, the adult's tone serves as a social reward. If this happens often, the baby will smile more frequently. If the infant's smile is consistently ignored, his or her smiling behavior will decrease. Likewise, when Carmen giggles out loud at a funny cartoon, her father laughs along with her. However, when she laughs at her brother who is struggling to play the violin, her father frowns slightly and shakes his head no, indicating that laughter is not an appropriate response in this circumstance.

In both cases, Carmen was given feedback regarding her emotional reaction. Scenarios like this are repeated many times throughout childhood. Based on the feedback they receive, children gradually come to know better as to where, when, and how to express their emotions.

Direct instruction. In many situations, adults give children specific instructions about how they should express their emotions. They do this when they point out appropriate and inappropriate reactions of others as well as when they tell children what is expected of them:

> "John did a good job of speaking up for himself at the meeting. He was angry, but he didn't lose his temper."

"You shouldn't laugh at people in wheelchairs."

"You just won first place. You should be smiling."

Rules such as these may be formal or informal and are enforced using a variety of social costs and rewards. Because children vary in the lessons they learn, they also vary in their emotional expressiveness.

Variations in How Children Interpret Emotional Events

Just as children differ in their emotional expression, they also vary in how they interpret what they are feeling. Some of these variations are age-related and common to most children, whereas others are unique to each child. To illustrate this concept, consider children's changing notions of what is dangerous and, therefore, frightening.

Developmental changes in children's fears.

> *Yoko, age 2, becomes frightened by the loud noise when her mom turns on the vacuum cleaner. She runs from the room crying.*
>
> *Jason and Yuri, two sixth graders, one from Idaho and the other from the Ukraine are e-pals. In their most recent e-mail messages they have shared their anxiety over the final exams each must face at the end of the term.*

Both younger and older children experience fear, but they are not afraid of the same things. Yoko exhibited fear in the presence of loud sounds. Because of her immature thinking and limited experience, she interpreted this noisy but harmless event as dangerous. In a similar situation, Jason and Yuri could reason that sounds cannot hurt them and remain unafraid. On the other hand, the 2-year-old has no comprehension of the potential negative outcomes of a failed exam. As a result, she would be oblivious to the concerns that command Jason's and Yuri's attention.

Such developmental differences in what children fear are common all over the world (Yamamoto et al., 1987; Gullone & King, 1993; Mellon, Koliadis, and Paraskevopoulos, 2004). The emergence of relatively predictable sequences of fears are outlined in Table 5-4.

As shown in the table, children's **imaginary fears** (e.g., fear of loud sounds or monsters under the bed; see Figure 5-6) gradually give way to more **realistic fears** (e.g., fear of physical danger or fear of social embarrassment). This progression parallels a developmental shift in children's thinking.

That shift comes about from children's more mature understandings of cause and effect, their increasing ability to understand the difference between fantasy and reality, and the growing backlog of experiences they have to draw upon as they mature.

Learned fears.   All the variations in children's fears described so far have been age-related. They evolve out of children's developing capabilities and understandings. As such, they are common to most youngsters. However, many children experience special fears that are unique to them and that are primarily learned (Wogelius, Poulsen, Toft-Sorensen, 2003; Papalia, Olds, & Feldman, 2006). As an example, take 6-year-old Tessa's intense apprehension about visiting the dentist. Her fear may have arisen from actual experience (at an earlier visit, she had a tooth filled, and it hurt); she may have observed her mother becoming pale and anxious while settling into the dentist's chair and concluded that this was a frightening situation; or she may have been told directly, "If you're not good, the dentist will have to pull out all your teeth," a horrifying thought! Most likely, she experienced a combination of these influences and encountered them on more than one occasion. In this way she learned to be frightened of going to the dentist.

Another child in her place might have put together a different interpretation of these events as an outgrowth of his or her different experiential history. Age-related variations in children's interpretation of emotional events combine with what they have learned to produce certain emotional responses and interpretations.

This underscores the fact that children will vary in how they respond to the emotional situations they encounter each day. The formulation of mature, emotional concepts evolves slowly and is still incomplete as children move into adolescence. As a result, children may find dealing with emotions a challenging experience.

CHALLENGES CHILDREN ENCOUNTER WHEN DEALING WITH EMOTIONS

> *Martin is so excited about going to the zoo that he keeps interrupting his father, who is trying to get directions for the trip.*
>
> *Andrea has been waiting a long time to use the kite. Frustrated, she grabs it from Barbara, then dashes to the other side of the playground.*

Table 5-4 Childhood Fears From Birth Through Adolescence.

AGE	SOURCE OF FEAR
0–6 Months	Loss of physical support, loud noises, flashes of light, sudden movements
7–12 Months	Strangers; heights; sudden, unexpected, and looming objects
1 Year	Separation from or loss of parent, toilet, strangers
2 Years	Separation from or loss of parent, loud sounds, darkness, large objects or machines, unfamiliar peers, changes in familiar environments
3 Years	Separation from or loss of parent, masks, clowns, the dark, animals
4 Years	Separation from or loss of parent, animals, darkness, noises (especially noises at night), bad dreams
5 Years	Separation from or loss of parent, animals, bodily injury, the dark, "bad" people, bad dreams
6 Years	Separation from or loss of parent, the dark, ghosts, witches, bodily injury, thunder and lightning, sleeping or staying alone, bad dreams
7–8 Years	Separation from or loss of parent, the dark, ghosts, witches, sleeping or staying alone, life threatening situations
9–12 Years	Separation from or loss of parent, the dark, life-threatening situations, death, thunder and lightning, tests or examinations, school performances (e.g., plays, concerts, sporting events), grades, social humiliation (gossip, fear of failure)
Adolescence	Appearance, sexuality, social humiliation, violence (at home and in the street), war and terrorism

Sources: "The fears of youth in the 1990s: Contemporary normative data," by E. Gullone, and N. J. King, 1993 *Journal of Genetic Psychology*. June, 154 (2), 137–153. "What Do Children Worry About? Worries and Their Relation to Anxiety," by W. K. Silverman, A. M. LaGreca, and S.Wasserstein, 1995, *Child Development*, 66, 671–686; *A Child's World: Infancy Through Adolescence*, by D. E. Papalia and S. W. Olds, 2006, New York: McGraw-Hill.

> *Fred is worried about what will happen when his mother goes into the hospital. Rather than letting anybody know his fears, he pretends he doesn't care.*

None of these children are handling their emotions particularly well. That is, none of them are dealing with their emotions in a way that will lead to greater personal satisfaction, resolution of a dilemma, or increased social competence.

Difficulties Experienced by Children from Infancy Through Age 7

Children are not born knowing how to manage their emotions. As a result they sometimes rely on strategies that are not helpful to themselves or others. For instance, because of their lack of social skills and immature language capabilities, young children often act out how they feel. They may pout when angry or jump up and down when excited. In these situations, children expect others to interpret their

emotions accurately and to respond in supportive ways. Unfortunately, nonverbal expressions of emotions may be misunderstood. For instance, an adult may assume that a crying child is tired, when frustration is really the source of the child's distress. Putting the child to bed, which is a reasonable way to support tired children, is not the best strategy for helping children cope with frustration.

Another problem for youngsters 2 to 7 years of age is that they often choose inappropriate actions to show how they feel. Their poor choices may be due to poor modeling, lack of know-how, or immature understandings (Shapiro, 1997). Finally, even when young children are able to express how they feel in words, they still may not know what to do about it. Such a situation is demonstrated by Sam, a very talented child who was afraid of many things. See Figure 5-7.

Difficulties Experienced by Children Ages 7 to 12

Children in the later elementary years are more aware of their emotions and how to use words to

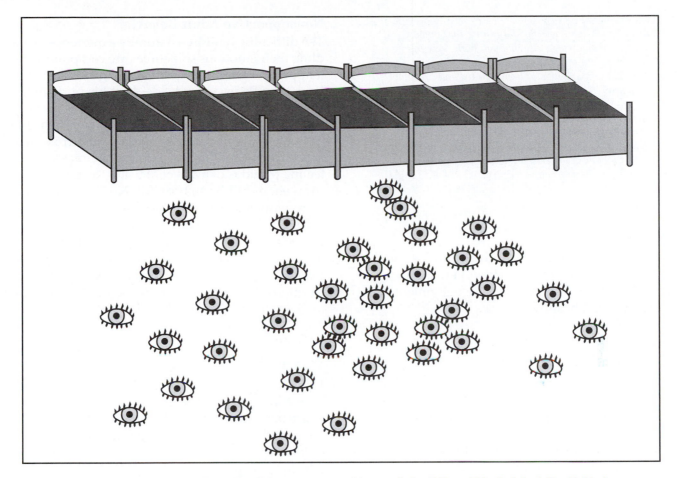

Figure 5-6 "The Monsters Under Erik's Bed." A computer rendition made by Erik and his dad depicting Erik's fear of the dark at age 4.6 years.

communicate them. However, they are less likely to be open about their emotions than are younger children. Children ages 7 to 12 may try to hide or minimize their emotions (Berk, 2006; Harter, 1998). This happens because they are very aware of the social rules governing emotional behavior and because they wish to avoid the negative social costs associated with expressing certain feelings. Unfortunately, the discrepancy between their real emotions and what they think those emotions should be causes great emotional distress. When children hide their emotions, they have no opportunity to discover that they have experiences in common with other people. This leads to feelings of isolation, self-doubt, and inferiority (Goleman, 1995). Youngsters in these circumstances come to think of their emotions as unnatural and different from anyone else's or the established norm. The more intense this perception, the more damaging the outcome. A dramatic example of the harm that can come from trying to hide

one's emotions is illustrated by Cathleen Brook's description of her life in an alcoholic home:

When I was growing up in an alcoholic home, one of the things that I was acutely aware of was that when I felt sad, or angry, or panicked, or hurt, there was no place—and no one—where I was safe enough to talk about how I felt.

I really believed that noise and upsetting and making people uncomfortable was what made things so bad in my house. So I spent my life trying never to make noise and always to be good, and never making anyone uncomfortable.

And it didn't work.

And then I found alcohol, and it worked.

It's amazing how well that stuff works. I spent 11 years of my life without it, and at 11 I put it in my body and I became who I had wanted to be. It was amazing. Alcohol was the only thing that made a great deal of sense to me. Had you been there to try to talk me out of using alcohol, I want to assure you that you would have been ignored and probably ridiculed.

But had you been there to tell me you cared what I was feeling you might have made all the difference. Had you been there to tell me you might even know a little bit of what I was feeling, I might have believed that there was some human being in the world I could count on.

(Woll, 1999, p. 1)

Not all children resort to drugs and alcohol to deal with their emotions. However, the fact that some do tells us that emotional development is not always an easy, healthy process.

Nonsupportive Adult Behavior

The difficulties children naturally experience in handling their emotions sometimes are compounded by inappropriate adult responses. Imagine what might happen to Pedro when he declares his pride in having won honorable mention in the writing contest. If his teacher responds with a comment like, "Cool!" or "You're really excited," Pedro's pride is acknowledged and he receives the message that feeling proud is okay. In contrast, if the teacher says, "You shouldn't be so boastful. No bragging!" such comments teach Pedro that feelings of pride and accomplishment are inappropriate. Being told that his feelings are bad may cause the child to evaluate himself negatively for having experienced them. Because children naturally experience a wide range of emotions, if this trend continues, Pedro may come to view a natural part of himself as unacceptable.

Four-year-old Sam was enrolled in a preschool for gifted and talented children. He was generally a happy child; however, Sam had many fears and often said he was afraid. Anticipation played a big part in Sam's fears. He worried about what was going to happen and how to avoid anything he thought might be bad. His teacher found that the following strategies helped Sam cope with his fearful feelings:

- Explain things to Sam in advance
- Give him a chance to participate in activities with an exit strategy in mind
- Give him scripts to express his feelings

Here are excerpts from notes his teacher sent to Sam's parents during the year to keep them informed about Sam's progress in relation to his fears:

Jan. 25—Sam cried during the story *Maia* (a chapter book about a dinosaur). He was afraid of the dinosaurs in the story, but stayed at group sitting close to an adult and was okay.

Jan. 26—Sam greeted me by saying he didn't want to hear Chapter 2 of *Maia*. We talked and I persuaded him to listen to part of it, saying he could bail out at any time. He stayed for the whole chapter.

Jan. 27—We did the Dinosaur Dance in the gym. Sam thought he'd be afraid, saying dinosaurs are big and scary. I told him he could stand near me if that happened, but it didn't. He had fun.

Jan. 28—I read another "scary" dinosaur book during large group today. Before I began reading, I talked about how funny it was going to be. Sam enjoyed it a lot.

Feb. 24—Outside, Mike P. was growling at Sam. Sam was "scared" at first. When Mike and I reminded Sam that Mike was playing dinosaurs again, he stopped being afraid and played dinosaurs with Mike most of the morning.

March 3—Sam is a little afraid of Erik, a loud child in our class who is very active. Erik also intrigues him. Outside today we practiced saying loudly, "Stop it. I don't like that." Of course, after one successful use, Sam wanted to say it often—not always when called for. The whole group talked a little about thumbs up and thumbs down as another signal to help each other know when something was getting to be too intense or uncomfortable. We all agreed to try this. Sam said it was a good plan.

Figure 5-7 The Story of Sam.

Source: Sam's Story was adapted with permission from a case study included in: *Children with Special Needs: Lessons for Early Childhood Professionals* written by Kostelnik, Onaga, Rohde and Whiren in 2002 and published by Teachers College Press (pp. 100–119).

When children arrive at such conclusions, they often choose maladaptive ways of coping. Pedro may become boastful as a way of bolstering his sagging confidence. He may reject compliments in an effort to adhere to an expected code of emotional conduct. Pedro may stop trying to excel as a way to avoid pride and achievement. He may develop a headache or stomachache in response to situations in which he might otherwise feel proud, or he may continually put himself down in an effort to look modest. All of these strategies take away from Pedro's future happiness.

There are four ways of responding to children's emotions that are ineffective or potentially harmful. These include ignoring children, lying to children, denying children's feelings, and shaming children (Hyson, 2004; Katz & Windecker-Nelson, 2004; Marion, 2007). All of these strategies cause damage at the time they are used, and also eliminate the adult as source of future emotional support to children.

Ignoring children's emotions.   Sometimes adults assume that if they ignore children's emotions those emotions will simply go away. This does not happen. The emotions remain, but regrettably children have no better way of coping. To make matters worse, children are left with the impression that their feelings are unimportant. Neither outcome leads to greater social competence or positive self-esteem.

Lying to children about emotional situations. Sometimes, in an effort to "protect" children from difficult emotional experiences, adults tell untruths. For example, 3-year-old Nina is about to have her blood drawn at the clinic. She is teary and somewhat fearful. Even though the needle is sure to prick, the adult says, "This won't hurt a bit." Such lies fail to prepare children for the reality of the situations they are facing and damage the credibility of the adult. Bonds of trust, which take time to establish, are destroyed.

Denying children's emotions.   There are many ways in which adults deny children's emotions. Sometimes, adults actually forbid children to have certain feelings. Phrases like "Stop worrying," "Don't be angry," or "You shouldn't be so scared" are examples of denying. At other times, adults dismiss the importance of the emotion being expressed, as when Lucas cried, "Look, there's blood on my finger," and the adult responded: "It's just a little cut. You won't die." On other occasions, adults tell children they do

Selena hides her eyes when the firefighter puts on his hat and oxygen mask.

not really have the emotion they claim to be experiencing: "You know you aren't really mad at each other," "Let's see you smile," "No more tears!" When adults deny children's emotions, the message they are conveying is that these emotions are wrong and that children are bad for experiencing them. Neither of these messages is true or helpful.

Shaming children.   Making fun of children or attempting to shame them out of their emotions is a destructive practice. Adults demoralize children when they say things like: "What are you crying for? I can't believe you're being such a baby about this," "All the other kids are having a good time. Why are you being so difficult?," or "Manny isn't afraid. What makes you such a scaredy-cat?" As with lying and denying, shaming makes children feel doubtful, guilty, or inferior. It certainly does not cause them to respond positively or make them feel better. For this reason, it has no place in a helping professional's collection of skills.

Adults who resort to ignoring, lying, denying, and shaming often are trying to avoid a scene or comfort children by minimizing the intensity of the moment. Such strategies have the opposite effect. They not only make matters worse, they prevent children from learning more effective ways to handle emotional situations.

In place of such destructive practices, adults can use a variety of strategies to promote children's feelings of trust, competence, and worth, and help them increase their skills in dealing with emotions.

APPROPRIATE WAYS OF RESPONDING TO CHILDREN'S EMOTIONS

To help youngsters cope more effectively with their emotions, adults have a variety of strategies available to them. Rather than trying to eliminate or restrict children's feelings, adults should accept them, even as they attempt to change the behaviors children use in emotional situations. Such an approach is synonymous with the idea of acceptance described in Chapters 1 and 4. Adults are better able to do this when they keep in mind the following facts:

1. Children's emotions are real and legitimate to them.
2. There are no right or wrong emotions. All feelings stem from the primary emotions, which occur naturally.
3. Children are not adept at regulating their emotions, nor can they simply change their emotions on command.
4. All emotions serve useful functions in children's lives.

Words are satisfying, more precise ways to express emotions and frequently are appropriate substitutes for physical action. Thus, in working with either preschool or school-age children, one obvious way to address the challenges children experience in handling emotions is to encourage them to talk more openly about what they are feeling.

Talking to Children About Their Emotions

There is strong evidence that when adults talk with children about their emotions, children's emotional competence increases (Hyson, 2004; Lagattuta & Wellman, 2001). Such conversations can take place throughout the day in a variety of contexts. A simple way to get emotion-focused conversations started is

for adults to simply identify the emotions children are expressing (Laible & Thompson, 2000). Because children learn best from firsthand experience, they benefit when emotions are named and described to them as they happen. For instance, if Matt is angry and an adult identifies his emotion ("Matt, you look angry"), the child has a hands-on experience with the concept of anger. Not only does Matt find out that his emotional state can be described, but he also becomes more aware of the internal and situational cues related to that emotion. Teachable moments such as these combine all three elements of mature emotional understanding—a situation, a physical reaction, and an interpretation. A basic strategy adults can use to name and describe children's emotions in day-to-day situations is called an affective reflection.

Affective Reflections

Affect refers to people's feelings or moods. **Affective reflections** are similar in form and intent to the behavior and paraphrase reflections presented in Chapter 4. They involve recognizing the emotions a child may be experiencing in a given situation and then using a reflection to name the emotions.

SITUATION A: Barry has climbed to the top of the jungle gym. With a big smile on his face, he announces, "Hey, everybody, look at me!"

> The adult says: You're proud to have climbed so high. (Or, either of the following: It feels good to be at the top; you made it! That's exciting.)

SITUATION B: Marlene complains that she had to clean up before her turn was over.

> The adult says: You wish you didn't have to clean up just yet. (Or: You didn't get to finish your turn; that's annoying; It's frustrating to be interrupted.)

SITUATION C: Earl is embarrassed about having to take a shower with the other boys after gym class.

> The adult says: It makes you uncomfortable to take a shower in public. (Or: You wish you didn't have to take your clothes off in front of everybody; it really seems unbelievable to you that this is required.)

Affective reflections such as these acknowledge and help to define children's emotions. In each situation, the adult's words and voice tone matches the emotional state being described, enhancing the completeness of the message.

How children benefit when you use affective reflections. Labeling children's emotions using affective reflections makes abstract, internal states

Take advantage of teachable moments to name children's emotions. What might these children be feeling?

more tangible; that is, naming something helps it to become more concrete (Berk & Winsler, 1995; Gergen, 2001). In addition, known events are easier to comprehend than unknown ones. Labels allow sensations to become more familiar. Because emotions cannot be touched or held and have elements that are not directly observable, labeling them is a particularly important strategy.

Verbal labels also are the primary means by which people recognize and recall past events (Shaffer & Kipp, 2006; Vygotsky, 1978). An irritated child who has heard irritation described in the past is better able to identify her or his current emotional state. This recognition helps her or him draw from past experience to determine a possible course of action.

Furthermore, language labels help to differentiate emotions that are perceptually similar but not entirely the same (Cutting & Dunn, 1999). On hearing the words "annoyed," "disgusted," and "enraged," you think of slightly different emotional states. All of these are variations on anger, yet are distinctive in their own right. Hearing different affective reflections enables children to be more precise in understanding what they are feeling. Moreover, as youngsters hear alternate feeling words, they adopt many of them for their own use. The broader their vocabulary, the more satisfied children are in using feeling words to express their emotions to others. They also are likely to exhibit more varied emotional reactions. Annoyance, disgust, and rage, for instance, may cause a child to envision different behavioral responses. Support for this line of reasoning comes from language research that shows that as people learn new words, their understanding of experience and ability to categorize events is strongly influenced by speech (Berk & Winsler, 1995).

When adults acknowledge children's emotions using affective reflections, they exhibit sensitivity and caring in a way children understand. This acknowledgment makes children feel heard and accepted (Dowling, 2005; Seligman, 1995). Not only do youngsters recognize that their emotions are respected by the adult, but as they hear their own and other people's emotions being described, they discover that their emotions are not so different from anyone else's. This reduces the chance that they will view their own emotional experiences as out of the ordinary. Affective reflections help children comprehend that all emotions, both pleasant and unpleasant, are an inevitable part of living. The many benefits of using affective reflections with children are summarized in Figure 5-8.

BENEFITS OF REFLECTING CHILDREN'S EMOTIONS

Affective reflections:

Help children better understand what they are feeling.

Make it easier for children to draw on past emotional learning.

Help children differentiate one emotion from another.

Enhance children's vocabulary.

Demonstrate adult caring and respect.

Show children that emotions are a normal part of living.

Figure 5-8 The value of using affective reflections with children.

Affective reflections are fundamental to enhancing children's emotional development. They can be used with children of all ages and in a wide array of circumstances. At times, the adult's purpose in using this skill is to focus more closely on the emotional aspects of an interaction. At other times, affective reflections are used to acknowledge the child's feelings while also dealing with other kinds of issues, such as making a rule or enforcing a consequence. Use of this skill contributes to a positive verbal environment. Finally, as you progress through this book, you will see that affective reflections are a foundation on which many other skills are based.

Helping Children Use Words to Express Their Emotions to Others

In addition to helping children recognize emotions through affective reflections, adults can also help children talk about their emotions and express them in acceptable ways. Children who are able to describe their emotions in words make it easier for others to know what they are feeling. Miscommunication is less likely, and the chances of gaining necessary support are better.

This type of emotional sharing is often referred to as **self-disclosure** and is considered a basic interpersonal skill. Interaction theories that stress open and honest communication all describe skills similar to or synonymous with this concept (Gazda, Balzer, Childers, & Nealy, 2005). This is because there is strong evidence that the degree to which people are able to express their emotions to others influences their ability to maintain close personal ties (Salovey & Mayer, 1990; Saarni, 1999). Also, when children learn to use words, they are less likely to resort to physical means to express negative feelings. Children who learn to say, "I'm angry" gain satisfaction from being able to capture their feelings in words. They also come to realize that they do not have to shove or hit to make their emotions known.

Children become better skilled at describing emotions when adults provide appropriate information about what people are feeling and why, rather than expecting children to know these things automatically (Landy, 2002). Younger children benefit from information related to expressive and situational cues (e.g., "Corine sure looks excited. She is laughing and jumping," or "Rafe dropped the ball. He seems upset"). Older children profit from input related to people's internal affective states (e.g., "Esther is still upset about the score from yesterday," or "Keisha, you enjoyed describing our picnic last year"). Additionally, children increase their social competence by learning actual phrases and scripts to use in emotional situations (Herrera & Dunn, 1997; Hyson, 2004). For instance, phrases such as, "I'm still working on this," or "You can have it when I'm finished" give children tools to express their needs when they do not want to give something up. Youngsters who have no such tools may resort to less acceptable physical actions or give way unnecessarily, leaving them frustrated or upset. Likewise, scripts such as, "I want a turn," or "I'm next," make it easier for children to negotiate in highly charged situations such as deciding who gets the next turn on the tricycle or the computer.

Children in intense emotional circumstances become more adept at coping when, in addition to helping them acknowledge their own feelings, adults instruct them in how to make such situations more manageable. This can be accomplished either by teaching a child a specific skill or by remaining supportive to children who are working out such issues for themselves. The following section describes more specific ways to implement these strategies.

SKILLS FOR SUPPORTING CHILDREN'S EMOTIONAL DEVELOPMENT

 Formulating Affective Reflections

1. Observe children carefully before saying anything. The context of a situation is important to its meaning. Pay close attention to children's facial expressions, voice tone, and posture as well as their actual words. Because younger children tend to be more open about what they are feeling, the behaviors they display may be easier to interpret than those exhibited by older children. With older children, pay particular attention to nonverbal cues. A child who is talking "happy" but looking "distressed" most likely is distressed.

2. Be sensitive to the wide range of emotions children exhibit. Children manifest numerous emotions. Some are extreme, some are more moderate; some are positive, some are negative. All emotions are important. If you only take time to notice intense emotions, or focus solely on the negative ones, children soon learn that these are the only emotions worth expressing. They get a broader perspective when all sorts of emotions are noticed and described.

3. Make a nonjudgmental assessment of what the child is experiencing. Form your impression of the child's feelings using only evidence about which you are certain. Avoid jumping to conclusions about why children feel the way they do. For instance, you may observe Jack entering the room crying. It is obvious that he is either sad or angry, but why he is so distressed may not be evident.

Although you may assume that he is missing his mother, he might really be upset about having to wear his orange sweater. Because you cannot be sure what is bothering him, an appropriate affective reflection would be "You look sad," rather than "You're sad

continued

SKILLS FOR SUPPORTING CHILDREN'S EMOTIONAL DEVELOPMENT—continued

Elena, a fourth grader, is invited to read to children in the preschool. How might she be feeling?

because you miss your mom." Opening the interaction with the first statement is potentially more accurate than using the second one.

4. Make a brief statement to the child describing the emotion you observed. Keep your reflection simple. Do not try to cram everything you have noticed about the child's emotional state into one response. Young children understand short sentences best. This also is true for children for whom English is not their home language. Older children will appreciate longer sentences or combinations of phrases, but will resent being overwhelmed with too much adult talk.

5. Use a variety of feeling words over time. Employ many different words to describe children's emotions. This expands children's vocabulary of feeling words and makes your responses more interesting.

Begin by naming the primary emotions (happy, mad, sad, afraid). Gradually, branch out to include related words that make finer distinctions. Next, think in advance of two or three words you have not used recently and plan to try them on a given day. Each time a situation arises for which one of your words is suited, use it. Repeat this process with different words on different days.

Finally, when you reflect using one of the more common feeling words in your vocabulary, follow it with a second reflection using a slightly different word ("You seem sad. It sounds like you're disappointed because the model didn't fly").

6. Acknowledge children's emotions even when you do not feel comfortable with them. At times, children express emotions adults find unreasonable, hard to understand, or uncomfortable to address. For instance, Shavette comes to the recreation center, furious. Snarling through clenched teeth, she hisses, "I hate that teacher. All she knows how to do is give homework, and there's no time for anything else." At this point, it is tempting to do any of the following:

> *Lecture:* "I've told you never to say 'hate.' That's not a nice way to feel about anyone."
>
> *Rationalize:* "Well, she really has to do that so you'll learn your math."
>
> *Deny:* "You couldn't hate anybody, could you?"
>
> *Ignore:* "Well, enough of that. Go pick out a video game to play."

Unfortunately, all of these responses disregard Shavette's perspective and make it less likely that she will share her feelings with you in the future. Additionally, such responses may cause her to react defensively or

SKILLS FOR SUPPORTING CHILDREN'S EMOTIONAL DEVELOPMENT

resort to more extreme measures to make her true emotions clear. Her impression probably will not be changed, and she has not learned constructive ways of handling her rage. A better response would be: "It doesn't seem fair to have to do so much homework," or "It sounds like you had a rotten day at school." Affective reflections like these prompt you to get beyond your own emotions and help you to recognize a viewpoint very different from your own. This must be accomplished if children are to trust you and give you access to their private selves.

7. Revise inaccurate reflections. Affective reflections are tentative statements of your perceptions of the child's emotional state. If you reflect, "You seem worried," and the child says something like "No" or "I'm just thinking," accept the correction gracefully: "Oh, I misunderstood you," or "I'm sorry. I didn't mean to interrupt."

 Common Questions About Using Affective Reflections

The mechanics of formulating an affective reflection are not difficult. However, when adults begin to practice them, they often have questions about real-life situations. We have identified the most common of these questions and have provided answers that should enhance your ability to use this skill more effectively.

1. Do children really correct inaccurate affective reflections? Expect that there will be times when your interpretation of a child's emotional state does not exactly match the child's perception. Initially, children may not know enough about their emotions to correct you. However, it is likely that there will be other times when your reflection is accurate. As children come to identify both the internal and situational cues that match the label you have applied, they will become more sensitive to your occasional inaccuracies.

Once this happens, most children will not hesitate to correct a mislabeled emotion. Correcting inaccurate reflections will come more easily to children once they become more familiar with your use of reflective responses and recognize that all reflections are tentative statements. You reiterate this point when you say "You seem pleased" or "You look sad" rather than "You must be pleased" or "I know you are sad."

2. How do I introduce feeling words that I'm not sure children already know? One way to help children understand new feeling words is to use your body, face, and voice to illustrate the affective state to which you are referring. For example, if Annice seems to be frustrated, say, "You look very frustrated," and accompany the words with a serious tone, a frown, and a shrug of the shoulders. A second approach is to tell Annice what it is about her behavior that leads you to believe she is frustrated: "You seem frustrated. Your body is very tense and you are frowning." Another effective strategy is to use the unfamiliar word in a short reflection and then follow it with a second sentence defining the word you have used: "You seem frustrated. It can be discouraging to work and work and still the pieces don't fit," or "You're disappointed. You wish we didn't have to stay inside because of the rain."

3. Why use an affective reflection, rather than just asking children about their feelings? At times it may seem easier to simply inquire: "How are you feeling" or "Are you feeling sad?" or "Why are you so angry?" Children sometimes answer well-meaning questions like these, but many times they do not. When you are involved in emotional situations, remember that children are not always sure what they are feeling or why.

Also, they may not be ready to give you the answer you are seeking. In either case, children's discomfort may be increased by a direct inquiry. It is more supportive to first let children know that you are simply trying to recognize their emotional state. This is best

continued

SKILLS FOR SUPPORTING CHILDREN'S EMOTIONAL DEVELOPMENT—continued

communicated through an affective reflection, to which the child does not have to respond, and which is correctable.

Children are more likely to answer questions after you have reflected first. Thus, it is appropriate to say: "You look sad. What happened?" In this situation, the child has the option of accepting your help or not. Regardless of what the child does, he or she knows you are available.

4. What if, after I reflect, the child still doesn't talk to me? Children do not always answer your reflection. For instance, you might reflect: "That looks like fun. You seem excited." The child makes no response. At times like these, remember that the purpose of any reflection is to indicate your interest in children without intruding on them. Once children understand this purpose, they frequently say nothing. Thus, lack of response may indicate that you are using the skill well. If your reflection is accurate, there is no need for youngsters to confirm your interpretation. It is not likely that you will hear: "You noticed that I'm excited. Yes, I'm having a wonderful time!" or "You're right."

Children often do not talk because they are absorbed in what they are experiencing and prefer to focus on that, rather than on you. Yet, even in circumstances such as these, they have the opportunity to hear their feelings defined and to know that you are interested in what is happening to them. Both of these factors have a positive influence on children's emotional development. When children obviously are distressed but do not want to talk, it can be effective to say: "You seem pretty angry. It looks like you don't want to talk about it right now. I'll be around if you want to talk later," or "I'll check back with you to see if you change your mind."

5. What if I cannot tell what the child is feeling? Emotions that are not extreme sometimes are difficult to interpret. Additionally, some children are less expressive than others. Both circumstances may interfere with your ability to immediately recognize what a child is feeling. As you get to know individual children, you will become more adept at identifying the behaviors they use when they are experiencing certain emotions. Iris flexes her fingers rapidly when she is nervous; Phil makes long pauses between his words when confused; Justin becomes belligerent when frightened.

If you do not know the child well, or there are no outward signs to guide you, use a behavior or paraphrase reflection as an opening to the interaction. Wait, and then use an affective reflection after you have considered, via words and gestures, what the child may be feeling. If no such opportunity arises, ask children directly; they may or may not be willing or able to tell you. If none of these strategies have worked, continue to observe and remain supportive, but do not force children to pursue a conversation.

 Promoting Children's Understanding and Communication About Emotions

1. Use stories, books, and songs to prompt discussions about emotions. Read a book such as Judith Viorst's *Alexander and the Terrible, Horrible, No Good, Very Bad Day* (Macmillan, 1987) or *Blizzard of the Blue Moon* by Mary Pope Osborne (Random House Books for Young Readers, 2006). Point out emotions experienced by characters in the story. Ask children to identify emotions they observe or to explain the source of a character's emotions or to predict how a character might feel in a certain situation. Any kind of story can serve as a prompt for this type of discussion, ("Goldilocks was pretty frightened," or "Laura Ingalls felt excited about going to town with her pa"). Refer to the Web site for this textbook for an initial list of relevant books for children of different ages. Make sure to address both positive and negative emotions.

SKILLS FOR SUPPORTING CHILDREN'S EMOTIONAL DEVELOPMENT

Songs can provide similar resources for expanding children's understandings and vocabulary. Consider the following adaptation of the song "If You're Happy and You Know It," as an example.

If You're Happy and You Know It

*If you're happy and you know it say, I'm glad.
I'm glad.
If you're happy and you know it say, I'm glad.
I'm glad.
If you're happy and you know it then your words
will surely show it,
If you're happy and you know it say, I'm glad.
I'm glad.*

*If you're angry and you know it say, I'm mad.
I'm mad.
If you're angry and you know it say, I'm mad.
I'm mad.
If you're angry and you know it, then your words
will surely show it,
If you're angry and you know it say, I'm mad.
I'm mad.*

2. Set an example for talking about emotions by bringing them up yourself. Include emotions in your casual conversations. Talk about how everyday events affect you ("What a great day. I'm so happy to see the sun out," or "I hate it when this plumbing keeps backing up"). Discuss events in terms of how they will affect people's feelings ("It sounds like if we don't have macaroni for lunch, everyone will be disappointed," or "If we were to leave without telling Ms. Jones, she might be worried"). Ask children how they might feel about particular events as they arise ("Oh, it's raining. Who here likes rain? Who here doesn't like rain?"). Discuss emotions experienced by people children know or people they have heard about in the news ("Mr. Sanchez, our principal, feels really good today. He became a grandfather," or "It was scary for the people along Spring Creek when the flood came").

3. Help children recognize opportunities to describe their emotions to others. Children often mistakenly believe that what they are feeling is obvious to everyone around them. Explain this is not always true ("You're disappointed that Melinda didn't help you like she'd promised. She doesn't know that's how you are feeling. Tell her so she'll know," or "You didn't want Claudia to take the hammer just yet. She didn't know. Say that to her").

4. Provide children with sample scripts to help them talk about their emotions. Sometimes, children fail to express their emotions verbally because they lack the words or they are too emotionally involved to think of them. If this happens, do one of the following:

a. **Suggest words to the child that fit the situation.** In other words, offer a verbal script (Kathy could be advised to say: "Claudia, I wasn't finished with the hammer," or "Claudia, I don't like it when you grab"). Younger or less experienced children benefit from brief phrases. Older or more experienced youngsters are better able to consider longer sentences and more than one potential script. Once children become more comfortable and adept at using the scripts you provide, help them think of some of their own ("You're upset with Claudia. Tell me words you could use to let her know that").

b. **Ask children questions that prompt them to describe how they feel.** Begin with simple yes-and-no questions ("Marco took your pliers. Did you like it when he did that?") Over time, advance to more open-ended inquiries ("Marco took your pliers. How did that make you feel?").

5. Help children figure out how another person is feeling based on that person's actions. Children are not always aware of what other people are feeling, nor are they completely accurate in their interpretations. Point out specific signs of people's emotional expression to toddlers and less experienced preschoolers ("Pearl is crying. That means she is unhappy"). Prompt older, more experienced youngsters to notice these cues for themselves ("Look at Pearl. Tell

continued

me what she is doing and what she might be feeling"). If a relevant answer does not follow, provide the appropriate information yourself.

6. Draw children's attention to situational cues that contribute to people's emotions. Tell toddlers and preschoolers what features of a situation triggered an emotion ("Julie and Chris both wanted the last cupcake. They decided to split it. They're pretty happy. People feel good when they can work things out," or "Garland, you had been waiting a long time to use the easel, and now it's all drippy. You look disappointed about that"). Ask older children to tell you what it was about a situation that they thought prompted the emotional reaction. This strategy can be applied both to situations in which the child is an observer and to those in which the child is directly involved.

In addition, point out similarities and differences in children's reactions to the same event ("You both saw the same movie, and it sounds like each of you enjoyed it," or "You both saw the same movie. Emma, it sounds like you really thought it was funny. Janice, you're not so sure").

7. Help children sort out mixed emotions. Begin by listening to the child describe the situation. Acknowledge each of the emotions you hear or observe when multiple emotions are evident. Tell children that it is normal to have different feelings at the same time. Also, point out discrepancies between the child's words and what he or she might be expressing in nonverbal ways ("You're telling me everything is fine, but you look miserable").

8. Make deliberate efforts to talk with both boys and girls about their emotions. As mentioned earlier in this chapter, this is not something adults do automatically and there is a tendency to talk more with girls than with boys about emotions. Pay attention to your remarks during the day. If possible, keep a simple tally of the number of times you use emotion-talk with the males and the females in your group. Adjust your interaction patterns as necessary

to include everyone and to cover the full range of emotions children experience.

9. Learn more about the cultural variations in emotional expression represented by the children and families within your group. Do this by observing how children and adults in the family/culture express emotions. Read journal articles or books that describe cultural communication. A good resource is *Developing Cross-Cultural Competence: A Guide for Working with Young Children and Their Families*, written by Eleanor Lynch and Marci Hanson, published by Paul H. Brookes Publishing Company in 2004. Recognize that children will utilize different display rules depending on their age and what they have learned at home. Respect these differences. Avoid trying to make children react in uniform ways and do not ignore signs of affect that may differ from what you grew up learning.

 Helping Children Cope with Strong Emotions

1. Acknowledge children's strong emotions. Stop destructive behaviors. Begin with an affective reflection followed by a statement in which you make clear that hurtful actions are not allowed. Suggest or demonstrate a more appropriate strategy children could use to express their feelings. For instance, "You're really angry. I can't let you hit. Hitting hurts. Say, 'I don't like that,' " or, "You're excited. I'm worried you are choking the gerbil and it could stop breathing. Hold it gently like this." (More about this type of intervention will be presented in later chapters.)

2. Comfort children who are sad or afraid. Offer physical as well as verbal consolation.

3. Redefine events to help children manage strong emotions. Sometimes children react strongly because they have misinterpreted other people's actions or intents. New information, delivered on the spot, can help children reconsider or moderate intense responses. Point out

SKILLS FOR SUPPORTING CHILDREN'S EMOTIONAL DEVELOPMENT

facts about a situation children may have misjudged or overlooked: "You thought Andrew was making fun of you. He was laughing at a joke he just heard, not at you," or, "You thought Melba was pushing ahead in line. She's been waiting a long time and it's really her turn now."

4. **Anticipate new situations that may cause some children to feel insecure, prompting intense reactions.** Talk with children about new or potentially difficult circumstances and describe what to expect. Offer explanations for events as children experience them. "When you hear the fire alarm it will make a loud sound. Some of you said you didn't like it being so noisy. The bell is loud like that so no matter where we are in the building, we can hear it. That alarm tells us to leave. We will walk outside quickly and quietly all together. I'll be with you the whole time."

5. **Allow children to approach feared situations gradually.** Help children find ways to make the fear more manageable. For example, a child who is afraid of dogs could benefit from going through the following steps:

a. Looking at pictures of dogs
b. Watching a DVD about a dog
c. Playing with a plush toy dog
d. Observing other children playing with dogs
e. Observing a puppy being held in the lap of an adult
f. Touching a puppy being held by an adult
g. Holding a sleeping puppy on his or her lap

There is no one right way to carry out such a process. Be sensitive to the cues children exhibit and introduce a new, harder step only after a child has comfortably mastered the current one. Youngsters vary in how long the process takes and how elaborate it must be. Impatience only adds to children's anxiety and negates potential benefits.

6. **Teach children self-regulating strategies they can use to manage their emotions more effectively.** Do this directly through conversations, on-the-spot coaching, and demonstrations.

When you observe children using effective strategies independently, bring them to their attention, either at the time or later in the day. This reinforces children's developing skills and helps them to recognize successful strategies in relevant situations.

Sample strategies include:

a. **Restricting sensory input.** Covering their ears or eyes to blunt emotional arousal. Looking away. Distracting themselves with something else.
b. **Watching others manage in situations that prompt strong emotions in themselves.** Noting the coping strategies other children use in fearful or angry encounters.
c. **Talking to themselves:** "Mom will be back soon." "The water is fun." "I can do this." "Stop. Take a breath. Relax."
d. **Changing their goals.** Deciding to play something else after being told there's no room for them in a game or that it isn't their turn.
e. **Problem solving.** A child who is frightened about going to a new school draws a map showing the way from the main office to her room. A child who is easily angered plans to take three deep breaths before responding to peers who are teasing him.
f. **Redefining difficult situations in more optimistic terms:** "Things could be worse." "I'll get another chance tomorrow." "She isn't the only one who could be my friend." More strategies aimed at supporting children in stressful situations are described in Chapter 6.

7. **Give children many opportunities to experience joy, happiness, and humor.** All children need opportunities to have pleasant emotional experiences. Happiness is contagious and promotes children's sense of well-being.

Take time to laugh with children. Play games, tell jokes, and act silly, engage in spontaneous merriment. Joyful experiences like these build up children's resilience and help them to see that the emotional world is not entirely bleak. When children see joy in your face as you interact with them, they

continued

SKILLS FOR SUPPORTING CHILDREN'S EMOTIONAL DEVELOPMENT—continued

also get a message that they are enjoyable companions and that the difficult emotions they have experienced are not the only lens through which you see them.

 Communicating with Family Members About Emotions

1. Provide information to family members about the emotions children experience during their time with you. Focus on everyday affective happenings; do not wait for a crisis or for something extraordinary to prompt messages home from you ("Jamal built a city with all the blocks today. He was excited to have found a way to use every single block," or "Today, Ted was very absorbed in writing in his journal about his time in New Jersey. Later he read his entry to the group. The other children asked him a lot of questions about his trip. He seemed pleased with their interest"). Such information can be shared in person, through short written notes, or through periodic calls home. Make it a goal to communicate with every family in your group at least once a month in this regard. Keep an informal record of your communications to make sure you are not giving a lot of information to some families and very little to others.

2. Elicit information from family members about children's emotional lives at home. Stay attuned to changes in children's home lives. Day-to-day events such as a disrupted night's sleep, an anticipated trip to the store after school, or a friend coming over later in the afternoon prompt emotional reactions in children. Likewise, more dramatic happenings such as an impending divorce, mom being away on a trip, dad's girlfriend moving in, or an upcoming family event influence how children feel during their time with you. Let families know that this kind of communication enables you to respond with greater understanding to the children.

3. Help family members better understand typical facets of children's emotional development. Mr. Ramirez mentions that his seemingly happy 3-year-old became hysterical at the sight of a clown giving out balloons at the mall. He wonders what might have prompted such a strong reaction. During a parent conference, a mother remarks that her fourth-grade daughter is in a quandary about an upcoming dance recital. The parent says, "One minute she's excited; the next minute she's terrified. She seems so moody." Use what you have learned in this chapter to help parents recognize that such behaviors have their roots in child development. For instance, explain that it is normal for young children to become wary of masks and dramatic makeup during the preschool years. Likewise, having mixed emotions is a common circumstance during the elementary years and one that children often find confusing. Hearing that their child's behavior is developmentally based often gives family members welcome assurance. If the circumstances seem appropriate, convey to families some strategies you have learned to deal with emotional situations like these.

4. Pay attention to the emotions family members express. The grown-ups in children's lives experience many emotions. These may be communicated through words and nonverbally. Watch for these cues and use affective reflections as appropriate. ("You look excited today," or "You seem upset").

Follow up with a question. ("Would you like to talk about it?" or "Is there something I can do to help?") Wait for the person to respond. Do not try to push parents or other family members into talking further.

Respect their right of privacy. If a response is forthcoming, listen carefully and use the skills you have learned in Chapters 4 and 5 to convey interest, acceptance, and empathy.

5. Accept family member emotions, even when those emotions make you uncomfortable. There will be times when the emotions family members express are at odds with your own or with what you believe their reactions should be. For instance, when telling a mother

SKILLS FOR SUPPORTING CHILDREN'S EMOTIONAL DEVELOPMENT

about her son's excitement in using certain art materials, a kindergarten teacher was surprised that the mother reacted with irritation saying, "I don't want him wasting his time making pictures. I want him to concentrate on learning to read." A scout leader felt dismay when a parent announced with pride that his 10-year-old son had "thrashed a cousin good." An infant/toddler teacher became upset when a parent asked that the staff keep her 14-month-old child away from another toddler who experiences epileptic seizures. In cases such as these, your first task is to demonstrate understanding by paraphrasing or acknowledging directly the feelings expressed. ("You'd rather Hyuk Jun not paint," or "It sounds like Raymond really stood up for himself," or "You're worried about Jessie having too much contact with Ronda"). Acknowledging the parent's perspective in a matter-of-fact way requires you to put aside your own feelings for the moment and concentrate on the parent's point of view. This may be difficult, but it is crucial if family members are going to trust you and feel comfortable expressing themselves honestly in your presence. Information about how to follow up on your reflection and how to remain true to your values while demonstrating respect for family positions is presented in Chapter 15.

6. Put a check on defensive reactions when family members express anger aimed at you or the program. A parent angrily confronts you in the hall: "I told you to keep Jessie away from Ronda, but I just saw them playing together in the housekeeping area. Don't you people know how to listen?" You answer a furious telephone call from a grandmother: "This is the third time Teisha has come home with paint on her sleeves. She's ruining all her good clothes. I don't have money to keep buying new things. Why aren't you paying more attention to what happens in your program?"

When you receive family messages like these, you may feel attacked, and it is natural to feel defensive.

This defensiveness is sometimes translated into dismissing family concerns, immediate

rationales and justifications, or counteraccusations. After all, you only have the children's best interests at heart. How could parents judge your intentions so poorly? How could they be so narrow-minded in their thinking? How can they expect you to be responsible for everything?

When you begin to experience these kinds of reactions, take a moment to gather your thoughts and gain control of your response. Try to reinterpret the situation from the family's point of view—the feelings behind such accusations are often focused on protecting the child or furthering the child's opportunities. Considered in this light, the feelings are justified—a parent made a request, which she perceived as having been ignored; it does create a hardship when children come home with soiled or damaged clothing.

In these situations, it is best to acknowledge the family member's sense of anger or injustice, and then work to resolve the issue in ways that are mutually beneficial. Even when the source of familial anger is difficult to fathom or seems unreasonable, remember that family members are entitled to their emotions. Moreover, they cannot be expected to always express anger in ways that avoid hurting your feelings. On the other hand, as a professional it is expected that you will respond with respect and understanding despite the circumstances. This is a hard job, but it is part of the ethical code of conduct that separates professionals from laypersons.

The first step in any angry encounter is to move from an impulsive, quick reaction to a more measured one. If possible, take a moment to cool off before responding. Second, try to see things from the family's perspective. This is best accomplished if you treat the family member's remarks as a source of information about his or her point of view instead of as a cue to defend your behavior. Third, approach the problem by accepting the family members' rights to have their own feelings. Finally, move into a problem-solving mode, as described in Chapter 15.

PITFALLS TO AVOID

Regardless of whether you are responding to children's emotions individually or in groups, informally or in structured activities, there are certain pitfalls you should avoid. These pitfalls also apply to your communication with adults.

Sounding "all-knowing."

"You must be feeling sad."

"I know you're feeling sad."

"You're feeling sad, aren't you?"

All of these phrases make you sound all-knowing. They make it more difficult for children to correct a mistaken reflection. Because reflections are supposed to be tentative and correctable, phrases such as these should not be used.

Accusing children. Words like vicious, stubborn, uncooperative, nasty, greedy, manipulative, and belligerent are not feeling words, even when used in the form of an affective reflection. They are accusatory terms based on adult evaluations of child behavior rather than accurate interpretations of children's emotions, and should be avoided. For instance, a child who wants all of something may feel justified, wishful, or entitled, but certainly not greedy, which implies getting more than he or she deserves. Likewise, a youngster who remains fixed on doing something a certain way may feel determined, but would not identify his or her feelings as stubborn, meaning obstinate. If you find yourself employing such a word, stop. Observe what the child is really trying to communicate, and then restate your reflection nonjudgmentally.

Coercing children into talking about their emotions. In an effort to show concern, adults may probe into children's emotional states, ignoring signs that such inquiries are frustrating for the child or unwelcome. With preschoolers, repeated questions such as "Are you disappointed?" or "Why are you so upset?" may be beyond the child's ability to answer, creating pressure that children find stressful. Similarly, older children may find these probes intrusive, preferring to keep their reactions to themselves.

The best way to avoid such negative circumstances is to remain alert to actions by children indicating they are not ready to talk. Turning away, pulling back, vague answers, mumbled replies, increased agitation, and verbal statements such as "I don't know" or "Leave me alone" should be respected.

SUMMARY

Emotions are an important part of children's lives. Positive emotions, such as joy and affection, feel good. They encourage children to reach out and to be receptive to people and experiences. Negative emotions, such as fear and anger, feel bad, inducing children to avoid, escape from, or surmount difficulties. Emotions are universal. They are triggered by events to which the body responds. People interpret what they are experiencing and take action based on their interpretation.

Emotions develop in a predictable sequence and arise from such primary emotions as joy, anger, sadness, and fear. Clusters of related emotions and combinations of them emerge over time to form more complex emotional reactions. The events that prompt particular clusters of emotion are essentially similar over the life span. Cognitive maturity and experience affect an individual's interpretation of these stimulus events.

People are thought to work through a series of emotional tasks over the course of their lives. Optimal growth occurs when the balance is toward the positive of the opposite poles in each stage. The developmental stages during which children work through emotional tasks are known as trust versus mistrust, autonomy versus shame and doubt, initiative versus guilt, and industry versus inferiority. In addition, changes in how children think about their emotions as they mature influence their emotional development. The youngest children believe that only one emotion can be experienced at a time; 5- and 6-year-olds begin to recognize that two emotions can be experienced simultaneously (but about different things); and 10- to 12-year-olds begin to identify multiple reactions to the same event. Children's recognition of emotions in others follows a similar trend. However, even older children may not be accurate interpreters of others' emotions because similar behavior cues may represent different feelings, and the same stimulus may prompt varying responses among different people or within the same individual at different times. Adults are the most significant teachers of what emotions society values and appropriate emotional expression.

Children encounter difficulties dealing with their emotions. They often rely on others' recognition of their nonverbal cues, which may be overlooked or misinterpreted; they may choose inappropriate actions to show how they feel; and they may try to hide, minimize, or avoid their emotions.

Inappropriate adult responses such as ignoring, lying, denying children's emotions, or shaming children compound these problems. It is more supportive and helpful to talk to children about their emotions by using affective reflections. Affective reflections involve recognizing the emotions a child may be experiencing, then using a reflection to name them. Affective reflections make abstract, internal states more concrete. Verbally labeling emotions helps children recall past events, helps them to differentiate emotions that are similar but not identical, allows adults to demonstrate caring and understanding, and contributes to a positive verbal environment.

Other ways to help children cope with their emotions are to use strategies that prompt them to talk with others about emotions and deal with strong emotions, and to communicate with family members regarding the emotional aspects of children's lives.

KEY TERMS

affective reflections	imaginary fears	self-disclosure
emotional IQ	primary emotions	social referencing
expressive style	realistic fears	

DISCUSSION QUESTIONS

1. Discuss the role of emotions in children's lives. Give examples based on your own childhood, or on your observation of young children, as to how this process actually works.

2. Malcom is 3 years old and his brother, William, is 10. Discuss how each of them probably thinks about his own emotions and to what extent he is likely to be aware of his brother's emotional reactions.

3. Describe each of the emotional tasks of childhood and identify children's behaviors that would be characteristic of each stage. What implications do these tasks have for adult practices?

4. Describe the developmental and learned aspects of children's fears. Discuss these in relation to your own fearful childhood experiences or the experiences of children you know.

5. Describe at least three ways in which affective reflections benefit children's emotional development.

6. Discuss specific ways in which you could make your own affective reflections more effective.

7. In each of the following situations, describe:
   a. What emotions the children involved might be experiencing.
   b. How you would use the strategies presented in this chapter to help the children become more aware of their own feelings and the feelings of others, and how you would help them cope effectively with the situation.

   SITUATION A: Calvin and George are playing in the sandbox. Calvin wants George's pail, so he takes it. George begins to cry, but Calvin continues to play, unperturbed. George comes running to you, saying, "He took my pail!"

   SITUATION B: Sandy has been standing watching the others jump rope. It seems as if she'd like to join in, yet she makes no move to do so.

   SITUATION C: Curtis has a dilemma. He was just invited to a barbecue at Steven's house, but his best friend, Travis, has not been asked to come.

8. Describe typical problems children experience in dealing with their emotions. Identify corresponding strategies adults can employ to help youngsters cope more effectively.

9. Take five minutes to write down as many affective words and phrases as you can think of. Compare your list with one or two classmates' lists.

10. Read the following scenario. Refer to the NAEYC Code of Ethical Conduct presented in Appendix A. Find the sections of the code that provide insight into the ethics of the teacher's behavior in the following situation.

> SITUATION: When Mrs. Huong, a parent, tells the teacher she is worried about her son sucking his thumb, the teacher offers her an article about thumb-sucking to read. The teacher also refers her to another parent who had that same concern last year.

FIELD ASSIGNMENTS

1. Keep a record of all the affective reflections you use when working with children. When you have a chance, record at least four of your responses. Identify what the child was doing or what the child said and your response. Write at least two alternate reflections you could have said in that circumstance.

2. Describe one pitfall you have encountered using the skills presented in this chapter. Brainstorm ideas with classmates about how to deal with the problem in the future.

3. Describe a situation in which a child expressed his or her emotions. Discuss how you or another adult responded and the child's reaction. Critique the effectiveness of the adult's approach. If it was ineffective, what strategies might have been better?

4. Identify one family communication strategy you heard or observed related to children's emotions. Describe the circumstances in which it was used and the family member's reaction. Provide an assessment of the practitioner's effectiveness.

Chapter 6

SUPPORTING CHILDREN IN STRESSFUL SITUATIONS

OBJECTIVES

On completion of this chapter, you should be able to describe:

- The nature of stress.

- Sources of children's stress.

- Children's physical, psychological, and behavioral reactions to stress.

- Strategies for helping children cope more effectively when they are under stress.

- Strategies for communicating with families of highly stressed children.

- Pitfalls to avoid in dealing with stressed children.

David is entering fifth grade at Hambly Middle School. He's never experienced a school as large as Hambly and is worried about remembering his locker combination, finding all of his classrooms, and undressing in front of everyone for gym. Lately, he feels dizzy and shaky and wonders if everyone else knows how he's feeling inside.

Three-year-old Karen has begun following her mother closely and crying inconsolably whenever they are separated. She thinks about the violent fights her mother and father have had and knows that is why her father doesn't come home anymore. She wonders if her mother will go away, too.

Kevin, who is 6, has come to dread going to school and especially fears reading time. He has a hard time doing what his teacher wants him to do—he would do the work if he could, but he can't. He wonders how other kids can make sense of the letters and words in the reader. His stomachaches are becoming frequent.

Although David, Karen, and Kevin differ with respect to gender, age, family situation, and many other characteristics, they do have one thing in common: **childhood stress.** This involves any unusual demand—something new or different—that forces children to draw on energy reserves that exceed what they would normally require for dealing with ordinary events in their lives (Aldwin, 2007).

Not all stress is harmful. Sometimes it is exactly what is needed to push us toward responding successfully to a challenge. The same is true with children. Moderate levels of stress can function to motivate them toward more mature behavior or make them more appropriately wary of danger in certain situations. Childhood tensions range from normative stresses (someone making fun of them, not being chosen for a role in the school play, the birth of a sibling) to the natural fear responses that caution them not to tease the neighbor's dog.

Experts agree that growing up in today's world is getting tougher. As many as 25% of all children are at risk of academic failure because of physical, emotional, or social problems and less able to function well in the classroom because they are hungry, sick, troubled, or depressed. Children seem to have fewer sources of adult support than in the past, and many are being pressured to grow up faster.

Over the last 20 years, there has been a profound transformation in the way children look and act. There are soccer teams for 3-year-olds, a view among some that recess is wasted time, growing obesity, and fewer chances to play freely with friends in the neighborhood. Increasing numbers of parents are involved in "greedy" occupations that siphon off their time and energy. Some, unfortunately, come to view their children as an added burden or an obstacle to personal fulfillment. To others who divorce and rarely see their offspring, children can quickly become an economic liability. The outcome is increasing numbers of children being medicated for extreme behaviors, as well as greater numbers who are experiencing school failure, psychosomatic upsets, and emotional problems.

Why Be Concerned? There are two reasons to be concerned about childhood stress. First of all, we know more about both the short-term and long-term effects of stress. Evidence suggests that undischarged stress that is prolonged and/or especially intense leads ultimately to disease and can trigger both behavioral disorders and increased psychological vulnerability.

Secondly, it is believed that a child's stress-coping responses are learned early in life through watching how their parents, siblings, extended family members, teachers, and peers cope when under pressure. These behaviors then become ingrained through habitual practice.

When learned coping patterns are positive and useful, they become lifelong resources for a child; when negative, they serve only to increase the demand in a child's life, making the child more vulnerable to stress.

Thus, a preventive approach must be twofold: (1) eliminating or modifying undue stress early in children's lives and (2) teaching children positive stress-management techniques before they learn negative coping patterns—and before the effects of stress have begun to take their physical and psychological tolls.

THE NATURE OF STRESS

Perception of an event as a stressor is extremely important. It is only when individuals perceive that a demand is greater than their resources to handle it that they become "stressed" and experience feelings of being overwhelmed or out of control. Also, incidents that we come to associate mentally with particularly negative events can generate stress in the form of anxiety or fear. In these cases, individuals can become hyper-aroused and aggressive toward others, seemingly for "no reason." For example, if a child has been frequently abused, she may perceive another's quick movement toward her as threatening, when no threat is intended. Another child who has not experienced such abuse would probably perceive the event entirely differently. As a result, the event immediately produces quite different physical, psychological, and behavioral responses. The child who does not feel threatened simply assimilates the adult's movement into the general scheme of things; the child who feels threatened, however, is involuntarily moved to behave in some way, perhaps flinching, moving away, shuddering, or actually striking out.

Childhood is often looked on as a period of life that is less demanding, making it easy to forget that children can feel overwhelmed with accumulated stress. They are called on daily to make an extraordinary number of adaptations—at home, in the classroom or child care setting, and in the peer group. Unlike adults, children often must do so with severely limited resources and experience.

SOURCES OF CHILDREN'S STRESS

The Child's Own Personality in Generating Stress

Why some children march to the left while almost everyone else seems to be moving to the right is a question that puzzles many who interact on a regular basis with young children. These are children who do not appear to be comfortable in any program, no matter how wide the range of offerings. They have noticeable trouble getting along with their family members, peers, and people in general. As they grow older, they often continue to struggle with poorly developed social skills, difficult personal interactions, and low self-esteem. Whether such children are "just born that way" or whether their personalities develop as a result of poor socialization techniques on the part of the significant adults in their lives continues to receive considerable attention from researchers in the field of personality development.

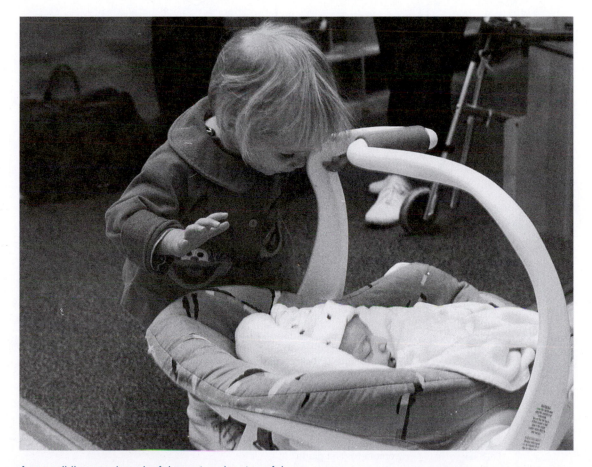

A new sibling can be a joyful event and a stressful one.

Family Stressors

Young children today are living in fairly complex ecosystems, as can be seen in the ecomap of Kelsey, the 7-year-old depicted in Figure 6-1. Family life can serve as a buffer for children or it can be a source of considerable stress for them. The ordinary aspects of family life may pile up to create demands for children that can range from mildly stressful to overwhelming. The birth of a sibling, the death of a pet, breaking a favorite toy, getting caught stealing or lying, carelessly spilling milk, losing a grandparent, or bringing home a bad report card—all can be either opportunities for growth or highly negative experiences, depending on the responses of significant adults.

Separation and divorce. The divorce of their parents is one of the most confusing and disturbing events most children will ever experience. Over 1 million children a year continue to go through this pain. Pre-divorce family stress can go on for long

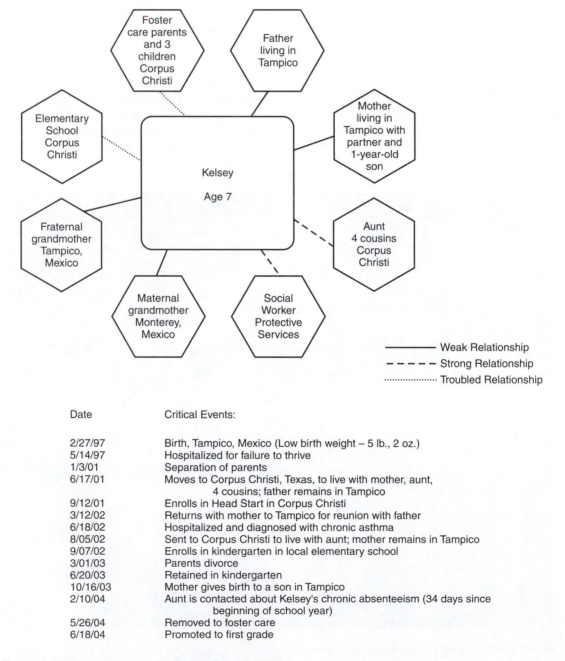

Date	Critical Events:
2/27/97	Birth, Tampico, Mexico (Low birth weight – 5 lb., 2 oz.)
5/14/97	Hospitalized for failure to thrive
1/3/01	Separation of parents
6/17/01	Moves to Corpus Christi, Texas, to live with mother, aunt, 4 cousins; father remains in Tampico
9/12/01	Enrolls in Head Start in Corpus Christi
3/12/02	Returns with mother to Tampico for reunion with father
6/18/02	Hospitalized and diagnosed with chronic asthma
8/05/02	Sent to Corpus Christi to live with aunt; mother remains in Tampico
9/07/02	Enrolls in kindergarten in local elementary school
3/01/03	Parents divorce
6/20/03	Retained in kindergarten
10/16/03	Mother gives birth to a son in Tampico
2/10/04	Aunt is contacted about Kelsey's chronic absenteeism (34 days since beginning of school year)
5/26/04	Removed to foster care
6/18/04	Promoted to first grade

Figure 6-1 Ecomap of Kelsey, a 7-year-old, September 12, 2004.

periods before one or both adults finally make a decision to end the marriage. Accompanying these changes are all the problems associated with the breakdown, breakup, and restructuring of the relationships involved: loneliness; poor coping skills on the part of the adults; fractured ties with siblings, peers, neighbors, schools, churches, and extended family members; and greater complexity in the maintenance of significant relationships.

Two myths seem to persist about children's views of their parents' divorce. The first is that they are probably just as relieved to see the end of a bad marriage as are their parents; the second is that so many of their friends' parents are divorcing that the trauma probably has been reduced considerably. Neither of these ideas is true. Young children are unable to intellectualize divorce. Their focus tends to be on their own families, not on the record high numbers of families "out there" whose foundations are crumbling. Although seeing their parents argue is tremendously stressful for children, being separated from a parent ranks even higher as a stressor, particularly before the age of 5 (see Figure 6-2).

Because attachments at early ages often are intense, fear of abandonment may cause a child to

Figure 6-2 "I don't want my mom and dad to get divorced."
Drawn by a third grader.

cling to the remaining parent. The child may throw an unexpected tantrum about going to school or to the child care center and may begin tagging after the custodial parent, not wanting to allow him or her out of sight (see Figure 6-3).

Much of this tension in children is caused by uncertainty about what the separation or divorce means with respect to their own security. Will they get up in the morning and find the other parent gone, too? Does the separation mean that they will have to move

Figure 6-3 "I have bad dreams about my parents leaving me."
Contributed by a third grader in a school program
for children with divorced parents.

to another neighborhood or go to a different school? Will the parent who left come back and take the dog? Did the parent leave because she or he is mad at the child? Parents add to children's stress when they fail to sit down with their children and explain, in an age-appropriate way, the changes that are in store for the family because of the change in the spousal relationship.

Because children's thinking at early stages tends to be egocentric and "magical" in nature, children younger than 6 years of age tend to feel somewhat guilty about certain events that happen in family life. Some children believe they may have caused their parents' separation or divorce by something *they* did—because of naughty behavior or wishing a parent away for one reason or another.

Children's problems are intensified when parents are unable to successfully restructure family life following divorce. Parents may continue to hurl insults at each other when possible, using their children as an audience. Children may be used as hostages to obtain child-support payments, as spies to find out what the ex-spouse is doing, or as messengers to carry information back and forth. Young children can become confused when they are forced to adjust to the different lifestyles or parenting approaches they encounter when moving between two households. Additional pressure is felt by both the parent and child who may want visitations to go perfectly. Neither may feel comfortable about "just hanging around" with each other, as ordinarily happens in intact families. A feeling often exists that, in order to maintain the relationship, the time spent must be "high quality" because there now is so little of it.

Tension also can be created by what "can't be talked about." Children wrestle with the dilemma of feeling disloyal to one parent if they appear loyal to the other. When a parent is openly hostile about the other parent, discusses the "sins" of that parent with the child in an attempt to vent some of his or her own feelings, or asks the child to keep certain information from the other parent, additional stress is induced as the child is forced unfairly to deal with the worry and guilt of handling adult-size problems (Soderman, 2003).

Even more stressful for some children, however, is the lack of opportunity to see the noncustodial parent or related grandparents because of continued hostility on the part of the custodial parent or severed affection by noncustodial family members. Adults who terminate relationships in an attempt to reduce their own pain can seriously add to a child's loss of self-esteem and loss of support networks.

Frequently, the transition time needed for most families to equilibrate following divorce is at least two years. During this period and afterwards, we know that it is not the event of the divorce itself that harms a child, but rather the continued conflict between parents that results in childhood problems such as anger, depression, and poor grades. When parents can learn to set aside their own conflicts, increase their awareness about how divorce can affect their children, and restructure their family relationships in a new and healthy way, the future for their children has been proven to be happier and more secure.

Almost all children, however, even those whose parents handle the transition well, manifest some signs of **psychological disequilibrium.** For this reason, divorce has been targeted as the single largest cause of childhood depression.

Stress caused as a function of the dissolution of the family is confounded by the tendency of large numbers of households to drop into poverty because the income once shared by all is not available to the custodial parent.

Low-income families.   One of the greatest sources of stress for children is the lack of family income. According to the National Center for Children in Poverty (NCCP), the more income a family has, the better. Everyday poverty significantly compromises the well-being of children, and we have good evidence that children in economically disadvantaged families are less able to function well, academically, socially, and physically. Despite this, almost 12 million children in the U.S. (16%) live in poverty, and another 5 million (7%) live in extreme poverty (Luthar & Sexton, 2007). As many as 100,000 of these children are homeless. It is estimated that if all were gathered in one city, they would represent a larger population of Atlanta or Denver. However, because they are "scattered over a thousand cities, they are easily unseen."

They live in families that are typically plagued with higher levels of substance abuse, domestic abuse, and mental health problems. Not surprisingly, poor children are more inclined to have developmental delays and behavioral and disciplinary problems than other children. They experience malnutrition, health problems, and below average school performance. Many need psychiatric help (Kozol, 2006, p. 3).

Children in mother-only families are among the most impoverished demographic group in the nation, with approximately 60% of children in these families falling below the poverty line as compared with only

11% in two-parent families (Kirby, 2004). The stress a child encounters while living in a single-parent family clearly has less to do with the marital status of the parent than with the resources available to the family. Of the children who are living with single parents, some will suffer little stress. They are the children of parents who have the necessary resources to cope effectively with single parenthood—positive self esteem, financial security, a supportive network of family and friends, parenting skills, and, in many cases, a workable relationship with their ex-spouse.

As would be expected, child health, emotional, and cognitive outcomes are deeply embedded in social and economic factors, such as family income and structure, parental employment and education, child care, and housing (Fass & Cauthen, 2006). Children engulfed in poverty are exposed to a variety of adversities: poor health and dental care, high mobility rates that negatively affect school performance, and a lack of material resources in a consumer-conscious world that causes them to become ashamed of how they are dressed and the way they live. Their parents are less likely to advocate for them, may suffer more frequent crises than middle-class families, and may experience poorer mental health (Shipler, 2005). There is little doubt that families in poverty are struggling to do the best they can for their children. Sometimes, however, their best will not be enough.

Blended families. Today of marriages ending in divorce, the average marriage in the United States lasts only seven years. Because 75% remarry, 1,300 new **blended families** are formed every day. Multiple problems that predictably beset blended families include those connected with weakened sexual taboos, biological ties that predate the new spousal ties, different life histories, matters of loyalty and affection, and difficulty in deciphering roles. Also, the competition between natural parents and stepparents and between stepsiblings can be problematic.

These families often do not have the luxury of time to develop attachments between nonbiological parents and children. Occasionally, children can be blunt about seeing the stepparent as an intruder. Stepparents, on the other hand, often view stepchildren in much the same way—as driving a wedge into the marital relationship.

Major stressors that children encounter in a stepfamily situation have to do with feelings of insecurity and jealousy that crop up between them and other members of the newly formed family. The child who has formed an overly close relationship with a single parent may resent having to share that parent with a stepparent and/or stepsibling. He or she may view the stepparent as having contributed to the breakup of the parents' marriage (which may or may not be the case). A child may constantly compare the stepparent with the biological parent who has been "lost" through death or divorce. Often, this parent is idealized to such a degree that only time and a reorganized perspective on the child's part can allow the child to accept anyone else.

Children may feel that their identity in a family is gone. For example, the oldest child may no longer be the oldest or the youngest child no longer the youngest. An "only child" may instantly have two or three siblings with whom he or she must now share the parent's attention. Resentment over a stepparent's efforts to discipline a child can be fierce, both by the child and the biological parent.

Stepparents can add pressure to the situation when their expectations of a stepchild are unrealistic or incompatible with previous expectations. Sometimes, expectations are based on experience with their own children's personalities and abilities; a stepchild's inability to be responsive may be viewed as insubordinate and uncooperative behavior when the child simply is at a loss about what the stepparent wants.

Barriers to open communication about natural parents can be highly damaging. For example, Roy, who had just returned from seeing his natural mother, innocently began telling his stepmother about the garage sale his mother was planning. He was startled at the fury in his stepmother's voice as she told him: "I'm sick and tired of hearing about your mother's financial problems. She probably told you that she has to have a garage sale in order to eat this week, didn't she? We don't want to hear anything about what she's doing. Just keep it to yourself!"

Educators frequently assume that a parent's remarriage is more beneficial to children than living in a single-parent home. It is thought that the potentials of shared child-rearing, additional income, and the provision of a gender role model that is missing can bring greater stability into a child's life. However, it should be recognized that remarriage also brings with it a myriad of ongoing adjustments for children and may contribute to the stress, anxious behavior, and unhappiness frequently seen in children with divorced parents.

Death as a stressor. Generally, teachers of young children do a good job of helping children develop healthy understandings about day-to-day events. However, many of these same professionals feel uncertain about how to comfort children who have experienced the loss of a beloved grandparent, parent, or pet. There are religious constraints on professionals as well, as the various beliefs of each family must be considered when answering children's spontaneous questions about death.

Before age 2, children understand very little about death. Beginning at about 3 years of age, however, there are three overlapping developmental stages through which children proceed before achieving a realistic view of death (see Table 6-1).

Because children's experience with loss is so limited, they may feel that their overwhelming feelings of sadness and the urge to cry will never end. Other intense feelings may include guilt, anger, and resentment, and children who realize that their visible hurt may be causing discomfort in adults may tend to hide their feelings. Children in these situations need caring and responsible adults who can help them understand that unhappy times have endings as well as beginnings.

Working parents. Whether children live in intact families, single-parent families, or blended families, an additional stressor today is the trend toward greater involvement in the workforce by parents. Today, 62% of mothers with young children are employed outside the home, most of them

Table 6-1 Stages in Children's Understanding of Death.

STAGE	CHARACTERISTIC THINKING	BEHAVIOR
Stage 1 3–6 years of age	Death is temporary and reversible, not final. People who are dead can become alive again. People who are dead still eat, sleep, and walk around. Death is like sleep or going away on a trip.	May not react immediately and may delay grief, with full understanding coming even years later. May appear to be through mourning before they actually are. There may be little crying, and the child may seem almost untouched. Children in this age group cannot yet grasp the permanence and extent of loss. They demonstrate great curiosity about the details, such as the funeral and coffin. They focus on what happens now instead of what led to the death and how it could have been prevented.
Stage 2 4–10 years of age	Realization that death is final and irrevocable. Do not recognize own mortality. Believe life is given and taken away by external forces and agents, such as fires, guns, cars. Death can be eluded if one is clever and careful. Continued confusion about what death truly means, despite more concrete understanding of the event.	May personify death in form of bogeyman, ghost, or angel of death. Children play games in which killing plays a role (ex. cops/robbers; soldiers/enemy; good guy/bad guy). May have nightmares in which death is confronted in some form.
Stage 3 9 years of age and older	See death realistically as personal, universal, inevitable and final. Understand all living things must die, including themselves. Realize that internal forces (old age, heart attacks, sickness) are also responsible for death in addition to external forces.	May become intrigued with meaning of life and develop philosophical views about life and death. Need greater support in event of death of a loved one since they understand irrevocable nature of death. Children in this age group are at greater risk for developing depression and other psychological impairment. Grief may be intense with unexpected death (Kastenbaum, 2004).

Children in the later elementary years develop philosophical views of life and death.

returning to work before their child is three months of age. Since this is a time when children's dependency needs are the highest, there is great potential for stress on both the working parent and the child.

Demands are growing for early childhood professionals, parents, and business and community leaders to work together to be responsive to the needs of children with working parents. Frantic juggling of family and work responsibilities often leaves parents feeling exhausted, anxious, and guilty.

Four-year-old Cameron and his 19-month-old sister, Amy, probably are not articulate enough to express their feelings about the quality-versus-quantity issue. They have become somewhat accustomed to the rushed exits in the morning and the noise and confusion in the child care setting where, from infancy, they have spent their days separated for long periods from their parents and from each other. They endure, sometimes not very graciously, the equally rushed times when they are picked up at 6:00 P.M. to make the trip home, often with stops at the supermarket, drugstore, and cleaners.

By 8:00 P.M., both children are in bed. Cameron and Amy's parents are genuinely concerned about the quality issue; in fact, it causes them a great deal

of stress. Their commitment to quality time with children, however, constantly is usurped. High-quality parenting competes with the needs for day-to-day living tasks such as taking care of the laundry, the report that has to be ready for a client the next day, a Tuesday night meeting at their church, a retirement dinner for someone at work, a flooded basement, and cleaning the bathroom.

Next door to Cameron and Amy, another family wrestles with the dilemma of fitting family life into demanding work schedules. They have decided this year that, rather than contending with the hassle of finding someone to come in before and after school, they will experiment with leaving 6-year-old Sammy by himself until they arrive home at 5:30 P.M. Sammy has found that he becomes afraid only occasionally in the morning after his parents leave and before he leaves for school; however, he has come to really dread the after-school period. Rather than tell his parents about his fears, he has begun a ritual of turning on all the lights and the television set as soon as he arrives home. He fantasizes about what he would do if a "burglar got in" and how he could escape.

There are at least 7 million children like Sammy in this country caring for themselves before and after school (Hymowitz, 2006). We now have some reliable evidence that self-care poses developmental risks for children, particularly those from low-income families. Studies of later primary children who have spent grades 1 to 3 largely unsupervised before or after school indicate that children in self care are less socially competent and obtain lower grades and achievement test scores than their classmates who are not in early self-care. However, some of the potentially negative impacts can be ameliorated (Riley & Sternberg, 2004). In many communities, efforts are expanding rapidly to offer all-day kindergartens and before- and after-school care for these children. Well-designed programs are tailored to the needs of the children and youth they serve, providing children with a comfortable environment and opportunities to move about and choose from a variety of games and activities. They have a safe place to learn new skills, interact with friends, read, do their homework, or just relax.

Where such resources are unavailable, or for children who prefer to go home after school, community and school professionals are providing information to children about self-help and safety procedures in case of emergency, hoping that such dialogue will minimize some of the strain children are feeling.

Children in abusive or neglectful families. The personal transitions that many adults face today, when coupled with the strains of parenting, can have devastating effects on children. Garbarino and Gilliam (1997) describe the case of an abusive or neglectful family.

> *Joan Higgins is a 23-year-old mother of three children, ages 5, 3, and 1. Her life is a bleak procession of work and children, which she must face alone. She no longer lives with the children's father. She has few friends and none who are doing much better than she is coping with day-to-day life. Her money goes for rent, cigarettes, beer, and whatever food she buys for her family. Each of her children show signs of neglect. Often unattended, they have the dull eyes of children whose emotional and physical diet is inadequate. They do not see a doctor regularly and have little contact with anyone outside the family. Joan often feels like giving up, and she sometimes does. On one such occasion, a neighbor called the police when the three children were left alone overnight with no food in the house. Much of the time, she is lonely and apathetic. Sometimes she is angry. This is nothing new. Her life has been this way as long as she can remember.*

In the United States, an estimated 3–10 million children are exposed regularly to **domestic violence**.

It happens in every segment of the population, and the children involved are at risk for short-term and long-term well-being, safety, and stability (Hamel & Nicholls, 2006). It is not something that children talk freely about to others because they feel ashamed, afraid, and feel uniquely alone. Living in an atmosphere of constant terror and tension, their home life is characterized by verbal abuse, insults, threats, rejection, humiliation, and disrespect. The physical aggression and beatings, which frequently result in psychological and behavioral problems, are the most frightening. Probably most damaging, however, is their developing sense that this is what home is like, and violence is the way you solve problems (Bancroft & Silverman, 2004).

In **multiproblem families**, abuse and neglect are major sources of stress for children. There are often concurring endemic problems such as substance abuse, poverty, lack of social support, emotional problems, a parental history of being mistreated as a child, and inadequate education. These interrelated problems then set the climate for abuse or maltreatment of children, including excessive use of force, sexual abuse, emotional rejection, or inadequate provision of essential nurturance. The problem is so far-reaching, and the professional's role in dealing with it so critical, that much of Chapter 15 serves to highlight it.

Children in foster care. Although there are currently no reliable figures on the numbers of children in foster care services, it is estimated that as many as 500,000 children are currently moving in and out of foster care. Although the provisions of the Adoption and Safe Families Act of 1997 mandated shorter time frames for making permanency decisions and facilitating adoption for children in foster care, most continue to be in foster care for a significant portion of their life (Mapp & Steinberg, 2007, p. 29). Foster families are, by definition, temporary, and professionals must recognize that foster children continually experience loss: loss of family members again and again; loss of clothing, toys, and personal belongings; and loss of housing, neighborhoods, and schools. These are children who may have experienced physical abuse, sexual abuse, maltreatment, or have parents who are unable to provide even minimally adequate care. Many of these children exhibit problem behaviors that result from short- or long-term family disruption and histories of neglect or abuse: picking fights with other children, an inability to form friendships with other children, attention-getting and disruptive classroom behavior, sadness, academic failure, school phobia, and truancy. In addition to a marked lack of appropriate social skills, foster children are over-represented among those who require special services.

Unfortunately, foster children often do not stay in one place long enough to receive the help they need. Also, because many of them bounce from place to place, foster care workers may have limited ability to understand or evaluate the child's behavior problems.

Caregivers who hold reasonable expectations and focus heavily on teaching problem solving and building self-esteem will make the greatest strides with these children. Tasks the children are given to complete must be developmentally appropriate rather than age appropriate; that is, expectations must be closely matched with the abilities and the capabilities children have at that particular time. Professional caregivers can be a powerful force in the lives of many of these children by making sure they receive proper assessment to diagnose needs, as well as speedy referral and follow-up when necessary (Golding, 2004).

Involvement with the child's foster family as a goal-seeking partner is critical. There must be acknowledgment that simply being in a foster family is a dilemma for many children. Professionals must keep the child's family status in mind when making arrangements involving family projects. They must be sensitive in selecting classroom materials—for example, books that represent children who live with others who are not biological relatives. When we look at children who are resilient and become successful adults despite tough childhood experiences, the one thing they share in common is a significant adult. Often, that person is a teacher.

Extrafamilial Stressors

As children move outward from the relative security of their family into the family's social networks (the neighborhood, the child care center, and formal school systems), stressors naturally will increase. In addition to familial stressors, children will encounter additional demands in the form of rules, expectations, and interaction patterns that are significantly different from those in their own family.

Other persons with whom children must interact frequently may not accept them as readily as their family does, resulting in decreased self-esteem and confidence. Infants and toddlers may react even more strongly to differences between the management techniques in their own family and those of a child care provider by developing fear or anxiety. Subsequently, they may resist being dropped off by crying or clinging to a parent. In moving between family and extrafamilial settings, children must

Children in high-quality child care experience far less stress than children who have poor-quality care.

adapt to differences between home and societal values, peer cultures, and the continuous pressure of exchanging the relative security of the family microsystem for the less secure realm of the outside world. There is evidence that children are having to make these adjustments at earlier and earlier ages.

Child care. The point should be made at the beginning of this discussion that high-quality developmental child care need not be stressful for children. In fact, for children who come from chaotic families, such care can often provide the structure, comfort, and adult nurturance that may be missing in their lives. However, we have not yet developed a universal, consistently good system of child care in the United States. Poor-quality child care contributes enormously to child stress.

According to a comprehensive study by the National Institute of Child Health and Development (NICHD), fewer than 12% of child care programs for children ages 6, 15, and 24 months meet the standards for quality programs outlined by the American Public Health Association (APHA) and the American Academy of Pediatrics (AAP). The standards include the ratio of adults to children, group size, teacher training, and college education. Almost 20% of the programs for 6- and 15-month-old children failed to meet any of these standards. In addition, as few as 34% of programs for 3-year-olds met these standards (NICHD, 2005; Gurian, 2006).

When the quality of care is assessed, three components are critical:

1. Child care providers must have training in child development and early childhood education, with continuing training each year. Increasingly, the minimum standards for this training are being regulated by some states. National organizations such as the National Association for the Education of Young Children (NAEYC), Head Start, and APHA/AAP are issuing recommendations in this area.
2. There should be low child-to-adult ratios and small group sizes, such as those recommended by NAEYC, APHA, and AAP.
3. Programs that provide high-quality care focus comprehensively on the general well-being of growing children and their families by providing educational, nutritional, and health information. Staffed by trained professionals, they provide parenting instruction in child development and experiences for children that promote social and educational development. Learning resources are abundant: they provide a variety of books and toys in good conditions, meet nutritional requirements, and offer medical care.

The number of hours that children spend in child care varies dramatically by ethnicity and income, with white non-Hispanics averaging the fewest hours of care and black non-Hispanics the most. Children from the lowest and highest income levels receive a higher quality of care than do children coming from the middle-income or near-poverty range, presumably because the latter do not qualify for subsidized care (McCartney, 2000).

What must be examined further are the long-term effects on children who are receiving less than adequate care: infants who have their needs met by any number of adults rather than a primary caregiver. Included are those environments in which children are placed in front of television sets for most of the day or where children become addicted to constant stimulation and rushing, spending 10 to 14 hours a day in crowded, noisy, and punitive environments. Also needing further attention are the stressful effects of limited family interaction: siblings growing up separated from one another and children and parents consistently spending little focused time with one another on a daily basis.

Although the growing acknowledgment of the importance of quality early care for young children is gratifying, the United States must do a better job of taking care of its children. We continue to be the only highly developed country in the world without a national child care policy. Current welfare reform efforts to move adults into employment must be accompanied by national child care and health care policies that protect children against mass warehousing while their parents work. It will take tax dollars to subsidize the caring environments needed by all children; however, if our society chooses not to meet that responsibility, those dollars will be spent later to mend the social problems that result when children's basic needs are ignored.

Stress in the school setting. Every fall, at least 10% of children entering school are not ready for what awaits them. Once they begin their formal education, most will spend 6 hours per day, 180 days per year for 13 years in educational settings. This amounts to roughly 14,000 hours for the 71% who will finish school. Although a few children function poorly in school because of the stress they bring with them from home or because they have lower than average intelligence, many more simply are not ready developmentally for what is expected of them academically. Such youngsters experience high levels of stress because they lack the intellectual, physical, or emotional resources they need to perform the tasks required in the classroom. We cannot view this as a problem in the child. Instead, it is our responsibility to be responsive to the needs and differences of the children entering our classrooms. Although both boys and girls are affected, the problem appears to be far more serious for boys, who later in life are over-represented in resource rooms for nonreaders and the emotionally impaired.

Although we need to be as rigorous as possible in guiding children's skillbuilding, we also need to be cautious about rushing young children academically. Often, when children struggle or fail because their cognitive development is not advanced enough to allow them to meet these demands, we move to "remediation" with them. Because we experience success with some children who are on the advanced end of the normal cognitive continuum, we have come to believe that all children can achieve the same success if they can only learn to "crack the code." Instead, it is the children who have begun to "crack" under pressure.

Physical and intellectual growth is more uneven in the early years than later. There are wider differences among children in the preprimary and primary years than will be found as this group of children moves into secondary schools. As children enter formal learning settings, these early differences may become more problematic in the following circumstances:

1. *A child is significantly younger than the other children.* Although chronological age by itself is not a reliable indicator of a child's school readiness, probably 80% of children experience similar patterns of development within a span of two years. Because boys are likely to be anywhere from 6 to 18 months behind girls developmentally in the early years and have less mature eye development, they are more likely to experience problems when entering school too early. Parents from low-income populations are more likely than affluent parents to send younger children to school because they cannot afford an additional year of child care.

2. *A child has not made the intellectual shifts (brain maturation) to reach new levels of learning that are required for formal schooling.* This does not necessarily mean that a child will experience learning difficulties in the future. Educational contexts in which teachers are trained to observe and plan for a range of developmental levels are likely to be less stressful.

3. *A child is emotionally unready for the pressure of moving into a large-group situation with unfamiliar adults and children.* The child may be overly attached to a parent because of fewer experiences than normal with people outside the family. Also, a child may be experiencing unsettling family difficulties such as parental divorce or death. Any of these could temporarily undermine a child's emotional stability and security, causing stress.

4. *A child has some organic condition that will require special education for at least a period of time.* Many of these conditions, including learning disabilities and other problems, are not discovered until a child enters a formal learning environment.

5. *The early primary curriculum is developmentally inappropriate, so that only the brightest and most mature kindergartners achieve success.*

The great diversity among young children in terms of chronological, cultural, primary language, gender, and experiential differences mandates that early childhood educators must continue efforts to apply developmentally appropriate practices (DAP) in the classroom. This approach holds the most promise for alleviating the stress that results from the mismatch between inappropriate educational expectations and children's ability to learn (Kostelnik, Soderman, & Whiren, 2007; Soderman, 2008).

Although young children may experience stress in adapting to the demands of formal education, children entering middle school also experience their share of distress. They must move from the more protective environment of the elementary school to one that demands increased independence, responsibility, and competence on the child's part. When expectations by adults about what children should be able to do are inappropriate, stress will be increased for children who are not up to the task.

More simply, preadolescent children may have concerns about very basic needs such as locating classrooms and lockers. The child may harbor fears about the use of the rest rooms, being picked on by older students, keeping personal possessions safe, and undressing in front of others in physical education classes. Belonging to a group, making at least one close friend, and learning to interact comfortably with the opposite sex become tremendously important as well as a source of stress in this age group.

Children at this age benefit greatly from empathic parents and teachers who recognize the potential insecurities of venturing out further toward independence. Providing the child with specific information about new expectations, locations, rules, regulations, and schedules can help to reduce anxiety. Adults also can provide positive reassurance that transitions sometimes are hard but can be weathered pretty well, given some time and experience.

Health-Related Assaults

Coping with poor health and health care is a stressor for growing numbers of children in the United States. The physical environments in which many children grow up can be a significant health hazard, leading to chronic disease. Increasingly, poor air quality, toxic chemicals, and other contaminants pose special risks to young children because their organs and immune systems are still developing.

Asthma now affects 4.8 million children in the United States. The disease, which is caused by obstruction in the airways of the lungs, producing difficulty in breathing, is the leading cause of school absence. Prevalence, hospitalization rates, and mortality are all on the rise, with black children more likely than white children to be affected and four times more likely to die. Triggers can be prolonged physical activity and stressful events such as test taking. Professionals who work with children prone to asthma must be knowledgeable about causes and signals that an attack is coming or already underway by the characteristic patterns of coughing and labored breathing. They should also be knowledgeable about administration of antihistamines that are used to treat the condition (Bowe, 2007). In the National Cooperative Inner-City Asthma Study (NCICAS), children with asthma were especially at increased risk for psychological/social maladjustment and death when their caretakers had less effective parenting styles, lack of social support, and significant life stress (Halterman et al., 2007). Our growing understanding of the lifelong penalties to vulnerable children because of environmental contaminants has led to important legislation to structure protective measures and tougher regulations. To protect children, these regulations must be monitored and enforced.

Other **chronic illnesses** experienced by children include cancer, sickle cell disease, cystic fibrosis, diabetes, hemophilia, and juvenile rheumatoid arthritis. Each of these chronic conditions differs with respect to the daily hassles, stress, trauma, and demand placed on the affected child and family. Pain, hospitalization, lengthy doctor visits, treatment side effects, and limitations imposed by the medical condition are among the challenges that must be faced along with the other developmental tasks experienced by typical healthy children (Gartstein, Short, Vannatta, & Nolt, 1999).

One of the greatest health threats to children today is a lack of exercise and inadequate nutrition. Childhood obesity, which has been linked to poor cardiovascular health (hypertension and increased cholesterol) and endocrine abnormalities (particularly type II diabetes and impaired mental health) now affects over 10% of children aged 2 to 5 and 15% of children 6 to 11 years of age (Gershoff, 2003).

Far more serious are the results of **vulnerable child syndrome** (VCS) that we continue to see from maternal substance use and abuse during pregnancy, including all the problems related to low birth weight, infections, pneumonia, congenital malformations, and drug **withdrawal** (Drotar et al., 2006). Fetal alcohol syndrome (FAS) is now the nation's leading known cause of mental retardation in children. The most severe cases leave children coping with physical malformations such as distinctive facial anomalies, short stature, and microcephaly.

Although facial characteristics associated with FAS become less distinctive as children approach adolescence and young adulthood, effects related to intellectual, academic, and adaptive functioning do not disappear. These include IQ scores of about 68, with only 6% of the children later able to function in regular classrooms without supplemental help. Average reading, spelling, and arithmetic grade levels average no higher than fourth grade, with arithmetic deficits most problematic. Socialization and communication skills and capabilities are notably deficient. Childhood stressors can arise from the child's failure to consider consequences of action, lack of appropriate initiative, unresponsiveness to subtle social cues, and lack of reciprocal friendships (Streissguth, 1997).

Because of a marked increase in cocaine and crack use among child-bearing adults, greater numbers of children are exposed in the prenatal period of their lives. However, initial concerns that arose in the 1990s about numbers of "crack babies" that were about to flood society and the problems that would bring to educators and care providers were somewhat overblown. Still, exposed children have been observed by professionals as being in constant motion, disorganized, impulsive and explosive, overly sensitive to stimuli, and generally less responsive to their environment. They have marked difficulty with transitions and are more inclined to test limits. Some refuse to comply and are less able to self-regulate their behavior. They have trouble making friends because smiling at others and eye contact are noticeably absent.

More seriously confounding the child's development are the interactional effects of the social environments in which these children are reared. Continued postnatal drug exposure may include passive inhalation, direct ingestion that is intentional or unintentional, or through breast feeding, resulting in a variety of neurobiological effects. Most problematic are the added problems related to parents' potential for continued addiction, leading to preoccupation with supporting their drug habits at the expense of the child's safety, home environment, nutrition, and intellectual and sensory stimulation (Bowe, 2007).

DeRamus (2000) tells the story of Eddie and Rita, two crack-addicted parents from southeast Michigan who found the strength to walk away from their crack habit—but not before they had returned their children's Christmas gifts for drug money:

> *Eddie and Rita now get up every morning and go to work. But some wounds remain as raw and painful as the cries of frightened children left alone while their parents hunted crack. The family's four daughters— Sharita, 11; Monet, 10; Talisha, 4; and Elise, 3—are now thriving at school instead of failing and falling apart. Yet the eldest girls have the eyes of children who have seen too much, eyes that will never forget the sight of their mother locking her bedroom door to smoke crack, or the looks on other children's faces as they yelled, "Your mama and daddy are crack heads!" Nor will the girls soon forget the shame of showing up at school with tangled hair and emotions, or the terror of being alone and frantically phoning relatives to come feed them and relieve their fear. (p. 118)*

The lucky few children who find their way early to supportive and nurturing families have a fairly good chance to develop positively. For those who are passed on from one foster care household to the next because of multiproblem social and academic development, however, the prognosis is far less satisfactory.

Rather than lamenting the source of the child's difficulties, it has been proven to be more useful to observe the child carefully to detect what triggers negative responses and what seems to work best to get that individual child focused and back on track. Direct instruction to teach behaviors that other children seem to pick up "naturally" is often necessary

and beneficial, as are specific tips and prompts for more socially rewarding behavior.

NATURAL DISASTERS, WAR, TERRORISM, AND VIOLENCE

As was seen with the numbers of families displaced by Hurricane Katrina, a young child's world can suddenly be turned upside down through natural disasters such as earthquakes, floods, fires, tornadoes, or hurricanes, causing loss of possessions, their home, or loved ones. Because children are thrown most out of balance when predictability and stability in their world is threatened, high levels of stress and anxiety caused by fear and ambiguity can result. Children's sense of place and well-being are replaced by profound feelings of disorientation and a need to get back into control.

Human-created social traumas, however, are much more frequent and increasingly affect more of our children. Some children live in communities that have been labeled war zones, where children become victims of or witness the use of weapons, rape, robbery, or assaults. These children have night terrors, become afraid to play outside, and come to believe early that life has little purpose and meaning or that they have no future. Anxiety, lack of impulse control, poor appetite, and poor concentration are characteristics of these children. School phobias and avoidance are also common.

Intervention can take place at several levels. In classrooms, professionals can be available to children who need to talk about worries or painful memories and to feel safe with a caring adult. Families can be helped to develop more appropriate coping strategies, and communities can be encouraged to upgrade services for children and families and to upgrade the quality of the neighborhood (Linares, 2004).

Even when children do not personally experience violent events, the stark reality of what such events can mean for young children is brought directly into their lives through television. They hear about situations such as the terrorist incident on September 11, 2001 that forever changed American lives and security and subsequent events in the Middle East and elsewhere. Children watch violent events displayed on TV, not understanding that they are replays being shown again and again. They hear adults discussing the shooting of a 6-year-old by another 6-year-old. Continually, they witness the gory details of the assassinations of political leaders, and the "scariness" of war in terms of extreme grief of family members, children made homeless, cold, hunger, disease, and the loss of limbs and eyes (see Figure 6-4). On milk cartons, they see pictures of children who have been abducted. They hear stories in the news about young children drowned by their own mothers and doctors who kill people.

It is commonly understood now that children spend more of their time involved with media than with school or their parents. Up to 80% of the primetime shows that they watch include beatings, shootings, and stabbings. *TV Guide* reports that during prime time, such incidents occur approximately every six minutes. Video games add another potentially unhealthy dose to the average child's daily intake of violence knowledge.

Child psychologists worry about a redefinition in children's minds about how we should treat others—that it is okay to "diss one another, push, shove, hit and kick" (Meriwether, 1996). In fact, the influence of this "normalization" of violence can be

Figure 6-4 Child's perception of war: "Dangerous, not funny, sometimes importan[t], always scary."

seen increasingly in the violence that young children, especially boys, bring to their play and in the kinds of toys they request. Later, it is again enacted in the growing rate of violent crime among American youths, now the highest in the industrialized world (Levin, 2004).

Table 6-2 depicts Levin's construction of a developmental framework for understanding the overall impact of this violence on younger children and how professionals can mediate the negative effects.

Other Assaults

Childhood historians believe we may be moving into a period in which children are less valued than in the past and distinctions between adulthood and childhood are becoming dangerously blurred. They remind us that in bygone centuries, adults held naive, even cruel, views regarding children and tended to ignore their needs. Others acknowledge the amount of stress, but see children as somehow immune from a fast-paced world that isolates them more and more from caring adults.

Garbarino (2005) goes as far as labeling these environments "socially toxic." There are numerous assaults on children today, including the kinds of food we are feeding them, the amount of television to which they are exposed, the usurping of play by adult-directed extracurricular activities, and the continuous and ominous early pushing that is taking place. Claims by commercial programs such as Baby Wow, Jumpstart, Baby Einstein, and Future Bright, which suggest their products can help children improve their discrimination, track patterns, and increase their attention span, simply have not been substantiated. Adults must serve as better gatekeepers, protecting the earliest developmental passages in

Table 6-2 A Developmental Framework for Understanding How to Counteract the Negative Effects of Violence.

HOW CHILDREN ARE AFFECTED BY VIOLENCE	HOW TO COUNTERACT THE NEGATIVE EFFECTS
• Sense of trust and safety is undermined as children see the world is dangerous and adults can't keep them safe.	• Create a secure, predictable environment, which teaches children how to keep themselves and others safe.
• Sense of self as a separate person who can have a positive, meaningful effect on the world without violence is undermined.	• Help children take responsibility, feel powerful, positively affect their world, and meet individual needs without fighting.
• Sense of mutual respect and interdependence is undermined—relying on others is a sign of vulnerability; violence is modeled as central in human interactions.	• Take advantage of many opportunities to participate in a caring community where people help and rely on each other and work out their problems in mutually agreeable ways.
• Increased need to construct an understanding of violent experiences in discussions, creative play, art, and storytelling.	• Provide wide-ranging opportunities to develop meanings of violence through art, stories, and play (with adult help as needed).
• Endangered ability to work through violence as mechanisms for doing so are undermined.	• Actively facilitate play, art, and language so children can safely and competently work through violent experiences.
• Overemphasis on violent content as the organizer of thoughts, feelings, and behavior.	• Provide deeply meaningful content that offers appealing alternatives to violence as organizers of experience.

Source: Adapted with permission from *Teaching Young Children in Violent Times* by Diane E. Levin © 2004 Educators for Social Responsibility, Cambridge, MA.

Sources of children's stress include:

- Child's own personality
- Intrafamilial stressors
  - Separation and divorce
  - Financial strain
  - Blended families
  - Working parents
  - Abuse/neglect
  - Foster care
- Extrafamilial stressors
  - Poor-quality child care
  - Cognitive/emotional pressure in school settings
  - Health-related assaults
  - National disasters, war, terrorism, and violence

Figure 6-5 Summary of sources of children's stress.

childhood. See Figure 6-5 for a summary of the sources of childhood stress.

CHILDREN'S REACTIONS TO STRESS

One in three children today suffers from chronic stress symptoms. In reality, growing up includes experiencing and learning to cope with the painful, complex emotions that define us as human beings. However, like adults who become overwhelmed when they are overloaded, understimulated, or faced with too much change, fear, or uncertainty, their responses to stress are highly individual. Personality characteristics, feelings of self-worth, learned coping skills, and the child's perception of how personally threatening any particular stressor is will affect each child's reaction when under pressure.

Physical Reactions

Highly stressed children often *look* stressed. When compared with more relaxed children, they frequently exhibit slumped posture or a noticeably rigid body carriage. The child may appear to be "charged up" (one or more body parts in constant motion) or peculiarly passive. Breathing is concentrated predominantly in the upper chest rather than in the lower abdomen. The voice may have an explosive or shrill quality, and speech may be accelerated. In children who have experienced prolonged or intense stress, the hair often is dull, and there may be dark

circles under the eyes (not usually seen in children). Frequency and/or urgency of urination may increase significantly, as do the numbers of somatic complaints such as headaches, stomachaches, and earaches. Appetite may increase or decrease dramatically, with accompanying gain or loss in weight. There may be vomiting, diarrhea, difficulty in swallowing, unexplained rashes on the face or other parts of the body, and frequent wheezing and/or coughing. The child may develop problems sleeping and be particularly susceptible to colds, flu, and other viral infections (Aldwin, 2007).

Psychological Reactions

When individuals are under prolonged or intense pressure, they are less able to concentrate or focus. There also is a marked inability to utilize information available in the environment. It becomes more difficult to make decisions. Those of us who have

Highly stressed children often look stressed and benefit from supportive adults.

ever found ourselves in a group setting in which we felt upset, inferior, or unprepared can understand this. We probably found ourselves unable to attend to the activity going on around us, or tremendously anxious and tense. Most likely, we had little to offer that was relevant to what was going on. Instead, we were directing all of our energy and thought only toward feeling less stressed. There is little reason to believe that young children feel any differently, although it often is difficult for them to articulate how they are feeling. Figure 6-6 summarizes children's reactions to stress.

How Children Cope with Stress

Coping with disturbing amounts of stress calls into play two different coping strategies: facing the stressor and adapting to it, or avoiding it. When the child feels he or she has the resources to assimilate or accommodate to the event, the stress that results is usually short lived. For example, having parents separate is obviously stressful; however, when parents work together to try to keep the child's life as stable as possible, are respectful and pleasant to each other, and focus on supportive parenting, the event loses its scariness. Similarly, if parents were always arguing and abusive toward one another, having an abusive parent leave may result in lessened stress. Though life is different, equilibrium and day-to-day normalcy return. Conversely, an inability to adapt usually involves the use of **defense mechanisms** such as repression, **denial,** displacement, **regression** to earlier behaviors, and these have been

observed in preschoolers. For example, a child may appear seemingly unaffected by something going on at home but may become more aggressive in the school setting. When asked about the behavior, the child may only report feeling "mad." Similarly, a child whose parents are divorcing may blatantly deny that to others, making up what sounds like a reasonable story about why one parent is no longer living in the home (Aldwin, 2007).

Young children may also use **withdrawal** or **impulsively act out** to protect themselves from stressful situations. In withdrawal, they take themselves physically or mentally out of the picture. They run from the stressful environment or become quiet and almost invisible. They concentrate their attention on pets and inanimate objects or lose themselves in daydreams to escape mentally when they cannot escape physically. Their efforts bring them respite from tension for the time being. Children may also act impulsively and often flamboyantly to avoid thinking either of the past or of the consequence of their current actions. They conceal their misery by making others angry with them. They seek quick and easy ways to stop their pain. In the process, they draw attention to themselves and find ways of momentarily easing their feelings of stress. However, in the long run, impulsive acting out (and the other coping strategies previously listed) is almost guaranteed to be self-destructive.

Children's more serious responses to stress. When the above strategies fail to reduce the psychological disequilibrium being experienced, a child may manifest other symptoms, such as panic, increased irritability, depression, agitation, dread, forgetfulness, distractibility, and sleep disturbances (including frequent nightmares). More serious symptoms of emotional distress may include children pulling out their hair, repeatedly inflicting pain on themselves or others (including animals), frequently annoying others to draw attention away from themselves, having severe temper tantrums, running away, defying authority often, stealing repeatedly, and expressing excessive or indiscriminate affection toward adults.

Children in even more severe trouble may express the feeling that they are no good, hear voices, or see things that are not there, often think people are trying to hurt them, have many unusual fears, or be preoccupied with death. They may refuse to respond when others talk to them and refuse to play with their peers. While it is normal for children

---

Children's Reactions to Stress

Physical
  Posture
  Breathing
  Speech
  Somatic complaints
  Appetite changes
  Sleep problems
  Susceptibility to illness

Psychological
  Attention deficits
  Inability to apply information
  Difficulty making decisions
  Anxiety and tension

Figure 6-6 Summary of children's reactions to stress.

to demonstrate a few of these characteristics during childhood, it is more likely that these signs may be symptomatic of typical growing pains or of the process of wrestling with a temporarily troublesome problem. However, multiple signals, lasting for a period of time and evident even when there is no apparent cause, may be a signal that undue stress is threatening the well-being of the child. In extreme cases, the well being of others may eventually be threatened as these children move toward adulthood. For example, Cho Seung Hui, the Virginia Tech student who went on a deadly shooting spree, had provided plenty of clues during childhood that he was unable to cope with growing anger and loneliness. Eventually, he built a wall around himself and his increasingly dangerous misperceptions of reality, rejecting any approach from others trying to befriend him.

Stress Coping: Developmental Aspects and Learned Behavior

The age of a child is extremely important in evaluating the child's ability to cope with stress. Frontal lobe development required for executive functioning shifts significantly around 18–20 months, allowing the child to orient more greatly toward the external environment and to anticipate events. It is not until then that children can begin to represent their world symbolically through the use of language. Continued brain development up to 30 months is accompanied by the older toddler's rapid development of control, emotional regulation, and ability to express his or her emotions. Preschoolers and elementary school children obviously have a more advanced range of resources for coping with problems. They are more aware of the social environment, are better able to balance their need for autonomy with the need for cooperation, and better understand what works better with some people or situations than others. Between the ages of 6 and 9, most children can verbalize and differentiate their feelings; they are also much more adept at calming themselves down in adverse situations (Aldwin, 2007).

Learned behavior is the other part of the stress-coping equation. People are not born with coping skills. Some of us were lucky enough to have had important adults around us—parents, teachers, or someone else we liked a lot—who modeled effective coping skills when they were under pressure. We watched what they did when things weren't going so well for them or when things were going

extremely well for them, and we sorted out those behaviors that seemed to yield the best payoffs in certain situations.

Some children rarely see effective coping strategies being used. They are reared in authoritarian settings in which power and striking out pays off, at least in the short run. Others spend their days in laissez-faire settings in which no one really cares what they do so long as they are not bothering someone, or in overprotective environments in which they become extremely vulnerable to peer pressures or to the exploitive behaviors of others.

Other children are reared in confusing environments in which parents and/or teachers react to them according to the adult's mood at that particular moment. If things are going well, the children are treated permissively; if things aren't so rosy, the atmosphere becomes more threatening. These children try to become good at "reading" the given moment.

One of the most critical elements in a child's ability to deal positively with strain and pressure is his or her self-concept. This develops in tandem with stress-coping abilities. The children who spend a great deal of their time with supportive and authoritative adults develop both high self-esteem and the best coping strategies because they become aware that the way their life goes has a great deal to do with some of the choices they make and that there are consequences attached to those choices. They also learn that some consequences are more unpleasant than others and that those caring adults are a little cooler toward them when reasonable expectations have not been met. They discover that outcomes are not necessarily always in their control, but tend to be generally more positive when they have observed the limits set for them by others. In addition, they learn to see other people as predictable and are able to see strengths and weaknesses in both themselves and others.

These "styles of coping" do not happen randomly. They are the cumulative results of children's continuous observation, reflection, action, and interaction with other important people in their lives—people who ultimately have tremendous influence on how each child will approach life's events.

We have become increasingly aware that not all children are traumatized in highly stressful situations, nor do effects become lifelong in some cases. Why some children have lasting scars and others are quite resilient has been the focus of longitudinal research by psychologist Emmy Werner and others who report that approximately two-thirds of the people they followed since 1955 were not able to overcome circumstances enough to be successful later in life; on the other hand, one-third were able to skirt the learning and behavior problems, delinquency, mental health problems, and early pregnancies found in the others. Protective factors may include the following (Monahon, 1997):

- easygoing response pattern to minor stresses
- biological endowment of an easy temperament that allows adaptability
- generally more satisfying experiences in school
- higher self-esteem and basic self-confidence
- perception that a person can have an impact on the course of his or her life
- tendency to master difficult situations with more ease
- connections and greater support outside the family

There is evidence that the number of risk factors (e.g., poverty, large families, absent fathers, drug infested neighborhoods) is an important factor in predicting whether there will be a "self-righting" of the individual or recovery in the long term. When there are eight or nine risk factors operating, nobody does well, according to Arnold Sameroff, a developmental psychologist .

What Adults Can Do to Help Children Manage Stress

For adults to be effective in helping stressed children, they need a combination of knowledge, appreciation, skill, and self-awareness (Brenner, 1997). They must build a strong knowledge base about the variety of demands children face, their typical ways of responding, and the effects of particular stressors on children and families. Helping professionals also need to become familiar with the legal issues related to any action they might take on behalf of a child and/or family and the kinds of resources that are available in the community.

Appreciation involves respecting children's viewpoints as well as their coping modalities, including any negative strategies they currently employ in lieu of something more positive. This is where empathy becomes important, enabling the adult to see the stressor through the child's eyes. Moreover, a holistic look at the stressor in terms of what other demands the child and family are facing is necessary in order to avoid simplistic "solutions." Skill in approaching children about the way they are responding to a stressor is of paramount importance in allowing both the adult and the child to progress toward stress reduction. This requires that adults respond to children in warm, nonthreatening, friendly, and helpful ways.

Caregivers must honestly examine their own biases and belief systems in regard to each kind of stressor and each kind of child and family. No matter how adept children become at coping with stress, it never is possible for them to be completely successful, to avoid all negative consequences, and to be able to take everything that comes. Children cannot cope with stress on a daily basis without help and support from at least one caring adult. For some children, a child care center or school may be the only place where they can find such help. Following are suggestions that may be useful in supporting children's development of positive stress management.

SKILLS FOR HELPING CHILDREN COPE WITH STRESS

 Developing General Stress-Reduction Skills

1. Be alert for early signs of excessive stress and observe children's coping skills. Watch for the withdrawn child as well as for the child who more openly displays negative feelings. Both may require tremendous patience on your part, since initial attempts to make them more comfortable may be met with resistance. The withdrawn child may become more in-

tensely avoidant; the angry, aggressive child may refuse, at first, to work at controlling hostile behavior. Giving in to or ignoring such behaviors, rather than guiding these children toward more productive coping, only reinforces their feelings of insecurity.

2. Use nonverbal attending skills. Focus on the child's feelings as much as on what the child is saying in situations in which children obviously are experiencing difficulty. Carefully observe changes in posture, expression, tone of

SKILLS FOR HELPING CHILDREN COPE WITH STRESS

voice, and other paralinguistic characteristics, as these communicate affect. Use your own body language to demonstrate interest and concern. Keep your own emotions and behavior under control.

Do not jump to conclusions or try for a "quick fix" when you do not fully understand the situation. Accept the fact that a child's stress can be very distressing for you as well as for the child. The child's greatest need, at first, is to know that someone understands and cares.

3. Use effective behavior and affective reflections. Let the child know that you are earnestly involved in helping and also in guiding him or her toward more effective coping. Use reflections to encourage adequate self-disclosure. Verbalize your perceptions of the situations to check for accuracy. Communicate clearly and directly, using the skills learned in Chapters 4 and 5. Do not tell the child that he or she will "outgrow" the problem or that the problem is essentially insignificant. If it is stressful for the child, the problem is important from his or her perspective.

4. Use children's artwork as a way to understand their perspectives about trauma-inducing events. In addition to their products providing caring adults a window into their thoughts and emotions about confusing and frightening events, children obtain a sense of organization, control, and mastery by ascribing human thoughts and emotions to animals and objects they depict. Adults should avoid asking "what" and "why" questions; instead, they should make their own observations about the picture and offer comments, such as, "I wonder what the people in the picture are feeling" (Looman, 2006).

 Creating a Safe, Growth-Enhancing Environment

1. Evaluate your teaching practices carefully to determine if there is anything in the environment that is causing or unnecessarily contributing to stress. Is the room crowded, disorganized, and messy? Is there bullying going on in the classroom or on the playground? Is there a provision for quiet and active periods during the day and opportunities for vigorous exercise?

Do you break down lessons into component parts to optimize children's probability for success? Do you avoid hurrying or pressuring children to "get through" parts of the curriculum they find especially challenging? Have you adjusted the pace of the schedule by either speeding up or slowing down regularly occurring programmatic intervals? If several children exhibit signs of stress within 60 to 90 minutes of arriving at school, then it is possible that the source of their stress is in the program itself.

2. Intervene immediately in aggressive encounters. Do not allow children to express tension by harming others. Stop children who are hurting other children. Reassure an injured child. Use the skills outlined in Chapter 12. Develop rules that promote an esprit de corps or a sense of "we-ness" when possible, by encouraging prosocial behavior. Praise children's efforts when they demonstrate respect for one another and when they behave empathically.

3. Make every child the object of daily focused attention. The younger the child, the more important it is to have a particular caregiver working consistently on a one-to-one basis with the child. Children never outgrow their need for individualized attention, however brief it may be. Keep a daily journal that you fill out after the children leave for the day. Briefly record your thoughts about the children with whom you recall having encounters.

Reread the journal after multiple entries have been made. Evaluate your pattern of comments on children; determine if there are some children who rarely are mentioned.

Make additional efforts to attend to those children; observe their behavior more closely.

continued

SKILLS FOR HELPING CHILDREN COPE WITH STRESS—continued

Another way to evaluate your performance is to go over a list of the children's names and mentally describe some aspect of their development such as motor skills or the ability to maintain peer relationships. If you cannot spontaneously recall information about a particular child, pay more consistent attention to that child.

4. Accept the child's choice of a play theme (death, divorce, violent episodes, fearful events). Do not try to direct play or determine how the details of play should be carried out. Play allows children to gain a sense of control when they are feeling fearful or uncertain. In the context of play, children can reduce their problems to manageable size and work at understanding them and themselves. For example, children commonly play "hospital" when they have just experienced hospitalization. Rarely are these children interested in being the patient. Instead, they prefer to play the role of doctor, making sure they are "in control" of the situation. It also is common for children to play at death: falling down "dead," "zapping" a playmate, telling spooky stories, or pretending to be in a casket. Play is a safe and appropriate avenue through which death can be explored. Do not intervene when you see this kind of play even though you may feel it is morbid or unhealthy. In fact, playing out difficult concepts and situations is the child's way of making them manageable.

5. Eliminate unnecessary competition. Protect preschool children, who are especially vulnerable to competitive activities. For example, "musical chairs," a game that may be highly enjoyed by 8-year-olds, creates distress for younger, egocentric children. Select cooperatively based group activities for grade-school children when possible. Focus on group achievement and developing team spirit rather than on individual performance.

6. Build relaxation breaks into the program. Plan for periodic relaxation breaks in which everyone takes part in activities such as the stretching, tensing, and relaxing of muscle groups, aerobic exercise, or exercises designed to relax breathing. Children who participate in these activities are better able to concentrate and spend more time on assigned tasks. Take children on "fantasy vacations." Ask them to close their eyes and depart together on an imaginary journey. Use sensory vocabulary to encourage more elaborate **imagery**. Sometimes, ask children to pretend that they are going to attempt a challenging task, and ask them to pretend each step while breathing deeply. Help them to envision themselves as an actor, a doer, one who can face the challenge.

7. Allow children to participate in decision making and conflict resolution. Children should be included in the solving of real, genuine problems. This skill is developed fully in Chapter 9.

8. Use teaching materials, strategies, and resources that promote divergent as well as convergent thought. Promote the consideration of alternative solutions to problems by saying: "How else do you think we could use these materials?" or "If we use these another way, the end result may be very different. Let's try it!" Choose textbooks or other curricular materials that depict males and females doing a variety of tasks. Select materials that depict variations in family structures and situation without implying that one family form or another is somehow deviant. A variety of cultural and racial groups should be depicted in positive terms.

9. Teach alternative strategies to inappropriate behavior. Although every effort should be made to respect individual differences, behaviors that are destructive to the child's own growth and/or destructive to others should be modified, if possible. Support the child while she or he is learning new behaviors. Say: "I know this is hard for you. I'll be right here to help." Acknowledge even the smallest effort at self-modification. Praise each modest success. If destructive behaviors

SKILLS FOR HELPING CHILDREN COPE WITH STRESS

are significantly difficult for you to change even after consistent effort, seek advice and/or assistance from other professionals who are more highly skilled.

 Developing Preventive Stress-Coping Behaviors in Children

1. Teach children how to cope with stress *before* they find themselves in a highly stressful situation. Behaviors that develop habits of exercise and good nutrition, when combined with self-understanding and good coping strategies, enhance children's abilities to deal with short- and long-term stressors.

2. Coach children on what to do in potentially frightening situations or emergencies. Prepare children for these encounters through discussion and role play (Jarratt, 1994). For example, ask, "What would you do if you got separated from your parents in a department store?" or "What would you do if someone older and bigger than you tried to take your lunch money away?"

3. Expand children's vocabulary to facilitate communication of troubling feelings and thoughts. Read children's books that depict stressful situations for the characters, or suggest titles for independent readers. Use precise vocabulary when making affective reflections ("You're so enthusiastic today!" or "I sense that you're pretty disappointed"). Help children formulate descriptions of what they are feeling when under stress. Remember, stress can be produced by a very happy event, such as a party, as well as an unhappy event, such as the death of a pet.

4. Allow children to experience the positive and negative consequences of their decisions unless doing so would endanger their safety or physical or emotional health. Tell children that mistakes are one useful way to discover better ways of doing something. Ask them to generate other alternatives that might have

led to different consequences. Do not intervene unless there is a clear risk to the child.

5. Provide opportunities for vigorous daily exercise. Teach children that regular exercise reduces the natural stress on the body and maintains health. Do not assume that children are getting enough exercise; this frequently is not true. Children and adults need at least 20 minutes of vigorous activity each day. Demonstrate the relationship of stress and activity: "I was feeling 'logy' because I've had such a hard day. Now that I've had a chance to do aerobics, I feel better! How do you feel?"

6. Teach children specific relaxation techniques. Encourage children to practice exercises such as deep muscle relaxation and relaxed breathing daily so they become habitual. Have children do some just before going home so they do not arrive there tense. One teacher asked children to investigate their own bodies to find out where all their "hinges" were (neck, elbow, wrist, waist, pelvis, knees, ankles). She had the children practice "bending" these hinges, then "locking them up" to develop an awareness of how their bodies felt when tense and when loose. She taught them to "turn themselves into floppy dolls" who become increasingly limp as they unlock one hinge after another. This game, and others she developed, allowed children to contrast tense and relaxed feelings.

7. Teach children to practice *positive self-talk* in tense situations by counting to 10 or telling themselves to take it easy or calm down and to sit quietly before responding to a situation. Young children may need to say these things out loud: "I am in control," "I can stay calm," "I'm scared, but I can handle this," or "I can breathe in and out very slowly to help myself stay calm." In contrast, discourage children from saying how stupid, incompetent, or helpless they are when in the middle of a stressful situation. Children cannot con-

continued

SKILLS FOR HELPING CHILDREN COPE WITH STRESS—continued

trol their feelings, but they can learn to control their behavior. First, they must believe that they have control. Help them to develop positive self-talk that is appropriate to the particular problems that they experience: "I can get really mad, but I don't have to hit," "I can choose to yell instead of hitting," or "I can tell them what they did that made me so angry." Self-talk contributes to self-control and decreases impulsiveness, which sometimes escalates a stressful event.

8. Use *encouraging responses* to help children feel better about themselves. When children have developed the habit of focusing verbally or mentally on the negative aspects of an experience ("I'm so dumb," "I knew everyone would laugh at me," "I can never remember anything!"), positive behavior changes can be facilitated by offering encouraging responses that verbalize positive aspects. These encouraging statements should not deny children's feelings ("You shouldn't feel that way," "It's not that bad"). Rather, they should be used to point out the potential benefits or good in a situation. For instance, after missing the word chaotic in a spelling bee, Chris sits down, saying, "I'm not any good at spelling anyway." At this point, you could say: "You're disappointed that you missed a word. You lasted for five rounds. That's pretty good."

9. Help children practice imagery. Children who have very limited skills in a particular area or poor self-esteem often foresee themselves as performing poorly in a particular situation before they even begin. This tends to decrease their potential for performing at least adequately, if not well. Suggest that children curtail this by having them pretend that they are going to perform very well in the particular task that worries them. Teach them to begin the task in their minds and go through it step by step until it is successfully "completed." Have the children pretend with all their senses; for example, they might imagine themselves preparing for an oral presentation, reading, writing note cards,

walking to the front of the group, and seeing classmates listening attentively. Encourage them to envision success and competence for this potentially threatening experience. Tell children to use this technique whenever they have to do something that worries or frightens them.

10. Use ordinary experiences and daily activities to discuss feelings, thoughts, and behaviors that people can use when they are afraid, uncertain, faced with change, or overwhelmed by what is happening to them. Discuss current events seen in newspapers, television shows that children watch, and experiences others share with the class. Highlight the coping techniques that were used. Explain to younger children how difficult the experience was for the person who went through it. For example, if a residence caught fire in the area, children will talk about it. Use this opportunity to discuss how frightening it was for the family and what they or their neighbors did to help. Stories also can be used as opportunities to play out some dramatic event. Do not deliberately try to frighten children; focus instead on positive steps they can take in similar situations.

 Providing Support for Children Coping with Loss

1. Use appropriate vocabulary when discussing death and dying. Use the words "dead," "dying," and "died" when talking about death. Avoid analogies such as "dying is like going to sleep" or euphemisms like "passed on," "lost," or "gone away." Children are literal in their interpretation of language. Thus, words that are meant to soften the blow may actually make the situation more difficult for them to understand.

2. Describe death in terms of familiar bodily functions. In describing what it means to be dead, point out that normal body functioning stops: The heart stops beating; there is

SKILLS FOR HELPING CHILDREN COPE WITH STRESS

no more breathing, no more feeling, no more emotions, no more loving, no more thinking, no more sleeping, and no more eating. Death is not like anything else. It is not like sleeping, resting, or lying still, and parallels to these activities should not be made. Children who overhear statements such as "She looks so peaceful, as if she were sleeping" may dread going to sleep themselves for fear that they will not wake up. This is particularly true for children in the first or second stages of conceptualizing death, who still think that death may be temporary and reversible.

3. Explain why the death has occurred, giving children accurate information. Eventually, children ask, "Why did he (or she) die?" When talking to a child about a person or an animal who died as a result of illness, explain that all living things get sick sometimes. Mostly, of course, they get better again. But there are times when they are so terribly sick that they die because their body wears out and cannot function anymore. When talking to children about a death that has occurred as a result of an accident or injury, help them differentiate between mortal injury and everyday cuts and scrapes from which we all recover.

4. Explain death rituals as a means by which people provide comfort to the living. Children often are confused by the mixed messages that funeral customs communicate. For instance, children who have been told that a dead person feels nothing may find it disconcerting that soft, satin blankets and pillows have been provided. In their minds, these props are objects of comfort, and their presence reinforces the notion that death is like sleep. Adults can point out that articles such as these are for the aesthetic benefit of the mourners.

5. Answer children's questions about death matter-of-factly. There is great value in teaching children about death before they actually experience it in their lives (Hopkins, 2005). Help children understand the details of death by responding calmly to queries about

cemeteries, coffins, cremations, embalming, tombstones, skeletons, ghosts, and angels. Accept their questions nonjudgmentally. Answer simply and honestly. Sometimes, children's questions seem morbid, insensitive, or bizarre, such as "When are you going to die?" or "Do worms eat the eyeballs, too?" If you recoil in shock or admonish the questioner, you add to children's perception that death is a secret topic, not to be discussed or explored. Things that cannot be talked about can be frightening to children, adding to the stress of the situation. Remember, too, that children learn through repetition, so they may ask the same questions over and over again. Each time they hear the answer, they are adding a new fragment of information to their store of knowledge. Frequent questions do not necessarily indicate stress or fear, but rather, can reflect normal curiosity.

6. Respect the family's prerogative for giving children religious explanations about death. Avoid religious explanations. As a helping professional, you will work with children and families whose beliefs vary widely. It is your responsibility to respect those differences by allowing parents to tend to the spiritual needs of their own child. Be sensitive to the cultural mores of the families in your group. Insensitivity or ignorance can have disastrous results for children because your explanation may undermine what they have been told by a parent.

The only exception to this rule is if you have been hired by a specific religious group to promote its philosophy. Then, because parents have chosen to send their child to you for religious teaching, it is appropriate for you to reiterate the philosophy of the institution. However, keep in mind children's age and level of comprehension when giving explanations.

7. Provide support for children who have chronic or potentially life-threatening disease, such as cystic fibrosis or cancer, without overprotecting them. Children who are

continued

SKILLS FOR HELPING CHILDREN COPE WITH STRESS—continued

in remission or well enough to attend school may need some privileges not accorded to other children related to the need for additional rest, medication, and nutritional limitations.

Like other children, they need understanding, consistent limits on behavior, appropriate and reasonable academic expectations, and occasional help in forming classroom friendships.

8. Provide accurate information to other children who may be confused or frightened at having a health-impaired member of the group. For example, a child recovering from chemotherapy may not have much hair. This condition is not catching, and when children understand the course of treatment better, they are more likely to accept the health-impaired child in their social activities. Parents or health professionals can provide the requisite information.

9. Be alert for negative reactions to children who are siblings of a health-impaired child. Some children may be reluctant to play or work with them for the same reasons they are reluctant to do so with the health-impaired child. Providing correct information will help them to be more sensitive to and supportive of children who have an ill brother or sister.

10. For children experiencing their parents' divorce, explain that divorce is the result of "grown-up problems." Tell children that adults get divorced because they can no longer find happiness in being together. Reassure youngsters that they are not responsible for the divorce, nor is it possible for them to bring their parents back together. Explain that although family members will be living in different households, they are still family, and the mother and father are still the child's parents.

11. Acknowledge the pain that divorce inevitably brings to children. Offer physical comfort; reflect children's emotions; remain available to children who wish to talk.

Remember that the **grieving process** takes a long time, and children will vary in their reactions to it. Lay a foundation for helping children cope with potential stressors such as death or divorce by using books dealing with such events even when they have not occurred in your classroom.

 Mediating Children's Stress Through Family Communication Strategies

1. Collaborate with parents to reduce childhood stress. Once children move into a situation in which they receive a significant portion of their care from adults other than their parents, all of the adults then become linked in the delicate responsibility of guiding their socialization. For this link to be effective the adults must be willing to share information that they believe the others need to know about a child in order to best support the child's needs. This calls for frank, open communication that is conducted in a nonthreatening, nonjudgmental manner, even when parents' behavior in a stressful situation has been less than optimal. When one adult seeks to place blame or to unfairly criticize another adult's genuine attempts to be supportive, the thread that links them together is weakened significantly. Professionals can be helpful to parents when they:

- let them know when a child is manifesting signs of undue stress.
- remain alert for signs of parental stress.
- share information with parents about the effects of childhood and adult stress through seminars or newsletters.
- listen empathically to parents when they speak of their own stress.
- let parents know they want to work cooperatively with them to support them and their child during stressful times.
- acknowledge parents' efforts to work cooperatively to reduce a child's level of distress.

SKILLS FOR HELPING CHILDREN COPE WITH STRESS

2. Talk to separating or divorcing parents about the importance of explaining to children how divorce will affect their daily living. Parents who are caught up in a divorce may not realize that children benefit from knowing such concrete details as where they will eat and sleep, with whom they will live, and how much they will be able to see the noncustodial parent. Draw parents' attention to these facts and help them think of ways to explain the issues to their children.

3. Share tips with parents about moderating the influence of the media on their children. The following are guidelines provided by the American Academy of Pediatricians:

- Don't allow the bedroom to be a media center with TV, video games, and Internet access.
- Limit media time to 1 to 2 hours of quality programming.
- Discourage TV viewing for children younger than 2 years (believing that at this age, there is more to be learned from a 3-dimensional world than a 2-dimentional one regardless of content).
- View and discuss content together.
- Turn off the TV when no one is watching and during meals.
- Be a good media role model (Shifrin, 2006, pp. 449–450).

4. Assist parents of young children who are exhibiting stress when being dropped off. Very young children sometimes have conflicting emotions about having their parents leave, particularly when they are first being introduced to a formal group setting, during periods when the family is going through a significant change (mother entering the workforce, father leaving because of divorce), and often following holiday recesses.

Children balk because they're feeling insecure about what may happen while they're in the program. Also, parents are the most significant persons in their lives and, quite frankly, they enjoy being around their parents more than anyone else. Also, children new to an educational setting do not know how much "fun" school can be, so it does little good for the parents or professional to plead that case. Children only know that they are in a place they would rather not be and that their "security person" is leaving them with unfamiliar people who cannot, at least at that moment, quite fill the void.

Parents who are introducing children to a new setting and new people should plan, if possible, on spending some time in the setting with the child to help her or him become more secure. Though not all parents can rearrange their work schedules, the possibility ought to be suggested at the parent orientation meeting held prior to the opening of the center or school.

Personality differences in children make it difficult to design foolproof guidelines for separating, but the following list provides useful information to share with parents:

a. Give parents ideas about how to help their children prepare for their participation in the program. Suggest that they visit the building together, play on the playground, or drive or walk past the program site prior to the first day. Advise parents to tell the child that he or she will be attending the center or class and to describe in detail some of the things that will be going on each day. Encourage parents to bring the children to any orientation that might be offered.

b. Give parents specific guidelines for how to initiate the separation process once they arrive at the center or classroom. The first step is for parents to find a material that looks interesting to them and to begin playing with it. This shows children that the setting is a fun, safe place to be. Have parents avoid asking, "Do you want to paint a picture?" or "Do you want to build with blocks?" Youngsters often perceive such questions as pressure to separate and therefore resist

continued

SKILLS FOR HELPING CHILDREN COPE WITH STRESS—continued

the invitation. After 5 or 10 minutes, if children have not become involved, parents can include them by saying something like: "I can't decide just where to put this block. What do you think?"

c. Encourage parents to gradually remove themselves from direct interaction with their child. This step involves having the parent say something like: "You're having a really good time here. I have to write a letter (read this book, work on a paper). I will sit on that bench (near the door but inside the room). I'll be there if you need me." If the child follows the parent to the chosen spot, a compromise is possible. The parent might say: "I'll work here for 5 minutes. Then, I will join you." When the child becomes able to play comfortably for 20 minutes without checking on the parent, the parent can tell the child that he or she is going to the "secretary's office" for 5 minutes. It is important for the parent to then leave, even if the child protests, emphasizing that he or she will return. The parent must then reappear at the appointed time. This lets even the unhappy child know that the parent will do what he or she has promised to do. Parents can then spend an increasingly lengthy time away from the room.

Once children can participate for at least 30 minutes without crying the whole time, parents can plan to leave their children at the appointed hour and pick them up when the program is over. Tell parents to anticipate the need for additional time to work through any separation problems with their child. Adapt the preceding routine to the parents' time constraints as necessary. Some may not have the luxury of working through the process. Do not try to coerce parents into spending more time than they are able or make them feel guilty if they cannot stay as long as you might like.

d. Encourage parents to leave promptly once they have said goodbye. Lingering departures or unexpected reappearances heighten children's anxiety by making the environment unpredictable. Escort parents to the door, if need be, and assure them that you will call them later in the day to explain how the child is getting along.

e. Physically intervene if necessary to help parents and children separate. Frequently, parents wait for children to give them permission to leave. They try to obtain this permission with statements like: "Don't you want to stay here with all your friends?"; "You don't want me to lose my job, do you?"; or "You want me to be proud of you, don't you?" Children seldom cooperate in this effort. At this point, you should step in and say: "Carla, your mom is leaving now. I'll help you find something to do." Then, take the child to an activity. Assure the parent that this is part of your job and that you expect that eventually the child will become happily involved.

f. Caution parents to resist the temptation to sneak away as soon as the child becomes involved with an activity. This damages the child's confidence in the parent and reinforces the idea that the school or center is not a place to be trusted. It can create a real sense of abandonment and terror in a child and may later trigger a fresh and more intense outburst.

g. Alert parents to potentially harmful ways of dealing with separation. Some of these include pressuring children, shaming them, or denying their feelings. Sometimes, parents admonish their children to "behave themselves," "be good," or "act nice." These cautions, although well intended, put pressure on children at a time when they least need additional worries. It is better for parents to say: "Have fun!," "Have a nice

SKILLS FOR HELPING CHILDREN COPE WITH STRESS

day," or "I love you. See you after outdoor time!" In addition, children's anxiety increases when adults say: "Mommy will feel bad if you don't stop crying," "I feel sad when you don't like the school," or "Nobody likes to play with a crybaby." These tactics do nothing to relieve the child's despair. Children who are sad or angry about separation should not be burdened with the additional responsibility of making other people feel better. Finally, phrases like "Don't worry" or "Don't cry" intensify rather than soothe children's feelings of distress. Such statements indicate that the child's feelings are wrong or unimportant, rather than helping him or her find a constructive way to cope. It is better to acknowledge a child's true feelings, no matter what they are.

h. Agree to telephone distraught parents to reassure them when their child has adjusted to the separation, if necessary. Occasionally, the parent has more difficulty leaving the child than the child has in leaving the parent. The procedure outlined thus far may be accomplished in half an hour or one day, or it may take several weeks. Some children will enter a room confidently, wave goodbye to their parents, and immediately settle into an activity. When they do not, these guidelines can be activated.

i. Support the parent and the child as needed in other transitions. Separating from children is not the only point at which parents experience problems with children in the program. Sometimes, the same kinds of behaviors are seen in children when parents participate in the setting (e.g., in a cooperative nursery) or return to take them home. When this happens, the behavior probably springs from other causes. A child may show off or become aggressive or clinging when his or her parent is working for the day, simply not

wanting to share the parent with other children. At pickup times, the child may be involved in an activity and not want to be interrupted. The child may be cranky, tired, out of sorts, and even angry with the parent for leaving. At times like this, it is not helpful for professionals to make comments like: "I can't understand why Sammy is acting this way. He's an angel when you're not here" or "He's been so good all morning." These are "killer" statements that can make parents feel extremely upset. Parents may worry that they have less control over their children than do other parents or professionals or that the bond they have with their child is being weakened by their absence. Professionals should reassure parents that this behavior is normal in children. End-of-the-day transition procedures, such as caregivers alerting children that their parents are present and that they can get ready immediately or play for five more minutes, are helpful to parents. Some schools or centers even offer a lounge where parents can have a cup of coffee and relax for a moment while the child and his or her belongings are readied for departure.

5. In cases where their children are frightened by events of terrorism or violence, Hamblen (2007) offers the following tips to share with parents:

a. Create a safe environment and keep children's routines as regular as possible. Children find comfort in having things be consistent and familiar.

b. Provide children with reassurance and extra emotional support. Create an environment where children feel safe enough to ask questions, express feelings or just be themselves. Ask them what they have heard and how they feel about it. Reassure them that they are safe and that they won't be abandoned.

continued

SKILLS FOR HELPING CHILDREN COPE WITH STRESS—continued

c. Be honest with them about what happened. Provide accurate, developmentally appropriate information. Very young children may not be aware that something bad has happened, but school-age children will need help understanding it. They can be told that a terrible accident has happened in which many have been hurt or killed. With older children who are seeing reports of the incident on TV, watch with them and discuss it.

d. Tell children what the government is doing. Explain that the state, federal government, police, firefighters, and hospitals are doing everything possible across the country and that other countries will also help if needed.

e. Be aware that children will often take on the anxiety of the adults around them. Adults often become frightened and insecure themselves during terrorist attacks, experiencing feelings of revenge, anger, and worry; these are reactions they must deal with before helping children. It helps to share that while adults are experiencing some of the same emotions felt by children, it's good to talk about ways to cope and how family members can help each other.

f. Try to put the event in perspective. Let children know that terrorist attacks are rare and that the world is generally a safe place.

PITFALLS TO AVOID

All children and all families experience stress. As has been pointed out, reactions to stressors will depend heavily on individual and familial assessment of resources to meet demands. Following are a few of the pitfalls experienced by caregivers in working with children and families under stress.

Stereotyping of families.   Caregivers, who as individuals carry with them their own perceptions and possibly very different resources, must be careful not to stereotype families based on composition, ethnicity, or financial resources. Much of a family's response in a stressful situation will depend on how they perceive a particular demand or crisis together with what they feel they can do to maintain their balance.

Remember that, although some individuals and families make what seem to be terribly poor decisions, they are doing the best they can given their current perceptions of their options and resources. In other words, people do not purposely or consciously "mess up" their lives.

Skewed and inappropriate responses.   Because withdrawn children cause us fewer problems in the classroom, there often is a tendency for helping professionals to see the aggressive or overly dependent child as the one who most needs help. In these cases,

we probably are responding as much to our own needs as to the needs we see in the children. Their behavior increases our own stress levels, prompting us to do something about it.

The children who suffer quietly may be particularly vulnerable, and we need to be alert for the subtle cues they present. These children need help in dealing with overwhelming thoughts and feelings; they will need particular help in learning to communicate what is bothering them and in learning to cope with these stressors rather than run away from them.

Problems in the educational setting occur when we see only the irritating behavior in a child, not the child's distress. When we find ourselves getting angry about a child's negativism, we need to remember that this is the child's strategy for coping with a particular situation. Although we will want to guide the child toward finding a more positive strategy, we must remember that effective behavior changes do not occur overnight. They require patience, consistency, and firmness on the adult's part and the development of trust on the child's part. A sensitive approach to troubled children need not be seen as a "soft" approach. Children do feel safer with a strong adult; what they do not need, however, is a punitive adult who strips them of their faulty defense mechanisms without providing anything more effective. This only makes an already vulnerable child feel more bankrupt and out of control.

Dictating "appropriate" responses. Although everyone experiences the same range of feelings, reactions to particular situations vary among individuals. Situations arise in which you expect a certain reaction, such as remorse, sadness, or tension. When the person does not respond in the expected manner, the reaction may be perceived as "inappropriate." Remember, there are no right or wrong feelings. Your role is not to tell children or members of their family how to feel, but rather to help them learn constructive ways of making their feelings known to others.

If a child or family rejects your offer for help, you may feel annoyed and unappreciated. Keep in the back of your mind that, in most cases, an individual's response is based on his or her reaction at the moment and has nothing to do with you. Children often show their distress through their behavior rather than through words. Although talking can help a troubled child, it must take place when the child is ready. Children vary in the time it takes them to reach this point.

Thus, adults can let children know they are available, but should not pressure them into talking or make them feel obligated to talk in order to obtain the adult's approval. You can say things like "If you want to talk, I'll be around," or "Sometimes people feel better when they talk about their feelings." If a child seems hesitant or expresses a desire to be left alone, respect his or her need for privacy by following up with a statement like "I'll still be here if you want to talk later; and, if you don't, that's all right, too."

Making a perfunctory diagnosis of a child's behavior. When helping professionals know that a child and his or her family are going through a stressful time, they may erroneously assume that all of the child's inappropriate behavior is a direct result of a particular stressor. For example, adults often are quick to say: "He's biting because his mother went back to work," "She has trouble making friends because her parents are divorced," or "She's complaining about an upset stomach—it must be because of jealousy over the new baby." Although the stressful situation at home may be contributing to these behaviors, there is a chance that other factors are involved. It is necessary to carefully consider the range of possibilities. For instance, the child who is biting may not know an alternative way of getting what he wants; the friendless child may not recognize other children's attempts to make contact, or may lack basic conversational skills; and the child

with the stomachache may, in fact, be simply reacting to something she ate.

Looking for a "quick fix" or a superficial solution. When we feel we do not have the time, the energy, or a ready solution to a particular problem, we sometimes fall into the trap of trying to get the situation over with as quickly as possible. This can be difficult for children because the adult's notion of a solution may not match the child's real need. For example, all of us, at one time or another, have seen adults trying to cajole or shame a crying child into being quiet. When this strategy fails, it is not unusual to hear the adult say coercively, "Either you stop crying, or I'll give you something to cry about!" At other times, adults may force children to prematurely confront a situation in the mistaken belief that this will make the child "get over" feelings of fear, revulsion, or unhappiness. Statements like "There's nothing to be afraid of," "Just get in there and do it," and "You'll get over it" are typical of this approach. In any case, the child's real feelings are neglected, and the adult is focusing on his or her own convenience. Helping others is not always convenient and providing emotional assistance takes time and energy. In addition, solutions do not necessarily come about within one encounter and may require repeated effort.

Failing to recognize your own limitations. It is not always within your power to eliminate the source of a child's distress. Although you perform an important function when you provide emotional support, it may not be possible to alter the child's environment or to change the behaviors of others in the child's environment who are negatively affecting the child. It's also important for professionals to know where their sphere of influence ends and when it is time to link families with other helping professionals.

Forgetting that parents have other roles that require their time and energy. The reaction of young children who run into their teachers at the supermarket or elsewhere in the community is often amusing to adults. The children seem absolutely amazed that the teacher can be anywhere but in the classroom and in the role of teacher. Ironically, professionals and parents hold like perspectives, unless they happen to travel in similar social circles that allow them to meet one another frequently outside the educational setting. Parents and professionals tend to think of one another narrowly and only in terms of the role each plays in their interactions. Thus, when parents think of helping professionals, they may forget that these people also are parents, spouses, adult children, voters, and homeowners. Similarly, helping professionals can forget that although parents may play the parenting role 24 hours a day, other roles can and do become more dominant in their lives during that 24-hour period. They, too, experience the pressure of meeting job demands, maintaining a home, nurturing intimate relationships with persons other than their children, furthering their education or training, responding to their own parents' needs, and performing a wide variety of community obligations.

Being inflexible and/or insensitive to the needs of financially troubled parents, working parents, single parents, teenage parents, divorced parents, stepparents, parents of handicapped children, and bilingual or migrant families. Professionals sometimes are seen as distant and unfeeling about the pressures many parents face in their everyday lives. Notices arrive home regularly reminding parents to put their children to bed early; to provide a quiet place to study, and to be sure that children eat a balanced diet. Parents whose homes are small and crowded, those who are unemployed, and those who are going through painful marital transitions or other unexpected crises must experience additional distress when receiving these reminders. In order to be sensitive to the total ecosystem or context in which children are developing, learn about each family. Understanding, flexibility, and insightfulness can ease their burdens.

Overreacting to negative parents. The less confident we are of our own position regarding a controversial issue, the more we will tend to become defensive when our views are challenged. As experience and continuing education allow us to integrate what we know about children and families with what others know, we will become more relaxed and open when others present a different, even hostile viewpoint. When we overreact to a critical and negative parent, we exhibit our fear of being proven wrong, our uncertainty, and our confusion.

A parent can make an important point, one that is based on very good intentions and might truly be helpful; however, she or he may deliver it in such a negative manner (blaming, sarcastic, derisive) that we fail to really listen. A message delivered in such a way that it puts the receiver in a highly charged emotional state often fails to be heard. Professionals need to

work hard to stay calm in such a situation, to actively listen and to perhaps reflect to the parent: "You're really angry. I think we need to talk about that, but I am hearing what you're saying about the need for a better information-delivery system, and I believe you're right." Occasionally, hostile remarks and behavior by a parent may have little to do with the professional or with what is really going on in the program. The parent may be feeling overwhelmed or out of control in other important areas and may see no other outlet for expressing his or her frustrations. Some careful probing, combined with understanding responses, sometimes can help such a person to understand what is happening and reevaluate his or her behavior.

SUMMARY

There is growing concern about increasing levels of childhood stress. Two reasons for that concern are that we now believe that undischarged stress and prolonged periods of stress lead ultimately to disease, and that stress-coping styles are learned in childhood. Childhood stressors range from mild to severe. However, even a number of seemingly mild stressors can be cumulative enough to cause a child extreme discomfort. Moreover, what may seem insignificant to an older child or adult with more experience can be perceived by a younger child as insurmountable and highly stressful.

Sources of childhood stress include the child's own personality as well as familial stressors such as death of a family member, marital transitions, intense workforce involvement of all adults in the family, and abuse. Also significant are extrafamilial stressors such as negative child care experiences, stress experienced in the formal educational arena, and stress experienced in natural disasters and other traumatic and violent events, including what is learned from the media.

Children react to stress physically, psychologically, and behaviorally. They learn positive or negative coping styles by watching significant adults in their environment. There are a variety of strategies that can be used to build coping skills in children. This depends on how threatening or demanding the child perceives the stressor to be, the personal resilience of the child, the types of support or resources available for modifying the stressor, and the coping skills that have been internalized by the child in previous experiences.

Stress is inevitable. As our world grows more and more complex, our ability to adapt positively to both negative and positive stimuli also must grow more sophisticated. Childhood is the period during which much of that critical learning will take place—or not take place. Because today's children spend much of their time in child care and educational settings, the influence of helping professionals working in those settings will be enormous. Although we cannot always improve a child's environment, we can provide every child with more effective tools for mastering that environment.

KEY TERMS

blended families
childhood stress
defense mechanisms
domestic violence

encouraging responses
grieving process
impulsive acting out
multiproblem families

perception of an event as a stressor
positive self-talk
psychological disequilibration
vulnerable child syndrome

DISCUSSION QUESTIONS

1. With three or four of your classmates, compare one another's most common physical, emotional, and behavioral reactions when under pressure. How are your reactions similar? How are they dissimilar?

2. A parents' group requests that you bring a speaker to discuss childhood stress. What aspects of the topic do you believe ought to be covered if the speaker has only an hour?

3. In your own childhood years, were there any significant stressors that you can remember, such as the death of a pet, parental divorce, or loss of a friendship? Discuss your own reaction or the type of support you received from significant others around you. Were their responses helpful or not helpful? If the response was poor, what could the person(s) have done to improve the outcome?

4. Discuss (a) as many aspects of poverty as possible that you believe can contribute, either directly or indirectly, to increased stress in children's lives, and (b) aspects of middle-class children's lives that differ from the experience of poverty but that also may create stress.

5. A coworker tells you: "All this stuff you read about children's stress is tiresome. We had stress growing up, too. Why make so much of it?" Share what you know about the importance of coping more effectively with stress.

6. You are eating lunch with several professional colleagues. One of them begins discussing the older brother of a child you have in your classroom, inserting negative remarks about the child's family. She asks you if you have had similar experiences with the parents and younger child. Refer to the NAEYC Code of Ethical Conduct in Appendix A and cite the section that is relevant in forming a response to her question.

7. Often, professionals focus on children of divorced families as children who may be distressed. Discuss the kinds of significant stressors that may exist in families that are intact but troubled—stressors that may be somewhat hidden.

8. Brainstorm with another person about the different kinds of helping agencies and professionals in your community that can provide support to distressed families and children. What are some factors that could limit a family's ability to get help from these resources?

9. Talk about aspects of a preprimary or primary program with which you are familiar that you believe are stress-producing or stress-relieving aspects for the children in that program.

10. You have a child who is not adjusting very well to his mother leaving him each morning. The child is at a table putting together a puzzle but keeping a wary eye on his mother. She says to you, "Is it all right if I leave now?" What do you say?

FIELD ASSIGNMENTS

1. Having books available or reading to children about difficult situations that others have experienced is a highly positive way to enhance their understanding of such crises, whether or not they have personally experienced them. Using a nearby library that features a children's reading section, identify a book (title, author, publisher, date of publication) at the preschool, early elementary, and later elementary levels for the following: children's fears; parents' separation, divorce, or remarriage; death; handicaps/illness.

2. Review the skills for helping children cope with stress. Observe closely one situation in which an adult is working with a distressed child. Evaluate whether the adult's responses toward the child have a calming or stress-heightening effect and why. Note the following:

   a. What was the child doing or saying?
   b. How did the adult respond?
   c. How did the child(ren) react?
   d. If the situation were to come up again, would you recommend that it be handled in the same way or that the approach be changed? Why?

3. When children respond inappropriately under stress, they are coping in the best way they know. When we want to eliminate such behavior, we must replace the child's present coping strategy with a more effective and appropriate one. This calls for observation of the behavior to see how often it happens and under what conditions, identification of a reasonable alternative, and effective communication with the child about substituting the new skill. It also calls for follow-up to see whether the child is able to adopt the alternative behavior successfully. Choose a child who needs supportive intervention for altering behavior and implement the procedure just outlined. Keep a journal of sequential steps and outcomes until the child successfully adapts with more appropriate responses.

4. Professionals need to have ready a list of other helping professionals to link needy or stressed families with community resources. Identify a helping agency that would be supportive to a parent if:

   a. The family was struggling with resources for food, shelter, or heat because of unemployment.
   b. Someone in the family has a chemical abuse problem.
   c. A family member is being physically or sexually abusive.
   d. Someone in the family is suffering from emotional anxiety or depression.
   e. A parent is considering separation or divorce.

   Include the name of the helping agency, address, telephone number, services provided, fees charged, and name of a contact person.

5. Describe the stress-reduction strategies that practitioners use in a particular early childhood setting. What special routines/strategies do they use in helping children make the transition from home to program? What day-to-day events/routines in the setting are sometimes stressful to children? What do practitioners do to reduce children's stress in these settings?

6. Describe three things you do to reduce the stress in your own life.

For additional resources, visit our Web site
www.EarlyChildEd.delmar.com

Chapter 7

ENHANCING PLAY

OBJECTIVES

On completion of this chapter, you should be able to describe:

- The relation of play to other aspects of development.

- Developmental trends in various types of play.

- How play contributes to each of the elements of social competence.

- The role of the adult in facilitating children's play.

- Communications with parents about children's play.

- Pitfalls to avoid in facilitating children's play.

SITUATION: *Two children are playing family roles of husband and wife.*

Anne: (Looking at rocking horse) Gotta go.

Phillip: Go?

Anne: Gotta go to work.

Phillip: No, you cook.

Anne: Can't cook, gotta go to work. (Climbs on the horse and begins to rock)

Phillip: No, you cook and stuff. I'll go to work. (Holds the reigns of the rocking horse)

Anne: Gonna be late for work. You stay and cook.

Phillip: Don't you know? You cook and I go to work.

Anne: (Trying unsuccessfully to rock) Drop you off on my way to work.

Phillip: (Mounts the horse behind her)

The play of these two children nearly floundered for lack of a shared meaning for the roles that they were playing. Fortunately, they were able to agree on the notion of both riding the horse to work even though they did not fully realize the difficulty of their differing perceptions of the roles of wives. Anne's mother had been employed throughout Anne's four years of life, and Phillip's mother was a full-time homemaker. These two children discovered a means for coping with their differing points of view. They continued the play, which they both enjoyed, even though they did not understand their differences in perspective or family backgrounds.

Play is both common and complex. Frequently, adults take it for granted, referring to this exciting activity of childhood as "just play." Play is a predominant social activity in early childhood, and it continues to provide common ground for informal social exchange as children mature. Therefore, adults who guide the social development of children need to understand the nature and function of play.

THE NATURE OF PLAY

Any definition of play must take into account the gleeful game of chase a toddler plays while running from his mother, the intense dramatization of an irate father played out in the nursery school, the boisterous and rough horsing about of young boys on the playground, the concentrated practice of a 10-year-old shooting basket after basket in the gym, the chanting cadence of the jump-rope rhyme, and

the patience and strategy of the school-age child accumulating wealth in a Monopoly game.

Play, although not easily defined, has certain definitive characteristics (Klein, Wirth, & Linas, 2004; Segal, 2004). Play is essentially *enjoyable*; although players may not be actively laughing, they are having fun. Children are *actively engaged*; they are deeply involved and not easily distracted. Play is *intrinsically motivated*; there are no extrinsic goals. It is essentially an unproductive activity in which the *process is more important than the ends.* Play is *voluntary*; to be play, the activity must be freely chosen by the child. Play is also *nonliteral*. It is not serious or does not "count" from the child's perspective.

Play is determined as play by the players. This means that the player may begin, end, or alter the activity in progress without consulting anyone but the other players. Adults do not order children about in play. Such behavior would make the episode unplayful. Helping professionals may be asked why they allow children to play and what benefits play provides for the child. Therefore, the relationship of "play" to "nonplay" aspects of development is briefly described. These relationships are graphically illustrated in Figure 7–1.

Genetic Foundations

Play is a species behavior (Power, 2000). All primates, including humans play. Adaptability, behavioral flexibility, and physical fitness have had great survival value for humans and are practiced and enhanced throughout play. Overall, individual animals of many species that play a lot appear to be more socially adjusted to their group and in better physical condition (McDonald, 1995). This play in animals has its own distinct communication signals and social conventions. Similar object play, play-fighting, and play-chasing behaviors are common among children as well (Power, 2000).

Defined this way, work and play are not necessarily opposites. Rather, the opposite of play is reality, or seriousness, rather than work. People can play at their work, enjoying it thoroughly, and may work hard at developing play skills necessary for a sport. Six- and 7-year-old children readily distinguish between work and play yet describe "in between" characteristics of play that are more worklike and work that is fun (Wing, 1995).

Cognition

Children tend to play in ways that are consistent with their cognitive development. Toddlers delight in sensory activity and toys that make noise or move

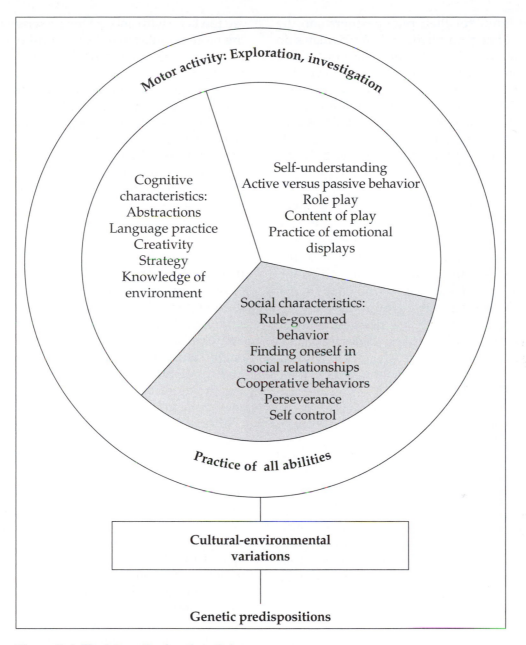

Figure 7–1 The integrative function of play.

as a result of their activity. Three- to 7-year-olds test their understanding of the social world through pretend play. A wide variety of cognitive skills are enhanced by play during the preschool years including measurement, equivalency, balance, spatial concepts, conservation, decentration, reversibility, memory and logical classification, mental representations, and creativity (Hughes, 1999; Bodrova & Leong, 2004). Play with other children and with materials calls forth the need to use these skills and to practice them. Older youngsters pursue a variety of games having complex rules, learning strategy, skill, and the ability to cope with chance.

Play is also the context for learning about interpersonal relationships among the children. They construct concepts about social play through observation, imitation, and trial and error, as well as from receiving information and feedback from other players. Play facilitates cognitive decentering, or the ability to take another's point of view or coordinate one's own understanding with those of others (Bodrova & Leong, 2004). Within the context of play, children of all ages learn how to initiate, maintain, and terminate play events. They also learn to suggest play ideas and to accept others' notions of how to play as well as to negotiate the themes or games in which to engage.

Children set limits for their play partners and the consequences of noncompliance when playmates do not play within the rules of the play episodes. These and many more ideas of how to play with each other emerge out of their experiences with other players. Adults may also provide children with direction, information, demonstrations, coaching, and discussions if the peer group is unable to figure out how to handle a problem that emerges from their experience.

Language

Language is used systematically in play and can be the subject of play. Almost all levels of organization of language are potential play material (Garvey, 1990). Children play with sounds and make up words, imitate adults or other children in amusing voices, and repeat their own statements with rhythm and rhyme. Certain occurrences, such as a group of 4-year-olds chanting "Delicious, nutritious, delectable juice" with great glee and accenting the syllables by pounding the table with cups or hands when faced with the detested apricot nectar, are a playful variation of the adult's words. Older children base jokes on the multiple meaning of words, and use all aspects of speech such as noises, intonation, and pauses as they play. In fact, the general level of cognitive functioning in self-directed play may be far above the level expected of the same children in academic subjects in school.

Perceptual-Motor Development

Strength, endurance, dynamic balance, flexibility, agility, and speed are gradually improved throughout childhood through play. The fundamental motor skills such as running, throwing and catching, climbing, dodging, kicking, and striking are usually acquired before the age of 8 and are eventually combined in games. With maturity and experience, children increase in efficiency as well as the number and scope of their basic movement competencies. Both boys and girls engage in vigorous play, though boys tend to be more boisterous and noisy. Successful children are frequently engaged in group games and sports and are seen by their peers as persons who are very desirable play partners. Success in physical play develops increased confidence, emotional stability, independence, and self-control in older children. Vigorous physical play also serves to reduce stress engendered in other aspects of life in a socially acceptable way.

Emotional Development

Children who enjoy playing, and who play more, seem to be happier than those who play less. They are fun to be with and are the preferred playmates or are more popular than less skillful players. Fantasy play allows for the personal integration of temperament, experience, and concepts that help the child understand the all-important question, "Who am I?" and thereby become a mentally healthy person.

Children's role selections display their concerns with nurturer/provider relationships, with the aggressor/victim dichotomy, with good and evil, with romance, and for older children, with their fearful fantasies. Through play the small and helpless child may become strong and powerful; the timid child can be very brave; and the most compliant child might pretend to be the monster. Children explore emotionally laden issues while attaining some degree of distance from the self.

Play supports emotional growth as typical children cope with conflicts or demands within the undemanding context of play. Youngsters either demonstrate or acquire some understanding of emotions and how they are appropriately displayed and regulated. Practice in reading and interpreting the emotional displays of others during the play process enhances their emotional competence (Wilson, 2004). In pretend play, they can enact sorrow, rage, worry, fear, love, and dismay with impunity. Play allows children to become active in shaping their own experiences and to explore alternatives and possibilities before choosing solutions to problems. As they play with each other, youngsters develop a capacity for relatedness within the setting where they are safe and nothing is "really for real" (Gitlin-Weiner, 1998). Children develop a sense of power and control when they manipulate objects and events to suit themselves. The direct feedback from others and from their success with materials contributes to the development of self-identity as a person who has an impact on the world.

Social Development

Gary saw Charles enter the 3- to 4-year-olds' playroom with anticipation and excitement. He ran toward him, eager to play, and tackled him around the knees, sending him to the floor with a crash. Charles cried and sought to get away from Gary. In dismay, Gary noted, "He don't want to play with me."

Linda entered the school playground holding a rope long enough for two others to swing for jumping rope. She told the other girls that she had learned how to jump doubles from her older cousins. As Olivia and Angeline twirled rope, Linda started to jump and invited Kathleen to join her. With many stops and starts and Linda's coaching and encouragement, the girls finally began the rhythmic jumping together. Franny stood by, waiting and watching. Her turn would be soon. After a long jumping sequence, Kathleen made a misstep and Franny got her turn. Angeline and Olivia turned the rope more smoothly at an even, slow pace. Franny started a jumping sequence right away without all of the missteps that Kathleen made at the beginning.

Fergus and Paul were at the water table in the kindergarten room. Pouring water into containers holding 8 ounces of fluid, Fergus noticed that Paul kept pouring water into an overflowing salad dressing bottle and said, "When it's full, it's full. You can't fuller it no more. Dump it or use another one." Paul noticed his full bottle, dumped it, and began filling it again.

Gary has learned from the consequences of his own behavior that a tackle is not a suitable approach to initiate play. Linda has realized how to coach and encourage others as they attempt new skills and also how to keep the interest of several other players engaged. Olivia and Angeline are cooperating in twirling the rope, delaying gratification in anticipation of their own turns. Franny has observed the others playing and has learned how to move into the jumping sequence from the errors of Kathleen. Fergus has learned that he can give information that can help another, and Paul has learned to accept help.

Each child in these examples has either learned a new social skill or practiced one in these very ordinary play events. Play and learning have a complex relation, with new learning being both generated in the context of play and practiced on other play occasions. Play leads development and calls forth opportunities for new competencies to be explored, modified, practiced, or even discarded for more effective strategies.

Children enjoy their play and desire to maintain it. With this strong motivation, they learn to become more effective communicators both verbally and nonverbally. They demonstrate empathy to others within the roles of pretend play and learn how to display and read others' pretend and real emotions. They negotiate roles, rules of games, and cooperate in group pretend play and the formation of competitive games.

As children mature, they recognize fair and unfair treatment of others. They plan ahead for their play, as Linda did when she brought the long jump rope to school with her. Ultimately, they learn to control themselves and influence their playmates so that the play continues smoothly. Spontaneous play of

children is influenced by the children's gender, their ability to play socially, and their status in the playgroup. Each of these will be explored more fully.

Gender Differences in Children's Play

There appear to be no gender differences in object manipulation in infants in the first two years (Power, 2000). Once children establish their gender identity and can reliably identify other boys and girls, the nature of their play changes forever (Fagot & Leve, 1998). The amount of play by boys and girls does not differ, but the **style** of play and the choices of themes diverge. Most boys, like other male primates, tend to play more vigorously and more aggressively than girls. They also range further from adults in their play than do girls. Social culture for boys tends to be organized into competing groups or coalitions, whereas the social culture for girls is consistently more communal. Girls tend to focus on relationships and social support, demonstrating more nurturing and empathy in their play (Geary, 2004). These naturally occurring gender differences are reinforced through social learning. While children are growing up, family members, the media, and other social institutions provide clear cues as to appropriate

Within the roles of pretend play, children learn how to demonstrate empathy to others and how to display and read others' pretend and real emotions.

gender behavior. Thus, boys and girls receive strong messages about what constitutes appropriate play for a child of their sex. Through words and actions, adults let children know what is expected. Moreover, parents (and fathers in particular) punish the play of both daughters and sons that falls outside of gender stereotyped roles (although greater latitude is offered for girls to play with trucks than for boys to play with more typically feminine toys or roles) (Honig, 1998). Media and toy manufacturers reinforce stereotypical gender-related behavior in the play materials created for this age-group as well (Klugman, 1999; Willis, 1999).

As a result of these influences, it doesn't take long for children to begin to prefer to play with certain toys, in certain ways and with same-sex peers. Girls tend to practice social roles most often, whereas boys tend to choose roles embodying power relationships. Girls participate more frequently in housekeeping settings and boys engage in pretend play in garage, spaceship, or work-related settings (Howe, Moller, Chambers, & Petrakos, 1993). Preschool children have no difficulty in discriminating sex-stereotyped toys for boys and girls, even though they may not choose to restrict themselves to the toys intended for their gender (Eisenberg, 1983). It is also interesting to note that both boys and girls view exclusion of other children solely on the basis of gender as wrong, based on it not being "fair," even when the materials to be used in the activity are stereotypical (Theimer, Killen, & Strangor 2001).

School-age children continue the trend in role selection but often incorporate media or literary figures into their role-play. One common characteristic of the gender role portrayal of children over 6 is the clarity and distinctiveness between the male and female portrayals. Children's knowledge of sex stereotypes and awareness of gender constancy become uniform during the elementary school years. Increasingly children have more detailed information about the specific characteristics of their appropriate sex role and how to act accordingly (Bem, 1985).

In general, girls' play activities generate rule learning, imitation, task persistence, bids for recognition, compliance, remaining close to adults, and help-seeking behaviors, whereas boys' play activities force them into creative problem-solving behaviors, exploration, and the restructuring of prior learning (Block, 1979). These behaviors usually are considered by society to be typical for the sex role of children. Still, there remain substantial individual differences—healthy male children often engage in nurturing and communal behavior and healthy female children often participate in the assertive vigorous physical play most often associated with boys.

Categories of social participation. Social participation is important if children are to practice socializing with other children. Interacting with other children is more difficult than interacting with a parent or other adult. Clearly, watching others play is easier than coordinating one's behavior with one or more other players. The types of social participation described in the following list once were thought to represent increasing degrees of ability, but it is now recognized that, although acquired in sequence, each type of participation has independent, important characteristics (Parten, 1932):

1. **Unoccupied behavior.** The child is not engaged in any task or social participation. She or he spends most of the time looking around or wandering around, but is occupied with no specific task.
2. **Onlooker.** The child watches other children and sometimes talks with them. The child is actively engaged in observing specific activities.
3. **Solitary play.** The child plays with toys alone and independently, without interacting with others. Children use their intelligence and problem solving abilities to engage with objects or to pretend alone (Bornstein, 2007).
4. **Parallel activity.** The child plays independently, but the chosen activity brings him or her among other children who are engaged in the same activity. Two children putting puzzles together on the same table is typical of this type of play. Certain levels of maturity are required for both solitary and group play, and most preschool children participate in both types.
5. **Associative play.** The child plays with other children and interacts with them around a similar, but not identical, activity. For example, Niki rides his truck back and forth near a block construction where Dennis and Mark are working together. Occasionally, he stops to comment and then continues his "deliveries."
6. **Cooperative or organized supplementary play.** The child plays in a group that is organized to make some material product or to strive for some common goal. A simple game of ring-around-a-rosy is **cooperative play**, as is the previously mentioned play of Dennis and Mark, who are engaged in building.

Certain levels of maturity are required for both solitary and group play, and most preschool children participate in both types.

Solitary play and the various forms of group play are not hierarchical categories for young children. Certain levels of maturity are required for each type of play. In fact, it has been suggested that solitary play fosters the formation of novel behavior patterns and exercises creativity, whereas social play serves to enhance the bonds between individuals (Dolgin, 1981). Solitary play is the most common form of play for toddlers, partly because they lack experience and opportunity to interact with peers and partly because there is a point in their development at which toddlers switch from treating peers as objects to treating them as people Midway through the second year, toddlers are capable of mutual involvement, turn taking, and repetition in playful activities between two children (Hay, Ross, & Goldman, 2004).

Overall, the adult may see various forms of social participation in play. For example, the onlooker, although not socially involved, may be acquiring the knowledge that later will enable him or her to participate more directly. Some children may need time to wander through the play setting to see what their choices are before making a decision. Parallel play frequently occurs prior to an episode of cooperative play. Therefore, each kind of social participation has something to contribute to the child's development.

Social status. When children play together, they invariably learn about status in the group, dominance roles, and other power relationships. Their play provides a safe way to explore their own position in the group and also to indirectly comment on the existence of power relationships (Pellegrini, 2004). Children also may resort to applying specific classroom rules in situations where another player might thwart their wishes. For example, a child might call forth the rule of "no guns" when another child has constructed a weapon and playmates are intrigued. Such assertions as "Only four can play," "Take care of what you get out," and "First come, first served" may be recalled and applied by 4- and 5-year-old children only when they serve the purposes of the child calling on the rule (Jordan, Cowan, & Roberts, 1995). Other less overt strategies are equally effective. For example, Toby, who faces Jeanette and announces, "Let's play house," is communicating her desire to play but also is excluding Marie, on whom she has turned her back. This message is equally clear to all concerned. Toby has established her role of leader by

initiating the play activity and may continue by defining the ongoing play.

Like Toby, children who have high status in the group tend to direct their messages to specific players. Often they do this with more than one playmate, each in turn. Preferred players, though, must also be contingently responsive to other children and act so as to maintain the play. Even when rejecting a play idea, the high-status child may offer an explanation or an alternative rather than an outright rejection, thus continuing the interaction (Hazen & Black, 1989).

Competent school-age children behave in ways that are relevant to the ongoing activity and are sensitive to the nonverbal cues of playmates and responsive and appropriate to the social initiations by their peers. Less effective children have poor emotional regulation and situation knowledge, are less attentive to social cues, and are much more likely to engage their peers in aggressive or coercive cycles. They are frequently rejected or isolated by their playmates. These lower-status youngsters appear to be less connected to the group and unable to "read" the social situations or the emotional tenor of the group in order to coordinate their activities with others (Pettit & Harrist, 1993).

TYPES OF PLAY

Exploratory Behavior

Renzell, age 4, picked up a stethoscope, blew into the bell, looked at the earpieces, put the earpieces in his ears, tapped the bell, then walked over to a doll and announced that he was a doctor. He played out this role with several dolls, listening to their bodies all over. When Michael walked into the area, Renzell said, "I think you are sick," and began to listen to Michael's arm. Michael told him, "Listen right here," pointing to his chest. Renzell listened to Michael's chest and said the thing didn't work. He then listened to Michael's chest in different places, asking, "Can you hear that?" every now and then. He also listened to the radiator, to the hamster, and to other children, momentarily forgetting his doctor role.

The manipulation and examination of objects often has been lumped into the category of play, although in some ways it differs from true play. Children engaging in exploratory behavior are scanning the environment, scrutinizing, feeling, smelling, mouthing,

The first step in learning about objects and problem solving is investigative exploration.

children become more systematic and apparently develop a plan to investigate the novel objects (Power, 2000).

The **complexity** of the objects explored seems to be closely related to the time it takes to manipulate and investigate the object. Complexity increases with the number of parts (consider the variety of puzzles or model cars), responsiveness or pliability (sand or water is more pliable than a toy truck), and the number of possible uses (a ball is more versatile than a hockey stick). **Novelty** is also a major factor, with children showing wariness of objects that are too novel. Children still engage in exploratory behaviors when they encounter the same object after a substantial time interval or objects that are similar to more familiar ones. Computer games incorporate both novelty and complexity with the many options built within some of the software stimulating both exploration of the software program and game play.

Adults should attend to youngsters' need to explore materials when they engage in hands-on activity, although the time needed to do this on the first exposure is generally much greater than on later exposures. Keeping in mind the relationships of novelty and complexity, successful opportunities may be provided for all age groups with little or no confrontation between children and adult, as youngsters will explore the objects whether or not adults have planned for this.

Babies explore with mouths, hands, and feet using all their senses. During the preschool years, children explore paste by tasting, smelling, and smearing before using it to adhere pieces of paper. Water and sand are poured, patted, tasted, and smelled. Paper is crumpled, torn, cut, and chewed. All of these are simple exploratory behaviors. Six- to 7-year-olds are likely to use their fingertips than the palms of their hands and to engage in careful visual or auditory exploration as well. For example, when they encounter a manual potter's wheel, children will swirl it around with their fingers, examine it closely to see how it works, and try it out with a bit of clay before trying to make something with the wheel.

Exploration becomes play when the child shifts from the question, "What does this object do?" to a slightly different question, "What can I do with this object?" The object itself ceases to be the major focus of concern. Children incorporate objects into their play, where they determine the meanings and

shaking, hefting, moving, operating, probing, or otherwise investigating the nature of the objects at hand. Exploratory play generally consists of three general patterns: object procuring, manual investigation, and asking questions (Power, 2000). The questions being addressed are: What can this do? How does it work? What is the nature of this object or situation? Exploratory behavior of novel objects precedes true play behavior (Hutt, 1971). Investigative exploration also is the first step in learning about objects and in solving problems.

Exploration takes time. However, children use this interval efficiently for understanding their world. Infants and toddlers find that every object is new; every event is novel. This is why young children seem so busy, getting into one thing after another, and why safety is such a concern, as very young children are as likely to mouth or bite an electrical cord as they are a new food.

The amount of exploratory play with novel objects remains consistent but studies suggest that the nature of exploration shows developmental change over time. In general, with increasing age, uses of the artifact. Like Renzell and his stethoscope, children shift from exploration to play repeatedly during a single episode of using an object.

Play with Objects

Children use a variety of toys, materials, and other objects in their play. The novelty of an object attracts attention and stimulates exploration. However, the complexity of an object is more important in sustaining interest. This is true of all objects for all ages (Weilbacher, 1981). Children will play with anything: real things (utensils, furnishings, leaves and sticks, animals); reconstruction materials or instructional materials (memory games, puzzles, stacking toys); construction materials (blocks, paints, clay, cardboard); fluid materials (water, sand, snow); or toys (cars, dolls, and other miniature replicas). Play behavior can occur anywhere: in the car, yard, playground, nursery school, living room, classroom, or hallway. The play context including space, materials, time, and other people influences the selection of play. The experiences of all the children engaged in the play as well as the terrain, plants, or other objects in the physical space suggest content and type of play (Reifel & Yeatman, 1993). In addition, the quality of the play context is highly associated with children's social problem solving in child care and other settings (Goelman, 2005). Therefore, the space, playthings, and other elements of the context may be constructed to promote the safety of children and desirable social behaviors and to minimize undesirable behaviors.

Toys are objects that are designed to be attractive to children, to stimulate their interest, and to be safer than the real-object counterparts. They may be reduced in size and simplified such as a toy stove, replicated such as a toy truck, or structured to make basic concepts clear such as a set of various-size colored rings on a cone-shaped holder. Toys are also symbolic: they represent family relationships, provide cues for appropriate sex-role behavior, symbolically represent the child's own personality or self-concept, and transmit cultural values. For example, children can learn that other children from around the world play with toys that they enjoy as well.

The designs of playthings vary from realistic to abstract. Toddlers need realistic materials to pursue a play theme. They simply do not have enough experience or knowledge of what to do with abstract pieces. However, school-age children will play

This little person is engaged in solitary play and problem solving using the reconstruction toy of stacking cups.

longer and engage in more complex play with abstract toys (Trawick-Smith, 1990). Children between 2 and 6 years of age play with less structured materials like sand, water, blocks, and dough for substantial periods of time, but they seem to need more realistic props for complicated dramatic play.

Attractiveness, complexity, safety, and design of equipment similarly influence playground activity. Solitary play and more movement play occur with stationary equipment. Less equipment tends to encourage more social contacts and more aggression. On the other hand, movable equipment tends to elicit a greater variety of pretend play than would the same pieces if immobile. Children use the immobile equipment with a greater variety of movements and are more likely to initiate group games unrelated to the equipment (Weilbacher, 1981).

Children's motor competence, cognitive functioning, and social skills affect the manner with which the child engages in object play. Once some of the basic competencies of early childhood have been achieved, play becomes more refined, more challenging, and more elaborate.

Developmental changes in the use of objects. Object play in infancy shifts from rhythmic motor behavior, such as banging the top of the table with the hand, to repetitive action on objects, such as dropping the spoon to the floor over and over. In the last quarter of the first year, babies explore, and by the end of the first year use objects realistically though out of context. For example, drinking motions are used with a cup. Longer exploration of combining objects and actions, such as putting the cup on a saucer or pretending to stir in it with a spoon, soon follow. By the end of the second year, toddlers use longer sequences of action related to the functions of the objects, such as stirring in a cup with a spoon, feeding a doll, combing its hair, and putting it to bed. By the time the child reaches the third year, he or she can assign to the doll the role of actor. In other words, the doll is made to "pick up the spoon" and "eat." The shift from simple manipulation of objects to dramatic play is made during the second year. Children learn to make this shift from the literal use of objects to pretend play as a result of their interactions with adults or more skilled children. What general sequences occur? The following list is a sequential summary of the play behaviors that occur as the very young child develops play with objects:

1. Repetitive motor behavior, mouthing.
2. Systematic exploration of objects.
3. Actions begin to be appropriate for objects.
4. Objects that have functional relationships are combined.
5. Action patterns are combined to form larger sequences (stirring in, pouring from, and washing a bowl).
6. Action patterns are applied to self (may be simple pretending—e.g., eating or sleeping).
7. Action patterns are applied to others or to replicas (doll "eats").
8. The ability to act is attributed to replicas (doll "feeds" teddy bear).
9. Objects that are not present but are needed to complete a logical sequence are "invented" (pretends a spoon to stir with).
10. Objects are transformed for use in sequences (uses pencil for spoon).

The term **transform** means to substitute one object for another. For example, a 3-year-old might use a pencil, a stick, a tongue depressor, or a screwdriver in the absence of a spoon to stir a drink or to feed a doll.

The first six behavior patterns are sometimes combined and practiced in order to gain mastery over an object. Mastery play or practice play is repetitious, but may have slight variations until the properties of the object and what it can do have been thoroughly mastered. One 2-year-old manipulated a set of seven nesting cubes in 30 different ways. Each cube was combined with one, two, and three other cubes, in addition to the full set. She also tried stacking the cubes. Mastery play, as well as exploratory behavior, is common when people of any age encounter objects that are novel and complex. Older children engage in similar play with newly introduced technologies.

Individual differences. Some children respond to the symbolic potential of objects more readily than others. Their play style has been called the **dramatist style**. However, other children respond to other attributes of objects; they are more interested in the color, texture, shape, form, and other physical characteristics of the materials. They are the **patterners**. The dramatist approaches materials with the question, "What story can I tell with these things?" The patterner approaches the materials with the question, "How can I arrange these things so that they are beautiful?" Patterners differ in their approach to materials in that between the ages of 2 and 3, these children communicate meaning by the spatial location of objects. For example,

Gieshala poked holes into a wad of tissue paper to represent eyes for her snowman, which needed to see. The dramatist simply would have pretended the eyes.

By 3 years of age, patterners tend to communicate meaning mostly by spatial location. They also are concerned with design elements and the functions of the structures or arrangements that they make. A child who is a patterner may use all the trucks and arrange them by size, color, function, or other criteria. Adults who do not recognize this style of play sometimes expect the child to give up some of the trucks to other players, who could be satisfied with using one in the dramatic style. However, the removal of several units of the design would totally disrupt the purpose of the play. For the patterner, the objects themselves are the significant elements of the play. Children's play style appears to develop early and to carry on as a preferred mode of play throughout childhood (Shotwell, Wolf, & Gardner, 1979).

Between 2 and 3 years of age, both patterners and dramatists will build with blocks in horizontal and vertical axes. The dramatist, however, builds more simply, just enough to construct the house or store where the people live and shop. The patterner of the same age combines blocks in larger, more complex, more elaborate structures, experimenting with line and balance.

Observant adults who supervise children should note which style the child appears to be using before insisting that children divide up the materials and share them. A better approach to a patterner is to suggest the sequential use of materials. A dramatist is unlikely to be disturbed by sharing the material as long as there is enough to enact the story he or she has in mind.

Dramatic Play

Dramatic play, or pretend play, probably is one of the most apparent forms of play seen in young children. Pretend play may begin at about 1 year of age, and the amount of time spent at it peaks between the ages of 5 and 6 then drops off as children are in school for longer periods of time. Pretend play with others or **sociodramatic play**, in which children share goals, a theme, and materials is possible by age 3 if children have acquired the skills to do so and will continue throughout childhood. Onset of this challenging form of play is delayed for those children whose opportunities are more limited. There are differences in style

If given the opportunity to play with others, young children will often engage in sociodramatic play, in which they share goals, a theme, and materials.

with which children enact events in their pretend play, as detailed in Table 7–1 (Rosenberg, 2001). Style refers to features of the behavior that occur independent of the content of the play. As with object play, style tends to be consistent over time with a player. Some children use both styles or do not appear to have a preferred mode.

When interrupted for a transition in a group setting, the **pragmatist** simply stops and complies with adult requests. The **fantasizer**, however, has difficulty leaving the imaginative mode and may resist change by ignoring the adult, incorporating the adult request into the fantasy, and may appear distracted or distressed at the interruption when forced to comply. Such children need sufficient warning to complete their imaginative episode prior to transition.

Older children also participate in pretend play, but school and group games take more of their time. They may use either style, and if time and opportunity permits, maintain the story line over several days or weeks.

In a recent review of cultural influences on social play, there appeared to be variations in the timing of skill development and in the preferences for particular themes in cross-cultural studies as well as those of subpopulations inside the United States (Power, 2000; Gaskins, Haight & Lancy, 2007). When play is understood as a cultural activity, it is easier to see the relationship of the child's culture (economic conditions, characteristics of the community, the value placed on play by adults, and child rearing practices) influence both the skills of the players and the content of the play (Göncü, Jain, & Tuermer, 2007).

Table 7–1 Dramatic Styles of Children in Imaginative Play

	CHARACTERISTIC TRAITS
Fantasizer	1. Child is thoroughly into the imaginative play. She cannot be distracted, has no concern about failure, and lacks self-consciousness. She is focused and riveted.
	2. There is an internal locus of control with a lack of concern for the adult leader or supervisor, who seem to be ignored.
	3. There is self-talk during the play where the child appears to have conversations with his "other self." He may take multiple roles.
	4. She usually has vivid images with details drawn from her own experience, but frequently imagines what has never happened. She oscillates between memory and fantasy with the memories providing a stimulus for elaboration.
	5. Fantasizers jump right into the activity and begin to play or they choose not to participate.
	6. They seem to be very sensitive to sensory cues and won't engage when there is a bad smell or they do not feel well.
Pragmatist	1. This child is concerned with the real world around her and can be distracted by nearby activity.
	2. There is a concern for the audience. He may seek approval and may need to be encouraged by the caregiver.
	3. She may ask for clarification or permission from the adult in the midst of play then start up again. The play is less intense.
	4. He engages in self-talk but it is generally self-evaluative or a comment on what he has done, "I really don't like this hat."
	5. The pragmatists enact what has happened in their lives. Their imagery is general, such as any cat, rather than a specific cat.
	6. She will play under more adverse conditions and does not appear to be concerned with the temperature or sensory characteristics of the space.
	7. She tries hard to find a useful procedure to carry out the activity, is predictable, and seeks adult approval.

Apparently pretend play is more sensitive to instruction and encouragement from the adults in the environment than are other forms of play (Smith, 2005). However, there appears to be little difference in the types of play children choose when all types of play available (Ramsey, 1998).

Youngsters' play may not flourish if the setting is not culturally similar or sensitive (Nourot & Van Hoorn, 1991). Pretend play is learned from adults who coach children in using symbols with words, actions, situations, and objects. Many families tend to do this without thinking about it, and others tend not to think of doing it at all.

Object substitution. Children need to develop several skills before they can easily pretend play with other children. First, they must acquire the ability to substitute one object for another, or transform one object into another. The closer the substituted object resembles the object needed for the dramatization, the more likely the child will be to use it. A shell can be substituted for a cup, but not for a bat. Between 2 and 3 years of age, children can substitute one object in their play, but not two. For example, an abstract wooden object might be used for a horse and a cup for a drinking trough, but the play breaks down if the child is given the abstract wooden object and a shell. In the third year, children will substitute a cup for any container: potty-chair, bowl, hat, or dish. Adults know the child is substituting because the object is renamed or because the action with the object is clearly an action appropriate for the object being substituted for. However, 4-year-olds tend to use objects more realistically (Trawick-Smith, 1990). They are more likely to engage in group pretend play, or sociodramatic play, in which all the players must agree on the meaning of each pretend object. There are obvious complications in having many substituted objects during group play.

Object invention. Next, children need to be able to invent an object—to imitate its use through actions even when no object is at hand. **Object invention** is simple pantomime, and in its simplest form, only one pretend object at a time is used. A child may use a stirring action above a bowl to invent a spoon, or twirl an arm above the head to symbolize a rope. Younger children find it very difficult to mime without a placeholder object (a real object that takes the place of another real object, such as a stone used as a car). Between 3 and 4 years of age,

they pretend with nothing to hold onto. School age children do it readily.

Children who have not learned how to pretend may approach toys in an exploratory mode and then respond to them as if they were real. In one preschool room, Emily entered the housekeeping area and examined the model stove, turning the knobs, gingerly touching the burners, and opening the oven to peer inside. Then, she pulled the stove from the wall and examined the back. Putting her hands on her hips in great disgust, she addressed the teacher, "This damned stove won't work!" She was upset when the adult responded that the toy stove was not supposed to work like a real stove.

Changes of time and place. Children also learn to transform time and settings. They might substitute a climber for a spaceship in flight or pretend that the sandbox is a beach during the period when prehistoric animals lived. Players are very aware of this convention and tend to play consistently with it. For example, Debbie, the "baby," climbed out of her bed to iron on the ironing board. Her "mother" admonished her that babies can't iron or they'll get burned. Debbie climbed back into her bed, said: "Grow, grow, grow. I'm the big sister now," and returned to the ironing board, condensing many years into a few seconds. Time and place have no restrictions except in the information of the players. In addition, children who have no knowledge or experience of objects such as buses and airplanes are unable to initiate play situations involving them.

Role-playing. The young player must learn to take on a role. The simplest kind of role is the **functional role** or behavioral role (Watson & Fisher, 1980). The child becomes a person who is driving a truck. This role does not contain a permanent identity or personality but is defined by the person in the present situation. A child taking on a **character role**, however, engages in many behavioral sequences appropriate for the part. Character roles include family roles (mother, father, sister), occupational roles (firefighter, doctor), and fictional roles (superhero, witch). Family roles are played with much more detail than the others. Younger children tend to limit themselves to roles with which they have had direct experience (baby, parent), but older preschoolers are more likely to act out roles that they have observed (husband, wife) and try more occupational roles. Lastly, preschool children are able to portray multiple roles. One 30-month-old girl was observed playing "mother" to "baby" and "wife" to "husband" while coaching "husband" in how to perform the role of "father" (Miller & Garvey, 1984). Older children and adults are capable of assuming a broad variety of character roles. Role and action representations initially are affected by the availability of realistic props.

Cultural and experiential differences in children.   Children bring to the play experience their cultural background and lifestyle as sources of information. For example, one child tried to bounce an orange. He had never eaten an orange, but had played with balls. Because of the orange's roundness, he treated it as a ball. This is not a situation for a reprimand, but for information.

Some children play out life experiences that are completely foreign to their teachers, such as being evicted, gang fighting, family violence, and burglaries, as well as explicitly sexual activities. On one hand, adults may not want this play in the group, but on the other, children may need to play out their experiences. Children may be redirected into other aspects of role behavior such as going to work or cleaning house. They should not be scolded or shamed about theme or role depiction.

The ways boys and girls establish common ground necessary for sociodramatic play are quite different. Boys tend to use statements about themselves or about what they are going to do to define a common play situation: "I am the bus driver," acclaimed Milton as he manipulated chairs and blocks to form a bus. Other boys joined the play theme by either assisting in the construction of the bus or sitting in it. On the other hand, girls usually focus on the group or the relationship and frequently establish the relationships between players as a means to begin play. "Let's pretend we are lost and scared," quivered Jean to her companion. The girls took hands and hid under the table. Style of play varies by social class as well.

Children in predominantly Euro-American, middle-class preschool programs are easily upset when peers deny them friendship or threaten them. African-American and Hispanic youngsters in a Head Start Program use a lot more teasing and oppositional and competitive talk with each other and are not upset by it (Ramsey, 1998). Both groups of children are able to form social cohesion within their classrooms, establish play frames, and maintain and terminate play using their own interaction patterns. Clearly, their approach is characterized by children's expectations of how one behaves when playing in the group. Needless to say, it is easier for children to play with members of their own groups, as it is easier for adults to supervise play of children who share their culture group.

Acceptance in play of all the cultural elements that might be expected in a group of children is basic to accepting the children. Race, ethnicity, religion, age, gender, family composition, lifestyle, economic circumstances, presence of disabling conditions, sexual preferences of familiar adults, as well as specifics related to the local community may appear in children's play content. One 11-year-old sought information about what to call the grandchildren of her father's second wife by her first husband and whether or not they should be invited to the wedding that she was enacting with adult figures. Adult responses of surprise, shock, or confusion can usually be reduced when such adults seek to understand the cultural milieu of all the children. Play behavior is built on variations of nonplay behavior, then repeated, combined in a number of ways, reduced to unimportance through humor, or magnified through play ritual. Children, of course, must use what they know, regardless of content. As in all other behavior, experience is important in determining how children play. Less experienced children usually play like younger children until they acquire the skills that others of the age group demonstrate. Experienced, knowledgeable adults take gender and cultural expectations into account when setting up and guiding play in a social environment.

Rules children construct for themselves in social pretend play.   Between 2 and 6 years of age, children gradually generate rules to allow them to engage in pretend play in groups. Two- and 3-year-olds do not see the need for the rules until they begin to engage in increasingly more sophisticated themes and stories or with more players. Some who have difficulty in entering and maintaining complex social play have not yet perceived the need for some rules, do not know the rules, or have not quite understood how to put the rules into operation. There may also be variations among groups of children as they develop the social rules. Needless to say, children need time and opportunity to interact with each other in supportive play settings in order to construct or modify the internal rules of social play (see Figure 7–2).

Explicit Rules:	Implicit Rules:
1. A child who is first to arrive in the dress-up area, or who first proposes an idea for a game, becomes the director of the play.	1. Children maintain the distinction between fantasy and reality while operating within the fantasy context.
2. All children must ask to play.	2. Unless playing alone, children engage others in the pretend game in progress.
3. All children must take on some role within the story.	
4. All children must play fairly (although what is fair is not clearly defined; it is usually used in the context of taking turns, sharing, and not being bossy).	3. Children maintain the pretend sequence by creating and continuing an adequate story line and by accepting the fantasy proposals of others. (Curran, 1999, p. 49)

Figure 7–2 Explicit and implicit rules.

Peer communication about pretend play. **Metacommunication**, a communication about communications, are either statements or actions that explain messages about how a behavior should be interpreted (Farver, 1992). They indicate if the behavior should be taken seriously or playfully. Verbal metacommunications often set the scene or conditions for play: "Let's pretend this fire is real." Nonverbal metacommunications are less explicit, such as a child "shoveling snow" in the middle of summer. Metacommunications explicitly separate the real from the pretend and work frequently to maintain the play (Göncü, Patt, & Kouba, 2004). Even when players step out of the play frame or outside the adopted roles to provide information or a rebuke, other players do not seem to experience confusion (Dockett, 1998).

These messages frame play so that it is socially defined as play and is not, therefore, "for real." To maintain play, some messages must be said "out of frame" in order to share information so that the play can continue.

The **play frame** encompasses the scope of the play event. Included in the play frame are all the objects and people relevant to the play scenario. Players within the frame are linked by communication and by their shared goals. For example, if a child is involved in an episode where he or she must leave the "restaurant" to get some more "food" from across the room, the child is still in the frame. If a photograph were taken of the pretend play episode described at the beginning of the chapter, the photographer would automatically move back to include the children and the rocking horse. This

would be so, even though other persons might be in either the foreground or background of the photo. Persons and objects nearby, but not linked by communication and common goals that further the play, are out of the play frame.

Metacommunications begin and end play, but also are used in planning and negotiating the content and direction of play and in coordinating role enactment. Helping professionals support and promote skill development when they demonstrate or suggest typical metacommunication devices to children who are less skillful (Table 7–2).

Some statements are *procedural*, such as "Do you want to play house?" or "It's my turn." Other statements that serve to initiate play are statements about role, objects, or setting, or about planning the theme. Children mention another's role ("You can be the daddy"), their own role ("I'll be the nurse"), or a joint role ("We can be neighbors"). Children mention objects, *transforming* them into something else ("This is the car," while arranging four chairs in a square) or inventing an object ("Here is the menu. What do you want?" while handing a pretend menu to a patron).

Children *transform settings* ("This here [pointing to some blocks] is the boat on the ocean") and also invent settings ("We are lost kids in the forest," while standing in the middle of the play yard).

Children *make plans* about the behavior or feelings of another character ("Pretend you are lost and scared"), about their own actions ("I gotta go shopping and I'm in a hurry"), or about joint plans ("We better build a big house so the monster won't get us").

Table 7–2 Purpose of Metacommunications About Play with Verbal and Nonverbal Examples

CHILD'S PURPOSE	VERBAL COMMUNICATION	NONVERBAL COMMUNICATION
Initiating the play	"Wanna play?" "Let's run."	Enters a play setting and engages in behaviors that start the play such as "cooking" or "offering" blocks to another child.
Establishing a theme	"Let's pretend we are in space and we get lost." "I am the doctor. Is your baby sick?"	Uses props that suggest a theme such as a menu for a restaurant or a cash register for a store.
Transforming settings or inventing them	"It's night, and dark here." "This can be my house and over there is your house." "Mission control is at the table."	Engages in actions that suggest a setting, such as making water-flow noises while aiming a hose.
Establishing a role	"I'm the mom." "I'll get this ship working." "This will be the biggest building I ever did!"	"Comforts" a doll. Carries the "tool box" over to the ship. Builds with blocks.
Establishing another's role	"You better watch where you are going "You be the daddy."	Hands another child the objects to be used, such as the flowers in a "flower shop." (Used only with children who play together frequently)
Establishing joint roles	"We are just kids and we are running away." "You get to be the monster, then I do."	Child acts as though experiencing great pain and falls to the ground in front of another player.
Transforming objects or inventing them	"Take this ship to Mars" (while sitting in a nest of large blocks). "Here is the money" (while the child gestures only)	Uses a teacup to feed or water model animals in the "farm" constructed of blocks.
Making plans about the feelings or the behavior of another	"Let's say you are really mean."	Uses facial expressions and gestures to convey feelings.
Making plans about his or her own feelings or behavior	"This place is really scary so I better hide."	
Establishing their joint feelings or behavior	"We can put this fire out really fast. Get another hose."	
Terminating play with communication about theme, role, props, or settings	"I don't want you to chase me anymore." "Let's play . . ." "Put the stuff in the box and let's have a snack."	Walks away. Looks away, attends to something else. Shakes head or uses other gestures to indicate disengagement.

Some statements *terminate the play*. These statements can be about the role ("I'm not the daddy anymore"), about actions ("I'm not chasing you"), or about settings ("Let's say we left the city") (Garvey, 1990).

Influencing the direction of play.   Preschool children tend not to expose their pretend illusion unnecessarily. If possible, they keep their communications "within frame," but metacommunications lie on a continuum from deeply within frame to completely out of frame (Griffin, 1984).

Children use **ulterior conversations**, which might appear to be role enactment but do alter the course of the play. The query "Is it nighttime?" from the "baby" effectively initiates a caregiving sequence from the "mother."

Underscoring provides information to other players (for example, "I'll get the dinner now," spoken in character voice). Underscoring also is used to "magic" something: "Grow, grow, grow. Now I am big." Another common example is "Wash, wash, wash" for dishes or laundry. This making of "magic" is done in a rhythmic, singsong voice.

Storytelling frequently is couched in the past tense and often is spoken in cadence. It allows for the development of more elaborate plots: "Let's say this spaceship went up, way up . . . and the computer went out . . . and the moon wasn't there."

Prompting is a technique in which one player instructs another on how to act or what to say, often in a stage whisper or a softer voice: "I'm ready for breakfast now; . . . (whispering) no, you have to cook the eggs first before I eat."

Formal pretend proposals sometimes are embedded into ongoing play, as in "Let's pretend the family goes to the beach." The suggestion for play variation usually is used when the play scenario is becoming repetitive or falling apart. Usually, the more indirect methods are preferred once a play sequence is begun. These are summarized in Table 7–3.

When children pretend using small figures and blocks or a dollhouse, nearly all of the story line is provided by narrative rather than by action of the dolls. When children themselves are the actors, however, they are more able to use nonverbal communicators as well to supply the content of the play.

Role selection.   The social relationships in a group of children are reflected in their play. High-status children can join ongoing play by imperiously adopting a role or defining an activity ("I'll be the aunt, coming to visit"). Lower-status children must ask permission to join the play ("Can I be the sister?") and may be restricted to particular roles. Often, higher-status children will assign lower-status children to the roles they may play ("You can be Grandma, who's sick").

Table 7–3 Summary of Strategies Children Use to Redirect Play Within the Play Frame

STRATEGIES	DESCRIPTION	EXAMPLE
Ulterior conversations	Statements that are a part of pretend play and also suggest what the other players should do next	"These children are really very hungry."
Underscoring	Statements made by one player to inform the others about what they are doing. These are usually used when nonverbal enactments may not work.	"I will go to work. Then I will come home again"
Storytelling	Statements that elaborate the theme or those that set up a problem that must be solved within the theme.	"Smoke! Smoke! The house is on fire and we gotta get out of here fast!"
Prompting	One player informs another on what to do or say. This is often in a stage whisper, but may be mimed or communicated through gestures.	(Whispered) "That's the bride, hat. If you want a hat, put on this one for the groom."
Formal pretend proposals	One player suggests a major shift in the play to the other players. The intent is to remain in the play sequence with all the players but change the theme.	(During house play) "What do you say that this family goes on a vacation to the beach?"

The roles assigned may reflect actual status in the group. Play leaders also use rejection statements ("You can't play here" and counter defining statements ("We aren't in a forest—we're in a jungle").

The role-play of children is very complex. They must participate as writer-directors of their imaginative play from outside the play frame and enact make-believe roles and events within the play frame.

Children tend to resist certain kinds of make-believe. They are much more willing to change generations than to change gender. Boys prefer male roles, whether they are baby or grandparent roles, and will not readily take mother roles. High-status children tend to resist taking a lower-status role in the make-believe play, preferring to be the parent rather than the baby, the captain rather than the seaman, and so on. When one player refuses to play an unsatisfactory role, she or he usually is incorporated into the more desirable role. For example, a child unwilling to be the victim becomes one of two monsters, and the victim is invented.

Children resist interrupting pretend play with reality. For example, if a child trips and falls down, he or she is likely to pretend a hospital-doctor sequence rather than interrupt the flow of the play to seek help from an adult. The child simply incorporates the event into the play if at all possible.

Combining the pretend play skills.   Once children have become skillful players, they modify and extend their pretend play. Children first use the pretend skills in short sequences then combine them into more complex sequences. These **play schemes** are named by topic such as "cooking," "playing babies," or "driving the car." Generally, these schemes combine pretend play with action or object and role play into action-based portrayals of real-life situations (Roskos, 1990). As children gain in maturity and skill, they join a group of related play schemes and transform the play into a more elaborate **play episode** that is socially organized and has a specific problem to solve inherent to the plot. It could be a family going on vacation with no suitcases. Episodes are tied together through the topic and rely on language to integrate and hold the play sequence together.

An episode is played out in stages. First, the children ready the play area by handling the materials and moving the props. Second, children share directing the course of play when the roles are determined, the ground rules are established, the problem is stated or implied, and the story is narrated (Roskos, 1990).

Both schemes and episodes are commonly called sociodramatic play or thematic play and may portray a variety of topics. However, in the episode, there will be a problem to resolve. Problems such as relatives coming to visit (but there are not enough beds), playing store (where no one comes to buy), or playing post office (where there is an insufficient number of stamps) are typical. Favorite schemes such as "comforting the baby" could appear in all of these, and often do, as children signal each other to repeat a preferred sequence. Episodes tend to have a storylike structure with a clear beginning, development of the problem, resolution of the problem, and an end. When children know each other well, have many shared play schemes, and have had the opportunity to develop all of the skills mentioned in this section, the pretend play can extend for substantial periods of time.

School-age children play more elaborately, with more characters, and with more detail when they are in an environment that allows them to pretend (Curry & Bergen, 1987). They also select more dramatic problems such as capture and rescue. Seven to 12-year-olds are able to increase the layers of pretend play, such as when their episode is that of writers and actors performing in the theater. The pretend play of rehearsal and script writing may take much longer than "the play" they are producing. They may also engage in improvisational contests or act out storybook or television themes. The pretend play of children requires cooperation, coordination of effort, organization of resources, and complex social interactions.

Construction Play

Children play with objects for the purposes of pretend play, but they also play with them for the purposes of manipulating them based on their physical properties alone. Some aspects of this have previously been described as children's handling of objects as dramatists or as patterners. **Construction play** occurs when children make or build something. Solitary, parallel, and cooperative play are all very common.

Young children.   During the second half of the first year of life, children can bang on objects and twist, turn, push, pull, open, and shut them. Between 1 and 2 years of age, children acquire the abilities to empty and fill objects, to hammer a peg into a pegboard, and to separate play dough. Real construction begins during the second year when the child learns to connect objects together (such as threading beads or attaching the pieces of a train) and develops the corresponding ability to disjoin objects (such as snap beads). Children also learn to stack and knock down blocks and to build both vertically and horizontally with them.

Between 2 and 3 years of age, children make constructions and name them "houses" and may combine various construction materials, such as mixing blocks with cars or toys. This often is done for the purpose of initiating pretend play. Given the guidance of supporting adults, they also will learn tool use, such as knives and rollers for clay, cookie cutters, scissors, and hammers and nails. At this age, children's constructions are very simple; they are more interested in the process than the product.

By the time children are 4, their constructions become more detailed and elaborate. They might construct a house of blankets and boxes and blocks, or a toy world with miniature dolls, trucks, and soldiers. They also make music in time, particularly with percussion instruments. They begin to show interest in their paintings as products and to cut paper designs. Their strategies are more organized.

Between 5 and 7 years of age, children have sufficient small-muscle control to plan and make a variety of things. Constructions are increasingly elaborate and often require social collaboration. They can do simple sewing and weaving; they can use potholders and cook simple dishes. At this time, they also begin to make costumes or other supplementary props for their pretend play.

Older children. Children in elementary school may be interested in model construction, handicrafts, weaving, woodworking, metalworking, bookbinding, basketry, carving, and a variety of other projects. They also construct some of their own games and do creative writing. Skillful pretend players also build sets, make costumes, and put on their own plays; the planning of script, actors, action, props, and sets may take hours, days, or weeks, whereas the production itself may be less than 10 minutes long. This also is the period of collecting and hobbies. School-age children extend their interests in constructions using a wide variety of materials, becoming increasingly scientific and experimental (Johnson, 1998).

Children who are inexperienced in social settings, or who seem to have difficulty getting along with others often find parallel play with construction materials satisfying. It provides for conversation

School-age children extend their interests using a wide variety of materials.

now and then and does not demand the integrated social skills of pretend play in a group.

Play with Movement

Adults are familiar with the joyous running, jumping, and laughing of children coming outside for recess. Most physical games are composed of fundamental motor skills in combinations that improve strength, endurance, balance, and coordination. Youngsters also acquire these attributes through informal play as they mature. For example, maintaining balance and just hanging on is the first stage of swinging. Children imitate peers in repeated attempts, but their movements are not synchronized and they have limited success, usually "stomaching" the swing. Eventually, they adapt their strategies to suit their own abilities and limitations, frequently kicking the ground to increase their swinging speed. Then the timing improves so the swing may be pumped, with unskillful jumping from the moving swing attempted. With practice, they delight in demonstrating their prowess to their peers, sometimes competing, even though optimum amplitude is not achieved. Refinement and efficiency of movement occurs as youngsters eventually attain security in their own skills and become capable of experimenting with "bumping" or other possibilities with the motion or the swing itself (Fox & Tipps, 1995). In a safe setting, with opportunities to observe more skilled players, and with practice and time, children attain skills in many movement activities.

The feeling of sheer splendor experienced by a preschooler racing down a hill, feet thudding on turf, wind blowing through the hair and on the skin; the careful placement of each step as a timid child threads the way up to the top of the climber; the amazingly empty feeling in the stomach of a child on a zooming sled: these all involve play with motion itself. The children may or may not laugh, but they are exquisitely satisfied and pleased with their performance. Less-abled children are often most successful in movement play with age-mates where demands for emotional regulation, language, and social skills are lessened.

Play with movement begins in infancy and continues throughout adulthood, as is evidenced in the popularity of swimming pools, ski resorts, and bowling alleys. Helping professionals, themselves players, usually are sensitive to the more mature forms of play with movement. Four aspects of movement play will be addressed that will illuminate the safe supervision of children's play: practice play, challenge, risk taking, and **rough-and-tumble play**.

Respecting repetitious activity. Practice play, sometimes called exercise play begins in infancy and continues throughout childhood. Quite simply, it is a behavior repeated over and over. For example, Esther, age 5, wanted to try the high slide in the park. An adult went with her and offered to catch her the first time. Hesitant and timid at first, Esther went up the slide and down with growing satisfaction and pleasure. She took 21 turns on the slide without ever repeating exactly her previous performance. She varied the placement of hands and feet; went down on belly, bottom, and back; climbed up the slide forward and backward; went down feet first and head first. The adult observed her, commented on her performance, and stood close to the slide when concerned for Esther's safety. This child, who began hesitantly, left the experience with satisfaction and greater confidence in her ability.

From infancy to adolescence, what the child practices varies but the process remains much the same. In the second year, toddlers walk, run, march, throw, climb, and dance. Between 2 and 3 years of age, they jump from low heights, hop on one foot, balance on a beam, and hang by their arms. Between the ages of 3 and 4, they begin to catch balls, climb jungle gyms, and ride tricycles. Between 4 and 5 years of age, they roller skate, swim, ride scooters and other vehicles, dance to music, bounce balls, and play catch. Between 5 and 7 years of age, they can use stilts, swing and pump the swing, and jump rope. Older children are likely to practice for specific sports. Exercise play contributes to physical fitness and to brain development (Smith, 2005). Skilled performance is often a means of engaging in social interactions that might otherwise be unavailable. It requires technique, memory, practice, and, as children are older, competition, which by its nature requires cooperation.

Maintaining interest in movement play. The selection of a play activity usually is based on its potential challenge for the child. The challenges undertaken are those that require slightly greater skill than the child already possesses. Usually, the child observes the action, tests his or her ability to do it, seeks instruction or help if necessary, and then practices the skill until it has been mastered. Children who are obese, clumsy, or disabled find the natural movements of much younger children challenging and need additional support and encouragement to attempt even those simpler skills (Javernik, 1988).

Because play is not "for real," children are free to drop a task that is too difficult for them without loss of self-respect. Sometimes, this is verbalized as "just playing around." Interest in the action remains high until mastery is complete. If a mastered skill, such as dribbling a ball, can be varied and incorporated into other skills, such as evading and running, interest may remain with the activity for long periods of time. In this sense, challenge comes from within the players and is a test of their own skills. At its best, challenging play helps children to understand themselves and their competencies and to recognize their own accomplishments against the background of previous behavior.

Understanding risk. There frequently is some risk in play with motion. Skiing is definitely more risky than running. Some youngsters seem like monkeys, climbing high into trees; others of the same age are frightened of simple climbing frames with padded mats beneath. Temperament and previous experience influence the willingness of children to take risks in play. Toddlers have little sense of potentially dangerous situations and must be protected. Preschool children, however, should be provided many opportunities to try skills in supervised play to learn just how competent they are.

By the age of 7, most children can judge the risk involved in any activity and are unlikely to go beyond their ability unless urged to do so. For example, Gwendolyn was well coordinated for a 7-year-old, was an excellent swimmer, and could ride a two-wheel bike. Jeff, only two weeks younger, moved easily enough but couldn't swim or do gymnastics. He spent more of his time at indoor activities. When the children were playing together outside, Gwendolyn climbed a tree and invited Jeff up. After being urged and called a scaredy-cat, Jeff attempted the climb. He fell three times because he couldn't catch the branch with his hands and pull himself up by his arms as Gwendolyn could. Bruised and shaken, he clung to the trunk once Gwendolyn had pulled him up. Apparently realizing that the tree was too risky for Jeff, Gwendolyn swung down and procured a ladder to help his descent. Children frequently assume that an activity that is easy for them will be easy for an age-mate and may need guidance in recognizing the difference between being supportive to peers and challenging them to perform potentially dangerous activities. Children

rarely attempt feats that are beyond their abilities unless pressured to do so.

Supporting social and physical testing. Many children participate in rough motor play, which increases both the challenge and the risk. At a high pitch of activity, children run, hop, jump, fall over, chase, flee, wrestle, hit, laugh, and make faces which is sometimes embedded in superhero play (Pellegrini, 2007).Usually played in a group, **rough-and-tumble play** differs from aggression, which includes such behaviors as pushing, taking things, grabbing, frowning, and staring down another (Pellegrini, 2004).

Play fighting is similar to rough-and-tumble play in that the participants know it's not real. Play fighting is carried out in interrupted sequences or in incomplete actions. For example, a child will say "Bam!" while striking at another but without following through with physical contact. Play fighting has clear metacommunication signals to let the participants know that it is play and not aggression. For example, one third-grade child passed a note to another girl, making her intentions quite clear (see Figure 7–3).

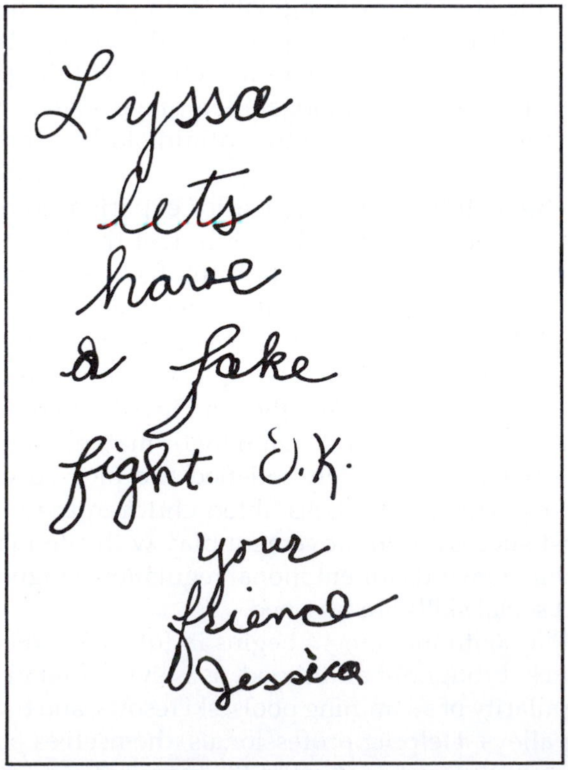

Figure 7–3 A written play signal for rough-and tumble play that was passed between two nine year-olds in school.

All preschool children engage in rough-and-tumble play, although boys do so more often than girls. Boys tend to play in this way in larger groups at the perimeter of the play yard and girls are more likely to carry out rough-and-tumble play near equipment and in a more restricted areas. Shrieks, shouting, howling, and laughter accompany this play. Rough-and-tumble play at this age frequently is combined with character roles of superheroes. Usually, young children spend more time watching this kind of play than participating in it.

School-age children usually play with children of the same sex, unless the play specifically requires a member of the opposite sex. One game, called "kiss or kill," requires one player to chase another of the opposite sex, get him or her down, say, "Kiss or kill?" and proceed with the kiss or the "strike" as the downed player prefers. Rough-and-tumble play is most likely to occur after the children have been engaged in set tasks or after prolonged sedentary activity. When older children participate in rough-and-tumble play, it most frequently flows into games with rules, not aggression (Pellegrini, 2004). Children generally play this with friends peaking in frequency during middle childhood (Smith, 2005). Tag or other running games often follow rough-and-tumble chasing. Interestingly, rough-and-tumble play is closely associated with social competence and high status in older boys. Unpopular boys, on the other hand, don't seem to be able to discriminate between aggression and rough-and-tumble play. Apparently, they have not learned to distinguish the appropriate cues and respond to playful acts with aggressive ones (Pellegrini, 2004).

Both children and helping professionals must be able to discriminate between real aggression and rough-and-tumble play or play fighting. The differences often are apparent only in facial expression, such as a smile, a silly face, or a frown. Laughter and noisemaking (such as "monster sounds") often signify that an activity is playful. Other play signals also are used to indicate the intent to play rough-and-tumble, such as "Let's play chase!" The adult's task is to help children indicate to peers whether or not they want to play ("Don't chase me—I'm not the dragon anymore," or "I'm not playing"). Often, safety zones must be established to avoid inadvertent involvement of unwilling players.

Three social functions are served through rough-and-tumble play, especially for boys. Children engaged in rough-and-tumble play are usually laughing, smiling, and joyous. Though rough-and-tumble play does not build friendships, it does contribute to maintaining them. In addition, children establish and maintain dominance within their groups during rough-and-tumble play, which in the long run contributes to reducing conflict by clearly defining the social structure. Lastly, such roughhouse play contributes to children's abilities to accurately read the nonverbal messages and subtle cues from others (Boyd, 1997). Rough-and-tumble play also contributes to motor training, particularly in physical fitness and strength, which in turn enables the children to be successful in game play during adolescence (Pellegrini, 2007).

Adults usually want to squelch rough-and-tumble play, perceiving it as aggression. Experienced helping professionals note that children not allowed rough-and-tumble play in one setting (school yards, recreational settings) do so in others (bus, neighborhood, backyards). It is better to supervise this play to minimize the risks to children's safety.

Violent combinations of dramatic and rough-and-tumble play.   Not all children's play is pleasant, cooperative, or peaceful. Violent content comes from several sources. First of all, children imitate violent adult behavior that they observe in the home, neighborhood, and school. Second, violence is portrayed in all news media as a result of natural events such as storms, volcanic eruptions, and earthquakes, as well as other catastrophes such as car accidents, firestorms, war, and crime. The third source of violence is related to children's inner needs to cope with their feelings of aggression and helplessness. Play is a vehicle for expressing strong feelings and attaining mastery over situations beyond a child's control. Youngsters are able to work out a variety of solutions to terrifying situations in play, thus developing some control of their feelings (Kostelnik, Whiren, & Stein, 1986). Even children whose contact and knowledge of violence and unpleasantness from the surrounding community is limited are likely to respond to these inner pressures. Fourth, some children enact scripts that they see on television or in electronic games. Finally, there is **masked play** in which the child plays for the purpose of behaving aggressively against others without having to be responsible for the consequences of the serious aggressive act.

Professionals are responsible for guiding children's play into channels that lead to social competence and to positive mental health. Adults may observe enactments of physical abuse as a part of the role of spouse, parent, or sibling. Simple redirection or discussing alternative ways to get people to cooperate is sufficient for imitative play of this sort. Prolonged, repetitive, detailed enactments of violence on another may be an indicator that the child is living in an unwholesome environment that requires additional attention.

The roles of rescuer, superhero, or soldier are all powerful ones that enable the child to explore many facets of the fearful situation. A "superhero" may be selected by a young child as a protector and used in new or potentially threatening situations. Adults help most when they provide accurate information about real incidents and when they provide reassurance to the players that they are safe and the environment is stable. Often other children will portray roles of nurturer, comforter, or offer reassurance.

Television and electronic games have increased in the number and intensity of violent incidents in programs. Play that is purely imitative with little elaboration based on the child's imagination, cooperation among players, or the use of problem solving and verbalization appears to be of the "hit and flit" variety and does not emerge as more advanced forms of sociodramatic or rough-and-tumble play. Characters may be stereotypic, racist (usually toward beings of strange colors or mutants), and sexist and hopefully would not be emulated by youngsters.

Young children also do not appear to comprehend the "moral lesson" usually delivered at the end of the program and tend not to perceive that the fantasy heroes are particularly helpful, kind, or gentle (French, 1987). Helpful strategies in organized programs for children are restricting access to television, guiding and redirecting play into more productive forms, and limiting the time and place for superhero play. Also helpful are eliminating superhero toys and weapons, providing other sociodramatic play opportunities and information for alternatives, and assessing the individual needs of children that make superhero play so attractive (Kostelnik et al., 1986; Ritchie & Johnson, 1988). Teasing and bullying are not related to play; both are acts of aggression and are discussed in the chapter on aggression.

Games

Games involve other players, have rules, and are eminently social. Games develop gradually as children's social skills mature, from the simple turn taking of toddlers to the complex games of older children. What makes a game fun? Movement play in the game, a sense of inclusion with other players,

and often the element of surprise or chance enhances the enjoyment of children between ages 3 and 8. Seven- to 12-year-olds are pleased to show off their skills and physical or mental competence and actually winning becomes increasingly important as children mature. They achieve acclaim and status through performance.

Older preschool children can play hide and seek or any number of games with a central person, like tag. They are able to take turns if the wait isn't too long. With more experience, they become able to change roles, playing various versions of hide and seek such as "kick-the-can." Between 5 and 7 years of age, children play games of acceptance and rejection, such as "farmer in the dell," and of attack and defense, such as snowball fighting. Seven- to 9-year-olds add games of dominance and submission such as "Mother may I," card and board games, and sandlot sports such as modified forms of softball and kickball. Older children, more concerned with outcomes, enjoy intellectual games such as charades or trivia and are more likely to participate in organized teams. The roles older children take in games are likely to depend on special skills they may have, such as playing guard in a basketball game.

Games may be based on chance (most dice games), skill (baseball), or strategy (checkers). Many games of motor skill have become sports in which the play is administered and directed by adults rather than by the children. Both the content of the rules and the process of playing are external to the children. In this book, we will focus on the informal games in which children can follow, make, modify, or change the rules themselves.

Adults who guide the social development of children should understand that young children do not approach a game in the same way that adults and older children might. Young preschool children play games in much the same fashion that they participate in movement play. They observe a particular way to move and imitate it. They are, in fact, frequently confused. In the game of tag, for example, a young child will run to avoid getting caught but is likely to have difficulties if tagged and declared to be "It." At this point, a very young child may refuse to play or may just stand there. If older players are willing, they may allow the little one to tag them so the game can go on.

Older preschool children frequently perceive rules as an interesting example of how to play rather than a required behavior. When playing together, they sometimes have difficulties regulating sequential turn taking. Nor are they concerned with what other players do; they simply are interested in their own actions. Each player is on his or her own. This is not the same as cheating, although adults observing young children playing a simple board game might interpret it as such.

Seven- and 8-year-olds begin to be concerned with problems of mutual control, winning, and losing. They are likely to discuss the rules before play but may have conflicting notions on what the "real" rules are. Conflicts may break out; these can be handled as discussed in Chapter 8. Children of this age often regard rules as sacred and untouchable, emanating from adults and lasting forever (Piaget, 1976; Sutton-Smith & Sutton-Smith, 1974). Rules may vary for some games, especially those that are passed on verbally by children themselves. The game rules may be followed, changed, ignored, enforced, and invented according to the context of the game or what children think is fun, fair, or acceptable. Usually no single person is in control of the rules, and group consent to alter the play is necessary. For example, if all the skilled players are on one side in a softball game, some may switch in the middle, as there is no real competition. How play rules are altered also contributes to the social hierarchy of children's groups and establishes

ideas of what is and is not acceptable (Freie, 1999). Children develop skill in negotiation as they decide among themselves what the rules are to be.

Games are varied and are combined with many other forms of play. There are singing and dancing games, games using a variety of objects, movement games, games associated with dramatics (charades), language games (Scrabble), and games that involve construction (Bug). Fortunately, most public libraries have good collections of books on games suitable for children to play in groups or individually.

The adult role is surprisingly similar for all ages in supporting informal game play. Adults provide materials, space, and time for children to play. They may teach the game by explaining how it is played and what the rules are as well as demonstrating as necessary to show children how to play. Playing as one of the players is also very helpful in the earlier phases of learning the game. Once the children seem to have the idea, effective adults take on an observer's role, preferably at some distance, but within sight of the action. They may help children identify the problem when there are different interpretations of the rules, and ensure the safety of youngsters (such as when a ball rolls into a street or parking lot). Otherwise children should play fairly independently.

Rules and strategy are hallmarks of older children's games.

Humor

Adults usually do not find the humor of young children very amusing, if they even recognize that the child is trying to joke. Children's humor is limited by their experience and their cognitive development, so what they perceive as funny is altogether too obvious for the adult. Children are not likely to find adult humor funny either, especially if they do not get the point of the joke. Understanding the development of children's use of incongruity for humor will help adults appreciate attempts at humor by the very young (McGhee, 1979).

Incongruity in children's humor. When an arrangement of ideas, social expectations, or objects is incompatible with the normal or expected pattern of events, it is incongruous. Although incongruity is not the only ingredient in humor, it may be the most common element in children's humor. Incongruity does not always elicit amusement, however. Children may react with interest, curiosity, anxiety, fear, or amusement.

Humor, like other play forms, is framed by clear play signals. The younger the child, the clearer the play signals need to be—laughter or a traditional joke opening such as "Knock, knock"—if the incongruous statement is to be treated as humor. Otherwise, the child will ignore it or treat it with curiosity.

Exaggeration is the enlarging of the story or motion so that it is beyond belief. Children often engage in slapstick actions or draw gigantic ears on a dog and laugh at their own joke or at others antics. Older children use exaggeration in their verbal jokes, such as when a 10-year-old imitated the "announcement voice" from a public speaker at school: "Will the person with the license plate BL 72958109936210 please remove it from the parking lot? It is blocking the drive."

Humor also is social. Children laugh longer in a group than when alone. Humor is dependent on the ability of the child to pretend and to have a playful orientation toward the situation in which humor occurs. If children do not have a playful orientation, they may enjoy exaggeration or incongruity but not find it funny. Children also try to share their jokes with people with whom they already have a close bond. Playful attitudes or moods are more easily maintained in a social group than when alone, as well. Parents often are the ones selected to hear a joke, as Chukovsky (1976, p. 601) reports:

> *One day in the twenty-third month of her existence, my daughter came to me, looking mischievous and embarrassed at the same time—as if she were up to some intrigue. . . . She cried to me even when she was still at some distance from where I sat: "Daddy, oggiemiaow". . . And she burst out into somewhat encouraging, somewhat artificial laughter, inviting me to laugh at this invention.*

Developmental trends in children's humor. Humor, like other aspects of development, proceeds sequentially. In the second year, the child simply uses an object in a way known to be inappropriate. For example, picking up a parent's shoe and using it as a telephone might lead to laughter if the child is in a playful frame of mind—the fantasy is known to be at odds with reality.

The second stage of children's humor frequently overlaps with the first as language is used to create the incongruity with an object or event. Children simply give names to objects or events that they know to be incorrect. For example, young children delight in calling a cat a dog or an eye a foot. In initiating this type of humor, however, adults should remember that the confidence of very young children in the naming of objects is not great; if a joke is made without clear play signals, a 2-year-old may think that new information is being presented. Between the ages of 3 and 4, children delight in exaggeration. For example, a drawing of a cat with no ears is funny. The distortion must be clear, but enough normal elements must be present for the child to recognize the familiar object. Another form of humor typical of this stage is to call someone by the wrong name. Older preschoolers who have mastered gender-related concepts may find it funny to call a girl a boy. However, this is threatening to some children and may be taken as an insult.

Preschoolers are perceptually oriented. A drawing of a bicycle with square wheels or stories of a "backwards day" or an elephant sitting on a nest all are perceived as funny. In the same way, young children are likely to laugh at people with disproportionate facial features, disfigurements, or noticeable handicapping conditions. They also laugh when someone falls in a funny way. Because of their cognitive limitations (very young children are unable to empathize), it is not intended to be cruel. Children who are very active and have short attention spans tend to initiate behavioral humor, or slapstick. This period also is the beginning of producing nonsense words from regular words: "Doggie, loggie, moggie," "Lyssa, missa, rissa," "Hamburger, samburger, ramburger" or inventing new nonsense words. For example, children might set out to capture a "torkel" with great glee.

The fourth stage in the development of humor, when children understand multiple meanings of words, starts at about age 7. This is the beginning of humor that is most similar to adult humor. Puns or simple play with the meaning of words begins.

> *"Why are ghosts like newspapers?"*
>
> *"Because they appear in sheets."*

Incongruous actions also are incorporated into the question-format joke.

> *"What goes 'Zzub! Zzub!'?"*
>
> *"A bee flying backwards."*

Jokes dealing with "what is it" questions and "knock, knock" jokes also appear:

What's black and white and red all over?	
A sunburned zebra. (older children)	
A newspaper. (younger children)	
Knock, knock.	*Knock, knock.*
Who's there?	*Who's there?*
Ether.	*Stella.*
Ether who?	*Stella who?*
Ether Bunny.	*Stella 'nother Ether Bunny.*

Older school-age children, having well-developed cognitive abilities, are able to enjoy humor based on illogical behavior, such as a person buying a cat when they don't like cats so they can use up the cat shampoo that they got on sale. Younger children imitate older ones in attempts to generate humor. However, they frequently forget the punch line or substitute a logical answer to the question, thereby "destroying" the joke.

Humor also may be used as a means for gratifying sexual aggression or inappropriate desires. For example, young children often use words related to bowel or bladder functions shortly after control has been established. Helping professionals usually have witnessed young children saying, "Pooh, pooh," "Pee, pee," or "Doo, doo," to the merriment of their peers. Older youngsters find jokes about any dichotomy funny, such as gender role confusion (man obviously walking funny in high heels), power problems of authority figures (the hapless policeman or adults outwitted by children), and continued enjoyment of immensely incongruous humor that is typical of slapstick. They are also able to enjoy humor in poetry and literature (Fuhler, Farris, & Walther, 1999).

Valuing children's humor.   Adults who understand the developing child's attempts at humor listen attentively and smile or laugh at their jokes. Admonishing children to stop being silly or quit fooling around inhibits the development of humor. Because children frequently imitate humor, adults who also use simple exaggeration or incongruity humor during the day provide a model to emulate. Humor is a social experience for children. It helps define the child as a member of a group, enhance the member's position in the group, or increases morale. In the early phases, children's humor isn't recognizable to many adults, who may then ignore, suppress, or even reprimand children for attempts at humor. Although the content of humor changes as the individual matures, the skill and confidence that children develop in this area enables them to participate successfully in a variety of social situations. Even though each type of play has its own sequence of development in childhood, all require the support and guidance of caring adults if the quality of the play is to become optimal for each child.

SKILLS FOR SUPPORTING, ENHANCING, AND EXPANDING CHILDREN'S PLAY

 Setting the Stage for Children's Play

1. Stand or sit near children at play. Keep children in view from a little distance. Be outside the play area, but adjacent to it for children of all ages. Avoid hovering over children because it stifles their play. However, do not stand at one end of the play yard while children are dispersed far away from you.

2. Pay attention to what the children are playing and what they say and do. Observe carefully; concentrate. Listen, and begin to remember the play preferences and styles of

continued

SKILLS FOR SUPPORTING, ENHANCING, AND EXPANDING CHILDREN'S PLAY—continued

individuals within the group. Note their narratives and the content of directions that they give each other.

3. Ensure the safety of all children. Involve children in determining rules for keeping safe in their environment to prevent physical and psychological injury for themselves and for others. Encourage children to paint, tell stories, or deal with issues of violence that emerge in their play in nonthreatening ways.

4. Provide adequate materials and space for the number of children playing. Match the number of children, the quantity of play materials, and the amount of space in which the children can play. A board game for four players requires enough space for the children to play without interruption or congestion. In addition, a sense of privacy is essential if children are to develop quality dramatic play. Block play and movement play usually require a large play area.

5. Provide quality playthings for all types of play. Children will play with anything, and some of the most interesting playthings, such as sand, water, and mud, are not toys. Provide materials for construction, such as bristle blocks, unit blocks, and paints of various types, paper, musical instruments, clay, and dough. Give young children realistic props; offer older children less realistic materials. Offer jump ropes, balls of various sizes, and other appropriate materials such as tricycles, ice skates, or basketball hoops for movement play. Provide different types of games: those that require cooperation (lifting one child in a parachute); those that encourage competition; some that are played in small groups indoors, such as checkers; and others that are played in larger groups outdoors, such as volleyball.

6. Encourage exploration of materials. Use nonverbal strategies such as smiling, watching, and offering or accepting materials. Assume that children may do anything with the materials that is not expressly prohibited by the setting, unless the well-being of others is at stake or property could be damaged. Delay any demonstration of material use until children ask for assistance. Refrain from setting limits until children actually misuse the materials. Point out new or interesting uses of materials by other children when appropriate.

7. Provide the props, materials, and the necessary information for children to create a variety of sociodramatic play scenarios. Offer props that support play themes that revolve around family activities (camping, gardening, traveling), community activities (postal services, hospital, veterinarian clinics), and literary characters (Three Pigs, Goldilocks, or Madeline). Read and reread good children's literature and information books that provide the background for play. Tape favorite stories so that children can listen independently. Provide specific props critical to the stories. Children who have a rich source of play materials will not be so dependent on electronic sources of stimulation for their play episodes.

8. Provide varied venues for play. Use parks, natural or wild settings as well as prepared playgrounds. Allow children to play alone, in small groups, or in larger groups both inside and outside.

 Maximizing the Play Potential of the Materials Available

1. Offer a variety of materials to encourage exploration and imagination (Klein, Wirth, & Linas, 2004). Include materials not usually offered at home such as finger paint and large hollow blocks. Incorporate materials from the natural environment (feathers, stones, sticks, etc.) as well as commercial ones. Use real things such as dishes, hammers, and baby blankets in the pretend play area. Provide open-ended materials such as balls, blocks, and dough. Include culturally relevant materials for the children in your group.

SKILLS FOR SUPPORTING, ENHANCING, AND EXPANDING CHILDREN'S PLAY

2. Mix unrelated toys together. Put water or play dough in the housekeeping area. Place the furnishings of the dollhouse in a box in the block area. Fasten butcher paper onto the wall of the building outdoors where children usually ride tricycles, and provide paints. Put Lego® blocks and other small construction toys into a pretend play area set up as an office or hospital. Think of all the possible, then the not-so-possible recombinations of materials. Materials need not have any obvious relationship. Stimulate the creative potential of the children.

3. Introduce novel toys and materials slowly. Avoid putting out all the new things at the same time. The stimulus value of each one competes with the others, becoming stale too soon.

4. Rotate playthings. Remove some play materials. When brought out again, they will generate increased interest. Similar to simple rotation is the practice of having a special set of toys in the childcare center that are used only in the late afternoon. The "new" materials, although similar to those used in the morning, generate much better play than would the same materials played with earlier.

5. Provide culturally relevant materials. Select play materials related to the occupations in the community, the family traditions of children, the geographic location of the community, or the group membership of children in the program. For example, preschool children in fishing villages will find more play potential in fishing-related objects than children from the southwestern plains. Make sure that the culturally relevant materials from all groups are represented over time (Jones, 2004).

6. Arrange the materials to encourage interaction between children. Set out two sets of Lego blocks instead of one. Place several puzzles on a large table rather than one on a small table. Have enough dress-up clothes for several children to play. When too many children want to play in the housekeeping area, suggest that some of them construct a home next door so that they can play neighbors. Other children are by far the most novel, interesting, and complex resources for play. Older children enjoy many of the new games that emphasize cooperation and working together. As children mature, they are able to play in larger groups, and materials such as cards and board games can be played with as many as six players. Make materials for such activities available and arrange them so that several children can play at once.

7. Suggest new uses for materials or ask other children to do so. Help children identify problems with their play and to seek information or help from peers. For instance, "It seems your car does not roll very far on the carpet. Ask Soo-Jin what she thinks might be used to make it go further." Soo-Jin might suggest a cardboard runway, boards, or movement of the car to a harder surface or the adult might do this. Let the children try things out, even if they try something like a scarf, which you already know will not work. Make a general request for new play ideas: "Angelo needs some money. Does anyone have an idea of what to use?"

8. Add writing and literacy materials to all play centers. Use blueprints of buildings in the block area and provide the appropriate paper, pencils, straight edge and other related tools. Use grocery list note pads in the kitchen area as well as real cookbooks. There are many kinds of writing implements and papers than can be incorporated into children's play.

 Helping Children Acquire Skills Through Your Direct Involvement as a Player

1. Play with materials. Children love to see adults smear the finger paint, work with a paintbrush on an easel with drippy paint, or

continued

SKILLS FOR SUPPORTING, ENHANCING, AND EXPANDING CHILDREN'S PLAY—continued

build in the sandbox. Comment on your play, saying things like: "I'm smearing my paint all over," or "I'm glad the sand is wet so my house stays up." Then, wait for children to comment on what they are doing. When modeling, respect your own play. Bring your play to some closure: flatten the sand castle, finish the painting, or announce that you are through. Children should not expect you to give way to them automatically when they want to play or when they just grab your materials. Simply tell them, "I'm nearly finished, and then you can have this place," as you complete whatever you are doing.

2. Use verbal or nonverbal prompts from outside the play frame. Mime the action that might be appropriate to the child once you have caught his or her eye. This is especially useful for children who are about to move to another level of play on their own or to those who really do not want adults to interfere. Such actions are "batting" or "throwing" in movement play, big smiles in a humorous situation, or a physical enactment in pretend play. Using a stage whisper for giving direction or prompting also is helpful for some children.

3. Take a role to encourage pretend play. Select either a behavioral role, such as saying "Varoom, varoom" as you "drive" a truck down a block highway, or a character role, such as becoming the parent, the baby, or the spaceship captain. Use a variety of techniques to influence the direction of the play, such as engaging in ulterior conversations or storytelling. Respond to the role cues of other children, and remain in character while in the play frame. Remember that you can't get out of the play frame to give directions without some clear signal that you are not playing any more. Gradually take a less active part until you can exit the play frame altogether.

4. Enter into play imaginatively when play between children appears to disintegrate (Jones, 2004). Take action and use scripts to enter the play. For instance, knock on the door and say, "I am a traveler and am lost and hungry."

5. Demonstrate movements as necessary. If you should see a 2-year-old attempting to jump down a step but walking it instead, the most playful thing to do is to jump yourself, with feet together, landing with knees slightly bent and using your arms for balance. Demonstrate jumping, hopping on one foot, or striking with a bat or hockey stick. This provides information, and if briefly and playfully done, it can be a part of the ongoing play. Give promps, such as "Bend your knees when you land," then resume the game or movement play.

6. Participate fully in the game. Play by the rules as you understand them and participate fully, taking turns, running, or whatever is required. Children learn some games, especially games of strategy, only by observing a better player. Chinese checkers is an example, as are Risk, chess, and Monopoly. Discuss the play as other players do, pointing out what you did and why, if appropriate. Be careful not to become so engrossed in your play that you forget that your goal is to support the play of the children.

 Helping Individual Children Change the Level of Social Participation in Play

1. Observe the child at play; note patterns of play alone and with others. Determine the appropriateness of the level of play that is influenced by age, experience, and culture. For example, if a child between 24 and 30 months spent most of the time watching older children play, this level of play is very appropriate. Encourage children to observe other more skilled children at play, "See how Laurie moves the pieces of the puzzle around." Promote social play between children who share similar abilities or interests. For example, a child with outstanding musical ability

SKILLS FOR SUPPORTING, ENHANCING, AND EXPANDING CHILDREN'S PLAY

might best pursue that area independently and be matched with another player with similar motor abilities for movement play.

2. Focus on the process of play so that the play may be extended or elaborated (Klein et al., 2004). Use statements, such as, "Is this baby crying?" or "What will happen to these animals when it rains?" to provide the child with additional information or clues for imaginative play.

3. Observe the child for cues that the present level of participation is inadequate. Cues indicating that children may need help in increasing their level of participation might be: prolonged observation of a group at play (more than 10 minutes); following more skillful players from one activity to another; forceful crossing of the play boundaries or disruption of others' group play; crying, complaining, or stating that they want to play too. Allow children who appear to be satisfied with their level of participation to continue if they appear to be relaxed, happy, and fully involved in what they are doing.

4. Match the activity to the child's level of skill. Observe children carefully so you know what level of skill is typical for them. Allow children to practice playing alone or in parallel play until they are comfortable. Notice when individuals shift from parallel play to short episodes of greater social interaction. Usually, parallel play is unstable and will shift into more direct interaction or solitary play. Again, select a potential playmate based on similar levels of competence in a particular area.

5. Play with the child yourself. Less skilled players perform more easily with a predictable, responsive adult than with other children. Give clear play signals and use a variety of metacommunications.

6. Invite the child and a second, less skilled player to play with you, and then ease yourself out of the situation. Do not try to match the best player or the most popular child with the least skilled player. The disparities in skill may be too great for the play to continue. Remember that children are sensitive to social status in developing their play roles.

 Escalating the Level of Play Gradually by Varying Your Play Performance or by Giving Cues Through Play Signals or Metacommunications

1. Extend object play by imitating what the child is doing, then vary the activity a little. Incorporate the child's ideas into your modeling. Use the same object in a slightly different way, such as tapping a maraca with your hand instead of shaking it, or talking to a doll in an emotionally expressive tone of voice instead of a normal tone or monotone.

2. Suggest that children use specific play signals to initiate or sustain play. Tell the least skillful player what to say to indicate the play: "Tell James, 'I'll be a policeman.'" This active approach is more likely to lead to success than the more general question, "Do you want to play?" Select the type of play signal that is commonly used by other players in the group. Consider ulterior conversations, underscoring, storytelling, prompting, or formal pretend proposals. The less skillful player will then have your prompting as well as opportunities to observe other children as a means of improving his or her skills. For example, when one player seems exasperated with the inability of another to play a role correctly, lean over the props and stage whisper directions: "Whisper to the mail carrier that she is supposed to give the letters to other people, not read them herself." Or perhaps if the play theme seems to be floundering, note the materials of interest and suggest the storytelling approach to one of the players: "Think what would happen if there were an earthquake and the city had to be rebuilt. Tell the story."

Demonstrate how to use nonverbal play signals when they would facilitate the play,

continued

SKILLS FOR SUPPORTING, ENHANCING, AND EXPANDING CHILDREN'S PLAY—continued

especially if they will enable less skilled players to enhance their skills. For instance, show a child how to "fall ill" just outside the pretend hospital by making moans and holding a part of the body as if in pain. Show a child how to portray being a sad "baby" outside the housekeeping area as a way to get a response from other players. Some children may need much more support and direction than others, but play skills can be learned and enhanced.

3. Withdraw from the play and resume the role of observer once the play is well underway. Think of a way to exit the game gracefully. ("Let's pretend that I am teacher and I have to go to work now") or step out of the play and state clearly that you aren't playing anymore. If you have a central role, such as pitcher in a softball game, you might just say that your turn is up, and ask who would like to pitch.

 Becoming Directly Involved in Children's Playfulness

1. Demonstrate a nonliteral approach to resources. Playfully respond to the environment and to commonplace situations. For example, Mr. Phipps used to sing little songs or make up verses about ordinary things as they occurred during the day: the rain on the windowsill, blocks falling down, parents going to work, or children not wanting naps. He did this quite unconsciously to amuse the children. No one noticed until parents commented that their children could make up songs and poetry by themselves and wondered what the school was doing to promote such creativity.

Another way to do this is to propose impossible conditions: "I wonder what if . . .?" What would happen if so much snow fell that the houses were covered? What would happen if all the girls grew wings and could fly? Encourage children to be expansive and to try to imagine all the possibilities. This often generates a lot of laughter. Show your interest in each child's contribution regardless of how silly it is.

2. Be accepting of young children's humor. Smile and show interest even if you do not have the least idea of what the joke is. When group glee strikes, with every child laughing uproariously, laugh along with it. They will quiet themselves down eventually. It is not at all unusual for the children not to know what they are laughing at either.

3. Explain that a child was only joking when someone misinterprets the meaning of what was said or did not recognize a play signal. Help less mature children recognize play signals. For example, to call a boy a girl is a serious insult, except in a joke, which would be common for older preschool or kindergarten children. Nonsense names or other names used to address people may be very distressing to children not in on the joke or too young to understand it. Tell them that is a joke and point out the play signal if necessary.

4. Use affective reflections when preschool children laugh at disfigurement, falls, or handicapping conditions; then, provide brief but accurate information. Say, for example: "You thought Mr. North walked very funny. He cannot help that because one leg is shorter than the other. People who cannot help the way they walk feel sad when other people laugh at them."

 Coaching Children Occasionally from Outside the Play Frame

1. Suggest a related theme. Extend the theme by suggesting that children go on a picnic, movie, go on vacation, or engage in some other family-related activity if the housekeeping play is disintegrating.

2. Add a necessary prop. Children "going on a vacation" need a suitcase, and the play may break down without it. Go to the storage area, get the suitcase, and place it near the play area. Do not leave children unsupervised for long periods of time while you search for materials, but when possible, make such impromptu additions to enhance their play.

SKILLS FOR SUPPORTING, ENHANCING, AND EXPANDING CHILDREN'S PLAY

3. Introduce new players from outside the play frame. Say something simple and direct, like "Mary has been watching you play and would like to play, too." The children participating in the play may or may not accept Mary. It's their choice. Should they not want Mary to play at this time, help Mary find another place to play, providing several alternatives. Small-group games and pretend play are much more difficult to enter than are activities such as artwork or block construction, because the children in play with an ongoing theme have already established roles and relationships. Do not force acceptance of another player; the play may completely disintegrate if established roles, themes, and relationships are disrupted. Play, by definition, is child directed and voluntary.

Offer a new character role for a player joining the group ("Here is the grandmother, coming to visit"). Additions of mail carriers, meter readers, relatives, guests to a party, and so on, can be incorporated into the ongoing play. Do not give the entering child a role that overshadows the other players, such as a spaceperson landing in the yard. The new player is likely to be "killed off" or rejected.

4. Teach players to use a clear signal when leaving the play frame. Say: "Tell Sarah you don't want to be the monster anymore," or "John doesn't know you don't want to chase him. Tell him that." Such suggestions will allow children to exit the play and will reduce the likelihood of the nonplaying child responding to rough-and-tumble play with aggression.

5. Make suggestions to further the goals of children, such as pointing out a problem or restating game rules. Offer specific help when it is needed to keep a game going. For example, if a child's block construction is wobbling, point out the area where the problem is occurring if the child does not see it. If children are confused about how a game should proceed, restate the relevant rules. When children are involved in superhero play, suggest that they think about the problem and talk about the characteristics of the true hero. Identify ways other than physical might to solve problems, or remind them to identify children who are and are not playing.

6. Talk about play events that disintegrate for older children who are rejected playmates or isolated by their peers. Assist them in identifying the social cues that they misinterpreted and suggest alternative behaviors. Ask them to tell you what they think happened. Probe for details. Correct misinterpretations and point out the behaviors that would lead to more acceptable responses and the maintenance of play. Initiating the social interactions, entering an ongoing play frame, and participating during rough-and-tumble play are particularly difficult for many youngsters.

7. Teach children games when necessary. Have all materials set up, and know the rules yourself. Invite the children to participate. Then, give brief directions, one at a time. For example, in the game of "Duck, duck, goose," say, "Take hands" (to form a circle). You may have to help by giving more specific directions, such as, "Jacob, hold Susan's hand." When the children are in a shoulder-to-shoulder circle, ask them to sit down. Once they are all seated, stand up and announce that you will be "It" the first time. Walk around the circle, tapping heads and saying "Duck, duck, duck, goose!" When the word "goose" is said, direct the child to chase you, then run around the circle, sitting in the child's empty space. Then, direct the standing child to be "it." With very young children, go with the child who is "It" for the first time as he or she taps heads and says, "Duck, duck . . . goose," and then run with the child to the empty space of the new person who is "It." Give directions and demonstrate in alternating patterns. With young children, don't give all the directions at once.

Allow the children to play until all have had a turn or their interest diminishes. Repeat the directions as necessary each time you play

continued

SKILLS FOR SUPPORTING, ENHANCING, AND EXPANDING CHILDREN'S PLAY—continued

the game until the children can play it by themselves.

8. Encourage children to solve their own problems and create their own rules during pretend play or with informal games. Use behavioral and affective reflections learned earlier to help children clarify social conflicts or problems. Frequently the problems stem from different perspectives: "Barbara, you think that everyone should play the game the same way; Jason thinks that the rules should be changed a little for the younger children because they cannot run as fast. Tell me how you think you can work this out." Respect children's decisions as they interpret, comply with, alter, or create rules for pretend play and games that may be different than the ones that are familiar to you.

 Guiding Children's Rough-and-Tumble Play

1. Decide whether rough-and-tumble play is to be allowed, and if so, when, where, and under what conditions such play will be permitted. Make your expectations clear and consistent. Some people limit rough-and-tumble play to outdoors in early childhood programs or to recess and do not allow it in the classrooms. Consider limiting such play to a specific area or space as is allowing it only during specified periods of the day. Once clear limits as to time and place for rough-and-tumble play are made, adults can use the following guides to help children toward more pleasant experiences.

2. Decrease the violence in all play instead of trying to eliminate rough-and-tumble play. Do not display or provide any weapons. Avoid toys that suggest violence or suggest themes that lead to violence in the enactment of play. When children "make" weapons of blocks, sticks, wads of paper, or anything else, remind them that they may not "kill" anyone or shoot, stab, or use a weapon. Use

videos that are information rich and avoid cartoons and television programs that are violent. Treat threats and verbal violence similarly to physical portrayals of violence.

3. Ask children to use specific, verbal play cues to initiate rough-and-tumble play. All children must agree to be players in order to minimize being frightened or feeling that they are being attacked. Individuals have a right to say no to this type of play.

4. Coach children in how to say no to play. Give scripts to children who do not care to engage in rough-and-tumble play. "No," "I don't want you to chase me," or "I want to play something else," are all statements that children can be taught to use in order to decline play.

5. Provide for a "safety zone" so that when a child enters the zone, rough-and-tumble play stops. This is similar to tag games where some object becomes a "safe" place. Children who are playing rough-and-tumble sometimes frighten themselves and need an easy way to stop playing.

6. Provide information about heroes. Frequently, superhero play focuses on the most violent aspects of fantasy character dramas. Point out the protection of the victim, the plot, and the array of nonviolent characters in the media portrayal. Helping, protecting, and honorable motives are central to superheroes, but young children often omit these aspects. If children portray real superheroes, their play resembles pretend play with bouts of chasing. Provide information about real heroes and the obstacles that they have overcome can provide for similar play that may meet the needs of the children for power and control.

7. Suggest that the villain or victim be imaginary. This way all of the children can be runners and no one needs to be chased.

8. Remain in close physical proximity to children engaging in rough-and-tumble

SKILLS FOR SUPPORTING, ENHANCING, AND EXPANDING CHILDREN'S PLAY

play. Move toward the action if you see three or four youngsters running in a pack, distant from the other children and the play equipment, because this is probably the beginning of a rough-and-tumble play sequence. The episode is more likely to remain playful than degenerate into overt aggression when an adult is close by.

9. If the rough-and-tumble play ceases to be fun, and someone is hurt or frightened, stop the behavior. It is no longer play. Playing must be fun and voluntary for everyone. Protect the children from hurting others or being hurt themselves. Strategies for doing this are discussed in Chapters 4, 5, 10, and 11.

 Demonstrating Awareness of Individual Differences

1. Accept the young child's approach to games with rules. Little children are not cheating or committing a moral error if they don't play precisely by the rules. Simply restate the rule in question and go on with the game. Children learn to play games with rules by playing with better players who know the rules.

2. Match the play activity to the skills of the players. Provide the time, materials and coaching that each child needs to improve his or her performance. All children should begin with simple games, roles, and constructions and move on toward more challenging activities as their skills develop. Use the developmental information provided in this chapter to help you match the level of play to the skills of the players.

3. Gradually assist less skillful players to enter social play. Allow some of the less skilled players to move into the play setting or attain play equipment for outdoor play from time to time. This will enable them to initiate the social play experience and make them less likely to be excluded from the play. Coach individuals on what to say or do as

they ask permission to enter the play frame of ongoing social play and support them if they are unsuccessful. (All children are unsuccessful some of the time.)

4. Accept the child's play-style preferences. Both patterners and dramatists engage in high-quality play. Encourage all children to experience construction and role play. Allow all players to use the preferred styles of play. Both children with strong fantasy and those with a more pragmatic approach benefit from their pretend play. Observe the play style of children from cultural groups that are different from your own before intervening. If the children are joyful and socially engaged in a nonviolent way, refrain from trying to change it.

5. Provide support for younger boys when girls outperform them in movement play. Girls' motor skills often develop faster than do that of boys until the later elementary grades, when the trend is reversed. Boys may be vulnerable to feelings of failure when the girls run faster, jump farther, and ride bikes earlier. Reassure them that they too will be able to do all of these things soon. Use similar strategies for developmentally delayed children.

6. Support children in their choice of play activities; do not limit play to sex stereotyped choices. Encourage children to explore a wide array of materials and roles. Respect playmate choices whenever possible as both boys and girls develop sex role–related skills in their play. Avoid assigning children to teams based on gender. Pitting the boys against girls is not fair. Instead count out the teams so that they are evenly balanced.

7. Respect cultural and experiential differences in children. Allow children to explore play themes that might be unfamiliar to you. Encourage children to freely express their ideas and emotions in their play. Refrain from responses that automatically reject or diminish others' cultural experience.

continued

SKILLS FOR SUPPORTING, ENHANCING, AND EXPANDING CHILDREN'S PLAY—continued

 Adapting Play Experiences for Children with Special Needs

In addition to using all of the skills previously mentioned, the following skills will assist you in supporting children who have special needs (Sandall, 2004).

1. Use information from parents and specialists and from your observations to identify the child's competencies. Avoid focusing on what the child cannot do. Use previously suggested strategies to find a co-player, select materials and guide play.

2. Simplify activities. Break down activities into component parts, reduce the number or complexity of the materials used, simplify directions and vocabulary, or adjust the way the activity is carried out. For example, reduce the number of cards in a memory game that has a total of 40 pairs to 5 or 10 pairs of cards. Use a pictograph of a sequence of steps to paint; this is easier for some children to understand than a series of oral directions.

3. Provide a psychologically safe environment in which to play. Use explanations such as, "Dakin has not learned to do that, yet," to explain why a child cannot do everything others can do. Note carefully that the child with special needs is not systematically excluded from play. Intervene as appropriate, providing assistance and support. Maintain similar expectations for the use of materials. For example, a child who has difficulty hearing should be expected to pick up toys and wait for the use of materials until others are finished (Sluss, 2005).

4. Encourage the children to play with preferred materials. If a child has an interest in trains, alter the nature of the activity over time by adding materials (train tracks or tickets), or encouraging other players to also play with trains. Incorporate trains one way or another in a variety of play opportunities.

5. Use special equipment to enable the child to gain access to peers and materials. Obtain a beanbag, which will allow a child typically in a wheelchair to be at the same level of other players. Help typically developing children to understand specialized equipment used by one child such as a hearing aide. Incorporate samples of special tools into exploratory play when possible.

6. Encourage peer support. Assign a job as helper for the day. Eric could not grasp the die or markers or move his marker when it was his turn. Ned was his partner for the day and would place the die in Eric's hand, then move the marker as indicated looking back at Eric for approval. Eric played and Ned helped.

7. Provide the time and repetition for all children to achieve success.

 Sharing Information with Parents and other Adult Family Members about Children's Play

1. Respond with information about the value of play to children's overall development when family members ask, "Why do they spend time playing?" Provide information and then follow it up with specific details relevant to the child's development in your program. Remain and calm and present your response with logical statements. Respect the right of the parent to have a different perspective than your own.

2. Write notes about children's success in a play episode informally throughout the time the child is in the program. Label paintings with the child's narrative. Share photos of children's constructions with a few comments about the developmental significance of the event. Write glad notes when a child finally participates successfully in a game with others. Let adult family members know where budding friendships might be encouraged through discussion at home. Describe a play event that illuminates the child's comprehension of ideas.

3. Provide information about suitable play materials for the age group with whom you

SKILLS FOR SUPPORTING, ENHANCING, AND EXPANDING CHILDREN'S PLAY

are working. Written resources are available from your state cooperative extension service through the county extension agent, as well as from the Association for Childhood Education International and the National Association for the Education of Young Children. In addition, many good articles are published in family magazines in November of each year.

4. Encourage families to participate in community-wide events that support children's play informally for all age groups. Send information about events in the community home during breaks or holidays. When other agencies or groups participate in park cleanup days, attend yourself and ask families to join you.

5. Ask about the child's play at home and in other settings, as well as what the child mentions about play in your setting. Parents and other adult family members know a lot about their own children. Their observations are likely to be very useful to you and may help in the planning and supervision of each child at play.

PITFALLS TO AVOID

When people are trying to use the skills described here, sometimes certain attitudes and behaviors may interfere with their ability to carry them out in a truly playful spirit.

Believing that children learn only what they are taught.   Learning is something that children do for themselves. Adults may structure the learning, but the information learned by direct instruction is limited compared with the information children acquire from the environment, from their families and friends, and at play. Adults can facilitate children's learning to play, but they should not require children to perform to specification. Facilitation requires that the adult truly believes that the children have the capacity to learn, to perform, and to be competent within themselves.

Organizing play primarily to meet academic ends.   Children learn from all of their play experiences. Adults should not try to limit the songs they sing to number songs and alphabet ditties. Play is only play when it belongs to the children, is voluntary, and is fun. If children choose to put together an alphabet puzzle, fine; however, a clown puzzle is just as good from a playful perspective.

Watching for mistakes.   Play is not serious, so mistakes in play simply do not count. By all means, assist a child when asked to do so, but never point out mistakes to a playing child. Let the child discover the error independently. Many interesting products were invented out of mistakes that someone played with.

Making demands for specific responses. Children do need to learn specific information about their world, and these tasks are organized into lessons. Lessons about materials, for example, should not be substituted for play with materials. For example, adults may present a lesson on the effects of mixing paint colors and ask the child to predict the color to be produced. The scientific approach to light and color has its place. However, it should be separated from the creative activity of painting a picture, in which some colors might become mixed. Answer questions if asked, otherwise, leave the child alone to manage the situation without giving instruction. The distinction between curious investigation from a scientific perspective and playful exploration often is not clear.

The best criterion to help distinguish between the two is to determine who has control of the situation. If the child does, and the adult only responds to inquiries, then the adult is behaving appropriately. However, if the child is passive and the adult is talking quite a bit, requiring answers from the child, or giving a series of directions, then this is a lesson, not play.

Expecting the play performance to be the same within a group.   Cultural differences become apparent in play. So do differences in style.

Though there are general differences between boys and girls, the range of individual differences are very great. Having uniform expectations of children is not appropriate.

Setting too many restrictions. Children cannot play if they are expected to maintain silence, not move, create no disorder, never touch one another, remain clean and tidy, and never create a mess. Play requires action. Action inevitably leads to disorder, messes, noise, joy, conversation, and, usually, jostling about. When adults set unreasonable restrictions on play, they simply are trying to prohibit play altogether. Of course, even the youngest player can be expected to clean up after the play, but that is a task in social responsibility, not play itself.

Squelching the creative use of materials. Consider whether there actually are reasons of safety or economics that restrict the use of a particular material. For example, poker chips make better money to carry in purses than do puzzle pieces, most children would rather use them, and puzzles are ruined if pieces are missing. However, the same thing does not apply to macaroni, strings, Lego blocks, or other small items that might be used in role-play. The challenge is in planning to manage the proper return of the items once play is finished for the day. One teacher maintained a pail for small items, and children deposited them there whenever they were found. Later, they were returned to the appropriate storage area.

Having no constraints at all. Play is planned disorder, or organized, rule-governed interactions that do not fit adult predetermined conceptions. Play simply does not flourish when there are no rules or means of controlling its scope or parameters. Rules regarding safety, rights and feelings of others, and other necessities of group living are essential prerequisites of quality play. Children who do not have limits spend most of their time in social testing to see just where the boundaries of acceptable behavior are rather than in productive play. You will learn about setting limits in Chapters 10, 11, and 12.

Ignoring play. Given the right conditions, play probably will develop without adult prodding. However, quality play—that which stretches the imagination and the social and cognitive abilities of the player—does not develop in a vacuum. Writing lesson plans, cleaning cupboards, planning menus, or chatting with other adults unrelated to the ongoing activity while the youngsters are engaged in play is inappropriate. Save these activities until the session is over or for when the children are asleep.

Directing play or games too soon. Children learn from the process of deciding on rules or setting up a fantasy play situation. It may take longer to do these tasks than adults think is necessary. Unfortunately, adults often move in too soon and usurp the planning and organizational functions. Unless children ask for help, or unless conflict erupts that the children are unable to resolve themselves, adults should show interest but remain uninvolved.

Asking children to explain their humor. This quickly kills all the fun of a joke. If one does not "get it," using a social smile, social laughter, or a simple pleasurable expression is an appropriate response.

Admonishing children to be quiet or to quit being silly when engaged in humor. Sometimes, adults are annoyed by children's laughter, especially if it occurs in the wrong time and place. In such cases, let children know you understand their merriment ("You kids are having a great time telling jokes") and then explain why their humor is inappropriate ("I'm concerned that I won't be able to drive safely in this traffic with all the distraction"). Do not just set limits on children's humor in a general, disapproving way.

Becoming too involved in the play. You may find yourself having so much fun playing that you forget that the purpose of participation is to stimulate children's high-quality play. Play should go on nicely once you have ceased to be so active. If it does not, you might have been dominating the play, the activity might have been above the children's level, or the role you had chosen might have been so central to the theme that the play cannot continue without it. Facilitate rather than dominate.

Restricting the activity of children with special needs to "lessons" or ignoring these children as they play. All children benefit from play and children learn from engaging in play with more skilled peers. Some children may need assistance or coaching during play and some activities may need to be adapted. Plan for individual needs for play.

Play is one area that most children can experience some success.

Omitting all mention of play performance when conferencing with parents.   Parents are interested in the social relationships of their children, which are typically displayed during play. They can best support their child's development if they understand what skills their children do or do not have.

SUMMARY

Play is a normal part of childhood, allowing children to practice skills in motor coordination, language, reasoning, social behavior, and in learning to cope with emotionally challenging problems. It is pleasurable, voluntary, and valued for the process of play from the players' perspective rather than for any useful product.

There are several types of play: play with movement and objects, construction play, and imaginative play. Within each play form, sequences of development were suggested through which children pass before they become skillful players. Most of these sequences occur in early childhood, with older children using early skills in new combinations for more complex forms of play.

The rules children create to further their play and the strategies that they use to initiate, develop, or change their play were discussed as well as some suggestions as to how adults might use their understanding of play to assist less skilled children.

Individual differences in the ways in which children play, were highlighted. The strategies that children use to frame the play, move the story forward, and terminate play were described. Humor is an additional aspect of playfulness and contributes to the child's social position in the group.

The role of the adult is to facilitate play for all the children in the group. This means that the adult must establish an atmosphere conductive to play, provide appropriate materials and facilities, and guide the skill development of the children toward increasing levels of performance. Responsiveness to children's observed behaviors is essential to this role, as is communication with children's parents. Several pitfalls were identified so that you can avoid them as you begin to support children's play.

KEY TERMS

associative play
character role
complexity
construction play
cooperative play
dramatic play
dramatist style
exaggeration
fantasizer
formal pretend proposals
functional role
games

masked play
metacommunication
novelty
object invention
object substitution
onlooker
parallel activity
patterners
play episode
play frame
play schemes
practice play

pragmatist
prompting
rough-and-tumble play
sociodramatic play
solitary play
storytelling
style
transform
ulterior conversations
underscoring
unoccupied behavior

DISCUSSION QUESTIONS

1. Why is it unlikely that play can ever be eliminated as a human behavior?
2. What is the impact of play in the overall development of children?
3. Describe the characteristics of play and give examples of playful and nonplayful behavior.
4. Why aren't the concepts of work and play opposites? Why is it more accurate to contrast play with seriousness than with work? Use your own life experience to elaborate on this topic.
5. List the skills needed for children to participate in dramatic play. Give examples of each skill.
6. Describe style differences in construction and pretend play.

7. What does metacommunication mean? Describe play signals that are nonverbal and those that are spoken.

8. When a young child starts to tell a joke but forgets the punch line and then laughs, how should you respond?

9. When a group of school-age children of mixed ages are playing softball and are not following the Little League rules on their own, how should you respond?

10. When older children are fully involved in play and everything is running smoothly, what should you do?

11. Explain the contribution of play to the six elements of social competence (social values, positive self-identity, interpersonal skills, self-regulation, planning and decision making, and cultural competence). Use your own life experience for examples or observations from children's play.

12. Referring to Appendix A, NAEYC Code of Ethical Conduct, determine if the following situations pose an ethical dilemma. Identify the section that influences your answer.
   a. A teacher leaves the children unattended on the playground with the intent of watching them from a window and assumes that, if there is an emergency, one of the children will come to get her.
   b. Three children are having a noisy confrontation while engaged in dramatic play. The teacher does nothing.
   c. One teacher complains to a colleague that Ms. Gace (another colleague) runs a room that is just too structured and the children don't get any real play time.
   d. A little girl is playing house and another child comes in and wants to be the mother. The children agree to have two mothers playing in one house. The adult intervenes and insists that families have one father and one mother in each house.

FIELD ASSIGNMENTS

1. Using simple, direct statements that you would use with the children, write out the directions to a game.

   Indicate where you would demonstrate what to do or play along with the players in order for them to get the idea of the game. Then try out the game with a group of children. How well were they able to follow your directions? What would you do differently?

2. Observe a group of young children over several days. Record whether or not you have observed the following behaviors for each child:
   a. Substitutes an object for another during pretend play
   b. Invents objects and uses gestures or movements to indicate existence
   c. Transforms time or age of player(s) or self
   d. Transforms place
   e. Takes on a behavioral or functional role
   f. Takes on a family or fantasy character role

   Now arrange to play with these children and devise strategies to encourage the development of these skills. What materials will you need? How will you coach them? If they can perform the basic skills, what should your role be?

3. Collect materials that would be useful to parents in making toy selections for specific age groups.

4. Become directly involved in play with children. Use the techniques suggested in the text to influence the direction of play. Note the effect that your participation has on the children.

For additional resources, visit our Web site
www.EarlyChildEd.delmar.com

Chapter 8

SUPPORTING CHILDREN'S PEER RELATIONSHIPS AND FRIENDSHIPS

OBJECTIVES

On completion of this chapter, you should be able to describe:

- Reasons that peer relationships and friendships are important to children.

- Variables that influence children's abilities to form relationships.

- Methods that children use to discern and describe friends over time.

- Variables that influence children's friendship choices.

- States of friendship: making contact, maintaining positive interactions, negotiating conflicts, and ending relationships—and the skills involved within these.

- Behaviors that differentiate children who make friends easily from those who have difficulty making friends.

- Strategies to increase children's friendship skills.

- Methods to help family members understand and facilitate children's friendships.

- Pitfalls to avoid in supporting children's friendships.

"Glad to have a friend like you...Fair and fun and skippin' free!
Glad to have a friend like you! And glad to just be ME!"
From: Free to Be . . . You and Me
Marlo Thomas

This song from *Free to Be You and Me* by Marlo Thomas echoes for children one of the most important tasks and valued accomplishments of childhood . . . the establishment of friendships and an acceptance among peers that *frees* children up to be themselves (Caspi & Shiner, 2006). Through peers, children come to better understand who they are and how they fit into their "own skin."

Once upon a time it was believed that friends just happened. We now know that adults can support children as they try to establish friendly relations with peers and help them increase their chances for success at future long-term, mature relationships and overall social competence (Erwin, 1998; Rubin, Bukowski, & Parker, 2006).

The ability to make and keep friends is one indicator of children's social competence. In fact, the complex process of locating, contacting, interacting with, and maintaining a friendship incorporates all six components of social competence discussed in Chapter 1. Thus, when adults focus on supporting children in friendships, they are actively increasing children's potential for social competence.

RELATIONSHIPS AND INTERACTIONS

The terms interactions, relationships, and friendships all refer to different levels of associations between people. **Interactions** describe a two-way exchange that is reciprocal in nature. Something may be gained from the interaction, but not necessarily. **Relationships** are much more. They infer a sense of belonging. They are established over time through a series of interactions that are filled with shared meaning, evolving expectations, and emotion. All relationships, however, are not defined as friendships. **Friendships** are voluntary associations in which each member recognizes and shares responsibility for the relationship. They are marked by a reciprocity of affection. In true friendship, both parties characterize the other as a friend and are much more committed to resolve conflicts to continue the relationship than in a non-friendship relationship (Rubin et al., 2006).

Children are involved in multiple types of relationships: with parents, teachers, siblings, and peers. Only the latter is typically the pool from which friendships eventually emerge. Thus, Jillian may see Maria, Dakota, Juanita, and Miss Cheryl at school, but only consider Juanita a true friend.

Adult–Child Relationships

Society has defined certain expectations for adult–child relationships. The interactions between adults and children are characterized by differences in status. For instance, Jillian loves Miss Cheryl, the lunchroom aide. She likes to talk with her and sings her songs she has just learned. Though Jillian may call Miss Cheryl her friend, it is not a true friendship. They do not play the same roles in their interactions.

Whether the relationship involves teacher and child, coach and player, or parent and child, it is expected that the adult will be the expert/leader and the child will be the learner/follower. Although such relationships serve important functions and may be marked by love and respect, they are unequal.

Peer Relationships

Peers are typically age-mates (Santrock, 2006b). Most often, peers share a common activity or interest and meet at regularly scheduled intervals to engage in these mutual interests. However, beyond the activity that has drawn them together, little or no contact occurs outside the scheduled event. Peers can be found nearly anywhere that children gather, such as neighborhoods, soccer leagues, or classrooms. Thus, Jillian and Dakota are in the same class, but outside of school they have no contact. They are peers.

As children mature from age 2 through age 12, they spend more and more time in the company of peers (Rubin, 2003). It is in the peer group that children achieve a sense of belonging. **Friends** are often selected from this social network based on "what feels right" (Hartup & Abeccassis, 2004).

Peers serve important socializing functions for children. Through peer relationships, children are able to develop a greater understanding of self and others. They establish a sense of social identity, a sense of where they fit into the social structure. Children in elementary school are able to better perceive themselves through their comparisons with the characteristics and abilities of peers (Harter, 2006). In the company of peers, children try on different roles and learn what is acceptable social behavior and what is not (Gest, Graham-Bermann, & Hartup, 2001).

Peer relationships also provide an opportunity for children to learn new skills and refine current ones.

Children learn quickly from the reactions of peers about the importance of regulating their emotions and actions. Those better able to regulate emotions and behavior are more popular among peers and are likely to be leaders (Rubin et al., 2006). These children recognize what is relevant to other children and are able to offer support and guidance in areas often overlooked or disdained by adults. For example, the ability to spit between the teeth, make silly faces, or build ramps and jump bikes are examples of accomplishments children value. Peers can teach things to one another without self-consciousness and without the total disparity in status that marks the adult–child relationship. Peer relationships offer children the unique opportunity of interacting in a context of relatively balanced equality and power (Erwin, 1998).

Friendship Relationships

As with peer relationships, friendships offer an opportunity for equal partnerships and so much more. Whereas peers come together at periodic intervals for common activities, friends choose to be with one another as specially chosen playmates outside of and in addition to peer activities. Friendships offer countless benefits for those involved.

Benefits of friendship.   Friends offer unique opportunities and benefits for children to develop their social competence. Participants are motivated to solve their conflicts peacefully through childhood diplomacy. They practice the difficult task of balancing their personal wants and desires with those of others, or community shared goals (Rubin et al., 2006). In turn, children with better social competence do better at making and keeping friends (Vaughn et al., 2000). Friendships support the development of prosocial skills such as cooperation and altruism (Sebanc, 2003). Children are more likely to behave in a positive manner when in the company of friends (Simpkins & Parke, 2002). With friends, children demonstrate higher levels of emotional competence (Rubin, et al., 2006). Friendships also provide a place for children to practice their social problem-solving skills. These skills include communicating, managing conflict, creating and maintaining trust, and establishing intimacy. Such skills, in turn, prepare children for future intimate relationships in adulthood (Erwin, 1998; Shaffer, 2006).

Friendships provide a source of security and social support (Shaffer, 2006). Friends are able to discuss attitudes and compare skills. These discussions and comparisons provide children with validation for their

Peer relationships provide an opportunity for children to achieve a sense of belonging.

Children without friends are more likely to be lonely and less likely to be able to initiate and maintain play with peers.

attitudes, ideas, and skills and help them feel more socially adept with a better awareness of self (Harter, 2006). Friendships may offer children a distraction from less pleasant assignments and responsibilities, making certain situations more fun (Erwin, 1998).

These special relationships also serve as an emotional buffer against stress in the children's lives (Wasserstein & LaGreca, 1996). Children with at least one friend are less likely to fall victim to aggression from peers. They are also more likely to have less externalizing problems, such as violence and aggression with one mutual best friend (Rubin, et al., 2006). Children who have friends are more likely to be self-confident and less lonely than those without friends. They are more often accepted by peers and experience less rejection. In addition, children with friends appear to perform better academically in school (Ladd, 1999; Newcomb & Bagwell, 1996; Sebanc, 2003).

Costs of not having friends. For all the wonderful benefits that friendships provide, you might wonder, what about the children who have few, if any, friends? Unfortunately, the situation is not at all pleasant. Research shows that even one friend is better than no friend. Without a best friend, children are likely to be victimized and lonely (Brendgen, Vitaro, & Bukowski, 2000). Children without friends are more likely to be troubled (Newcomb & Bagwell, 1996). They are less likely to be able to initiate and maintain play with peers (Howes, Matheson, & Wu, 1992). They are more likely to suffer academically and have more negative attitudes toward school (Ladd, 1990). Children who do not have friends miss the opportunity to practice the important social skills necessary for maintaining social attachments throughout life, thus they develop or fail to develop these appropriate life skills (Rubin et al., 2006). Therefore, friendless children are more likely to suffer lifelong internalizing problems such as depression, mental illnesses, heart disease, and hypertension in adulthood (Lawhon, 1997; Ladd & Troop-Gordon, 2003). In addition, friendless children are more likely than their counterparts, who have friends, to become juvenile delinquents, drop out of school, receive a dishonorable discharge from the military, experience psychiatric problems, and commit suicide. Although completely friendless children are rare, many youngsters grow up wishing they had more friends. For most children, however, the critical factor is not how many friends they have, but the quality of the friendships they establish.

VARIABLES THAT INFLUENCE CHILDREN'S FRIENDSHIPS

There is a body of research that indicates that children's own behavior greatly influences how they are accepted by peers (Rubin, et al., 2006). Children's interaction patterns, for the most part, are a primary factor in determining whether others will perceive them as desirable or undesirable as companions. Before looking at each one, please refer to Figure 8-1.

As demonstrated in Figure 8-1, there are multiple aspects influencing children's peer relationships and ability to make friends: their social understanding/social cognition, their ability to regulate their emotions, their play experiences and abilities, their language abilities, and the adult support received in support of peer relationships. The grounding influence for all of these is the cultural values of each child, which springs from the family. Finally, it is the child's view of self that filters each of these influences and paves the way for a child to believe in his or her ability to make friends or not.

Social Cognition

Children with greater social cognitive abilities along with emotional maturity are better able to make friends. Further, the more social cognition a child demonstrates, the more popular and sought out as a playmate that child will be (Rubin, et al., 2006).

Figure 8-1 Variables that influence children's peer relationships and friendships.

You'll recall from Chapter 4 that social understanding and cognition stems from children's ability to think about someone else's inner ideas, beliefs, and emotions in relation to their actions and to be able to generate appropriate actions or reactions. Thus it is important to be able to predict what will make someone want to be a friend and then take appropriate actions to make this happen. The capacity to do this takes time. Children who can imagine the thinking of others are more accepted by peers and seem to possess greater social competence (McElwain & Volling, 2002). These children can imagine things that are pleasing to others and act on them in a manner consistent with social expectations. This ability increases through interactions with peers.

Emotional Regulation

To do well with friends, children must learn to regulate not only their own behavior, but also their emotions (Hay, Ross, & Goldman, 2004). Children who better understand their own emotions and can adjust these emotions to fit the social situation properly, demonstrate better social behavior, experience more positive feedback from others, and become more sought after peers than those who find it difficult to regulate their emotions (Rubin, et al., 2006). When children can recognize and label their own emotions, are able to read another's emotional expression, and then respond well, they open themselves up to more social possibilities. (See Chapter 5 for more on emotional development.) Overall, the quality of the friendship is linked with children's ability to show and to regulate their emotions, which in turn is linked with their developing social understanding of self and others (McDowell, O'Neil, & Parke, 2000).

Play Experiences

One of the best places to practice talking about the emotions and thoughts of others and taking appropriate action is in pretend play (Dunn, Cutting, & Fisher, 2002). Within the boundaries of play, children are able to practice sharing and negotiating. Consequently, it has been found that pretend imaginative play is an important force in forming early friendships (Dunn et al., 2002; Rubin, 2003). This is true no matter what the culture (Farver, Kim, & Lee-Shim, 2000). Play is so vital to friendship formation that, when pretend play is not supported, it can interfere with "harmonious peer relations" (Hay et al., 2004, p. 90). See Chapter 7

for more on the importance of play for promoting social competence.

Language

In pretend play with peers and friends, children develop conversation competence as they give and receive information that sustains the play. Language also impacts their success and overall acceptance with peers in other situations (Hay et al., 2004). Children listen very carefully to messages. If they possess a good understanding and use of language, they are better able to respond to the content of messages of others. Children with strong language skills are also more able to construct responses that describe their emotions and point of view to the other children. Children's responses to peers in conversation predicts their social status (Kemple, Spermanza, & Hazen, 1992). Those with language difficulties are often reported as having a more difficult time with friendship (Pavin, 2001). In all areas of friendship—initiating, maintaining, negotiating conflict, and ending the relationship—language is vital. When adults talk with children about their interactions with others, when they label the emotions of others and reasons for reactions of others, they are supporting children in both their language and social competence (Thompson, 2006).

Adult Support

Beyond scaffolding children's language, many other things that children experience are directly related to or controlled by the adults in their environment. Early experiences with adults set the stage for the type of interaction that children expect from others, including peers, in their social world (Thompson, 2006). When children experience positive interactions with the adults in their world, they come to expect good things out of future interactions with others. The opposite is also true.

The responsibility to create or administer social experiences for children rests with the adults in their lives. When the adults set up early play experiences with other children and assist the children in learning to play with these other children, they are scaffolding potentially positive early peer relationships. However, when adults bring children together but do not assist in the social experience and leave children to "be children"—such as when 3-year-olds are expected to work out their disagreements over toys on their own—they are putting the children at a distinct disadvantage. Just as with so many other things, young children can do some things on their own, but benefit greatly with an interpreter to help them understand what can be done to improve the experience. Adults who assist children in reading the situations, understanding the social cues and emotions of others and the causes behind the emotions, help children become more socially accepted. When social encounters are seen as opportunities to teach how to get along with others, the children are likely to become more socially competent and thus be more sought after as future play partners and friends (Saarni, Campos, Camras, & Witherington, 2006).

The expectations adults have for children's behavior also plays a large role in their peer relationships and potential friendships. Children's temperament is known to influence their peer interactions. However, temperament cannot be blamed for things "not working" with peers. When adults blame children's behavior on their temperament or find other reasons to excuse or brush off socially inappropriate behaviors, they are not likely to assist children in improving their behavior. Instead, when adults acknowledge the differences in children and work to improve children's social competence, positive behaviors can emerge (Rubin et al., 2006).

Finally, the amount of security in the form of warmth and support that children experience in their relationships with adults directly influences their potential for other relationships. If children experience a high sense of security in their relationships with adults, they are likely to experience greater closeness and intimacy in their future relationships with teachers and friends (Thompson, 2006). Unfortunately the opposite is true also. The role of adults in children's socialization of relationships cannot be understated.

Cultural Values

Adults are the ones that introduce and socialize children into their culture. It is within the culture that behaviors towards peers and between friends are socialized. Some distinct differences in children's understanding of friendship and their corresponding interactions are based on culture. For instance, in the United States and Western Europe, friends are seen as an emotional support and a source for intimacy. In more sustenance economies, friendships are valued for the instrumental aid they provide each other in daily life (Rubin et al., 2006). Also, the role of the family in any given culture contributes to one's perception of the importance of friends. In cultures where much of the power and

authority rests with the family system, there is less dependence and worth placed on friendships than in cultures where the family is not as important (French, 2004).

CHILDREN'S IDEAS ABOUT FRIENDSHIP

What exactly is a friend in the eyes of a child? Do children see their friends in the same way adults view theirs? What many adults may not know is that children's concept of friendship—their notion of how it works, their expectations, and the rules that govern their actions toward friends—changes over time.

Five children, ages 3, 6, 9, 11, and 13 were asked to draw themselves with their friends. Notice in Figures 8-2 through 8-6 the features of friendship each child added to his or her drawing. Without any prompting, the children represented varying stages of friendship quite succinctly. Their pictures demonstrate the progression of friendship in children.

The Emergence of Friendship

Friends are important from the first days of life. Observe any two 6-month-olds together and you will see why babies enjoy interacting with other babies (Vandell & Mueller, 1995). By 18 months of age, children will imitate other children and play simple social games such as peek-a-boo or look-for-the-toy (Howes & Matheson, 1992). Children as young as 2 proudly proclaim of another child, "She's my friend." Researchers have studied children's friendships for the past 20 years and have devised a hierarchy of how children develop friendship as they mature. In this book we refer to this as the **Friendship Framework**.

This framework begins around the age of 3 and coincides with children's development of empathy and their understanding of other people's perspectives or Theory of Mind (Selman & Schultz, 1990). Within each of the five levels of the Friendship Framework, you will notice that children's understanding of what a friend is, the value they place on friendship, and the **friendship skills** required to make and keep friends changes (Selman, Levitt, & Schultz, 1997).

In the early levels of friendship, children are preoccupied with their own emotions, with the physical characteristics of their companions, and with what is happening here and now. In the later levels, children are more sensitive to the desires and concerns of others, they appreciate psychological traits such as humor and trustworthiness, and they think about the future of their relationships as well as the present. Children progress from the first level to the last as a result of age; increasing intellectual, physical, and language abilities; social understanding; and accumulated experience.

Many children have temporary difficulties when their ideas about friendship lag behind or move far beyond those of their peers. These problems are reduced once children and their age-mates catch up to one another. In the meantime, children may choose to associate with younger or older peers who are in the same stage of thinking. Adults cannot necessarily accelerate children's progress through the sequence in the friendship framework, but they can attempt to understand children's behavior by knowing more about their friendship understanding, friendship skills, and friendship valuing at each level to better plan for ways to assist the children in their development.

The Friendship Framework

Level Zero—Momentary playmates: Ages 3 to 6. Young children call "friend" those peers with whom they play most often or who engage in similar activities at a given time. This was evident in 3-year-old Maddie's answer to the question about her friendship drawing: Why are they your friends? "Because we play Polly Pockets together and all wear pink dresses" (see Figure 8-2). In this way, children define their friends by proximity ("He's my friend; he lives next door"). Friends are also valued for their possessions ("She's my friend; she has a Barbie doll") or because they demonstrate visible physical skills ("He's my friend because he runs fast").

Because children of this age are egocentric, they think only about their own side of the relationship. Consequently, they focus on what they want the other child to do for them. The thinking is in the here and now, within the activity at hand, so whoever the child is playing with at this very moment is the friend. They have no thought of their own duties to the relationship and so do not consider how to match their behaviors to the other child's needs. Moreover, it is common for youngsters to assume that friends think just the way they do. If this proves false, they become very upset.

Level Zero youngsters are better at initiating an interaction than they are at responding to others'

Figure 8-2 Maddie and her friends.

overtures. Hence, they may inadvertently ignore or actively reject other children's attempts to join their play. We have observed that this phenomenon happens most often once the play has been established. By that time, a solitary player or group of children has centered on carrying out the play episode in a particular way, which includes only those currently involved. It then becomes difficult for the players to expand their thinking to envision how the newcomer could be included. The refusal to allow another child access to their play is a cognitive dilemma, not a deliberate act of cruelty.

Level One—One-way assistance: Ages 5 to 9. At Level One, children identify those age-mates as friends whose behavior pleases them. As 6-year-old Veronica drew the friends walking dogs together, she smugly explained that her friend Kelly in the picture was going to get her a Barbie for her birthday party (see Figure 8-3). For some children, good feelings are engendered by a playmate who will give them a turn, share gum, offer them rides on the new two-wheeler, pick them for the team, save them a seat on the bus, or give special birthday presents. For others, pleasure comes from having another child accept the turn, the gum, the ride, the invitation to join team, the seat, or the present. Because each friend is concerned about whether his or her wants are being satisfied, neither necessarily considers what to do to bring pleasure to the other. If, by chance, their individual wants and behaviors are compatible, the friendship lasts. If not, the partners change in short order. Another characteristic of Level One is that children try out different social roles: leader, follower, negotiator, instigator, comic, collaborator, appeaser, or comforter. As part of this process, they experiment with a variety of behaviors that may or may not match their usual manner. Thus, it is normal for children who are practicing their roles to manifest extreme examples of them. That is, a child who wants to be more assertive may become bossy and overbearing; a child who discovers the benefits of comedy may become silly or outrageous.

By the time youngsters reach this level, their desire to have a friend is so strong that many prefer to play with an uncongenial companion rather than play alone. They will try almost anything to initiate a relationship and may attempt to bribe or coerce another child to like them by saying: "If you'll be my friend, I'll invite you to my party," or "If you don't let me have a turn, I won't be your friend." Children who resort to such tactics are not malicious, but are merely experimenting with what works and what does not. Level One also is notable for the fact that boys play with boys and girls play with girls (Fabes, Martin, & Havish, 2003). This occurs because children continue to focus on outward

Figure 8-3 Veronica and Kelly on their play date.

similarities, and gender is an obvious way of determining likeness. School age friends are observably similar to each other (Rubin et al., 2006).

Although youngsters concentrate much of their energy on the friendship process, they have difficulty maintaining more than one close relationship at a time. An outgrowth of their struggle to identify friends is that they become preoccupied with discussing who is their friend and who is not. This is when children can be overheard to say, "You can't be my friend; Mary's my friend." Pairs often change from day to day and frequently are determined, by what people are wearing, by a newfound common interest, or by convenience (who shows up first). However, some friendship pairs remain relatively stable over time, as long as the two children see each other frequently (Park & Waters, 1989). There is also evidence that some friendships begun in preschool may last throughout kindergarten and even beyond and that these stable friendships predict future success for both children in their peer relationships (Hay et al., 2004; Rubin, et. al, 2006).

Level Two—Two-way, fair-weather cooperation: Ages 7 to 12.   The thinking of children at

Level Two has matured to the point at which they are able to consider both points of view in the friendship. This leads to a notion of justice that dictates how the relationship should proceed. Children expect friends to be "nice" to each other and often trade favors as a way of helping each other satisfy their separate interests: "You helped me yesterday—I'll help you today"; "We're playing my game first and then your game." They recognize that each person should benefit from the relationship and that the friendship will break up if this does not occur: "If you call me names again, I won't be your friend"; "That's not fair! I waited for you yesterday." Friends are concerned about what each thinks of the other and evaluate their own actions as they feel the other might evaluate them: "Steve will like me if I learn to catch better"; "Nobody will like me with this doofy haircut." It is at this level that conformity in dress, language, and behavior reaches a peak as children try to find ways to fit in with the group. As a result, it becomes very important for children to carry a lunch box decorated with the latest movie cartoon character, wear their hair in special ways, or take swimming lessons.

As can be seen from these examples, the emphasis throughout this period is similarity. Forming clubs

Katrina reads to Mae: A great example of one-way assistance benefiting both children.

is a natural outgrowth of this. Clubs, although short lived, have elaborate rules, and the major activity involves planning who will be included and who will be excluded (see Figure 8-4 for Cauleen's Cool Cat Club). To further confirm their unity, friends share secrets, plans, and agreements.

Friendships tend to develop in pairs. In particular, groups of girlfriends are loose networks of best friend partnerships; male friendship occurs in groups, characterized by an activity or sport with fewer best-friend relationships (Fabes et al., 2003).

Within both male and female groups, friends are very possessive of each other, and jealousy over who is "friends" with whom is quite pronounced. As children are concerned about belonging to groups and gaining acceptance, gossip begins and increases throughout middle childhood. It is through the gossip that children's membership to a group is valued and tested. The gossip demonstrates adhering to the group's beliefs and behaviors and seems to foster friendship closeness (Kuttler, Parker & LaGreca, 2002).

Level Three—Intimate, mutually shared relationships: Ages 8 to 15.   Level Three marks the first time that children view friendship as an ongoing relationship with shared goals, values, and social understanding (Rubin et al., 2006). Now, children are more willing to compromise rather than simply cooperate. This means they are not concerned with the tit-for-tat reciprocity that marked the previous level; rather, they become involved in each other's personal lives and have a stake in each other's happiness. They gain satisfaction from the emotional support they enjoy within the relationship. On this basis, friends share feelings and help each other solve personal conflicts and problems. To each other they reveal thoughts and emotions that they keep from everyone else.

Friendship has now become intimate and the best-friend relationship is a crucial one. Because this is such an intense learning experience, children often only focus on one best friend at a time, as evident in Michael's picture (see Figure 8-5). It is natural for them to become totally absorbed in each other. Such friendships are both exclusive and possessive. In other words, friends are not supposed to have another close friend, and they are expected to include each other in everything. Friends do share approved **acquaintances** but are not allowed to

Figure 8-4 The Cool Cat Club. Who's in—who's not!

At Level Two, children have matured to the point at which they are able to consider both points of view in the friendship. These two friends are able to cooperate as they share in a common activity.

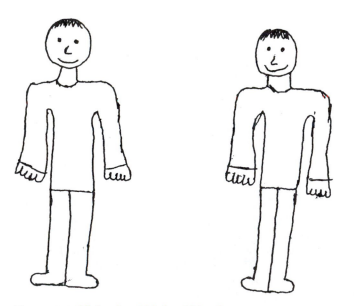

Figure 8-5 Michael and his best friend.

pursue a relationship with someone one of them does not like. The greatest betrayal comes when someone breaks these rules. Only after children have developed friendship to this point are they able to branch out and have close ties with more than one peer at a time.

Level Four—Mature friendships: Ages 12 and older. For persons at the mature-friendship level, emotional and psychological benefits are the most valued qualities of friendship. Friends are not as possessive of each other as they were in previous levels; they can have some dissimilar interests and can pursue activities separately. Children at this level are able to allow their friends to develop other close relationships as well. Thus, they can have more than one friend at a time and can have friends who are not friends with each other. In this way, friendship becomes a bond that involves trust and support. These elements sometimes are attained by coming together and somvetimes by letting go. As a result, friends now are able to remain close over long distances, over long periods of time, and in spite of long separations (noted by Siobhan's picture of friends talking on the phone; see Figure 8-6).

Figure 8-6 Long distance.

Friendship Selection

Eric and Sandy are like two peas in a pod; they dress alike; they talk alike; they act alike. They are the best of friends.

Sasha and Tabitha are as different as night and day. One is short, one is tall; one is boisterous, one is quiet; one likes cats, one likes dogs. Still, they are inseparable.

No matter what the age of a child (or adult), friendships are dynamic and continually in a process of change (Hansen, Nangle, & Ellis, 1996). Adults often wonder why children choose the friends they do. Name, physical appearance, race, gender, age, ability, and attitudes all are cues children consider in selecting a potential friend (Hartup, 1996). Children

are more likely to choose friends who they think are similar to them. Even in middle childhood and adolescence, children are attracted to those who resemble them in age, gender, ethnicity, and behavioral states (Hartup & Abeccassis, 2004).

Physical appearance. One factor that contributes to children's friendship selection is personal appearance. Children are naturally attracted to those who look like them (Kupersmidt, DeRosier, & Patterson, 1995). Children who are overweight, mentally impaired, disabled, slovenly, or physically unattractive are less likely to be chosen as friends than are youngsters who fit children's concept of beauty (Hartup, 1996). Interestingly, the same standard of beauty is held by children of all ages and cultures and fits many of the stereotypes promoted through the popular media (Harter, 2006). Children attribute the positive qualities of friendliness, intelligence, and social competence to those they consider attractive. Likewise, they associate negative attributes with peers they think of as unattractive.

Race. Children also pick their friends based on race and are most likely to choose friends from their own racial group (Hartup & Abeccassis, 2002). However, parental attitudes do influence how children feel about making friends with someone of another race or culture. If children perceive their parents as accepting of racial differences, they are more likely to include children of different racial or ethnic backgrounds among their friends.

Gender. Gender is another dominant consideration in who is "friends" with whom. There is an expectation in children for how one should act based on gender. When children do not follow the stereotype, girls, the "tomboys," seem to fare well and are liked irregardless, but boys are likely to be disliked and shunned (Rubin et al., 2006).

Children prefer same-sex playmates throughout childhood and even at a very early age tend to exclude the opposite sex. At 2, girls prefer to play with girls. By 3, boys begin to prefer to play with boys, although this preference is not set until age 5 (Smith & Inder, 1993). Girls tend to play in pairs and small groups; boys tend to form packs and engage in group activities (Fabes et al., 2003). Females tend to share personal information whereas males tend to engage in physical activities that do not require personal sharing (Rubin, et al, 2006). When the best friend of a boy is a girl, more sharing of personal information and emotional intimacy occurs (Zarbatany McDougall, and Hymel, 2000). Although friendships between males and females do occur, same-sex friendships tend to be more lasting and stable over time, with male relationships more stable than female (Benenson & Christakos, 2003). This is due in no small measure to the reinforcement children receive from adults and peers for choosing friends of their own gender. The segregation between the sexes can be reduced through adult facilitation and encouragement (Erwin, 1998).

Children prefer same-sex playmates throughout childhood, and even at an early age tend to exclude the opposite sex.

Age. Children are also more likely to select friends who are close to their own age. When friendships develop between children of different ages, it usually is because the participants are developmentally similar in some ways. For instance, shy children who have less confidence in their interaction skills may seek out younger friends with whom they feel more comfortable socially (Zimbardo & Radl, 1982).

Behavior characteristics. The likelihood that two children will become friends can be closely linked to the number of behavioral attributes they share (Kupersmidt et al., 1995). In both Western and Eastern cultures, similarities between friends can be found with regard to level of: prosocial behavior, antisocial behavior, shyness, depression, popularity, and achievement (French, Jansen, Riansari, & Setiono, 2000). Friends also may resemble one another in terms of physical or cognitive skill, and degree of sociability (Bukowski, Sippola, & Boivin, 1995). Consequently, it is not unusual to see children choose as friends those who share their love of sports, reading, chess, or stamp collecting. Nor is it uncommon for bright, agile, impulsive, or outgoing children to seek friends much like themselves.

In addition to searching for likenesses, youngsters often choose as friends those peers whose characteristics complement their own personality and capacities (Rubin et al., 2006). This often involves attributes that they themselves lack and for which the other child can serve as a model. Thus, loud children and quiet children, active children and passive children, serious children and "class clowns" may choose one another as friends. Yet, even when this occurs, one must remember that these youngsters have found enough common ground that they see more similarities than differences in each other. Children are not attracted to those whom they view as opposites (Hartup & Abeccassis, 2004).

Play behaviors. Children are likely to seek out friends with similar styles of play (Rubin, Lynch, Coplan, Rose-Kransor, & Booth, 1994). In addition, children are more likely to play with someone with a style of play that resembles another friend (Dunn, Cutting, & Fisher, 2002).

Attitudes. When children who are dissimilar in some fashion discover that they share like attitudes, they feel more positive about one another. This awareness facilitates friendly relations between children who initially perceive themselves as totally different. Such knowledge has been found to promote increased friendships among children of differing races and between nondisabled and disabled youngsters (Bukowski et al., 1995).

Adults who want children to experience the rewards of friendships with children of the opposite sex, of another race, or whose abilities do not match their own must provide opportunities for the children to recognize more subtle similarities. Specific strategies for achieving this aim are presented in the skills section of this chapter.

ADULT CONCERNS ABOUT FRIENDSHIP
Uncomfortable Friendship Choices

Adults sometimes express concern about children's friendship choices when they observe what seems to be an unequal relationship between two youngsters. For instance, 5-year-olds Lily and Carmen play together every day. Carmen appears to dominate. She chooses where they will play, what they will play with, and who else is allowed to play with them. Carmen is often perceived as bossy and Lily is viewed as helpless and compliant. From the children's point of view, however, the situation appears to be quite different. Lily may choose to play with Carmen because Carmen has lots of ideas and takes responsibility for directing the play. Lily is happy because she can play without having to think about what to do next. Carmen also is satisfied because there is no question as to who is in charge. Over time, as Lily has a chance to observe how Carmen asserts her will, she too may venture to test her own assertiveness. In the meantime, Carmen may grow tired of such a passive playmate. If the girls do not respond to each other's changing needs, chances are that each will select a new companion. While they are in the process of working out their relationship, adults can help each child express her changing desires to the other, as well as aid them in exploring new potential friendships. Usually, it should be left up to the children, not the adults, to judge the best time to change the nature of their association or to move on to others. However, it is important to note that early peer relationships with prosocial friends seem to set up a positive pattern for successful social behaviors with others in the future (Dunn et al., 2002). The early company you keep does matter.

Another issue of concern to adults is what is sometimes referred to as "peer pressure." This influence occurs most frequently by middle and later childhood. During those years, children's expanding social horizons cause them to be aware of the opinions of friends and other youngsters in their peer group to an even greater degree than was true of early childhood. Thus, in an effort to be accepted, older children in groups are likely to yield to the norms that the group has established, even if the norm is against family or other microsystem beliefs. Professionals who work with children at this phase of development must recognize that they cannot eliminate peer pressure. However, they can influence the values that children bring to their social interactions. Professionals can help children sort out their beliefs with respect to particular behaviors, such as honesty. Furthermore, adults can be valuable resources in offering support and suggesting alternative responses that children can use when confronted by pressures from peers that are incompatible with those beliefs. In addition, helping professionals can help groups of children to establish and maintain a positive group image. Finally, it is important to note that while the peer group has a greater effect on children's behavior in middle childhood than in early childhood, parents and teachers continue to be powerful and important socializing influences as well (Santrock, 2000b). In addition, having a high-quality friendship seems to lessen children's tendency to imitate less socially accepted behaviors of peers (Berndt, 2002).

Unsuccessful Types of Peer Interactions

Unsuccessful peers fall into two categories: peer neglected and rejected. Adults must intervene in both situations because children who experience persistent difficulties with peers are more likely to experience later psychological dysfunction (Ladd & Troop-Gordon, 2003). Skillful adults can help to prevent further negative impact on children (Dodge et al., 2003).

Peer neglected children. Peer neglected children are typically shy and passive. They are not talkative. They make very few attempts to enter play and dislike being the focus of attention (Harrist, Zaia, Bates, Dodge, & Pettit, 1997). It is not that these children are necessarily less socially skilled than their peers; they just perceive themselves to be so (Rubin, Bukowski, & Parker, 1998). Often children are neglected simply because they do not know or do not use socially accepted ways of attracting other children's attention (Rubin, 2003). As a result of the developing expectation for neglect, these children

back away further from interactions, thus missing out on opportunities with peers and any future positive interaction.

This leaves **peer neglected** children feeling even more isolated (Rubin, 2003; see Figure 8-7). For example, Rudy watches Steven and Jamie play space rangers under the jungle gym. His caregiver, Mr. Rogers, suggests that Rudy go play too. Rudy replies, "Nah, I'm no good at that game," and backs away. Rudy doesn't believe that he can enter the play and would rather not even try.

Peer rejected children.   Children who experience rejection from peers are more likely to become aggressive, especially if they already have a tendency towards aggression. The combination of early aggression and rejection is likely to lead to antisocial behavior (Dodge et al., 2003). These children are motivated to be social based on the desire to get even or to defeat their peers. Clearly, both are not useful for promoting social relationships (Rubin et al., 2006).

Peer rejected children seem to follow two patterns: rejected withdrawn or rejected-aggressive. Each comes with its own set of baggage.

Rejected-withdrawn children are socially awkward. They display immature or unusual behavior and are insensitive to their peer group expectations. These children expect to be rebutted. They know that they are not liked by others (Downey, Lebolt, Rincon, & Freitas, 1998; Harrist et al., 1997). For instance, Janelle, age 6, observes her peers playing house. She wants to play too, but she does not think the others will let her. Instead of asking to play, she gets on all fours and barks her way into the scene, irritating the others and disrupting the play. The children give her dirty looks and proceed to ignore her. Rejected-withdrawn children are lonely. They possess low self-esteem, depression, negative social-emotional functioning and other emotional disorders . These children are targets for bullies, frequently falling victim (Rubin et al., 2006).

Rejected-aggressive children are just the opposite. They often are the bullies. Rejected-aggressive children alienate themselves from their peer group through the use of force. They try to dominate interactions, are critical of others, and typically are uncooperative (Newcomb, Bukowski, & Pattee, 1993). They see the behavior of others as hostile toward them. For example, Josh wants to play soccer with the neighborhood boys. He approaches the

Figure 8-7 The pattern of neglected children. Source: Rubin, 2003.

game on his bike. When no one invites him to join, he rides his bike through the middle of the game. He gets off on the other side, letting his bike fall onto the edge of the field, knocks another player down, and kicks the ball away, making a field goal. Part of the difficulty lies in their level of social cognition. These children cannot grasp the consequences of their own behavior on others and the corresponding peer reactions. Because they don't make the connection, they fail to take responsibility for their actions, believing that the fault is with everyone else (Rubin, et al., 2006). While rejected-withdrawn children expect others to dislike them, rejected aggressive children believe themselves to be socially popular when they are in fact the opposite (Zakriski & Coie, 1996). These children are more likely than all others to become chronically hostile, develop conduct disorders, and engage in

criminal violence (Hay et al., 2004). Whether withdrawn or aggressive, rejected children, without intervention, are likely to continue their rejection patterns throughout life (Cillessen, van Ijzendcorn, van Lieshout, & Hartup, 1992).

Both neglected and rejected children seem to possess an inaccurate perception of others. They are not necessarily lacking in social understanding, but are truly misreading or misunderstanding the social cues of other children much more often than others (Hay et al., 2004). This leads to very lonely children.

All children experience some degree of loneliness at some point in time (Pavin, 2001; see Figure 8-8). Children who persistently receive negative feedback for their peer interactions are more likely to experience loneliness (Kochenderfer-Ladd & Wardrop, 2001). Of the children who experience

Figure 8-8 I'm lonely.

peer interaction difficulties, rejected-withdrawn children report having the greatest amount of loneliness (Asher & Paquette, 2003).

Children with difficulties with peer interactions and friendship may encounter difficulty at one or many points in the four states of friendship. Recognizing the tasks within each one serves to prepare adults to better assist children successfully through these states.

STATES OF FRIENDSHIP

Making Contact

Before a friendship can "get off the ground," one person must make an approach and another must respond. How this contact is carried out influences each child's perception of the other. Children make good impressions when they engage in the following actions (Coie, Dodge, & Kupersmidt, 1990; Shapiro, 1997):

- Smile and speak "Hi" or "Hey!" pleasantly or offer "What's up?" greetings.
- Ask for information. "What's your name?" or "Where's the cafeteria?"
- Respond to others' "I'm new too" or greetings and "Come with me. I'll show you."
- Offer information: "My name's Rosalie. This is my first day at Central."
- Invite participation: "Wanna play catch?" or "You can be on our team."

By these signals, children are able to let others know that they want to be friends. Often, though, children try to make contact once the play has already begun. In this case, children should learn to watch, listen, move closer, and ease into the situation (Rubin, 2003). Depending on the age of the child, another behavior widely interpreted as a friendly overture by younger children is imitation. However, this technique used alone may not lead to success. Children also should ask to enter into the play (Rubin, 2003).

From this discussion, it can be seen that youngsters who are cordial elicit positive reactions and are better accepted by their age-mates (Goleman, 1995). This is true whether the child is the initiator or the respondent. Although polite prosocial actions may seem obvious strategies to adults, many youngsters fail to make the connection. These are children whose timing is off or who have the right idea but an inappropriate way of showing it. They may be truly unaware of the importance of such strategies or may fail to recognize how or why their behavior affects others as it does. Whatever the explanation, such children often attempt to make contact by grabbing, pushing, barging in, whining, threatening, ignoring, begging, criticizing, or being bossy (Shapiro, 1997).

Children who rely on these approaches are rejected frequently. As their lack of success becomes more habitual, they tend to withdraw or become hostile. Both reactions exacerbate their difficulties (Erwin, 1998). Over time, they develop a reputation of being unfriendly or undesirable as a playmate, and the downward spiral for neglected/rejected children will occur. In cases such as these, adults can help children learn to make more positive contacts and hence improve their chances of finding a friend.

Maintaining Positive Relationships

The positive behaviors that characterize successful beginnings continue to be important as the relationship grows. Popular children of all ages are described by peers as sensitive, kind, flexible, and fun to be with (Rubin et al., 2006). In particular, how well youngsters communicate both verbally and nonverbally influences their likeableness. So, children who speak directly, are attentive to everyone involved in specific situations, respond interestedly to and acknowledge the play signals of others, and who offer many alternatives are sought after as playmates

(Hazen & Black, 1989). The following techniques characterize their interactions with others:

- **Expressing interest:** smiling, nodding, establishing eye contact, asking related questions.
- **Cooperating:** taking turns, sharing, working together.
- **Expressing acceptance:** listening to another child's ideas, adopting another child's approach to a play situation.
- **Expressing affection:** hugging, holding hands, or saying: "I like you" or "Let's be friends."
- **Expressing empathy:** "That's a neat picture you made," "You look sad; want me to sit with you while you wait?"
- **Offering assistance and helpful suggestions:** "If you like, I can hold the box while you tie it. It may need some string on top of the tape."

Popular children of all ages are described as fun to be with.

- **Praising playmates:** "That was a great hit," "Neat idea! I think it'll work," "You're pretty."

Children who use these tactics actively demonstrate respect and affection for others. This has the happy outcome of making them desirable companions because people seek out friends who are enjoyable (Rubin et al., 2006). Thus, it is true that positive behaviors elicit positive responses, which in turn reinforce children's efforts and prompt them to continue their successful actions.

In the same way that positive cycles are established, so, too, are negative ones. Children who are aggressive or uncooperative or who act silly, show off, or display immature behavior may irritate, frustrate, and offend their peers. They tend to further isolate themselves by daydreaming or escalating their negative behavior (Erwin, 1998).

Similar problems arise when children try to act appropriately but misjudge how to do it. They may rely on insincere flattery, express their affection too roughly (giving bear hugs), or communicate their appreciation too effusively. Others miss the mark by constantly correcting rather than suggesting or taking over instead of merely helping. In any case, these behavior patterns sabotage children's efforts to maintain friendships over time.

Negotiating Conflict

Perhaps the most severe test of a relationship occurs when the friends disagree. How the conflict is managed on both sides determines to a large extent whether the friendship will continue or be abandoned. Children who use constructive ways of resolving differences while still meeting their own needs are most successful in pursuing lasting relationships (Goleman, 1995). This is because they are able to preserve their dignity and at the same time take into account another person's perspectives. Children who are so passive that they never stand up for themselves lose self-respect and, eventually, the respect of peers. Those who respond aggressively also are rejected. Neither extreme is conducive to eliciting positive reactions (Rubin et al., 2006).

There is a strong correlation between children's effective use of **negotiation skills** and their ability to communicate accurately (Holden, 1997). Successful conflict negotiation depends on all parties having a common idea of the source of the problem and being able to express to others their ideas for a solution. Children who use threats, shame, or coercion to force a solution violate these fundamental requirements. Consequently,

other children begin to avoid them or retaliate in kind. Successful negotiators are children who implement the following strategies (Stocking, Arezzo, & Leavitt, 1980):

- **Express personal rights, needs, or feelings:** "I want a chance to pick the movie this time."
- **Listen to and acknowledge others' rights and feelings:** "Yeah, you have been waiting a long time to see that movie."
- **Suggest nonviolent solutions to conflicts:** "Let's flip for it."
- **Explain the reasoning behind a proposed solution:** "This way, we each get a chance."
- **Stand up against unrealistic demands:** "No, you got to pick the last time. Now it's my turn."
- **Accept reasonable disagreement:** "Okay, I hadn't thought of that."
- **Compromise on solutions:** "Let's see both, or go swimming instead."

Ending Relationships/Friendships

In most situations, children are interested in establishing friendships; however, at times in every child's life a relationship or friendship will end. As with all other components of the friendship process, ending relationships also can be a natural event. Not all friendships continue. Sometimes friendship termination is determined by family transitions such as moving to another neighborhood or to another child care environment. Sadness, loneliness, and longing to play with a friend are not unusual; over time children acquire new friends. Children must learn how to deal graciously with the ending of a relationship (Levinger & Levinger, 1986). How well a child is able to leave a relationship and move on to another requires three skills: creating and/or acknowledging the separation, verbalizing the goodbye or termination, and locating alternative people and/or activities to replace the ended relationship.

ADULT STRATEGIES TO SUPPORT THE IMPROVEMENT OF CHILDREN'S PEER RELATIONSHIPS AND FRIENDSHIPS

Because the distinction is so clear between successful friendship-making strategies and those that are not, you may wonder why any child would choose techniques doomed to fail. Children are not born automatically knowing the best ways to make friends. They must learn by observing others, by practicing, by experimenting with a variety of social behaviors, and by experiencing the consequences of their actions (Erwin, 1998). Children who are better observers and more accurate evaluators of what is effective and what is not acquire friends more easily than those who make poor observations and assessments or those who have poor role models at home or among peers. This does not mean the children who experience difficulty have no chance for improvement.

On the contrary, there is encouraging evidence that children can learn how to make productive contacts, maintain positive relationships, manage conflicts constructively, and end relationships successfully (Erwin, 1998; Selman, Levitt, & Schultz 1997). Several studies point to the improved **friendship-making skills** of some neglected and some rejected children who underwent a specific course of study designed to increase their awareness, teach them particular behaviors, and decrease their aggressive responses (Coie & Koeppl, 1990; Erwin, 1998; Murphy & Schneider, 1994; Selman et al., 1997).

When considering how to assist children with friendship, it is important to pay attention to the child's developmental understanding of friendship as well as the multiple influences discussed in earlier the chapter that impact friendship. Beyond the role of the adult (which in this case is yours), these include: social cognition/social understanding, emotional regulation, play experiences, language ability, cultural values, and child's view of self. Often the difficulty with friendship lies in either a mismatch between children's developmental understanding and expectations for friendship or in a poor grasp of one or more of the six influences of friendship.

In addition, within any phase of the friendship process, children may experience difficulty in one of the following three areas: knowing what is appropriate behavior, knowing what behavioral skills to use or how to use them, or monitoring and modifying one's own behavior to meet specific situations (Erwin, 1998). For many children this last area, adapting behavior, is most cumbersome.

Methods to Use with All Children to Improve Social Interactions

From the research, there appear to be six strategies successfully used with all children to improve

their friendship process. These include shaping, modeling, coaching, peer teaching, social problem solving, and **cooperative activities**. As helping professionals, you may choose to use one or a combination of many to meet the needs of the children with whom you work. When selecting a method, keep in mind that some of these techniques are more effective with certain ages. For instance, *modeling* is more effective with 2- to 6-year-olds because it is less cognitively complex, whereas *coaching*, which requires higher cognitive abilities, is more effective with 6- to 12- year-old children (Schneider, 1992).

Shaping.   **Shaping** is among the most powerful of intervention tools to help socially isolated children (Schneider, 1992). It involves using rewards to maintain or encourage a desired behavior a little bit at a time. For instance, if Jeremy requires assistance with initiating contact with peers, each time he says, "Hello, I'm Jeremy," his teacher rewards his contact with a smile or a comment such as, "That is a friendly way to meet others, by saying hello." The teacher does not wait for him to carry out this greeting perfectly the first time. Instead she shapes Jeremy's behavior by rewarding him for increasingly more appropriate greetings. If it is not obvious to the child how to go about the target behavior, modeling may be a better beginning intervention.

Modeling.   **Modeling** is the process of demonstrating a skill in action. One way to model friendly behavior is through friendship skits, in which a specific aspect of friendship is enacted using puppets, dolls, or people. It also can be accomplished through assisted observation, in which an adult points out effective behaviors to the child as the adult and child watch other children play. This kind of modeling is most effective if the value-reward of the target behavior is emphasized as the act occurs and when the model is similar in age and gender to the child who is being taught (Erwin, 1998).

Coaching.   **Coaching** works well with children in elementary and later grades. It involves directly telling the child how to perform the skill or strategy, helping the child practice it, and giving feedback to the child to help improve performance. It has been demonstrated that coaching can improve children's knowledge of social strategies (Mize & Ladd, 1990). Typically, coaching occurs in a one-on-one situation, with the helping professional working directly with one child; however, it also can be used effectively in small groups in which the peers can be coached on how to interact with the child in need of assistance (Erwin, 1998). A coaching "session" includes discussion, demonstration of the skill, practice, and evaluation.

Peer teaching. A fourth method of assisting children in the friendship process is **peer teaching** or pairing. Simply put, it is the act of putting a more friendship-able child with a less able child. Such pairings have been found to improve the social skills and status of neglected children (Morris, Messer, & Gross, 1995). Often, socially neglected children do not know how to keep up with their age-mate peers. For this reason, it is sometimes useful to pair them with younger children to help them gain practice using appropriate behaviors (Rubin, 2003). These social behaviors then can be transferred to age-mate peers (Erwin, 1998). These pairings can be accomplished by giving classroom assignments to teacher-selected pairs, working in a buddy system such as a third grader reading to a second grader, or by special jobs that pairs conduct together such as collecting the scouting dues and reporting the results to the pack.

Increasing social problem-solving skills. The ability and skill to solve social problems has been associated with many positive social outcomes including the ability to make and keep friends. Teaching social problem-solving skills has been identified as a powerful method for improving elementary school children's abilities in the friendship process (Erwin, 1998). Using discussions and role-playing of friendship skills, children can practice social problem-solving skills. In a role-play situation, children take turns acting out social situations while their peers observe. The children then debrief. They discuss the emotions felt while playing the characters as well as the observations of the audience. All are able to participate in solving social problems in a "risk-free" situation. Through the **role-playing**, the children are also able to obtain concrete examples of social behavior that are easier to recognize than those offered through discussion alone.

Initiating cooperative activity and play. Finally, cooperative activities and play can serve as powerful places for teaching the phases of the friendship process. Group friendship activities that call for cooperation have been found to be effective for preschoolers as well as elementary school children (Cooper & McEvoy, 1996; Siner, 1993). The key is to structure both daily and special activities to foster cooperative interactions between children, with minimal, if any, focus on competition.

Peer Relations and Children with Special Needs

There are many situations in which children need some extra assistance to interact with peers to build relationships and friendships. These situations occur in all children at various times—in children with and without special needs. However, particularly for children with special needs, sometimes children's desires for a friend are not deemed as important as assisting them with acquiring specific academic skills. Given all of the powerful benefits that peer relationships and friendship can provide for children, it seems that finding a friend should rank among the top in priorities. See Figure 8-9 for a brief look at how the multiple influences on friendship relate to some types of special needs in children.

The good news is that for all children, adults are able to provide assistance with peer relationships through multiple avenues. No matter what level of special need, all children can benefit from adults skilled in supporting friendship.

HOW CHILD DEVELOPMENT & EXPERIENCE INFLUENCE THE FRIENDSHIP SKILLS OF CHILDREN WITH SPECIAL NEEDS

Influence on Friendship	Autistic Children	Language Impaired Children	Gifted Children	Neglected and Abused Children
Social Cognition	Autistic children may have difficulty: reading social cues (verbal intonations, facial expressions, body language); using appropriate social cues to match situations (such as waving hello); seeing cause and effect in social interactions/ relationships.	Language impaired children etc may have difficulty relating cause and effect, thus misinterpreting social events. They may also avoid eye contact and conversations with others and be delayed in other social behaviors.	Children who are gifted may relate well to peers, or may get utterly frustrated with peers' lower-level understanding of social situations and therefore have difficulty relating to them.	Neglected children tend to see themselves as deserving to be ignored. They are not experienced at reading social cues nor in promoting their own ideas. They expect others to be angry with them and assume their encounters with peers will be negative. As a result, abused children may approach others in an aggressive manner.
Emotional Regulation	Autistic children may not demonstrate appropriate facial expressions to match the situation at hand or their expressions and emotional reactions to events may be more extreme than their peers. They may also be oblivious to the feelings of others.	Language impaired children may not be able to describe their own emotions accurately or clearly for others to understand and experience high levels of frustration.	Gifted children may be overly sensitive to criticism. They may have a heightened awareness of the emotions of those around them and 'overwork' to please others. They may also become so caught up in reflecting on their own emotions that they do not notice those of others.	Neglected children have difficulty recognizing and discriminating emotions in others. Children who have been abused are not typically not very good at understanding the connection between facial expressions and emotional explanations.

Figure 8-9 Considering the multiple influences of friendship with special needs children—*continued*

Language Ability	Autistic children may experience a range of language abilities. They may have good talking ability, but be unaware of the give and take of conversations, sounding. They may have speech that is difficult to understand They also may not respond to the communication attempts from others.	Children with language problems may be difficult to understand or very stilted in their use of language. They may use more nonverbal signs to communicate than words. They may not answer questions appropriately or engage in conversations willingly.	Gifted children typically have early developing language abilities. They may acquire language quickly and use vocabulary above that of their peers, causing a disconnect between peers and child.	Children who experience neglect and or abuse may have language ability issues. These will depend on each child's specific situation or experiences.
Play Experiences	Autistic children may have difficulty coming up with imaginative ideas or ways to respond to others in play. They frequently play alone.	Since play relies so much on language and communication, language impaired children are at a disadvantage. Language impaired children may have a close friend with whom they play frequently but may appear less willing to deviate from the 'safe' person to interact with others.	Gifted children may have many interesting play ideas and be appealing to peers as a play partner. They also may be at such advanced level in their thinking that the play falls apart when both parties cannot understand the intentions of the play.	Neglected and abused children may not have many experiences of play with peers that have been supported by adults, thus they may be less-abled play participants.
Self Esteem	The spectrum for autism is highly varied. Children's experiences and the reaction of those around them influence their resulting self esteem.	Children with language impairments often experience difficulties not only socially but also academically. Their self esteem is likely to suffer from the multiple unsuccessful encounters they have with peers.	Gifted children may be especially critical of themselves and set high standards for themselves that are impossible to achieve. They also may be well rounded and comfortable. Self esteem varies from child to child.	Neglected children often possess a low view of self, with little sense of competence, worth, or control. Abused children often possess a lowered sense of self value and see themselves as powerless in social situations.

Figure 8-9 Considering the multiple influences of friendship with special needs children—*continued*

Sources: Paasche et al., 2004; Saarni et al., 2006; Thompson, 2006.

SKILLS FOR SUPPORTING CHILDREN'S FRIENDSHIP

 Encouraging and Facilitating Friendships

Children vary in the degree to which they will find adult support necessary and beneficial. However, all children profit when adults create an environment in which their friendships are respected and encouraged. The following guidelines will help you create such an environment for the children with whom you work.

1. Provide informal peer opportunities. Opportunities to talk, to play, and to enjoy one another's company are necessary. Develop a daily routine that includes planned times when children can respond to one another freely. Planned opportunities include both structured activities and unstructured times. Both provide rich opportunities for children to practice social skills and to learn more about themselves.

2. Pair children together for various activities. Pairing children gives them a chance to practice their friendship-making skills in a relatively risk-free situation. Assign children to do jobs together or have them carry out a joint project as a way to create common interests. Children feel closer when they see themselves working toward a collaborative goal. Finally, encourage parents to arrange play dates to help children see similarities and further develop relationships.

3. Pair a shy child with a younger playmate who is less sophisticated socially. Begin by pairing him or her with a younger child of the same gender (Rubin, 2003). Gradually, include age-mates of the same and opposite sex. This arrangement enables the shy child to practice social skills with a non-threatening, often openly approving younger admirer.

4. Take children's friendships seriously. Listen when children talk about their friends. Reflect their involvement and concerns. Ask questions to show your interest.

5. Lead discussions that focus on children's self-discovered similarities. First, set the scene by having children discuss their reaction to an adult-posed condition, for instance, "Things I like best." Then invite each child to answer a question such as "Paul and I both like . . . " or "I like the Mets and so does . . ." This tactic helps children recognize peers with whom they share similar attitudes, interests, and concerns.

6. Help children learn each other's names. Because names are a basic form of recognition, children feel most comfortable making contact with peers whose names they know. Less common names can become familiar if you refer to each child by name. Make sure you know how to pronounce every child's name correctly and that you do not avoid using names that are unfamiliar or unattractive to you. Use children's names when you praise them as a way to create a positive image of each child to the group.

7. Point out the friendly intentions between peers as they occur. Children often overlook or misinterpret the friendly advances of other youngsters because they are so involved in what they are doing that they are unable to recognize the positive nature of the approach. Instead, they may interpret the newcomer as a potential competitor for space or materials and thus feel threatened rather than pleased. Be alert for such occurrences. Step in if you see a child rebuff another without giving a reason. Paraphrase the newcomer's positive aim. Then, let the child decide for him or herself whether the contact is welcome. Children will often be more receptive to another's overtures once the friendly intentions are made clear. For example, Matt was an active 4-year-old who longed for a friend. He frequently talked with teachers about who his friends might be. Yet, his actions often contradicted his words. One day, he had the entire block area to himself. He worked for a long time building a bus. As he was busily "driving to Chicago," Courtney arrived on the scene and asked if she could go, too. Matt scowled and said, "No." Courtney repeated her request and was again rebuffed. This time she said: "Well, I'll just stand here on the corner until someone gets off. Then, I'll get on."

continued

Matt looked confused. At this point, an adult approached and said: "Matt, you're having fun driving to Chicago. Courtney is telling you she would like to play. She wants to be a passenger on your bus. That way, she can be your friend." Matt looked pleased and relieved. He had not recognized the cues Courtney was using to signify her interest in his game. Information provided by the adult put a whole new light on the situation, and the two children played "bus" for most of the morning.

8. Help children recognize how their behavior affects their ability to make friends. Frequently, children are unaware of the link between what they do and how other people react. Offer information to make this association more clear. For instance, Steven pushed Daisy to get her attention. She stalked off. He became angry when she rejected him. The adult noted Steven's surprise, took him aside, and said: "It seems as if you want to be friends with Daisy. Pushing hurts. When you push her, it makes her so angry that she doesn't want to play with you. Friends don't hurt each other. Next time, you could say her name and tell her what you want." The adult gave Steven important information that he had not picked up very well on his own. This information would have to be repeated several times and in several different circumstances before Steven could really follow the advice. If the negative pattern persisted, Steven would be a likely candidate for the coaching strategies found in this chapter. Information need not only be confined to corrections. Tell children about the positive skills they exhibit so they can repeat them at another time. For instance, if you notice children sharing, taking turns, smiling at each other, or coming to a compromise, point out the positive effects these actions have on their relations with one another: "You two figured out a way that you could both wash the blackboards. That was a friendly way to settle your disagreement."

9. Help children recognize the emotional reactions in themselves and in others. Use affective reflections with children to help them recognize and label their emotional reactions.

When children hear the emotions of others as they see the cues on their faces, it will help them better comprehend these in the future. Take time to point out how the intentions of others may be different than their intentions and how it makes each party feel. "You were really thrilled that we were going outside today, so you yelled loudly. Jonah was very disappointed—the clouds scare him and, when you yelled, it surprised and frightened him."

10. Get children involved at the beginning of a play episode. Children who hang back before attempting to join a group often are penalized because, once the group has been established, it is difficult for its members to imagine any other configuration. If you notice that certain children are hesitant to become involved and subsequently are shut out, try one of the following approaches.

First, plan ahead with the child and help her or him identify an activity to choose as soon as playgroups begin to form. In this way, the child will not have to cross any social barriers but instead will be an initial participant. If this is too difficult for the child, an alternative is to help her or him move into the group with you. To do this, you might choose a potential role and approach the activity within the role. For instance, if several children are pretending to fly to the moon, you could walk toward them, saying: "Carol and I will be Mission Control. We'll talk to you up in the spacecraft." Then back out of the play gradually as Carol becomes more comfortable and the group becomes more accepting of her. Do not be surprised if at first Carol walks out when you do. With your continued support, she eventually will feel more relaxed and be able to maintain her membership in the group on her own.

A second tactic is to advise a hesitant child to play near the desired group and at the same type of activity. Gradually, the group may allow that child to join them and become their friend. An alternative to this approach is to help the child build a new group by inviting other children to draw, build, compute, or cook with her or him.

SKILLS FOR SUPPORTING CHILDREN'S FRIENDSHIP

11. Help children endure the sorrows of friendship. When a potential friend rejects them, an old friend snubs them, or a good friend moves away, children have a real sense of loss. Their feelings range from misery to frustration to fury—all of which are normal reactions. As an adult, you cannot protect the child's feelings, no matter how much you would like him or her to be spared. You can accept the child's emotions, reflect them, and talk about them, if the child so desires. You also can offer your condolences: "I'm sorry you and Tricia weren't able to patch up your differences. It's really sad to lose a friend."

12. Assist children in developing conversation skills. Children who are successful at making friends are likely to use conversation or information exchange in their interactions with others (Ladd & Coleman, 1993). Two- to 6-year-old children are just learning how to talk comfortably with one another. To hold a successful conversation and keep it going, children must identify a topic of mutual interest, stay on the same subject, and share information (Sharp, 1988). It helps if they look at each other and take turns talking. The more children practice this skill, the better they get.

Help children link their dialogue by referring children's questions and comments to one another. For example, if Jeremy approaches the block area where other children are working and says to you, "Can I build?" refer his question to one of the builders. "Jeremy, you want to build. Tell Russell." Provide a script if necessary: "Say, ' I'm ready to help you.'" If Russell fails to respond, offer information to one child or the other to help the interaction along. "Jeremy, Russell didn't hear you. Get closer to him and tell him again." Or "Russell, Jeremy is trying to tell you something. Stop, look at him, and listen to his words."

If children become engaged in a conversation, avoid interrupting, but stay nearby to help as needed. Intervene when the conversation falters. If, for example, children lose track of the topic and no longer seem to be connecting, help them refocus. "Jeremy and Russell, you were talking about how to get the arch to balance. Russell, tell Jeremy what you discovered." Sometimes, children who are not yet conversant benefit from having their rudimentary language interpreted by the teacher to the other children. Thus, when Melissa asks Jane, "Do you want orange juice?" and Jane responds, "Ju," Melissa may not understand. Pause to see if she responds. If Melissa seems confused, paraphrase Jane's words, "She said, ' Juice.'" On the other hand, if Melissa addresses a question to Jane, "How about some juice?" and Jane does not answer, again, act as an interpreter. "Jane, did you hear Melissa's words? Look at her and she'll ask you again." Once children begin talking to one another, bow out of the conversation, lest you become the focus of their attention.

Older children, ages 6 to 12, may need guidance in initiating a conversation topic or in attending while another child is speaking. Suggest that he or she comment on the object or event with which a potential playmate is engaged, using an observation or asking a question. Well-informed, talkative children may need help attending to what another child wants to say. Coach these children to listen attentively with comments such as, "Try to remember the details of what Tessa is saying" or "Watch Lydia's face and hands while she is talking so you can tell how she's feeling." Later, ask the child whether he or she was able to implement these strategies successfully and how the strategies might fit similar situations in the future.

13. Conduct discussions highlighting facts about friendship. Refer to Table 8-1 for examples of friendship facts. Introduce one or two items at a time for children to explore. You may stimulate their thinking by reading a book, telling a story, or showing them pictures that relate to the ideas you have chosen. Prompt discussion through the use of open-ended questions such as "How does it feel when a good friend moves away?" or "What can you do when a friend hurts your feelings?" or "How can you let someone know you want to be friends?" Listen carefully. Reflect children's answers.

continued

SKILLS FOR SUPPORTING CHILDREN'S FRIENDSHIP—continued

Offer relevant information as openings in the conversation occur. Do not be concerned with obtaining a "correct" answer or reaching consensus. Instead, focus on allowing children to explore each idea in their own way. Provide every youngster with an opportunity to contribute, but avoid pressuring children into talking if they prefer not to. Summarize key points of the discussion, either aloud or on paper, for the children to refer to later.

14. Assist peer neglected or rejected children to develop satisfying relationships. Observe children carefully to determine whether they are neglected or rejected children. If you decide

a child is neglected, concentrate on helping the other youngsters discover that individual, using the strategies outlined in the chapter. When dealing with a rejected child, focus first on direct intervention with that child, using the on-the-spot coaching techniques outlined later.

15. Assist children in ending relationships/ friendships. There are two general situations in which relationships and friendships are terminated: those that are under the control of the child and those that are not. Although the coaching that an adult may use in each situation will follow the same steps, the scripts for each case would obviously be different.

Table 8-1 A Partial Listing of Friendship Facts for Children Ages 2–12

Friends Defined
1. Friends are people who like you and whom you like.
2. Some friends are members of your family; some are outside your family.
3. Friends may be like you in many ways and different from you in others.
4. Friends often spend time together doing the same or similar things.
5. Friends share ideas, play, work, and share secrets and feelings with each other.
6. People experience a variety of feelings about each other, some positive and some negative.
7. Sometimes friends hurt each other's feelings.
8. Sometimes friends can forgive each other, and sometimes they cannot.
9. Sometimes friendships end.
10. Having a friend:
    a. Makes people feel good.
    b. Gives people someone with whom to share ideas, play, and work.
    c. Gives people someone with whom to share secrets.
    d. Gives people someone with whom to share feelings.
11. It can be sad or confusing when someone no longer wants to be your friend.
12. People can make new friends.

Making and Keeping Friends
1. People's behavior affects their ability to make and keep friends.
2. People use their bodies to express friendly emotions such as smiling, playing near someone, and looking at them when they speak.
3. People use words to express friendly emotions, such as conversing, listening to their ideas, inviting them to play, and exchanging thoughts and feelings.
4. People feel friendly toward those who act positively toward them.

SKILLS FOR SUPPORTING CHILDREN'S FRIENDSHIP

Steps to assist children with the process of ending relationships and friendships:

- Acknowledge the child's feelings about the current relationship.
- Help the child explore the possibilities of what will happen if the friendship ends.
- Be factual with the child. Discuss the possible reaction of the other child in the friendship.
- Give the child scripts to assist with the goodbye. Help the child rehearse these.
- Debrief with the child after the goodbye has occurred.
- Discuss the child's current feelings, labeling emotions where necessary for the child.
- Brainstorm new activities and/or people to replace the terminated friendship.

As with any other early childhood situation, when the children cannot control the termination of the friendship it is important to provide them with forewarning when possible. It is also important not push children into new relationships before they are ready.

16. Talk to families about the loss of children's friendships as a result of family transition. When families are in the process of relocating, parents and guardians are often caught up in the logistics of the move and may not have considered the impact of the move on their children's friendships. Assist these adults in helping their children anticipate and deal with the end of their current friendships. Refer to the strategies in skill 15 for assistance with this.

 Designing Skits That Demonstrate Friendship Skills

Even the youngest of children enjoy skits. Younger children (2- and 3-year-olds) benefit most when professionals simply act out a scene and then explain it. Older preschoolers and grade-schoolers benefit from additional group discussion as well.

1. Choose a friendship skill to teach. It usually is best to focus on only one skill at a time. This way, children can more easily identify the exact behavior being demonstrated.

2. Choose the medium through which the skill will be demonstrated. Dolls, pictures, and puppets all are good choices. Children learn best from concrete examples that include props they can point to, handle, and discuss.

3. Outline a script that consists of five parts. The script should include the following:

a. Demonstration of the skill
b. Demonstration of lack of the skill
c. An explanation by the adult
d. Discussion by the children
e. An opportunity for children to use the props to make up their own version of the skit

The best skits are only a few lines long.

4. Write out the statements and questions you will use to stimulate discussion. Discussion should revolve around which character was demonstrating the skill and which was not, how viewers arrived at their conclusions, and what skill they would suggest the characters use the next time.

5. Rehearse the skit. Gather your props. Practice the skit, privately or with friends. Revise the skit until you can do it from memory and feel comfortable about carrying it out.

6. Present your skit. Present your skit to children either in a group situation or in a one-to-one interaction. Speak clearly and with expression. Elicit group discussion. Listen carefully and accept children's answers nonjudgmentally. If children are way off track, give them information that will clarify the situation and make a mental note to revise your skit to make the point more clear next time. Praise children as they watch and again as they discuss what they have seen.

7. Evaluate how well your skit got the point across. Do this later in the day. If it seemed that children were interested and were able to

continued

SKILLS FOR SUPPORTING CHILDREN'S FRIENDSHIP

generate relevant conversation about the selected topic, plan to repeat the same skit using different props and dialogues the next time. Over time, gradually introduce new information for youngsters to consider. If children were uninterested, determine whether things in the environment distracted them or whether your activity was unappealing. Observe children carefully or ask their opinions as a way to find out. Children will not be attentive if the skit is too advanced or too babyish, if you fumble or seem tense, or if you press too hard for one "right" answer. A sample of a type of skit that can be effective with young children is outlined in Table 8-2. It illustrates a scenario designed to teach friendship-initiation skills. Such vignettes could be adapted to illustrate any of the friendship skills discussed in this chapter.

8. Encourage older children to make up skits of their own that dramatize a problem with friends. Sometimes, children between 10 and 12 years of age will be willing to enact their skits for peers or for younger children. The same procedures just discussed apply, regardless of the age of the skit planner.

 Teaching Children to Role-Play

Most children ages 4 through 12 enjoy role-playing. However, it cannot be assumed that they automatically know how to do it. Rather, helping professionals must teach youngsters how to take on a role prior to expecting them to benefit from enacting a vignette or from watching one carried out by others. This can be accomplished using the following strategies.

1. Explain role-playing. Define it as a particular way of pretending in order to present a lesson. Describe roles as parts children play in a scene. Tell youngsters they may now act out how they would feel in a given situation or how they think another person might feel under those circumstances. Point out to the children that for each role-play episode, some youngsters will be taking on roles while others watch, and everyone will have a chance to discuss the

results. Show them the boundaries of the physical area in which the enactment will take place as well as any props available to the actors.

2. Set the scene. Present a theme, script, or problem. You may also suggest certain emotions for them to portray. Give each child a specific role to play and a few hints about related actions or words that might characterize their role.

3. Help the role-players get into character. Allow youngsters to select a prop or costume item as a way to further establish their roles. This step is critical for children younger than 7 years of age who otherwise might have difficulty enacting and sustaining a role. Young children may need to hang a picture or symbol around their neck if the role is abstract or a good prop is not available.

4. Observe attentively. Applaud the efforts.

5. Discuss events in the role-play. Elicit comments both from the participants and the observers. Refer to the friendship facts presented in Table 8-1 as a way to support and extend the discussion.

6. Ask children to develop alternate scenarios. Have youngsters act these out, then discuss the varying outcomes.

7. Summarize the key points of the discussion. Identify similarities in their thinking as well as differences. Highlight the one or two major points that seemed most important to the group.

 Carrying Out Friendship Coaching

Coaching begins when you have determined that a child has fallen into a destructive pattern of interactions or is unhappy with his or her inability to make friends and seems at a loss for what to do next. Coaching consists of short, regularly scheduled sessions with the child in which you work on particular friendship skills together. Your approach is very similar to that suggested for use with children in groups.

continued

Table 8-2 Sample Skit for Teaching a Friendship Skill

General Instructions

Seat children in a semicircle facing you. Make sure everyone can see your face and hands and the space directly in front of you. If you are sitting on the floor, it is useful to kneel so you are more easily visible to the children. If you are sitting in a chair, a low bench or table can be used to display the props. As the script unfolds, manipulate the dolls in corresponding actions. Be expressive with your face and your voice. Use dialogue for the characters that seems appropriate for the situation; use different voices for each character.

Materials

Two dolls (or puppets); several small, colored blocks

Procedure

Adult: Today, we are going to talk about friends. Here are two dolls. We are going to pretend that these dolls are real children just like you. Their names are Max and Gus. They are 4 years old and go to a school just like ours. Watch carefully and see what happens when Gus and Max try to be friends. (Set up one doll [Gus] as if "playing" with several blocks. Place second doll [Max] facing Gus but at least a foot away.)

Adult: Here is Gus. He is playing alone with the blocks and is having a good time. Max sees Gus and would really like to play with him, so he watches Gus very carefully. Gus keeps playing; he doesn't look up. Max feels sad. He thinks Gus doesn't want to be friends.

Question for discussion:

1. Tell me what Gus was doing.

2. Tell me what Max wanted to do.

3. Did Gus know Max wanted to play? How do you know?

4. What else could Max do to let Gus know he wanted to play?

As children answer these questions, provide information to help in their deliberations: "Gus was so busy playing, he didn't look up. That means he never even saw Max standing there. He didn't know Max wanted to play. Watch again and see what Max does differently this time."

Adult: Here is Gus. He is playing alone with the blocks and is having a good time. Max sees Gus and really would like to play with him. So, he watches Gus very carefully. Gus keeps playing. He doesn't look up. Max walks over to Gus and says: "Hi. I like your building. I'll help you get some more blocks."

Questions for discussion:

1. What was Gus doing?

2. What did Max want to do?

3. Did Gus know Max wanted to play?

4. How could he tell?

5. What will Gus do next?

6. Let's think of some other ways Max could let Gus know he wants to play.

As children suggest ideas, paraphrase them and write them down where all the children can see them. Accept all ideas regardless of originality, correctness, or feasibility. If children have difficulty thinking of ideas, prompt them by providing information: "Sometimes, when people want to play, they can say: 'Hi. I want to play,' or they can ask a question like,' What are you building?' This lets the other person know they want to be friends. What do you think Max could do?" Once children have suggested their ideas, replay the scene using each suggestion, one at a time. Ask the children to predict how Gus will react in each case. Play out the scene as they suggest. Provide further information as appropriate: "John, you said Max could help Gus build. Let's try that." (Maneuver the dolls and provide appropriate dialogue.) "Tell me what you think Gus will do now."

SKILLS FOR SUPPORTING CHILDREN'S FRIENDSHIP—continued

The difference is that you are working with one child at a time and giving that child specific, on-the-spot feedback about his or her performance. Some children may need considerable help with several skills, and others may progress rapidly with more limited intervention. In addition, you may use children as friendship coaches. Select child trainers on a volunteer basis and have them practice what they will say to a targeted child and how they will give feedback on the child's response. Follow the procedure as outlined next, whether it is you or a child who is acting as the coach.

1. Select a "skill for improvement." Identify a friendship skill that will address the child's particular difficulty. It can be challenging to narrow your choice to one skill if you see a child who seems to be doing "everything" wrong: ignoring peers, rejecting them, grabbing, pushing, interrupting, taking over, teasing. It is tempting to plan a complete makeover. However, trying to do too much all at once usually ends in frustration and failure. A better approach is to work on one problem area at a time. In this way, both the child and you experience success each step of the way. This encourages continued efforts and may ease the way for learning in related areas.

2. Initiate coaching. Experts emphasize the importance of selecting a neutral time to begin coaching rather than immediately following a disagreeable encounter. Otherwise, the targeted child may feel singled out and react defensively. Your goal is to have children perceive these sessions as enjoyable activities, not as the negative consequence of their behavior. Initiate the coaching session by taking the child aside at some dispassionate time and saying: "Robert, today you and I are going to have a special time together. Come with me and I'll tell you all about it."

3. Describe the skill to the child. Introduce the skill you are going to focus on, such as expressing acceptance, by describing it in observable terms rather than generalizations.

Appropriate: "When you want someone to be your friend, it is important to listen to his (her) ideas. That means looking at him (her) and not talking while he (she) is trying to tell you something."

Inappropriate: "When you want someone to be your friend, you should act more interested."

4. Demonstrate the skill. Model the behavior or point it out in other children who are playing so the child can actually see what you are talking about: "Here, I'll show you. Tell me one way we could play with these puppets and I will listen to your idea" or "Look at Jeremy—he's listening very carefully to what Sondra is saying."

5. Give the child a reason for why the new behavior is important: "When you listen to people's ideas, it makes them feel good. That helps them to like you better."

6. Practice the skill. Have the child rehearse the skill with you. It usually is helpful if the child can first differentiate between examples of good and poor skill usage. It helps to demonstrate with puppets and dolls: "Here are two puppets, Rollo and Gertrude. Rollo is telling Gertrude an idea. Watch and listen. Tell me how well Gertrude shows Rollo she wants to be friends." After several demonstrations, Robert can then rehearse the new behavior by role-playing with you or another child or by manipulating the dolls and puppets himself. Time to practice helps children feel more comfortable with their new skills. They can more experience what it is like to be both the recipient and the initiator of varying social behaviors. From this, children may suggest their own ideas about other ways to demonstrate the skill. They also have a chance to ask questions and discuss their emotions and reactions.

7. Evaluate the child's use of the skill. Praise children's efforts and improved performance throughout the practice session. Point out instances of the child's appropriate use of the skill. Commend the child for trying. Provide

SKILLS FOR SUPPORTING CHILDREN'S FRIENDSHIP

physical support through smiles and hugs. In addition, offer corrective feedback aimed at improving the child's use of the skill. Focus on behaviors: "You listened to some of my ideas. You didn't hear them all. Let's try again."

8. Repeat the coaching procedure several times. Change the props and the hypothetical circumstances more than once. Remember that children vary in the rate at which they learn new behaviors. Some will progress quickly; others will move at a much slower pace. As you see each child increase his or her use of the targeted skill in day-today interactions, you should praise their efforts and offer some on-the-spot information that will help them polish their performance. With improvement, plan to introduce a new skill for the child to work on or gradually fade out the coaching sessions.

Coaching should not be ended abruptly at the first signs of progress. Children need the continued feedback and reinforcement such sessions offer in order to maintain their use of each skill. As they experience more and more success with peers, the natural environment will become rewarding enough that the coaching sessions are no longer the child's primary source of reinforcement. Children who need coaching are those who have not acted on the subtle cues present in the everyday environment; therefore, the adult must make those cues more explicit and focus the child's attention on them. The professional's role goes beyond discussing and pointing out appropriate skills to include the elements of practice and evaluation. These latter steps are critical, both in the session and outside of it.

 Communicating with Children's Families

Help family members understand and support children's friendships using the following strategies:

1. Make yourself available to families. Talk with parents and guardians about the normal course of children's friendships. Listen carefully to what they have to say and reflect their thoughts and emotions. Provide information to them by explaining the characteristics of the particular friendship stage their child is experiencing. This enables adults to view their children's behavior in the context of expected development. Simply knowing that most children find making and maintaining friendships a rocky road may give family members comfort and assurance. When children say such things as, "You can't be my friend," or "I'll be your friend if you invite me to your birthday party," parents and other adults are frequently appalled at the child's insensitivity. Suggest strategies cited earlier in this chapter so parents can better understand where children's attempts are coming from and can deal more effectively with unacceptable behaviors in positive and supportive ways. Explore other issues with family members as they arise, such as having "best friends" or the disappointment of failed friendships. Offer suggestions in terms of the ideas presented in this book. For instance, instead of offering children advice, suggest families engage in active listening; give parents a brief "script" in which you outline this technique. Older children's parents are frequently concerned about the groups their children are participating in and the pressure for conformity within those groups. If this or other issues arise repeatedly in your discussions with parents, think of ways to initiate a parent workshop on the subject.

2. Help families facilitate children's friendships beyond school time. As children mature, the frequency of requests for "someone to come over to play" increases markedly. Such opportunities provide an important link between the family and the peer social system. Interestingly, the extent to which parents engage in this form of peer management may vary, with the families of more popular children taking less initiative than do families of less popular or shy children. Mutual home visiting is easy to arrange within a small and

continued

SKILLS FOR SUPPORTING CHILDREN'S FRIENDSHIP—continued

close neighborhood, where families tend to know one another and are familiar with each other's parenting styles. Visiting can be somewhat more involved when the children are friends at school, but their families do not especially know one another. Several situations that families encounter in the process of finding and keeping friends may arise:

a. Sometimes adult family members are looking for a new friend for their youngster. Suggest to them the names of other children in the group who you believe might be potential friends. Use the criteria suggested in the beginning of this chapter in determining which children might be suitable friends for a particular individual. The children's age, gender, proximity, relationship in the program, interests, and stage of friendship are all attributes for you to consider.

b. Parents appreciate help in figuring out ways to make visits between children go more smoothly. They wonder whose "rules" should govern a "guest's" behavior, whether their child should have to share everything, or what to do when host and visiting children get into an argument. Work with families to establish "helpful hints" for parents, so that daytime and, in the future perhaps, overnight visits will be fun for children and livable for adults.

3. Establish a policy for out-of-school party invitations. For example, a kindergarten classroom had a policy that unless all children in the group were to be asked, invitations to parties were to be offered by mail or phone, so as not to hurt other children's feelings and to avoid the confusion of a message getting into the wrong child's hands.

4. Initiate classroom events that enable families to get to know one another. Parents and guardians may be understandably hesitant to invite a child to their home or to allow their child to visit a family with whom they are unfamiliar. This deprives children of an important aspect of friendship development that of shared activities outside the program. One

solution is to invite family members to a singalong or potluck dessert function. This kind of experience offers families the opportunity to "break the ice," as the children can introduce their families to each other. Casual conversation helps people feel more comfortable and may result in "play dates" for the children. This strategy is especially helpful if the program draws families from an area wider than the few blocks around the program site.

5. Talk to adult family members about their peer-neglected or rejected children. Sometimes children experience more than the usual pains of friendship. When parents describe their children in ways that lead you to believe that their lack of friends is the result of serious dysfunction, or when you have made similar observations, speak openly and compassionately with the adults in a private setting. Listening carefully to what they say is an essential part of your determination and will guide you in offering helpful advice. Respond to their anguish or uncertainty using affective reflections. Inquire about the child's friendships beyond the school setting and within the family (siblings, cousins, etc.). Be aware that some children have strong friendships out of school; they do not feel the desire to have a special school friend. Keep this in mind in your conversations with parents. Document examples of the child's unsuccessful attempts at friendship making or his or her rebuffs of the overtures of others. Try all the strategies suggested in the text. If, over a sufficient period of time (weeks or months), the child fails to move forward, take the issue seriously and recommend intervention. Use the guidelines in Chapter 15 to help you recognize and deal with this aspect of extreme behavior. Help families seek community resources, such as counselors, social workers, or psychologists, who might be available to give assistance. Sometimes group therapy in a protected setting with a skilled facilitator can provide the youngster with the appropriate feedback from peers. Actions such as these may head off grave consequences.

PITFALLS TO AVOID

Regardless of whether you are supporting children's friendships individually or in groups, informally or in structured activities, there are certain pitfalls you should avoid.

Barging in too quickly. When adults see children struggling over friendship issues, it is tempting to step in as a mediating figure immediately. No one likes to see children suffer. Unless there is some physical danger that should be dealt with quickly, it is important to take a moment to observe the situation and to thoughtfully determine what form of intervention is best. At times, simply moving physically closer to the situation defuses it. In other instances, direct use of the strategies described in this chapter is more appropriate. Regardless of which course you follow, remember that the more children practice friendship skills with the least help from you, the more quickly they will learn how to be successful in their interactions with peers. Children benefit when they have an opportunity to try out strategies and solutions on their own.

Missing opportunities to promote friendly interactions among children. Adults sometimes become so centered on interacting with the children themselves that they fail to recognize opportunities to help children increase their friendship skills with peers. For example, an adult who is carrying on a conversation with one child may view the arrival of a second child as an interruption or may carry on two separate conversations simultaneously. A better approach would be to use reflections or provide information that would help the children talk to each other as well as to the adult:

> *Juan: We went to the store last night.*
>
> *Anita: We had pizza for dinner.*
>
> *Adult: You both did interesting things last night. Juan, tell Anita what you saw at the store.*

Insisting that everyone be "friends." Although it is natural for adults to want children to like each other, it does not always turn out that way. Instead, children in groups tend to form close relationships with only a few children at a time. Insisting that everyone like each other not only is unrealistic but also denies children's real emotions. In every group, there are people who rub each other the wrong way. Part of what children can learn is how to interact constructively with the people they like best and the people they like least. Adults must show children alternative acceptable ways of making their preferences known.

Requiring everyone to be together all the time. It is a mistake to think that friendship is built on constant companionship. Although familiarity does breed common interests, forcing children to play together when they do not really want to detracts from, rather than enhances, their relationships. With this in mind, adults are cautioned to allow children opportunities to engage in solitary activity and to help each child to constructively explain his or her desire for privacy to curious or well-meaning peers. In addition, adults should aid the child who is rebuffed by a peer who would rather be alone. This can be accomplished by explaining the other's desire for privacy and by helping the youngster who is turned away to find an alternate activity or companion.

Breaking up children's friendships. At any time in the preschool and early elementary years, a child will develop a best-friend relationship. During this time, the two children involved become inseparable. Adults often worry that this closeness is interfering with the children's ability to develop other friendships. As a result, adults frequently decide to intervene by limiting the children's time together. This is a mistake. As children begin to develop "special relationships," it is natural for them to center on the object of their admiration. It must be remembered that when children first become interested in making friends, their main goal is simply to be included in group activities.

However, once this has been accomplished, children begin to want to have an influence on their relationships. In other words, they want others to listen to their ideas, accept their suggestions, and involve them in decision making. From the children's viewpoint, this is a relatively risky process. So, they seek the security of a one-to-one relationship within which to test their skills. In friendship pairs, risks are reduced because the two children involved come to know each other well and therefore are more accurate in predicting another's reaction. In addition, they build up a history of good times, which helps them weather the bad times that are sure to occur. It takes a long time for children to work through these needs. When adults interrupt the process, they deprive children of important opportunities to learn the true meaning of friendship. Adults should allow children to experience this important phase of relationship building.

Failing to recognize children's friendship cues. Children may use inappropriate behaviors in their efforts to make friends. For instance, children may taunt to initiate an interaction, physically force other children out of an area to have exclusive access to a favored peer, or try to coerce a friend into rejecting another as a way of confirming their own friendship bond. On the surface, these may appear to be straightforward limit-setting situations. However, an observant adult will recognize that the issue relates to friendship and will seize the opportunity to help the erring child learn more constructive friendship skills such as better ways of making contact or expressing affection.

SUMMARY

Peer relationships and friendships with peers are important events in the lives of children. They offer children unique opportunities to develop socially, emotionally, and intellectually. Both peer relationships and friendships serve as places to practice social competence skills. Some children make friends easily; others do not. The repercussions of not having a friend or of being dissatisfied with the relationships one does have represent severe difficulties in childhood, which can last through adulthood. Completely friendless children are rare; however, evidence does indicate that many children wish they had more or better friends. Children's success with peer relationships and friendships depends on many

variables. These include their social cognition/social understanding abilities, emotional regulation, play experiences, language ability, adult support, cultural values, and of course, how they view themselves.

Adults may wonder whether children really understand what friendship means. Although children's ideas about what constitutes friendship are different from adults' and change as children mature, it is clear that even very young children are interested in having friends who are like them in age and experience and who share their intellectual and physical abilities. Children progress from an egocentric view of relationships to one of mutual support and caring. When first choosing a friend, children focus on obvious attributes such as name, physical appearance, race, gender, age, ability, and attitudes. In general, it can be said that children seek out friends whom they perceive as being similar to themselves. At times, these likenesses are apparent only to the children involved.

The social skills children display also have a major impact on their ability to make and keep friends. Making friends is not an automatic or magical process. Children who "win friends and influence people" know how to make contact, maintain positive relationships, negotiate the inevitable conflicts that arise, and gracefully end unfruitful relationships. These are skills that some children learn on their own but with which many children need help.

Adults can play a vital role in increasing children's friendly behavior. This can be accomplished through informal, day-to-day techniques, planned activities, or structured coaching sessions. Family members may also be involved in promoting children's friendships both in and out of the formal group setting. Professionals can be of great help in supporting them in their efforts.

KEY TERMS

acquaintances
coaching
cooperative activities
friends
friendships
friendship-making skills
Friendship Framework

friendship skills
interactions
modeling
negotiation skills
peers
peer neglected
peer teaching

peer rejected children
rejected-aggressive children
rejected-withdrawn children
relationships
role-playing
shaping

DISCUSSION QUESTIONS

1. A Chinese proverb states, "One can do without people, but one has need for a friend." React to this statement, discussing the reasons why people need friends.

2. Think about a childhood friend. Describe what attributes made that person important to you.

3. Describe how children's ideas of friendship change over time. Describe children you know who fit into each stage and explain your conclusions.

4. Describe two children you know—one who seems to have many friends and one who seems to have no friends. Discuss what variables might be influencing each child's situation.

5. As a group, develop a friendship skit aimed at teaching children how to make contact with a potential friend. In addition, generate at least five discussion questions.

6. Pretend you have been invited to a parent meeting to describe friendship coaching. Outline what you might say to parents regarding the rationale for this technique as well as its component parts.

7. Referring to Appendix A, NAEYC Code of Ethical Conduct, judge the ethics of the following situation: You and your best friend work in the same program. One evening your friend tells you that sometimes when the children are happy she goes outside for a cigarette, leaving the children unattended.

8. Identify a child you know who might benefit from friendship coaching. Describe the area in which coaching would be most useful and explain how you would implement the coaching procedure.

9. Pretend that a child's parent has spoken with you about concerns regarding his or her child's peer relationships. What information would you require in order to give an appropriate response? What suggestions could you make to the parent to help foster this child's friendships outside of school?

10. Identify the pitfall in this chapter to which you think adults are most susceptible and describe ways to avoid it.

FIELD ASSIGNMENTS

1. Discuss three situations in which you supported children's friendships. Describe what the children were doing.

    Next, talk about what you did, making specific reference to the skills you have learned in this chapter.

    Explain how the children reacted to your approach. Conclude by evaluating your skill usage and describing any changes you might make in future situations that are similar.

2. Choose a friendship skill. Design an activity through which you will teach the skill to children. Write down your plan in detail. Also, include a description of how you expect children to react to the activity. Carry out the activity with a small group of children.

    Evaluate in writing your presentation, state any unexpected outcomes, and describe any changes you would make if you were to repeat this activity in the future.

3. Select three children. Describe their interactions with peers. Using Figure 8-1, describe each variable as it relates to these children. Discuss how your observations relate to the content from the chapter. Suggest one thing that could be done with each child to improve his/her peer relationships.

For additional resources, visit our Web site
www.EarlyChildEd.delmar.com

INFLUENCING CHILDREN'S SOCIAL DEVELOPMENT BY STRUCTURING THE PHYSICAL ENVIRONMENT

OBJECTIVES

On completion of this chapter, you should be able to describe:

- What structuring is and how structuring can enhance children's social competence.

- How to use time, space, and furnishings to enhance children's social development.

- How to work within the daily schedule.

- How to select and organize materials to promote social development.

- How to help children become decision makers and managers of their own environment.

- How to communicate with parents about structuring to support children's social development.

- Pitfalls to avoid in structuring the physical environment.

Jerry, 3-and-a-half years old, sits quietly on the rug placing blocks carefully on a tower. His friend walks past carrying a sign saying "CLEAN UP 5 minutes" and ringing a small hand bell. Jerry surveys his structure and then carefully removes the blocks, replacing them on open shelves that are marked with the silhouette of each shape.

Mitsy, age 5, hurries to her cubby and removes her one-piece snowsuit. Spreading it out on the floor, she promptly sits in the middle. With quick efficiency she puts on her clothing and prepares to go outside announcing, "The snow will pack (for snowballs) today!"

Edward, age 7, scans his long pictograph to be sure that he has completed all of the starred activities for the week. Now that it is Thursday, he smiles because all of the required activities have been completed and he can do whatever he chooses. He watches other children for several minutes, then moves into the science area where one of his friends is looking through a microscope at something. He marks the science pictograph with a crayon to record his participation and begins to examine the materials placed in the center.

Each of these children is functioning independently in an environment designed to foster their autonomy. The open storage for blocks with the shelves clearly marked enabled Jerry to put away his materials. Convenient coat storage and instruction in putting on outer wraps enabled Mitsy to move efficiently from the indoors to outside. The use of a pictograph facilitated record keeping for Edward and provided the necessary information he needed to plan his day at school. In every case, the physical environment positively influenced these children's social competence. This did not happen by chance. Adult management of the environment was indirect but deliberate. This aspect of guiding children's social development and learning is called structuring.

Structuring is the management of time, space, and materials aimed at promoting children's social competence. Other aspects of child development and skills are also influenced by environmental factors. However, in this chapter we will focus only on the social domain.

There are three reasons why early childhood professionals structure the physical environment. First, adults try to anticipate children's behavior and then prepare the setting before children arrive or become involved in a particular activity in order to promote desirable actions and minimize undesirable ones.

This is the most common form of structuring. It requires adults to consider in advance what social goals to emphasize with the children and how time, space, and materials might best be arranged to help children pursue those goals. Secondly, adults structure on the spot to resolve problems as they arise. This strategy minimizes frustration and conflict among and between children as well as between adults and children. A quick environmental adjustment may alter the context sufficiently to minimize children's difficulties and improve social outcomes. Finally, adults structure to teach the children how to make decisions themselves. They support children in making decisions, forming plans, implementing them, and evaluating their usefulness. Adults give directions, provide opportunities, and assist children in the process and sometimes comfort them when they are unsuccessful. Used in these ways, structuring can enhance all six elements of social competence described in Chapter 1. Examples are presented in Table 9-1.

STRUCTURING SPACE AND MATERIALS

One of the ways that adults prepare the surroundings to promote desirable social behavior is by structuring space and materials. Buildings, furnishings, materials, and elements of the natural environment are concrete, visible resources that can be managed to facilitate the social development of children. The physical environment in which children play and learn has much to do with the presence or absence of disruptive behavior. Many "discipline problems" in classrooms can be traced directly to the arrangement and selection of furnishings and materials (Weinstein & Mignano, 2007). On the other hand, self-control develops in a well-designed and well-arranged physical space. Friendships flourish in cozy, comfortable rooms where informal exchange is planned for. The general consensus of researchers and theorists is that a well-designed environment creates a positive, supportive setting for the group using it (Levin, 2003). Overall, professionals want the spaces that children work and play in to provide a sense of belonging and connection to others in the group. A flexible space with many open-ended materials that can be used to meet a multitude of goals is desirable. In addition, natural materials engage the senses and generate a sense of wonder and curiosity in the most effective spaces (Curtis & Carter, 2003).

Table 9-1 The Relationship between Social Competence Goals, Forms of Structuring, Teaching Goals, and Adult-Structuring

ELEMENT OF SOCIAL COMPETENCE	FORM OF STRUCTURING	GOAL FOR THE CHILDREN	STRUCTURING EXAMPLE
Social Values	Structuring in advance	Children will take care of the materials that they use.	The adult organizes storage so that children have easy access to it.
Positive Self-Identity	Structuring in advance	Children will have opportunities to contribute to the group and be recognized.	The adult provides display space for all children's work, projects, or art.
Interpersonal Skills	Structuring on the spot	Children will work together toward a common goal.	More children want to help with the collage than the teacher originally anticipated. The adult adds additional supplies to accommodate the larger group rather then turning children away from the activity.
Self-Regulation	Structuring on the spot	Children will pay attention during whole-group efforts.	Children are distracted by materials on a nearby shelf during group time. The adult turns the shelf around to lessen the distraction.
Planning and Decision Making	Structuring for decision-making	Children will choose between competing materials or activities.	The adult provides appropriate alternative materials or activities from which children may choose.
Cultural Competence	Structuring in advance	Children will become aware of people having various cultural backgrounds.	The adult adds pictures of people of varying backgrounds and abilities to learning centers throughout the room.

Building and Grounds

Architects, landscape designers, interior designers, and program administrators have the responsibility to build or modify a building to meet the appropriate standards for the intended use. Safety, convenience, durability, maintenance, beauty, accessibility, and specific adaptations for use are all considerations in this process. For example, very small toilets are appropriate in a child care center serving toddlers but not for a public school where the youngest child is 5.

Playgrounds usually need fencing. All states have standards for safety and health for those facilities that serve children. Although the facilities have impact on children's social development, practitioners who are working within programs cannot alter or change facilities easily by themselves.

Maintaining health and safety.   Children and adults alike have responsibility to maintain the physical environment to promote health and safety.

Children can engage in the stages of an activity based on cues provided by the environment.

Adults prepare the environment to promote desirable outcomes.

Mr. Barkley quickly pulled the blood spill kit from the shelf and hurried over to Andrew, who was having a nose-bleed. He put on protective gloves and used a cold towel to apply pressure to stop the bleeding. After reassuring Andrew, he sprinkled the blood with absorbent material and scooped it into the orange bag for disposal. The tissues and other bloody refuse were also placed in the bag that would later be disposed of appropriately. He washed the floor, table, and chair thoroughly and used a disinfectant before throwing his gloves into the orange bag.

As a part of a unit on ecology, Mrs. Goldstein took the children outside where they picked up all of the trash that had accumulated on the grounds. She later asked the children to weigh this trash and discuss personal responsibility for the environment and the consequences to other people in the community.

Ms. Leitner felt like leaving the basket of book bags in the hallway outside the door because it would be so

much easier. She knew that this could interfere with children leaving the building quickly if there was a fire so she distributed the book bags into each of the lockers in the hallway instead.

The infant room was hot, stuffy, and odorous. Ms. Youngblade opened the top and bottom windows.

Each of these adults was demonstrating social responsibility as well as maintaining the physical environment. Mr. Barkley had prepared in advance, accurately anticipating the probability of a child bleeding at some time in the room. Mrs. Goldstein used instructional strategies to help children understand social responsibility. Ms. Leitner anticipated the need for safe exit from the building. Ms. Youngblade made an on-the-spot decision to open windows. In taking such actions, these adults used standards for cleanliness, order, safety, and consideration of others. Children learn these social values through exposure to adults who practice safe and healthy maintenance procedures.

Observe individual children carefully and provide clear directions as the first steps in eliciting social cooperation.

Adjusting interior spaces to promote social development.   Many schools and hospitals have been constructed using "hard" architecture. The interiors are similar to those of a factory, with easy maintenance enjoying the highest priority. Frequently, the spaces are unattractive, make people feel closed in, allow limited movement, and reverberate with sound. Fortunately, modifications can be made to make spaces more homelike or more hospitable. The image of a comfortable, child-centered home rather than an institutional setting is more desirable for programs for children under 6.

If elements of the space itself are creating challenges for children in the setting or are interfering with the social goals of the programs, then these spaces should be modified to meet the needs of children and adults using the space. Most of these alterations are done as a part of the preparation of the environment, though opportunities do occasionally occur for on-the-spot changes.

Walls are permanent. Color hue and intensity influence the atmosphere and set the stage for interaction. The walls themselves do not change, and regular painting is at long intervals. However, adults can modify the wall space by adding bulletin boards or corkboard strips to display children's work, placing furniture against the walls, or by hanging appropriate prints or other displays in the spaces. Children feel that the space is their own when they see simple, uncluttered displays of their own work as well (Clayton, 2001). In addition, wall-hung shelves improve storage and may decrease noise, while at the same time displaying children's three-dimensional projects.

Artificial lighting and the placement of windows are often considered immutable to change. However, adults can readily turn the lights off to reduce heat during hot weather and adjust blinds to increase or decrease the amount of natural light and adjust them to diminish glare. Lower lighting and lighting dispersed around the room are most conducive to social interaction (Meers, 1985). Adding lamps and turning some overhead lighting off will have this effect in institutional spaces.

Floors frequently are of either carpet or a hard surfaced, easy-to-clean material. Even though the floor itself cannot be changed, rugs and carpets can be added to decrease noise or removed so that cleanup of messy activities is easier. Variation in vertical space may be achieved by adding a loft, an indoor climber with platforms, or ramps leading to elevated structures. These structures separate spaces and provide interest and possibilities for enclosures for personal spaces as well.

Sound control.   Soft materials like carpet, draperies, ceiling and wall tile, stuffed furniture, and pillows absorb noise. A certain level of noise is to be expected as children talk and move about. However, reverberating noise is not desirable. One way to determine if the environment needs changing is to listen carefully as children and adults are behaving appropriately. If the room still seems too noisy, additional sound-absorbing, soft materials should be added.

Variation in texture usually influences the sound level and tends to humanize the environment. Hard surfaces on floors are useful in art areas, kitchens, bathrooms, and entrances and where children play in sand or water. Carpets are easier to sit on and are softer to land on if a child falls from an indoor climber. In the block corner, a firm-surfaced carpet reduces

Adults prepare the environment to promote desirable outcomes.

noise without reducing the stability of blocks. One enterprising teacher hung three tumbling mats on a cement wall. This solved the problem of storing the mats when they were not in use, decreased the reverberation of noise in the basement room, and added color and texture to the wall. Most administrators will allow staff to bring additional rugs into such settings. Some examples of adjusting the interior are in Table 9-2.

Adjusting Exterior Spaces to Promote Social Development

All children from infancy to adolescence need opportunities to play outdoors. Human beings need contact with the natural environment to maintain their mental health. Quite often, a child's judgment of self-competence in movement is acquired outside and constitutes part of the sense of self-efficacy and body image. Freedom of movement in a safe environment allows children of all ages to explore what they can do as they investigate nature and practice their motor skills. Outdoor play spaces, like other areas, should be developmentally appropriate, scaled to the size of the children, and designed to promote success and independence. Often young children are able to compare their skills with children of the same age, imitate others who are more skillful, and engage in play in noncompetitive ways. Such activity, while challenging one child, is a source of personal power to another who serves as the model.

Children have opportunities to help and encourage their peers in outdoor play (Hearron & Hildebrand, 2004). Often the social constellation of children changes as the activities outdoors bring forth their various competencies. For example, boys tend to engage in more pretend play when outdoors than when inside. Leadership and play groups may change in the outdoor spaces.

To enable all children adults should plan multiple opportunities for small and large motor play, construction play, and pretend play as well as other program activities (Bilton, 2002). Indoor activities can be moved outdoors and natural materials

Table 9-2 Adjusting Aspects of the Facility to Influence Children's Behavior

DIMENSION	CONDITION OBSERVED	ADJUSTMENT	IMPACT ON CHILDREN
Safety (Temperature)	Hot and stuffy room	Open windows and doorways.	Children experience less stress and greater comfort.
	Drafty or unusually cool room	Press towels or diapers on window sills until permanent insulators are installed.	
(Cleanliness)	Water droplets on bathroom floor	Wipe up water.	Prevents adults and children from slipping
(Equipment)	The latch on the play yard gate leading to the playground is broken.	Tie a rope around the gatepost and keep the gate closed and/or stand at the gate to let children and adults through until repairs are made.	Prevents children from dashing into areas where moving cars might injure them
Interior design (Walls)	Walls are clean, plain, dull yellow.	Mount children's paintings in a single color and cover one area of the wall.	Children are proud to have their artwork displayed, especially if it's adding to the aesthetics of their classroom.
	Children don't play in the manipulative toy area.	Cover the room divider with a bright hue (cherry or orange) construction paper using two-way tape so the "papering" is temporary.	Children are attracted to bright colors and will more likely move into the area.
Sound control	Children are hammering on the "Pound a Peg" toy that is resting on a table.	Place a folded section of newspaper under the toy.	The child who is pounding can continue to enjoy the activity without distracting others.
Lighting	Bright sunny day.	Turn off electric lights and use lighting from windows alone. or Adjust blinds or drapes to prevent glare in the eyes of people.	Dimmer lighting tends to encourage quiet interpersonal interactions. Glare increases eye fatigue and children are not able to do close visual work in these conditions.

moved inside (Oliver & Klugman, 2005). Active adult planning and supervision is as important outdoors as indoors, as failure to do so may result in having youngsters afraid to go out to play, behavior outdoors becoming more aggressive and often unacceptable, boredom, or having children cling to adults (Bilton, 2002).

Ground surfaces can be modified over time with less cost involved than in interior alterations. For example, grass clippings and wood chips added to a spot will eventually improve the soil so that plants will be more likely to thrive. Gravel or sand may be used to fill in a low area that becomes muddy. Paving bricks are relatively inexpensive and may be added to a pathway to improve accessibility for wheelchairs, if needed. Often parents and volunteers contribute in this way in modifying the grounds.

Plants are an important feature in the outdoor environment. Sod absorbs some of the stress when children are running or falling and is ideal for group games or rough-and-tumble play. Hedges around the perimeter reduce traffic noise and dust, and provide increased privacy at the same time. Sometimes practitioners add grass or clover seed to areas getting a lot of hard use. Children can contribute to the beauty of the environment while cooperating in developing a garden. Adult guidance is needed so that only nonpoisonous plants are put in the garden and plants such as poison ivy are removed. Shade trees provide excellent group meeting spaces and some groups of children have planted seedlings as part of their learning experiences. A thoughtful arrangement of bushes can provide enclosed places for small groups of children to play. Yard fencing is excellent to support pole beans, squash, or trumpet vines. With variations of climate and soil type, the modifications to the outdoor play space using plants is very large in scope and other professionals or master gardeners may need to be consulted. Additionally, planning for these modifications may require consultation with those who share the space, but adding and deleting plants is quite possible.

A permanent climbing apparatus is a feature of many playgrounds in schools, parks, and child care environments. Although the structure itself cannot be changed readily, adults often must redistribute the impact-absorbing material beneath it to maintain safety. Movable outdoor equipment such as ladders, crates, and boards encourages cooperative play, and play spaces with many movable pieces allows children to alter their environment themselves (Felstiner, 2004).

Toys and equipment are readily added or deleted according to the plans of the day and the developmental competence of children. Sleds replace tricycles during the winter. During pleasant weather any toy or material that is typically indoors may be used outdoors. The principles discussed in upcoming sections in this chapter may also be applied to exterior environments.

Generally speaking, the strategies for supporting social interaction outdoors are the same as those indoors. A few adaptations of nonverbal communications might be needed as children move more quickly and farther away when outside. Additionally, it is sometimes difficult to hear directions and guidance given the distances involved.

Structuring the indoor and outdoor facilities minimizes the numbers of limits that adults must set to keep children safe. In a well-structured place, interactions between adults and children are supportive, positive, and focused on achieving social and intellectual competence.

Arranging Furnishings and Equipment

A supportive environment allows children to control their surroundings when appropriate and permits and encourages movement so that children can interact freely with objects and people (Marion, 2007). Because safety always is of highest priority, adults should plan environments to minimize risk for children.

A supportive environment is arranged into **learning centers**, or areas that provide for individual, small-group, or large-group activities (Bilton, 2002). When these are organized, physical limits are clear and regulate the use of materials and the behavior of children. Conflict between children is reduced, and conditions for high-quality learning or play are established. The needs of children with disabilities must be kept in mind so that those children are able to function independently as much as possible (Sutterby & Frost, 2006).

The number and kinds of areas needed are determined by the age of the children and the size of the group. If an **activity space** is defined as that occupied by a child using a material, then the number of activity spaces for a block area may be 4 or 6 because that number of children could reasonably use the blocks at one time. To prevent waiting, it is recommended that there be roughly one-third more activity spaces than there are children (Marion, 2007). A minimum of 27 activity spaces for a group of 20 children would be needed. Realistic estimation based on the physical space and the children's age is necessary to attain the desired outcome. Generally speaking, preschool children play more successfully in groups of 2 to 4 and school-age children may organize some of their play in slightly larger groupings. When individual materials are involved, such as a puzzle or watercolor materials, then the number estimated should match exactly the number of materials. Do not count sharing except when the supply of materials is large, such as with blocks. Most manipulative sets of construction materials are suitable for 1 or possibly 2 children, so multiple sets are needed if you intend for more children to play. Activity spaces can be estimated as follows:

Pretend play	4
Blocks	4–6
Six puzzles	6
Board game	2–4
Listening center with six headphones	6
Writing center	1–4
Reading area	2–4
Easel painting	1–2

Similar planning for outdoor play is necessary. The numbers for each zone, enclosure, or play area should be estimated carefully because they vary greatly. Some simple structures are suitable for one or two children; other complex combinations of equipment provide play space for many children.

Private space.   A **private space** is an area designed for one child, or maybe two, to which the child can retreat from social interaction. In one second grade classroom, the teacher had painted an old bathtub red and filled it with pillows. A child in that area, usually reading or simply watching others, always was left undisturbed. A private area of this type is not to be used for punishment or time-out but to provide a sense of relaxation, comfort, and privacy in the midst of a public environment. The use of private space may reduce stress and eventually help a child attain higher levels of self-control. Children can briefly escape the noise and activity to a space that provides comfort and security (Frost, Wortham & Reifel, 2005).

Small-group space.   A **small-group space** is designed for fewer than eight children. In most programs for young children, four to six children may be playing together (housekeeping, blocks, water play) or engaged in studying (insect collections, number lotto, weighing cubes). A small-group work area should have spaces for sitting and a surface for working. Primary-school teachers generally conduct reading groups in a small-group area with the children sitting in a circle or around a table. Some areas of this type, such as an art area, are specialized so that materials may be stored on adjacent shelves. Other small group spaces need easy access to water or electricity and should be placed in the room where these are easily accessible. Areas are more flexible when their use is not predetermined and materials may be brought into or removed from the area. Opportunities for social interaction abound in small-group settings.

Large-group space.   Most settings have a **large group space** that can accommodate all of the children at one time. Usually this space has bulletin boards, large book easels, and audio-visual equipment. This type of indoor space is normally used for a variety of activities: language arts, creative dance, group discussion, games, and music. Participation in large-group activities helps children to see themselves as a part of the larger social network.

Boundaries and activity areas.   Clear, physical **boundaries** tend to inhibit running, provide cues to where the child is supposed to participate, curb intrusions and interruptions, and designate appropriate pathways for children to move throughout the room. Usually, furnishings and low room dividers are used to mark separations in areas. Most youngsters under age 8 forget or ignore unclear boundaries, such as those formed by floor tape, or those described verbally such as telling the children not to play with the trucks when the area is used for large group activity. Placing fabric over the shelf housing the trucks is a clearer restriction. Each learning center may be further defined by distinctive materials, such as books and cushions in one area and childsize tables and chairs with board games in another.

The large-group area may have different types of learning centers at different times, with block play one day and a climber on another if there is not sufficient space to have them both. In addition, two learning centers may be side by side, and deliberately left permeable to encourage small groups of children to interact (Schickedanz, Pergantis, Kanosky, Blaney, Ottinger, 1997)

Areas also should be arranged within the room so that activities do not conflict with one another or offer distractions. Quiet activities should be separated from more vigorous ones. For example, it is better to locate a study carrel near a work area or the independent reading area than near the block or game area to avoid setting limits for children who unintentionally intrude. The number, type, and arrangement of activity areas are within the control of the helping professional. Activity areas can be added, removed, or relocated to facilitate the achievement of program goals.

Activity areas are as useful outdoors as indoors. Usually, boundaries are established outdoors by varying the surface. Asphalt may be used on a ball court or a tricycle path, grass on the playing or running field, and sand or other resilient materials under climbing equipment. Resilient surfaces promote safety, decreasing the frequency of adult cautions and limit setting. Constructed boundaries, like fences and pathways, are clear to children and provide them with clues to appropriate behaviors, as well as providing greater safety. Within well-defined areas, adults can influence social interaction by the use of mobile equipment and materials, such as the addition of water or shovels and pails to a digging area. Temporary boundaries may be added as needed to diminish reprimands and reminders, such as when orange traffic cones mark off a big puddle of rainwater on the playground.

Pathways. Activity areas also must be arranged so that movement between areas is easily accomplished without interfering with the activities in progress. Such pathways need to be sufficiently wide to allow children to pass one another without physical contact. Usually, 30 to 36 inches is adequate indoors; outdoors, wider pathways are necessary to avoid collisions where children run. Pathway width may need adjustment if a child needs a walker or a wheelchair. In some rooms, the area designated as the large-group area also serves as a means of access to other activity areas.

Sometimes, the pathway is like a hallway without walls, with the large-group area at one end and small-group and private spaces arranged on either side of a central pathway. This arrangement may encourage running by toddlers but a central pathway may be more effective for older children.

Storage. Storage is essential to all programs. It promotes responsibility for the materials and encourages children to care for their environment independently. Effective storage supports children's independent behavior and promotes

appropriate handling of materials and equipment. Stored items should be sorted, placed at the point of first use, and arranged so that they are easy to see, reach, and grasp and easy to replace by those who use them most often (Berns, 2007). Like items should be together.

Storage units should be planned to enable even young children to be successful in using them. Tall storage units should be bolted to the floor or wall. Low mobile storage cupboards equipped with casters can be used to set boundaries. Materials that are used regularly should be readily accessible from pathways or activity areas. Storage of equipment and materials used outdoors should be suitable in size and accessible from the playground areas.

Adult storage space that is inaccessible to children also is desirable for safety. Cleaning compounds, medicines, power tools, and potentially harmful substances and equipment should be stored in locked cupboards where children cannot get to them. Sharp pointed scissors, electric fry pans, and other potentially hazardous materials should be stored out of childrens' reach. Such items are sometimes stored centrally for a number of classrooms, outside of areas used by children.

Controllable Dimensions

The physical setting is composed of a number of **dimensions** involving the facility, the furnishings, and the materials used by children: **soft–hard, open–closed, simple–complex, intrusion–seclusion,** and **high mobility–low mobility** (Jones, 1981). The particular combination of these dimensions varies according to the type of program (hospital, playroom, YMCA recreation area) as well as the goals of the program and the philosophy of the adults. These dimensions determine the overall comfort and atmosphere communicated by the physical environment. The dimensions are briefly defined with typical examples seen in many programs in Table 9-3.

Qualities of the physical environment have a continuing impact on the quality of interpersonal interaction within it. **Hardness** usually is associated with efficiency and formality, and **softness** is associated with relaxation and comfort. Younger children are more at ease in a softer setting and gradually learn how to behave in the more formal hard settings. When a material is **closed,** there is only one way to use it, but when it is **open** neither

Teachers and caregivers must take into consideration the number of children that will play in each area when structuring the physical environment.

Planning for outdoor play and the number of children using the equipment is also necessary when structuring the physical environment.

the alternatives nor the outcomes are limited. More open settings encourage curiosity, exploration, and social interaction, and completely closed settings prohibit such behavior altogether. The **simple–complex** dimension describes the material in terms of the number of alternatives that can be generated. Children tend to play cooperatively with complex and super units more frequently than with simple units, which often elicit solitary or parallel play activity. Complexity encourages deep exploration, and variety encourages broad exploration. Formal group settings need some of each so that children will focus on an activity for an extended period of time, which is more likely with complex activities, but also can move to other alternatives for a change of pace. The **intrusion–seclusion** dimension describes the permeability between the program and the things and people outside it and the boundaries between people and things inside the program. Many classrooms have no seclusion within them and may be very fatiguing to young children. Children who are overcome by the stress of continuous interaction in a large group act up, cry, or daydream to escape for short periods. Private areas, as described earlier, are spaces in which children

can have a degree of seclusion. Small-group spaces are partially secluded and enable the child to moderate their level of seclusion. Children who have the opportunity to choose some sedentary activities and some active pursuits usually choose both in the course of the day. Prolonged sedentary activity causes children to wiggle to ease their muscles and to become bored and restless regardless of the interest or importance of the activity. They frequently engage in inappropriate behavior, irritating peers and adults and necessitating limit setting. To prevent this, daily **schedules** should provide for a balance between vigorous movement, moderate activity, and more quiet pursuits. When children's need for mobility is taken into account, the selection of equipment and the use of space usually are changed.

Each of the dimensions varies by degrees and may vary over the course of a year or within a single day. Each dimension affects the social relationships of children in the setting. An open, moderately secluded, soft environment with **low-to-moderate mobility** is a conversation area, much like a living room, in which children can relax and interact informally.

Table 9-3 Controllable Dimensions in the Physical Environment

DIMENSION & DEFINITION	ONE EXTREME	MIDDLE	OTHER EXTREME
Softness: responsiveness of the texture to touch	**Soft:** Pillow Upholstered chair	**Malleable materials:** Sand, water & dough Grass or lawn	**Hard:** Cement Tricycle Walls
Openness: degree to which the material itself restricts its use	**Open:** Blocks, toy stove Clay, ball	**Semiopen/semiclosed:** Accessible cabinet with doors, playing cards	**Closed:** Puzzle, tracing patterns, form boards
Complexity: the number of components and their variety	**Simple:** Ladder, wind-up car Doll dress	**Moderately complex:** Jump rope Simple toy car Unit blocks Erector set	**Complex:** Large climber with multiple possible activities Computer
Seclusion: permeability between boundaries	**Seclusion:** Study carrel; private space learning center Single stall toilet with door Large block building with roof A box or tent where children can close themselves in	**Semisecluded:** Bushes where children play but adults can see easily Climber where toddler can crawl under and peek out Sunglasses or mask	**Intrusion:** Open windows in a classroom; sounds of children moving outside the room Lab schools with visitors
Mobility: degree of opportunity for children to physically move their bodies in a learning center	**High mobility:** Gym; playground; tricycle; indoor climber; indoors during transitions	**Moderate:** Garden with pathways and boundaries Most early childhood classrooms; pretend play area; block area; often science areas	**Low mobility:** Nailed-down seats in a room; writing center; reading center; sometimes math center

Continuous evaluation of the effectiveness of the space to support children's social development requires flexible thought. Sometimes adults continue in ineffective settings simply because the classroom or playground has "always been this way." Sit at the child's eye level and appraise the environment from various perspectives when children are using it and when it is empty. Table 9-4 provides guidelines for evaluating the effectiveness of the child care setting.

Choosing Appropriate Materials

Adults can promote competent and independent behavior in children by providing a moderately rich assortment of exploratory materials (Dodge, Colker, & Heroman, 2002). The goal in careful selection, maintenance, display, and storage of materials is to have resources that children can use in cooperative or independent activity. Carefully selected materials that meet the interests of children and support program objectives contribute to overall functioning, emotional adjustment, the development of self-concept and self-control (Frost, Wortham, and Reifel, 2005). The physical resources that children use also affects the level of social interactions when they play (Sutterby & Frost, 2006).

Developmentally appropriate materials. Materials should reflect the goals and levels of competence

Table 9-4 Evaluating the Effectiveness of the Space

Health and safety	**Outdoors** • Are the gates closed? • Is the ground free of trash especially beverage containers, broken glass, metal, or cigarette butts? • Do children participate in cleaning up the yard? • Is equipment in good repair, or set aside for repair? • Are there appropriate materials under climbing equipment to absorb force from falls? • Is there provision for children with special needs in the program? **Indoors** • Are medicines, sharp objects, or electrical appliances out of reach of children? • Are the tables, counters, cots, and chairs clean? • Are kitchens, toilets, and drinking fountains sanitized regularly?
Promotion of social development	• Is the light appropriate for the activities of the children? • Are there hard surfaces under easel and water play areas and carpeting in areas where there is noise produced or where children sit on the floor? • Is there a variety of learning centers indoors and out? • Are centers maintained and supervised? • What behaviors or affective moods have you noticed in each of the areas of the room? Boredom–interest? Engagement with others–aggression? • Do displays reflect the children in the program? • Is the classroom clean, orderly, and organized consistent with program goals? • Are centers appropriate for the abilities of all children so that both success and challenge are experienced? • Can you see all of the space when children are present? • Is there evidence that the children in the group "own" this place?
Sound control	• Is the room noisy when children are behaving appropriately? • Are there soft, absorbent textures in various noisy activity areas? • What is the nature of the sounds from the environment that you hear when the children are not there?
Variety and adequacy of interest areas	• Is each interest area adequately equipped for the planned activities? • Are there duplicate materials available for younger children? • Do children have to wait long to use materials or equipment? • Are there at least one-third more play spaces than children indoors and out? • Is there at least one private space indoors and out? • Is the size of each small-group space adequate for the children to engage in the activities planned successfully with other children? • Are the activity spaces located near the resources that they need (water, electricity, light)? • Does the large-group space accommodate all of the children without crowding? • Are the boundaries between activities clearly and concretely marked? • Are the quiet activities located together and generally separated from the areas where vigorous activities occur?
Pathways	• Are children able to move from one activity to another without interrupting the learning of other children? • Do the boundaries of activities mark the pathway so that children do not inappropriately expand into a pathway? • Do the children move in and out of centers easily and at an appropriate pace?

Table 9-4 Evaluating the Effectiveness of the Space—continued

Storage	• Do movables have containers that are clearly marked so that children can put materials away? • Is the storage space marked with pictures, pictographs, or words so that children can put things away correctly? • Are similar things stored together? Are they always in the same place? • Is storage at the point of first use? • Is the storage adequate both indoors and outdoors? • Is the storage appropriate for what is stored? Pegs for hanging things, drawers or shelves as needed?
Controllable dimensions	• Is the space inviting and comfortable? • Are the hard aspects of the structure softened? • Is there a balance between open-ended materials to use flexibly and those where the use is specific? • Is there someplace that is restful (or sometime where a place is set up to be restful and secluded)? • Are children able to move about freely as appropriate for the activity? Is there sufficient opportunity for physical activity? • Is the overall space pleasant, beautiful, and appealing?

of children in the program. Adults would think it strange if someone gave a chemistry set to a 5-year-old. Not only would the child be at risk of swallowing some of the chemicals, but also in all probability, the set would quickly be destroyed and the child frustrated with failure. However, the same set given to a 12-year-old could provide hours of pleasure and instruction. Frequently, materials intended for older children create potential risks and failure for younger ones. In addition, when older children use equipment and materials designed for young children, they lose interest because there is no challenge, and they find new, often destructive ways to use them.

Structurally safe materials. Materials should be examined for potential safety hazards. Sturdiness, durability, craftsmanship, and appropriate construction materials all contribute to safe products. For example, a metal climbing frame may be a sensible, safe purchase for 3- to 5-year-olds, but a wooden one would be much safer for toddlers and young preschoolers in cold climates. Young children tend to put their tongues on the metal in winter and can become stuck to it and badly injured. Tricycles available in local stores are not as sturdily constructed as those designed specifically for use by groups of children. Maintenance of equipment is necessary to ensure continued safety. Eventually,

even sturdy toys break down. Care also should be taken to see that materials are not likely to cause choking. If an object is small enough to get into a toddler's mouth and has a diameter between that of a dime and a quarter, it might get stuck in the throat.

Materials that work. Children become frustrated when equipment and materials do not operate, which sometimes leads to disruptive behavior. The wheels of trucks should turn; scissors should cut; finger paint should be thick, and the paper heavy enough or glossy so that it doesn't fall apart. It is nearly impossible to trace accurately through standard typing paper; tracing paper and paper clips make the job much easier. Children cannot use basketballs, kick balls, or volleyballs that are under-inflated. Seeing that all materials are usable is the responsibility of the adult.

Complete materials that are ready to use. Puzzles should have all their pieces. If one gets lost, it can be replaced by molding in some plastic wood (available in most hardware stores) to fit the hole. One 10-year-old was extremely upset when, after working on a hooked pillow cover for weeks, she discovered that there was insufficient yarn in the kit

Sand provides protection from falls as well as opportunities for children of all ages to play. Because it is loose and malleable, it is excellent as a learning material as well.

to complete it. Incomplete materials lead to unnecessary feelings of failure and frustration and loss of self-esteem.

In addition, when materials need to be brought out by an adult for a demonstration or for children's use, they should be assembled in advance so that children do not have to wait while the adult rummages around in a cupboard or drawer for a pair of scissors or a bit of wire. Waiting children usually lose interest or become disruptive. Complete preparation by the adult includes some plan for cleaning up, so having a damp sponge in a pan would be appropriate preparation for a messy activity. In this way, the adult never needs to leave the group of children and can offer continuous guidance.

Organizing materials storage.   Storage should be where the material is most frequently used or where it is first used and located in logical areas. If children know where something is located, they can go and get it to complete a project, especially common items such as paper, crayons, and scissors. Materials also should be stored so that children can take care of them. For example, taping shapes of unit blocks on the back of a cupboard so that children

know where to put each size and shape encourages independence. Materials that have many pieces, like beads, small math cubes, or Cuisenaire® rods, should be placed in sturdy containers such as clear plastic shoeboxes or tiny laundry baskets because the cardboard boxes soon wear out. In this way, children can keep all materials that go together in one place.

Attractively displayed materials.   Neatness and orderliness are aspects of attractiveness. Materials are easier to find and more inviting if they are not crammed into a crowded area. Young children simply have difficulty in selecting materials on crowded shelves.

Materials that are displayed in a moderately empty space on the shelf are most likely to be used. Some materials should be available to children and displayed on low, open shelves. Puzzles in a puzzle rack or laid out on a table ready for use are more appealing than a large, heavy stack of them.

Appropriate size of equipment and materials. Tables, chairs, desks, or other equipment add to the comfort and decrease the fatigue of children if they are sized correctly. Adults also should have at least one chair that fits them to sit on occasionally.

Fewer problems are encountered at mealtime if preschool children are offered 6-inch plates, salad forks, and 4- or 5-ounce glasses to use. Serving dishes (soup bowls) with teaspoon servers would enable children to serve themselves amounts of food that they can reasonably consume. Using small, unbreakable pitchers for milk and juice encourages independence as well. When children determine portion size for themselves, there is less wasted. Children who are entering the growth spurt around the ages of 11 or 12 might reasonably use large, divided trays that can hold substantial servings.

Young children spend much time in adult-sized environments. Therefore, in programs designed for them, the environment and all the materials should be appropriate for their sizes. Long mirrors in a toddler room should be mounted horizontally, slightly above the molding on the wall; for preschoolers, mirrors can be set vertically, but again, low. The height of sinks, toilets, and drinking fountains can be adjusted by building platforms around adult-sized facilities, or child-sized fixtures can be installed. If materials, equipment, and furnishings are appropriate in size, children can act more independently and develop good habits.

Quantities appropriate to the number of children.   If there are enough materials for a particular activity, children can work without conflict. If there is an insufficient supply, either the number of materials should be increased or the number of children using them decreased. For example, if a third-grade teacher has 12 books and 14 children, she can either hold two consecutive sessions of 7 children and use the books on hand or get 2 more books. Either solution is better than having children rush to the reading area in order to get a book for themselves. Toddlers as well as some inexperienced preschool-aged children do not comprehend sharing. In addition, a toy being played with by another child is more appealing than one on a shelf. Duplicate toys allow the desires of the toddler to be met without conflict.

Adequate supplies of materials are necessary for any program regardless of the children's age if children are to be reasonably successful. Materials should be accessible to all children as well. This fosters independent action and allows children to play together peacefully.

Adding or Removing Materials and Childproofing the Environment

Purchasing materials and equipment and the initial furniture arrangement or materials storage is usually the responsibility of administrators in the organization. Selecting specific materials appropriately and organizing and displaying them carefully are strategies teachers use to prevent frustration, interpersonal conflict, property damage, and physical risk. These strategies are the result of advanced planning with ultimate goals of supporting positive social interactions and appropriate behavior. Helping professionals, who are working directly with the children, structure the specific materials to meet the immediate needs of the children and ensure that the physical environment is conducive to the development of social competence of the children (Kostelnik, Soderman, & Whiren, 2007). In addition, supervising adults must make adjustments based on individual or group needs as children interact within the space, use equipment, and engage in the activities with materials in meaningful ways. The most common adjustments that adults make to the environment in support of children's interpersonal engagement are to add materials, take them away, or childproof the environment.

Adding to the environment.   There are many ways adults add to the environment. A photograph of each child's family or of the local community might be hung and discussed with the children. An artifact or an article of clothing representative of the cultural heritage of one of the children might be brought in to share. Fresh flowers or living plants and animals might be added temporarily in the setting to soften the environment and to add interest.

These additions are typical of the general strategy of preparing the environment. However, on-the-spot adjustments of adding to the environment occur daily. For example, if two children want to look at one picture book about trains, offer a second book with pictures of trains. If children are waiting a long time to use glue sticks, provide either school paste or glue. If Alyce is arguing with Theresa about leaving the store without "paying," ask them what they think could be used for money and then help them to obtain the material if necessary. Such on-the-spot actions usually rectify the situation sufficiently for the children to move forward in their social interactions as well as support their problem solving skills.

Taking away from the environment.   Removing a container from the library area and putting it back in the water table where it belongs would be appropriate if the object is not being used for play. Removing splinters of wood from the guinea pig cage or moving a frog from someone's pocket into a terrarium until it can be returned to a more suitable place would protect the lives of these animals. Sometimes the removal is temporary, but necessary, such as moving all the chairs away from a table so children can cook, or putting materials out of sight so they do not distract children from group times.

On-the-spot removals are also frequent. If Teddy drops materials in the toilet, remove them right then. If six youngsters are pushing and crowding around a table, remove one or two of the chairs to indicate that only four to five children may use this center at a time. If a wheel is wobbly on a tricycle, remove it from the play area and label it for repair so that children experience success rather than frustration.

Generally the adding or deleting of materials are done to enhance play, minimize potentials for frustration or conflict, and to promote cooperation and self-control. The environments in which we live and work affect our mood and our behaviors with each other and are relatively easy to change either before the program is in session or during it.

Childproofing the environment.   Adding materials, taking them away, and altering them are necessary for childproofing the environment. Childproofing means providing the necessary adjustments to ensure the safety of the children. It is usually done before children enter the environment but may occur when safety risks are fist detected. Several examples of this are illustrated in Table 9-5.

The amount of space necessary may have been incorrectly estimated for an activity. For example, Mr. Bongard placed an indoor climber about 18 inches from an open, screened window one hot summer day because he thought that the vigorous activity would benefit from the potential air circulation. However, as he was watching Brad and Doug climb to the top between the window and the climber, they attempted to stand on the nearby windowsill. He hastily lifted Brad down and asked Doug to climb down before he moved the climber at least 3 feet away from the window. The quick adjustment to increase safety was essential.

Other adjustments.   Sometimes space should be limited instead of increased. Miss Adkins took her kindergarten children to the gym to run simple relay races. At first, she set the activity up so that children would run the length of the gym. She noticed that they were quickly tired and restless, as they had to wait so long for a turn. She then shifted to running a second group of relay races across the width of the gym, which still gave ample room to run but cut down the waiting time. Adjustments by

Table 9-5 Examples of Adjusting Materials to Increase Safety

OBSERVATION WHEN CHECKING	ACTION TAKEN
A toddler is poking at the electrical outlet in the hallway.	Add an outlet cover and remove child from hallway.
A 3-year-old has put on the hot water at full force to wash her hands.	Adjust the water temperature and flow.
A group of 7-year-olds are filling balloons with water and throwing them in the hall.	Stop the balloon throwing. Give children a mop and pail and show them how to clean up the mess.
The cord to the coffee pot is hanging over the edge of a table in the teachers' area, but it is in sight of youngsters.	Fold the cord loosely and fasten it with a wire twist or rubber band.
Pointed, adult scissors are left on the activity table in the kindergarten.	Take away the scissors and put them out of children's reach.
A rung of the wooden ladder is broken.	Take away the ladder.
A mother gave the child a sack with medications and directions for administering them and sent her into the primary classroom.	Take the medicine from the child and place it in a safe spot.

moving equipment or by increasing or decreasing space most appropriate for an activity are fairly typical of most child-centered programs.

Sometimes adjustments are made in the ways in which directions are given. At the beginning of this chapter, Edward used a pictograph so that he could assess whether he was free to choose completely on his own what he should do. Using sequenced photographs or drawings for routine activities such as washing hands, tying shoes, or taking off outdoor clothing are easy structuring strategies that support directions already given to children on how to do the task. In addition, individual children may not understand the directions on the use of equipment or materials, so additional explanations and demonstrations may be necessary for each person to be successful. For example, having a classroom computer with a variety of programs as one of the learning centers is not useful if the children do not know how to operate the machine. One demonstration to the group is generally inadequate. Mr. Rock discovered that children were hesitant to attempt independent use. He therefore adjusted his strategy of encouragement to one of training a few of the children in the kindergarten to use the machine and then asking those children to give demonstrations to their peers. This "each one teach one" adjustment also supported social interaction and contributed to the prosocial goal of helpfulness.

Occasionally, a center is adjusted by simply closing it. Mrs. Perry temporarily closed the thematic play center "Seed Store" when children were just throwing the seeds around instead of engaging in productive play. Upon close appraisal, she decided that the children didn't have the necessary understandings about seeds, their use, or how they were bought and sold to engage in the play. Once children learned more about shopping for seeds the center was reopened successfully several days later.

Most frequently, adjustments are very simple behaviors that make the children more likely to be successful in learning and in their interactions with each other.

Miss Peabody noticed that the four children at the table were pushing each others' materials around and arguing as they tried to place large pieces of paper on the table. A basket with lots of scissors was in the middle, so Miss Peabody removed enough scissors for each child from the basket, placed them on the table, and put the basket on a nearby shelf, where it was still accessible; this adjustment left enough space for each child and eliminated the cause of conflicts.

Mr. Turkus responded to the frustrated cry of 3-year-old George, who slapped his painting with the paintbrush and exclaimed, "Is not red." The red drippings on the outside of the jar did not match the muddy, purplish red color of the paint inside. Mr. Turkus showed George how to rinse the brushes and jars, and provided a small amount of the three primary colors. He then demonstrated how to keep the red paint red by using a separate brush for each color. George resumed painting happily.

Ms. Polzin noticed Nicholas riding his truck through the block area and ramming into block structures that Claire and Raphael were building. When they moved to hit him, he seemed oblivious to the cause of their anger. Once a settlement between the children was complete, Ms. Polzin used masking tape to mark off a road for the truck where block structures could not be built.

Miss Clark attended to a child who got a sliver in his hand from the edge of the climber. She then sanded the rough place to make it safe.

In each of these instances, the adults added, took away materials, or childproofed the environment to enhance the success of the children in their care. Each adjustment was made as a result of the adults **checking** on children's activities and assessing the nature of the problem to be solved by the presence, absence, or condition of the appropriate materials or equipment.

Structuring the furnishings, equipment, and materials of the physical environment prepares the setting before children arrive. Likewise, adults plan in advance for the use of time in programs and an orderly, predictable sequence of events for children. This sets the stage for the quality of interpersonal experiences adults and children have in the physical environment.

STRUCTURING TIME

Adults value time as a resource and are concerned with helping children to function within the cultural definitions of time that adults use. One way adults help children to use time efficiently is by teaching them a habit, for activities that are repetitious and are used regularly (e.g., washing hands). Sometimes, adults become angry with children when they are slow to develop a desired habit. At such times, the child either may not know an appropriate sequence of behaviors, or the sequence is so new that he or she must concentrate closely on each action in the sequence.

A typical example of not knowing an appropriate sequence is when a kindergarten child puts on boots before the snow pants, or when the first garment put on by the child is the mittens.

Adults sometimes become irritated when such incidents make the group wait, mostly because they do not realize that the situation requires teaching rather than demanding and limit setting. Another way adults help children learn the cultural meaning of time is by organizing events into predictable sequences or routines.

The Daily Schedule

Schedules are organized time segments related to the program. These blocks of time are arranged in a certain order, with children moving from one activity to another in an unsurprising pattern. The daily schedule or routine supports children's ability to act autonomously. Events can be predicted; expectations for behavior are clear. Healthy habits regarding hand washing, toileting, and tooth brushing are routines in many early childhood programs are formed with clear directions, consistent practice, an understanding of their purpose, and can be learned well enough to become routine (Oshikanlu, 2006). All routines contribute to the children's sense of safety. The need for constant guidance in what to do and how to do it is minimized, so children's dependence on adult direction is decreased.

Some schedules are more flexible than others. When a child first enters a formal group setting, the familiar patterns developed within the family often must be altered to fit the new situation. This change results in distress and confusion and often is referred to as the initial adjustment to the program. The problems of adjustment are reduced as children and families incorporate the new pattern into their behavior.

Routines, however, must be learned. Adults first must adapt to the toddler's schedule then gradually teach children to function within a group schedule. Young children take longer to learn routines than older ones do. They simply have more difficulty remembering. Children under 6 years of age may take as long as a month to adapt to a new daily schedule. Children in the elementary grades often adjust in two weeks or less; at this age, a pictorial chart or written schedule may help them to adjust more quickly. Routines may be flexible, allowing a little more time to finish an activity if the change is compatible with the requirements of other program segments. Sometimes, however, as when large groups of children must use the same resources, schedules must be quite rigid. The use of the swimming area in a summer camp requires that all children must arrive, enter, and leave the water in an orderly fashion if standards of safety are to be maintained; every group must operate on clock time if all groups are to be able to swim each day. In contrast, in an after-school family child care program, children may move indoors and outdoors whenever adult supervision is available; a rigid clock-time schedule is unnecessary.

The predictability of a routine offers emotional security to young children. After a distressing encounter with another child, Cara, age 4, chanted the daily schedule several times: "First we play, then we wash, then we have a snack, then we hear a story, then we go outside, and then my mama comes to take me home." After each repetition, she appeared more cheerful and ultimately was able to participate comfortably for the rest of the day. Young children also will comprehend the sequence of the daily routine before understanding the concept of time. Ross, 3 1/2 years old, was distressed when his mother left him at the child care center. He played for about 45 minutes, and then asked if the children could go outside. This was a drastic change of schedule—usually, outside play was the last activity of the day—but the teacher allowed Ross and two other boys to go outside with an assistant. Ross played happily for a few minutes, and then informed the adult that his mother would be there soon to pick him up! He had erroneously inferred that playing outside caused his mother to arrive because of the contiguity of the events.

Transitions.   A good schedule is continuous, fluid, and goal directed. Blocks of time allow children to finish tasks and provide for individual differences in speed. Waiting is minimal, and the transitions in which the whole group must participate are as few as possible. A group **transition** occurs when one time block is finished and another begins. These transitions usually occur when children move from one room to another or when there is a complete change of materials. In Cara's verbalization of her routine, she located all the group transitions by saying "then." In public schools, transitions occur before and after recess and lunch and also may occur between activities, such as between math and social studies. An individual transition is when a child is finished with one activity and moves on to another within a scheduled time block.

Generally, there is a marked increase in the number of interaction problems between children and between adults and children during group transitions. Children may be confused about how to behave after one activity is over and before another begins. Sometimes youngsters deliberately run, call out to friends, or wander during a transition. Older school-age children use this time for conversation and play, with a resulting increase in noise. Therefore, decreasing the number of transitions results in the lower probability of interaction difficulties.

Short attention spans and differences in working speed can be managed by grouping a variety of activities together in a larger time period and allowing children to change activities individually. For example, in a second-grade room, a teacher combined reading groups, workbook activities, and selected games involving one or two children into one block of time. In programs for very young children, a large variety of materials usually is available at any one time. Individual transitions are generally smoother, with children most successful if they have decided what to do next. In general, the schedule should be adapted to the length of time children need to complete tasks rather than to rigid periods, with particular attention to the age of children and time of year. Youngsters tend to focus on their tasks longer as they mature, and from fall to spring have a longer attention span.

In any case, the goal is to meet the individual needs of children; strategies and standards for doing so differ according to program demands. However, there are nine general guides that will help support transitions for all age groups.

- Plan carefully so that you consider just what each child is supposed to do and how they are supposed to do it. Teach repeating transitions carefully so that each child develops relevant habits related to that transition. Entering the building is one of these regular transitions that can be taught so well that it becomes a habit. For example, children should know which door to enter and which staircase (if you use one) to use, which side of the staircase to walk on, how to walk safely with using the handrail, how to remove outdoor wear and where to put it, and to wash and dry their hands (reduces transmitting colds), and where in the room to congregate or what the first activity should be. This kind of instruction with appropriate ongoing supervision tends to reduce problems like running in hallways, fooling around in stairwells, and congregating in bathrooms or locker areas. Treat transition as a skill to be taught.
- Provide enough time so that the transition can me accomplished without rushing, yet eliminate waiting as much as possible (Lamm, Grouix, Hansen, Patton & Slaton, 2006). Children can use

sign up sheets when more youngsters want a material than can be accommodated. Specific materials such as picture books might be used while children gather for a group experience.

- Give clear, precise directions. Some adults write them out so that they use the same directions daily until all learn the task. They should be specific, direct, with three or fewer directions stated at one time. For example, when it was time for a group transition from learning centers to another group setting or activity, one effective adult approached a small group who had been using a lot of blocks and said, "Put each block on the shelf where it matches the shape" (pointing to the silhouette). She stayed nearby to make sure these young children understood. Then she said, "Place *all* of the blocks on the shelves." Seeing the children engaged, she moved on to another area to give directions to those children using paints. If necessary, this adult would return to the block area to give the same directions or a demonstration if needed.
- Alert children that a transition is coming soon so that they can either complete an activity or organize the materials so that completion is possible later. Use the same signal every day such as having the helper carry around a sign that reads "5 minutes to play."
- Plan for the movement of children through pathways when the whole group is in transition. Dismiss children in small groups or individually to avoid congestion in bottleneck areas such as doorways. Consider the size of the pathway and whether one child will be walking past other children. In spacious outdoor areas, small groups of older children may pass each other without physical contact, but even then, rough-and-tumble play might begin through "accidental" contact.
- Tell children what is coming next if it is a group transition or ask children what they plan to do next if it is an individual transition. This helps children to develop planning skills and increases their ability to predict what will happen sequentially.
- When children are engaged in a free-choice activity, start the transition to cleaning up the room by the whole group gradually. Ask small groups of children with the greatest number of materials to take care of to begin cleanup before the other children. Then move to other small groups so that the whole group finishes about the same time.
- Always send children to something or someone that is prepared for them. Aimless wandering or dabbling with numerous materials is not desirable

during individual or group transitions. Assure that each child knows where to be and what he or she should be doing at the end of the transition. Ambiguity in this often leads children to fear and uncertainty and contributes to over-stimulation or perception that things are out of control.

- Assist unengaged children to find some way to contribute to the group effort during clean-up time if they are unable to identify opportunities for helping by themselves.

All whole group transitions are noisy. Books are closed. People move from place to place. Children interact with one another. Transitions take longer during learning and are much shorter once the specific transition habit is acquired. However, if children are milling around, pushing and shoving, engaged in boisterous play and generally disorganized, then the adult should take immediate action. When this happened in Ms. Haden's group, she flicked the light, asked all of the children to lie on the floor where they were until the room was quiet. Then said, "Lie still until I ask to stand up. You will be quiet as mice and not touch anyone. When I touch you, stand up and put away the materials you have been using and come sit in the group area." She paused, then asked them to stand up and move quietly like mice. Her voice was soft and firm. Later she provided an opportunity for children to discuss what happened during that transition. She discouraged blaming others and helped children to think about what they did to contribute to the bedlam. She neither shamed nor scolded. Later, she evaluated her instructional strategies, directions, and transition planning.

> *Bruce was a 5- year-old child with autisim. His language skills were delayed and what speech he had was mono-tone. He avoided eye contact and had difficulty in most social interactions. He was very skillful in solitary play and showed superior problem solving skills when working with his hands. When the group transitions occurred in the classroom, he withdrew to the book reading area, often covering his ears, though the transition was generally smooth. Dismissal was from the gym where four groups of children gathered for music just before being picked up by their parents. The sound bounced in this hard space and it was unusually noisy, though orderly and controlled. When Bruce first experienced this setting, he ran in large circles screaming in a very high-pitched voice. The characteristics of the space had made the sound overwhelming and terrifying to Bruce. By agreement, Bruce's parent arrived about 5 minutes early to pick up Bruce from another area of the building.*

Bruce was extremely sensitive to sound. Yet the transition in the setting was quick, efficient, and orderly for the program. To meet Bruce's specific needs, the timing and conditions of the transition were altered to provide him with a less stressful experience and, at the same time maintain an effective group transition for others in this preschool program.

Rate and Intensity of Programs

The speed, rate, or pace of a program may be described by the number of transitions per unit of time. For example, some children may experience three or more transitions in 1 hour. This is a fast pace with a rapid rate of change, providing only 15 to 20 minutes for each segment. A moderate pace would have at least one activity period of 45 to 60 minutes and others of varying length of time. A low-pace program would have few group transitions and two long periods in a half-day program.

The intensity of the program generally refers to the amount of change within a time segment and the degree to which children must attend to an adult. High-intensity programs have three to five novel experiences per week with fewer opportunities to repeat or practice skills. The adult–child interaction is high and the number of adult-initiated activities greater. In low-intensity programs, children have one or two novel activities per week and many opportunities to repeat and vary familiar activities; the role of the adult is that of observer and facilitator. Children may be over-stimulated, rushing from one thing to another, or they may be bored with a very low-intensity program. In either extreme, children find it difficult to have congenial, easygoing interactions with their peers. Either over-stimulation or boredom might generate fatigue which limits children's ability to cope with social interactions. A child who is able to solve interpersonal problems when rested may simply cry or become distraught if required to face the same situation when tired.

Fatigue. The following are possible explanations for fatigue:

1. Bodily changes that might be the result of "running hard" for a long time
2. Frustration with one's inability to cope with a situation
3. Boredom with the activity
4. The normal wear and tear of life due to stress

It is quite possible to have some children in a program frustrated, others bored, and still others exhausted from the stress of working under pressure to keep up. Factors that influence the rate at which children can function are motivation, health, knowledge, skill, practice, age, stamina, habit, and the number of people involved in an activity (Berns, 2007). Crowded conditions are more tiring than those in which the density is lower. Interacting continuously with someone is more tiring than sporadic contact during the day. Interruptions lead to frustration and to fatigue. In a child care center, if the pace and intensity of the schedule are low to moderate, children are more likely to experience only the normal fatigue that is the result of daily activity, which is reduced by napping, and will be able to engage in more pleasant social experiences during the rest of the day.

COACHING CHILDREN IN DECISION MAKING, PLANNING, IMPLEMENTING, AND EVALUATING

Even the youngest children express their needs. Babies cry when they are in pain, hungry, bored, or tired. Toddlers point to the refrigerator when hungry or the faucet when thirsty. Preschoolers express their wants and needs for affiliation (relating to others) rather directly. These are usually expressed very simply: "I want to play with Jake." Young children are very concrete and adults must infer the broader social competencies from what the child says and does.

Children's Goals for Themselves

> *Diane went happily out to the playground after finally zipping her jacket. Running over to the paved area, she stopped suddenly, noticing that all of the trikes were occupied. With determination, she walked over to the supervising adult and said, "I want to ride a trike." Mrs. Sturgeon reflected, "You would like a turn. When Natalie slows down, ask her if you could ride when she is finished."*

Diane stated her objective simply and directly and Mrs. Sturgeon responded with the recognition of her objective and during the course of the morning assisted her with the interpersonal skills necessary to approach another child, ask for a turn, and wait until the other child was finished riding to achieve it. Other young children may need assistance

in recognizing or identifying their objectives. When youngsters watch other children play with materials, they are showing an interest in those materials and may need assistance in identifying their objective. A simple inquiry, "Would you like to work a puzzle, too?" or an invitation to participate, "There is plenty of room for you at the puzzle table" can be helpful in clarifying the child's own objective. Both of these statements about materials and space are instances of helping children to recognize their objectives related to environmental resources.

Older children who have developed more social understanding and skill are more articulate in their objectives. They are very clear in recognizing unfair play and injustice applied to themselves and others, or verbalizing difficulties in self-regulation: "I don't want to wait to use the computer tomorrow. I want to do it now." Older children are also able to recognize that there is nearly always a scarcity of resources in the physical environment and that there are processes for the distribution and use of these resources.

Helping Children Make Decisions

Children practice **decision making** from toddlerhood on. When adults offer them choices, children feel good about themselves and have an opportunity to practice decision making skills: generating alternatives, seeking information, considering consequences, and eventually accepting responsibility for the outcome (Hendrick & Weissman, 2006).

Adults who try to understand the youngster's own goals and then offer simple either/or choices between two acceptable alternatives support young children in the decision making process. Between ages 2 and 3, children are able to select playthings from an array of toys and play contentedly. By the time youngsters are 4, they might be able to generate some of the alternatives themselves when confronted with the problem of not having enough shovels in the sandbox. About this age, Karouko asked an adult for spoons, scoops, or little cans so everyone could play, "Cause then I don't have to give her the red shovel." The adult's role is to demonstrate, explain, and guide the process. Children learn to make choices by doing it and are more likely to "own" the decisions they themselves make. Involved children are less likely to resent the consequences of decisions that turn out to be less desirable than anticipated when they have made them themselves.

All children need close guidance in learning to make decisions. The younger children are, the more difficulty they have with understanding that

What choices might you offer this child?

their goals are not the same as other peoples' goals. Perspective taking is most difficult with scarce resources, especially when the goal of another child is in conflict with the child's own purposes. However, children usually are more satisfied if they have participated in the decision making process than when an adult has made the decision for them. As children mature, they are increasingly able to understand the purposes of another person and, by virtue of greater experience in making decisions, they often are able to generate more alternatives to dilemmas.

The link between making choices and the consequences of these choices develops gradually over time. Decisions regarding their own goals are easiest to make and those regarding others are more difficult (see Chapter 13). Youngsters' success and comfort with decision making is dependent upon the guidance and opportunities to practice making small decisions earlier.

> *Ms. Fawcett offered Paul, who is almost 2 years old, two identical pairs of socks. Paul chose one and proceeded to put them on himself without any resistance. In previous instances, Paul had simply refused to put on the socks that had been chosen for him, curling up his toes and feet and protesting mightily.*

> *Dolly, age 3, needed help in deciding whether to eat one or two pieces of Halloween candy on that holiday and save the rest for later. She was surprised when all the candy was gone after choosing two pieces for many days in a row.*

> *By age 8, Peggy successfully planned to carry out her learning activities in a second grade room: "See, these are the ones you gotta do (pointing to a list on the chalkboard). So I always start with two on Monday and then I do something else and I work with anybody I want to. Then on the rest of the days, I start with one of the ones that have to be done, too. If we have all the ones we gotta do done on Friday, me and my friends do whatever we like and that's okay."*

Paul was developing independence and autonomy and, when given little opportunities to exercise this autonomy, made choices and was satisfied. Dolly initially experienced surprise at the consequences of her choices, but with guidance, developed strategies for making choices and understanding the consequences. Peggy had personal criteria for making choices in organizing her time and effort.

Group decision making takes more time than individual decision making, and supporting the process with a group of children takes even longer.

When adults decide to let the children choose as a group, they also have committed a substantial time resource to the process. Extensive communication is required in order to arrive at a decision. However, the time is well spent because children are more committed to a course of action if they have participated in determining it. Some decisions that groups of children might make are which song to sing, which game to play, whether to participate in a fund-raising activity, or how a holiday should be celebrated. Some groups of children are allowed to participate in choosing displays to make, rearranging furniture, and organizing storage. Children who experience making simple decisions gradually develop the ability to make more decisions and to live with the consequences of them.

Helping Children to Plan, Carry Out, and Implement Plans Themselves

Two- and 3-year-olds are capable of making short-term, simple plans when asked what they might like to play with or do. The time between choice and action is a few moments. Four- and 5-year-olds might verbalize about the blocks they want to use in building a structure, about the colors to select for a painting, or about the choice of play partners for climbing on the outdoor structure. These are the beginnings of plans. As children mature, if given some experience in making plans, they will increase their planning for longer time periods and further into the future. The plans will be for increasingly complex tasks as well. Whereas a 4-year-old can participate in making and implementing a plan to share riding vehicles outdoors, 12-year-olds who have had many previous planning experiences are capable of creating a plan for a full camp evening activity using a variety of materials and equipment.

Both age groups require supportive and informative adults to assist them in thinking about the consequences of each decision and anticipating how the action will be implemented. In order to do this, adults must help children clearly do the following:

- define problem (or what the goal will be)
- obtain information about the resources available
- generate possible alternatives
- make choices among the alternatives and stick to them
- gather materials and equipment as necessary and arrange the physical environment
- carry out the plan
- discuss and evaluate the activity

Ms. Seaman holds a greeting time for a few minutes with the 3- and 4-year-old children in her group. As a part of this time, she describes the choices available in each center so that children will know the alternatives. She helps children plan daily which activity they will choose first before dismissing the children from the group setting.

Eventually, children learn that there is time to participate in some but not all activities and that many activities are available regularly. As time goes on they tend to plan where they are going to play or with whom. Preschool children also learn that if they do not choose to paint during the time that painting is offered, then they will not have a painting to carry home. Ms. Seaman comforts disappointed children while assuring them that they can make plans for the following day right then.

Older children may be led through the planning process formally. Teachers who use centers ask primary children to plan which centers they are going to use and then follow this up with a daily assessment. These adults assist children in the full process of planning, choosing, and evaluating. Other formal planning experiences with children over 6 might include choosing among various recreational or learning activities in a camp setting and then evaluating one day while planning another. A group of third grade children made board games that included developing the playing boards, the rules for play, and the social rules to guide behavior. After playing several of the board games, children made modifications in their games. They also discussed what made a game fun (evaluation criteria). Children learn these skills gradually through the guidance of adults who provide them opportunities to manage some appropriate tasks.

Helping Children Evaluate and Develop Standards

Children learn self-expectations and standards from their interactions directly with the environment as well as from adults and other children. The consequences of their behavior become clear as children engage in their programs. Materials not returned to the correct shelf are difficult to find. Youngsters who are distracted by materials during whole-group activities are themselves distractions to others. When adults organize the physical environment so that positive outcomes are obvious when social expectations are met, children will make the attempt to comply with these expectations because, in the long run, it is to their advantage to do so.

Both adults and children are able to recognize that the age and experience of a child must be taken into account when considering how good is good enough. Very young children can express what they like or prefer and what they dislike. Older youngsters and more experienced ones may account for differences in standards within the group by indicating, "Gracie hasn't learned how to do that yet," regarding a youngster whose intellectual development is not as rapid as her peers, while insisting that the same behavior in a more competent child is unacceptable.

Adults help children learn about standards by setting reasonable standards for the children, communicating expectations, providing directions and appropriate guidance, demonstrating these behaviors themselves, and providing reasons for the standards to children. Some children set their standards too high and never seem to experience satisfaction and acquire the self-worth that comes from accomplishment. Others set standards so high that they are fearful of failing their attempt to meet the objective. A few children only attempt tasks when they are almost assured of easy success before they begin. Unfortunately, some children have had little experience of appropriate standards and have not yet learned to judge with accuracy what might be appropriate in a specific situation. All children benefit when adults structure activities so that goals can be achieved gradually, but are challenging enough to promote growth (Vygotsky, 1978).

Probably the best recognized learning opportunity for children to develop standard-setting skills is when they select their "best work" or "best picture" to be included in their portfolios or for display. When discussing the reasons for their selection, young children may initially be very idiosyncratic in their reasoning. Older children who have discussed standards for their products with others will actually state more objective criteria. Children of all ages may have more difficulty in expressing the idea of "good enough" related to more obviously social problems. When Jason, who had four cars, was asked if he was satisfied with the distribution of cars with Brian, who had seven cars, he affirmed that he was and continued playing. He glanced at the teacher when she noted the difference in number and ignored her comment with a shrug.

The ability to plan and implement decisions using limited resources is an essential social competence. Children learn to anticipate the potential consequences for themselves as criteria for decision making and, as they mature, they take into account the consequences for others. By the end of childhood, youngsters are capable of generating rules for the use and preservation of limited resources such as how to make a limited supply of glue last for the year. With guidance, children learn to organize space, materials, and time to achieve their own goals.

Opportunities to manage materials and events appropriate to the child's age help children feel they are competent and have some control over their immediate environment. These feelings of autonomy and confidence contribute to positive self-esteem and eventually to greater social competence.

SKILLS FOR INFLUENCING CHILDREN'S SOCIAL DEVELOPMENT BY STRUCTURING THE PHYSICAL ENVIRONMENT

Arranging the Room to Support Social Development

Classrooms, playrooms, gymnasiums, and other spaces are used for children's activities. Following are some general guidelines for initially setting up a room. However, the nature of the program and the nature of the space will greatly influence the specifics.

1. Survey the space. Note the placement of potential hazards such as electrical outlets, probable pathways such as doorways, water sources, windows, and electrical outlets. Sit on the floor and look around. Is the space inviting or attractive? Does it stimulate curiosity and promote order?

2. Imagine how children might move within this space and try to predict the problems

SKILLS FOR INFLUENCING CHILDREN'S SOCIAL DEVELOPMENT BY STRUCTURING THE PHYSICAL ENVIRONMENT

they might encounter that are likely to require setting limits. Can children change from one play space to another easily? Is it likely that children will walk? Is the space organized to prevent hazards? Spilling or dripping paint is not unusual. Extension cords are a trip hazard for children and adults. Even older youngsters have poked things into electrical outlets (that should have been covered). Surfaces next to areas where children form lines are usually touched, leaving dirty fingerprints. Young people frequently run and mill about during arrival and dismissal as well as other scheduled transitions.

3. Arrange the furnishings in the room so that the need to set limits is minimized and children are safe, comfortable, and as independent as possible. Consider all of the dimensions of the space so that children are most likely to interact together appropriately and are less likely to interrupt each other or come into conflict. Some specific suggestions are as follows:

- Place quiet activities, such as looking at books, away from the more active areas of the room.
- Place cubbies or lockers near doorways, electrical equipment near outlets, paints near a water source.
- Place messy activities on hard-surface floors and potentially noisy activities (blocks, workbench) on carpets.
- Attach fabric to the open shelf units with Velcro™ fasteners so that the shelves may be closed off during group time.
- Interrupt long pathways that invite running by placing interesting activities partway down them that would require children to turn right or left.
- Use shelving that allows storage and display of materials such as paper, glue, pencils, crayons, and scissors to be readily accessible and near where they would be used; this prevents children from having

to move across areas of the room repeatedly. If necessary, have writing supplies for older children in all centers.

4. Evaluate the placement of furnishings in terms of social development goals. If peer conflict regularly occurs in the same place, consider reorganizing the space. Are children able to move through the space with confidence and ease without interrupting someone else? Where do most of the limit-setting instances occur? Use the answers to these questions to help you restructure the area.

5. Use furnishings of appropriate size only.

6. Adapt the room arrangement as needed to meet the needs of children experiencing physical or mental challenges. Children in wheelchairs must have more space in pathways than children who are independently mobile. Children with broken limbs who are temporarily experiencing limitations in mobility may also require space adjustments so they may do what they can for themselves. Children with sensory or mental impairments may require greater attention to maintaining clear walkways or opportunities for seclusion from time to time. Parents and specialists usually can provide suggestions for meeting the special needs of individuals. In principle, adults structure the environment to enable the successful participation of all the children within it.

7. Adjust furnishing and equipment as necessary to support children's social behavior on the spot. Move tables or other large equipment a few inches so that youngsters can move freely without interfering with another person. Observe for pushing, shoving, loud voices with protest, or other disruptions and consider alternatives in the physical environment to change the conditions before setting limits. Change the location of the activity if it is too close to other activities that interfere with the children's success and enjoyment.

continued

SKILLS FOR INFLUENCING CHILDREN'S SOCIAL DEVELOPMENT BY STRUCTURING THE PHYSICAL ENVIRONMENT—continued

8. Add or subtract objects in the physical environment to achieve specific goals related to children's social development.

9. Share your observations of children's use of space and room arrangement with program leaders if children's interactions indicate a consistent or ongoing problem. Cooperate with fellow team members by discussing structuring issues. As a group, view the room at the level of the children and evaluate whether or not it supports the social competence of the children or if it generates potential problems for them.

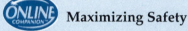 **Maximizing Safety**

The safety of children is every adult's responsibility, regardless of role. Usually, the adults in charge of a program will check the environment and childproof it so it is safe. Occasionally, however, people overlook less obvious risks or forget to follow through in making the adjustments.

Therefore, all adults must make it a habitual part of daily practice to apply the principles of childproofing the environment. Taking simple precautions is much better than telling children to be careful or scolding them for playing near something hazardous. You always have the option of inquiring about a situation you think is unsafe.

1. Scan the environment inside and out for potential safety hazards when supervising children. Look at the spaces you habitually use so that hazards can be removed. People may throw glass bottles or cans into children's play spaces. Sometimes, when other people use space during other time periods, materials and equipment are left out that may pose a danger to the children. Remove these promptly.

2. Keep safety in mind when supervising activities. Some materials are potentially hazardous if used improperly but otherwise are safe. A stapler used properly is safe, but little fingers can get under the staple. Large blocks usually are safe, but a tall construction may require an adjustment of a lower block to ensure balance of the whole structure. Remain alert and observant throughout the day.

3. Act promptly when a safety hazard is noticed. Do not delay if you perceive a hazard to children. Act conservatively and, if your judgment is at fault, it is better to be more protective than less protective in an ongoing program for children. For example, if some 8-year-olds taste the fruit of a bush near the play yard with which you are unfamiliar, remove the fruit and the children from the area and contact the local poison control center according to program procedures. If the plant turns out to be harmless, consider it a fortunate event rather than being embarrassed that you inquired. If three preschool children are at the top of a slide all trying to come down at once, climb the slide, help one child to go down at a time and monitor the number that are able to get to the top to take a turn. Hesitancy to act may increase the risk to children.

4. Review any actions during the program day with other adults so adjustments that can be implemented before the children arrive may be completed. For example, plants not known to be safe can be removed from the environment or these areas can be protected by fencing. Adults who are not with the children for the full time they are in session also need information so that the same hazardous situation does not reoccur.

5. Know the local and state legal guidelines and periodically check that they are being maintained.

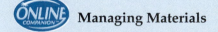 **Managing Materials**

Organizing according to the following guidelines can minimize problems with cleanup done by children.

SKILLS FOR INFLUENCING CHILDREN'S SOCIAL DEVELOPMENT BY STRUCTURING THE PHYSICAL ENVIRONMENT

1. Store materials to be used by children in durable containers near the point of first use and so that they are easy to reach, grasp, and use. Help children place materials in the correct storage container, if necessary.

2. Establish a specific location for materials so that children will know where to put them. Maintain the storage area in an orderly fashion so that children will know what it is supposed to look like. Mark storage areas with words, symbols, or pictures as needed to identify materials that should be located there.

3. Check equipment and materials to be sure they are complete, safe, and usable.

4. Demonstrate the proper care of materials. If necessary, tell the children exactly what to do while demonstrating step-by-step, and then take the materials out again so that the children can imitate the behavior. A camp leader may need to demonstrate the cleaning and folding of a tent several times before children learn to do it correctly.

5. Give reasons for the standards that you set. For example, say: "Put the pieces in the puzzle box before putting it in the rack. That way, the pieces won't get lost." You might ask older children to read the numbers on the spine of a book and replace it exactly so that another reader can find it.

6. Supervise the process of putting materials away, giving reminders as necessary; praise children who are achieving the standard and those who are helping others to do so. Allow children to choose between two or three tasks. If they are unwilling to choose which task to do, assign a task and support the child through the process. Check periodically to see that there has been follow through. (These skills are discussed in Chapters 10 and 11.)

 Arranging Space and Materials so Children Have Clues for How to Behave

1. Provide only enough chairs for the maximum number of children that can participate in an activity. Children become confused if there are five chairs at a table, but only three children may participate in the activity. To avoid this problem, remove extra chairs.

2. Use signs, labels, or pictographs placed so that children understand what is expected. For example, put one colored cube in a plastic bag and tape it to the exterior of the opaque bin that holds the cubes. Place a label on the container as well. Then draw a cube, color it, and label the shelf where the bin is stored. Children will know how and where to place the cubes when pickup time occurs. Use more floor area for larger groups and less space for smaller groups. For example, the computer, table, and two chairs can be placed in a small area near the library comfortably. However, the thematic play space should be three to four times larger as more children are likely to play there. Usually children move through large open space or bring materials into the space to use them there.

3. Make all activities appear to be appealing and attractive. Add color to attract children such as placing blue construction paper under a puzzle, much like a placemat. Beginning to engage in an activity also may attract children, such as painting at the easel. Opening a few books with lovely illustrations and arranging them so that children can see them from afar might draw children into the library area. Where excessive clustering occurs, sit on the floor or in a small chair and really look to see if all of the activity areas are equally appealing.

continued

SKILLS FOR INFLUENCING CHILDREN'S SOCIAL DEVELOPMENT BY STRUCTURING THE PHYSICAL ENVIRONMENT—continued

4. Encourage children to personalize their space making room decorations, using the bulletin boards, or having a display area. Keep written messages, pictures, and photographs at children's eye level. Put pictures of the young child on the locker or cubby or place family photos on bulletin boards where children may talk about their families to each other.

5. Provide for appropriate activities for a private space. Plan activities that children may do alone. Permit the child who needs some seclusion an opportunity to behave appropriately while withdrawing from the main flow of action.

6. Provide materials that are developmentally appropriate. Avoid offering activities that are too simple or too difficult. Modify the planned activity if necessary for children to participate. Use information available from other professionals and from the literature if you are uncertain about the appropriateness of an activity.

7. Have all the materials ready and all the equipment and furnishings in place when the program begins. Supervise the children continuously rather than leaving to get supplies. Survey the areas you are supervising, check the materials for usability, quantity, and safety, and confer with the leader, if necessary, to ensure the smooth functioning of activities. Then you are free to interact with the children.

8. Organize materials so that physical work is minimized both for children and for you. Observe children and other adults for ways to eliminate or simplify unnecessary work. For instance, use a tray to carry several items instead of making many trips. Make suggestions to help children make their own work much more efficient.

9. Send children to an activity or an area rather than away from one. Give children a clear notion of what alternatives they may pursue. Give a direction, such as "Put away

your books and come to the large-group area," or ask the child what he or she plans to do next. Avoid ending a statement by saying things like "You should finish up" or "You're all done." Neither statement helps the child decide what activities are open for him next.

 Minimizing Potential Conflict Over Materials

1. Provide materials in an appropriate number for the task and situation. In an open classroom, use the ratio of 1.5 to 2.5 play spaces per child. Check the number of spaces and the amount of materials available when mobility is excessive or when child-to-child conflict occurs. Either too many or too few activities can produce this effect. Either add or remove activity areas and play units, based on your assessment.

2. For young children, especially toddlers, provide duplicate or near-duplicate play materials. Substitute a duplicate or similar object for the one under contention.

3. Arrange the space so children can get materials and take care of them without interfering with other children. Place furnishings so children can move to and from storage without bumping into other people or asking them to move their activity.

 Supporting and Working Within the Daily Schedule

1. Know the time schedule for your work or participation hours and be on time. Check the environment when you arrive to be sure it is acceptable for children and the necessary materials that you need are there. Notify the program if you are going to be late or absent due to illness. Then others can make appropriate adjustments to their plans.

SKILLS FOR INFLUENCING CHILDREN'S SOCIAL DEVELOPMENT BY STRUCTURING THE PHYSICAL ENVIRONMENT

2. Know the children's daily schedule and the schedules for any other groups of children when common spaces or equipment are shared. Make sure that you understand where you are supposed to be at any given time. Find out about any anticipated changes in the schedule for special events.

3. Remind children of the daily schedule as necessary to aid them in making decisions about their activities. For example, if there is less than 10 minutes until cleanup, the child who has decided to carry a tub of digging equipment to the sandbox may need guidance: "I notice that you want to use some digging tools. It is nearly time for cleanup. Maybe you should only take out one shovel and one pail. Then there will be less to put away." The ordinary expectation is that children could play with a variety of scoops and containers. Another example in a camp setting is when the adult leader blows her whistle 15 minutes before the group leaves the tent area for breakfast so that children have time to finish dressing and to make their beds. She also blows it again 5 minutes before leaving.

4. Be on time to the activity area or learning center and begin immediately. End on time. In general, lead the children. Either enter an activity with them or before them in time, particularly when groups share space such as a gym or playground. If only one group can use the space at a time, and if you are delayed in leaving or arriving, you may be decreasing the opportunities of another group of children to use the resource. In addition, the other group may have to wait until you exit, which is generally a time of disruption and restlessness among children.

5. Know how normal routines are implemented in the program. Learn the typical ways of handling arrival or departure, diapering or toileting, meals, naps or rests, movement in hallways, all group assemblies, and other regular program events.

Adhere to established routines as much as possible. Once children learn the routines and understand the behavioral expectations they are most likely to behave in socially appropriate ways. When children do not recognize a routine, give directions for the expected behavior and provide children the time and opportunity to practice it until each child can participate successfully. For example, Scottie, age 3, began to run into the parking lot where cars were moving as well as stationary when he saw his parent's car. Ms. Shinn grasped his hand and admonished him, "You are really excited about seeing your parents. You wait until either your parents or a teacher takes you by the hand to your car." Explain the routines to children who do not comply with them, especially new children and very young ones.

6. Make on-the-spot adjustments as needed to support children's appropriate behavior. Refrain from rushing or hurrying children during transitions. Instead, start the cleanup or the beginning of the transition sequence earlier than the scheduled time if the activity is obviously going to take longer than is normal. Make small adjustments on your own. Anything greater than 5 to 10 minutes should be checked with the head teacher.

 Supporting Children's Attempts to Plan, Implement Plans, and Assess Them Using Environmental Resources

Children have their own social goals and their own ideas of how, when, where, and with whom resources should be made available. This means that there are many opportunities for adults to help children in making plans throughout the day and from day to day in their programs. Planning for the use of resources is one of the most useful skills that children can develop.

con

SKILLS FOR INFLUENCING CHILDREN'S SOCIAL DEVELOPMENT BY STRUCTURING THE PHYSICAL ENVIRONMENT—continued

1. Identify opportunities for children's participation in planning. Guide children into planning experiences commensurate with their experience. Help children identify their problems in the course of daily activity. Let them solve these dilemmas for themselves when they cannot endanger themselves or others. Consider the following examples as you read the remaining suggestions.

> *Manuel is getting ready to leave for the day and begins to cry, "I wanna picture, too."*
> *He had happily played in the blocks, used the computer, investigated some seashells, and spent a pleasant day in the program.*
>
> *Kendal and Erica were putting train tracks down that ran into the pathway where other children were passing.*
>
> *"I want to play ball with Jake and Toby," commented Will to the teacher, who had planned other outdoor games for the day.*

Assist them to reflect on their choices and the consequences of what they have chosen to do.

2. Use affective and behavior reflections to help children clarify the problem. Use reflections to assist children in sorting out the feelings of the moment, which get in the way of children's clear thinking. Observe, listen, and consider what the children's purposes are and construct your reflections accordingly.

3. Assist children in identifying possible alternatives. Use open-ended questions as necessary. "What ideas do you have?" "What do you think we can do about this?" "How long do you think that will take?" "What other people might like to do this or play?" "Is there another alternative?" and "How much more room do you need to do that?" are examples of open-ended questions. Avoid contributing your ideas to the solution of their problem. Do not take the initiative and the ownership of the problem away. Help children to identify

possible alternatives. Listen respectfully to their ideas, even the unlikely ones.

Kendra and Erica suggested several alternative ideas to the congestion in the pathway:

- Continue building as they had, but let others step over their train.
- Move a table to deflect the people traffic around them.
- Make signs about a railroad crossing and put them on chairs on either side of the intersection.
- Change the direction of the railroad to avoid getting in the pathway.

4. Encourage children to make specific plans to implement their decisions. Ask leading questions such as: "How will you accomplish this?" or "What materials will you need?" or "Are there other ways to accomplish the same thing?" or "What steps will you need to take to be able to do this?"

5. Provide sufficient time for children to cooperate in planning group efforts or making complex plans. Listen attentively to ideas; avoid rushing to completion. Structure planning time into the day to avoid the sense of being hurried. Make decisions yourself if there is not time for the group to carry out the process. Avoid imposing your choices on children when you have told them that they can choose.

6. Once children have generated alternatives and determined the plan of action, review the plan with them. If there are several hours between planning and implementation, review it again. Write down what they are planning to do. Draw a plan if space and furnishings are involved. Such drawings are very rough, but can convey the idea. For example, some 4-year-olds want two "houses" to play neighbors. When they ask the teacher, she asks them to share their ideas with her and eventually with the larger group of children. To do this, they sketch a map of where things might be put.

SKILLS FOR INFLUENCING CHILDREN'S SOCIAL DEVELOPMENT BY STRUCTURING THE PHYSICAL ENVIRONMENT

Manuel's teacher reminded him, "You asked me to remind you to choose painting this morning so that you would have a picture to take home." He happily walked over to the art area and stayed briefly to produce his picture.

Ask older youngsters to write out a plan to correct their own behavior when they have difficulty with their social interactions with others. Assist them to organize and think through a course of action in regard to their behavior and to develop a concrete map to follow.

7. Use reflections and open-ended questions to support children's evaluations of their plans. For example, was the child satisfied with the process? ("You figured out a way to . . .") Did the outcome meet his or her expectations? ("You have rearranged the playhouse into two playhouses. Tell me how you think that is working.") Consider the process successful if the plan is satisfying to the children and the implementation of it meets the needs that generated it "well enough" for them. Accept their plans, even though they are not likely to be what you imagine. Assist the child in the group who is less satisfied than another. This, too, is typical of any planning group. Allow older children more time to assess their plans.

 Helping Children Make Decisions

1. Offer many different choices to children each day. Anticipate situations in which choices could be offered, and plan what those choices will be. For instance, if you know you will be reading a story to the group, consider giving children a choice about where to sit, whether they would like to follow up the story by writing a poem or drawing a picture, or what character they would like to portray in a reenactment of the tale.

2. Take advantage of naturally occurring situations in which to offer choices. Ask if the child would pass out plates or napkins. Even if materials all look the same, give children a choice of which one to use, or ask children which side of the table they would like to sit on. Let a child decide whether he or she will put away the large blocks or the small blocks first.

3. Offer choices using positive statements. Give children acceptable alternatives rather than telling them what they cannot choose. It would be better to say "You can use the blocks to make something like a road, a house, or a rocket" than to say, "You can make anything except a gun." The former statement helps children to recognize what alternatives are available; the latter directs children's attention to the very thing you do not want them to consider.

4. Offer choices for which you are willing to accept either alternative the child selects. Pick alternatives with which you are equally comfortable. If you say, "You can either water the plants or feed the fish," you should be satisfied with either choice the child makes. If what you want is for the child to water the plants, do not make plant watering optional. Instead, offer a choice within the task, such as watering the plants in the morning or just after lunch. These choices are presented as either-or statements or "you choose" statements. For example, "You can water either the big plants or the little plants first" or "You choose: big plants or little plants first?" Avoid the tag question, "OK?" to a statement for which a child has no choice. It implies a choice and the child may say "NO!"

5. Allow children ample time to make their decisions. When making choices, children often vacillate between options. Allow them time to do this rather than rushing them.

continued

SKILLS FOR INFLUENCING CHILDREN'S SOCIAL DEVELOPMENT BY STRUCTURING THE PHYSICAL ENVIRONMENT—continued

Give youngsters a time frame within which to think: "I'll check back with you in a few minutes to see what you've decided," "While you're finishing your painting, you can decide which area to clean up," or "I'll ask Suzy what she wants to do, and then I'll get back to you."

6. Allow children to change their minds if the follow-through on the decision has not yet begun. If Camille is trying to decide between the blue cup and the red cup and initially chooses the blue one, she should be allowed to switch to the red cup as long as her milk has not already been poured into the blue one or the red cup has not been given to someone else.

7. Allow children to carry out and complete the implementation by themselves. Permit children to act on their choices. Provide the necessary demonstration but still ask the child to complete the follow through of the plan. For example, a child chooses a book by picking it up, chooses a play partner by offering to share materials, and so on. Avoid doing tasks for children that they can do for themselves as it implies that the child is not competent and undermines self-esteem.

8. Assist children in accepting responsibility for the choices they make. Once children have made a decision and it is in process, help them stay with and follow through on their choice. For example, Kent decided he wanted to water the plants after lunch; a gentle reminder on his return that afternoon may help him to act on his decision if it seems that he has forgotten. Use a neutral tone and neutral language; say: "Kent, earlier you decided to water the plants after lunch. It's about time to do that now" rather than "Kent, how are you ever going to learn to be responsible if you don't follow through on your decisions?" Similarly, if you had already poured the milk into the cup Camille had chosen but she wanted to switch at that point,

your role would be to help her live with the consequences of the decision. Reflect: "You changed your mind" or "You're disappointed that the red cup is gone." Talk about how the child may choose differently another time: "Today, you chose the blue cup. Tomorrow, you'll have another chance to choose. If you still want the red cup, you can choose it then." Comfort children who are unhappy about the results of their decision.

9. Help children learn to evaluate their own accomplishments. Focus on what has been accomplished compared to what was intended. "Did this picture turn out the way you planned?" You may also point out that the child could do something, given the effort, "You tried twice to get those boots on, but you did it in the end." Sometimes children need to have **feedback** on how to assess if they have accomplished the task. Ask them in advance questions such as, "How will you know if the dishes are really clean?" Ultimately, children will learn to provide feedback to themselves, but this takes much practice and experience. Avoid comparisons between children.

 Supporting Children's Social Competence Through Careful Supervision

1. Maintain a global perspective of all people in the environment as well as those closest to you. Observe all children carefully by rapid scanning, being alert to noise and smell. Note all children and adults present before focusing in on the children nearest you. Watch for children having difficulties with materials or other children. Note the needs of other adults as they are engaged in interactions so that you may supply materials or give assistance as needed. Try to avoid daydreaming or other intruding ideas when supervising children as needs arise quickly that require your attention.

SKILLS FOR INFLUENCING CHILDREN'S SOCIAL DEVELOPMENT BY STRUCTURING THE PHYSICAL ENVIRONMENT

2. Situate your body so that you can view the whole space and all of the children. Usually have your back to a wall, a corner, or a boundary. If seated in an area where visibility is limited, stand up occasionally. Reorient when you hear unusual noise or notice unexpected movement.

3. Take action if necessary to protect children. Adjust the blocks if they appear to be unstable. Retrieve a toddler if the child has managed to open a gate and go through. Ask unfamiliar adults if you can help them if they remain in the vicinity of the playground awhile. (The person may or may not be a threat to the children.) If safety is the issue always act without delay. If another adult is closer and is moving into the situation, return to your place, scan the whole area, and continue your activity. If an accident should occur, reassure the other children and continue with the program.

4. Check carefully that all adults and children are present and accounted for during inclement weather drills and fire drills. Count them before you leave the classroom to move to a safer area and when you get there. (When children are frightened, they may hide in a place that makes them feel secure rather than moving with the group.) Regular drills enable children to predict the sequence of events.

5. Modify the use of materials, space, or equipment as needed to support social goals for children. There are only three things you can do: You may add materials, equipment, or space. You may remove or limit materials. You may alter the space in some way.

a. Adding to the environment. Add more dough to the table if it appears that children need more to play successfully. Offer the children an alternative (additional) activity perhaps with sand or water if there is no more dough. Add a "house plan" diagram from a homemaking magazine and suggest they build it if the block area play appears to become disruptive. Either move adjacent furniture a few inches or shift the activity elsewhere if the space appears too congested. (Note: If you add space in one area, you are limiting it by the same amount in an adjacent area.)

b. Removing material from the environment. Remove furnishings to other locations, put materials away, or close cupboards. For example, if children are consistently having conflicts with peers as they throw balls into the basket, provide feedback to them and give a warning. If the inappropriate behavior continues, take the hoop away. This can be done during the session as well as later in the day and is a logical consequence of the children's actions. Remove access to distracting material rather than actually shifting the location. Limit the number of place settings and chairs at each table if children appear to be bumping and shoving at lunch. (Note that another table would need to be added or the eating divided into two sessions so that everyone can be served.)

c. Adjusting the physical environment. Substitute a less complex puzzle for one that is proving too difficult and challenging to a child. Add flour to play dough that is too sticky. Blow up sports balls with insufficient air to make play fun. Simplify an activity using the same materials but different directions so that children who have special needs or who a1re less mature may participate with success. Enhance the complexity to an activity by modifying the directions for children who need more challenge. Alter the pathways of the room to wider, straighter spaces when children who have crutches or walkers are added to the group. Consider both the challenge and the success as you make alterations.

continued

SKILLS FOR INFLUENCING CHILDREN'S SOCIAL DEVELOPMENT BY STRUCTURING THE PHYSICAL ENVIRONMENT—continued

ONLINE COMPANION **Sharing Ideas About Structuring the Physical Environment with Families**

1. Apply structuring strategies to behavioral problems that parents bring to your attention. Structuring the environment to promote appropriate behaviors is applicable to many situations that parents encounter during the child-rearing years. Strategies that are used for children in groups may be modified and applied to family situations. Following are some fairly typical experiences with some structuring possibilities that might make family life more pleasant.

- **Toileting accidents.** Can the child easily walk to the toilet, remove clothing, and get on and off the toilet easily and independently? Do these accidents generally occur at the same time of day or in the same conditions, such as when they are outside? Modify clothing, add a small stool, or monitor the reminders given children.

- **Rough-house-play or noisy interaction in the car.** This behavior is very distracting and potentially dangerous. Family members may add something for the children to do. There are numerous small games that children can play while riding.

- **Sibling fighting or older children hitting younger ones.** This usually occurs when the younger child intrudes on the older child's space or possessions. Parents can clarify which things are personal possessions, which belong to both, and where each is stored. They also can provide opportunities in which either child is free from intrusion.

- **Cleaning up play space.** Principles related to storage and schedules apply here. Children need a warning that play is finished at home as well as school and are able to learn a standard that is acceptable for the

home. Young children should help, and eventually they will learn how to do this if they can see where things are to be placed. Open shelves and plastic containers at home work well.

2. Communicate with family members about any major changes in the child's group membership, room arrangements, daily schedule, or major changes in equipment and furnishings. When parents know about changes in advance, they are able to reassure the child. They are also less likely to experience distress than if they discover the changes all on their own. In child care settings, when older toddlers move from the comfortable room they know into a new group of preschool children, both the children and the parents should be part of this transition. Adding a loft to a kindergarten in the middle of a semester is stressful, although usually it is seen very positively. Usually changes that involve the group are communicated in a newsletter, and changes that involve an individual are communicated in person or on the phone.

3. Tell family members how structuring is used to support the children's appropriate behavior in the group setting. After listening to your ideas parents can adapt them at home. They know that the adults in the program are taking some responsibility to promote acceptable behavior. For example, seating in a classroom often supports friendship. Noting this effect of physical closeness, parents might consider inviting children who live nearby to come to their homes for play. Separating materials for older and younger children is another easily transferable idea.

4. Structure family members' arrival, observation or participation, and dismissal so that they and their children have a successful experience. Some mothers breastfeed their infants in workplace child care programs; therefore, a secluded area and a

SKILLS FOR INFLUENCING CHILDREN'S SOCIAL DEVELOPMENT BY STRUCTURING THE PHYSICAL ENVIRONMENT

chair with armrests are most comfortable. New parents may wish to observe their children, whereas others may want to visit the program for short periods and leave again. Parents who volunteer in grade school may want to observe their child during a session. Regardless of parental needs, professionals should structure these events so that parents, children, and staff are all comfortable with the plan.

Transitions between home and programs are often rushed, hectic, and full of opportunities for adult/child stress or conflict. The physical facility, adjacent parking, traffic problems, and the timing of when children arrive and leave influence how the process should be structured. With plenty of parking, parents may bring children into a building, but with very limited parking or when children leave at the same time, adults may deliver the children to their parent's cars. Each program should follow principles of structuring to minimize the stress and increase the comfort of everyone involved.

 Engaging Family Members in Structuring the Physical Environment

1. Invite parents to participate in events that contribute to the maintenance and beauty of the facility. Periodic yard cleanup days or paint-and-fix days (held for three or four hours, two to four times a year) contribute to the quality of the program at a lower cost than if carried out by contractors or employees. These events are usually done by nonprofit organizations but may also be implemented by public schools or public parks. If carefully structured, adults enjoy themselves and feel very positive about contributing to their child's program.

2. Ask family members to contribute materials or equipment to the program. Paper rolls, fabric scraps, wood scraps, plastic food trays, baby food jars, film canisters, wrapping paper, holiday cards, and many other materials that some people discard can be used by programs for young children. Dress-up clothing, computers, toys in good repair, or surplus household items that might be sold may also be willingly contributed. If you are soliciting contributions, write a very specific request to parents.

- State clearly the acceptable conditions such as "a doll carriage in good working order," "clean baby food jars with the labels removed," or "clean, squeaky baby toys in good condition."
- Accept all contributions with thanks, gracefully and individually. Avoid making an issue of contributions for children whose families were unable to participate.
- Provide a written thank-you for the contribution of items that might be sold so that parents may use the contribution in their income taxes. You do not have to state the dollar value of the gift.

PITFALLS TO AVOID

In structuring the physical environment to enhance children's social development, there are certain pitfalls you should avoid.

Making too many changes at once.   Children need security and predictability. Even though you can think of several major alterations to make, such as altering the daily schedule and rearranging the room, do them gradually. Younger children are more upset than older children by major changes.

Evaluating too soon.   Sometimes, when new materials are added, rooms changed, or schedules altered, you will anticipate an immediate positive result. Young children usually are very active as they refamiliarize themselves with the area. Increased noise and confusion can be expected immediately, with improvements more discernible after three weeks.

Failing to supervise.   Never leave children unattended by an adult. Children may misuse materials usually considered safe. Even if you are just gone for a minute, a situation that could endanger a child may occur at that time. In addition, children may lose interest and behave inappropriately.

Planning inadequately.   Do not initiate major adjustments in the daily schedule or room arrangement on the spur of the moment. Of course, you can add materials, such as plants, books, or toys. But impulsive major changes upset children, especially younger ones. Follow the guidelines. Sketch major furnishings on a floor plan before moving heavy items. If they do not fit, you will have to move them again, thereby increasing your fatigue and frustration.

Adhering rigidly to the plan.   When you have evaluated the situation and it is clear that the plan won't work, either adjust the plan, modify it, or give it up. Sometimes, the very best plans don't work out as anticipated and must be adjusted.

Directing rather than guiding when supervising children.   Occasionally adults are more focused on the product than on the children doing the activity. Therefore, they tend to make all the decisions, establish the standards of what is good enough, and tell children what to do and how to do it at all points. **Directing** is only the best choice when an issue of health or safety is involved. If adults direct too much, they diminish children's autonomy, confidence, and feelings of competence.

Inserting your own alternatives for decisions or contributing too much to children's planning too early.   Adults tend to take over the process of the planning from children by offering too much help too soon. Wait for the children to ask, then review some of their ideas and ask for other ideas. Let them develop and discard unworkable solutions. Approach this knowing that lots of ideas can be considered, even those that are unlikely to work. Taking over undermines children's self-confidence and their trust in you.

Giving unnecessary or over-detailed directions.   Adults tend to give directions when children are already competent to do the task. This may lead to youngsters tuning out the adult. Keep directions simple and direct. When in doubt, ask children if they know how to do the task.

Confusing situations that require setting limits with those that require giving directions.   If a child knows how to do a task or knows the expectations of behavior and chooses not to follow through, then limit-setting is appropriate. Do not give directions repeatedly as a means of trying to achieve compliance; however, if the child does not appear to know how to do the task, give directions. The key here is to judge the child's previous experience and knowledge. For example, a child who is new to the program wanders in the hallway. Perhaps she is lost and needs directions as to where to go. Another child who has been in the program for weeks also wanders in the hallway. This child needs to have clear limits set.

Assuming that a child knows how to do a routine.   Learn to distinguish whether a child does not know how to do something or is refusing to do it. Children do not automatically know how to dress, undress, wash, put away materials, get food in a school cafeteria, or clean cupboards. If you are supervising a child, teach the child how to do a task correctly rather than criticizing the child's best effort. Comments such as "Didn't your mother teach you anything?" "If you can't do it right, don't do it at all" or "Can't you even wipe a table? I'll do it myself" are all inappropriate. Instead, use comments like "You are having a hard time with that. I'll show you how and you can finish it."

Assuming that the observations of support staff are not important.   Support staff members are usually working near the children and can see how they are functioning in an area and with the materials. It is their responsibility to share this information with the group leader who then can work toward more effective planning. If you are the head teacher, encourage support staff to share what they observe and find ways to make this a regular part of the program. If you are in a support role, be observant and share your observations with your head teacher or others in charge.

Assuming that nothing can be done. Sometimes, you may go into a room and assume that the present arrangements cannot be improved. You may not be able to do much, but most spaces can at least be made attractive and can be personalized. When you do not know whether the materials, furnishings, or decorations can be changed, ask someone in authority. Usually, an extra pillow or small table is no major problem. Such things may be available.

Failing to communicate your plans to other adults and to children. When engaging in any aspect of the structuring process, change is involved. This requires communication to all parties. Everything will run more smoothly if adequate preparation of children and adults has been accomplished.

Allowing children complete freedom to choose. No one can do whatever he or she wants to do. There are limits to all things. Children need to collaborate and be involved in decisions, but giving them complete freedom places a burden on them that they are not yet prepared to carry. Children who are given the opportunity to "do anything" may not even be able to generate choices. This complete freedom of choice is stressful for children, and they will become confused and distressed. This distress usually is accompanied by noise and disorder as all the children try to determine if you really mean that they can do anything.

Assuming that family members understand the principles of decision making and know how to structure decisions for their children. Though professionals learn specifics about decision making and can teach this to children, parents may not even think of providing their smallest children with simple choices such as which sock to put on first. Sharing such strategies supports the continuity between home and school.

SUMMARY

The processes of structuring to achieve the goals of social competence were discussed in this chapter. Preparing a physical environment that is efficient and pleasant reduces fatigue and promotes independent behavior in children. Organizing the materials, furnishings, and equipment can minimize interpersonal conflict in the group as well as support safe learning opportunities. Making choices permeates the structuring process and can be taught to even the youngest children. Planning and implementing change that is goal-directed may be time consuming but leads to satisfaction for both children and adults.

General structuring processes were applied specifically to time management in programs for children. Special consideration was given to the importance of predictability and routine for children's sense of security and emotional adjustment to the environment. Transitions are generally unsettling for children but there are strategies to promote appropriate behavior.

Principles of structuring also were applied to the selection, storage, and use of materials and to the arrangement of space. The quality of the environment influences social interaction among children and adults. Skills were described for establishing and changing room arrangements, supervising children, and promoting efficient use of materials. Techniques were presented for adding to or subtracting from the environment as a means to facilitate social interaction.

Finally, skills were described for helping children to become responsible decision makers and participants in the planning process. Suggestions were made to help parents use structuring to support their childrearing practice and to organize opportunities for parents to donate time and materials to the program.

KEY TERMS

activity space	intrusion–seclusion dimension	simple–complex dimension
boundaries	large-group space	small-group space
decision making	learning centers	soft–hard dimension
directing	open–closed dimension	structuring
feedback	private space	transition
high mobility–low mobility	schedules	

DISCUSSION QUESTIONS

1. Describe the structuring process as simply as you can so that someone who does not know the vocabulary would understand.

2. Describe how you would apply the structuring process to the problem of disruptive, noisy, or difficult transitions from free play to a story-listening experience.

3. Why might the standards of order and efficiency differ among similar kinds of programs in different settings?

4. Why do adults involve children in the decision making process? How does it influence their social development?

5. Explain the role of communication between adults who rearrange a room or make major changes in the schedule of the day. Identify various strategies by which ideas can be shared, and situations in which the adult-to-adult communication about structuring might be problematic.

6. Why would a decision rule such as "The job at hand is less important than the child doing it" become widely accepted among professionals and be frequently repeated to professionals in training?

7. Explain how the management of time and of the daily schedule is related to children's social and emotional development. Is it important throughout childhood? Why?

8. Explain the importance of having a private space in programs for groups of children.

9. Select any activity for children and identify all the opportunities for children to make choices in carrying out the activity. Identify alternatives that are unacceptable to you, and state your reasons.

10. Think back over your own childhood and recall instances in which you were denied opportunities to make choices. How did you feel? How did you behave? Did the adults make explanations to you? How did they behave?

11. Write a letter that could be sent to family members asking for materials for the program or asking them to participate in a volunteer workday. Make the letter friendly and inviting, as well as very specific. Exchange your letter with a classmate and discuss the differences and reasons for those differences.

12. Referring to Appendix A, NAEYC Code of Ethical Conduct, determine which of the situations listed here would constitute an ethical problem and identify the principles and ideals that influence your thinking.

    a. Showing up 20 minutes after you were expected without calling in advance in a program with young children.

    b. Failing to mention that the gate to the fenced playground is broken.

    c. Letting a preschool child carry a pot of very hot water.

    d. Scooping the pieces of many sets of materials together and dumping them in one container to make cleanup faster.

    e. Failing to have images of adults and children of all racial groups and some disabling conditions available to children.

    f. Moving a toddler from the infant/toddler room to a preschool room without informing the parent or preparing the child.

    g. Placing the cooking project on a table that is across the pathway where children walk and using an extension cord to connect the hot plate.

FIELD ASSIGNMENTS

1. Observe a professional working with children. Describe incidents in which children were offered a choice. Write how this choice was worded or how it was implemented. Describe incidents of children who are managing their own activity. What aspects of the situation or setting enable the children to act on their own with minimal support? Write out any errors you think the adult made and what corrections might be possible.

2. Supervise a group of children doing a simple activity. Later, write out a description of how you checked, adjusted the environment, and guided the children. Evaluate your own performance.

3. Observe any program for children and note the daily schedule as posted. Compare it to what actually happened. What adjustments were made and why? How did the children know when to make a transition? Describe in detail the transitions you observed, identifying what adults said and did and how children responded.

4. Make a visit to an early childhood program. Draw a detailed floor plan of one of the rooms. List the strengths and weaknesses of the room arrangement in relation to children's social development. Suggest improvements in the physical layout.

Chapter 10

FOSTERING SELF-DISCIPLINE IN CHILDREN: COMMUNICATING EXPECTATIONS AND RULES

OBJECTIVES

On completion of this chapter, you should be able to describe:

- What self-discipline is and how it comes about.

- How development and experience influence self-discipline in children.

- How different adult guidance styles affect children's personality and behavior.

- What personal messages are and when to use them.

- Guidelines for creating personal messages.

- Strategies for communicating with families about childhood expectations and rules.

- Pitfalls to avoid when using personal messages.

Cross at the light.

Catch your sneeze in your sleeve.

Pet the puppy gently.

Wait your turn.

These are typical expectations that children encounter growing up. Although no one standard of behavior is universal, all societies have behavior codes to keep people safe and to help them get along (Berns, 2006). Adults have the primary responsibility for teaching children how to act in ways that are acceptable to the community and culture in which they live. People often refer to this as teaching children to behave. Socialization is another term we use to describe this process. Adults socialize children to carry out desirable actions like sharing, answering politely, and telling the truth. They also socialize children to avoid inappropriate behaviors such as shoving, tattling, spitting on the sidewalk, or taking all the chocolate-covered cherries for themselves. Lessons like these touch on every aspect of social competence: values, culture, self-identity, interpersonal skills, decision making, and self-regulation.

How well children learn to adapt their behavior to societal expectations influences how well they function at home, at the center, in school, and in the community at large. Initially, we expect adults to play a major role in teaching children right from wrong. Eventually, however, we hope children will figure things out on their own and regulate their actions appropriately. In other words, we hope children will become self-disciplined.

WHAT IS SELF-DISCIPLINE?

In this situation, both boys were tempted to disregard the sign. Casey gave in to that temptation because

Casey and William, both third-graders, rush to get to a ball game at the Y. On the way, they come to a huge patch of ground that has been freshly seeded and covered with straw. A large sign announces, "PLEASE STAY OFF THE GRASS." Casey looks around. He's anxious to get to the game, but doesn't want to get in trouble for disobeying a rule. Seeing no adults in sight, he quickly cuts across the newly seeded area.

William is in a hurry too. He also notices that no one is around, but reasons that stepping on the newly planted grass could damage it. Although he is tempted to take the shortcut across the seeds, he suppresses the impulse and walks around, even though it takes a little more time.

no one was there to enforce the rule or to help him choose a better response. His reasoning and actions demonstrated his inability to practice self-regulation. William, on the other hand, controlled his desire to dash across the new grass. He made a decision to go around, based on his personal sense of what was right, not because his actions were being monitored by anyone else. This kind of thinking and behaving illustrates self-discipline.

As you can see, children who are self-disciplined judge what is right and what is wrong based on reasoning, concern for others, and an understanding of acceptable and unacceptable conduct. Such children do not rely on someone else to make them do the right thing or to forbid them from behaving inappropriately.

Instead, they consider other people's needs and feelings while simultaneously adapting their actions to fit the rules of society (Newman & Newman, 2003). This involves initiating certain behaviors and inhibiting others. Consequently, self-disciplined children carry out positive social interactions and implement constructive social plans without having to be told they must. They also resist temptation, curb negative impulses, and delay gratification independent of supervision (Bronson, 2000; Mischel, 1996). Refer to Table 10-1 for examples.

How Self-Discipline Evolves

Self-discipline emerges gradually throughout childhood in an "outside" to "inside" developmental process (Marion, 2007). Initially, children depend on others to regulate their behavior for them. With time and practice, they eventually demonstrate greater degrees of self-regulation. In this text, we describe this sequence as advancing from an amoral orientation to internalization.

Amoral Orientation (No Regulation)

Babies have no concept of right or wrong; they are **amoral**. That is, they are *not able* to make ethical judgments about their actions or consciously control their behavior in response to moral demands. For instance, baby Leroy reaches for his mother's glasses as they sparkle close by. He does not think about the potential pain he might cause her if he is successful in pulling them off. Nor can he end his investigation merely because his mother frowns or warns him to stop. Leroy has not yet learned to interpret these parental behaviors or to adjust his actions in response.

Gradually, through maturation and experience, this complete lack of self-monitoring begins

Table 10-1 Signs of Self-Discipline

BEHAVIOR	EXAMPLES
Children carry out positive social interactions	Walter comforts Latosha who is sad over missing her mom.
	Michael shares his headphones with a newcomer to the listening center.
Children implement constructive social plans	Marcus wants a turn with the watercolors. He figures out a strategy for getting some, such as trading chalk for paint, and then tries bargaining with another child to achieve his goal.
	Courtney recognizes that Graham is struggling to carry a dozen hula hoops down to the gym. She helps Graham by taking several hoops from his arms and walking with him downstairs.
Children resist temptation	Woo-Jin walks all the way over to the trash can to dispose of her sandwich wrapper, although she is tempted simply to drop the crumpled paper on the ground.
	Juan turns in a change purse he found in the hallway, even though he is tempted to keep it for himself.
Children curb negative impulses	Ruben suppresses the urge to strike out in anger when Heather accidentally bumps into him in the hallway.
	LaRonda refrains from teasing Richard about the "awful" haircut he got over the weekend.
Children delay gratification	Carla waits for Tricia to finish talking to the scout leader before announcing that she is going to Disney World.
	Lionel postpones taking another brownie until everyone gets one.

to change. Most toddlers and young preschoolers learn to respond to external cues supplied by parents, caregivers, and teachers to guide their actions. This type of regulation is called **adherence**.

Adherence (External Regulation)

Adherence is the most superficial degree of self-discipline and occurs when people rely on others to monitor their actions for them. Early in life, children need physical assistance in learning how to behave appropriately. Here are some examples:

Baby Leroy's mother puts her glasses beyond the child's reach. Leroy can no longer pull at them.

Three-year-old Nary is running in the classroom. The teacher takes her hand and walks with her to the block area, helping her to slow down.

The playground supervisor separates two kindergartners who are pushing to get on the swing next. The children stop pushing.

Gradually, children also learn to respond to verbal cues about what to do and what not to do. For example:

When Gary, age 4, takes three cookies at snack, the provider says, "Remember each person may have two cookies to start." Gary puts one cookie back.

When Nary runs in the classroom, the teacher reminds her to walk. Nary slows down.

The teacher's aide provides Morris with a script he can use to tell another child he wants a turn on the swing instead of pushing. Morris says, "Can I go next?"

In each of these situations, adults provided controls children were unable to supply completely on their own.

Another form of adherence occurs when people follow a rule or expectation simply to gain a reward or to avoid negative consequences (Hoffman, 1988; Kohlberg, 1976; Shaffer & Kipp, 2006).

For instance, 3-year old Hannah has had numerous "sharing lessons" in her short lifetime. She has been rewarded with smiles and praise when she voluntarily hands a toy to a peer or sibling and she has experienced the negative consequences of being admonished for failing to share with playmates. Based on episodes like these, Hannah is slowly beginning to differentiate desirable and undesirable behaviors. This is an important first step on the road to self-discipline. However, rewards and consequences alone do not provide enough information for Hanna to acquire all the reasoning she will need for self-regulation. At adherence, she has no real understanding of why sharing is good; she simply knows it is expected. When she does share it is based on her own self-interests, not empathy for another child. As a result, Hanna is most likely to share when an adult is present. However, if mom or the teacher is out of sight, Hanna has no rationale of her own for sharing, and may resort to hitting or grabbing to protect her toys or get what she wants (Turiel, 1998). This is because children at adherence need constant support and supervision to behave appropriately.

Identification (Shared Regulation)

A more advanced degree of self-discipline occurs when children adopt certain codes of behavior so they can be like someone they admire. Through the process of **identification,** children imitate the conduct, attitudes, and values of the important people in their lives (Kohlberg, 1976; Charlesworth, 2008; Putman, 1996). Children's compliance with certain expectations may also be a strategy for establishing or preserving satisfying relationships with those persons.

Identification happens for several reasons. (Kagan, 1971). First, children want to be like the people they revere. For instance, Fiona admires her swimming coach and wants to follow in her footsteps. Second, children assume they are like the model. Fiona believes that she and her swimming coach share many traits in common—a drive to win, a sense of fair play, and sensitivity to others. Other people affirm this identification with comments such as, "I can tell you're one of Coach Zimmer's girls. You know how to give it your all." Third, children experience emotions similar to those they observe in the model. In this case, when the coach

These children identify with their teacher and try to clean the brushes just like she showed them.

expresses sadness over the death of her dog, Fiona shares the coach's grief, not for a pet she didn't know, but because the coach's sadness makes her feel sad too. Finally, children act like the people they admire. They adopt their mannerisms, their words, and their ways of behaving. Typically children identify with parents or other family members. Helping professionals in formal group settings are also sources of identification. In every case, the persons with whom youngsters identify are nurturing, powerful people—usually adults or older children (Howoritz, Darling-Hammond & Bransford 2005; Berk, 2006).

Identification is important to children's development. It moves them beyond the simple formula of rewards and punishments and provides them with many of the ideas and standards they will carry with them into adulthood. However, children who share things as a result of identification use sharing as a way to further their own aims—confirming their similarity to an admired person who advocates sharing or pleasing that person through their actions. They still do not recognize the inherent fairness in sharing or the real needs of the person to whom they lend something briefly. Also, children governed by identification rely on second-guessing how someone else might behave in a given situation. If they have never seen the model in a similar circumstance, children may not know what to do and may lack the means to figure it out on their own.

Internalization (Internal Regulation)

Internalization is the most advanced degree of self-discipline. When people treat certain expectations as logical extensions of their own beliefs and personal values, we say they have internalized those expectations (Kochanska, 1993; Shaffer, 2005). It is this internal code that guides their actions from one circumstance to another. The course of action they choose in each situation is aimed at avoiding self-condemnation rather than acquiring external rewards or gaining approval from others. People whose behaviors fall within the internalization category understand the reasons behind certain behavior standards and feel a moral commitment to act in accordance with those standards. They also recognize how specific actions fit into larger concepts such as justice, honesty, and equity. Individuals who reason according to internalized beliefs take into account the impact their behavior will have on others. For instance, Mariah, who has internalized the value of sharing, will offer to give another child some of her crayons, not because the teacher said so or because anyone else is watching, but because sharing seems the appropriate thing to do. Engaging in this positive action makes Mariah feel good. She enjoys knowing another child will have a chance to draw too.

Once children have internalized an expectation, they have a guide for how to behave appropriately in all kinds of circumstances, even unfamiliar ones. Understanding the reasons for certain rules gives children the ability to weigh the pros and cons of alternate actions and to choose behaviors that match their ideals. This eliminates the need for constant supervision. Children can be depended on to regulate their own behavior. Most importantly, internalized behaviors are long lasting. Children who adopt beliefs in justice, honesty, or fairness as their own will abide by those ideals long after their contacts with certain adults are over and in spite of temptation or the opportunity to break the rule without being discovered (Newman & Newman, 2003). Thus, Mariah may eventually adopt additional prosocial behaviors beyond sharing (such as cooperating or comforting) because helping others feels like the "right" thing to do.

Internalization should not be confused with unquestioning adoption of others' rules and practices (Turiel, 1998). At times, remaining true to a particular ideal such as justice or honesty may prompt people to go against current conventions or to question some behavior expectations advocated by elders or significant peers. This is exemplified by a child who refuses to discriminate against a classmate based on the child's gender, even though such actions are advocated by some important people in the child's world. True internalization, therefore, requires people to think for themselves and to regulate their actions in accordance with the ideals they value. When this happens, we can truly say a person is demonstrating self-discipline.

Figure 10-1 provides a summary of the amoral, adherence, identification, and internalization orientations to self-discipline just described.

Internalization evolves gradually. It takes many years for children to develop an internalized code of conduct. Consequently, preschoolers show lesser degrees of self-discipline than do children in the upper elementary grades. Although toddlers are able to comply with simple requests and commands, they mostly rely on external controls to guide their actions. As children form relationships with nurturing

Figure 10-1 Orientations to self-discipline.

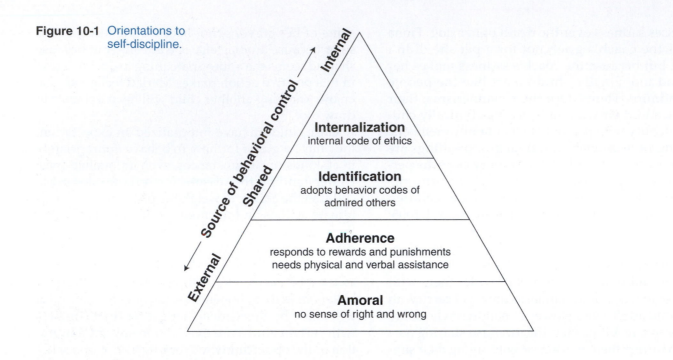

adults, identification gradually becomes a more significant factor in what motivates children to behave in certain ways. With time (there is no way to predict exactly how much), increasing numbers of children demonstrate internalization of commonly held rules, such as taking turns at the snack table or walking in the hallway. By the later elementary years, children's capacities for self-regulation have expanded greatly, and they are better able to monitor their own actions in both typical and novel situations (Bugental & Goodnow, 1998; National Research Council and the Institute of Medicine, 2000).

Children progress toward self-discipline at varying rates and in varying degrees. Even though we can expect children to demonstrate increased self-discipline as they mature, they do not move from an amoral orientation to higher levels of conduct according to a strict age-related timetable. Research supports the notion of a developmental progression but also indicates that children achieve greater self-discipline at rates and in degrees that vary from child to child (Kochanska, 1997; Metcalfe & Mischel, 1999; Goleman, 2006). For instance, 4-year-old Lucille may require physical support in order to share, while Sandra, also 4 years of age, may find verbal reminders enough to accomplish this aim. It may takes months or even years before Carl learns to curb his impulse to strike out at someone who teases him, whereas Joseph may grasp this notion much sooner. In young children, such behavioral differences are common. This means the children you encounter will vary widely in their progress toward self-discipline.

DEVELOPMENTAL PROCESSES THAT INFLUENCE SELF-DISCIPLINE

There are many reasons why children's capacity for self-discipline increases with age. The most notable of these are changes in children's emotional development, cognitive development, language development, and memory skills.

Emotional Development

Two emotions that strongly contribute to self-discipline are guilt and empathy (Eisenberg & Fabes, 1998; Kochanska, Gross, Lin & Nichols., 2002). **Guilt** feelings warn children that a current or planned action is undesirable. Guilt also prompts regret for past misdeeds.

Empathy, or feeling a little of what another person feels, conveys the opposite message. Empathy causes children to initiate positive actions in response to emotional situations. Children as young as 3 years old are capable of both guilt and empathy (Hoffman, 2000; Zahn-Waxler & Robinson, 1995). However, these emotions are aroused by different events for younger and older children.

Guilt.   The situations that arouse guilt evolve from simple, concrete incidents in toddlerhood to abstract, complex situations in later adolescence (Baumeister, 1998; Williams & Bybee, 1994: Mills, 2005). Initially, children feel guilty over their transgressions—actions that violate known rules and the expectations of others.

Spilling their milk, damaging a toy while using it, or stealing something from a classmate are examples of the actions children might feel guilty about during the early childhood period. In the later elementary years, children report feeling guilty when their inaction leads to distress for others. Thus, Thomas, a fifth grader, might feel guilty when classmates tease a child on the playground and he does nothing to stop it. By middle school an increasing number of children report feeling guilty over neglecting responsibilities, such as forgetting to let the dog out before leaving for school or failing to attain ideals they have set for themselves like making the track team or achieving a certain grade-point average (Hoffman, 1990). As children mature, the main things that make people feel guilty are related to personal standards, rather than failing to satisfy other people's expectations. This gradual shift in focus contributes to the inner controls needed for self-regulation.

Empathy.   The beginnings of empathy are also present early in life (Hoffman, 2000; Goleman, 2006). Empathic feelings occur when children identify with another person's emotions and feel those emotions themselves.

Infants express empathy to other children by simply mimicking their distress. For instance, many babies cry upon hearing or seeing the cries of other babies. Between 1 and 2 years of age, infants' global reactions grow into more genuine feelings of concern for a particular person. At this age, children also recognize that some action is required as part of their response. This is demonstrated when one toddler pats another who is crying as a result of falling down. In the later preschool and early elementary years, children make more objective assessments of other people's distress and needs (Miller, Partch, Solomon & Hepworth, 1995). They begin to recognize emotional reactions different from their own, and they become more adept at responding in a variety of ways to provide comfort and

Ramone mirrors Jemma's delight in spinning the dial. This is an example of empathy.

support. By the time children reach the age of 10 to 12 years, they demonstrate empathy for people with whom they do not interact directly—the homeless, the disabled, the victims of a disaster. This increased sensitivity to the plight of others is a contributing factor in children's development of self-discipline.

Cognitive Development

Children's ability to distinguish between appropriate and inappropriate behavior evolves in conjunction with changes in their cognitive powers. As children's cognitive capacities expand so does their ability to regulate their behavior internally. These evolving capabilities are influenced by *changing notions of right and wrong,* the degree to which children *comprehend the perspective of other persons* and the cognitive characteristics of *centration and irreversibility.*

Children's notions of right and wrong. In toddlerhood, children tend to use rewards and punishments as their primary criteria for figuring out if their actions or those of another child are right or wrong. They determine that sharing is "good" when such actions are praised and they find out that writing in picture books is "wrong" when they are corrected for such behavior. As these lessons unfold, children also discover that not all transgressions are treated equally (Nucci & Wever, 1995). By 3 and 4 years of age, children realize that punching your sister elicits a much stronger negative reaction from adults than does something like coming to the table with dirty hands. As a result of many such experiences, preschoolers begin to make distinctions between **moral violations** (lying, stealing, hurting others) and **social-conventional infractions** (poor table manners, greeting someone improperly, speaking rudely, and other problems regarding social etiquette; Turiel, 1998; Yan & Smetna, 2003). By the time they reach kindergarten age, children classify actions as "very wrong" if they result in physical harm to people or property (hitting people or breaking things) or if they violate people's rights such as someone missing a turn or not getting an equal share of something (Tisak & Block, 1990). On the other hand, children categorize actions that disrupt the social order of the group, such as forgetting to say "please" or not putting toys away as "not very wrong." In both cases, children's focus is on the here and now, and they do not routinely think about how their current actions might impact people or property in the future.

Older children (ages 8 and up) use more sophisticated reasoning in thinking about rules and expectations. They expand their definitions of hurtful behavior beyond physical actions to include psychological impacts such as hurting people's feelings, betraying secrets, or violating another person's trust. They recognize the need for maintaining some form of social order to protect the rights of individuals and the group. Children at this stage also take into account long-term as well as immediate outcomes in judging if an action is right or wrong. Thus, fourth graders recognize that cheating at a game may yield a short-term positive result such as winning, but ultimately lead to dishonor for yourself and for your team, making cheating a "wrong" choice.

Refer to Figure 10-2 to see how children's thinking about right and wrong relates to their day-to-day behavior.

Children's perspective-taking abilities. To interact effectively with others and to make accurate judgments about what actions would be right or wrong in particular situations, children must understand what other people think, feel, or know. Called **perspective-taking,** this capacity is not fully developed in young children. Youngsters 5 years of age and younger often have difficulty putting themselves in another person's shoes. That dilemma is a result of being unable, rather than unwilling, to comprehend or predict other people's thoughts (Berkowitz, 2002; Berk, 2006).

Thinking and Doing are Not the Same!

At circle time, Ms. Wilson asks a group of 3-year-olds, "Is it okay to hit people to get what you want?" The children answer in chorus, "NO!" Ms. Wilson makes another query. "Is it a good idea to share?" In unison, the whole group shouts, "YES!" The children clap their hands in approval.

Conversations like this show that even very young children recognize the desirability of moral standards such as human welfare, justice, and preserving people's rights. In fact, these are moral orientations children share worldwide (Turiel, 1998; Neff & Helwig, 2002). Yet, early in life, knowing what is right and doing what is right are not synonymous. Young children are impulsive; their actions are not always guided by rational thought. What is easy for them to state in the relaxed atmosphere of circle time is quickly forgotten in the heat of an action-filled encounter. This makes the link between moral thinking and moral action weak for preschoolers and children in the early elementary years. As children mature and gain the developmental understandings and skills described in this chapter, the tie between thinking right and doing right becomes much stronger.

Figure 10-2 The link between moral thinking and moral behavior.

Young children may have trouble recognizing other peoples' viewpoints, especially when those views conflict with their own. They erroneously assume that their interpretation of events is universal. Frequently, such differences must be brought to children's attention before they begin to recognize that their perspective is not shared. This lack of skill is sometimes called egocentrism and refers to the challenge children have in recognizing differing points of view.

Youngsters between 6 and 8 years of age are more likely to realize that someone else's interpretation of a situation may be different from their own. However, they cannot always recognize what the differences are without assistance. Even when differences are pointed out to them, children this age may assume that variations in perspective have occurred simply because each person has different information or is in a different situation. It is not unusual for youngsters this age to go to great lengths trying to convince others of the validity of their view. The seemingly endless arguments and rationales they generate are an outgrowth of their immature reasoning, not tactics deliberately aimed at frustrating you or someone else they are trying to persuade to see the situation exactly as they do.

Nine- and 10-year-olds recognize that their own thoughts and the thoughts of another person are different and may even be contradictory. They understand that two people can react to the same circumstance in opposite ways or that the same person can have a mixed reaction. However, they tend to think about their own view and other people's views alternately, making it hard for them to address multiple perspectives within the same situation on their own.

Eleven- and 12-year-olds are able to differentiate their own perspective from that of other people and are able to consider the two perspectives simultaneously. They can also speculate about what other people currently are thinking or what they might think in the future. These abilities help children determine how to behave in an increasingly varied number of situations.

Centration influences children's social conduct. Throughout early childhood, children tend to direct their attention to one primary attribute of a situation, ignoring most others (Charlesworth, 2008). This phenomenon, known as **centration**, restricts children's ability to see the big picture and to generate alternate solutions to problems they

encounter. Thus, young children have a limited rather than comprehensive perception of events. Centration causes them to overlook important details relevant to their actions and the behavior of others and to persist in using a singular approach to achieve their aims. This explains why youngsters may try the same unsuccessful strategy repeatedly and why they have difficulty shifting their attention from one facet of an interaction ("She knocked over my blocks" or "He has all the gold glitter paint") to another ("She was trying to help me stack the blocks higher" or "There are several other colors of glitter paint from which to choose").

Even when youngsters recognize that actions such as grabbing or striking are inappropriate, they may be unable to generate suitable alternate behaviors at the moment such thinking is needed. The younger the child, the more this is so. Likewise, the more emotional the situation is for the child, the more difficult it is for him or her to think about other approaches. Decentering occurs only gradually, as children are confronted with multiple perceptions and methods of resolution. Adults enhance the process when they point out options to children and when they help youngsters brainstorm suitable alternatives as relevant circumstances arise (Kostelnik, Soderman & Whiren, 2007). Such supports continue to be helpful well into adolescence.

Irreversibility affects children's efforts to comply. Toddlers and preschoolers do not routinely mentally reverse actions they initiate physically (Berk, 2006). In other words, their thinking is irreversible. This means they are not proficient at readily thinking of an opposite action for something they are actually doing. If they are pushing, it is hard for them to pull instead; if they are reaching for something, it's a challenge to draw back. Young children also have difficulty spontaneously interrupting an ongoing behavior. For example, if a child is in the act of hitting, she might complete the hitting action before reversing it either by taking her hand away or dropping it to her side.

> *Jennifer, a 3-year-old, was busy gluing dry leaves to her collage. In her effort to get to the bottom of the glue bottle, she tipped it upside down, and the glue ran all over. The caregiver said, "Don't tip the bottle." Jennifer continued gluing and the glue kept on dripping.*

When the adult called out her warning, she assumed Jennifer knew how to reverse tipping the bottle. To the adult, it was obvious that returning the jar to an upright position was the reverse of holding it upside down. However, she should not have anticipated that Jennifer would know this. Young children have not had enough experience to picture in their minds how to transpose a physical action. For this reason adults must help preschoolers reverse inappropriate acts by showing them or telling them how to do it. The same holds true for older children in unfamiliar situations. For instance, elementary-aged children are better able to halt or slow down if an adult says, "Don't run in the hall"; they are less likely to respond successfully in a situation that is new to them or that takes place in unfamiliar surroundings.

Language and Memory Development

Not only is the capacity for self-discipline affected by children's emotional development and cognitive capabilities, but language, private speech, and memory play roles in the process too.

Language. The phenomenal rate of language acquisition during the childhood years plays a major role in children's development of internal behavior controls. This is because language contributes to children's understanding of why rules are made and gives them more tools for attaining their goals in socially acceptable ways. By the time they are 3 years old most children have command of a well-developed receptive vocabulary and the ability to express their basic needs. However, they are not always successful at responding to verbal directions or at telling others what they want.

As a result, it is not unusual for preschoolers to resort to physical actions to communicate. They may grab, jerk away, fail to respond, push, or hit rather than use words to express themselves. Gradually, children learn to use language more effectively.

They become more successful at telling others what they want and better equipped to understand and respond to the verbal instructions, requests, explanations, and reasoning used by others as guides for behavior (Marion, 2007; Schultz, 2003). Consequently, they find words more satisfactory and precise to communicate. When this occurs, their physical demonstrations become less frequent and intense.

Private speech. Children also use **private speech** as a means for self-regulation (Winsler, De Leon, Wallace, Carlton & Wilson-Quale, 2003; Mischel, 1996). That is, they talk out loud to themselves as a way to reduce frustration, postpone rewards, or remind themselves of rules. While putting on her shoes and socks, Molly says to herself in a singsong voice, "One shoe, one sock, one foot." Olga sits down in the writing center and says to no one in particular, "Hmmm, what do I need? I know: paper, pens, and tape." When Abdul begins losing patience putting a model together, he quietly repeats to himself, "Slow down, take your time. You'll get it." This kind of talk is common in early and middle childhood, accounting for 20 to 60% of what children say (Kochanska, 1993; Papalia, Olds & Feldman, 2006). The normal developmental progression is for toddlers and 3-year-olds to repeat audible rhythmic sounds. Children ages 4 to 7 or 8 years "think out loud" in conjunction with their actions. They generate whole phrases to plan strategies and monitor their actions. Children in the later elementary years mutter single words in barely discernable tones (Frauenglass & Diaz, Winsler, et al., 2003). Studies of

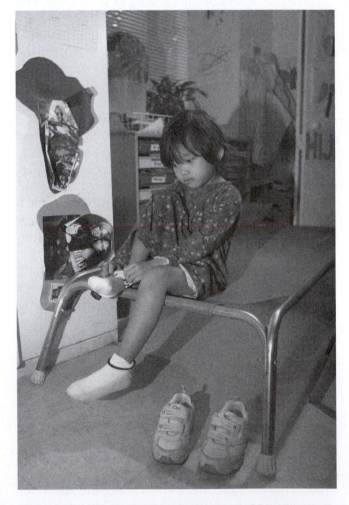

Mia uses private speech to remind herself of how to put on her socks and shoes.

children's behavior in problem solving situations indicate that they rely on private speech most when a task is difficult. Moreover, children's performance typically improves following the self-instruction they provide themselves (Bailey & Brookes, 2003; Winsler, et al., 2003). In adolescence, audible private speech becomes the silent, inner speech that people use throughout their lives to organize and regulate day-to-day activities. Although private speech is a naturally occurring phenomenon, it appears that children also can be taught to use "self-talk" as a deliberate means for self-regulation.

Memory skills.   Memory is another variable that influences self-discipline. Although scientists have not yet determined whether memory actually increases from one year to the next, it does seem that as children grow older, they become better able to use the information they have stored in their memory as a resource

for determining future behavior. Consequently, they become less dependent on others to show or tell them how to respond to each new situation. Instead, they use remembered information to guide their actions (Coie & Dodge, 1998; Lucariello, 1998). This means helping professionals working with children in formal group settings should expect that children will periodically "forget" the rules. Also, youngsters may be unsure of how to respond in unfamiliar circumstances. From toddlerhood through 8 to 9 years of age, children often need frequent reminders about rules and procedures and clear explanations about what to expect when routines change or new activities are introduced.

Older children benefit from periodic reviews of the rules, but are better able to remember them without continual adult support. See Figure 10-3 for a summary of all the developmental influences just discussed.

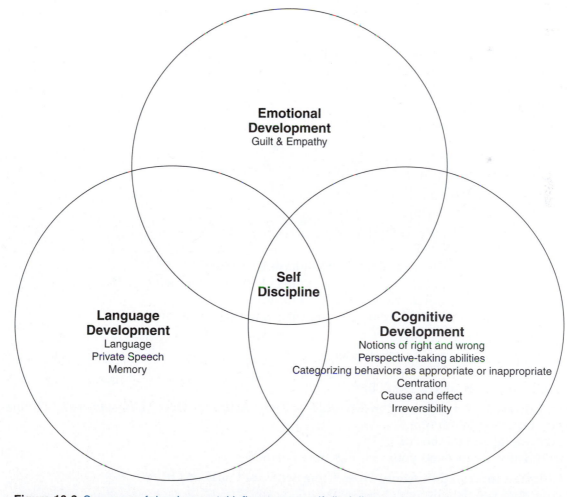

Figure 10-3 Summary of developmental influences on self-discipline.

Source: Adapted from "Current Patterns of Parental Authority," by D. Baumrind, 1971, Developmental Psychology Monographs, 4, no. 1, pt. 2; and Social and Personality Development, by D. R. Shaffer, 2005, Pacific Grove, CA: Brooks/Cole Publishing Co.

HOW EXPERIENCE INFLUENCES SELF-DISCIPLINE

Because most young people experience the developmental changes just discussed and thus acquire some of the basics for internalization, the reasons why they vary in their compliance with societal expectations can best be attributed to differences in experiences. Children learn the rules of society from others through direct instruction, observation, reinforcement and negative consequences, and attribution (Landy, 2002). Infants and preschoolers are chiefly responsive to parents and other adults with whom they have a positive relationship; grade-school children are also influenced by peers.

Direct Instruction

As mentioned earlier in this chapter, adults regulate children's behavior using physical and verbal controls. These are forms of **direct instruction**. At first, adults rely mainly on bodily intervention to keep youngsters safe and help them get along. They separate squabbling siblings, remove dangerous objects from reach, extract forbidden items from children's grasp, and restrain them from dashing across busy streets. These actions usually are accompanied by brief verbal commands such as "Stop," "No," "Give me that," or "Wait for me." Gradually, physical interventions give way to greater reliance on verbal directions and warnings, to which children become increasingly responsive. Typical adult instructions usually fall into the categories outlined in Table 10-2. Verbal instructions are the quickest way to let children know what the appropriate, inappropriate, and alternate behaviors are. They are particularly effective when combined with modeling.

Table 10-2 Modes of Adult Instruction

Telling Children What Is Right and What Is Wrong
"It hurts the cat when you pull her tail."
"Share your toys."
"Stealing is bad."

Informing Children of Expected Standards
"Pet the cat gently."
"Put your toys away."
"Give Grandma a kiss."

Restricting Certain Behaviors
"Five more minutes on the swing."
"Put on a smock before you start painting."
"Use this tissue, not your sleeve."

Advising Children About How to Meet the Standards They Set
"You could stack all the big plates on one side and the little plates on the other, like this."
"You could use the ball together or you could take turns."
"If you think about something else, that will make the waiting go faster."

Redirecting Children's Behavior
"Go outdoors. Don't bounce that ball inside."
"That spoon is too big. Try this one."
"You can tell him you're angry. Don't bite."

Providing Children with Information About How Their Actions Affect Themselves and Others
"He hit you because you hit him."
"Every time you tease her, she cries."
"Mr. Martin really appreciated your helping him rake the leaves."

Giving Children Information About How Their Behavior Looks to Others
"Comb your hair. People will think I don't take good care of you."
"When you don't say 'Hi' back, he thinks you don't like him."
"When you forget to say 'Thank you,' people don't know you appreciated what they did."

Modeling

Adults **model** a code of conduct through their own actions (Zahn-Waxler & Robinson, 1995; Garbarino, 2006). Returning library books on time, helping an injured animal, or resisting the urge to eat a candy bar before supper all convey messages to children about desirable behaviors.

Setting a good example is an important way of teaching children right from wrong. However, although it is true that children imitate much of what they see, modeling is most effective when the model's behavior is obvious to children. This means youngsters are best able to imitate a model with whom they can interact or whose behavior is pointed out to them (Shaffer & Kipp, 2006). This helps children to recognize important details that they might otherwise not notice. Thus if the object is to demonstrate gentle handling of animals, it is best to work directly with the child and demonstrate the task. It is also useful to say, "See, I'm picking up the chicks very gently so I don't hurt them or crush their feathers. Look at how loosely I'm bending my fingers." Simply showing children the proper procedure without direct explanation may not cause them to imitate the appropriate behavior themselves at a later time.

Verbal descriptions of modeled behaviors are especially valuable when the adult hopes children will recognize that a person they are watching is resisting temptation or delaying gratification (Hetherington, Parke, Gauvin, & Otis-Locke, 2005). Children may not recognize what the person is doing unless told. Statements such as the following assist children in recognizing someone's efforts to delay gratification: "Raymond really wants to use the unabridged dictionary, even though the college dictionary is available now. He has decided to wait until Karen has finished with it so he can use it next." Children also benefit when an adult model clearly states a rule he or she is following and the rationale for not committing a certain act. For example, explaining that the guinea pigs are eating and that it is important to let them finish before picking them up illustrates this technique. Children who watch a model delay action and understand what they are seeing are better able to postpone gratification in subsequent situations themselves (Bandura, 1991).

Unfortunately, modeling not only accentuates positive actions; children also learn from the negative models they observe. For instance, children who see others act aggressively with no negative consequences sometimes imitate those same aggressive behaviors in future interactions.

Reinforcement and Negative Consequences

In addition to instructing children about how to act and modeling particular behaviors themselves, adults reinforce desirable deeds and penalize those they consider unacceptable. **Reinforcement** involves providing some consequence to a behavior that increases the likelihood the child will repeat that behavior in similar situations. **Negative consequences** are ones that reduce the probability of a particular behavior being repeated. Although the principles of reinforcement and negative consequences are relatively straightforward, appropriate use is complex. For this reason, Chapter 11 is devoted entirely to this subject. For now, it is important merely to recognize that children experience both reinforcement and negative consequences as a result of their behavior and that these play a major role in their acquisition of self-discipline.

Integrating Development and Experience

The individual interactions children experience each day help them create a unique mental map of the social environment (Coie & Dodge, 1998; Goleman, 2006). That is, children mentally chart their experiences and make note of which behaviors make them feel guilty, which make them feel good, which are rewarded, and which are not, and under what circumstances those conditions apply. Gradually, this map grows in breadth and complexity. Over time, children catalogue a growing number of experiences and make finer discriminations among events. They draw on information gleaned from these episodes to fit their behavior to situational demands rather than depending on other people to direct them at that moment. In addition, their increased developmental competence enables them to interpret more accurately the cues they receive and to envision more varied responses to those cues. As a result, they become progressively more successful in monitoring their own behavior.

Gradually, peers also contribute to children's understanding of what constitutes desirable and undesirable behavior. The combined experiences with adults and age-mates lead to greater self-discipline. Interactions with adults teach children about obligations, responsibility, and respect; peer relations give children firsthand experience with cooperation and justice (Shaffer & Kipp, 2006). This difference in perspective is a result of children's general interpretation that positive behavior with adults means obedience, and positive behavior with peers involves reciprocal actions such as sharing or taking turns. This chapter

Adults help children learn about obligations, responsibilities, and respect in their daily interactions with peers.

and the next concentrate on the adult's role in helping children achieve self-discipline. Chapter 8 describes how peers influence this process as well.

HOW ADULT BEHAVIOR AFFECTS CHILDREN'S BEHAVIOR

All adults rely on instruction, modeling, rewards and negative consequences to teach children how to behave. However, the combination of techniques they use and the way in which they apply them differ. Such variations have been the subject of research for the past four decades. It has been found that the blend of socialization strategies parents and helping professionals adopt has a major influence on children's personality development and whether children follow rules because of adherence, identification, or internalization. Both short-term and long-range effects have been noted (Kochanska et al., 2002; Kuczynski & Kochanska, 1995). Although most research has focused on the parent–child relationship, other adult–child interactions, including ones between children and teachers or other helping professionals, have been examined. Much of this work has yielded similar results.

In a series of landmark studies, researchers identified four common adult discipline styles—authoritarian, permissive, uninvolved, and authoritative (Baumrind, 1967, 1973, 1991; Maccoby & Martin, 1983). These four styles continue to be the standard for comparison today (Hetherington, Parke, Gauvin, & Otis-Locke, 2005). Each is characterized by particular adult attitudes and practices related to the dimensions of control, maturity demands, communication, and nurturance.

Control refers to the manner and degree to which adults enforce compliance with their expectations. **Maturity demands** involve the level at which expectations are set. **Communication** describes the amount of information offered to children regarding behavior practices. **Nurturance** refers to the extent to which adults express caring and concern for children.

Differences among the four styles of discipline are reflected in differing combinations of these dimensions and are depicted in Figure 10-4. Authoritarian adults are high in control, high in maturity demands, low in clarity of communication, and low in nurturance. Permissive adults are low in control, low in maturity demands, low in communication

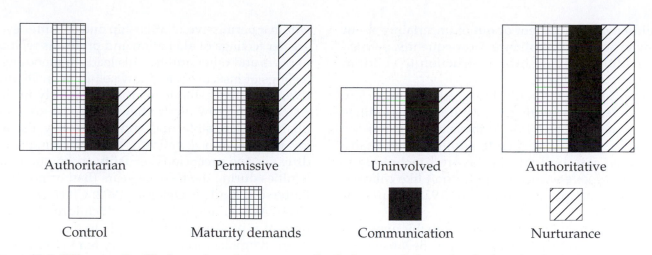

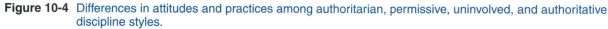

Figure 10-4 Differences in attitudes and practices among authoritarian, permissive, uninvolved, and authoritative discipline styles.

clarity, and high in nurturance. Uninvolved adults are low in every category. Adults high in all four dimensions are described as "authoritative." Although no adult uses only the few strategies representative of a particular category, behaviors do tend to cluster according to one pattern or another. Understanding the characteristics of each discipline style and its impact on children is important knowledge for helping professionals to have. It enables them to assess their use of discipline in the formal group setting and provides insights as to why children respond as they do.

The Authoritarian Discipline Style

"Do what I tell you," and *"Do it because I said so!"*

Demands such as these typify the **authoritarian discipline style**. Adults who display this style value children's unquestioning obedience above all else. They put all of their energy into the action dimension of socializing children's behavior and spare little time for relationship building. To achieve the high standards they have for children's conduct, adults become vigilant rule enforcers. Explanations and reasoning do not fit into their view of themselves as the ultimate authority. Broken rules are dealt with swiftly and forcefully, most often through ridicule, shame, or physical punishment. Not too surprising, authoritarian adults have cold, distant relationships with children. Youngsters view them as harsh taskmasters who focus more on finding

mistakes than on recognizing their attempts to comply (Kochanska et al., 2002; Shaffer & Kipp, 2006). This approach, sometimes referred to as power-assertive discipline, keeps children at the adherence level of moral reasoning (Laible & Thompson, 2002; Newman & Newman, 2003). Youngsters follow rules out of fear or blind obedience, not out of empathy or concern for others. This hampers their ability to develop the reasoning skills and emotional sensitivity necessary for internalization. In addition, children who interact mostly with authoritarian adults generally become unfriendly, suspicious, resentful, and unhappy. They tend to be underachievers, to avoid their peers, and to exhibit increased incidents of misconduct, as well as more extreme acting-out behaviors (Keenan & Shaw, 1995; Pratt, Arnold, Pratt, & Diessner, 1999; Kochanska et al., 2002).

The Permissive Discipline Style

Adults who display a **permissive discipline style** have warm relationships with children, but establish few boundaries on children's behavior. Consequently, permissive adults are the opposite of the authoritarian adults just described. They emphasize relationship building at the expense of the action dimension of the socialization process. Permissive adults see themselves as loving resources to children but not as active agents responsible for shaping children's present or future behavior. They accept a wide range of children's actions based either on the conviction that external controls thwart children's development or out of uncertainty about how to achieve compliance. Consequently, permissive adults provide little instruction to children about how to behave.

They ignore children's transgressions, make few demands, and seldom give children opportunities to assume responsibility. At those infrequent times when they feel compelled to administer a penalty for gross misconduct, the favored technique is temporary love withdrawal ("I don't like children who hurt people") (Baumrind, 1978; Shaffer & Kipp, 2006).

Unfortunately, children subjected to this approach show few signs of internalization. Because they receive almost no cues about which behaviors are socially appropriate and which are not, they fail to develop mental guidelines or strategies to draw on in their day-to-day social encounters. Moreover, they have little chance to develop feelings of empathy for others because cause-effect relationships are not explained. Peers and adults often view their unrestrained behavior as immature, inconsiderate, and unacceptable. Such negative perceptions contribute to children's feelings of anxiety and low self-esteem.

As a rule, children whose world is dominated by permissive adults tend to be withdrawn, unproductive, and unhappy. In adolescence, this style is frequently associated with delinquency and poor academic performance (Laible & Thompson, 2002; Haith & Miller; Siegel, 1999; Patterson & Stouthamer-Loeber, 1984).

The Uninvolved Discipline Style

Uninvolved adults are indifferent to the children in their care. They do not put any energy into relating to children or into guiding children's social behavior (Hetherington and Clingempeel, 1992; Lamborn, Mounts, Steinberg, & Dornbusch, 1991; Siegel, 1999). Thus, acting within the **uninvolved discipline style,** they decline to use both facilitation and action-related strategies. These grownups are self-absorbed, focusing on their own needs at the expense of the children's. Their extreme egocentrism is often a result of depression or stress (Kochanska, 1991; Patterson & Capaldi, 1991). Whatever the cause, neglectful adult behavior leads to many of the same outcomes described for children subjected to a permissive approach.

Those problematic results are compounded by the fact that children lack the warmth enjoyed within a permissive relationship and so suffer even greater feelings of alienation and problems relating to peers and other adults. This leads to moodiness, feelings of insecurity, and low self-esteem. Disruptive, detached behavior is the norm early in life. As children grow older, they tend to be noncompliant, irresponsible, and immature. They also are low performers academically. Truancy, delinquency, drug use and precocious sexuality are common difficulties during the teenage years (Baumrind, 1991; Patterson, Reid, & Dishion, 1992; Clark & Gross, 2004). As you might guess, such children lack important experiences that could help them move toward internalization and so they tend to remain at the amoral or adherence stages of moral regulation.

The Authoritative Discipline Style

Adults who adopt an **authoritative discipline style** combine the positive attributes of the authoritarian and permissive discipline styles, while avoiding the negative ones. They respond to children's needs with warmth and nurturance; they have high standards and establish clear behavioral expectations (Bukatko & Daehler, 2004). Authoritative adults also rely on additional strategies that permissive and authoritarian adults fail to use altogether. In this way they address both the facilitation and the action dimensions of the helping relationship. Thus, helping professionals who exemplify an authoritative style are friendly and affectionate toward children. They make children feel important by allowing them to assume appropriate responsibility and acknowledging their accomplishments. They also teach children relevant social skills to help them meet their needs in socially acceptable ways.

Simultaneously, authoritative adults establish high standards for children's behavior, but gear their expectations to match children's changing needs and abilities. Although quick to respond to children's misbehavior, they use explanations, demonstrations, suggestions, and other types of reasoning as their primary socialization strategies (Hoffman, 2000; KerrLopez, Olson & Sameroff, 2004). These adults use discipline encounters as opportunities for discussions related to guilt and empathy and as a means for teaching lessons about which behaviors to choose, which to avoid, and which to try instead. This nonpunitive form of behavior regulation is sometimes called *inductive discipline* because adults induce children to regulate their behavior based on the impact their actions will have on themselves and others.

Authoritative adults combine the positive attributes of the authoritarian and permissive discipline styles while avoiding the negative ones.

The authoritative discipline style is the one most strongly associated with the development of self-discipline in children (Turiel, 1998; Vasta, Haith & Miller et al., 2004). Children know what is expected of them and how to comply. Moreover, they become sensitive to the needs of others, happy, cooperative, resistant to temptation, and socially responsible. They are also better able to initiate and maintain tasks on their own and are less likely to engage in health risk behaviors such as heavy drinking and illicit drug use (Baumrind, 1991; Adalbjarnardottir & Hafsteinsson, 2001; Clark & Gross, 2004). Their behavior is the most socially competent of the four patterns described in this chapter. For these reasons, young children benefit when the adults in their lives display an authoritative discipline style.

Refer to Table 10-3 for a summary of all four discipline styles and the corresponding patterns of child behavior with which they are associated. Recent evidence not only supports the relationships depicted but also indicates that these outcomes tend to endure from early childhood into later maturity (Baumrind, 1988, 1995; Pratt, Skoe & Arnold, 2004).

Implications

The behavior outcomes associated with the four dominant patterns of adult supervision show that each has a profound impact on children's immediate and long-term development. Heavy-handed discipline tends to produce children who are compliant, afraid, dependent, and angry (Kochanska et al., 2002). Coercive tactics, such as physical force, shame, and dictatorial demands cause youngsters to act out of fear or blind obedience, not out of empathy or concern for others. This interferes with their ability to develop the reasoning and caring that is necessary for internalization. Thus, control exerted without explanation or affection does not help children become

Table 10-3 Discipline Styles and Associated Patterns of Child Behavior

DISCIPLINE STYLE	CHILDREN'S BEHAVIOR PROFILE
Authoritarian	Aimless Fearful, apprehensive Hostile Low self-reliance and low self-control Moody, unhappy Suspicious Unfriendly Withdrawn Aggressive
Permissive	Aggressive Aimless Domineering Immature Impulsive Low achiever Low self-reliance and self-control Rebellious Unhappy Withdrawn
Uninvolved	Aggressive Immature Impulsive Insecure Irresponsible Low achiever Low self-esteem Low self-reliance and low self-control Moody Noncompliant
Authoritative	Cooperative Curious Empathic Friendly Goal oriented Happy High achiever High self-reliance and high self-control

self-disciplined. Instead, they maintain an external orientation and remain at adherence.

Likewise, internalization does not occur when adults are affectionate but fail to provide children with direction or predictable expectations, or when they ignore children altogether. In these situations, children have few opportunities to receive accurate feedback about how other people perceive them and how their behavior affects others. With so few cues about what is socially appropriate, they are unable to create a realistic foundation of experience to serve as a guide for future behavior. For them, the world often is unfriendly because other adults and peers who do not share the same permissive standards find their unrestrained behavior unacceptable. The resulting rejection contributes to feelings of anxiety and low self-esteem. Unfortunately, such children also are less likely to develop feelings of empathy for others (Goleman, 1995; Hoffman, 1983). These omissions add up to a dismal prognosis for youngsters who are the product of either the permissive or the uninvolved discipline styles.

Obviously, the adult behavior pattern that is most likely to lead to internalization is the authoritative style. Authoritative adults effectively address all three factors contributing to self-discipline: emotions, cognition, and experience.

When adults are able to convey acceptance to children while at the same time making it clear that they have expectations for their conduct, children feel secure knowing that people care about them and that they have a resource for determining how to behave. Discipline encounters provide an opportunity for discussions about guilt and empathy, two emotions not easily acknowledged by a child who is defensive or hostile as a result of power assertion or concerned over love withdrawal (Bell, Carr, Denno, Johnson, & Phillips, 2004; Kohn, 1996).

Reasoning with children also contributes to their cognitive development because they are exposed to moral judgments other than their own. This is an important element in developing higher levels of thinking about what is right and what is wrong. In addition, children acquire precise information about which behaviors to choose again, which to avoid, and which alternatives to consider. This increases the breadth and depth of their cognitive map of the social environment. Finally, when adults reason with children they model language that children can use in the future to regulate their own behavior. When this happens youngsters maximize the potential successes available to them because they have learned to satisfy their needs within guidelines established by adults.

From the children's point of view.   If children were to rate the various discipline styles just described, how might they judge each one? That was the question posed, using simple scenarios, to children ages 4 through 18 (Siegal & Cowen, 1984). Authoritative methods were the disciplinary strategies children of all ages overwhelmingly rated as "right" or "very right," regardless of the discipline styles they experienced at home. Physical punishment came in as the second-best approach, with love withdrawal being favored by no one. In fact, all the children studied said that outright permissiveness was "wrong or very wrong." Children in more recent studies echo these sentiments, indicating that telling children to stop fighting or to share candy is "right," especially when adults use rationales related to kindness or fairness to back up their demands (Kim, 1998; Kim & Turiel, 1996). Results like these underscore the fact that young children see a need for adults to intervene and guide their social behavior and that authoritative methods make the most sense to them.

> *Jessie is a quiet 3-year-old, somewhat fearful of new situations and timid with people. In terms of temperament, she could be described as slow to warm up.*
>
> *Raelynn, on the other hand, is impulsive and fearless in her social interactions. She is a contentious child, who many would call temperamentally difficult.*

The Dynamic Interaction Between Children's Temperament and Adult Discipline Styles

Evidence based on differences in temperament show that children like Jessie find it easier to exercise self-discipline than do children like Raelynn (Kochanska, 1995, 2002). This does not mean that Jessie will achieve self-discipline automatically nor that Raelynn will never develop self-control. It does mean that the road toward internalization is usually easier for the quiet, more reflective child than for the child whose approach to life is naturally impulsive, rebellious, and headstrong.

How adults approach the two girls will be a factor in the children's emerging self-regulatory capabilities as well. There should be similarities as well as some differences in how adults interact with each youngster to promote self-discipline (Kochanska, 1995, 1997). For instance, Jessie is likely to respond most favorably to gentle, psychological strategies that emphasize nurturance and communication with a modest focus on maturity demands and control. Fearful youngsters like her are highly anxious and often burst into tears at the slightest hint of a reprimand. When this happens it is difficult for them to absorb desired moral lessons. Thus, adults must tread lightly in helping Jessie learn the "rules." Addressing Raelynn's needs also requires a warm, secure relationship between adult and child. However, the mild directives that work best with fearful children may be insufficient to capture a fearless child's attention. Thus, Raelynn will also need clear and firm (not harsh) messages of what is expected and how to best maintain the warm, mutually cooperative relationship she has with the significant adults in her life. As you can see, these varying approaches are simply variations on the authoritative discipline style.

Authoritarian techniques, on the other hand, are not likely to work well with either girl. Clearly, such strategies would overpower Jessie, causing her to withdraw even more. Children with difficult temperaments like Raelynn tend to act out when power assertion is used. That reaction typically prompts adults to increase their demands for control with increasingly poor results (Kochanska et al., 1996, 2002; Lytton, 1990). In both instances, adults and children have contributed to a counterproductive cycle that is hard to break and could contribute to increased behavior problems later.

The most favorable outcomes occur when adults strive to maintain a corresponding fit between their discipline styles and children's dispositions (Grusec, Goodnow, & Kuczynski, 2000). Adults who are able to accommodate the fearful child's need for loving support and modest demands promote the emergence of self-discipline and their own feelings of competence in working with the child. Those who strive to maintain positive relationships with difficult children in spite of children's irritable contentious demeanors find that the going gets better over time. Difficult children, treated with patience, warmth, and firm guidance, become better able to moderate their reactions and develop self-regulating mechanisms associated with social competence. When a corresponding fit between temperament and adult style is absent, both children and adults suffer.

A cross-cultural perspective. Some people wonder whether the authoritative approach to discipline represents the needs and best interests of people of varying ethnic/cultural and socioeconomic backgrounds. To date, research with Euro-American children, children of color, middle-class children, and children from lower socioeconomic backgrounds indicates that the principles of combining warm, affectionate relationships with high standards, clear expectations, and reasonable boundaries on child behavior are associated with children's development of positive self-esteem and self-discipline regardless of background (Baumrind, 1995). In addition, the link between authoritative discipline and children's development of high self-esteem and greater self-control is much the same in Taiwan, Korea, and Australia as it is in the United States and Canada (Chen, 1998; Kim, 1998; Scott, Scott, & McCabe, 1991). However, readers are reminded that each child lives in a contextual niche unique to that child. The details of how relationships are established and how compliance is achieved vary.

Alternative life conditions may call for techniques that differ in form but correspond in concept to those associated with an authoritative perspective. For instance, the Green family lives in a housing project riddled with drugs and violence. Mrs. Green is faced with having to keep her son safe in a hostile environment. She may demand quicker compliance and more absolute obedience in that environment than she would if she lived elsewhere. Moreover, what children and the significant adults in their lives interpret as warm and supportive depends on past experiences and current interpretations (Deater-Deckard & Dodge, 1997). This means one child may interpret teasing from adults as a positive relationship building strategy, whereas another views teasing as a strategy of rejection. Likewise, sarcasm may be understandable to some children as a gentle admonition to be taken seriously ("Go ahead, make me tell you a second time"), whereas other children would miss the message entirely. Children's comprehension is tied to the customs of speech and interaction with which they are familiar. For this reason, helping professionals are cautioned not to judge other adults' socialization styles too narrowly, and to seek ways to adapt their skills

to meet the needs of children and families whose backgrounds vary widely. The skills provided later in this chapter fit these criteria.

Becoming Authoritative

Once it was thought adults were instinctively authoritarian, permissive, or authoritative. We now know that although some people's personality or temperament seem more aligned with one style or another, through training and practice any adult can learn to be more authoritative (Charney, 1998). Authoritative adults think of themselves as teachers. They assume that "teaching" children to behave is as natural as teaching them anything else (See Figure 10-5).

To assume an authoritative teaching role, you must pay attention to how you establish relationships with children and to how you communicate your expectations and rules to children. Skills presented in previous chapters have focused on relationship enhancement. Thus, you have already learned one component of the authoritative style. The skills presented in this chapter will help you with component two expectations and rules.

STATING YOUR EXPECTATIONS

One of the best ways to express expectations and rules for children's behavior is through a **personal message**. A personal message consists of three parts. In step one you will use a reflection to acknowledge

When children don't know how to wash their hands,

we teach them.

When children don't know how to say the alphabet,

we teach them.

When children don't know how to multiply,

we teach them.

When children don't know how to dance,

we teach them.

When children don't know how to behave,

we teach them.
          Adapted from T. Herner (1998), p. 2.

Figure 10-5 Becoming an authoritative adult.

the child's point of view. In the second portion, you will identify your emotional reaction to the child's behavior, name the specific action that prompted those feelings, and explain why. The third segment, used only in situations in which behavior change is desired, involves describing an alternate behavior for the child to pursue. This last step is, in fact, a statement of a rule that the child is expected to follow for that situation. Here is an example:

The ultimate aim of using personal messages is to give children the information they need for both current and future reference. Personal messages help children better understand how their actions

> *Three-year-old Kayla is using a plastic butter knife to cut a banana for fruit salad. Playfully, she begins swiping the air with the knife as though it were a pretend sword. The teacher worries that Kayla might hurt herself or another child and so he says,*
>
> *"Kayla, you're having fun. I'm worried someone could get hurt when you wave the knife around. Keep the knife low like this." (The teacher demonstrates what to do.)*

affect others and provide them with cues about desirable and undesirable behaviors.

In favorable circumstances, personal messages tell children what they are doing right so they can repeat the behavior in subsequent interactions. For instance, an adult who values cooperation may acknowledge two children's efforts to share by saying: "You're working together. It makes me feel happy to see you sharing. Sharing is one way to cooperate." In problem situations, personal messages set the stage either for children to comply on their own or for the adult to impose consequences when children fail to obey. For example, adults who want to redirect a child's anger away from hitting and toward talking could say: "You're angry. It upsets me when you hit. Hitting hurts. Tell Stuart what he did that made you so mad." For now, we will turn our attention to personal messages aimed at changing problem behaviors, later, we will consider how to use them in positive situations.

Knowing When Behavior Change Is Necessary

Every day, adults are faced with situations in which they must decide whether or not a child's behavior is appropriate. If a behavior is not acceptable, they must also determine what conduct would be more

suitable. In order to make these decisions, the following questions must be asked:

1. Is the child's behavior unsafe either for self or others?
2. Is the child's behavior destructive?
3. Does the child's behavior infringe on the rights of someone else?

If the answer to any of these questions is yes, it is a clear sign that the adult should intervene (Galambos-Stone, 1994; Malott & Suarez, 2004). If the response is no, then demands for behavior change are unnecessary.

For example, concern about safety is the reason why children are stopped from running with scissors, prevented from dashing across a busy street, or kept from playing with matches. Similarly, the sanctions adults impose on graffiti or writing in library books are aimed at protecting property. When children are rebuked for copying from someone else's paper or for bullying a timid classmate, adults are making an effort to teach children respect for others' rights. In all of these situations, there are legitimate grounds for trying to alter children's behavior.

Finally, adults must decide whether a problem behavior is important enough to warrant persistent attention (Bell et al., 2004; MacKenzie, 2003). This can be described as the principle of importance. In other words, is the behavior serious enough to deal with each and every time it happens? When a behavior meets these criteria, a personal message is in order.

For example, when Mr. Smith sees children throwing rocks on the playground, he takes action to stop it regardless of when he sees it or how tired or preoccupied he is. Because rock throwing is so dangerous, preventing it is a top priority for Mr. Smith. In this case, a personal message that forbids rock throwing is appropriate.

On the other hand, it annoys Mr. Smith when children pile their backpacks on the floor rather than hanging them up on the hooks provided. Some days, he makes and enforces a rule that all backpacks have to be up off the floor and on the hooks so people won't trip over them. However, if he has a headache or has put in a long day, Mr. Smith pretends not to see the backpacks on the floor rather than dealing with the problem. The intermittent nature of Mr. Smith's attention to the backpack standard is a sign that it is not important enough, at least for now, to warrant a personal message.

Is behavior change needed here?
How will you decide?

The standards of safety, property, and people's rights are simple and all encompassing. They provide basic guidelines by which to judge children's behavior and are applicable to children of varying ages and abilities. (See Figure 10-6.)

Because adults differ, their interpretations vary as to what constitutes a dangerous situation or a potential threat to another's self-esteem. People's personal standards are uniquely influenced by past experience, family, community, and culture. This means that no two adults' standards match exactly. However, when adults relate the standards they set to at least one of the principles just described, they minimize major variations, which are confusing to children.

An assessment regarding all of these criteria must be made prior to making your standards known. This is true both when thinking about what rules might apply to upcoming situations as well as when confronted with the need to set limits on-the-spot. With so many factors to consider, you may wonder if prompt action can ever be taken. Experienced professionals consider all these points quickly and intervene in a timely fashion. It may take the novice slightly longer to decide if a personal message is appropriate. Refer to Figure 10-7 for a brief review of the critical dimensions to use in determining whether or not to intervene using a personal message.

Part One of the Personal Message

To successfully teach children how to achieve their aims appropriately, adults must first understand what children are trying to accomplish. Once this has been established, it is easier to determine an acceptable alternate behavior that will satisfy both the adult and the child. Based on this rationale, the first step of the personal message is to recognize and acknowledge the child's perspective using a behavior, paraphrase, or affective reflection.

There are several reasons why a personal message begins with a reflection. First, in problem situations, adults and children often have very different points of view. For example, when 4-year-old Allison lifts her dress up over her head in the supermarket to show off her new panties, she feels proud, but her mother is mortified. At times like these, adults wish children would act differently, so it is common for them to center on this desire and forget that children's emotions are legitimate, although contrary to their own. Reflecting helps adults avoid this pitfall.

Four-year-old Rosie Carmassi attends preschool with other typically developing children her age in the morning and a special education program in the afternoon. Rosie was born with cerebral palsy. She is an intelligent little girl who enjoys music, storybooks, and dress up play with scarves and hats. Currently, Rosie can't walk, can't talk, and can't voluntarily control any part of her body other than her eyes and her lips.

Over the year Rosie became an integral member of the preschool group, participating fully in classroom life and making friends. However, it took some time for her teachers to figure out that Rosie needed limits as much as she needed other learning opportunities each day.

Rosie's morning teacher tells about early efforts to help Rosie learn to behave in the classroom.

Rosie could make some limited sounds, but didn't have enough control so that she could use them to communicate. She really depended on her eyes. She could roll her eyes upward for yes and downward for no. She could also move them left and right to signal direction and look at something to make her needs known.

Initially, Rosie had a picture board that we used. It was a circular board with pictures displayed in wedges, kind of like a pie. She had a few pictures of typical things she might need or want in the classroom, such as water or the toilet, and some pictures for areas in the room, such as blocks or pretend play. The board was always available, and she would look at a part of it to indicate what she wanted.

We had some frustrating times early in the year. Rosie would want something and neither the teachers nor the children would know what it was. Then she'd get frustrated and cry or shriek. She also did this whenever she didn't want to do something. At first, when Rosie got upset about things, all the adults in the classroom would try to give her anything she wanted. Everyone just felt so sorry for this little girl in the wheelchair, who couldn't talk or move about freely. As a result, Rosie was getting rewarded for some very inappropriate behavior, and it was getting worse. One day at our before-school meeting I said, "We are not helping Rosie when we give in to her every whim." I asked them if they would say "yes" to some of the things she wanted if other children asked for them (such as not washing her hands before snack or not waiting her turn with a hat). Everyone agreed they wouldn't. Then I said, "We are here to help Rosie. The way we are going to help her is to not let her behave like that." We decided to use the principles of *safety* and *protecting property and rights* (just as we did with the other children) to guide our decision-making when it came to determining expectations for Rosie We worked hard at making those expectations clear and consistent. It was challenging for all of us, but within weeks we saw a change in Rosie. She was more relaxed and more successful in the classroom. She knew what the boundaries were and that we cared enough to keep her safe and treat her like the other kids. This was an important lesson for all of us.

[1] Rosie's Story was adapted from a case study included in: *Children with Special Needs: Lessons for Early Childhood Professionals* written by Kostelnik, Onaga, Rohde and Whiren in 2002 and published by Teachers College Press, pp. 32–48.

Figure 10-6 Meet Rosie.

It compels them to remember that each child has a unique perception that must be considered prior to subsequent action.

Another advantage of reflecting first is that the reflection is a clear signal to the child that the adult is actively attempting to understand his or her position. Children are more willing to listen to adult messages when they think their own messages have been heard. Even when children have chosen a physical means to express their desires, knowledge of adult awareness reduces their need to escalate the behavior in order to make their feelings known. For instance, if Sam is angry, he may be ready to fling a book across the room to make his point. When the adult reflects, "Something happened that really upset you," Sam may not feel so compelled to throw the book to show his anger because someone has already acknowledged it.

A third value of reflecting first is that it is a way to mentally count to 10 before committing yourself to a particular line of action. It offers a moment in which adults can sort out their emotions, organize their

PROTECT SAFETY
PROTECT RIGHTS
PROTECT PROPERTY

If you need to address one or more of these dimensions, prepare to intervene.

IMPORTANCE

If it is important enough to address this problem every time it happens, INTERVENE.

Figure 10-7 The critical dimensions of intervention.

Benefits of Reflecting First

Helps you see child's point of view

Signals child you are trying to understand

Helps you mentally count to 10

Shows respect for child

Figure 10-8 Why reflections come first in the personal message.

thoughts, or readjust their approach. It reduces the risk of overreacting or responding thoughtlessly. For instance, from across the room, Ms. Romano notices Danny painting a picture with tempera dripping all over the floor. Her first reaction is one of annoyance.

She hurries to the easel, a reprimand on her lips. However, as she approaches, she becomes aware of Danny's obvious pride in his work and his total absorption in his painting. By reflecting, "You're really excited about your painting," she is able to put a check on her initial response. Instead of blurting out, "How many times have we talked about keeping the paint on the paper," she is able calmly to provide him with important information. "Some paint dripped on the floor. I'm worried someone might slip and get hurt. Get a sponge and we'll clean it up." In this way, the reflection served as a reasoned entry into what could have been an emotionally charged situation.

Finally, reflecting is a way for adults to show respect and caring for children. This demonstration of positive regard must continue, particularly when disciplinary action is in order. When used in conjunction with the other portions of the personal message, reflecting unites the two components of the authoritative style: affection and clear behavioral expectations.

All of the reasons for reflecting before acting are summarized in Figure 10-8. To summarize, in problem situations, the child has one perspective, the adult another. In order for a resolution to take place, each must accurately and correctly take into account the other's attitudes. This mutual understanding forms the basis for a shared response that will join the two separate lines of thought. The reflection represents the adult's effort to assess the

child's attitude; the second portion of the personal message is aimed at helping the child recognize the adult's perspective.

Part Two of the Personal Message

The second portion of the personal message describes the adult's emotions, identifies the child's behavior that led to those feelings, and gives a reason for why this is so:

"I feel annoyed when you hit. Hitting hurts."
"It upsets me when you interrupt. I keep losing my place."

Why adults should talk about their emotions. Helping professionals often have an emotional reaction to children's behavior. They feel pleased when children cooperate, distressed when they fight, annoyed when they procrastinate. Emotions are just as natural for adults as they are for children. Experienced practitioners learn to use their own emotions as a guide to interacting more effectively with children. They do this by talking about their emotions as they happen.

When adults disclose their emotions to children, they illustrate the universality of feelings. They demonstrate that at different times, everyone feels unhappy, pleased, frustrated, worried, proud, satisfied, or angry. This helps children realize that all human beings experience emotions and, as a result, makes them more willing to accept feelings in themselves and to recognize them in others (Hendrick and Weissman, 2006). Talking about emotions also aids children in learning that people have different reactions to the same situation. They find out that what makes them happy may prompt sadness in others, or that an event that causes them anxiety is welcomed by someone else. Children do not automatically know this and instead may assume that their current feelings are shared by everyone else. As they hear more about other people's emotions, they gradually become aware that this is not always the case. Another advantage is that adults serve as a model for using words to express emotional states. Children discover that people can have a variety of reactions and still be capable of verbalizing how they feel. Eventually, children find that emotions can be put into words and that words offer a satisfying way to communicate with other people.

Adults who wish to maintain positive relationships with children also should keep in mind that sharing their feelings with children promotes closer ties. People who talk honestly about their emotions are considered more trustworthy and helpful by the persons with whom they interact than people who avoid such conversations (Gazda, Balzer, Childers & Nealy, 2005). When adults risk revealing something personal about themselves, children see it as a demonstration of the regard in which they are held. In addition, when such revelations are the norm, children find it less threatening to reveal their own emotions. This leads to greater mutual understanding and respect.

Finally, children are interested in how the significant adults in their lives react to what they say and do. They care about how adults feel and are responsive to their emotions. In fact, adults who describe their own disappointment or disapproval regarding a particular child's behavior place that child in an optimal state of arousal for receiving the rest of the information contained in their message (Goodnow, 1992; Hoffman, 2000). Without this type of sanction, children will not be induced to seriously consider the adult's reasoning. On the other hand, adults who depend on power assertion or love withdrawal as a way to communicate concern provoke such strong reactions in children that they are unable to attend to the specific content of the message. Thus, when children refrain from hitting because it would upset their teacher, or when they share materials because the caregiver has advocated cooperation, they are demonstrating identification. It is from this base that they eventually begin to internalize some of the behavior expectations adults think are important.

Focusing on children's behavior.   Once adults have described their emotions, it is important that they tell the child which behavior has caused them to react. Children often do not know which of their behaviors is prompting the adult's reaction. This means identifying by name the undesirable behavior that the child is displaying. This helps children pinpoint actions to avoid (Newman & Newman, 2003; Malott & Suarez, 2004). For example, a personal message that includes the statement "It bothers me when you keep jumping out of your seat" tells the child what behavior prompted the adult's irritation and describes an issue that can be resolved. On the other hand, remarks such as "It annoys me that you're showing off" or "I get upset when you're such a slob" are accusations that attack a child's personality and do not further mutual respect and understanding.

Behaviors are actions you can see. Taking turns, hitting, kicking, and coming on time are all visible, objective ways to describe children's conduct. On the other hand, descriptors such as lazy, uncooperative, hyperactive, stubborn, greedy, hostile, nasty, and surly are all subjective and accusatory labels. They make children feel defensive without giving them clear cues as to which specific actions are the focus of your message. If such labels are used, children may become hostile or think that satisfying the adult is beyond their capability. In either case, effective behavior change is more difficult to achieve. To avoid such adverse reactions, use objective words to describe children's actions rather than subjective labels when talking to children about problem behaviors.

The importance of giving children reasons. Children are better able to understand and respond to adult expectations when these expectations are accompanied by reasons (Bugental & Goodnow 1998; Larzelere, Schneider, Larson, & Pike, 1996).

This is why the second portion of the personal message also includes giving children an explanation for the adult's reaction.

> Why are adults upset when children hit?
>> Because hitting hurts.
> Why are they frustrated when children dawdle?
>> Because they may be late for something important.
> Why do they become annoyed when children interrupt a story over and over again?

Because interrupting interferes with their train of thought, or makes it difficult for others to concentrate.

Although such conclusions may be perfectly clear to adults, they are not so obvious to many children. When adults give children reasons for their expectations, they help them to recognize that behavior standards have a rational rather than arbitrary base.

Reasons help children see the logic of expectations that they might not discover on their own. In addition, reasons offer children information about the effect their behavior has on others. This increases their understanding of interpersonal cause and effect, that is, the relationship between their own acts and the physical and psychological well-being of another person (Landy, 2002; Larzelere et al., 1996). Reasons make the connections among actions clearer. See Figure 10-9.

When children hear reasons over and over again, they gradually make connections that help them determine for themselves whether certain actions are acceptable or not. This is illustrated by the child who thinks to herself, "Hitting is inappropriate because it hurts people. Then biting must be inappropriate because it hurts people too." In this way, children eventually use reasons to guide their judgments about what is right and what is wrong (Shaffer & Kipp, 2006). Likewise, a child who says to himself, "I shouldn't eat a candy bar before supper because it will spoil my appetite" is relying on reasons he has heard previously to self-regulate his current behavior.

Reasoning is the hallmark of the authoritative adult. Youngsters who see adults model reasoning as a way to resolve problem situations demonstrate more self-discipline and less aggression than do children for whom such models are not available (Baumrind, 1995; Hoffman, 2000). In addition, children can only internalize standards that make sense to them and that help them to predict the possible aftermath of the things they do or say. Reasoning fulfills these criteria and leads to the establishment of long-term behavior controls. Stating a reason for why a rule is necessary also helps adults determine if that rule is important enough to implement and enforce.

Matching reasons to children's understanding. A child's current developmental level has an impact on what types of reasons will make the most sense to him or her. For instance, preschoolers are most responsive to demonstrable, object-oriented rationales, such as "Be careful with the magnifying glass. It's fragile and it might break". They also understand reasons that emphasize the direct physical effects of their actions: "If you keep pushing him, he'll fall down and cry" (Hoffman, 1983, 2000). Young children are less able to comprehend explanations that focus on ownership or the rights of others, such as "That's Timmy's magnifying glass from home. Ask him first before you touch it." On the other hand, children 6 years of age and older are more receptive to reasoning that focuses on the rights, privileges, and emotions of other people.

The most effective reasons at this age emphasize the psychological effects of children's actions ("He feels sad because he was proud of his tower and you knocked it down") as well as explanations that focus on the fairness of the child's actions in terms of someone else's motives ("Wait before you holler—he was only trying to help"; Hoffman, 2000; Killen, 1991). A depiction of the developmental differences in what reasons make sense to young children is shown in Figure 10-10.

Variations in part two of the personal message. As we have discussed, the second portion of the personal message consists of a statement of the adult's emotion, a reference to the child's behavior, and a reason for this reaction. These three components can be arranged in any sequence after the reflection. Adults should always reflect first and then proceed with the second part in a way that seems most comfortable for them. There is no one correct order. For

---

Reasons Strengthen Connections!

Toddler Mia stuck her finger into the electrical outlet. Her dad told her that her fingers would get hurt and to keep them away from the outlet. Then she touched the outlet with her elbow; Dad moved closer, repeating the reason and the limit. Then she turned around and put her bottom on it! He scooped her up and talked firmly to her about keeping every part of her body away from the electricity.

Mia treated each body part and each action as a separate event. Although her dad understood that fingers, elbows, and bottoms all fell under the category: "Keep away from outlets," Mia did not see the connection among them. Her dad offered a reason, getting hurt, to make that connection for her. Adults who use reasons to point out the similarities among different actions (e.g., fingers poking and elbow touching are both unsafe), help children make such associations more easily.

Figure 10-9 Reasons Strengthen Connections!

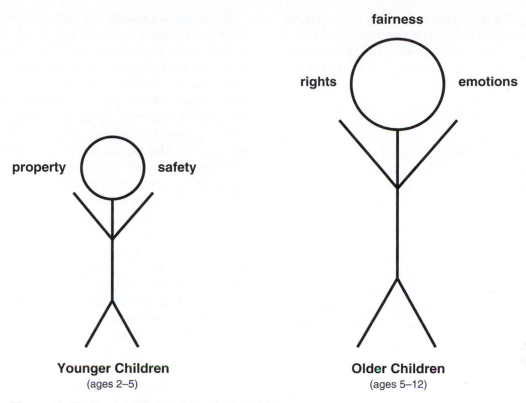

Figure 10-10 Reasons that make sense to children.

example, in the case of Allison, who was lifting her dress over her head in a proud display of her underwear, more than one response is appropriate:

OPTION 1. "Allison, you're proud of your new panties. Underwear is very personal clothing. It's not meant for everyone to see. It upsets me when you lift your dress so high."

OPTION 2. "Allison, you're proud of your new panties. It upsets me when you lift your dress over your head. Underwear is very personal clothing and is not meant for everyone to see."

How adults decide to articulate the second part of the personal message will depend on what they think of first and their own individual style. What matters is that all the components are included.

In addition, individuals are not all alike in their reactions. Some adults may have felt amused at Allison's performance, some would be indignant, and others might be embarrassed. Personal messages are ideally suited to account for these variations. They enable adults to respond to each situation individually based on their own impressions, without having to second-guess how someone else might respond in their place. Instead, the adult's emotions serve as a guide for how they will proceed. In

the situation just discussed, if the adult is amused, she or he may do nothing but smile; if the adult is indignant or embarrassed, she or he probably will tell Allison to put her dress down. In the latter case, depending on which emotion is involved, explanations for why the child is required to assume a more modest demeanor will differ somewhat, thus enabling each adult to express personal views.

Finally, if the adult uses a behavior reflection as an introduction to the personal message, the behavior does not have to be mentioned again in the second portion. For instance: "Allison, you're lifting your dress up over your head. That upsets me. Underwear is very personal clothing; it is not something everyone should see." In this case, the reflection specified the behavior in question, making it unnecessary to repeat.

Part Three of the Personal Message

Telling children an appropriate course of action for a particular circumstance is the function of the third portion of the personal message. Due to children's relative lack of experience and the influence of centration and irreversible thinking, it is not enough to tell them which behaviors are unacceptable. They must also be told what to try instead (Curwin & Mendler, 2000). This appropriate substitute behavior serves as a rule for children to follow. Thus, the "rule" portion of the personal message is a guide for behavior—it tells children what to do (Miller, 2007).

Some examples are:

"Walk."

"Keep your dress down."

"Turn your homework in as soon as you get to school."

"Share the jump ropes."

"Talk quietly in the lunchroom."

Rules make the world more predictable because they help children recognize what they can and cannot do. This knowledge enables them to be more successful in interacting with both peers and adults (Marzano, 2003). When children are not sure what the rules are, they are less likely to know how to get what they want in ways that enhance rather than interfere with their relationships with others. In addition, if the rules they must follow are arbitrary, unreasonable, or inappropriate for their developmental level, youngsters may be unable or unwilling to comply. Thus, how rules are set has much to do with how well children are able to follow them. Therefore, it pays for adults to learn the specific attributes that characterize good rules.

Rules must be reasonable.   Reasonable rules are rules children are capable of following. Being capable means having both the ability and the knowledge necessary to carry out the desired behavior. To create reasonable rules, adults must take into account children's development, their past experiences, their current abilities, and the type of task required (Bredekamp & Copple, 1997). For example, if a child is expected to put the design blocks back in the box according to shape and color, it must first be determined whether he or she has the skills necessary to perform the task. In this case, a child would have to be able to manipulate the blocks, distinguish color, know that like pieces go together, and also know that all of the blocks should lie flat and in the same direction. If the child lacked know-how in any of these areas, the expectation would have to be revised to correspond to what the child could do. This might mean telling the child to simply gather the blocks, or to pile them in the box randomly, or to work with another person to collect the materials.

Rules must benefit the child.   Rules must have long-term positive effects that *benefit the child, not just the adult* (Katz & Chard, 2000). Hence, adults must decide whether a rule enhances a child's development or hinders it. Development is enhanced when expectations promote significant increases in children's interpersonal, academic, or life skills. Development is hindered when adults fail to take into account children's individual needs and abilities or when they prohibit children from engaging in constructive activities. Such instances occur when adults set standards indiscriminately or solely for their own convenience. Thus, forbidding all the children in a mixed-age group from climbing on the high jungle gym because the youngest ones are afraid, preventing a crying child from clutching a blanket for comfort because the adult thinks it is high time she grew up, forbidding a boy from using a loom because the leader sees weaving as too feminine, or demanding that children be silent during lunchtime because the principal wants to make sure they do not yell across the table are all growth-inhibiting measures. These are all examples of depriving children of potentially beneficial experiences.

Adults avoid such problems when they recognize that each child is an individual and that although some standards are appropriate for a group (such as walking rather than running inside), others are best applied on a child-by-child basis. For instance, because physical mastery is important for everyone, younger children could be encouraged to tackle a low climber, while older youngsters could attempt a more challenging apparatus. Moreover, adults should examine their own attitudes for biases that curtail children's exposure to a wide range of opportunities. Intolerance and sexism, as illustrated in the preceding blanket and loom incidents, are examples of these. Additionally, in an effort to deal with definite problem behaviors, such as shouting during lunch, adults must be careful not to exact a standard that is unnecessarily extreme. Because children benefit from peer interaction, they should be encouraged to talk informally with classmates. Teaching youngsters to monitor the volume of their voices is a better approach to the problem of too much noise than eliminating conversation altogether. Finally, adults must continually reexamine their rules in an effort to keep them up to date. A rule that is appropriate for a child of 4 may be inhibiting at age 6.

Rules must be definable.   Rules are **definable** when both the adult and the child have the same understanding of what the rule means (Malott & Suarez, 2004; Miller, 2007). Good rules specify the exact behavior that adults value and find acceptable. It is confusing to children when adults use language that is open to many interpretations. This is exemplified when adults tell children to "behave," "act nice," "be good," or "act like a lady." Such phrases mean different things to different people. The child may construe these generalizations in one way, the adult in another. Youngsters who make genuine attempts to carry out the instructions become frustrated when their efforts fall short of the expected standard. For example, the teacher's notion of "nice" might mean sitting quietly with hands in lap, while the fidgeting child thought that he was complying by not spitting at a teasing classmate.

The difficulty is compounded when adults assume that because they use the same phrases over and over, children must know what they mean. For instance, a teacher tried to stop two children from fighting. She said: "You're angry. I get upset when you fight. Someone could get hurt. Use your words." Following her directions, one child said to the other, "Okay, . . . you!" The adult did a quick double take . . . she certainly didn't mean those words! Adults who want children to use words to express their emotions, who want children to cooperate, or who want children to stop acting up must tell them a specific way to accomplish these things.

Rules must be positive.   Children are most successful at following **positive rules** that tell them what to do rather than what not to do or what to stop doing (Marion, 2007). In other words, it is easier for children to respond appropriately when they are told "Put your hands in your pockets" rather than "Stop pushing"; "Walk" rather than "Don't run"; and "Eat your food" rather than "Don't play with your food." One reason why preschoolers are slow to respond to inhibiting commands is that they pay little attention to the words don't and stop. Rather, they focus on the verb in each directive as a guide for what to do (Luria, 1961). Thus, the child who is told, "Don't play with your food," hears "Play with your food." This problem is intensified when the adult speaks forcefully because children respond to the tone or physical energy of the message and are actually stimulated to continue. Also, although school-age children are more aware of the importance of listening to all the words of an instruction, it is not unusual for them

to miss the "don't" or the "stop" in unfamiliar or highly emotional situations (Gordon, 1992).

Finally, adults are reminded that the irreversible aspects of children's thinking also make negative commands difficult for them to comprehend. Children are much more successful in following rules that help them redirect an action, rather than reversing or interrupting ongoing behaviors.

The steps that make up a complete personal message are summarized in Figure 10-11. A shorthand method for remembering all the necessary components is to think of each personal message as containing three parts and four R's: part one—Reflect, part two—React and give a Reason, and part three—state the Rule.

Articulating the Entire Personal Message—The Four R's

The following situations illustrate the integration of all three parts of the personal message, including all four R's.

SITUATION 1:   A child is poking Mr. Kee in order to get him to listen to her story.

> *Adult:* You're anxious to tell me something. I don't like it when you poke me to get my attention. It hurts. Call my name or tap my shoulder lightly.

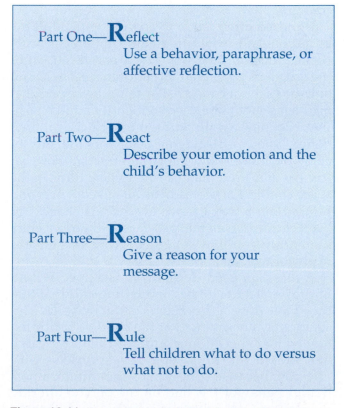

Part One—**R**eflect
Use a behavior, paraphrase, or affective reflection.

Part Two—**R**eact
Describe your emotion and the child's behavior.

Part Three—**R**eason
Give a reason for your message.

Part Four—**R**ule
Tell children what to do versus what not to do.

Figure 10-11 Creating a complete personal message.

SITUATION 2: Several children have left their gym towels scattered about the locker room.

> *Adult:* You're in a hurry to get back to class. It bothers me when you leave your dirty towels all over the locker room because then I have to pick them up. Put them in the laundry basket before you leave.

SITUATION 3: It is a hot, humid day. The class is restless and children are beginning to fidget and whisper while a classmate is reporting on the life of Sojourner Truth.

> *Adult:* You're hot and uncomfortable. It's distracting to Karl when you whisper while he's giving his report. I'm concerned his feelings will be hurt. He worked hard to find this information. Sit quietly until he is finished.

Messages such as these can be given to individual children or to groups. In addition to being used to correct children's behavior, personal messages should also be implemented as a way to reinforce appropriate actions.

Positive Personal Messages

A positive personal message contains only parts one and two of the format just described. Our previous emphasis on problems should not be taken to mean that you should expect children to engage only in negative behavior. In reality, the evidence is to the contrary.

Children often strive to comply with adult expectations and, in fact, frequently initiate constructive actions on their own. As a result, not all of the emotions prompted by children's behavior are ones of anger or concern. For this reason, personal messages should be used to identify adults' positive reactions as well. Adults must "catch" children being "good"—displaying behaviors that are socially desirable—and tell children what those behaviors are: "You made a rule to take turns in the space shuttle. I'm pleased you all talked it over and figured out a way to give everyone a chance" or "You cleaned up all the art scraps without anybody reminding you. I'm delighted. Now, this table is ready for making popcorn."

A message used in this way is a special kind of praise. Adults go beyond telling children that they have done a "good job" or "great work." Instead, they are saying that the child's specific behavior had special meaning for them. Research has shown that this type of response is very effective because it describes the impact a particular behavior has had on the person offering the praise. General terms such as good, nice, or pretty soon lose their meaning for both children and adults if they are used over and over again or applied indiscriminately. Moreover, children interpret effusive remarks that glorify them, rather than their behavior, as insincere or "too gushy." Thus, it is more effective to say: "You worked hard on your essay. I really liked it. It made me want to know more about Harriette Tubman" than to say, "You are a born writer." In the same vein, children learn more about their behavior from a statement such as "You're trying to comfort Andrew. It makes me feel good that you noticed he was so sad. He needs a friend right now" than from a comment like "You're a terrific kid." When adults identify behavior they are pleased to see children display and tell them why, they encourage youngsters to repeat those actions another time. All too often, adults take children's proactive behaviors or compliance for granted; they simply expect children to do as they are told or to automatically behave in an appropriate fashion. When this happens, adults have failed to recognize that it takes effort for children to achieve these productive outcomes.

Positive personal messages share many of the characteristics cited earlier regarding effective praise. Both are useful tools for helping children recognize the positive behaviors they demonstrate. The difference between the two is in who evaluates the child's behavior, the child or the adult. Effective praise prompts self-evaluation by the child because the adult acknowledges the effort or accomplishment solely from the child's viewpoint, without offering any opinions about it. Positive personal messages, on the other hand, offer a more direct way for adults to tell children what they think about children's appropriate behavior. These are most useful when children are first learning how to behave in a particular circumstance and are looking to adults for specific cues in this regard. As children become more adept at complying with rules on their own, most positive personal messages should give way to effective praise statements. This allows children to judge for themselves the extent to which their conduct is in keeping with the internalized codes they are beginning to develop. However, it is always appropriate for grownups to let children know when their behavior has affected the adult personally and positively. Children appreciate hearing statements such as, "You helped me shelve a lot of books. I appreciate it. That saved me hours of work" or "You remembered I had a hoarse

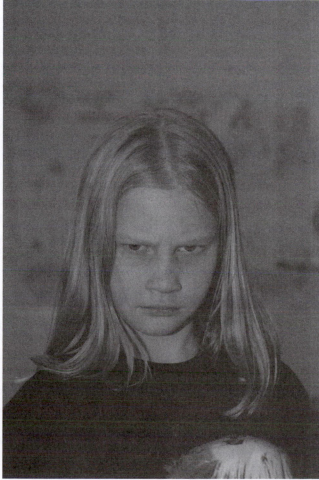

Emily has been working on a craft project for most of the morning.

When the Clean-up bell rings, she does not want to clean up. The teacher says:

R1   You're not quite finished.

R2   I'm concerned that if you keep working,

R3   you'll miss time outside.

R4   Find a spot on the shelf to keep your project until tomorrow.

voice and were very quiet while I read the story. I'm glad. That made it easier for me to talk."

Stating positive personal messages. Positive personal messages begin with a reflection. This step clarifies the situation from the child's point of view and alerts children that the adult has noticed what they are doing. Next, the adult identifies a personal emotion regarding the child's action and gives a reason for it. In addition, the specific behavior that prompted the adult's emotional reaction is described.

This may seem like a lot of words when a simple "Thank you" or "Good" would do. However, the purpose of a positive personal message is to teach children which behaviors they should retain for future use. Thus, positive personal messages

help children internalize the constructive behaviors they display. Again, the emphasis is on helping children move from adherence to higher levels of social conduct.

Children need reasons why they should behave in certain ways as much as they need to know why they should not engage in particular actions. They also need to know that the adults with whom they identify are sources of approval as well as correction.

At this point, you have learned about parts one, two, and three of the personal message. Rationales for each component have been offered and suggestions made for how to use personal messages in both positive and negative situations. Following are specific guidelines for how to carry out effective personal messages.

SKILLS FOR EXPRESSING EXPECTATIONS AND RULES TO CHILDREN

 Reflecting in Problem Situations

1. Observe children carefully before talking. Consider what the child may be trying to achieve and why.

2. Use reflections to accurately describe the child's perspective. Maintain a nonjudgmental stance as you strive to capture the child's point of view. Try reflections such as, "You wanted another turn at bat." Or, "You don't think you had a fair turn." Avoid thinly veiled accusations, such as "You just don't want to cooperate today" or "You thought you could pull a fast one."

3. Remind yourself to describe the child's point of view before your own. In problem situations it is natural to want to express your reaction immediately. As we've discussed, this is not effective. To avoid this reaction, take a deep breath prior to speaking. That breath will serve as a cue that the reflection comes first. If you catch yourself skipping the reflection, stop and begin again. Later, think of alternate reflections you might use should the situation arise another time. This type of mental practice will help you in future encounters.

4. Pay attention to children's age when deciding which type of reflection to use. Affective reflections generally are most effective with children under eight. For instance, if two first graders have come to blows over who will get the next turn at bat, it would be accurate to say, "You're hitting," and then proceed with the rest of the personal message. However, it is closer to the mark to reflect: "You're really angry. You each thought it was your turn next." This acknowledges what the children consider to be the real problem (the dispute over turns) and provides a more helpful introduction to the subsequent message. On the other hand, older children sometimes resent having an adult interpret their feelings in front of others. It seems too personal. In such cases, the more neutral behavior reflection or paraphrase reflection is more appropriate.

5. Avoid using "but" as a way to connect the reflection to the rest of the personal message. The word "but" means "on the contrary." When it is used to connect two phrases, the second phrase contradicts the first. For example, if a friend were to meet you on the street and say, "You look wonderful, but . . ." you would know that the initial praise was a perfunctory introduction to what the person thought was really

SKILLS FOR EXPRESSING EXPECTATIONS AND RULES TO CHILDREN

important. The same is true when it comes to the personal message. Adults who say, "You wish the story would end, but I want to finish it" are telling children that their feelings do not count. This betrays the true spirit of the reflection.

 Expressing Your Emotions to Children

1. Identify the emotions you experience. State your emotions clearly to the child. Do not rely on nonverbal cues alone. Adults sometimes tap their fingers to show irritation, wrinkle their nose to convey disgust, or sigh to indicate exasperation. Children often misinterpret these signs or miss them altogether. They do not automatically know how you feel and, in fact, are often surprised to find that your feelings may be quite different from their own. Subtle hints will not get your message across. Children benefit from the explicit communication that words provide. Words are specific and to the point. They help children know how you feel and why you feel that way:

"I feel pleased . . ."
"It makes me angry . . ."
"I'm annoyed . . ."
"It's important to me . . ."
"I wish . . ."

2. Become sensitive to your own internal cues that signal a particular emotion. Perhaps your cheeks get hot when you start to feel angry, your stomach gets jumpy when you are anxious, or your head seems heavy when you are overwhelmed. At first, it will be the more extreme emotions, like anger, fear, or excitement that will be the easiest to discern and express. Eventually, you will become better able to recognize and talk about more moderate emotions such as contentment, irritation, discomfort, or confusion.

3. Use a wide range of feeling words of differing intensities. Purposely select an assortment of feeling words. The greater the vocabulary at your disposal, the more likely you are to be attuned to the array of emotions these words represent. If you find yourself using the same few words over and over, select variations to use in the future and then do it.

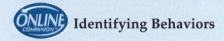 **Identifying Behaviors**

1. Name the behavior that is affecting you. Be specific. Describe actions you can see or hear. Avoid generalities that clump several behaviors together or that are open to misinterpretation. Rather than saying, "I get upset when you do mean things," say: "I get upset when you (hit me; throw things; tease Jacquie; punch Frank)." Both you and the child must know exactly what you find acceptable or unacceptable.

2. Describe the behavior, not the child. It is inappropriate to tell children that they are "not nice," bad, nasty, a hard case, hyper, or that they should know better. All of these descriptions attack children as persons and should not be used.

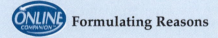 **Formulating Reasons**

1. Give children specific reasons for why you approve or disapprove of their behavior. Link those reasons to safety, protecting property, or protecting people's rights. Rationales such as "Because I said so," "Because I want you to," "Because it's important," "Because it's not nice," "Because that's the rule," or "Because that's how we do things around here" are not effective. They do not clearly relate to any of the criteria for deciding when behavior change is appropriate. Adults often use phrases like these when they cannot think of anything else to say. If you cannot think of a legitimate reason for your reaction, reexamine the situation to determine whether your expectations really are appropriate.

continued

SKILLS FOR EXPRESSING EXPECTATIONS AND RULES TO CHILDREN—continued

2. Phrase reasons in terms children understand. Use familiar language and short, simple sentences. Focus on one main idea rather than offering an explanation that incorporates several ideas.

3. Give reasons every time you attempt to change a child's behavior. Do not assume that because you gave an explanation yesterday for why running is prohibited, the children will remember today. Children often forget the rationale or may not realize that the reason still exists after a lengthy time lapse. They must hear the same reasons repeatedly before they are able to generalize from one situation to another.

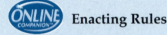 **Enacting Rules**

1. Study child development norms. Learn what behaviors and understandings might realistically be expected for children of a particular age. Become familiar with the knowledge and skills of children younger and older than those with whom you are working so you will have an understanding of the wide range of children's abilities that are apt to be represented in the group. This also will help you realize what sequence of skills and concepts children must master to move from one to the next. Know what actions and concepts are clearly beyond the capability of most of your children.

2. Get to know the children in your group as individuals. Recognize differences in interaction style, reactions to new situations, mood, level of involvement, tolerance for frustration, and attention span. Identify specific abilities exhibited by each child as well as those concepts and skills they have yet to master. Consider all these factors as you develop rules for the classroom.

3. Only implement legitimate rules. Use the criteria of safety, protection of property, and respect for others and the principle of importance to determine whether a rule is appropriate for a given situation. If the child's behavior cannot be linked to any of these, reconsider making a rule.

4. Tell children what the rules are. Rules should be explicit rather than implicit. Do not assume that children know a rule just because you know it, or that they remember it from past experience. Remind children of what the rules are at times when the rules are not an issue. Calm, rational discussions of why certain rules are enforced help children understand the value of and reasons for specific expectations. Also, remind children of the rules in situations in which those rules apply. For instance, it is more effective to say in part three of the personal message, "Remember to walk in the classroom," when a child is caught running than to say, "How many times have I told you about running indoors?" The latter remark assumes that the child knows that the rule is "walk." Although the child may recognize that running is not allowed, there is no guarantee that he or she remembers the rule that specifies what to do instead.

5. Reward children's approximations of the rule. Do not expect children to comply perfectly with all rules every time. Recognize behaviors that show that children are attempting to follow the rule, although they may not be totally successful. For instance, if the rule is that children must raise their hands and wait to be called on in order to talk in a group, you should not expect perfect silence as you survey the waving hands before you. That would be too much for children to accomplish all at once. At first, it is likely that raised hands will be accompanied by excited vocalization as children attempt to gain your attention. Rather than focusing on the infraction of talking, it would be better to praise them for remembering to raise their hands. Gradually, with time and many reminders, fewer children will call out when they raise their hands to speak.

SKILLS FOR EXPRESSING EXPECTATIONS AND RULES TO CHILDREN

6. Use positive personal messages thoughtfully. When children follow a rule or act in other appropriate ways, draw their attention to their desirable acts with a personal message. Point out to them the favorable effect their behavior had in terms of safety or preserving people's rights or property. These on-the-spot observations are memorable to children and make it more likely that they will remember the rule in the future. As children demonstrate increasing skill at following rules independently, shift to more frequent use of effective praise.

7. Use positive attribution to promote children's favorable self-impressions and to increase their repertoire of socially acceptable behaviors. Look for situations in which children demonstrate delay of gratification, control over their impulses, resistance to temptation, or the ability to carry out prosocial plans. Identify these instances for them. Label the behavior, not the child.

> "You're waiting patiently."
> "You wanted that extra cupcake, but you let Carol have it instead. That was hard to do and you did it."
> "You put a check on yourself when you were going to hit Anthony. That took a lot of control."
> "You remembered the guinea pigs had no water. It was very responsible of you to come back over lunchtime to fill their water bottle."

8. Revise unreasonable rules. If you become aware that a child is not able to follow a rule as you have stated it, do not press on in the mistaken notion that rules must be absolute. It is better to revamp the rule at a level at which the child is able to comply. For example, this would mean changing a rule from "Everyone must raise his or her hand and wait quietly to be called on before speaking" to "Everyone must raise his or her hand in order to be called on." The "wait quietly" portion of the rule should be added only after most children have demonstrated an ability to raise their hand.

9. Use language that is clear and to the point. Identify a specific behavior that you wish the child to carry out—walk, put the ball down, turn in your homework first-thing in the morning, wait until the speaker is finished talking. Avoid generalizations, such as "be nice," "don't be mean," "don't act up," "act your age," "make me proud of you," "behave yourself," "be good at school," "don't make me ashamed of you," or "mind your manners." Not only are these expressions vague, but children's interpretation of what they mean may differ from yours.

10. Determine whether children have the same understanding of the rule that you do. Ask children to repeat the rule in their own words, or get them to demonstrate their comprehension in some manner. Watch to see how well they follow through.

11. When in doubt, assume that children have not understood, rather than concluding that they are deliberately breaking the rule. If children have not understood your rule, you will have to do something to make your rule clearer. Some things you can try are:
a. Repeating your words more slowly and articulating more clearly.
b. Rephrasing your message in simpler, more familiar language and emphasizing key words.
c. Restating your message using a combination of gestures and words.
d. Taking the child to an area where there is less interference from noise and other distractions.
e. Emphasizing your message using physical prompts such as pictures or objects in combination with gestures.
f. Demonstrating what you want by doing it yourself.

12. Practice thinking about what you want children to do as well as what you wish they would stop doing. Anticipate potential problem situations and the positive actions children could take to avoid or remedy them.

continued

SKILLS FOR EXPRESSING EXPECTATIONS AND RULES TO CHILDREN—continued

13. Catch yourself saying "No" or "Stop." Rephrase your negative instruction as a positive statement. This may mean interrupting yourself in the middle of a sentence. Also, couple negative instructions with positive ones, such as saying: "Don't run. Walk."

14. Tell younger and less experienced children what to do instead. Let older or more experienced children generate alternatives for themselves. If a young child is pushing to get out the door, you could say:

> "You're anxious to get outside. I'm worried that when you push, someone will get hurt. Take a giant step back away from the door and we'll try again."

The message to an older child might be:

> "You're anxious to get outside. I'm worried that when you push, someone will get hurt. Let's think of a way everyone can get outside safely."

Select one response or the other by considering children's previous experience and their potential readiness to negotiate. Two-year-olds, a fifth grade class that has come together for the first time, or a group of youngsters frenzied with excitement probably will have neither the skill, the patience, nor the trust necessary to work out a compromise.

However, youngsters who have had lots of practice generating ideas and alternatives and who are calm are more likely to rise to the challenge.

15. Talk and act simultaneously. Immediately stop children's actions that may be harmful to themselves or others. Use physical intervention if necessary. For example, if two children are fighting, stop the hitting by grasping their hands or separating them. If a child is about to jump off a too-high step, move quickly to restrain him or her. If children are using the saw inappropriately, gain control of it. Once the dangerous situation has been neutralized, youngsters are better able to hear what you have to say. It

is at this point that personal messages have their greatest impact.

16. Ask children to help make the rules. Gather the children in a group and ask them to help create rules for the group or a particular activity. Record their ideas on paper and post them for all to see. Refer back to the children's rules as the year goes by. Periodically discuss whether or not revisions are necessary. Participating in the self-governance of the group increases children's understanding of rules and promotes their feelings of internal control. They receive clear evidence that their ideas are worthwhile and that they can influence events in the classroom.

17. Follow the rules yourself. Children learn by watching you. Abide by the rules you make. Avoid sitting on tables, chewing gum, using put-downs to make a point, and so forth.

 Communicating with Families

1. Become familiar with overall program rules related to child and family participation. All early childhood programs have guidelines or expectations for family behavior relative to their involvement in the program. These often are communicated to families through written program policies. Know what these policies are. For instance, there may be guidelines for when children are too ill to attend, requirements that families sign permission slips for field trips, restrictions on the kind of toys children may bring from home, or requirements that children have an emergency card on file in order to remain in the program. Your awareness of these expectations will support program functioning and keep families from receiving mixed messages, which would happen if staff members varied in their application of such rules.

2. Find out what expectations families have for their children's behavior. Every family has certain ways in which they expect their

SKILLS FOR EXPRESSING EXPECTATIONS AND RULES TO CHILDREN

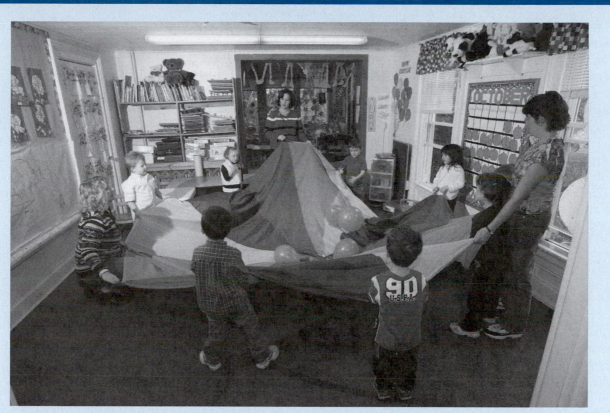

What rules might you and the children create for playing with the parachute?

children to act at home and away from home. Knowing what these expectations are helps early childhood professionals to better understand individual families and to support families in their child-rearing role. Obtain such information through individual and group discussions held during the year, ask families to complete a brief written form on which they identify some of the "home rules" they have for their children, and talk with families informally as related circumstances arise. Remain open and accepting. Avoid making judgments regarding the merit of certain family rules.

3. Communicate your discipline approach to families. Families have a right to know how you plan to carry out discipline in the formal group setting. This includes the kinds of rules you will enforce with children and how that enforcement will take place.

Such information may be shared with families at an introductory orientation, in a parent handbook, in newsletters sent home, at conference time, or in informal conversations with family members.

4. When talking to family members whose discipline style differs from the authoritative one you are learning, emphasize similarities rather than concentrating on differences in philosophy. Professionals sometimes believe they have little in common with family members who hold nonauthoritative attitudes toward discipline.

Likewise, family members who espouse more authoritarian or permissive philosophies may question the authoritative techniques you use. Under these circumstances, the most effective approach is to emphasize the common ground between these approaches, not the discrepancies (Bolin, 1989).

continued

SKILLS FOR EXPRESSING EXPECTATIONS AND RULES TO CHILDREN —continued

With this in mind, remember that authoritarian and authoritative styles both advocate firm control and high standards; permissive and authoritative styles promote warm, accepting relationships between children and adults. Discussing authoritative strategies in terms of how they support these overarching principles provides some common ground between them. For instance, family members with more authoritarian attitudes may believe that reasoning is unnecessary or undesirable because youngsters should simply do as they are told. To help such persons feel more comfortable with your giving reasons to children, point out that you will establish boundaries on the child's behavior by stating a rule and that you are prepared to enforce that rule as necessary. Further explain that the reasons you offer children will help them make sense of the rule at the time and be better able to follow the rule in the future. This explanation combines an authoritative value (helping children think through a problem) with an authoritarian one (achieving compliance) and builds a bridge between the two.

PITFALLS TO AVOID

Regardless of whether you are fostering children's self-discipline individually or in groups, informally or in structured activities, there are certain pitfalls you may fall into at first, but which you should eventually avoid.

Talking in paragraphs. Effective personal messages are brief and to the point. However, beginners who are struggling to include all four R's often add extra words or sentences. An awkward example would be: "You seem really unhappy about not getting a turn. I'm sorry you didn't get a turn but you are hitting Tanya with a stick. When you hit her with a stick, I'm afraid she could get hurt. I'd like you to hand the stick to me." Children are not likely to pay attention to all this talk. They cannot distinguish the main point, and may forget what was stated in the beginning. Laborious personal messages are ones children ignore. They get tired of listening and tune out.

When first learning this skill, talking too much is better than forgetting an important element. If adults find themselves delivering a particularly long personal message, they should think afterward of a more concise way of expressing it. For instance, the preceding example could have been condensed to: "You're upset. It worries me that if you hit Tanya with a stick, you could hurt her. Hand the stick to me."

Failing to use the personal message for fear of making a mistake. Adults may become tongue-tied at moments when a personal message would be appropriate. They dread stumbling over the words, getting the order wrong, or forgetting parts. Unfortunately, the more adults remain quiet, the less practice they get, and so improvement and comfort with the skill does not develop. The only remedy is to make fledgling attempts whenever the opportunity arises. It often is easier to begin with positive personal messages because there is less risk involved. Once these flow smoothly, corrective messages seem less difficult.

Talking about personal feelings only in problem situations. Some adults have a tendency to focus primarily on children's mistakes. They are quick to express their dissatisfaction, and focus on admonishing children who fall short of their expectations. This outlook fails to recognize that behavior change is not solely a product of telling children what they are doing wrong but is also a function of strengthening positive behaviors children already display. Thus, in order for children to keep certain behaviors in their repertoire, they must hear that adults feel pleased, excited, amused, appreciative, comforted, or supported by their actions.

Giving up midway. Children do not always wait patiently to hear an entire personal message. They may turn their heads or simply walk away. Sometimes when this happens, adults become flustered and give up. A better approach is to use the nonverbal strategies presented in Chapter 3. Adults should lightly hold onto an uninterested child or pursue youngsters who dash off in an attempt to avoid confrontation. This does not mean jerking children around or forcing them to establish eye contact.

It does mean trying to gain the child's attention for the entire duration of the message. It also is important for children to be told that adults become annoyed when children do not listen. "You don't want to hear what I'm telling you. It upsets me when you walk away while I'm talking. Stand still and listen."

Focusing on short-term rather than long-term goals. In problem situations, adults sometimes find it easier to simply say "No" or "We don't do that here." Occasionally, these shortcuts have the desired effect: children stop what they are doing. Unfortunately, such success usually is temporary because it does not prompt children's internalization of the rule. Instead, adults have to repeat their admonitions over and over again. Moreover, children may not comply without direct supervision. Personal messages are worth the time they take because they contribute to increased self-discipline.

Making expectations known from a distance. When adults see children in threatening situations, their first impulse is to shout a warning: "Look out! You'll drop the fish tank" or "Watch it! The floor is slippery." In cases such as these, children frequently ignore the message because they do not realize it is directed at them. The adult's loud voice may cause alarm or stimulate children to become louder or more active themselves. In either case, the adult's message is not received adequately. A better approach is to move quickly over to the child and state expectations in a face-to-face interaction. The benefits of such a direct approach outweigh the seconds lost to achieve it.

Waiting too long to express your emotions. In an effort to avoid committing themselves to a line of action, some adults refrain from expressing less intense emotions and allow their emotions to build up over time. When they do react, it is often when they have reached the limit of their endurance. Then, their irritation explodes into fury, concern blossoms into real anxiety, or confusion escalates into panic. None of these are constructive responses because they are so intense that rational action becomes difficult. In addition, children usually are shocked at such extreme reactions and are genuinely uncertain as to what led to the eruption. Adults who rely on this approach also model that only extreme emotions are worth expressing. They should not be surprised when children copy their example. This pitfall can be forestalled by discussing your emotions when first aware of them.

Disguising expectations. When adults feel nervous about telling children what to do, they often disguise their rules. The most common tactic is to phrase the rule as a question. Instead of saying, "It's time to clean up," they cajole: "Don't you want to clean up, now?"; "Clean up, okay?"; "You wouldn't want us to have a messy room would you?"; or "We want a clean room, right?"

In every case, adults are hoping children will see things their way. Yet, children usually interpret these messages not as rules that they are obligated to follow, but as questions, which are optional and that can be answered with either "Yes" or "No." Adults who are unwilling to hear "No" eliminate ambiguity when they phrase their rules as statements: "Start cleaning up"; "It's time to clean up."

A final error that obscures rules is for adults to include themselves in the rule when they have no real intention of following it. For instance, adults say, "Let's wipe our bottom until it is clean," when what they mean is, "Wipe your bottom," or they say, "Let's brush our teeth," rather than "Brush your teeth." Adults who do this imply that children should look to them as a model of the behavior in question. When this does not mirror reality, the statement is confusing.

Adults who use disguising tactics limit children's chances to be successful. Rules should be phrased as statements rather than questions, using words with precise, rather than ambiguous, meanings, and in a way that leaves no doubt as to who is expected to follow them.

SUMMARY

All children must learn to behave in accordance with the expectations of their culture if they are to be accepted by society. Adults are responsible for teaching children what those expectations are, and they spend much of their time engaged in this role. Their ultimate aim is to help children develop the ability to regulate their own behavior. Self-discipline is composed of several capabilities: curbing initial impulses that might be damaging to self or others, resisting temptation, postponing gratification, implementing plans of action, and initiating appropriate social behaviors. How children feel about their behavior, how they think about it, and their previous experiences affect children's ability to achieve self-discipline. Guilt and empathy are emotional factors influencing this capacity. The development of moral reasoning, role-taking abilities, impulse control, desire for independence, language, memory, and understanding of how events are related to one another are cognitive processes that influence children's achievement of self-control.

It is generally agreed that children become more self-disciplined as they grow older; however, even in adulthood, people exhibit a wide range of behavior ranging from no self-control to self-discipline.

Amoral, adherence, identification, and internalization are terms used to describe these variations. Individuals' behaviors generally fall into one or another of these categories, although it should be noted that everyone at different times and in different circumstances may display any of them.

Children learn the values and expectations of society through direct instruction, observation, and reward and inhibiting consequences. Adults tell and show children what is expected of them—explicitly in words and implicitly by their own behavior. Different discipline styles—authoritarian, permissive, uninvolved, and authoritative—have been linked to emotional and behavioral outcomes in children. The authoritative mode produces children who feel good about themselves and are most likely to internalize standards of behavior. Therefore, it is the style of interaction we recommend adults adopt in this text.

Authoritative adults may express their expectations through a personal message. This consists of a reflection acknowledging the child's point of view, a statement to the child that describes the adult's reaction to a specific behavior of the child and the reason for the reaction, and, finally, an alternative, desirable behavior in which the child is to engage. This last step is used only in situations focusing on behavior change and serves as a rule that governs the child's behavior for that situation. Circumstances under which rules are appropriate deal with safety, protection of property, and the rights of others. The rule portion of the personal message must be reasonable, beneficial to a particular child, definable, and positive. Personal messages are also used to reinforce children's constructive behavior. Difficulties students encounter when first learning how to formulate personal messages can be overcome by paying close attention to the rationale for this particular skill.

Finally, it is important to communicate with families regarding program-related approaches to discipline. Elicit information from families and provide information to them as appropriate. Strive to develop a working partnership with family members aimed at enhancing children's development of self-discipline as well as family involvement in the formal group setting.

KEY TERMS

adherence
amoral
authoritarian discipline style
authoritative discipline style
centration
communication
control
definable rules
direct instruction
empathy

guilt
identification
internalization
maturity demands
model
moral violations
negative consequences
nurturance
permissive discipline style
perspective-taking

personal message
positive rules
private speech
reasonable rules
reinforcement
self-discipline
social-conventional infractions
uninvolved adults
uninvolved discipline style

DISCUSSION QUESTIONS

1. Define self-discipline and describe its component parts.

2. Jamal is a preschooler. His brother Ahmed is 10 years old. Discuss how guilt and empathy would figure into each child's thinking.

3. It has been shown that children become more capable of self-discipline as they mature. Explain the developmental changes that contribute to this increased capacity.

4. Define amoral, adherence, identification, and internalization. Then, discuss which behavior cues tell you when a person is operating at any one of these levels.

5. Name three rules you had to follow as a child. Talk about whether your compliance with each rule was at the adherence, identification, or internalization level.

6. Describe all of the things you could do in relation to instruction and modeling to teach a child how to handle guinea pigs safely. Make sure you take into account children's varying levels of maturity.

7. Think about a teacher you had while growing up. Describe that person's behavior to someone else, keeping in mind the four discipline styles discussed in this chapter. See if the listener can categorize the teacher's behavior based on your description. Then, discuss the effect that style had on your learning.

8. Describe what changes you might have to make in your own interaction style to make it more authoritative.

9. With classmates, identify the three parts of the personal message and provide no less than three reasons per part why each is included.

10. Refer to the NAEYC Code of Ethical Conduct presented in Appendix A. Find sections that address the following situations related to rules.

   a. The Brown family and the Smith family both have children in your class. Mrs. Brown approaches you, saying that she doesn't want her child to interact with the Smith child. She expects you to enforce this rule.

   b. One of the families in your group is from another country. The father approaches you, saying he wants his 4-year-old daughter to learn to act in the ways of her culture. This means she must be very deferential in her interactions with adults. He is disturbed that she calls out at group time, seems bossy in her play, and makes decisions such as where to play. In all of these cases, he believes that she should be more submissive. He wants you to support his family's expectations.

FIELD ASSIGNMENTS

1. Keep a record of the personal messages you use in your field placement. When you have a chance, record at least three of your responses. Begin by describing what the child(ren) said or did to prompt your remarks.

   Next, write the exact words you used. Critique your effectiveness and correct any inaccurate personal messages.

   Finally, record two alternate personal messages you could have tried in each situation. Make sure to identify both personal messages used to change children's behavior and ones used to reinforce positive actions.

2. Describe a situation in which your use of a personal message was effective, both from your point of view and the child's. Next, describe a situation in which your use of a personal message was ineffective. Analyze what went wrong and how your response could be improved in the future.

3. Identify a situation involving the children with whom you work, in which it may be necessary for you to establish a rule. Write out your rule. Record how well it fits the criteria for an effective rule described in this chapter. If necessary, change your rule to make it more appropriate. Next, talk about what you will do and say to remind children of the rule and to enforce it as necessary.

   Later, discuss whether or not you had to use the rule you made. Describe any changes you enacted in carrying out the rule and why. Conclude by describing the children's reactions to your rule.

4. Read program materials designed to acquaint families with program policies regarding their participation and that of the child (e.g., enrollment materials, program handbook, introductory newsletter). List at least five rules, policies, or expectations for families and describe the reasoning behind these. If the reasoning is not obvious to you, talk to someone in the program to find out more about why the policies have been made.

For additional resources, visit our Web site
www.EarlyChildEd.delmar.com

FOSTERING SELF-DISCIPLINE IN CHILDREN: IMPLEMENTING SOLUTIONS AND CONSEQUENCES

OBJECTIVES

On completion of this chapter, you should be able to describe:

- Typical reasons why children engage in inappropriate behavior.

- Ways adults can change their behavior to help children follow rules more successfully.

- Four kinds of consequences.

- The difference between consequences and punishments.

- How to combine personal messages and consequences effectively.

- Appropriate and inappropriate uses of time-out.

- Family communication strategies related to consequences.

- Pitfalls to avoid in implementing consequences.

Adult: *You're enjoying the easel. It's time to clean up now and get ready for lunch. Please cap the paints or tag the projects that are already dry.*

Child 1: *No.*

Child 2: *I don't want to.*

Child 3: *(Says nothing; continues to paint at the easel.)*

USING CONSEQUENCES TO PROMOTE SOCIAL COMPETENCE

Learning to voluntarily comply with reasonable rules and requests is a major component of social competence. Yet, as everyone knows, there are times when children refuse to do what they are asked to do, when they behave inappropriately, or when they fail to follow a given rule. What to do in such situations is a common concern of teachers, caregivers, and parents (Charles, Seuter, & Barr, 2005). On the one hand, adults want children to comply; on the other hand, they are often unsure of how to achieve obedience in developmentally appropriate ways. This chapter will address such concerns.

Everything you read will be based on three assumptions. First, children are novices when it comes to social behavior. Although they generally want to act in ways that adults and peers find acceptable, they are not always successful. Second, learning the rules of society is a complex process that takes time and practice to master. It is not automatic nor is it easy. Third, children make mistakes.

Such mistaken behavior can come about for several reasons:

1. Children are not sure of what the rules are or how to follow them.
2. Children know that certain behaviors are inappropriate, but they do not know what to do instead.
3. Children are not capable of following a particular rule.
4. Children have difficulty controlling impulsive behavior.
5. Children have mistaken perceptions about how to gain acceptance.
6. Other significant adults, siblings, or peers advocate certain behaviors that are counter to the rule.

7. Children think that the rule is unjustified or unnecessary.
8. Children have no ownership of the rules and no investment in following them.
9. Children have learned that unacceptable behaviors are usually ignored or that following the rule makes no difference.
10. Children are testing the adult to see how far he or she will bend in relation to the rule and how consistently the rule will be enforced.

In most instances, any one or a combination of these reasons may be why children act inappropriately. Such problems often improve when adults make changes in their own behavior.

BEHAVIOR PROBLEMS AND THEIR SOLUTIONS

Problem 1: Children Are Uncertain About What the Rules Are and How to Follow Them

Problem 2: Children Can't Figure Out What Actions to Substitute for Unacceptable Ones

Problem 3: Adults Have Inappropriate Expectations for Children's Behavior

These three problems result from poor rule making (MacKenzie, 2003). In each case, children make mistakes because they are incapable of following a particular rule rather than because they are unwilling. In essence, ineffective rules predict children's failure because children lack the guidance necessary to succeed. If this experience is repeated frequently, children may stop trying to comply, convinced that their efforts are hopeless. What began as a problem related to inappropriate rule setting may escalate as children continue to rely on ineffective strategies.

Solution. As described in Chapter 10, effective rules are ones children are capable of following. They also tell children appropriate behaviors to substitute for inappropriate ones (this is the fourth R of the personal message). Rules that are reasonable, definable, and positive meet these criteria and make it less likely that children will continue mistaken behavior.

Problem 4: Acting on Impulse

At times, children act without thinking: an idea or desire pops into their heads, and they are in motion; they see something they want and grab for it; they think something and blurt it out (Berk, 2006; Calkins, 1994). Impulsivity decreases with age, and by 6 years of age most children can inhibit their impulses relatively well. However, there are youngsters who remain impulsive because that is their cognitive style. These children continue to act immediately on their desires, in contrast to their peers whose cognitive approach is to respond more thoughtfully (Reed, 1991; Hyson, 2004).

Solution. Impulsivity may be a function of temperament or may represent lack of maturity and skill. It is not deliberate misbehavior. Knowing this, helping professionals can assist children as young as 3 in learning how to wait and respond more thoughtfully (Mischell, 1996). For example, impulsive children benefit when adults literally help them to slow down (Educational Productions, 1993; Marion, 2007).

Slowing children down may involve physical intervention, verbal strategies, or a combination of the two. For instance, Manny bumps and bangs into children outdoors. A grown-up takes him aside, holds his hands, tells him to catch his breath, and then talks to him about hurting the other children. After Manny has regained his composure and can repeat aloud the rule about playing without hurting people, he is allowed to rejoin the other children. Oksana hurries through an assignment, doing it poorly. Her teacher asks her to repeat the task, one step at a time, promoting a more reflective, thorough response.

In addition, children can learn self-instructional strategies as a way to inhibit impulses and resist temptation (Zins, Weissberg, Wang, & Walberg, Grunwald & Pepper, et al., 2004). For instance, children who are taught to say to themselves "It is good if I wait" will find it easier to hold back than youngsters who do not have such training. The same is true when adults tell children to repeat relevant rules to themselves, such as "I shouldn't touch the stove." Such self-talk is most effective when children talk to themselves about the task in which they are involved rather than focusing on a possible reward for their behavior. Thus, it is more useful to teach them to say "I am putting away the books" rather than "When I'm through, I'll get to go outside."

Problem 5: Children's Mistaken Perceptions
Some children engage in unacceptable behavior because they have an erroneous perception of how to achieve status. There are three common perceptual errors. Certain children mistakenly believe that the only time they are valued is when they are the center of attention. Others are sure they must have power over peers and adults in order to be important. Still others

conclude that there is no point to behaving appropriately because no one cares about them or what they do (Carr et al., 2000; Greenspan & Salmon, 1996). These children can be described in turn as attention seekers, power seekers, and hopeless children. Regardless of which perception prompts their behavior, such youngsters are unable to consider the needs of those with whom they interact and are incapable of recognizing the destructive impact of their actions. As a result, they tend to perpetuate the negative interaction patterns that support their mistaken conclusions.

For instance, *attention seekers* demand constant, undue notice by playing the clown, bragging, badgering, demanding continual praise, or deliberately breaking known rules in order to elicit a reaction. Adults inadvertently encourage these problem behaviors by responding to inappropriate demands for attention and/or by failing to recognize appropriate behaviors.

Power seekers exert their power blatantly, using brute force, or more subtly by resisting other's requests. This often results in power struggles in which the child's goal is to outwit the adult. Children who have no legitimate power over their lives are most likely to succumb to this maladaptive pattern.

Hopeless children have given up all prospects of gaining attention or power. They may feel so completely rejected that their only gratification comes from hurting others as a way to be noticed (Dreikurs et al., 1998). Children in this state of mind sometimes are violent or vengeful. They make it their business to discover the vulnerability of the people with whom they come in contact and take advantage of this knowledge. This counterproductive approach gains them the notoriety they seek.

Not all hopeless children resort to hurtful behavior, however. Some act completely helpless in an effort to discourage anyone from expecting too much of them (Pomerantz & Ruble, 1997). They avoid any situation in which there is a chance for failure. Their perception of absolute inadequacy is reinforced when adults focus primarily on their mistakes or take over rather than allowing them to do things for themselves.

Solution. Changing children's perceptions is no easy matter; yet, in situations like these, it is the key to making permanent improvements in their behavior. Adults must first recognize and acknowledge misconceptions, then make a conscious effort to help children learn alternative ways of establishing their self-worth (Seligman, 1995; Dowling, 2005).

Attention seekers The positive behaviors of attention seekers should be rewarded by personal messages and effective praise. When a child engages in inappropriate actions, the adult can choose either of two options. The first is to ignore minor eruptions and wait for the child to choose a more appropriate action before giving attention. The second option, better suited to more severe bids for notice, involves reflecting the child's desire for attention, explaining that it will not be given until he or she demonstrates more desirable behavior, then following through with this plan (Dreikurs et al., 1998; Greenspan & Salmon, 1996).

Power seekers Power-seeking youngsters should have an opportunity to experience legitimate power. Giving children choices, allowing them to make decisions, and requesting their participation in planning are effective and appropriate ways to achieve this. When power struggles occur, the key to defusing them is to remain calm, to refrain from fighting, and to refuse to give in (Dowling, 2005). The exact ways in which adults can get themselves out of these entanglements will be described later in this chapter.

Hopeless children Hopeless youngsters need nurturing relationships with adults as well as opportunities to experience meaningful success in order to alter their self-perceptions (Curwin & Mendler, 2000). It is particularly important that adults not reinforce children's dismal assessments of their capacities by becoming punitive or detached. Instead, they must see through children's defenses and show the children that there are some things about them that are likable and worthy. It often takes imagination and effort to identify such qualities, but it is obvious that if adults cannot see them, children never will.

Problem 6: Contradictory Rules

It is not unusual for the influential people in children's lives to have differing ideas about how children should behave. As a result, they may actively support conflicting codes of conduct. For instance, school personnel may tell children to settle disagreements peacefully, but family members may encourage them to "defend themselves." In this situation, the school's main focus is on teaching children harmonious group living, and parents are interested in teaching them self-defense skills. Both goals have merit, but are different. This puts children in a dilemma. In an effort to obey one set of expectations, they may violate another.

Solution. We must remember that our expectations are not the only appropriate ones, nor are they the only ones with which children are expected to comply. Consequently, helping professionals must work with the other members of children's mesosystems to minimize the dilemmas youngsters face. How this can best be accomplished is described in Chapter 15, Making Ethical Judgments and Decisions.

Furthermore, when adults use personal messages, they help children realize that people have differing reactions to their behavior. This enables helping professionals to stress that certain standards may be situation specific: "You're upset. At home you don't have to pick up. It bothers me when the puzzles are all over the floor. We could lose the pieces. Here at school everybody helps. There is a puzzle for you to put away."

Problem 7: Silly Rules

Problem 8: No Ownership of the Rules

Children often reject rules that seem silly or unnecessary (Kohn, 1996). Rules that make no sense from the child's point of view and rules that seem arbitrary are ones children are less likely to follow. Similarly, rules mandated by adults alone elicit less support than expectations and solutions that involve child input.

Solution. Adults minimize children's rejection of rules when they give reasons for their rules and requests. As mentioned in Chapter 10, the reasons that make sense to young children are ones that focus on keeping people safe and those that protect property. Eventually protecting people's rights also becomes an understandable rationale for certain expectations.

In addition, children are most willing to adopt a code of behavior in which they have some say (Landy, 2002). Young children benefit from participating in discussions about problem situations in the classroom and their potential solutions. Such discussions often highlight why rules are important to groups of people living and working together and what rules the children think should be observed (Hendrick & Weissman, 2006; Rightmeyer, 2003). When children have opportunities to define problems they would like to see resolved as well as identify rules to abide by, they perceive those rules as legitimate social agreements and themselves as partners in those agreements. This prompts children to become invested in helping create an environment in which such rules are honored.

See Figure 11-1 for an example of how one first-grade class put this solution into practice.

PROBLEM SOLVING IN A WHOLE-CLASS MEETING	
ROUTINE	IN PRACTICE
1. A child experiencing a problem writes it on the agenda for discussion at class meeting.	Joshua writes "Blocks—Joshua" on the agenda.
2. At class meeting, the teacher asks a class member to bring the agenda to the group.	"Hope, would you please bring the agenda to the rug?"
3. The teacher reads the first problem on the agenda.	"It says here 'Blocks—Joshua.' Joshua, will you please explain what the problem is?"
4. The student who listed the item explains why it is a problem for him or her.	"Well, yesterday I had blocks for my cleanup job, and when I went in there, every block was on the floor and there was no one left to help me. I had to put all the blocks back by myself."
5. If needed, the teacher helps the child clarify the problem and make it explicit for the other children.	"Why is that a problem, Joshua?" "It's a problem because I had to do it by myself." "What's the problem with that?" "Because it's too much work for one person. I didn't even play in blocks!" "So you don't like it when you have to put away someone else's blocks all by yourself, is that it?" "Yeah, that's right."
6. The children suggest solutions to the problem.	"We should have four people clean up blocks." "The people who play blocks should clean them up." "The people who play blocks should clean them up for five minutes, and then one person should do the rest of the job." "The people who play in blocks should clean them up for four minutes and then two people finish the job." "We should close blocks for a week." "We should have two people clean the blocks."
7. The person with the problem chooses one of the solutions. If none are acceptable, that person invites one.	"What do you think we should do, Joshua?" "I think we should clean up our own spot for five minutes, and then four people do blocks."
8. The teacher repeats the solution to check for accuracy and writes it in the solutions book. The solution is tried for a week.	Written in the Book of Solutions: "January 30. At cleanup time, first clean up your own spot for five minutes; then do your assigned job."

Figure 11-1 Example of how children can participate in problem solving and rule creation.
Source: Reprinted with permission from "Democratic Discipline: Children Creating Solutions," by E. C. Rightmeyer, 2003, *Young Children*, 58(4), 40.

Problem 9: Mixed Messages

Even when a rule is appropriately stated to children, adult actions may undermine it. This happens when adults fail to reward compliance, ignore broken rules, or give in to noncompliance (MacKenzie, 2003; Miller, 2007). Such acts create an unpredictable environment in which children cannot be sure what the real expectations are. For example, a rule in the mixed-age preschool room is that children should wear a smock to paint at the easel. Some days, adults enforce the rule regularly; on other days adults pay little attention and many children paint without smocks. It is not surprising that children are unsure of the rule and seldom remember to use a smock on their own. Similarly, at Roosevelt Elementary School, it is expected that children will eat their lunch at a moderate pace. Youngsters are understandably confused when, on the days they eat slowly, no one notices.

Additionally, on some days they are scolded for gobbling their food, but on other days they are urged to eat faster (adults are running late), and on still other days they are ignored when they wolf down their sandwiches (adults are too tired to cope). Adult actions have made enforcement of the rule arbitrary. Over time, youngsters conclude that the rule has no real meaning and do not feel obliged to uphold it.

Problem 10: Testing the Limits

Children constantly try to determine what constitutes in-bounds and out-of-bounds behavior. The only way they can discover these differences is to test them out by repeated trial and error (Bell, Carr, Denno, Johnson, & Phillips, 2004). Because adults vary in their willingness to obtain compliance, children test each adult with whom they come in contact to discover that person's limits. Both forms of testing frequently result in inappropriate behavior.

Solution. The way to resolve behavior problems related to mixed messages and limit testing is to enforce rules consistently through the use of consequences. The following portion of this chapter focuses on this important skill.

CONSEQUENCES

Consequences are events that make a particular behavior more or less likely to happen in the future. Positive consequences increase the chances that behaviors will be repeated, and inhibiting consequences reduce them.

Consequences That Increase Desirable Behaviors

Positive consequences are ones that reward children for maintaining a rule or encourage them to repeat a positive behavior in the future (Marzano, 2003). One of the most common and most effective is to reinforce children's behavior with a positive

When the children put the blocks away, their behavior could be reinforced with a positive personal message.

personal message. For instance, when Mr. Moore says: "LaTisha, you remembered to raise your hand before talking. I'm pleased. That gave me a chance to finish what I was saying," his message is highlighting the child's appropriate behavior in a way that will make an impression on LaTisha. In addition, it acknowledges that following the rule took effort.

When adults affirm children's compliance using personal messages, children are likely to comply again in the future. This is because positive personal messages remind children of rules and their rationale at times when children have demonstrable proof that they are able to follow it. This type of confirmation is beneficial to children of all ages.

Another positive consequence, with which readers already are familiar from Chapter 4, is effective praise. An example is when the adult points out, "You've been reminding yourself to bring your homework every day this week. You've made it to

Thursday already with homework every day." This nonevaluative acknowledgment of children's rule-related behavior underscores their growing ability to act in socially acceptable ways.

Similarly, when adults acknowledge the accumulated benefits of following a rule over time, they promote children's feelings of self-satisfaction and pride in their own performance. For instance, if the rule were "practice the piano every day," the adult might say: "You were a big hit at the recital. All of your practicing really paid off."

Positive consequences can take the form of earned privileges too. For instance, if the rule is "handle library books carefully," when children can demonstrate this skill, they are permitted to use the books without adult assistance. This type of reward actually formalizes the natural aftermath of their positive behavior. It also emphasizes the positive outcomes that result from their actions. When this information is articulated, the link between behavior and outcome becomes more evident.

Finally, there are times when positive consequences take the form of tangible rewards such as stickers or stars on a progress chart. For example, a child may receive a sticker for each day she is able to get through the morning without hitting another child. Such tangible rewards serve as concrete evidence of positive behavior and help some children recognize their accomplishments. Though tangible rewards are not used in every setting, they are used in some situations, with beneficial outcomes.

Consequences That Reduce Mistaken Behaviors

Social scientists commonly refer to all consequences that reduce problem behaviors as punishments. However, research shows that some uses of punishment are effective in promoting self-discipline and others are not. To clearly distinguish between the two, we will label strategies that enhance self-control as **inhibiting consequences** and strategies that detract from self-control as **punishments**. There are significant differences between the two. These are summarized in Table 11-1.

Punishments. Punishments such as hitting children, yelling at them, or shaming them make children suffer in order to teach them a lesson (Kohn, 1996). These are harsh, unreasonable actions that rely on power and force to change children's behavior or get them to do something. They may be carried out with no warning or in a threatening manner that frightens or humiliates children. As described in Table 11-1, punishments focus on making children "pay" for their misdeeds, rather than teaching them how to behave more appropriately. Punishments do not emphasize reasoning or the development of empathy for others. Nor do they teach children desirable alternatives to their misbehavior (Coie & Dodge, 1998). Consequently, children who are punished on a regular basis tend to adopt the coercive demeanor to which they have been subjected, becoming increasingly defiant and hostile (Beaudoin & Taylor, 2004; Strassberg, Dodge, Pettit, & Bates, 1994). Much of their time also is spent figuring out how to do what they want without getting caught (Newman & Newman, 2003). For all these reasons, punishments lead to short-term compliance only. Children remain at adherence because they do not acquire the tools necessary for internalization (empathy, reasoning, new behaviors).

Inhibiting consequences. The rule in Ms. Vigna's classroom is that children must roll up their sleeves to work with the clay. As Julia approaches the clay table, she is reminded to roll up her sleeves. When she fails to do so, Ms. Vigna intervenes. She calmly talks to the child about why her long sleeves could get smeared with clay. Then she helps Julia step back from the clay table to roll up her sleeves. The act of rolling up her sleeves with the teacher's help enables Julia to rehearse the desired behavior and may remind her to roll up her sleeves in the future. As such, it acts as an inhibiting consequence.

Inhibiting consequences are constructive actions aimed at helping children recognize the impact their behavior has on themselves and others. They are implemented with the long-term goal of teaching children self-discipline. Inhibiting consequences help children learn acceptable conduct from the experience of being corrected. They enable children to approximate desired acts. They also serve as practice for the future and make it more likely that children will succeed in repeating appropriate behaviors independently (Bell et al., 2004). When properly applied, inhibiting consequences encourage children to think about characteristics of problem situations, which may be useful to them in future encounters. For example, what prompted the episode, how and why did people react to the child's behavior, and what acceptable alternatives were suggested? This self-analysis is possible because inhibiting consequences do not elicit intense feelings of fear or

Table 11-1 Differences Between Inhibiting Consequences and Punishments

INHIBITING CONSEQUENCES	PUNISHMENTS
Children are accepted, even when their behavior is not	Children are rejected
Are instructive—they teach children how to correct problem behaviors	Are not instructive—they inform children that a problem has occurred, but do not teach them how to correct it
Focus on mistaken behavior	Focus on "bad" child
Have a clear link to the mistaken behavior	Have no relationship to the mistaken behavior
Are thoughtfully imposed	Are arbitrary and demeaning
Communicate that children have the power to correct mistaken behaviors	Communicate the personal power of the adult
Enable children to change their own behavior	Require adults to assume the entire responsibility for behavior change
Focus on prevention of future mistakes	Focus on retaliation for mistakes
Are applied matter-of-factly	Are applied with obvious resentment, anger, indifference or contempt
Are applied in proportion to the severity of the mistaken behavior	Are severe and exceed the severity of the mistaken behavior
Rely on reasoning	Rely on coercion

Sources: From *Discipline Without Tears*, by R. Dreikurs and P. Cassel, 1992, New York: Hawthorn Books; *Discipline with Dignity*, by R. L. Curwin and A. N. Mendler, 1999, Reston, Virginia: Reston Publishing Co.; and *A Guidance Approach to the Encouraging Classroom*, by D. Gartrell, 2007, Clifton Park, NY: Delmar Learning.

shame, both of which interfere with children's ability to reason.

Another attribute of inhibiting consequences is that they make the children's world more predictable; children know exactly what will happen when a rule is broken. Infractions are dealt with matter-of-factly and consistently, no matter who the perpetrators are or how often they have broken the rule before. This makes it easier for children to recognize the link between actions and reactions and to gradually internalize an acceptable code of conduct.

Types of Inhibiting Consequences

Inhibiting consequences come in three varieties: natural, logical, and unrelated.

Natural consequences. Natural consequences happen without intervention by an adult (MacKenzie, 2003). They are a direct result of the child's behavior alone. As such, natural consequences signal children that their actions matter and that they have the power to influence outcomes. For instance, if children fail to put their jackets in their cubbies, the natural consequence may be a lost jacket. Children who come late for lunch may experience the natural consequence of eating cold food or eating alone because everyone else is finished. Natural consequences are most effective when they are obvious to children and when children care about the outcome: wanting to wear the lost jacket; not wanting to eat cold food or by themselves. Eventually children will learn to put their jackets away if they want to find them easily or come on time for lunch if they prefer warm food or eating with friends.

Logical consequences. When Jamie draws on a tabletop in her classroom, an adult talks with her about her actions and their impact on classroom materials. Then she helps Jamie gather what she needs to scrub the table clean. Scrubbing helps Jamie restore damaged property and makes an obvious connection between the inappropriate behavior of drawing on the table and the consequence of cleaning it (Bell et al., 2004; MacKenzie, 2003). This makes scrubbing the table a logical consequence. **Logical consequences** generally take one of three forms:

- Rehearsal (children approximate or practice a desired behavior)

- Restitution (children make genuine amends for their misbehavior)
- Temporary loss of privilege (for a brief time, children forfeit a privilege they have abused)

Rehearsal   If Rudy is running down the hall, a logical consequence would be to have him go back and walk. The act of walking serves as a more relevant reminder of the rule than would scolding him or making him sit out for several minutes. Walking actually enables Rudy to "rehearse" the appropriate behavior he is expected to use in the future. Having children practice rules you want them to remember increases their likelihood of following the rule another time on their own.

Restitution   At times rehearsals are not feasible, and so restitution is more appropriate. This was demonstrated by Jamie, who drew on the table, then scrubbed away the marks, returning the table to its original condition. Similarly, the logical consequence

when children throw food on the floor is to insist that they clean it up prior to getting anything else to eat. This act restores the situation to a more acceptable state and shows children that the unacceptable behavior of throwing food will not be tolerated. In this way, restitution improves a problem situation or repairs damage done.

Rehearsal and restitution are the most common forms of logical consequences (Charles, Seuter & Barr, 2005; Charney, 2002). They support the development of self-control among children of all ages and are well suited for most situations in which consequences are needed. Because they are so tangible, rehearsal and restitution dominate our work with toddlers and children whose thinking is characteristically described as preoperational. As children begin to think more abstractly, temporary loss of privilege is another form of logical consequence that can help children develop greater powers of self-regulation.

The logical consequence for smearing the table with jelly is to clean it up.

The logical consequence for forgetting to flush the toilet is to go back and flush the toilet.

Temporary loss of privilege   Raymond keeps dumping the sand out of the sand table. After being warned of what will happen if he continues to throw the sand, he is asked to leave the area for a while, thereby briefly losing the privilege of playing there.

Later in the day he is allowed to return to try to play again without dumping sand. In Mr. Li's class, the children are allowed to go into the hall unaccompanied to retrieve things from their lockers. When Corinne begins wandering the corridors while getting her backpack, the teacher temporarily revokes her privilege to be in the hall on her own. She is given another chance the next day to see if she can assume the privilege responsibly. Playing at the sand table and going into the hall unsupervised involve both privilege and responsibility. When children demonstrate that they are not capable of handling the two successfully, a logical consequence interrupts the problem behavior and helps children recognize that if they wish to have certain privileges, they will have to assume the responsibilities that go with them.

Alternately, forbidding children to play outside for a week is not a logical consequence for fighting with peers over the ball. Although this penalty temporarily halts the dispute, it does not teach children how to deal with the issue more effectively in the future. A better solution would be to tell children they must take turns if they wish to continue to play, and then help them carry out this plan if they are unable to do so on their own. This proposal teaches children that sharing can be a viable solution and gives them practice doing it.

An important benefit of using logical consequences is that they teach children behaviors that are incompatible with problem behaviors children are displaying (Wolfgang, 2005). For instance, cleaning a table is incompatible with drawing on it, cleaning food off the floor is incompatible with throwing it there. As incompatible responses like these are strengthened through practice and positive consequences, the less desirable behaviors that they replace are weakened.

Hence, children who must go back and walk each time they run down the hall are rehearsing walking in the specific situation in which it is called for. This rehearsal makes it more likely that they will remember to walk on their own once in a while. If such instances are noted and praised, eventually youngsters learn to replace the taboo behavior (running) with the more desired action (walking). Further

examples of logical consequences are described in Table 11-2.

Unrelated consequences.   The third type of inhibiting consequence is an **unrelated consequence**. As the name implies, these consequences are not the natural outgrowth of a child's behavior, nor do they enable children to approximate desired behaviors or rectify less desirable ones. Instead, they are outcomes manufactured by the adult in response to children's misbehavior. Examples might include forbidding Lisa to watch television until she brushes her teeth or to choose a learning center until she hangs up her coat. Brushing teeth has nothing to do with watching television, so denial of television neither teaches Lisa how to brush her teeth nor improves her unclean mouth. However, if Lisa really values her time in front of the set, she will quickly learn that watching television is contingent on tooth brushing. The same is true regarding the coat. Forbidding Lisa to choose a workstation does not give her practice in hanging up her coat. What it does do is create an aversive situation that the child can make more positive by doing what is required.

Unrelated consequences involve the introduction of a penalty unrelated to the offense. It is the unrelated nature of the penalty that distinguishes these consequences from the loss of privilege variation of logical consequences. Because they have no relation to the broken rule, adults must take particular care to enforce these in the true spirit of consequences, not punishments. Furthermore, the most beneficial unrelated consequences are those that, although dissimilar in content, are linked in time to the infraction. For instance, it is more effective to withhold the next event in a sequence than one far in the future. Therefore, it is better to deprive Lisa of participating in some portion of the free-choice period for forgetting to hang up her coat than to keep her in from recess several hours later. Of the three types of inhibiting consequences described here, unrelated consequences are used least often. However, there are times when they are appropriate. How to decide when to use each type will be discussed next.

Deciding Which Inhibiting Consequences to Use

Inhibiting consequences are important instructional tools that have the power to teach children right from wrong, to help them distinguish appropriate from inappropriate behavior, and to demonstrate

Table 11-2 Examples of Logical Consequences

PROBLEM BEHAVIOR	LOGICAL CONSEQUENCE	FORM OF LOGICAL CONSEQUENCE
Lacey knocks over another child's blocks.	Lacey helps rebuild the block structure.	Restitution
Lindsey makes a mess.	Lindsey cleans it up.	Restitution
Chris hits another child in anger.	Chris gets a tissue to soothe the victim's tears.	Restitution
	Chris is separated from the victim and must remain near an adult to be reminded not to hit.	Rehearsal
	Chris must develop a plan for what to do when angry rather than hitting.	Rehearsal
	Adult provides Chris with a script to use in lieu of hitting and has Chris practice using it.	Rehearsal
	Chris looks up potential words to use for "angry scripts" in lieu of hitting.	Rehearsal
Taylor rips pages out of a book.	Taylor repairs the book.	Restitution
	Taylor replaces the book.	Restitution
	Taylor helps pay for the book.	Restitution
Gena says she finished her work so she can go to another activity, but she really didn't.	Instead of moving from one activity to another independently, Gena must show her finished work to the adult before moving on.	Temporary loss of privilege
Jennifer keeps slamming the computer keys.	Jennifer practices striking the computer keys gently (this could be on her own or with help from a peer or adult).	Rehearsal
	Jennifer must give up using the computer for a short while.	Temporary loss of privilege
Leah keeps talking to her friends during an assembly.	Leah must sit apart for a while and practice focusing on the speaker.	Rehearsal
	Leah sits next to an adult who helps her focus on the speaker.	
Cora pushes to get ahead in line.	Cora must go to the back of the line.	Restitution
	Cora must leave her newfound spot and practice waiting at the back of the line with an adult.	Rehearsal
Anthony speaks rudely to the after-school caregiver.	Adult walks away after explaining that he/she will not respond when a child uses a rude tone and rude words.	Temporary loss of privilege
	Anthony may approach the caregiver when he is ready to speak more politely.	Rehearsal
Karla knocks another child to the ground.	Karla helps the child get up.	Restitution
	Karla gets a wet paper towel and band-aid to soothe the victim's injury.	Restitution

to them the potential impact of their behavior on themselves and on others. With so many valuable lessons to offer, they cannot be carelessly applied. Rather, adults must thoughtfully formulate the consequences they use. The three types of inhibiting consequences should be considered in order, from natural to logical to unrelated.

Step one. When considering natural consequences, it is important to determine three things:

Is the outcome acceptable to you?
Will the child recognize that a consequence has occurred?
Does the consequence matter to the child?

Obviously, a consequence that would result in physical harm to a child is unacceptable. The natural aftermath of a child drinking poison or playing in traffic are clear examples. Yet, things other than safety also influence acceptability. What might be acceptable to one adult might be unthinkable to another. As mentioned earlier, the natural consequence for children who arrive late for a meal is to eat cold food or eat alone. Some caregivers might view these outcomes as reasonable; others would find themselves reheating the meal or keeping the child company. If adults know they will be unable to sustain a hands-off policy, the natural consequence is not the consequence of choice. The same is true if the consequence is so subtle the child will never notice it happened (e.g., family members always eat independently, so this time is no different) or if the consequence is one the child doesn't care about (child prefers eating alone.) All of these conditions diminish the power of the natural consequence to inhibit children's behavior in the future. This makes a logical or unrelated consequence more suitable.

Step two. If the natural consequence is unsuitable, logical consequences should be considered next. These can be tailored to fit any situation. Adults should think about ways in which the rule could be reenacted (such as repeating an action correctly or carrying out the behavior with adult help) or ways in which a problem situation might be rectified. Although logical consequences take more imagination than do unrelated penalties such as sitting in isolation, going to detention, or being sent to the principal's office, they are much more effective in helping children learn appropriate alternate behaviors (Landy, 2002).

Step three. As a last resort, unrelated consequences can be implemented. These must be used sparingly because their primary value is in curtailing behavior for the moment. For long-term change to occur, children must learn acceptable substitutes for which logical consequences are preferable. Unrelated consequences should be implemented only when no logical consequence is available. See Figure 11-2 for an explanation of how the consequences described here relate to one another.

Implementing Inhibiting Consequences

Several children are crowded around the water fountain.

They begin to push and shove. Seeing that someone could get hurt, Mr. Wilson decides to intervene.

When children are engaged in potential problem situations like this, adults begin by reminding them of the rule in a matter-of-fact tone (Charles, Seuter, & Barr, 2005). The rule portion of the personal message serves as this reminder. In this case, Mr. Wilson says, "It looks like everyone wants a drink at the same time. I'm worried someone will get hurt when you are pushing like this. Take turns. One person at a time at the front." Often, such prompting is all that is needed for children to comply. If children obey at this point, they should be reinforced with effective praise. However, if they continue to disregard the rule, the adult must implement an appropriate inhibiting consequence.

The consequence is first stated to the child in the form of a warning (Curwin & Mendler, 2000). The **warning** is phrased as an either-or statement that repeats the rule and then tells the child what will happen if he or she does not follow it. Mr. Wilson's rule is "Take turns. One person at a time at the front." He might state a warning such as, "Either wait your turn, or you will have to go back to the end of the line." This warning gives children an opportunity and an incentive to change their behavior in accordance with adult expectations. It also notifies children that this is the last chance for them to comply prior to the further adult intervention.

The warning is not intended to be frightening, abusive, or threatening. Rather, it is a plain statement of fact. This means adults warn children calmly. They do not yell at children or use threatening gestures to make their point.

Once the warning is stated, the adult pauses to give children an opportunity to comply. Children's

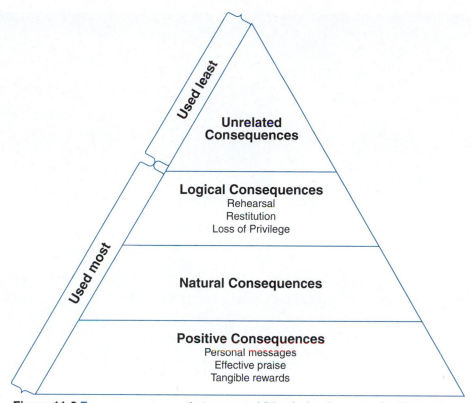

Figure 11-2 Four consequences that support children's development of self-discipline.

reaction times are somewhat slower than adults sometimes wish. Adults have to take care not to jump in before the child has had time to respond. For instance, Alexia continues to push in the line at the water fountain. Mr. Wilson tells her to wait her turn or go to the end of the line. It may take Alexia several seconds to decide what to do. Alexia's delay poses no real threat to those around her, and so it can be tolerated for a few moments to give her a chance to abide by the rule on her own.

On the other hand, there are times when safety is jeopardized. These circumstances call for immediate physical intervention, even as the warning is being stated. For example, if Marla is about to throw a stone, the adult should quickly catch her hand while saying, "You can either put the stone down yourself, or I will take it from you." Even here, a moment's pause is necessary to give Marla a chance to drop the rock herself.

The adult should maintain a grasp on Marla's hand and try to sense her intention, based on whether she remains tense or begins to relax, as well as by what she might be saying. If Marla were capable of releasing the stone herself, she would be displaying a little self-control. If she were not, the adult would exert the maximum external control by taking the stone away from her. This last step is a follow-through on the stated consequence and is very important.

Following Through on Inhibiting Consequences

It is not enough simply to tell youngsters what the consequences of their actions will be. Adults must enforce consequences if children do not comply (Bell et al., 2004; MacKenzie, 2003). This is called the **follow-through**. Based on this step, if Alexia continues to push in line at the water fountain, Mr. Wilson will follow-through by escorting her to the back of the line, as noted in the warning. The follow-through is a critical part of the discipline process because it involves the enactment of the inhibiting consequence.

Because appropriate inhibiting consequences are instructive, this step provides children with valuable information about how to redirect inappropriate behavior. It also demonstrates that adults mean what they say and that there is a limit to the amount of out-of-bounds behavior they will tolerate. From social encounters such as these children begin to build an accurate picture of their effect on the world and its reaction to them.

When adults find themselves in situations that demand a follow-through, there are certain things they must say so that the reasoning behind their

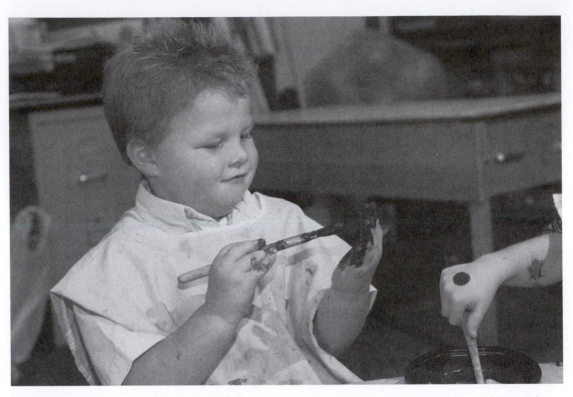

Mark enjoys making hand prints. He wants to keep the paint on all day. The teacher uses a personal message to remind him that the rule is, "Wash your hands before lunch."

The teacher warns Mark that he can "either wash his hands on his own or she will help him." When he does not comply, she gently leads him to the sink.

actions is clear to the child. It is important for children to recognize that inhibiting consequences are a result of their own behavior; they are not arbitrary or vengeful actions on the part of the adult.

The follow-through begins with a brief reflection that summarizes the situation from the child's point of view. Next is a sentence that restates the warning. This often is prefaced by the words "Remember, I told you . . ." Then, the adult repeats the consequence as a statement of what will happen next as a result of the child's behavior. This statement often begins with "now." Thus, a typical follow-through might sound like this: "Alexia, you're still anxious to get ahead in line. Remember, I told you, either wait your turn or go to the back. Now, go to the back." While this is being said, Mr. Wilson might have to escort Alexia to the back of the line as a way to physically affirm his words.

When to Implement Inhibiting Consequences

Two key factors influence how well children learn from the consequences they experience: consistency and timing. Consistency involves how often the rule is enforced. Timing refers to the period between when the rule is broken and enforcement is initiated. Rule enforcement must be consistent (Malott & Suarez, 2004; Charney, 2002). Every time the rule is broken, the adult must be prepared to enact appropriate inhibiting consequences to ensure compliance.

Rules that are administered one day and neglected the next are ineffective. Because children cannot be sure whether or not the rule is in operation, they are not likely to follow it. As a result, youngsters who experience erratic rule enforcement tend to demonstrate more incidents of mistaken behavior than do children whose experience has been more regular. Because consistency is so important, adults are cautioned to insist on only a few rules at a time. It is better to unwaveringly enforce one or two important rules than to half-heartedly attempt many rules.

In addition to being consistent, rule enforcement must be immediate. Long delays between the moment when the child breaks the rule and the moment when the follow-through takes place weaken the impact of the consequence (O'Leary, 1995). In other words, it would be ineffective for Mr. Wilson to tell Alexia that if she continued to push at the water fountain, she wouldn't get a treat later in the day.

Moving to the back of the line soon after the pushing occurred helped Alexia focus more clearly on the problem behavior and its logical solution. Children must have an opportunity to associate their inappropriate behavior with an immediate consequence. The further removed the consequence is in time from the act itself, the more difficult it is for children to make a connection. For these same reasons, consistency and immediacy are important to the implementation of positive consequences as well.

COMBINING THE WARNING AND FOLLOW-THROUGH WITH THE PERSONAL MESSAGE

Up to this point, we have focused on the appropriate use of both positive and inhibiting consequences. Yet, consequences do not stand alone. Rather, the follow-through stage of rule enforcement represents the final step in a sequence of skills aimed at enhancing children's development of self-control. This sequence consists of a personal message succeeded by a warning and then, if necessary, a follow-through. The sequence is illustrated in the following situation.

SITUATION: Mr. Howard, a student teacher, enters the bathroom to find Alan stuffing several paper towels down the toilet. Water and towels are all over the floor. The child does not see the adult come in.

PERSONAL MESSAGE: Mr. Howard quickly approaches Alan and stands close to him. He catches Alan's hand just as the child reaches for another towel. Mr. Howard says, "Alan, you're having fun. I'm worried that with this water all over the floor, someone will slip and get hurt. Start cleaning up this mess." Mr. Howard pauses a moment and waits for Alan to comply. Instead, Alan tries to move toward the door. Mr. Howard stops him.

WARNING: "You'd rather not clean up. Either you figure out where to start cleaning, or I'll tell you where to start." Again, Mr. Howard waits a few seconds in the hope that Alan will begin. The child just stands there. Mr. Howard calmly hands Alan a bucket and a sponge.

FOLLOW-THROUGH: "It's hard for you to make a choice. Remember, I said either you choose, or I'd choose. You can start in this corner." Mr. Howard places the sponge in Alan's hand and edges him toward the puddle.

Skill-Sequence Rationale

By combining a personal message with a warning and follow-through, Mr. Howard was using a step-by-step sequence designed, in the short run, to change Alan's unacceptable behavior. Its long-range objective is to provide a structure through which Alan eventually learns self-regulation.

Short-term benefits. The immediate advantages to both Mr. Howard and Alan of the sequential use of a personal message, warning, and follow through are outlined in Table 11-3.

Long-term benefits. The skills just described offer short-term advantages to adults and children; they provide long-term benefits as well. Combining a personal message, a warning, and a follow-through helps adults deal with children's inappropriate behaviors consistently, both for the same child over time and among different children. This consistency enables helping professionals to establish an authoritative pattern of interaction with youngsters in formal group settings. In addition, the time adults initially invest in using the sequence with children pays off later in fewer future mistaken behaviors (Bell et al., 2004).

Children also profit when their confrontations with adults are eventually reduced. They feel more

Table 11-3 Short-Term Benefits of the Sequential Use of a Personal Message, Warning, and Follow-Through

	SHORT-TERM BENEFITS FOR MR. HOWARD	SHORT-TERM BENEFITS FOR ALAN
Step 1a: Personal Message	Has a way to enter the situation calmly and rationally	Is treated with respect and acceptance
	Has a means of communicating respect and acceptance of the child, but disapproval of the behavior	Is alerted that his behavior is inappropriate and is told why
	Has a blueprint for what kinds of information to provide the child initially	Is informed via the rule of what to do instead (clean up the mess)
Step 1b: Pause	Has a chance to see if Alan can comply before he exerts further external control	Is given a chance to change the inappropriate behavior on his own, thereby exercising internal control
	Has a moment to think of an appropriate consequence to use if necessary	
Step 2a: Warning	Has a constructive way to exert increased external control over Alan's behavior	Is reminded of the rule
	Establishes a legitimate foundation for carrying out the follow-through if necessary	Gains a clear understanding of what will happen if he does not comply
Step 2b: Pause	Has a chance to see if Alan can comply before he exerts further external control	Is given a chance to change the inappropriate behavior on his own, thereby exercising internal control
Step 3: Follow-through	Has an authoritative way to resolve the situation without becoming abusive or giving in	Is able to rehearse an acceptable behavior he was not able to carry out on his own
	Has been able to stop the negative behavior as well as remedy the problem situation	Has evidence that the adult means what he says and is predictable in his actions
	Has had an opportunity to demonstrate that he means what he says, increasing his predictability in the eyes of the child	

successful and better able to satisfy their needs in ways that result in social rewards rather than social costs. The resulting positive self-appraisal enhances their feelings of self-esteem. Moreover, as children experience this sequence on a variety of occasions, they gradually shift from complete dependence on external, adult control, as embodied in the follow-through, to greater internal control, as prompted by the personal message and warning.

When the sequence is first introduced, most youngsters will test the adult's predictability and resolve by proceeding all the way to the follow-through. As children become more familiar with both the adult and the sequence of steps described here, they often respond to the warning without having to experience the follow-through directly. This happens because they have learned that the adult means what he or she says and that a warning indicates that a follow-through is forthcoming unless the behavior is changed. Behavior change at this point shows that children are beginning to exercise some self-regulation. They are at the adherence level, focused on avoiding a consequence or gaining the benefits of compliance.

Eventually, children reach a point at which a personal message is all that is needed to guide their actions. In this way, they begin to exert greater control over their behavior, while the adult exerts less. Initially, this change occurs because children respond to the emotions of the adult with whom they identify. Gradually, however, they take into account the reasoning behind the expectation and, as a result, consider the effects their actions have on those around them. Such reasoning ultimately leads to internalization.

As this occurs, it is the child who assumes the greatest responsibility for his or her conduct, not the adult. Thus, the adult's use of the skill sequence in any given situation will match the child's ability to exercise inner control. If the child is able to comply based on the reasoning of the personal message, further intervention is unnecessary. However, should a youngster need more support, it is provided. The relationship between children's degree of self-discipline and the skill sequence is depicted in Table 11-4.

Successive Use of the Skill Sequence

It is not unusual for children to resist complying by attempting to divert the adult's attention from the issue at hand. Shouting, protesting, escalating the problem behavior, or running away are common strategies children may use. All of these tactics are aimed at getting the adult to forget about enforcement, allowing the child to escape consequences. Unfortunately, if adults give up, they are teaching

Table 11-4 Four Types of Compliance

TYPE OF COMPLIANCE	DEFINITION	SOURCE OF BEHAVIOR CONTROL	STAGE OF THE SKILL SEQUENCE THAT APPLIES
Amoral	Children have no sense of right or wrong.	External to child	Child requires a follow-through
Adherence	Children respond to rewards and punishments; they often anticipate these and behave accordingly.	Shared between others and the child—primary responsibility remains with adult	Child responds to warning
Identification	Children attempt to adopt behavioral codes of admired others; they second-guess how that person might behave in varying situations and act likewise.	Shared between others and the child—child assumes greater share of responsibility	Child responds to personal message
Internalization	Children govern their behavior using an internal code of ethics created from their own values and judgments.	Internal to child	Child monitors self

children that these tactics work. As a result, children begin to rely on inappropriate strategies more and more frequently.

This dilemma must be avoided at all costs because the more ingrained an inappropriate behavior becomes, the more difficult it is to change. The best way to deal with such situations is to defuse them right at the start. This means always following through once a warning has been stated and the child has failed to demonstrate compliance. For example, if the warning is "Either walk, or I will help you," that is exactly what must happen. If Ginger runs away, she must be retrieved; if Vince curses, it is best to ignore his words; if Saul become stiff or goes limp, his feet should be shuffled along. Even a few steps is enough to make the point.

Sometimes one problem behavior will lead to another. For instance, 4-year old Linda climbs to the top of the bookcase as part of her superhero play. The helping professional approaches and goes through the sequence to the warning, which is "Either come down by yourself, or I will take you down." Linda laughs and shouts, "You can't get me!" Grasping the child's foot, the adult begins to follow through. As she takes the child into her arms, Linda starts to kick. Kicking represents a new problem behavior and is treated as such. The adult initiates the sequence again. This time, the warning is "either keep your feet still, or I will hold your feet until you do." The adult then follows through until Linda becomes less agitated. In this way, the adult has demonstrated that he or she will follow through over and over again until the negative behaviors diminish. When adults enforce their rules as illustrated here, they create a predictable, stable environment for children and leave no doubt in children's minds as to what will happen when rules are followed or broken. This type of consistency is absolutely necessary if children are to learn that there is no behavior they can display to which adults are unable to respond rationally and fairly.

GUIDING THE SOCIAL BEHAVIOR OF CHILDREN WITH SPECIAL NEEDS

Based on everything you have read in this chapter, you might consider intervening in these situations, reminding each child of the appropriate rules and applying consequences as necessary. Would any of that change if you were to learn that one or more of these children had some type of disability—a

At greeting time, the teacher reviews the steps for painting at the easel, including putting on a paint smock. As soon as free-choice starts, 3-year-old Kenyon begins painting without a covering up first. He continues painting even after the teacher reminds him of the rule.

What should the teacher do?
In the kindergarten, Devonne has difficulty sitting through group time. She frequently interrupts the story, stands up in front of the other children, and laughingly pokes at children nearby.

What should the teacher do?
Gerald, a third grader, is reading a book and saying "hoooy boy" over and over, sometimes loudly and sometimes under his breath. His actions could distract the other children.

What should the teacher do?

hearing impairment, Down Syndrome, or Tourette Syndrome? It is common for teachers-in-training to wonder if skills they are learning are also applicable to working with children who have disabilities. At no time is this more true than when addressing the subject of helping children develop self-discipline.

All young children need to learn limits, sharing, turn taking, as well as appropriate behavior for different settings. This includes children with disabilities, though in some instances it will take them longer to learn and consistently apply these skills (Paasche, Gorrill & Strom, 2004). Most of the guidance strategies you are acquiring through this textbook can be applied universally. However, adaptations may be necessary to accommodate children's special needs. Some accommodations will be tailored to meet the unique characteristics of each child's condition. For instance, certain strategies you would use to support a child with a hearing impairment are different from others you might use to guide the behavior of a child with a visual impairment or traumatic brain injury.

Specific ideas about how to work with a child who has a particular special need can be developed by consulting with family members and specialists in the field, by reading, and by contacting professional organizations dedicated to supporting people with particular conditions. In addition, there are

- Observe children carefully.
  Determine if there are sights, sounds, smells, sensations, people, routines, or times in the day that seem to trigger a child's misbehavior or make it more difficult for him or her to behave successfully.
  Determine what delights each child and what he or she might view as a positive consequence.
- Head off problem behaviors in advance.
  Reduce sensory overload.
  Make adjusts in environments, routines and schedules to avoid triggers that prompt mistaken behavior.
  Increase supervision and social support as necessary.
- Get children's attention before stating rules and consequences.
- Use repetition to enhance children's understanding of rules and consequences.
  Create predictable routines that enable children to follow rules more successfully.
  Repeat the same few rules often.
  Use the personal message, warning and follow-through consistently.
- Break rules/expectations into manageable steps.
  Teach one step at a time.
  Reward small steps.
  Do not expect 100% compliance 100% of the time.
- Give children ample time to respond to rules and warnings.
  Become familiar with each child's response pattern.
  Avoid demanding instant compliance.
- Apply demands for compliance wisely.
  Ignore some behaviors that are annoying, but that do not threaten safety, property, or rights.
  Choose logical consequences that help a child and those around him or her be more successful in doing what needs to be done.
  Avoid shame as a consequence to get children to behave.

Figure 11-3 General strategies for implementing rules and consequences with children who gave special needs.

Adapted from: Klein, M. D., Cook, R. E. & Richardson-Gibbs, A. M. (2001). *Strategies for Including Children with Special Needs in Early Childhood Settings*. Albany, NY: Delmar/Thomson Learning; Stephens, T. J., (2006). *Discipline Strategies for Children with Disabilities*. School of Medicine & Health Sciences, Center for Disabilities, University of South Dakota, Sioux Falls, SD.

a number of generic strategies that can be used effectively with any child who has special needs or who may need extra help for any reason in learning to comply with classroom rules. Some of these are listed in Figure 11-3.

Now that you have reviewed general strategies to guide the social behavior of children with special needs, let us revisit Kenyon, Devonne, and Gerald in their classrooms.

Kenyon has a hearing impairment. This makes it difficult for him to respond to verbal communication. He is better able to get the message through visible communication such as pictographs, demonstrations, sign language or Cued Speech (using hand signals in combination with mouth movements to make the sounds of spoken language look different from each other) (National Dissemination Center for Children with Disabilities, 2004). Initially, Kenyon's

teacher uses visible communication to make sure Kenyon is aware of the rule (drawing his attention to the steps for painting shown in a pictograph and physically offering him a smock to put on). If Kenyon continues to paint without a smock, the teacher warns Kenyon that if he doesn't put on a smock he will have to leave the easel until he does. If Kenyon ignores the warning, the teacher leads the child away from the easel and helps him put on a smock (rehearsal) before he is allowed to continue.

Devonne has Down Syndrome. This disorder, caused by a chromosomal anomaly, involves a combination of birth defects including some degree of mental retardation and often visual as well as hearing impairments (March of Dimes Birth Defects Foundation, 2007). Devonne's interruptions at group time are good natured, but disruptive to the other children. Her teacher establishes a few important rules for everyone—sit on your bottom and keep your hands to yourself. She repeats these before and during each group time. An aide sits near Devonne. When Devonne gets up, the aide quietly reminds her of the rule in an abbreviated form (Devonne, remember the rule is "sit" so everyone can see.) If Devonne continues to stand, she is warned that she will have to sit at the back of the group with an adult where she can practice listening without disturbing the others (rehearsal). The aide follows through as necessary. In addition, Devonne's kindergarten teacher and the after-school child care teacher have collaborated on this strategy, so Devonne experiences the same rule and consequences in her kindergarten classroom as in her after-school child care setting.

Gerald has Tourette Syndrome, a neurological disorder characterized by tics—involuntary, sudden motions or vocalizations, which are completely meaningless, but which the child experiences as irresistible urges that must be expressed (National Institute of Neurological Disorders and Stroke, 2005). Although children can control such tics (from seconds to hours at a time) with great effort, suppressing them may merely postpone more severe outbursts. Tension increases the rapidity and severity of children's tics; tics are less pronounced when children are relaxed. Knowing this, Gerald's teacher does not make a rule forbidding Gerald from expressing his verbal tic "hoooy boy" and provides him a private study area in a quiet part of the room during reading so as to be less distracting to others. At the same time, she helps Gerald work on more controllable social behaviors such as taking turns and collaborating on projects by coaching him and by making rules and enforcing them as she would with any child.

These examples have illustrated some ways in which rules and consequences can be used to help children with disabilities become more socially competent. Chapters 14 and 15 offer more information about working with children with special needs.

TIME-OUT

One consequence early childhood educators have mixed feelings about is time-out. **Time-out** involves removing a child from a situation or activity for a brief period of time in order to help the child regain control of his or her emotions. Another reason adults use time-out is to interrupt a harmful series of child behaviors, allowing the child to regroup and start over on a more positive note (Kazdin, 2001; Nelson, 1999). When used appropriately, time-out is a logical consequence that supports children's development of self-discipline.

Inappropriately applied, time-out can become a punishment that demeans children and detracts from their ability to learn better ways of handling difficult situations. Let's take a few moments to consider the difference between effective uses of time-out and poor uses of the technique.

What Is Time Out and When Is It Appropriate to Use?

To call for a time-out in a sporting event signifies the need for a rest or a break from the action. During time-outs in a game, players have a chance to rethink how they might approach a situation or regain their composure following a particularly intense interaction. Time-outs with children can serve a similar purpose. When an adult removes a child from a highly charged situation, it helps that child calm down or reconsider his or her actions in a new light. This makes it more likely that the adult and child can eventually talk about what happened calmly and resolve the problem (Ucci, 1998; Nelson, 1999). In this text, we recommend using time-out for two specific kinds of problem behaviors: temper tantrums and habitual antisocial behavior.

Most people know a **temper tantrum** when they see one. There is no mistaking the physical signs: red face, flailing arms and legs, screaming, and crying. Although such behavior is disconcerting to adults, it is important to remember that a temper tantrum is such an intense emotional and physical response that children's normal thought processes are no longer available to them. The impassioned child cannot hear or respond to adult directions or efforts to comfort; cannot think out a logical, more socially appropriate sequence of actions; and can no longer gauge the effect his or her behavior has on self or others. Any child, at any time, may become involved in a tantrum, and although such behavior is most common in toddlers, older preschoolers as well as school-age children may, on occasion, resort to these volcanic outbursts.

Children have tantrums for several reasons. Tantrums initially appear when urgent wants are not immediately gratified. Later, tantrums may occur because adults have previously given in to children's tantrums, because children are fatigued, because they are stressed from multiple demands in their day, because they receive little attention for positive behavior, because they are continually subjected to unrealistic adult demands, or because rule enforcement is unpredictable (Brooks, 2006).

The best way to avoid temper tantrums is to make sure children's physical needs are met, acknowledge children's feelings before they become intense, establish predictable routines, teach children alternate ways to get what they want, respond positively to children's appropriate behavior, and make reasonable rules and enforce them consistently (Harrington, 2004). Yet, children occasionally will resort to temper tantrums in spite of all these precautions. When this happens, the goal is to help them regain their self-control. In the case of toddlers, whose outbursts are extreme but short lived, the best way to restore calm is to ignore their outrageous behavior and let them quiet down in their own way and time. Older children, whose emotional states are longer lasting, benefit from the logical consequence: time-out.

Habitual antisocial behavior. At times, all children engage in some antisocial behaviors, such as kicking, hitting, or biting. These occasional bouts of mistaken behavior are best dealt with using personal messages and the consequences described earlier. For some children, however, reliance on harmful actions becomes habitual—they repeatedly engage in these negative behaviors because they have learned that punching, pushing, or pinching gets them the attention they want, intimidates others to give in, or enhances their prestige with some members of the group by allowing them to gain power over others. When adults recognize that children have established a pattern of **habitual antisocial behavior**, they must work at stopping the problem behavior as well as interrupting the pattern of positive reinforcement that has allowed it to continue. Here again time-out is an appropriate consequence to consider.

Implementing Time-Out

Time-out means time away from the mainstream of group activity. It should be carried out in a place that is safe, has minimal distractions, and is easily supervised. An adult should accompany the child to the time-out place and/or remain close by. Children should never be put in complete isolation (Ucci, 1998). The usual length of time-out ranges from only a minute or two for preschoolers to five minutes or so for older, more experienced children.

Refer to Appendix B for a more complete outline of the steps involved in the effective use of time-out.

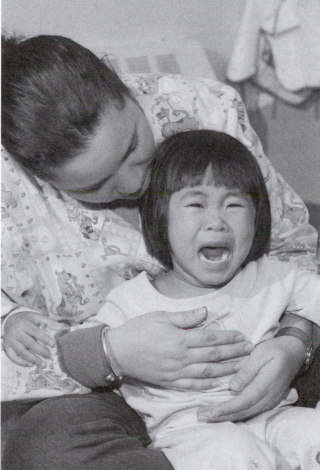

Temper tantrums are so intense that children are not able to reason while they are happening.

After the Child Leaves Time-Out

One question often asked is whether children who have just been through time-out should be required to comply with the adult expectation that may have triggered it. In other words, should Cecily have to put away the materials she didn't want to put away earlier, or should Harley be made to finish all the problems on page 2? For children who have resorted to a tantrum, it must be remembered that time-out was implemented as a consequence for out-of-control behavior, not as a consequence for failing to clean up or for not finishing an assignment. Self-control is a prerequisite to achieving the other desired behaviors. If self-control has been regained, the child has learned a big lesson. It is up to the adult to decide whether the child will benefit from attention to the secondary goals at this point. In considering this, adults should never become so caught up in their own immediate desires (cleanup rules, completed assignments) that they lose sight of their long-term goals for children.

When youngsters have gone through a time-out for habitual antisocial behavior, a good follow-up is to have them perform an act of kindness for the victim sometime during the day. This does not mean making the child apologize; rather, it involves some positive behavior, such as helping the victim do something (Bell et al., 2004). Restitution reduces the chances of the victim feeling a need to retaliate, and helps teach the erring child a substitute form of interaction.

Variations on Time-Out

Time-out can be implemented as described here with both preschool and school-age children. However, it is most suitable for children ages 3–5, when tantrums are at their peak (Harrington, 2004). Sometimes adults use time-out in response to a child's actions, sometimes children initiate time-out themselves because they are on the verge of losing control. When this happens, helping professionals should be sure to use positive personal messages and effective praise to underscore children's efforts to control their own behavior. At other times, it is not the child who needs a time-out from the tensions of the formal group setting, but the adult. All of us have experienced the rising feelings of anxiety that occur when the pace of the day seems too frantic or we think we cannot possibly cope with one more disaster. At times like these it can be hard to maintain composure. If that begins to happen, it is best to take a time-out yourself for a few minutes to calm down. Something as simple as taking a deep breath, getting a drink of water, or moving to another part of the room for a few minutes may be all it takes to reduce the tension. Asking another adult to help you in a particularly difficult situation or to take your place for a little while as you walk outside or sit alone for a few moments are other examples of adult versions of time-out.

Time-Out Versus Sitting Apart

It is worth noting that the procedure outlined for time-out is not the same as simply having children sit apart from the group for a while (Reynolds, 2008). **Sitting apart** involves temporarily removing a child from an activity or group time because he or she is causing harm or disruption, but is not having a temper tantrum or engaging in habitual antisocial behavior. The following scenario illustrates sitting apart.

During circle-time, Elka is enjoying tapping Brandon's back with her feet. She has been told to scoot back and keep her feet still. She refuses. Her kicking is becoming more vigorous and Brandon is becoming more unhappy. In this case, the adult might say, "Either keep your feet still or you'll have to sit away from the group so you can't kick Brandon any more." Elka continues her kicking game. The adult follows through. Elka is moved a little ways from the circle to a spot where she can still see the story but where she has no physical contact with the others in the group. She is told she may return when she can sit without kicking.

Elka will remain there until she signals that she is ready to return or the story is over, whichever comes first. Thus, she is able to practice the desired behavior in a setting in which she will have success. Sitting apart used in this manner is a way to rehearse sitting without kicking people, making it a logical consequence.

Besides the differences in behavior that prompt the two different consequences, sitting apart differs from time-out in the following ways. First, when sitting apart, children are usually kept in the same area as the rest of the group and are permitted to return as soon as they are ready or when a new activity begins. Secondly, children may initiate the procedure themselves, sitting apart for awhile (e.g., in their cubby or in the story corner) as a way to collect their thoughts or reduce stimulation for a brief time.

We expect that sitting apart will be used much more often than will time-out because time-out is reserved for only the most extreme behaviors.

Alternatives to the Misuse of Time-Out

Unfortunately, what is basically a sound practice—giving children an opportunity to gain control of their own behavior—is frequently misused. Such misuse is not only ineffective but may be damaging to children (NAEYC, 1996b). This has caused child development experts to warn against the inappropriate use of time-out (Gartrell, 2007). Following are examples in which time-out is misapplied and alternate strategies that would be more appropriate.

- **It is not appropriate to use time-out for every infraction of classroom rules.**

  EXAMPLE: Ms. Hannah uses time-out a lot. When children push in line, the consequence is time-out; when children refuse to put on their coats to go outdoors, the consequence is time out; when children are involved in a squabble over a toy truck, the consequence is time-out.

BETTER PRACTICE: Each of these circumstances would be better addressed using natural, logical, or appropriate unrelated consequences. When time-out is overused, it loses its effectiveness and violates the understanding that time-out should only be implemented when children have a temper tantrum or engage in habitual antisocial behavior.

- **It is not appropriate to use time-out as a threat.**

EXAMPLE: "Roberto, one more remark like that, young man, and you go into time-out." The teacher's threatening words clearly imply that if Roberto does not comply he will be banished from the room. The focus here is on coercing the child to obey rather than on teaching him how to do so.

BETTER PRACTICE: Threats undermine trust between adults and children. They damage children's feelings of worth and are incompatible with an authoritative approach to discipline. Time-out is only effective when it is treated as a coping mechanism, not as a form of punishment. A better consequence might be to ignore the child's words until he speaks appropriately.

- **It is not appropriate to use time-out to humiliate children.**

EXAMPLE: When Margie, a third grader, acts silly in class, she is sent for time-out to the kindergarten room. The teacher says, "If you want to act like a kindergartner then you can go and sit with the kindergartners until you're ready to act your age."

BETTER PRACTICE: In this situation, time-out became a punishment, not a logical consequence. As a result it encompasses all the negative features of punishment outlined in Table 11-1. Time-out should help children to feel better about themselves. An alternative consequence could be for Margie to sit near the teacher as she carries out her work.

- **It is not appropriate to use time-out in lieu of helping children learn better alternatives to problem behaviors.**

EXAMPLE: Jamal and Wally are arguing over who will get the next turn on the computer. They have had several disagreements already today.

The teacher marches over and tells the children, "Take a time-out!"

BETTER PRACTICE: Although it can be frustrating to adults, children need many opportunities to practice appropriate social skills. Each disagreement the boys have is an opportunity to teach them alternate ways of getting what they want. Coaching the boys through their dispute or using a logical consequence such as having them plan together a way to share the computer would teach them more of what they need to know than does time-out. Time-out should only be implemented when no other appropriate strategies are available.

- **It is not appropriate for time-out to last longer than the time it takes for children to calm down.**

EXAMPLE: Roger had a time-out when he became hysterical over the fact that his boots would not go on easily. The classroom aide was keeping an eye on him but gradually became caught up in what was happening in the classroom. The next time she thought about Roger, he had been in time-out for 30 minutes, even though he had quieted down 15 minutes ago.

BETTER PRACTICE: Time-out is not simply a means for getting "problem children" out of the way. It takes time for children to calm down. However, once that has happened, the purpose of timeout has been accomplished, and children should return to the mainstream of classroom activity. Time-out should be used as cool-down time only. It should end when children are ready to return to the group. This means adults have to keep an eye on the child and an eye on the clock, remembering to have children leave time-out as soon as appropriate.

- **It is not appropriate to place children in time-out simply for adult relief.**

EXAMPLE: Amidst gales of laughter, Morgan and Sheldon have been purposely passing gas for the last several minutes. The after-school provider has talked to them twice about their behavior. Walking over to the children she announces, "Okay, you two, time-out!"

BETTER PRACTICE: At times, adults feel like they cannot tolerate children's misbehavior for even a minute more. It may be tempting on these occasions to put children into time-out simply to get them "out of your hair" for a while. This violates the purpose of time-out. A better solution is for adults to take time-out themselves to regain their composure. Even a few minutes can make a difference. Adults who work in teams can relieve one another as needed. Those who work on their own can practice short relaxation exercises they can do themselves or with the class as a whole to change the atmosphere in the room. Having something beautiful or relaxing to look at (such as a picture or aquarium) can also offer a momentary respite.

It is clear from these examples that time-out can be mishandled and even abused. To prevent such misuse, some professionals avoid using time-out altogether. Unfortunately, that deprives children of a potentially beneficial consequence for the extreme situations in which they sometimes find themselves.

Although we believe all other avenues should be explored before instituting time-out, we also think that time-out can prove helpful for children who lose control or who have well-established patterns of antisocial behavior. Even in those circumstances, we caution that time-out is effective only if used sparingly and in the spirit of helping children develop internal controls.

WHERE CONSEQUENCES FIT IN YOUR REPERTOIRE OF GUIDANCE STRATEGIES

Consequences help children to maintain or change their actions in response to rules and expectations. This makes them valuable tools for guiding children's social behavior. To use them effectively, it is best to consider the context in which consequences are applied. Sometimes, children's behavior is so clearly unsafe, or damaging to people or property, that immediate adult intervention is necessary. In situations like these you will use the skill sequence (personal message, warning, follow through) described in this chapter. At other times, problem behaviors are less pressing and it is possible to rely on more subtle means of adult intervention to guide children toward more positive actions. Several of these have been described in previous chapters in this text. Thus, there is a continuum of intervention strategies focused on solving behavior problems in the classroom. These range from ones in which children behave constructively with minimal adult support to ones in which adults exert greater control through the enforcement of consequences. The continuum is illustrated in Figure 11-4.

SKILLS FOR IMPLEMENTING CONSEQUENCES

 Creating Appropriate Consequences

1. Anticipate consequences that fit the rules you make. Think ahead about possible consequences for common rules you expect to make. For example, if you are working with preschoolers, think about the consequences you could use to enforce rules about sharing, sitting through group time, and keeping quiet at nap time. If the children in your group are older, decide on consequences for resolving playground conflicts with peers and to enforce rules for paying attention, turning assignments in on time, and doing one's own work. These are all typical situations in which rule enforcement may be necessary. Think first of the natural consequences you might use. Then, consider possible logical

consequences. Figure out an unrelated consequence last. Generate ideas for positive consequences as well; consider forms of praise as well as earned privileges.

2. Give children opportunities to generate their own ideas for solutions to problems or potential consequences. Just as children benefit from formulating some of the rules that govern their lives, they can also learn from helping to generate potential solutions and consequences. Introduce potential problem situations at a time when mistaken behavior is not an issue, and help children consider open-ended questions such as "What should we do when people knock down other people's blocks?" or "What should we do when people keep wandering around the room and interrupting those who are working?" When youngsters weigh out the value of the rule

continued

THE INTERVENTION CONTINUUM

Greatest Self Regulation

1. **Watch and listen.** Observe children from nearby. Make yourself available if children want to come to you, but let them work things out for themselves if they can.

2. **Add or take something away** to make it easier for children to manage on their own. For instance, too few objects for children at the art table could lead to arguments. Adding a few more might be all that is needed for children to share more successfully. On the other hand, too many objects on the table might make it difficult for children to work without getting in one another's way. Removing a few items could make it easier for them to use the materials cooperatively.

3. **Describe what you see:** "It looks like two people want to use the scissors at the same time." Or, "You decided to share the glitter. I'm pleased you found a way to work together."

4. **Provide information.** "You thought she spilled the glue on your picture on purpose. She was trying to get the glue back into the bottle and some spilled out. It was an accident." Or, "Sometimes when two people want the same thing at the same time, they decide to share or take turns."

5. **Pose questions.** "What could you do to solve this problem?" Or, "What could you do instead of hitting her to show you're angry?"

6. **Give choices.** "John is using the skinny paintbrush now. You may use the thick brush or the charcoal" Or, "It's clean-up time. You may put away the smocks or stack the trays."

7. **Physically intervene.** Stop hurtful actions such as hitting by catching the child's hands. Hold onto a wiggling child to help him or her hear what you are saying. Separate two children who are pushing.

8. **Help children negotiate problems.** Serve as a translator in the situation. "Did you like it when he pushed you? What could you say to him about that?" Or, "Kali, you think it would be okay to take turns. What do you think, Melanie?" (You will read more about this strategy in Chapter 12.)

9. **Remind children of rules using a personal message.** "You really wanted the glitter. It bothers me when you grab to get what you want. Someone could get hurt. Ask Lisa for a turn next."

10. **Connect actions to consequences via a warning or effective praise.** "Either take turns with the glitter or you'll have to choose something else to work with." Or, "You decided to trade the glitter shaker for the glue. That solved the problem."

11. **Enforce logical consequences.** "You're having a hard time remembering to share the glitter cans. Let's find another material for you to use." Or, "You accidentally dripped glue on Morgan's picture. Let's get some towels and blot it off."

12. **Use time-out with children who are having a temper tantrum or who engage in habitual anti-social behavior.** "You're very upset. I can't talk to you when you're kicking and screaming like that. Either calm down here or we will have a time-out."

Greatest External Regulation

Figure 11-4 The Intervention Continuum

SKILLS FOR IMPLEMENTING CONSEQUENCES—continued

and what action might lead to better compliance, they are directly experiencing the causal relationship between behavior and outcome. They also have an opportunity to explore why the rule is important and to discuss the role of consequences. It is not unusual for such talks to begin with children suggesting unkind or totally unfeasible penalties. Do not reject these outright, but include them for analysis along with the other suggestions. Experience has shown that once the novelty of such outrageous notions has worn off, children settle down to serious discussion.

In addition to discussions prompted by you, encourage children to identify whole-group problems they would like to see resolved. As children generate ideas, post them on a list specified for this purpose (John wants to talk about problems in the block area. Jamal wants to talk about people calling names). Create a forum, such as a daily class meeting, in which to discuss such issues. Avoid naming any individual wrongdoers or developing consequences for a particular child. Instead talk about ways any child in the group might respond to such problems in the future. Record potential solutions on chart paper or in a notebook to which children have continual access. Encourage children to make a sustained effort to try the solution for a week, and then evaluate how the solution is working. Make revisions as necessary.

3. State consequences in the form of a warning. Link the rule and the consequence in an either-or statement to the child: "Either choose your own place in the circle, or I will help you choose one," "Either put that puzzle together, or you won't be allowed to get another off the shelf," "Either stop whispering, or I'll have to separate you."

4. Give warnings privately. Children who are preoccupied with saving face as a result of public humiliation are not inclined to comply with rules. When giving warnings, move close to the child and stoop down to his or her level. Use a firm, quiet voice to explain what will happen should the misbehavior continue.

5. Point out the natural consequences of children's actions. Provide information to children about the natural consequences of their behavior in a matter-of-fact, nonjudgmental tone. Children benefit from factual information such as, "When you shared the paste with Tim, he was willing to share the glitter with you" or "When you forgot to feed the fish, it meant they went hungry all day." Children tune out when they catch a hint of "I told you so" in your words or demeanor. Resist the temptation to tell children how smart you were all along. They will learn more from supportive explanations of the facts. Thus, instead of saying: "See. Those were never intended to go every which way in the box," say, "You've discovered that when the pieces go every which way, they don't fit in the box."

6. Use the personal message, warning, and follow-through in order. Stick with the sequence and keep all the steps. Skipping parts invalidates both the short-term and long-term benefits described earlier in this chapter.

7. Allow children enough time to respond to each step of the sequence. Approach discipline encounters with the idea of spending at least a few minutes. At each phase of the sequence, wait at least several seconds so children have time to comply if they are able. In situations you consider dangerous, stop the action physically and watch for signs that the youngster will obey. In less pressured circumstances, a time lapse of a few minutes between personal message and warning, then warning and follow-through may not be too long. For instance, Mr. Gomez, the social worker, has decided it is time for Lou Ellen to choose a workstation rather than flitting in and out, disrupting everyone. He says: "Lou Ellen, you haven't found an activity that really interests you yet. It bothers me when you wander around because it is distracting. Pick one spot where you would like to work. I'll check on you in a minute or two to see which you decide on." Three minutes later, Mr. Gomez checks and finds that Lou Ellen still is unoccupied. Approaching her,

SKILLS FOR IMPLEMENTING CONSEQUENCES

he says: "Lou Ellen, you're still looking for something to do. You can either select a station now, or I'll pick one for you." He stands by the child for 30 seconds or so. She does not move. At this point, Mr. Gomez enforces the rule by stating: "You still can't decide. Remember, I said you choose, or I'd choose. Now, we'll try bird calls." Mr. Gomez takes Lou Ellen by the hand and heads in the direction of the birdcall station.

Notice that in the prolonged interaction, a reflection prefaced each portion of the sequence. Reflecting helped to reclarify the situation each time and provided continuity from one step to the next.

Helping professionals who work in a team should be alert to fellow team members who are caught up in a limit-setting situation. When this occurs, other adults should provide supervision to the group until the follow-through has been completed. Professionals who work alone may have to follow through while simultaneously maintaining a global view of the room throughout the procedure. In addition, they should be prepared to tell other children in the group what to do until the situation is resolved. ("Dolores and I have to work this out. Keep working on the 'word wall' until we are through.")

8. Finish the follow-through once you begin it. Although it is important to give children enough time to respond, it also is critical to enforce rules once you progress to the follow-through phase of the sequence. If you have begun to say, "Remember, I told you . . ." and the child vows never to do it again or says, "Okay, okay, I'll do it," continue to implement the consequence calmly and firmly. Do not get sidetracked at this phase by other issues. Reflect the child's concern or promise, thereby acknowledging it, and then point out that the consequence is for current behavior, not future actions.

9. Communicate with other adults regarding rule enforcement. Sometimes, children push the limits with one adult and then move on to someone else when a follow-through is forthcoming. In this way, the same child may engage in problem behavior all over the room with no real enforcement. Prevent this from happening by alerting other adults about the warning you have given a certain child. Do this within the child's hearing so that she or he is aware that the warning remains in effect even though the location has changed. Be receptive when other adults advise you of their warnings. Follow through on their warning if necessary. For example, if Kathleen has been warned that if she pushes another child on the playground one more time, she will have to sit on the side for five minutes, tell other adults that this is the case. Thus, anyone seeing Kathleen push again can enforce the consequence. This creates a much more predictable environment for Kathleen in which she will learn that pushing is unacceptable. As other children hear and see you enforce consequences fairly and predictably, they come to trust you and rely on you to create a safe, predictable environment.

10. Avoid power struggles.

Adult: *Yes, you will.*

Child: *No, I won't.*

Adult: *Yes, you will.*

Child: *No, I won't.*

This is the common language of a power struggle. It typically occurs when adults try to implement consequences and children refuse to comply (Kurcinka, 2000; Charney, 2002). The situation escalates when both become more adamant about their positions. Power struggles usually involve a verbal battle and often happen in front of an audience. Unfortunately, there are no winners—both parties stand to lose something. The adult may gain temporary adherence, but may well have lost the respect of the child. On the other hand, if the child gains superiority for the moment by having the adult back down, he or she may suffer future repercussions from an adult who feels thwarted or ridiculed.

continued

SKILLS FOR IMPLEMENTING CONSEQUENCES—continued

Don't rush children through the sequence. Give them time to respond to your words.

There are a number of strategies you can use to avoid this problem:

   a. Avoid making unnecessary rules.

   b. Do not embarrass children in public—keep all communication between you and the child private.

   c. Remain calm.

   d. Avoid contradicting children's assertions.

For instance, if the warning is "Either take a drink without snorting, or I will take your straw" and the child snorts, reach for the straw. If the child says, "But I didn't mean it," do not debate the purposefulness of the act. Instead, acknowledge the child's contention with the words, "That may be . . .," and continue to implement the consequences: "You didn't snort on purpose. That may be. Remember, I told you, any more animal sounds and I would take the straw away. Now, I'm taking the straw."

   e. Stick to the main issue. Do not allow yourself to become involved in an argument over extraneous details.

   f. Discuss the power struggle privately with the child. This strategy is particularly effective with older children who have learned some methods of compromise.

Tell the child directly that a power struggle seems to be developing and that you would like to work out the issue in another way.

   g. Avoid entrapment. When children begin to argue, refuse to become involved. You can do this either by quietly repeating the rule and the consequences and then resuming your normal activity, or by telling the children that you would be willing to discuss it later when you all are calmer.

11. Help children understand legitimate differences between home rules and your expectations for their behavior in the program. Sometimes, there are real differences in expectations for what children do at home and what is required in the formal group setting. When this occurs, acknowledge the

SKILLS FOR IMPLEMENTING CONSEQUENCES

child's confusion or distress and point out that certain standards may be situation specific. "You're upset. At home you don't have to put things back on the shelf when you're through. That may be. It bothers me when there are puzzles all over the floor. Pieces could get lost. Here at the center everybody is expected to help clean up. Now please find a puzzle to put away."

12. Teach children self-instruction strategies. Help impulsive children exert greater self control by teaching them to tell themselves "I can wait," "I am patient," "I am picking up the books, one at a time." Support youngsters' attempts at self-regulation with reflections of your own: "You waited very patiently," "You're picking up the books, one at a time."

13. Acknowledge children's compliance with rules. Use positive personal messages, effective praise, and earned privileges to help children recognize and repeat socially acceptable conduct. Do this for all children in the group, especially those who frequently misbehave. These latter youngsters need confirmation that they are indeed capable of achieving success in this regard.

14. Actively attempt to alter children's mistaken perceptions. Give attention seekers appropriate attention. Provide power seekers with legitimate power. Confer on hopeless children your affirmation of their worth. Refer to the earlier portions of this chapter for ideas on how to accomplish these goals.

15. Use time-out only with children who are having a temper tantrum or who exhibit habitual antisocial behavior. Remember that time-out is a logical consequence only in these two circumstances. Avoid implementing it indiscriminately. Do not use it when another, logical consequence could better teach the child how to follow the rule. For instance, if Benny forgets to raise his hand before blurting out an answer, it would be better to tell him that he won't be called on until he does raise his hand than to send him into the hall for time-out.

 Communicating with Families

1. Listen empathically to family members who express frustration about their children's misbehavior. There are times when parents and guardians need a chance to talk about their children's negative behavior without feeling guilty or embarrassed. At other times, they benefit from the opportunity to explore their concerns and to determine the relative seriousness of certain behavior problems they are encountering. In all of these circumstances, your role is to listen. Use the skills you learned associated with the facilitation dimension to provide support and convey your interest and concern. Refrain from giving advice. Sometimes, family members just need to talk things through. Refer really troubled family members to program personnel whose job responsibilities include counseling.

2. Help family members recognize signs that their children are achieving greater self-control. Provide information to parents and guardians illustrating children's increasing abilities to delay gratification, resist temptation, curb their impulses, and carry out positive plans. Short notes home or brief verbal comments are ideal ways to convey such messages. "Today, Leanne offered her turn at the easel to a child who was anxious to paint before time ran out. She decided this all on her own. I thought you'd enjoy hearing about her growing awareness of the needs of others," or "Perry was very angry that our field trip was canceled. He wrote about this in his journal and suggested that our class develop a backup plan for next time. I was impressed that he used such constructive strategies to deal with his frustration and just wanted you to be aware that he is making great progress in this regard."

3. Clarify who will enforce rules when both family members and staff members are present. Family members and professionals often feel uncertain about who should step in

continued

SKILLS FOR IMPLEMENTING CONSEQUENCES—continued

when both witness an incident in which the family member's child engages in disruptive behavior, such as refusing to cooperate during a "family night" program, resisting coming out of the bedroom during a home visit, or hitting another child in frustration. To avoid such confusion it helps to have pre-established guidelines for what to do when these things happen. Many families and professionals have found the following guidelines both fair and useful:

a. Parents are in charge of the "home front." In other words, when a professional is making a home visit or meets a parent and child in a public setting such as a store or at a concert, parents are in charge of their own children and should take action as necessary.

b. Program staff are in charge during program hours in program-related environments, including field trip sites.

c. Parents who are acting as volunteers or aides in the program take responsibility primarily for children other than their own and leave the handling of their own children to another volunteer or the professional.

If this is an accepted procedure in the program, adults should be quick to attend to problems involving another volunteer's child. For example, if Mrs. Sanchez is attempting to read a story to a group of children and her own child continually interrupts, the professional or another volunteer should move swiftly to deal with the situation.

Be aware of the policies for your program and follow them. If no such policies exist, discuss this topic with fellow staff members and generate ideas about how to handle such incidents before the need arises.

When confronted with a situation in which you must intervene with a family member's child in that person's presence, act matter-of-factly and use the skills you have learned in this chapter. Say something to alert the person to your intentions if the conditions seem appropriate for such a remark. For instance, if Jeremiah is trying to follow his mom out

the door as she is leaving, you might say to his mom, "I'll help Jeremiah find something fun to do. We'll stay together here in the classroom." Give Jeremiah a personal message and a warning. If you must proceed to the follow-through, calmly help him remain in the classroom, even if he is crying hard. Thank the parent and assure her that you will let her know how Jeremiah is doing later in the day.

4. Answer family members' questions about program-related discipline strategies honestly and openly. Sometimes family members wonder, "How can you expect children to listen to all that talk," or "Why don't you make children apologize every time they hurt someone?" Answer such questions directly rather than trying to ignore them or responding in a defensive manner. One way to convey acceptance is to say something like, "A lot of parents ask about that," or "That's a common thing people want to know." Then proceed with your response. Refer to scientific evidence as well as personal philosophy. This helps people recognize there is an expert knowledge base to the profession and that we use it to guide our actions in the field. Thus, you might answer a parent's query regarding too much talk in the following manner. "That's a good question. All of the adults in our classroom are trying to help children develop self-control. Our goal is for children to learn to obey rules without constant adult monitoring. It's quicker to just say, 'no' and sometimes children even listen, for the moment. Unfortunately, that is usually short-lived. We have pretty good scientific evidence that shows that children learn self-control best when adults reason with them. That means we have to talk about emotions, give reasons for rules, and point out what to do instead of focusing on what not to do. That is a lot of talk. But based on our understanding of child development and from results we've seen with children here in the center, we know it works. As the year goes on, let me know how you think it's going."

SKILLS FOR IMPLEMENTING CONSEQUENCES

Recognize that family members may or may not agree with your response. However, they will have a better idea of why you do what you do and that your actions are based on more than personal opinion. In addition, you have kept the door open for further conversation in the future.

5. Discuss with family members mutual ways to help children achieve self-control. Interact with family members to identify strategies for use both at home and in the formal group setting to promote children's positive behaviors and to address problematic ones. Ask if such behaviors occur at home and what family members do about them. Make note of these strategies and whenever possible use them in creating a plan for working on the behavior in the formal group setting. If the behavior is not evident at home, talk with family members about what is happening in the program, describe current strategies, and ask for feedback and/or

additional recommendations. Similarly, listen attentively when family members describe behaviors they observe in their children. Talk about the extent to which such actions appear away from home and what people in the program may be doing about them. Agree on one or two common strategies that family members and program professionals will use. Discuss a timetable for checking in with one another to determine progress and alterations. If you are the professional in charge, carry out your plan. Confirm the results with family members and make adjustments as necessary. If you are a student participant and a family member mentions such an instance to you, acknowledge the person's concern and say that you will bring the matter to the attention of the head teacher or some other appropriate person in the program. Follow through on your conversation. Later, get back to the family member, letting him or her know that you informed the appropriate person as promised.

PITFALLS TO AVOID

Regardless of whether you are fostering children's self-discipline individually or in groups, informally or in structured activities, there are certain pitfalls you should avoid.

Reluctance to follow through.

> Jonathan, you're having a good time up there. I'm worried you might fall. Climb down, please.
>
> Jonathan, I mean it: climb down.
>
> Jonathan, I really mean it this time.
>
> Jonathan, how many times do I have to tell you to climb down?
>
> Jonathan, am I going to have to get angry?
>
> Jonathan, I'm getting mad.
>
> OK, Jonathan, I'm really mad now—climb down.
>
> Jonathan, that's it! I'm going to carry you down.

This scenario illustrates a common problem for many adults: their reluctance to follow through on the limits they set. In an effort to avoid a confrontation, they may find themselves repeating a warning or some variation of it numerous times. This confuses children. They have no way of telling when adults finally mean what they say. In Jonathan's case, will that point be reached after the third warning, the fifth, or the sixth? Perhaps yesterday, the adult waited until the fifth warning; tomorrow, he or she may stop at the second. Children are not mind readers and cannot predict when the adult's patience may run out. The one way to avoid this situation is always to follow through after you give the first warning. In this way, children learn that the description of the consequence is a cue for them either to change their behavior or to expect the consequence to happen.

Relying on convenient or familiar consequences rather than finding one best suited to the situation. Some adults utilize the same consequence over and over. Frequently, they choose an unrelated consequence, like removing children from a situation or having them lose a particular privilege.

Although such consequences may stop the behavior for the moment, they do not teach appropriate alternatives for children to use in future situations. Over time, children may learn to anticipate the consequence and may decide that certain misbehaviors are worth it. This problem can be avoided by varying consequences to fit the situation at hand.

Ignoring natural consequences. Sometimes adults fail to recognize that a natural consequence has taken place and so institute additional, unnecessary consequences. For instance, Peggy accidentally stepped on her guinea pig. She was terribly distressed over the possible injury and attempted to soothe the animal. Her distress was the natural consequence of her error. The 4-H leader completely missed the importance of the natural consequence and proceeded to scold Peggy for being so careless. Then told her she was not to hold the guinea pig for the next hour, even though the child already had recognized the negative results of her actions. Because the purpose of a consequence is to make children aware of the impact of their behavior, no further penalty was called for. Instead, the adult could have talked with Peggy about ways to avoid future injuries.

Unfortunately, many adults do not think the natural aftermath of a child's mistake is enough. They cannot resist the desire to drive the point home by lecturing, moralizing, or instituting more drastic consequences. However, children who feel victimized are less able to change their behavior. Adults who ignore natural consequences by intervening either prematurely or unnecessarily fail to provide children with opportunities to learn from their own actions. The best way to avoid this pitfall is to survey the situation carefully and note any natural consequences that may have occurred. If these are evident, no further consequences should be imposed.

Demanding cheerful compliance. When adults follow through with a consequence, they should not expect children to comply cheerfully. This means that a child may pout, complain, mutter, or stomp as he or she adheres to the rule. Adults must keep in mind that the aim of the follow-through is to enforce the consequence. It is too much to insist that a child also put a smile on his or her face when doing something he or she really does not want to do. Adults create unnecessary confrontations when they insist that youngsters obey with pleasure. Although it may be annoying when children show their obvious distaste for the rule, attitude is not something over which adults have control, and it should not become a major issue in adult–child interactions.

Harboring grudges. After imposing a consequence, the adult's motto should be "forgive and forget." It is counterproductive to allow feelings of anger, resentment, or hostility for past actions to color present interactions. Once a consequence has been imposed, that is the end of it. Treat each new day as a fresh start. Furthermore, if on a particular day, one adult has had continual confrontations with the same child or is feeling frustrated or overwhelmed, she or he should take a break, or, in a team-teaching situation, ask someone else to deal with the child for a while.

Insisting that children apologize. Frequently, adults think that if they can just get children to say they are sorry, the problem is solved. With this in mind, they may force children to say "sorry" even when they do not really mean it. Unfortunately, this causes children to conclude that apologizing takes care of everything. They figure they can engage in any behavior they like as long as they are prepared to express their regret at the end. They also learn that insincerity is okay. Sorrow and remorse are emotions. We cannot make children experience these emotions on demand.

Children can, however, be taught to make restitution for a wrong they have committed. This may involve having the child soothe the victim, get a wet cloth to wash the victim's bruised knee, or repair a broken object. Research has shown that children definitely grasp the concept of restitution prior to understanding the true significance of an apology (Hendrick, 2003). As a result, concrete restitution has the most meaning for children. Only when children feel genuine remorse should they be encouraged to express their regret using the words, "I'm sorry."

SUMMARY

There are times when children do not follow the rules set by adults. They may engage in mistaken behavior because they lack the capability or the understanding to follow the rules because adults have given mixed or unclear messages or because they believe the rule is unnecessary. On other occasions, youngsters act inappropriately because they are impulsive or because they have developed faulty self-perceptions.

Adults can avoid or counteract these problems by making rules that take into account children's development, by clarifying or rephrasing their expectations, and by helping children develop positive, appropriate alternative behaviors. In addition, adults can monitor their own behavior so that their words are congruent with their actions, offer explanations for rules, and provide opportunities for children to become part of the rule-making process.

Adults enforce rules through the use of positive or inhibiting consequences. These help children recognize the impact of their behavior on self and others. Positive consequences reinforce appropriate behavior. Inhibiting consequences reduce children's mistaken behavior. They are instructive, rely on reasoning, and are humanely and matter-of-factly administered. They are categorized as natural, logical, or unrelated. Natural consequences happen without direct adult intervention, logical consequences are directly related to a particular rule, and unrelated consequences are manufactured by adults. The latter should be used sparingly and be linked, at least in time, to the rule infraction. Adults must carefully weigh many factors in deciding which consequences to use in particular situations.

Adults implement inhibiting consequences by reminding children of the rule. If children do not comply, the adult repeats the rule and states a warning as an either-or statement. Adults pause long enough to give children an opportunity to correct their behavior on their own. If children do not, adults follow through with the consequence. All consequences should be implemented consistently and immediately.

Personal messages combined with the warning and follow-through allow adults to help children to learn to regulate their own behavior. As children become more accustomed to this process, they learn to respond to earlier phases in the sequence, decreasing the necessity for adults to go through all three steps.

At times, when one problem behavior leads to another, adults must exercise patience and implement appropriate consequences for each problem behavior. The logical consequence of time-out is used infrequently and only when children are out of control or exhibit habitual antisocial behavior. In addition to working directly with the children to foster self-discipline, it is important to join with parents as partners in helping children develop self-control.

KEY TERMS

follow-through	natural consequences	temper tantrum
habitual antisocial behavior	positive consequences	time-out
inhibiting consequences	punishments	unrelated consequences
logical consequences	sitting apart	warning

DISCUSSION QUESTIONS

1. Describe six reasons why children misbehave and their corresponding solutions.

2. Discuss the mistaken perceptions that may prompt children's misbehavior. Describe (without naming) a child you have observed whose behavior might indicate that such a perception was in operation. Explore strategies that might be employed to alter the child's perception.

3. Discuss the similarities and differences between positive consequences, inhibiting consequences, and punishments.

4. Generate ideas for positive consequences and for natural, logical, and unrelated consequences for the following rules:
   a. Walk, don't run, down the hall.
   b. Throw the ball, don't kick it.
   c. Only use your own gym towel.
   d. Handle the computer keyboard gently.
   e. Walk on the sidewalk, not in the flower bed.
   f. Tell someone when you need help.
   g. Call people by their real names, don't mock people's names.

5. Discuss the importance of following through on consequences as well as the results of not doing so.

6. Referring to the NAEYC Code of Ethical Conduct in Appendix A, identify the principles or ideals that will help you determine an ethical course of action in the following situations:

    a. A parent is walking with her child to the car. Suddenly the child dashes away from her into the busy parking lot. The parent, obviously frightened, grabs the child and smacks her three times saying, "You scared the life out of me. Never do that again." You are getting out of your car nearby when this happens and witness the interaction.

    b. You notice a colleague in the hallway arguing with her own child (4 years old) who is enrolled in the program. The child is screaming and trying to pull away as the adult escorts him toward the door. Suddenly the adult turns the child around and gives him two swats on the bottom. You and several children from your class see the incident.

    c. A large group of third graders are playing T-ball on the playground. Another adult comes to you and says, "I have to go in now. I told Jeff he couldn't play T-ball any more today because of his fighting. Please make sure he doesn't play T-ball." The adult goes inside. There are 20 minutes left to play. A few minutes later Jeff, who has been watching from the sidelines, is called into the game by his friends. He looks to you and says, "I've learned my lesson. Can't I play?"

7. How would you respond to another helping professional who said: "The skill sequence takes too long. Besides, children can't respond to so much talking. Just tell them what's not allowed and be done with it"?

8. Identify any difficulties you have had in implementing the skill sequence described in this chapter. With classmates, brainstorm ways to improve.

9. Describe a time-out you have observed. Discuss why it was done, how it was done, and what its effect was.

10. Pretend you have been assigned to describe your center's use of time-out to a group of parents. Give a five-minute presentation to a group of your classmates. Then, generate a list of questions parents might ask and discuss how you would respond.

FIELD ASSIGNMENTS

1. Briefly describe a situation in which you will be working with children in the coming week. Identify any potential behavior problems that could arise within that circumstance. Using the entire skill sequence discussed in this chapter, write out the step-by-step process you would go through should such a problem actually occur. Later, record whether or not the issue came up. If it did, discuss how you handled it. Talk about any changes that were made in your original script and why they were made. Identify ways you will improve your performance the next time.

2. Write down three situations in which, as you worked with children, you did or could have used the entire sequence of skills from personal message to warning to follow-through. Begin by describing what the child(ren) said or did to prompt your response. Then, record your exact remarks (regardless of their correctness). Briefly discuss the child's reaction. Next, discuss the strengths and weaknesses of your approach. Conclude by describing an alternate strategy that might fit the situation or another way you could have phrased your message.

3. Observe another adult in your field placement handle a child's inappropriate behavior. Describe the situation and how it was addressed. Describe the adult's approach and discuss how it compared with the strategies you have been learning about in this book.

4. Discuss your use (or that of a supervisor or colleague) of one of the family communication strategies listed in this chapter. Describe what you (or he or she) did, the role of the family member, and the outcome of the situation. Critique how the skill was used. Suggest how you would handle the same situation if it were to happen again.

For additional resources, visit our Web site
www.earlychilded.delmar.com

OBJECTIVES

On completion of this chapter, you should be able to describe:

- Four types of aggression.

- Differences between assertiveness and aggression.

- Factors that contribute to aggressive behavior.

- Adult actions that increase childhood aggression.

- Techniques that reduce children's aggression.

- Strategies for communicating to families about childhood aggression.

- Pitfalls to avoid in addressing childhood aggression.

HEY! You wrecked it!

No, I didn't!

Yes, you did!

Slam! Bang! Hit!!

Teacher, he hit me!

He started it!

Scenes like this happen in early childhood settings. After all, children are just learning the skills they need to get along. However, these days it is not uncommon to hear adults say things like,

> *"I'm spending more and more time helping children settle disputes. Many kids seem to have fewer skills than the children I had 15 years ago when I started teaching. More kids hurt kids as soon as they can't get their way." (Levin, 2003, p. 53)*

Research confirms these impressions. Increasing numbers of children are demonstrating aggressive behaviors at younger ages and at higher levels than ever before (Phillips, Hensler, Diesel & Cefalo, 2004). Left unchecked, aggression hurts people, damages property, disrupts daily activities, and creates negative group environments. Furthermore, children who display high rates of unrestrained aggression when they are young are very likely to experience future problems getting along and feeling competent at home, at school, and in the community (Campbell, Shaw & Gilliom, 2000; Cote, Zoccolillo, Tremblay, Nagin & Vitaro, 2001; Garbarino, 2006). All of this makes childhood aggression a significant early childhood issue.

WHAT AGGRESSION IS

Aggression is antisocial behavior that damages or destroys property or that results in physical or emotional injury to a person or animal. It can be verbal or physical (Dodge, Coie & Lyman, 2006). Slapping, grabbing, pinching, kicking, spitting, biting, threatening, degrading, shaming, snubbing, gossiping, attacking, teasing, and demolishing are all examples of aggressive actions. Although each of these behaviors has negative outcomes, children engage in them for different reasons.

Types of Aggression

In this chapter you will learn about four types of aggression: accidental, expressive, instrumental,

and hostile. Effective strategies for responding to each type vary. Knowing their similarities and differences will enhance your ability to respond effectively when children are aggressive.

Accidental aggression. Often, without thinking, children hurt others in the process of their play. This is **accidental aggression**. Stepping on someone's fingers while climbing the monkey bars, tagging a friend too hard in hide and seek, or telling a joke that unexpectedly hurts someone's feelings, are all circumstances in which damage occurs, but there is no conflict or harmful intent. The hurtful behavior happens by chance.

Expressive aggression. Expressive aggression is a pleasurable sensory experience for the aggressor. It occurs when a child derives enjoyment from a physical action that unintentionally hurts others or interferes with their rights (McCauley, 2000). The aggressor's goal is not to get a reaction from the victim or to destroy something; instead, he or she is preoccupied with the enjoyable physical sensation of the experience. For instance, when Roger knocks down Sammy's building, he feels satisfaction in a well-placed karate chop; when Marvin rams his bike into the back of Jack's wagon, he likes the sudden jolt he receives. Expressive aggression as depicted in these examples is marked by the absence of angry, frustrated, or hostile emotions for the perpetrator. It involves playful or exploratory physical acts that cause unintentional unhappiness for someone else (Sammy is upset that his building fell down; Jack protests when his wagon is crunched).

Instrumental aggression. There are times when children are so intent on getting what they want or defending something that their physical actions inadvertently result in someone getting hurt. This is called **instrumental aggression**. For instance, when Marsha and Celeste struggle over a rolling pin, their pushing and shoving leads to Marsha being smacked in the eye and Celeste having her fingers smashed. The outcome is two unhappy children, both of whom have been injured. Neither child started out trying to hurt the other; each simply wanted the rolling pin for herself.

Unfortunately, they relied on force to stake their claims. In this case, the resulting aggression was a byproduct of the girls' interaction, not its main purpose. Lack of premeditation and lack of deliberate intent to harm are the two factors that distinguish instrumental aggression from the purposeful attempts to hurt people or reduce their self-esteem we will describe later in this chapter (Berk, 2006). Most instrumental aggression is prompted by quarrels over objects, territory, or rights.

- *Instrumental aggression over objects:* Jessica and LaTesha both run to the swing at the same time. Each wants it for herself. Soon they are shoving and pushing over who will get it. The goal of the children's actions is to gain possession of the swing. In the process of their struggle, aggression results.
- *Instrumental aggression over territory:* Raymond has taken over a large part of the block area to build his airport. He becomes upset when other children's structures edge into his space. In the subsequent dispute over who can build where, children start hitting. Although the goal of the children's actions is to simply establish control over territory in the block area; the unfortunate result is that children get hurt.
- *Instrumental aggression over rights:* An argument breaks out as several children rush to the door to go outside. Each wants to be "line leader." In this situation, the children's main goal is to establish who will have the right to be first in line. The aggression that comes about is a by-product of their efforts to achieve that goal.

Hostile aggression.   Children who display **hostile aggression** want to inflict pain on others (Shaffer & Kipp, 2006). Their hurtful actions or words are purposeful attacks aimed at retaliating for prior insults or getting a victim to do what the aggressor wants. Hostile aggression is expressed in two different ways:

1. *Overt aggression*—harm to others through physical injury or the threat of such injury.
2. *Relational aggression*—damage to another person's status or self-esteem, through gossip, lies, or other forms of social manipulation.

In both cases, the purposeful nature of hostile aggression differentiates it from the three other forms of unintentional aggression identified earlier.

> SITUATION: *Several fourth-graders are rushing to get to their lockers before the bell rings. In her effort to get in and out on time, Jean accidentally knocks Claudia into the wall. Before anyone can respond, Claudia, red-faced, jumps up and runs into the classroom. Later, as the children line up at the water fountain, Claudia shoves Jean and says, "There, see how you like it."*

Initially, Jean's behavior was an example of accidental aggression. However, Claudia interpreted it as a deliberate blow to her ego, which required her to retaliate later in the day. By pushing Jean, Claudia felt they were "even," and her honor was restored. In this case, the act of pushing Jean was a purposeful attempt to hurt her, making it an example of hostile aggression. The same would be true if Jean retaliated against Claudia's shove by telling everyone on the playground, "Don't let Claudia play, she's no good."

The four types of aggression we have just discussed are summarized in Figure 12-1.

Assertiveness Versus Aggression

A socially acceptable alternative to aggression is being assertive. Children display **assertiveness** when they express themselves or protect their rights while respecting the rights and feelings of others (Hegland & Rix, 1990; Slaby et al., 1995; Ostrov, Pilat & Crick, 2006). Assertive children do the following:

- Resist unreasonable demands: "No, I won't give you the eraser yet. I still need it."
- Refuse to tolerate aggressive acts: "Stop calling me names" or "No pushing."
- Stand up against unfair treatment: "You forgot my turn" or "Hey, no fair cutting in line."
- Accept logical disagreements: "Okay, I see what you mean."
- Suggest solutions to conflict: "You can have it in a minute" or "I'll use it again when you're through."

Children demonstrate greater social competence and develop positive feelings about their abilities when they can express themselves and when they can exert some control and influence over others.

As children mature they try out many strategies to express that influence. However, because they are just learning the social skills necessary to get along, children's efforts to be assertive are sometimes unsuccessful. They may even take the form of aggression. Ultimately, through observation, instruction, feedback, and practice, children can gradually learn the more constructive, socially acceptable behaviors associated with assertion. How to best support the emergence of assertion is more easily understood if you first know why and how aggression develops.

TYPE OF AGGRESSION	MOTIVATION	OUTCOME
Accidental	Unintentional.	Someone gets hurt or property is damaged.
Expressive	Enjoys physical experience. Unaware that victim is unhappy.	Someone gets hurt or property is damaged.
Instrumental	Goal is to get or protect an object, territory, or right. Aggression is a by-product of the interaction.	Someone gets hurt or property is damaged.
Hostile	Deliberate effort to hurt someone or to achieve power through intimidation.	Someone gets hurt or property is damaged.

Figure 12-1 The four types of aggression.

These children are learning assertiveness as they practice making suggestions and listening to each others' ideas.

WHY CHILDREN ARE AGGRESSIVE

In explaining the roots of aggression, scientists do not agree on how much can be attributed to biology and how much is a result of learning (Coie & Dodge, 1998). However, there is general agreement that, from infancy onward, both shape children's aggressive behavior.

Biology

In the mid-twentieth century, some scientists hypothesized that human beings are biologically programmed to be aggressive, particularly when safety or other basic needs are threatened (Lorenz, 1966). More recently, the presence of high levels of androgen and testosterone (male sex hormones) have been linked to physical aggression and aggressive impulses (Archer, 1994; Tremblay et al., 1997). Temperament may also play a role in people's aggressive tendencies (Hetherington, Parke, Gauvain & Locke, 2005; Loeber, Farrington, Stouthamer-Loeber, Moffitt & Caspi, 1999). For instance, children who are temperamentally noisy, active, and distractible and who have difficulty adjusting to changes in routine more often resort to aggression than children whose temperaments are more mellow. Such children tend to interact physically by hitting, touching, and grabbing objects from peers. Their quieter classmates stay more physically distant, avoiding interactions that may lead to aggressive outcomes. Findings like these help us see that biology contributes to childhood aggression, but that it is not the only factor involved.

The Frustration-Aggression Hypothesis

For some time, it was widely thought that frustration was the source of all aggression (Berkowitz, 1965). Today we still believe that a frustrated child is more likely to be aggressive than one who is contented, but we also know that other variables like biology and learning contribute to aggressive behavior. Moreover, frustrated people do not always act aggressively. For instance, children may react to frustrating experiences by trying harder, requesting help, simplifying the task, giving up, or taking a break. Thus, frustration contributes to aggression, but it is not the only source and it does not guarantee that aggression will occur.

The Distorted-Perception Hypothesis

Some children see hostile intent where none exists. For instance, a ball hits Trevor from behind as he walks across the play yard. He assumes that someone hit him on purpose even though the action was really the result of a wild throw. He responds with a yell and an aggressive gesture. Any child could react to accidental aggression in this way. However, some children are more prone than others to respond as though others' actions are deliberate and hostile. Such youngsters are generally poor social observers. They find it difficult to accurately interpret other children's expressive cues, such as facial expressions or words that would help them to understand no harm was intended (Crick & Dodge, 1996; Zins, Weissberg, Wang & Walberg, 2004).

Even if the other children apologize for the wild throw, Trevor may feel obligated to retaliate. That aggressive response could then trigger counter-aggression from the other children. This reinforces Trevor's impression that peers are hostile toward him. A vicious cycle becomes established, increasing the antagonism that exists between Trevor and the children with whom he must interact each day. Additionally, as Trevor's reputation for aggression becomes more firmly established, classmates may become less patient in dealing with him and be quicker to resort to physical force than they would with a less aggressive peer. This promotes increased aggression among all the children involved.

Direct Instruction

In some cases, adults or older peers instruct children to use aggression to resolve a problem situation or obtain their approval. Such instruction has a powerful effect on children's behavior. For example, in an early experiment involving children 6 to 16 years of age, 75% of them carried out an aggressive action in order to comply with adult expectations (Shanab & Yahya, 1977). "Hit her back," "Stick up for yourself," and "Don't be a sissy," were common commands. Today, tactics like these continue to contribute to childhood aggression (Herbert, 1998; Zins et al., 2004).

Reinforcement

There is convincing evidence that reinforcement plays a key role in shaping and maintaining aggressive behavior in children (Herbert, 1998; Frick et al., 2003). For instance, children may hit, bite, scratch, taunt, or threaten in order to get their way. When other children or adults give in by withdrawing from the conflict or yielding to the aggressor's wishes, the child's aggression is rewarded. Situations like these teach both aggressors and victims that hurtful actions are effective. If such behavior continues to be rewarded, children who demonstrate aggression develop feelings of power that further reinforce their negative actions. Aggressors may even achieve a certain notoriety that underscores the value of behaving aggressively. All of these factors reinforce rather than inhibit aggressive actions.

Modeling

Another explanation for why children behave aggressively is that they learn how to be aggressive by watching others (Patterson, 1997; Garbarino, 2006). The models they observe may be adults or peers in their family, at the center, at school, or in the community. Such models may be live or in the media. For instance, children see television programs in which disputes are settled by violence; they observe Aunt Martha shake Tony in order to make her point; they watch peers and siblings use physical power as a successful means of getting what they want. Children experience aggression directly when they are smacked, shaken, or shoved as punishments for misbehavior.

All of these examples illustrate to children that aggression is an effective way to assert one's will. They also break down any inhibitions children may have regarding the use of force (Garbarino, 2006). It makes little difference that adults frequently admonish youngsters not to resort to violence or advise them to "act nice." For children, "seeing is believing." Unfortunately, children exposed to aggressive models retain the effects of that modeling long after a particular incident is over. They remember what they see and hear and are able to imitate it months later (Bell & Quinn, 2004). All of these factors contribute to the enormous influence aggressive models have on children's lives.

Lack of Knowledge and Skills

Children sometimes resort to aggression because they don't know what else to do when their goals are blocked or when they come under attack by another child. Children may resort to physical violence after they run through their entire repertoire of social skills and still fail to get what they want or protect something important to them (Herbert, 1998; Goleman, 2006). Immaturity contributes to this problem, but so does lack of experience. Children who have few opportunities to practice nonviolent strategies or to learn the skills associated with assertiveness are most likely to be aggressive (Levin, 2003).

THE EMERGENCE OF AGGRESSION

As you can see, the sources of aggression are varied and complex. Any combination of the factors just described may result in antisocial behaviors. How children express aggression and the amount of aggression they exhibit is further influenced by age, experience, and gender.

Changes in Aggression over Time

There are two trends that characterize childhood aggression from the time children are toddlers through middle childhood:

- Younger children often resort to physical force to get their way. Older children rely more on verbal tactics.
- Younger children most often engage in instrumental aggression. Hostile aggression becomes more common in later childhood.

These developmental shifts occur for several reasons.

Aggression during early childhood.   Toddlers and preschoolers are impulsive. When they want something, they go after it immediately. Children this age also have immature language skills and

Young children need adult support to resolve instrumental conflicts.

know only a few strategies for getting what they want. If their limited tactics fail, they often resort to physical force to get what they need or to defend whatever they believe is theirs. In addition, when toddlers and preschoolers are asked to share, their egocentric view of the world makes it hard for them to give up objects. All of these developmental characteristics increase the likelihood that young children will hit, grab, kick, or bite to resolve disputes over sharing and ownership. As a result, there is a high rate of instrumental aggression among children this age. In fact, instrumental aggression is so prevalent in early childhood that most youngsters will experience more aggressive encounters during the preschool years than at any other time in their lives (Bell & Quinn, 2004). Fortunately, this form of aggression peaks around 30 months and then begins a gradual decline over the next several years (Garbarino, 2006).

Interestingly, although preschoolers' arguments over objects tend to be highly emotional, such disagreements usually blow over quickly. Young children's less developed memory skills keep them from holding a grudge. For them, once a dispute has been resolved, the episode is over. Peers who a few minutes earlier were in the throws of conflict, can resume playing side by side with few ill effects. They do not see an argument as a challenge to their honor and feel little need to retaliate or "get even" in the future (Shaffer & Kipp, 2006). Thus, hostile aggression is relatively rare among preschool-aged children. This condition begins to change as children enter elementary school.

Aggression throughout the elementary years.   The good news in grade school is that as children ages 6 to 12 expand their verbal and cognitive skills, their ability to resolve instrumental disputes amicably increases. They become more adept at negotiating conflict and find problem solving an effective way to achieve goals they previously addressed through more forceful means (Levin, 2003). As a result, the overall rate of aggression becomes less with every ensuing grade (Shaw, Gilliom, Ingoldsby & Nagin, 2003). Unfortunately, advances in language and cognition also contribute to more frequent rates of hostile aggression among some children during this time (Bell & Quinn, 2004; Loeber & Hay, 1993).

For instance, based on past experience, older children shift from physical to verbal strategies to get what they want. At the same time, they become more adept at incorporating verbal ridicule, teasing, and name calling into their arsenal of aggressive strategies (Coie & Dodge, 1998; Shaffer & Kipp, 2006). With practice, the verbal taunt becomes a satisfying weapon that leaves no visible traces and is often harder for adults to discern or control.

Cognitively, children more clearly recognize the negative intents of others and have well-developed memory skills that help them remember angry encounters long after they are over. Because children are now more aware of the reciprocal nature of relationships, they also are more likely to value "getting even." This is particularly true of 6-, 7-, and 8-year-olds, who have great difficulty differentiating accidental from intentional acts. It is not unusual for children this age to respond to hurtful behavior as if it were purposeful, regardless of whether or not

it actually was (Coie, Dodge, Terry & Wright et al., 1991; Hubbard et al., 2002).

The probability for hostile aggression also intensifies as rivalry among peers increases. Children between the ages of 8 and 12 spend much of their time comparing themselves with peers. Consequently, it becomes more common for them to feel threatened by the accomplishments of age-mates and to try to build themselves up by tearing others down. Minor disagreements or misunderstandings can quickly escalate to expressions of hostile aggression through insults, baiting, or rejection (Goleman, 1995; Garbarino, 2006). Such interactions can last days or even months as children "get even" over and over again (Nelson, Robinson & Hart, 2005). On top of all this, grade-school children (particularly boys) are reluctant to condemn retaliatory acts they believe are justified or necessary to maintain "face" with one's peers (Shaffer & Kipp, 2006). As a result, although physical fighting lessens during the elementary school years, verbal disputes and covert manipulation increase.

Gender Differences in Aggression

Who tends to be more aggressive—boys or girls? At one time, the common answer was that boys were more aggressive from the earliest days onward. Today, researchers are revisiting that assumption. A summary of current thinking in the field is presented in Figure 12-2.

As Figure 12-2 illustrates, all children are aggressive at one time or another and males and females are equally capable of aggression. Consequently, both boys and girls need support in learning effective ways to meet their needs more constructively.

How well children learn alternatives to aggression depends a great deal on adult intervention. Most adults agree that this is an important responsibility for them to assume, but they often are at a loss about what to do. As a result, they may unwittingly choose strategies that stimulate or prompt aggression rather than diminish it. Thus, helping professionals must learn not only which strategies are useful, but also which ones are not. Fortunately, there are substantial research data that clearly differentiate effective techniques from those that are detrimental. We will explore each of these, beginning with those that should be avoided. In that category are physical punishment, ignoring aggression, displacement, and inconsistency.

MALE/FEMALE DIFFERENCES IN AGGRESSION

- In their first year, little girls and little boys are equally aggressive
- Between 15 months and 2 years, sex-linked differences in aggression become apparent. Both boys and girls are aggressive, but they express their aggression in different ways.
- Males are more overtly aggressive than females. They use physical force and verbal threat more often than females do and are more likely to strike back when aggression is aimed at them.
- Similar differences in **overt aggression** are found between the sexes across social classes and cultures world-wide
- Females are more relationally aggressive than males. They are more likely to gossip, snub or ostracize a peer, or say mean things to assert their power or respond to insult/injury
- Relational aggression by females appears at levels equal to the overt aggression more typical of males
- Sex-related differences in aggression are related to:
  Biology (males' greater concentrations of testosterone, physical strength, and more vigorous motor impulses may contribute to higher levels of physical aggression)
  Social learning (physical aggression is more approved and reinforced for boys than girls. Alternately, it is more socially acceptable for girls to manipulate and sabotage an adversary's self-esteem or status)
  Both males and females who display high levels of aggression tend to be rejected by their peers.

Figure 12-2 Sex-related differences in childhood aggression.

Sources: Archer, J. (1994). Testosterone and aggression: A theoretical review. *Journal of Offender Rehabilitation*, 21, 3–9; Crick, N. R. & Dodge, K. A. (1996). Social information processing mechanisms in reactive and proactive aggression. *Child Development*, 67, 993–1002; Garbarino, J. (2006). *See Jane Hit: Why girls are growing more violent and what we can do about it.* NY: Penguin Group.; Rys, G. S. & Bear, G. G. (1997). Relational aggression and peer relations: Gender and developmental issues. *Merrill Plamer Quarterly*, 43, 87–106; Ruble, D. N. & Martin, C. L. (1998). Gender development. In N. Eisenberg (Ed.) & W. Damon (Series Ed.) *Handbook of child psychology: Vol 3. Social, emotional and personality development* (5th editon), pp. 933–1016. New York: Wiley.

INEFFECTIVE STRATEGIES ADULTS USE TO REDUCE CHILDREN'S AGGRESSIVE BEHAVIOR

Physical Punishment. Many adults adhere to the old adage "Spare the rod and spoil the child." Their response to children's misbehavior, including those instances when youngsters exhibit aggression, is to resort to aggression themselves through strong physical punishment. They assume that children will learn to adapt their behavior to adult standards in order to avoid the pain of a spanking (Dobson, 1996). However, that notion is not supported by research.

In fact, evidence shows that routine use of physical punishment promotes rather than lessens childhood aggression (Slaby, Rodell, Arezzo & Hendrix et al., 1995; Straus, Sugarman & Giles-Sims, 1997; Society for Adolescent Medicine, 2003). Such effects are also long lasting. The more frequently and the more severely children experience physical punishment when they are young, the more aggressive they are as adolescents (Coie & Dodge, 1998; Gershoff, 2002). Several factors contribute to these outcomes. Let us consider the interaction between

Ms. Johnson and 4-year-old Olivia to better understand what they are.

> **SITUATION:** *Ms. Johnson tried many things to get 4-year-old Olivia to stop pinching other children when she became upset. The adult talked to Olivia, made her sit out, scolded her, and warned her that her peers would not want to play with her, but Olivia continued to pinch. Finally, in exasperation, Ms. Johnson said: "Olivia, you don't seem to understand how much pinching hurts. There (pinching Olivia hard). Now, you see what I mean. Every time you pinch, I'll pinch you like that to remind you of how it feels!"*

Ms. Johnson hoped that by pinching Olivia, the child would learn important lessons (that pinching hurts and that she shouldn't pinch anyone again). Unfortunately, Olivia did learn some lessons, but they were not the ones Ms. Johnson intended.

Lesson 1: Here's How to be Aggressive
Ms. Johnson gave Olivia an "up close and personal" lesson in how to be aggressive. From what we know about aggressive modeling, Olivia is more likely to mimic these same hurtful actions and attitudes than to abandon them (Zahn-Waxler & Robinson, 1995;

Goleman, 2006). If Ms. Johnson continues her pinching campaign, Olivia's aggressive behavior could therefore escalate rather than diminish.

Lesson 2: Aggression Gets Your Message Across

Ms. Johnson demonstrated that "might makes right." In other words, physical power rather than reasoning is the way to make one's point. In addition, powerful people can use aggression against weaker people to enforce their ideas (Herbert, 1998; Riak, 1994). In the future Olivia may aim her pinching at younger, smaller or weaker children rather than abandoning the tactic altogether.

Lesson 3: There are No Satisfactory Alternatives to Aggression

Olivia is using pinching to express frustration. Unfortunately, Ms. Johnson's approach to the problem doesn't give Olivia a nonaggressive alternative that will satisfy her needs. With no clear idea of what to do instead, it is likely that Olivia will continue to rely on hurtful behaviors to express upset feelings (Malott & Suarez, 2004).

Lesson 4: Watch Out for Number #1

When Ms. Johnson pinches her, Olivia becomes absorbed in her own reactions (pain, the desire to save face, and/or anger). In this state, she is less likely to take into account other children's needs or to develop empathy for her victims. Without those emotions to guide her actions, it will be harder for Olivia to achieve the more advanced levels of thinking and feeling that lead to reduced aggression. Making matters worse, physical punishment triggers strong feelings of self-preservation that translate into thinking about how to "get even" or how to establish one's power more absolutely (Society for Adolescent Medicine, 2003). Such thinking contributes to a more aggressive mind set, not a more peaceful one.

Lesson 5: Don't Get Caught!

Physical punishment is aversive. To avoid it, children may cease acting out in one situation only to continue their negative behavior elsewhere. Thus, Olivia may stop pinching at the center, but shift to pinching children at home or in her dance class. Alternately, she may become covert in her actions, focused more on avoiding detection then on finding constructive ways to interact with others (Malott & Suarez, 2004). In either case, Olivia will be functioning at the adherence level of self-regulation. Continual adult surveillance will be required to ensure Olivia's obedience. Ms. Johnson's pinching

consequence did not help Olivia internalize values inconsistent with aggression, making it probable the aggression will continue.

Negative outcomes such as these make physical punishment a poor choice to counter childhood aggression. Unfortunately, even though few helping professionals advocate striking children in anger, adult aggression is practiced and even mandated in many formal group settings under policies of corporal punishment.

Corporal punishment in the United States. **Corporal punishment** refers to the intentional application of physical pain as a method for changing behavior. It includes behaviors such as hitting, slapping, pinching, and shaking (Society for Adolescent Medicine, 2003). Although corporal punishment has been banned in prisons, in the military, and in mental hospitals, it is still practiced in some child care programs, elementary, middle, and high schools in the United States (Fathman, 2006). Currently, 22 states permit school personnel to use "reasonable force" against children to maintain discipline (U.S. Department of Education, 2006). Most commonly, that discipline involves some form of paddling. Children most likely to be paddled are those in kindergarten and the early elementary grades, children with learning and mental disabilities, children of color and children from low-income families (U.S. Department of Education, 2000; Zirpoli, 1990). The majority of programs that permit spanking require written permission from a child's parents prior to corporal punishment being used with that child. Many parents provide this consent.

With so much support from government, schools, and parents, you might conclude that corporal punishment effectively reduces aggression in school. That turns out not to be true.

The case against corporal punishment in formal group settings. The consensus among medical, psychological, and educational researchers is that corporal punishment in schools and child care centers yields negative outcomes (American Academy of Pediatrics, 2006; National Coalition to Abolish Corporal Punishment in Schools, 2002). There is strong evidence that children subjected to institutionalized corporal punishment become more aggressive, coercive, and destructive over time (Hyman, 1990; Gershoff, 2002). In addition, schools in which corporal punishment is used generally experience higher incidents of vandalism, attacks against teachers and more disruptive student behavior than is true for schools in which it is not practiced (Society for Adolescent Medicine, 2003).

Why, then, is corporal punishment still practiced anywhere? The answer involves a complex amalgamation of politics, social beliefs regarding the value of "old-fashioned" discipline and lack of awareness of how else to control children's behavior and maintain order in the classroom (Hyman, 1990; Lynnette, 2001). Fortunately, factual evidence regarding the impact of corporal punishment on children's development and behavior is gradually reducing the reliance on physical punishment in U.S. schools and early childhood programs. As of 2007:

- More than half (28) of U.S. states ban corporal punishment in the public schools (See Figure 12-3).
- Many public school districts, even in states in which corporal punishment is legal, prohibit its use.
- The overall number of school paddlings declined from a high of 1.5 million in 1976 to 342,000 (still too many, but heading in the right direction!).
- Corporal punishment is banned in every Catholic Dioscesan School System in every state.
- More than 50 U.S. learned societies and professional organizations have created position statements urging the complete elimination of

corporal punishment in formal group settings (NCACPS, 2002; Society for Adolescent Medicine, 2003).

Our understanding of how to counter childhood aggression and how to manage children's behavior more productively in the classroom is expanding all the time. Although each program that bans corporal punishment has its own way of approaching these issues, most are characterized by the following practices (Marzano, 2003; Taylor-Greene & Kartub, 2000; Zins et al., 2004):

- Family members are welcome in the program and there is clear communication between home and center/school.
- Children, staff, and family members work together to create a common approach to discipline.
- Family members and school personnel have high standards for children's behavior.
- Behavioral expectations are defined.
- Behavioral expectations are taught.
- Appropriate behaviors are acknowledged.
- Behavioral mistakes are corrected immediately and proactively.
- Children have opportunities to learn how to express their emotions constructively.

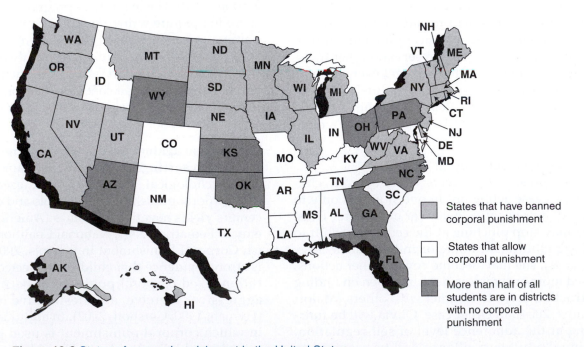

Figure 12-3 Status of corporal punishment in the United States.
Source: Elementary and Secondary School Civil Rights Report, U.S. Department of Education, 2000.

- Programs are characterized by a positive verbal environment.
- Problem solving and mediation are used to resolve conflicts.
- Problem settings (e.g., playground, unsupervised bathrooms, etc.) are restructured.
- The education program is relevant to children.
- Therapeutic approaches are used in response to some behavior problems.

Other effective techniques involve developing well planned alternative school programs, in-school suspension, the appropriate use of time-out, and peer and cross-age counseling.

Given the damaging outcomes of corporal punishment and the viable alternatives available, the authors maintain that there is no justifiable reason for helping professionals to slap, spank, or otherwise inflict physical pain on children in an effort to control their behavior in any early childhood setting. This view is echoed in the NAEYC Code of Ethical Conduct (See Figure 12-4).

> The NAEYC Code of Ethical Conduct states ". . . we shall not harm children. We shall not participate in practices that are disrespectful, degrading, dangerous, exploitative, intimidating, psychologically damaging, or physically harmful to children."

Figure 12-4 Excerpt from the NAEYC code of ethical conduct.

Ignoring Aggression

Sometimes, adults ignore children's aggressive acts in the hope that those behaviors eventually will go away. This is a mistake. Research shows that when adults ignore children's antisocial behavior, aggression increases (Espelage & Swearer, 2004) Ignoring aggression creates a permissive atmosphere in which both the aggressor and victim learn that aggression has its rewards (Herbert, 1998; Slaby et al., 1995). Aggressive children continue unabated, and children who cannot depend on a protective adult eventually give up or counterattack. As children's counterattacks become more successful and they are less frequently victimized, they begin to initiate aggressive acts towards others. In this way, unchecked aggression in a group setting not only perpetuates itself, but actually escalates.

Displacement

There are those who think that the way to deal with children who are angry and aggressive is to have them displace their emotions from the original source of anger to some unrelated target. For instance, they would encourage a youngster who was frustrated with a playmate to leave that situation and pound some clay or punch a pillow, as a way to express his or her feelings. Once these actions were carried out, the adult would assume that the child's anger was resolved and that his or her need to express that anger had been satisfied. The evidence is to the contrary.

Children who are taught that **displacement** is the ultimate means of handling angry feelings do not learn how to deal with the real source of their emotions (such as lack of cooperation from a peer) (Berkowitz, 1993). They also fail to develop strategies for confronting problems constructively or for preventing future problems. It is not surprising that such children eventually become frustrated at never having an opportunity for direct resolution and so become increasingly hostile.

Additionally, as children mature, they may shift the "safe target" chosen by an adult to one of their own choosing, such as a child down the street, a family pet, or a younger sibling. Although displacement of angry feelings from a person or animal to an inanimate object is an appropriate first step in teaching some children how to cope with their emotions, it is not an adequate solution in and of itself (Slaby et al., 1995).

Inconsistency

A fourth ineffective means of dealing with children's aggressive behavior is to be inconsistent. Adults who are haphazard in their approach promote increased aggression (Cohen & Brooks, 1995; Stormshak, Bierman, McMahon, Lengua & the Conduct Problems Prevention Research Group, 2000). "Coming down hard" on one child while avoiding confrontation with another, or sticking with the rules today and ignoring them tomorrow, leads to confusion and frustration for children. Since adult reactions follow no stable pattern, the only way children can tell if their aggressive activities will be ignored or addressed is to carry them out and see what happens each time.

The four strategies we have just discussed, physical punishment, ignoring aggression, displacement, and inconsistency, all contribute to, rather than reduce, aggressive behavior in children (see Figure 12-5).

STRATEGY	ADULT THINKS	CHILD LEARNS	OUTCOME
Physical Punishment	This will show the child that aggression is wrong.	Aggression works. Might makes right. Watch our for #1. Don't get caught.	Aggression increases
Ignoring	Maybe the aggression will go away.	This must be okay. It doesn't matter what I do.	Aggression increases
Displacement	This will help the child calm down.	There's no way to fix the real problem. People shouldn't deal directly with the people or things that upset them.	Aggression increases
Inconsistency	(Day 1)—I've got to be firm about stopping aggression. (Day 2)—I'm too tired to deal with this today. (Day 3)—I've had too many run-ins with this child. I'll look the other way today. (Day 4)—I've got to be firm about stopping aggression.	I don't know what will happen until I try it!	Aggression increases

Figure 12-5 Ineffective strategies for addressing childhood aggression.

Such methods fail because they allow the aggression to continue and/or because they fail to provide children the opportunity to learn acceptable alternatives for future use.

EFFECTIVE STRATEGIES ADULTS USE TO REDUCE CHILDREN'S AGGRESSIVE BEHAVIOR

Effective strategies for decreasing children's aggression are ones that teach children how to meet their needs peacefully as well as how to respond assertively to the aggression of others. Just as children learn to be aggressive through modeling, reinforcement, and instruction, they can learn to be nonaggressive through these same channels. Such learning takes place whether a child is in the role of aggressor, bystander, or victim. In all cases, the key to reducing children's aggressive behavior is to help them internalize values and methods of interacting that are incompatible with violence (Levin, 2003; Slaby et al., 1995).

Modeling

There are two ways adults can influence what behaviors children imitate. First, they can model nonaggression through their own behavior. For instance, when children see adults talking about problems, reasoning with others, and making compromises, they are likely to view these approaches as desirable alternatives to aggression (Bandura, 1989; Hyson, 2004). Second, when adults treat children calmly and rationally regardless of the situation, youngsters gain firsthand experience by watching someone adopt a nonaggressive solution to a problem. In both cases, adult modeling provides a standard of peaceful conduct for children to emulate.

Reinforcement

As with any other behavior, children are more likely to repeat nonaggressive strategies for making their desires known when those strategies are rewarded. One type of reinforcement adults can use is to acknowledge children's efforts with positive personal messages or other forms of effective praise. Positive personal messages are especially helpful because they identify specific behaviors and give children a reason for why such behaviors are desirable. Adult praise gives youngsters the important information that their peaceful behavior is both appropriate and effective.

Another way children find such behavior rewarding is when it helps them to successfully reach their goals. Hence Pablo, who asks for a turn with the kite rather than grabbing it, and who ultimately gets a chance to use it, is likely to incorporate asking into his future repertoire of social behaviors. Even though he occasionally is turned down, if, over time, his requests are honored more often than not, he will learn that asking is a useful approach.

Direct Instruction

The following are a number of instructional techniques adults can use to minimize children's aggressive behavior.

Reducing the frustration in children's lives. Because frustration makes aggression more likely to occur, its reduction leads to fewer aggressive incidents. Appropriate structuring of the physical environment is an excellent way to reduce potential frustration. For example, children are less aggressive when there are sufficient materials for them to use and when the physical environment allows freedom of movement without overcrowding or interference among activities. Routines that eliminate excessive waiting and sitting lessen frustration too. Children are less likely to experience frustration when adults keep rules to a minimum as well as warn them in advance about changes in the daily routine. Frustration also is reduced in classrooms where cooperation is emphasized

over competition. Finally, children are less likely to resort to physical force when adults provide sufficient support during free-choice times or in physical areas where aggression is likely to occur, such as in the block area, on the playground, in the hallways, in the bathrooms, or in the cafeteria (Herbert, 1998; Slaby et al., 1995).

Helping children feel more competent. Children who feel they have some control over their lives are less likely to resort to aggression as a way to establish power. When adults give children choices, help them to develop their skills, and avoid insisting on perfection, they influence children to be less aggressive (Hendrick & Weissman, 2006).

Fostering empathy among children. Aggressive children are often unconcerned about or unaware of the harmful effects their behaviors have on others. However, such youngsters can be taught to recognize people's emotions, to imagine how victims feel, and to identify the negative consequences of their aggressive actions. When this happens children are less likely to hurt one another or to gain pleasure from the discomfort of a victim (Hyson, 2004). The strategies identified in Chapter 5, Supporting Children's Emotional Development, are effective measures to achieve these aims.

Teaching children prosocial behaviors. Kindness, helpfulness, and cooperation are incompatible with aggression. When adults actively teach children these behaviors, aggression diminishes (Marion, 2007). Because this is such a powerful strategy, all of Chapter 13 is devoted to prosocial behavior.

Making it clear that aggression is unacceptable. When physical or verbal aggression occurs, adults must intervene before children experience the satisfaction of getting what they want through negative means (Beaudoin & Taylor, 2004). Interrupting aggression takes away the reward of such behavior and provides a perfect opportunity for adults to help children identify and carry out appropriate alternative actions.

When helping professionals establish that aggressive behavior will not be tolerated and when they reason with children and point out the harmful effects of aggression, violence diminishes (Berkowitz, 1993; Malott & Suarez, 2005). See Brian's Story, presented in Figure 12-6 for an example of one teacher's use of this strategy.

BRIAN'S STORY[1]

Brian's Teacher Narrates

Brian entered my classroom as a 3-year-old, having been identified as needing special education for speech and language. His official diagnosis was apraxia of speech. This meant it was difficult for him to produce language. Because of brain damage or lack of brain development he had to consciously work (both mentally and physically) at making sounds that come naturally to most children.

In the classroom, if someone had a toy Brian wanted, he took it. He would pinch. Or, he would step on somebody's foot. This kind of aggression was frequent. By closely observing him, I realized that these hurtful acts were related to Brian's inability to communicate. His actions were saying, "I have no way to communicate with you. I have no way of getting your attention or getting you to do what I want."

Goals and Strategies for Brian

One goal I had in working with Brian was to help him become less aggressive. A second was to enhance his communication skills. These two goals were complementary.

Strategy 1: Intervening Whenever Brian Was Aggressive

Whenever Brian would hurt someone, I interceded. I would take his hand, draw him close to the other child and say, "Look, look what you did! See her face. She is crying. You hurt her. Did you want to tell her something?" Next, I suggested words that I thought he wanted to say, e.g., "I want it." At first, Brian would try to pull away. However, as time went on, he'd squeeze up against me during these little conversations. He'd make sounds and point to things he wanted. I made sure to repeat the same few words over and over again. At first, it felt like this was all my aide and I were doing all day long.

Over time the other children came to realize that hurting people was not what Brian wanted to do. He was just going after something he wanted. Even so, we didn't want them to feel like perpetual victims. So, we gave them gestures (putting their hands up to ward off his grabbing) and simple scripts to let Brian know how they felt and what he could do instead. They became more adept at anticipating his needs and at telling him "no" if he began to hurt them. This empowered them and interrupted his aggressive actions.

Other strategies we used included: establishing consistent expectations for Brian's behavior (coming to group time, sharing toys, staying in the classroom), introducing sign language (signs for more, and want came first and were especially useful), combining signs and sounds, rewarding tiny improvements, intensive speech therapy, and working with Brian's mom and dad to ensure consistency between home and school.

Epilogue

Brian's aggression did not stop immediately. His behavior change was gradual. It took a year for the aggression to pretty much disappear. Today Brian is in a class for 4-year-olds with special needs. His aggression appears only sporadically. Childhood apraxia is not something children grow out of. However, with proper intervention early in life, children like Brian can learn to speak more clearly and to communicate more effectively.

[1] Brian's Story was adapted from a case study included in: *Children with Special Needs: Lessons for Early Childhood Professions* written by Kostelnik, Onaga, Rohde and Whiren in 2002 and published by Teachers College Press, pp. 120–135.

Figure 12-6 Brian's story.

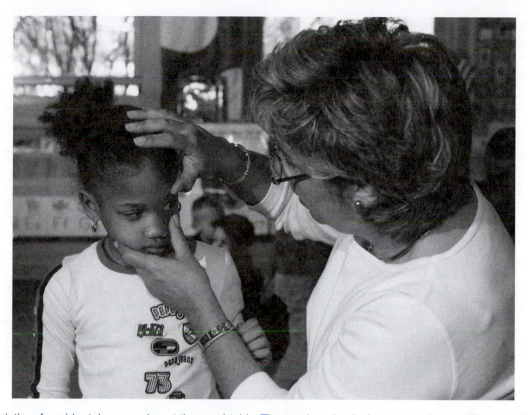

Tina is a victim of accidental aggression at the sand-table. The teacher checks her eye and says, "That surprised you. It's no fun to have sand in your face. Joe didn't mean to hurt you. It was an accident."

Helping children recognize instances of accidental aggression. Frequently, victims of accidental aggression react as though the aggression was intentional. Providing accurate information changes the child's view of the purposefulness of the act and reduces the necessity for retaliation (Herbert, 1998; Holden, 1997). Adults defuse the situation when they identify the victim's feelings and clarify the accidental nature of the incident ("You were surprised to get hit. It hurt. He wasn't trying to hurt you; he was trying to keep the ball from going out of bounds").

This kind of information does not excuse the aggression but rather attempts to explain its unintentional nature. Added benefits occur when adults point out to the aggressor the impact that the action had on the victim, and, when possible, enlist the aggressor's aid in repairing the damage: "When you jumped for the ball, you knocked Jesse over. His knee is scraped. Come with us and we'll fix it up together." Using this approach helps both victim and aggressor better understand the context of the incident and gives them a constructive way to resolve it.

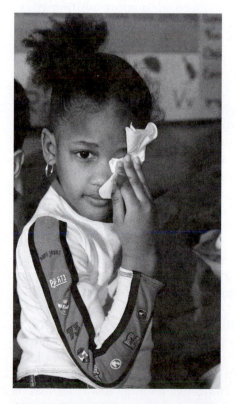

Joe gets Tina a tissue to make amends.

Rechanneling children's expressive aggression. When carried out safely, kicking, pounding, throwing, and knocking down are appropriate physical activities for children. Youngsters derive satisfaction from mastering the environment and their bodies by kicking or throwing a ball as hard as they can, from pounding at the workbench, or from crashing down something they have built.

Problems arise when children go beyond these safe situations to gain pleasure from ones that are potentially damaging to people or property. Thus, Rodney may become so engrossed in his play that he fails to notice that the ball he is throwing is interfering with other children's games. Likewise, when he chases Joel, he may assume that Joel, in spite of his protests, is experiencing the same thrill that he is. Because of their potentially destructive outcomes, these circumstances represent expressive aggression and require adult intervention.

The focus of that intervention should be on allowing the child to continue the pleasurable physical movement while structuring the situation so it becomes harmless. This is accomplished through substitution. Substitution consists of replacing the unacceptable target of the child's expressive aggression with one that is more suitable (Landy, 2002). Rodney could be redirected to throw the ball away from the group or to chase a more willing playmate. Rodney is still allowed to throw the ball or play chase, but in an acceptable way. Thus, the alternative offered by the adult continues to support the child's activity but redirects his actions more suitably.

At this point, you may notice some similarities between substitution and the ineffective strategy of displacement discussed earlier in this chapter. Both attempt to redirect children's inappropriate behavior. However, there is an important difference between the two. Substitution is used only with children engaged in expressive aggression. Such children are happy, not frustrated or angry. Their actions are acceptable, but the target of their actions is not. The redirection that takes place teaches them what they need to know in the situation. For instance, children learn that throwing something is allowable, but what you throw must be considered carefully. Displacement strategies, on the other hand, do not teach children what they need to learn in difficult situations: how to deal with the source of their anger or frustration. A child who is redirected from expressing his angry feelings toward someone does not learn a better way to confront that person.

Pounding clay or painting an angry picture are unrelated activities that fail to teach children appropriate assertiveness skills. For instance, if Rodney were chasing Joel because Joel had done something to upset him, the displacement technique of telling Rodney to "work out" his anger by pounding the clay would be ignoring his need to confront Joel directly.

Helping children de-escalate potentially aggressive play. Frequently, play episodes that begin as positive social interactions escalate at a rate and in a way children do not intend or expect. This may lead to accidental aggression, which in turn may develop into an angry confrontation. Adults can head off the development of purposeful aggression by keeping an eye on children as they play and by watching for early signs of difficulty. When youngsters stop laughing, when their voices become upset or complaining, when their facial expressions show fear, anger, or distress, and when words move out of the realm of pretend into real-life menace, aggression is likely. If such signs become apparent, adults should intervene immediately by redirecting the play or by becoming involved in the play themselves. For example, in a game of chase, if a child shows signs of angrily turning on her pursuers, the helping professional could defuse potential problems by laughingly becoming the object of the chase.

Similarly, there are times when children's solitary play escalates into aggression due to frustration. Children become angry when a toy does not work, when they are unable to produce the picture they envision, or when something interferes with the accomplishment of a goal they have in mind. At times like these, children may lash out, throw something, or explode in fury. Alert adults can de-escalate aggression by helping children to cope directly with the source of their frustration rather than simply criticizing them for acting inappropriately: "You're upset! That model keeps falling apart. The glue you're using works better on paper than it does on plastic. Let's look for a different kind of glue." Such intervention may involve giving children information, offering assistance, helping them reevaluate their goals, breaking the task into more manageable steps, or taking a break before resuming the project.

Teaching children alternatives to gun play. In the United States real guns are highly visible and widespread. There are almost 200 million guns in public hands (National Association of Federally Licensed Firearms Dealers and Professional Gun Retailers Association, 2001) and approximately one in four households in the country contain at least one handgun (National Rifle Association, 2001). Thus, many children live in or visit homes containing a gun. Unfortunately youngsters cannot be counted on to differentiate pretend guns from real ones or to know how to handle real weapons safely. The tragedy that results from children's mistakes is evident from the accidental shootings that often make the headlines (Children's Defense Fund, 2005). Consequently, both gun rights advocates and gun control supporters agree that children should be taught to treat all guns as potentially real and therefore dangerous (Center to Prevent Handgun Violence, 2006; National Rifle Association, 2001). For all these reasons, it is best to discourage children from bringing toy guns to the program and to tell those who do bring such items from home to "check" them at the door until the session is over. During the session, children who use other objects such as sticks or fingers as gun substitutes should be redirected into less violent play themes or into discussions of alternate means for resolving their make believe differences.

In each case, it is important for adults to explain to children that guns are serious business and are not to be treated as toys. Moreover, even pretending to kill people or animals is not in keeping with the nonaggressive goals of a developmentally appropriate classroom (Kuykendall, 1995).

Teaching children to generate potential responses to the aggression of others. Many children become frustrated because they do not know what to do when someone teases them, hurts them, or calls them names. They may either yield to the aggressor or counterattack. Neither strategy is desirable because both lead to further aggression.

Adults who take children's complaints of aggression seriously and intervene directly or model appropriate ways of handling problem situations contribute to a reduction in the aggressive behavior of younger children. For instance, Mr. Monroe notices Callie calling Georgio "Georgio-porgio." She is laughing, enjoying the sound of the words. Scowling, Georgio rushes at her to make her stop. The adult intervenes quickly and says, "Georgio, you're upset that Callie is calling you names. I'm worried if you knock her down she'll get hurt. Tell her how you feel." Mr. Monroe remains with the children,

Stories can be used to illustrate the skills related to assertiveness and negotiation.

helping Georgio figure out the words he will use to express his displeasure to Callie. The child eventually says, "I don't think you're very funny. My name is Georgio." This kind of coaching helps victims learn skills they need to handle such situations more effectively in the future. It also reduces the likelihood that they will use aggressive means to resolve the problem.

With older children, direct intervention may lead to later reprisals by the aggressor. Indirect approaches, such as discussing possible motives behind the aggressor's behavior or brainstorming with children about the potential advantages and disadvantages of various responses, are more effective (Horne, Orpinas, Newman-Carlson & Bartolomucci, 2004). Some children also appreciate having an opportunity to rehearse what they are going to say or do before actually trying it out.

It also is useful to help identify other children with whom a victim of continued aggression could establish a relationship. Perpetual victims tend to feel isolated and so are likely to tolerate continued aggression directed at them, thus reinforcing it. It is especially common for young children not to recognize alternate playmates but instead to center on maintaining their interaction with the aggressor. Helping them to recognize others as potential choices breaks this nonproductive cycle. Finally, the comfort and information offered by a caring adult goes a long way toward helping children feel that they do indeed have some power within the situation.

Teaching alternatives to aggression through planned activities. Children who are unable to generate alternate solutions to conflict situations may resort to aggression instead (Landy, 2002). On the other hand, children who can envision a wide range of possibilities are less apt to resort to violence (Beaudoin & Taylor, 2004). Fortunately, there is growing evidence that even very young children can increase their repertoire of appropriate options through planned activities (Zins et al., 2004; Wittmer & Honig, 1994). One approach is to have group discussions with children. These can center on effects of aggression, nonviolent ways to get what they want, how to resolve problem situations, and how to respond to the aggression of others. Another strategy involves teaching children specific skills related to assertiveness and negotiation (Levin, 2003; Slaby et al., 1995). Adults can use puppets, storybooks, flannel boards, skits, or open-ended vignettes to illustrate skills and stimulate conversation.

Helping professionals who use these techniques on a regular basis report that children improve in their ability to identify, describe, and suggest socially appropriate alternatives to aggression (Mize & Ladd, 1990b; Zins et al., 2004). This makes planned activities an effective introduction to teaching children how to substitute positive behaviors for aggressive ones.

Teaching alternatives to aggression through conflict mediation. Even when youngsters are able to talk about sharing and taking turns in planned activities, they sometimes forget and resort to instrumental aggression in the heat of real-life confrontations. At times like these, adults may be tempted to simply separate the children or remove the disputed object. Although such tactics halt the aggression, they do not teach children better ways to handle conflict. A more effective strategy is to use such occasions to help children practice nonviolent approaches to conflict resolution (Levin, 2003; Wheeler, 2004). In this process, your role is to support children as they attempt to resolve their differences.

To do this effectively, it helps to remember that conflict is not necessarily negative. Differences of opinion and ways of doing things are normal aspects of community living. In fact, conflict offers children a natural means for improving their social competence. Sometimes children are able to work out solutions without direct adult intervention.

Keeping this in mind, allow children to argue as long as their actions do not turn to violence. If a resolution comes about, use positive personal messages to identify children's appropriate behaviors and bring them to their attention. However, if aggression occurs or children seem at a loss for what to do next, you can become directly involved as a conflict mediator.

Conflict mediation. This involves walking children through a series of steps beginning with problem identification and ending with a mutually satisfactory solution. The adult provides more or less direction as necessary until some conclusion is reached. The aim of the process is not for adults to dictate how children should solve their problem, but to help them figure out a solution of their own. Children experience several benefits from working through their differences in this way (deVogue, 1996; Wheeler, 2004). **Conflict mediation:**

- contributes to more peaceful program environments

- builds trust among children and between children and adults
- teaches constructive ways of dealing with highly emotional situations
- teaches children problem-solving strategies
- encourages positive actions instead of fighting
- promotes friendliness among children
- promotes feelings of competence and worth among children

During conflict mediation children learn the skills necessary to reach peaceful resolutions. These skills involve communication, compromise, the ability to see how different aspects of a dispute are related, and the ability to consider their own perspective as well as that of another person (Levin, 2003). At first, children need a lot of support to proceed all the way to a negotiated settlement. The mediator provides this support, serving as a model and as an instructor. As children learn problem-solving procedures and words, they become increasingly capable of solving problems for themselves. There is also evidence that these childhood learnings are maintained into adulthood (Goleman, 1995).

As with any other social skill, children require numerous opportunities to practice conflict resolution under the guidance of a more experienced person (Beane, 2005; Wheeler, 2004). In most cases, this is an adult. However, over the past decade 10-, 11- and 12-year-olds have been taught to mediate peer conflicts on the playground and in the lunchroom. Regardless of whether the mediator is an adult or older child, most conflict resolution models involve similar steps. Let us turn our attention to a practical, systematic model that can be used to mediate children's disputes while teaching them appropriate problem solving skills.

A MODEL FOR CONFLICT MEDIATION

From the far end of the yard, Mrs. Woznawski, the after-school supervisor, hears Sarah shout, "Give me that pogo stick—I need it!" Bianca screams back: "Use something else! I'm not done." Alerted to the difficulty, the adult watches from a distance as the children continue their argument. However, as the dispute heats up, the children begin to grab and pull on the pogo stick. This is an opportune time for Mrs. Woznawski to begin conflict mediation.

Step One: Initiating the Mediation Process

The first step in approaching a conflict situation is to assume the role of mediator. Stopping the aggressive behavior, separating the combatants, and defining the problem accomplishes this: "You both want the pogo stick at the same time. It looks like you each have different ideas about what to do." You may have to position yourself between the children as you help them focus on the mutual problem rather than on the object or territory they are defending. It is helpful to neutralize the object of contention by temporarily gaining control of it and assuring the children that it will be safe until the conflict is resolved: "I will hold the pogo stick until we can decide together what to do." This procedure stops the children from continuing to hit or grab, helps them to hear you and each other, and sets the stage for them to approach a highly emotional situation more objectively.

Step Two: Clarifying Each Child's Perspective

Clarifying the conflict based on the children's perspective is the focus of step two. Ask each child in turn to state what he or she wants from the situation. It is important to allow each child ample opportunity, without interruption, to state his or her ultimate desire. This might involve possession of a toy or getting a turn. Some sample statements might include: "You both seem very angry. Sarah, you can tell me what you want. Bianca, you can tell me what you want when Sarah is finished." This step is critical for you to be an effective mediator, the children must trust you not to make an arbitrary decision in favor of one child or the other. You establish neutrality by withholding any evaluation of the merits of either child's position. Paraphrasing each child's view to the other child is also important in this step. This ensures that you correctly understand each child's point of view and helps the children to clarify both positions. Children who are very upset or quiet may require several opportunities to describe their position. It must be emphasized that, depending on the level of the children's distress, this step may take several minutes. Children may need help articulating their desires. Try to be as accurate as possible in paraphrasing, checking back with the children at each turn.

Step Three: Summing Up

The third step occurs when you have enough information to understand each child's perception of the conflict. When this happens, define the problem in mutual terms, implying that each child is responsible for both the problem and its solution: "Sarah and Bianca, you each want to play with the pogo stick all by yourself. We have a problem. It is important that we find a solution that will satisfy each of you." In other words, state that a problem exists and that a solution must be found.

Step Four: Generating Alternatives

Generating several possible alternative solutions takes place in the fourth stage of mediation. Suggestions may be offered by the children themselves or may be volunteered by bystanders. Each time a possible solution is offered, you will paraphrase it to the children directly involved: "Jonathan says you could share." At this point, each child is asked to evaluate the merits of the recommendation: "What do you think, Sarah? What do you think, Bianca?" Elicit as many divergent ideas as possible and have no stake in which solution is eventually selected. Each child should be a willing participant in the outcome and no alternative should be forced on any child. It is typical during this phase for children to reject certain possibilities that they may later find acceptable.

Therefore, when a suggestion is repeated, present it again rather than assuming it will be rejected a second time. If the children are not able to originate alternatives, help them out by saying something like: "Sometimes when people have this problem, they decide to use it together, take turns, or trade toys back and forth. What do you think?" Sometimes during this step, children tire of the process and one or the other says something like, "I don't want it anymore" or "It's okay, she can have it." Other times, one of the children will simply walk away. If this happens, reflect and provide information, "This is hard work" or "You're getting tired of trying to solve this problem. Working things out can take a long time." If the child insists that he or she would like to solve the problem by giving up, respect his or her wishes. With practice, children increase their skills and are better able to tolerate the time involved in reaching a negotiated settlement. In the meantime, both children have witnessed the mediation process up to a certain point, and each will have a better idea of what to expect the next time it is used.

Step Five: Agreeing on a Solution

Children will reject certain suggestions outright and will indicate that others seem more acceptable. The ultimate aim of the fifth step is to get the children to agree on a plan of action that is mutually satisfying. Your job as mediator is to help the children explore the possibilities that seem most acceptable to them. The plan should not include any alternatives that

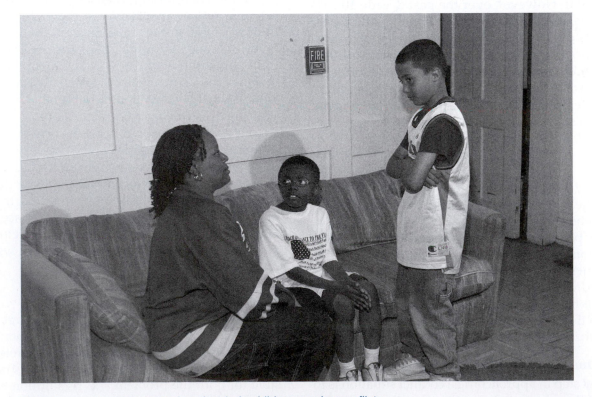

Mediators must remain neutral as they help children resolve conflicts.

Table 12-1 Summary of Conflict Mediation Model

Step one: Initiating the mediation process	Establish the mediator role and neutralize object, territory, or right.
Step two: Clarifying each child's perspective	Clarify conflict based on each child's perspective.
Step three: Summing up	Define dispute in mutual terms; make clear each child has responsibility for both the problem and its solution.
Step four: Generating alternatives	Ask for suggestions from the children involved and from bystanders.
Step five: Agreeing on a solution	Help children create a plan of action that is mutually satisfying.
Step six: Reinforcing the problem-solving process	Praise children for developing a mutually agreed on solution and for solving process working hard to achieve it.
Step seven: Following through	Help children carry out the terms of the agreement.

either child vehemently opposes. The final agreement usually involves some concessions on the part of each child and so may not represent the action the child would take if she or he did not have to consider another person's point of view. Eventually, the children will exhibit behaviors that indicate that each can find a way to accept one or a combination of ideas.

Continue the mediation process until the possibilities have been narrowed down to a workable solution. When this finally occurs, it is important to identify that a resolution has been achieved. For example: "You think you can use the stick together. It sounds like you've solved the problem! Try out your idea."

Step Six: Reinforcing the Problem-Solving Process

The purpose of the sixth stage of mediation is to praise the children for developing a mutually beneficial solution. The message to be conveyed is that the process of reaching the solution is as important as the solution itself. The way to achieve this is to acknowledge the emotional investment each child had in the original conflict and the hard work involved in reaching an agreement: "It was important to each of you to have the pogo stick. You worked hard at figuring out how to do that without hurting each other."

Step Seven: Following Through

The conclusion of the mediation process involves helping the children to carry out the terms of the agreement. This is accomplished by reminding the children what the terms were and, if necessary, physically assisting or demonstrating how to comply. At this point, an adult should remain in the vicinity to determine the degree to which children carry out the agreement. If the plan begins to falter, the children should be brought together again to discuss possible revisions. The seven steps involved in conflict mediation are summarized in Table 12-1.

Conflict Mediation in Action

The following is a transcript of an actual conflict between two children, both 5 years old, in which the helping professional used the model just described.

Step one

Angela: Mr. Lewin, Evan and Aaron are fighting.

Adult: Aaron and Evan, you're both trying to put on that stethoscope. (Restrains the two children, who are pulling on the stethoscope, crouches to the children's level, and turns each child to face him.) I'll hold it while we're deciding what to do about it. I'll hold it. I'll make sure it's safe. I'll hold on to it. (Removes the stethoscope from the children's grasp and holds it in front of him.)

Step two
Aaron: I wanted that!

Adult: You wanted the stethoscope. How about you, Evan?

Evan: I want it.

Adult: You wanted the stethoscope, too. (Another child offers a stethoscope.)

Evan: I don't like that kind.

Aaron: I want it.

Adult: Aaron says he really wants that stethoscope. What about you, Evan?

Evan: I want it!

Step three
Adult: You want it, too. Evan and Aaron, you both want to play with one stethoscope. We have a problem. What can we do about it? Anybody have any ideas?

Step four
Aaron: He can have Angela's.

Adult: You think he can have Angela's. It looks like Angela still wants hers. (Angela backs away.)

Evan: I still want mine, too.

Adult: Evan, you want yours, too. Sometimes when we have a problem like this, we can figure out a solution. Sometimes we share it, sometimes we take turns. Anybody have any ideas?

Another child: Share it.

Adult: Shanna thinks you can share it. What do you think Aaron?

Aaron: Take turns.

Adult: Aaron thinks we should take turns. What do you think, Evan?

Evan: Unh uh. (Shaking his head from side to side.)

Adult: You don't think we should take turns.

Evan: Then I just want it.

Adult: Then you just really want it, hmm. That's still a problem.

Aaron: I want it.

Adult: You really want a turn with it. How about you, Evan? What do you think?

Step five
Evan: No. Aaron can have one turn.

Adult: You think Aaron can have one turn.

Evan: Yes, guess so.

Step six
Adult: Thank you, Evan.

Evan: Not a long turn.

Adult: Not a long turn. You want to make sure that you get it back. Aaron, Evan said you could have one turn, and then you'll give it back to him.

Evan: A short turn.

Adult: A short turn. Aaron, you may have a short turn. Thank you very much, Evan. That was really hard to do.

Step seven
Adult: It's about five minutes' till it's cleanup time. So Aaron can have a two-minute turn, and you can have a two-minute turn.

Adult: (Two minutes later.) Aaron, two minutes are up. Now, it is time for Evan's turn. Thank you, Aaron. You kept your part of the bargain, and Evan kept his.

How Children Think About Conflict Resolution

Conflicts are a natural part of human interaction. It is through differences of opinion that we learn to recognize and value other people's views of the world and to rethink our own. Thus, disagreements are not necessarily bad and children do not automatically use aggression to resolve every conflict. In fact, over time children become capable of generating a variety of solutions to disagreements over objects, rights, and territory. The nature of the solutions they select is determined largely by how they perceive conflict in general. Thus, children's concept of conflict resolution evolves as their understanding of relationships becomes more sophisticated.

Initially, very young children see force or withdrawal as the most likely solutions to a disagreement (Wheeler, 2004). This simplistic view can be summed up as "fight or flight." When two toddlers fight over a toy they might try grabbing or hitting to resolve the situation or simply give up if a peer refuses to yield a favored item.

As children mature, their ability to understand the needs of others increases. This helps them to take into account other children's perspectives when objects or rights are in dispute. However, they also expect peer interactions to be balanced (Berk, 2006). If a peer uses aggression to approach a problem, that aggression creates an imbalance, which must be resolved. Although children as young as 5 years old disapprove of random aggression, when arguments break out, their philosophy becomes "an eye for an eye." In the view of older preschoolers and some elementary-aged children, the most common equalizer is for the victim to return the aggression in kind. Thus, children justify aggressive solutions by saying things like, "He hit me first," or "I had it." Children's need for equity at this age also contributes to the feeling that victims must get some restitution from the offending party for the conflict to be ended satisfactorily. Successful resolution depends on the aggressor taking responsibility for restoring harmony. This can take the form of an apology or some action to reverse the hurtful words or deeds. For instance, it is common to hear children shout "Say you're sorry" or "You take that back!" as evidence of this kind of thinking.

Eventually, children's reasoning evolves to where they recognize that both participants bear some responsibility for the conflict and will benefit from a mutually satisfying settlement (Wheeler, 2004). They also understand that more than one solution may be possible. Arrival at these notions depends on cognitive maturation and experience.

The mediation model presented here helps children move in this direction: They have an opportunity to observe problem solving in action and experience the consequences of nonviolent resolution while benefiting from the guidance of a supportive adult. When models like this are used with preschoolers, most children suggest some form of alternative action as a solution. Taking turns, trading objects, replacing one object with another, and dividing the materials are the most common ideas offered.

Grade-school children often decide to use materials simultaneously or to select an altogether new

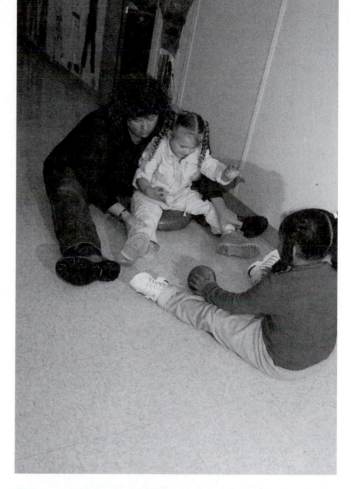

Children sometimes need assistance in the follow-through phase of conflict mediation.

material. Older children sometimes forego their claim to a right or possession if the other child acknowledges the error of his or her aggressive approach (e.g., "I didn't mean to push you" or "I'm sorry I took it away before you were finished.").

Does Conflict Mediation Work?

At this point, you may be wondering whether using a model like the one just described actually reduces children's aggression and expands their ability to resolve conflicts on their own. Studies do indeed show that children who participate in conflict mediation on a regular basis improve in their ability to engage in that process. Over time, children increase the number and variety of solutions they suggest and decrease the amount of time they need to negotiate a settlement (Evans, 2002). In addition, as the negotiation process becomes more familiar, the number of onlookers increases. These children, along with the disputants, become more actively involved in suggesting ideas and reasons for a particular course of action. Gradually, children also become better able to resolve conflicts on their own without the help of a formal mediator (Wheeler, 2004). Finally, there is promising evidence that in groups in which mediation is used, not only does aggression diminish, but positive, prosocial behaviors increase (Lopes & Salovey, 2004; Holden, 1997). This type of instruction, combined with the other strategies suggested in this chapter, will go a long way toward decreasing children's aggressive social interactions.

The mediation model outlined here can be adapted for use with children as young as 3 or as old as 12 years of age. The steps of the model are similar to many mediation programs currently available commercially as well as others described in the literature. It can be adapted for use by an adult in a single classroom, by an entire program staff, and by children serving as peer mediators in formal group settings. Conflict mediation is most effective for dealing with incidents of instrumental aggression. Hostile aggression requires additional skills.

WHEN AGGRESSION BECOMES HOSTILE

Four-year-old Selena has developed a pattern of picking on Cammy, a younger, physically smaller child in her child care home. The provider notes that Selena seems angry much of the time and that she hits anyone who disagrees with her; she is especially aggressive toward Cammy. Selena calls Cammy names and physically torments her.

Cammy has begun to exhibit signs of anxious behavior, such as crying when her mother leaves in the morning and clinging to the caregiver throughout the day.

Tristan's parents are thinking about pulling him out of Elmwood School. The fourth-grader complains that a certain group of boys continually threaten him in the hallways and on the playground. They play cruel pranks such as trashing his locker or spilling food on him in the cafeteria.

The boys tell him that he smells bad and warn other children not to associate with him. They make fun of his family, his culture, and his abilities. Their tactics have made life miserable for Tristan, yet his teacher does not feel comfortable intervening. She believes adult intervention will only make things worse and has told Tristan he will have to "work things out for himself."

All children have times when they exhibit aggressive behavior. However, some children routinely and deliberately use hurtful actions such as rejection, name calling, or physical intimidation to exert power over others. Such incidents go beyond the simple altercations common among children; they represent prolonged misuse of influence by one person or group of persons over another. This form of hostile aggression is traditionally called **bullying**.

Bullying is most prevalent in the later elementary years; yet even preschoolers can exhibit early signs of hostile behavior (Alsaker & Valkanover, 2001; Beane, 2005; Tremblay, 1994). Bullying takes its toll on victims, on aggressors, and on those who witness it. Children as young as 3 years of age talk about bullying and recognize it as

Deliberate	"He did it on purpose"
Imbalanced	"Unfair—the bully is bigger or more powerful than the victim."
Continuous	"It happens a lot."

These concepts are illustrated in Figures 12-7 and 12-8, children's drawings of bullies.

Victims of Bullying

It is estimated that as many as 80% of all children experience bullying sometime during early or middle childhood (Hanish, Kochenderfer-Ladd, Fabes, Martin & Denning, 2004). Approximately 10 to 20% of these children become chronic victims. Such victims tend to be the children least able to respond effectively to taunts and physical assaults. This involves youngsters possessing limited language abilities and few social skills, children who are socially isolated, and ones who are physically weak. Low self-esteem is another distinctive characteristic of chronically victimized children (Olweus, 1993). Such children think of themselves as failures, and feel stupid and unattractive. Most are **passive victims**. They seldom initiate the hostile attack and rarely assert their rights when it happens. However, a few can be described as **provocative victims**. They incite aggressive reactions by crying easily, by becoming very defensive or angry when it is not appropriate, or by misinterpreting joking or teasing as verbal aggression when that is not the intent (Roffey, Tarrant & Majors, 1994). Regardless of the cause, each time victims become involved in aggressive incidents, their ineffective responses reinforce the bully's behavior, prompting the cycle of aggression to continue.

Generally, chronic victims of bullying tend to be disliked and elicit little sympathy from peers who

Draw A Bully

Figure 12-7 S. Swearer (2005). Children's Depictions of Bullies. University of Nebraska, Lincoln.

Draw A Bully

Figure 12-8 S. Swearer (2005). Children's Depictions of Bullies. University of Nebraska, Lincoln.

observe their predicament (Boivin & Hymel, 1997; Perry, Willard & Perry, 1990). For instance, victims who provoke attack through ineffective or irritating behaviors are often viewed as "getting what they deserve" (Society for Adolescent Medicine, 2003). In addition, both aggressive and nonaggressive children anticipate potential rewards from interacting with chronic victims in terms of getting what they want. In other words, classmates see victims as patsies who can be easily taken advantage of and made to give up coveted items. It is no surprise, then, that victims of bullying experience a severely diminished sense of competence and worth. They may express their discomfort through lack of appetite, disturbed sleep, real or imagined illnesses, inability to concentrate, increased fear of facing others, unexplained bouts of crying or extremely anxious behavior, reluctance to go to the formal group

setting, or unusually aggressive behavior toward others (often younger peers, siblings, or pets; Egan & Perry, 1998; Hodges Malone, & Perry, 1997; Ladd, Kochenderfer & Coleman, 1996).

Bullies

The most common type of bully is fearless, coercive, and impulsive. Such children often have high self-esteem based on their powerful status. Other bullies feel inferior and insecure. They use aggression to mask these feelings and dominate others. All bullies value aggression and the power it gives them over other people. They expect aggression to get them what they want and feel justified using hostile acts to assert their will (Horne et al., 2004). A look into their background sometimes reveals that they have been victims of bullying themselves in another time and place, making them bully/victims. Some bullies are youngsters who have experienced few boundaries, gaining an impression that they can do anything they like. Other children become bullies as a result of attributing hostile intent to peers and then believing their hostile outbursts are justified as a means of maintaining their rights. A fourth scenario involves children who experience some overwhelming life event that leaves them angry and confused. Unable to control the situation, they try to control the behavior of others through coercion. Rather than risk expressing their anger toward those close to them, such children find a "safe" target among their peers. Finally, children who are the product of a coercive home life often exhibit bullying behavior with peers (Coie et al., 1991; Essa, 2003; Roffey et al., 1994).

Regardless of what has prompted it, bullying that goes unchecked in the preschool and early elementary years manifests itself as delinquency and academic failure by middle school (Offard, 1992; Tremblay, 1994). Moreover, children for whom bullying becomes a standard mode of conduct are four times more likely as adults to be involved in violent crime, be imprisoned, be involved in domestic violence, abuse their children, and be unable to hold a job (Brendtro & Long, 1995; Society for Adolescent Medicine, 2003).

Witnesses

Besides the bully and the victim, other children frequently observe bullying episodes. Such witnesses are affected by this hostile aggression, even when they are not directly involved. Witnesses see bullying modeled and reinforced. They may develop feelings of fear, frustration, hopelessness, or anger based on what they see. They may feel guilty about not doing more to help another child or tangentially powerful if they support the bully's behavior from the sidelines. They may fear for their own safety or worry that they will become targets of the harassment (Beaudoin & Taylor, 2004). Conversely, witnesses can influence what happens when bullying takes place. They may function as supporters of the bully or supporters of the victim. If they ignore what is happening they send a message to bully and victim that bullying is okay with them or that there is nothing that can be done to change the situation. Consequently, witnesses play an important role in determining to what extent bullying is accepted or rejected as a way of life in formal group settings.

The Role of Adults in Bully Prevention

Both victims and bullies are vulnerable people whose long-term prognosis for social and academic success is negative. Witnesses are also impacted negatively.

The adults in children's lives must take such destructive behavior seriously. Children cannot be left to their own devices to "simply work things out." Proactive strategies can be enacted with victims and tormentors, as well as on a program-wide basis. Thus intervention (when bullying is happening) must be combined with prevention (creating a bully-free program) to have the greatest impact. Both helping professionals and family members can contribute to this effort.

Working with victims. Children are less likely to be victimized if they possess verbal assertiveness skills with which to establish their desires and protect their rights (Horne et al., 2004; Slaby et al., 1995). All children need support in developing these skills, but this is especially true for youngsters who lack general language proficiency and social skills. Early evidence from continuing research would appear to suggest that assertiveness training is among the most effective types of intervention in reducing bullying behavior (Roffey et al., 1994). Teaching children what they might do to appear more confident can also reduce their vulnerability. Victims often behave in ways consistent with the distorted-perception hypothesis described in the early pages of this chapter. Their misinterpretation of benign behavior as aggression may prompt a cycle of aggression from which it is difficult to extract themselves. Adult coaching regarding the accurate interpretation of social cues is an effective countermeasure (Goleman, 1995). Finally, children who have friends seem to cope better against assaults by bullies, demonstrating fewer adjustment problems than those with no friends. Helping children form friendships and develop friendship skills goes a long way toward breaking their victim image (Hodges, Boivin, Vitaro & Bukowski, 1999; Zins et al., 2004). The skills presented in Chapter 8, Supporting Children's Friendships, are useful in this regard.

Dealing with bullies. Bullies cannot simply be shunned or ignored by adults in formal group settings. Such tactics push them beyond the bounds of normal social circles, reinforcing their defiant style. Thus, clear boundaries and consistent expectations are key ingredients for working with perpetrators of hostile aggression. Children must be told that such behavior will not be tolerated. Hostile youngsters must also be helped to control their angry impulses (Essa, 2003). Strategies such as self-talk, identification of emotions, figuring out behavioral cues that tell how others are feeling, and logical consequences have been described in previous chapters and are effective tools related to impulse control.

Children with friends are better able to cope with bullies.

Interestingly, many aggressors also benefit from the same strategies that support victims—assertiveness training and coaching related to more accurate interpretations of social encounters. For instance, in one program, aggressive grade-schoolers benefited from targeted training in which they were taught to see how some of the social cues they interpreted as hostile (e.g., being jostled in the hall) were in fact neutral or friendly. They also practiced taking the perspective of other children, to get a sense of how they were being perceived when they resorted to coercion. Another facet of the training involved learning to monitor their angry feelings—to recognize what prompted those feelings and to find alternatives (such as humor, assertion, walking away, or counting to 10) rather than lashing out when those feelings arose. After only 6 weeks, their behavior showed significant signs of improvement. These positive results lasted well into their teenage years (Lochman, 1994).

Working with other children in the program.
Any child may witness bullying at any time, so

every child needs to know there are protections in place so they will not be victimized themselves or left feeling helpless in the face of hostile aggression. Most important, witnesses need to know what to do when they see or learn about someone bullying someone else. The first and most important step is to "break the code of silence" that surrounds bullying (Beane, 2005). That is, practitioners must talk about bullying openly and find ways to involve all the children in helping to create a bully-free environment. Children who are witnesses can be empowered to support victims in a variety of ways, to find new approaches to interacting with bullies, and to help create an inclusive program in which no one feels threatened or left out.

The notion of inclusion was the basic tenet of Vivian Paley's celebrated book, *You Can't Say, You Can't Play*, in which children from kindergarten through fifth grade decided that rejecting another child's bid to play was a form of hostile aggression (Paley, 1992). They agreed to create a rule, "You can't say, You can't play," meaning that no one could be left out of group activities and group games based on how they looked, how they talked, or because they were not a favorite or appealing peer. This rule came about after much discussion among the children and adults about how to create a safe, nurturing environment in which all children would feel valued. Simply formulating the rule was not enough. Together the children and their teacher explored its meaning, practiced following it, and continually discussed the impact the rule was having on their lives as individuals and on the climate in their classroom overall. In time, the climate improved and instances of rejection were reduced.

This example illustrates that hostile aggression can be effectively addressed when many children are involved in creating a new environment and when bully-prevention techniques move beyond the bullies and victims alone. In addition, though the individual strategies described so far are effective, they are most powerful when combined in a comprehensive approach to bully prevention that includes children and adults in the program as well as children's families. Thus, our best means for reducing the hostile aggression of bullying is to work out program-wide solutions.

Program-wide solutions to bullying. Willow Creek School and Walnut Hills School look very much the same from the outside, but inside there is a significant difference between them.

> There is very little bullying at Walnut Hills and when it does happen, children and adults know what to do to make things safer for everyone.

Willow Creek School and Walnut Hills School have chosen different approaches to dealing with bully-

> *At Willow Creek School there is little talk about bullying. Students seldom tell adults if they are bullied. They believe it won't make a difference; they fear it will make things worse. Adults don't act on what they learn or they tell children to "work things out for themselves." Bullying takes place in the hallways, the bathrooms, and on the playground. When asked if there is a problem with bullying at their school, everyone is quick to say, "no." But the truth is, several children are bullies; more are victims; and even more children witness bullying every day.*
>
> *The picture is different at Walnut Hills School. The focus here is on prevention. Children, staff, and family members talk about bullying and what they might do to reduce bullying in the program. In every classroom there is a Bully Buster poster that summarizes the philosophy at Walnut Hills.*

> *Bullying is not cool at our school.*
>
> *We don't tease, call names, or put people down.*
>
> *We don't hit, shove, kick, or punch.*
>
> *If we see someone being bullied, we speak up and stop it (if we can) or go for help right away.*
>
> *When we do things as a group, we include everybody and make sure no one is left out.*
>
> *We have the power to stop bullying! We are working together!*

ing in their programs. The outcomes are quite different as well. Such results could be predicted by the research (Espelage & Swearer, 2004). Bullying is most likely to occur when

- children are frequently left unsupervised
- behavior expectations are unclear and inconsistent
- adults rely on autocratic or permissive discipline strategies
- adults ignore bullying behavior
- no preventative measures are taken to address bullying
- children and adults lack the knowledge and skills to be bully-free
- there is poor communication between home and the formal group setting

Programs characterized in this way tend to be "bully laboratories," in which everyone suffers (Beane, 2005; Roffey et al., 1994). On the other hand, bully-free programs incorporate the same elements that characterize schools implementing alternatives to corporal punishment. These are listed on pages 418 and 419 of this chapter. The emphasis in such programs is on authoritative discipline strategies that demonstrate respect for children and require them to take responsibility for their actions. Staff members model the behaviors they wish children to adopt, are consistent in their approach to discipline, and provide adequate supervision for children at all times. Strong home–program partnerships are valued and nurtured.

Most importantly, bullying is taken seriously. Adults and children join forces to confront bullying in constructive ways and to create a bully-free environment. Many of the strategies you have learned about in this text support that goal. How to implement these effectively is further described in the skill sections that follow.

SKILLS FOR HANDLING CHILDREN'S AGGRESSIVE BEHAVIOR

Dealing with Aggression in Formal Group Settings—General Strategies

1. Model nonaggressive behavior. Use the skills you have learned thus far to present a calm, rational model for children to imitate. Even when confronting children or adults whose behavior angers or frustrates you, keep your voice level and firm, your movements controlled, and your gaze directed at them. Do not scream or make threatening gestures.

2. Eliminate aggressive materials from your setting. Forbid children to bring aggressive toys to the program. If youngsters arrive with toy weapons, temporarily confiscate them and send them home with the child at the end of the day. Inform parents of this policy. In addition to monitoring weapons at your site, monitor books, pictures, DVDs, computer programs, and other instructional aids for violent images and content.

3. Structure the classroom environment to minimize potential frustration among children. Check equipment to make sure that it works. Determine whether materials are appropriate for the children's developmental stage. If they are not, revise them. If a piece of equipment does not function, repair it or replace it with something else. Have enough materials that youngsters do not have to wait for long periods of time to gain access to them. Allow children to have things long enough so that they feel satisfied.

Alert children to upcoming changes in routine so that they are not surprised when such changes occur. Warn them prior to transitions between activities so they can finish what they are doing before going on to the next thing. Keep rules to a minimum, and explain their purposes with personal messages. Provide options throughout the day so that children do not feel regimented and can gain a sense of autonomy. Periodically present new things for youngsters to work with or revamp old activities so children perceive the program as interesting.

Arrange classroom furniture to give children easy access to functional activity spaces. Make these areas large enough for more than one child to occupy comfortably. Provide walkways through the classroom and exits from one area to another so children can move about freely without accidentally bumping into peers or objects or otherwise interfering with one another's activities.

4. Remain alert to children for whom frustration is building. Watch children for signs of frustration. When it is evident that a child is becoming distressed, intervene. Offer comfort, support, information, or guidance as befits the situation. If circumstances allow, ask the child in question what he or she can think to do—take a break, get help from another child, go to another resource for information, watch someone else for a while, and so on. Support children when they attempt one of these solutions. If the child is stumped, ask other children to suggest a way to resolve the dilemma: "Raul is feeling frustrated. The paint is soaking all the way through his paper and spoiling his picture. Sam and Carlos, what do you think Raul could do about this problem?" In this way children have a chance to turn frustrating situations into more positive encounters.

5. Provide children with opportunities to feel competent. Assign them age-appropriate responsibility: watering the plants, feeding the fish, checking that the computer is turned off at the end of the day, and so forth. Give children chances to make choices and to try a variety of tasks and experiences independently. Structure these so children feel challenged but not so overwhelmed that success is unlikely. Teach children the skills they need to achieve their goals: how to use tools, how to play games, and how to work with others.

continued

SKILLS FOR HANDLING CHILDREN'S AGGRESSIVE BEHAVIOR—continued

6. Reinforce children's behaviors that are incompatible with aggression. Acknowledge their helpful, cooperative, empathic responses. Make a special effort to note such behaviors in youngsters who are typically aggressive. Although all children benefit from positive reinforcement, more aggressive children particularly need to hear that they are capable of appropriate behavior. It is all too easy to get into the rut of expecting aggression from certain children and failing to recognize the more positive things they do. Avoid this by assigning yourself the task of purposely looking for nonaggressive behaviors and telling children your favorable observations.

7. Rechannel group play in which children are pretending to shoot one another with guns. When you observe children pretending to use blocks, sticks, or their fingers as weapons, step in immediately and redirect the play. Say something like: "You're having fun. You're using the stick as a gun. It upsets me when you pretend to shoot someone else. Guns are dangerous. They are not toys. Use the stick to dig with. You may not use it as a weapon." Do not be sidetracked by children's protestations that they were "just pretending." Reflect their assertion: "You weren't shooting each other for real. That may be. It makes me feel sad when children pretend at hurting others. There are better games to play. Let's figure one out."

8. Help children learn assertive language. Plan discussions and formulate activities to highlight sample words children might use when they want to express themselves or maintain their rights assertively. Take advantage of teachable moments throughout the day to teach these same lessons. Chapter 8 provides examples of how skits might be used to teach such scripts. Refer to Chapter 13 for guidelines about how to plan activities and use on-the-spot coaching with similar aims in mind. Sample scripts include: "I'm still using this," "I want a turn," "When will I know that your turn is over?" "Stop calling me names," "Please stop grabbing," and "I'm not ready yet."

9. Set consistent limits on children's aggressive behavior. Stop aggressive behavior, relying on physical intervention if necessary. Acknowledge the aggressor's emotions, express your concern, and explain why the behavior is unacceptable. Suggest specific alternative behaviors for younger children to pursue; help older children generate their own ideas for a solution to the problem. Clearly state the consequences for continued aggression, and follow through immediately should children persist. This approach can be employed in response to accidental, expressive, and instrumental aggression as well as those incidents of hostile aggression that obviously have been provoked by another child's actions. Given a case of accidental aggression, if the aggressor fails to stop after being told the victim's acts were unintentional, use the personal message, warning, and follow-through skills you have learned. Do the same if a child engaged in expressive aggression does not accept the preferred substitute. Implement similar strategies in response to cases of instrumental aggression in which children are developmentally unable to negotiate or there is no time to do so. Use the same tactic when you observe children using hostile aggression as a way to "save face." For example, children who shove in reaction to being jostled themselves, or those who get into a teasing interchange, are exhibiting signs of having been provoked and will benefit from having their point of view acknowledged while at the same time hearing that their behavior is forbidden.

10. Attend to the victims of aggression. Comfort the victim in front of the aggressor and help the child generate ideas for how to respond to similar aggressive acts in the future. "You're upset. Jeanna hit you. The next time she tries that, put up your hand and say, 'Stop.'" In addition, whenever possible,

SKILLS FOR HANDLING CHILDREN'S AGGRESSIVE BEHAVIOR

Comfort victims of aggression.

involve the aggressor in helping the victim as well. Avoid humiliating the aggressor or coercing her or him to apologize in your attempt to assuage the victim's distress.

11. Praise children when they attempt non-aggressive solutions to difficult situations. Use positive personal messages and effective praise when you observe children settling a potential dispute, refraining from hitting to resolve a conflict, or coming to the aid of a victim of hostile aggression. Compliment children's efforts to be nonviolent even if their approach has been rebuffed by others. Offer comfort and suggestions for how their performance could improve in the future.

12. Explore alternatives to corporal punishment if it is practiced in your setting. Most schools and centers do not require that all helping professionals use corporal punishment, even though some on the staff may. Prior to accepting a position, ascertain whether you will be expected to paddle children. If this is a requirement of the job, consider seeking another. If it is not, discuss with your supervisor ways in which you can use your disciplinary approach within the confines of the system.

 Handling Accidental, Expressive, and Instrumental Aggression

1. Intervene when accidental aggression occurs. Comfort the victim and explain the accidental nature of the aggression. If the aggressor does not realize the results of his or her actions, point them out in concrete, nonjudgmental ways: "Look at Susan. She is crying. When you knocked over the chair it hit her in the back. That hurt." Teach the aggressor to use such phrases as "It was an accident," "I didn't mean it," or "It wasn't on purpose." When appropriate, assist the aggressor in finding ways to make restitution. This is a good time to teach the words, "I'm sorry" if the aggressor truly regrets his or her actions. Sometimes victims can contribute ideas for restitution as well: "Susan, what could Kathleen do to help you feel better?"

2. Use substitution to respond to children's expressive aggression. When working with toddlers, acknowledge the aggressor's perspective. Point out firmly the inappropriateness of the behavior and provide a substitute object for his or her use: "Geoffrey, it's fun to crash blocks. Those are Brian's—here are some you can play with." Move the aggressor away from the victim to focus his or her attention on the substitute object. Comfort the victim and help him or her repair the damage. When working with older children,

continued

SKILLS FOR HANDLING CHILDREN'S AGGRESSIVE BEHAVIOR—continued

include the aggressor in the reparations before offering the substitution. Help the victim articulate a reaction to the aggressive act as a way of making the perpetrator more aware of the inadvertent impact of his or her violent behavior.

3. Give children practice sharing, taking turns, trading, bargaining, and negotiating to get what they want. Accomplish this through games, on-the-spot coaching, role-playing, and skits. Use a variety of strategies and use them often. Offer waiting lists so children can hold a place in activities that are popular or too crowded for everyone to try at once.

4. Mediate children's conflicts. When incidents of instrumental aggression occur, utilize the conflict mediation model described in this chapter. Carry out each step in order:

    a. Initiate the mediation process.
    b. Clarify each child's perspective.
    c. Sum up the situation.
    d. Assist children in generating alternatives.
    e. Help children agree on a solution.
    f. Reinforce the problem-solving process.
    g. Aid children in following through on their agreement.

Make sure you allow yourself enough time to work through the entire process. If you have less than five minutes available, do not begin negotiation. Implement the strategies of the personal message and inhibiting consequences presented in Chapters 10 and 11 instead.

 Responding to Hostile Aggression

1. Talk about bullying. Define bullying with the children. Share stories about bullying. Give children opportunities to draw pictures, write in their journals, or read stories about bullies to provide an opening to discuss these matters. Invite children to describe what bullying looks like and how it feels to

be a victim, a bully, or a witness. Use one or more of the many on bullying to guide the conversation.

2. Make specific rules about bullying and follow through on them. Rules communicate that bullying is unacceptable and that it is everyone's responsibility to create a bully-free setting. Ask the children to help you create rules similar to the ones written by the children at Walnut Hills School (described earlier in this chapter). Establish a few simple rules that children describe in their own words. Talk about what will happen if people break the rules. If you see bullying, follow through on the rules you set. If you hear about bullying in your program, intervene. Work with bullies, victims, and witnesses to increase their skills and to follow the rules. Conduct a variety of conversations with children one-on-one, in small groups, and with the group as a whole to gauge to what extent you are maintaining a bully-free environment.

3. Help children distinguish between tattling and telling about bullying. Key to establishing a bully-free environment is for everyone to join forces to stop bullying. Because much bullying occurs when and where adults can't see it and intervene, children who see bullying need to tell a trusted grown-up that bullying is happening. Allan Beane (2005) has created the following rules to help children understand the importance of telling adults about bullying (p. 43):

If you see someone being bullied, tell the teacher.

If you know that someone is being bullied, tell the teacher.

If you think someone is being bullied, tell the teacher.

If you do nothing about bullying, you're saying bullying is okay with you.

We have the power to stop and prevent bullying in our classroom, but we have to work together.

SKILLS FOR HANDLING CHILDREN'S AGGRESSIVE BEHAVIOR

Though younger children often feel comfortable telling a teacher when problems arise, older children will need to be reminded of the distinction between tattling and telling. Define tattling as pointing out behaviors that are not dangerous. Describe telling as letting adults know about dangerous situations such as bullying, thereby enabling them to address the problem.

4. Help children explore ways to avoid becoming victims of bullying and what to do if they are victimized. Conduct group discussions as well as individual coaching sessions as appropriate. Explore such strategies as: staying away from bullies, looking confident, taking a big breath before responding to verbal aggression, walking away, saying "Stop," telling a grown-up, asking for help, and bunching together with friends.

5. Help children develop a repertoire of strategies for what to do if they witness bullying. Just as onlookers can support children involved in conflict mediation, so too can witnesses support children who are being bullied. Some strategies bully-prevention experts recommend include (Beane, 2005; Jackson, 2003; McCain, 2001): refusing to join in with the bullying, speaking out and saying that bullying is not okay, reporting bullying that witnesses know about or see, inviting the person who is being bullied to join the witness and his or her friends, offering support to the victim in the presence of the bully, supporting a victim in private, and gathering several witnesses together to protect a victim.

6. Coach children who engage in bullying in how to control their angry impulses. Talk with children about their strong feelings—what those feelings are and what prompts them. Work with children to recognize signs that their emotions are escalating beyond their control. Teach children self-talk to help them maintain their composure. Point out the feelings of victims to assist angry children in empathizing with people who are hurt, unhappy, or angry too. Teach children relaxation

techniques. Consider short-term use of tangible rewards to assist children in recognizing and practicing nonaggressive responses in provocative circumstances. These strategies and others described in Chapters 5 and 6 encourage children's development of impulse control.

7. Help bullies and victims learn to more accurately interpret social cues. Provide children with practice recognizing social cues such as voice tone, facial expressions, and words that differentiate aggressive actions from nonaggressive ones. Pose hypothetical situations, enact short skits with puppets, or use role-play to demonstrate these variations. Next, ask children to interpret what they have observed. Point out that there may be more than one interpretation for each event: "You think he bumped her because he didn't like her. Another reason might be that there were too many people crowded around the table. There wasn't room for everybody to stand without touching each other." Encourage children to practice taking the perspective of the victim, to get a sense of how aggressors are perceived when they resort to coercion: "How do you think Marvin felt when Geraldine shoved him and yelled at him?" Once they become somewhat accurate in their conclusions, invite children to generate nonaggressive reactions to the scenarios you pose. "When Marvin stepped on Geraldine's foot, what could she do instead of shoving him so hard?" or "What would happen if she did that?" or "What will happen next?" Make sure to have the children critically evaluate each proposed response. "Why do you think that is a good idea?" or "Why don't you think that will work?" or "Which of our ideas seems best?" This final step helps children move beyond generating random suggestions to consciously weighing the merits of disadvantages of each—a skill they must possess to be successful at controlling aggression in real-life circumstances.

After children have become relatively successful at interpreting and creating

continued

SKILLS FOR HANDLING CHILDREN'S AGGRESSIVE BEHAVIOR—continued

nonaggressive responses to hypothetical situations, help them transfer the skills they have learned to their daily interactions with peers (Slaby et al., 1995). Use on-the-spot coaching in actual social situations to help typically aggressive children go through the steps just described (recognizing cues, interpreting them accurately, generating nonaggressive responses, choosing a response, enacting it). Refer to Chapter 8 for more information about such coaching. Notice when children put a check on initial aggressive impulses or react in nonaggressive ways at times when formerly they may have responded with aggression. Use effective praise to help children recognize the progress they are making.

 Communicating with Families

1. Communicate to family members how you intend to deal with aggression in your setting. Explain what you will do as well as what you will not do. Provide a rationale for your choices. Do not try to coerce parents into adopting your methods for themselves, but do make it clear that in your setting, certain adult practices are acceptable and others are inappropriate. If parents tell you to spank their children if they misbehave, say something like: "You're really anxious for your child to behave at school. That's important to me, too. I will be making it clear to children what the rules are, and I will be using consequences to enforce them. However, paddling is not one of my consequences." Briefly describe a sample disciplinary encounter, using the skills you have learned, to demonstrate what you mean.

2. Listen thoughtfully if family members report that other children are bullying their child. Respond with appropriate action. It has been reported that commonly when parents mention that their child is being bullied, program personnel minimize the importance of this problem, maintain that such predicaments are beyond their jurisdiction, or shift

the conversation to other difficulties the child might be having (Roffey et al., 1994). The denial that surrounds bullying is detrimental to child development. That is, adults who pretend bullying is not happening or who think of it as mere child's play are not doing all they can to help bullies and victims develop more appropriate interaction strategies. If you become aware that a child is being bullied, talk with parents about possible ways to address the issue, both at home and in the program. If a child or parent complains of bullying about which you have been unaware, promise to observe the situation more closely. Develop a plan for how you will respond using strategies outlined in this chapter. Address concerns related both to the victim and the bully. Ask family members for input and ways the plan might be generalized for home use. Carry out the plan, offering and getting periodic feedback from home. Support parents as they express their frustration or concern throughout the process. Keep family members apprised of children's progress.

3. Talk with families of children who engage in bullying behavior. If a child is beginning to establish a pattern of bullying behavior in the program, bring this to his or her parents' attention. Ask if they have observed similar actions at home. Using the strategies outlined in this chapter, work with family members to create a plan to address the child's aggression. Check in with parents periodically to discuss the child's progress. Maintain a helpful, supportive manner throughout the process.

4. Support children who may witness or experience violence in their families. Help children sort through the intense emotions such incidents elicit. If the aggression is vicarious (e.g., aimed at someone else or the result of violent television or older sibling play), work with the child and the family to figure out coping strategies he or she can use. When the child appears to be the victim of aggression, follow the procedures outlined in Chapter 15 regarding child abuse.

PITFALLS TO AVOID

The major pitfalls in handling children's aggressive behavior have already been covered in the section on ineffective strategies (e.g., physical punishment, ignoring aggression, displacement, and inconsistency). However, conflict mediation is a new skill for many people and there are several pitfalls one can fall into when first learning to mediate. The following section therefore focuses on common mistakes adults make when mediating children's conflicts.

Failing to lay the groundwork. Prior to initiating conflict mediation, the adult must have established himself or herself in the children's eyes as someone who cares about them, who will keep them safe, and who is predictable in reacting to children's actions. It is on these primary elements of adult–child relationships that the model is founded. Failure to establish these conditions undermines the spirit of the process. Therefore, the mediation model is most effectively implemented only after children are comfortable and familiar with their caregivers, the surroundings, and the daily routines.

Ignoring developmental considerations. In order to successfully participate in conflict mediation, children must be able to indicate acceptance or rejection of proposed alternatives. Children whose age or development has not reached the point at which they can state their desires, or children who do not speak the same language as the mediator, are not yet ready to engage in this model. Children can communicate verbally or by using an effective substitute such as signing.

In addition, adults who try conflict mediation are cautioned to remain sensitive to children's tolerance for frustration. Not all children are ready to go through all of the steps at once. Most children calm down as mediation proceeds. Those whose behavior becomes increasingly agitated are demonstrating a lack of readiness. At that point, the procedure should be terminated, with the adult enforcing a limit to resolve the original conflict: "You both want the stethoscope. I can't let you hurt each other as a way to decide who gets it, so I will have to decide. Evan, you can have the stethoscope for two minutes, and then Aaron, you can have a two-minute turn." At the same time, children should be praised for their hard work up to that point: "Evan and Aaron, you worked hard at telling me what you wanted. That helped a lot." Gradually, children will be able to proceed further in the process.

Skipping mediation altogether. Adults sometimes avoid conflict mediation because they feel uncomfortable taking their attention away from an entire group to focus on only one or two children. They worry that the mediation process requires more time than they can spare. Instead, they may separate children, remove the disputed toy, and dictate an expedient solution. This approach undoubtedly works in the short run. However, it does not provide an opportunity for children to practice problem-solving strategies. As a result, over time, the adult continues to bear the primary responsibility for conflict resolution rather than gradually transferring this responsibility to the children.

It is important to consider the fact that mediation takes place where the conflict occurs; disputing children are not removed from the group. As a result, children who are not directly involved in the conflict frequently participate as observers or advisors. In this way, the teaching that is taking place affects several children at once. Also, because children become so engrossed in the process, another conflict rarely erupts elsewhere in the room during this time.

Denying children's legitimate claims. In his or her zeal to reach a compromise, a helping professional may inadvertently deny a child's legitimate right to maintain possession of a desired object. The mediator may hear such statements as "I had it first," or "She took it from me." When this occurs, the focus shifts to helping the perpetrator generate appropriate strategies, such as asking, trading, or bargaining, to achieve his or her goal. There also will be times when a child has used an acceptable strategy for obtaining the object and the child in possession refuses. In these cases, the mediator can help the children develop a suitable time frame for the exchange to take place. If the mediator does not know who has the legitimate claim, this can be stated in a personal message that also stresses the inappropriateness of any violent solution to a difference of opinion.

Laying blame. Sometimes when adults hear a commotion, their first impulse is to say: "Okay, who started it?" or "Haven't I told you not to fight?" Children's responses to these queries frequently take the form of denial or accusation, neither of which leads to clarification or constructive problem solving. It is better to approach the conflict saying "You both seem very upset" or "It looks like you both want the stethoscope at the same time." These statements focus on the problem that exists between the children rather than attributing sole responsibility to either child.

Taking sides. In order to establish credibility and be accepted as a mediator, the adult must be perceived as impartial. For this reason, she or he should avoid indicating initial agreement or disagreement with any position that is stated. This means strictly avoiding giving nonverbal cues such as nodding, frowning, and finger tapping as well as refraining from verbal indications of support, sympathy, disdain, or revulsion.

Denying a child's perspective. There will be times during conflict mediation when a child expresses a point of view that seems ludicrous or untrue. In those circumstances, it is tempting for the adult to try to correct the child's perception: "You know you really don't hate John," or "You shouldn't be so upset about having to wait your turn," or "You should feel pleased that John wants to play with you at all after the way you've been acting." Although any one of these statements may seem accurate to the adult, they do not correspond to the child's perception of the situation.

As a result, what began as mutual problem solving will end in fruitless argument. As hard as it may be, it is the adult's responsibility to exercise patience and allow children to work through their own feelings about the problem under discussion.

Masterminding. It is natural for adults to want to resolve conflicts quickly. Sometimes, to accelerate the mediation process, they step in with their own solution rather than permitting children to work out the problem themselves. A related tactic is to force children toward a preconceived conclusion by asking such questions as "Don't you think . . . ?" or "Doesn't it seem that you should . . . ?" or "Wouldn't it be nice if we . . . ?" If the teacher has chosen to initiate the mediation process, he or she should allow it to proceed to a mutual resolution. Otherwise, children become frustrated at being led to believe that they are responsible for reaching a decision when in reality, they must acquiesce to the teacher's conclusion.

When this occurs, the chances for continued conflict are high because children do not feel a real commitment to an approach that is dictated to them. In addition, coercive strategies do not help children

to practice the problem-solving skills they will need to reconcile future disagreements. Finally, the use of such autocratic techniques seriously jeopardizes the adult's credibility in subsequent attempts to mediate children's conflicts.

SUMMARY

Aggression is any verbal or physical behavior that injures, damages, or destroys. Four types of aggression have been identified: accidental, expressive, instrumental, and hostile. The first three categories are unintentional by-products of an interaction; hostile aggression is a purposeful act. Assertiveness and aggressiveness are two different things. Although both involve exerting influence over others, assertion does not include any intent to injure or demean. There is no single factor that causes violent behavior in children.

Current research shows that aggression is influenced by biology and is learned through modeling, direct instruction, and reinforcement as well. The way children express aggression changes over time due to cognitive maturation and experience. Hostile aggression becomes more evident as children mature. Both boys and girls demonstrate aggressive behavior, although the tactics they use are somewhat different. Males tend to be more overt and physically abusive, and females rely on relational and verbal strategies. Adults have tried different ways to reduce children's aggression. Physical punishment, ignoring aggression, displacement, and inconsistency actually increase children's antisocial behavior. Effective preventive techniques include serving as a model of self-control and limiting the aggressive toys, films, books, pictures, and television programs to which children are exposed in the formal group setting. Helping children to recognize their own competence while reducing the frustration in their lives also is beneficial.

When adults teach children prosocial behaviors and praise them for nonaggressive action, aggression is replaced with more appropriate conduct. When children do exhibit aggression, adults can assist them in changing their behavior by explaining instances of accidental aggression, by using substitution to rechannel expressive aggression, by helping children learn the language of assertiveness, and by intervening to de-escalate aggressive play. At the same time, it is important for adults to create an environment in which children know that aggression is unacceptable. Setting limits on hurtful behavior and following through on those limits is an important tactic for accomplishing this aim. Children also benefit when they have an opportunity to explore potential responses to the aggression of others. It is difficult for some children to shift from violent to peaceful strategies all at once. Adults must gradually introduce a logical sequence of steps to help children move in this direction. Children can learn alternatives to aggression through planned activities. In addition, they can be taught to negotiate their differences through on-the-spot conflict mediation.

When hostile aggression occurs, adults must be quick to respond with firm limits and strategies aimed at teaching children how to curb angry impulses, interpret social cues more accurately, and replace their aggressive reactions with less violent ones. Attention must be paid to bullies, their victims and any witnesses to aggression. Program-wide strategies for dealing with hostile aggression are also important to develop. Finally, working with family members is essential for reducing childhood aggression of all kinds.

KEY TERMS

accidental aggression
aggression
assertiveness
bullying
conflict mediation

corporal punishment
displacement
expressive aggression
hostile aggression
instrumental aggression

overt aggression
passive victims
provocative victims
relational aggression

DISCUSSION QUESTIONS

1. Describe the four types of aggression. Discuss behaviors that differentiate them from one another. Present examples of behavior you have witnessed that fit into a particular category.

2. Describe an interaction in which you have observed either a child or an adult being aggressive. Discuss what changes in that person's behavior would have made the actions assertive instead.

3. Choose a fictional character or a public figure you consider aggressive. In a small group, identify some of that person's characteristics. Apply your knowledge of learned aggression to offer some explanation for the person's behavior.

4. Describe the emergence of aggression in children. Discuss how maturity and experience influence the types of aggression children display at different ages.

5. In this book, we have taken a strong stand against corporal punishment in professional settings. Discuss your reactions to that position.

6. Describe the differences between displacement and substitution. Identify instances from your own experience in which you have seen these techniques used. Talk about the outcomes you observed.

7. Describe an aggressive behavior exhibited by a child without revealing the child's identity to the group. Use the strategies and skills outlined in this chapter to assist you in formulating a plan for reducing the unwanted behavior.

8. Two children come to the program with toy light sabers they got over the weekend. They want to play with them in the classroom. Using the content of this chapter as background, discuss what you would do in this situation.

9. When Mr. Clark, a parent, drops the children off at school, he mentions that he noticed some bruises on Timmy, one of the children in the carpool. The child told him his older brother had smacked him around when their parents were out. The teacher thanked Mr. Clark and then said, "Oh, I'm sure there's nothing to worry about. Timmy tends to exaggerate." Find the place in the NAEYC Code of Ethical Conduct (Appendix A) that offers professional guidelines in such a situation. Based on your understanding of the code, decide whether the teacher's behavior was ethical or unethical.

10. Share with the group your experience in attempting the conflict mediation model presented in this chapter. Describe children's reactions, your own reactions, and the eventual outcome. Brainstorm with classmates ways to improve your technique.

FIELD ASSIGNMENTS

1. Describe an incident of childhood aggression that occurred in your field placement. Discuss how another adult handled it. Evaluate the effectiveness of the approach that was used. Next, describe how you handled an aggressive incident involving a child in your setting. Evaluate the effectiveness of your approach.

2. Interview two community professionals who work with young children. Obtain information from them regarding the strategies they use to help children who exhibit aggressive behavior. Report your findings.

3. Describe a situation in which you were involved in conflict mediation. Begin by discussing what prompted the conflict. Next, talk about the children's reactions to the mediation process and what final outcome occurred. Identify two things you did well during the process and one thing you would like to improve the next time such a situation arises. Conclude by discussing your reaction to your role as a mediator.

4. Watch a child's television show (cartoon) or movie and record the frequency of aggressive or violent acts. Discuss possible effects on children.

5. Review the parent handbook for the program in which you are participating. Identify policies and procedures aimed at reducing childhood aggression.

Chapter 13

PROMOTING PROSOCIAL BEHAVIOR

OBJECTIVES

On completion of this chapter, you should be able to describe:

- Examples of prosocial behavior.

- Benefits of prosocial behavior (and how children benefit when they act prosocially).

- What motivates children to be prosocial.

- The steps involved in acting prosocially.

- Factors that influence prosocial behavior.

- Strategies to increase children's prosocial behavior.

- Family communication strategies related to prosocial behavior.

- Pitfalls to avoid in promoting children's prosocial behavior.

PROSOCIAL BEHAVIOR AND CHILDREN

Helping	Sharing
Sacrificing	Aiding
Sympathizing	Encouraging
Volunteering	Giving
Reassuring	Inviting
Rescuing	Defending
Cooperating	Comforting
Donating	

All of these terms describe prosocial behaviors and represent positive values of society. They are the opposite of antisocial conduct, such as selfishness and aggression. **Prosocial behaviors** occur in response to the well-being of others and are carried out either proactively or as a response to a noticed need (Hastings, Utendale & Sullivan, 2007). They often are executed without the doer's anticipation of cost or benefit (Grusec, Davidov & Lundell, 2004). At times, they also involve some risk to the individual performing them, such as when a person defends a friend in a situation that is either physically or socially dangerous. The disposition to engage in such actions is learned and practiced as a child, eventually carrying over into adulthood (Eisenberg, 2003). Evidence suggests that the roots of caring, sharing, helping, and cooperating are in every child (Hoffman, 1988). Although older children demonstrate a wider range of prosocial behaviors, even very young children have the capacity to demonstrate prosocial responses in a number of different settings (Eisenberg, Fabes & Spinrad, 2006).

Prosocial behavior is a significant component of social competence. Regardless of age, children's interactions tend to be more positive than negative. For instance, data suggest that the ratio of children's prosocial behaviors to antisocial acts is no less than 3:1 and may be as high as 8:1 (Moore, 1982). This means that for every negative behavior, children average three to eight positive actions. This proportion remains relatively stable throughout the preschool and elementary years. Thus, childhood is an optimal period for the development of prosocial attitudes and conduct.

Although it is obvious that children benefit when acts of kindness are directed toward them, youngsters who help, share, cooperate, comfort, or rescue also benefit (Saarni et al., 2006).

Benefits of Acting Prosocially

There are social, emotional, and academic advantages for behaving prosocially. Children who engage in prosocial acts develop feelings of satisfaction and competence from assisting others. When youngsters help with the family dishes, share information with a friend, comfort an unhappy playmate, or work with others to achieve a final product, they come away thinking: "I am useful. I can do something. I am important." The resulting perception of being capable and valuable contributes to a healthy self-image (Trawick-Smith, 2005). Kindness also serves as a sign of affection and friendship. It contributes to positive feelings in both doers and receivers, providing entry into social situations and strengthening ongoing relationships (Hartup & Moore, 1990).

Children whose interactions are characterized by kindness maximize the successful social encounters they experience. This increases the likelihood that their kind acts will continue in the future. In fact, children's natural sharing behavior at age 4 has been linked with predicted prosocial behavior into adulthood (Eisenberg, Fabes, Shepard, Cumberland & Carlo, 1999). Prosocial behavior also increases children's chances for receiving help or cooperation when they need it. Children who are more prosocial are more likely to be on the receiving end of prosocial acts (Cassidy, Werner, Rourke, Zubernis & Balaramun, 2003; Persson, 2005).

Children who are the beneficiaries of any type of prosocial action get a closer look at how such behaviors are carried out. Each episode serves as a model from which they derive useful information to apply to future encounters. Recipients also have chances to learn how to respond positively to the kindness that others extend to them. Individuals who never learn this skill eventually receive fewer offers of comfort and support.

Children who behave prosocially are more likely to be in supportive peer relationships (Lerner, Lerner, Almerigi, Theokas, Phelps, Gestsdottir, et al., 2005). They tend to have at least one or two friends, engage in less aggression and conflict with others, and are more popular with peers (Eisenberg et al., 2006). Adults often describe prosocial children as socially skilled (Cassidy et al., 2003).

Finally, there is clear evidence that early prosocial behavior strongly predicts current and future academic achievement (Caprara, Barbaranelli, Pastorelli, Bandura & Zimbardo, 2000). This may be because children who are prosocial are more able to ask for assistance from peers and adults, further developing their cognitive abilities and thus creating a more positive school climate for themselves (Bandura, 1997). Table 13-1 summarizes the benefits of prosocial behavior.

Table 13-1 Benefits of Engaging in Prosocial Behavior

1. Creates feelings of satisfaction
2. Builds perceptions of competence
3. Provides entry into social situations
4. Promotes ongoing relationships
5. Increases popularity among peers
6. Increases chances of receiving help or cooperation
7. Increases academic performance
8. Leads to positive group atmosphere

Besides benefiting the individual, prosocial behavior has advantages for groups as well. Group settings in which children are encouraged to be cooperative and helpful result in more friendly interactions and productive group efforts than settings in which little attention is paid to these values (Gazda, Balzer, Childers & Nealy, 2005). Moreover, routine or tedious chores, such as cleanup, are more easily managed. When everyone pitches in, tasks are quickly accomplished and no one person feels overly burdened. An added benefit is that youngsters begin to develop a positive group image in which they view both themselves and other group participants as genial and competent (Marion, 2007).

Children's Motivation to Act Prosocially

There are multiple reasons that children behave prosocially. Some may be acting to prevent harm (inviting a child to play so her feelings aren't hurt). Others react spontaneously to an event (Jerome falls off of the swings, Fred runs over yelling, "Are you O.K.?"). Still others act prosocially to make up for the distress their own behavior caused (Kurt knocked Jeremy aside to get the robot he wanted first. He then notices that Jeremy is near tears and hands over a second robot smiling, "You can have this one"). A prosocial behavior may occur because someone has directed the child ("Give her some of your blocks, please"). A plea for help may be yet another reason for prosocial behavior ("Could you please get the teacher for me?"). Finally, a child may act simply for the benefit of someone else, no strings attached (Hastings et al., 2007).

The motivation to act prosocially is influenced by developmental factors such as age, the ability to think of others, and the child's level of moral development. It is also influenced by experience—observing prosocial acts, experiencing kindness, and experiencing reactions to their own efforts to be prosocial. In the early years, children practice kind acts with mom and dad and then peers, Preschoolers and early elementary students use self-centered or needs-oriented reasons for action, selecting behaviors to make themselves feel better (to stop the crying, or to get praise from adults). This reasoning decreases in the later elementary years. Over time, the reasons for prosocial behavior become more abstract, relying on principles and moral standards as a guide for taking action (Eisenberg et al., 2006).

Steps to Acting Prosocially

At one time, it was thought that if children could be taught to think prosocially, the appropriate actions would automatically follow. Unfortunately, kind thoughts have not been significantly linked to prosocial acts. Although even preschoolers can explain that sharing, taking turns, and working together are good things to do, they do not necessarily act in these ways when doing so would be appropriate. For example:

> While pretending to be a police officer, Brian would look his teacher in the eyes and clearly state: "The rule is: Keep your hands to yourself. Hitting other children hurts." He would then walk away from this recitation, see someone doing something he interpreted as wrong, grab the block from his belt (his billy club), and conk the offender over the head.

Children must get beyond simply thinking about what is right; they have to go through a series of steps that move them from thought to action. These include (1) becoming aware that sharing, help, or cooperation is needed; (2) deciding to act; and (3) carrying out the prosocial behavior (see Figure 13-1).

Step One: Awareness

Youngsters must first become aware that someone would benefit from a prosocial response (Honig & Wittmer, 1996). To do this requires accurately interpreting what they see and hear. This means recognizing typical distress signals such as crying, sighing, grimacing, or struggling—as well as correctly identifying verbal cues: "This is too much for me to do all by myself," or "If we work together, we'll finish faster." How easily children recognize such cues depend on how clear they are. Ambiguous or subtle signals are more difficult for children to interpret than direct ones (Horowitz & Bordens, 1995). For instance, if Patty observes Duwana fall and moan, it may not be clear to her that Duwana

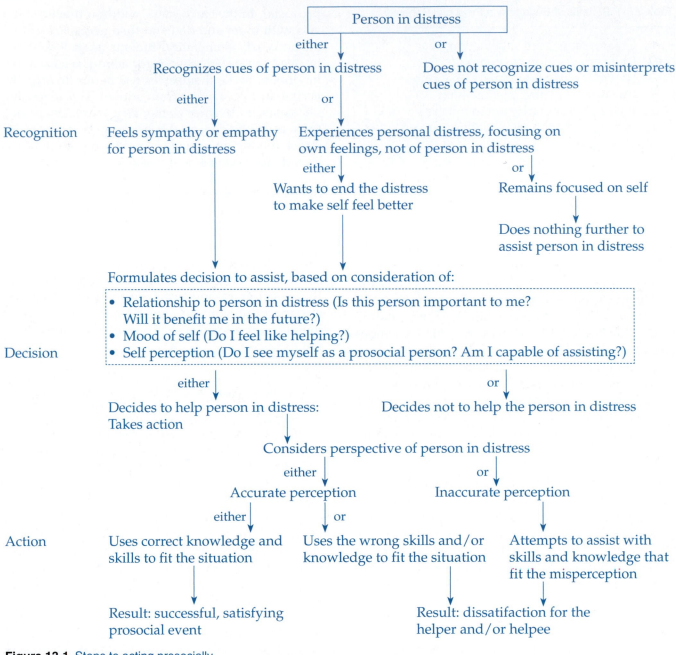

Figure 13-1 Steps to acting prosocially.

needs assistance. However, if Duwana cries and calls for help, Patty will comprehend her distress more easily. Likewise, Patty might enter the awareness phase of prosocial behavior if an adult pointed out to her the signs of distress exhibited by Duwana. In most cases, people who come upon a problem situation look both to the victim and the reactions of others nearby to determine if a real problem exists.

This is especially true when the situation is ambiguous or vague. If onlookers appear unfazed, a potential helper may remain unaware that intervention

is needed. This is illustrated when Abdul's construction crashes to the floor. Abdul appears unhappy but makes no sound. Several children nearby look up, but seeing no tears or other overt signs of distress, return to their play. Roger, observing the entire scene, may also assume that assistance is unnecessary because no one else made a move to help. He might think differently if an adult or other child said something like, "Are you okay?" or "That's too bad your tower fell." These comments prompt awareness that the situation could indeed be distressing to Abdul.

All children benefit from direction to notice those who could use some help. For young children who are hearing impaired and do not hear cues of distress, adult intervention is particularly useful. Each year, Ms. Eppinger teaches her entire class of preschoolers the American Sign Language signs for "stop" and "look" and uses these daily to point out helping opportunities with peers. Whenever a potential situation occurs, she says the word while simultaneously signing, "Stop. Look." This benefits all students in her room.

As children become aware of cues that someone is in distress, they may feel sympathy or empathy for that person; or, they may feel personal distress over the situation. Feeling distress for the other person is more likely to lead to prosocial action, whereas feeling distress for one's self is less likely to lead to such action. Initially, a very young child's emotional reaction is to mimic the distress signals by crying or sighing. As children mature, they become more able to feel empathy and are more adept at coupling their emotional response with some gesture of assistance. In fact, the more empathy and sympathy a child feels for the person, the more likely they are to take action (Eisenberg et al., 2006).

Step Two: Decision
Once children identify a person in need, they are faced with the decision of whether or not to act. Three factors that influence this decision include children's relationship to the person in need, their mood, and whether they think of themselves as basically prosocial beings.

Relationship.   Children of all ages are most likely to respond prosocially to people they like and with whom they have established relationships (Eisenberg et al., 2006). Although children may react compassionately to people they do not know, friends are more often kinder to one another than they are to strangers. Prosocial acts such as sharing are also more likely to occur if the recipient is someone who has shared with the giver previously or if sharing will require the receiver to do likewise in the future (Eisenberg & Fabes, 1998). Under these circumstances, children feel obligated to one another based on their notions of fairness and reciprocity.

Mood.   Mood also affects whether or not children decide to pursue a prosocial course of action. Children of all ages who are in a positive frame of mind are more likely to act prosocially than those in a negative or neutral mood (Carlson, Charlin & Miller, 1988). When youngsters are happy, they become optimistic about the outcome of their efforts. They may even undertake difficult or costly prosocial actions with the expectation of ultimate success. On the other hand, children who are angry or sad often cannot see beyond their own unhappy circumstances to aid others, or they may believe that their actions will fail anyway. Exceptions to this rule occur when older children who are in a bad mood perceive that behaving prosocially will actually improve their state of mind. Their subsequent acts of kindness may be carried out in the hope of making themselves feel better. However, if they see no self-serving benefits to their actions, such children will decide not to engage in prosocial activities.

Self-perception.   A child's decision of whether to behave prosocially may also hinge on how kind the child considers herself or himself to be. Children who frequently hear themselves described as cooperative or helpful believe they are and often choose to act in ways that support this self-image (Baron & Bryne, 1993; Paley, 1999). Youngsters who have no such self-perceptions may shy away from deciding to carry out a prosocial act because such behaviors do not fit the way they see themselves in relation to others.

Step Three: Action
If children assume responsibility for sharing, helping, or cooperating, they must then select and perform a behavior they think is appropriate to the situation. Their conduct in such circumstances is influenced by two abilities: perspective-taking and instrumental know-how (Berk, 2006).

In **perspective-taking**, children recognize what would be useful to someone else whose needs may not mirror their own at the moment. Toddlers who offer Mommy their well-chewed cracker as a way to ease her distress over the mess made by the puppy mean well, but do not understand what is truly needed to rectify the situation. Their ineffectiveness is not surprising because they have limited role-taking skills. As these abilities emerge, preschoolers and youngsters in the lower elementary grades become better equipped to help and to cooperate in situations in which the setting is familiar or the circumstances of distress resemble something they themselves have experienced. Eventually, children 10 years of age and older also become able to project appropriate responses in unfamiliar situations.

Instrumental know-how involves having the knowledge and skills necessary to act competently (Goleman, 1991). Children who have many skills at their disposal are the most effective in carrying out their ideas. Those who have few skills may have good intentions, but their efforts often are counterproductive or inept. Moreover, younger children who are the most prosocial also are the most likely to engage in some antisocial behaviors. Due to their inexperience, they cannot always discriminate appropriate actions from inappropriate ones. Gradually, children become more aware of what differentiates these two types of behavior and become better able to initiate actions that are useful and appropriate.

Children may experience difficulty in proceeding through any one of the three steps just described. For instance, youngsters may overlook or misinterpret cues that convey another person's need for a prosocial response. They also may choose an inappropriate action when trying to help. A child who is trying to comfort may shove a favorite storybook in another child's face; hug so hard that it hurts, or say something lacking tact, like "Well, you don't smell that bad." Young helpers may miss the mark by adding water to the acrylic paint to make it go further or by using toothpaste to scrub the windows because they have heard that it cleans so well. In a similar vein, youngsters attempting to defend someone may become aggressive or "catty" as a way to show their favor. At times, children may assume that cooperation means giving up all of one's own ideas or settling for mediocrity in an effort to please everyone. These are all natural mistakes children make in learning how to be kind to one another. As children mature and gain experience, these become less frequent.

INFLUENCES ON CHILDREN'S PROSOCIAL BEHAVIOR

What wisdom can you find that is greater than kindness?

Jean-Jacques Rousseau, 1712–1778

What makes one person act with kindness and another not? As with many other areas of development, scientists have tried to determine the factors that contribute to prosocial behavior beyond daily interactions with peers. The list continues to expand. As might be expected, it includes elements of biology, social-cognitive understanding, language, social experiences, cultural expectations, and adult behaviors.

Biology and Prosocial Behavior

Prosocial behavior may due in part to biology (Grusec et al., 2004). Studies provide evidence for biological links to the development of empathy, sympathy and prosocial behavior (Eisenberg, 2003; Hastings, Zahn-Waxler & McShane, 2005).

Temperament. From the research, it appears that the combination of temperament, sensitivity to emotions of self and others, and the regulation of emotions is connected with an individual's ability to react to situations in a prosocial manner (Eisenberg et al., 2006). For instance, children who are more prone to have pleasant dispositions, which recognize the distress of others but are not overly upset by this distress, are more likely to react in a prosocial manner. A child who sees the world in a bleak manner and who is likely to become more distressed by someone else's dismay is more caught up in worry over herself than the other child in need and is not likely to take appropriate helpful action.

Children who can regulate their emotions but are prone to intense emotions are more prone to sympathy for others (Eisenberg et al., 2006). However, it is not necessarily the intensity of emotions that is most important; instead it is the control of the emotions and regulation of the action that counts. Prosocial children tend to be those who are able to regulate their emotions and take action (Eisenberg et al., 2006).

Gender. The majority of studies have shown no gender differences in children's willingness to engage in prosocial behavior. It would seem that both boys and girls have an equal capacity to be prosocial. Some research has found there is a difference in gender in the *occurrence* of prosocial behavior. Girls have been found to engage in prosocial behaviors more often than boys (Keane & Calkins, 2004; Russell, Hart, Robinson & Olsen, 2003). Others have found no difference (Hastings, Rubin & DeRose, 2005). Age also can make a difference in the extent to which children are prosocial and in the reasoning they use to guide their actions.

Age. Simply growing older does not guarantee that a person will become more prosocial. However, it generally can be said that children's capacity for prosocial behavior expands with age (Eisenberg et al., 2006). The first signs begin early in life. Infants and toddlers seem to recognize and often will react to a companion who is crying or in obvious distress (Thompson, 2006). Behaviors such as sharing, helping, cooperating, donating, comforting, and defending become much more common as children mature (Pratt, Skoe & Arnold, 2004).

Social Cognitive Understanding and Prosocial Behavior

Social cognitive understanding includes thinking about how others are thinking and feeling. To do this, one must have some degree of empathy, perspective-taking, and theory of mind. Each is linked to prosocial behavior (Eisenberg et al., 2006; Hastings, 2007). Thus, children who can understand the emotions of others are more likely to behave prosocially and with greater overall social competence (Hart, Burock, London, Atkins, 2003; Saarni et al., 2006).

Language and Prosocial Behavior

Language is powerful. Children's ability to understand and to use language is very important in communicating needs and getting those needs met. In particular, as children expand their use of emotion words, they learn more about themselves, come to better understand the behavior of others, and respond empathically and sympathically to others (Saarni et al., 2006).

Sharing.   Sharing provides a good example of the combination of the influence of biology, social cognitive understanding, and language in children's growing prosocial development. In a typical early childhood program that serves toddlers and preschoolers, you are bound to see examples of children sharing. Children 18 months–24 months old are not too likely to share. Yet companions as young as 2 years old, offer playthings to one another (Hay, Castle, Davies, Demetriou & Stimson, 1999). They find sharing with adults easier, but their frequency of sharing is relatively low compared with older children. This is because younger children are by nature territorial and egocentric (Reynolds, 2006). They highly prize the possession of the moment, making it difficult for them to relinquish objects, even when they are no longer using them. This explains why 4-year-old Michael, who rides the tricycle and then runs off to dig in the sand, protests loudly when

Dramatic play is a great place to practice sharing. These boys are sharing the task of cooking.

another child gets on the tricycle. To Michael, the tricycle is his and he dislikes giving it up even though he had lost interest in it.

Additionally, younger children lack the verbal negotiation skills necessary to resolve disputes over possessions or to strike bargains with people that satisfy each party. Consequently, their initial reasons for sharing focus on self-serving interests, such as sharing now so the recipient will be obliged to share with them in the future or to appease a peer who threatens, "I won't be your friend if you don't gimme some."

Throughout the later preschool and early elementary years, children come to realize that sharing leads to shared activity and that playing with another person is often more fun than playing alone (Reynolds, 2006). During this time children's peer interactions increase and their sharing abilities become greater. The most dramatic changes occur between 6 and 12 years of age (Honig & Wittmer, 1992).

There are several reasons why older children share more easily. First, their more advanced intellectual abilities enable them to recognize that it is possible for two people to legitimately want the same thing at the same time, that possessions shared can be retrieved, and that sharing often is reciprocated (Berk, 2006). They also understand that there is a difference between sharing (which means temporary loss of ownership) and donating (which is permanent), and they can understand, as well as make clear to others, which of the two is intended. In addition, they have more skills at their disposal that allow them to share in a variety of ways. If one approach, such as taking turns, is not satisfactory, they have such options to fall back on as bargaining, trading, or using an object together. These youngsters also have had the opportunity to learn that those around them view sharing favorably, so they may use this strategy to elicit positive responses (Eisenberg et al., 1995b). Finally, older children find it easier to part with some items because they differentiate among the values of their possessions.

Children in the early elementary years are also motivated to share by a desire for acceptance from others. Prosocial acts such as sharing are seen as good, making it more likely that children who engage in such behavior will enjoy the approval of their peers. The self-sacrifice that comes with sharing is compensated for by that approval.

Gradually, as children mature, their reasoning also becomes influenced by the principle of justice. Sharing becomes a way to satisfy that principle. At first children define justice as strict equity, meaning that everyone deserves equal treatment regardless of circumstance. When sharing is called for, children figure that each person must have the same number of turns, that each turn must last the same amount of time, and that everyone must receive the same number of pieces. There is much discussion among peers at this age about fairness.

Eventually, children come to believe that equity includes special treatment for those who deserve it—based on extra effort, outstanding performance, or because of disadvantaged conditions (Damon, 1988). Under these circumstances, children decide that sharing does not have to be exactly the same to be fair. They recognize that a person who has fewer chances to play may require a longer turn or reason that someone who worked especially hard on a project deserves to go first. This reasoning is sometimes evident in children as young as 8 years of age, but for others it appears much later. In either case, such thinking deepens children's understanding of prosocial behavior, leading to more frequent instances of kindness than is possible earlier in life.

The differences between older and younger children in their ability to share underscore changes in their general development and reasoning abilities.

Thus children gradually move from self-oriented rationales ("He'll like me better if I share") to other-oriented reasoning ("She'll be unhappy if she doesn't get a turn") and from concrete rationales ("I had it first") to more abstract ideals ("She needs it"). Ultimately, children become better able to "put themselves in another person's shoes" and do so to support their self-respect. The latter achievement tends to occur in later adolescence and is seldom seen in children younger than 12 years of age. Finally, there is evidence that the levels of reasoning described here relate to the actual behaviors children display (Eisenberg et al., 2006). Youngsters who are more mature moral reasoners display a bigger repertoire of prosocial skills and are more likely to engage in prosocial behavior than children who reason at less mature levels (see Table 13-2). Children's maturity is determined by their own biological clock and by their social and cultural experiences.

Social Experiences and Prosocial Behavior

The experiences children have in the social environment of family, peers, and school plays a role in their prosocial development. In the family, as early as birth, the environment begins to impact prosocial behavior. The emotional attachment that occurs

Table 13-2 Influence of Age on Sharing

YOUNGER (AGES 2 TO 6)	OLDER (AGES 6 TO 12)
1. Self-oriented motives	1. Other-oriented motives
2. Recognize own claim	2. Recognize legitimacy of others' claims
3. Prize the possession of the moment	3. Differentiate value among objects
4. "Here and now" thinking	4. Thinking of future benefits; past experience may be used to guide behavior
5. Few verbal skills with which to bargain or negotiate	5. Well-developed verbal skills
6. Some difficulty seeing more than one option	6. Many alternative solutions

between baby and parent is believed to be the basis for prosocial development (Saarni et al., 2006). Also, the conversations that parents have with young children are linked with the development of empathy (Thompson, 2006). In the later years, in homes where children are given chores to do and in which everyone works to help for the good of the family, children demonstrate increased prosocial behavior (Eisenberg et al., 2006).

Children learn from each other. Thus peers provide great opportunities for both giving and receiving prosocial behavior. Most importantly, interacting with age-mates offers chances to practice positive acts of all kinds. Simply being exposed to prosocial peers has been shown to produce children who are more prosocial in the future (Fabes, Moss, Reesing, Martin & Harish, 2005). Further, having at least one reciprocal friendship is related to higher levels of prosocial behavior (Wentzel, Barry & Caldwell, 2004). Also, participating with peers in youth activities and community service opportunities are linked to later prosocial behaviors, particularly volunteerism (Youniss & Metz, 2004).

Finally, the overall quality of the school environment, particularly the human interactions between teacher and child and child and child, are linked to children behaving in more or less prosocial ways. For instance, the higher the quality of care children receive in childcare the greater the amount of prosocial behavior they exhibit (NICHD, 2002). Further, there is an association between the quality of the school and children's self regulation, empathy, and social competence (Eisenberg et al., 2006). It takes thoughtful purposeful action to create quality interactions that promote prosocial behavior.

Cultural Expectations and Experiences and Prosocial Behavior

Cultures differ in the emphasis they place on prosocial behaviors such as sharing, helping, or cooperating.

Some emphasize competition and individual achievement, whereas others stress cooperation and group harmony. Some have a high tolerance for violence; others do not. In any case, cultural influences play a role in the extent to which kindness is a factor in human interactions.

These influences are expressed in laws, in economic policies, through the media, and in the institutions people create. The ways in which members of the society think about children, how children spend their time, what they see and hear, how they are treated at home and in the community, and the expectations people have for children's behavior are all culturally based. Children growing up in societies that value kindness, helpfulness, and cooperation are apt to internalize those values and display corresponding behaviors in their daily living. Additionally, cultures that promote warm, loving relationships between adults and children, as well as the early assignment of tasks and responsibilities that contribute to the common good are likely to produce prosocial children (Hastings et al., 2007). The most common place in which societies' youngest members encounter these cultural teachings is in the microsystems of home and formal group settings such as the school or child care center. Adults are major players in these settings. In fact, the influence of adults strongly influences whether children become more or less prosocial.

Adult Behavior and Prosocial Behavior

Adults have a major impact on the degree to which children learn to be helpful and cooperative. One way they do this is through the relationships they develop with children. When adults are warm and supportive, children become more securely attached to them and are more likely to behave prosocially (Hastings et al., 2007). Another way is by creating microsystems that either facilitate or inhibit the development of children's prosocial behavior (Honig & Wittmer, 1996). In group settings, the atmosphere most likely to promote nurturing, sharing, cooperating, and rescuing has the following characteristics (Cummings & Haggerty, 1997):

1. Participants anticipate that everyone will do his or her best to support one another.
2. Both adults and children contribute to decisions made, practices, and procedures.
3. Communication is direct, clear, and mutual.
4. Individual differences are respected.
5. Expectations are reasonable.
6. People like one another and feel a sense of belonging to the group.
7. There is an emphasis on group as well as individual accomplishments.

Adults shape such an environment by using an authoritative discipline style, modeling prosocial behavior, rewarding children's attempts at prosocial actions, instructing children in prosocial values or skills, and providing children with practice of prosocial behaviors.

Discipline strategies. The authoritative approach to discipline espoused in this text can be a positive and powerful component to learning to behave in a prosocial manner (Hastings et al., 2007; Laible & Thompson, 2007). Talking through situations and giving rational reasons for reactions and compliance leads to internalized values in children (Eisenberg et al., 2006). When adults maintain high expectations for children to engage in prosocial behavior and enforce rules that support this philosophy, kind and fair behavior towards peers not only occurs in the here and now but in the years that follow (Pratt, Hunsberger, Pancer & Alisat, 2003). However, when adults use withdrawal of love or assertion of power techniques, the results can be quite different. See Chapters 10 and 11 for more on these approaches and their results.

Modeling. Youngsters who frequently observe people cooperating, helping, sharing, and giving are most likely to act in those ways themselves (Hastings et al., 2007). Thus, adults who model such actions, either with other adults or with children, help to increase children's prosocial conduct now and into the future (Eisenberg & Fabes, 1998). Children are likely to glean even more from the model if there is a simultaneous conversation focusing on how the act will benefit the other person (Hastings et al., 2007). Saying, "This will really make Janet feel better to know that we took the time to make her a

get-well card," instead of "It is kind to send a card," puts the focus on the other person, not on the self.

Children emulate those models in their lives that are skilled in their behavior, are considered to be of high status by the observer, are helpful and friendly, and are in a position to administer both rewards and consequences (Schickedanz, 1994). Models that are aloof, critical, directive, punitive, or powerless commonly are ignored. In addition, prosocial modeling has its greatest impact when what adults say is congruent with what they do (Shaffer, 2006). Researchers have found that when there is inconsistency between words and deeds, the model is less credible and may even prompt children to engage in fewer prosocial acts. This follows the old adage "Actions speak louder than words." Hence, adults who urge children to lend one another a hand but seldom offer assistance themselves or do so grudgingly, show children that helping is not really a high priority. Furthermore, adults who insist that children always be truthful yet tell "little fibs" when it is convenient for them show children that lying is acceptable even when they say it is not.

The result in all cases is that children become less inclined to help or cooperate. On the other hand, when children observe adults acting prosocially and deriving obvious pleasure from their actions, imitation becomes more likely (Bandura, 1989). Even characters on television could serve as models for prosocial behavior. Studies have shown that children who view prosocial behavior on television will engage in such behavior in real-life situations at a later time (Bernstein, 2000).

Prosocial attribution. As mentioned earlier, people's self-definition of how helpful they are is another factor that influences how prosocially they behave. Thus, the more kind, generous, or compassionate children believe themselves to be, the more kindly, generously, and compassionately they will behave toward others (Baron & Bryne, 1993). Therefore, one way to promote prosocial acts is to encourage children to think of themselves in these ways using **prosocial attributions** (also called **character attributions** or **dispositional attributions**). A prosocial attribution is a statement to a child in which the adult attributes a prosocial behavior to a child, such as "You shared because you like to help others" (Wittmer & Honig, 1994). Such prosocial attributions make it more likely that children will incorporate these actions and motivations into their images of whom they are and what they can do.

These make future prosocial behavior more likely. Attributions must be specific and closely related to what the child has done or said. In addition, they should refer to the child's dispositional kindness or internal motives, rather than simply labeling the actions as a positive thing (Eisenberg et al., 2006). For instance, stating, "You are a good helper" or "You helped put away the toys" is not as effective as saying, "You put away the toys because you are a helpful person." Using simple praise without the internal attribution makes it less likely that the behavior will transfer to new situations in the future (Eisenberg et al., 2006).

Rewarding prosocial behavior.   A prosocial environment is one in which such conduct is likely to be rewarded. When children's prosocial behaviors are reinforced, they are likely to increase their use of such actions within the same environment, so that they can be seen and rewarded again (Eisenberg et al., 2006). Technically, all adults have to do is watch for instances of children being kind and then enact positive consequences. Yet, adults commonly fail to make the most of this strategy. This happens when they take children's prosocial behaviors for granted and do not reward them adequately or often enough. It also happens when adults inadvertently reward actions that actually counteract helpful or cooperative behavior. Finally, candy or stickers, used as rewards for kind acts, may actually lower the occurrence of prosocial behavior.

To avoid these problems, adults must remember that prosocial behaviors are learned and are subject to the same conditions that characterize other learning episodes. That is, children must be motivated to learn and to feel successful. Neither of these criteria is met when adults ignore children who are trying to figure out what the positive expectations are or spend the majority of their time correcting them. Instead, adults must take as much care to enact positive consequences as they do to follow through with corrective ones.

These children are working as a team to create a block structure.

Cooperation. Cooperation among children will be undermined if adults rely on competition as their primary means for motivating children. Youngsters are encouraged to compete rather than cooperate when they are told: "Let's see who can put the most blocks away," "Whoever gets the most words right gets a star"or "The nicest picture will go in the showcase." In each instance, youngsters are quick to determine that there will be only one winner and that helping or cooperating with someone else will sabotage their own chances for coming out on top. On the other hand, such situations could be modified to make it easier for the youngsters to cooperate by focusing on group accomplishments rather than on individual achievement: "Let's see how well we can all work together to put these blocks away," "I'll check the board to find out if the class got more words right today than it did yesterday," or "When you're finished painting your pictures, we'll go out and hang them in the hall." These conditions clear the way for youngsters to come to one another's assistance or to work together as appropriate.

In addition, group-administered rewards encourage children to work as a team to achieve a common aim. Putting a star up for each book read by the group or for each act of kindness helps keep track of the children's progress as a whole and directs their attention to what the entire group can achieve. Thus, it is effective to monitor the group's progress and then enact positive consequences when certain benchmarks are obtained rather than always rewarding youngsters individually. This approach has been found to lead to friendlier, more cooperative behavior among the participants (Fabes, Fultz, Eisenberg, May-Plumlee & Christopher, 1989). When adults try to administer tangible rewards to encourage prosocial behavior among children, the results are usually counterproductive. Children who are bribed in these ways attribute their actions to the tangible rewards rather than to the needs of others or their own inclinations to treat others kindly.

Direct instruction. Children's prosocial behavior also increases when they have been trained to think and act prosocially (Cummings & Haggerty, 1997; Seefeldt, 1995). Such training focuses on the individual skills that lead to helping and cooperating. Recognizing prosocial behavior when it is displayed, identifying the needs of another, anticipating the consequences of acts, and generating multiple solutions to interpersonal problems are all prosocial skills. A variety of strategies have been

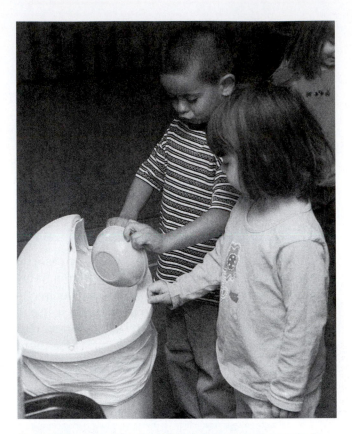

Creating opportunities for children to help or cooperate in real-life situations enhances their prosocial behavior.

used to teach these skills to children of varying ages. Some include:

1. Discussing the value of prosocial behavior and giving examples of how children themselves can act prosocially.
2. Telling stories that illustrate prosocial principles.
3. Demonstrating prosocial behavior using small figures, dolls, puppets, televised vignettes, or live models.
4. Getting children to reenact previously observed prosocial actions.
5. Having children role-play situations in which they take on the behaviors of helper and helpee.
6. Teaching children games that promote cooperation and awareness of others.
7. Creating opportunities for children to help or cooperate in real-life situations.

Youngsters who actively participate in tasks or situations that enable them to rehearse prosocial skills demonstrate the greatest instances of such behaviors in similar circumstances (Honig & Wittmer, 1996). These findings hold true from preschool through preadolescence, particularly for children younger than 6 years of age. The opportunity to physically reenact appropriate behaviors in relevant situations helps children better remember both the behavior and the cues that signal what conditions apply in a given circumstance (McGinnis & Goldstein, 1990). For example, when Heidi watches a skit in which she must use a variety of cues to decide which puppet needs help, she is better equipped to recognize when help is needed in a real-life situation.

Thus, the most productive approach for direct instruction is to combine verbal descriptions and explanations with practice of corresponding actions.

Practice with prosocial behavior. Actual participation in prosocial activities seems to foster prosocial behavior in the future (Eisenberg et al., 2006). Many researchers believe that for children to develop a future interest in behaving in a prosocial manner, they must actually engage in the behavior and experience firsthand the empathic rewards it can offer. When children practice behaving prosocially, they also experience the satisfaction of social approval from adults. Finally, participation in prosocial acts also helps children feel more competent at engaging in helping behaviors, which can assist them in seeing themselves as helpful.

SKILLS FOR PROMOTING PROSOCIAL BEHAVIOR IN CHILDREN

 Creating a Prosocial Environment

Using the skills you have learned in previous chapters will help you create an atmosphere that is conducive to the development of prosocial behavior. Some additional strategies include the following.

1. Label prosocial acts as they occur naturally. When children clean the guinea pig's cage, tell them they are showing concern for the animal's well-being. When Theresa announces that she received a get-well card during her recent absence, point out that sending the card was the way someone chose to comfort her. Explain that youngsters who remain quiet while a peer gives a report are helping him or her to concentrate. When children take turns, mention that this is a way of cooperating with one another. All of these instances enable you to highlight prosocial behavior rather than lecturing or moralizing about it.

2. Point out instances in which an unintentional lack of kindness was shown and describe an alternate, prosocial approach. Through inexperience or thoughtlessness, people sometimes are inconsiderate, selfish, uncooperative, or uncharitable. When this happens, point out to children the effects that behavior had on the person to whom it was

directed and describe a more appropriate action. Rather than labeling the child as "selfish," say, "When you didn't give her any, it hurt her feelings." Thus, if youngsters laugh when one of them trips and drops his or her lunch tray, say, "It embarrassed Sam when you laughed. He feels really uncomfortable. Help him to pick up the tray."

3. Create opportunities for children to cooperate. Each day, include projects and routines that require the efforts of more than one person. Consider the tasks that you may normally do and identify ones that teams of children could assist with, such as feeding classroom pets or setting up experiments. Encourage children to help one another as occasions arise. Be sure to ask special needs children to assist their more abled peers whenever the opportunity arises. When children ask you to help, try instead to find another child who could fulfill that role.

4. Use prosocial reasoning when talking with children. Offer explanations for classroom expectations that are prosocially motivated. For instance, explain that turn taking gives everyone a chance to try a new object or experience. Point out that comforting a friend in distress makes the unhappy child feel better and often makes the comforter feel better too. Focus on other-oriented rationales

continued

as well as benefits to the doer. Discuss the special needs represented by each child and how fairness requires taking into account individual circumstances. Ask children to talk about the prosocial reasons behind certain activities in the classroom, such as why people wait to tell their idea until after another person has finished. Set aside time to talk with children about specific incidents in which they and their peers were kind to one another. Reflect on these circumstances and encourage children to discuss how prosocial acts make people feel.

5. Reward prosocial behavior. Remain alert to children's attempts to be helpful, cooperative, or kind. Avoid taking these actions for granted or waiting for dramatic episodes before administering a reward. Instead, acknowledge small kindnesses, such as when children move out of the way, help to carry something, play together without bickering, share an idea, or offer encouragement to someone else. Show approval and appreciation by smiling and using positive personal messages and prosocial attributions.

6. Administer group rewards. Think of situations that have the potential for children to work together. These may be newly introduced conditions (such as a special project) or circumstances that traditionally have focused more on individual achievement. For instance, if you have emphasized each child taking care of his or her own area or materials, plan to change this routine to encourage youngsters to work together to clean up a larger area. Implement your plan. Afterward, praise children for their cooperation and helpfulness.

7. Demonstrate a variety of prosocial behaviors. Carefully examine your own behavior with children and with other adults and then set an example for children to follow. Although it may seem easiest to comfort, rescue, or help children, do not forget to share and cooperate as well.

8. Demonstrate constructive ways of responding to other people's prosocial behavior. Regardless of whether you are interacting with children or adults, and in spite of whether you want help, a positive response contributes to the prosocial environment. If you desire the help that is offered, say, "Thank you" with a pleased expression on your face. If you would rather do something on your own, or if the proposed assistance would not be helpful, do not simply brush the child or adult aside. Instead, acknowledge the kindness and explain that this is something you would like to do yourself or describe an action that would be more useful. In both cases, you are modeling appropriate ways of either accepting or declining help.

9. Be positive when engaging in prosocial behavior. Because children tend to imitate adults who seem to enjoy giving help and cooperation, exhibit obvious pleasure in prosocial situations. Smile and say things like, "It makes me feel good to help you."

10. Point out the prosocial behaviors modeled by yourself and others. Children are better able to understand the prosocial models they see when their model's behavior is explained. Provide children with such information by saying things like: "Arthur was having a hard time coming up with words for his song, so Lamont is helping him by making a list of some words that rhyme," or "Randi and Mike have decided to use the workbench together. Randi will use the hammer while Mike uses the saw. Then, they'll trade."

11. Use positive attribution to increase children's prosocial self-images. Say specific things, such as, "Elke, you were really helpful to Danielle when you reached up high for the dictionary she needed," or "Lonny and Javon, you were cooperative when you worked together on the diorama. That made the work easier for both of you," or "Jackson, you showed a lot of kindness when you wiped your sister's tears. It made her feel better knowing you were concerned about her."

SKILLS FOR PROMOTING PROSOCIAL BEHAVIOR IN CHILDREN

 **Giving Direct Instruction
Related to Prosocial Behavior**

Receiving direct training in helping and co-operating leads to an increase in children's prosocial behavior. Such instruction can be provided through on-the-spot teaching in naturally occurring situations or through pre-planned activities. In both cases, the role of the adult is to teach children basic facts about kindness, to demonstrate applications to real life situations, and to give children a chance to rehearse related skills. Each approach has certain elements in common but also unique characteristics that must be understood in order to implement them successfully.

 **Providing On-the-Spot
Instruction**

As you will recall, there are three steps involved in behaving prosocially: awareness, decision making, and action. The main focus of on-the-spot instruction is to assist children at any point beyond which they seem unable to proceed.

1. Observe children for signs of prosocial behavior. Watch children carefully. Take note when they show consideration for another person, when they attempt to assist someone, or when they join forces, even briefly.

2. Ask children directly to help you. This is particularly important when working with preschoolers who have not yet developed the observational skills to accurately recognize when help is needed. Pointing out your need for assistance gives them practice in recognizing situational cues and performing corresponding behaviors related to kindness.

3. Make children aware when someone else needs help or cooperation. There are times when children fail to recognize distress signals or other signs that indicate that help or cooperation is desired. Rectify this by giving children relevant information to assist them in becoming more attuned to the circumstances at hand. If Marianne seems oblivious to Barney's struggle to carry a heavy board, say: "Look at Barney. He's working awfully hard. He looks like he could use some help." Likewise, if children are outside trying to pick teams and several youngsters are laughing at a private joke, it may be difficult for others to hear whose name is being called. As a result, those who are straining to listen may try to elicit cooperation by telling the jokesters to "pipe down," or "shut up." Such language could easily be misinterpreted by those to whom it is directed or even seen as a challenge to continue. Information from you at this point would be useful: "You are having a good laugh. It's hard for other people to hear. They're just asking you to cooperate by being a little quieter."

4. Teach children signals they might use to elicit help or cooperation from others. In the preceding example, youngsters who were trying to get their loud age-mates to cooperate used an antagonistic strategy, which could have back-fired. They, too, could benefit from some basic information, such as: "When you yelled at them, it just made them get louder. It might have been better to walk over and explain why you wanted them to be quiet." Toddlers and preschoolers, as well as youngsters in highly charged situations, respond best to direct suggestions. Offer these in the form of a script or sample words that they might use: "Tell Marianne, 'This board's too big for me to carry alone.'" With your support and encouragement, most school-age children who are not passionately involved in a situation will be able to generate their own ideas for what to say.

5. Point out situations in which people could decide to help or cooperate. At times, children are aware that someone needs their help or cooperation, but don't know what to do next. This is when you can highlight that a prosocial decision can be made by saying

continued

SKILLS FOR PROMOTING PROSOCIAL BEHAVIOR IN CHILDREN—continued

something such as: "Janice looks like she needs your help. We can decide to help her," or "Mr. Crouch wants us all to work together on this project. We'll have to decide whether or not to do that."

6. Discuss situations in which it would be best to decide not to cooperate. Help children sort out the reasons for such decisions. These would involve circumstances in which people or property are endangered or moral codes are violated. For example, joining together for the purpose of stealing, cheating on an exam, or spray-painting the lavatory walls would be inappropriate cooperative efforts. With school-age children, discuss peer pressure and generate strategies and scripts children might use to cope in uncomfortable peer-related circumstances.

7. Assist children in determining what type of help or cooperation is most suitable for a particular situation. Once children show some signs of wanting to help or cooperate, aid them in deciding what action to take. Provide information for them to consider, such as: "Sometimes, when people are unhappy, it helps when someone hugs them or says nice things to them," or "Sometimes, people feel satisfaction from attempting to do something that is difficult, and their pleasure is spoiled if another person takes over."

Demonstrations also are useful. Showing a child how to unlock the wheelchair of a classmate in need, illustrating to children how one person can steady a doll while another puts on the clothes, or demonstrating how it takes two people to make the computer game work are all ways to make these types of discussions more concrete. In addition, discuss ways children can support another person's effort without offering direct, physical assistance.

Point out the importance of a reassuring smile, the "thumbs-up" sign, or cheering from the sidelines. These are all ways children can provide comfort and encouragement. Finally, teach children to ask questions such as: "Do you want help?" "How can I help you?" "What do you need?" and "What would you like me to do?" This enables children to acquire information about what kind of behavior another person might perceive as helpful or cooperative in a given situation.

8. Teach children how to share. Teaching children how to share is not the same as telling them to do it. Children often need some guided experience with sharing before they will readily share objects and materials. Use planned activities and on-the-spot instruction to acquaint children with many different ways to share materials and territory such as: taking turns, using an object/place simultaneously, dividing materials/territory, finding a substitute object/place, or compromising.

Strategies to teach children to share include:

1. Demonstrating what sharing looks like
2. Suggesting multiple options from which children might choose
3. Pointing out instances of sharing as they occur
4. Reading stories that illustrate ways to share as discussion starters
5. Giving children sample scripts to use in asking for something, as well as for expressing their desire to finish using something.
6. Helping children negotiate the sequence for using an item; for instance, "I get it next, then Mary gets a turn."

Another strategy is to teach children who are waiting for a turn to ask, "How will I know when your turn is over?" This requires the child in possession of an item to designate a signal for completion and gives the waiting child something specific to look for. Older children appreciate being able to say, "Okay, but I get it next." Establishing their turn in the order of possession satisfies their need for some control in the situation.

Finally, help children recognize legitimate instances in which sharing can be expected (e.g., using class materials) and other times when sharing cannot be expected (e.g., using someone else's private property). All of these

SKILLS FOR PROMOTING PROSOCIAL BEHAVIOR IN CHILDREN

techniques touch on nuances of sharing that cannot be conveyed by simply demanding that children "share."

9. Work at increasing children's perspective-taking skills. For children to understand when help or cooperation is needed or when an act of kindness is called for, they must learn to put themselves in the place of another person. Although this skill will often emerge around age 6, it can be taught to children who are as young as 3, 4, and 5 years of age, and it can benefit people of all ages. Promote children's conscious understanding of prosocial behavior by using open-ended questions, such as "How did you know that would happen?" or "What made you think of trying that?" Promote children's consequential thinking by asking such questions as, "What will happen if . . . ?" or "What will happen next . . . ?" Finally, promote children's alternative thinking with such statements as, "William wants to finish the project himself. What could you do to help him do that?" or "What's another way you could help?"

10. Provide opportunities for children to increase their instrumental know-how. Teach children these strategies: (1) Help children put feelings into words so they are able to express their own emotions and understand the expression of other people's emotions. (2) Provide numerous formal and informal opportunities for children to make decisions in the classroom. This gives children practice in generating alternatives to problems and in developing confidence in their abilities to find positive solutions. (3) Finally, give children chances to learn useful skills. Sorting and organizing materials in the classroom, holding doors while others carry things, and using actual tools to fix broken toys are only some of the possibilities.

11. Work with children to evaluate the results of their actions. Children learn a lot from taking a retrospective look at what they have done as close to the event as possible: "Did jumping on the box solve the problem?"

"Were there enough of you, or did you need more people to work on that project?" "Were you able to give Raymond all the information he needed?" or "How do you think it worked out for everybody to have a five minute turn with the microscope?"

If children are unable to assess their own performances, offer some information yourself or help them gather information from others. This evaluation could be conducted during a private conversation with a child or as a group assessment of group effort. Regardless of how well their prosocial venture worked out, praise children for attempting it.

12. Encourage children to accept kindness from others. Sometimes, children are unaware of or misinterpret other children's attempts at prosocial behavior. Thus, Tricia may not realize that when Audrey takes over, she is actually trying to help, nor may she understand that Sam's apparent lack of decisiveness is his way of trying to cooperate. In situations like these, point out what is really taking place.

In addition, there are children who, wanting to be independent or self-sufficient, actively reject assistance, reassurance, or sympathy. Frequently, they neither cooperate nor expect cooperation from others. Their rationale is that they expect nothing and give nothing. In reality, such youngsters often fear rejection or "taking a chance" on someone. These children need to experience kindness before they can extend it to those around them. Because their actions put other children off, it is you who must reach out.

Do not fail to provide unreceptive youngsters with the same courtesies or offers of help and encouragement that you might grant to a more appreciative child. This is the first step in helping them become more accepting of prosocial behavior from someone else.

13. Support children when their attempts at kindness are rebuffed. At times, children's enthusiasm is dashed if their offer of help is refused or an action they thought was helpful

continued

SKILLS FOR PROMOTING PROSOCIAL BEHAVIOR IN CHILDREN—continued

turns out not to have been. If this happens, acknowledge the child's disappointment or frustration and discuss the situation. Offer information that might assist the child in understanding the outcome. If you do not know why their attempt failed, be supportive and sympathetic.

All of the preceding strategies can be used individually, on separate occasions, or in combination. Which specific technique is called for depends on the particular circumstance in which you are involved. This is illustrated in the following real-life scenario.

SITUATION: Kenton and Josh, two 6-year-olds, are playing with a construction toy that has many interconnecting pieces. Josh builds an elaborate vehicle, which Kenton admires.

Kenton: Make me one like yours.

Josh: Well, if I make it, it'll be mine.

Kenton: But I want one. Make me one.

Josh: Then it'll be mine!

Kenton: I can't get the pieces to fit.

At this point, it is obvious that Kenton is unsuccessfully trying to elicit Josh's help. Now is when the adult intervention is appropriate.

Adult: Josh, Kenton is asking you for help. Sometimes, when people help, they do the job for someone. However, it sounds like you think if you make the car for Kenton, it will have to be yours. Another way people help is by showing someone how to do it. That way, Kenton can make his own with your help How does that sound to you?

Josh: Okay.

Kenton: Yeah.

Josh demonstrated how his car went together. Once this was well underway, the adult commented briefly on the boys' cooperative behavior as well as on Josh's willingness to help a friend.

In this situation, the adult enabled one child to become aware of another child's signals and

provided information about a possible course of action. She also rewarded the children for demonstrating prosocial behavior. Later in the day, she could take a moment to informally talk with Kenton and Josh about their reactions to the helping episode. Another type of direct instruction involves teaching prosocial behavior through planned activities.

 Coordinating Planned Activities

Planned activities are lessons adults develop in advance and carry out with children individually or in groups. The best activities are not necessarily the most elaborate; rather, they are those that have been well prepared and then implemented in ways that are sensitive to children's interests and needs. The following list illustrates how best to accomplish this.

1. Decide what prosocial skill you want to teach. Choose one of the skills described in this chapter, such as becoming aware that someone needs help, deciding to help, or taking action to help.

2. Consider multiple optional lessons for the skill. Lessons that include both discussion and active participation are the most effective. Active participation means getting children physically involved in the activity by handling props, moving about, and talking rather than simply listening. Some examples of successful activities include:

a. Reading and telling stories that have a prosocial theme.

b. Dramatizing prosocial situations through skits or through use of puppets, dolls, or stand-up figures.

c. Discussing with the children prosocial events that have occurred in the formal group setting.

d. Role-playing prosocial episodes. Sample topics might include how to ask for help or cooperation, how to decide whether help or cooperation is needed, determining

SKILLS FOR PROMOTING PROSOCIAL BEHAVIOR IN CHILDREN

what type of action would be most helpful or cooperative, and how to decline unwanted help.

e. Discussing scenes from magazines, books, or posters. The discussion might involve identifying who was helped, who provided help, and how the help was carried out or pointing out cooperative and uncooperative behaviors.

f. Playing cooperative games such as ring-around-the-rosy with toddlers or carrying out a scavenger hunt with older children in which groups of children search for things as a team rather than competing as individuals.

g. Turning traditionally competitive games such as bingo into cooperative group efforts.

To adapt this game, have one card for every two or three children. The object is to help one another find the matching numbers or pictures rather than competing to be the first to complete a card. When one group's card is complete, those youngsters may move to another group to help them. Several game books are on the market that emphasize cooperative efforts.

h. Creating group projects, such as a class book or mural, to which everyone contributes.

3. Select one of your activity ideas to fully develop. Make a realistic assessment of what props are available, how much time you will have, the physical setting, and the number of children you will be working with at one time. For instance, do not choose a story that takes 20 minutes to read if you only have 10 minutes in which to work. Likewise, if the only setting available is a bustling waiting room, or the only time available is when children may be hungry or preoccupied with other responsibilities, it is not appropriate to plan activities that require intense concentration.

4. Develop a plan of action that outlines the prosocial activity from start to finish. Write this plan down as a way to remember it and further think it through. Include what you will say to introduce the activity, any instructions you may have to give, how you will handle materials, how you will have children use them, the sequence of steps you will follow, and how you will close. Anticipate what you will say or do if children seem uninterested or unable to carry out your directions. See Table 13-3 for a sample activity plan.

5. Gather the materials you will need. Make any additional props that are necessary.

6. Implement your plan. Utilize skills you have learned in previous chapters related to nonverbal and verbal communication, reflecting, asking questions, and playing to enhance your presentation.

7. Evaluate your activity in terms of immediate and long-term prosocial outcomes. Typical evaluation questions include: Who were the children who participated? What did children actually say or do in this activity? How did children demonstrate interest or lack of interest? Later in the day, did children refer either to the activity or the prosocial skill covered in the activity in their conversation or play? Over time, do children spontaneously demonstrate prosocial behaviors highlighted by the activity?

8. Repeat the same prosocial activity, or a variation of it, at another time. Children learn prosocial concepts through repeated exposure over time. Therefore, do not expect to see immediate behavior change or the adoption of prosocial skills in their everyday interactions after just one or two presentations of a particular skill.

 Communicating with Children's Families

Children's prosocial behaviors within the family setting can and should be encouraged by family members. Following are some strategies that will enable you to join forces with parents and other significant people in

continued

Table 13-3 Sample Activity to Promote Prosocial Behavior

Activity Name:	Sharing a Lump of Clay
Goal:	To help children share
Materials:	A 2-pound lump of clay, a table with five chairs (one for an adult, four for children), one plastic knife, one pair of scissors, one 12-inch length of wire.

Procedure:

1. Place a lump of clay in the center of the table.

2. Neutralize the clay by keeping one hand on it. Say: "I have one big ball of clay, and there are four children who want to use it. Tell me how everyone can have a chance."

3. Listen to children's ideas; elicit suggestions from everyone.

4. Clarify each child's perspective by paraphrasing his or her ideas to the group. Follow up with, "And what do you think of that?"

5. Remain impartial throughout this process. Do not show disapproval of any child's idea, regardless of its content.

6. Remind children as necessary that the first step in playing with the clay is deciding how that will take place.

7. If children become bogged down, repeat pertinent helping facts and principles.

8. Summarize the solution when it has been achieved.

9. Praise children.

10. Carry out the agreed-upon solution.

SKILLS FOR PROMOTING PROSOCIAL BEHAVIOR IN CHILDREN—continued

children's lives to promote children's prosocial behavior.

1. Communicate your classroom philosophy of cooperation to families. Cooperative activities, group projects, and individual work give children a message that each person in the classroom has an important role in the smooth functioning of that setting. Communicate your philosophy to parents in the form of a newsletter in which you describe what prosocial behavior is and how it is encouraged in the classroom.

2. Initiate and model cooperative activities in the program that include family members. There are many tasks to be done in a classroom such as special maintenance of computers, washing door and window frames, sterilizing toys, planting bushes or trees on school grounds, or fundraising for new play equipment that may provide logical opportunities to involve family members. Infrequent but regular "work parties," during which adult and child family members have important roles in classroom or school improvement are a useful way of including families. Such tasks as the ones described require varying degrees of expertise, thus providing opportunities for a wide range of participation. The work party time focuses on building community among the teachers, children, and their families, as well as accomplishing the necessary work. In all cases, families are actively involved in the planning and the execution stages of the project. Professionals work with family members to break down the tasks into manageable components, so that everyone can be successful

SKILLS FOR PROMOTING PROSOCIAL BEHAVIOR IN CHILDREN

and to ensure that all necessary materials and equipment are ready to be used. An essential feature of projects such as this one is that all the professionals are modeling the cooperative behavior they are asking of others. On a smaller scale, you may wish to choose one special project that will involve families in an active, cooperative way. Work with other professionals in your setting to select the project and to organize family involvement. Remember to point out to the children the helpful actions carried out by their family members. Be sure not to make comparisons, but simply make children aware of the help that was offered.

3. Invite parents and other family members to help in the formal group setting. Expand the old concept of "room mothers" to include every member of the child's family. At the beginning of the program year, send out a "family interest survey" eliciting information about things adult family members are interested in doing, such as repairing toys, sewing, accompanying field trips, designing bulletin boards, or telling stories. Among the most valuable contributions families can make to the classroom are activities that represent their cultural heritage that may be unfamiliar to many students,. Families may be reluctant to respond in writing, so carry out conversations with parents at informal times as a way of both finding out information and encouraging them to participate.

Some adults may be more comfortable helping "behind the scenes," whereas others may be able to take advantage of working directly with the children. Provide an opportunity for all kinds of participation, and be sure to acknowledge all help in writing and verbally. Children will benefit from sending a "thank you" note to the family.

4. Answer families' questions about the role of competition and cooperation in their children's lives. At the same time that cooperation is being fostered in the classroom, some parents may express concern that in

order to be "successful in life" their children need to feel competitive.

Hold discussions with family members on this topic or introduce it as part of a newsletter to families. Encourage parents to express their views and acknowledge their perceptions. Point out some of the differences between "doing one's best" and "beating the opposition." For example, give families some specifics as to how children's achievement may be measured in many ways such as reviewing how much better they did this time than last. Suggest keeping journal entries regarding the emotions of the individual when working toward an identified goal. Help parents understand how to support their children through the disappointments and hard times that inevitably come with competition and comparisons. Rather than denying their children's perceptions of "failure," aid parents in understanding how to use affective reflections and continuing responses to encourage children to reveal and, therefore, better understand their emotions at such times. Point out developmental norms with regard to how children at various ages assess their success or failure. In addition, mention, if appropriate, that while some children become more motivated to do as the adult wishes when prompted by a competitive statement or challenge, friction among children also increases.

5. Assist adults in figuring out how their children can be helpful at home. In many families, certain routine chores are assigned to the youngest members. Jobs such as making one's own bed in the morning, clearing dishes from the table, meal planning, and even simple meal preparation are well within the abilities of most children. Responsibility for these tasks gives children a sense of contributing to the life of their family, as well as increasing their self-perceptions of competence and worth.

Encourage adult family members to have discussions with their offspring as to the

continued

SKILLS FOR PROMOTING PROSOCIAL BEHAVIOR IN CHILDREN—continued

ways in which the children can be helpful at home. Suggest that the family draw up a list of chores to be done and let young family members choose from among the list. Sometimes children prefer doing the same task over and over; at other times, they would rather change jobs frequently. Suggest that the family make a decision about this, and explore the possibility that the same strategy need not necessarily apply to every child. In other words, some children in a family may hold the same responsibility while others may switch. Offer a visible means of letting everyone know that a job is done, such as a chart with stars or other stickers that the children are responsible for marking.

Caution parents against fostering competition among their children. Negative comparisons have the effect of discouraging rather than encouraging participation. Suggest instead that

some chores may be more efficiently handled when several people cooperate. Also include standards for completion in order to avoid misunderstandings. For example, in one family, 8-year-old Aaron was to sweep the kitchen after dinner. His father was cross with him for not returning the broom and dustpan to the closet. After some discussion, both parties realized that although the adult assumed that putting things away was part of the job, the child did not see that as part of his responsibility. As a consequence, the chore was changed to sweeping the floor and putting away the tools.

Finally, explain to adults the importance of not taking children's work for granted. Children are more likely to continue their efforts when their assistance has been acknowledged and the positive influence of their contributions on the operations of the family has been appreciated.

PITFALLS TO AVOID

Whether you are teaching children prosocial behavior by creating an atmosphere that is conducive to acts of kindness, providing on-the-spot instruction, or using planned activities, there are certain mistakes to avoid.

Failing to recognize children's efforts to behave prosocially. Children who are just learning to help and cooperate may be awkward in their attempts or may initially pursue a course of action that at first bears little resemblance to kindness. When this happens, adults may misinterpret these behaviors as purposefully uncooperative or unhelpful. Harmful behavior should be limited, but children should receive support for their good intentions as well as information on how to improve their performance. This means it will be necessary to ascertain what a child was trying to achieve before taking corrective action. Thus, if children are adding water to the acrylic paint or scrubbing the window with toothpaste, don't automatically assume that their motives are to ruin the materials or to strike out at you. Instead, ask questions such

as: "What were you trying to do?" "What did you think would happen?" or "Why are you . . .?" If they give an indication that their intent was to be helpful, acknowledge their efforts and explain why they aren't helpful, suggesting alternative actions that would be useful. Make sure that your voice tone is sincerely questioning and not accusatory.

These same strategies can be employed in any situation in which a child is attempting to help, cooperate, comfort, or rescue via some inappropriate means. There will be occasions when you do set a limit or enforce a consequence only to discover later that the child truly was trying to help. If this happens, go back to the child, explain that you now understand what he or she was trying to do, and discuss why corrective action was necessary. Give the child specific ideas about what to do instead.

Bringing a prosocial model's behavior to a child's attention through negative comparison or through competition. As has been stated previously, children are more likely to imitate models whose behavior is pointed out to them. However, adults should not use these situations to make unfavorable comparisons between the model's behavior and that of the child. Statements like, "Look at Roger. He's so polite. Why can't you be more like that?" make the child feel defensive rather than receptive and do not make imitation likely. A better approach would be to say: "Roger accidentally bumped into Maureen, so he said, 'Excuse me.' That was a very polite thing to do." This latter statement provides factual information in a nonjudgmental way.

Coercing children to engage in insincere pro-social behavior.   It is not uncommon for adults who are trying to teach children consideration to manipulate them into expressions of kindness that the youngsters do not really feel. These is illustrated by the parent who insists that 12-year-old Raymond "be nice" and give Aunt Martha a kiss, even though the child has protested that he doesn't like to do it. He complies, not to be kind to Aunt Martha, but to avoid trouble. Similar difficulties arise when children are prodded into saying they are sorry when in fact they are not. They learn that apologizing is the quickest way out of a dilemma rather than a sincere expression of remorse. Likewise, children who are urged to bestow false compliments on others as a way to charm them are learning that hypocrisy is acceptable.

To avoid these undesirable outcomes, adults must refrain from being preoccupied with the outer trappings of kindness at the expense of helping children develop the empathy that is necessary for true kindness to occur. Hence, it would be better to give the child information about the other person that might prompt empathic feelings: "Aunt Martha is glad to see you. She loves you very much. It would make her feel good to know that you care about her, too," "When you were trying to practice with your crutches, you banged Jerry in the leg. That hurt a lot," or "You told me you thought Carrie's spider was neat. She'd probably like to hear that from you."

Making children share everything, all the time.   There is no doubt that sharing is an important interpersonal skill that children should learn about. Unfortunately, there are times when adults promote this virtue too enthusiastically. They make children give up items that they have really not finished using as soon as other children want them. For instance, Elizabeth was using three grocery bags to sort the food in her "store." One bag was for boxes, one was for cans, and one was for plastic fruit. She needed all three bags. Helen approached

and asked if she could have one of the bags to make a "dress." Elizabeth protested, but the adult insisted that Helen be given a bag. The adult dumped out the fruit and gave a sack to Helen.

In this case, Elizabeth had a legitimate right to finish using the bag. It would have been easier for her to share it willingly once her game was over. A better approach would have been to say: "Elizabeth, when you are finished playing your game, Helen would like a chance to use a bag. Tell her when you are ready." A variation of this problem occurs when adults arbitrarily regulate turn taking as a way to get children to share. For example, as soon as a child gets on a tricycle, the adult admonishes, "Once around the yard, and then you'll have to get off so someone else can have a turn." This approach is utilized in a well-meaning effort to avoid conflict or to be fair. However, it often ends up with no child feeling truly satisfied. Furthermore, it requires constant adult monitoring.

Instead, allow children to fully use the materials to which they have access. It would be better, if at all possible, to expand the amount of equipment available so that youngsters are not pressured into having to give up something with which they are deeply involved. If this is not possible, prompt empathic feelings by pointing out that others are waiting and would like a turn, too. Finally, remember to praise children when they finally relinquish what they have been using to someone else. Point out how their actions pleased the child who wanted to be next.

SUMMARY

Youngsters who behave prosocially develop feelings of satisfaction and competence, have many successful encounters, and get help and cooperation from others in return. Groups in which prosocial behavior is fostered are friendlier and more productive than those in which it is ignored.

To behave prosocially, children first must become aware of situations in which such acts would be beneficial. Then, they have to decide if and how they will act and finally, take the action (or lack of action) they have decided on. Desiring to act prosocially and knowing how best to do it are not necessarily learned at the same time. As children mature and gain experience, they become more proficient at matching their prosocial actions to the needs of others. Children's abilities to take on another's perspective also affect their prosocial behavior; that is, children with good role-taking abilities are generally more prosocially inclined. This link becomes stronger with age. Gender, age, family, peers, school and culture influence children's prosocial behavior.

Particular societal characteristics either promote or inhibit prosocial conduct. The most profound influences on children's helpful and cooperative behavior are the adults: the warmth of their relationship with children, the discipline strategies, the behaviors they model, the behaviors in children they reward, and the prosocial values and the skills they teach. Teaching children kindness can be accomplished through creating an atmosphere conducive to prosocial actions, through on-the-spot instruction, and through planned activities. Partnerships between the family and the professionals who work with the children enhance children's intentions and skills toward prosocial behavior.

KEY TERMS

character attributions
dispositional attributions

instrumental know-how
perspective-taking

prosocial attributions
prosocial behavior

DISCUSSION QUESTIONS

1. Identify several aspects of prosocial behavior. Discuss their similarities and differences using examples from real life.

2. In small groups talk about the benefits and risks of behaving prosocially. When appropriate, tell about some personal instances in which you did or did not behave prosocially and the consequences of those behaviors.

3. Geraldo is working hard at constructing a bridge out of tongue depressors. He seems to be having difficulty getting it to stay up. Patrick is watching.

   a. Describe the steps Patrick will go through in acting prosocially toward Geraldo.

   b. Discuss all the possible choices Patrick will have to make and the potential outcomes of each decision.

4. Describe the influence of age on children's prosocial behavior. Discuss the emergence and the increase or decline of particular types of prosocial behaviors as children get older. Give reasons based on your understanding of children's development.

5. Discuss cultural influences on children's prosocial behavior. Describe experiences in your own upbringing to illustrate. Describe particular family or social values that had an impact.

6. Describe the attributes of the atmosphere of a formal group setting that facilitate the development of children's prosocial behavior. Discuss specifically how the discipline strategies you have learned thus far contribute to this atmosphere.

7. Describe six ways in which adults can model cooperation in the formal group setting and in the home. Discuss how children can translate these techniques into their own behavior.

8. Using examples from the formal group setting in which you work, describe instances in which adults:

   a. rewarded children's prosocial behavior.

   b. overlooked children's prosocial behavior.

   c. inadvertently punished children's prosocial behavior.

   Discuss any aftermath you observed, either immediately or within a short time.

9. Discuss the role of direct instruction on children's prosocial behavior. Relate specific skills that foster helping and cooperating to particular strategies for teaching these skills.

10. Referring to Appendix A, NAEYC Code of Ethical Conduct, find the principles and ideals to use in judging the ethics of the following situation: Two teachers in your program are excited about an activity they heard about at a recent workshop. Each time children do a kind act they earn a point. The child with the most points at the end of the week is named "kindness kid" for a day.

FIELD ASSIGNMENTS

1. Choose a prosocial skill. In a few sentences, describe an activity you will use to teach children about the behavior you have selected. Carry out your plan with children. Describe how you carried out your plan and how the children responded. Briefly talk about how you might change or improve your plan for repetition in the future.

2. Identify a job you ordinarily carry out yourself in your field placement. Describe at least three ways you could get children involved in helping you. Implement one of your strategies. Then describe what actually happened. Discuss what it is about your plan that you might repeat in the future and what you might change.

3. Focus on modeling prosocial behavior. Describe a prosocial behavior that you modeled and how you did it. Next, discuss a situation in which you pointed out prosocial modeling by yourself or by another person. Write the words you used.

4. Select a prosocial skill to teach children. Use the on-the-spot strategies identified in this chapter. Document children's progress over time.

5. Describe a conversation between you (or another professional) and an adult family member in which a child's prosocial behavior was discussed. Outline the nature of the behavior as well as any strategies that were suggested to encourage the prosocial actions. Write a brief evaluation based on the material covered in this and earlier chapters.

Chapter 14

SUPPORTING CHILDREN'S DEVELOPMENT: SEXUALITY, ETHNICITY, AND EXCEPTIONAL NEEDS

OBJECTIVES

On completion of this chapter, you should be able to describe:

- Children's psychosexual development.

- Outcomes related to the development of ethnic identity, preferences, and attitudes in young children.

- Issues surrounding inclusion of children with exceptional needs in formal group settings.

- Characteristics of precocious or excessively shy children.

- The impact of shyness and difficult temperament on children's individuality.

- Skills for effective handling of developmental issues related to children's sexuality, ethnicity, exceptional needs, and other differences.

- Strategies for communicating with families about children's individual differences.

- Pitfalls in the handling of issues related to variations in children's development.

A 4-year-old boy in the housekeeping area of a large child care center suddenly announces that the dolls are "going to make a baby." Putting one doll on top of the other, he tells two other children who are playing nearby, "Watch this!" and proceeds with a fairly demonstrative performance. The other two children watch with obvious fascination. As the teacher approaches, the child quickly picks up one of the dolls, purposefully ending the play episode.

Several young children begin arguing over selection of a variety of dolls representative of different ethnic groups. The hands-down favorites are the white and Asian dolls. An adult cheerfully suggests that no one has chosen any of the black dolls lying on the bottom of the box. "We can't! They're dirty and bad," responds one of the children. The adult is particularly surprised because the statement is made by an African-American child.

Kathy, a student who is visually impaired, is being mainstreamed into a fifth-grade classroom. She watches tensely as two teams are chosen for kickball during recess. When she is not chosen by either team, the teacher announces, "Kathy will want to play, too." There is an embarrassing silence, but no offer is made by either team to have Kathy join them.

Episodes like these commonly arise as children navigate the social environment. How we respond to them influences the lessons children learn and how children feel about themselves and others in the process. At times, we may feel genuine embarrassment, irritation, discomfort, and uncertainty in handling sensitive situations such as these. Because of personal emotions that automatically arise in response to our own moral sensibilities and past experiences, we may find ourselves reacting too intensely, avoiding or ignoring negative behaviors, or feeling momentarily confused about what might be the most effective response.

Occasionally, we may misinterpret a child's intentions. For example, a 6-year-old boy in a North Carolina classroom gained national attention for kissing a classmate. He was charged with sexual harassment and isolated by his teacher from other children, causing him to miss out on a coloring activity and an ice cream party as a consequence. When questioned about what he understood relative to sexual harassment, the child was at a loss for an explanation, simply saying, "She's my friend." A serious by-product of excessive adult anxiety, discomfort, rejection, or avoidance in such situations is the potentially negative effect on children's development—primarily the production of guilt, loss of self-esteem, or the reinforcement of negative attitudes, misinformation, and maladaptive behavior.

Conversely, when adults are able to maintain a sensitive, nonreactive, and matter-of-fact approach in handling sensitive issues, positive psychosocial development and competence are promoted in the child. By structuring discussions, answering children's questions honestly and thoughtfully, and providing experiences that teach self-awareness and counter **biases**, professionals promote development of **social competencies** in children—values of social justice, healthy attitudes toward sexuality, and the ability to interact effectively with people of varying cultural, ethnic, and racial backgrounds. Over time, children who develop strength in social competence become adults who are better able to read social situations accurately, give and receive emotional support, and develop a positive self-identity.

CHILDREN'S PSYCHOSEXUAL DEVELOPMENT

Gender-Role Development

As children develop a sense of themselves, it's important for them to feel comfortable about their sexuality. Here, we want to distinguish at the outset the difference between **gender identity** (biological, male–female identification) and **gender-role identification**, which refers to the behaviors, abilities, and characteristics associated with a particular gender. Gender typing is a psychosocial developmental process by which children obtain not only a gender identity, but also the motives, values, and behaviors considered appropriate in their culture for members of their biological sex. This begins a great deal earlier than previously thought and continues even into adulthood (Berk, 2006). Gender-role development is highly complex, with both cognitive and social variables being highly influential. Parents play a particularly important role, but so do teachers, peers, and siblings.

Children progress through a series of stages in acquiring gender-typed behavior (see Table 14-1), and we see it reflected in their choice of playmates, selection of playthings, and later gender segregation. The sequence remains the same for all children but is dependent also on the experiences they have and their intellectual maturity.

Observations of children's play shows that they are fully aware of socially defined behaviors and attitudes associated with being male or female, and this knowledge is reflected in their "gender-doing." We hear them make comments in their play: "Daddies

Table 14-1 Overview of Gender Typing.

AGE IN YEARS	GENDER IDENTITY	GENDER STEREOTYPING	GENDER-TYPED BEHAVIOR
0–2½	Ability to discriminate males from females emerges and improves. Child accurately labels the self as a boy or a girl.	Some gender stereotypes emerge.	Gender-typed toy/activity preferences emerge. Preferences for same-sex playmates emerge (gender segregation).
3–6	Conservation of gender (recognition that one's gender is unchanging) emerges.	Gender stereotyping of interests, activities, and occupations emerges and becomes quite rigid.	Gender-typed play/toy preferences become stronger, particularly for boys. Gender segregation intensifies.
7–11		Gender stereotyping of personality traits and achievement domains emerges. Gender stereotyping becomes less rigid.	Gender segregation continues to strengthen. Gender-typed toy/activity preferences continue to strengthen for boys; girls develop (or retain) interest in some masculine activities.
12 & beyond	Gender identity becomes more salient, reflecting gender intensification pressures.	Intolerance of cross-sex mannerisms increases early in adolescence. Gender stereotyping becomes more flexible in most respects later in adolescence.	Conformity to gender-typed behaviors increases early in adolescence, reflecting gender intensification. Gender segregation becomes less pronounced.

Source: Shaffer, 2005.

are strong," "Mommy cooks the dinner," and "I get to be the nurse because I'm a girl." Also seen in preschoolers is an ability to use "gender-bending" in their play dynamics when necessary. However, as children grow older, they exhibit more discomfort in taking on roles of the opposite gender. This signals that they are no longer in process of exploring "gender-doing" because this part of their social learning has become more inflexible. This is true for boys earlier than for girls (Hyun & Choi, 2004).

Gender-role development has a major effect on children's understanding of their place in society as a male or female and also in the roles they take on to express their maleness or femininity. However, identity and role taking also are shaped by children's environments and their experiences within those environments. For example, there is evidence that abused children may develop significant difficulties in their gender identification, as in the following case study:

> *Isolated from his peers and disinterested in the normal activities of typical boys . . . , he enjoyed making clothes for his Barbie dolls, with which he played for hours on end. In the laboratory he often folded his arms high on his chest in an attempt, he said, to imitate breasts. Like many of the other abused children, he appeared anxious, forlorn, and frightened. . . . Under an early barrage of abuse from the outside world, he—and many of the other young victims—seemed to have lost his sense of identity and to have entered a prolonged and unresolved sexual crisis. (Segal & Yahres, 1979, p. 182)*

The Development of Sexual Attitudes

From infancy, all human beings have sexual feelings. A positive attitude toward sexuality means accepting

"Girls don't but women do have breasts. Boys never do, not even when they're men."

Figure 14-1 An example of developing gender segregation.

Source: From "Psychosexual Development in Infants and Young Children, by A. S. Honig, September 2000, Young Children, 55(5), 71. Reprinted with permission from the National Association for the Education of Young Children.

these sensual feelings and urges as natural rather than shameful. Children's subsequent ability to handle such feelings depends on their earliest experiences. Early encounters involving psychological intimacy with significant others teach a child that interpersonal involvement is safe or dangerous, pleasurable or not pleasurable. Similarly, children develop positive or negative attitudes toward their own bodies and bodily functions depending on adults' verbal and nonverbal reactions as they help

children with everyday functions such as bathing, dressing, and elimination.

If adults use words such as nasty or dirty to describe genital areas or elimination, children are apt to develop feelings that there is something unacceptable about them. In essence, children learn about sexuality just as they learn about everything else: through words, actions, interactions, and relationships. Some children will express more interest in sexual words, touching genitalia, or in masturbation than do others (Chrisman & Couchenour, 2004).

Masturbation.   Although childhood masturbation is a fairly universal human experience, eliciting major concern in some adults, most children discover their genital areas quite by accident during infancy as they become acquainted with their own bodies through poking into openings and exploring their own extremities. Young children can be seen occasionally rubbing or patting their genitals prior to napping, while adults are reading to them or when watching television. This is usually little more than normal, self-soothing activity. At other times, children seek to derive comfort or enjoy similar sensations by stroking other less provocative body parts such as their noses and ears, twisting locks of their hair, or rubbing pieces of soft material between thumb and finger.

Children between the ages of 3 and 5 years of age often experience growing emotional attachment to the opposite-sexed parent and express residues of these feelings by leaning their bodies against a favored adult, sitting very close, touching, combing or brushing his or her hair, or playing tickling games. At any age, children may engage in masturbation consciously or unconsciously, as a source of comfort when feeling tired, tense, anxious, stressed, bored, or isolated from others; when needing to go to the bathroom; to get attention; or because it simply feels pleasurable. Young boys often unknowingly clutch at their genitals when worried, tired, or excited.

The time to be concerned about masturbatory play or self-manipulation is when it goes on for a large part of the day, when there is infection in the genital area, or when children are being exposed to adult sexual activity, pornography, or sexual abuse. Adults who view masturbatory behavior as abnormal or precocious sexual behavior, and therefore wrong, may actively attempt to discourage such exploration through shaming, threatening, or punishing the child. Instead, what is called for is good observation skills to document the frequency and normalcy of the behavior (Honig, 2000).

Sex play.   By 3 to 5 years of age, children have learned that there is an opposite sex. Most also have discovered that this opposite sex is equipped with different genitalia, which are interesting not only because of their markedly different appearance but also because they are used in a different way for elimination.

Because children are curious beings as well as sexual beings, it should come as no surprise that they may want to explore these differences and that they commonly do so during the course of playing "house," "doctor," and other childhood games. At this stage of development, children show interest in adult heterosexual behavior. Those who are exposed to media depictions of sexuality or real-life encounters occasionally use dolls and other toys to reconstruct remembered acts. If they have witnessed the actual birth of a younger sibling or watched representations of a birth on television, they sometimes extend sex play to act out the birth process.

A potentially serious problem can occur when children sometimes choose to insert objects into each other's genital openings as part of their sex play. Although adults should acknowledge children's curiosity in such situations, they also should explain the harm that can be caused by putting objects into body openings, including other openings such as the eyes, mouth, nose, and ears. Adults should calmly set limits about sex play and redirect inappropriate behavior to another activity.

Children's curiosity about the human body should not be dismissed, and adults can help satisfy children's natural desires to learn more about their bodies and the bodies of others by answering questions in a simple and forthright manner. Some excellent picture books that provide satisfactory answers to many of the questions children pose about sexual differences and where babies come from include Patricia Pearse's *See How You Grow*, Angela Rayston's very simple *Where Do Babies Come From?*, or the more explicit book by Peter Mayle, *Where Did I Come From?* These and others can be suggested for use by parents. Using correct terminology (e.g., penis rather than wee-wee) is also an important part of teaching physiological facts and takes away the aura of secrecy about sexual differences.

Peeping or voyeurism by children.   Often considered in the category of "sexual disturbances," voyeurism usually occurs when children's natural curiosity about sexual differences has been seriously stifled. Some children who do not have opposite sexed siblings (a natural laboratory for learning about sex differences) may use the child care center or school bathroom to satisfy some of their curiosity. For this reason, directors of preprimary centers often purposely choose to leave the doors off toilet stalls.

This can be upsetting for some parents who feel that such practices promote precocious interest in sexuality, although there is evidence to the contrary. Also, young children who have been taught that toileting should take place in absolute privacy may be somewhat stressed. For this reason, at least one stall should have a door.

Peeping and other deviant behaviors also can occur in children who have been sexually abused or chronically over-stimulated sexually by witnessing adult sexual activity. These children may go beyond covert behavior and become more openly aggressive sexually. When such behavior occurs in very young children, it can be shocking to adults, particularly when they view such children as entirely "innocent" and incapable of such thoughts and actions. A child care aide described the experience of having a 4-year-old boy begin unbuttoning her blouse as he sat on her lap listening to a story she was reading. When she asked him to stop what he was doing, he grinned and told her, "I want to see your boobies." She notes: "I was amazed and shaken that this little 4-year-old knew exactly what he was saying and doing. I'm still having a hard time dealing with it, and I find myself avoiding him."

Responding to unexpected behaviors.   Although adults can be thrown temporarily off balance when children unexpectedly display behaviors such as exhibitionism, peeping, public masturbation, homosexual acts, and sexually explicit language, several "rules of response" should be kept in mind. These are summarized in Figure 14-2 and elaborated on later in the skills section of this chapter.

Troublesome Aspects of Children's Psychosexual Development

In addition to behaviors related to normal sexual development and those that appear to be outcomes of sexual disturbances in children, there may be aspects of **psychosexual development in children** that can be problematic for some adults. Perhaps most troublesome is the behavior of the effeminate boy or excessively tomboyish girl. At the other end of the continuum, however, are those children who seem to play extremely stereotypical and rigid sex roles at the expense of developing a wider range of androgynous behaviors—that is, behaviors that are viewed as non-sex-specific. For example,

1. Maintain a calm demeanor when responding to children's sex play.

2. Redirect children's behavior that may be perfectly normal but makes others feel uncomfortable.

3. Express clear expectations for future behavior and reasons why a particular behavior is not appropriate.

4. Investigate when you suspect negative influences on the child that may be taking place in other environments in which the child plays and lives.

5. Use correct vocabulary when referring to body parts.

6. Provide natural opportunities for children to learn more about their sexual development.

Figure 14-2 Responding to unexpected behaviors.

an androgynous male would not see child care as solely a woman's responsibility; similarly, an androgynous female would view learning how to change a tire as beneficial and appropriate rather than as "masculine." Adults who themselves hold more androgynous views and see these as appropriate may be uncomfortable seeing children developing what they feel are narrow psychosexual viewpoints. There is evidence that no matter how carefully parents guard against their children developing traditional male/female stereotypes, 4- and 5-year-old children move in that direction anyway. Their determination seems fueled by gender stereotypes that continue to be promoted on television, in books, and in all of the many contexts in which children develop.

Myths about feminine and masculine psychological differences, such as that girls are more social or "suggestible" than boys, have lower self-esteem, are better at role learning, and are less analytical, have not been substantiated by research. Four gender differences that do appear to hold up under scrutiny are the following (Berk, 2006):

1. Girls have greater verbal ability than boys, particularly beyond the age of 11 years.

2. Boys excel in visual-spatial ability, a finding more consistently present in adolescence and adulthood than in early childhood.

3. Boys excel in mathematical ability, particularly from age 12 on.

4. Males are more aggressive, both physically and verbally; girls are more emotionally sensitive, compliant, and dependent.

In addition, there is evidence that prior to about age 7 or 8, males are behind females in emerging literacy skills and concepts. These differences are manifested later in better reading scores in females, seemingly a world phenomenon (Pfile, Connor, & Livingston, 1999; Soderman, Chikara, Hsiu-Ching, & Kuo, 1999; Soderman, Kauppinen, & Laakkonen, 2000).

The difference in male/female aggressive behavior seems to be the most troublesome to deal with. Adults who do not support such a viewpoint or who are particularly threatened by a lot of vigorous activity may tend to suppress boys' natural vigor rather than providing effective outlets for their energy. The fact that boys are more energetic and often harder to control than their sisters "does not mean that masculinity itself is pathological. What boys need is clear moral guidance and healthy outlets for their natural energy and competitiveness" (Charen, 2000).

One third-grade teacher made wrestling and chasing games off-limit activities on the playground for the boys in her class. No other suggestions were made about what might replace such play, and when two of the boys in the class continued wrestling, she would order them to stand quietly against the building until they could think of something else to do other than "bully one another." Other children in the class who had been more compliant soon began to tease the two boys, who became labeled as the "bullies," with no intervention on the teacher's part. When one of the boys' parents expressed concern over the reputation her son was earning, the teacher countered with the explanation, "If other children can control themselves and find more acceptable outlets for their energy in using the playground equipment provided, so can these boys." This unwillingness or inability of classroom teachers to deal with boisterous behavior has contributed to the overrepresentation of boys in special-education classes for the emotionally impaired and learning disabled. Males consistently outnumber girls in such programs by a ratio of 3:1 and, in some school districts, the ratio is as high as 20:0 (Soderman, Gregory, & McCarty, 2005).

Effects of Parental Absence on Psychosexual Development

Whether children's gender identity is negatively affected by the absence of the same-gendered parent has received serious attention by researchers. Because the majority of children continue to be cared for by their mothers, almost all studies have examined the father's absence. Cross-cultural studies indicate that an early lack of opportunity for young boys to form an identification with their fathers was associated later with a higher frequency of aggression and violence and an almost total rejection of femininity in every form. It was almost as if these so-called masculine characteristics—physical strength, dominance, toughness, aggression—were being worn as badges in an "overboard" attempt to prove their masculine identity. The result is that boys today, who more frequently grow up in the absence of their fathers, may be substituting the traditional masculine attributes with more aggressive attributes such as dominance, toughness, aggression, daring behavior, and even violence (Hoffman, 1995). Conversely, boys who spend considerable time involved with their fathers become significantly more empathic and compassionate adults than those males with little father involvement (Parke & Brett, 1999).

Studies of girls whose fathers had been absent revealed a tendency for these girls to have trouble with later heterosexual behavior, manifested by extreme **shyness** and anxiety about sex, or sexual promiscuousness and inappropriately assertive behavior with male peers and adults. Shyness and anxiety were more likely to be found in girls whose fathers had died, and sexually assertive behavior was found more often in girls whose fathers were absent because of divorce (Cherlin, Kiernan, & Chase-Lansdale, 1995; Hetherington, 1999).

For children whose sexual behavior or gender role identification seems to be on a divergent track, helping professionals must sort out those behaviors that seem to be consistent with normal development and those that are not. When behavior is inappropriate, the child will need understanding as well as supportive intervention. Adults who are unsure about how to evaluate a child's behavior objectively or provide necessary guidance need to consult professionals who have additional expertise in this area.

Although we are living in an era of significant change regarding sexual values and roles, the restructuring of male-female concepts does not call for the abandonment of all current social definitions constituting masculinity and femininity. Helping professionals must, however, be aware of how their own personal convictions may affect their responses to children and their program planning for them.

ETHNIC IDENTITY, PREFERENCES, AND ATTITUDES IN CHILDREN

Just as gender-role development appears to be age and stage specific, so is the development of **ethnicity**, cultural awareness and sensitivity. Sometimes, we are caught off guard by disparaging remarks children may make about a person of differing racial or ethnic origin. Such remarks can be quite innocent in nature, simply reflecting the child's lack of experience and information, or they may be more intentionally hostile, such as when they demonstrate the development of a style of "humor" that debases different races, nationalities, or religions. This type of humor depends on a negative conceptualization of the disparaged group and cannot succeed unless the child has learned to think in terms of "good guys" and "bad guys." There also are conscious slurs that result from a child's developing **ethnocentrism**, the exaggerated preference for one's own group and a concomitant dislike of other groups (Wolpert, 1999).

Because of their own ethnocentrism, professionals may occasionally find themselves fighting feelings of mild dislike or even strong hostility toward children, parents, or colleagues who belong to other racial or ethnic groups. These feelings can also stem from socioeconomic differences. Whatever the source, such feelings affect our interactions, causing patronizing behavior, avoidance, or even aggressiveness.

Polakow (1994) describes a scenario in which three African-American preschoolers were constantly and exclusively singled out as "Mrs. Naly's black (and deviant) troublemakers":

> *Jomo goes over to the piano and sounds a note. Mrs. Naly rushes over. "Can you tell me what that says?" she says, roughly pulling Jomo so that he turns and faces a hand-lettered sign that has a frowning face. "No playing," he says, squirming under her grasp. "Right," she responds and walks back to the art table. Danny and Ryan, who are playing on the floor, tickle Jomo and he falls on top of them laughing. The three boys roll on the*

floor giggling and tickling each other, and Ryan's foot catches a shelf with stacking blocks. The blocks fall on top of the boys, and more giggling ensues as Ryan says, "Quit it man—I'm building," and starts to build a structure on the floor. As the other two follow, Mrs. Naly approaches from the other side of the room. "You three are misbehaving again— you're just going to have to learn to settle down, and until you do, you'll be in trouble with me—no outside time today!" For the third day that week, the three "troublemakers" are kept inside while the other children go out.

Mrs. Naly tells me that none of those three is ready for kindergarten: "They're real problem kids and their families are a mess." (Polakow, p. 125)

Because children's developing self-concept is heavily influenced by the interactions they have with others, including peers and nonfamilial adults, the attitudes others hold about the child's racial group, social class, or religious sect will be critical. As soon as children achieve a basic sense of self as distinct from others (15 to 18 months), they are capable of being shamed and feeling ashamed (York, 2003). As a result, when children perceive they have negative social status, basic feelings of self-worth will suffer.

How we develop racial and ethnic preferences and dislikes has received a great deal of attention since the Supreme Court's desegregation efforts of the 1950s. It is believed that factors that lead to the development of racist attitudes clearly have their origin in early childhood and include elements of direct learning, personality, cognition, perception, communication from the media and the important people in children's lives, and reinforcement of behavior (Bernal & Knight, 1993). As early as 2 or 3 years of age, children begin to notice differences in the way people look and the way they behave. Early positive or negative attitudes tend to increase with age, clearly showing more consensus and reliability at 4 years of age than at 3 and becoming fairly well ingrained in all children by the age of 6 (see Table 14-2).

As children respond to their observations, they receive verbal feedback from others that is both informational and evaluative. For example, Martin became very friendly with Eugene, a light-skinned African-American classmate. When he asked his mother if Eugene could come home to play after school, she responded negatively, saying she preferred that Martin not invite black children home. Martin, later appealing again to his mother, challenged her statement that Eugene was black, noting that he didn't have black skin. "Yes," replied his mother. "But that isn't the only way you can

tell someone is black. He has very broad lips and a black person's hair. He's black, all right. You just play with your own kind." Thereafter, Martin began looking at Eugene and children like Eugene in a different way. A very different scenario is found in the home of Chi Yun, whose parents actively encourage her friendships with children from several ethnic groups. Their goal is that she grow to value people based on shared interests and respect, rather than on family class or birth place.

Usually at about 5 years of age, the child begins to develop an established concept of "us" and "them" related to racial cues. This is a time when children begin to expand their perception of the differences that characterize particular groups. At the same time, intragroup differences become less important. For example, children may focus on the general differences between African-Americans, European-Americans, and different Asian groups in terms of skin color, eye color and shape, hair texture, shape of lips, and other facial characteristics and become less discerning about the wide variations among individuals within these outgroups, helping to build later faulty perceptions that "they all look alike." It is also at this age that a "rejection" stage begins, when children begin to rationalize their feelings and preferences aloud. Children of this age can be very rule bound and rigid in their behavior (York, 2003). As a result, they are likely to choose friends that are alike in gender and race. Verbal aggression increases but can be effectively moderated by engaging 5- and 6-year-olds in discussions about fairness.

It is difficult to gauge the ratio of prejudicial (i.e., preconceived hostile attitudes, opinions, feelings or actions against another person or race) and nonprejudicial experiences a child may have when developing particular racial and ethnic concepts. Unless more opportunities for positive examples are actively provided, children can become victims of a pileup of negative experiences. An African-American educator noted that "many black children spend all day long in environments where they feel they are not valued. But when they get home and back in their own neighborhoods, they know they're accepted, that they're all right." There is evidence that what goes on in the classroom in the relationships between teachers and certain students may either reinforce negative attitudes about minority-group membership or modify them in a positive direction.

Native American children may experience more difficulty. Research indicates that by the age of 10, a third of the children still assert that they are white and evaluate themselves more negatively than do

Table 14-2 Acquisition of Racial Awareness.

AGE	CHARACTERISTICS/BEHAVIORS OF RACIAL AWARENESS
2–3	More aware of others' physical characteristics and cultural behaviors, as different from themselves May be afraid of others who are different in skin color or who exhibit physical disabilities
4	Growing curiosity about how they are like or different from other children Think about and develop reasons for the cultural/physical differences they see Can be confused about what "goes together" ("Why are children called black when their skin isn't black?" "Girls are supposed to have girl names, so how can 'Sam' be a girl?") Beginning to classify people by physical characteristics (gender, color, appearance) Growing interest in cultural difference related to lives of children and adults they know (where they live and work, who is in the family, what language is spoken) Thinking and behavior become more reflective of societal norms, interaction with others, and learned negativity/fears related to differences ("If I play with the child who has a disability, I might catch it too." "Hispanics talk funny.")
5	Deepening awareness of "general, racial, ethnic, and ability differences and similarities" Growing awareness of socioeconomic class, age, aging Heightened awareness of themselves and others as members of a family ("How come Sara doesn't have a daddy?") Continue to think about reasons why people differ from one another Greater absorption and use of stereotypes "to define others and to tease or reject other children"
6	Likely to share family's classification for people but may still be uncertain about why "specific people are put into one category or another" Exercise discrimination against others, based on identities Beginning to understand own emerging group identity and that others have an ethnic and lifestyle identity as well
7–8	Increased interest in others' religions, lifestyles, and traditions Beginning "to appreciate deeper structural aspects of culture" (i.e., human connection to land, influence of the past on current ways of life) "if presented concretely through stories about real people" Growing cognition allows understanding that there are different ways to meet common human needs Increased in-group solidarity May experience tension or conflict with others based on gender, race, ethnic identity, socioeconomic class, as well as biases against certain groups because of disabilities, ethnic, religious, socioeconomic differences

Source: Adapted from Derman-Sparks, 1989, *Anti Bias Curriculum: Tools for Empowering Young Children*. Washington, D.C.: National Association for the Education of Young Children.

other minority cultures. It is thought that the subordinate role of the children's parents in white society, as well as negativity and repressed hostility in the parents, are "caught" by the children, who respond with self-deprecation and passive, apathetic, and ambivalent attitudes toward white people. Because most Native Americans do not believe in a "melting pot" theory, they struggle to remain separate but equal. As a result, their children often experience a conflict of cultures, knowing they must become part of the mainstream in order to be successful; at the same time, however, they must also respect their heritage in the Indian culture to affirm their own identity (Sample, 1993).

There is little research that looks at the effects of "transplanting" single children from one culture to another, as has been the case with many Korean children. Questions must be asked about the timing and effect of interrupting the sequence of development of ethnic identity and racial attitudes in such children, many of whom find themselves members of what ordinarily would constitute an outgroup. Increases in the numbers of adoption cases involving African-American children and their Caucasian adoptive parents raise similar questions.

In summary, the child's development of ethnic and racial identity and outgroup attitudes begins in infancy as soon as the child becomes perceptually aware of physical differences in people. It then proceeds through a sequence in which children label and classify people, develop opinions, and begin to value particular attributes, persons, or lifestyles over others.

Prejudice can be the outcome as the child's attitudes and preferences grow more rigid. However, children can emerge into adolescence and young adulthood free of the limiting and distorted perspectives that ultimately lay the foundation for hurtful social behavior. To do so, they must be challenged appropriately to examine their feelings and attitudes, remain open to new information, and have opportunities to become familiar with a variety of people.

Children form racial concepts through their interactions with peers and adults in the classroom.

INCLUSION OF CHILDREN WITH EXCEPTIONAL NEEDS

Another potentially vulnerable group of children in many educational and child care settings are those who are disabled in one way or another, but not to a degree that would make them ineligible for membership in mainstream society. Although it has been estimated that approximately 10% of all children have exceptional needs, disabilities, and/or developmental delays, it is difficult to determine an exact number. Some **disabling conditions,** such as Down syndrome, cerebral palsy, missing body parts, and severe visual or speech impairments, are easy to spot. Others, such as mild or moderate emotional impairment or learning disabilities, are more difficult to determine. When including children with exceptional needs in the everyday classroom, it is often the latter disabilities—those that are more "invisible"—that are not as readily embraced by other children and adults in the setting.

Because of the remarkable advances in medical technology, greater numbers of children born with disabling conditions are surviving and eventually entering our child care and educational systems, many requiring special services. Although all children have unique needs, children with exceptional needs are those whose well-being, development, and learning would be compromised if particular and expertly designed attention is not provided in the early years. A special focus must be directed toward specifically organized and adjusted environments. Moreover, these children need professionals who are sensitive to their general needs but also highly competent in promoting learning.

A study of teacher candidates' perceptions about inclusion (Aldrich, 2002, p. 172) indicated that they held positive self-perceptions about their beliefs, attitudes, and knowledge related to inclusion of children with disabilities, but that they did not feel trained to implement inclusive practices in the regular classroom. Indeed, one of the first steps in professional preparation to provide for effective inclusion is to be aware of our own stereotypes. Are we inclined to look negatively on those who are overweight, too short, more ragged and dirty than other children, who speak "funny," are timid, physically weak, pimply, or "too" smart? What about our reaction to children who are not yet toilet-trained, those who take longer to catch on to simple information or routines, or who come from "problem" families (Honig, 2004)?

Given the comprehensive services provided today to children with disabling conditions, it is difficult to believe that prior to 1975, many American children with impairments were denied enrollment in public schools. Between 1960 and 1975, various states in the United States had begun to recognize the benefits of providing early intervention and were pushing for federal support. This came in the form of Public Law 94-142, the Education for All Handicapped Children Act (later renamed in 1990 as the Individuals with Disabilities Education Act or IDEA). It provides services for children between the ages of 3 and 21, but focuses largely on children 6 years of age or older. In 1986, Public Law 99-457 was enacted, enlarging the scope of P.L. 99-142 with a downward extension that now ensures services for all children with disabilities, including at-risk infants and toddlers with handicapping conditions and special needs (Part H) and preschoolers in need of services (Part B). Also, in 1990, PL 101-476 added the categories of autism and traumatic brain injuries for the purposes of part B.

Assistance for Education of Children with Disabilities mandates the following:

1. That the state will guarantee a free, appropriate public education to all eligible children with disabilities "including children with disabilities who have been suspended or expelled from school"

2. That the state will ensure that each child with a disability receives an Individualized Education Program (IEP)

3. That state and local education agencies will place children with disabilities in settings that also serve children without disabilities to the extent that such placements do not compromise the right of children with disabilities to receive an appropriate education that meets their unique needs

4. That the state will act to protect the due-process rights of children with disabilities and their parents

5. That the state will take whatever steps are necessary to ensure an adequate supply of special educators and related services personnel

6. That the state will set "performance goals and indicators" for improving special education, particularly in the areas of district wide assessments of academic performance (Bowe, 2007, p. 117)

Developing Individualized Family Service Programs (IFSPs) and Individualized Education Programs (IEPs). Like other families, those who have children with exceptional needs have hopes and aspirations for their children that need to be encouraged and enabled. An **individualized family service program (IFSP)** developed for children from birth to 3 years is meant to do just that. It requires a highly collaborative process between the family and a service coordinator to identify and organize the most effective resources available to support a child's optimal development. If the plan is to

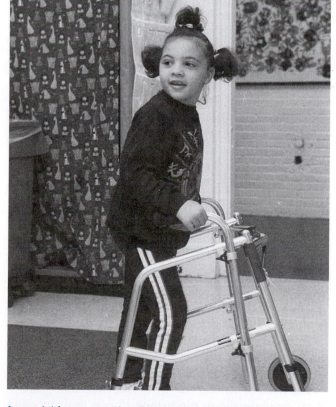

A special focus must be directed toward specifically organized and adjusted environments for children with special needs.

fulfill its promise, it must include a family-directed assessment of the family's resources, priorities, and concerns. At every step in the ongoing process, it must also be respectful of the family's beliefs and values (Cook, Tessier, & Klein, 2004).

Forms for the IFSP differ from state to state and area to area but usually include outcome statements for each of the following:

- family's strengths and preferred resources (e.g., a preference for home-based services versus center-based services)
- family's concerns and priorities
- child's strengths and present levels of development
- IFSP outcomes (e.g., goals the family would like to work on in the next six months that are directly related to their stated priorities and concerns)
- a transition plan to the next set of services
- statement of eligibility
- family permission for implementation of the plan (signatures)
- a list of the IFSP participants

An **individualized education program (IEP)**, a written plan for children older than 3 years of age, broadens the collaboration beyond family members, the service coordinator, and those persons directly providing services to the child. It usually includes a multidisciplinary assessment team to determine the appropriate educational goals and objectives for a child. Usually included are at least one general education teacher (if the process is based on inclusion), at least one special education teacher or provider, any other member of the school staff required to meet the child's unique needs, an individual who can match evaluation outcomes to specific instructional strategies, the school administrator, and other individuals whose expertise is valued by the parent or school, such as a child care provider.

Required contents of an IEP are as follows:

- a statement of the child's present levels of educational performance (based on results of norm-referenced and criterion-referenced tests)
- a statement of annual goals and related benchmarks or short-term behavioral objectives
- a statement of the specific education and related services and supplementary aids to be provided for the child, and a statement of the program modifications or supports for school personnel that will be provided
- an explanation of the extent, if any, that the child will not participate with typically-developing peers in the regular classroom

- the projected dates for initiation of services and the anticipated frequency, location, and duration of services
- the appropriate objective criteria and evaluation procedures
- the schedule for determining whether the short-term instructional objectives are being achieved (each child's program must be reevaluated at least once each year) (Cook et al., 2004).

Categories of Disabling Conditions

A disability is not necessarily a handicap and becomes one only when the child experiences a problem functioning or interacting in the environment because of the impairment. It should be emphasized that children with exceptional needs are individuals with as much variety in ability and personality as typically developing children. Also, because they may have more than one disability, impairment, or compromised health condition, precise diagnosis is often difficult. **Disabling conditions** are categorized in various ways depending on whether the categorizing group is medically, educationally, or legislatively oriented. The major categories that seem most useful to teachers, parents, and child care personnel are **learning disabilities, developmental disabilities, mental retardation, serious emotional disturbance, speech and language disorders**, and **physical or sensory disabilities** (see Table 14-3).

Children with attention-deficit/hyperactivity disorder (ADHD).   ADHD, a neurobehavioral syndrome, is the most common reason for referral of children to pediatricians, educational specialists, and child mental health professionals (Stein, Efron, Shaff, & Glanzman, 2002). Without a doubt, there has been a dramatic and troubling increase in the numbers of young children diagnosed in this category, with over 4 million children being seen in pediatric clinics and almost 2 million taking stimulant medication to control their behavior.

Although ADHD is hypothesized to be a neurological disorder, a specific cause has not been firmly established, and it is not listed as a disability under the IDEA. A biochemical theory suggests that there may be a problem in the reticular activating system of the brain so that neurotransmitters fail to fire unless medication is given to stimulate them. Because it is often seen in parent and child, there is some evidence of a genetic link. Little evidence supports theories that diet is an important factor or that psychogenic or family dynamics cause the disorder.

Table 14-3 Major Categories of Disabling Conditions.

CATEGORY	DESCRIPTION
Learning Disabilities (LD)	Learning disabilities, although difficult to define, are said not to be due to visual, hearing, or physical disabilities, mental retardation, or emotional disturbance. Included conditions relate to brain injury, perceptual-motor impairment, dyslexia (difficulty in reading), or developmental aphasia (impaired ability to use and understand words). This category may include as many as 51% of K-12 students served under IDEA and 5% of all children in our public schools. Increased awareness of the existence of these disabilities, ambiguous definitions, and an inability of regular education to accommodate individual differences account for much of the steady growth in this category.
Developmental Disabilities (DD)	As defined by federal legislation, the category of DD includes the following conditions: Mental retardation, cerebral palsy (CP), epilepsy, or other adverse neurological condition Treatment needed similar to that required for the mentally retarded Evidence of the disability before the age of 18 Expectation that the disability is long term and will continue on indefinitely Children with neurological impairments have specific, identifiable central nervous system disorders or damage. CP, a nonprogressive disorder, usually is characterized by motor or movement dysfunction and some impairment of intellectual and perceptual development. As many as 70 to 80% of children with cerebral palsy experience multiple disabling conditions, including speech and hearing problems and some aberration of motor dysfunction (spasticity, paralysis, muscle weakness, lack of coordination). Epilepsy is characterized primarily by seizures, either the more common and severe grand mal type, or the milder petit mal type, which is characterized by brief staring episodes, eyelid fluttering, or lapses in speech fluency. There may be frequent seizures, severe visual impairment, and/or other disabilities for some children, whereas others are only mildly disabled and able to function without help. Although children who are hyperactive or hyperkinetic often are classified as neurologically impaired, it should be noted that rarely do active children have (central nervous system) CNS disorders or damage.
Mental Retardation	Mental retardation is defined by significantly below-average intellectual functioning (an IQ score of 70 or below, divided into subcategories of moderate, severe, profound) existing concurrently with deficits in adaptive behaviors (developmentally appropriate skills displayed by a child in taking care of his or her own needs and carrying out social responsibilities). These children constitute 11% of IDEA-eligible children, and African-American children are twice as likely as Caucasians to be diagnosed because of poverty and cultural bias.
Serious Emotional Disturbance	Emotionally disturbed (approximately 9% of IDEA-served children) may display frequent or intense temper tantrums, inability to tolerate frustrations, moodiness, and withdrawal, difficulty in making friends, or "school phobia." Severe emotional disturbance also includes the conditions of infantile autism (extreme withdrawal from normal interaction and exhibition of unusual or bizarre behaviors) and childhood schizophrenia (a cluster of psychotic or severely inappropriate or deranged behaviors).
Speech and Language Disorders	This category makes up an additional 22% of children eligible for services under IDEA. Most have a speech disorder involving articulation. Approximately half of the children have language impairments that include problems with comprehension, expression, word-finding, and/or auditory discrimination.

continued

Table 14–3 Major Categories of Disabling Conditions—continued

CATEGORY	DESCRIPTION
Physical or Sensory Disabilities	This category makes up another 7% of eligible children, including those with hearing or visual impairment, orthopedic impairment, or traumatic brain injury. Some children's vision is so limited that it cannot serve as a channel for learning. Although it is rare for a child to be totally blind, an individual is considered legally blind when keenness of vision does not exceed 20/200 in the better eye with correcting lenses. Hearing losses may be present that range from partial to severe. Individuals considered deaf are those whose hearing loss was so severe at birth or during the period of language development that normal language comprehension and expression have not been acquired.

Source: Data from Behrman, R. E. "Special education for students with disabilities: Analysis and Recommendations." *The Future of Children*, 1996, (6) 4–24.

These children are twice as likely to be diagnosed as learning disabled (LD), making them eligible for special education, and others are made eligible for services under Section 504 of the Rehabilitation Act. According to the American Psychiatric Association's Diagnostic and Statistical Manual of Mental Disorders (DSM-IV, 1994), the essential feature of ADHD is a "persistent pattern of inattention and/or hyperactivity-impulsivity that is more frequent and severe than is typically observed in individuals at a comparable level of development." Four criteria for diagnosis are:

- some symptoms must have been present before age 7.
- some impairment must be present in at least two settings (e.g., home/school).
- there must be clear evidence of interference with developmentally appropriate social, academic, or occupational functioning.
- the disturbance does not occur exclusively during the course of other specific disorders.

Symptoms of inattention include difficulty in organizing task and activities, being easily distracted, or inability to sustain attention. To the degree that it is maladaptive and inconsistent with a child's developmental level, symptoms of hyperactivity may include such characteristics as constant "on the go" behavior, extreme restlessness or fidgeting, and talking excessively. Behavior-altering medication is now prescribed for as many as one million children, 3–5% of all young children in the U.S. (U.S. Department of Health and Human Services, 2007). Concern about misdiagnosis of the condition is warranted, as there are a number of medication contraindications including loss of appetite and weight, sleep difficulties, stomachaches, headaches, tics, Tourette's syndrome association, emotional liability and cloudy cognitive ability, height and growth impairments, generalized anxiety, and abuse of the drug.

Overall, in addition to the need for sensitive child care practitioners, a child's future is more positive if hyperactivity and aggression are a minimal part of the condition, if IQ is higher, and if family strengths are well developed. Social skills will be an important and powerful predictor of the child's ability to cope and be successful.

It is important to remember that children continue behaviors that work; they are not motivated to alter strategies if the current behavior is "working" for them in achieving their goals. Such behaviors have a purposeful communication function: "You're asking me to do something that is too difficult. . . . I don't understand what you want. . . . I want a certain thing, and I want it now. . . . I'm bored; pay some attention to me" (Cook et al., 2004).

Children with autism spectrum and Asperger syndrome disorders. The rise in incidence and prevalence of autism has been called "startling," with the Centers for Disease Control and Prevention reporting that autism spectrum disorders occur about five times per 1,000 live births; ten years ago, the figure was one in 2,000 births (Bowe, 2007). Earlier, there was suspicion that growing rates of autism were linked to vaccines given to children, specifically because the vaccines contained thimerosal, which is 50% ethyl mercury, However, mercury has now been removed from the vaccines, and there has been no corresponding decline in the rates of autism (Gurian, 2007). Tragically, we do not currently have an answer, either to the cause of autism or to the apparent increase.

Though the major causative factor is yet to be determined, research points strongly toward a genetic predisposition and neurological disorder. What is known is that it is a complex, severe pervasive developmental disorder that usually becomes apparent between 18 months and 3 years of age. It is manifested in difficulty in social interaction, communication skills, ritualistic/compulsive behavior, and almost always in impaired intellectual functioning. Found more frequently in males, symptoms vary widely from child to child, making it difficult to design an educational approach. In the social realm, red flags include an inability of a child to read nonverbal clues, not responding when called by name, lack of eye contact, inappropriate responses, a lack of play skills, unreasonable fears in new situations, a resistance to change, a preference for isolated play, little recognition of cause/effect, and lack of facial expression. The child may wander off, unaware of being separated from the group, may not develop empathy for others, and may be aggressive and/or destructive toward self and others, and throw unexplained tantrums.

Professionals working with children who exhibit the disorder are more successful when they ease the child into new situations, strategize to capture the child's attention without forcing it, teach and model social and play skills purposefully, redirect swiftly by giving clear verbal signals, and distract the child away from negative behaviors, fixations, and withdrawal from others by encouraging involvement in more acceptable activity.

Children with Asperger syndrome disorder, which is often not diagnosed until about age 6, often share many of the same communication, physical/motor, and social/emotional adaptive behaviors as children with autism. However, with Asperger's, there do not appear to be significant intellectual or language delays. Self-help skills and social development also are more likely to be on target (Paasche, Gorrill & Strom, 2004).

Inclusion

The severity of any of these disabling conditions and the availability of community, school, and family resources will determine whether a child will attend a special school or be included in the social, recreational, and educational activities that other children experience. The purpose of inclusion is twofold: (1) to enhance their social competence so they can later live more comfortably and successfully in the mainstream of society and (2) to promote the acceptance of children with disabilities through reduction

and removal of social stigma. Making this a reality requires a collaborative approach with constructive attention to ensuring access to services, developing and enforcing quality assurance standards, and training personnel and administrators in appropriate strategies for meeting the needs of extremely diverse populations of children (Sexton et al., 1993).

Personnel in public school, child care centers, and other programs for children have made great strides in making these mandated "least restrictive environments" as available as possible to children with a variety of disabling conditions. Architectural barriers and problems with transportation and toilet facilities have dramatically improved despite the expense involved. Formal preparation and in-service education for professionals who work primarily with typically developing children now regularly include information and skill training regarding disabling conditions, strategies for supporting the social integration of children, and techniques for modifying curricula for children with exceptional needs. In-service programs to upgrade professional knowledge and skills are increasingly directed toward enhancing professional competencies in classroom management of children with exceptional needs, screening and evaluation, interpretation of clinical reports, agency referral, and the structuring of IEPs and IFSPs.

The challenges encountered by helping professionals involved in the inclusion of children with disabilities often are similar to those attempting racial integration: successfully melding those who are different from the majority into the mainstream. Some children accomplish this with few problems; others experience increased conflict, isolation, and accompanying loss of self-esteem. Placing a student with exceptional needs into the regular classroom can result in both opportunities and risks for the child who is being integrated. If the process is well monitored and structured by knowledgeable professionals, it can result in the growth of true understanding and friendships between nondisabled children and the child with exceptional needs. If the process is not well structured and monitored, the child may become the victim of inattention, be stereotyped, or be treated in a paternalistic manner—all of which are worse than not including the child in the first place.

When skilled professionals truly value inclusion, there is good evidence that all children in the setting—both with exceptional needs and without—have positive experiences in planning and learning with those who one day will be their coworkers and neighbors.

Children's Perceptions of Disabling Conditions

Social acceptance by other children depends not so much on a child's limitations as on individual characteristics such as independence, friendliness, and other social skills. Successful integration also will depend on the helping professional's ability to structure the environment, paying as much attention to the social dynamics of the integration as to physical facilitation and curricular aspects. As pointed out earlier, young children are keenly aware of differences in other children and react in a variety of ways when they encounter a child who acts, moves, looks, speaks, or thinks differently. Because young children are still learning the "rules" of life, and generalize about the rest of the world from their own experience, they often are strict conformists about what is acceptable and what is not. They tend to explain disabilities in terms of what they already know. Sometimes, their attempts to resolve their own curiosity result in their identifying with the child who has a disabling condition ("When I was a baby, I didn't have any fingers on my hands, either"); creating explanations for a disability (in reference to a 4-year-old classmate who could not walk, "When Cierra grows up, then she'll be able to walk!"); and handling fears about their own intactness by avoiding other children with a disability or making statements such as, "My legs might get broked, too."

Children's Attitudes Toward Peers Who Have Special Needs

Young children who have not learned negative social attitudes toward disabling conditions will not automatically reject a child simply on the basis of a disability. They are open to social models portrayed by adults and more apt to learn positive attitudes toward disability when a positive model is provided through adults' actions, words, nonverbal behaviors, and explanations.

Negative attitudes toward atypical peers exhibited by children aged 5 and older often exist before these children have experiences with mainstreaming. These are natural responses to first impressions and to the labeling process that fosters stigmatization. Acceptance results from mutual interaction and experiences where: (1) children have to depend on one another for assistance; (2) feelings of psychological safety are present and rejection and threat are absent; (3) differences are seen realistically and

accepted as natural and okay; and (4) perceptions about working and playing with one another in the setting—no matter what the existing differences—are upbeat and generally rewarding rather than distasteful and unpleasant.

An actual observation of the process of peer acceptance over a period of time was made by a researcher when Chris, a preschooler with a moderate-to-severe hearing loss, was being mainstreamed into a university preschool setting. To date, he had not been well accepted by the other children. Because he chanced to begin a spontaneous play episode that caught the interest of some of the children, he eventually "earned" his way into the group:

> *March 2. Chris spots a purple cape hanging in the dramatic play area. He puts it on and begins pretending he is a vampire, moving about the room flapping his wings and "scaring" other children. He draws the attention of several other children who decide they, too, want capes so they can be vampires.*

"Vampire play" grew in popularity for several days afterward. The head teacher allowed the children to wear the capes about the room instead of confining their play to the dramatic-play corner, which usually was encouraged.

> *March 7. Cameron takes Chris up to a student teacher, telling her, "I have a whole team of vampires. He's (pointing to Chris) on my team." Cameron then "attacks" a helping adult standing nearby. Chris copies him. Cameron spreads his "wings" over Chris, catching him and saying, "Gotcha, little vampire." He takes him to a locker and puts him inside roughly. Chris tries to "break out." Cameron indicates the other children to Chris and says, "Let's suck their blood." They are joined by David. Cameron catches Chris again, saying to David, "I caught the little bat; I caught the little vampire!" He then lets Chris go, saying to Chris and David, "C'mon, team. We're a whole team."*

Chris is definitely a member of the team now and, thus, is on his way to becoming an integrated, mainstreamed member of the class. Should the head teacher have insisted that the play be maintained in the dramatic-play area or asked the boys to play something else "nicer" than vampire play, the moment may have been lost. The fragile nature of the process, chance happenings, and sensitivity on the part of the supervising adults can be seen in a subsequent observation and example of expectations for reworking future interaction with classmates:

> *March 8. Chris has his "bat cape" on again. It is precious to him, and he searches for it as soon as he enters the room. It has been his key to getting into the group. When he attempts to climb on some larger equipment with it, a student teacher asks him to remove the cape because of safety. He declines to play on the equipment, rather than give up the cape. The student teacher is aware of the cape's importance and does not push the issue. If Chris takes the cape back to the dramatic-play corner while he climbs, someone else may take it, and he will have lost his key.*

Guidelines for Integrating Children with Disabling Conditions into Formal Group Settings

The quality of the integrative process will differ significantly depending on the extent to which professionals make the additional effort needed to go beyond the mere maintenance of students with exceptional needs in the nonspecialized setting.

The skills every teacher must master in dealing with common variations among typically developing children are needed even more when dealing with those who have exceptional needs. Each situation may be so different that it will call for the professional to educate himself/herself on the disability, perhaps seeking advice from a consultant teacher. However, there are some very general considerations for supporting commonly experienced disabilities, as can be seen in Figure 14-3. There is no set formula for successful inclusion. What is clear is that it must be made a priority by the administrators, parents, and professionals who are involved.

Other Differences

Advanced and precocious children. Over the years, Harvard psychologist Howard Gardner has made us more sensitive to children's multilearning capabilities and the fact that some children will be more highly developed than others in any one of the eight multiple intelligences described in Chapter 1. Such individuals may be termed **precocious children.** These individual differences may result in noticeable limitations, average abilities, or advanced development because of a rich variety of educational and family experiences, precocious development, or "gifted and talented" characteristics.

Teachers may need to consult with other professionals about particular disabilities or special needs.

Orthopedic Impairments and Developmental Disabilities

The pace of classroom activity may need to be adjusted.

Position children so they can feel as secure, comfortable, and involved as possible in activities and routines.

Make space adjustments as necessary to address safety issues and facilitate freedom of movement.

Support, encourage, and facilitate interactions with materials and equipment while accepting levels of interaction that are appropriate for each individual.

Protect children who are not mobile or cannot speak from loud noises and other sensory discomforts.

Adapt materials, toys, and utensils for easier use (e.g., nonskid materials, larger handles, Velcro or magnetic blocks).

Visual Impairments

Minimize clutter.

Familiarize the child with the environment.

Help the child use auditory or tactile clues to increase independence.

Support, encourage, and facilitate interactions with peers.

Place materials within reach and increase cues such as texture, smell, and high contrast to make toys and objects more identifiable.

Hearing Impairments

Use multisensory cues (tactile, visual, good lighting, picture cues) and optimal positioning of materials for sight.

Check hearing aids and batteries daily.

Capitalize on residual auditory abilities (e.g., use a bell).

Use simple sign language with all children in the room.

Emotional/Behavioral Challenges

Teach clear, consistent, predictable limits.

Make explanations brief and direct.

Model behaviors you want to establish.

Provide "retreat" spaces.

Provide very concrete cues for transitions.

Build children's vocabularies to express feelings.

Observe interactions and behaviors closely to prevent provocations.

Reduce noise and movement as necessary and be aware of individual stimulation thresholds.

Children's Strengths

Support successes by giving approval without distracting the child from a task.

Break tasks into smaller steps and scaffold learning.

Provide for open-ended play and exploration but be ready to model, stimulate, and encourage.

Support child–child interaction and facilitate child–object involvement.

Allow for extra time to complete tasks and for practice.

Encourage children to stay engaged while working toward mastery of a task.

Figure 14-3 Supporting commonly experienced disabilities.

Source: Based on Gonzales-Mena, 2004, pp. 110–113.

Giftedness has been defined as the ability to solve the most complex problems in effective, efficient, elegant, and economical ways (Maker & Nielson, 1996). Adults can use the following guidelines when trying to assess whether a child is truly gifted, talented, or has some kind of outstanding potential (Gage & Berliner, 1998):

- talent in performing or creating
- a wide variety of interests and information

- ability to concentrate on a problem, task, or activity for long periods
- ability to engage in abstract thinking and to construct relationships between problems and solutions
- independent thinking characterized by creative ideas
- extensive curiosity
- early reading ability
- use of a large vocabulary
- rapid learning of basic skills

Not all children who seem advanced are truly gifted or talented, but practitioners must be alert for children who demonstrate the above characteristics. Because young children are in the process of developing their abilities and capabilities in many areas, there is a real danger that children may be tagged as either "slow" or "advanced" when time and further observation of their development may prove the diagnosis is untrue (McAfee & Leong, 2007). In addition, cognitive "gifts" in one area may occasionally come at the cost of proficiency in other developmental areas. Some of the world's brightest and most talented individuals, including Albert Einstein, Thomas Edison, Lewis Carroll, Winston Churchill, and William Butler Yeats, were, in fact, thought to be seriously "learning disabled" in their early years. None of these individuals' strong interests and needs as children were recognized; instead, they were overlooked by adults who equated intellectual prowess, giftedness, and talent with conformity, neatness, good behavior, rapid learning, and early maturation (West, 1998).

When children appear truly advanced in one area, there is always the temptation to believe they are generally advanced in all areas, and this may not be so. Children who are large for their age, have well-developed vocabularies, or who are more cognitively sophisticated than their peers are sometimes expected by adults to excel in all areas and are reprimanded when they fall short.

Rather than placing advanced and precocious children in specialized settings, heterogeneous grouping that allows for diverse abilities and variety in developmental growth patterns, cultures, languages, temperaments, and individual needs is the strongest model for nurturing human development (Maker & King, 1996). The best approach for supporting the potential of any child with special needs, whether delayed or advanced, is to pair that child with a professional who is highly knowledgeable about child development and skill emergence in young children, and also well trained in developing effective programming for a range of abilities in a group of young children. Best practice—whether for children with special needs, average abilities, or advanced capabilities—involves providing engaging, interdisciplinary experiences in all areas of developing intelligences and respecting the experiential and developmental differences children bring with them into any context.

Excessively shy children.   Almost all children will exhibit shyness at some point in their lives. About 20% of children are inherently shy, however, and another 20% develop shyness because of situational happenings in family life such as a divorce or a move. Thus, it is a personality style shared by a sizeable number, ranging on a spectrum from only moderately shy to severely shy (Swallow, 2000). Children who have this personality style are fairly easy to spot. They may avoid eye contact in order to reduce the tension they feel in being around others who are unfamiliar. They may hide or cry when encountering a new situation or act as if the situation does not even exist—or occasionally explode into an unpredictable temper tantrum to release their anxiety. Though normally talkative around family and friends with whom they are comfortable, they can "shut down" almost completely in less familiar contexts, refusing to speak or answering only in monosyllables to questions from others. Shy children may go without what they need or want, rather than summon up the courage to make a simple request. They experience a variety of uncomfortable responses when they feel they are "onstage"—flushing of their skin, dry mouth, stomachaches, and stage fright that may be so severe that it interferes with their ability to demonstrate their true abilities.

Shy children may also be hypersensitive to even the smallest slights from others, whether imagined or real; while they would like to escape from others in social situations, they also long to be as well liked and socially competent as other children. Unfortunately, their tendency to misinterpret social signals from others often leads to feelings of being left out, incorrect perspectives about how others view them, and eventually true shunning by other children.

Although it may be impossible to eliminate shyness altogether in such children, it is useful to help them become more aware of the connections between self-talk and their emotional responses. Self-talk is the constant "background talk" that goes on in the brain in any particular situation, and it can range from highly negative to highly positive. Shy children and adults tend to bombard themselves with negative self-talk in negotiating stressful events. When we experience any kind of perceived threat or demand, within milliseconds we automatically connect it to our perceived resources to handle it. Thus, the child who has to give a report in front of his classmates and realizes he is anxious and inhibited about it can be taught to recognize when negative self-talk is taking over ("I can't do this because I'll forget what I'm saying and everyone will laugh at me!"), setting up increased anxiety and diminishing his self-confidence in the situation.

Learning to imagine or pretend and practice thinking about successful outcomes rather than dwelling on the worst possible scenario are also helpful. Shy children can be given helpful scripts that can get them through the initial stages of situations that are particularly stressful for them—entering an

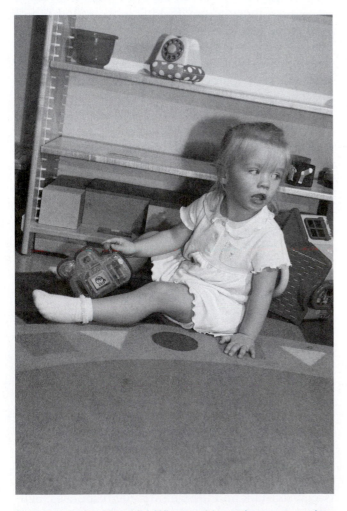

Selena is a very shy child. What could you do to support her social competence?

ongoing playgroup, meeting new people, and asking for what they need. It is also important to debrief about situations that were particularly difficult for them, to focus on any successes they had, and to plan for ways they can restructure similar experiences in the future in order to be more comfortable, thereby increasing their self-confidence and social competence (Swallow, 2000).

Temperament and individuality. As children become increasingly aware of ways in which they differ from others, they begin to evaluate the meanings of these differences through a value-plus and value-deficit lens. Evolving self-identity depends a great deal on self-esteem. This, in turn, results from clues received from others in response to their behavior and developing abilities.

Children who are perceived by others to be difficult or less socially competent often have temperamental characteristics that place them at extreme ends of a normal continuum of behavior responses. They appear predisposed to be more negative in mood, more impulsive or unpredictable, and given to more intense reactions when under stress. They may also have a tendency to withdraw when confronted with unfamiliar people, activities, or stimuli. These unique characteristics, which begin as inherited traits, may be somewhat modified over time in a more positive direction or become established behavioral patterns that place such children in a special-needs category. The outcome will depend on the particular combination of difficult traits and how long an established pattern has existed. Turecki (2000) describes Adam, a very difficult child:

When Adam Johnson was born, his mother Marjorie anticipated an experience similar to that of raising his brother, Jeremy. . . . She had some trouble feeding Adam during the hospital stay; later, at home, he didn't get onto a schedule as easily as Jeremy had. He always seemed fretful when he was with her, and he would fall into short catnaps from which he would awaken easily with a start, accompanied by loud cries. He seemed louder than Jeremy, but his mother felt this was because she was used to a quieter, older child (Jeremy was 3). Adam's father, Stephen, was proud of his new son and called this behavior "feisty" and "tough," predicting that Adam would be "a little pisser." Neither parent could have anticipated what was to happen to Adam and to their family. Adam

Johnson's problems with eating, sleeping, and crying were only the beginning. His fretful, cranky, erratic behavior continued to increase. . . . Marjorie felt inadequate and helpless as her mother questioned her closely and told her she was doing things wrong. Her mother had been overly involved with her raising of Jeremy as well, but the advice hadn't bothered Marjorie as much since he had been a "good baby." Now she felt her mother was right; she was doing something wrong. She was a "bad mother," or at least "not as good a mother as my own was."

By the time Adam was 3, life in the Johnson home revolved around him. He was often wild and never seemed to listen. Repeated power struggles would usually end in tantrums. He slept a great deal or very little, without any predictable pattern. He could not be easily fed, for it was hard to get him to sit still at the table and even harder to find foods he liked. He refused to wear any clothes he called "itchy," which included anything new, and he liked to sleep in what he was wearing. He never wore pajamas. He never sat still to play with games or puzzles, but only to watch MTV with its flashy, loud rock videos running continuously. His father hated this and tried to get Adam interested in watching sports. But Adam had no patience for baseball and would scream for MTV until his father, in disgust, changed the channel. . .

The constant battles were taking their toll on Adam as well as his family. Adam was becoming fearful at night and clinging more to his mother. In nursery school he was somewhat calmer but certainly a handful. On the positive side, Adam, when not angry or upset, seemed to have a cheerful disposition. And his father enjoyed roughhousing with him and was proud of Adam's "toughness." His mother liked his "creativity." He loved drawing colorful pictures of flowers and cars. On an ordinary day in the life of the Johnson family, Adam was always at center stage, and his parents, brother, grandparents, friends, schoolmates, and teachers were all supporting players. It sometimes seemed to his mother that the world revolved around her difficult child and his bad behavior, and in a sense it did—for everyone reacted to his actions, which were often negative and which left a string of negative reactions in their wake. (Turecki, 2000, pp. 86–90)

Children who have difficult temperaments have greater potential to be classified as having ADHD, due to their more extreme responses. Some scientists question the desirability of labeling children "difficult." They maintain that such identification may not be valid; it can, in fact, be damaging, given a caregiver's resulting expectations for such children. Reality reminds us, however, that although serious issues continue to surround valid assessment of difficult temperament, there is no question that certain children are more difficult to deal with than others. Whether their difficulties are a reflection of their own constitutional characteristics, disturbed caregiver–child interactions, or other environmental stressors, the fact remains that difficult traits do appear early in some young children. Equally important is our knowledge that difficult behavior may be modified or intensified by life experiences. The child, as an active agent in his or her own socialization, plays an important part in flavoring those experiences.

Important "others" in a child's life also play ongoing roles in the dynamic unfolding of his or her individual personality. This concept of mutual influence is important. When children are difficult to handle, less confident caregivers often develop self-doubts, feelings of guilt, and anxiety over what the future holds for the child and their relationship with the child. Unless difficult behaviors, or caregivers' perceptions of those behaviors, can be satisfactorily modified, a sense of helplessness often begins to pervade all interactions with the child. Dreams of being a competent parent or teacher may yield to the hard reality that the child is unhappy, out of control, and moving in a negative direction developmentally. Attitudes toward the difficult behavior may move swiftly from early amusement or pride over a child's "assertiveness" to disapproval and even rejection by the adult.

Adult responses, in turn, have a marked effect on whether additional stress will be imposed on the child or whether the child will be guided successfully toward developing more positive coping behaviors. Positive, respectful interaction, which builds resiliency and inner strength in all children, is absolutely essential for children who have difficulty with adaptive interaction. Caregivers who acknowledge that diverse temperament patterns do exist but who persist in encouraging healthier behaviors in a sensitive and supportive way bolster children's protective factors that enhance their development. They help children understand cause and effect, become better problem solvers, and view themselves and others in a more positive light (Gonzales-Mena & Eyer, 2007).

SKILLS FOR SUPPORTING CHILDREN'S DEVELOPMENT RELATED TO SEXUALITY, ETHNICITY, AND EXCEPTIONAL NEEDS

 Adapting Skills to Support Children's Development

1. Become acquainted with persons of varying cultural, religious, racial, and developmental backgrounds. Participate in community, social, or cultural events that represent different groups and find ways to become personally acquainted with at least one family of each racial and cultural group in your community. Go beyond seeking information only related to foods and holidays. Find out as much as possible about subtle social conventions that sometimes cause irritation when not understood: concepts of family, time, nature, gender roles, aesthetics, ecology, dress, and safety (Trawick-Smith, 2005). Take advantage of opportunities to broaden your familiarity with other groups through ethnic festivals, community-awareness programs involving those with disabilities, or open events sponsored by religious groups other than your own. In addition, seek out establishments in your area, such as stores and restaurants, that offer artifacts and food representative of particular cultures. Look for organizations and institutions in your community that focus on international programs. Visit a medical supply store that caters to the disabled and examine the different equipment that some individuals use to function more effectively. Finally, volunteer in programs in which you are likely to interact with people who are different from yourself. Use these experiences to broaden your understanding.

2. Evaluate your own responses to the individual differences described in this chapter. Explore your own background and culture. Relate your differences to those of other groups in order to better understand and value similarities and differences. Pay careful attention to your nonverbal behaviors as well. If you find yourself drawing away, making a face, or avoiding eye contact with a child who falls into any of the categories discussed or to one who brings up sensitive subjects, stop. Remember that in your professional role, you are obligated to treat all children with respect and sensitivity.

Watch out for any tendency on your part to blame whole groups of people for what individuals do, and demand proof when you hear children repeat rumors that reflect on any group; do not tell stories, however funny, that reflect on any group, and do not laugh when others tell them. Show disapproval when others use hateful terms that slur any group. In addition, monitor your verbal responses, making sure you do not dismiss or deny children's feelings and verbal expressions of these feelings. It may also be useful to discuss situations that are difficult for you with a colleague or classmate as a way to clarify your own attitudes as well as to elicit further suggestions.

3. Build a positive social climate in which both similarities and differences are valued. Emphasize that each person has something valuable and unique to contribute to the group. Take advantage of the many children's books about individual differences as well as puppet play, films, videotapes, and filmstrips to promote growth in the understanding of others. Utilize resource people from the community, including those with varying racial and ethnic origins and disabling conditions. Take advantage of video technology to allow children to visit other countries and explore differing lifestyles without leaving the classroom (Winter, 1995).

Foster positive attitudes and attitude changes in school-age children through role-playing and disability simulations. For example, wheelchairs can be borrowed from equipment companies to allow students to understand the difficulty involved in maneuvering a wheelchair. Glasses can be made with layers of yellow cellophane to simulate visual impairment. In addition to focusing on the religious, racial and ethnic, and developmental differences that can be found in others, it is necessary also to discuss similarities between

SKILLS FOR SUPPORTING CHILDREN'S DEVELOPMENT RELATED TO SEXUALITY, ETHNICITY, AND EXCEPTIONAL NEEDS

people. We all need friends, we all have similar emotions, and all people have both positive and negative qualities.

4. Build a cooperative rather than competitive spirit within the group. Encourage children to rely on one another and to seek each other's help in solving problems rather than depending on the adults in the setting. Use small, heterogeneous groups to foster the development of acceptance, rapport, and mutual understanding among children of different racial, ethnic, and developmental backgrounds. Structure activities in which children have opportunities to establish eye contact, talk with one another, and develop common goals. Provide needed support to guide these groups toward success.

Purposely plan activities that will highlight, at one time or another, the skills of all children in the program. For example, one paraprofessional had a student who was visually impaired demonstrate her ability to get around the room and explain the kinds of cues in the room on which she relied for help. Students then were blindfolded and, with the help of another student to keep them safe, tried their luck at negotiating the same path, relying not on their sight but on the cues their classmates had identified.

5. Address children's stereotypical remarks directly and in a nonjudgmental manner. When children make stereotypical remarks such as, "Only boys can be doctors," help them develop more accurate understandings by using the following strategies:

- Challenge children by using open-ended questions. ("Why do you think only boys can be doctors?")
- Provide accurate information in matter-of-fact ways. ("Some doctors are men; some doctors are women.")
- Point out examples to counter children's mistaken ideas. ("Daniel said his doctor is a woman." or "Here is a picture of a woman doctor.")

- Talk over children's ideas in class meetings. ("Jimmy thinks only boys can be doctors. What do you think?")
- Use props that counter stereotypes (e.g., puzzles, pictures, books, and dress-up clothes for both genders).
- Follow up with field trips or visitors. (Visit a female doctor's office or have a female doctor visit the classroom.)

6. Respond thoughtfully to children's questions about sexuality, ethnicity, disabling conditions, and other differences. Listen carefully to determine what it is they really want to know. Clarify the question by reflecting before answering. For example, if a child asks the question "Is Timmy still a baby?" about a 7-year-old who cannot walk, you would want to clarify with, "You mean, 'How come Timmy can't walk yet?'" After determining the child's purpose, answer the question at a level he or she can understand. Often, in an effort to be comprehensive, adults give children more information than they need or can manage. Give short, precise, clear answers in language that the child understands. Use simple phrases and familiar analogies. Then, check to see what the child thinks you have said by asking him or her to paraphrase your answer. "Tell me in your own words why Sandy talks the way she does." Work from there to expand the child's understanding, if necessary. Do not give more information than children ask for; allow them time to assimilate what already has been said.

Reassure children when they seem to be overly concerned. Watch for evidence that the child is more comfortable once he or she has been given an explanation. You may have to answer the same question several times for very young or overly fearful children. When questions about another child's physical, ethnic, or developmental differences are repeatedly asked in that child's presence, redirect the curious child to discuss the issue with you privately.

continued

SKILLS FOR SUPPORTING CHILDREN'S DEVELOPMENT RELATED TO SEXUALITY, ETHNICITY, AND EXCEPTIONAL NEEDS—continued

7. Use correct vocabulary when referring to body parts, cultural groups, or disabling conditions. Words like vagina, penis, and breast describe specific parts of the body, which should be as accurately labeled as other body parts. To do otherwise demeans the body and teaches children that genital organs are not natural but are things to be ashamed of. Likewise, certain cultural groups prefer to be called by a particular name. For instance, some people prefer to be known as Black Americans, others as African-Americans or people of color; some as Indians, some as Native Americans; and some prefer the term Latino whereas others favor Hispanic or Mexican-American. If you are not sure about the preferences of the families in your group, find out. Similarly, describe a child as having a hearing impairment rather than saying that her ears are broken. In each of these situations, it is better to be truthful and precise when speaking with children than to try to sidestep the sensitive arenas through euphemisms or inaccurate terminology.

8. React calmly to children's sex play. Reflect children's interest in their own bodies and the bodies of others. Give them information that will satisfy their curiosity, such as the names of their body parts and how they function. Set limits on behavior that is inappropriate or dangerous, such as fondling another child's genitalia, masturbating in public, or putting something in a child's vagina or anus. For instance, if in the course of playing doctor, a child tries to take the rectal temperature of a classmate by poking him with a pipe cleaner under his pants, step in immediately. Reflect, "You're pretending to be a doctor," and continue with a personal message: "I'm worried that you will hurt him with the pipe cleaner. It is important not to put objects inside of someone's body. You can pretend to take his temperature like this." (Demonstrate an appropriate alternative.)

9. Provide natural opportunities for children to learn more about their sexual development. For very young children, the bathroom at the preschool or child care center is an ideal place to ask questions, observe similarities and differences, and learn that body parts and body functions do not have to be hidden behind closed doors. Allow preschoolers to use the bathroom in one another's presence if they wish. Also, provide dolls with anatomically correct genitalia for them to play with. With parents' permission, use books to communicate information to older children. Act as a resource for answering their questions honestly and clearing up misunderstandings.

10. In your day-to-day treatment of children, be as gender fair as possible and actively nurture "opposite gender" characteristics to encourage full human development—gentleness, nurturance, cooperation, communication in males and courage, competence, and independence in females. Be aware of and avoid adult tendencies that have been documented—that is, tendencies to interrupt girls more frequently when they are speaking and/or providing boys with more help, attention, information, and encouragement to solve problems. To encourage a wide range of development in both boys and girls, present important concepts in many diverse ways and repeatedly. Encourage visual-spatial activity and logicomathematical experiences in early childhood for girls (mazes, maps, blocks, geo-boards, and more practice in noting likenesses and differences). These may be helpful in shoring up abilities that are often needed later in fields where few women excel (Schlank & Metzger, 1997). Similarly, boys may benefit from more active involvement in language activities and experiences, as well as help in stress and conflict management, intrapersonal, and interpersonal skill building.

11. Remain alert for valuable learning experiences that may be created spontaneously by the children. Be flexible enough to let them progress without interruption. At times, children's interactions with materials and with one another capture their interest to such an extent that our own best-laid curricular

SKILLS FOR SUPPORTING CHILDREN'S DEVELOPMENT RELATED TO SEXUALITY, ETHNICITY, AND EXCEPTIONAL NEEDS

plans are usurped. When this happens, assess whether allowing children to deviate from intended activities will allow other learning or needed social adaptations to occur. Sometimes, as illustrated by the following example, a spontaneous event can be far more valuable than the planned one:

A student teacher commented to her head teacher that although the children were not very socially accepting of a young classmate with a hearing impairment, they certainly were curious about the hearing aid she wore. In response, the head teacher suggested that the student prepare a "lesson" for the children to teach them how a hearing aid worked.

Subsequently, the student teacher set up on one of the tables a display of vibrating objects, including a tuning fork and xylophone, which she invited the children to examine. While she was working with some of the children and the tuning fork, the child with the hearing impairment began looking at the xylophone, which also was a wheeled toy that could be pulled with a string. Instead of using the striking mallet on the toy, the child put the xylophone on the floor and began pulling it across the room, marching as she went. Several nonhandicapped children fell in line after her, marching and singing, "Down by the station, early in the morning . . ." The children who had been observing the tuning fork activity also fell in line, leaving the student teacher and her carefully constructed display of vibrating objects in favor of the march.

Later, at a follow-up session in which the teachers were discussing the success of the lesson, the student teacher explained that the display had been somewhat dismantled with the loss of the xylophone and departure of her "audience" but that she felt the children had more to gain by joining the march. When asked to elaborate on the reasons why, the student noted that the social interaction of the child with a disability with her nondisabled peers, although a primary objective in the inclusion of the child, had not been going well. "I just thought it was a great opportunity to let the children take care of something

that's had me stumped." Much to the student's relief, her head teacher congratulated her on her rationale and her ability to capture the "teachable moment."

12. Help children develop pride in their own cultural heritage and appreciation for our diverse heritage as a society. Pronounce a child's name as his or her family pronounces it rather than anglicizing it. Honor differences in language and traditions. Serve foods that are familiar to the children's particular backgrounds, asking for suggestions and recipes. Allow children to bring in articles that are used in family celebrations and to explain to the group how they are used. Include dress-up clothes from a variety of cultures. As a part of the daily routine, sing songs, tell stories, play games, and engage in other activities that relate to the cultures represented by the children and staff in your group. If your group is homogeneous, introduce other customs anyway. It may be best to begin with groups that can be found in the wider community rather than cultures with whom children are unlikely to interact. It is better to integrate such activities into the ongoing curriculum rather than to occasionally have a "Mexico Day" or "Black American Week." The latter approach sensationalizes and makes artificial what, to the culture itself, is just a natural part of living.

13. If children reject other children because of their gender, ethnicity, or special needs, deal with the situation calmly, using one or more of the following strategies:

Reflect the victim's feelings: "You look really upset, Jerome. It hurt your feelings when Samuel called you a name."
Express empathy: "Jerome, I know it hurts when people call us names."
Protest: "Samuel, I don't like it when you call Jerome 'four-eyes.' That hurts his feelings."
Give accurate information: "Jerome is wearing glasses to help him see better."

continued

Describe alternate strategies for expressing feelings: "You were upset because Jerome bumped into what you were building. It's hard to remember what to say when you're angry.

> Say, 'I'm angry' instead of calling Jerome the name 'four-eyes.'"

> Describe the behavior you expect: "In our room, we are respectful toward one another. You may tell other people how you feel about something they've done, but you may not call one another hurtful names."

14. Utilize rules and consequences to let children know that purposeful slurs and unkind references to particular children or groups will not be tolerated. If youngsters seem to be using terms such as "homo," "wop," or "honky" without knowing what they mean, provide pertinent rationales for why such behavior is unacceptable to you. When children deliberately use such tactics to wound the self-esteem of another, they are engaging in hostile aggression. This should be stopped with a personal message, warning, and follow-through as necessary, carried out in a calm, matter-of-fact, and firm tone.

15. Monitor all teaching materials and activities for racial, cultural, gender-role, religious, and developmental stereotypes. Continuously watch for ways in which the curriculum may influence children's perceptions of their own or others' roles and abilities. Encourage them to participate in a wide range of enriching activities on the basis of their interests and skills rather than on outmoded ideas.

16. Assess your classroom environment for anti-bias and culturally relevant materials. Ask yourself:

- What groups are represented by pictures and photographs displayed (e.g., race, culture, gender, family structures, lifestyles, age, physical disabilities)? Is any one dominant? Do they represent real or stereotyped

individuals? Are they contemporary or historical?
- What genders and cultures are included in music activities, displayed artwork (prints, sculpture, textiles, artifacts), dress-up area, and reading corner?

Make adjustments to provide more balance and broader representation as appropriate.

17. Interview family members to explore their culture, asking about special days and family celebrations. Ask how they guide behavior and recognize special achievement or rites of passage. Plan whole-family events such as potluck dinners and activities that are fun for all ages. Take pictures and display them where children and their parents can look at them together. Honor or highlight each family individually in your newsletter, providing them with an opportunity to share a favorite family story with others in the program.

18. Respond professionally and compassionately to children who are challenging (Stephens, 1996, p. 47) and children with disabling conditions (Graves, Gargiulo, & Sluder, 1996, p. 427):

- Maintain a predictable daily schedule. Privately warn children of changes in routine, as problems are most likely to occur during transitions. Rehearse any changes that can be anticipated (e.g., role-play procedures that will be followed for a field trip). Adjust the schedule of the day to accommodate the specific differences in your group of children.
- Give children simple, step-by-step directions when guiding them through activities or routines. Allow ample time for completing tasks and be patient.
- Establish a minimum of classroom rules that set limits and clearly define expectations in a positive fashion (usually focused on health and safety). Involve children in structuring these rules.
- Because some children become overwhelmed when given too many choices,

SKILLS FOR SUPPORTING CHILDREN'S DEVELOPMENT RELATED TO SEXUALITY, ETHNICITY, AND EXCEPTIONAL NEEDS

limit the number of activities offered at one time. Work in small groups as much as possible. Make a concerted effort to keep the classroom from being overly stimulating. Rotate toys and materials, leave more white space on the walls, and keep noise and voice levels steady. If children begin losing control, provide more structure by offering fewer choices and more specific directions to follow.

- Make sure all activities are developmentally appropriate. Remember that successful experiences with hands-on materials are especially important. Use activities and materials relevant to the child's life experiences. Incorporate multisensory approaches to learning and include movement activities whenever possible.

- Document problematic behaviors in a daily log. Analyze log entries. Can you identify what triggers antisocial behavior such as hitting, kicking, or having tantrums? Can the classroom be further modified to eliminate or reduce the triggers?

- Create quiet, secluded corners so that children can remove themselves when necessary from the over-stimulation of group interaction. Provide access to less distracting areas of the classroom when children are expected to complete tasks requiring close attending skills.

- Coach children toward self-control. Every child can be impulsive, but especially high-spirited children. Teaching them self-discipline is imperative. Helping them master language for expression of feelings and desires will help them gain positive social skills. Apply positive discipline techniques consistently and provide numerous instances of positive reinforcement.

- Remember that establishing good rapport with children before implementing consequences is critical. Forms of positive attention, such as genuine praise, a smile, nod, or pat on the back are some of the most basic but powerful management tools.

- Involve parents; encourage them to be partners in their child's experience. Hold frequent conferences to coordinate classroom practices with home practices. Keep family members fully informed.

- Make and maintain connections to special education personnel when a child's behaviors impact negatively on classroom performance.

- When working with children diagnosed with ADHD, deliver rules and instructions in a clear, brief, and highly visible way (e.g., display on wall; have a child repeat out loud when following through). Provide consequences for negative behavior consistently and swiftly, as delays reduce or degrade efficiency.

- Teach to the child, not the disability label; instructional strategies appropriate for typical children are usually effective (with some modification) for children with exceptional needs.

- When you become overwhelmed and drained, seek the counsel of a supportive friend or coworker. Find someone you trust who will just listen and can give you the release you need to face the next day with an optimistic attitude.

 Communicating with Families About Children's Individual Differences

1. Actively listen to family members to discover their agenda and wishes concerning their child's experience in the program. For example, an African-American mother was concerned that there were no other minority children in the program. A father expressed worry about his young son's gender orientation because of the amount of time the child spent dressing up in feminine clothing in the pretend play area. Parents of a bright 4-year-old asked what you were doing to

continued

teach her how to read. Be clear about the parent's thoughts and feelings. Explore what they believe your responsibility is in relation to their concerns.

2. Respond with empathy and honesty to family members' concerns. Realize that parents or grandparents often are seeing a problem in terms of what it means for the future of a child, whereas you may be more concerned about the child's present functioning and behavior. Often, the two most common concerns of family members of children with disabilities are the social acceptance and future of the child.

Professionals can gain a great deal of insight into how a child functions by learning more about the parents' feelings, thoughts, behaviors, and values. How do they feel about this child? Are they proud or disappointed? What are their hopes for him or her? Let parents know that their concerns are important to you before outlining intervention strategies you believe best match their child's needs. Follow through responsibly in giving parents the information they need on an ongoing basis.

3. When integrating children with exceptional needs, utilize the family as a primary resource. With respect to at least one child in the program, each parent is an unqualified expert. You can make this concept work for you and the child by forming partnerships with parents and other family members. As well as providing advice to them when they ask, you can ask their advice when having a difficult time figuring out what to do with their child (e.g., "How do you get Jenny to hang up her coat? I'm having a tough time helping her remember to do that!"). With especially shy children, most of the year could go by before you get a handle on the child's likes, dislikes, and interests.

A parent often can provide a valuable shortcut to a workable strategy.

4. Be supportive and responsive to family members of typically developing children who have questions and concerns about the presence of children with exceptional needs in the group. Such concerns are to be expected. Parents or grandparents may worry that their own child may not get enough attention or will regress in his or her own development. If you become defensive or intimidating or make parents feel guilty for having "negative" feelings, you probably will construct unwanted barriers. Respond as honestly as possible to both open and hidden concerns.

For example, a parent might ask, "Are things going pretty smoothly this year with all the changes?" If you were to respond, "Not bad," leaving it there, you may cut off an opportunity to have the parent share his or her concerns. If, however, you respond: "Not bad. How are parents looking at the changes?" you leave an opening for the parent to bring up a concern with a general response.

Make yourself available to answer questions and invite parents into the classroom to observe for themselves. Let family members know you are interested in their questions and feedback and that you value openness.

5. Stick to the issue when challenging parents who are advocating nonacceptance of others to their children, based on bias. If you have direct evidence that a family member is actively teaching nonacceptance based on ethnic/racial or disability differences or is blaming every negative occurrence on race or disability, ask to have a private discussion about the situation. Stick to the issue and, without being argumentative, firmly provide reasons why bias is harmful and cannot be tolerated in a developmentally appropriate learning context where respect is essential.

PITFALLS TO AVOID

When utilizing the skills described, there are common pitfalls to avoid.

Overprotecting the child who is atypical or from a minority group.   Whenever helping adults give special privileges to one child and not to others, they run the risk of alienating other children and hampering the potential development of the favored child. Rules should be changed to accommodate individual children only when there are safety issues involved, when the child's learning modes are inadequate for the task at hand, or when children are not emotionally able to meet the challenge set before them. When rule changes are necessary, simple, matter-of-fact explanations can be given to other children. In addition, they can be drawn into a discussion about how to make the rule change palatable, given the circumstances. Children's sense of fairness, particularly when they are asked their opinion about a problem, almost always inclines them toward helpfulness. When rules are changed arbitrarily, however, and without apparent fairness, children can become resentful, rejecting, and hostile toward the other child and/or the supervising adult.

Failing to see negative interactions because they are not part of the success picture you have in mind.   It can be tempting to overlook negative incidents that happen or to make light of them because we want to build a positive picture that everything in the classroom is going well. However, honest, ongoing evaluations of inclusiveness are essential. Incidents in which a child is being exploited, manipulated, isolated, or harmed (physically or psychologically) by children or adults in the setting must be addressed immediately by (a) interrupting the incident; (b) acknowledging the emotions of all individuals involved; (c) stating that exploitive and harmful behavior is not allowed under any circumstances; and (d) structuring alternatives that will lead not only toward promoting interaction and feelings of psychological safety but also toward positive acceptance of one another.

Inadvertently using stereotypical language. All people have phrases in their vocabulary that they use unthinkingly. Some of these may be unintentionally offensive. Referring to someone as an "Indian giver," describing the haggling process as "Jewing someone down," saying you'll go out

"Dutch" with someone, or asking children to sit "Indian style" are examples. In addition, referring to workers as "firemen," "postmen," and "salesgirls" reinforces sex-role stereotypes. More egalitarian terminology would include "firefighters," "postal workers," and "salesclerks." Similarly, beware of segregating males and females unnecessarily. It is not constructive to pit boys against girls in games or have children retrieve their art projects by having one gender go before the other. Use other attributes to designate subgroups, such as "Everyone with green socks may get their coats" or "All the people at this table may be dismissed."

Failing to plan for and evaluate student progress effectively.   Children's programs almost always have an evaluation component attached to them. Usually, these are summative in nature and

Randy refuses to share the camera with Rosalie. He says, "Only boys can be cameramen." What will you do?

based on predetermined, normative criteria, measuring how much a child is able to accomplish against a given standard in a given period of time. However, children who have ability deficits for one reason or another are certain to measure up poorly unless they are given reasonable mastery objectives based on their own ability. Similarly, children who consistently need more challenging activities than most of the children must have their progress evaluated more frequently to make sure they are progressing.

Failing to seek the support of administrators, family members, other professionals, and community members. Just as children work within a team situation in the classroom, professionals are part of a larger team of adults who affect what goes on in the program. If you are working with children who require additional resources, such as more time, understanding, patience, staff, and materials, you many have to justify those needs to other adults who are in positions to help. Often, without additional support, there will be a tendency toward burnout and a feeling of being overwhelmed and inadequate in meeting the children's needs. When there is effective communication between helping professionals and the other adults with expertise, these feelings can be minimized.

Responding only to the needs of family members with whom you feel comfortable and avoiding those with different values or differing racial, ethnic, or cultural backgrounds. Family members who are different from the majority of the other families or who do not speak fluent English may shy away from becoming involved because they feel they have little to offer or that what they have to offer will not be valued. Some may sense, fairly or unfairly, a condescending or standoffish attitude on the part of the professional. For example, one young woman who applied for a Head Start position was excited about working with "those" children.

What she failed to consider was that her job also required her to work with "those" parents. Armed with some of her best ideas from a parent–teacher interaction class she had taken in college, she came in the first evening, excited to share some of her expertise. The parents had not come prepared to receive it and had other things on their minds. She said the next day to one of her colleagues, "All they wanted to do was sit and talk and drink coffee!"

She and the parents never were able to get beyond that, and the young woman lasted only the rest of the year in that position. Instead of working to meet parents where they needed her to meet them, she indignantly waited for them to "show some interest in their kids." However, their need to talk to one another about their concerns had to come first. Professionals who have had few personal experiences with certain ethnic groups and cultures can gain new understandings by making a genuine effort to study ethnic groups and cultures different from their own.

SUMMARY

Sensitive issues surrounding children's sexuality, ethnicity, exceptional needs, and personality differences sometimes can cause us discomfort, irritation, embarrassment, or confusion in choosing the most effective ways to support children and their families. When these feelings lead to avoidance, rejection, aggressiveness, or overprotectiveness, our ability to support children's development and competency building is significantly diminished.

Sexual behavior in children such as public masturbation, sex play, peeping, sex-oriented language, and sexually assertive moves toward an adult should be handled as matter-of-factly as possible, with the adult calmly guiding the child toward more appropriate behavior. Apparent deviations in psychosexual development, although sometimes troublesome to adults, may not be subject to alteration and call instead for understanding and a more thorough knowledge of the child's perspective. Severe sexual deviations should be handled by seeking the expertise of other professionals.

Children's attitudes toward other racial and ethnic groups, such as gender-role development, appear to be age and stage specific. Adults who work with children and parents of other racial and ethnic origins or socioeconomic status occasionally may find themselves dealing with negative feelings based on their own ethnocentrism and experiences. Unless they can rise above these feelings, their professional effectiveness will be undermined or negatively affect children's self-esteem and developing ethnic attitudes. Conversely, positive behaviors on the part of the adult serve as an important prerequisite to prejudice prevention and reduction.

Inclusion of children with exceptional needs into formal group settings also is an area requiring additional sensitivity on the part of the adult. The objective of integrating children with disabling conditions is twofold: to promote acceptance of atypical children through stigma reduction and removal, and to enhance their social competence so they can later live more comfortably and successfully in the mainstream of society. The challenge for professionals involved in inclusion efforts is similar to that encountered by those attempting racial integration—that is, melding those who are different from the majority successfully into the mainstream. This potential for qualitatively improving the lot of the child with exceptional needs through inclusion carries a greater risk of increased stigmatization, stereotyping, and rejection if the helping professional is not able to facilitate supportive interaction in the group between typically developing children and children with exceptional needs. Success will depend on the adult's own commitment to successful integration, his or her ability to structure the environment, and the attention he or she pays to the developing social dynamics in the learning context.

Respecting the uniqueness of all persons is a positive statement confirming our ability to be truly human toward one another. Adults who interact on a day-to-day basis with children have the responsibility to surround those children with an accepting, nurturant, growth-enhancing environment—one that allows children to see themselves and others as fully functioning, competently developing human beings.

KEY TERMS

biases
developmental disabilities
disabling conditions
ethnicity
ethnocentrism
gender identity
gender-role identification
giftedness

individualized education program (IEP)
individualized family service program (IFSP)
learning disabilities
mental retardation
physical or sensory disabilities

precocious children
psychosexual development in children
serious emotional disturbance
shyness
social competencies
speech and language disorders

DISCUSSION QUESTIONS

1. The parent board of an all-white cooperative nursery school is considering offering a scholarship to an African-American preschooler for the coming year. What advantages and disadvantages do you see in such an arrangement? What kinds of preparation do you feel should be made prior to implementing such a procedure?

2. You have a Korean-American child in your third-grade classroom and find that he is being harassed on the way home by three of the more popular boys in the classroom. You arrange to meet with the three boys. How do you begin your discussion with them? Role-play this situation with three classmates who can take the part of the students.

3. You are teaching in a large, urban middle school. An 11-year-old girl approaches you during lunch hour, saying that a young male security guard in the school tried fondling her and has been asking her if he can take her home after school. How do you respond to her? What action, if any, do you take?

4. You are holding an open house for parents. The father of a 5-year-old boy approaches you and asks you what you think about letting boys play with dolls. He also asks, "How early can you tell whether or not a male is going to be gay?" State your initial response to him exactly as you would make it. Review the normative sequence in the development of gender identity as you might relate it to the father.

5. You have observed that one of the parents who has volunteered to tutor children with reading problems appears to be highly impatient with Kevin, a second-grader. This morning, you overhear her saying to him: "Your problem is laziness. That's why a lot of you black children aren't able to ever finish school. Is that what you want to happen to you?" How do you handle this situation?

6. As you round the corner into the "quiet" area reserved for reading, you discover two 5-year-old boys examining each other's genitals. What are your initial thoughts? What do you say to the boys? Do you take any further action? If so, what?

7. One of the boys in your Cub Scout group appears to be extremely nervous. On picking him up after a meeting, his mother notices him touching his genitals. In front of the other boys, she crudely quips: "For crying out loud, Terry, quit playing with yourself. You're going to make it fall off!" You ask her if you can talk privately with her for a moment. What do you say to her?

8. You see one of the white preschoolers vigorously rubbing the arm of a black aide. When you ask about it, the aide laughs and says, "He's trying to rub off the dark color of my skin." How do you respond?

9. In the middle of the morning's activity, one of the children unexpectedly has a grand mal seizure. Following the episode, the rest of the children are visibly shaken, and some are crying. What do you say to them?

   Afterward, with the potential of it happening again, how do you prepare the classroom and the children for the possibility?

10. Children in the child care center are having a snack of raisin toast and peanut butter. The student teacher has been instructed to serve only one piece to each child until all children have been served. You notice that Kendra, a child with Down syndrome, has been sitting at the table for quite a long time and is on her second piece of toast. When you ask the student about the situation, she says, "I know the rule, but I feel sorry for her." Verbalize your response exactly as you would make it to the student teacher.

11. Read the following ethical scenario. Refer to the NAEYC Code of Ethical Conduct presented in Appendix A. Find the section(s) that provides insight into the professional responsibilities related to the following situation:

    Jessica, a child with cerebral palsy, uses a wheelchair. She attends Maple Avenue Child Development Center. During outdoor time, she is wheeled into the teachers' lounge and left there to watch television while the other children play outside. Her caregiver explains, "TV is a good activity for her because there's nothing for her to do on the playground. This way, she doesn't get hurt."

12. If you were to assess your own personality type based on the brief discussion of temperament in this chapter, would you say you were an easy child to raise, a slow-to-warm-up child, or a difficult one? If someone were to interview your family, what kinds of specific examples might they provide to support or dispute your conclusions?

FIELD ASSIGNMENTS

1. To become more skillful in handling others' responses, it is important to examine your own feelings about the sensitive areas that are the focus of this chapter. Respond as honestly as possible to the following:

   With respect to your own sexuality, differing ethnic, religious, racial persons or groups, and disabled persons or populations:

   a. cite any negative childhood experiences you had.

   b. identify any faulty or stereotypic information you remember being given.

   c. on a scale of 1 to 10, 10 being most comfortable, describe how comfortable you are related to your own sexuality and interaction with people different from you.

   d. describe any negative adult experiences you have had related to these areas.

   e. have your beliefs and thinking about individual differences changed during your adult years? If so, how?

   f. what social changes do you think need to take place in order to have less biased behavior related to these issues?

2. Professionals who work on a day-to-day basis with children should become familiar with some of the screening tools used to assess growth and development. These are tools that can be simply administered without specialized knowledge or clinical experience. They are available through universities, colleges, intermediate school districts, hospitals, and clinics. The ESI (Early Screening Inventory) and DDST II (Denver Developmental Screening Test II) are two examples. Arrange to obtain one of these tools and use it to test three different children in the age range indicated. Obtain permission from the child's parents prior to testing the child. Because you are probably not experienced in assessment at this point, do not

share the results of the test with the child, the child's parents, or other professionals. Remember to keep the results confidential.

3. We need to constantly monitor teaching materials and classroom activities for racial, cultural, gender-role, sexual, religious, and developmental stereotypes. Examine the materials and activities in your classroom for any unnecessary stereotyping that can be found in the following:

- textbooks or children's books
- assessment tools
- religious holidays observed in programming
- foods served
- responsibilities delegated to children for care and management of the environment
- activities planned onsite and off
- rules and regulations
- resource people invited to participate in the program
- makeup of professional and paraprofessional staff

4. Adapt a previously developed lesson plan for a particular child with exceptional needs and carry out the modified plan. What modifications were necessary? What additional modifications would you make if using the adapted plan for a child with a different set of exceptional needs?

For additional resources, visit our Web site
www.EarlyChildEd.delmar.com

Chapter 15

MAKING ETHICAL JUDGMENTS AND DECISIONS

OBJECTIVES

On completion of this chapter, you should be able to describe:

- The difference between simple decision making and ethical judgments.

- How program goals, strategies, and standards relate to ethical judgments.

- Variables that influence how judgments are made.

- The principles involved in making ethical judgments.

- Ethical judgments that must be made about children's extreme behavior.

- Ethical codes of conduct related to children's extreme behavior and child abuse and neglect.

- Ethical dimensions of working with families.

- Skills for making ethical judgments.

- Pitfalls to avoid in making ethical judgments.

The children in the hospital playroom are reminded that at the end of the session, everything must be put back where they found it. When cleanup time is announced, all the children pitch in to help. When they proclaim the job finished, Mr. Walters, the child life specialist, surveys the room. He notices that although tables are clean and everything has been put away, the cupboards are disheveled, and not all of the markers have been capped. Looking at the children's beaming faces, he ponders, "Should I make them do more, or should I accept the job they've done?"

Two children in an English-immersion preschool are playing with blocks together. They are speaking French to one another, their primary language. Andy, a Korean 5-year-old, approaches and stoops down, intending to get involved. "Only French or English to play here!" says Julian. Andy speaks neither French nor English very well but understands from Julian's body language and tone that he's not welcome. The teacher, overhearing, knows that an intervention is called for but wonders what the most effective approach would be.

On the playground, Myron drops a hard line-drive. "Oh, damn," he says, looking embarrassed that he has dropped the ball. He is seemingly unaware of the epithet. Miss Delmar, who overhears this, considers many options: lecturing Myron, having him apologize for using a curse word, sending him off the field, or ignoring the incident.

For the second time this month, Stuart comes to the center badly bruised. When asked what happened, he claims that he fell down the stairs. The director muses, "Is this really the result of an accident, or could it be a sign of abuse?"

Every day, professionals working with children and families are faced with making sound, sensitive decisions and **ethical judgments** such as these. Some of the situations they encounter demand on-the-spot decision making; others allow time for longer deliberation. Some call for maximum intervention, others for only minimal interference or none at all.

While our day-to-day decision making usually involves simply making a choice between alternatives, making ethical judgments require us to sort out conflicting values we may have relative to the situation and to prioritize them. When these choices affect others, we draw on what we believe about right and wrong, honesty, justice, kindness, reciprocity, and respect for others. This is the essence of ethical decision making.

Essentially, the best ethical judgments are those that we make consciously and involve the same series of

steps found in any decision-making model. In Table 15-1, we see how Mr. Walters, the teacher who opened our chapter, reached his decision to praise the children for a less-than-perfect cleanup job.

Formulating an ethical judgment carries with it certain risks and no guarantees. Yet, as uncertain as the process is, we're more likely to make a better choice when we do so consciously, rather than in an arbitrary fashion. Going through these steps makes it more likely that our actions will match our aims. Furthermore, evaluating the outcomes that actually occur once an option is carried out provides additional information that can be used as input for future judgments we make.

Ethical judgments are influenced both by the situation and by the person who is deciding how to proceed. Any two persons faced with formulating a choice about the same circumstance might make entirely different, yet equally good or equally poor, decisions. Because ethical judgments are so personal and so situation specific, it would be unwise here to suggest prescribed answers to a variety of scenarios. Rather, our goal in this chapter is to point out what variables to consider when making a sound judgment as well as how to think through the process involved in making ethical judgments.

How Program Goals, Strategies, and Standards Relate to Ethical Judgments

Situations that call for sensitive judgments usually involve the enacting of goals, strategies, or standards.

Goals. One of the **goals** we have in almost all programs involving children is that of enhancing children's social competence. Typical goals include fostering their self-regulation, interpersonal skills, positive self-identity, social values, cultural competence, and their planning and decision-making skills. Each of these represents a desired outcome: the achievement of increased social competence. None are wholly attained within the setting or time period during which we work with a particular child. However, when adults establish goals, their interactions with children gain purpose, and there is usually progress. There is an end result to work toward, rather than operating haphazardly with no purpose in mind. Goals can be general or specific, long range or short range, more or less important, and independent of or interdependent with other aims (Goldsmith, 2004). Furthermore, we develop goals for individual children as well as goals for the entire group. Sometimes these multiple aims are

Table 15-1 Steps in Making an Ethical Decision.

PROCEDURE	WHAT MR. WALTERS DOES TO REACH HIS DECISION
1. Assess the situation.	Mr. Walters formulates a picture of what is happening, taking into account the children's lack of familiarity with the hospital playroom, the anxiety many of them are feeling at being in a hospital setting, his supervisor's desire for neatness, the importance of what's been left undone, the children's display of pride, his knowledge that no one will be using the playroom again until tomorrow, and his own feelings of pleasure that the children have worked together.
2. Analyze possible strategies in response to it.	Mr. Walters thinks about the possible responses. Some of these include accepting the children's work without comment, having them redo the work, singling out particular children on the basis of their contributions, scolding them all for not doing enough, and praising the children for working together willingly. He takes into consideration whether making the children redo the work would seem reasonable to them or make them feel defeated. He considers the fact that he is unfamiliar with the youngsters and doesn't know how they will react to a scolding. He wonders if he praises the children for their efforts, some will recognize the discrepancy between their performance and a really clean room and view his words as false.
3. Selecting and implementing a strategy or combination of strategies.	On the spot, Mr. Walters chooses to praise the children for their cooperation in working together.
4. Evaluating the outcome.	Mr. Walters is satisfied that his response best supports his overall aim that children feel comfortable in the hospital environment and that they have made an earnest effort to replace materials.

compatible; sometimes they are in direct opposition to one another, resulting in our having to make many ethical judgments regarding the goals. Some of the questions related to goal setting include:

What are the appropriate goals for each child?
Is a goal that is appropriate for one child also suited for another?
What should be done when pursuit of a goal for an individual runs counter to one established for the group?
Is a particular goal still valid?
What should be done when one goal for a child seems incongruent with another?
What factors necessitate changing a goal?
What makes one goal more important than another?

Mrs. Torez must consider questions such as these when, during a class discussion, Jesse blurts out an answer without raising his hand. Her goal for the group has been for children to exercise greater impulse control and demonstrate it by waiting to be called on. Yet, Jesse is a shy child whom Mrs. Torez has been encouraging to become more assertive. Should her response be geared toward supporting the group goal or the one established for Jesse? Is there a way to address both goals without compromising either? What Mrs. Torez does will be based on her judgment of the situation.

Strategies.   In order to pursue their goals for children, adults implement particular **strategies**. Some of these involve determining the following:

Which strategy is best suited to achieving a particular goal?
Is the strategy that is most potentially effective actually feasible?
How compatible are the strategies implemented for one goal with those for another goal?
How long should a strategy be continued before judging its effectiveness?
Can a planned strategy be carried out as originally intended?

Can a strategy stand alone or should it be carried out in conjunction with other strategies?

A situation in which an ethical judgment about strategies must be made arises when Mr. Chvasta considers T. J.'s persistent antisocial behavior in the group. For the past several months, he has been trying to get T. J. to handle his frustration in a more constructive manner. Though Mr. Chvasta has tried several options, none has had the desired effect.

Recently, he has begun to wonder whether he has used too many different approaches, too rapidly. He also wonders whether his efforts to contend with T. J. have led him to neglect other children, prompting them to act out. The conclusions Mr. Chvasta reaches and what he will do about them depend on the soundness of the judgments he makes.

Standards.   Success in accomplishing goals is assessed using **standards**. People establish standards when they decide that a certain amount of a behavior or a certain quality of behavior represents goal attainment. Behaviors that do not meet these criteria are indications that the goal has not yet been achieved. The measurement of standards may be formal or informal, known by children or unknown by them, and purposeful or intuitive on the part of the adult. Questions that focus on ethical judgments about standards are as follows:

What standards should be established?
Should the same standard apply to all children?
When or why should a standard be changed?
When competing standards exist, which standards should prevail?
How well does a child's behavior meet a given standard?

Think back to Mr. Walters, the child-life specialist. He was making an ethical judgment about standards when deciding whether the children's definition of a clean room was good enough to accept. Ms. Heller, a first-grade teacher, is also thinking about standards when she tries to determine whether to accept Gavin's second attempt at editing the story he is writing. Her dilemma is whether to hold Gavin to the standards she usually has for her first-graders at this time in the school year or to consider the improvement he has made and the considerable effort it took for Gavin to produce the work. In each case, final determinations regarding an acceptable level of performance will come about as the result of adult judgments.

VARIABLES THAT AFFECT ETHICAL JUDGMENTS

Goals, strategies, and standards must continually be evaluated. Goals that are accomplished are replaced by other goals, and those that obviously are unattainable or no longer fit are revised; strategies that are outmoded or ineffective are updated. Because none of these remains constant forever, helping professionals continually make ethical judgments about them. Their judgments are influenced by three variables: their values, their knowledge of how children learn and grow, and their assessment of the situation at hand. Let's examine each of these influences more closely.

Values

Underlying each ethical judgment are personal values. **Values** are the qualities and beliefs a person considers desirable or worthwhile (Berns, 2007). As such, values are deeply internalized feelings that direct people's actions. For instance, adults for whom honesty is a value set goals for children with that value in mind. Some of these might include telling the truth, not cheating on tests, and completing one's work without copying.

To achieve these goals, these adults implement related strategies such as rewarding children who tell the truth, separating children who are taking tests, and teaching children appropriate sources for getting help as a substitute for copying. In addition, they apply related standards to determine how well their goals have been met. For instance, an adult might allow a preschooler to tell a tall tale, but refuse to accept a fabrication from a fifth-grader. He or she might expect 100% of the students to keep their eyes on their own papers during an exam and monitor students' homework to determine that none of their answers were exactly the same. Not only do adults' values influence their goals for children, but they also affect how adults interpret and appraise children's behavior. As a result, an adult may view children who tell tall tales with less favor than children who refrain from such practices.

Because values cannot be seen, their presence can only be inferred from what people do (Goldsmith, 2004). For instance, Linda Hong frequently reminds children about the value of telling the truth and doing their own work. She often carries out activities in which children must discriminate between fact and fancy. She reveals her emotions rather than hiding them, and she encourages children to describe their true reactions even when they are in opposition to

Eventually, the children and adults will have to decide: Is our room clean enough? This is a question of standards.

her own. If a child copies another's work, he or she is told to do it over. Based on her actions, you might conclude that the value of honesty is important to her. On the other hand, were she to ignore minor incidents of cheating, tell fibs herself, or attempt to deny children's emotions, her behavior would indicate that honesty was not critical to her. Even if she were to say that it was, her actions would belie her words.

How values develop.   Values are a product of socialization. Families, society, culture, teachers, religion, friends, professional colleagues and organizations, and the mass media all contribute to one's belief system. In this way, every facet of a person's environment has a direct or indirect impact on his or her thinking. Because value acquisition starts in infancy, it is the family that has the first and most profound influence on this process.

Family members, through their day-to-day interactions, contribute to the fundamental dispositions of young children. As people mature, these beliefs are supplemented by inputs from all of the contexts in which they live, work, and play with others. These combine to form a particular orientation

that individuals internalize and that guides them throughout their lives.

Because each person's ecological milieu is unique, no two people have exactly the same value system. Values differ across cultures, between families in the same culture, and among individual family members. This means there is no one correct set of values to which all persons subscribe.

Prioritizing values.   People develop a system of values that often is hierarchical, ranging from most critical to least important. The order of importance is determined by whether a person treats a particular value as basic (a value that is absolute regardless of context) or relative (one that depends on context for interpretation). **Basic values** usually take priority over **relative values**, and relative values take on more or less importance, depending on the situation (Deacon & Firebaugh, 1988). In Linda Hong's case, for example, the basic value of honesty pervades everything she does. Therefore, when she must choose between being forthright, circumspect, or deceitful, she usually selects the first option.

However, a value's hierarchy is not always so linear, with each value being placed above or below another. Rather, several values may occupy the same level of importance at the same time. These values may be compatible or contradictory. The similar weight shared by a cluster of competing values explains why people sometimes experience value conflicts. For instance, a person may equally value honesty and kindness. At times, he or she may be caught in the dilemma of whether to tell the truth, perhaps hurting someone's feelings, or to be less than honest based on the person's judgment in that particular circumstance.

Recognizing our own values.   The more we are consciously aware of our own personal values, the better we are able to examine them. Only then can we determine when conflicting values exist within ourselves or between ourselves and others and then take systematic steps to resolve the dilemmas that result.

Additionally, it is possible for us to determine whether our actions are congruent with the values we espouse. This makes it more likely that we will be consistent in our interactions with children and their families. For all of these reasons, clarifying our values is an important facet of professional life.

Knowing the values supported by your profession.   In addition to personal values, values espoused by the profession at large provide useful guides for making judgments. Such values are usually identified in the ethical codes of conduct adopted by professional organizations or societies.

A code of ethical conduct to which members are committed represents the collective wisdom of the field regarding common values, required practices that support those values, and prohibited practices that undermine them. In other words, a code of ethics provides a tangible framework for thinking about professional values and how those values might influence our behavior in the formal group setting. When we keep that code in mind at all times, we then have a credible foundation for the judgments we will have to make.

Respecting clients' values.   It's important to be sensitive to the differing values held by the children and families with whom we work. We cannot expect clients' values to exactly mirror or always be compatible with our own and may be confronted with dissimilarities between our values and those of our clients. If so, our task becomes one of finding ways to work with others that demonstrate respect

for their belief systems, regardless of what action is eventually taken.

Separating values from goals, strategies, and standards.   Occasionally, professionals mistake differences in goals, strategies, and standards for value conflicts. In reality, it is possible for dissimilar goals, strategies, and standards to be applied in response to the same value.

For example, Mrs. Williams values competence and has a goal for her son, DeRon, to be able to handle social situations with greater skill. She teaches him to establish his rights through physical force and considers his winning a fight as a positive indication of his abilities. Mrs. Pritchard, his teacher, shares the same value and goal, but her tactics and standards differ. She teaches DeRon to use words to establish his rights and views his avoidance of physical confrontation as a measure of achievement.

In this case, the dissimilar approach between parent and teacher is based not on conflicting values, but on differing means. Although values are almost impossible to debate, strategies can be negotiated. The two adults do have common ground. If Mrs. Pritchard recognizes this, she will have a positive base from which to approach the parent. If she does not see this shared perspective, her efforts to influence the parent could result in failure. In addition to an understanding of values, there are two other variables that affect the ethical judgments helping professionals make. The first involves how well they take into account children's current level of functioning; the second is whether they look at each situation in context.

Knowledge of child development and learning.   When adults make ethical judgments about goals, strategies, and standards related to children's behavior, they must weigh such variables as the child's age, what the child's current level of comprehension might be, and what experiences the child has had.

Although age is not an absolute measure of a youngster's capabilities and understanding, it does serve as a guide for establishing appropriate expectations. For instance, adults who know that preschoolers do not yet have a mature grasp of games with rules would not view a 4-year-old who spins twice or peeks at the cards in a memory game as a cheater. Subsequently, they would not require very young children to adhere to the rules of a game in

Helping professionals must be sensitive to the differing values held by the children and families with whom they work.

the same way they might expect grade-schoolers to. Likewise, awareness that 7- and 8-year-olds normally spend lots of time talking about who is and is not in their friendship circle keeps adults from moralizing to children when they hear such discussions going on. Rather, their strategy for improving peer relations might consist of group discussions aimed at encouraging children to discover similarities with others in the group.

The types of previous knowledge and skills a child brings to a situation should also be taken into account. Obviously, children with little or no exposure to a particular situation or skill should not be expected to pursue exactly the same goals or perform at the same level of competence as youngsters whose backlog of experience is greater. For instance, goals for a field trip to a farm for children from the inner city would be different from those established for youngsters from a rural area. Standards related to dressing independently would be different for a 2-year-old from those for a 6-year-old, not only because of differences in age, but because the older child has had more practice.

Furthermore, a child who has lived all her life in Florida would not initially be expected to demonstrate the same degree of skill in putting on a snowsuit as would a child from a northern climate, where such clothing is commonplace. In instances such as these, helping professionals use children's development and experience to guide their ethical judgments.

The Situational Context

Adult judgments do not take place in a vacuum. Rather, they are made within an ecological milieu, which is influenced by several factors. Some of these include time, human resources, material resources, the physical environment, and the specific details of the behavioral episode itself. The goals, strategies, and standards finally decided on are all affected by these constraints. For instance, under normal circumstances, Ms. Omura's goal is to foster independence among the children in her class. Ordinarily, children are given the time to make their own decisions, to repeat a task in order to gain competence, and to do as much as possible for themselves. However, these goals and strategies have to be modified during a tornado drill, when the goal of safety supersedes that of independence. Under such circumstances, children have no choice about taking shelter, nor can they take their time dressing themselves.

As a result, slow dressers get more direct assistance than is customarily provided. Similarly, Mr. Ogden might think that the best strategy for helping an impulsive child is constant, one-to-one monitoring by an adult. Yet, he concludes that he would be unable to implement this approach because of demands on his own time and the lack of other adults who might serve in this role.

The impact of contextual factors also is evident when a social worker who ordinarily advocates sharing, but who also knows that Michelle has recently become a stepsister, allows her to keep all of the watercolors to herself one day. He realizes that this child already is sharing many things for the first time—attention at home, her room, and even some of her things. In his judgment, asking her to share on this occasion is unnecessarily stressful, so he does not oblige her to follow the rule for now. Physical resources and available time also affect ethical judgments. This explains why the presence of a huge mud puddle on the playground could be viewed as either a place to avoid or an area of exploration. Which judgment is made depends in part on what kind of clothing the children are wearing, whether soap and water are available for cleanup, whether it is warm enough to go barefoot, and whether there is enough time for children to both play in the mud and get cleaned up before the next activity period.

As you can see, values, knowledge of child development and learning, and the situational context all influence the kinds of ethical judgments we make. These variables affect sensitive judgments about ethical behavior, judgments involving one's priorities, judgments about extreme behavior, and judgments related to child abuse and neglect.

JUDGMENTS ABOUT ETHICAL BEHAVIOR

Helping professionals continually confront ethical dilemmas in their daily work:

- Ms. Skegel, a cooperative nursery teacher, runs into a parent in the local grocery store who asks her how well the "situation is going" with the inclusion in the classroom of a child with autism.
- Craig DeLong, who teaches first grade at Challenger Elementary School, has been asked to give the children in his classroom a group-administered standardized test, which he knows will produce inordinate stress in the children.

- Ms. Satton, an aide in a kindergarten classroom, watches as the teacher passes out worksheets to the children; she knows these take up a lot of the children's time but produce little real learning.
- The new administrator of a child care program learns that the building is in violation of the state fire code, but is told by the board president that it would be too expensive to remedy the situation and that his cooperation would be appreciated.
- Three-year-old Tomeko Kenyon's mother asks Ms. Levinger not to allow Mr. Kenyon to pick Tomeko up after school because the parents are separated, and he is abusive. When Ms. Levinger asks if she has a court order to support this, Mrs. Kenyon says, "No, but I know you'll help me out for Tomeko's sake."

Concerns arise from incidents professionals witness directly, as well as ones they hear about. These predicaments can affect children, families, colleagues, supervisors, or other community members. Ultimately, the basic judgments to be made center on which actions are right and which ones are wrong.

These are moral judgments, with no middle ground, requiring the application of one's professional code of ethics. In this text, we have used the NAEYC Code of Ethical Conduct as a guide for professional behavior. Up until this point, however, our primary focus has been on recognizing circumstances addressed by the code. Although familiarity with the code is essential, it is not sufficient to ensure that practitioners will always act ethically. For this to occur, ethical principles and codes must be embedded into all professional thinking (Newman, 2002). Effectively utilizing the code is a skill that can be learned just as other skills are learned through direct instruction, modeling, and positive reinforcement.

Personal reflection on ethical dilemmas (both hypothetical and real) and conversations with colleagues about such dilemmas are essential strategies for building a strong foundation on which to make future professional judgments. Time must be set aside during pre-service classes, staff meetings, or other training sessions to talk about the components involved in building a strong conceptual framework of the knowledge, skills, and dispositions involved in making ethical judgments (see Figure 15-1).

The ability to make a sound professional judgment also involves establishing priorities from

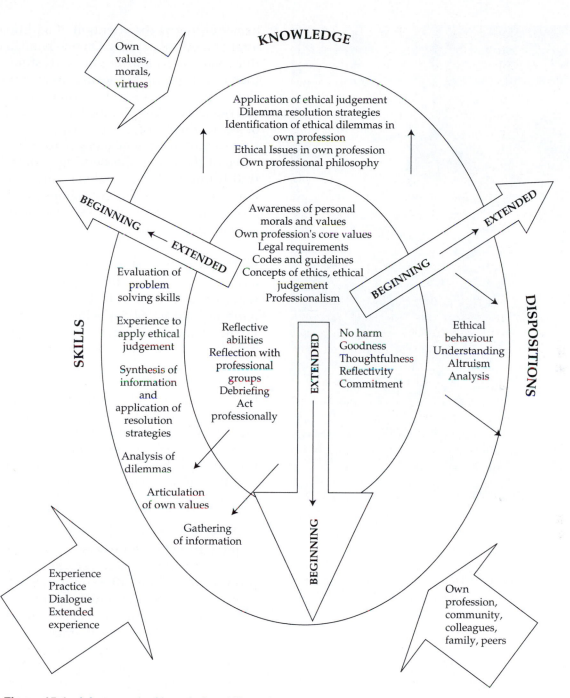

Figure 15-1   A framework of knowledge skills and dispositions for making ethical judgments.

Source: Newman (2002).

among competing interests. Some of these include self-interest versus children's interests, individual interests versus group interests, and the interests of one person versus those of another. People also may experience conflicts within their own value system that cloud their ability to make a definitive judgment. Although there are no absolute rules for distinguishing among these, there are some general

principles helping professionals can use when faced with difficult decisions.

Priority Principles

Seven principles are arranged in a hierarchy in Table 15-2, from most to least important. Each one has higher priority than those that follow it. All of them serve as guideposts for which priorities take precedence in a

It's cleanup time. These boys have newly discovered one another and are engrossed in their conversation. What judgment principles apply here?

given circumstance. These principles came about as a result of our experiences with families and children and through discussions with helping professionals representing a variety of backgrounds.

Using the priority principles just described is an effective way of thinking through an ethical judgment process. These principles can be applied to a wide range of scenarios involving both on-the-spot decision making and longer-term deliberations. Moreover, they are valid in dealing with issues of varying magnitude. For this reason, we feel they can be generalized to most of the day-to-day sensitive judgments helping professionals have to make.

ETHICAL CONSIDERATIONS ABOUT CHILDREN'S EXTREME BEHAVIOR

Sometimes, helping professionals find themselves in a dilemma, trying to decide whether a child's behavior merits the attention of additional behavioral or medical experts. On one hand, a child's actions may be so baffling or so dysfunctional that the adult fears that ignoring them could have serious consequences. On the other hand, he or she worries about alarming the family, offending them, or asking them to commit to what may be a significant outlay of time or money. Torn between both sides of the issue, the helping professional may find it impossible to make a conscious decision. Fortunately, there are guidelines available to enable professionals to make such ethical judgments with more assurance.

What Constitutes Extreme Behavior

Criteria have been developed for determining what behaviors should be considered extreme (Guerney, 2004). Some behaviors are extreme by virtue of their mere presence. Others are designated as extreme because they exceed the normal boundaries you would expect in relation to a child's age. How intense a behavior is and how generalized it becomes are additional factors that must be taken into account when determining whether behavior is extreme. Other variables that influence decision making include the effect the behavior has on the child's present or future functioning and how resistant the behavior is to modification.

Presence of self-destructive behaviors and cruelty to others/animals. Self-destructive acts are danger signs. Their very appearance should prompt immediate intervention. Self-destructive acts are those that children inflict on themselves and that result in physical injury or mental damage. This is exemplified by the youngster who disfigures herself by scratching; by the child who bangs his head, causing contusions; and by the child who deliberately courts danger as a thrill-seeking device. In each case, the behavior is too serious to be allowed to continue.

Similarly, children who repeatedly engage in unprovoked acts of cruelty toward others and/or the animals in their lives are displaying antisocial behaviors that are more often than not linked to serious future problems. As many as half of all sex offenders self-report a history of animal cruelty and in most incidents of recent school shootings, the juveniles involved had documented histories of animal cruelty. Though childhood animal cruelty does not inevitably lead to later violence toward

Table 15-2 Priority Principles.

PRIORITIZED PRINCIPLES	EXAMPLE OF APPLICATION OF PRINCIPLE
Principle 1. Children's safety takes precedence. The overriding concern of every helping professional is children's physical and mental welfare. If you must choose between an option in which a child's health and well-being can be maintained and other, more efficient easier, or less involved options in which safety is a question, there is no choice. You are ethically and morally obligated to pursue the safest alternative.	The fifth-grade science class is doing an experiment with heat that involves the use of Bunsen burners. The children, working in small groups, are running behind schedule in their task. Another class is to arrive in five minutes. While surveying the room, the teacher notices that a few children, still working, have taken off their protective goggles. The adult feels caught between wanting them to get the experiment over with in time and feeling that she should enforce the safety standards. Even though there are only a few minutes remaining, and making the children don the goggles will cause a delay, the appropriate course is clear, as mandated by principle 1: safety first.
Principle 2. Give priority to the approach that promises the most positive and the least negative outcomes. Although all goals, strategies, and standards have some benefits and some drawbacks, it is best to eliminate the most negative options and choose from among those that are most favorable. Sometimes, the best option has the largest number of benefits. Sometimes, an option is best because its negative aspects are less detrimental than the other alternatives under consideration.	During a conference with the director of the child care center, Mrs. Leeper (a parent) reveals that her father is terminally ill and is not expected to live much beyond the new year. She has not yet shared the news with her children and has approached the center director for advice. Together, they identify the benefits of telling the children about the situation right away, such as giving the children lead time to deal with the tragedy, a chance to say goodbye to their grandfather, and an opportunity to share in a family experience; a chance for Mrs. Leeper to gain family support; and the relief of not having to keep it a secret. Drawbacks to telling the children include causing everyone to feel sad during the holiday, as well as the difficulty of introducing a topic about which Mrs. Leeper feels uncomfortable and with which her children have had little experience. The two adults also explore the pros and cons of not telling. Favorable aspects of postponing the disclosure are that the children probably will have an uninterrupted holiday and that the mother will not have to deal with the issue right away. The negative aspects of this approach include the mother's growing anxiety, her inability to share a very traumatic period of her life with her loved ones, the potential shock to the children, and their probable distress over sensing that something is wrong but not knowing what it is. Taking all of these factors into account, Mrs. Leeper makes the judgment that it is better to tell them than to remain silent. In her opinion, the benefits of telling right away outweigh both the benefits of not telling and the negative aspects of making the announcement.
Principle 3. When a child's needs and an adults' needs differ, give priority to the child's needs whenever possible. Children's interests always take higher priority, unless the adult would find pursuit of those needs unlivable or contrary to his or her basic values.	Children at the Jefferson School are rehearsing for a spring concert. The music teacher is especially eager for the youngsters to put on a good show because music teachers from several other districts are in the audience. While listening to the opening number, she realizes that Sandra is singing loudly and enthusiastically, but is off key. She debates whether to allow the child to sing. She knows that other teachers have told such youngsters to mouth the words without making a sound. At the same time, she is aware of how much Sandra is anticipating singing at the concert. Based on her understanding of principle 3, she rejects restricting Sandra's participation in favor of allowing her to sing, putting Sandra's needs before her own.

continued

Table 15-2 Priority Principles—continued

PRIORITIZED PRINCIPLES	EXAMPLE OF APPLICATION OF PRINCIPLE
Principle 4. When goals of equal weight conflict, give priority to the goal that is least often addressed in day-to-day encounters. Often, situations arise in which it is possible to concentrate on reinforcing only one of several competing goals. When this happens, it is best to pursue the goal that is less often addressed.	Jorge received $10 from his grandmother for his birthday. He took the entire amount and bought his mother a change purse painted with a half-naked woman in a suggestive pose. He is proud of his purchase and pleased to be giving his mother a gift. His mother is touched that he so selflessly used his money for someone other than himself, but she is also concerned with his poor choice and lack of fiscal awareness. She realizes that she must focus on one aspect of the situation or the other. If she tries to deal with both by thanking him and then having him return the inappropriate purchase, she would, in fact, diminish the genuineness of her praise. She must choose between the value she places on prosocial behavior and her value related to money management. After much though and following the premise of principle 4, she thanks Jorge for the change purse and says nothing about the inappropriate image or the way he spent the money. She decides that she will have many future opportunities to teach fiscal responsibility but fewer chances to reward Jorge's generosity.
Principle 5. When a strategy supports a short-term objective but interferes with long-term goals, give priority to pursuing the long-term goal.	Children from the center have been on a walking field trip. They are tired, and the adults want to get back. It's been a long afternoon. The group reaches the middle of the block. The center is right across the street, and no traffic is in sight. The leader considers jaywalking, but realizes that such an action would detract from her long-range goal of teaching children the safe way to cross the street. Her decision to have the children walk several extra yards to the corner is based on her understanding of principle 5.
Principle 6. When group and individual needs compete, give priority to the approach that best satisfies each. This may involve a compromise that addresses both sets of needs simultaneously. If this is not possible, competing needs may have to be addressed sequentially, knowing that the final result may not be completely satisfactory to all. In either case, strive to achieve win-win solutions, as opposed to outcomes in which either the individual or the group is perceived as a "winner" or a "loser."	Vito has little self-confidence. The one area in which he excels is building with blocks. Day after day, he builds elaborate structures and then begs that they remain standing, undisturbed. At first, the adult honors Vito's wishes, even though it limits other children's access to the blocks. She reasons that it is more important for Vito to feel good about an accomplishment than for the group to use the materials. However, over time, the adult notices that the youngsters are becoming increasingly upset and feeling short-changed about their limited opportunities to build. Using principle 6, the adult decides to limit how long a structure can remain standing, as well as Vito's monopolization of the blocks. She offers him a choice of using the blocks exclusively for a few minutes or using them for a longer time in conjunction with other children.

people, early displays of such behavior require speedy consultation with a behavior expert. This is especially true when children claim that such acts are accidental or put the blame on others, all the while seeming to enjoy the havoc that results. If such actions become customary, either at home or in the program, the child is exhibiting signs of extreme behavior.

Sudden drastic changes in behavior patterns. Another cause for concern is a child's normal behavior pattern changing suddenly or radically. A generally happy, responsive child who becomes withdrawn and fearful, a habitually mild-mannered child who overnight becomes volatile, and a child who begins complaining of unrelenting stomachaches are all showing evidence of extreme behaviors. Because these actions are so out of character, they signal a need for closer scrutiny.

Age-atypical behavior. Frequently, a behavior is considered extreme if it reappears or continues to exist long after one would expect a child to have outgrown it. Although it is typical for 2-year-olds to have temper tantrums, even frequent ones, 9-year-olds do not usually behave this way. Thus, if a 9-year-old repeatedly resorted to explosive outbursts, it would be obvious that the behavior should be categorized as extreme. Likewise, if an 8-year-old suddenly begins bed-wetting, after having been dry at night since toddlerhood, this would deserve serious attention.

Intense behavior.   Problem behaviors are generally considered normal if they appear only occasionally or briefly. However, they are labeled extreme if they occur frequently or if they last for prolonged periods of time. For instance, it is not unusual for preschoolers to periodically seek the comfort of blanket and thumb when frightened or tired. On the other hand, were 3-year-old Michael to spend the majority of his waking hours pacifying himself in this manner, the behavior would be considered extreme. Likewise, everyone has times when they want to "sneak" an extra cookie or snack item. However, the child who regularly steals or hoards food is exhibiting signs of extreme behavior. Whether parents or the professional with whom the child comes in regular contact should seek outside help would depend on how long the problem lasts. There are times when extreme behaviors are short lived. That is, they appear for a few days, and then children gradually return to their original behavior patterns. Such instances are viewed as temporary crises that require adult support but not necessarily outside intervention. However, should the behavior endure, some serious exploration of the child's situation, with the help of an expert in such matters, would be in order.

Indiscriminate and pervasive behavior.   Certain actions that might be considered normal if their appearance were limited become abnormal when they pervade all aspects of a child's life. For instance, it is common for youngsters aged 4 through 9 to tell untruths to protect themselves in incriminating situations or to make themselves seem more interesting. Although hardly exemplary, their resorting to lies under duress or in moments of self-expansiveness should not be categorized as extreme.

On the other hand, there are a few children who rely on falsehoods in virtually all situations, regardless of whether they are in obvious trouble or in a circumstance in which absolute adherence to the facts is unimportant. These youngsters tend to lie about many things even when the truth would serve them better. In these cases, a behavioral expert should be consulted to determine how it could be modified.

Behaviors that hamper children's functioning.   Behaviors that have the potential to hamper children's growth or development should be treated as extreme. This is exemplified by children who repeatedly force themselves to throw up after eating, those who are so hostile or lacking in affect they do not let anyone get close to them, and youngsters who become so centered on getting good grades that they resort to cheating, lying, and sabotage of others' work to better their own standing. Likewise, diabetic children who deliberately avoid their medication or habitually eat forbidden foods fall into this category. Young people who are so shy or standoffish that they literally have no friends or acquaintances also are enmeshed in extreme, counterproductive patterns of behavior. In each case, consultation with parents and behavioral experts is recommended.

Resistance of the behavior to change.   Resistance for more than a short time (usually several weeks) to reasonable efforts to correct a common, everyday problem is a sign that the behavior has become extreme. "Reasonable efforts" refer to adult use of relevant, constructive strategies aimed at eliminating negative actions while simultaneously promoting desirable alternate behaviors. It also implies consistency. That is, the problem behavior must receive attention on a predictable basis, and the strategies employed must be used often enough and long enough that a behavior change is likely.

Within this definition, a child who periodically experiences negative consequences for being out of his seat, but who at other times is inadvertently rewarded for wandering, is not demonstrating resistant behavior but rather the effects of the adult's unpredictable responses. Conversely, were the child to experience appropriate consequences over a two-month span but still habitually wander the room, this is evidence that the behavior has become extreme.

Similarly, a developmental task for all young children is to become toilet trained. Although the optimal period for this to occur varies among individuals, it is accepted that by about 3 years of age, most children will have begun this training. Yet, some children resist learning to use the toilet. Initial resistance is common and should not be a signal for alarm. However, there are youngsters whose resistance continues to mount such that bladder or bowel control is still not achieved into the grade-school years. Under these conditions, the behavior can appropriately be described as extreme.

Frequently Reported Sources of Extreme Behavior

When adults are confronted with children's extreme behavior, they often wonder where it comes from and why it occurs. Although the variables influencing any single child may differ widely, three of the most commonly reported sources include physiological factors, childhood fears, and childhood depression (Goleman, 2007).

Physiology.   It has been suggested that some children who exhibit extreme behavior do so as a result of protein, vitamin, or mineral deficiencies in their diet (Santrock, 2005). For instance, children who are deprived of essential B vitamins have impaired concentration, resulting in a shorter attention span and a lack of task commitment. Over the past several years, scientists also have hypothesized that some genuinely extreme, noncompliant behavior is related to neurological dysfunction. Hyperactive behavior, sometimes

diagnosed as attention deficit disorder or attention deficit/hyperactivity disorder, is the most common of these. Brain damage, which may result from birth complications or a later head injury, can also make it difficult for a child to sit still, and chemical imbalances in the brain may interfere with the transfer of signals from one cell to another. Either way, brain dysfunction may contribute to a child's need for constant motion and an inability to relax (Berger & Thompson, 2005).

Another extreme behavioral problem that results from neurological difficulties is Tourette's syndrome. Children with this condition display tics (repeated involuntary movements, such as eye blinking), which may be accompanied by the shouting of obscenities and the production of loud and/or strange noises. All of these behaviors are actually beyond the child's ability to control. When related to bioneurological dysfunction, assistance from specially trained professionals is necessary.

Childhood fears.   Another source of extreme behavior in children is fear. All children at one time or another become afraid of certain places, people, things, or events. Even if extreme in intensity for days or sometimes weeks, these fearful episodes usually are of a relatively short duration. (Refer to

It is important to communicate concerns to the child's family about potentially extreme behaviors.

Chapter 5 for a review of typical childhood fears and what to do about them.) Time, along with adult empathy and support, will dissipate most of these. Yet, there are times when fears persist for such long periods and permeate so many areas of a child's life that they interfere with the child's ability to function. Such extreme fears are called **anxiety disorders**. They are persistent, unfounded, out of proportion to the actual danger or threat, and lead to maladaptive behavior (Berns, 2006).

Most often, this maladaptation takes the form of extreme withdrawal. For example, 7-year-old Veronica reached a point where she was terrified at the mere prospect of coming in contact with anything fuzzy. Initially, Veronica had expressed a fear of mice. Gradually, her fear extended to encompass most fuzzy objects, such as stuffed animals, blankets, and the fur collar on her coat. As time went on, she became hysterical at the touch of a cotton swab and when asked to use yarn in a weaving project. Ultimately, her anxiety prompted her to resist leaving the sanctuary of her home, from which most of the offending items had been eliminated.

A common anxiety disorder during the grade school years is known as school refusal, or **school phobia** (Papalia, Olds, & Feldman, 2006). Although many youngsters experience some anxiety about school, about 16 of every 1,000 develop such severe anxieties that they become physically ill at the prospect of going to school each day (Gelfand & Drew, 2003). Their resistance to school becomes extreme: Screaming, crying, and tantrums are common, as are severe stomachaches, headaches, and sore throats. The child's distress may be directly related to incidents at school (inability to perform the work expected or being made fun of by other children). It also may be caused by other factors not so easily discernible, such as fears that develop from a misunderstood conversation or the chance remark of another child. In either case, the child's reaction is to attempt to withdraw from all school contacts.

Occasionally, rather than trying to resolve fear through withdrawal, some youngsters try to master it directly. In the process, they often overreact, engaging in potentially harmful activities. For example, following a period of extreme fear of fire, some children set fires. They reason that their ability to produce a flame at will and to extinguish it themselves demonstrates their power over it.

Another worrisome way that some children cope with fear is to develop an obsession or a compulsion. Undesired recurring thoughts are called **obsessions**.

These are persistent preoccupations or ideas children cannot get out of their heads. Impulses to repeatedly perform certain acts are called **compulsions** (Berns, 2006). Everyone exhibits some obsessive or compulsive behavior at some time, and in their mildest forms, neither of these is a problem.

However, if a compulsion or obsession begins to interfere with a person's functioning and is one from which he or she derives no pleasure or social benefits, it is judged extreme. For instance, 10-year-old Jessica was obsessed with the thought of having to urinate even though there was no physical basis for her concern. Her obsession caused her to make as many as 50 trips to the bathroom each day. Often, once she got there, she was unable to produce even a drop. When Jessica was denied access to the bathroom as often as she wanted, her anxiety over a possible accident drove her to tears. She became so preoccupied with this one biological function that she was able to think of little else. As with other fear-related circumstances that exceed the bounds of normalcy, behaviors such as Jessica's require the attention of a behavioral expert.

Childhood depression.   A source of extreme behavior that has become increasingly prevalent in children ages 2 to 12 is childhood depression (Papalia, Olds, & Feldman 2006). Behaviors associated with this phenomenon range from affective ones, like sadness, continual crying, withdrawal, inability to concentrate, lack of interest in life, and feelings of defeat, to physical manifestations such as severe and frequent stomachaches or headaches for which there seems to be no physiological basis. Sometimes, extreme misbehavior can be a symptom of depression as well. It shows itself in such acting-out behaviors as stealing, fighting, or defiance.

These and other destructive acts are characterized by excessive disobedience and unrelenting resistance to change. It must be remembered that all children occasionally disobey for a variety of reasons and that noncompliance does not, in and of itself, mean that a child is suffering from depression. Rather, outside help is warranted when unremitting, intense, hostile disobedience occurs over a long period of time.

ETHICAL JUDGMENTS REGARDING CHILD ABUSE AND NEGLECT

When helping professionals believe that a child in their care has suffered the trauma of child abuse or neglect, their emotions may run high. Initially, they may experience disbelief, horror, anger, or panic. If they allow these feelings to dictate their reaction, their response will not be constructive. Incredulity may cause them to ignore a serious problem; shock may immobilize them; rage may prompt them into a destructive mode of action; and panic could detract from their ability to deal with the situation coherently. At times like these, helping professionals must be able to control their emotions and make a calm, rational judgment about whether there is a possibility of child abuse. In order to make such a judgment, they first must understand the nature of child abuse and the signs to look for.

Defining Abuse and Neglect

The mistreatment of children includes both abuse—actions that are deliberately harmful to a child's well-being—and **neglect**—failure to appropriately meet children's basic needs (Berger & Thompson, 2006). Legally, every state has its own definition of these acts. However, there is general agreement that abuse and neglect most often take the following forms.

Physical abuse. These are assaults on children that produce pain, cuts, welts, bruises, broken bones, and other injuries. Whipping children, tying them up, locking them in closets, throwing them against walls, scalding them, and shaking them violently are common examples.

Sexual abuse. This includes molestation, exploitation, and intimidation by an adult (95% of reported cases are by men) to dominate or control a child. **Sexual abuse** is accomplished through force, coercion, cajoling, enticement, and threats and, because children generally trust, respect, and love the adults in their lives, they are easy to manipulate (Crosson-Tower, 2005). Children who are sexually abused may also be subjected to obscene phone calls or sexually explicit language; they may be made to exhibit themselves or to watch the exhibition of an adult.

Physical neglect. Neglect includes failure of adults to provide adequate food, clothing, shelter, medical care and supervision for children. Neglected children starve because they are not fed, freeze when they are left without clothing in frigid temperatures, and may perish in fires when left unsupervised (Papalia, Olds, & Feldman, 2006).

Emotional abuse. Abuse includes actions that deliberately destroy children's self-esteem. Such abuse is usually verbal and may take the form of scapegoating, ridiculing, humiliating, or terrorizing children.

Emotional neglect. This means failure of adults to meet children's needs for affection and emotional support. Emotionally neglected children are ignored or subjected to cold, distant relationships with adults.

In each of these cases, children's current levels of functioning are damaged and there is a potential threat to their future well-being. At one time it was thought that such negative acts occurred rarely and were perpetrated by a few "sick" people in our society. We now know better.

Medical neglect. Adults might fail to meet children's need for medical attention in cases of acute or chronic disease.

Other maltreatment. Abuse and neglect includes cases where there is abandonment, threats of harm, and congenital drug addiction.

Scope of the Problem

Child abuse is a very serious problem, which is more widely recognized today than ever before. Figure 15-2 shows substantiated cases of abuse and neglect documented by the National Child Abuse and Neglect Data System (NCANDS). Note: Percentages add up to more than 100% because many children suffer more than one type of maltreatment and are coded more than once. It is estimated that 12.1 of every 1,000 children in the United States are abused (47.3% boys; 50.7% girls) and that each year, over 1,000 children die as a result of abuse and neglect. Children under 1 were the most vulnerable and accounted for 40.9% of all the fatalities; 3/4ths of all children neglected are under age 3 (NCANDS, 2005). These figures are based on reported cases, with 24.3% of the cases reported by teachers; the real numbers undoubtedly are higher because much abuse is never brought to the attention of the authorities.

Such data suggest that at least 1 of every 10 young people will experience violation of their person during the childhood years. According to the law of averages, this means that a helping professional may come in contact with about two or three such children during a 12-month period. This is not to say that an abused child will

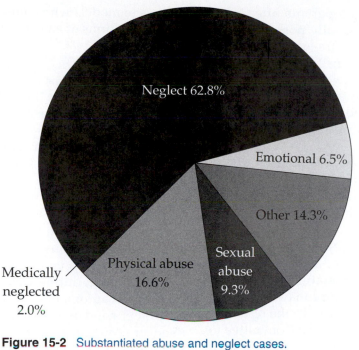

Figure 15-2 Substantiated abuse and neglect cases.
Source: NCANDS (2003).

be found in every formal group setting. It does underscore the fact that sometime during their career, helping professionals will have to make a judgment about whether a child is a victim of abuse. In fact, the problem has become so widespread that all 50 states now have laws requiring that suspected cases of child abuse be reported by doctors, teachers, and other helping professionals who work with children. Furthermore, in most states, helping professionals are legally responsible for any injury to a child that comes about because the professional failed to make such a report.

The Abusers

Who would beat, bash, burn, choke, neglect, starve, rape, sodomize, or otherwise assault a child? Are the perpetrators of such hideous deeds psychopathic monsters?

Overwhelmingly, the evidence says no. Rather, they are ordinary people who, for any number of reasons, subject children to humiliating or physically injurious acts. Child abuse cuts across all ages, both genders, all races, all social classes, all family structures, and all socioeconomic groups.

There are no characteristics that infallibly separate abusers from nonabusers, victims from nonvictims. Although certain conditions may be more or less highly related to abuse, their existence alone is not an absolute indicator of whether or not abuse will occur. Rather, it is a combination of variables that determines actual outcomes.

Physical abusers. Physical abuse is most likely to occur at the hands of the natural parent. Parents who physically abuse their children are not crazy people. Only 10% actually suffer from a serious psychotic disorder (Berger & Thompson, 2005). The remainder are adults who claim to care for their children although the care they offer frequently is marred by violence or neglect.

Abusive parents frequently have unrealistic expectations about what children should be able to do at a particular age. For instance, a parent might become incensed when an infant does not stop crying on demand or when a 2-year-old continues to wet or soil his pants. These parents also inaccurately assume **intentionality** in their children's behavior, believing that the child is uncooperative or "misbehaving" just to be difficult. Thus, a mother may be convinced that a school-age child who fell down and scraped her knee did so deliberately, just to upset her. Physically abusive parents also tend to have a "spare the rod and spoil the child" philosophy about physical punishment; they are afraid that their children will be out of control unless they spank them, even for small infractions.

Unfortunately, because these parents often have a low tolerance for stress, usually possess a poor repertoire of life skills, and are frequently unhappy being a parent, their intentions to be an effective parent result in physical abuse of their children. In an overwhelming number of these cases, the adults have experienced poor relationships with their own parents, often having been abused as children themselves (Goleman, 2007).

Finally, situational factors within and outside the family play a significant role in the likelihood of abuse occurring. For example, abuse is most common in families in which finances are severely strained (regardless of socioeconomic status). Other stressful life events such as divorce, unemployment, family conflict, overcrowding, lack of a support system, or drastic changes in status and role create the conditions in which abuse may eventually take place (Berk, 2006). Most recently, the results of a nationwide survey by the National Committee to Prevent Child Abuse also linked child abuse with homelessness and substance abuse by parents (Children's Defense Fund, 2005). Abusive families frequently are isolated families; that is, they have little access to parenting information that might be of use to them or to potential resource people and have no real means of social comparison, either for their children or for themselves. This isolation heightens, and sometimes causes, many of the problems they experience.

Increasingly, scientists believe that abuse occurs as a result of an interactive effect among all of the variables just described: the adult's personality, lack of parenting skills, unrealistic expectations, situational characteristics, and lack of community support services (Papalia, Olds, & Feldmen 2006). The volatile nature of the encounter may be heightened by the child's own attributes, such as temperament or physical appearance. How and why this occurs will be discussed shortly.

Neglectful parents.   Parents who fail to meet their children's basic physical, emotional, or educational needs typically are isolated individuals who have difficulty forming relationships or carrying on the routine tasks of life (Crosson-Tower, 2005). They also lack the basic skills necessary to organize a safe, warm home environment. As a result they ignore their children's needs. Again, such parents are likely to have been poorly nurtured themselves and to have stressful relationships with other significant adults in their lives. Thus, they often do not have

access to models who could demonstrate more appropriate forms of engagement with children.

Sexual abusers.   For many years, parents and helping professionals have warned children to stay away from strangers. Most often, the child molester has been portrayed as a classic "scary person": an unfamiliar, middle-aged male in a raincoat who hangs around parks or schools waiting to tempt a lone child with candy. Unfortunately, this scenario does not cover the most common situations in which children are at risk. In reality, in 80% of child sexual abuse cases, the child knows the offender, and more frequently than not, the offender is a member of the child's own household. When sexual abuse by strangers does occur, it is most likely to happen in a single episode, during warm-weather months, outside, in an automobile, or in a public building. On the other hand, abuse perpetrated by family members or acquaintances is apt to occur repeatedly, at any time, and at home (Shaffer & Kipp, 2006). In these cases, force or bribery seldom is used. Instead, the child may submit to the adult's requests in deference to the adult's perceived status in the family or from a desire to please.

Families in which the father or father figure abuses a daughter represent the most common incidents of abuse. These families often are plagued by dysfunctional relationships, especially between spouses. The adult male frequently has low self-esteem and is weak and resentful rather than virile or oversexed as is the common stereotype. Most mothers are aware of the situation but are unable to face their predicament and so must deny what is happening. In fact, once the abuse becomes known, it is not uncommon for family members to turn against the victim, blaming her for the disruption. Circumstances such as these can go on for years if no intervention is forthcoming.

The Victims

The majority of physical-abuse cases are initiated during the preschool years. Though the phenomenon has been tied to abuse in future generations, it is important to point out that individuals who were abused or neglected do not necessarily grow up to abuse or neglect their own children. Though it is true that many of those who abuse children were abused themselves as children, it does not hold true that because a child is abused, he or she will automatically become an abuser in the future. Other myths often attached to children who are abused and neglected are that they become deviant adults who are involved in crime, drugs, or prostitution, or that the effects of abuse or neglect are irreparable and render victims incapable of leading a fulfilling and happy life (Crosson-Tower, 2005).

Individuals can and do break the cycle of earlier maltreatment, and that is most likely to occur if there is early detection, support from a nonabusive adult during childhood (and therapy when indicated), and when they later have a satisfying, nonabusive relationship with a spouse (Shaffer & Kipp, 2006).

Although 10% of all victims of sexual abuse are younger than 5 years of age, the majority are school children between the ages of 9 and 12 (Santrock, 2005). Although females are primary targets, it should not be forgotten that boys also are victims of abuse and that adult females can be abusers. Unlike physical abuse, child sexual abuse often extends to more than one victim within the same family.

These sexual encounters frequently begin with innocent touching and progress to fondling and then to overt sexual stimulation. Forcible rape rarely occurs. Instead, there often are pleasurable overtones to the interactions, which contribute to children's confusion over what is happening to them. The most likely victims are those who lack information about sexual abuse and what to do if it occurs. Children who have low self-esteem and those who are physically weak and socially isolated are the most likely candidates for victimization.

Effects on victims. An obvious outcome of either physical or sexual abuse is injury. For example, it has been reported that abusive acts are the fourth most common cause of death in children 5 years of age and younger (Children's Defense Fund, 2005). Other problems include fractures, lacerations, internal injuries, pregnancy, and venereal disease. In addition, we can only begin to calculate the cost to society of caring for victims, incarcerating perpetrators, and the loss of productive family functioning. Because of the close contact helping professionals enjoy with the children in their care, they play an important role in identifying victims of abuse.

Signs of Abuse

Several signs may indicate possible child abuse. Some relate to the child's appearance, others to the child's behavior, and still others to what the child says. Certain family indicators also should be considered. For example, does the child receive a lot of spankings at home or complain that the parents are always angry?

Does the child come to school early and find reasons to stay after school as long as possible? Abused children may role-play behaviors displayed by abusive parents when they are involved in dramatic play or they may represent the abuse in drawings they make. They may abuse younger children, exhibit aggressive behavior, be self-abusive, or express suicidal ideas. There may be frequent absences from school with no explanation (Driscoll & Nagel, 2004).

The presence of one sign alone does not automatically signal abuse. However, if one or more are present, they should be interpreted as a warning that additional attention is warranted (Berk, 2006). More specific signs are summarized in Table 15-3 and Figure 15-3.

Reporting Child Abuse

Early childhood professionals are required by law to report any evidence of suspected child abuse. Such reports signal only the suspicion that abuse has occurred. However, when there are clear signs of abuse, helping professionals who document and relay them to the proper authorities act as an advocate for the child. Often, there may be no one else in the child's life who is willing to do so.

The reporting process is straightforward. Although particular institutions and government jurisdictions have their own individual procedures, most include:

1. A disclosure of the suspicion to a designated person within the program: social worker, principal, director.
2. A verbal report to the social agency responsible for children's protective services in a particular community. This report is conveyed either directly by the individual who has the suspicion or indirectly through a designated spokesperson. In either case, the identity of the person who originally suspected abuse is kept confidential and is revealed only with his or her consent.
3. A written report to the social agency with which verbal contact was initiated. This usually occurs within two to three days. The written statement contains essential information, usually is brief, and is written in the person's own words rather than in legalistic terms.
4. An interview with the child. This is most common when sexual abuse is suspected. Youngsters usually are interviewed in the presence of someone they trust; in many cases, this is the helping professional in whom they confided.

Table 15-3 Signs of Child Abuse and Neglect: Physical, Behavioral, Verbal, and Family Indicators.

PHYSICAL ABUSE AND NEGLECT

Physical Indicators

Bruises

    Bruises on the face, lips, or mouth; on large areas of the back, torso, buttocks, or thighs; on more than
      one side of the body

    Bruises of different coloration, indicating that they occurred at different times

    Bruises that are clustered

    Bruises that show the imprint of a belt buckle, coat hanger, strap, or wooden spoon

Welts

Wounds, cuts, or punctures

Burns

    Rope burns on arms, legs, neck, face, or torso

    Burns that show a pattern (cigarette, iron, radiator)

    Burns on the buttocks or genitalia

    Caustic burns

    Scalding-liquid burns

Fractures

    Multiple fractures in various stages of healing

    Any fracture in a child younger than 2 years of age

Bone dislocations

Human-bite marks

Neglect

    Child is consistently dirty, hungry, or inappropriately dressed for the weather

    Child has been abandoned

    Child has persistent medical problems that go unattended

Behavioral Indicators

The child:

    Is wary of physical contact with adults

    Flinches when adults approach or move

    Exhibits a dramatic change in behavior

    Shows extreme withdrawal or aggression

    Indicates fear of parents or caregivers

    Consistently arrives early and stays late

    Is consistently tired or falls asleep during the day

    Is frequently late for school or absent

    Is under the influence of alcohol or drugs

    Begs or steals food

    Shows a limited capacity for experiencing pleasure or enjoying life

Verbal Indicators

The child:

    Reports injury by parents or caregiver

    Offers inconsistent explanations for injuries or condition

    Offers incredible explanations for injuries or condition

    Makes comments such as: "Can I come and live with you?", "Do I have to go home?", "My mom/dad
      doesn't like me"

    Reports not having a place to sleep and/or enough to eat

Family Indicators

The family:

    Maintains a filthy home environment

Table 15-3 Signs of Child Abuse and Neglect: Physical, Behavioral, Verbal, and Family Indicators.

Is socially isolated from the rest of the community

Is extremely closed to contacts with school or child's friends

Refuses to allow child to participate in normal school activities (physical education, social events)

Offers inconsistent, illogical, or no explanation for child's injury or condition

   Shows lack of concern about child's injury or condition

Attempts to conceal child's injury or condition

Describes the child as evil, monstrous, or incorrigible

Reports or uses in your presence inappropriate punishments (denial of food, prolonged isolation, beating)

Consistently speaks demeaningly to the child

Abuses alcohol or drugs

Reacts defensively to inquiries regarding the child's health

SEXUAL ABUSE

Physical Indicators
The child:

   Is pregnant

   Shows signs of venereal disease

   Has blood in urine

   Has genitals that are swollen or bruised

   Shows presence of pus or blood on genitals

   Has physical complaints with no apparent physical cause

   Has torn or stained underclothing

   Shows rectal bleeding

Behavioral Indicators
The child:

   Persistently scratches genital area

   Has difficulty sitting on chairs or play equipment (squirming, frequently readjusting position, frequently leaving seat)

   "Straddle walks" as if pants were wet or chafing

   Suddenly loses appetite

   Suddenly reports nightmares

   Shows extreme withdrawal or aggression

   Shows wariness of contact with adults

   Shows inappropriate seductiveness with adults or other children

   Shows a sudden lack of interest in life

   Withdraws into fantasy behavior

   Regresses to infantile behavior such as bed-wetting, thumb sucking, or excessive crying

   Shows limited capacity for enjoying life or experiencing pleasure

   Is promiscuous

   Runs away

   Is frequently truant

   Exhibits knowledge of sexual functions far beyond other children in his or her peer group

   Suddenly withdraws from friends

Verbal Indicators
The child:

   Complains of pain in the genital area

   Reports incidents of sexual contact with an adult or older child

   Reports having to keep secret a game with an adult or an older child

continued

Table 15-3 Signs of Child Abuse and Neglect: Physical, Behavioral, Verbal, and Family Indicators—continued

> Expresses fear of being left alone with a particular adult or older child
> Reports: "She/he fooled around with me," "She/he touched me," or "My mother's boyfriend/my father/my brother/my aunt does things to me when no one else is there"

Family Indicators

The family:
> Exhibits an obvious role reversal between mother and daughter
> Is socially isolated from the rest of the community
> Is extremely closed to contacts with school or child's friends
> Demonstrates extreme discord
> Refuses to allow child to engage in normal social interactions

EMOTIONAL ABUSE AND NEGLECT

Physical Indicators
> None

Behavioral Indicators

The child:
> Does not play
> Is passive and compliant or aggressive and defiant
> Rarely smiles
> Has poor social skills
> Is socially unresponsive
> Avoids eye contact
> Seeks attention constantly and always seems to want and need more
> Relates indiscriminately to adults in precocious ways
> Shows reluctance to eat or fascination with food
> Is prone to rocking, thumb-sucking

Verbal Indicators

The child:
> Reports problems sleeping
> Continually describes self in negative terms
> Is reluctant to include family in program-related events

Family Indicators

The family:
> Conveys unrealistic expectations for the child
> Seems to rely on the child to meet own social and emotional needs
> Shows indifference or lack of interest in child
> Lacks basic knowledge and skills related to child rearing
> Describes child in primarily negative terms
> Seems focused more on meeting own needs than those of the children
> Blames child

5. Continued investigation. From this point on, the case falls within the jurisdiction of a protective service worker. Although contact with the helping professional is desirable, the burden of responsibility has now shifted to the protective service worker.

Despite the fact that professionals must report suspected child abuse, doing so is always stressful, often confusing, and even traumatic. Some of the unfortunate realities that accompany the tough judgments that caretakers make in these situations, and sometimes cause professionals to second-guess

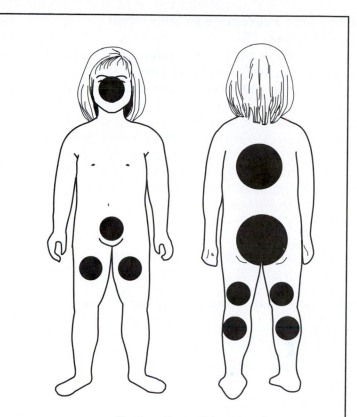

Bruises that usually result
from children's play.

Bruises that seldom result
from children's play.

Figure15-3 Comparison of the location of typical and suspicious bruising areas.
Source: Head Start Bureau, 1977.

themselves, are described by Nunnelley and Fields (1999, p. 75):

Chindwin, a new employee in a child care facility, discovered what appeared to be cigarette burns on a toddler assigned to her room. She showed them to the director who informed her that she didn't want to hear about such incidences (because it would mean loss of the child's weekly tuition). . . . Chindwin felt bewildered and confused. She knew she should report the problem, but she wanted to keep her job.

Tarrissa was concerned about one of the girls in her first grade class. The child was somewhat obsessed with keeping her hands clean and was reluctant to ever go to the bathroom with other children. Following the established procedure in her school, Tarrissa discussed her concerns with the school counselor. Unfortunately, the information became buried on the

counselor's desk, and Tarrissa's suspicions of sexual abuse were never reported.

Renaldo, a teaching assistant in a special program for children with profound disabilities, discovered multiple bruises all over one child's back. Renaldo became physically ill at the sight and enraged that anyone would do such a thing to someone so vulnerable. The abuse was reported, and the child was immediately removed from the home. Renaldo never saw the boy again, and he often wondered what had happened to him.

Margaret, the owner of a family child care home, had worked for months with a family experiencing domestic violence. After a particularly bad incident, the mother sought refuge in a shelter and, fearing for her children's lives, sent the police to retrieve her daughters from Margaret's care. The girls were terribly frightened to go with the officers and cried and clung to Margaret. The experience was traumatic for everyone.

Child Abuse Prevention in the Formal Group Setting

Less than 2% of all substantiated cases of child abuse occur in formal group settings (Lung & Daro, 1996). Although this is a relatively small portion of the total cases, we must do all we can to reduce the possibility that abuse will happen when children are in our care. Hiring procedures for new staff and policies focused on day-to-day operations and family communication can all be designed with child abuse prevention in mind. A summary of strategies that make abuse less likely to occur on the job is presented in Table 15-4.

This chapter has focused on factors that influence ethical judgments helping professionals make. We have concentrated on ethical judgments in day-to-day encounters, considerations about children's extreme behavior, and those regarding child abuse and neglect. Suggestions for working ethically with family members, specific skills for making ethical decisions, and pitfalls that should be avoided follow.

ETHICAL DIMENSIONS OF WORKING WITH FAMILIES

Family members should be welcome at all times. Success of a program depends on communicating with families regularly and establishing warm, caring relationships with parents and other

Table 15-4 Preventive Strategies that Reduce the Probability of Child Abuse in Formal Group Settings.

Hiring Practices

Applicants are carefully screened. This includes all staff members, substitutes, and volunteers—people who work with the children directly and those who provide support services to the programs such as cooks and custodians.

Screening strategies include signed written applications, personal interviews, on-site observations with children, verification of personal and professional references and education qualifications, criminal record checks, and signed declarations related to previous convictions of any crime against children or other violent crime. A person's failure to fully disclose previous convictions is cause for automatic dismissal.

New employees are oriented to the job and are informed of the child abuse prevention procedures to follow.

Mandatory probation periods for new employees are instituted, during which time they are paired with seasoned employees who provide modeling and consultations. New employees are observed frequently to assess their interactions with children.

Day-to-Day Operations

The program's discipline policies are clearly defined.

Programs create conditions that alleviate staff fatigue and burnout, such as limiting the number of children for which each adult is responsible, keeping group sizes within established bounds, providing adequate breaks, and offering refresher training related to discipline, classroom management, parent relations, staff conflict, and child abuse prevention.

Programs are structured to avoid the possibility of private, hidden opportunities for child abuse to occur. All early childhood spaces are regarded as public. Daily routines and the physical environment (both indoors and outdoors) are reviewed to eliminate the possibility that staff members have solitary access to children with no possibility of being observed by others. Program policies encourage parental drop-in visits and provide ongoing supervision by qualified personnel throughout the day.

Source: Data adapted from Position Statement on the Prevention of Child Abuse in Early Childhood Programs and Responsibilities of Early Childhood Programs to Prevent Child Abuse, NAEYC, 1996; Administration of Programs for Young Children, by P. M. Click, 2007, Clifton Park, N.Y.: Delmar Learning; and *Intervening with New Parents: An Effective Way to Prevent Child Abuse*, 1996, Chicago: National Committee for the Prevention of Child Abuse.

family members. Families need information on all components of a program, including philosophy, goals, discipline strategies used, child abuse prevention measures taken by the program, and methods for reporting suspected child abuse. They should also understand that in the interest of keeping their children safe, they will only be released to parents, legal guardians, and the people parents have designated in writing.

Despite every effort to communicate well with families, teachers do encounter ethical situations with families. When surveyed about the most frequent ones, they have reported the following:

- How to handle cases of possible child abuse and neglect
- Challenges created by the custody disputes of parents who are divorcing
- Parents' demands to treat children in ways that teachers, in their professional judgment, believe are harmful
- Requests to share information that they fear parents may use as justification to harshly punish their children
- Encounters with parents who expect special treatment for their children
- Demands that make the teacher vulnerable to burnout or even disciplinary action (Freeman & Swick, 2007, p. 164)

Undoubtedly, one of the thorniest situations in dealing with families is that of filing a child abuse report. Still, if you find it necessary to do so, ethical behavior mandates that you contact the family after it has been made. The purpose of this contact is not to humiliate them or to try to get them to repent, but to indicate that you respect them enough that you would not do something behind their backs.

Inform them that you suspect that their child has been subjected to physical or sexual abuse. Explain that you are legally bound to report such suspicions and that you wanted them to know you had done so. Indicate that you would like to be supportive of the family in any way they might find acceptable. Expect a hostile or incredulous reaction, particularly if the parents themselves have been involved in the abuse.

Avoid berating the family or spending a great deal of time trying to justify your actions to them. Should parents choose to respond to you, either in defense of their actions, to explain extenuating circumstances, or to accuse you of misrepresenting them, listen nonjudgmentally. Use the reflective listening skills you have learned to accomplish this.

Keep confidential all matters related to the case. Do not gossip or disclose tantalizing tidbits to other parents or to staff members who are not directly involved. Refuse to answer questions from curious people who have no legitimate right to the information.

If you are in a situation that requires continued contact with the family, treat them casually and civilly. Acknowledge their presence, speak to them, and be genuine in your interactions. This means not being effusive or more friendly than you have been in the past. Talk about day-to-day affairs rather than "the case."

In all situations that call for considering ethical decision-making with families, professionals must move beyond their own moral and idiosyncratic reactions to a particular situation and rely explicitly on the professional code of conduct, "using the 3Rs of parental relationship: respecting, responding, and reflecting on the strengths, hopes, and dreams of each family" (Freeman & Swick, 2007, p. 169).

SKILLS FOR MAKING ETHICAL JUDGMENTS

 How to Make Ethical Judgments

1. Identify situations that have ethical implications. This may encompass both hypothetical and real circumstances. Refer to the journal *Young Children* for sample cases illustrating ethical dilemmas. Think about ways to approach these. Refer to the sample answers in each issue, comparing your response to those of others in the field. In addition, keep a journal of your experiences with children and families. Catalog examples from real life to discuss with colleagues in an appropriate setting.

2. Become familiar with the NAEYC Code of Ethical Conduct. Review the code. Know what it contains. Refer to it often when faced with perplexing situations that challenge your personal and professional values.

continued

SKILLS FOR MAKING ETHICAL JUDGMENTS—CONTINUED

3. Practice using the NAEYC Code of Ethical Conduct in response to ethical dilemmas. You may find that some circumstances are easily categorized as ethical or unethical because they clearly support or run counter to the code. Others are not so obvious. This may be due to their complexity or the subtle nature of the incident. In either case, practice will improve your skills and confidence using the code. Both students in training and practitioners in the field report that such practice is most beneficial when carried out regularly and in small groups of colleagues.

- First, decide what makes a troubling situation an ethical dilemma. Remember, not all worrisome situations are ethical in nature. Ethics implies right and wrong.
- Identify signals that alert you to potential ethical issues. Listen carefully to the signals other people say they use. Compare these with your own and add or subtract ones that would be helpful for future use.
- Next, sort out matters that must be addressed by different people. The response to an ethical dilemma may require varying actions by more than one person. Explore what these responses might be.
- Finally, refer to the code for help in thinking about priorities and responsibilities in determining a plan to address the situation.

The point is not to achieve unanimous agreement on a single course of action, but to generate one or more strategies that support ethical approaches to the problem. Identify those strategies that seem most congruent with your own thinking. Consider what you would say and do to carry out your plan.

Keep a record of typical responses to hypothetical circumstances. In real-life situations in which you are involved, carry out your plan. Then make note of the outcomes for future reference.

4. Refer to the code when talking about why you carry out certain practices in your work and why you refrain from using others. Such conversations may be with parents,

colleagues, or laypersons. Explaining to others that we have a code of ethics is a valuable sign of professionalism. It also provides justification for judgments and decision making that goes beyond intuition. For instance, the reason early childhood professionals do not deprive children of food or use of the toilet as a means of punishment is that such behavior is unethical according to principles set forth in the code. As a profession we have agreed that ethical behavior requires us to inform parents of accidents involving their child and to maintain family confidentiality.

These expectations are outlined in the code. Referencing the code periodically is a good way to keep its standards in the forefront of your thinking.

 How to Make Day-to-Day Judgments

1. Become aware of values that are important to you. Think about decisions you have made in your own life in terms of the values they represent. Try to determine what basic beliefs govern your interactions with children and their families. Figure out if there are discernible patterns to the kinds of choices you make. Discuss your ideas with friends and colleagues. Compare your reactions with theirs, and try to articulate why you have chosen a particular path. Take advantage of formalized opportunities to engage in values clarification.

2. Comprehensively assess situations in which a judgment must be made. Make an initial survey that includes the following factors: recognition of the child's perspective, awareness of your own affective state, consideration of the child's age and past experiences, and an analysis of the situational context.

If you are in a situation in which you are an observer and in which safety is not in question, take a few moments to sort out the issues prior to acting. Should you be in a

SKILLS FOR MAKING ETHICAL JUDGMENTS

circumstance in which an immediate response is expected, use an affective reflection and the middle portion of the personal message (that is, your emotions and the reasons for them) to identify aloud the child's perspective and your own. If, at that point, you need a few more moments to think, tell the children, "Let me think about it for a minute, and then I'll decide what to do."

3. Consider alternative strategies in terms of their potential outcomes. Imagine various responses to a particular situation. Predict the possible impact of each on the child, on yourself, and on others. Think about how each outcome would either support or impede your current goals for all parties.

4. Select and implement a strategy or combination of strategies that supports your overall goals for children and that is based on your priorities for the situation. Keep in mind the goals you are working toward for each child and for the group as a whole. In addition, use the priority principles outlined in this chapter to help you sort out what is most important in a given instance. Use the goals and priorities you identify as the basis for action.

5. Include nonintervention as a strategy option. Taking no action in a situation can be the result of a considered judgment on your part. Some incidents, particularly when they have no effect on others, do not require a response.

6. Adopt standards that take into account children's age and experience. Apply your understanding of child development and learning to your expectations for children's performance. Do not expect children to perform perfectly the first few times. Allow them to make mistakes. Observe youngsters carefully to determine what they can and cannot do, then set your standards accordingly. As they become more adept, increase your expectations gradually.

7. Reassess situations in light of new information. Remember that you can make different judgments regarding your goals, strategies, and standards as you acquire new knowledge. This may mean selecting an option you had previously discarded or developing an entirely new one.

8. Evaluate the ethical judgments you make. Take time to assess the effectiveness of your thinking and of corresponding actions. Consider whether the potential outcome became reality. If so, ask yourself whether it contributed to progress toward a desired goal. If the anticipated effect did not occur, reflect on what contributed to the incongruous result and what might be done instead. Discuss your deliberations with a colleague or supervisor.

9. Learn from judgment errors. Sooner or later, you will make a judgment that you will come to regret. When this happens, mentally review the circumstances under which you made it. Consider what prompted your response and what other options were available to you at the time. Try to determine what went awry, and figure out what you might do if you had the decision to make again. Sometimes, you will conclude that you made a bad judgment and that another option would have been better. On other occasions, you will deduce that the judgment was right at the time, even though the outcome was negative or stressful. Mentally catalogue relevant information for future use. Then, move on. It is counterproductive to unceasingly agonize over a past judgment.

10. Support colleagues who have made poor judgments. When fellow staff members have made a judgment and it has turned out poorly, offer comfort and encouragement. Be available as a sounding board and listen to their evaluation of what went into their decision. Help them sort out what went wrong and brainstorm remedial strategies or alternate approaches for the future.

11. Identify values you and colleagues or parents hold in common when differences in goals, strategies, and/or standards exist. Talk over conflicts in approach that arise. Explore

continued

SKILLS FOR MAKING ETHICAL JUDGMENTS—CONTINUED

thoroughly the other person's perceptions by asking him or her to describe his or her understanding of the situation and overall purpose within it. Listen carefully and quietly, avoiding jumping to conclusions, interrupting, or giving your opinion prematurely.

Use the reflective listening skills you have learned to convey interest and acceptance. Look beyond the details of what people are saying to the essence of their message.

Find common aims at this level. Then, proceed to negotiate the goals, strategies, and standards that might be acceptable to both of you. In most cases, this type of clarification should contribute to mutual understanding and a more unified approach. If you recognize that you have a true conflict in values, acknowledge this state of affairs. Then, determine what you will have to do to make the situation livable.

 How to Deal with Children's Extreme Behavior

1. Get to know the children in your group prior to making a judgment that any one of them is exhibiting extreme behavior. Although the mere presence of some behaviors is enough to signal a problem, it is important that you give yourself enough time to determine what is typical or atypical for each child.

2. Make a concerted effort to change a behavior by using appropriate guidance techniques before judging it extreme. Use the skills you have learned in previous chapters as your initial means of addressing problematic behavior. Be consistent in your approach, and allow enough time (usually several weeks) for your strategies to have a fair chance of success. Ask a colleague to review your plan and/or to observe its implementation in order to judge whether it is appropriate and whether you are carrying it out effectively. If you discover that a child's continued exhibition of a problem behavior is the result of a faulty plan or ineffective implementation, make the corresponding revisions.

3. Confirm your judgment that a child's behavior is extreme. Make an objective record of the child's behavior over time. Then, refer to resources that describe age or behavioral norms. If the behavior appears to be inappropriate, carefully observe how often it can be seen in other children of comparable age while they are both active and quiet. If no other children manifest the behavior in question, talk to an experienced and trusted colleague who has worked with many children effectively. Also, consult your supervisor or other coworkers whose job responsibilities encompass this type of consultation. If others agree that the behavior seems extreme, seek out a reputable professional for consultation.

4. Communicate to the family your concern that their child's behavior is extreme. When making the initial contact, whether in person, by telephone, or by written message, express your concern matter-of-factly and request a meeting with the parent(s). Avoid going into elaborate detail or sounding secretive and mysterious in the initial contact with parents so that you do not alarm them or make them feel defensive. You might say something like: "I've been observing Charles for the last several days and have become concerned about his sudden lack of interest in interacting with the other children. Normally, he's quite outgoing, and his withdrawal has persisted for some time. I'd like to set up a time to discuss this with you in more detail."

When the meeting takes place, be prepared to provide concrete examples of the behavior in question. Find out if the same behavior occurs at home and whether or not the parent considers it atypical. If, as the conference proceeds, you reach the conclusion that indeed, the behavior is extreme, share this concern with the parent(s) and provide a rationale for your judgment. Be prepared to suggest specific courses of action the parent(s) could take.

SKILLS FOR MAKING ETHICAL JUDGMENTS

5. Seek out or recommend the type of professional who could deal most appropriately with a particular problem. Determine with the family who will contact the consulting professional. If the behavior may be physically based, as in problems with eating, elimination, sleeping, too much or too little energy, or obvious depression, the family should first contact a physician. If an extreme behavior is obviously unconnected to physical sources, begin with a behavioral expert trained in dealing with the behavior of concern. Such an expert is more likely to be familiar with behavioral problems than would many physicians. Further, reputable, competent behavioral specialists would be aware of conditions to which physical difficulties could contribute and would suggest medical consultation in such instances.

Check on potential community resources such as child guidance clinics, college psychological clinics, school guidance counselors, community mental health agencies, social service agencies in your area, intermediate school districts (umbrella agencies that offer special services across school districts), and programs specializing in youngsters whose problems are similar to the one you have tentatively identified for a particular child. Even when an individual program may not exactly suit your needs, personnel there may be able to direct you to a more appropriate source.

6. Provide emotional support to families who are seeking outside help for their child's extreme behavior. The referral process often takes a long time, resulting in anxiety or frustration for families. Offer words of encouragement or sympathy, and be willing to listen to familial complaints and lamentations. Use reflective listening skills to communicate your understanding. Take additional action, if possible, to speed up the process.

7. Follow up on your recommendation that a child or family receive outside services. If you have agreed to provide a contact for a medical or behavioral expert, do so promptly.

Make the contact directly or through the channels dictated by your agency or program. Periodically check on the progress of your referral and make sure that contact actually is made. Should the family assume primary responsibility for seeking help, communicate with them regularly to ascertain what has happened.

8. Provide accurate, relevant information to the consulting professional. Share your observations of the child's behavior, either verbally or in writing. Make available records you have kept regarding his or her behavior pattern, or summarize them in a report.

Invite the outside expert to observe the child within the formal group setting. Offer to meet with him or her and the family.

9. Coordinate the way you deal with the child's extreme behavior in the formal group setting with the way it is being handled by the family and by the consultant to whom the child has been referred. Find out what action has been recommended. Discuss with the consultant and the family the feasibility of adapting your program to the consultant's recommendations as well as ways in which your actions can complement theirs. For instance, if it has been decided that certain behaviors will be rewarded and others ignored at home and in the therapy session, follow the same guidelines, if possible.

Provide feedback to all adults involved in the plan regarding the child's progress in your setting. Make relevant suggestions for changes and revisions in the plan. Also, ask for feedback regarding your own performance. Maintain periodic contact with both the consultant and the family throughout this time.

 How to Deal with Child Abuse and Neglect

1. Find out the appropriate procedures for reporting child abuse and neglect. Read the laws of your state regarding child abuse and

continued

SKILLS FOR MAKING ETHICAL JUDGMENTS—CONTINUED

neglect, including what constitutes abuse, the persons or agencies to whom such cases should be referred, who is legally obligated to report abuse, and what safeguards exist for those reporting. Although all 50 states mandate reporting suspected cases and protect helping professionals from legal prosecution when making reports in good faith, the specifics of who is bound to report, who is notified, and how it is done vary. For example, the Michigan Child Protection Law requires all school administrators, teachers, counselors, social workers, nurses, physicians, dentists, audiologists, law enforcement officers, and duly regulated child care providers to make an oral report of suspected child abuse or neglect to the local department of social services.

In addition to obtaining this legal knowledge, find out the reporting protocol of the formal group setting in which you are employed. If you are required to make a report through a designated person, determine how you will be apprised that your report has been filed. Also, ask what role you are expected to play in subsequent action. Should the policy require that you report your suspicions directly to the authorities, find out who they are. (Often, these are described as "children's protective services.") If you are unable to locate the authorities in your community, contact one of the nationwide emergency numbers provided in Appendix B.

2. Watch for signs of child abuse and neglect. Use the physical, behavioral, verbal, and family indicators outlined in Table 15-2.

Pay attention to children. Look at them. Listen to what they say. Disclosure may be accidental or embedded in statements they make about other events (Austin, 2000). Be alert for changes in a child's physical condition or demeanor. Believe children when they persistently complain that they are hungry, that they "hurt down there," or that cousin Billy beat them with a strap (Hendrick & Weissman, 2006). Most children do not make up stories about abuse or molestation.

3. Document your suspicions. Keep written notes about the sign that caused you to suspect child abuse or neglect and the date on which it occurred. If more than one sign is present, record each of them.

4. Respond appropriately when children disclose abuse, as follows:

  a. Remain calm and reassuring, maintaining an open, relaxed posture.

  b. Take the child to a private space to talk out of the earshot of others.

  c. Use language appropriate to the child's developmental level and do not use words that the child has not already used. Begin with general, open-ended questions or statements. Refrain from asking "why" questions. "What" and "how" questions are preferable.

  d. Use reflective listening and minimal prompts ("um hmm," "I see.").

  e. Take the child seriously.

  f. Allow the child feelings (e.g., guilt, shame, fear, ambivalence) and let the child know that such feelings are normal.

  g. Assure the child that he or she is not alone and that you are willing to help. However, do not make false promises (e.g., "It will be all right." "Nothing bad is going to happen.").

  h. Obtain only the information necessary to make a report.

  i. Reassure the child that the abuse is not his or her fault. Thank the child for confiding in you about the problem.

  j. Do not condemn the alleged abuser.

  k. Help the child devise a safety plan if the abuse happens again by telling a trusted adult. (Austin, 2000, pp. 3–5)

5. Promptly report suspected cases of child abuse or neglect. Should a child or family display a combination of signs that you have been trained to recognize as indicative of child abuse, report it. Do not delay in the hope that conditions will change or that you were wrong. Do not vacillate about what to do. Once the suspicion is there, the subsequent action is clear.

SKILLS FOR MAKING ETHICAL JUDGMENTS

6. Reassure children who have revealed that they are victims of abuse or neglect. Say something like: "It was hard for you to tell me about this" or "You're upset your momma knocked your tooth out. I'm really glad you told me." Let them know that you believe what they have said and that no harm will come to them from you for reporting the incident. Reflect their feelings of confusion, worry, anger, or guilt. Allow them to talk out their feelings and to describe individual incidents with as much or as little detail as they want. Remain receptive and supportive of abused children no matter how uncomfortable or distressed you may feel.

On the other hand, avoid pumping children for details that are beyond their capacity or willingness to reveal at a given time. Express your sympathy about what has happened, but at the same time, do not berate the child's family. Even youngsters who have been ill treated often feel a loyalty to family members. They may withdraw if they perceive that they must defend their family to you.

Many children feel guilty regarding their role in the abusive situation. They may conclude that because they are "no good" or "ugly" or "so bad," the adult had no choice but to abuse them. Attempt to rectify these misperceptions by stating that what happened was not the child's fault. Instead, it was the adult's behavior that was inappropriate.

Explain that sometimes, adults become angry, confused, or lonely, but that beating children, tricking them, or subjecting them to unwanted fondling is wrong.

7. Talk to children about physical touching. Begin with infants, and continue throughout the childhood years, to use feeling words to describe physical interactions. Provide children with information about how touching affects them and others. Say things like: "A hug feels good," "Pinching hurts," "You were happy when Jeremy scratched your back," or "You didn't like it when Marion hit you." Such statements form the foundation for a "touch vocabulary" that can be expanded as children develop.

Familiarizing children with these specialized words is the first step in teaching personal safety.

8. Teach children personal safety. It is widely believed that children benefit when they are taught ways to avoid exploitive touching. Refer to the personal safety terms, facts, and principles in Appendix C for ideas on relevant and accurate facts to present to children. Use these facts and principles as the basis for discussions with children and to give you ideas about appropriate material for activities and skits. Review Chapters 8 and 13 for guidelines on how to construct these. Adapt your presentation to match children's understanding and experience. For example:

a. Initiate a discussion in which children talk about touches that make them feel good and touches that make them feel bad. Introduce the idea of confusing touches: those that start out feeling good but that eventually become uncomfortable (tickling, bear hugs, petting). Point out that no one has the right to use bad touch or confusing touch with another person. Tell children that if someone tries to touch them in ways they do not like, they can say "No," get away, and then tell someone they trust.

b. Set up a skit in which one character tries to trick another character into doing something. With very young children or older youngsters who have had little prior training, begin with obvious tricks unrelated to sexual abuse. As the children begin to understand the notion of a trick, introduce skits that address inappropriate touching (e.g., bribery, keeping a "secret," or flattery). Emphasize the point that it is not okay for people to force children to touch them or to trick children into touching them. Teach children that if a person tries to trick them into touching him or her or into doing things the child does not understand, the child can say, "No, get away!" and tell someone he or she trusts.

continued

SKILLS FOR MAKING ETHICAL JUDGMENTS—CONTINUED

c. Play the "What if . . . ?" game as a way to check children's understanding of how to respond in dangerous situations. Make up pretend episodes, such as "What if the man down the street asks you to come in and see the new puppies?" "What if your babysitter asks you to keep a secret, especially from your mom and dad?" or "What if you have a fight with your friends in the park and a nice lady you don't know offers you a ride home?" Reflect children's answers and provide accurate information as appropriate. Ask open-ended questions to further extend the discussions.

9. Treat families with sensitivity even when child abuse is suspected or has occurred. Be aware of help available in your community for parents who indicate they are on the brink of abuse. Promising studies show that many abusing parents can be helped so that they no longer resort to physical violence (Shaffer, 2005). This is an indication of how important it is to refer parents to people and programs designed to assist them. Find out as much as you can about such support programs in your area. Identify short-term alternatives such as hotlines, sources of respite care, parent groups, educational opportunities, and workshops. In addition, keep a file of long-term options including local individual and family therapists, mental health agencies, and religious and social service programs, as well as such nationally recognized groups as Parents Anonymous and National Committee to Prevent Child Abuse (see Appendix B).

PITFALLS TO AVOID

There are many guidelines to remember in deciding how to make an ethical judgment. The skills just covered describe the behaviors you should exhibit. The pitfalls that follow describe behaviors you should avoid.

Failing to make a conscious judgment because of time pressures. Sometimes, helping professionals are so rushed that they think they cannot take the time to figure out what to do. Instead, they react instinctively. Occasionally, their intuitive responses are correct and fit well into a comprehensive approach to the child and the group. More often, they satisfy short-term ends but do not comprehensively address long-term goals. Although it is not always feasible to ponder over what to do, it is possible to incorporate the ethical judgment process somewhere in the situation. Even if this can be done only in retrospect, assessing your judgment is a valuable professional skill. Moreover, unless safety is the issue, it is better to postpone your reaction in order to think it out than to respond haphazardly. Frequently, time spent in an initial assessment that leads to a successful approach is less than that accumulated over time in failed efforts.

Staying with a poor judgment too long. At times, people become wedded to a selected option because they have invested so much time and energy in making that judgment. They fail to recognize signs that a goal or standard does not fit, that a strategy useful under other circumstances is not effective in this instance, or that a plan simply is not working. If they continue to ignore these cues, the situation will deteriorate. The best way to avoid this pitfall is to keep alert to changes in the situational context and to remain receptive to new information. Continual reevaluation of judgments made also is essential, as is a willingness to let go of unproductive approaches.

Failing to recognize your limitations. Helping professionals err when they imagine themselves as the only person capable of helping a child even when the child's problems call for skills beyond their own. This mind-set can be the result of any of the following:

1. They may think they are the only ones who care enough to handle the child appropriately or who understand the child well enough to know what to do.
2. They may jealously guard their role in the child's life and perceive other helping professionals as interlopers.

3. They may not recognize the seriousness of the child's situation.
4. They may interpret consultation with an outside expert as an indication of their own inadequacy.
5. They may think they possess skills that, in fact, they do not.

In any case, this type of thinking is not conducive to creating the most favorable climate for the child's development. Helping professionals who find themselves resisting making a referral, even when all signs indicate that doing so is in the best interest of the child, must examine their attitudes. If they find that their lack of enthusiasm relates to any of the reasons just described, reconsideration is in order.

Neglecting to clarify your own role in relation to the consulting professional.   Working with an outside consultant requires a coordination of efforts.

Children benefit most when they are handled consistently. This means that professionals in the formal group setting must have a clear understanding of what expectations, if any, the consultant has for their performance. It is not enough to have a vague picture of what is required. Instead, one must develop a precise list of expectations. It is therefore important to clarify mutual goals and the strategies and standards that will support them.

Not following the recommendation of a consultant long enough to allow it to work.   One of the most common pitfalls in working with an outside consultant is to prematurely abandon a mutually agreed-on plan. Having finally taken the step of calling in an outsider, the helping professional may expect instant results. When these are not forthcoming, he or she gives up in disappointment. To avoid succumbing to this form of disillusionment, it is best to formulate, in conjunction with the consultant, a timeline along which progress will be measured. Knowing that a particular approach might have to be employed for several weeks or even months before a change can be expected increases your patience and makes setbacks easier to bear.

Ignoring signs of abuse.   Sometimes, in an effort to avoid dealing with a difficult situation or because they wish it were not so, helping professionals overlook obvious cues that abuse has occurred. If a child exhibits bruises and reports that his mother beat him, the professional may think, "Oh, all children get paddled sometimes." When a

youngster's vagina is raw and bleeding, the adult attributes it to masturbation. Should a child continually be dirty and smell bad, the adult passes it off as typical of that cultural group or social class.

Children are not served well when adults reach these conclusions, which are based not on the facts but on their own psychological and emotional defenses. Every sign that could indicate abuse must be taken seriously. Children should not be made to suffer because adults are afraid to face reality.

Threatening families you suspect of child abuse.   Occasionally, rather than reporting a case of probable child abuse, helping professionals try to intervene directly with the family. They confront family members, saying things like: "If you do this again, I'll have to report you" or "Promise me you'll stop, and I won't report you." Their motives may be self-serving (wishing to avoid legal entanglements) or well-meaning (hoping to save the family embarrassment).

In either case, these tactics are ill advised and should not be used. Rather, helping professionals should follow the procedures outlined in the child abuse section of this chapter.

Purposely frightening children as a way to teach personal safety.   Adults who are trying to teach children to be careful about strangers and exploitive touching may deliberately overgeneralize their warnings so that youngsters become fearful of everyone and all forms of physical contact. Describing in lurid detail horrible incidents of abuse, treating all situations as unsafe, and failing to distinguish "good touch" from "bad touch" contributes to this negative perception. It is not healthy for young people to feel always in jeopardy. Instead, they must be exposed to a balanced view in which caution is promoted, but complete terror and distrust is avoided.

Assuming personal safety training will automatically protect children from sexual abuse. Even with personal safety training, many children will have trouble saying "No" to adults, especially people with whom they have a close relationship. Young children should not be expected to handle the full burden of protecting themselves. Treat personal safety training as one potential tool children have at their disposal, not as a one-time inoculation against all potential abuse. Throughout childhood, children continue to need the support of caring adults. Remain alert to signs of sexual abuse regardless of whether or not children have had any training in this regard.

SUMMARY

Helping professionals continually make ethical judgments for and about the children with whom they work. These encompass long- or short-range judgments, those which adults have time to evaluate carefully and others that must be made immediately, and judgments that have profound or relatively minor effects. All ethical judgments must be made consciously.

In making any ethical judgment, helping professionals go through several steps. First, they assess the circumstance; next, they think about possible actions in response; eventually, they must select one or a combination of strategies, which they then put into action. Finally, helping professionals evaluate the results of their decisions and use this information to guide future judgments. Although no outcome can be guaranteed, following this process makes a measured judgment more likely. Furthermore, the probability is greater that the adult's goals, strategies, and standards for children will be congruent.

Goals represent milestones on the path toward achieving social competence. Strategies are the specific practices adults employ to pursue their goals for children. Standards are used to determine the degree to which goals have been achieved. Developing, implementing, and evaluating goals, strategies, and standards calls for a multitude of judgments.

Several variables affect the ethical judgments people make. Among these are their values. Understanding your own values leads to more conscious behavior and helps individuals to respect the values of others as well as to separate values from goals, strategies, and standards. A second variable that affects ethical judgments helping professionals make is their knowledge of child development and learning. A third is the context of the situation in question. Deciding which professional behaviors are right and which ones are wrong is a function of ethical judgment. Helping professionals refer to their ethical codes of conduct in making such determinations.

Other judgments involve establishing priorities from among a range of possibilities; it is important to adopt and follow principles for how to set these priorities. Such principles range from putting safety first to making choices based on personal preferences.

The preceding discussion has dealt with everyday kinds of ethical judgments. Two arenas require specialized judgments: children's extreme behavior and child abuse or neglect. The judgment to be made in each case is whether the condition exists. Once this is determined, there are specific actions helping professionals should follow. The factors that go into a judgment of whether children's behavior is extreme are the presence of self-destructive acts or a sudden shift in a child's functioning; inappropriate behavior for the child's age; persistently intense behavior; indiscriminate evidence of particular behaviors; impairment of a child's present or future functioning; and resistance of the behavior to change. Extreme behavior often can be attributed to physiological causes, children's fears, and childhood depression.

Ethical judgments about suspected child abuse or neglect are critical for children's health and well-being. Physical abuse is a non-accidental injury that results from acts of omission or commission by a family member, guardian, or caregiver. Sexual abuse exists when youngsters are forced or persuaded to engage in sexual activity by an older child or adult.

Effects of abuse on its victims are injury, truancy, dramatic behavior changes, psychological distress, guilt, and anger. The need for early intervention is critical, so helping professionals must become familiar with the signs of abuse. For each type, there are physical, behavioral, verbal, and family indicators.

All states have specific reporting guidelines that helping professionals must learn. There are specific skills helping professionals can learn to enable them to make ethical day-to-day judgments, some involving children's extreme behavior and others concerning child abuse and neglect. In addition, there are behaviors that helping professionals should avoid when making these types of judgments.

KEY TERMS

anxiety disorders	intentionality	sexual abuse
basic values	neglect	standards
compulsions	obsessions	strategies
ethical judgments	relative values	values
goals	school phobia	

DISCUSSION QUESTIONS

1. Discuss the relationship between helping professionals' values and their goals, strategies, and standards for children. Give some examples from your own life.

2. In a small group, discuss a value that you hold. As best you can, trace its origin and how it has affected a judgment you have made.

3. Consider the following cases. Use the NAEYC Code of Ethical Conduct (Appendix A) to help you make a judgment about the ethics or lack of ethics displayed. First, identify parts of the code that pertain to each case. Next, determine whether the person(s) acted in an ethical or unethical way. Finally, discuss possible responses.
   a. Kevin Matthews was recently hired as assistant teacher in the 3-year-old room at the McMillan Child Care Center. His room is next to the toddler room. He notices that although the legal ratio is one adult for every four toddlers, the twelve children are frequently left with one adult in attendance. When he mentions this concern to the director, she says, "You pay attention to what goes on in your room. I'll worry about the rest." Kevin observes no change in the supervision pattern for toddlers over the next several weeks.
   b. The parent council for a cooperative nursery school decides not to interview James Beck for the job of head teacher in the toddler group because they believe women are the best caregivers for children that age.
   c. The State of Michigan is reviewing Public Act 116—State Regulations for Child Care. Mr. Kowalski, a second-grade teacher, volunteers to be on the review panel.

4. Discuss the priority principles outlined in this chapter. Make comments either in support of or in opposition to:
   a. The order in which they are presented
   b. A specific principle or principles
   c. How they should or should not be applied

5. Define what is meant by extreme behavior. Describe four factors that must be taken into account when making an ethical judgment about whether a behavior is extreme. Discuss three pitfalls to avoid in making this kind of judgment.

6. Discuss how a child's fear may result in extreme behavior. Describe the ethical judgments a helping professional must make in such a case.

7. Define what is meant by physical abuse and neglect. Discuss who are the most likely victims and the most likely perpetrators. Discuss what you would do if you suspected physical abuse.

8. Define what is meant by sexual abuse. Discuss who are the most likely victims and the most likely perpetrators. Discuss what to do if you suspect sexual abuse.

9. You help a 3-year-old with toileting and notice what appear to be welt marks on her buttocks and legs. Find the place in the NAEYC Code of Ethical Conduct (Appendix A) that offers professional guidelines in such a situation. What should you do, based on the code?

10. Discuss the similarities and differences in ethical judgments you would make on a day-to-day basis and those you would make when dealing with extreme behavior or child abuse.

FIELD ASSIGNMENTS

1. Interview an early childhood professional about ethical decisions he or she has made. Without betraying the rule of confidentiality, ask the person to describe a situation requiring an ethical judgment in which he or she was involved. Ask: What made it an ethical dilemma? How was the situation handled? Looking back on the outcome, would he or she do anything differently if the same circumstance arose again?

2. Describe at least two situations that occurred during your field placement in which you made a conscious judgment using the priority principles identified earlier in this chapter. Describe each situation and what you did. Identify the priority principle(s) you used. Discuss your response with classmates. Would you handle the situation the same way again? Why or why not?

3. Name the person in your field placement to whom you would report a suspected case of child abuse. Outline the child abuse reporting procedures required in your agency or state. Name the governmental agency responsible for dealing with child abuse in your community. Identify at least three agencies, services, or programs available to parents who are on the brink of child abuse or who have committed child abuse.

4. Look up the law of your state regarding the reporting of child abuse and neglect.

Appendix A

CODE OF ETHICAL CONDUCT AND STATEMENT OF COMMITMENT

A position statement of the
National Association for the Education of Young Children
Revised April 2005

PREAMBLE

NAEYC recognizes that those who work with young children face many daily decisions that have moral and ethical implications. The NAEYC Code of Ethical Conduct offers guidelines for responsible behavior and sets forth a common basis for resolving the principal ethical dilemmas encountered in early childhood care and education. The Statement of Commitment is not part of the Code but is a personal acknowledgement of an individual's willingness to embrace the distinctive values and moral obligations of the field of early childhood care and education. The primary focus of the Code is on daily practice with children and their families in programs for children from birth through 8 years of age, such as infant/toddler programs, preschool and prekindergarten programs, child care centers, hospital and child life settings, family child care homes, kindergartens, and primary classrooms. When the issues involve young children, then these provisions also apply to specialists who do not work directly with children, including program administrators, parent educators, early childhood adult educators, and officials with responsibility for program monitoring and licensing. (Note: See also the "Code of Ethical Conduct: Supplement for Early Childhood Adult Educators.")

Core Values

Standards of ethical behavior in early childhood care and education are based on commitment to the following core values that are deeply rooted in the history of the field of early childhood care and education. We have made a commitment to:

- Appreciate childhood as a unique and valuable stage of the human life cycle
- Base our work on knowledge of how children develop and learn
- Appreciate and support the bond between the child and family
- Recognize that children are best understood and supported in the context of family, culture,* community, and society
- Respect the dignity, worth, and uniqueness of each individual (child, family member, and colleague)
- Respect diversity in children, families, and colleagues
- Recognize that children and adults achieve their full potential in the context of relationships that are based on trust and respect

Conceptual Framework

The Code sets forth a framework of professional responsibilities in four sections. Each section addresses

> * *Culture* includes ethnicity, racial identity, economic level, family structure, language, and religious and political beliefs, which profoundly influence each child's development and relationship to the world.

an area of professional relationships: (1) with children, (2) with families, (3) among colleagues, and (4) with the community and society. Each section includes an introduction to the primary responsibilities of the early childhood practitioner in that context. The introduction is followed by (1) a set of ideals that reflect exemplary professional practice and (2) a set of principles describing practices that are required, prohibited, or permitted.

The **ideals** reflect the aspirations of practitioners. The **principles** guide conduct and assist practitioners in resolving ethical dilemmas.* Both ideals and principles are intended to direct practitioners to those questions which, when responsibly answered, can provide the basis for conscientious decision making. While the Code provides specific direction for addressing some ethical dilemmas, many others will require the practitioner to combine the guidance of the Code with professional judgment. The ideals and principles in this Code present a shared framework of professional responsibility that affirms our commitment to the core values of our field. The Code publicly acknowledges the responsibilities that we in the field have assumed and in so doing supports ethical behavior in our work. Practitioners who face situations with ethical dimensions are urged to seek guidance in the applicable parts of this Code and in the spirit that informs the whole. Often, "the right answer"—the best ethical course of action to take—is not obvious. There may be no readily apparent, positive way to handle a situation. When one important value contradicts another, we face an ethical dilemma. When we face a dilemma, it is our professional responsibility to consult the Code and all relevant parties to find the most ethical resolution.

SECTION I: ETHICAL RESPONSIBILITIES TO CHILDREN

Childhood is a unique and valuable stage in the human life cycle. Our paramount responsibility is to provide care and education in settings that are safe, healthy, nurturing, and responsive for each child. We are committed to supporting children's development and learning; respecting individual differences; and helping children learn to live, play,

---

* There is not necessarily a corresponding principle for each ideal.

---

and work cooperatively. We are also committed to promoting children's self-awareness, competence, self-worth, resiliency, and physical well-being.

Ideals

I-1.1—To be familiar with the knowledge base of early childhood care and education and to stay informed through continuing education and training.

I-1.2—To base program practices upon current knowledge and research in the field of early childhood education, child development, and related disciplines, as well as on particular knowledge of each child.

I-1.3—To recognize and respect the unique qualities, abilities, and potential of each child.

I-1.4—To appreciate the vulnerability of children and their dependence on adults.

I-1.5—To create and maintain safe and healthy settings that foster children's social, emotional, cognitive, and physical development and that respect their dignity and their contributions.

I-1.6—To use assessment instruments and strategies that are appropriate for the children to be assessed, that are used only for the purposes for which they were designed, and that have the potential to benefit children.

I-1.7—To use assessment information to understand and support children's development and learning, to support instruction, and to identify children who may need additional services.

I-1.8—To support the right of each child to play and learn in an inclusive environment that meets the needs of children with and without disabilities.

I-1.9—To advocate for and ensure that all children, including those with special needs, have access to the support services needed to be successful.

I-1.10—To ensure that each child's culture, language, ethnicity, and family structure are recognized and valued in the program.

I-1.11—To provide all children with experiences in a language that they know, as well as support children in maintaining the use of their home language and in learning English.

I-1.12—To work with families to provide a safe and smooth transition as children and families move from one program to the next.

Principles

P-1.1—Above all, we shall not harm children. We shall not participate in practices that are emotionally damaging, physically harmful, disrespectful, degrading, dangerous, exploitative, or intimidating to children. *This principle has precedence over all others in this Code.*

P-1.2—We shall care for and educate children in positive emotional and social environments that are cognitively stimulating and that support each child's culture, language, ethnicity, and family structure.

P-1.3—We shall not participate in practices that discriminate against children by denying benefits, giving special advantages, or excluding them from programs or activities on the basis of their sex, race, national origin, religious beliefs, medical condition, disability, or the marital status/family structure, sexual orientation, or religious beliefs or other affiliations of their families. (Aspects of this principle do not apply in programs that have a lawful mandate to provide services to a particular population of children.)

P-1.4—We shall involve all those with relevant knowledge (including families and staff) in decisions concerning a child, as appropriate, ensuring confidentiality of sensitive information.

P-1.5—We shall use appropriate assessment systems, which include multiple sources of information, to provide information on children's learning and development.

P-1.6—We shall strive to ensure that decisions such as those related to enrollment, retention, or assignment to special education services, will be based on multiple sources of information and will never be based on a single assessment, such as a test score or a single observation.

P-1.7—We shall strive to build individual relationships with each child; make individualized adaptations in teaching strategies, learning environments, and curricula; and consult with the family so that each child benefits from the program. If after such efforts have been exhausted, the current placement does not meet a child's needs, or the child is seriously jeopardizing the ability of other children to benefit from the program, we shall collaborate with the child's family and appropriate specialists to determine the additional services needed and/or the placement option(s) most likely to ensure the child's success. (Aspects of this principle may not apply in programs that have a lawful mandate to provide services to a particular population of children.)

P-1.8—We shall be familiar with the risk factors for and symptoms of child abuse and neglect, including physical, sexual, verbal, and emotional abuse and physical, emotional, educational, and medical neglect. We shall know and follow state laws and community procedures that protect children against abuse and neglect.

P-1.9—When we have reasonable cause to suspect child abuse or neglect, we shall report it to the appropriate community agency and follow up to ensure that appropriate action has been taken. When appropriate, parents or guardians will be informed that the referral will be or has been made.

P-1.10—When another person tells us of his or her suspicion that a child is being abused or neglected, we shall assist that person in taking appropriate action in order to protect the child.

P-1.11—When we become aware of a practice or situation that endangers the health, safety, or well-being of children, we have an ethical responsibility to protect children or inform parents and/or others who can.

SECTION II: ETHICAL RESPONSIBILITIES TO FAMILIES

Families* are of primary importance in children's development. Because the family and the early childhood practitioner have a common interest in the child's well-being, we acknowledge a primary responsibility to bring about communication, cooperation, and collaboration between the home and early childhood program in ways that enhance the child's development.

---

* The term *family* may include those adults, besides parents, with the responsibility of being involved in educating, nurturing, and advocating for the child.

Ideals

I-2.1—To be familiar with the knowledge base related to working effectively with families and to stay informed through continuing education and training.

I-2.2—To develop relationships of mutual trust and create partnerships with the families we serve.

I-2.3—To welcome all family members and encourage them to participate in the program.

I-2.4—To listen to families, acknowledge and build upon their strengths and competencies, and learn from families as we support them in their task of nurturing children.

I-2.5—To respect the dignity and preferences of each family and to make an effort to learn about its structure, culture, language, customs, and beliefs.

I-2.6—To acknowledge families' childrearing values and their right to make decisions for their children.

I-2.7—To share information about each child's education and development with families and to help them understand and appreciate the current knowledge base of the early childhood profession.

I-2.8—To help family members enhance their understanding of their children and support the continuing development of their skills as parents.

I-2.9—To participate in building support networks for families by providing them with opportunities to interact with program staff, other families, community resources, and professional services.

Principles

P-2.1—We shall not deny family members access to their child's classroom or program setting unless access is denied by court order or other legal restriction.

P-2.2—We shall inform families of program philosophy, policies, curriculum, assessment system, and personnel qualifications, and explain why we teach as we do—which should be in accordance with our ethical responsibilities to children (see Section I).

P-2.3—We shall inform families of and, when appropriate, involve them in policy decisions.

P-2.4—We shall involve the family in significant decisions affecting their child.

P-2.5—We shall make every effort to communicate effectively with all families in a language that they understand. We shall use community resources for translation and interpretation when we do not have sufficient resources in our own programs.

P-2.6—As families share information with us about their children and families, we shall consider this information to plan and implement the program.

P-2.7—We shall inform families about the nature and purpose of the program's child assessments and how data about their child will be used.

P-2.8—We shall treat child assessment information confidentially and share this information only when there is a legitimate need for it.

P-2.9—We shall inform the family of injuries and incidents involving their child, of risks such as exposures to communicable diseases that might result in infection, and of occurrences that might result in emotional stress.

P-2.10—Families shall be fully informed of any proposed research projects involving their children and shall have the opportunity to give or withhold consent without penalty. We shall not permit or participate in research that could in any way hinder the education, development, or well-being of children.

P-2.11—We shall not engage in or support exploitation of families. We shall not use our relationship with a family for private advantage or personal gain, or enter into relationships with family members that might impair our effectiveness working with their children.

P-2.12—We shall develop written policies for the protection of confidentiality and the disclosure of children's records. These policy documents shall be made available to all program personnel and families. Disclosure of children's records beyond family members, program personnel, and consultants having an obligation of confidentiality shall require familial consent (except in cases of abuse or neglect).

P-2.13—We shall maintain confidentiality and shall respect the family's right to privacy, refraining from disclosure of confidential information and intrusion into family life. However, when we have reason to believe that a child's welfare is at risk, it is permissible to share confidential information with agencies, as well as with individuals who have legal responsibility for intervening in the child's interest.

P-2.14—In cases where family members are in conflict with one another, we shall work openly, sharing our observations of the child, to help all parties involved make informed decisions. We shall refrain from becoming an advocate for one party.

P-2.15—We shall be familiar with and appropriately refer families to community resources and professional support services. After a referral has been made, we shall follow up to ensure that services have been appropriately provided.

SECTION III: ETHICAL RESPONSIBILITIES TO COLLEAGUES

In a caring, cooperative workplace, human dignity is respected, professional satisfaction is promoted, and positive relationships are developed and sustained. Based upon our core values, our primary responsibility to colleagues is to establish and maintain settings and relationships that support productive work and meet professional needs. The same ideals that apply to children also apply as we interact with adults in the workplace.

A—Responsibilities to co-workers
Ideals

I-3A.1—To establish and maintain relationships of respect, trust, confidentiality, collaboration, and cooperation with co-workers.

I-3A.2—To share resources with co-workers, collaborating to ensure that the best possible early childhood care and education program is provided.

I-3A.3—To support co-workers in meeting their professional needs and in their professional development.

I-3A.4—To accord co-workers due recognition of professional achievement.

Principles

P-3A.1—We shall recognize the contributions of colleagues to our program and not participate in practices that diminish their reputations or impair their effectiveness in working with children and families.

P-3A.2—When we have concerns about the professional behavior of a co-worker, we shall first let that person know of our concern in a way that shows respect for personal dignity and for the diversity to be found among staff members, and then attempt to resolve the matter collegially and in a confidential manner.

P-3A.3—We shall exercise care in expressing views regarding the personal attributes or professional conduct of co-workers. Statements should be based on firsthand knowledge, not hearsay, and relevant to the interests of children and programs.

P-3A.4—We shall not participate in practices that discriminate against a co-worker because of sex, race, national origin, religious beliefs or other affiliations, age, marital status/family structure, disability, or sexual orientation.

B—Responsibilities to employers
Ideals

I-3B.1—To assist the program in providing the highest quality of service.

I-3B.2—To do nothing that diminishes the reputation of the program in which we work unless it is violating laws and regulations designed to protect children or is violating the provisions of this Code.

Principles

P-3B.1—We shall follow all program policies. When we do not agree with program policies, we shall attempt to effect change through constructive action within the organization.

P-3B.2—We shall speak or act on behalf of an organization only when authorized. We shall take care to acknowledge when we are speaking for the organization and when we are expressing a personal judgment.

P-3B.3—We shall not violate laws or regulations designed to protect children and shall take appropriate action consistent with this Code when aware of such violations.

P-3B.4—If we have concerns about a colleague's behavior, and children's well-being is not at risk, we may address the concern with that individual. If children are at risk or the situation does not improve after it has been brought to the colleague's attention, we shall report the colleague's unethical or incompetent behavior to an appropriate authority.

P-3B.5—When we have a concern about circumstances or conditions that impact the quality of care and education within the program, we shall inform the program's administration or, when necessary, other appropriate authorities.

C—Responsibilities to employees
Ideals

I-3C.1—To promote safe and healthy working conditions and policies that foster mutual respect, cooperation, collaboration, competence, well-being, confidentiality, and self esteem in staff members.

I-3C.2—To create and maintain a climate of trust and candor that will enable staff to speak and act in the best interests of children, families, and the field of early childhood care and education.

I-3C.3—To strive to secure adequate and equitable compensation (salary and benefits) for those who work with or on behalf of young children.

I-3C.4—To encourage and support continual development of employees in becoming more skilled and knowledgeable practitioners.

Principles

P-3C.1—In decisions concerning children and programs, we shall draw upon the education, training, experience, and expertise of staff members.

P-3C.2—We shall provide staff members with safe and supportive working conditions that honor confidences and permit them to carry out their responsibilities through fair performance evaluation, written grievance procedures, constructive feedback, and opportunities for continuing professional development and advancement.

P-3C.3—We shall develop and maintain comprehensive written personnel policies that define program standards. These policies shall be given to new staff members and shall be available and easily accessible for review by all staff members.

P-3C.4—We shall inform employees whose performance does not meet program expectations of areas of concern and, when possible, assist in improving their performance.

P-3C.5—We shall conduct employee dismissals for just cause, in accordance with all applicable laws and regulations. We shall inform employees who are dismissed of the reasons for their termination. When a dismissal is for cause, justification must be based on evidence of inadequate or inappropriate behavior that is accurately documented, current, and available for the employee to review.

P-3C.6—In making evaluations and recommendations, we shall make judgments based on fact and relevant to the interests of children and programs.

P-3C.7—We shall make hiring, retention, termination, and promotion decisions based solely on a person's competence, record of accomplishment, ability to carry out the responsibilities of the position, and professional preparation specific to the developmental levels of children in his/her care.

P-3.C.8—We shall not make hiring, retention, termination, and promotion decisions based on an individual's sex, race, national origin, religious beliefs or other affiliations, age, marital status/family structure, disability, or sexual orientation. We shall be familiar with and observe laws and regulations that pertain to employment discrimination. (Aspects of this principle do not apply to programs that have a lawful mandate to determine eligibility based on one or more of the criteria identified above.)

P-3C.9—We shall maintain confidentiality in dealing with issues related to an employee's job performance and shall respect an employee's right to privacy regarding personal issues.

SECTION IV: ETHICAL RESPONSIBILITIES TO COMMUNITY AND SOCIETY

Early childhood programs operate within the context of their immediate community made up of families and other institutions concerned with children's welfare. Our responsibilities to the community are to provide programs that meet the diverse needs of families, to cooperate with agencies and professions that share the responsibility for children, to assist families in gaining access to those agencies and allied professionals, and to assist in the development of community programs that are needed but not currently available. As individuals, we acknowledge our responsibility to provide the best possible programs of care and education for children and to conduct ourselves with honesty and integrity. Because of our specialized expertise in early childhood development and education and because the larger society shares responsibility for the welfare and protection of young children, we acknowledge a collective obligation to advocate for the best interests of children within early childhood programs and in the larger community and to serve as a voice for young children everywhere. The ideals and principles in this section are presented to distinguish between those that pertain to the work of the individual early childhood educator and those that more typically are engaged in collectively on behalf of the best interests of children—with the understanding that individual early childhood educators have a shared responsibility for addressing the ideals and principles that are identified as "collective."

Ideal (Individual)

I-4.1—To provide the community with high-quality early childhood care and education programs and services.

Ideals (Collective)

I-4.2—To promote cooperation among professionals and agencies and interdisciplinary collaboration among professions concerned with addressing issues in the health, education, and well-being of young children, their families, and their early childhood educators.

I-4.3—To work through education, research, and advocacy toward an environmentally safe world in which all children receive health care, food, and shelter; are nurtured; and live free from violence in their home and their communities.

I-4.4—To work through education, research, and advocacy toward a society in which all young children have access to high-quality early care and education programs.

I-4.5—To work to ensure that appropriate assessment systems, which include multiple sources of information, are used for purposes that benefit children.

I-4.6—To promote knowledge and understanding of young children and their needs. To work toward greater societal acknowledgment of children's rights and greater social acceptance of responsibility for the well-being of all children.

I-4.7—To support policies and laws that promote the well-being of children and families, and to work to change those that impair their well-being. To participate in developing policies and laws that are needed, and to cooperate with other individuals and groups in these efforts.

I-4.8—To further the professional development of the field of early childhood care and education and to strengthen its commitment to realizing its core values as reflected in this Code.

Principles (Individual)

P-4.1—We shall communicate openly and truthfully about the nature and extent of services that we provide.

P-4.2—We shall apply for, accept, and work in positions for which we are personally well-suited and professionally qualified. We shall not offer services that we do not have the competence, qualifications, or resources to provide.

P-4.3—We shall carefully check references and shall not hire or recommend for employment any person whose competence, qualifications, or character makes him or her unsuited for the position.

P-4.4—We shall be objective and accurate in reporting the knowledge upon which we base our program practices.

P-4.5—We shall be knowledgeable about the appropriate use of assessment strategies and instruments and interpret results accurately to families.

P-4.6—We shall be familiar with laws and regulations that serve to protect the children in our programs and be vigilant in ensuring that these laws and regulations are followed.

P-4.7—When we become aware of a practice or situation that endangers the health, safety, or well-being of children, we have an ethical responsibility to protect children or inform parents and/or others who can.

P-4.8—We shall not participate in practices that are in violation of laws and regulations that protect the children in our programs.

P-4.9—When we have evidence that an early childhood program is violating laws or regulations protecting children, we shall report the violation to appropriate authorities who can be expected to remedy the situation.

P-4.10—When a program violates or requires its employees to violate this Code, it is permissible, after fair assessment of the evidence, to disclose the identity of that program.

Principles (Collective)

P-4.11—When policies are enacted for purposes that do not benefit children, we have a collective responsibility to work to change these practices.

P-4.12—When we have evidence that an agency that provides services intended to ensure children's well-being is failing to meet its obligations, we acknowledge a collective ethical responsibility to report the problem to appropriate authorities or to the public. We shall be vigilant in our follow-up until the situation is resolved.

P-4.13—When a child protection agency fails to provide adequate protection for abused or neglected children, we acknowledge a collective ethical responsibility to work toward the improvement of these services.

NAEYC has taken reasonable measures to develop the Code in a fair, reasonable, open, unbiased, and objective manner, based on currently available data. However, further research or developments may change the current state of knowledge. Neither NAEYC nor its officers, directors, members, employees, or agents will be liable for any loss, damage, or claim with respect to any liabilities, including direct, special, indirect, or consequential damages incurred in connection with the Code or reliance on the information presented.

Statement of Commitment*

As an individual who works with young children, I commit myself to furthering the values of early

childhood education as they are reflected in the ideals and principles of the NAEYC Code of Ethical Conduct. To the best of my ability I will

- Never harm children.
- Ensure that programs for young children are based on current knowledge and research of child development and early childhood education.
- Respect and support families in their task of nurturing children.
- Respect colleagues in early childhood care and education and support them in maintaining the NAEYC Code of Ethical Conduct.
- Serve as an advocate for children, their families, and their teachers in community and society.
- Stay informed of and maintain high standards of professional conduct.
- Engage in an ongoing process of self-reflection, realizing that personal characteristics, biases, and beliefs have an impact on children and families.
- Be open to new ideas and be willing to learn from the suggestions of others.
- Continue to learn, grow, and contribute as a professional.
- Honor the ideals and principles of the NAEYC Code of Ethical Conduct.

Glossary of Terms Related to Ethics

Code of Ethics   Defines the core values of the field and provides guidance for what professionals should do when they encounter conflicting obligations or responsibilities in their work.

Values   Qualities or principles that individuals believe to be desirable or worthwhile and that they prize for themselves, for others, and for the world in which they live.

Core Values   Commitments held by a profession that are consciously and knowingly embraced by its practitioners because they make a contribution to society. There is a difference between personal values and the core values of a profession.

Morality   Peoples' views of what is good, right, and proper; their beliefs about their obligations; and their ideas about how they should behave.

Ethics   The study of right and wrong, or duty and obligation, that involves critical reflection on

---

* This Statement of Commitment is not part of the Code but is a personal acknowledgement of the individual's willingness to embrace the distinctive values and moral obligations of the field of early childhood care and education. It is recognition of the moral obligations that lead to an individual becoming part of the profession.

morality and the ability to make choices between values and the examination of the moral dimensions of relationships.

Professional Ethics   The moral commitments of a profession that involve moral reflection that extends and enhances the personal morality practitioners bring to their work, that concern actions of right and wrong in the workplace, and that help individuals resolve moral dilemmas they encounter in their work.

Ethical Responsibilities   Behaviors that one must or must not engage in. Ethical responsibilities are clear-cut and are spelled out in the Code of Ethical Conduct (for example, early childhood educators should never share confidential information about a child or family with a person who has no legitimate need for knowing).

Ethical Dilemma   A moral conflict that involves determining appropriate conduct when an individual faces conflicting professional values and responsibilities.

Sources for Glossary Terms and Definitions

Feeney, S., & N. Freeman. 1999. Ethics and the early childhood educator: Using the NAEYC code. Washington, DC: NAEYC.

Kidder, R.M. 1995. How good people make tough choices: Resolving the dilemmas of ethical living. New York: Fireside.

Kipnis, K. 1987. How to discuss professional ethics. *Young Children* 42 (4): 26–30.

Appendix B

IMPLEMENTING TIME-OUT APPROPRIATELY

A specific sequence of steps must be followed in order to implement time-out correctly:

1. The child is warned, and if the behavior continues, he or she is removed to a suitable time-out area (safe, minimal distractions, is NOT completely isolated).

   a. When a child is in the midst of a tantrum, warn him or her of the consequences of such behavior: "You're very upset. I can't talk to you when you're screaming (kicking or biting) like this. Please stop. Either calm down here or we will have a time-out." If the child continues the tantrum, follow through by saying, "Now, we will have a time-out," and then lead the child to the time-out place. This often is easier said than done. You may have to bodily remove the child by using a firm grasp and possibly lifting the child and carrying him or her. Children should never be jerked, pulled, or shoved as you attempt to move them along. One effective method of physically handling a struggling child is to position yourself behind the child, crossing the child's arms across the body and holding on. Simultaneously, spread your legs so the child's kicks will not be harmful. In this position, sidle out of the room. This is a safe approach regardless of the child's size or physical movement.

   b. In the case of a child who demonstrates habitual antisocial behavior, you have already warned the child that time-out will take place if the behavior is repeated. If it is, immediately initiate time-out by saying: "Lila, you pinched. Time-out." Lead the child to the time-out area. If the child resists, proceed as in step 1a.

2. Once in the time-out area, reflect the child's feelings and provide basic information so that he or she will know what to expect: "You're still very angry. When you're more quiet we can talk about what's bothering you," or "You pinched. You will have time-out for three minutes."

3. Hold to the stated limit before allowing the child to leave the time-out area. One to two minutes of quiet is appropriate for children between the ages of 3 and 6; five minutes is satisfactory for older school-age youngsters. This means a prescribed period of calm. Any time the child spends screaming is not included.

4. Remain with the child in the time-out area. Children should never be left alone. If the child tries to leave the area before calming down, return him or her to the area.

5. Throughout the time-out process, remain silent. This is not the time for a lecture. Talking only aggravates the situation. First, it may prolong the time-out because the child may not yet be

at a point at which she or he is able to focus on what is being said. Second, talking teaches the child that one way to get undivided adult attention is to engage in unacceptable behavior.

6. Any attempts to harm you or self must be stopped immediately. Hurting an adult can lead to later feelings of guilt and fear that the child may find hard to overcome. In addition, you will find it extremely difficult to react rationally and calmly if you have been injured. Also, a child cannot be allowed to inflict self-harm. One way to prevent injury is to physically restrain the child. Physical restraint involves holding the child in a passive "bear hug" to keep the child from harming himself or herself or anyone else (Gartrell, 2007). Wrapping your arms around the child's arms and your legs around the child's legs is the easiest way to accomplish this.

Some adults prefer to sit with the child on a chair, others sit in a "pretzel" position on the floor. In either case it is best to have the child facing away from you to reduce stimulation.

Restraint calms some children and further incites others. Unfortunately, you do not always know in advance how a child will react. If you learn that holding a child will add to his or her distress, physical restraint should be avoided, if possible. If the situation seems potentially unsafe, it helps to say: "You don't want me to hold you. I will only hold you if it looks like you could get hurt. If not, I will stand here, but I won't touch you."

7. If peers seem curious about what is going on, reflect their concerns and remind them about time-out. It should be emphasized that the child went into time-out to feel better again. Assure children that the child is unharmed and that he or she will be returning to the group when he or she is ready.

8. Children who have had a tantrum should leave time-out when they are ready to rejoin the group. Children who have gone to time-out because of habitual antisocial behavior must satisfy the stated conditions (e.g., three minutes). Children should never remain in time-out beyond these brief time periods.

9. Following time-out, children should have an opportunity to discuss the incident and to make decisions or plans about future behavior. This discussion should not take place in the time-out area; in this way, the child will learn that problems can be solved in the regular group setting rather than only in a special place. Some children will not want to discuss the incident at this time. If that is the case, the child should be allowed to resume his or her place in the group without being forced into conversation.

10. A child who has completed time-out as the result of a tantrum should be praised for the hard work he or she put into calming down.

11. Later in the day, the adult who implemented time-out should have a pleasant contact with the child to reassure him or her of the adult's continuing affection. When you maintain a nurturing relationship with the child, she or he becomes better able to exercise control in subsequent situations.

Glossary

abusive or neglectful families Families who maltreat children by way of psychological, physical, or sexual abuse or who do not provide for children's basic needs.

acceptance To value children with no strings attached.

accidental aggression Unintentional harm to things or people that happen as a part of everyday life.

acquaintances People whom children meet and with whom they may or may not have much interaction.

action dimension The process of teaching children to maintain or change their behavior.

activity space Area occupied by one child using a material.

adherence Following a rule merely to gain a reward or avoid a punishment; relying on others to monitor one's personal actions.

affect Emotions, mood.

affective reflections Nonjudgmental statements that describe the emotion of the child or adult.

aggression Any behavior that results in physical or emotional injury to persons, or any behavior that leads to property damage or destruction.

amoral Having no concept of right and wrong.

antisocial behavior Inappropriate problem behavior.

anxiety disorders Persistent unfounded fears that are out of proportion to the actual threat or danger and lead to maladaptive behavior.

appreciation of children's stress Respecting children's viewpoints as well as their coping strategies.

assertiveness Purposeful action used to express self or protect rights while respecting the rights and feelings of others.

associative play A situation in which a child plays with other children and interacts with them sporadically in similar but not identical activities or in activities that are loosely associated.

attachment Reciprocal, enduring relationship between infant and caregiver, each of whom contributes to the quality of the relationship.

authenticity Genuineness; being truthful while still being reasonable and encouraging.

authoritarian discipline style Adults vigilantly enforcing the rules typically without explanation or reasons. Punishments occur swiftly and forcefully, often using ridicule, shame, or physical means.

authoritative discipline style Adults respond to children's needs with warmth and nurturance with high standards and expectations for behavior. Emphasis is on teaching the children to take responsibility and make good decisions. Consequences with explanations, demonstrations, suggestions, and discussions are used instead of punishments.

autobiographical memory A memory, created by a child, that is based on his or her specific perceptions of events.

axial space   Physical space that extends to the outer reach of the arms and legs.

baby talk   Stylized speech usually having an atypical voice pitch, in which adults use diminutive word forms, sound substitutions, and use pronouns improperly. Children do not talk like this.

basic values   Values that are absolute, regardless of the situation or context.

behavior reflections   Nonjudgmental statements made to children that describe their attributes or their roles in activities in which they are engaged; begin with the child, not "I," and are descriptive in nature.

behavioral state   Degree of arousal. Muscle tone, activity, respiration, position of the eyelids, and alertness vary in each state (i.e., sleeping or crying).

biases   Inclinations toward prejudging persons or situations not based on fact or the current situation.

blended families   Families that are reconstituted as a result of divorce and/or death; bi-nuclear families.

boundaries   Physical or psychological barriers.

bullying   Routinely using hostile aggression to exert power over others.

catharsis   A technique in which opportunities are provided for children who are not currently behaving aggressively to engage in controlled aggression in an attempt to "drain off" aggressive tendencies with the goal of reducing chances for future aggression.

centration   Directing attention to only one attribute of a situation while ignoring all others.

channel of communication   A mode of nonverbal communication (i.e., voice tone, facial expression, gesture, body position and orientation, and use of clothing or furnishings).

character attribution   Verbally assigning particular characteristics to children such as "you are kind" or "you are giving;" a verbal strategy used to affect how children think about themselves.

character role   Child takes on the behaviors and responsibilities of another role within the play scenario; may be family roles, work roles, or roles based on fantasy.

childhood stress   Things of any type that place unusual demands on a child's ability to cope with life events.

closed-ended questions   Questions that call for a one- or two-word answer, and effectively close the door on future conversations.

coaching   An intervention tool that involves an adult working directly with a child to instruct him or her on specific skills that can be used to make and keep friends.

communication   Verbal messages.

communicative gestures   Child points to or physically signals the caregiver to look at something. Infant checks to see if the adult is responding.

competence   The belief that one is able to accomplish tasks and achieve goals.

complexity   State of having two or more parts or multiple uses; having interrelated parts; complicated.

compulsions   Impulses to repeatedly perform certain acts.

conflict mediation   A strategy used to diffuse conflict between parties in order to come to a mutually agreed-upon solution to the conflict.

construction play   Occurs when children build something.

contingent behavior   Actions that respond to another person's action.

control   The manner and degree to which adults enforce compliance with their expectations.

control (as related to self-esteem)   The feeling on the part of individuals that they can influence the outcomes and events in their world.

cooperative activity   Activity in which participants work together to complete a group goal. It is the opposite of competitive activity.

cooperative play   Two or more children maintain play that is focused on some common goal or play theme. Actions and communication are coordinated.

corporal punishment   Formalized approach to physical punishment used by some institutions such as schools and prisons and regulated by laws and institutional rules.

creative questions   Questions which invite respondent to direct the conversation, to select the content of response. These questions invite responses greater than one or two words. Also known as **open-ended questions.**

defense mechanisms   Strategies used to temporarily regain a sense of balance.

definable rules   Rules in which both children and adults have the same understanding of what behavior is expected.

denial   Acting as if stress does not exist.

developmentally appropriate practices   The early childhood teaching behaviors that result when adults take into account children's age, their individual needs, and the context in which children live.

dimension of high–low mobility   The degree of opportunity for the physical movement of children's bodies within a space.

direct instruction   Specific directions used by adults to regulate children's behavior through physical and verbal controls.

directing   Supervising by efficient, effective means to attain a goal; speaking or acting clearly, explicitly; telling someone what to do and how to do it; utilizes the action dimension heavily.

disabling conditions   A blanket categorization that refers to a child's special need, which may fall under any one or more of the following categories: learning disability, developmental disability, mental retardation, serious emotional disturbance, speech and language disorders, or physical or sensory disability.

displacement   A technique in which children who are behaving aggressively are given another source at which to aim their aggression so as to rid themselves of the aggression.

display rules   Unspoken expectation of nonverbal behavior in response to a situation.

distal space   Physical space from the outer edges that the arms and legs can reach to the furthest that the eye and ear can perceive.

dramatic play   Pretend play; a storylike performance of a player taking on an imaginary role.

dramatist style   A mode of play during which constructions or materials are used mostly to support pretend play and intrinsic design is less important.

duration   A period of time.

easy child   generally happy, friendly, predictable, and adaptable.

effective praise   Praise that is selective, specific, and positive.

emblems   Specific cultural gestures that have a direct verbal referent.

emotional IQ   Measure of a person's adeptness at understanding his or her own emotions and the emotions of others.

emotions   Display of affect.

empathy   Recognizing and understanding another person's perspective.

encouraging responses   Statements from another person (parent, teacher, or peer) that point out the potential benefits or good in a situation to counter a child's habit of focusing verbally or mentally on negative aspects.

English language learners   Those whose first language is not English.

ethical judgments   Decisions focused on ethical codes of conduct.

ethnicity   Ethnic classification or affiliation.

ethnocentrism   Focus on only ethnicity of self.

exaggeration   An overstatement; something that has been embellished or amplified.

exosystem   People and settings that indirectly affect what happens in the microsystem.

expansions   A type of paraphrasing in which the respondent fills in or enhances what the child has just said.

expressive aggression   Unintentional harm to things or people that happens as a result of a physical action that is a pleasurable sensory experience for the aggressor.

expressive speech   Words about emotional content.

expressive state   The typical manner in which an individual expresses his or her emotions.

expressive style   Children's patterns of emotional responsiveness.

facilitation dimension   The process of creating emotionally supportive relationships with children; the basis for any successful interaction with children. Composed of five elements: empathy, warmth, respect, acceptance, and authenticity.

fantasizer   A person who uses a narrative, story, or situation as a point of reference.

feedback   Information provided about performance. It includes what was done correctly, what was incorrect, and what to do next time.

feelings   Interval affective states.

follow-through   Enforcing the negative consequence set up in the warning. It is used when the child does not comply with the warning, and includes a reflection of the child's current action, emotion, or statement, followed by a reminder of the warning and implementation of the negative consequence.

formal pretend proposals   A straightforward request to play or to change the direction of the play within the play scenario.

friendship framework   the ways in which children think about friends and friendship from the earliest years through their maturity.

friendship-making skills   Specific skills needed to acquire and keep friends.

friendship skills   Specific skills that are used to make and keep friends.

functional role   Simple role-play in which the child becomes the actor in the present situation; may be the role of truck driver while moving a truck around or the "motor" of the truck with appropriate sounds.

games   Group-rule governed play; usually includes a winner and loser.

gaze   Infant looks at the caregiver's face then orients to the same location.

gender identity   Biological, male–female identification.

gender-role identification   The behavior and characteristics associated with a particular gender.

gestures   The movements of hands, arms, or body that accompany speech used to illustrate words, give emphasis, or replace words.

giftedness   The ability to solve complex problems in an effective, efficient, elegant, and/or economical way.

goals   A desired end toward which effort is directed; an end that can be attained.

goodness of fit   The degree to which the adult temperament fits the temperament of the infant.

grieving process   Behaviors used in coping with loss, including denial, bargaining, depression, and acceptance of the event.

guidance   Adult interaction with children which involves both discipline and instructional approaches.

guiding   Leading, explaining, suggesting a course of action toward a goal; problem solving; utilizes the facilitation dimension heavily; goal is helping the child learn the task or process.

guilt   A feeling that warns that a current or planned action is undesirable and provokes regret for past misdeeds.

habitual antisocial behavior   Destructive behavior carried out without thought.

hesitations   A pause, often vocalized.

high or low mobility   A person's physical activity level.

hostile aggression   Intended harm to things or people in which the aggressor experiences satisfaction with the harmful outcome.

identification   Following a rule to imitate or gain the approval of an individual one admires.

illustrator gestures   Movements of the hands or body that depict an object or event.

imagery   Purposefully imagined pictures in the mind.

imaginary fears   Unfounded fears that are very real to children, such as monsters under the bed.

imitative learning   Repetition of the acts of others.

impulsive acting out   Acting impulsively and often flamboyantly to avoid thinking of either the past or the consequence of current actions to conceal true feelings of misery and pain.

individualized education program (IEP)   A written plan developed for children older than 3 years to provide the most effective resources to support the child's development.

individualized family service plan (IFSP)   A plan developed for children, birth to age 3, under P.L. 99–457, to identify and organize the most effective resources to support the child's development.

individuation   Process by which the self or identity is developed.

inhibiting consequences   Consequences that reduce the probability of problem behaviors being repeated.

interactions   a two way exchange that is reciprocal in nature.

inhibition   Tendency to repress, or show restraint.

instrumental aggression   Unintentional harm to things or people that happens as a result of the aggressor trying to get or protect something using force. Often occurs over objects, territory, or rights.

instrumental know-how   Having the knowledge and skills to act competently.

intensity   Frequency per unit of time; strength.

intentionality   Uncooperativeness or misbehavior thought to be designed by a child in order to be difficult.

internal space   Physical space from the center of the body to the surface of the skin.

internalization   Following rules based on an internal code of ethics; the same as self-discipline.

intrusion–seclusion dimension   Permeability of the boundaries between spaces; particularly permeable between the group and the things and people outside the group.

irreversible   Unable to mentally reverse actions that are initiated physically—not able to think of an opposite action for something one is doing; common among toddlers and preschoolers.

large-group space   A learning center for more than eight children, usually all of the children in the group.

learning centers A physical arrangement of furnishings and materials that is designed to promote learning.

linguistic diversity A term used to describe children enrolled in educational programs who speak a language other than English at home and who are variously proficient in English (NAEYC, 1996a).

logical consequences Consequences directly related to a rule; they are used to help a child learn what to do instead or repair what has been done, and include rehearsal of the appropriate action, restitution for the action, or temporary loss of privilege.

macrosystem Significant ideas, such as patterns of beliefs, laws, customs, and cultural traditions, that impact the microsystem, mesosystem, and exosystem.

masked play Aggressive or violent behavior in which the aggressor claims to have been playing.

mask smile The simple smile with an otherwise neutral expression.

maturity demands The level at which expectations are set.

mesosystem The combination of microsystems in which a person is directly involved.

metacommunication A communication about how to communicate or talking about how to speak; requires thinking about the way one communicates; in play, it sets the frame for the fact that play is going on or a statement is meant as a joke.

microsystem The entire array of people, activities, roles, and interpersonal relationships experienced by a child in a face-to-face setting such as home or school.

mixed message A communication in which the spoken words and one or more nonverbal channels communicate conflicting meanings.

modeling An intervention tool involving the process of demonstration of a skill "in action."

moral violations Lying, stealing, and hurting others.

narrative talk The language that is used in communication between adults that serves to create a story for the child of his/her life.

natural consequences Consequences that happen without any intervention.

negative affect Grumpiness in babies; global mood that is unhappy.

negative consequences Strategies used to help children change their behavior in ways that enhance children's self-control. Constructive actions aimed at helping children learn acceptable conduct from the experience of being corrected.

negative verbal environment The verbal atmosphere in which children feel unworthy, unlovable, insignificant, or incompetent as a result of what adults do or do not say to them.

neglect Failure to appropriately meet children's basic needs.

neglected children Children who are rarely or never selected as friend/play partner. These children believe themselves to be less skilled than others.

negotiation skills Specific skills which enable one to work out disagreements through dialogue.

nonlexical sounds Vocalizations without words such as throat clearing or yawning.

nonverbal communication Actions rather than words used to communicate.

novelty New; not resembling something known or previously used.

nurturance The extent to which adults express caring and concern for children.

object invention Imaginative creation of objects.

object substitution The act of substituting one object for another or transforming one object into another.

obsessions Undesired recurring thoughts.

onlooker The child who watches other children; actively observes; may briefly comment to them but does not engage with others.

open–closed dimension The degree by which the use of materials or equipment is restricted by their design.

open-ended questions Questions for which there are many possible answers; used to invite conversation and allow the speaker to direct the course of the conversation.

overt aggression Harm to others through physical injury or the threat of physical injury.

paralinguistics Vocalizations that are not words.

parallel activity The child plays in the presence of other children, often with the same or similar materials; nonverbal contact with other players is common.

paraphrase reflections Nonjudgmental restatements of something the child said, but not word for word.

passive victims Victims of bullying who do nothing to instigate the bullying. Passive victims seldom initiate the hostile attack and rarely assert their rights when it happens.

patterners   Children whose preferred style of construction or materials use is to build an aesthetically pleasing design or pattern as a desired end goal.

peer teaching   An intervention tool that involves putting a more abled child with a less abled child.

peers   Others who are around the same age level or maturity level as the person.

perception of a stressor   A child's understanding of a perceived stressor, whether the stressor is or not.

permissive discipline style   Emphasizes warmth and affection with little instruction on how to behave or expectations for behavior. Punishments often include love withdrawal.

personal message   A statement that expresses behavior expectations for children. It includes a reflection of what the child is doing, saying, or feeling; the adult emotional reaction and the reason for the reaction; and if it is used to change behavior, then also a direction for what to do instead (redirection).

personal space   Space within one's arm reach.

perspective-taking   The ability to think about how another person feels in a given situation.

pitch and tone   Characteristics of the voice that depict high or low and range of sound.

play episode   All of the materials and equipment, the theme, and all of the players involved in a prolonged, socially organized play event.

play frames   Defines the context (people, materials, space) of a particular play scenario.

play schemes   Short sequences of pretend play such as eating, waking up, or cooking that are used in combination in dramatic play.

poor-quality child care   Child care that fails to meet standards outlined by the APHA and AAP. Care where the providers are untrained, where child–adult ratios and group sizes are inappropriate, or care is based on low-quality programs.

positive consequences   Rewards for maintaining rules.

positive praise   Comments intended to praise a child which are stated in a positive manner.

positive rules   Statements that identify desired behaviors.

positive self-talk   Giving one's self messages to help self-manage a situation, such as "I can sit quietly" or "I can handle this calmly."

positive verbal environment   The verbal atmosphere in which children feel competence, worth, and control as a result of what the adults say and do not say to them.

practice play   Repetitive actions with materials in play; examples include repeatedly dropping balls in a container and dumping them out and repeatedly shooting hoops.

pragmatist   Focuses on the here and now, the direct and the concrete.

precocious children   Children who are more highly developed than usual.

primary emotions   The intense and relatively pure emotions that are the first to develop in infancy and from which other related emotions emerge; such emotions include joy, anger, sadness, and fear.

private space   A physical space designed for one or two children to occupy alone or together.

private speech   Talking out loud to one's self as a way to think through a problem, reduce frustration, postpone rewards, or remind self of rules. Commonly used by children for self-regulation.

professionals   People who use their skills and abilities to assist other people in improving the quality of their lives and who have access to specialized knowledge, demonstrated competence, standards of practice, continuing education, and a code of access.

prompting   A technique that children use to instruct another child on what to say or how to act.

prosocial attribution   Telling children that they have prosocial characteristics, such as "You shared because you noticed that she didn't have any dough and you like to help others." Also called **dispositional attributions**.

prosocial behavior   Acts that support, assist, or benefit others without external rewards.

provocative victims   Victims of bullying who prompt aggressive reactions from others by crying easily; by becoming defensive or angry when it is not appropriate; or by misinterpreting joking or teasing as verbal aggression when that is not the intent.

proximal space   Physical space from the surface of the skin to the outer edges of clothing, hair, or ornament.

psychosexual development   The development of children's cognitive beliefs about sexual matters and processes.

punishments   Penalties for misbehavior; actions taken against children whose behavior is disapproved of.

punishments   Detract from children's development of self-control.

realistic fear   Fear of actual things such as physical danger or social embarrassment.

reasonable rules Rules that a child is capable of following.

recasting A higher form of paraphrasing in which the adult restructures the child's sentence into a new, more complex form.

referential speech Words about objects, actions, and locations.

regression Acting younger than one's age and engaging in earlier-age behaviors.

reinforcement Providing some consequence to a behavior that increases the likelihood that the behavior will reoccur in a similar situation.

rejected-aggressive children Children whose attempts to enter play and make friends are rejected and who respond with aggression toward others as a typical means of interaction.

rejected children Children whose attempts to form friendships or enter play are usually rejected.

rejected-withdrawn children Children whose attempts to enter play and make friends are rejected. These children are typically socially awkward and insensitive to group expectations.

relational aggression Damage to another person's ego or relationships as happens when children gossip or tell lies about someone.

relative values Values that vary, taking on more or less importance depending on the situation.

resistance to control A temperamental approach that is negative in mood, independent and irritable.

respect Believing that children are capable of learning and making self-judgments.

responsive Reacts to nonverbal and verbal cues.

role-playing Fictional reenactments or creations in which participants each take on a role and act out a situation.

rough-and-tumble play Movement play in which the children run, hop, fall, chase, wrestle, or kick at other children while laughing or showing pleasant expressions; may include play fighting.

rhythm Predictable and regular timing.

scaffolding The process of linking what a person knows or can do with new information or skills he or she is ready to acquire.

schedule Planned sequence of events that are regular over a day and/or a week.

school phobia Anxiety about going to school.

selective praise Praise which is used judiciously, not on every child/case.

self-awareness An understanding that the self is separate from others in the environment.

self-concept The combination of attributes of the abilities, behaviors, attitudes, and values that one believes defines the self and sets the self apart from others.

self-discipline The ability to behave in acceptable ways of one's own choice rather than depend on others to guide and control one's behavior.

self-disclosure A type of emotional sharing; considered a basic interpersonal skill.

self-esteem The evaluation placed on one's definition of self; composed of three dimensions: worth, competence, and control.

self-regulate Act of internally controlling behavior.

sexual abuse Molestation, exploitation, and intimidation of children in order to engage them in sexual activity.

shaping Involves the gradual incremental use of rewards to maintain or encourage desired behaviors.

shared attention Focus of infant and caregiver is on the same thing or event; the infant may check on the caregiver's face to make sure he or she is looking at the object of interest to the infant.

shyness A personality style ranging from moderate to severe, resulting in social discomfort and avoidance.

shyness and inhibition Fearfulness, tendency to withdraw.

simple–complex dimension The number of alternative uses that can be generated from equipment or materials.

simultaneous bilingualism Acquisition of more than one language before age 2.

sitting apart Involves temporarily removing a child who is disruptive or causing harm from an activity or group time so that the child may regain self-control, and then allowing the child to reenter the group when calm or when the activity is done. During the sitting apart time, the child remains in the room close to the focus activity.

skills Observable actions that can be learned and evaluated.

small-group space A learning center for eight or fewer children (usually four to six children).

social cognition Knowledge and understanding of social acts.

social competence The ability to recognize, interpret, and respond appropriately in social situations.

social competencies Values of social justice, healthy attitudes toward sexuality, and the ability to interact effectively with people of varying cultural, ethnic, and racial backgrounds.

social-conventional infractions   Poor table manners, speaking rudely, greeting someone improperly.

social referencing   When a baby appraises a new situation by looking at the caregiver's facial expression and attending to his or her tone of voice and other nonverbal cues before responding; process becomes increasingly refined with age and experience.

social responsibility   Behavior which contributes to the common good.

social understanding   Comprehension of the manner in which the social world works.

socialization   Capacity to cooperate in a group, to regulate one's behavior according to society, and to get along with others.

sociodramatic play   Cooperative play that depicts a story line with extended communications among the players that move the story forward; a common theme and shared pretend sequences and objects.

soft–hard dimension   Responsiveness of the texture to touch.

solitary play   The child plays alone; no social interaction.

specific praise   Praise that provides explicit information about what is being praised.

standards   Method of assessing attainment of goals.

strategies   Methods used to pursue goals.

storytelling   A play strategy that provides a narrative about the situation, characters, past events, or unseen objects or events; usually it is used to set the stage for play and to state the problem to be resolved during the play.

structuring   Management of time, space, and materials aimed at promoting children's social competence.

style   Features of the behavior that occur independent of the content of play.

subjective time   Not related to clock or calendar time; instead it is a concept that things will occur when they are ready; readiness is determined by the people using this frame of reference.

successive bilingualism   Acquisition of second language after age 3.

temper tantrum   An intense physical and emotional response in which a child has no access to rational thought processes.

temperament   Describes the degree or intensity of emotional behavior and the timing and duration of response.

theory of mind   Children's evolving theory about their own and others' thoughts, desires, emotions, and beliefs.

time-out   A technique that involves the adult removing the child from an environment in which reinforcers for the undesirable behavior are available, to an environment where such reinforcers are absent. Used with children ages three and up who are engaged in a temper tantrum or habitual antisocial behavior.

transform   To change into something else; in play roles, objects, situations, time, and circumstances are transformed into something else as part of pretend play.

transition   A period of time between the ending of one segment in the schedule and the beginning of another.

ulterior conversations   Usually whispered directions or comments about the play to another player.

underscoring   Statements made by children whose pretend actions may not clearly communicate what the child is doing and how the role is being performed.

uninvolved adults   Those adults who ignore children and are indifferent to them.

unoccupied behavior   The child is not engaged in any talk, object manipulation, or social activity.

unrelated consequences   Consequences not related to the action but set up by an adult in response to child's misbehavior. Often involves loss of privilege unrelated to the problem behavior or the introduction of an unrelated penalty.

values   The qualities and beliefs a person considers valuable or worthwhile.

verbal environment   All of the verbal and nonverbal exchanges that take place within a given setting.

vulnerable child syndrome (VCS)   problems that result from maternal substance use and abuse during pregnancy, including all the problems related to low birth weight, infections, pneumonia, congenital malformations, and drug withdrawal.

warmth   Showing interest, being friendly, and being responsive.

warning   An either-or statement that repeats the rule and tells the child what will happen if he or she does not follow it.

withdrawal   Taking oneself mentally or physically out of the picture.

worth   The extent to which people value and like themselves as well as perceive that they are valued by others.

References

Adalbjarnardottir, S. & Hafsteinsson, L. G. (2001). Adolescent's perceived parenting styles and their substance abuse: concurrent and longitudinal analyses. *Journal of Research on Adolescence, 11*(4), 401–423.

Adamson, L. (1995). *Communication development during infancy*. Dubuque, IA: Brown & Benchmark.

Ainsworth, M. D. S. (1973). The development of infant–mother attachment. In B. M. Caldwell & H. N. Riccuti (Eds.), *Review of child development research* (Vol. 3). Chicago: University of Chicago Press.

Aldrich, J. E. (2002). Early childhood teacher candidates' perceptions about inclusion. *Journal of Early Childhood Teacher Education, 23*(2), 167–173.

Aldwin, C. M. (2007). Stress, coping, and development: An integrative approach (2nd ed.). New York: Guilford.

Alsaker, F. D., & Valkanover, S. (2001). Early diagnosis and prevention of victimization in kindergarten. In J. Juvonen & S. Graham (Eds.), *Peer harassment in school: The plight of the vulnerable and the victimized* (pp. 175–195). New York: Guilford.

American Academy of Pediatrics. (2006). Policy statement on corporal punishment in schools. *Pediatrics, 106*(2), 343.

American Medical Association. (1992). *Physicians' guide to media violence*. Chicago: AMA.

Andersen, P. A., Guerrero, L. K. & Jones, S. M. (2006), Nonverbal behavior in intimate interactions and intimate relationships, In V. Manusov & M. Patterson (Eds.), *The Sage handbook of nonverbal communication* (pp. 259–278). Thousand Oaks, CA: Sage Publications.

Anderson, G., Hilton, S., & Wouden-Miller, M. (2003). A gender comparison of the cooperation of 4-year-old children in classroom activity centers. *Early Education and Development, 5*(14), 441–451.

Archer, J. (1994). Testosterone and aggression: Atheoretical review. *Journal of Offender Rehabilitation, 21*, 3–9.

Ard, L., & Pitts, M. (Eds.). (1990). *Room to grow: How to create quality early childhood environments*. Austin: Texas Association for the Education of Young Children.

Asher, S. R., & Paquette, J. A. (2003). Loneliness and peer relations in childhood. *Current Directions in Psychological Science, 12*(3), 75–78.

Aslin, R. N., Jurczyk, P. W., & Pisoni, D. B. (1998). Speech and auditory processing during infancy: Constraints on and precursors to language. In W. Damon, D. Kuhn, & R. Siegler (Eds.), *Handbook of child psychology, Vol. 2: Cognition, perception, and language*. New York: Wiley.

Astington, J. W. (2001). The future of theory of mind research: Understanding motivational states, the role of language, and real-world consequences. *Child Development, 72*, 685–687.

Austin, J. S. (2000, Fall). When a child discloses sexual abuse. *Childhood Education, 77*(1), 2–5.

Badenes, L. V., Estevan, R. A. C., & Bacete, F. J. G. (2000). Theory of mind and peer rejection at school. *Social Development, 9,* 271–283.

Bailey, B. A. & Brookes, C. (2003). Thinking out loud: Development of private speech and the implications for school success and self-control. *Young Children, 58*(5), 46–52

Bailey, D. B., Jr. (2002). Are critical periods critical for early childhood education? The role of timing in early childhood pedagogy. *Early Childhood Research Quarterly, 17,* 281–284.

Bajgar, J., Ciarrochi, J., Lane, R. & Deane, F. P. (2005). Development of the levels of emotional awareness scale for children (LEAS-C). *British Journal of Developmental Psychology, 23* (4), 569–586.

Baker v. Owen, 39 F. Suppl. 294 (M.D.N.C. 1975), Off'd U.S.—96 S. Cet. 210.

Ball, J. (1989, February). The National PTA's stand on corporal punishment. *PTA Today, XIV,* 15–17.

Bancroft, L. & Silverman, J. G. (2004). Assessing abusers risks to children. In P. Jaffee, L. Boher, and A. Cunningham (Eds.), *Protecting children from domestic violence: Strategies for community intervention.* New York: Guilford.

Bandura, A. (1989). Social cognitive theory. In R. Vasta (Ed.), *Annals of child development* (Vol. 6, pp. 1–60). Greenwich, CT: JAI Press.

Bandura, A. (1991). Social cognitive theory of moral thought and action. In W. M. Kurtines & J. L. Gewirtz (Eds.), *Handbook of moral behavior and development* (Vol. 1, pp. 45–103). Hillsdale, NJ: Erlbaum.

Bandura, A. (1997). *Self-efficacy: The exercise of control.* New York: Freeman.

Barnet, A. B., & Barnet, R. J. (1998). *The youngest minds: Parenting and genes in the development of intellect and emotion.* New York: Simon & Schuster.

Baron, R. A., & Bryne, D. (1993). *Social psychology: Understanding human interaction* (5th ed.). Newton, MA: Allyn & Bacon, 1993.

Barr, R. G., & Gunnar, M. (2000). Colic: The transient responsivity hypothesis. In R. Barr, B. Hopkins, & J. Green (Eds.), *Crying as a sign, a symptom, and a signal* (pp. 41–66) London: Mac Keith Press.

Baumeister, R. F. (1998). Inducing guilt. In J. Bybee (Ed.), *Guilt and children* (pp. 185–213). San Diego: Academic Press.

Baumeister, R. F., Campbell, J. D., Krueger, J. I., & Vohs, K. D. (2003). Does high self-esteem cause better performance, interpersonal success, hap-

piness or healthier lifestyles? *Psychological Science in the Public Interest, 4*(1), 1–44.

Baumrind, D. (1967). Child care practices anteceding three patterns of preschool behavior. *Genetic Psychology Monographs, 75,* 43–88.

Baumrind, D. (1973). Current patterns of parental authority. *Developmental Psychology Monographs, 4,* 1.

Baumrind, D. (1978). Parental disciplinary patterns. *Youth and Society, 9,* 223–276.

Baumrind, D. (1988). *Familial antecedents of social competence in middle childhood.* Unpublished manuscript.

Baumrind, D. (1991). The influence of parenting style on adolescent competence and substance use. *Journal of Early Adolescence, II,* 56–95.

Baumrind, D. (1995). *Child maltreatment and optimal caregiving in social contexts.* New York: Garland.

Bavelas, J. B., Choril, N., Coates, L., and Roe, L. (1995). Gestures specialized for dialogue. *Personality and Social Psychology Bulletin, 21*(4), 394–405.

Bavelas, J. B. & Chovil, N. (2006) Nonverbal and verbal communication: Hand gestures and facial displays as part of language use in face to face dialogues, In V. Manusov & M. Patterson (Eds.), *The Sage handbook of nonverbal communication* (pp. 97–118). Thousand Oaks: Sage Publications.

Beane, A. L. (2005). *The bully free classroom.* Minneapolis, MN: Free Spirit Publishing.

Beane, J. (1991). Middle school: Natural home of integrated curriculum. *Educational Leaderships, 49*(2), 9–13.

Beaudoin, M., & Taylor, M. (2004). *Breaking the culture of bullying and disrespect, grades K–8.* Thousand Oaks, CA: Corwin Press.

Bee, H. (1999). *The developing child* (9th ed.). New York: Harper and Row.

Beebe, B., and & Stern, D. (1977). Engagement—disengagement and early object experiences. In N. Friedman & S. Grand (Eds.), *Communicative structures and psychic structures.* New York: Plenum.

Behrman, R. E. (Ed.). (1996). Special education for students with disabilities: Analysis and recommendations. *The Future of Children, 6,* 4–24.

Bell, S. H., Carr, V., Denno, D., Johnson, L. J., & Phillips, L. R. (2004). *Challenging behaviors in early childhood settings: Creating a place for all children.* Baltimore: Paul H. Brookes.

Bell, S. H., & Quinn, S. (2004). Clarifying the elements of challenging behavior. In S. H. Bell, V. Carr, D. Denno, L. J. Johnson, & L. R. Phillips (Eds.), *Challenging behaviors in early childhood settings* (pp. 1–19). Baltimore: Paul H. Brookes.

Bell, S. M., & Ainsworth, M. D. (1972). Infant crying and maternal responsiveness. *Child Development, 43*, 1171–1190.

Belsky, J., Friedman, S. L., & Hsieh, K. (2001). Testing a core emotion-regulation prediction: Does early attentional persistence moderate the effect of infant negative emotionality on later development? *Child Development, 72*, 123–133.

Bem, S. L. (1985). Androgyny and gender scheme theory: A conceptual and empirical integration. In T. B. Sondergregger (Ed.), *Nebraska Symposium on Motivation* (Vol. 32, pp. 1–71). Lincoln: University of Nebraska Press.

Benenson, J.F., & Christakos, A. (2003). The greater fragility of female's versus male's versus male's closest same-sex friendships. *Child Development, 74*, 1123–1129.

Berger, K. S. (2000). *The developing person through childhood.* New York: Worth.

Berger, K. S. (2005). *The developing person: Through childhood and adolescence* (7th ed.). New York: Worth.

Berger, K. S., & Thompson, R. A. (2005). *The Developing Person through Childhood and Adolescence.* New York: Worth Publishers.

Berk, L. (2006). *Child development* (7th ed.). Needham Heights, MA: Allyn & Bacon.

Berk, L. E., & Winsler, A. (1995). *Scaffolding children's learning: Vygotsy and early childhood education.* Washington, DC: National Association for the Education of Young Children.

Berkowitz, L. (1965) The concept of aggressive drive: Some additional considerations. In L. Berkowitz (Ed.), *Advances in experimental social psychology* (Vol. 2.), Orlando, FL: Academic Press.

Berkowitz, L. (1993). *Aggression: Its causes, consequences and control.* New York: McGraw-Hill.

Berkowitz, M. W. (2002). The science of character education. In W. Damon (Ed.), *Bringing in a new era of character education* (pp. 43–63). Stanford, CA: Hoover Institution Press.

Bernal, M. E., & Knight, G. P. (Eds.). (1993). *Ethnic identity: Formation and transmission among Hispanics and other minorities.* Albany: State University of New York Press.

Berndt, T. J. (2002). Friendship quality and social development. Current Directions in *Psychological Science, 11*(1), 7–10.

Berns, R. M. (1994). *Topical child development.* Clifton Park, NY: Thomson Delmar Learning.

Berns, R. M. (2006). *Child, family, school, community: Socialization and support* (7th ed.). Belmont, CA: Wadsworth.

Bernstein, L. J. (2000). Sesame bridge: Peace in the Middle East through television for children. In P. Senge, N. Cambron-McCabe, T. Lucas, B. Smith, J. Dutton, & A. Kleiner (Eds.), *Schools that learn: A fifth discipline field book for educators, parents, and everyone who cares about education* (pp. 519–526). New York: Doubleday.

Bilton, H. (2002). *Outdoor play in the early years: Management and innovation.* London: David Fulton Publishers.

Blanck, P., & Rosenthal, R. (1982). Developing strategies for decoding "leaky" messages: On learning how and when to decode discrepant and consistent social communications. In B. S. Feldman (Ed.), *Development of nonverbal behavior in children.* New York: Springer-Verlag.

Block, J. (1979). Personality development in males and females: The influence of differential socialization. In *Socialization influencing personality development.* Berkeley: University of California Press.

Block, J. (1993). Studying personality the long way. In D.C. Funder, R. D. Parke, C. Tomlinson-Keary, & K. Widama (Eds.), *Studying lives through time. Personality and Development,* (pp. 9–41). Washington, DC: American Psychological Association.

Bloom, L. (1998). Language acquisition in its developmental context. In D. Kuhn & R. Siegler (Eds.), *Handbook of child psychology: Vol. 2, Cognition, perception and language* (pp. 309–370). New York: John Wiley & Sons.

Bodrova, E., & Leong, D. (1996). *Tools of the mind: The Vgotskian approach to early childhood education.* Englewood Cliffs, NJ: Prentice-Hall.

Bodrova, E. & Leong, D.J. (2004) Chopsticks and counting chips: Do play and foundational skills need to compete for the teacher's attention in an early childhood classroom? In Koralek, D., (Ed.), *Young children and play* (pp. 4–11). Washington, DC: National Association for the Education of Young Children.

Boivin, M., & Hymel, S. (1997). Peer experiences and social self-perceptions: A sequential model. *Developmental Psychology, 33*, 135–145.

Bolin, G. G. (1989). Ethnic differences in attitude towards discipline among day care providers: Implications for training. *Child & Youth Care Quarterly, 18*(2), 111–117.

Boone, R. T., & Cunningham, J. G. (1998). Children's decoding of emotion in expressive body movement. The development of cue attunement. *Developmental Psychology, 34*, 1007–1016.

Bornstein, M. C. (2007) On the significance of social relationships in the development of children's earliest symbolic play: An ecological perspective, In A. Göncü & S. Gaskins (Eds.), *Play and Development: Evolutionary, sociocultural, and functional perspectives* (pp. 101–129). Mahwah, NJ: Erlbaum.

Bosacki, S. L., & Moore, C. (2004) Preschooler's understanding of simple and complex emotions: Links with gender and language. *Sex Roles: A Journal of Research.* 50 (9–10), 659–675.

Boukydis, C. F. Z. (1985). Perception of infant crying as an interpersonal event. In B. M. Lester & C. F. Z. Boukydis (Eds.), *Infant crying: theoretical and research perspectives.* New York: Plenum.

Bowe, F. G. (2007). *Early childhood special education birth to eight* (4th ed.) New York: Thompson Delmar Learning.

Boyd, B. (1997). Teacher response to superhero play: To ban or not to ban. *Childhood Education,* 74(1), 23–29.

Brackbill, Y. (1979). Obstetrical medication and infant behavior. In J. D. Osofsdy (Ed.), *Handbook of infant development* (pp. 76–125). New York: John Wiley & Sons.

Bray, J. H., & Kelly, J. (1999). *Stepfamilies.* New York: Broadway.

Brazelton, T. B. (1976). Early mother-infant reciprocity. In V. C. Vaughn, III and T. B. Brazelton, *The family—Can it be saved?* Chicago: Yearbook Medical Publishers.

Bredekamp, S., & Copple, C. (1997). *Developmentally appropriate practice in early childhood programs* (Rev. ed). Washington, DC: NAEYC.

Brendgen, M., Vitaro, F. & Bukowski, (2000). Deviant friends and early adolescents' emotional and behavioral adjustment. *Journal of Research on Adolescence, 10*(2), 173–189.

Brendtro, L., Brokenleg, M. & Van Bockern, S. (1992). *Reclaiming youth at risk: Our hope for the future.* Bloomington, IN: National Educational Service.

Brendtro, L., & Long, N. (1995). Breaking the cycle of conflict. *Educational Leadership, 52*(5), 52–56.

Brenner, A. (1997). *Helping children cope with stress.* San Francisco: Jossey-Bass.

Bretherton, I. et al. (1986). Learning to talk about emotions: A functionalist perspective. *Child Development, 57,* 529–548.

Bretherton, I. (2006) In pursuit of the internal working model construct and its relevance to attachment relationships. In E. Klaus, K. Grossman, E. Grossman, & E. Waters, (Eds.), *Attachment from infancy to adulthood* (pp. 13–14). Florence, KY: Taylor & Francis Group.

Bronfenbrenner, U. (1993). The ecology of cognitive development research models and fugitive findings. In R. H. Wozniak & K. W. Fischer. (Eds.), *Development in context* (pp. 3–44). Hillsdale, NJ: Erlbaum.

Bronson, M. B. (2000). *Self-regulation in early childhood: Nature and nurture.* New York: Guilford.

Brooks, J. B. (2006). *The process of parenting.* New York: McGraw Hill.

Brophy-Herb, H., Kostelnik, M. J., & Stein, L. C. (2001). A Developmental Approach to Teaching about Ethics Using the NAEYC Code of Ethical Conduct, *Young Children, 56*(1), 80–84.

Brown, J. D. (1998). *The self.* New York: McGraw Hill.

Brown, J. R., & Dunn, J. (1996). Continuities in emotional understanding from three to six years. *Child Development, 67,* 789–802.

Buck, R. (1982). Spontaneous and symbolic nonverbal behavior and the ontogeny of communication. In R. S. Feldman (Ed.), *Development of nonverbal behavior in children* (pp. 28–62). New York: Springer-Verlag.

Bugental, D., Caporael, L., & Shennum, W. A. (1980). Experimentally produced child uncontrollability: Effects on the potency of adult communication patterns. *Child Development, 51,* 520–528.

Bugental, D., Kaswan, J.W., & Love, L. R. (1970). perception of contradictory meanings conveyed by verbal and nonverbal channels. *Journal of Personality and Social Psychology, 16,* 647–655.

Bugental, D., Love, L. R., & Gianetto, R. (1971). Perfidious feminine faces. *Journal of Personality and Social Psychology, 17,* 314–318.

Bugental, D. B., & Goodnow, J. J. (1998). Socialization processes. In N. Eisenberg (Ed.), *Handbook of child psychology* (Vol. 3, pp. 389–462). New York: Wiley.

Bugental, D. B. & Grusec, J. E. (2006). Socialization Processes. In N. Eisenberg, W. Damon, & R.M. Lerner (Eds.), *Handbook of child psychology* (pp. 366–428). Hoboken, NJ: John Wiley & Sons.

Bukatko, D., & Daehler, M. (2004). *Child development: A thematic approach.* Boston, MA: Houghton Mifflin.

Bukowski, W. J. (1990). Age differences in children's memory of information about aggressive, socially withdrawn, and prosocial boys and girls. *Child Development, 61,* 1326–1334.

Bukowski, W. M., Sippola, L. K., & Boivin, M. (1995). *Friendship protects "At risk" children from victimization by peers.* Paper presented at the meeting of the Society for Research in Child Development, Indianapolis, IN.

Burgoon, J. K., & Saine, L. (1978). A communication model of personal space violations: Explanation and an initial test. *Human Communication Research, 4*(2) 129–142.

Burgoon, J. K. & Dunbar N. E. (2006) Nonverbal expressions of dominance and power in human relationships. In V. Manusov, & M. Patterson, (Eds.), *The Sage handbook of nonverbal communication* (pp. 279–298). Thousand Oaks: Sage Publications.

Burton, S., & Mitchell, P. (2003). Judging who knows best about yourself: Developmental change in citing the self across middle childhood. *Child Development, 74*(2), 426–443.

Bush, G., Luu, P., & Posner, M. I. (2000). Cognitive and emotional influences in anterior cingulated cortex. *Trends in Cognitive Sciences, 4*(6), 215–222.

Business Roundtable (2004). *Early Childhood Education: A call to action from the business community.* (pp. 1–9), Washington, DC: Corporate Voices for Working Families.

Butterfield, P. M., Martin, C., & Prairie, A. P. (2004). *Emotional connections: How relationships guide early learning.* Washington, DC: Zero to Three Press.

Caldera, V., Huston, A., & O'Brien, M. (1989). Social interaction and play patterns of parents and toddlers with feminine, masculine and neutral toys. *Child Development, 60,* 70–76.

Calkins, S. (1994). Origins and outcomes of individual differences in emotion regulation. In N. A. Fox (Ed.), *The Development of emotion regulation: Biological and behavioral considerations* (pp. 53–61). Monographs of the Society for Research in Child Development, 240(59), nos. 2–3.

Camaras, L. A., Malatesta, C., & Izard, C. E. (1991). The development of facial expressions in infancy. In R. S. Feldman & G. Rime (Eds.), *Fundamentals of nonverbal behavior.* Cambridge, U.K.: Cambridge University Press.

Campbell, S. B., Shaw, D. S., & Gilliom, M. (2000). Early externalizing behavior problems: Toddlers and preschoolers at risk for later maladjustment. *Development & Psychopathology, 12,* 467–488.

Campos, J. J. et al. (1983). Socioemotional development. In P. H. Hussen (Ed.), *Handbook of child psychology* (Vol. 2). New York: John Wiley & Sons.

Caprara, G. V., Barbaranelli, C., Pastorelli, C., Bandura, A., & Zimbardo, P. G. (2000). Prosocial foundations of children's academic achievement. *Psychological Science, 11*(4), 302–306.

Carkhuff, R. R. (2000). *The art of helping in the 21st century* (8th ed.). Amherst: MA: Human Resources Development Press.

Carlson, M., Charlin, V., & Miller, N. (1988). Positive mood and helping behavior: A test of six hypotheses. *Psychological Bulletin, 55,* 211–229.

Carpenter, M., Nagell, K., & Tomasello, M. (1998). Social cognition, joint attention, and communicative competence from 9 to 15 months of age. *Monographs of the Society for Research in Child Development, 63*(255), 4.

Carr, E. G., Levin, L. McConnachie, G., Carlson, J. I., Duane, C. Kemp & Smith, C. E. (2000). *Communication-based Intervention for Problem Behavior: A user's guide for producing positive change.* Baltimore: Paul H. Brookes.

Carson, J., Burks, V., & Parke, R. D. (1993). Parent–child physical play: Determinants and consequences. In K. McDonald (Ed.), *Parent–child play: Descriptions and implications* (pp. 197–220). Albany: State University of New York Press.

Case, R., & Okamoto, Y. (1996). The role of central conceptual structures in the development of children's thought. In *Monographs of the Society for Research in Child Development, 61*(2), serial no. 246. Chicago: University of Chicago Press.

Caspi, A. & Shiner, R.L. (2006). Personality development. In N. Eisenberg, W. Damon, & R.M. Lerner (Eds.), *Handbook of child psychology* (pp. 300–365). NY: Wiley.

Cassidy, D. J. (2003). Questioning the young child: Process and function. *Childhood Education, 65,* 146–149.

Cassidy, K. W., Werner, R. S., Rourke, M., Zubernis, L. S., & Balaramun, G. (2003). The relationship between psychological understanding and positive social behaviors. *Social Development, 12*(2), 198–221.

Center for the Study of Ethics in the Professions (2006). *Online Ethics Codes Project.* Chicago IL: The Center for the Study of Ethics in the Professions at Illinois Institute of Technology. http://csep.iit.edu/codes.

Center for Disease Control and Prevention (2006). Child Development. *Attention-Deficit/Hyperactivity Disorder (ADHD).* Atlanta, GA. http://www.cdc.gov/ncbddd/adhd/what.htm.

Center to Prevent Handgun Violence (2006). *Steps to Prevent Firearm Injury in the Home.* Washington, DC.

Cervantes, C. A., & Callanan, M. A. (1998). Labels and explanations in mother–child emotion talk: Age and gender differentiation. *Developmental Psychology, 34,* 88–98.

Chang, H. N. L., Muckelroy, A., & Pulido-Tobiassen, D. (1996). *Looking in, looking out.* San Francisco: California Tomorrow Publications.

Charen, M. (2000, April 24). Our boys could use some help. *Lansing State Journal,* 6A.

Charles, C. M., Seuter, G. W., & Barr, K. B. (2005). *Building classroom discipline.* White Plains, NY: Longman.

Charlesworth, R. (2008). *Understanding child development* (7th ed.). Clifton Park, NY: Thomson Delmar Learning.

Charney, R. S. (2002). *Teaching children to care: Classroom management for ethical and academic growth, K–8.* Greenfield, MA: Northeast Foundation for Children.

Chen, F. M. (1998). *Authoritative and authoritarian parenting of mothers with preschool children in Taiwan.* Unpublished doctoral dissertation, Michigan State University.

Chen, Z., Sanchez, R. P., & Campbell, T. (1997). From beyond to within their grasps: The rudiments of analogical problem solving in 10–13 month-olds. *Developmental Psychology, 33,* 790–801.

Chen, Z., & Siegler, R. (2000). Across the great divide: Bridging the gap between understanding of toddlers' and older children's thinking. *Monographs of the Society for Research in Child Development, 65*(2).

Cherlin, A. J., Kiernan, K. E., & Chase-Lansdale, P. L.(1995). Parental divorce in childhood and demographic outcomes in young adulthood. *Demography, 32,* 99–318.

Children's Defense Fund. (2005). *The State of America's Children.* Washington, DC: Children's Defense Fund.

Chipman, M. (1997). Valuing cultural diversity in the early years: Social imperatives and pedagogical insights. In J. P. Isenberg & M. R. Jalongo (Eds.), *Major trends and issues in early childhood education: Challenges, controversies and insights* (pp. 43–45). New York: Teacher's College Press.

Chrisman, K., & Couchenour, D. (2004, March/April). Healthy sexuality development in young children. *Child Care Information Exchange,* 34–36.

Chukovsky, K. (1976). The sense of nonsense verse. In J. S. Bruner, A. Jolly, & K. Sylva. (Eds.), *Play: Its role in development and evolution* (pp. 596–602). New York: Basic Books.

Cillessen, A. H. N., van Ijzendoorn, H. W., van Lieshout, C. F. M., & Hartup, W. W. (1992). Heterogeneity among peer-rejected boys: Subtypes and stabilities. *Child Development, 63,* 893–905.

Clark, C. & Gross, K. H. (2004). Adolescent Health-risk Behaviors: The effect of perceived parenting style and race. *Undergraduate Research Journal for the Human Sciences, 3,* 1–11.

Claussen, A. H., & Crittenden, P. M. (1991). Physical and psychological maltreatment: Relations among types of maltreatment. *Child Abuse and Neglect, 15,* 5–18.

Clayton, M. K. (2001). *Classroom spaces that work.* Greenfield, MA: Northeast Foundation for Children.

Click, P. M. (2007). *Administration of programs for young children* (7th ed.). Clifton Park, NY: Thomson Delmar Learning.

Clymen, R. B. et al. (1986). Social referencing and social looking among twelve-month-old infants. In T. B. Brazelton & M. W. Youeman (Eds.), *Affective development in infancy* (pp. 75–94). Norwood, NJ: Abex.

Cohen, P., & Brooks, J. S. (1995). The reciprocal influence of punishment and child behavior disorder. In J. McCord (Ed.), *Coercion and punishment in long-term perspectives* (pp. 154–164). Cambridge, U.K.: Cambridge University Press.

Coie, J. D., & Dodge, K. A. (1998). Aggression and antisocial behavior. In N. Eisenberg (Ed.), *Handbook of child psychology Vol. 3: Social, Emotional, and Personality Developement,* (6th ed., pp. 779–862). New York: Wiley.

Coie, J. D., Dodge, K. A., & Kupersmidt, J. B. (1990). Peer group behavior and social status. In S. R. Asher & J. D. Coie (Eds.), *Peer rejection in childhood* (pp. 17–59). New York: Cambridge University Press.

Coie, J. D., Dodge, K. A., & Lynam, D. (2006). Aggression and antisocial behavior in youth. In W. Damon (Series Ed.), & N. Eisenberg (Vol. Ed.), *Handbook of Child Psychology, Vol. 3: Social, Emotional, and Personality Development,* (6th ed., pp. 719–788). New York: Wiley.

Coie, J. D., & Koeppl, G. K. (1990). Adapting intervention to the problems of aggressive and disruptive rejected children. In S. R. Asher & J. D. Coie (Eds.), *Peer rejection in childhood.* New York: Cambridge University Press.

Coie, J. D., Dodge, K. A., Terry, R. & Wright. V. (1991). The role of aggression in peer relations: An analysis of aggression episodes in boys' play groups. *Child Development, 62,* 812–826.

Cole, P. M., Bruschi, C. J. & Tamang, B. L. (2002) Cultural differences in children's emotional reactions to difficult situations. *Child Development, 73,* 983–996.

Collins, W.A. & Steinberg, L. (2006). Adolescent Development in Interpersonal Context. In N. Eisenberg, W. Damon, & R. M. Lerner (Eds.), *Handbook of Child Psychology* (pp. 1003–1067). Hoboken, NJ: John Wiley & Sons.

Cook, R. E., Tessier, A., & Klein, M. D. (2004). *Adapting early childhood curriculum for children in inclusion settings* (5th ed.). Upper Saddle River, NJ: Merrill/Prentice-Hall.

Cooper, C. S., & McEvoy, M. A. (1996). Group friendship activities: An easy way to develop the social skills of young children. *Teaching Exceptional Children, 28*(3), 67–69.

Coplan, R. J., Bowker, A., & Cooper, S. M. (2003). Parenting daily hassles, child temperament and social adjustment in preschool. *Early Childhood Research Quarterly, 18*, 376–393.

Copple, C. and Bredekamp, S. (2006). *Basics of developmentally appropriate practice: An introduction for teachers of children 3 to 6.* Washington, DC: National Association for the Education of Young Children.

Cote, S., Zoccolillo, M., Tremblay, R. Nagin, D., & Vitaro, F. (2001). Predicting girls' conduct disorder in adolescence from childhood trajectories of disruptive behavior. *Journal of the American Academy of Child and Adolescent Psychiatry, 40*, 678–684.

Crary, E. (1993). *Without spanking or spoiling: A practical approach to toddler and preschool guidance.* Seattle, WA: Parenting Press.

Crick, N. R. & Dodge, K. A. (1996). Social information processing mechanisms in reactive and proactive aggression. *Child Development, 67*, 993–1002.

Crick, N. R., & Grotpeter, J. K. (1995). Relational aggression, gender, and social-psychological adjustment. *Child Development, 66*, 710–722.

Crockenberg, S., Jackson, S., & Langrock, A. M. (1996). In *At the threshold: The developing adolescence* (pp. 41–55). Cambridge, MA: Harvard University Press, New Directions for Child Development.

Crossette, B. (1996, February 29). Agency sees risk in drug to temper childhood behavior. *New York Times*, p. 14.

Crosson-Tower, C. (2005). *Understanding child abuse and neglect.* Boston: Allyn & Bacon.

Cummings, C., & Haggerty, K. (1997, May). Raising healthy children. *Educational Leadership, 54*(8) 28–30.

Cunningham, M. R. et al. (1990). Separate processes in the relation of elation and depression to helping: Social versus personal concerns. *Journal of Experimental Social Psychology, 26*, 13–33.

Curran, J. (1999). Constraints of pretend play: Explicit and implicit rules. *Journal of Research in Childhood Education, 14*(1), 47–55.

Curry, N., & Bergen, D. (1987). The relationship of play to emotional, social, and gender/sex role development. In D. Bergen (Ed.), *Play as a medium for learning and development: A handbook for theory and practice.* Portsmouth, NH: Heinemann.

Curry, N. E., & Johnson, C. N. (1990). Beyond self-esteem: Developing a genuine sense of human value. In *Research Monograph of the National Association for the Education of Young Children* (Vol. 4). Washington, DC: NAEYC.

Curtis, D. & Carter, M. (2003) *Designs for living and learning: Transforming early childhood environments.* St. Paul, MN: Readleaf. Development of the levels of emotional awareness scale for children (LEAS-C). *British Journal of Developmental Psychology, 23*(4), 569–586.

Curwin, R. L., & Mendler, A. N. (2000). *Discipline with dignity.* Reston, VA: Reston Publishing Co., Inc.

Cutting, A., & Dunn, J. (1999). Theory of mind, emotion understanding, language and family background: Individual differences and interrelations. *Child Development, 70*, 853–865.

Damon, W. (1988). *The moral child.* New York: Free Press.

Damon, W. (1995). *Greater expectations: Overcoming the culture of indulgence in America's homes and schools.* New York: Free Press.

Damon, W., & Hart, D. (1982). The development of self-understanding from infancy through adolescence. *Child Development, 53*, 841–864.

Day, M., & Parlkian, R. (2004). *How culture shapes social- emotional development: Implications for practice in infant-family programs.* Washington, DC: Zero to Three Press.

Deacon, R., & Firebaugh, F. (1988). *Family resource management: Principles and applications.* Boston: Allyn and Bacon.

DeAngelis, T. (1994, May). Homeless families: Stark reality of the '90s. *APA Monitor, 1*(38).

Deater-Deckard, K., & Dodge, K. A. (1997). Externalizing behavior problems and discipline revisited: Nonlinear effects and variation by culture, context and gender. *Psychological Inquiry, 8*, 161–175.

DeCapua, A. Wintergerst, A. (2007). *Crossing cultures in the language classroom.* Ann Arbor: University of Michigan Press.

Deci, E. L., & Flaste, R. (1995). *Why we do what we do: The dynamics of personal autonomy.* New York: Grossett/Putnam.

Deci, E. L., & Ryan, R. M. (2000). The what and the why of goal pursuits: Human needs and the selfdetermination of behavior. *Psychological Inquiry, 11*(4), 227–268.

DeLoache, J. S. (2000). Cognitive development in infants: Looking, listening, and learning. In D. Cryer & T. Harms (Eds.), *Infants and toddlers in out-of-home care*. Baltimore: Brooks.

Dennis, T., Bendersky, M., Ramsay, D. and Lewis, M. (2006). Reactivity and regulation in children prenatally exposed to cocaine. *Developmental Psychology, 42*, 688–697.

DeRamus, B. (2000, January). Back from crack. *Essence, 30*(9), 118–121.

Derman-Sparks, L. (1989). *Anti-bias curriculum: Tools for empowering young children*. Washington, DC: National Association for the Education of Young Children.

DeSpelder, L. A., & Strickland, A. L. (2001). *The last dance—encountering death and dying*. Mountain View, CA: Mayfield Publishing.

Dettore, E. (2002). Children's emotional growth: Adults' role as emotional archaeologists. *Childhood Education, 78*(5), 278–281.

DeVogue, K. (1996, March) *Conflict resolution with children in grade school*. Presentation to Forest View Elementary School Teachers, Lansing, MI.

DeWolfe, M. & Benedict, J. (1997). Social development and behavior in the integrated curriculum. In C. H. Hart, D. C. Burts, and R. Charlesworth (Eds.), *Integrated curriculum and developmentally appropriate practice, birth to age 8* (pp. 257–284). New York: State University of New York Press.

Dobson J. (1996). *The new dare to discipline*. Wheaton, IL: Tyndale House Publishers.

Dockett, S. (1998). Constructing understanding through play in the early years. *International Journal of Early Years Education, 6*(1), 105–116.

Dodge, D. T., Colker, L. J., & Heroman, C. (2002). *The creative curriculum for preschool*. Washington, DC: Teaching Strategies.

Dodge, K. A. (1986). Asocial information processing model of social competence in children. In M. Perlmutter (Ed.), *Minnesota symposia on child psychology* (Vol. 18). Hillsdale, NJ: Erlbaum.

Dodge, K.A., Coie, J.D. & Lynam D. (2006). Aggression and antisocial behavior in Youth. In N. Eisenberg, W. Damon, & R.M. Lerner (Eds.), *Handbook of child psychology* (pp. 719–788). Hoboken, NJ: John Wiley & Sons.

Dodge, K. A., Lansford, J. E., Lansford, B., Salzer, V., Bates, J. E., Pettit, G. S., Fontaine, R. & Price, J. M.

(2003). Peer rejection and social informationprocessing factors in the development of aggressive behavior problems in children. *Child Development, 74*(2), 374–393.

Doherty-Sneddon, G. (2004). *Children's unspoken language*. New York: Jessica Kingsley Publishers.

Dolgin, K. (1981). The importance of playing alone: Differences in manipulative play under social and solitary conditions. In A. Cheska (Ed.), *Play as context* (pp. 238–247). West Point, NY: Leisure Press.

Doll, B., Zucker, S. & Brehm, K. (2004). *Resilient Classrooms: Creating Healthy Environments for Learning*. NY: The Guilford Press.

Donnellan, M. B., Trzesniewski, K. H., Robins, R. W., Moffitt, T. E., Caspi, A. (2005). Low Self-Esteem is Related to Aggression, Antisocial Behavior and Delinquency. *Psychological Science, 16*(4), 328–335.

Donovan, W., & Leavitt, L. (1985). Physiology and behavior: Parents' response to the infant cry. In B. M. Lester and C. F. Z. Boukydis (Eds.), *Infant crying: Theoretical and research perspectives*. New York: Plenum.

Dowling, M. (2005). *Young Children's Personal, Social and Emotional Development*. London: Paul Chapman Educational Publishing.

Downey, G., Lebolt, A., Rincon, C., & Freitas, A. L. (1998). Rejection sensitivity and children's interpersonal difficulties. *Child Development, 69*, 1074–1091.

Dreikurs, R. (1991). *The challenge of child training: A parent's guide*. New York: Hawthorn Books, Inc.

Dreikurs, R., & Cassel, P. (1992). *Discipline without tears*. New York: Hawthorn Books, Inc.

Dreikurs, R., Grunwald, B. B. & Pepper, F. C. (1998). *Maintaining Sanity in the Classroom: Classroom management techniques*. Philadelphia, PA: Taylor and Francis.

Dreikurs, R., & Soltz, V. (1992). *Children: The challenge*. New York: Hawthorn Books, Inc.

Driscoll, A., & Nagel, N. G. (2004). *Early childhood education, birth–8*. Boston: Allyn and Bacon.

Drotar, D., Greenley, R., Hoff, A., Johnson, C., Lewandowski, A., Moore, M., Spilsbury, J., Witherspoon, D. and Zebracki, K. (2006). Summary of issues and challenges in the use of new technologies in clinical care and with children and adolescents with chronic illness, *Children's Health Care, 35*(1), 91–102.

Dundee University. (1999). *Promoting social competence: Curriculum-based project to enhance personal, social, emotional and behavioral competence*.

Dundee, U.K.: Department of Psychology, Dundee University.

Dunn, J., Brown, J. R., & Maguire, M. (1995). The development of children's moral sensibility: Individual differences in emotion understanding. *Developmental Psychology, 31,* 649–659.

Dunn, J., Cutting, A. L., & Fisher, N. (2002). Old friends, new friends: Predictors of children's perspective on their friends at school. *Child Development, 73*(2), 621–635.

Dunn, L., & Kontos, S. (1997). What have we learned about developmentally appropriate practice? *Young Children, 52*(5), 4–13.

Dunne, J. (1990, Spring). Clear Creek ISD trustee Margaret Snook speaks out. *P.O.P.S. News.* Houston: Newsletter of People Opposed to Paddling Students, Inc. Eaton, W. O., & Von.

Dwyer, K. P. (1997). Disciplining Students with Disabilities. *LD Online. Article 6182,* 1–8.

Eccles, J.S. (2007). Families, Schools, and Developing Achievement-Related Motivations and Engagement. In J. E. Grusec & P. D. Hastings (Eds.), *Handbook of Socialization: Theory and Research* (pp. 665–691). New York, NY: The Guilford Press.

Educational Productions Inc. (1993). *The child who is rejected: Play problem interventions.* Portland, OR: EPI (video format).

Educational Products, Inc. (1988). *Good talking to you.* Portland, OR: EPI (video format).

Egan, G. (2007). *The skilled helper* (8th ed.). Pacific Grove, CA: Brooks/Cole Publishing Co.

Egan, S. K., & Perry, D. G. (1998). Does low self-regard invite victimization? *Developmental Psychology, 334,* 299–309.

Eisenberg, N. (2006). *Handbook of child psychology* (pp. 1–23). Hoboken, NJ: John Wiley & Sons.

Eisenberg, N. (1983). Sex-typed toy choices: What do they signify? In M. Liss (Ed.), *Social and cognitive skills: Sex roles and children's play* (pp. 45–74). New York: Academic Press, Inc.

Eisenberg, N. (2003). Prosocial behavior, empathy, and sympathy. In M. H. Bornstein, L. Davidson, C. L. M. Keyes, & K. A. Moore (Eds.), *Well-Being: Positive development across the life course* (pp. 253–267). Lawrence Erlbaum Associates. Mahwah, NJ.

Eisenberg, N., & Fabes, R. (1998). Prosocial development. In N. Eisenberg (Ed.), *Handbook of child psychology* (Vol. 3, pp. 710–778). New York: Wiley.

Eisenberg, N., Fabes, R. A., Shepard, S. A., Cumberland, A., & Carlo, F. (1999). Consistency and development of prosocial dispositions: A longitudinal study. *Child Development, 70,* 1360–1372.

Eisenberg, N., Fabes, R.A., & Spinrad, T.L. (2006). Prosocial development. In N. Eisenberg, W. Damon, & R.M. Lerner (Eds.), *Handbook of child psychology* (pp. 646–718). Hoboken, NJ: John Wiley & Sons.

Eisenberg, N. et al. (1994). The relations of emotionality and regulation to children's anger-related reactions. *Child Development, 65,* 109–128.

Eisenberg, N. et al. (1995). Prosocial development in late adolescence: A longitudinal study. *Child Development, 66,* 1179–1197.

Eisenberg, N. & Spinrad, T. I. (2004). Emotion-related regulation: Sharpening the definition. *Child Development, 75,* 334–339.

Ekman, P. (2003). *Emotions revealed.* NY: Times Books.

Ekman, P., & Friesen, W. (1969). The repertoire of nonverbal behavior: Categories, origins, usage, and coding. *Semiotica, 1,* 49–98.

Ekman, P., Friesen, W., & P. Ellsworth, P. (1972). *Emotion in the human face: Guidelines for research and integration of findings.* New York: Pergamon Press, Inc.

Elfenbein, H. A. & Ambady, N. (2003). Universals and cultural differences in recognizing emotions. *Current directions in Psychological Science, 12*(5), 159–165.

Eliason, C., & Jenkins, L. (2003). *A practical guide to early childhood curriculum.* Upper Saddle River, NJ: Prentice Hall.

Elicker, J., & Fortner-Wood, C. (1997). Research in review: Adult–child relationships in early childhood settings. *Young Children, 51*(1), 69–78.

Eliot, L. (1999). *What's going on here?* London: Bantam Books.

El Konin, D. (1971). Symbolics and its functions in the play of children. In R. Herron & B. Sutton-Smith (Eds.), *Child's play* (pp. 221–230). New York: John Wiley & Sons, Inc.

Ellis, B. J. & Bjorklund, D. F. (Eds.). (2004). *Origins of the social mind: Evolutionary psychology and child development.* New York: Guilford Press, 219–244.

Erikson, E. H. (1950, 1963). *Childhood and society* (Rev. ed.). New York: W. W. Norton & Co., Inc.

Erwin, P. (1998). *Friendship in childhood and adolescence.* New York: Routledge.

Espelage, D. L., & Swearer, S. M. (2004). *Bullying in American schools: A social-ecological perspective on prevention and intervention.* Mahwah, NJ: Lawrence Erlbaum Associates.

Essa, E. L. (2003). *A practical guide to solving preschool behavior problems.* (5th ed.) Clifton Park, NY: Thomson Delmar Learning.

Evans, B. (2002). *You can't come to my birthday party: Conflict resolution with young children.* Ypsilanti, MI: High/Scope Press.

Exley, H. (1989). *What It's Like to Be Me* (p. 17). NY: Friendship Press.

Fabes, R. A., Fultz, J., Eisenberg, N., May-Plumlee, T., & Christopher, F. S. (1989). The effects of reward on children's prosocial motivation: A socialization study. *Developmental Psychology, 25,* 509–515.

Fabes, R. A., Martin, C. L. & Havish, L. D. (2003). Children at play: The role of peers in understanding the effects of child care. *Child Development, 74*(4), 1039–1043.

Fabes, R.A., Moss, A., Reesing, A., Martin C.L., & Hanish, L.D. (2005). *The effects of peer prosocial exposure on the quality of young children's social interactions.* Data presented at the annual conference of the National Council on Family Relations, Phoenix, AZ.

Fagot, B., & Leve, L. (1998). Gender identity and play. In D. Fromberg & D. Bergen (Eds.), *Play from birth to twelve and beyond: Contexts, perspectives and meanings* (pp. 187–192). New York: Garland Publishing, Inc.

Fathman, R. E. (2006). *2006 School corporal punishment report card.* Columbus, OH: . National Coalition to Abolish Corporal Punishment in Schools, 1–3.

Farver, J. (1992). Communicating shared meanings in social pretend play. *Early Childhood Research Quarterly,* 501–516.

Farver, J. A. M., Kim, Y. K., & Lee-Shim, Y. (2000). Within cultural differences; Examining individual differences in Korean-American and European-American preschoolers' social pretend play. *Journal of Cross-Cultural Psychology, 31,* 583–602.

Fass, S., & Cauthen, N. K. (2006). Who are America's poor children. National Center for Children in Poverty (NCCP). New York: Columbia University.

Feeney, S., & Freeman, N. K. (1999). *Ethics and the early childhood educator.* Washington, DC: National Association for the Education of Young Children.

Feldman, R. S. (1999). *Child development: A topical approach.* Upper Saddle River, NJ: Prentice Hall, 1999.

Feldman, R. S., Coats, E. J., & Philippot, P. (1999). Television exposure and children's decoding of nonverbal behavior in children. In P. Philippot, R. S. Feldman, and E. J. Coats. (Eds.), *The social context of nonverbal behavior.* Cambridge, England: Cambridge University Press.

Feldman, R. S., Jenkins, L., & Popoola, O. (1979). Detection of deception in adults and children via facial expressions. *Child Development, 50,* 350–355.

Felstiner, S. (2004). Emergent environments: Involving children in classroom design. *Childcare Information Exchange, 157,* 41–43.

Feyereisen, P., & deLannoy, J. (1991). *Gestures and speech: Psychological investigations.* Cambridge, England: Cambridge University Press.

Field, T. M., & Ignatoff, E. (1980). Interaction of twins and their mothers. Unpublished manuscript, University of Miami. As referred to by Campos et al. Socioemotional development in P. Mussenn (Ed.), *Handbook of child psychology* (Vol. 2, pp. 783–916). New York: John Wiley & Sons, Inc.

Fields, M. V., and C. Boesser. (2002). *Constructive Guidance and Discipline: Preschool and Primary Education,* 3rd ed. Upper Saddle River, NJ: Merrill.

Fogel, A. (1993). *Developing through relationships: Origins of communication, self, and culture.* Chicago: University of Chicago Press.

Fox, J., & Tipps, R. (1995). Young children's development of swinging behaviors. *Early Childhood Research Quarterly, 10,* 491–504.

Fox, L., Dunlap, G., Hemmeter, M. L. Joseph, G. E., & Strain, P. S. (2003). The teaching pyramid: A model for supporting social competence and preventing challenging behavior in young children. *Young Children, 58*(4), 48–52.

Fox, N. A. (Ed.). (1994). The development of emotion regulation: Biological and behavioral considerations. *Monographs of the Society for Research in Child Development, 240*(59), 2–3.

Franz, C. E., McClelland, D. C., & Weinberger, R. L. (1991). Childhood antecedents of conventional social accomplishment in mid-life adults: A 36 year prospective study. *Journal of Personality and Social Psychology, 60,* 586–595.

Freeman, N. K., & Swick, K. J. (Spring 2007). The ethical dimensions of working with parents. *Childhood Education, 83*(3), 163–169.

Freie, C. (1999). Rules in children's games and play. In S. Reifel (Ed.), *Play and contexts revisited. Play and culture studies* (Vol. 2, pp. 83–100). Stamford, CT: Ablex Publishing Co.

French, D. C. (2004). The cultural context of friendship. *ISSBD Newsletter, 28,* 19–20.

French, D. C., Jansen, E. A. Riansari, M., & Setiono, K. (2000). Friendships of Indonesian children: Adjustment of children who differ in friendship presence and similarity between mutual friends. *Social Development, 12*(4), 605–618.

French, J. H. (1987). *A historical study of children's heros and fantasy play*. Boise State University, Idaho: School of Education 1987.

Frey, K. S., & Ruble, D. N. (1990). Strategies for comparative evaluation: Maintaining a sense of competence across the life span. In R. J. Sternberg & J. Kolligan (Eds.), *Competence Considered* (pp. 167–169). New Haven, CT: Yale University Press.

Frick, P. J., Cornell, A. H., Bodin, S. D., Dane, H. E., Barry, C. T., & Loney, B. R. (2003). Callous-unemotional traits and developmental pathways to severe conduct disorders. *Developmental Psychology, 39,* 246–260.

Fridlund, A. L. & Russell, J. A. (2006). The functions of facial expressions: What's in a face. In V. Manusov & M. Patterson (Eds.), *The Sage handbook of nonverbal communication* (pp. 299–319). Thousand Oaks, CA: Sage Publications.

Frijda, N. (2000). The psychologist's point of view. In M. Lewis & J. M. Haviland-Jones (Eds.), *Handbook of emotions* (pp. 59–74). New York: Guilford.

Fromberg and D. Bergen (Eds.). (1998) *Play from birth to twelve and beyond: Contexts, perspectives and meanings* (pp. 187–192). New York: Garland Publishing, Inc.

Frost, J., Wortham, S., & Reifel, S. (2005). *Play and child development*. Upper Saddle River NJ: Merrill, Prentice Hall.

Fuhler, C. J., Farris, P. J., & Walther, M. P. (1999). Promoting reading and writing through humor and hope. *Childhood Education, 26*(1), 13–18.

Furnham, A., Cheng, H. (2000). Lay theories of happiness. *Journal of Happiness Studies, 1,* 227–246.

Gage, N. L., & Berliner, D. C. (1998). *Educational Psychology*. Boston: Houghton Mifflin.

Galambos-Stone, J. (1994). *A guide to discipline*. Washington, DC: National Association for the Education of Young Children.

Garbarino, J. (1995). *Children and families in the social environment* (2nd ed.). New York: Aldine de Gruyter.

Garbarino, J. (1999). *Lost boys: Why our sons turn violent and how we can save them*. New York, NY: Free Press.

Garbarino, J. (2001). *Understanding abusive families: An ecological approach to theory and practice*. San Francisco: Jossey-Bass.

Garbarino, J. (2005). *Growing up in a socially toxic environment*. CSREES-CYFAR conference. Washington DC: November.

Garbarino, J. (2006). *See Jane Hit: Why girls are growing more violent and what we can do about it*. NY: Penguin Group.

Garbarino, J., & Gilliam, G. (1997). *Understanding abusive families*. Lexington, MA: D. C. Heath & Company.

Gardner, H. (1999). *Disciplined mind*. New York: Basic Books.

Gardner, H. (2003, April 21). *Multiple intelligences after twenty years*. Paper presented at the American Education Research Association. Chicago, IL.

Gartrell, D. J. (2007). *A guidance approach to the encouraging classroom*. (4th ed.) Clifton Park, NY: Thomson Delmar Learning.

Gartstein, M. A., Short, A. D., Vannatta, K., & Nolt, R. B. (1999, June). Psychological adjustment of children with chronic illness—an evaluation of three models. *Developmental and Behavioral Pediatrics, 20*(3) 157–161.

Garvey, C. (1990). *Play*. Cambridge, MA: Harvard University Press.

Gaskins, S., Haight, W., & Lancy, L. F. (2007). The cultural construction of play. In A. Goncu & S. Gaskins (Eds.), *Play and development: Evolutionary, sociocultural, and functional perspectives* (pp. 179–202). Mahwah, NJ: Lawrence Erlbaum Ass.

Gazda, G. M., Balzer, F., Childers, W., Nealy, A., Phelps, R., & Walters, W. (2006). *Human relations development—a manual for educators* (7th ed.). Boston: Allyn and Bacon, Inc.

Geary, D. (2004). Evolution and developmental sex differences. In Junn, E. N. & Booyatzis, C. J. (Eds.), *Annual editions: Child growth and development* (pp. 32–36). McGraw Hill Contemporary Learning Series. Dubuque, IA: McGraw-Hill.

Gelfand, D. M. and Drew, C. J. (2003). *Understanding child behavior disorders*. Belmont, CA: Wadsworth.

Gelman, D. (1997). The miracle of resiliency. In K. L. Freiberg (Ed.), *Human development—annual editions*. Guilford, CT: Dushkin Publishing Group.

Genishi, C. (2002). Young English language learners: Resourceful in the classroom. *Young Children, 57*(4), 66–71.

Gergen, K. (2001). *Social construction in context*. London: Sage.

Gershoff, E. (2003, November). Living at the edge. *Research brief #4. Low income and the development of America's kindergartners*. New York: Columbia University, National Center for Children in Poverty.

Gershoff, G. T. (2002). Corporal punishment by parents and associated child behaviors and experiences: A meta-analytic and theoretical review. *Psychological Bulletin 128*, 539–579.

Gest, S. D., Graham-Bermann, & Hartup, W.W. (2001). Peer experience: Common and unique features of number of friendships, social network centrality, and sociometric status. *Social Development, 10*, 23–40.

Gestwicki, C. (2007). *Developmentally appropriate practice: Curriculum and development in early education.* (3rd ed.) Clifton Park, NY: Thomson Delmar Learning.

Gilness, J. (2003, November). How to integrate character education into the curriculum. *Phi Delta Kappan, 85*(3), 243–245.

Gitlin-Weiner, K. (1998). Clinical perspectives on play. In D. Fromberg & D. Bergen (Eds.), *Play from birth to twelve and beyond: Contexts, perspectives and meanings* (pp. 187–192). New York: Garland Publishing, Inc.

Gleason, J. B. (2004). *The development of language.* Boston: Allyn & Bacon.

Goelman, H. (1994). Conclusion: Emerging ecological perspectives on play and child care. In G. Goleman & E. Jacobs (Eds.), *Children's play in child care settings* (pp. 214–222). Albany: State University of New York.

Goffin, S. G. (1989). How well do we respect the children in our care? *Childhood Education, 66*(2), 68–74.

Golding, K. (2004). Providing specialist psychological support to foster carers: A consultation model. *Child and Adolescent Mental Health, 9*(2), 71–76.

Goldsmith, E. B. (2004). *Resource management for individuals and families* (3rd ed.). Belmont, CA: Wadsworth/Thompson Learning.

Goldsmith, H.H., Buss, A. H., Plomin, R., Rothbart, M. K., Chess, S., Hinde, R.A., & McCall, R.B. (1987). Roundtable: What is temperament? Four approaches. *Child Development, 58*, 505–529.

Goleman, D. (1991). *Psychology updates.* New York: HarperCollins.

Goleman, D. (1995). *Emotional intelligence: Why it can matter more than IQ.* New York: Bantam Books.

Goleman, D. (1999). *Working with emotional intelligence.* New York: Bantam.

Goleman, D. (2006). *Social Intelligence: The New Science of Social Relationships.* New York: Bantam Books.

Goleman, D. (2007). *Social Intelligence: The New Science of Human Relationships.* New York: Bantam Books.

Goncu, A., Jain, J. & Tuerner, U. (2007) Children's play as cultural interpretation, In A. Goncu & S. Gaskins (Eds.), *Play and Development: Evolutionary, sociocultural, and functional perspectives* (pp. 155–178). Mahwah, NJ: Lawrence Erlbaum Ass.

Göncü, A., Patt, M., & Kouba, E., Understanding young children's pretend play in context, In P. K. Smith & C. Hart (Eds.), *Blackwell handbook of childhood social development* (pp. 418–437). Malden, MA: Blackwell Publishers.

Gonzalez-Mena, J. (2001). *Foundations: Early childhood education in a diverse society.* Mountain View, CA: Mayfield Publishing.

Gonzalez-Mena, J. (2004). *The caregiver's companion. Readings and professional resources.* Boston: Mc-Graw-Hill.

Gonzalez-Mena, J., & Eyer, D.W. (2006). *Infants, toddlers and caregivers.* (7th ed.). Boston: McGraw Hill.

Goodnow, J. J. Analyzing Agreement between Generations: Do Parents' Ideas Have Consequences for Children's Ideas? In I. E. Sigel, A. M. McGillicuddy-DeLisi, & J. J. Goodnow (Eds.), *Parental belief systems* (pp. 293–317). Hillsdale, NJ: Erlbaum.

Goossens, F., & Ijzendoorn, M. (1990). Quality of infants' attachments to professional caregivers: Relation to infant–parent attachment and daycare characteristics. *Child Development, 61*(3) 832–837.

Gootman, M. (1988, November/December). Discipline alternatives that work: Eight steps toward classroom discipline without corporal punishment. *The Humanist, 48*, 11–14.

Gordon, J. (1990, April 23). Teaching kids to negotiate. *Newsweek*, 65.

Gordon, T. (1992). *Discipline that works: Promoting self-discipline in children.* New York: Plume Books.

Graves, S. B., Gargiulo, R. M., & Sluder, L. C. (1996). *Young children: An introduction to early childhood education.* Minneapolis: West Publishing Co.

Greenspan, S. I. & Salmon, J. (1996). *The challenging child.* New York: Perseus Books.

Griffin, H. (1984). The coordination of meaning in the creation of a shared make believe. In I. Bretherton (Ed.), *Symbolic play.* Orlando, FL: Harcourt Brace Jovanovich, Inc.

Griffin, S. (1992). Structural analysis of the development of their inner world: A neo-structural analysis of the development of intrapersonal intelligence. In R. Case (Ed.), *The mind's staircase* (pp. 198–206). Hillsdale, NJ: Erlbaum.

Grolnick, W. S., Bridges, L. J., & Connell, J. P. (1993). Emotional self-regulation in two-year-olds: Strategies and emotionality in four contexts. *Child Development, 67*, 928–941.

Grolnick, W. S., Bridges, L. J., & Connell, J. P. (1996). Emotion regulation in two-year-olds: Strategies and emotional expression in four contests. *Child Development, 67*, 928–941.

Grossman, K., Grossman, K., & Waters, E. (Ed). (2006). *Attachment from infancy to adulthood*. Florence, KY: Taylor & Francis Group.

Gruendel, J. M. (1977). Referential extension in early language development. *Child Development, 48*, 1567–1576.

Grusec, J. E., Davidov, M., & Lundell, L. (2004). Prosocial and helping behavior. In P. K. Smith & C. H. Hart (Eds.), *Blackwell handbook of childhood social development* (pp. 457–473). Malden, MA: Blackwell Publishing Ltd.

Grusec, J. E., Goodnow, J. J., & Kuczynski, L. (2000). New directions in analyses of parenting contributions to children's acquisition of values. *Child Development, 71*, 205–211.

Guerin, D.W., & Gottfried, A.W. (1994). Temperamental consequences of infant difficultness. *Infant Behavior and Development, 17*, 421–423.

Guerney, L. (2004). *Parenting: A skills training manual* (2nd ed.). State College, PA: Ideals.

Guerrero, L. K. & Floyd, K. (2006). *Nonverbal communication in close relationships*. Mahwah, NJ: Lawrence Erlbaum Associates.

Gullone, E. & King, N. J. (1993). The fears of youth in the 1990s: Contemporary normative data. *Journal of Genetic Psychology, 154*(2), 137–153.

Gurian, M. (2006). The Wonder of Boys. New York: Jeremy P. Tarcher.

Gurian, M. (2007). *Nurture the nature*. San Francisco, CA: Jossey-Bass.

Gustafson, G. E., Wood, R. M., & Green, J. A. (2000). Can we hear the causes of infants' crying? In R. Barr, B. Hopkins, & J. Green (Eds.), *Crying as a sign, a symptom, and a signal* (pp. 8–22). London: Mac Keith Press.

Haith, M. M. (1983). Future-oriented processes in infancy: The case of visual expectations. In C. E. Grandrud (Ed.), *Visual perception and cognition in infancy*. Hillsdale, NJ: Erlbaum.

Halberstadt, A. G. (1991). Toward an ecology of expressiveness: Family socialization and a model in general. In R. S. Feldman & B. Rime (Eds.), *Fundamentals of nonverbal behavior*. New York: Cambridge University Press, 106–160.

Hall, E. T. (1966). *The hidden dimension*. Garden City, NY: Doubleday & Company, Inc.

Hall, E. T. (1981). *The silent language*. Garden City, NY: Anchor Press/Doubleday.

Hall, J. (1996, Spring). Touch, status, and gender at professional meetings. *Journal of Nonverbal Behavior, 20*(1), 23–44.

Hall, J. (2006) Women's and Men's nonverbal communication: Similarity, differences, stereotypes, and origins. In V. Manusov & M. Patterson (Eds.), *The Sage handbook of nonverbal communication* (pp. 201–218). Thousand Oaks, CA: Sage Publications.

Halterman, J. S., Coon, K. M., Forbes-Jones, E., Fagano, M., Hightower, A. D., & Szilagyi, P. G. (2007). Behavior problems among inner city children with asthma: Findings from a community-based sample, *Pediatrics*, http://www.pediatrics.org.

Hamblen, J. (2007). *Terrorist attacks and children*. Washington, DC: U. S. Dept. of Veteran Affairs National Center for Posttraumatic Stress Disorder. http://www.ncptsd.va.gov/ncmain/ncdocs/fact_shts/fs_children_disaster.html.

Hamel, J. & Nicholls, T. (2006). *Family Intervention in Domestic Violence*. New York: Springer Publishing.

Hanish, L. D., Kochenderfer-Ladd, B. Fabes, R. A., Martin, C. L., & Denning, D. (2004). Bullying among young children: The influence of peers and teachers. In D. L. Espelage & S. M. Swearer (Eds.), *Bullying in American schools: A socialecological perspective on prevention and intervention* (pp. 141–159). Mahwah, NJ: Lawrence Erlbaum Associates.

Hansen, D. J., Nangle, D. W., & Ellis, J. T. (1996). Reconsideration of the use of peer sociometrics for evaluating social skills training. *Behavior Modification, 20*, 281–299.

Harrington, R. G. (2004). Temper tantrums: Guidelines for parents. *Helping Children at Home and School II: Handouts for Families and Educators*. Bethesda, MD: National Association of School Psychologists.

Harris, P. L. (1989). *Children and emotion: The development of psychological understanding*. New York: Basil Blackwell.

Harrist, A. W., Zaia, A. F., Bates, J. E., Dodge, K. A., & Pettit, G. S. (1997). Subtypes of social withdrawal in early childhood: Sociometric status and social-cognitive differences across four years. *Child Development, 68*, 278–294.

Hart, B & T. R. Risley, (2006). In W. Damon & N. Eisenberg (Eds.), *Handbook of child psychology: Vol. 3. Social, emotional, and personality development* (5th ed., pp. 553–618). New York: Wiley.

Hart, D., Burock, D., London, B., & Atkins, R. (2003). Prosocial tendencies, antisocial behavior, and moral development. In A. Slater & G. Bremmer (Eds.), *An introduction to developmental psychology* (pp. 334–356). Malden, MA: Blackwell.

Harter, S. (1998). The development of self-preservations. In W. Damon & N. Eisenberg (Eds.), *Handbook of child psychology, Vol. 3: Social, Emotional, and Personality Development* (5th ed., pp. 553–618). New York: John Wiley and Sons, Inc.

Harter, S. (1999). *The construction of the self: A developmental perspective.* New York: The Guilford Press.

Harter, S. (2006). The self. In N. Eisenberg, W. Damon & R.M. Lerner (Eds.), *Handbook of child psychology* (pp. 505–570). Hoboken, NJ: John Wiley & Sons.

Hartup, W. W. (1996). The company they keep: Friendships and their developmental significance. *Child Development, 67,* 1–13.

Hartup, W. W., & Abeccassis, M. (2004). Friends and enemies. In P. K. Smith & C. H. Hort (Eds.), *Blackwell handbook of childhood social development* (pp. 285–305). Malden, MA: Blackwell.

Hartup, W. W., & Moore, S. G. (1990). Early peer relations: Developmental significance and prognostic implications. *Early Childhood Research Quarterly 5*(1) 1–17.

Haslett, B. B., & Samter, W. (1997). *Children communicating: The first five years.* Mahwah, NJ: Erlbaum.

Hastings, P.D., Rubin, K.H., & DeRose, L. (2005). Links among gender, inhibition, and parental socialization in the development of prosocial behavior. *Merrill-Palmer Quarterly, 51,* 501–527.

Hastings, P.D., Utendale, W.T., & Sullivan, C. (2007). The socialization of prosocial development. In J.E. Grusec & P. D Hastings (Eds.), *Handbook of socialization: theory and research* (pp. 638–664), New York, NY: Guilford Press.

Hastings, P.D., Zahn-Waxler, C., & McShane, K. (2005). We are, by nature, moral creatures: Biological bases for concern for others. In M. Killen & J. Smetana (Eds.), *Handbook of moral development* (pp. 483–516). Hillsdale, NJ: Erlbaum.

Hay, D., Ross, H., & Goldman, B. D. (2004). Social games in infancy. In B. Sutton-Smith, (Ed.), *Play and learning* (pp. 83–108). New York: Gardner Press.

Hay, D.F., Castle, J., Davies, L., Demetriou, H., & Stimson, C.A. (1999). Prosocial action in very early childhood. *Journal of Child Psychology and Psychiatry and Allied Disciplines, 40,* 905–916.

Hay, D. F., Payne, A., & Chadwick, A. (2004). Peer relations in childhood. *Journal of Child Psychology and Psychiatry, 45*(1), 84–108.

Hazen, N. L., & Black, B. (1989). Preschool peer communication skills: The role of social status and interaction content. *Child Development, 60*(4) 867–876.

Head Start Bureau. (1977). *Child abuse and neglect: A self-instructional text for Head Start personnel.* Washington, DC: U.S. Government Printing Office.

Hearron, P. & Hildebrand, V. (2004). *Guiding young children.* Upper Saddle River, NJ: Merrill.

Hegland, S. M., & Rix, M. K. (1990). Aggression assertiveness in kindergarten children differing in day care experiences. *Early Childhood Research Quarterly, 5,* 105–116.

Heimann, M. (2003). *Regression periods in human infancy.* Mahwah, NJ: Erlbaum.

Hendrick, J. (2003). *Total learning.* New York: Macmillan.

Hendrick, J. & Weissman, P. (2006). *Total Learning: Developmental Curriculum for the Young Child.* Upper Saddle River N.J.: Prentice Hall.

Henley, N. (1977). *Body politics: Power, sex and nonverbal communication.* Englewood Cliffs, NJ: Prentice-Hall.

Herbert, M. (1998). *Clinical child psychology: Social learning, development and behavior* (2nd ed.). Chichester, U.K.: John Wiley & Sons.

Herner, T. (1998). Understanding and intervening in young children's challenging behavior. *Counterpoint.* Volume 1, Alexandria, VA: National Associaiton of Directors of Special Education, p. 2.

Herrera, C., & Dunn, J. (1997). Early experiences with family conflict: Implications for arguments with a close friend. *Developmental Psychology, 33,* 869–881.

Hetherington, E. M. (1999). *Coping with divorce.* Hillsdale, NJ: Erlbaum.

Hetherington, E. M., & Clingempeel, W. G. (1992). Coping with marital transitions: A family systems perspective. *Monographs of the Society for Child Development, 57,* 2, 3, serial no. 227.

Hetherington, E. M., Parke, R, Gauvin, M. & Otis-Locke, V. (2005). *Child psychology: A contemporary viewpoint.* Boston: McGraw-Hill.

Hinde, R. A. (2006). Ethological and attachment theory. In K. Grossman, E. Grossman, & E. Waters (Eds.), *Attachment from infancy to adulthood* (pp. 1–12). Florence, KY: Taylor & Francis Group.

Hodges, E. V. E., Boivin, M., Vitaro, F., & Bukowski, W. M. (1999). The power of friendship: Protection against an escalating cycle of peer victimization. *Developmental Psychology, 35,* 94–104.

Hodges, E. V. E., Malone, M. J., & Perry, D. G. (1997). Individual risk and social risk as interacting determinants of victimization in the peer group.*Developmental Psychology, 33,* 1032–1039.

Hoffman, C. D. (1995). Pre- and post-divorce father–child relationship and child adjustment: Non-custodial fathers' perspectives. *Journal of Divorce and Remarriage, 182*(3), 20.

Hoffman, M. (1983). Affective and cognitive processes in moral internalization. In E. T. Higgins, D. N. Ruble, & W.W. Hartup (Eds.), *Social cognition and social behavior: Developmental perspectives.* New York: Cambridge University Press.

Hoffman, M. L. (1988). Moral development. In M. H. Bornstein and M. E. Lamb (Eds.), *Developmental psychology: An advanced textbook.* Hillsdale, NJ: Erlbaum.

Hoffman, M. L. (1990). Empathy and justice motivation. *Motivation and Emotion, 14,* 151–172.

Hoffman, M. L. (2000). *Empathy and moral development.* New York: Cambridge University Press.

Holden, G. (1997). Changing the way kids settle conflicts. *Educational Leadership, 54*(8), 74–76.

Honig, A. (1992, November). *Mental health for babies: What do theory and research teach us?* Paper presented at the Annual Meeting of National Association for the Education of Young Children, New Orleans, LA.

Honig, A. (1993, December). *Toddler strategies for social engagement with peers.* Paper presented at the Biennial National Training Institute of the National Center for Clinical Infant Programs, Washington, DC.

Honig, A. (1998). Sociological influences on genderrole behaviors in children's play. In D. Fromberg & D. Bergen (Eds.), *Play from birth to twelve and beyond: Contexts, perspectives and meanings* (pp. 338–348). New York: Garland.

Honig, A. S. (1985, March). Compliance, control and discipline. *Young Children, 40*(3), 47–51.

Honig, A. S. (1998, April). *Create a prosocial plus cognitive curriculum for young children.* Paper presented at the Early Childhood Branch of the New York Public Library, New York.

Honig, A. S. (2000, September). Psychosexual development in infants and young children. *Young Children, 55*(5), 70–77.

Honig, A. S. (2004, March/April). How to create an environment that counteracts stereotyping. *Child Care Information Exchange,* 37–41.

Honig, A. S., & Wittmer, D. S. (1992). *Prosocial development in children: Caring, sharing, and cooperating: A bibliographic resource guide.* New York: Garland.

Honig, A. S., & Wittmer, D. S. (1996). Helping children become more prosocial: Ideas for classrooms, families, schools and communities. *Young Children, 51*(2), 62–70.

Hopkins, A. R. (2005). Children and grief: The role of the educator. In K. M. Paciorek & J. H. Munro (Eds.), *Early childhood education annual editions* (pp. 144–199). Dubuque, IA: McGraw-Hill/Dushkin.

Horne, A. M., Orpinas, P., Newman-Carlson, D., & Bartolomucci, C. L. (2004). Elementary school bully busters program: Understanding why children bully and what to do about it. In D. L. Espelage & S. M. Swearer (Eds.), *Bullying in American schools: A social-ecological perspective on prevention and intervention* (pp. 297–325). Mahwah, NJ: Erlbaum.

Horowtiz, F. D., Darling-Hammond, L. and Bransford, J. (2005). Educating teachers for developmentally appropriate practice. In L. Darling-Hammond and J. Bransford (Eds.), *Preparing teachers for a changing world* (pp. 88–125). San Francisco, CA: Jossey-Bass.

Horowitz, I. A., & Bordens, K. S. (1995). *Social psychology.* Mountain View, CA: Mayfield.

Hostetler, K. (1997). *Ethical judgment in teaching.* Boston: Allyn & Bacon.

Howe, N. et al. (1993). The ecology of dramatic play centers and children's social and cognitive play. *Early Childhood Research Quarterly, 8,* 235–251.

Howes, C., & Matheson, C. C. (1992). Sequences in the development of competent play with peers: Social and social pretend play. *Developmental Psychology, 28,* 961–974.

Howes, C., Matheson, C. C. & Wu, F. (1992). Friendships and social pretend play. In C. Howes, O. Unger, & C. C. Matheson (Eds.), *The collaborative construction of pretend.* Albany: State University of New York Press.

Hubbard, J. A., Smithmyer, C. M., Ramsden, S. R., Parker, E. H., Flanagan, K. D., Dearing, K. F., Relyea, N. & Simons, R. F. (2002). Observational, psychological, and self-report measures of children's anger: Relations to reactive versus proactive aggression. *Child Development, 73,* 1101–1118.

Hughes, F. (1999). *Children, play, and development.* Boston: Allyn & Bacon.

Hutt, C. (1971). Exploration and play in children. In R. Herron & B. Sutton-Smith (Eds.), *Child's play.* New York: John Wiley & Sons.

Hyman, I. A. (1990). *Reading, writing and the hickory stick: The appalling story of physical and psychological violence in American schools.* Boston: Lexington Books.

Hyman, I. A. (1997). *The case against spanking: How to discipline your child without hitting.* San Francisco, CA: Jossey Bass.

Hymowitz, K. S. (2006). *Marriage and caste in America: Separate and unequal families in a post-marital age.* Chicago: Ivan R. Dee, Publisher.

Hyson, M. (2004). *The emotional development of young children.* New York: Teachers College Press.

Hyun, E., & Choi, D. H. (2004). Examination of young children's gender-doing and gender-bending in their play dynamics. *International Journal of Early Childhood, 36*(1), 49–64.

Ingraham v. Wright, 95 S. Ct. 1401, at 1406, Citing 525 F.2d. 909 (1977), at 917.

Isabella, R., & Belsky, J. (1991). International synchrony and the origins of infant–mother attachment: A replication study. *Child Development, 62*(2), 373–384.

Isberg, R. S. et al. (1989). Parental contexts of adolescent self-esteem. *Journal of Youth and Adolescence, 18,* 1–23.

Izard, C. (1994). Innate and universal facial expression. Evidence from developmental and cross-cultural research. *Psychological Bulletin, 115,* 288–299.

Izard, C. E., Fantauzzo, C. A., Castle, J. M., Haynes, O. M., Rayias, M. F., & Putnam, P. H. (1995). The ontogeny and significance of infants' facial expressions in the first 9 months of life. *Developmental Psychology, 31,* 997–1013.

Jackson, J. S. (2003). *Bye-bye, Bully!: A kid's guide for dealing with bullies.* St. Meinrad, IN: Abbey Press.

Jalongo, M. R., & Isenberg, J. (2004). *Exploring your role: A practitioner's introduction to early childhood education.* Upper Saddle River, NJ: Merrill.

Jarratt, J. (1994). *Helping Children Cope with Separation and Loss.* Stockholm: Slussens Bokforlag.

Javernik, E. (1988). Johnny's not jumping: Can we help obese children? *Young Children,* 18–23.

Jenkins, J. M., Turrell, S. L., Kogushi, Y., Lollis, S., & Ross. H. S. (2003). A longitudinal investigation of the dynamics of mental state talk in families. *Child Development, 74*(3), 905–920.

Johnson, J. C., Ironsmith, M., Whitchler, A. L., Poteat, G. M., Snow, C. W. & Mumford, S. (1997). The development of social networks in preschool children. *Early Education and Development, 8*(4), 389–405.

Johnson, K. R. (1998). Black kinesics: Some nonverbal communication patterns in black culture. *Florida FL Reporter, 57,* 17–20.

Jones, E. (1981). *Dimensions of teaching–learning environments.* Pasadena, CA: Pacific Oaks.

Jones, E. (2004). Playing to get smart, In Koralek, D. (Ed.), *Young children and play* (pp. 25–27). Washington, DC: National Association for the Education of Young Children.

Jordan, E., Cowan, A., & Roberts, J. (1995). Knowing the rules: Discursive strategies in young children's power struggles. *Early Childhood Research Quarterly, 10,* 339–358.

Kagan, J. (1997). Temperament and the reactions to unfamiliarity. *Child Development, 68,* 139–143.

Kamii, C. (1994). Viewpoint: Obedience is not enough. *Young Children, 39*(4), 11–14.

Kasser, T., & Ryan, R. M. (1996). Further examining the American dream: Differential correlates of intrinsic and extrinsic goals. *Personality and Social Psychology Bulletin, 22*(3), 280–287.

Kastenbaum, R. (2004). *Death, society, and human experience.* Boston: Allyn and Bacon.

Katz, L. G. (1993). Distinctions between self-esteem and narcissism: Implications for practice. *Perspectives from ERIC/EECE. Monograph Series, 5,* Urbana, IL: Eric Clearinghouse on Elementary and Early Childhood Education. (ERIC Document Reproduction Service No. 363–452).

Katz, L. G., & Chard, S. C. (2000). *Engaging children's minds: The project approach.* Norwood, NJ: Ablex.

Katz, L. G., & McClellan, D. E. (1997). *Fostering children's social competence: The teacher's role.* Washington, DC: National Association for the Education of Young Children.

Katz, L. F. & Windecker-Nelson, B. (2004). Parental meta-emotion in families with conduct-problem children: Links with peer relations. *Journal of Abnormal Psychology, 32,* 385–398.

Kazdin, A. E. (2001). *Behavior modification in applied settings.* Belmont, CA: Wadsworth.

Keane, S. P. & Calkins, S. D. (2004). Predicting kindergarten peer social status from toddler and preschool problem behavior. *Journal of Abnormal Child Psychology, 32,* 409–423.

Kearney, M, (1999). The role of teachers in helping children of domestic violence. *Childhood Education, 75*(5), 290–296.

Keenan, K., & Shaw, D. S. (1995). The development of coercive family processes: The interaction between aversive toddler behavior and parenting factors. In J. McCord (Ed.), *Coercion and punishment in long-term perspectives* (pp. 165–180). New York: Cambridge University Press.

Kemple, K., Spermanza, H., & Hazen, N. (1992). Cohesive discourse and peer acceptance: Longitudinal relations in the preschool years. *Merrill Palmer Quarterly, 38*, 364–381.

Kenyon, P. (1999). *What would you do? An ethical case workbook for human service professionals.* Pacific Grove, CA: Brooks/Cole.

Kerr, D. C. R., Lopez, N. L., Olson, S. L. & Sameroff, A. J. (2004). Parental discipline and externalizing behavior problems in early childhood: The roles of moral regulation and child gender. *Journal of Abnormal Child Psychology, 32*, 369–383.

Kessler, J. W. (1972). Neurosis in childhood. In B. Wolman (Ed.), *Manual of child psychopathology.* New York: McGraw-Hill.

Key, M. R. (1975). *Paralanguage and kinesics.* Metuchen, NJ: Scarecrow Press.

Killen, M. (1991). Social and moral development in early childhood. In W. M. Kurtines & J. L. Gerwirtz (Eds.), *Handbook of moral behavior and development, Vol. 2: Research* (pp. 115–138), Hillsdale, NJ: Erlbaum.

Kim, J. M. (1998). Korean children's concepts of adult and peer authority and moral reasoning. *Developmental Psychology, 34*, 947–955.

Kim, J. M., & Turiel, E. (1996). Korean children's concepts of adult and peer authority. *Social Development, 5*, 310–329.

Kirby, J. (2004). *Single-parent families in poverty.* Columbus: Ohio State University.

Klaus, M. H., Kennell, J. H., & Klaus, P. H. (1995). *Bonding: Building the foundations of secure attachment and independence.* Reading, MA: Addison Wesley.

Klein, M. D., Cook, R. E. & Richardson-Gibbs, A. M. (2001). *Strategies for Including Children with Special Needs in Early Childhood Settings.* Albany, NY: Delmar/Thomson Learning.

Klein, T. P., Wirth, D., Linas, K. (2004). Play, children's context for development. In Koralek, D. (Ed.), *Spotlight on young children and play.* Washington, DC: National Association for the Education of Young Children.

Klugman, K. (1999). A bad hair day for G.I. Joe. In B. L. Clark & M. Higonnet (Eds.), *Girls, boys, books, toys* (pp. 169–182). Baltimore: Johns Hopkins University Press.

Knapp, M. L., & Hall, J. (2005). *Nonverbal communication in human interaction.* - Upper Saddle River, NJ: Thompson Learning.

Kochanska, G. (1991). *Affective factors in mothers' autonomy-granting to their five-year-olds: Comparisons of well and depressed mothers.* Paper presented at the Meetings of the Society for Research in Child Development, Seattle, WA.

Kochanska, G. (1993). Toward a synthesis of parental socialization and child temperament in early development of conscience. *Child Development, 64*, 325–347.

Kochanska, G. (1995). Children's temperament, mother's discipline, and security of attachment: Multiple pathways to emerging internalization. *Child Development, 66*, 597–615.

Kochanska, G. (1997). Multiple pathways to conscience for children with different temperaments: From toddlerhood to age 5. *Developmental Psychology, 33*, 228–240.

Kochanska, G., Padavic, D. L., & Koenig, A. L. (1996). Children's narratives about hypothetical moral dilemmas and objective measures of their conscience: Mutual relations and social antecedents. *Child Development, 67*, 1420–1436.

Kochanska, G., Gross, J. N., Lin, M. & Nichols, K. E. (2002). Guilt in young children: Development, determinants and relations with a broader system of standards. *Child Development, 73*, 461–482.

Kochanska, G., Padavic, D. L., & Koenig, A. L. (1996). Children's narratives about hypothetical moral dilemmas and objective measures of their conscience: Mutual relations and social antecedents. *Child Development, 67*, 1420–1436.

Kochenderfer-Ladd, B. J., & Wardrop, J. L. (2001). Chronicity and instability of children's peer victimization experiences as predictors of loneliness and social satisfaction trajectories. *Child Development, 72*, 134–151.

Kohlberg, L. (1976). Moral stages and moralization: The cognitive–developmental approach. In T. Lickona (Ed.), *Moral development and behavior.* New York: Holt, Rinehart & Winston.

Kohn, A. (1996). *Beyond discipline: From compliance to community.* Alexandria, VA: Association for Supervision and Curriculum Development.

Kontos, S., & Wilcox-Herzog, A. (1997). Teacher's interactions with children: Why are they so important? *Young Children, 52*(2), 4–12.

Kopp, C. B. (1994). *Baby steps: The "whys" of your child's behavior in the first two years*. New York: W. H. Freeman.

Kostelnik, M. (1987). *Development practices in early childhood programs*. Keynote address, National Home Start Day, New Orleans.

Kostelnik, M. J. (1987). *Evaluation of a communication and group management skills training program for child development personnel*. Ph.D. dissertation, The Pennsylvania State University.

Kostelnik, M. J. (1983, November). *Evaluation of an in-service multi-media training program in discipline skills for teachers of young children*. Paper presented at the Annual Meeting of the National Association for the Education of Young Children, Atlanta, GA.

Kostelnik, M. J., Onaga, E., Rohde, B. & Whiren, A. (2002) Rosie: The Girl with the Million Dollar Smile. In *Children with special needs: Lessons for early childhood professionals* (pp. 32–48). NY: Teachers College Press.

Kostelnik, M. J., Onaga, E., Rohde, B. & Whiren, A. K. (2002). Brian: Just bursting to communicate. In *Children with special needs: Lessons for early childhood professionals* (pp. 120–135). New York: Teachers College Press.

Kostelnik, M. J., Onaga, E., Rohde, B. & Whiren, A. (2002) Sam: A Complex Child. In *Children with special needs: Lessons for early childhood professionals* (pp. 100–119). New York: Teachers College Press.

Kostelnik, M. J., Soderman, A. K., & Whiren, A. P. (2007). *Developmentally appropriate programs in early childhood education*. Upper Saddle River, NJ: Prentice-Hall.

Kostelnik, M. J., & Stein, L. C. (1986, November 14). *Effects of three conflict mediation strategies on children's aggressive and prosocial behavior in the classroom*. Paper presented at the Annual Meeting of the National Association for the Education of Young Children, Washington, DC.

Kostelnik, M. J., Whiren, A., & Stein, L. (1986). Living with He-Man: Managing superhero fantasy play. *Young Children, 41*(4), 3–9.

Kozol, J. (2006). Rachel and her Children—*Homeless families in America*. New York: Three Rivers Press.

Krannich, C., & Krannich, R. (2001). *Savvy interviewing: The nonverbal advantage*. Manassas Park, VA: Impact Publications.

Kristal, J. (2005). *The temperament perspective: Working with children' behavioral styles*. New York: Paul H. Brookes.

Kuczynski, L., & Kochanska, G. (1995). Function and content of maternal demands: Developmental significance of early demands for competent action. *Child Development, 66*, 616–628.

Kuebli, J., Butler, S., & Fivush, R. (1995). Mother–child talk about past emotions: Relations of maternal language and child gender over time. *Cognition and Emotion, 9*, 256–283.

Kupersmidt, J. B., DeRosier, M. E., Patterson, C. J. (1995). Similarity as the basis for children's friendships: The roles of sociometric status, aggressive and withdrawn behavior, academic achievement, and demographic characteristics. *Journal of Social and Personal Relationships, 12*, 439–452.

Kurcinka, M. S. (2000). *Kids, parents and powers Struggles*. New York: Harper Collins.

Kuttler, A.F., Parker, J.G., & LaGreca, A.M. (2002). Developmental and gender differences in preadolescents' judgments of the veracity of gossip. *Merrill-Palmer Quarterly, 48*, 105–132.

Kuykendall, J. (1995). Is gun play OK here??? *Young Children, 50*(1), 56–59.

Labile, D. J., & Thompson, R. A. (2007). Mother–child discourse, attachment security; shared positive affect, and early conscious development. *Child Development, 71*, 1424–1440.

Labile, D. J. & Thompson, R. A. (2007). Mother–child conflict in the early toddler years: Lessons in emotion, morality and relationships. *Child Development, 73*, 1187–1203.

Ladd, G. W. (1990). Having friends, keeping friends, making friends, and being liked by peers in the classroom: Predictors of children's early school adjustment. *Child Development, 61*, 1081–1100.

Ladd, G. W. (1999). Peer relationships and social competence during early and middle childhood. *Annual Review of Psychology, 50*, 333–359.

Ladd, G. W. (2000). The fourth R: Relationships as risks and resources following children's transition to school. *American Educational Research Division Newsletter, 19*(1), 7, 9–11.

Ladd, G. W., & Coleman, C. C. (1993). Young children's peer relationships: Forms, features, and functions. In B. Spodek (Ed.), *Handbook of research on the education of young children* (pp. 54–76). New York: Macmillan.

Ladd, G. W., Kochenderfer, B. J., & Coleman, C. C. (1996). Friendship quality as predictors of young children's early school adjustment. *Child Development, 67*, 1103–1118.

Ladd, G. W., & Troop-Gordon, W. (2003). The role of chronic peer difficulties in the development of children's psychological adjustment problems. *Child Development, 74*(2), 1344–1367.

Lafrance, M., & Hecht, M. A. (1999). Option or obligation to smile: The effects of power and gender on facial expression. In P. Philippot, R. Feldman, & E. Coats (Eds.), *Social context of nonverbal behavior.* Cambridge, U.K: Cambridge University Press, 1999.

LaFrance, M., & Mayo, C. (1976). Racial differences in gaze behavior during conversations: Two systematic observational studies. *Journal of Personality and Social Psychology, 33*, 547–552.

Lagattuta, K. H. & Wellman, H. M. (2001). Thinking about the past: Early knowledge about links between past experience, thinking and emotions. *Developmental Psychology, 38*, 564–580.

Lagattuta, K. H., Wellman, H. M., & Flavell, J. H. (1997). Preschoolers' understanding of the link between thinking and feeling: Cognitive cuing and emotional change. *Child Development, 68*, 1081–1104.

Laible, D. J., & Thompson, R. A. (2000). Mother–child discourse, attachment security, shared positive affect, and early conscience development. *Child Development, 71*, 1424–1440.

Laible, D. J., & Thompson, R.A. (2007). Early socialization: A relationship perspective. In J. E. Grusec & P. D. Hastings (Eds.), *Handbook of socialization: Theory and research* (pp. 181–206). New York: Guilford.

Lamb, M. E. (1981). Developing trust and perceived effectance in infancy. In L. P. Lipsitt (Ed.), *Advances in infancy research* (Vol. 1, pp. 107–127). Norwood, NJ: Ablex.

Lamb, M. E., & Easterbrooks, M. A. (1981). Individual differences in parental sensitivity: Origin, components and consequences. In M. E. Lamb & L. R. Sherrod (Eds.), *Infant social cognition: Theoretical and empirical considerations* (pp. 127–154). Hillsdale, NJ: Erlbaum.

Lamborn, S., Mounts, N. S., Steinberg, L., & Dornbusch, S. (1991). Patterns of competence and adjustment among adolescents from authoritative, authoritarian, indulgent, and neglectful families. *Child Development, 62*(5), 1049–1065.

Lamm, S. Grouix, J. G., Hansen, C. Patton, M.M. & Slaton, A.J. (2006), Creating environments for peaceful problem solving, *Young Children. 61*(1), 22–28.

Landy, S. (2002). *Pathways to competence: Encouraging healthy social and emotional development in young children.* Baltimore: Paul H. Brooks.

Lareau, A. (2003). *Unequal childhoods: Class, race & family life.* Berkeley: University of California Press.

Larzelere, R. E., Schneider, W. N., Larson, D. B., & Pike, P. L. (1996). The effects of discipline responses in delaying toddler misbehavior recurrences. *Child & Family Behavior Therapy, 18*, 35–57.

Lawhon T. (1997, Summer). Encouraging friendships among children. *Childhood Education, 73*, 228–231.

Leary, M. R. (2004). The sociometer, self-esteem, and the regulation of interpersonal behavior. In R. F. Baumeister & K. D. Vohs (Eds.), *Handbook of self-regulation: Research, theory, and applications* (pp. 373–391). New York: Guilford.

Leary, M. R., Baumeister, R. F. (2000). The nature and function of self-esteem: Sociometer theory. *Advances in Experimental Social Psychology, 32*, 1–62.

Leary M. R., Baumeister R. F. (2000). The nature and function of self-esteem; sociometer theory. *Advances in Experimental Social Psychology, 32*, 1–62, *16*(4) 328–335.

Leary, M. R., & McDonald, G. (2003). Individual differences in self-esteem: A review and theoretical integration. In M. Leary & J. P. Tangney (Eds.), *Handbook of self and identity* (pp. 401–418). New York: Guilford.

Lee, L., & Charlton, J. (1980). *The hand book.* Englewood Cliffs, NJ: Prentice-Hall.

Legerstee, M. (2005). *Infants' sense of people: Precursors to a theory of mind.* New York: Cambridge University Press.

Lepper, M. R. & Henderlong, J. (2000). Turning "play" into "work" and "work" into "play": 25 years of research on intrinsic versus extrinsic motivation. In C. Sanson & J.M. Harackiewicz (Eds.), *Intrinsic and extrinsic motivation: The search for optimal motivation and performance* (pp. 257–307). New York: Academic Press.

Lerner et al., (2005). Positive youth development, participation in community youth development programs, and community contributions of fifth-grade adolescents: Findings from the first wave of the 4-H study of positive youth development. *Journal of Early Adolescence, 25*, 17–71.

Levin, D. (2003). *Teaching young children in violent times* (2nd ed.). Washington DC: National Association for the Education of Young Children.

Levin, D. E. (2004, April). *Children in violent times: Building a peaceable classroom* (2nd ed.). Washington, DC: National Association for the Education of Young Children.

Levine, L. J. (1995). Young children's understanding of the causes of anger and sadness. *Child Development, 66*, 697–709.

Levinger, G., & Levinger, A. C. (1986). The temporal course of close relationships: Some thought about the development of children's ties. In W. W. Hartup & Z. Rubin (Eds.), *Relationships and development*. Hillsdale, NJ: Erlbaum.

Lewis, D., & Carpendale, J. (2004). Social cognition. In P. K. Smith & C. H. Hart (Eds.), *Childhood social development* (pp. 375–393). Malden, MA: Blackwell.

Lewis, M. (1999a). Social cognition and the self. In P. Rochat (Ed.), *Early social cognition: Understanding others in the first months of life* (pp. 81–100). Mahwah, NJ: Erlbaum.

Lewis, M. (1999b). The role of the self in cognition and emotion. In T. Dalgleish & M. J. Powers (Eds.), *Handbook of cognition and emotion* (pp. 125–142). Chichester, U.K.: Wiley.

Lewis, M., Alessandri, S. M., & Sullivan, M.W. (1992). Differences in shame and pride as a function of children's gender and task difficulty. *Child Development, 63*, 630–638.

Linares, L. O. (2004). *Community violence: The effects on children*. New York: NYU Child Study Center.

Lochman, J. (1994). Social–cognitive processes of severely violent, moderately aggressive and nonaggressive boys. *Journal of Clinical and Counseling Psychology, 62*, 366–374.

Loeber, R., & Hay, D. F. (1993). Developmental approaches to aggression and conduct problems. In M. Rutter & D. F. Hay (Eds.), *Development through life: A handbook for clinicians* (pp. 488–516). Oxford, U.K.: Blackwell Scientific Publications.

Loeber, R. L., Farrington, D. P., Stouthamer-Loeber, M., Moffitt, T. E., & Caspi, A. (1999). The development of male offending: Key findings from the first decade of the Pittsburgh Youth Study. *Studies on Crime and Crime Prevention, 8*, 245–263.

Loew, R. (2006). *Last Child in the Woods*. Chapel Hill: Algonquin Books.

Lopes, P. N. & Salovey, P. (2004). Toward a broader education: Social, emotional and practical skills. In J. E. Zins, R. P., Weissberg, M. C. Wang, & H. J. Walberg (Eds.), *Building Academic Success on Social and Emotional Learning* (pp. 76–93). New York: Teachers College Press.

Lorenz, K. (1966). *On Aggression*. (M. K. Wilson, Trans.). New York: Harcourt Brace Jovanovich.

Lu, H. (2003, July). *Low income children in the United States*. Columbia University, New York: National Center for Children in Poverty.

Lucariello, J. (1998). Together wherever we go: The ethnographic child and the developmentalist. *Child Development, 69*, 355–358.

Lung, C. T., & Daro, D. (1996). *Current trends in child abuse reporting and fatalities: The results of the 1995 Annual Fifty States Survey*. Chicago: National Committee to Prevent Child Abuse.

Luria, A. R. (1961). *The role of speech in the regulation of normal and abnormal behavior*. London: Pergamon Press.

Lutz, S. E., & Ruble, D. N. (1995). Children and gender prejudice: Context, motivation and the development of gender conception. In R. Vasta (Ed.), *Annals of child development* (Vol. 10). London: Jessica Kingsley.

Lynch, E. W., & Hanson, M. J. (2004). *Developing cross-cultural competence: A guide for working with children and their families*. Baltimore: Paul H. Brookes.

Lynnette, R. (2001). Corporal punishment in American public schools and the rights of the child. *Journal of Law Education, 30*, 554–563.

Lytton, H. (1990). Child and parent effects in boy's conduct disorder: A reinterpretation. *Developmental Psychology, 26*, 683–697.

Maccoby, E., & Martin, J. A. (1983). Socialization in the context of the family: Parent–child interaction. In P. H. Mussen (Ed.), *Handbook of child psychology* (4th ed, Vol. 4). New York: Wiley.

Machotka, P., & Spiegel, J. (1982). *The articulate body*. New York: Irvington Publishers.

MacKenzie, R. J. (2003). *Setting limits in the classroom: Moving beyond the classroom dance of discipline*. Rocklin, CA: Prima Publishing.

Magid, K., & McKelvey, C. A. (1996). *High risk: Children without a conscience*. New York: Bantam Books.

Mahler, M., Pine, S., & Bergman, A. (1975). *The psychological birth of the human infant*. New York: Basic Books.

Maker, C. J. (1993). Creativity, intelligence, problem solving: Adefinition and design for cross-cultural research and measurement related to giftedness. *Gifted Educational International, 9*, 68–77.

Maker, C. J., & King, M. A. (1996). *Nurturing giftedness in young children*. Reston, VA: Council for Exceptional Children.

Maker, C. J., & Nielson, A. B. (1996). *Curriculum development and teaching strategies for gifted learners.* Austin, TX: Pro-Ed.

Malott, R. W., & Suarez E. T. (2004). *Principles of Behavior* (5th ed.). Upper Saddle River, NJ: Prentice-Hall.

Mapp, S., & Steinberg, C. (2007 Jan/Feb). Birth-families as permanency resources for children in long-term foster care, *Child Welfare, 86*(1), 29.

March of Dimes Birth Defects Foundation (2007). Down Syndrome. *Quick Reference & Fact Sheets for Professionals and Researchers, 681,* 1–4.

Marion, M. (2007). *Guidance of young children.* New York: Macmillan.

Marky, A., Szilagyi, P. G. (2006). Improved preventive care for asthma, *Arch Pediatr Adolesc Med.* 160:1018–1025.

Marsh, D. T., Serafica, F. C., & Barenboim, C. (1981). Interrelationships among perspective taking, interpersonal problem solving, and interpersonal functioning. *Journal of Genetic Psychology, 138,* 37–48.

Martin, J. G. (2000). Providing specialist psychological support to foster carers. New York: Grune and Stratton.

Marzano, R. J. (2003). *Classroom management that works: Research-based strategies for every teacher.* Alexandria, VA: Association for Supervision and Curriculum Development.

Masataka, N. (1993). Effects of contingent and non-contingent maternal stimulation on the vocal behavior of three- to four-month-old Japanese infants. *Journal of Child Language, 20,* 303–312.

Matsumoto, D. (2006) Culture and nonverbal behavior, In V. Manusov & M. Patterson (Eds.), *The Sage handbook of nonverbal communication.* Thousand Oaks: Sage Publications, 219–336.

Mayle, P. (2000). *Where Did I Come From?* New York: Coral Publishing Group.

McAfee, O., & Leong, D. (2007). *Assessing and guiding young children's development and learning* (3rd ed.) Boston: Allyn and Bacon.

McCain, B. R. (2001). *Nobody knew what to do: A story about bullying.* Morton Grove, IL: Albert Whitman & Company.

McCartney, K. (2000). NICHD Early Child Care Research Network. The relation of child care to cognitive and language development. *Child Development, 71,* 960–980.

McCay, L. O., & Keyes, D. W. (2002). Developing social competence in the inclusive primary classroom. *Childhood Education, 78*(2), 70–78.

McClellan, D., & Katz. L. (2001). *Assessing young children's social competence.* Champaign, IL: ERIC Clearinghouse on Elementary and Early Childhood Education. (ERIC Document Reproduction Service No. ED450953).

McClelland, M. M., & McCauley, C. (2000). Some things psychologists think they know about aggression and violence. *The HGF Review of Research, 5*(1), 1–5.

McDonald, K. (1995, January 13). The secrets of animal play. *Chronicle of Higher Education,* 8–9, 12–13.

McDowell, D. J., O'Neil, R., & Parke, R. D. (2000). Display rule application in a disappointing situation and children's emotional reactivity: Relations with social competence. *Merrill-Palmer Quarterly, 46,* 306–324.

McElwain, N. L., & Volling, B. L. (2002). Relating individual control, social understanding, and gender to child–friend interaction: A relationships perspective. *Social Development, 11*(3), 362.

McGhee, P. (1979). *Humor: Its origin and development.* San Francisco: W. H. Freeman.

McGinnis, E., & Goldstein, A. P. (1990). *Skillstreaming in early childhood: Teaching prosocial skills to the preschool and kindergarten child.* Champaign, IL: Research Press.

McGroarty, M. (1992, March). The societal context of bilingual education. *Educational Researcher, 21*(2), 7–9.

Meers, J. (1985). The light touch. *Psychology Today, 19*(9), 60–67.

Mehrabian, A. (1972). *Nonverbal communication.* Chicago: Aldin-Atherton.

Mellon, R., Koliadis, E. A., & Paraskevopoulos, T. D. (2004). Normative development of fears in Greece: Self-reports on Hellenic Fear Survey Schedule for Children. *Journal of Anxiety Disorders, 18*(3), 233–254.

Meriwether, H. (1996, September 15). Why doctors worry about media influence on kids. *Detroit Free Press,* p. 3F.

Messinger, D. S., Fogel, A. & Dickson, K. L. (2001). All smiles are positive, but some smiles are more positive than others. *Developmental Psychology, 37,* 642–653.

Metcalfe, J., & Mischel, W. (1999). A hot/cool-system analysis of delay of gratification: Dynamics of willpower. *Psychological Review, 106,* 3–19.

Meyer, J. (1992, Fall). The collaborative development of power in children's arguments. *Argumentation and Advocacy, 29,* 77–88.

Midgley, C. (2002). *Goals, goal structures, and adaptive learning.* Mahwah, NJ: Erlbaum.

Mill, D., & Romano-White, D. (1999). Correlates of affectionate and angry behavior in child care educators of preschool-aged children. *Early Childhood Research Quarterly, 14*(2), 155–178.

Miller, C. S. (1984). Building self-control: Discipline for young children. *Young Children, 40*(1), 15–19.

Miller, D. F. (2007). Positive child guidance (5th ed.) Clifton Park, NY: Thomson Delmar Learning.

Miller, L. C. (1983). Fears and anxiety in children. In C. E. Walker & M. C. Roberts (Eds.), *Handbook of clinical child psychology.* New York: Wiley.

Miller, P., & Garvey, C. (1984). Mother–baby role play: Its origins in social support. In I. Bretherton (Ed.), *Symbolic play: The development of social understanding* (pp. 101–130). New York: Academic Press.

Miller, P. A., Partch, J., Solomon, M., & Hepworth, J. (1995, March). *Assessing empathy and prosocial behaviors in early childhood: Development of a parental questionnaire.* Paper presented at the Biannual Meeting of the Society for Research in Child Development, Indianapolis, IN.

Mills, R. S. L. (2005) Taking stock of the developmental literature on shame. *Developmental Review, 25,* 26–63.

Mischel, W. (1996). From good intentions to will power. In P. M. Gollwitzer & J. A. Bargh (Eds.), *The psychology of action* (pp. 197–218). New York: Guilford.

Mize, J., & Ladd, G. W. (1990). A cognitive social learning approach to social skill training with low-status preschool children. *Developmental Psychology, 26*(3), 388–397.

Mize, J., & Ladd, G. W. (1990b). Toward the development of successful social skills training for preschool children. In S. R. Asher & J. D. Coie (Eds.), *Peer rejection in childhood.* New York: Cambridge University Press.

Monahon, C. (1997). *Children in trauma: A guide for parents and professionals.* San Francisco: Jossey-Bass.

Moore, S. G. (1982). Prosocial behavior in the early years: Parent and peer influences. In B. Spodek (Ed.), *Handbook of research in early childhood education* (pp. 65–81). New York: Free Press.

Morris, T. C., Messer, S. C., & Gross, A. M. (1995). Enhancement of the social interaction and status of neglected children: A peer-pairing approach. *Journals of Clinical Child Psychology, 24,* 11–20.

Morrison, F. J. (2003). The emergence of learning-related social skills in preschool children. *Early Childhood Research Quarterly, 18,* 206–224.

Morrison, G. (2006). *Early childhood education today.* Upper Saddle River, NJ: Prentice-Hall.

Murphy, K., & Schneider, B. (1994). Coaching socially rejected early adolescents regarding behaviors used by peers to infer liking: A dyad-specific intervention. *Journal of Early Adolescence, 14,* 83–95.

Nabuzoka, D., & Smith, P. (1995). Identification of expressions of emotions by children with and without learning disabilities. *Learning Disabilities Research & Practice, 10*(2) 91–101.

NAEYC. (1996a). *NAEYC position statement responding to linguistic and cultural diversity recommendations for effective early childhood education.* Washington, DC: NAEYC.

NAEYC. (1996b). Time out for time-out. *Early Years Are Learning Years, 15,* 1.

NAEYC. (1998). *Position statement on the prevention of child abuse in early childhood programs and responsibilities of early childhood programs to prevent child abuse.* Washington DC: NAEYC.

NASP. (2002). Social skills:Promoting positive behavior, academic success, and school safety. *NASP Center Fact Sheet on Social Skills 2002* (pp. 1–5). Bethesda, MD: National Association of School Psychologists, Bethesda, MD.

National Association of Federally Licensed Firearms Dealers and Professional Gun Retailers Association (2001). Firearm facts. *American Firearms Industry Magazine, 1,* 2001, 3–4.

National Center for Children in Poverty (1996). 6th Annual Report, (2), 1–7, New York: Columbia University.

National Coalition to Abolish Corporal Punishment in Schools. (2002). *Corporal punishment fact sheet.* Columbus, OH: NCACPS.

National Council for Teachers of English (NCTE). Literacy Standards (2003). Available online at http://www.ncte.org/collections/secell.

National Research Council and the Institute of Medicine. (2000). In J. P. Shonkoff and D. A. Philips (Eds.), *From neurons to neighborhoods: The science of early childhood development.* Washington DC: National Academy Press.

National Dissemination Center for Children with Disabilities (2004). *Deafness and Hearing Loss, Fact Sheet 3 (FS #3),* January, 1–5.

National Institute of Neurological Disorders and Stroke. (2005). *Tourette Syndrome Fact Sheet,* NIH Publication No. 05–2163, April, 1–6.

National Rifle Association. (2001). *A parent's guide to gun safety.* Washington, DC: NRA.

National Scientific Council on the Developing Child. (2006). Children's emotional development is built into the architecture of *their brains*. Working Paper #2. Waltham, MA: Brandeis University Press.

NCANDS. (2005). National Data Archive on Child Abuse and Neglect, Data Set 131, Ithica, NY: Cornell University Family Life Development Center.

Neff, K. D. & Helwig, C. C. (2002). A constructivist approach to understanding the development of reasoning about rights and authority within cultural contexts. *Cognitive Development, 17*, 1429–1450.

Nelson, D. A., Robinson, C. C. & Hart, C. H. (2005). Relational and physical aggression of preschool-age children: Peer status linkages across informants. *Early Education and Development, 16*, 115–139.

Nelson, J. (1999). *Positive time-out*. New York: Crown Publishing Co.

Nelson, K. (2003). Narrative and self, myth, and memory: Emergence of a cultural self. In R. Fivush & C.A. Haden (Eds.), *Autobigraphical memory and the construction of a narrative self: Developmental and cultural perspectives* (pp. 72–90). Mahwah, NJ: Erlbaum.

Nelson, K. & Fivush, R. (2004). The emergence of autobiographical memory: A social-cultural developmental theory. *Psychological Review, 111*, 48–511.

Newcomb, A. F., & Bagwell, C. (1996). The developmental significance of children's friendship relations. In W. M. Bukowski, A. F. Newcomb, & W. W. Hartup (Eds.), *The company they keep: Friendships in childhood and adolescence* (pp. 289–321). Cambridge, U.K.: Cambridge University Press.

Newcomb, A. F., Bukowski, W. M., & Pattee, L. (1993). Children's peer relations: A meta-analytical review of popular, rejected, neglected, controversial and average sociometric status. *Psychological Bulletin, 113*, 99–128.

Newman, L. (2002). Making the hard decisions: Student teachers moving toward ethical judgment. *Journal of Early Childhood Teacher Education, 23*(1), 19–26.

Newman, P. R., & Newman, B. M. (2003). *Childhood and adolescence*. Pacific Grove, CA: Brooks/Cole.

NICHD Early Child Care Research Network. (2001). Child care and children's peer interaction at 24 and 36 months: The NICHD study of early child care. *Child Development, 72*(5), 1478–1500.

NICHD Early Child Care Research Network. (2002). Child-care structure – process – outcome: Direct and indirect effects of child-care quality on young children's development. *Psychological Science, 13*, 199–206.

NICHD Early Child Care Research Network (Eds.). (2005). *Child care and child development: Results from the NICHD Study of Early Child Care and Youth Development*. New York: Guilford.

Nickell, P., Rice, A., and Tucker, S. (1976). *Management in family living*. New York: Wiley.

Nourot, P. M., & Van Hoorn, J. (1991). Symbolic play in preschool and primary settings. *Young Children, 46*(6) 40–51.

Nucci, L. P., & Wever, E. (1995). Social interactions in the home and the development of young children's perceptions of the personal. *Child Development, 66*, 1438–1452.

Nunnelley, J. C., & Fields, T. (1999, September). Anger, dismay, guilt, anxiety—the realities and roles in reporting child abuse. *Young Children, 54*(5), 74–79.

Oakes, L. M. (1994). The development of infant's use of continuity cues in their perceptions of causality. *Developmental Psychology, 30*, 869–879.

Offard, D. (1992). Outcome, prognosis, and risk in a longitudinal follow-up study. *Journal of the American Academy of Child and Adolescent Psychiatry, 31*, 55–63.

O'Hair, D., & Friedrich, G. (2001). *Strategic communication*. Boston: Houghton-Mifflin.

O'Hair, M. J., & Ropo, E. (1994, Summer). Unspoken messages: Understanding diversity in education requires emphasis on nonverbal communication. *Teacher Education Quarterly, 21*(3), 91–112.

O'Leary, S. (1995). Parental discipline mistakes. *Current Directions in Psychological Science, 4*, 11–13.

Oliver, S & Klugman E. (2005), Play and the outdoors: What's new under the sun? *Exchange* #164, 6–12.

Olweus, D. (1987, Fall). Schoolyard bullying: Grounds for intervention. *School Safety*, 4–11.

Olweus, D. (1993). *Bullying and school: What we know and what we can do*. Oxford: Blackwell Scientific Publications.

Oshikanlu, S. (2006). Teaching healthy habits to young children, *Exchange, #169*, 28–30.

Ostrov., J. M., Pilat, M. M. & Crick, N. R. (2006). Assertion strategies and aggression during childhood: A short-term longitudinal study. *Early Childhood Research Quarterly, 21*(4), 403–416.

Otto, B. (2006.) *Language development in early childhood*. Upper Saddle River, NJ: Pearson.

Paasche, C. L., Gorrill, L. & Strom, B. (2004). *Children with special needs in early childhood settings: Identification, intervention, inclusion.* Albany, NY: Delmar/Thomson Learning.

Paley, V. G. (1992). *You can't say, . . . you can't play.* Cambridge, MA: Harvard University Press.

Papalia, D., Olds, S., & Feldman, R. (2006). *A child's world* (10th ed.). Boston: McGraw-Hill.

Papousek, H., & Papousek, M. (1997). Mothering and the cognitive head start: Psychobiological considerations. In H. R. Schaffer (Ed.), *Studies in mother–infant interaction.* London: Academic Press.

Parfen, M. B. (1932). Social participation among preschool children. *Journal of Abnormal and Social Psychology, 27,* 243–269.

Park, K. A., & Waters, E. (1989). Security of attachment and preschool friendships. *Child Development, 60,* 1076–1081.

Parke, R., & Brett, A. (1999). *Throwaway dads: The myths and barriers that keep men from being the father they want be.* New York: Houghton-Mifflin.

Parke, R.D. & Buriel, R. (2006). Socialization in the family: Ethnic and ecological perspectives. In N. Eisenberg, W. Damon, & R.M. Lerner (Eds.), *Handbook of child psychology* (pp. 429–504). Hoboken, NJ: Wiley.

Parker, J. G., Rubin, K. H., Price, J., & DeRosier, E. (1995). Peer relations, child development, and adjustment. A developmental psycho-pathology perspective. In D. Cicchettia, & E. Cohen (Eds.), *Developmental psycho-pathology, Vol. 2: Risk, disorder and adaptation* (pp. 96–161). New York: Wiley.

Parsons, J. E., Kaczala, C. M., & Meece, J. L. (1982). Socialization of achievement attitudes and beliefs: Classroom influences. *Child Development, 53,* 322–339.

Patterson, G. R. (1997). Performance models for parenting: Asocial interactional perspective. In J. E. Grusec & L. Kuczynski (Eds.), *Parenting and children's internationalization of values* (pp. 193–26). New York: Wiley.

Patterson, G. R., & Capaldi, D. M. (1991). Antisocial parents: Unskilled and vulnerable. In P. A. Cowen & E. M. Hetherington (Eds.), *Family transitions.* Hillsdale, NJ: Erlbaum.

Patterson, G. R., Reid, J. B., & Dishion, T. J. (1992). *A social learning approach, Vol 4: Antisocial boys.* Eugene, OR: Castalia Press.

Pavin, S. (2001). Loneliness in children with disabilities. *Teaching Exceptional Children, 33*(6), 52–58.

Peisner-Feinberg, E. S., Burchinal, M. R., Clifford, R. C., Culkin, M. L., Howes, C., Kagan, S. L., & Yazejian N. (2001). The relation of preschool child-care quality to children's cognitive and social developmental trajectories through second grade. *Child Development, 72*(5), 1534–1553.

Pellegrini, A. (1991). Alongitudinal study of popular and rejected children's rough and tumble play. *Early Education and Development, 2*(3), 205–213.

Pellegrini, A. D. (1995). Boys rough-and-tumble play and social competence. In A. D. Pellegrini (Ed.), *The future of play theory* (pp. 107–126). Albany, NY: State University of New York Press.

Pellegrini, A. (2004). Rough-and tumble play from childhood through adolescence: Development and possible functions. In P. K. Smith & C. Hart (Eds.), *Blackwell handbook of childhood social development* (pp. 438–454). Malden, MA: Blackwell.

Pellegrini, A. (2007). The development and function of rough and tumble play in childhood and adolescence: A sexual selection theory perspective. In A. Goncu and S. Gaskins (Eds.), *Play and development.* Mahwah, N. J. Erlbaum.

Perry, D. G., Willard, J. C., & Perry, L. C. (1990). Peers perceptions of the consequences that victimized children provide aggressors. *Child Development, 61,* 1310–1325.

Persson, G.E.B. (2005). Young children's prosocial and aggressive behaviors and their experiences of being targeted for similar behaviors by peers. *Social Development, 14,* 206–228.

Pettit, G., & Harrist, A. (1993). Children's aggressive and socially unskilled behavior with peers: Origins in early family relations. In C. Hart (Ed.), *Children on playgrounds: Research perspectives and applications* (pp. 14–42). Albany: State University of New York.

Pfile, R., Connor, S., & Livingston, A. (Eds.). (2000). *The condition of education.* Washington, DC: National Center for Education Statistics.

Phillips, L. R., Hensler, J., Diesel, M., & Cefalo, A. (2004). Seeing the challenge more clearly. In S. H. Bell, V. Carr, D. Denno, L. J. Johnson, & L. R. Phillips (Eds.), *Challenging behaviors in early childhood settings* (pp. 67–96). Baltimore: Paul H. Brookes Publishing Co.

Piaget, J. (1962). *The origins of intelligence in children.* New York: W. W. Norton.

Piaget, J. (1976). The rules of the game of marbles. In J. Bruner, A. Jolly, & K. Sylva (Eds.), *Play: Its role in development and evolution* (pp. 411–441). New York: Academic Press.

Polakow, V. (1994). *Lives on the edge: Single mothers and their children in the other America*. Chicago: University of Chicago Press.

Pomerantz, E. M., & Ruble, D. N. (1997). Distinguishing multiple dimensions and conceptions of ability: Implications for self-evaluation. *Child Development, 68*, 1165–1180.

Pomerantz, E. M., & Rudolph, K. D. (2003). What ensues from emotional distress? Implications for competence estimation. *Child Development, 74*(2), 329–345.

Poole, S., & Magilner, D. (2000). Crying complaints in the emergency department. In R. Barr, B. Hopkins, & J. Green (Eds.), *Crying as a sign, a symptom, and a signal* (pp. 96–105). London: Mac Keith Press.

Power, T. (2000). *Play and exploration in children and animals*. Mahwah, NJ: Erlbaum.

Pratt, M.W., Hunsberger, B., Pancer, S.M., & Alisat, S. (2003). A longitudinal analysis of personal values socialization: Correlates of a moral self-ideal in late adolescence. *Social Development, 12*, 563–585.

Pratt, M. W., Arnold, M. L., Pratt, A. T., & Diessner, R. (1999). Predicting adolescent moral reasoning from family climate: A longitudinal study. *Journal of Early Adolescence, 19*, 148–175.

Pratt, M. W., Skoe, E. E. & Arnold, M. I. (2004). Care reasoning development and family socialization patterns in later adolescence. A longitudinal analysis. *International Journal of Behavioral Development, 28*, 139–147.

Puckett, M. & Black, J. (2004). *The young child: development prebirth through age eight*. Upper Saddle River, NJ: Pearson.

Putman, D. (1996). Integrity and moral development. *The Journal of Value Inquiry, 30*(1–2), 237–246.

Ramsey, P. (1998). Diversity and play: Influences of race, culture, class and gender. In D. Fromberg & D. Bergen (Eds.), *Play from birth to twelve and beyond: Contexts, perspectives and meanings* (pp. 23–33). New York: Garland Publishing.

Raver, C. (1996). Relations between social contingency in mother–child interaction and 2-year-olds' social competence. *Developmental Psychology, 32*(5), 850–859.

Reed, D. F. (1991). Preparing teachers for multicultural classroom. *The Journal of Early Childhood Education, 38*(12), 16–21.

Reifel S., & Yeatman, J. (1993). From category to context: Reconsidering classroom play. *Early Childhood Research Quarterly, 8*, 347–367.

Reproduction Service No. (ED 280–574 PS016–396)

Roberts, W., & Strayer, J. (1996). Empathy, emotional expressiveness, and prosocial behavior. *Child Development, 67*, 449–470.

Reynolds, E. (2006). *Guiding young children: A problemsolving approach*. (4th ed.) Mountain View, CA: Mayfield.

Riak, J. (1994). *Plain talk about spanking*. Alamo, CA: Parents and Teachers against Violence in Education.

Richmond, V., & McCroskey, J. (2003). *Nonverbal behavior in interpersonal relations* (2nd ed.). New York: Prentice-Hall.

Riggio, R. (2006). Nonverbal skills and abilities, In V. Manusov & M. Patterson (Eds.), *The Sage handbook of nonverbal communication* (pp. 79–96). Thousand Oaks: Sage Publications.

Rightmyer, E. C. (2003, July). Democratic discipline: Children creating solutions. *Young Children, 58*(4), 38–45.

Riley, D. & Steinberg, J. (2004). Four popular stereotypes about children in self care: Implications for family life educators. *Family Relations, 53*(1), 95–101.

Ritchie, K., & Johnson, Z. (1988, November 13–16). *From Scooby-Doo to Skeletor: Evolving issues in superhero play*. Paper presented at the Annual Conference for the National Association for the Education of Young Children. ERIC Document.

Rochat, P., & Striano, T. (1999). Social-cognitive development in the first year. In P. Rochat (Ed.), *Early social cognition: Understanding others in the first months of life* (pp. 3–34). Mahwah, NJ: Erlbaum.

Roffey, S., Tarrant, T., & Majors, K. (1994). *Young friends: Schools and friendships*. New York: Cassell Publishing.

Rogers, C. R. (1961). *On becoming a person*. Boston: Houghton Mifflin.

Rosenberg, H. (2001). Imagination styles of four and five year olds. In S. Golbeck (Ed.), *Psychological perspectives on early childhood education* (pp. 280–296). Mahwah, NJ: Erlbaum

Rosenberg, M. 1979. *Conceiving the self*. New York: Basic Books.

Rosenblith, J. (1992). *In the beginning: Development from conception to age two*. Newbury Park, CA: Sage Publications.

Roskos, K. (1990). A taxonomic view of pretend play activity among 4- and 5-year-old children. *Early Childhood Research Quarterly, 5*(4), 495–512.

Ross, H. S., & Conant, C. L. (1992). The social structure of early conflict: Interactions, relationships and alliances. In V. Shantz & W. W. Hartup (Eds.), *Conflict in child and adolescent development*. Cambridge, MA: Cambridge University Press.

Rothbart, M., & Bates, J. (1998). Temperament. In W. Damon & N. Eisenberg (Ed.), *Handbook in child psychology, Vol. 3: Social and emotional development* (5th ed.). New York: Wiley.

Rubin, K. H. (2003). The friendship factor: Helping our children navigate their social world and why it matters for their success and happiness. NY, NY: Penguin Group.

Rubin, K. H., Bukowski, W. M., & Parker, J. G. (1988). Peer interactions, relationships, and groups. In W. Damon & N. Eisenberg (Eds.), *Handbook of child psychology, Vol. 3: Social, emotional and personality development* (5th ed., pp. 619–700). New York: Wiley.

Rubin, K. H., Bukowski, W. M., & Parker, J. G. (1998). Peer interactions, relationships, and groups. In W. Damon & N. Eisenberg (Eds.), *Handbook of child psychology, Vol. 4: Socialization, personality and social development* (pp. 619–700). New York: Wiley.

Rubin, K.H., Bukowski, W.M., & Parker, J.G. (2006). Peer interactions, relationships, and groups. In N. Eisenberg, W. Damon, & R.M. Lerner (Eds.), *Handbook of child psychology* (pp. 571–645). Hoboken, NJ: Wiley.

Rubin, K. H., Burgess, K. B., Dwyer, K. M., & Hastings, P. D. (2003). Predicting preschoolers' externalizing behaviors from toddler temperament, conflict and maternal negativity. *Developmental Psychology, 39*, 164–176.

Rubin, K. H., Lynch, D., Coplan, R., Rose-Kransor, L., & Booth, C. L. (1994). Birds of a feather: Behavioral concordances and preferential personal attraction in children. *Child Development, 65*, 1778–1785.

Ruble, D. N. & Martin, C. L. (1998). Gender development. In N. Eisenberg (Ed.) & W. Damon (Series Ed.), *Handbook of child psychology: Vol 3. Social, emotional and personality development* (5th ed., pp. 933–1016). New York: Wiley.

Ruble, T. L. (1987). The acquisition of self-knowledge: A self-socialization perspective. In N. Eisenberg (Ed.), *Contemporary topics in developmental psychology*. New York: Wiley-Interscience.

Russell, A., Hart, C.H., Robinson, C.C., Olsen, F.F. (2003). Children's sociable and aggressive behaviour with peers: A comparison of the United States and Australia, and contributions of temperament and parenting style. *International Journal of Behavioral Development, 27*, 74–86.

Rys, G. S., & Bear, G. G. (1997). Relational aggression and peer relations: Gender and developmental issues. *Merrill Palmer Quarterly, 43*, 87–106.

Saarni, C. (1995). Socialization of emotion. In M. Lewis & J. M. Haviland (Eds.), *Handbook of emotions* (2nd ed., pp. 435–446). New York: Guilford.

Saarni, C. (1999). *The development of emotional competence*. New York: Guilford.

Saarni, C., Campos, J. J., Camras, L.A., & Witherington, D. (2006). Emotional development: Action, communication and understanding. In N. Eisenberg, W. Damon, & R.M. Lerner (Eds.), *Handbook of child psychology* (pp. 226–299). New York, NY: Wiley.

Saarni, C., Mumme, D. L., & Campos, J. L. (1998). Emotional development: Action, communication and understanding. In W. Damon & N. Eisenberg (Eds.), *Handbook of child psychology* (Vol. 3, pp. 237–309). New York: Wiley.

Saarni, C., & Weber, H. (1999). Emotional displays and dissemblance in childhood: Implications for self-presentation. In P. Philippot, R. Feldman, & E. Coats (Eds.), *Social context of nonverbal behavior*. Cambridge, U.K:. Cambridge University Press.

Sadurni, M., & Rostan, C. (2003). Reflections on regression periods in the development of Catalan infants. In M. Heimann (Ed.), *Regression periods in human infancy* (pp. 7–22). Mahwah, NJ: Erlbaum.

Salovey, P., & Mayer, J. D. (1990). Emotional intelligence. *Imagination, Cognition, and Personality, 9*, 185–211.

Sample, W. (1993). The American Indian child. *Exchange, 3*, 39–40.

Sandall, S.R. (2004). Play modifications for children with disabilities. In Koralek, D., (Ed.), *Young children and play* (pp. 44–45). Washington, DC: National Association for the Education of Young Children.

Sansone, A. (2004). *Mothers, babies and their body language*. London: Karnac.

Santrock, J. W. (2005). Child Development: An Introduction. New York: McGraw-Hill

Santrock, J. W. (2006a). *Children* (7th ed.) Boston: McGraw-Hill.

Santrock, J. W. (2006b). Child development (10th ed.). Dubuque, IA: Brown and Benchmark.

Scarr, S. (1984). *Mother care—other care*. New York: Basic Books.

Scheflen, A. (1972). *Body language and the social order*. Englewood Cliffs, NJ: Prentice-Hall.

Schickedanz, J. A. (1994). Helping children develop self-control. *Childhood Education, 70*(5), 274–278.

Schickedanz, J., Pergantis, M.L., Kanosky, J., Blaney, A., Ottinger, J. (1997). *Curriculum in early childhood*. Boston: Allyn & Bacon.

Schlank, C. H., & Metzger, B. (1997). *Together and equal*. Boston: Allyn & Bacon.

Schneider, B. H. (1992). Didactic methods for enhancing child's peer relations: A quantitative review. *Clinical Psychology Review, 2*, 363–382.

Schultz, E. W., & Heuchert, C. M. (1983). *Child stress and the school experience*. New York: Human Sciences Press.

Schultz, K. (2003). *Listening, listening, listening*. New York: Teachers College Press.

Schultz, R. L., & Schultz, L. H. (1990). *Making a friend in youth: Developmental theory and pair therapy*. Chicago: University of Chicago Press.

Scott, W. A., Scott, R., & McCabe, M. (1991). Family relationships and children's personality: A cross-cultural comparison. *British Journal of Social Psychology, 30*, 1–20.

Sebanc, A. M. (2003). The friendship features of preschool children: Links with prosocial behaviorand aggression. *Social Development, 12*(2), 249–265.

Seefeldt, C. (1995). Transforming curriculum in social studies. In S. Bredekamp & T. Rosegrant (Eds.), *Reaching potentials: Transforming early childhood curriculum and assessment* (pp. 109–124). Washington, DC: NAEYC.

Segal, J., & Yahres, H. (1979). *A child's journey*. New York: McGraw-Hill.

Segal, M. The roots and fruits of pretending. In E. F. Zigler, D. G. Singer, & S. J. Bishop-Josef (Eds.), *Children's play: The roots of reading*. Washington, DC: Zero to Three Press.

Seligman, M. E. P. (1995). *The optimistic child*. Boston: Houghton Mifflin.

Selman, R. L., Levitt, M. Z., & Schultz, L. H. (1997). The friendship framework: Tools for the assessment of psychosocial development. In R. Selman, C. L. Watts, & L. H. Schultz (Eds.), *Fostering friendship* (pp. 31–52). New York: Aldine De Gruyter.

Selman, R. L., Schultz, L. H. (1990). *Making a friend in youth: Developmental theory and pair therapy*. Chicago: University of Chicago Press.

Serbin, L. A., Moller, L., Powlishta, K., & Gulko, J. (1991, April). The emergence of gender segregation and behavioral compatibility in toddlers' peer preferences. In C. Leuper (Ed.), *Gender differences in relationships*. Symposium at the Society for Research in Child Development, Seattle, WA.

Sexton, D. et al. (1993). Infants and toddlers with special needs and their families. *Childhood Education, Annual Theme Issue, 278*–286.

Shaffer, D. R. (2005). (6th ed.). Belmont, CA: Wadsworth.

Shaffer, D. R., & Kipp, K. (2006). *Developmental psychology: Childhood and adolescence* (7th ed.). Pacific Grove, CA: Brooks/Cole.

Shanab, M. E., & Yahya, K. A. (1977). A behavioral study of obedience. *Journal of Personality and Social Psychology, 35*, 550–586.

Shapiro, L. (1997). *How to raise a child with a high EQ*. New York: HarperCollins.

Sharp, C. (1987). *Now you're talking: Techniques that extend conversations*. Portland, OR: Educational Productions.

Sharp, C. (1988). *Between you and me: Facilitating child-to-child conversations*. Portland, OR: Educational Productions.

Shaw, D. S., Gilliom, M., Ingoldsby, E. M. & Nagin, D. S. (2003). Trajectories leading to school-age conduct problems. *Developmental Psychology, 39*, 189–200.

Sherrod, L. (1981). Issues in cognitive–perceptual development: The special case of social stimuli. In M. E. Lamb & L. Sherrod (Eds.), *Infant social cognition: Empirical and theoretical considerations*. Hillsdale, NJ: Erlbaum.

Shifrin, D. (2006). Effect of media on children and adolescents. *Archives of Pediatric and Adolescent Medicine Vol. 160*, 448–450.

Shipler, D. K. (2005). *The working poor*. New York: Vintage Books.

Shirk, M. & Stangler, G. (2004). *On their own*. Boulder, CO: Westview.

Shonkoff, J. P., & Phillips, D.A. (Eds.) (2000). *From Neurons to Neighborhoods: The science of early childhood development*. Washington, DC: National Academy Press.

Shonkoff, J., & Hauser-Cram, P. (1987). Early intervention for disabled infants and their families: A quantitative analysis. *Pediatrics, 80*, 650–658.

Shotwell, J., Wolf, D., & Gardner, H. Exploring early symbolization: Styles of achievement. In B. Sutton-Smith (Eds.), *Play and learning* (pp. 127–156). New York: Gardner Press.

Siegel, D. (1999). *The Developing Mind:How relationships and the brain interact to shape who we are*. New York: Guilford.

Siegal, M., & Cowen, J. (1984). Appraisals of intervention: The mother's versus the culprit's behavior as determinants of children's evaluations of discipline techniques. *Child Development, 55,* 1760–1766.

Sifianou, M. (1995). Do we need to be silent to be extremely polite? Silence and FTAs. *International Journal of Applied Linguistics, 5*(1), 95–110.

Simms, M. D., Dubowitz, H., & Szilaqyl, M. A. (2000). Health care needs of children in the foster care system. *Pediatrics, 106,* 909–918.

Simons, K. J., Paternite, C. E., & Shore, C. (2001). Quality of parent/adolescent attachment and aggression in young adolescents. *Journal of Early Adolescence, 21,* 182–203.

Simpkins, S.D. & Parke, R.D. (2002). Do friends and nonfriends behave differently? A social relations analysis of children's behavior. *Merrill-Palmer Quarterly, 48,* 263–283.

Siner, J. (1993). Social competence and cooperative learning. *Educational Psychology in Practice, 9,* 170–180.

Slaby, R.G., Roedell, W., Arezzo, D., Hendrix, K. (1995). *Early violence prevention.* Washington, DC: NAEYC.

Sluss, Dorothy. (2005). *Supporting play birth through age eight.* Clifton Park, NY: Thompson.

Smith, A. B., & Inder, P. M. (1993). Social interaction in same and cross gender preschool peer groups: A participant observation study. *Educational Psychology, 13,* 29–42.

Smith, A. I. (1970). *Nonverbal communication through touch.* Ph.D. dissertation, Georgia State University.

Smith, P. (2005). Play: Types and functions in human development. In B. J. Ellis & D. F. Bjorklund (Eds.), *Origins of the social mind: Evolutionary psychology and child development* (pp. 271–291). New York: Guilford.

Smith, P. K. (1978). A longitudinal study of social participation in preschool children: Solitary and parallel play reexamined. *Developmental Psychology, 14,* 517–523.

Society for Adolescent Medicine (2003). Corporal punishment in schools: Position paper of the Society for Adolescent Medicine. *Journal of Adolescent Health, 32,* 385–393.

Soderman, A. (1985). Helping the school-age child deal with stress. *Focus, 10*(1), 17–23.

Soderman, A., & Phillips, M. (1986). The early education of males: Where are we failing them? *Educational Leadership, 44*(3), 70–72.

Soderman, A. K. (2003, August). *Divorce.* Paper delivered at the 13th Annual meeting of the European Early Childhood Education Research Association (EECERA). University of Glasgow, Scotland.

Soderman, A. K. (2008). *Creating literacy rich preschools and kindergartens.* Boston: Allyn & Bacon.

Soderman, A. K., Chikara, S., Hsiu-Ching, C., & Kuo, E. (1999). Gender differences that affect emerging literacy in first grade children: The U.S., India and Taiwan. *International Journal of Early Childhood, 31*(2), 9–16.

Soderman, A. K., Gregory, K. S., & McCarty, L. (2005). *Scaffolding emergent literacy: A childcentered approach, preschool through grade 5* (2nd ed.). Boston: Allyn & Bacon.

Soderman, A. K., Gregory, K. M., O'Neill, L. T. (2005). *Scaffolding emergent literacy.* Boston, NJ: Allyn & Bacon.

Soderman, A. K., Kauppinen, R., & Laakkonen, J. (2000, August). *Gender and cultural differences in emerging literacy: U.S.A. and Finland.* Paper delivered at the Tenth Annual European Early Childhood Research Conference, London.

Solomon, R. (1995). Pediatricians and early intervention: Everything you need to know but are too busy to ask, *Infants and young Children, 7,* no.3.

Sommer, R. (1974). *Tight spaces: Hard architecture and how to humanize it.* Englewood Cliffs, NJ: Prentice-Hall.

Sroufe, A. (1996). *Emotional development.* Boston: Cambridge University Press.

Sroufe, L. A., & Cooper, R. G. (1999). *Child development: Its nature and course.* New York: Alfred A. Knopf.

Stayton, D. J., Hogan, R., & Ainsworth, M. D. S. (1971). Infant obedience and maternal behavior: The origin of socialization reconsidered. *Child Development, 42,* 1057–1069.

Stein, M. A., Efron, L. A., Shaff, W. B., & Glanzman, M. (2002). Attention deficits and hyperactivity. In M. L. Batshaw (Ed.), *Children with disabilities* (5th ed.). Baltimore: Paul H. Brooks.

Stein, N., & Levine, L. J. (1999). The early emergence of emotional understanding and appraisal: Implications for theories of development. In T. Dalgleish & M. J. Powers (Eds.), *Handbook of cognition and emotion* (pp. 383–408). Chichester, U.K.: Wiley.

Steiner, J., & Whelan, M. S. (1995). *For the love of children: Daily affirmations for people who care for children.* St. Paul: Redleaf Press.

Stephens, K. (1996). Responding professionally and compassionately to challenging children. *Child Care Information Exchange, 9,* 44–48.

Stephens, T. J. (2006). *Discipline strategies for children with disabilities.* Sioux Falls, SD: Center for

Disabilities, School of Medicine & Health Sciences, University of South Dakota.

Stocking, S. H., Arezzo, D., & Leavitt, S. (1980). *Helping kids make friends*. Allen, TX: Argus Communications.

Stone, J. (1993). Caregiver and teacher language: Responsive or restrictive. *Young Children, 48*(4), 12–18.

Stormshak, E. A., Bierman, K. L., McMahon, R. J., Lengua, L. J., & the Conduct Problems Prevention Research Group. (2000). Parenting practices and child disruptive behavior problems in early elementary school. *Journal of Clinical Child Psychology, 29,* 17–29.

Strassberg, Z., Dodge, K., Pettit, G. S., & Bates, J. E. (1994). Spanking in the home and children's subsequent aggression toward kindergarten peers. *Development and Psychopathology, 6,* 445–461.

Straus, M. A., Sugarman, D. B., & Giles-Sims, J. (1997). Spanking by parents and subsequent antisocial behavior of children. *Pediatrics and Adolescents Medicine, 151,* 761–767.

Streissguth, A. P., Barr, H. M., Bookstein, F. L., Sampson, P. D., and Carmichael Olson, H. (1999). The long-term neurocognitive consequences of prenatal alcohol: a 14-year study. *Psychological Science 10*(3), 186–190.

Streissguth, A. P. (1997*). Fetal Alcohol Syndrome: A Guide for Families and Communities*. Baltimore: Paul H. Brookes Publishing Co.

Streissguth, A. P., Aase, J. M., Clarren, S. K., Randels, S. P., LaDue, R. A., & Smith, D. F. (1997). Fetal alcohol syndrome in adolescents and adults. *Journal of American Medical Association. 19,* 51–70.

Strom, S. (1989). The ethical dimension of teaching. In M. Reynolds (Ed.), *Knowledge base for the beginning teacher*. Oxford, U.K.: Pergamon Press.

Sullivan, M. W. & Lewis, M. (2003). Contextual determinants of anger and other negative expressions in young infants. *Developmental Psychology, 39,* 693–705.

Sutterby, J. & Frost, J. (2006). Creating play environments for early childhood: Indoors and out, In B. Spodek & O. N. Saracho (Eds.), *Handbook of research on the education of young children* (pp. 305–322). Mahwah, NJ: Lawrence Erlbaum Associates.

Sutton-Smith, B., & Sutton-Smith, S. (1974). *How to play with your child and when not to*. New York: Hawthorn Books.

Swallow, W. K. (2000). *The shy child*. New York: Warner Books.

Talwar V., & Lee, K. (2002). Emergence of white-lie telling in children between 3 and 7 years of age. *Merrill Palmer Quarterly, 48*(2), 160–181.

Tangney, J. P. & Dearing, R. (2002). *Shame and guilt*. New York: Guilford.

Taylor-Green, S. J. & Kartub, D. T. (2000). Durable implementation of school-wide behavior support: The high five program. *Journal of Positive Behavior Interventions, 2*(4), 233–235.

Theimer, C., Killen, M., & Strangor, C. (2001). Young children's evaluations of exclusion in genderstereotypic peer contexts. *Developmental Psychology, 37*(1), 18–27.

Thomas, A., & Chess, S. (1986). The New York longitudinal study: From infancy to early adult life. In R. Plomin & J. Dunn (Eds.), *Changes, continuities and challenges*. Hillsdale, NJ: Erlbaum, 1986.

Thompson, R. A. (1988). Early sociopersonality development. In N. Eisenberg (Ed.), *Handbook of child psychology* (Vol. 3, pp. 25–104). New York: Wiley.

Thompson, R.A. (2006). The development of the person: Social understanding, relationships, conscience, self. In N. Eisenberg, W. Damon, & R.M. Lerner (Eds.), *Handbook of child psychology* (pp. 24–98). Hoboken, NJ: Wiley.

Tice, D. M., Wallace, H. M. (2003). The reflected self: Creating yourself as (you think) others see you. In M. R. Leary & J. P. Tangney (Eds.), *Handbook of self and identity* (pp. 91–105). New York: Guilford.

Ting-Toomey, S. (1999). *Communicating across cultures*. New York: Guilford.

Tisak, M. S., & Block, J. H. (1990). Preschool children's evolving conceptions of badness: Alongitudinal study. *Early Education and Development, 4,* 300–307.

Toner, I. J., Parke, R. D., & Yussen, S. R. (1978). The effect of observation of model behavior on the establishment and stability of resistance to deviation in children. *Journal of Genetic Psychology, 132,* 283–290.

Tracy, R. L., & Ainsworth, M. D. S. (1981). Maternal affectionate behavior and infant–mother attachment patterns. *Child Development, 52,* 1341–1343.

Trainor, L. J. (1996). Infant preferences for infant-directed versus non-infant directed play songs and lullabies. *Infant Behavior and Development, 19,* 83–92.

Trawick-Smith, J. (1990). The effects of realistic versus nonrealistic play materials on young children's symbolic transformation of objects. *Journal of Research in Childhood Education, 5*(1), 27–36.

Trawick-Smith, J. (2005). *Early childhood development: A multicultural perspective* (4th ed.) Columbus, OH: Merrill.

Tremblay, R. (1994, September). Predicting early onset of male antisocial behavior from preschool behavior. *Archives of General Psychiatry, 51,* 732–739.

Tremblay, R. E., Schaal, B., Boulerice, B., Arseneault, L., Soussignan, R., & Perusse, D. (1997). Male physical aggression, social dominance, and testosterone levels at puberty: A developmental perspective. In A. Raine & P. A. Brennan (Eds.), *Biological bases of violence.* NATO ASI Series A: Life Sciences (Vol. 292, pp. 271–291). New York: Plenum.

Trepanier-Street, M. L. (1991). The developing kindergartner: Thinking and problem solving. In J. S. McKee (Ed.), *The developing kindergarten: Programs, children, teachers.* East Lansing, MI: Michigan Association for the Education of Young Children.

Turecki, S. (2000). *The difficult child.* New York: Bantam.

Turiel, E. (1998). The development of morality. In N. Eisenberg (Ed.), *Handbook of child psychology, Vol. 3: Social, emotional, and personality development* (pp. 863–932). New York: Wiley.

Turnbull, A. P., Turnbull, H. R., Erwin, E.J., & Soodak, L.C. (2006). *Families, professionals and exceptionality: A special partnership* (5th ed.). Columbus, OH: Merrill/Prentice-Hall.

Ucci, M. (1998). Time-outs and how to use them. *Child Health Alert, 1,* 2–3.

U.S. Bureau of the Census. (1995). *Statistical abstract of the United States* (15th ed.). Washington, DC: U.S. Government Printing Office.

U.S. Bureau of the Census (2000). www.census.gov.

U.S. Department of Education. (2006). *2006 elementary and secondary school civil rights compliance report.* Washington, DC: Office for Civil Rights.

Vandell, D. L., & Mueller, E. C. (1995). Peer play and friendships during the first two years. In H. C. Smith, A. J. Chapman, and J. R. Smith (Eds.), *Friendship and social relations in children* (pp. 181–208). New Brunswick, NJ: Transaction.

Vargen, D. (1981). Asynchronous development of gender understanding in preschool children. *Child Development, 52,* 1020–1027.

Vasta, R., Haith, M. M., & Miller, S. A. (2004). *Child psychology.* New York: Wiley.

Vaughn, B. E., Azria, M., Krzysik, L., Caya, L., Newell, W., & Kazura, K. L. (1999). A longitudinal analysis of social competence in a sample of preschool children attending Head Start: Construct and index indicators. In B. E. Vaughn & K. K. Bost (Eds.), *Measurement and implications of social competence for preschool children* (pp. 56–71). Monograph submitted for publication.

Volkmar, F. R., & Siegel, A. E. (1982). Responses to consistent and discrepant social communications. In R. Feldman (Ed.), *Development of nonverbal behavior in children* (pp. 231–256). New York: Springer-Verlag.

Vygotsky, L. (1978). *Mind in society: The development of higher psychological processes.* Cambridge, MA: Harvard University Press.

Walden, T. A., & Ogan. T. A. (1988). The development of social referencing. *Child Development, 59,* 1230–1240.

Walton, G. L., Bower, N. J. A., & Bower, T. G. R. (1992). Recognition of familiar faces by newborns. *Infant Behavior and Development, 15,* 265–269.

Wasserstein, S. B., & LaGreca, A. M. (1996). Can peer support buffer against behavioral consequences of parental discord? *Journal of Clinical Child Psychology, 25,* 177–182.

Watson, M. W., & Fisher, K. W. (1980). Development of social roles in elicited and spontaneous behavior during the preschool years. *Child Development, 18,* 483–494.

Weilbacher, R. (1981). The effects of static and dynamic play environments on children's social and motor behaviors. In A. Cheska (Ed.), *Play as context* (pp. 248–258). West Point, NY: Leisure Press.

Weinberg, M. K., Tronick, E. Z., Cohn, J. F., & Olson, K. L. (1999). Gender differences in emotional expressivity and self-regulation during early infancy. *Developmental Psychology, 35,* 175–188.

Weinberger, L., & Starkey, P. (1994). Pretend play by African American children in Head Start. *Early Childhood Research Quarterly, 9,* 327–343.

Weinreb, M. L. (1992, January). Be a resiliency mentor. You may be a lifesaver for a high-risk child. *Young Child, 52*(2), 14–20.

Weinstein, C. S., & Mignano, A. J. (2007). *Elementary classroom management: Lessons from research and practice.* New York: McGraw-Hill.

Wellman, H. M., Cross, D. & Watson, J. (2001). Meta analysis of theory of mind development: The truth about false belief. *Child Development, 72,* 655–684.

Wellman, H. M., & Liu, D. (2004). Scaling theory of mind tasks. *Child Development, 75*(2), 523–541.

Wentzel, K.R., Barry, C.M., & Caldwell, K.A. (2004). Friendship in middle school: Influences on motivation and school adjustment. *Journal of Educational Psychology, 96*, 195–203.

Werner, E., & Smith, R. (1992). *Overcoming the odds: High risk children from birth to adulthood.* Ithaca, NY: Cornell University Press.

West, T. G. (1998). *In the mind's eye: Visual thinkers, gifted people with learning difficulties, computer images, and the ironies of creativity.* Buffalo, NY: Prometheus Books.

Wheeler, E. J. (2004). *Conflict resolution in early childhood.* Upper Saddle River, NJ: Pearson.

Whitesell, N. R., & Harter, S. (1989). Children's reports of conflict between simultaneous opposite—valence emotions. *Child Development, 60*, 673–682.

Widen, S. C. & Russell, J. A. (2003). A closer look at preschoolers' freely pronounced labels for facial expressions. *Developmental Psychology, 35*, 232–245.

Wieder, S., & Greenspan, S. I. (1993). The emotional basis of learning. In B. Spodek (Ed.), *Handbook of research on the education of young children* (pp. 77–104). New York: Macmillan.

Willatts, P. (1990). Development of problem solving strategies in infancy. In D. F. Bjorklund (Ed.), *Children's strategies.* Hillsdale, NJ: Erlbaum.

Williams, C., & Bybee, J. (1994). What do children feel guilty about? Developmental and gender differences. *Developmental Psychology, 30*(5), 617–623.

Willis, S. (1999). Imagining dinosaurs. In B. L. Clarke & M. Higonnet (Eds.). *Girls, boys, books, toys* (pp. 183–195). Baltimore: Johns Hopkins University Press.

Wilson, R. (2004). The role of emotional competence in the development of the young child. In K. M. Paciorek & J. H. Munro (Eds.). *Annual Editions: Early Childhood Education* (pp. 63–66). Guilford CT: McGraw-Hill.

Wing, L. (1995). Play is not the work of the child: Young children's perceptions of work and play. *Early Childhood Research Quarterly, 10*, 223–247.

Winsler, A., De Leon, J. R., Walace, B. A., Carlton, M. P. & Wilson-Quayle, A. (2003). Private speech in preschool children: developmental stability and change, across-task consistency, and relations with classroom behavior. *Journal of Child Language, 30*(3), 583–608.

Winter, S. M. (1994/1995). Diversity: A proposal for all children. *Childhood Education, 71*(2), 91–95.

Wintre, M. G., & Vallance, D. D. (1994). A developmental sequence in the comprehension of emotions: Intensity, multiple emotions, and valence. *Developmental Psychology, 30*(4), 509–514.

Witherington, D. C., Campos, J. J. & Hertenstein, M. J. (2001). Principles of emotion and its development in infancy. In G. Bremner & A. Fogel (Eds.). *Blackwell Handbook of Infant Development* (pp. 427–464). Madden, MA: Blackwell.

Witkin, G. (1999). *Kid stress.* New York: Penguin Books.

Wittmer, D. S., & Honig, A. S. (1994, July). Encouraging positive social development in young children. *Young Children*, 4–12.

Wogelius, P., Poulsen, S. & Toft-Sorensen, H. (2003). Prevalence of dental anxiety and behavior management problems among six to eight year old Danish children. *Acta Odontologica Scnadinavica, 61*(3), 178–183.

Wolfe, L. (1992). Reaching potentials through bilingual education. In S. Bredekamp & T. Rosegrant (Eds.), *Reaching potentials: Appropriate curriculum and assessment for young children* (Vol. 1, pp. 139–145). Washington, DC: NAEYC.

Wolff, P. H. (1969). The causes, controls, and organization of behavior in the neonate. *Psychological Issues, 5*(1), 7–11.

Wolfgang, C. H. (1996). *The three faces of discipline for the elementary school teacher.* Boston: Allyn and Bacon.

Wolfgang, C. H. (2005). *Solving discipline and classroom management problems: Methods and models for today's teachers.* New York: Wiley.

Woll, P. (1999). Children of chemical dependency: Respecting complexities and building on strengths. *Prevention Forum, 11*(1), 1.

Wolpert, E. (1999). *Start seeing diversity.* St. Paul: Redleaf Press.

Woolmore, A., & Richer, J. (2003). Detecting infant regression periods: Weak signals in a noisy environment. In M. Heimann, (Ed.), *Regression periods in human infancy* (pp. 23–41). Mahwah, NJ: Lawrence Erlbaum Associates.

Yamamoto, K, Abdalla Soliman, Jmes Parsons, O. L. Davies Jr. (1987). Voices in unison: Stressful events in the lives of children in six countries. *Journal of Child Psychology and Psychiatry, 28*(6), 855–864.

Yan, J. & Smetana, J. G. (2003). Conceptualizations of moral, social-conventional, and personal events among Chinese preschoolers in Hong Kong. *Child Development, 74*, 647–658.

York, S. (2003). *Roots and wings.* St. Paul, MN: Redleaf Press.

Youniss, J. & Metz, E. (2004). *Longitudinal gains in civic development through school-based required service.* Manuscript submitted for publications.

Zahn-Waxler, C., & Robinson, J. (1995). Empathy and guilt: Early origins of feelings of responsibility. In J. P. Tangney & K.W. Fischer (Eds.), *Self-conscious emotions* (pp. 143–173). New York: Guilford.

Zakriski, A. L., & Coie, J. D. (1996). A comparison of aggressive-rejected and non aggressive-rejected children's interpretations of self-directed and other-directed rejection. *Child Development, 67,* 1048–1070.

Zarbatany, L., McDougall, P., Hymel, S. (2000). Gender-differentiated experiences in the peer culture: Links to intimacy in preadolescence. *Social Development, 9,* 62–79.

Zimbardo, P. G., & Radl, S. L. (1982). *The shy child.* Garden City, NJ: Doubleday.

Zins, J. E., Weissberg, R. P., Wang, M. C., & Walberg, H. J. (Eds.). (2004). *Building Academic Success on Social and Emotional Learning.* New York, NY: Teachers College Press.

Zirpoli, T. J. (1990). Physical abuse: Are children with disabilities at greater risk? *Intervention, 25*(1), 6–11.

Zuckerman, J., Driver, R., & Guadagno, N. (1985). Effects of segmentation patterns on the perception of deception. *Journal of Nonverbal Behavior, 9*(3), 160–168.

Zuckerman, M. et al. (1981). Controlling nonverbal cues: Facial expressions and tone of voice. *Journal of Experimental Social Psychology, 17,* 506–524.

Index